About Pearson

Pearson is the world's learning company, with presence across 70 countries worldwide. Our unique insights and world-class expertise comes from a long history of working closely with renowned teachers, authors and thought leaders, as a result of which, we have emerged as the preferred choice for millions of teachers and learners across the world.

We believe learning opens up opportunities, creates fulfilling careers and hence better lives. We hence collaborate with the best of minds to deliver you class-leading products, spread across the Higher Education and K12 spectrum.

Superior learning experience and improved outcomes are at the heart of everything we do. This product is the result of one such effort.

Your feedback plays a critical role in the evolution of our products and you can contact us - reachus@pearson.com. We look forward to it.

CRYPTOGRAPHY AND NETWORK SECURITY

PRINCIPLES AND PRACTICE

SEVENTH EDITION

William Stallings

Pearson

For Tricia: never dull, never boring, the smartest and bravest person I know

Credits and acknowledgments borrowed from other sources and reproduced, with permission, in this textbook appear on page 753.

The right of William Stallings to be identified as the author of this work has been asserted by him in accordance with the Copyright, Designs and Patents Act 1988.

All trademarks used herein are the property of their respective owners. The use of any trademark in this text does not vest in the author or publisher any trademark ownership rights in such trademarks, nor does the use of such trademarks imply any affiliation with or endorsement of this book by such owners.

Authorized adaptation from the United States edition, entitled *Cryptography and Network Security: Principles and Practice, Global Edition,* 7th Edition, ISBN 978-1-292-15858-7 by Stallings, William, published by Pearson Education, Inc, Copyright © Pearson Education Limited 2017.

Indian Subcontinent Adaptation
Copyright © 2017 Pearson India Education Services Pvt. Ltd

All rights reserved. This book is sold subject to the condition that it shall not, by way of trade or otherwise, be lent, resold, hired out, or otherwise circulated without the publisher's prior written consent in any form of binding or cover other than that in which it is published and without a similar condition including this condition being imposed on the subsequent purchaser and without limiting the rights under copyright reserved above, no part of this publication may be reproduced, stored in or introduced into a retrieval system, or transmitted in any form or by any means (electronic, mechanical, photocopying, recording or otherwise), without the prior written permission of both the copyright owner and the publisher of this book.

ISBN 978-93-325-8522-5

First Impression , 2017
Second Impression , 2018

This edition is manufactured in India and is authorized for sale only in India, Bangladesh, Bhutan, Pakistan, Nepal, Sri Lanka and the Maldives. Circulation of this edition outside of these territories is UNAUTHORIZED.

Published by Pearson India Education Services Pvt. Ltd, CIN: U72200TN2005PTC057128, formerly known as TutorVista Global Pvt. Ltd, licensee of Pearson Education in South Asia.

Head Office: 15th Floor, Tower-B, World Trade Tower, Plot No. 1, Block-C, Sector 16, Noida 201 301, Uttar Pradesh, India.
Registered Office: 4th Floor, Software Block, Elnet Software City, TS-140, Block 2 & 9, Rajiv Gandhi Salai,Taramani, Chennai 600 113, Tamil Nadu, India.
Fax: 080-30461003, Phone: 080-30461060
in.pearson.com , Email: companysecretary.india@pearson.com

Printed in India by India Binding House

CONTENTS

ONLINE CHAPTERS AND APPENDICES[1]

[1]Online chapters and appendices are available via the access card at the front of this book.

NOTATION

Symbol	Expression	Meaning
D, K	D(K, Y)	Symmetric decryption of ciphertext Y using secret key K
D, PR_a	D(PR_a, Y)	Asymmetric decryption of ciphertext Y using A's private key PR_a
D, PU_a	D(PU_a, Y)	Asymmetric decryption of ciphertext Y using A's public key PU_a
E, K	E(K, X)	Symmetric encryption of plaintext X using secret key K
E, PR_a	E(PR_a, X)	Asymmetric encryption of plaintext X using A's private key PR_a
E, PU_a	E(PU_a, X)	Asymmetric encryption of plaintext X using A's public key PU_a
K		Secret key
PR_a		Private key of user A
PU_a		Public key of user A
MAC, K	MAC(K, X)	Message authentication code of message X using secret key K
GF(p)		The finite field of order p, where p is prime.The field is defined as the set Z_p together with the arithmetic operations modulo p.
GF(2^n)		The finite field of order 2^n
Z_n		Set of nonnegative integers less than n
gcd	gcd(i, j)	Greatest common divisor; the largest positive integer that divides both i and j with no remainder on division.
mod	$a \bmod m$	Remainder after division of a by m
mod, $\equiv$	$a \equiv b \pmod{m}$	$a \bmod m = b \bmod m$
mod, $\not\equiv$	$a \not\equiv b \pmod{m}$	$a \bmod m \neq b \bmod m$
dlog	$\mathrm{dlog}_{a,p}(b)$	Discrete logarithm of the number b for the base a (mod p)
φ	$\phi(n)$	The number of positive integers less than n and relatively prime to n. This is Euler's totient function.
Σ	$\sum_{i=1}^{n} a_i$	$a_1 + a_2 + \cdots + a_n$
Π	$\prod_{i=1}^{n} a_i$	$a_1 \times a_2 \times \cdots \times a_n$
$\|$	$i\|j$	i divides j, which means that there is no remainder when j is divided by i
$\|,\|$	$\|a\|$	Absolute value of a

Symbol	Expression	Meaning
$\|$	$x \| y$	x concatenated with y
$\approx$	$x \approx y$	x is approximately equal to y
$\oplus$	$x \oplus y$	Exclusive-OR of x and y for single-bit variables; Bitwise exclusive-OR of x and y for multiple-bit variables
$\lfloor, \rfloor$	$\lfloor x \rfloor$	The largest integer less than or equal to x
$\in$	$x \in S$	The element x is contained in the set S.
$\longleftrightarrow$	$A \longleftrightarrow (a_1, a_2, \ldots a_k)$	The integer A corresponds to the sequence of integers $(a_1, a_2, \ldots a_k)$

PREFACE

WHAT'S NEW IN THE SEVENTH EDITION

In the four years since the sixth edition of this book was published, the field has seen continued innovations and improvements. In this new edition, I try to capture these changes while maintaining a broad and comprehensive coverage of the entire field. To begin this process of revision, the sixth edition of this book was extensively reviewed by a number of professors who teach the subject and by professionals working in the field. The result is that, in many places, the narrative has been clarified and tightened, and illustrations have been improved.

Beyond these refinements to improve pedagogy and user-friendliness, there have been substantive changes throughout the book. Roughly the same chapter organization has been retained, but much of the material has been revised and new material has been added. The most noteworthy changes are as follows:

- **Fundamental security design principles:** Chapter 1 includes a new section discussing the security design principles listed as fundamental by the National Centers of Academic Excellence in Information Assurance/Cyber Defense, which is jointly sponsored by the U.S. National Security Agency and the U.S. Department of Homeland Security.
- **Attack surfaces and attack trees:** Chapter 1 includes a new section describing these two concepts, which are useful in evaluating and classifying security threats.
- **Number theory coverage:** The material on number theory has been consolidated into a single chapter, Chapter 2. This makes for a convenient reference. The relevant portions of Chapter 2 can be assigned as needed.
- **Finite fields:** The chapter on finite fields has been revised and expanded with additional text and new figures to enhance understanding.
- **Format-preserving encryption:** This relatively new mode of encryption is enjoying increasing commercial success. A new section in Chapter 7 covers this method.
- **Conditioning and health testing for true random number generators:** Chapter 8 now provides coverage of these important topics.
- **User authentication model:** Chapter 15 includes a new description of a general model for user authentication, which helps to unify the discussion of the various approaches to user authentication.
- **Cloud security:** The material on cloud security in Chapter 16 has been updated and expanded to reflect its importance and recent developments.
- **Transport Layer Security (TLS):** The treatment of TLS in Chapter 17 has been updated, reorganized to improve clarity, and now includes a discussion of the new TLS version 1.3.
- **Email Security:** Chapter 19 has been completely rewritten to provide a comprehensive and up-to-date discussion of email security. It includes:
  - New: discussion of email threats and a comprehensive approach to email security.
  - New: discussion of STARTTLS, which provides confidentiality and authentication for SMTP.

— Revised: treatment of S/MIME has been updated to reflect the latest version 3.2.
— New: discussion of DNSSEC and its role in supporting email security.
— New: discussion of DNS-based Authentication of Named Entities (DANE) and the use of this approach to enhance security for certificate use in SMTP and S/MIME.
— New: discussion of Sender Policy Framework (SPF), which is the standardized way for a sending domain to identify and assert the mail senders for a given domain.
— Revised: discussion of DomainKeys Identified Mail (DKIM) has been revised.
— New: discussion of Domain-based Message Authentication, Reporting, and Conformance (DMARC) allows email senders to specify policy on how their mail should be handled, the types of reports that receivers can send back, and the frequency those reports should be sent.

OBJECTIVES

It is the purpose of this book to provide a practical survey of both the principles and practice of cryptography and network security. In the first part of the book, the basic issues to be addressed by a network security capability are explored by providing a tutorial and survey of cryptography and network security technology. The latter part of the book deals with the practice of network security: practical applications that have been implemented and are in use to provide network security.

The subject, and therefore this book, draws on a variety of disciplines. In particular, it is impossible to appreciate the significance of some of the techniques discussed in this book without a basic understanding of number theory and some results from probability theory. Nevertheless, an attempt has been made to make the book self-contained. The book not only presents the basic mathematical results that are needed but provides the reader with an intuitive understanding of those results. Such background material is introduced as needed. This approach helps to motivate the material that is introduced, and the author considers this preferable to simply presenting all of the mathematical material in a lump at the beginning of the book.

PLAN OF THE TEXT

The book is divided into eight parts.

- Background
- Symmetric Ciphers
- Asymmetric Ciphers
- Cryptographic Data Integrity Algorithms
- Mutual Trust
- Network and Internet Security
- System Security
- Legal and Ethical Issues

The book includes a number of pedagogic features, including the use of the computer algebra system Sage and numerous figures and tables to clarify the discussions. Each chapter includes a list of key words, review questions, homework problems, and suggestions for further reading. The book also includes an extensive glossary, a list of frequently used acronyms, and a bibliography. In addition, a test bank is available to instructors.

INSTRUCTOR SUPPORT MATERIALS

The major goal of this text is to make it as effective a teaching tool for this exciting and fast-moving subject as possible. This goal is reflected both in the structure of the book and in the supporting material. The text is accompanied by the following supplementary material that will aid the instructor:

- **Solutions manual:** Solutions to all end-of-chapter Review Questions and Problems.
- **Projects manual:** Suggested project assignments for all of the project categories listed below.
- **PowerPoint slides:** A set of slides covering all chapters, suitable for use in lecturing.
- **PDF files:** Reproductions of all figures and tables from the book.
- **Test bank:** A chapter-by-chapter set of questions with a separate file of answers.

All of these support materials are available at the **Pearson Resource Center (PRC)** for this textbook, which can be reached through the publisher's Web site www.pearsoned.co.in/williamstallings.

PROJECTS AND OTHER STUDENT EXERCISES

For many instructors, an important component of a cryptography or network security course is a project or set of projects by which the student gets hands-on experience to reinforce concepts from the text. This book provides an unparalleled degree of support, including a projects component in the course. The PRC not only includes guidance on how to assign and structure the projects, but also includes a set of project assignments that covers a broad range of topics from the text:

- **Sage projects:** Described in the next section.
- **Hacking project:** Exercise designed to illuminate the key issues in intrusion detection and prevention.
- **Block cipher projects:** A lab that explores the operation of the AES encryption algorithm by tracing its execution, computing one round by hand, and then exploring the various block cipher modes of use. The lab also covers DES. In both cases, an online Java applet is used (or can be downloaded) to execute AES or DES.
- **Lab exercises:** A series of projects that involve programming and experimenting with concepts from the book.

- **Research projects:** A series of research assignments that instruct the student to research a particular topic on the Internet and write a report.
- **Programming projects:** A series of programming projects that cover a broad range of topics and that can be implemented in any suitable language on any platform.
- **Practical security assessments:** A set of exercises to examine current infrastructure and practices of an existing organization.
- **Firewall projects:** A portable network firewall visualization simulator, together with exercises for teaching the fundamentals of firewalls.
- **Case studies:** A set of real-world case studies, including learning objectives, case description, and a series of case discussion questions.
- **Writing assignments:** A set of suggested writing assignments, organized by chapter.
- **Reading/report assignments:** A list of papers in the literature—one for each chapter—that can be assigned for the student to read and then write a short report.

This diverse set of projects and other student exercises enables the instructor to use the book as one component in a rich and varied learning experience and to tailor a course plan to meet the specific needs of the instructor and students. See Appendix A in this book for details.

THE SAGE COMPUTER ALGEBRA SYSTEM

One of the most important features of this book is the use of Sage for cryptographic examples and homework assignments. Sage is an open-source, multiplatform, freeware package that implements a very powerful, flexible, and easily learned mathematics and computer algebra system. Unlike competing systems (such as Mathematica, Maple, and MATLAB), there are no licensing agreements or fees involved. Thus, Sage can be made available on computers and networks at school, and students can individually download the software to their own personal computers for use at home. Another advantage of using Sage is that students learn a powerful, flexible tool that can be used for virtually any mathematical application, not just cryptography.

The use of Sage can make a significant difference to the teaching of the mathematics of cryptographic algorithms. This book provides a large number of examples of the use of Sage covering many cryptographic concepts in Appendix B, which is included in this book.

Appendix C lists exercises in each of these topic areas to enable the student to gain hands-on experience with cryptographic algorithms. Appendix C includes a section on how to download and get started with Sage, a section on programming with Sage, and exercises that can be assigned to students in the following categories:

- **Chapter 2—Number Theory and Finite Fields:** Euclidean and extended Euclidean algorithms, polynomial arithmetic, GF(2^4), Euler's Totient function, Miller–Rabin, factoring, modular exponentiation, discrete logarithm, and Chinese remainder theorem.

- **Chapter 3—Classical Encryption:** Affine ciphers and the Hill cipher.
- **Chapter 4—Block Ciphers and the Data Encryption Standard:** Exercises based on SDES.
- **Chapter 6—Advanced Encryption Standard:** Exercises based on SAES.
- **Chapter 8—Pseudorandom Number Generation and Stream Ciphers:** Blum Blum Shub, linear congruential generator, and ANSI X9.17 PRNG.
- **Chapter 9—Public-Key Cryptography and RSA:** RSA encrypt/decrypt and signing.
- **Chapter 10—Other Public-Key Cryptosystems:** Diffie–Hellman, elliptic curve.
- **Chapter 11—Cryptographic Hash Functions:** Number-theoretic hash function.
- **Chapter 13—Digital Signatures:** DSA.

ONLINE DOCUMENTS FOR STUDENTS

For this new edition, a tremendous amount of original supporting material for students has been made available online.

Purchasing this new textbook also grants the reader access to the following reading materials:

- **Online chapters:** To limit the size and cost of the book, four chapters of the book are provided in PDF format. This includes three chapters on computer security and one on legal and ethical issues. The chapters are listed in this book's table of contents.
- **Online appendices:** There are numerous interesting topics that support material found in the text but whose inclusion is not warranted in the printed text. A total of 23 online appendices cover these topics for the interested student. The appendices are listed in this book's table of contents.

To access these online materials, follow the instructions mentioned in the inside front cover of this book.

ACKNOWLEDGMENTS

This new edition has benefited from review by a number of people who gave generously of their time and expertise. The following professors reviewed all or a large part of the manuscript: Hossein Beyzavi (Marymount University), Donald F. Costello (University of Nebraska–Lincoln), James Haralambides (Barry University), Anand Seetharam (California State University at Monterey Bay), Marius C. Silaghi (Florida Institute of Technology), Shambhu Upadhyaya (University at Buffalo), Zhengping Wu (California State University at San Bernardino), Liangliang Xiao (Frostburg State University), Seong-Moo (Sam) Yoo (The University of Alabama in Huntsville), and Hong Zhang (Armstrong State University).

Thanks also to the people who provided detailed technical reviews of one or more chapters: Dino M. Amaral, Chris Andrew, Prof. (Dr). C. Annamalai, Andrew Bain, Riccardo Bernardini, Olivier Blazy, Zervopoulou Christina, Maria Christofi, Dhananjoy Dey,

Mario Emmanuel, Mike Fikuart, Alexander Fries, Pierpaolo Giacomin, Pedro R. M. Inácio, Daniela Tamy Iwassa, Krzysztof Janowski, Sergey Katsev, Adnan Kilic, Rob Knox, Mina Pourdashty, Yuri Poeluev, Pritesh Prajapati, Venkatesh Ramamoorthy, Andrea Razzini, Rami Rosen, Javier Scodelaro, Jamshid Shokrollahi, Oscar So, and David Tillemans.

In addition, I was fortunate to have reviews of individual topics by "subject-area gurus," including Jesse Walker of Intel (Intel's Digital Random Number Generator), Russ Housley of Vigil Security (key wrapping), Joan Daemen (AES), Edward F. Schaefer of Santa Clara University (Simplified AES), Tim Mathews, formerly of RSA Laboratories (S/MIME), Alfred Menezes of the University of Waterloo (elliptic curve cryptography), William Sutton, Editor/Publisher of *The Cryptogram* (classical encryption), Avi Rubin of Johns Hopkins University (number theory), Michael Markowitz of Information Security Corporation (SHA and DSS), Don Davis of IBM Internet Security Systems (Kerberos), Steve Kent of BBN Technologies (X.509), and Phil Zimmerman (PGP).

Nikhil Bhargava (IIT Delhi) developed the set of online homework problems and solutions. Dan Shumow of Microsoft and the University of Washington developed all of the Sage examples and assignments in Appendices B and C. Professor Sreekanth Malladi of Dakota State University developed the hacking exercises. Lawrie Brown of the Australian Defence Force Academy provided the AES/DES block cipher projects and the security assessment assignments.

Sanjay Rao and Ruben Torres of Purdue University developed the laboratory exercises that appear in the PRC. The following people contributed project assignments that appear in the instructor's supplement: Henning Schulzrinne (Columbia University); Cetin Kaya Koc (Oregon State University); and David Balenson (Trusted Information Systems and George Washington University). Kim McLaughlin developed the test bank.

Finally, I thank the many people responsible for the publication of this book, all of whom did their usual excellent job. This includes the staff at Pearson, particularly my editor Tracy Johnson, program manager Carole Snyder, and production manager Bob Engelhardt. Thanks also to the marketing and sales staffs at Pearson, without whose efforts this book would not be in front of you.

ABOUT THE AUTHOR

Dr. William Stallings has authored 18 titles, and counting revised editions, over 40 books on computer security, computer networking, and computer architecture. His writings have appeared in numerous publications, including the *Proceedings of the IEEE, ACM Computing Reviews*, and *Cryptologia*.

He has 13 times received the award for the best Computer Science textbook of the year from the Text and Academic Authors Association.

In over 30 years in the field, he has been a technical contributor, technical manager, and an executive with several high-technology firms. He has designed and implemented both TCP/IP-based and OSI-based protocol suites on a variety of computers and operating systems, ranging from microcomputers to mainframes. As a consultant, he has advised government agencies, computer and software vendors, and major users on the design, selection, and use of networking software and products.

He created and maintains the *Computer Science Student Resource Site* at ComputerScienceStudent.com. This site provides documents and links on a variety of subjects of general interest to computer science students (and professionals). He is a member of the editorial board of *Cryptologia*, a scholarly journal devoted to all aspects of cryptology.

Dr. Stallings holds a PhD from MIT in computer science and a BS from Notre Dame in electrical engineering.

PART ONE: BACKGROUND

CHAPTER 1

COMPUTER AND NETWORK SECURITY CONCEPTS

LEARNING OBJECTIVES

After studying this chapter, you should be able to:

- Describe the key security requirements of confidentiality, integrity, and availability.
- Describe the X.800 security architecture for OSI.
- Discuss the types of security threats and attacks that must be dealt with and give examples of the types of threats and attacks that apply to different categories of computer and network assets.
- Explain the fundamental security design principles.
- Discuss the use of attack surfaces and attack trees.
- List and briefly describe key organizations involved in cryptography standards.

This book focuses on two broad areas: cryptographic algorithms and protocols, which have a broad range of applications; and network and Internet security, which rely heavily on cryptographic techniques.

Cryptographic algorithms and protocols can be grouped into four main areas:

- **Symmetric encryption:** Used to conceal the contents of blocks or streams of data of any size, including messages, files, encryption keys, and passwords.
- **Asymmetric encryption:** Used to conceal small blocks of data, such as encryption keys and hash function values, which are used in digital signatures.
- **Data integrity algorithms:** Used to protect blocks of data, such as messages, from alteration.
- **Authentication protocols:** These are schemes based on the use of cryptographic algorithms designed to authenticate the identity of entities.

The field of **network and Internet security** consists of measures to deter, prevent, detect, and correct security violations that involve the transmission of information. That is a broad statement that covers a host of possibilities. To give you a feel for the areas covered in this book, consider the following examples of security violations:

1. User A transmits a file to user B. The file contains sensitive information (e.g., payroll records) that is to be protected from disclosure. User C, who is not authorized to read the file, is able to monitor the transmission and capture a copy of the file during its transmission.
2. A network manager, D, transmits a message to a computer, E, under its management. The message instructs computer E to update an authorization file to include the identities of a number of new users who are to be given access to that computer. User F intercepts the message, alters its contents to add or delete entries, and then forwards the message to computer E, which accepts the message as coming from manager D and updates its authorization file accordingly.

3. Rather than intercept a message, user F constructs its own message with the desired entries and transmits that message to computer E as if it had come from manager D. Computer E accepts the message as coming from manager D and updates its authorization file accordingly.
4. An employee is fired without warning. The personnel manager sends a message to a server system to invalidate the employee's account. When the invalidation is accomplished, the server is to post a notice to the employee's file as confirmation of the action. The employee is able to intercept the message and delay it long enough to make a final access to the server to retrieve sensitive information. The message is then forwarded, the action taken, and the confirmation posted. The employee's action may go unnoticed for some considerable time.
5. A message is sent from a customer to a stockbroker with instructions for various transactions. Subsequently, the investments lose value and the customer denies sending the message.

Although this list by no means exhausts the possible types of network security violations, it illustrates the range of concerns of network security.

1.1 COMPUTER SECURITY CONCEPTS

A Definition of Computer Security

The NIST *Computer Security Handbook* [NIST95] defines the term *computer security* as follows:

> **Computer Security:** The protection afforded to an automated information system in order to attain the applicable objectives of preserving the integrity, availability, and confidentiality of information system resources (includes hardware, software, firmware, information/data, and telecommunications).

This definition introduces three key objectives that are at the heart of computer security:

- **Confidentiality:** This term covers two related concepts:

  Data[1] confidentiality: Assures that private or confidential information is not made available or disclosed to unauthorized individuals.

  Privacy: Assures that individuals control or influence what information related to them may be collected and stored and by whom and to whom that information may be disclosed.

---

[1]RFC 4949 defines *information* as "facts and ideas, which can be represented (encoded) as various forms of data," and *data* as "information in a specific physical representation, usually a sequence of symbols that have meaning; especially a representation of information that can be processed or produced by a computer." Security literature typically does not make much of a distinction, nor does this book.

- **Integrity:** This term covers two related concepts:

  Data integrity: Assures that information (both stored and in transmitted packets) and programs are changed only in a specified and authorized manner.

  System integrity: Assures that a system performs its intended function in an unimpaired manner, free from deliberate or inadvertent unauthorized manipulation of the system.

- **Availability:** Assures that systems work promptly and service is not denied to authorized users.

These three concepts form what is often referred to as the **CIA triad**. The three concepts embody the fundamental security objectives for both data and for information and computing services. For example, the NIST standard FIPS 199 (*Standards for Security Categorization of Federal Information and Information Systems*) lists confidentiality, integrity, and availability as the three security objectives for information and for information systems. FIPS 199 provides a useful characterization of these three objectives in terms of requirements and the definition of a loss of security in each category:

- **Confidentiality:** Preserving authorized restrictions on information access and disclosure, including means for protecting personal privacy and proprietary information. A loss of confidentiality is the unauthorized disclosure of information.
- **Integrity:** Guarding against improper information modification or destruction, including ensuring information nonrepudiation and authenticity. A loss of integrity is the unauthorized modification or destruction of information.
- **Availability:** Ensuring timely and reliable access to and use of information. A loss of availability is the disruption of access to or use of information or an information system.

Although the use of the CIA triad to define security objectives is well established, some in the security field feel that additional concepts are needed to present a complete picture (Figure 1.1). Two of the most commonly mentioned are as follows:

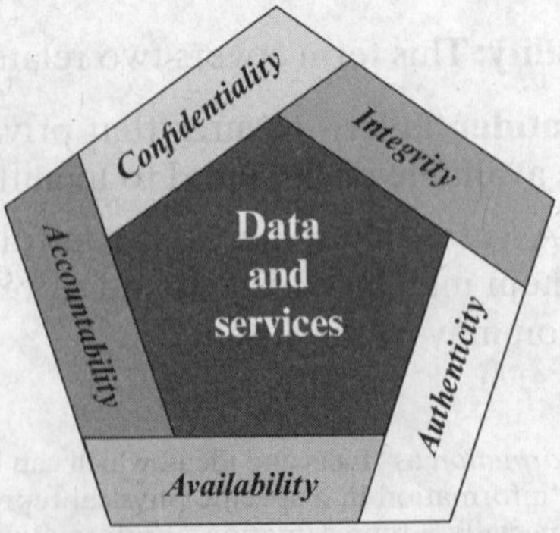

Figure 1.1 Essential Network and Computer Security Requirements

- **Authenticity:** The property of being genuine and being able to be verified and trusted; confidence in the validity of a transmission, a message, or message originator. This means verifying that users are who they say they are and that each input arriving at the system came from a trusted source.
- **Accountability:** The security goal that generates the requirement for actions of an entity to be traced uniquely to that entity. This supports nonrepudiation, deterrence, fault isolation, intrusion detection and prevention, and after-action recovery and legal action. Because truly secure systems are not yet an achievable goal, we must be able to trace a security breach to a responsible party. Systems must keep records of their activities to permit later forensic analysis to trace security breaches or to aid in transaction disputes.

Examples

We now provide some examples of applications that illustrate the requirements just enumerated.[2] For these examples, we use three levels of impact on organizations or individuals should there be a breach of security (i.e., a loss of confidentiality, integrity, or availability). These levels are defined in FIPS PUB 199:

- **Low:** The loss could be expected to have a limited adverse effect on organizational operations, organizational assets, or individuals. A limited adverse effect means that, for example, the loss of confidentiality, integrity, or availability might (i) cause a degradation in mission capability to an extent and duration that the organization is able to perform its primary functions, but the effectiveness of the functions is noticeably reduced; (ii) result in minor damage to organizational assets; (iii) result in minor financial loss; or (iv) result in minor harm to individuals.
- **Moderate:** The loss could be expected to have a serious adverse effect on organizational operations, organizational assets, or individuals. A serious adverse effect means that, for example, the loss might (i) cause a significant degradation in mission capability to an extent and duration that the organization is able to perform its primary functions, but the effectiveness of the functions is significantly reduced; (ii) result in significant damage to organizational assets; (iii) result in significant financial loss; or (iv) result in significant harm to individuals that does not involve loss of life or serious, life-threatening injuries.
- **High:** The loss could be expected to have a severe or catastrophic adverse effect on organizational operations, organizational assets, or individuals. A severe or catastrophic adverse effect means that, for example, the loss might (i) cause a severe degradation in or loss of mission capability to an extent and duration that the organization is not able to perform one or more of its primary functions; (ii) result in major damage to organizational assets; (iii) result in major financial loss; or (iv) result in severe or catastrophic harm to individuals involving loss of life or serious, life-threatening injuries.

[2]These examples are taken from a security policy document published by the Information Technology Security and Privacy Office at Purdue University.

Confidentiality Student grade information is an asset whose confidentiality is considered to be highly important by students. In the United States, the release of such information is regulated by the Family Educational Rights and Privacy Act (FERPA). Grade information should only be available to students, their parents, and employees that require the information to do their job. Student enrollment information may have a moderate confidentiality rating. While still covered by FERPA, this information is seen by more people on a daily basis, is less likely to be targeted than grade information, and results in less damage if disclosed. Directory information, such as lists of students or faculty or departmental lists, may be assigned a low confidentiality rating or indeed no rating. This information is typically freely available to the public and published on a school's Web site.

Integrity Several aspects of integrity are illustrated by the example of a hospital patient's allergy information stored in a database. The doctor should be able to trust that the information is correct and current. Now suppose that an employee (e.g., a nurse) who is authorized to view and update this information deliberately falsifies the data to cause harm to the hospital. The database needs to be restored to a trusted basis quickly, and it should be possible to trace the error back to the person responsible. Patient allergy information is an example of an asset with a high requirement for integrity. Inaccurate information could result in serious harm or death to a patient and expose the hospital to massive liability.

An example of an asset that may be assigned a moderate level of integrity requirement is a Web site that offers a forum to registered users to discuss some specific topic. Either a registered user or a hacker could falsify some entries or deface the Web site. If the forum exists only for the enjoyment of the users, brings in little or no advertising revenue, and is not used for something important such as research, then potential damage is not severe. The Web master may experience some data, financial, and time loss.

An example of a low integrity requirement is an anonymous online poll. Many Web sites, such as news organizations, offer these polls to their users with very few safeguards. However, the inaccuracy and unscientific nature of such polls is well understood.

Availability The more critical a component or service, the higher is the level of availability required. Consider a system that provides authentication services for critical systems, applications, and devices. An interruption of service results in the inability for customers to access computing resources and staff to access the resources they need to perform critical tasks. The loss of the service translates into a large financial loss in lost employee productivity and potential customer loss.

An example of an asset that would typically be rated as having a moderate availability requirement is a public Web site for a university; the Web site provides information for current and prospective students and donors. Such a site is not a critical component of the university's information system, but its unavailability will cause some embarrassment.

An online telephone directory lookup application would be classified as a low availability requirement. Although the temporary loss of the application may be an annoyance, there are other ways to access the information, such as a hardcopy directory or the operator.

The Challenges of Computer Security

Computer and network security is both fascinating and complex. Some of the reasons follow:

1. Security is not as simple as it might first appear to the novice. The requirements seem to be straightforward; indeed, most of the major requirements for security services can be given self-explanatory, one-word labels: confidentiality, authentication, nonrepudiation, or integrity. But the mechanisms used to meet those requirements can be quite complex, and understanding them may involve rather subtle reasoning.
2. In developing a particular security mechanism or algorithm, one must always consider potential attacks on those security features. In many cases, successful attacks are designed by looking at the problem in a completely different way, therefore exploiting an unexpected weakness in the mechanism.
3. Because of point 2, the procedures used to provide particular services are often counterintuitive. Typically, a security mechanism is complex, and it is not obvious from the statement of a particular requirement that such elaborate measures are needed. It is only when the various aspects of the threat are considered that elaborate security mechanisms make sense.
4. Having designed various security mechanisms, it is necessary to decide where to use them. This is true both in terms of physical placement (e.g., at what points in a network are certain security mechanisms needed) and in a logical sense (e.g., at what layer or layers of an architecture such as TCP/IP [Transmission Control Protocol/Internet Protocol] should mechanisms be placed).
5. Security mechanisms typically involve more than a particular algorithm or protocol. They also require that participants be in possession of some secret information (e.g., an encryption key), which raises questions about the creation, distribution, and protection of that secret information. There also may be a reliance on communications protocols whose behavior may complicate the task of developing the security mechanism. For example, if the proper functioning of the security mechanism requires setting time limits on the transit time of a message from sender to receiver, then any protocol or network that introduces variable, unpredictable delays may render such time limits meaningless.
6. Computer and network security is essentially a battle of wits between a perpetrator who tries to find holes and the designer or administrator who tries to close them. The great advantage that the attacker has is that he or she need only find a single weakness, while the designer must find and eliminate all weaknesses to achieve perfect security.
7. There is a natural tendency on the part of users and system managers to perceive little benefit from security investment until a security failure occurs.
8. Security requires regular, even constant, monitoring, and this is difficult in today's short-term, overloaded environment.
9. Security is still too often an afterthought to be incorporated into a system after the design is complete rather than being an integral part of the design process.

10. Many users and even security administrators view strong security as an impediment to efficient and user-friendly operation of an information system or use of information.

The difficulties just enumerated will be encountered in numerous ways as we examine the various security threats and mechanisms throughout this book.

1.2 THE OSI SECURITY ARCHITECTURE

To assess effectively the security needs of an organization and to evaluate and choose various security products and policies, the manager responsible for security needs some systematic way of defining the requirements for security and characterizing the approaches to satisfying those requirements. This is difficult enough in a centralized data processing environment; with the use of local and wide area networks, the problems are compounded.

ITU-T[3] Recommendation X.800, *Security Architecture for OSI*, defines such a systematic approach.[4] The OSI security architecture is useful to managers as a way of organizing the task of providing security. Furthermore, because this architecture was developed as an international standard, computer and communications vendors have developed security features for their products and services that relate to this structured definition of services and mechanisms.

For our purposes, the OSI security architecture provides a useful, if abstract, overview of many of the concepts that this book deals with. The OSI security architecture focuses on security attacks, mechanisms, and services. These can be defined briefly as

- **Security attack:** Any action that compromises the security of information owned by an organization.
- **Security mechanism:** A process (or a device incorporating such a process) that is designed to detect, prevent, or recover from a security attack.
- **Security service:** A processing or communication service that enhances the security of the data processing systems and the information transfers of an organization. The services are intended to counter security attacks, and they make use of one or more security mechanisms to provide the service.

In the literature, the terms *threat* and *attack* are commonly used to mean more or less the same thing. Table 1.1 provides definitions taken from RFC 4949, *Internet Security Glossary.*

---

[3]The International Telecommunication Union (ITU) Telecommunication Standardization Sector (ITU-T) is a United Nations-sponsored agency that develops standards, called Recommendations, relating to telecommunications and to open systems interconnection (OSI).

[4]The OSI security architecture was developed in the context of the OSI protocol architecture, which is described in Appendix L. However, for our purposes in this chapter, an understanding of the OSI protocol architecture is not required.

Table 1.1 Threats and Attacks (RFC 4949)

Threat A potential for violation of security, which exists when there is a circumstance, capability, action, or event that could breach security and cause harm. That is, a threat is a possible danger that might exploit a vulnerability.
Attack An assault on system security that derives from an intelligent threat; that is, an intelligent act that is a deliberate attempt (especially in the sense of a method or technique) to evade security services and violate the security policy of a system.

1.3 SECURITY ATTACKS

A useful means of classifying security attacks, used both in X.800 and RFC 4949, is in terms of *passive attacks* and *active attacks* (Figure 1.2). A passive attack attempts to learn or make use of information from the system but does not affect system resources. An active attack attempts to alter system resources or affect their operation.

Passive Attacks

Passive attacks (Figure 1.2a) are in the nature of eavesdropping on, or monitoring of, transmissions. The goal of the opponent is to obtain information that is being transmitted. Two types of passive attacks are the release of message contents and traffic analysis.

The **release of message contents** is easily understood. A telephone conversation, an electronic mail message, and a transferred file may contain sensitive or confidential information. We would like to prevent an opponent from learning the contents of these transmissions.

A second type of passive attack, **traffic analysis**, is subtler. Suppose that we had a way of masking the contents of messages or other information traffic so that opponents, even if they captured the message, could not extract the information from the message. The common technique for masking contents is encryption. If we had encryption protection in place, an opponent might still be able to observe the pattern of these messages. The opponent could determine the location and identity of communicating hosts and could observe the frequency and length of messages being exchanged. This information might be useful in guessing the nature of the communication that was taking place.

Passive attacks are very difficult to detect, because they do not involve any alteration of the data. Typically, the message traffic is sent and received in an apparently normal fashion, and neither the sender nor receiver is aware that a third party has read the messages or observed the traffic pattern. However, it is feasible to prevent the success of these attacks, usually by means of encryption. Thus, the emphasis in dealing with passive attacks is on prevention rather than detection.

Active Attacks

Active attacks (Figure 1.2b) involve some modification of the data stream or the creation of a false stream and can be subdivided into four categories: masquerade, replay, modification of messages, and denial of service.

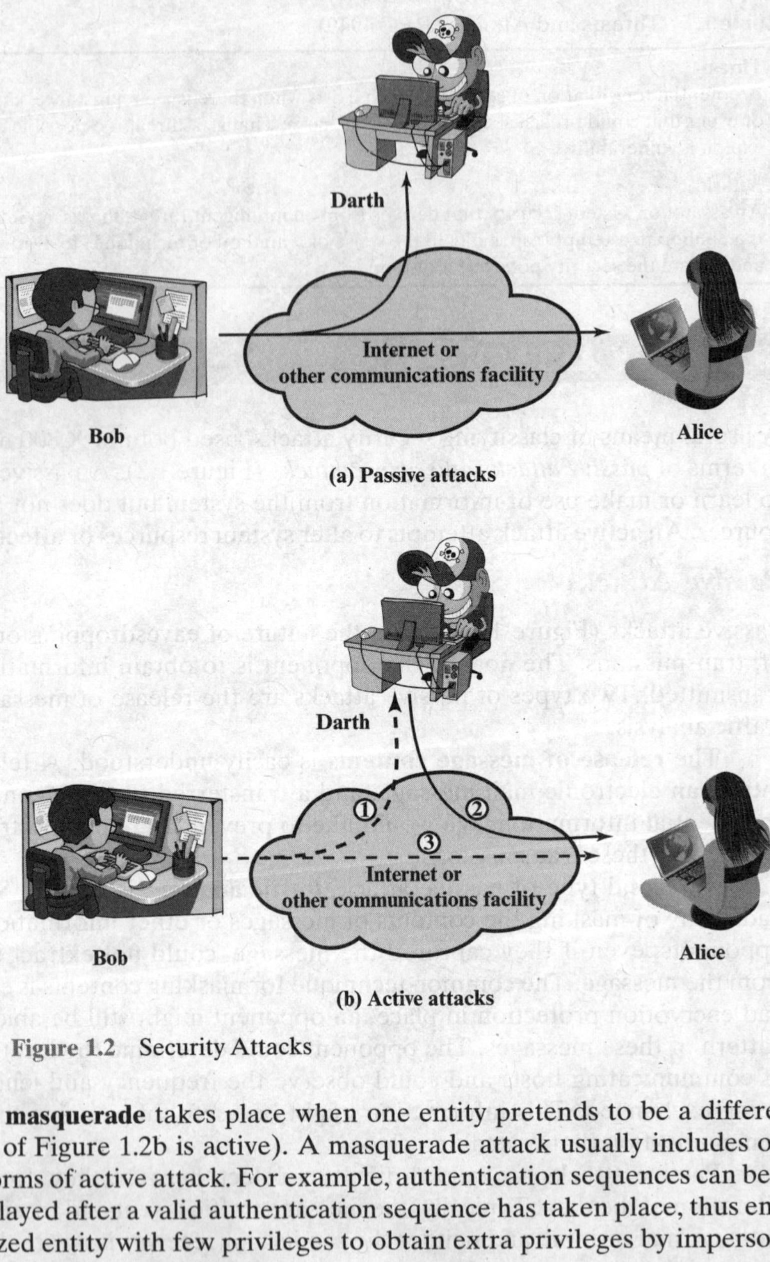

Figure 1.2 Security Attacks

A **masquerade** takes place when one entity pretends to be a different entity (path 2 of Figure 1.2b is active). A masquerade attack usually includes one of the other forms of active attack. For example, authentication sequences can be captured and replayed after a valid authentication sequence has taken place, thus enabling an authorized entity with few privileges to obtain extra privileges by impersonating an entity that has those privileges.

Replay involves the passive capture of a data unit and its subsequent retransmission to produce an unauthorized effect (paths 1, 2, and 3 active).

Modification of messages simply means that some portion of a legitimate message is altered, or that messages are delayed or reordered, to produce an unauthorized effect (paths 1 and 2 active). For example, a message meaning "Allow John Smith to read confidential file *accounts*" is modified to mean "Allow Fred Brown to read confidential file *accounts.*"

The **denial of service** prevents or inhibits the normal use or management of communications facilities (path 3 active). This attack may have a specific target; for example, an entity may suppress all messages directed to a particular destination (e.g., the security audit service). Another form of service denial is the disruption of an entire network, either by disabling the network or by overloading it with messages so as to degrade performance.

Active attacks present the opposite characteristics of passive attacks. Whereas passive attacks are difficult to detect, measures are available to prevent their success. On the other hand, it is quite difficult to prevent active attacks absolutely because of the wide variety of potential physical, software, and network vulnerabilities. Instead, the goal is to detect active attacks and to recover from any disruption or delays caused by them. If the detection has a deterrent effect, it may also contribute to prevention.

1.4 SECURITY SERVICES

X.800 defines a security service as a service that is provided by a protocol layer of communicating open systems and that ensures adequate security of the systems or of data transfers. Perhaps a clearer definition is found in RFC 4949, which provides the following definition: a processing or communication service that is provided by a system to give a specific kind of protection to system resources; security services implement security policies and are implemented by security mechanisms.

X.800 divides these services into five categories and fourteen specific services (Table 1.2). We look at each category in turn.[5]

Authentication

The authentication service is concerned with assuring that a communication is authentic. In the case of a single message, such as a warning or alarm signal, the function of the authentication service is to assure the recipient that the message is from the source that it claims to be from. In the case of an ongoing interaction, such as the connection of a terminal to a host, two aspects are involved. First, at the time of connection initiation, the service assures that the two entities are authentic, that is, that each is the entity that it claims to be. Second, the service must assure that the connection is not interfered with in such a way that a third party can masquerade as one of the two legitimate parties for the purposes of unauthorized transmission or reception.

Two specific authentication services are defined in X.800:

- **Peer entity authentication:** Provides for the corroboration of the identity of a peer entity in an association. Two entities are considered peers if they implement to same protocol in different systems; for example two TCP modules in two communicating systems. Peer entity authentication is provided for

[5]There is no universal agreement about many of the terms used in the security literature. For example, the term *integrity* is sometimes used to refer to all aspects of information security. The term *authentication* is sometimes used to refer both to verification of identity and to the various functions listed under integrity in this chapter. Our usage here agrees with both X.800 and RFC 4949.

Table 1.2 Security Services (X.800)

AUTHENTICATION The assurance that the communicating entity is the one that it claims to be. **Peer Entity Authentication** Used in association with a logical connection to provide confidence in the identity of the entities connected. **Data-Origin Authentication** In a connectionless transfer, provides assurance that the source of received data is as claimed. **ACCESS CONTROL** The prevention of unauthorized use of a resource (i.e., this service controls who can have access to a resource, under what conditions access can occur, and what those accessing the resource are allowed to do). **DATA CONFIDENTIALITY** The protection of data from unauthorized disclosure. **Connection Confidentiality** The protection of all user data on a connection. **Connectionless Confidentiality** The protection of all user data in a single data block. **Selective-Field Confidentiality** The confidentiality of selected fields within the user data on a connection or in a single data block. **Traffic-Flow Confidentiality** The protection of the information that might be derived from observation of traffic flows.	**DATA INTEGRITY** The assurance that data received are exactly as sent by an authorized entity (i.e., contain no modification, insertion, deletion, or replay). **Connection Integrity with Recovery** Provides for the integrity of all user data on a connection and detects any modification, insertion, deletion, or replay of any data within an entire data sequence, with recovery attempted. **Connection Integrity without Recovery** As above, but provides only detection without recovery. **Selective-Field Connection Integrity** Provides for the integrity of selected fields within the user data of a data block transferred over a connection and takes the form of determination of whether the selected fields have been modified, inserted, deleted, or replayed. **Connectionless Integrity** Provides for the integrity of a single connectionless data block and may take the form of detection of data modification. Additionally, a limited form of replay detection may be provided. **Selective-Field Connectionless Integrity** Provides for the integrity of selected fields within a single connectionless data block; takes the form of determination of whether the selected fields have been modified. **NONREPUDIATION** Provides protection against denial by one of the entities involved in a communication of having participated in all or part of the communication. **Nonrepudiation, Origin** Proof that the message was sent by the specified party. **Nonrepudiation, Destination** Proof that the message was received by the specified party.

use at the establishment of, or at times during the data transfer phase of, a connection. It attempts to provide confidence that an entity is not performing either a masquerade or an unauthorized replay of a previous connection.

- **Data origin authentication:** Provides for the corroboration of the source of a data unit. It does not provide protection against the duplication or modification of data units. This type of service supports applications like electronic mail, where there are no prior interactions between the communicating entities.

Access Control

In the context of network security, access control is the ability to limit and control the access to host systems and applications via communications links. To achieve this, each entity trying to gain access must first be identified, or authenticated, so that access rights can be tailored to the individual.

Data Confidentiality

Confidentiality is the protection of transmitted data from passive attacks. With respect to the content of a data transmission, several levels of protection can be identified. The broadest service protects all user data transmitted between two users over a period of time. For example, when a TCP connection is set up between two systems, this broad protection prevents the release of any user data transmitted over the TCP connection. Narrower forms of this service can also be defined, including the protection of a single message or even specific fields within a message. These refinements are less useful than the broad approach and may even be more complex and expensive to implement.

The other aspect of confidentiality is the protection of traffic flow from analysis. This requires that an attacker not be able to observe the source and destination, frequency, length, or other characteristics of the traffic on a communications facility.

Data Integrity

As with confidentiality, integrity can apply to a stream of messages, a single message, or selected fields within a message. Again, the most useful and straightforward approach is total stream protection.

A connection-oriented integrity service, one that deals with a stream of messages, assures that messages are received as sent with no duplication, insertion, modification, reordering, or replays. The destruction of data is also covered under this service. Thus, the connection-oriented integrity service addresses both message stream modification and denial of service. On the other hand, a connectionless integrity service, one that deals with individual messages without regard to any larger context, generally provides protection against message modification only.

We can make a distinction between service with and without recovery. Because the integrity service relates to active attacks, we are concerned with detection rather than prevention. If a violation of integrity is detected, then the service may simply report this violation, and some other portion of software or human intervention is required to recover from the violation. Alternatively, there are mechanisms available to recover from the loss of integrity of data, as we will review subsequently. The incorporation of automated recovery mechanisms is, in general, the more attractive alternative.

Nonrepudiation

Nonrepudiation prevents either sender or receiver from denying a transmitted message. Thus, when a message is sent, the receiver can prove that the alleged sender in fact sent the message. Similarly, when a message is received, the sender can prove that the alleged receiver in fact received the message.

Availability Service

Both X.800 and RFC 4949 define availability to be the property of a system or a system resource being accessible and usable upon demand by an authorized system entity, according to performance specifications for the system (i.e., a system is available if it provides services according to the system design whenever users request them). A variety of attacks can result in the loss of or reduction in availability. Some of these attacks are amenable to automated countermeasures, such as authentication and encryption, whereas others require some sort of physical action to prevent or recover from loss of availability of elements of a distributed system.

X.800 treats availability as a property to be associated with various security services. However, it makes sense to call out specifically an availability service. An availability service is one that protects a system to ensure its availability. This service addresses the security concerns raised by denial-of-service attacks. It depends on proper management and control of system resources and thus depends on access control service and other security services.

1.5 SECURITY MECHANISMS

Table 1.3 lists the security mechanisms defined in X.800. The mechanisms are divided into those that are implemented in a specific protocol layer, such as TCP or an application-layer protocol, and those that are not specific to any particular protocol layer or security service. These mechanisms will be covered in the appropriate

Table 1.3 Security Mechanisms (X.800)

SPECIFIC SECURITY MECHANISMS	PERVASIVE SECURITY MECHANISMS
May be incorporated into the appropriate protocol layer in order to provide some of the OSI security services.	Mechanisms that are not specific to any particular OSI security service or protocol layer.
Encipherment The use of mathematical algorithms to transform data into a form that is not readily intelligible. The transformation and subsequent recovery of the data depend on an algorithm and zero or more encryption keys.	**Trusted Functionality** That which is perceived to be correct with respect to some criteria (e.g., as established by a security policy).
Digital Signature Data appended to, or a cryptographic transformation of, a data unit that allows a recipient of the data unit to prove the source and integrity of the data unit and protect against forgery (e.g., by the recipient).	**Security Label** The marking bound to a resource (which may be a data unit) that names or designates the security attributes of that resource.
Access Control A variety of mechanisms that enforce access rights to resources.	**Event Detection** Detection of security-relevant events.
	Security Audit Trail Data collected and potentially used to facilitate a security audit, which is an independent review and examination of system records and activities.
Data Integrity A variety of mechanisms used to assure the integrity of a data unit or stream of data units.	**Security Recovery** Deals with requests from mechanisms, such as event handling and management functions, and takes recovery actions.

SPECIFIC SECURITY MECHANISMS

Authentication Exchange
A mechanism intended to ensure the identity of an entity by means of information exchange.

Traffic Padding
The insertion of bits into gaps in a data stream to frustrate traffic analysis attempts.

Routing Control
Enables selection of particular physically secure routes for certain data and allows routing changes, especially when a breach of security is suspected.

Notarization
The use of a trusted third party to assure certain properties of a data exchange.

places in the book. So we do not elaborate now, except to comment on the definition of encipherment. X.800 distinguishes between reversible encipherment mechanisms and irreversible encipherment mechanisms. A reversible encipherment mechanism is simply an encryption algorithm that allows data to be encrypted and subsequently decrypted. Irreversible encipherment mechanisms include hash algorithms and message authentication codes, which are used in digital signature and message authentication applications.

Table 1.4, based on one in X.800, indicates the relationship between security services and security mechanisms.

Table 1.4 Relationship Between Security Services and Mechanisms

SERVICE \ MECHANISM	Encipherment	Digital signature	Access control	Data integrity	Authentication exchange	Traffic padding	Routing control	Notarization
Peer entity authentication	Y	Y			Y			
Data origin authentication	Y	Y						
Access control			Y					
Confidentiality	Y						Y	
Traffic flow confidentiality	Y					Y	Y	
Data integrity	Y	Y		Y				
Nonrepudiation		Y		Y				Y
Availability				Y	Y			

1.6 FUNDAMENTAL SECURITY DESIGN PRINCIPLES

Despite years of research and development, it has not been possible to develop security design and implementation techniques that systematically exclude security flaws and prevent all unauthorized actions. In the absence of such foolproof techniques, it is useful to have a set of widely agreed design principles that can guide the development of protection mechanisms. The National Centers of Academic Excellence in Information Assurance/Cyber Defense, which is jointly sponsored by the U.S. National Security Agency and the U.S. Department of Homeland Security, list the following as fundamental security design principles [NCAE13]:

- Economy of mechanism
- Fail-safe defaults
- Complete mediation
- Open design
- Separation of privilege
- Least privilege
- Least common mechanism
- Psychological acceptability
- Isolation
- Encapsulation
- Modularity
- Layering
- Least astonishment

The first eight listed principles were first proposed in [SALT75] and have withstood the test of time. In this section, we briefly discuss each principle.

Economy of mechanism means that the design of security measures embodied in both hardware and software should be as simple and small as possible. The motivation for this principle is that relatively simple, small design is easier to test and verify thoroughly. With a complex design, there are many more opportunities for an adversary to discover subtle weaknesses to exploit that may be difficult to spot ahead of time. The more complex the mechanism, the more likely it is to possess exploitable flaws. Simple mechanisms tend to have fewer exploitable flaws and require less maintenance. Further, because configuration management issues are simplified, updating or replacing a simple mechanism becomes a less intensive process. In practice, this is perhaps the most difficult principle to honor. There is a constant demand for new features in both hardware and software, complicating the security design task. The best that can be done is to keep this principle in mind during system design to try to eliminate unnecessary complexity.

Fail-safe defaults means that access decisions should be based on permission rather than exclusion. That is, the default situation is lack of access, and the protection scheme identifies conditions under which access is permitted. This approach exhibits a better failure mode than the alternative approach, where the default is to permit access. A design or implementation mistake in a mechanism that gives explicit permission tends to fail by refusing permission, a safe situation that can be quickly detected. On the other hand, a design or implementation mistake in a mechanism that explicitly excludes access tends to fail by allowing access, a failure that may long go unnoticed in normal use. Most file access systems and virtually all protected services on client/server systems use fail-safe defaults.

Complete mediation means that every access must be checked against the access control mechanism. Systems should not rely on access decisions retrieved from a cache. In a system designed to operate continuously, this principle requires that, if access decisions are remembered for future use, careful consideration be given to how changes in authority are propagated into such local memories. File access systems appear to provide an example of a system that complies with this principle. However, typically, once a user has opened a file, no check is made to see if permissions change. To fully implement complete mediation, every time a user reads a field or record in a file, or a data item in a database, the system must exercise access control. This resource-intensive approach is rarely used.

Open design means that the design of a security mechanism should be open rather than secret. For example, although encryption keys must be secret, encryption algorithms should be open to public scrutiny. The algorithms can then be reviewed by many experts, and users can therefore have high confidence in them. This is the philosophy behind the National Institute of Standards and Technology (NIST) program of standardizing encryption and hash algorithms, and has led to the widespread adoption of NIST-approved algorithms.

Separation of privilege is defined in [SALT75] as a practice in which multiple privilege attributes are required to achieve access to a restricted resource. A good example of this is multifactor user authentication, which requires the use of multiple techniques, such as a password and a smart card, to authorize a user. The term is also now applied to any technique in which a program is divided into parts that are limited to the specific privileges they require in order to perform a specific task. This is used to mitigate the potential damage of a computer security attack. One example of this latter interpretation of the principle is removing high privilege operations to another process and running that process with the higher privileges required to perform its tasks. Day-to-day interfaces are executed in a lower privileged process.

Least privilege means that every process and every user of the system should operate using the least set of privileges necessary to perform the task. A good example of the use of this principle is role-based access control. The system security policy can identify and define the various roles of users or processes. Each role is assigned only those permissions needed to perform its functions. Each permission specifies a permitted access to a particular resource (such as read and write access to a specified file or directory, connect access to a given host and port). Unless a permission is granted explicitly, the user or process should not be able to access the protected resource. More generally, any access control system should allow each user only the privileges that are authorized for that user. There is also a temporal aspect to the least privilege principle. For example, system programs or administrators who have special privileges should have those privileges only when necessary;

when they are doing ordinary activities the privileges should be withdrawn. Leaving them in place just opens the door to accidents.

Least common mechanism means that the design should minimize the functions shared by different users, providing mutual security. This principle helps reduce the number of unintended communication paths and reduces the amount of hardware and software on which all users depend, thus making it easier to verify if there are any undesirable security implications.

Psychological acceptability implies that the security mechanisms should not interfere unduly with the work of users, while at the same time meeting the needs of those who authorize access. If security mechanisms hinder the usability or accessibility of resources, then users may opt to turn off those mechanisms. Where possible, security mechanisms should be transparent to the users of the system or at most introduce minimal obstruction. In addition to not being intrusive or burdensome, security procedures must reflect the user's mental model of protection. If the protection procedures do not make sense to the user or if the user must translate his image of protection into a substantially different protocol, the user is likely to make errors.

Isolation is a principle that applies in three contexts. First, public access systems should be isolated from critical resources (data, processes, etc.) to prevent disclosure or tampering. In cases where the sensitivity or criticality of the information is high, organizations may want to limit the number of systems on which that data is stored and isolate them, either physically or logically. Physical isolation may include ensuring that no physical connection exists between an organization's public access information resources and an organization's critical information. When implementing logical isolation solutions, layers of security services and mechanisms should be established between public systems and secure systems responsible for protecting critical resources. Second, the processes and files of individual users should be isolated from one another except where it is explicitly desired. All modern operating systems provide facilities for such isolation, so that individual users have separate, isolated process space, memory space, and file space, with protections for preventing unauthorized access. And finally, security mechanisms should be isolated in the sense of preventing access to those mechanisms. For example, logical access control may provide a means of isolating cryptographic software from other parts of the host system and for protecting cryptographic software from tampering and the keys from replacement or disclosure.

Encapsulation can be viewed as a specific form of isolation based on object-oriented functionality. Protection is provided by encapsulating a collection of procedures and data objects in a domain of its own so that the internal structure of a data object is accessible only to the procedures of the protected subsystem, and the procedures may be called only at designated domain entry points.

Modularity in the context of security refers both to the development of security functions as separate, protected modules and to the use of a modular architecture for mechanism design and implementation. With respect to the use of separate security modules, the design goal here is to provide common security functions and services, such as cryptographic functions, as common modules. For example, numerous protocols and applications make use of cryptographic functions. Rather than implementing such functions in each protocol or application, a more secure design is provided by developing a common cryptographic module that can be invoked by numerous protocols and applications. The design and implementation effort can then focus on the secure design and implementation of a single cryptographic module and including mechanisms to protect the module from tampering. With respect to the use of a modular architecture, each security mechanism should be able to support migration to new technology or upgrade of new features without requiring an entire system redesign. The security design should be modular so that individual parts of the security design can be upgraded without the requirement to modify the entire system.

Layering refers to the use of multiple, overlapping protection approaches addressing the people, technology, and operational aspects of information systems. By using multiple, overlapping protection approaches, the failure or circumvention of any individual protection approach will not leave the system unprotected. We will see throughout this book that a layering approach is often used to provide multiple barriers between an adversary and protected information or services. This technique is often referred to as *defense in depth*.

Least astonishment means that a program or user interface should always respond in the way that is least likely to astonish the user. For example, the mechanism for authorization should be transparent enough to a user that the user has a good intuitive understanding of how the security goals map to the provided security mechanism.

1.7 ATTACK SURFACES AND ATTACK TREES

In Section 1.3, we provided an overview of the spectrum of security threats and attacks facing computer and network systems. Section 22.1 goes into more detail about the nature of attacks and the types of adversaries that present security threats. In this section, we elaborate on two concepts that are useful in evaluating and classifying threats: attack surfaces and attack trees.

Attack Surfaces

An attack surface consists of the reachable and exploitable vulnerabilities in a system [MANA11, HOWA03]. Examples of attack surfaces are the following:

- Open ports on outward facing Web and other servers, and code listening on those ports
- Services available on the inside of a firewall
- Code that processes incoming data, email, XML, office documents, and industry-specific custom data exchange formats
- Interfaces, SQL, and Web forms
- An employee with access to sensitive information vulnerable to a social engineering attack

Attack surfaces can be categorized as follows:

- **Network attack surface:** This category refers to vulnerabilities over an enterprise network, wide-area network, or the Internet. Included in this category are network protocol vulnerabilities, such as those used for a denial-of-service attack, disruption of communications links, and various forms of intruder attacks.

- **Software attack surface:** This refers to vulnerabilities in application, utility, or operating system code. A particular focus in this category is Web server software.
- **Human attack surface:** This category refers to vulnerabilities created by personnel or outsiders, such as social engineering, human error, and trusted insiders.

An attack surface analysis is a useful technique for assessing the scale and severity of threats to a system. A systematic analysis of points of vulnerability makes developers and security analysts aware of where security mechanisms are required. Once an attack surface is defined, designers may be able to find ways to make the surface smaller, thus making the task of the adversary more difficult. The attack surface also provides guidance on setting priorities for testing, strengthening security measures, and modifying the service or application.

As illustrated in Figure 1.3, the use of layering, or defense in depth, and attack surface reduction complement each other in mitigating security risk.

Attack Trees

An attack tree is a branching, hierarchical data structure that represents a set of potential techniques for exploiting security vulnerabilities [MAUW05, MOOR01, SCHN99]. The security incident that is the goal of the attack is represented as the root node of the tree, and the ways that an attacker could reach that goal are iteratively and incrementally represented as branches and subnodes of the tree. Each subnode defines a subgoal, and each subgoal may have its own set of further subgoals, and so on. The final nodes on the paths outward from the root, that is, the leaf nodes, represent different ways to initiate an attack. Each node other than a leaf is either an AND-node or an OR-node. To achieve the goal represented by an AND-node, the subgoals represented by all of that node's subnodes must be achieved; and for an OR-node, at least one of the subgoals must be achieved. Branches can be labeled with values representing difficulty, cost, or other attack attributes, so that alternative attacks can be compared.

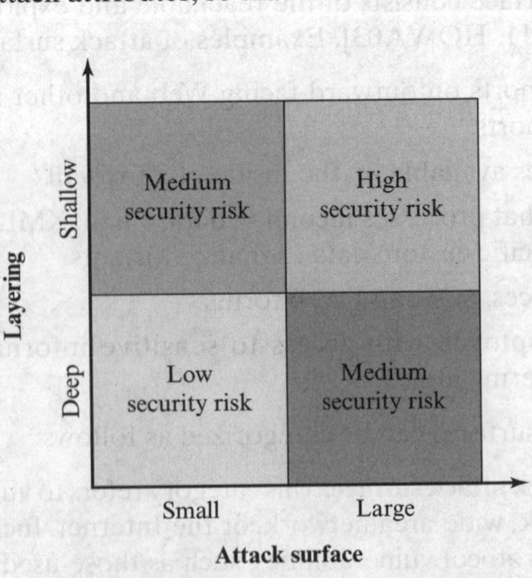

Figure 1.3 Defense in Depth and Attack Surface

The motivation for the use of attack trees is to effectively exploit the information available on attack patterns. Organizations such as CERT publish security advisories that have enabled the development of a body of knowledge about both general attack strategies and specific attack patterns. Security analysts can use the attack tree to document security attacks in a structured form that reveals key vulnerabilities. The attack tree can guide both the design of systems and applications, and the choice and strength of countermeasures.

Figure 1.4, based on a figure in [DIMI07], is an example of an attack tree analysis for an Internet banking authentication application. The root of the tree is the objective of the attacker, which is to compromise a user's account. The shaded boxes on the tree are the leaf nodes, which represent events that comprise the attacks. Note that in this tree, all the nodes other than leaf nodes are OR-nodes. The analysis to generate this tree considered the three components involved in authentication:

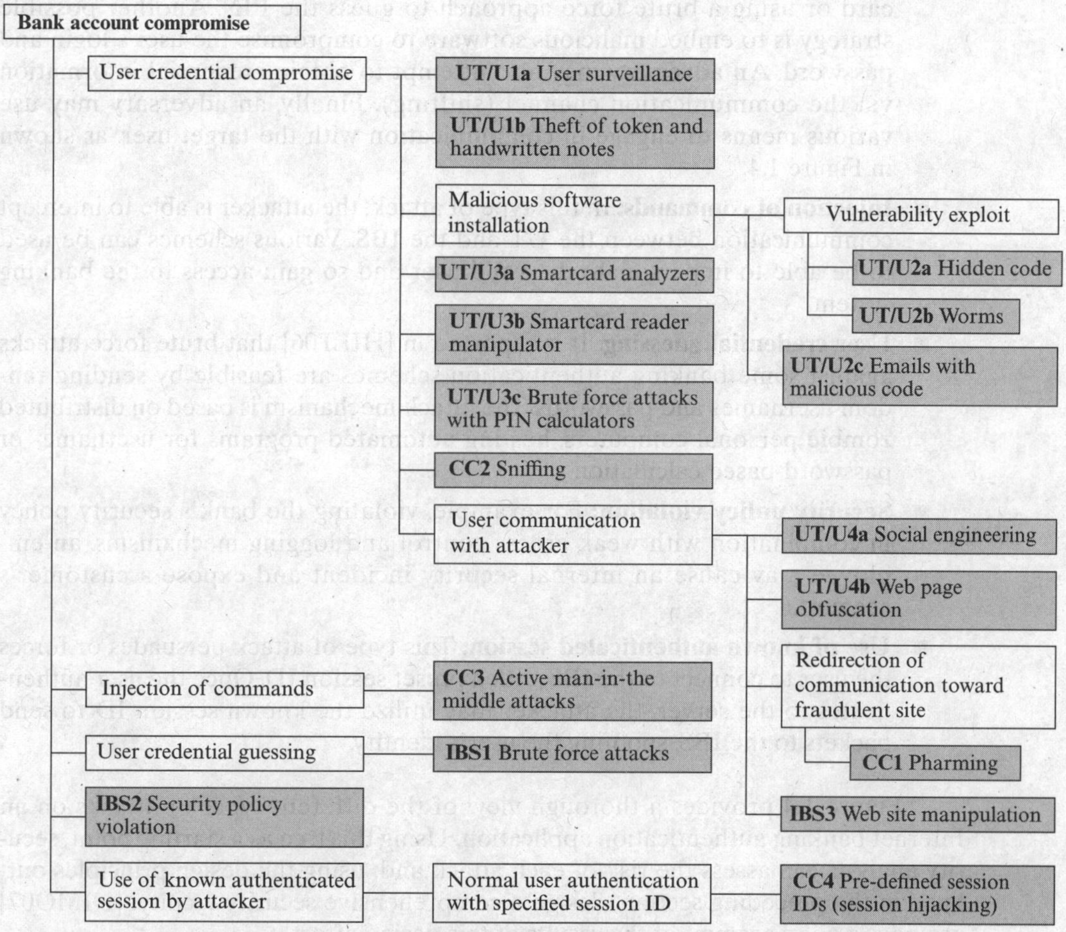

Figure 1.4 An Attack Tree for Internet Banking Authentication

- **User terminal and user (UT/U):** These attacks target the user equipment, including the tokens that may be involved, such as smartcards or other password generators, as well as the actions of the user.
- **Communications channel (CC):** This type of attack focuses on communication links.
- **Internet banking server (IBS):** These types of attacks are offline attacks against the servers that host the Internet banking application.

Five overall attack strategies can be identified, each of which exploits one or more of the three components. The five strategies are as follows:

- **User credential compromise:** This strategy can be used against many elements of the attack surface. There are procedural attacks, such as monitoring a user's action to observe a PIN or other credential, or theft of the user's token or handwritten notes. An adversary may also compromise token information using a variety of token attack tools, such as hacking the smartcard or using a brute force approach to guess the PIN. Another possible strategy is to embed malicious software to compromise the user's login and password. An adversary may also attempt to obtain credential information via the communication channel (sniffing). Finally, an adversary may use various means to engage in communication with the target user, as shown in Figure 1.4.
- **Injection of commands:** In this type of attack, the attacker is able to intercept communication between the UT and the IBS. Various schemes can be used to be able to impersonate the valid user and so gain access to the banking system.
- **User credential guessing:** It is reported in [HILT06] that brute force attacks against some banking authentication schemes are feasible by sending random usernames and passwords. The attack mechanism is based on distributed zombie personal computers, hosting automated programs for username- or password-based calculation.
- **Security policy violation:** For example, violating the bank's security policy in combination with weak access control and logging mechanisms, an employee may cause an internal security incident and expose a customer's account.
- **Use of known authenticated session:** This type of attack persuades or forces the user to connect to the IBS with a preset session ID. Once the user authenticates to the server, the attacker may utilize the known session ID to send packets to the IBS, spoofing the user's identity.

Figure 1.4 provides a thorough view of the different types of attacks on an Internet banking authentication application. Using this tree as a starting point, security analysts can assess the risk of each attack and, using the design principles outlined in the preceding section, design a comprehensive security facility. [DIMO07] provides a good account of the results of this design effort.

1.8 A MODEL FOR NETWORK SECURITY

A model for much of what we will be discussing is captured, in very general terms, in Figure 1.5. A message is to be transferred from one party to another across some sort of Internet service. The two parties, who are the *principals* in this transaction, must cooperate for the exchange to take place. A logical information channel is established by defining a route through the Internet from source to destination and by the cooperative use of communication protocols (e.g., TCP/IP) by the two principals.

Security aspects come into play when it is necessary or desirable to protect the information transmission from an opponent who may present a threat to confidentiality, authenticity, and so on. All the techniques for providing security have two components:

- A security-related transformation on the information to be sent. Examples include the encryption of the message, which scrambles the message so that it is unreadable by the opponent, and the addition of a code based on the contents of the message, which can be used to verify the identity of the sender.
- Some secret information shared by the two principals and, it is hoped, unknown to the opponent. An example is an encryption key used in conjunction with the transformation to scramble the message before transmission and unscramble it on reception.[6]

A trusted third party may be needed to achieve secure transmission. For example, a third party may be responsible for distributing the secret information

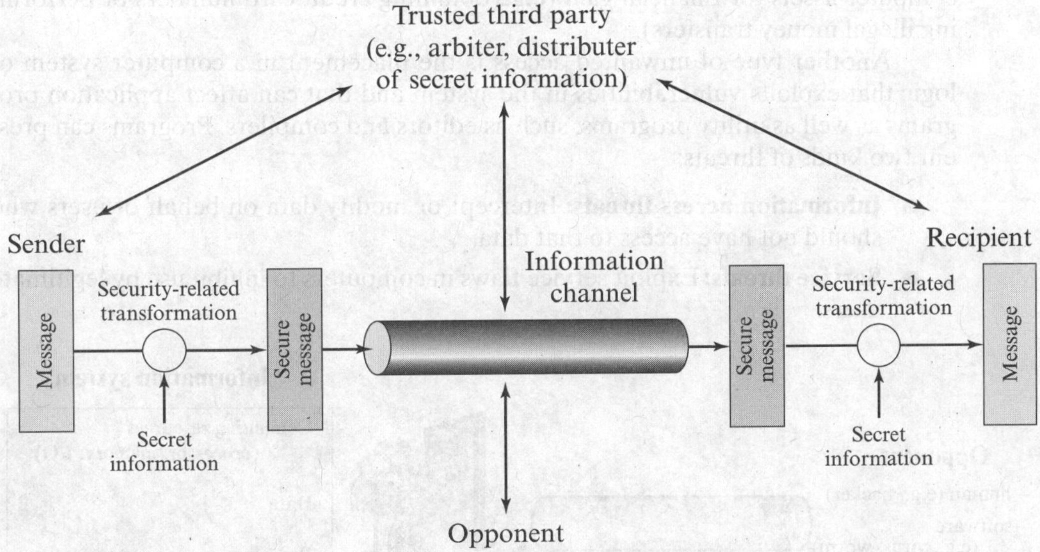

Figure 1.5 Model for Network Security

[6]Part Two discusses a form of encryption, known as a symmetric encryption, in which only one of the two principals needs to have the secret information.

to the two principals while keeping it from any opponent. Or a third party may be needed to arbitrate disputes between the two principals concerning the authenticity of a message transmission.

This general model shows that there are four basic tasks in designing a particular security service:

1. Design an algorithm for performing the security-related transformation. The algorithm should be such that an opponent cannot defeat its purpose.
2. Generate the secret information to be used with the algorithm.
3. Develop methods for the distribution and sharing of the secret information.
4. Specify a protocol to be used by the two principals that makes use of the security algorithm and the secret information to achieve a particular security service.

Parts One through Five of this book concentrate on the types of security mechanisms and services that fit into the model shown in Figure 1.5. However, there are other security-related situations of interest that do not neatly fit this model but are considered in this book. A general model of these other situations is illustrated in Figure 1.6, which reflects a concern for protecting an information system from unwanted access. Most readers are familiar with the concerns caused by the existence of hackers, who attempt to penetrate systems that can be accessed over a network. The hacker can be someone who, with no malign intent, simply gets satisfaction from breaking and entering a computer system. The intruder can be a disgruntled employee who wishes to do damage or a criminal who seeks to exploit computer assets for financial gain (e.g., obtaining credit card numbers or performing illegal money transfers).

Another type of unwanted access is the placement in a computer system of logic that exploits vulnerabilities in the system and that can affect application programs as well as utility programs, such as editors and compilers. Programs can present two kinds of threats:

- **Information access threats:** Intercept or modify data on behalf of users who should not have access to that data.
- **Service threats:** Exploit service flaws in computers to inhibit use by legitimate users.

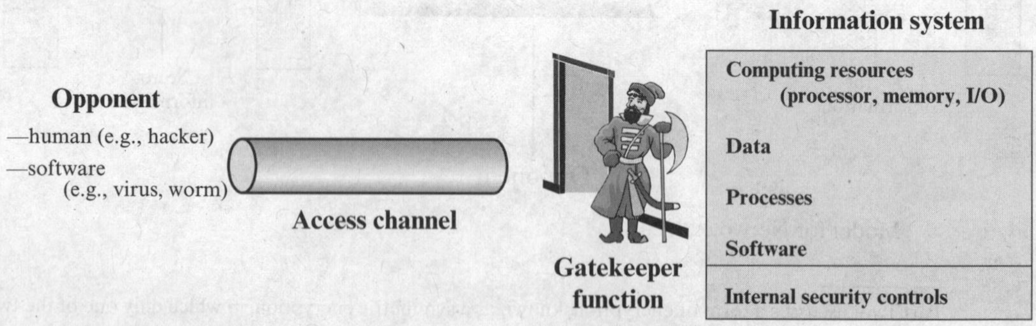

Figure 1.6 Network Access Security Model

Viruses and worms are two examples of software attacks. Such attacks can be introduced into a system by means of a disk that contains the unwanted logic concealed in otherwise useful software. They can also be inserted into a system across a network; this latter mechanism is of more concern in network security.

The security mechanisms needed to cope with unwanted access fall into two broad categories (see Figure 1.6). The first category might be termed a gatekeeper function. It includes password-based login procedures that are designed to deny access to all but authorized users and screening logic that is designed to detect and reject worms, viruses, and other similar attacks. Once either an unwanted user or unwanted software gains access, the second line of defense consists of a variety of internal controls that monitor activity and analyze stored information in an attempt to detect the presence of unwanted intruders. These issues are explored in Part Six.

1.9 STANDARDS

Many of the security techniques and applications described in this book have been specified as standards. Additionally, standards have been developed to cover management practices and the overall architecture of security mechanisms and services. Throughout this book, we describe the most important standards in use or that are being developed for various aspects of cryptography and network security. Various organizations have been involved in the development or promotion of these standards. The most important (in the current context) of these organizations are as follows:

- **National Institute of Standards and Technology:** NIST is a U.S. federal agency that deals with measurement science, standards, and technology related to U.S. government use and to the promotion of U.S. private-sector innovation. Despite its national scope, NIST Federal Information Processing Standards (FIPS) and Special Publications (SP) have a worldwide impact.
- **Internet Society:** ISOC is a professional membership society with worldwide organizational and individual membership. It provides leadership in addressing issues that confront the future of the Internet and is the organization home for the groups responsible for Internet infrastructure standards, including the Internet Engineering Task Force (IETF) and the Internet Architecture Board (IAB). These organizations develop Internet standards and related specifications, all of which are published as Requests for Comments (RFCs).
- **ITU-T:** The International Telecommunication Union (ITU) is an international organization within the United Nations System in which governments and the private sector coordinate global telecom networks and services. The ITU Telecommunication Standardization Sector (ITU-T) is one of the three sectors of the ITU. ITU-T's mission is the development of technical standards covering all fields of telecommunications. ITU-T standards are referred to as Recommendations.

- **ISO:** The International Organization for Standardization (ISO)[7] is a worldwide federation of national standards bodies from more than 140 countries, one from each country. ISO is a nongovernmental organization that promotes the development of standardization and related activities with a view to facilitating the international exchange of goods and services and to developing cooperation in the spheres of intellectual, scientific, technological, and economic activity. ISO's work results in international agreements that are published as International Standards.

A more detailed discussion of these organizations is contained in Appendix D.

1.10 KEY TERMS, REVIEW QUESTIONS, AND PROBLEMS

Key Terms

access control	denial of service	passive attack
active attack	encryption	replay
authentication	integrity	security attacks
authenticity	intruder	security mechanisms
availability	masquerade	security services
data confidentiality	nonrepudiation	traffic analysis
data integrity	OSI security architecture	

Review Questions

1.1 What is the OSI security architecture?

1.2 List and briefly define the essential network and computer security requirements.

1.3 List and briefly define categories of passive and active security attacks.

1.4 List and briefly define categories of security services.

1.5 Draw a matrix that shows the relationship between security services and security mechanisms.

1.6 List and briefly define the fundamental security design principles.

1.7 List and briefly define categories of attack surfaces.

Problems

1.1 Consider an automated cash deposit machine in which users provide a card or an account number to deposit cash. Give examples of confidentiality, integrity, and availability requirements associated with the system, and, in each case, indicate the degree of importance of the requirement.

1.2 Repeat Problem 1.1 for a payment gateway system where a user pays for an item using their account via the payment gateway.

---

[7]ISO is not an acronym (in which case it would be IOS), but it is a word, derived from the Greek, meaning *equal*.

1.3 Define the type of security attack in each of the following cases:

a. John gives a cheque of $14 to the shopkeeper to buy a book. Later he finds that the cheque was cashed for $140.

b. A student breaks into university's office to get a copy of exam paper to be held on the next day.

c. A person sends hundreds of e-mails every day to another person using a phony return e-mail address.

1.4 For each of the following assets, assign a low, moderate, or high impact level for the loss of confidentiality, availability, and integrity, respectively. Justify your answers.

a. A student maintaining a blog to post public information.

b. An examination section of a university that is managing sensitive information about exam papers.

c. An information system in a pathological laboratory maintaining the patient's data.

d. A student information system used for maintaining student data in a university that contains both personal, academic information and routine administrative information (not privacy related). Assess the impact for the two data sets separately and the information system as a whole.

e. A University library contains a library management system which controls the distribution of books amongst the students of various departments. The library management system contains both the student data and the book data. Assess the impact for the two data sets separately and the information system as a whole.

1.5 Draw a matrix similar to Table 1.4 that shows the relationship between security services and attacks.

1.6 Draw a matrix similar to Table 1.4 that shows the relationship between security mechanisms and attacks.

1.7 Develop an attack tree for gaining access to the contents of a physical safe.

1.8 Consider a company whose operations are housed in two buildings on the same property; one building is headquarters, the other building contains network and computer services. The property is physically protected by a fence around the perimeter, and the only entrance to the property is through this fenced perimeter. In addition to the perimeter fence, physical security consists of a guarded front gate. The local networks are split between the Headquarters' LAN and the Network Services' LAN. Internet users connect to the Web server through a firewall. Dial-up users get access to a particular server on the Network Services' LAN. Develop an attack tree in which the root node represents disclosure of proprietary secrets. Include physical, social engineering, and technical attacks. The tree may contain both AND and OR nodes. Develop a tree that has at least 15 leaf nodes.

1.9 Read all of the classic papers cited in the Recommended Reading section for this chapter, available at the Author Web site at WilliamStallings.com/Cryptography. The papers are available at box.com/Crypto7e. Compose a 500–1000 word paper (or 8–12 slide PowerPoint presentation) that summarizes the key concepts that emerge from these papers, emphasizing concepts that are common to most or all of the papers.

CHAPTER 2

INTRODUCTION TO NUMBER THEORY

LEARNING OBJECTIVES

After studying this chapter, you should be able to:

- Understand the concept of divisibility and the division algorithm.
- Understand how to use the Euclidean algorithm to find the greatest common divisor.
- Present an overview of the concepts of modular arithmetic.
- Explain the operation of the extended Euclidean algorithm.
- Discuss key concepts relating to prime numbers.
- Understand Fermat's theorem.
- Understand Euler's theorem.
- Define Euler's totient function.
- Make a presentation on the topic of testing for primality.
- Explain the Chinese remainder theorem.
- Define discrete logarithms.

Number theory is pervasive in cryptographic algorithms. This chapter provides sufficient breadth and depth of coverage of relevant number theory topics for understanding the wide range of applications in cryptography. The reader familiar with these topics can safely skip this chapter.

The first three sections introduce basic concepts from number theory that are needed for understanding finite fields; these include divisibility, the Euclidian algorithm, and modular arithmetic. The reader may study these sections now or wait until ready to tackle Chapter 5 on finite fields.

Sections 2.4 through 2.8 discuss aspects of number theory related to prime numbers and discrete logarithms. These topics are fundamental to the design of asymmetric (public-key) cryptographic algorithms. The reader may study these sections now or wait until ready to read Part Three.

The concepts and techniques of number theory are quite abstract, and it is often difficult to grasp them intuitively without examples. Accordingly, this chapter includes a number of examples, each of which is highlighted in a shaded box.

2.1 DIVISIBILITY AND THE DIVISION ALGORITHM

Divisibility

We say that a nonzero b **divides** a if $a = mb$ for some m, where a, b, and m are integers. That is, b divides a if there is no remainder on division. The notation $b|a$ is commonly used to mean b divides a. Also, if $b|a$, we say that b is a **divisor** of a.

The positive divisors of 24 are 1, 2, 3, 4, 6, 8, 12, and 24.
$13|182$; $-5|30$; $17|289$; $-3|33$; $17|0$

Subsequently, we will need some simple properties of divisibility for integers, which are as follows:

- If $a|1$, then $a = \pm 1$.
- If $a|b$ and $b|a$, then $a = \pm b$.
- Any $b \neq 0$ divides 0.
- If $a|b$ and $b|c$, then $a|c$:

$11|66$ and $66|198 \Rightarrow 11|198$

- If $b|g$ and $b|h$, then $b|(mg + nh)$ for arbitrary integers m and n.

To see this last point, note that

- If $b|g$, then g is of the form $g = b \times g_1$ for some integer g_1.
- If $b|h$, then h is of the form $h = b \times h_1$ for some integer h_1.

So

$$mg + nh = mbg_1 + nbh_1 = b \times (mg_1 + nh_1)$$

and therefore b divides $mg + nh$.

$b = 7$; $g = 14$; $h = 63$; $m = 3$; $n = 2$
$7|14$ and $7|63$.
To show $7|(3 \times 14 + 2 \times 63)$,
we have $(3 \times 14 + 2 \times 63) = 7(3 \times 2 + 2 \times 9)$,
and it is obvious that $7|(7(3 \times 2 + 2 \times 9))$.

The Division Algorithm

Given any positive integer n and any nonnegative integer a, if we divide a by n, we get an integer quotient q and an integer remainder r that obey the following relationship:

$$a = qn + r \qquad 0 \leq r < n; q = \lfloor a/n \rfloor \tag{2.1}$$

where $\lfloor x \rfloor$ is the largest integer less than or equal to x. Equation (2.1) is referred to as the division algorithm.[1]

[1]Equation (2.1) expresses a theorem rather than an algorithm, but by tradition, this is referred to as the division algorithm.

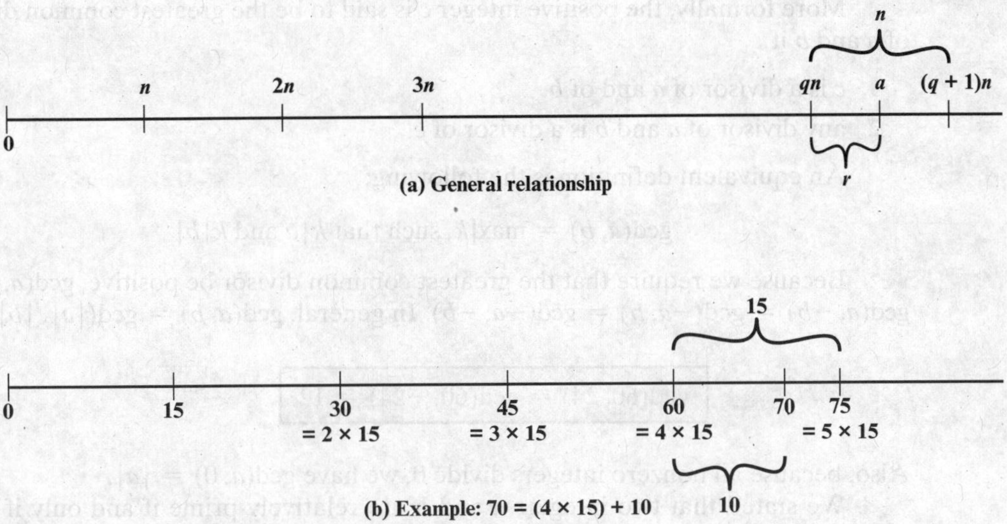

Figure 2.1 The Relationship $a = qn + r; 0 \leq r < n$

Figure 2.1a demonstrates that, given *a* and positive *n*, it is always possible to find *q* and *r* that satisfy the preceding relationship. Represent the integers on the number line; *a* will fall somewhere on that line (positive *a* is shown, a similar demonstration can be made for negative *a*). Starting at 0, proceed to *n*, 2*n*, up to *qn*, such that $qn \leq a$ and $(q + 1)n > a$. The distance from *qn* to *a* is *r*, and we have found the unique values of *q* and *r*. The remainder *r* is often referred to as a **residue**.

$a = 11; \quad n = 7; \quad 11 = 1 \times 7 + 4; \quad r = 4 \quad q = 1$

$a = -11; \quad n = 7; \quad -11 = (-2) \times 7 + 3; \quad r = 3 \quad q = -2$

Figure 2.1b provides another example.

2.2 THE EUCLIDEAN ALGORITHM

One of the basic techniques of number theory is the Euclidean algorithm, which is a simple procedure for determining the greatest common divisor of two positive integers. First, we need a simple definition: Two integers are **relatively prime** if and only if their only common positive integer factor is 1.

Greatest Common Divisor

Recall that nonzero *b* is defined to be a divisor of *a* if $a = mb$ for some *m*, where *a*, *b*, and *m* are integers. We will use the notation gcd(*a*, *b*) to mean the **greatest common divisor** of *a* and *b*. The greatest common divisor of *a* and *b* is the largest integer that divides both *a* and *b*. We also define $\gcd(0, 0) = 0$.

More formally, the positive integer c is said to be the greatest common divisor of a and b if

1. c is a divisor of a and of b.
2. any divisor of a and b is a divisor of c.

An equivalent definition is the following:

$$\gcd(a, b) = \max[k, \text{ such that } k|a \text{ and } k|b]$$

Because we require that the greatest common divisor be positive, $\gcd(a, b) = \gcd(a, -b) = \gcd(-a, b) = \gcd(-a, -b)$. In general, $\gcd(a, b) = \gcd(|a|, |b|)$.

> $\gcd(60, 24) = \gcd(60, -24) = 12$

Also, because all nonzero integers divide 0, we have $\gcd(a, 0) = |a|$.

We stated that two integers a and b are relatively prime if and only if their only common positive integer factor is 1. This is equivalent to saying that a and b are relatively prime if $\gcd(a, b) = 1$.

> 8 and 15 are relatively prime because the positive divisors of 8 are 1, 2, 4, and 8, and the positive divisors of 15 are 1, 3, 5, and 15. So 1 is the only integer on both lists.

Finding the Greatest Common Divisor

We now describe an algorithm credited to Euclid for easily finding the greatest common divisor of two integers (Figure 2.2). This algorithm has broad significance in cryptography. The explanation of the algorithm can be broken down into the following points:

1. Suppose we wish to determine the greatest common divisor d of the integers a and b; that is determine $d = \gcd(a, b)$. Because $\gcd(|a|, |b|) = \gcd(a, b)$, there is no harm in assuming $a \geq b > 0$.
2. Dividing a by b and applying the division algorithm, we can state:

$$a = q_1 b + r_1 \qquad 0 \leq r_1 < b \qquad \textbf{(2.2)}$$

3. First consider the case in which $r_1 = 0$. Therefore b divides a and clearly no larger number divides both b and a, because that number would be larger than b. So we have $d = \gcd(a, b) = b$.
4. The other possibility from Equation (2.2) is $r_1 \neq 0$. For this case, we can state that $d|r_1$. This is due to the basic properties of divisibility: the relations $d|a$ and $d|b$ together imply that $d|(a - q_1 b)$, which is the same as $d|r_1$.
5. Before proceeding with the Euclidian algorithm, we need to answer the question: What is the $\gcd(b, r_1)$? We know that $d|b$ and $d|r_1$. Now take any arbitrary integer c that divides both b and r_1. Therefore, $c|(q_1 b + r_1) = a$. Because c divides both a and b, we must have $c \leq d$, which is the greatest common divisor of a and b. Therefore $d = \gcd(b, r_1)$.

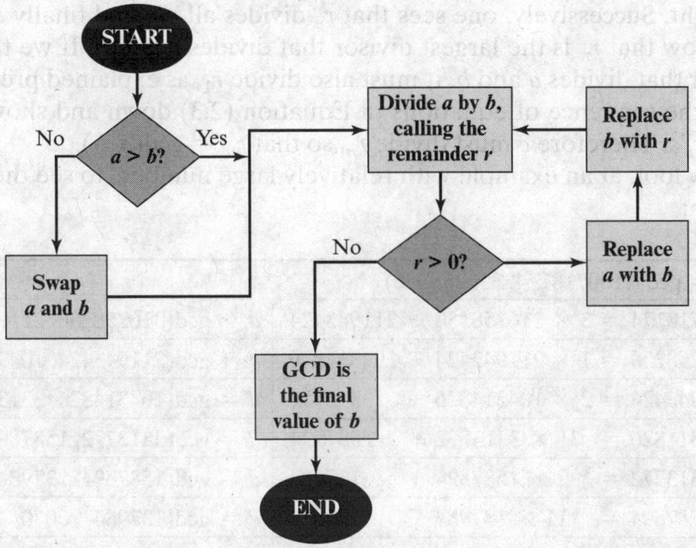

Figure 2.2 Euclidean Algorithm

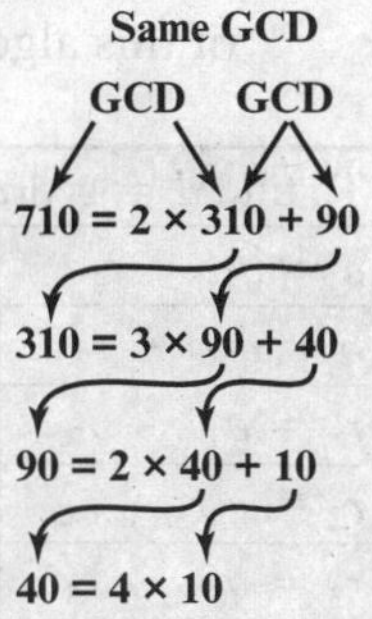

Figure 2.3 Euclidean Algorithm Example: gcd(710, 310)

Let us now return to Equation (2.2) and assume that $r_1 \neq 0$. Because $b > r_1$, we can divide b by r_1 and apply the division algorithm to obtain:

$$b = q_2 r_1 + r_2 \qquad 0 \leq r_2 < r_1$$

As before, if $r_2 = 0$, then $d = r_1$ and if $r_2 \neq 0$, then $d = \gcd(r_1, r_2)$. Note that the remainders form a descending series of nonnegative values and so must terminate when the remainder is zero. This happens, say, at the $(n + 1)$th stage where r_{n-1} is divided by r_n. The result is the following system of equations:

$$\left.\begin{array}{ll} a = q_1 b + r_1 & 0 < r_1 < b \\ b = q_2 r_1 + r_2 & 0 < r_2 < r_1 \\ r_1 = q_3 r_2 + r_3 & 0 < r_3 < r_2 \\ \bullet & \bullet \\ \bullet & \bullet \\ \bullet & \bullet \\ r_{n-2} = q_n r_{n-1} + r_n & 0 < r_n < r_{n-1} \\ r_{n-1} = q_{n+1} r_n + 0 & \\ d = \gcd(a, b) = r_n & \end{array}\right\} \qquad (2.3)$$

At each iteration, we have $d = \gcd(r_i, r_{i+1})$ until finally $d = \gcd(r_n, 0) = r_n$. Thus, we can find the greatest common divisor of two integers by repetitive application of the division algorithm. This scheme is known as the Euclidean algorithm. Figure 2.3 illustrates a simple example.

We have essentially argued from the top down that the final result is the gcd(a, b). We can also argue from the bottom up. The first step is to show that r_n divides a and b. It follows from the last division in Equation (2.3) that r_n divides r_{n-1}. The next to last division shows that r_n divides r_{n-2} because it divides both terms on the right. Successively, one sees that r_n divides all r_i's and finally a and b. It remains to show that r_n is the largest divisor that divides a and b. If we take any arbitrary integer that divides a and b, it must also divide r_1, as explained previously. We can follow the sequence of equations in Equation (2.3) down and show that c must divide all r_i's. Therefore c must divide r_n, so that $r_n = \gcd(a, b)$.

Let us now look at an example with relatively large numbers to see the power of this algorithm:

To find $d = \gcd(a, b) = \gcd(1160718174, 316258250)$		
$a = q_1 b + r_1$	1160718174 = 3 × 316258250 + 211943424	$d = \gcd(316258250, 211943424)$
$b = q_2 r_1 + r_2$	316258250 = 1 × 211943424 + 104314826	$d = \gcd(211943424, 104314826)$
$r_1 = q_3 r_2 + r_3$	211943424 = 2 × 104314826 + 3313772	$d = \gcd(104314826, 3313772)$
$r_2 = q_4 r_3 + r_4$	104314826 = 31 × 3313772 + 1587894	$d = \gcd(3313772, 1587894)$
$r_3 = q_5 r_4 + r_5$	3313772 = 2 × 1587894 + 137984	$d = \gcd(1587894, 137984)$
$r_4 = q_6 r_5 + r_6$	1587894 = 11 × 137984 + 70070	$d = \gcd(137984, 70070)$
$r_5 = q_7 r_6 + r_7$	137984 = 1 × 70070 + 67914	$d = \gcd(70070, 67914)$
$r_6 = q_8 r_7 + r_8$	70070 = 1 × 67914 + 2156	$d = \gcd(67914, 2156)$
$r_7 = q_9 r_8 + r_9$	67914 = 31 × 2156 + 1078	$d = \gcd(2156, 1078)$
$r_8 = q_{10} r_9 + r_{10}$	2156 = 2 × 1078 + 0	$d = \gcd(1078, 0) = 1078$
Therefore, $d = \gcd(1160718174, 316258250) = 1078$		

In this example, we begin by dividing 1160718174 by 316258250, which gives 3 with a remainder of 211943424. Next we take 316258250 and divide it by 211943424. The process continues until we get a remainder of 0, yielding a result of 1078.

It will be helpful in what follows to recast the above computation in tabular form. For every step of the iteration, we have $r_{i-2} = q_i r_{i-1} + r_i$, where r_{i-2} is the dividend, r_{i-1} is the divisor, q_i is the quotient, and r_i is the remainder. Table 2.1 summarizes the results.

Table 2.1 Euclidean Algorithm Example

Dividend	Divisor	Quotient	Remainder
a = 1160718174	b = 316258250	q_1 = 3	r_1 = 211943424
b = 316258250	r_1 = 211943434	q_2 = 1	r_2 = 104314826
r_1 = 211943424	r_2 = 104314826	q_3 = 2	r_3 = 3313772
r_2 = 104314826	r_3 = 3313772	q_4 = 31	r_4 = 1587894
r_3 = 3313772	r_4 = 1587894	q_5 = 2	r_5 = 137984
r_4 = 1587894	r_5 = 137984	q_6 = 11	r_6 = 70070
r_5 = 137984	r_6 = 70070	q_7 = 1	r_7 = 67914
r_6 = 70070	r_7 = 67914	q_8 = 1	r_8 = 2156
r_7 = 67914	r_8 = 2156	q_9 = 31	r_9 = 1078
r_8 = 2156	r_9 = 1078	q_{10} = 2	r_{10} = 0

2.3 MODULAR ARITHMETIC

The Modulus

If a is an integer and n is a positive integer, we define $a \bmod n$ to be the remainder when a is divided by n. The integer n is called the **modulus**. Thus, for any integer a, we can rewrite Equation (2.1) as follows:

$$a = qn + r \qquad 0 \le r < n; q = \lfloor a/n \rfloor$$

$$a = \lfloor a/n \rfloor \times n + (a \bmod n)$$

$11 \bmod 7 = 4; \qquad -11 \bmod 7 = 3$

Two integers a and b are said to be **congruent modulo** $\boldsymbol{n}$, if $(a \bmod n) = (b \bmod n)$. This is written as $a \equiv b \pmod{n}$.[2]

$73 \equiv 4 \pmod{23}$;	$21 \equiv -9 \pmod{10}$

Note that if $a \equiv 0 \pmod{n}$, then $n \mid a$.

Properties of Congruences

Congruences have the following properties:

1. $a \equiv b \pmod{n}$ if $n \mid (a - b)$.
2. $a \equiv b \pmod{n}$ implies $b \equiv a \pmod{n}$.
3. $a \equiv b \pmod{n}$ and $b \equiv c \pmod{n}$ imply $a \equiv c \pmod{n}$.

To demonstrate the first point, if $n \mid (a - b)$, then $(a - b) = kn$ for some k. So we can write $a = b + kn$. Therefore, $(a \bmod n) =$ (remainder when $b + kn$ is divided by n) $=$ (remainder when b is divided by n) $= (b \bmod n)$.

$23 \equiv 8 \pmod{5}$	because	$23 - 8 = 15 = 5 \times 3$
$-11 \equiv 5 \pmod{8}$	because	$-11 - 5 = -16 = 8 \times (-2)$
$81 \equiv 0 \pmod{27}$	because	$81 - 0 = 81 = 27 \times 3$

The remaining points are as easily proved.

---

[2]We have just used the operator *mod* in two different ways: first as a **binary operator** that produces a remainder, as in the expression $a \bmod b$; second as a **congruence relation** that shows the equivalence of two integers, as in the expression $a \equiv b \pmod{n}$. See Appendix 2A for a discussion.

Modular Arithmetic Operations

Note that, by definition (Figure 2.1), the (mod n) operator maps all integers into the set of integers $\{0, 1, \ldots, (n - 1)\}$. This suggests the question: Can we perform arithmetic operations within the confines of this set? It turns out that we can; this technique is known as **modular arithmetic**.

Modular arithmetic exhibits the following properties:

1. $[(a \bmod n) + (b \bmod n)] \bmod n = (a + b) \bmod n$
2. $[(a \bmod n) - (b \bmod n)] \bmod n = (a - b) \bmod n$
3. $[(a \bmod n) \times (b \bmod n)] \bmod n = (a \times b) \bmod n$

We demonstrate the first property. Define $(a \bmod n) = r_a$ and $(b \bmod n) = r_b$. Then we can write $a = r_a + jn$ for some integer j and $b = r_b + kn$ for some integer k. Then

$$\begin{aligned}(a + b) \bmod n &= (r_a + jn + r_b + kn) \bmod n \\ &= (r_a + r_b + (k + j)n) \bmod n \\ &= (r_a + r_b) \bmod n \\ &= [(a \bmod n) + (b \bmod n)] \bmod n\end{aligned}$$

The remaining properties are proven as easily. Here are examples of the three properties:

11 mod 8 = 3; 15 mod 8 = 7
[(11 mod 8) + (15 mod 8)] mod 8 = 10 mod 8 = 2
(11 + 15) mod 8 = 26 mod 8 = 2
[(11 mod 8) − (15 mod 8)] mod 8 = −4 mod 8 = 4
(11 − 15) mod 8 = −4 mod 8 = 4
[(11 mod 8) × (15 mod 8)] mod 8 = 21 mod 8 = 5
(11 × 15) mod 8 = 165 mod 8 = 5

Exponentiation is performed by repeated multiplication, as in ordinary arithmetic.

To find $11^7 \bmod 13$, we can proceed as follows:

$$\begin{aligned}&11^2 = 121 \equiv 4 \pmod{13} \\ &11^4 = (11^2)^2 \equiv 4^2 \equiv 3 \pmod{13} \\ &11^7 = 11 \times 11^2 \times 11^4 \\ &11^7 \equiv 11 \times 4 \times 3 \equiv 132 \equiv 2 \pmod{13}\end{aligned}$$

Thus, the rules for ordinary arithmetic involving addition, subtraction, and multiplication carry over into modular arithmetic.

Table 2.2 provides an illustration of modular addition and multiplication modulo 8. Looking at addition, the results are straightforward, and there is a regular pattern to the matrix. Both matrices are symmetric about the main diagonal in conformance to the commutative property of addition and multiplication. As in ordinary addition, there is an additive inverse, or negative, to each integer in modular arithmetic. In this case, the negative of an integer x is the integer y such that $(x + y) \bmod 8 = 0$. To find the additive inverse of an integer in the left-hand column, scan across the corresponding row of the matrix to find the value 0; the integer at the top of that column is the additive inverse; thus, $(2 + 6) \bmod 8 = 0$. Similarly, the entries in the multiplication table are straightforward. In modular arithmetic mod 8, the multiplicative inverse of x is the integer y such that $(x \times y) \bmod 8 = 1 \bmod 8$. Now, to find the multiplicative inverse of an integer from the multiplication table, scan across the matrix in the row for that integer to find the value 1; the integer at the top of that column is the multiplicative inverse; thus, $(3 \times 3) \bmod 8 = 1$. Note that not all integers mod 8 have a multiplicative inverse; more about that later.

Properties of Modular Arithmetic

Define the set Z_n as the set of nonnegative integers less than n:

$$Z_n = \{0, 1, \ldots, (n - 1)\}$$

Table 2.2 Arithmetic Modulo 8

+	0	1	2	3	4	5	6	7
0	0	1	2	3	4	5	6	7
1	1	2	3	4	5	6	7	0
2	2	3	4	5	6	7	0	1
3	3	4	5	6	7	0	1	2
4	4	5	6	7	0	1	2	3
5	5	6	7	0	1	2	3	4
6	6	7	0	1	2	3	4	5
7	7	0	1	2	3	4	5	6

(a) Addition modulo 8

×	0	1	2	3	4	5	6	7
0	0	0	0	0	0	0	0	0
1	0	1	2	3	4	5	6	7
2	0	2	4	6	0	2	4	6
3	0	3	6	1	4	7	2	5
4	0	4	0	4	0	4	0	4
5	0	5	2	7	4	1	6	3
6	0	6	4	2	0	6	4	2
7	0	7	6	5	4	3	2	1

(b) Multiplication modulo 8

w	$-w$	w^{-1}
0	0	—
1	7	1
2	6	—
3	5	3
4	4	—
5	3	5
6	2	—
7	1	7

(c) Additive and multiplicative inverse modulo 8

This is referred to as the **set of residues**, or **residue classes** (mod n). To be more precise, each integer in Z_n represents a residue class. We can label the residue classes (mod n) as [0], [1], [2], . . . , [n – 1], where

$$[r] = \{a: a \text{ is an integer}, a \equiv r \pmod{n}\}$$

> The residue classes (mod 4) are
> $[0] = \{\ldots, -16, -12, -8, -4, 0, 4, 8, 12, 16, \ldots\}$
> $[1] = \{\ldots, -15, -11, -7, -3, 1, 5, 9, 13, 17, \ldots\}$
> $[2] = \{\ldots, -14, -10, -6, -2, 2, 6, 10, 14, 18, \ldots\}$
> $[3] = \{\ldots, -13, -9, -5, -1, 3, 7, 11, 15, 19, \ldots\}$

Of all the integers in a residue class, the smallest nonnegative integer is the one used to represent the residue class. Finding the smallest nonnegative integer to which k is congruent modulo n is called **reducing k modulo n.**

If we perform modular arithmetic within Z_n, the properties shown in Table 2.3 hold for integers in Z_n. We show in the next section that this implies that Z_n is a commutative ring with a multiplicative identity element.

There is one peculiarity of modular arithmetic that sets it apart from ordinary arithmetic. First, observe that (as in ordinary arithmetic) we can write the following:

$$\textbf{if } (a + b) \equiv (a + c) \pmod{n} \textbf{ then } b \equiv c \pmod{n} \qquad \textbf{(2.4)}$$

> $(5 + 23) \equiv (5 + 7)(\text{mod } 8); 23 \equiv 7(\text{mod } 8)$

Equation (2.4) is consistent with the existence of an additive inverse. Adding the additive inverse of a to both sides of Equation (2.4), we have

$$((-a) + a + b) \equiv ((-a) + a + c)(\text{mod } n)$$
$$b \equiv c \pmod{n}$$

Table 2.3 Properties of Modular Arithmetic for Integers in Z_n

Property	Expression
Commutative Laws	$(w + x) \bmod n = (x + w) \bmod n$ $(w \times x) \bmod n = (x \times w) \bmod n$
Associative Laws	$[(w + x) + y] \bmod n = [w + (x + y)] \bmod n$ $[(w \times x) \times y] \bmod n = [w \times (x \times y)] \bmod n$
Distributive Law	$[w \times (x + y)] \bmod n = [(w \times x) + (w \times y)] \bmod n$
Identities	$(0 + w) \bmod n = w \bmod n$ $(1 \times w) \bmod n = w \bmod n$
Additive Inverse ($-w$)	For each $w \in Z_n$, there exists a z such that $w + z \equiv 0 \bmod n$

However, the following statement is true only with the attached condition:

if $(a \times b) \equiv (a \times c)(\text{mod } n)$ **then** $b \equiv c(\text{mod } n)$ **if** a is relatively prime to n **(2.5)**

Recall that two integers are **relatively prime** if their only common positive integer factor is 1. Similar to the case of Equation (2.4), we can say that Equation (2.5) is consistent with the existence of a multiplicative inverse. Applying the multiplicative inverse of a to both sides of Equation (2.5), we have

$$((a^{-1})ab) \equiv ((a^{-1})ac)(\text{mod } n)$$
$$b \equiv c(\text{mod } n)$$

To see this, consider an example in which the condition of Equation (2.5) does not hold. The integers 6 and 8 are not relatively prime, since they have the common factor 2. We have the following:

$$6 \times 3 = 18 \equiv 2(\text{mod } 8)$$
$$6 \times 7 = 42 \equiv 2(\text{mod } 8)$$

Yet $3 \not\equiv 7 \ (\text{mod } 8)$.

The reason for this strange result is that for any general modulus n, a multiplier a that is applied in turn to the integers 0 through $(n - 1)$ will fail to produce a complete set of residues if a and n have any factors in common.

With $a = 6$ and $n = 8$,

Z_8	0	1	2	3	4	5	6	7
Multiply by 6	0	6	12	18	24	30	36	42
Residues	0	6	4	2	0	6	4	2

Because we do not have a complete set of residues when multiplying by 6, more than one integer in Z_8 maps into the same residue. Specifically, $6 \times 0 \text{ mod } 8 = 6 \times 4 \text{ mod } 8$; $6 \times 1 \text{ mod } 8 = 6 \times 5 \text{ mod } 8$; and so on. Because this is a many-to-one mapping, there is not a unique inverse to the multiply operation.

However, if we take $a = 5$ and $n = 8$, whose only common factor is 1,

Z_8	0	1	2	3	4	5	6	7
Multiply by 5	0	5	10	15	20	25	30	35
Residues	0	5	2	7	4	1	6	3

The line of residues contains all the integers in Z_8, in a different order.

In general, an integer has a multiplicative inverse in Z_n if and only if that integer is relatively prime to n. Table 2.2c shows that the integers 1, 3, 5, and 7 have a multiplicative inverse in Z_8; but 2, 4, and 6 do not.

Euclidean Algorithm Revisited

The Euclidean algorithm can be based on the following theorem: For any integers a, b, with $a \geq b \geq 0$,

$$\gcd(a, b) = \gcd(b, a \bmod b) \qquad \textbf{(2.6)}$$

$$\gcd(55, 22) = \gcd(22, 55 \bmod 22) = \gcd(22, 11) = 11$$

To see that Equation (2.6) works, let $d = \gcd(a, b)$. Then, by the definition of gcd, $d|a$ and $d|b$. For any positive integer b, we can express a as

$$a = kb + r \equiv r \pmod{b}$$
$$a \bmod b = r$$

with k, r integers. Therefore, $(a \bmod b) = a - kb$ for some integer k. But because $d|b$, it also divides kb. We also have $d|a$. Therefore, $d|(a \bmod b)$. This shows that d is a common divisor of b and $(a \bmod b)$. Conversely, if d is a common divisor of b and $(a \bmod b)$, then $d|kb$ and thus $d|[kb + (a \bmod b)]$, which is equivalent to $d|a$. Thus, the set of common divisors of a and b is equal to the set of common divisors of b and $(a \bmod b)$. Therefore, the gcd of one pair is the same as the gcd of the other pair, proving the theorem.

Equation (2.6) can be used repetitively to determine the greatest common divisor.

$$\gcd(18, 12) = \gcd(12, 6) = \gcd(6, 0) = 6$$
$$\gcd(11, 10) = \gcd(10, 1) = \gcd(1, 0) = 1$$

This is the same scheme shown in Equation (2.3), which can be rewritten in the following way.

Euclidean Algorithm	
Calculate	**Which satisfies**
$r_1 = a \bmod b$	$a = q_1 b + r_1$
$r_2 = b \bmod r_1$	$b = q_2 r_1 + r_2$
$r_3 = r_1 \bmod r_2$	$r_1 = q_3 r_2 + r_3$
• • •	• • •
$r_n = r_{n-2} \bmod r_{n-1}$	$r_{n-2} = q_n r_{n-1} + r_n$
$r_{n+1} = r_{n-1} \bmod r_n = 0$	$r_{n-1} = q_{n+1} r_n + 0$ $d = \gcd(a, b) = r_n$

We can define the Euclidean algorithm concisely as the following recursive function.

```
Euclid(a,b)
    if (b=0) then return a;
    else return Euclid(b, a mod b);
```

The Extended Euclidean Algorithm

We now proceed to look at an extension to the Euclidean algorithm that will be important for later computations in the area of finite fields and in encryption algorithms, such as RSA. For given integers a and b, the extended Euclidean algorithm not only calculates the greatest common divisor d but also two additional integers x and y that satisfy the following equation.

$$ax + by = d = \gcd(a, b) \tag{2.7}$$

It should be clear that x and y will have opposite signs. Before examining the algorithm, let us look at some of the values of x and y when $a = 42$ and $b = 30$. Note that $\gcd(42, 30) = 6$. Here is a partial table of values[3] for $42x + 30y$.

x / *y*	−3	−2	−1	0	1	2	3
−3	−216	−174	−132	−90	−48	−6	36
−2	−186	−144	−102	−60	−18	24	66
−1	−156	−114	−72	−30	12	54	96
0	−126	−84	−42	0	42	84	126
1	−96	−54	−12	30	72	114	156
2	−66	−24	18	60	102	144	186
3	−36	6	48	90	132	174	216

Observe that all of the entries are divisible by 6. This is not surprising, because both 42 and 30 are divisible by 6, so every number of the form $42x + 30y = 6(7x + 5y)$ is a multiple of 6. Note also that $\gcd(42, 30) = 6$ appears in the table. In general, it can be shown that for given integers a and b, the smallest positive value of $ax + by$ is equal to $\gcd(a, b)$.

Now let us show how to extend the Euclidean algorithm to determine (x, y, d) given a and b. We again go through the sequence of divisions indicated in Equation (2.3), and we assume that at each step i we can find integers x_i and y_i that satisfy $r_i = ax_i + by_i$. We end up with the following sequence.

$$\begin{array}{rlrl}
a &= q_1 b + r_1 & r_1 &= ax_1 + by_1 \\
b &= q_2 r_1 + r_2 & r_2 &= ax_2 + by_2 \\
r_1 &= q_3 r_2 + r_3 & r_3 &= ax_3 + by_3 \\
&\vdots & &\vdots \\
r_{n-2} &= q_n r_{n-1} + r_n & r_n &= ax_n + by_n \\
r_{n-1} &= q_{n+1} r_n + 0 & &
\end{array}$$

[3]This example is taken from [SILV06].

Now, observe that we can rearrange terms to write

$$r_i = r_{i-2} - r_{i-1}q_i \tag{2.8}$$

Also, in rows $i - 1$ and $i - 2$, we find the values

$$r_{i-2} = ax_{i-2} + by_{i-2} \quad \text{and} \quad r_{i-1} = ax_{i-1} + by_{i-1}$$

Substituting into Equation (2.8), we have

$$\begin{aligned} r_i &= (ax_{i-2} + by_{i-2}) - (ax_{i-1} + by_{i-1})q_i \\ &= a(x_{i-2} - q_i x_{i-1}) + b(y_{i-2} - q_i y_{i-1}) \end{aligned}$$

But we have already assumed that $r_i = ax_i + by_i$. Therefore,

$$x_i = x_{i-2} - q_i x_{i-1} \quad \text{and} \quad y_i = y_{i-2} - q_i y_{i-1}$$

We now summarize the calculations:

Extended Euclidean Algorithm			
Calculate	**Which satisfies**	**Calculate**	**Which satisfies**
$r_{-1} = a$		$x_{-1} = 1; y_{-1} = 0$	$a = ax_{-1} + by_{-1}$
$r_0 = b$		$x_0 = 0; y_0 = 1$	$b = ax_0 + by_0$
$r_1 = a \bmod b$ $q_1 = \lfloor a/b \rfloor$	$a = q_1 b + r_1$	$x_1 = x_{-1} - q_1 x_0 = 1$ $y_1 = y_{-1} - q_1 y_0 = -q_1$	$r_1 = ax_1 + by_1$
$r_2 = b \bmod r_1$ $q_2 = \lfloor b/r_1 \rfloor$	$b = q_2 r_1 + r_2$	$x_2 = x_0 - q_2 x_1$ $y_2 = y_0 - q_2 y_1$	$r_2 = ax_2 + by_2$
$r_3 = r_1 \bmod r_2$ $q_3 = \lfloor r_1/r_2 \rfloor$	$r_1 = q_3 r_2 + r_3$	$x_3 = x_1 - q_3 x_2$ $y_3 = y_1 - q_3 y_2$	$r_3 = ax_3 + by_3$
• • •	• • •	• • •	• • •
$r_n = r_{n-2} \bmod r_{n-1}$ $q_n = \lfloor r_{n-2}/r_{n-1} \rfloor$	$r_{n-2} = q_n r_{n-1} + r_n$	$x_n = x_{n-2} - q_n x_{n-1}$ $y_n = y_{n-2} - q_n y_{n-1}$	$r_n = ax_n + by_n$
$r_{n+1} = r_{n-1} \bmod r_n = 0$ $q_{n+1} = \lfloor r_{n-1}/r_n \rfloor$	$r_{n-1} = q_{n+1} r_n + 0$		$d = \gcd(a, b) = r_n$ $x = x_n; y = y_n$

We need to make several additional comments here. In each row, we calculate a new remainder r_i based on the remainders of the previous two rows, namely r_{i-1} and r_{i-2}. To start the algorithm, we need values for r_0 and r_{-1}, which are just a and b. It is then straightforward to determine the required values for x_{-1}, y_{-1}, x_0, and y_0.

We know from the original Euclidean algorithm that the process ends with a remainder of zero and that the greatest common divisor of a and b is $d = \gcd(a, b) = r_n$. But we also have determined that $d = r_n = ax_n + by_n$. Therefore, in Equation (2.7), $x = x_n$ and $y = y_n$.

As an example, let us use $a = 1759$ and $b = 550$ and solve for $1759x + 550y = \gcd(1759, 550)$. The results are shown in Table 2.4. Thus, we have $1759 \times (-111) + 550 \times 355 = -195249 + 195250 = 1$.

Table 2.4 Extended Euclidean Algorithm Example

i	r_i	q_i	x_i	y_i
−1	1759		1	0
0	550		0	1
1	109	3	1	−3
2	5	5	−5	16
3	4	21	106	−339
4	1	1	−111	355
5	0	4		

Result: $d = 1; x = -111; y = 355$

2.4 PRIME NUMBERS[4]

A central concern of number theory is the study of prime numbers. Indeed, whole books have been written on the subject (e.g., [CRAN01], [RIBE96]). In this section, we provide an overview relevant to the concerns of this book.

An integer $p > 1$ is a prime number if and only if its only divisors[5] are ± 1 and $\pm p$. **Prime numbers** play a critical role in number theory and in the techniques discussed in this chapter. Table 2.5 shows the primes less than 2000. Note the way the primes are distributed. In particular, note the number of primes in each range of 100 numbers.

Any integer $a > 1$ can be factored in a unique way as

$$a = p_1^{a_1} \times p_2^{a_2} \times \cdots \times p_t^{a_t} \qquad \textbf{(2.9)}$$

where $p_1 < p_2 < \ldots < p_t$ are prime numbers and where each a_i is a positive integer. This is known as the fundamental theorem of arithmetic; a proof can be found in any text on number theory.

$$91 = 7 \times 13$$
$$3600 = 2^4 \times 3^2 \times 5^2$$
$$11011 = 7 \times 11^2 \times 13$$

It is useful for what follows to express this another way. If P is the set of all prime numbers, then any positive integer a can be written uniquely in the following form:

$$a = \prod_{p \in \mathrm{P}} p^{a_p} \quad \text{where each } a_p \geq 0$$

---

[4]In this section, unless otherwise noted, we deal only with the nonnegative integers. The use of negative integers would introduce no essential differences.

[5]Recall from Section 2.1 that integer a is said to be a divisor of integer b if there is no remainder on division. Equivalently, we say that a divides b.

Table 2.5 Primes Under 2000

2	101	211	307	401	503	601	701	809	907	1009	1103	1201	1301	1409	1511	1601	1709	1801	1901
3	103	223	311	409	509	607	709	811	911	1013	1109	1213	1303	1423	1523	1607	1721	1811	1907
5	107	227	313	419	521	613	719	821	919	1019	1117	1217	1307	1427	1531	1609	1723	1823	1913
7	109	229	317	421	523	617	727	823	929	1021	1123	1223	1319	1429	1543	1613	1733	1831	1931
11	113	233	331	431	541	619	733	827	937	1031	1129	1229	1321	1433	1549	1619	1741	1847	1933
13	127	239	337	433	547	631	739	829	941	1033	1151	1231	1327	1439	1553	1621	1747	1861	1949
17	131	241	347	439	557	641	743	839	947	1039	1153	1237	1361	1447	1559	1627	1753	1867	1951
19	137	251	349	443	563	643	751	853	953	1049	1163	1249	1367	1451	1567	1637	1759	1871	1973
23	139	257	353	449	569	647	757	857	967	1051	1171	1259	1373	1453	1571	1657	1777	1873	1979
29	149	263	359	457	571	653	761	859	971	1061	1181	1277	1381	1459	1579	1663	1783	1877	1987
31	151	269	367	461	577	659	769	863	977	1063	1187	1279	1399	1471	1583	1667	1787	1879	1993
37	157	271	373	463	587	661	773	877	983	1069	1193	1283		1481	1597	1669	1789	1889	1997
41	163	277	379	467	593	673	787	881	991	1087		1289		1483		1693			1999
43	167	281	383	479	599	677	797	883	997	1091		1291		1487		1697			
47	173	283	389	487		683		887		1093		1297		1489		1699			
53	179	293	397	491		691				1097				1493					
59	181			499										1499					
61	191																		
67	193																		
71	197																		
73	199																		
79																			
83																			
89																			
97																			

The right-hand side is the product over all possible prime numbers p; for any particular value of a, most of the exponents a_p will be 0.

The value of any given positive integer can be specified by simply listing all the nonzero exponents in the foregoing formulation.

> The integer 12 is represented by $\{a_2 = 2, a_3 = 1\}$.
> The integer 18 is represented by $\{a_2 = 1, a_3 = 2\}$.
> The integer 91 is represented by $\{a_7 = 1, a_{13} = 1\}$.

Multiplication of two numbers is equivalent to adding the corresponding exponents. Given $a = \prod_{p \in \mathrm{P}} p^{a_p}$, $b = \prod_{p \in \mathrm{P}} p^{b_p}$. Define $k = ab$. We know that the integer k can be expressed as the product of powers of primes: $k = \prod_{p \in \mathrm{P}} p^{k_p}$. It follows that $k_p = a_p + b_p$ for all $p \in \mathrm{P}$.

> $k = 12 \times 18 = (2^2 \times 3) \times (2 \times 3^2) = 216$
> $k_2 = 2 + 1 = 3$; $k_3 = 1 + 2 = 3$
> $216 = 2^3 \times 3^3 = 8 \times 27$

What does it mean, in terms of the prime factors of a and b, to say that a divides b? Any integer of the form p^n can be divided only by an integer that is of a lesser or equal power of the same prime number, p^j with $j \leq n$. Thus, we can say the following.

Given

$$a = \prod_{p \in \mathrm{P}} p^{a_p}, \; b = \prod_{p \in \mathrm{P}} p^{b_p}$$

If $a|b$, then $a_p \leq b_p$ for all p.

> $a = 12$; $b = 36$; $12|36$
> $12 = 2^2 \times 3$; $36 = 2^2 \times 3^2$
> $a_2 = 2 = b_2$
> $a_3 = 1 \leq 2 = b_3$
> Thus, the inequality $a_p \leq b_p$ is satisfied for all prime numbers.

It is easy to determine the greatest common divisor of two positive integers if we express each integer as the product of primes.

$$300 = 2^2 \times 3^1 \times 5^2$$
$$18 = 2^1 \times 3^2$$
$$\gcd(18{,}300) = 2^1 \times 3^1 \times 5^0 = 6$$

The following relationship always holds:

$$\text{If } k = \gcd(a, b), \text{ then } k_p = \min(a_p, b_p) \text{ for all } p.$$

Determining the prime factors of a large number is no easy task, so the preceding relationship does not directly lead to a practical method of calculating the greatest common divisor.

2.5 FERMAT'S AND EULER'S THEOREMS

Two theorems that play important roles in public-key cryptography are Fermat's theorem and Euler's theorem.

Fermat's Theorem[6]

Fermat's theorem states the following: If p is prime and a is a positive integer not divisible by p, then

$$a^{p-1} \equiv 1 \pmod{p} \tag{2.10}$$

Proof: Consider the set of positive integers less than p: $\{1, 2, \ldots, p - 1\}$ and multiply each element by a, modulo p, to get the set $X = \{a \bmod p, 2a \bmod p, \ldots, (p - 1)a \bmod p\}$. None of the elements of X is equal to zero because p does not divide a. Furthermore, no two of the integers in X are equal. To see this, assume that $ja \equiv ka(\bmod p))$, where $1 \leq j < k \leq p - 1$. Because a is relatively prime[7] to p, we can eliminate a from both sides of the equation [see Equation (2.3)] resulting in $j \equiv k(\bmod p)$. This last equality is impossible, because j and k are both positive integers less than p. Therefore, we know that the $(p - 1)$ elements of X are all positive integers with no two elements equal. We can conclude the X consists of the set of integers $\{1, 2, \ldots, p - 1\}$ in some order. Multiplying the numbers in both sets (p and X) and taking the result mod p yields

$$a \times 2a \times \cdots \times (p - 1)a \equiv [(1 \times 2 \times \cdots \times (p - 1)](\bmod p)$$
$$a^{p-1}(p - 1)! \equiv (p - 1)! \pmod{p}$$

We can cancel the $(p - 1)!$ term because it is relatively prime to p [see Equation (2.5)]. This yields Equation (2.10), which completes the proof.

[6]This is sometimes referred to as Fermat's little theorem.

[7]Recall from Section 2.2 that two numbers are relatively prime if they have no prime factors in common; that is, their only common divisor is 1. This is equivalent to saying that two numbers are relatively prime if their greatest common divisor is 1.

$a = 7, p = 19$
$7^2 = 49 \equiv 11 \pmod{19}$
$7^4 \equiv 121 \equiv 7 \pmod{19}$
$7^8 \equiv 49 \equiv 11 \pmod{19}$
$7^{16} \equiv 121 \equiv 7 \pmod{19}$
$a^{p-1} = 7^{18} = 7^{16} \times 7^2 \equiv 7 \times 11 \equiv 1 \pmod{19}$

An alternative form of Fermat's theorem is also useful: If p is prime and a is a positive integer, then

$$a^p \equiv a(\text{mod } p) \qquad \textbf{(2.11)}$$

Note that the first form of the theorem [Equation (2.10)] requires that a be relatively prime to p, but this form does not.

$p = 5, a = 3 \qquad a^p = 3^5 = 243 \equiv 3(\text{mod } 5) = a(\text{mod } p)$
$p = 5, a = 10 \qquad a^p = 10^5 = 100000 \equiv 10(\text{mod } 5) \equiv 0(\text{mod } 5) = a(\text{mod } p)$

Euler's Totient Function

Before presenting Euler's theorem, we need to introduce an important quantity in number theory, referred to as **Euler's totient function**. This function, written $\phi(n)$, is defined as the number of positive integers less than n and relatively prime to n. By convention, $\phi(1) = 1$.

Determine $\phi(37)$ and $\phi(35)$.

Because 37 is prime, all of the positive integers from 1 through 36 are relatively prime to 37. Thus $\phi(37) = 36$.

To determine $\phi(35)$, we list all of the positive integers less than 35 that are relatively prime to it:

1, 2, 3, 4, 6, 8, 9, 11, 12, 13, 16, 17, 18
19, 22, 23, 24, 26, 27, 29, 31, 32, 33, 34

There are 24 numbers on the list, so $\phi(35) = 24$.

Table 2.6 lists the first 30 values of $\phi(n)$. The value $\phi(1)$ is without meaning but is defined to have the value 1.

It should be clear that, for a prime number p,

$$\phi(p) = p - 1$$

Now suppose that we have two prime numbers p and q with $p \neq q$. Then we can show that, for $n = pq$,

Table 2.6 Some Values of Euler's Totient Function $\phi(n)$

n	$\phi(n)$
1	1
2	1
3	2
4	2
5	4
6	2
7	6
8	4
9	6
10	4

n	$\phi(n)$
11	10
12	4
13	12
14	6
15	8
16	8
17	16
18	6
19	18
20	8

n	$\phi(n)$
21	12
22	10
23	22
24	8
25	20
26	12
27	18
28	12
29	28
30	8

$$\phi(n) = \phi(pq) = \phi(p) \times \phi(q) = (p - 1) \times (q - 1)$$

To see that $\phi(n) = \phi(p) \times \phi(q)$, consider that the set of positive integers less than n is the set $\{1, \ldots, (pq - 1)\}$. The integers in this set that are not relatively prime to n are the set $\{p, 2p, \ldots, (q - 1)p\}$ and the set $\{q, 2q, \ldots, (p - 1)q\}$. To see this, consider that any integer that divides n must divide either of the prime numbers p or q. Therefore, any integer that does not contain either p or q as a factor is relatively prime to n. Further note that the two sets just listed are non-overlapping: Because p and q are prime, we can state that none of the integers in the first set can be written as a multiple of q, and none of the integers in the second set can be written as a multiple of p. Thus the total number of unique integers in the two sets is $(q - 1) + (p - 1)$. Accordingly,

$$\begin{aligned}\phi(n) &= (pq - 1) - [(q - 1) + (p - 1)] \\ &= pq - (p + q) + 1 \\ &= (p - 1) \times (q - 1) \\ &= \phi(p) \times \phi(q)\end{aligned}$$

$\phi(21) = \phi(3) \times \phi(7) = (3 - 1) \times (7 - 1) = 2 \times 6 = 12$
where the 12 integers are $\{1, 2, 4, 5, 8, 10, 11, 13, 16, 17, 19, 20\}$.

Euler's Theorem

Euler's theorem states that for every a and n that are relatively prime:

$$a^{\phi(n)} \equiv 1(\text{mod } n) \qquad \textbf{(2.12)}$$

Proof: Equation (2.12) is true if n is prime, because in that case, $\phi(n) = (n - 1)$ and Fermat's theorem holds. However, it also holds for any integer n. Recall that

$\phi(n)$ is the number of positive integers less than n that are relatively prime to n. Consider the set of such integers, labeled as

$$R = \{x_1, x_2, \ldots, x_{\phi(n)}\}$$

That is, each element x_i of R is a unique positive integer less than n with $\gcd(x_i, n) = 1$. Now multiply each element by a, modulo n:

$$S = \{(ax_1 \bmod n), (ax_2 \bmod n), \ldots, (ax_{\phi(n)} \bmod n)\}$$

The set S is a permutation[8] of R, by the following line of reasoning:

1. Because a is relatively prime to n and x_i is relatively prime to n, ax_i must also be relatively prime to n. Thus, all the members of S are integers that are less than n and that are relatively prime to n.
2. There are no duplicates in S. Refer to Equation (2.5). If $ax_i \bmod n = ax_j \bmod n$, then $x_i = x_j$.

Therefore,

$$\prod_{i=1}^{\phi(n)} (ax_i \bmod n) = \prod_{i=1}^{\phi(n)} x_i$$

$$\prod_{i=1}^{\phi(n)} ax_i \equiv \prod_{i=1}^{\phi(n)} x_i \pmod{n}$$

$$a^{\phi(n)} \times \left[\prod_{i=1}^{\phi(n)} x_i\right] \equiv \prod_{i=1}^{\phi(n)} x_i \pmod{n}$$

$$a^{\phi(n)} \equiv 1 \pmod{n}$$

which completes the proof. This is the same line of reasoning applied to the proof of Fermat's theorem.

$a = 3; n = 10; \phi(10) = 4; \quad a^{\phi(n)} = 3^4 = 81 = 1(\text{mod } 10) = 1(\text{mod } n)$
$a = 2; n = 11; \phi(11) = 10; \quad a^{\phi(n)} = 2^{10} = 1024 = 1(\text{mod } 11) = 1(\text{mod } n)$

As is the case for Fermat's theorem, an alternative form of the theorem is also useful:

$$a^{\phi(n)+1} \equiv a(\text{mod } n) \tag{2.13}$$

Again, similar to the case with Fermat's theorem, the first form of Euler's theorem [Equation (2.12)] requires that a be relatively prime to n, but this form does not.

[8]A permutation of a finite set of elements S is an ordered sequence of all the elements of S, with each element appearing exactly once.

2.6 TESTING FOR PRIMALITY

For many cryptographic algorithms, it is necessary to select one or more very large prime numbers at random. Thus, we are faced with the task of determining whether a given large number is prime. There is no simple yet efficient means of accomplishing this task.

In this section, we present one attractive and popular algorithm. You may be surprised to learn that this algorithm yields a number that is not necessarily a prime. However, the algorithm can yield a number that is almost certainly a prime. This will be explained presently. We also make reference to a deterministic algorithm for finding primes. The section closes with a discussion concerning the distribution of primes.

Miller–Rabin Algorithm[9]

The algorithm due to Miller and Rabin [MILL75, RABI80] is typically used to test a large number for primality. Before explaining the algorithm, we need some background. First, any positive odd integer $n \geq 3$ can be expressed as

$$n - 1 = 2^k q \qquad \text{with } k > 0, q \text{ odd}$$

To see this, note that $n - 1$ is an even integer. Then, divide $(n - 1)$ by 2 until the result is an odd number q, for a total of k divisions. If n is expressed as a binary number, then the result is achieved by shifting the number to the right until the rightmost digit is a 1, for a total of k shifts. We now develop two properties of prime numbers that we will need.

Two Properties of Prime Numbers The **first property** is stated as follows: If p is prime and a is a positive integer less than p, then $a^2 \bmod p = 1$ if and only if either $a \bmod p = 1$ or $a \bmod p = -1 \bmod p = p - 1$. By the rules of modular arithmetic $(a \bmod p)\,(a \bmod p) = a^2 \bmod p$. Thus, if either $a \bmod p = 1$ or $a \bmod p = -1$, then $a^2 \bmod p = 1$. Conversely, if $a^2 \bmod p = 1$, then $(a \bmod p)^2 = 1$, which is true only for $a \bmod p = 1$ or $a \bmod p = -1$.

The **second property** is stated as follows: Let p be a prime number greater than 2. We can then write $p - 1 = 2^k q$ with $k > 0$, q odd. Let a be any integer in the range $1 < a < p - 1$. Then one of the two following conditions is true.

1. a^q is congruent to 1 modulo p. That is, $a^q \bmod p = 1$, or equivalently, $a^q \equiv 1 (\bmod p)$.
2. One of the numbers $a^q, a^{2q}, a^{4q}, \ldots, a^{2^{k-1}q}$ is congruent to -1 modulo p. That is, there is some number j in the range $(1 \leq j \leq k)$ such that $a^{2^{j-1}q} \bmod p = -1 \bmod p = p - 1$ or equivalently, $a^{2^{j-1}q} \equiv -1 (\bmod p)$.

Proof: Fermat's theorem [Equation (2.10)] states that $a^{n-1} \equiv 1 (\bmod n)$ if n is prime. We have $p - 1 = 2^k q$. Thus, we know that $a^{p-1} \bmod p = a^{2^k q} \bmod p = 1$. Thus, if we look at the sequence of numbers

$$a^q \bmod p, a^{2q} \bmod p, a^{4q} \bmod p, \ldots, a^{2^{k-1}q} \bmod p, a^{2^k q} \bmod p \qquad \textbf{(2.14)}$$

[9]Also referred to in the literature as the Rabin-Miller algorithm, or the Rabin-Miller test, or the Miller–Rabin test.

we know that the last number in the list has value 1. Further, each number in the list is the square of the previous number. Therefore, one of the following possibilities must be true.

1. The first number on the list, and therefore all subsequent numbers on the list, equals 1.
2. Some number on the list does not equal 1, but its square mod p does equal 1. By virtue of the first property of prime numbers defined above, we know that the only number that satisfies this condition is $p - 1$. So, in this case, the list contains an element equal to $p - 1$.

This completes the proof.

DETAILS OF THE ALGORITHM These considerations lead to the conclusion that, if n is prime, then either the first element in the list of residues, or remainders, $(a^q, a^{2q}, \ldots, a^{2^{k-1}q}, a^{2^k q})$ modulo n equals 1; or some element in the list equals $(n - 1)$; otherwise n is composite (i.e., not a prime). On the other hand, if the condition is met, that does not necessarily mean that n is prime. For example, if $n = 2047 = 23 \times 89$, then $n - 1 = 2 \times 1023$. We compute $2^{1023} \bmod 2047 = 1$, so that 2047 meets the condition but is not prime.

We can use the preceding property to devise a test for primality. The procedure TEST takes a candidate integer n as input and returns the result `composite` if n is definitely not a prime, and the result `inconclusive` if n may or may not be a prime.

```
TEST (n)
1. Find integers k, q, with k > 0, q odd, so that
     (n - 1 = 2k q);
2. Select a random integer a, 1 < a < n - 1;
3. if aq mod n = 1 then return("inconclusive");
4. for j = 0 to k - 1 do
5.    if a^(2^j)q mod n = n - 1 then return("inconclusive");
6. return("composite");
```

Let us apply the test to the prime number $n = 29$. We have $(n - 1) = 28 = 2^2(7) = 2^k q$. First, let us try $a = 10$. We compute $10^7 \bmod 29 = 17$, which is neither 1 nor 28, so we continue the test. The next calculation finds that $(10^7)^2 \bmod 29 = 28$, and the test returns `inconclusive` (i.e., 29 may be prime). Let's try again with $a = 2$. We have the following calculations: $2^7 \bmod 29 = 12$; $2^{14} \bmod 29 = 28$; and the test again returns `inconclusive`. If we perform the test for all integers a in the range 1 through 28, we get the same `inconclusive` result, which is compatible with n being a prime number.

Now let us apply the test to the composite number $n = 13 \times 17 = 221$. Then $(n - 1) = 220 = 2^2(55) = 2^k q$. Let us try $a = 5$. Then we have $5^{55} \bmod 221 = 112$, which is neither 1 nor $220(5^{55})^2 \bmod 221 = 168$. Because we have used all values of j (i.e., $j = 0$ and $j = 1$) in line 4 of the TEST algorithm, the test returns `composite`, indicating that 221 is definitely a composite number. But suppose we had selected $a = 21$. Then we have $21^{55} \bmod 221 = 200$; $(21^{55})^2 \bmod 221 = 220$; and the test returns `inconclusive`, indicating that 221 may be prime. In fact, of the 218 integers from 2 through 219, four of these will return an inconclusive result, namely 21, 47, 174, and 200.

Repeated Use of the Miller–Rabin Algorithm How can we use the Miller–Rabin algorithm to determine with a high degree of confidence whether or not an integer is prime? It can be shown [KNUT98] that given an odd number n that is not prime and a randomly chosen integer, a with $1 < a < n - 1$, the probability that TEST will return `inconclusive` (i.e., fail to detect that n is not prime) is less than 1/4. Thus, if t different values of a are chosen, the probability that all of them will pass TEST (return inconclusive) for n is less than $(1/4)^t$. For example, for $t = 10$, the probability that a nonprime number will pass all ten tests is less than 10^{-6}. Thus, for a sufficiently large value of t, we can be confident that n is prime if Miller's test always returns `inconclusive`.

This gives us a basis for determining whether an odd integer n is prime with a reasonable degree of confidence. The procedure is as follows: Repeatedly invoke TEST (n) using randomly chosen values for a. If, at any point, TEST returns `composite`, then n is determined to be nonprime. If TEST continues to return `inconclusive` for t tests, then for a sufficiently large value of t, assume that n is prime.

A Deterministic Primality Algorithm

Prior to 2002, there was no known method of efficiently proving the primality of very large numbers. All of the algorithms in use, including the most popular (Miller–Rabin), produced a probabilistic result. In 2002 (announced in 2002, published in 2004), Agrawal, Kayal, and Saxena [AGRA04] developed a relatively simple deterministic algorithm that efficiently determines whether a given large number is a prime. The algorithm, known as the AKS algorithm, does not appear to be as efficient as the Miller–Rabin algorithm. Thus far, it has not supplanted this older, probabilistic technique.

Distribution of Primes

It is worth noting how many numbers are likely to be rejected before a prime number is found using the Miller–Rabin test, or any other test for primality. A result from number theory, known as the prime number theorem, states that the primes near n are spaced on the average one every ln (n) integers. Thus, on average, one would have to test on the order of ln(n) integers before a prime is found. Because all even integers can be immediately rejected, the correct figure is 0.5 ln(n). For example, if a prime on the order of magnitude of 2^{200} were sought, then about $0.5 \ln(2^{200}) = 69$ trials would be needed to find a prime. However, this figure is just an average. In some places along the number line, primes are closely packed, and in other places there are large gaps.

> The two consecutive odd integers 1,000,000,000,061 and 1,000,000,000,063 are both prime. On the other hand, 1001! + 2, 1001! + 3, . . . , 1001! + 1000, 1001! + 1001 is a sequence of 1000 consecutive composite integers.

2.7 THE CHINESE REMAINDER THEOREM

One of the most useful results of number theory is the **Chinese remainder theorem** (CRT).[10] In essence, the CRT says it is possible to reconstruct integers in a certain range from their residues modulo a set of pairwise relatively prime moduli.

> The 10 integers in Z_{10}, that is the integers 0 through 9, can be reconstructed from their two residues modulo 2 and 5 (the relatively prime factors of 10). Say the known residues of a decimal digit x are $r_2 = 0$ and $r_5 = 3$; that is, $x \bmod 2 = 0$ and $x \bmod 5 = 3$. Therefore, x is an even integer in Z_{10} whose remainder, on division by 5, is 3. The unique solution is $x = 8$.

The CRT can be stated in several ways. We present here a formulation that is most useful from the point of view of this text. An alternative formulation is explored in Problem 2.33. Let

$$M = \prod_{i=1}^{k} m_i$$

where the m_i are pairwise relatively prime; that is, $\gcd(m_i, m_j) = 1$ for $1 \le i, j \le k$, and $i \ne j$. We can represent any integer A in Z_M by a k-tuple whose elements are in Z_{m_i} using the following correspondence:

$$A \leftrightarrow (a_1, a_2, \ldots, a_k) \qquad \textbf{(2.15)}$$

where $A \in Z_M$, $a_i \in Z_{m_i}$, and $a_i = A \bmod m_i$ for $1 \le i \le k$. The CRT makes two assertions.

1. The mapping of Equation (2.15) is a one-to-one correspondence (called a **bijection**) between Z_M and the Cartesian product $Z_{m_1} \times Z_{m_2} \times \ldots \times Z_{m_k}$. That is, for every integer A such that $0 \le A < M$, there is a unique k-tuple $(a_1, a_2, \ldots, a_k)$ with $0 \le a_i < m_i$ that represents it, and for every such k-tuple $(a_1, a_2, \ldots, a_k)$, there is a unique integer A in Z_M.
2. Operations performed on the elements of Z_M can be equivalently performed on the corresponding k-tuples by performing the operation independently in each coordinate position in the appropriate system.

Let us demonstrate the **first assertion**. The transformation from A to $(a_1, a_2, \ldots, a_k)$, is obviously unique; that is, each a_i is uniquely calculated as $a_i = A \bmod m_i$. Computing A from $(a_1, a_2, \ldots, a_k)$ can be done as follows. Let

[10] The CRT is so called because it is believed to have been discovered by the Chinese mathematician Sun-Tsu in around 100 A.D.

$M_i = M/m_i$ for $1 \le i \le k$. Note that $M_i = m_1 \times m_2 \times \ldots \times m_{i-1} \times m_{i+1} \times \ldots \times m_k$, so that $M_i \equiv 0 \pmod{m_j}$ for all $j \ne i$. Then let

$$c_i = M_i \times (M_i^{-1} \bmod m_i) \qquad \text{for } 1 \le i \le k \tag{2.16}$$

By the definition of M_i, it is relatively prime to m_i and therefore has a unique multiplicative inverse mod m_i. So Equation (2.16) is well defined and produces a unique value c_i. We can now compute

$$A \equiv \left(\sum_{i=1}^{k} a_i c_i \right) \pmod{M} \tag{2.17}$$

To show that the value of A produced by Equation (2.17) is correct, we must show that $a_i = A \bmod m_i$ for $1 \le i \le k$. Note that $c_j \equiv M_j \equiv 0 \pmod{m_i}$ if $j \ne i$, and that $c_i \equiv 1 \pmod{m_i}$. It follows that $a_i = A \bmod m_i$.

The **second assertion** of the CRT, concerning arithmetic operations, follows from the rules for modular arithmetic. That is, the second assertion can be stated as follows: If

$$A \leftrightarrow (a_1, a_2, \ldots, a_k)$$
$$B \leftrightarrow (b_1, b_2, \ldots, b_k)$$

then

$$(A + B) \bmod M \leftrightarrow ((a_1 + b_1) \bmod m_1, \ldots, (a_k + b_k) \bmod m_k)$$
$$(A - B) \bmod M \leftrightarrow ((a_1 - b_1) \bmod m_1, \ldots, (a_k - b_k) \bmod m_k)$$
$$(A \times B) \bmod M \leftrightarrow ((a_1 \times b_1) \bmod m_1, \ldots, (a_k \times b_k) \bmod m_k)$$

One of the useful features of the Chinese remainder theorem is that it provides a way to manipulate (potentially very large) numbers mod M in terms of tuples of smaller numbers. This can be useful when M is 150 digits or more. However, note that it is necessary to know beforehand the factorization of M.

To represent 973 mod 1813 as a pair of numbers mod 37 and 49, define

$$m_1 = 37$$
$$m_2 = 49$$
$$M = 1813$$
$$A = 973$$

We also have $M_1 = 49$ and $M_2 = 37$. Using the extended Euclidean algorithm, we compute $M_1^{-1} = 34 \bmod m_1$ and $M_2^{-1} = 4 \bmod m_2$. (Note that we only need to compute each M_i and each M_i^{-1} once.) Taking residues modulo 37 and 49, our representation of 973 is $(11, 42)$, because $973 \bmod 37 = 11$ and $973 \bmod 49 = 42$.

Now suppose we want to add 678 to 973. What do we do to $(11, 42)$? First we compute $(678) \leftrightarrow (678 \bmod 37, 678 \bmod 49) = (12, 41)$. Then we add the tuples element-wise and reduce $(11 + 12 \bmod 37, 42 + 41 \bmod 49) = (23, 34)$. To verify that this has the correct effect, we compute

$$\begin{aligned}(23, 34) \leftrightarrow a_1M_1M_1^{-1} &+ a_2M_2M_2^{-1} \text{ mod } M \\ &= [(23)(49)(34) + (34)(37)(4)] \text{ mod } 1813 \\ &= 43350 \text{ mod } 1813 \\ &= 1651\end{aligned}$$

and check that it is equal to (973 + 678) mod 1813 = 1651. Remember that in the above derivation, M_i^{-1} is the multiplicative inverse of M_1 modulo m_1 and M_2^{-1} is the multiplicative inverse of M_2 modulo m_2.

Suppose we want to multiply 1651 (mod 1813) by 73. We multiply (23, 34) by 73 and reduce to get (23 × 73 mod 37, 34 × 73 mod 49) = (14, 32). It is easily verified that

$$\begin{aligned}(14, 32) &\leftrightarrow [(14)(49)(34) + (32)(37)(4)] \text{ mod } 1813 \\ &= 865 \\ &= 1651 \times 73 \text{ mod } 1813\end{aligned}$$

2.8 DISCRETE LOGARITHMS

Discrete logarithms are fundamental to a number of public-key algorithms, including Diffie–Hellman key exchange and the digital signature algorithm (DSA). This section provides a brief overview of discrete logarithms. For the interested reader, more detailed developments of this topic can be found in [ORE67] and [LEVE90].

The Powers of an Integer, Modulo *n*

Recall from Euler's theorem [Equation (2.12)] that, for every a and n that are relatively prime,

$$a^{\phi(n)} \equiv 1 \pmod{n}$$

where $\phi(n)$, Euler's totient function, is the number of positive integers less than n and relatively prime to n. Now consider the more general expression:

$$a^m \equiv 1 \pmod{n} \tag{2.18}$$

If a and n are relatively prime, then there is at least one integer m that satisfies Equation (2.18), namely, $m = \phi(n)$. The least positive exponent m for which Equation (2.18) holds is referred to in several ways:

- The order of a (mod n)
- The exponent to which a belongs (mod n)
- The length of the period generated by a

To see this last point, consider the powers of 7, modulo 19:

$$\begin{aligned}
7^1 &\equiv && 7 \pmod{19} \\
7^2 &= 49 = 2 \times 19 + 11 &\equiv\ & 11 \pmod{19} \\
7^3 &= 343 = 18 \times 19 + 1 &\equiv\ & 1 \pmod{19} \\
7^4 &= 2401 = 126 \times 19 + 7 &\equiv\ & 7 \pmod{19} \\
7^5 &= 16807 = 884 \times 19 + 11 &\equiv\ & 11 \pmod{19}
\end{aligned}$$

There is no point in continuing because the sequence is repeating. This can be proven by noting that $7^3 \equiv 1(\text{mod } 19)$, and therefore, $7^{3+j} \equiv 7^3 7^j \equiv 7^j(\text{mod } 19)$, and hence, any two powers of 7 whose exponents differ by 3 (or a multiple of 3) are congruent to each other (mod 19). In other words, the sequence is periodic, and the length of the period is the smallest positive exponent m such that $7^m \equiv 1(\text{mod } 19)$.

Table 2.7 shows all the powers of a, modulo 19 for all positive $a < 19$. The length of the sequence for each base value is indicated by shading. Note the following:

1. All sequences end in 1. This is consistent with the reasoning of the preceding few paragraphs.
2. The length of a sequence divides $\phi(19) = 18$. That is, an integral number of sequences occur in each row of the table.
3. Some of the sequences are of length 18. In this case, it is said that the base integer a generates (via powers) the set of nonzero integers modulo 19. Each such integer is called a primitive root of the modulus 19.

More generally, we can say that the highest possible exponent to which a number can belong (mod n) is $\phi(n)$. If a number is of this order, it is referred to as a **primitive root** of n. The importance of this notion is that if a is a primitive root of n, then its powers

$$a, a^2, \ldots, a^{\phi(n)}$$

are distinct (mod n) and are all relatively prime to n. In particular, for a prime number p, if a is a primitive root of p, then

$$a, a^2, \ldots, a^{p-1}$$

are distinct (mod p). For the prime number 19, its primitive roots are 2, 3, 10, 13, 14, and 15.

Not all integers have primitive roots. In fact, the only integers with primitive roots are those of the form 2, 4, p^α, and $2p^\alpha$, where p is any odd prime and α is a positive integer. The proof is not simple but can be found in many number theory books, including [ORE76].

Table 2.7 Powers of Integers, Modulo 19

a	a^2	a^3	a^4	a^5	a^6	a^7	a^8	a^9	a^{10}	a^{11}	a^{12}	a^{13}	a^{14}	a^{15}	a^{16}	a^{17}	a^{18}
1	1	1	1	1	1	1	1	1	1	1	1	1	1	1	1	1	1
2	4	8	16	13	7	14	9	18	17	15	11	3	6	12	5	10	1
3	9	8	5	15	7	2	6	18	16	10	11	14	4	12	17	13	1
4	16	7	9	17	11	6	5	1	4	16	7	9	17	11	6	5	1
5	6	11	17	9	7	16	4	1	5	6	11	17	9	7	16	4	1
6	17	7	4	5	11	9	16	1	6	17	7	4	5	11	9	16	1
7	11	1	7	11	1	7	11	1	7	11	1	7	11	1	7	11	1
8	7	18	11	12	1	8	7	18	11	12	1	8	7	18	11	12	1
9	5	7	6	16	11	4	17	1	9	5	7	6	16	11	4	17	1
10	5	12	6	3	11	15	17	18	9	14	7	13	16	8	4	2	1
11	7	1	11	7	1	11	7	1	11	7	1	11	7	1	11	7	1
12	11	18	7	8	1	12	11	18	7	8	1	12	11	18	7	8	1
13	17	12	4	14	11	10	16	18	6	2	7	15	5	8	9	3	1
14	6	8	17	10	7	3	4	18	5	13	11	2	9	12	16	15	1
15	16	12	9	2	11	13	5	18	4	3	7	10	17	8	6	14	1
16	9	11	5	4	7	17	6	1	16	9	11	5	4	7	17	6	1
17	4	11	16	6	7	5	9	1	17	4	11	16	6	7	5	9	1
18	1	18	1	18	1	18	1	18	1	18	1	18	1	18	1	18	1

Logarithms for Modular Arithmetic

With ordinary positive real numbers, the logarithm function is the inverse of exponentiation. An analogous function exists for modular arithmetic.

Let us briefly review the properties of ordinary logarithms. The logarithm of a number is defined to be the power to which some positive base (except 1) must be raised in order to equal the number. That is, for base x and for a value y,

$$y = x^{\log_x(y)}$$

The properties of logarithms include

$$\log_x(1) = 0$$
$$\log_x(x) = 1$$

$$\log_x(yz) = \log_x(y) + \log_x(z) \qquad \textbf{(2.19)}$$

$$\log_x(y^r) = r \times \log_x(y) \qquad \textbf{(2.20)}$$

Consider a primitive root a for some prime number p (the argument can be developed for nonprimes as well). Then we know that the powers of a from

1 through $(p - 1)$ produce each integer from 1 through $(p - 1)$ exactly once. We also know that any integer b satisfies

$$b \equiv r \pmod p \text{ for some } r, \text{ where } 0 \le r \le (p - 1)$$

by the definition of modular arithmetic. It follows that for any integer b and a primitive root a of prime number p, we can find a unique exponent i such that

$$b \equiv a^i \pmod p \quad \text{where } 0 \le i \le (p - 1)$$

This exponent i is referred to as the **discrete logarithm** of the number b for the base $a \pmod p$. We denote this value as $\text{dlog}_{a,p}(b)$.[11]

Note the following:

$$\text{dlog}_{a,p}(1) = 0 \text{ because } a^0 \bmod p = 1 \bmod p = 1 \quad \textbf{(2.21)}$$

$$\text{dlog}_{a,p}(a) = 1 \text{ because } a^1 \bmod p = a \quad \textbf{(2.22)}$$

Here is an example using a nonprime modulus, $n = 9$. Here $\phi(n) = 6$ and $a = 2$ is a primitive root. We compute the various powers of a and find

$$\begin{array}{ll} 2^0 = 1 & 2^4 \equiv 7 \pmod 9 \\ 2^1 = 2 & 2^5 \equiv 5 \pmod 9 \\ 2^2 = 4 & 2^6 \equiv 1 \pmod 9 \\ 2^3 = 8 & \end{array}$$

This gives us the following table of the numbers with given discrete logarithms (mod 9) for the root $a = 2$:

Logarithm	0	1	2	3	4	5
Number	1	2	4	8	7	5

To make it easy to obtain the discrete logarithms of a given number, we rearrange the table:

Number	1	2	4	5	7	8
Logarithm	0	1	2	5	4	3

Now consider

$$x = a^{\text{dlog}_{a,p}(x)} \bmod p \qquad y = a^{\text{dlog}_{a,p}(y)} \bmod p$$
$$xy = a^{\text{dlog}_{a,p}(xy)} \bmod p$$

[11]Many texts refer to the discrete logarithm as the **index**. There is no generally agreed notation for this concept, much less an agreed name.

Using the rules of modular multiplication,

$$xy \bmod p = [(x \bmod p)(y \bmod p)] \bmod p$$
$$a^{\mathrm{dlog}_{a,p}(xy)} \bmod p = [(a^{\mathrm{dlog}_{a,p}(x)} \bmod p)(a^{\mathrm{dlog}_{a,p}(y)} \bmod p)] \bmod p$$
$$= (a^{\mathrm{dlog}_{a,p}(x) + \mathrm{dlog}_{a,p}(y)}) \bmod p$$

But now consider Euler's theorem, which states that, for every a and n that are relatively prime,

$$a^{\phi(n)} \equiv 1(\bmod n)$$

Any positive integer z can be expressed in the form $z = q + k\phi(n)$, with $0 \leq q < \phi(n)$. Therefore, by Euler's theorem,

$$a^z \equiv a^q(\bmod n) \qquad \text{if } z \equiv q \bmod \phi(n)$$

Applying this to the foregoing equality, we have

$$\mathrm{dlog}_{a,p}(xy) \equiv [\mathrm{dlog}_{a,p}(x) + \mathrm{dlog}_{a,p}(y)](\bmod \phi(p))$$

and generalizing,

$$\mathrm{dlog}_{a,p}(y^r) \equiv [r \times \mathrm{dlog}_{a,p}(y)](\bmod \phi(p))$$

This demonstrates the analogy between true logarithms and discrete logarithms.

Keep in mind that unique discrete logarithms mod m to some base a exist only if a is a primitive root of m.

Table 2.8, which is directly derived from Table 2.7, shows the sets of discrete logarithms that can be defined for modulus 19.

Calculation of Discrete Logarithms

Consider the equation

$$y = g^x \bmod p$$

Given g, x, and p, it is a straightforward matter to calculate y. At the worst, we must perform x repeated multiplications, and algorithms exist for achieving greater efficiency (see Chapter 9).

However, given y, g, and p, it is, in general, very difficult to calculate x (take the discrete logarithm). The difficulty seems to be on the same order of magnitude as that of factoring primes required for RSA. At the time of this writing, the asymptotically fastest known algorithm for taking discrete logarithms modulo a prime number is on the order of [BETH91]:

$$e^{((\ln p)^{1/3}(\ln(\ln p))^{2/3})}$$

which is not feasible for large primes.

Table 2.8 Tables of Discrete Logarithms, Modulo 19

(a) Discrete logarithms to the base 2, modulo 19

a	1	2	3	4	5	6	7	8	9	10	11	12	13	14	15	16	17	18
$log_{2,19}(a)$	18	1	13	2	16	14	6	3	8	17	12	15	5	7	11	4	10	9

(b) Discrete logarithms to the base 3, modulo 19

a	1	2	3	4	5	6	7	8	9	10	11	12	13	14	15	16	17	18
$log_{3,19}(a)$	18	7	1	14	4	8	6	3	2	11	12	15	17	13	5	10	16	9

(c) Discrete logarithms to the base 10, modulo 19

a	1	2	3	4	5	6	7	8	9	10	11	12	13	14	15	16	17	18
$log_{10,19}(a)$	18	17	5	16	2	4	12	15	10	1	6	3	13	11	7	14	8	9

(d) Discrete logarithms to the base 13, modulo 19

a	1	2	3	4	5	6	7	8	9	10	11	12	13	14	15	16	17	18
$log_{13,19}(a)$	18	11	17	4	14	10	12	15	16	7	6	3	1	5	13	8	2	9

(e) Discrete logarithms to the base 14, modulo 19

a	1	2	3	4	5	6	7	8	9	10	11	12	13	14	15	16	17	18
$log_{14,19}(a)$	18	13	7	8	10	2	6	3	14	5	12	15	11	1	17	16	4	9

(f) Discrete logarithms to the base 15, modulo 19

a	1	2	3	4	5	6	7	8	9	10	11	12	13	14	15	16	17	18
$log_{15,19}(a)$	18	5	11	10	8	16	12	15	4	13	6	3	7	17	1	2	14	9

2.9 KEY TERMS, REVIEW QUESTIONS, AND PROBLEMS

Key Terms

bijection	Euler's theorem	modulus
composite number	Euler's totient function	order
commutative	Fermat's theorem	prime number
Chinese remainder theorem	greatest common divisor	primitive root
discrete logarithm	identity element	relatively prime
divisor	index	residue
Euclidean algorithm	modular arithmetic	

Review Questions

2.1 What does it mean to say that b is a divisor of a?

2.2 List some simple properties of divisibility for integers.

2.3 What is the difference between modular arithmetic and ordinary arithmetic?

2.4 When are the two positive integers said to be relatively prime?

2.5 What is Euler's totient function?

2.6 Write the Miller-Rabin algorithm to test a number for primality.

2.7 What is a primitive root of a number?

2.8 What do you mean by discrete logarithm?

Problems

2.1 Reformulate Equation (2.1), removing the restriction that a is a nonnegative integer. That is, let a be any integer.

2.2 Draw a figure similar to Figure 2.1 for $a < 0$.

2.3 For each of the following equations, find an integer x that satisfies the equation.

a. $3x \equiv 4 \pmod 5$
b. $9x \equiv 3 \pmod 7$
c. $7x \equiv 6 \pmod 9$

2.4 In this text, we assume that the modulus is a positive integer. But the definition of the expression a mod n also makes perfect sense if n is negative. Determine the following:

a. 5 mod 3
b. 5 mod −3
c. −5 mod 3
d. −5 mod −3

2.5 A modulus of 0 does not fit the definition but is defined by convention as follows: $a \bmod 0 = a$. With this definition in mind, what does the following expression mean: $a \equiv b \pmod 0$?

2.6 In Section 2.3, we define the congruence relationship as follows: Two integers a and b are said to be congruent modulo n if $(a \bmod n) = (b \bmod n)$. We then proved that $a \equiv b \pmod n$ if $n|(a - b)$. Some texts on number theory use this latter relationship as the definition of congruence: Two integers a and b are said to be congruent modulo n if $n|(a - b)$. Using this latter definition as the starting point, prove that, if $(a \bmod n) = (b \bmod n)$, then n divides $(a - b)$.

2.7 What is the smallest positive integer that has exactly k divisors? Provide answers for values for $1 \leq k \leq 6$?

2.8 Prove the following:

a. $a \equiv b \pmod n$ implies $b \equiv a \pmod n$
b. $a \equiv b \pmod n$ and $b \equiv c \pmod n$ imply $a \equiv c \pmod n$

2.9 Prove the following:

a. $[(a \bmod n) - (b \bmod n)] \bmod n = (a - b) \bmod n$
b. $[(a \bmod n) \times (b \bmod n)] \bmod n = (a \times b) \bmod n$

2.10 Find the multiplicative inverse of each nonzero element in Z_{10}.

2.11 Show that an integer N is congruent modulo 9 to the sum of its decimal digits. For example, $723 \equiv 7 + 2 + 3 \equiv 12 \equiv 1 + 2 \equiv 3 \pmod 9$. This is the basis for the familiar procedure of "casting out 9's" when checking computations in arithmetic.

2.12 **a.** Determine gcd(72345, 43215)
b. Determine gcd(2740, 1760)

2.13 The purpose of this problem is to set an upper bound on the number of iterations of the Euclidean algorithm.
a. Suppose that $m = qn + r$ with $q > 0$ and $0 \le r < n$. Show that $m/2 > r$.
b. Let A_i be the value of A in the Euclidean algorithm after the ith iteration. Show that

$$A_{i+2} < \frac{A_i}{2}$$

c. Show that if m, n, and N are integers with $(1 \le m, n, \le 2^N)$, then the Euclidean algorithm takes at most $2N$ steps to find gcd(m, n).

2.14 The Euclidean algorithm has been known for over 2000 years and has always been a favorite among number theorists. After these many years, there is now a potential competitor, invented by J. Stein in 1961. Stein's algorithms is as follows: Determine gcd(A, B) with $A, B \ge 1$.

STEP 1 Set $A_1 = A, B_1 = B, C_1 = 1$

STEP 2 For $n > 1$, (1) If $A_n = B_n$, stop. gcd$(A, B) = A_nC_n$
(2) If A_n and B_n are both even, set $A_{n+1} = A_n/2$, $B_{n+1} = B_n/2$, $C_{n+1} = 2C_n$
(3) If A_n is even and B_n is odd, set $A_{n+1} = A_n/2$, $B_{n+1} = B_n$, $C_{n+1} = C_n$
(4) If A_n is odd and B_n is even, set $A_{n+1} = A_n$, $B_{n+1} = B_n/2$, $C_{n+1} = C_n$
(5) If A_n and B_n are both odd, set $A_{n+1} = |A_n - B_n|$, $B_{n+1} = \min(B_n, A_n)$, $C_{n+1} = C_n$

Continue to step $n + 1$.
a. To get a feel for the two algorithms, compute gcd(6150, 704) using both the Euclidean and Stein's algorithm.
b. What is the apparent advantage of Stein's algorithm over the Euclidean algorithm?

2.15 **a.** Show that if Stein's algorithm does not stop before the nth step, then

$$C_{n+1} \times \gcd(A_{n+1}, B_{n+1}) = C_n \times \gcd(A_n, B_n)$$

b. Show that if the algorithm does not stop before step $(n - 1)$, then

$$A_{n+2}B_{n+2} \le \frac{A_nB_n}{2}$$

c. Show that if $1 \le A, B \le 2^N$, then Stein's algorithm takes at most $4N$ steps to find gcd(m, n). Thus, Stein's algorithm works in roughly the same number of steps as the Euclidean algorithm.
d. Demonstrate that Stein's algorithm does indeed return gcd(A, B).

2.16 Using the extended Euclidean algorithm, find the multiplicative inverse of
a. 550 mod 1769
b. 7465 mod 2464
c. 42828 mod 6407

2.17 The purpose of this problem is to determine how many prime numbers there are. Suppose there are a total of n prime numbers, and we list these in order: $p_1 = 2 < p_2 = 3 < p_3 = 5 < \ldots < p_n$.
a. Define $X = 1 + p_1p_2 \ldots p_n$. That is, X is equal to one plus the product of all the primes. Can we find a prime number P_m that divides X?
b. What can you say about m?
c. Deduce that the total number of primes cannot be finite.
d. Show that $P_{n+1} \le 1 + p_1p_2 \ldots p_n$.

2.18 The purpose of this problem is to demonstrate that the probability that two random numbers are relatively prime is about 0.6.

a. Let $P = \Pr[\gcd(a, b) = 1]$. Show that $P = \Pr[\gcd(a, b) = d] = P/d^2$. *Hint:* Consider the quantity $\gcd\left(\frac{a}{d}, \frac{b}{d}\right)$.

b. The sum of the result of part (a) over all possible values of d is 1. That is $\Sigma^{d \geq 1}\Pr[\gcd(a, b) = d] = 1$. Use this equality to determine the value of P. *Hint:* Use the identity $\sum_{i=1}^{\infty}\frac{1}{i^2} = \frac{\pi^2}{6}$.

2.19 Why is $\gcd(n, n + 1) = 1$ for two consecutive integers n and $n + 1$?

2.20 Using Fermat's theorem, find $3^{201} \bmod 11$.

2.21 Use Fermat's theorem to find a number a between 0 and 92 with a congruent to 7^{1013} modulo 93.

2.22 Use Fermat's theorem to find a number x between 0 and 37 with x^{73} congruent to 4 modulo 37. (You should not need to use any brute-force searching.)

2.23 Use Euler's theorem to find a number a between 0 and 9 such that a is congruent to 9^{101} modulo 10. (*Note*: This is the same as the last digit of the decimal expansion of 9^{100}.)

2.24 Use Euler's Theorem to find a number x between 0 and 28 with x^{85} congruent to 6 modulo 29. (You should not need to use any brute-force searching.)

2.25 Notice in Table 2.6 that $\phi(n)$ is even for $n > 2$. This is true for all $n > 2$. Give a concise argument why this is so.

2.26 Prove the following: If p is prime, then $\phi(p^i) = p^i - p^{i-1}$. *Hint:* What numbers have a factor in common with p^i?

2.27 It can be shown (see any book on number theory) that if $\gcd(m, n) = 1$ then $\phi(mn) = \phi(m)\,\phi(n)$. Using this property, the property developed in the preceding problem, and the property that $\phi(p) = p - 1$ for p prime, it is straightforward to determine the value of $\phi(n)$ for any n. Determine the following:

a. $\phi(27)$ **b.** $\phi(41)$ **c.** $\phi(440)$ **d.** $\phi(231)$

2.28 It can also be shown that for arbitrary positive integer a, $\phi(a)$ is given by

$$\phi(a) = \prod_{i=1}^{t}[p_i^{a_i-1}(p_i - 1)]$$

where a is given by Equation (2.9), namely: $a = P_1^{a_1}P_2^{a_2}\ldots P_t^{a_t}$. Demonstrate this result.

2.29 Consider the function: $f(n)$ = number of elements in the set $\{a: 0 \leq a < n$ and $\gcd(a, n) = 1\}$. What is this function?

2.30 Although ancient Chinese mathematicians did good work coming up with their remainder theorem, they did not always get it right. They had a test for primality. The test said that n is prime if and only if n divides $(2^n - 2)$.

a. Give an example that satisfies the condition using an odd prime.

b. The condition is obviously true for $n = 2$. Prove that the condition is true if n is an odd prime (proving the **if** condition).

c. Give an example of an odd n that is not prime and that does not satisfy the condition. You can do this with nonprime numbers up to a very large value. This misled the Chinese mathematicians into thinking that if the condition is true then n is prime.

d. Unfortunately, the ancient Chinese never tried $n = 341$, which is nonprime $(341 = 11 \times 31)$, yet 341 divides $2^{341} - 2$ without remainder. Demonstrate that $2341 \equiv 2 \pmod{341}$ (disproving the **only if** condition). *Hint:* It is not necessary to calculate 2^{341}; play around with the congruences instead.

2.31 Show that, if n is an odd composite integer, then the Miller–Rabin test will return `inconclusive` for $a = 1$ and $a = (n - 1)$.

2.32 If n is composite and passes the Miller–Rabin test for the base a, then n is called a *strong pseudoprime to the base a*. Show that 2047 is a strong pseudoprime to the base 2.

2.33 A common formulation of the Chinese remainder theorem (CRT) is as follows: Let $m_1, \ldots, m_k$ be integers that are pairwise relatively prime for $1 \le i, j \le k$, and $i \ne j$. Define M to be the product of all the m_i's. Let $a_1, \ldots, a_k$ be integers. Then the set of congruences:

$$x \equiv a_1 (\text{mod } m_1)$$
$$x \equiv a_2 (\text{mod } m_2)$$
$$\vdots$$
$$x \equiv a_k (\text{mod } m_k)$$

has a unique solution modulo M. Show that the theorem stated in this form is true.

2.34 Use the CRT to find x for the following equations:

$x \equiv 3 \pmod 7$
$x \equiv 3 \pmod{13}$
$x \equiv 0 \pmod{12}$

2.35 Six professors begin courses on Monday, Tuesday, Wednesday, Thursday, Friday, and Saturday, respectively, and announce their intentions of lecturing at intervals of 3, 2, 5, 6, 1, and 4 days, respectively. The regulations of the university forbid Sunday lectures (so that a Sunday lecture must be omitted). When first will all six professors find themselves compelled to omit a lecture? *Hint:* Use the CRT.

2.36 Find all primitive roots of 13.

2.37 Given 5 as a primitive root of 23, construct a table of discrete logarithms, and use it to solve the following congruences.

a. $3x^5 \equiv 2 \pmod{23}$
b. $7x^{10} + 1 \equiv 0 \pmod{23}$
c. $5^x \equiv 6 \pmod{23}$

Programming Problems

2.1 Write a computer program that implements fast exponentiation (successive squaring) modulo n.

2.2 Write a computer program that implements the Miller–Rabin algorithm for a user-specified n. The program should allow the user two choices: (1) specify a possible witness a to test using the Witness procedure or (2) specify a number s of random witnesses for the Miller–Rabin test to check.

APPENDIX 2A THE MEANING OF MOD

The operator mod is used in this book and in the literature in two different ways: as a binary operator and as a congruence relation. This appendix explains the distinction and precisely defines the notation used in this book regarding parentheses. This notation is common but, unfortunately, not universal.

The Binary Operator mod

If a is an integer and n is a positive integer, we define a mod n to be the remainder when a is divided by n. The integer n is called the **modulus**, and the remainder is called the **residue**. Thus, for any integer a, we can always write

$$a = \lfloor a/n \rfloor \times n + (a \bmod n)$$

Formally, we define the operator mod as

$$a \bmod n = a - \lfloor a/n \rfloor \times n \quad \text{for } n \neq 0$$

As a binary operation, mod takes two integer arguments and returns the remainder. For example, 7 mod 3 = 1. The arguments may be integers, integer variables, or integer variable expressions. For example, all of the following are valid, with the obvious meanings:

7 mod 3

7 mod m

x mod 3

x mod m

$(x^2 + y + 1) \bmod (2m + n)$

where all of the variables are integers. In each case, the left-hand term is divided by the right-hand term, and the resulting value is the remainder. Note that if either the left- or right-hand argument is an expression, the expression is parenthesized. The operator mod is not inside parentheses.

In fact, the mod operation also works if the two arguments are arbitrary real numbers, not just integers. In this book, we are concerned only with the integer operation.

The Congruence Relation mod

As a congruence relation, mod expresses that two arguments have the same remainder with respect to a given modulus. For example, $7 \equiv 4 \pmod 3$ expresses the fact that both 7 and 4 have a remainder of 1 when divided by 3. The following two expressions are equivalent:

$$a \equiv b \pmod m \qquad \Leftrightarrow \qquad a \bmod m = b \bmod m$$

Another way of expressing it is to say that the expression $a \equiv b \pmod m$ is the same as saying that $a - b$ is an integral multiple of m. Again, all the arguments may be integers, integer variables, or integer variable expressions. For example, all of the following are valid, with the obvious meanings:

$7 \equiv 4 \pmod 3$

$x \equiv y \pmod m$

$(x^2 + y + 1) \equiv (a + 1)(\text{mod } [m + n])$

where all of the variables are integers. Two conventions are used. The congruence sign is $\equiv$. The modulus for the relation is defined by placing the mod operator followed by the modulus in parentheses.

The congruence relation is used to define **residue classes**. Those numbers that have the same remainder r when divided by m form a residue class (mod m). There are m residue classes (mod m). For a given remainder r, the residue class to which it belongs consists of the numbers

$$r, r \pm m, r \pm 2m, \ldots$$

According to our definition, the congruence

$$a \equiv b \pmod{m}$$

signifies that the numbers a and b differ by a multiple of m. Consequently, the congruence can also be expressed in the terms that a and b belong to the same residue class (mod m).

PART TWO: SYMMETRIC CIPHERS

CHAPTER 3

CLASSICAL ENCRYPTION TECHNIQUES

LEARNING OBJECTIVES

After studying this chapter, you should be able to:

- Present an overview of the main concepts of symmetric cryptography.
- Explain the difference between cryptanalysis and brute-force attack.
- Understand the operation of a monoalphabetic substitution cipher.
- Understand the operation of a polyalphabetic cipher.
- Present an overview of the Hill cipher.
- Describe the operation of a rotor machine.

Symmetric encryption, also referred to as conventional encryption or single-key encryption, was the only type of encryption in use prior to the development of public-key encryption in the 1970s. It remains by far the most widely used of the two types of encryption. Part One examines a number of symmetric ciphers. In this chapter, we begin with a look at a general model for the symmetric encryption process; this will enable us to understand the context within which the algorithms are used. Next, we examine a variety of algorithms in use before the computer era. Finally, we look briefly at a different approach known as steganography. Chapters 4 and 6 introduce the two most widely used symmetric cipher: DES and AES.

Before beginning, we define some terms. An original message is known as the **plaintext**, while the coded message is called the **ciphertext**. The process of converting from plaintext to ciphertext is known as **enciphering** or **encryption**; restoring the plaintext from the ciphertext is **deciphering** or **decryption**. The many schemes used for encryption constitute the area of study known as **cryptography**. Such a scheme is known as a **cryptographic system** or a **cipher**. Techniques used for deciphering a message without any knowledge of the enciphering details fall into the area of **cryptanalysis**. Cryptanalysis is what the layperson calls "breaking the code." The areas of cryptography and cryptanalysis together are called **cryptology**.

3.1 SYMMETRIC CIPHER MODEL

A symmetric encryption scheme has five ingredients (Figure 3.1):

- **Plaintext:** This is the original intelligible message or data that is fed into the algorithm as input.
- **Encryption algorithm:** The encryption algorithm performs various substitutions and transformations on the plaintext.
- **Secret key:** The secret key is also input to the encryption algorithm. The key is a value independent of the plaintext and of the algorithm. The algorithm will produce a different output depending on the specific key being used at the time. The exact substitutions and transformations performed by the algorithm depend on the key.

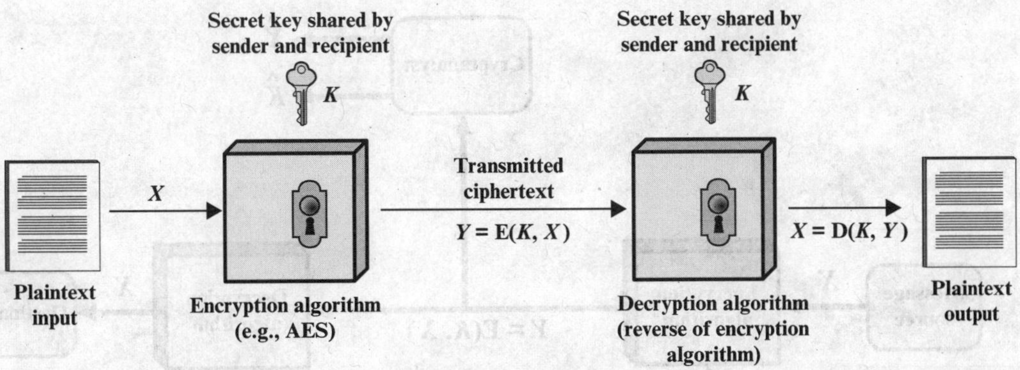

Figure 3.1 Simplified Model of Symmetric Encryption

- **Ciphertext:** This is the scrambled message produced as output. It depends on the plaintext and the secret key. For a given message, two different keys will produce two different ciphertexts. The ciphertext is an apparently random stream of data and, as it stands, is unintelligible.
- **Decryption algorithm:** This is essentially the encryption algorithm run in reverse. It takes the ciphertext and the secret key and produces the original plaintext.

There are two requirements for secure use of conventional encryption:

1. We need a strong encryption algorithm. At a minimum, we would like the algorithm to be such that an opponent who knows the algorithm and has access to one or more ciphertexts would be unable to decipher the ciphertext or figure out the key. This requirement is usually stated in a stronger form: The opponent should be unable to decrypt ciphertext or discover the key even if he or she is in possession of a number of ciphertexts together with the plaintext that produced each ciphertext.
2. Sender and receiver must have obtained copies of the secret key in a secure fashion and must keep the key secure. If someone can discover the key and knows the algorithm, all communication using this key is readable.

We assume that it is impractical to decrypt a message on the basis of the ciphertext *plus* knowledge of the encryption/decryption algorithm. In other words, we do not need to keep the algorithm secret; we need to keep only the key secret. This feature of symmetric encryption is what makes it feasible for widespread use. The fact that the algorithm need not be kept secret means that manufacturers can and have developed low-cost chip implementations of data encryption algorithms. These chips are widely available and incorporated into a number of products. With the use of symmetric encryption, the principal security problem is maintaining the secrecy of the key.

Let us take a closer look at the essential elements of a symmetric encryption scheme, using Figure 3.2. A source produces a message in plaintext, $X = [X_1, X_2, \ldots, X_M]$. The M elements of X are letters in some finite alphabet. Traditionally, the alphabet usually consisted of the 26 capital letters. Nowadays,

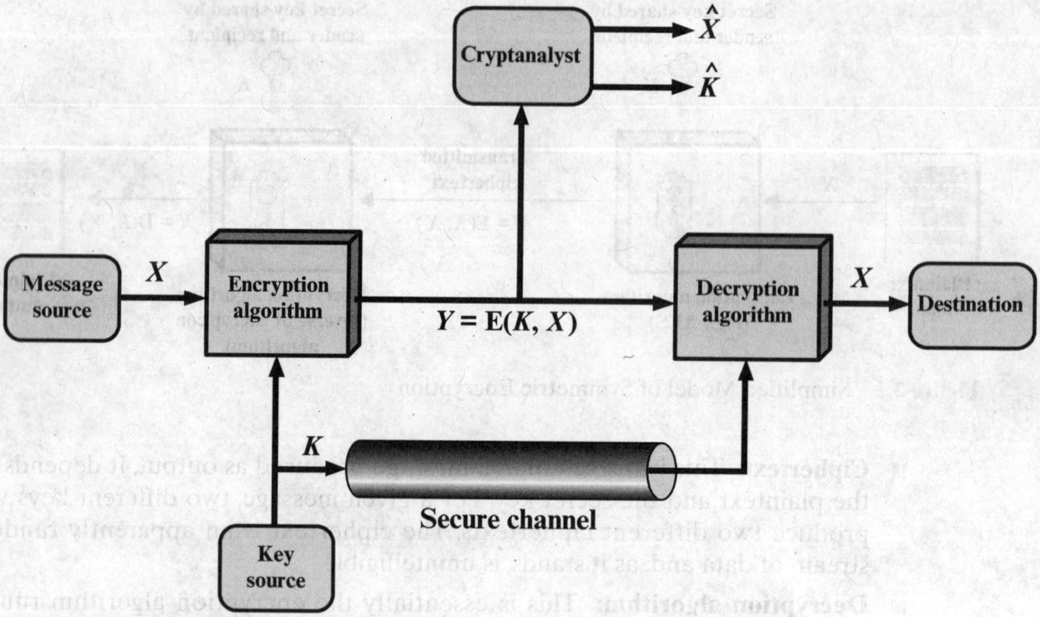

Figure 3.2 Model of Symmetric Cryptosystem

the binary alphabet {0, 1} is typically used. For encryption, a key of the form $K = [K_1, K_2, \ldots, K_J]$ is generated. If the key is generated at the message source, then it must also be provided to the destination by means of some secure channel. Alternatively, a third party could generate the key and securely deliver it to both source and destination.

With the message X and the encryption key K as input, the encryption algorithm forms the ciphertext $Y = [Y_1, Y_2, \ldots, Y_N]$. We can write this as

$$Y = \mathrm{E}(K, X)$$

This notation indicates that Y is produced by using encryption algorithm E as a function of the plaintext X, with the specific function determined by the value of the key K.

The intended receiver, in possession of the key, is able to invert the transformation:

$$X = \mathrm{D}(K, Y)$$

An opponent, observing Y but not having access to K or X, may attempt to recover X or K or both X and K. It is assumed that the opponent knows the encryption (E) and decryption (D) algorithms. If the opponent is interested in only this particular message, then the focus of the effort is to recover X by generating a plaintext estimate $\hat{X}$. Often, however, the opponent is interested in being able to read future messages as well, in which case an attempt is made to recover K by generating an estimate $\hat{K}$.

Cryptography

Cryptographic systems are characterized along three independent dimensions:

1. **The type of operations used for transforming plaintext to ciphertext.** All encryption algorithms are based on two general principles: substitution, in which each element in the plaintext (bit, letter, group of bits or letters) is mapped into another element, and transposition, in which elements in the plaintext are rearranged. The fundamental requirement is that no information be lost (i.e., that all operations are reversible). Most systems, referred to as *product systems*, involve multiple stages of substitutions and transpositions.
2. **The number of keys used.** If both sender and receiver use the same key, the system is referred to as symmetric, single-key, secret-key, or conventional encryption. If the sender and receiver use different keys, the system is referred to as asymmetric, two-key, or public-key encryption.
3. **The way in which the plaintext is processed.** A *block cipher* processes the input one block of elements at a time, producing an output block for each input block. A *stream cipher* processes the input elements continuously, producing output one element at a time, as it goes along.

Cryptanalysis and Brute-Force Attack

Typically, the objective of attacking an encryption system is to recover the key in use rather than simply to recover the plaintext of a single ciphertext. There are two general approaches to attacking a conventional encryption scheme:

- **Cryptanalysis:** Cryptanalytic attacks rely on the nature of the algorithm plus perhaps some knowledge of the general characteristics of the plaintext or even some sample plaintext–ciphertext pairs. This type of attack exploits the characteristics of the algorithm to attempt to deduce a specific plaintext or to deduce the key being used.
- **Brute-force attack:** The attacker tries every possible key on a piece of ciphertext until an intelligible translation into plaintext is obtained. On average, half of all possible keys must be tried to achieve success.

If either type of attack succeeds in deducing the key, the effect is catastrophic: All future and past messages encrypted with that key are compromised.

We first consider cryptanalysis and then discuss brute-force attacks.

Table 3.1 summarizes the various types of **cryptanalytic attacks** based on the amount of information known to the cryptanalyst. The most difficult problem is presented when all that is available is the *ciphertext only*. In some cases, not even the encryption algorithm is known, but in general, we can assume that the opponent does know the algorithm used for encryption. One possible attack under these circumstances is the brute-force approach of trying all possible keys. If the key space is very large, this becomes impractical. Thus, the opponent must rely on an analysis of the ciphertext itself, generally applying various statistical tests to it. To use this

Table 3.1 Types of Attacks on Encrypted Messages

Type of Attack	Known to Cryptanalyst
Ciphertext Only	■ Encryption algorithm ■ Ciphertext
Known Plaintext	■ Encryption algorithm ■ Ciphertext ■ One or more plaintext–ciphertext pairs formed with the secret key
Chosen Plaintext	■ Encryption algorithm ■ Ciphertext ■ Plaintext message chosen by cryptanalyst, together with its corresponding ciphertext generated with the secret key
Chosen Ciphertext	■ Encryption algorithm ■ Ciphertext ■ Ciphertext chosen by cryptanalyst, together with its corresponding decrypted plaintext generated with the secret key
Chosen Text	■ Encryption algorithm ■ Ciphertext ■ Plaintext message chosen by cryptanalyst, together with its corresponding ciphertext generated with the secret key ■ Ciphertext chosen by cryptanalyst, together with its corresponding decrypted plaintext generated with the secret key

approach, the opponent must have some general idea of the type of plaintext that is concealed, such as English or French text, an EXE file, a Java source listing, an accounting file, and so on.

The ciphertext-only attack is the easiest to defend against because the opponent has the least amount of information to work with. In many cases, however, the analyst has more information. The analyst may be able to capture one or more plaintext messages as well as their encryptions. Or the analyst may know that certain plaintext patterns will appear in a message. For example, a file that is encoded in the Postscript format always begins with the same pattern, or there may be a standardized header or banner to an electronic funds transfer message, and so on. All these are examples of *known plaintext*. With this knowledge, the analyst may be able to deduce the key on the basis of the way in which the known plaintext is transformed.

Closely related to the known-plaintext attack is what might be referred to as a probable-word attack. If the opponent is working with the encryption of some general prose message, he or she may have little knowledge of what is in the message. However, if the opponent is after some very specific information, then parts of the message may be known. For example, if an entire accounting file is being transmitted, the opponent may know the placement of certain key words in the header of the file. As another example, the source code for a program developed by Corporation X might include a copyright statement in some standardized position.

If the analyst is able somehow to get the source system to insert into the system a message chosen by the analyst, then a *chosen-plaintext* attack is possible. An example of this strategy is differential cryptanalysis, explored in Appendix S.

In general, if the analyst is able to choose the messages to encrypt, the analyst may deliberately pick patterns that can be expected to reveal the structure of the key.

Table 3.1 lists two other types of attack: chosen ciphertext and chosen text. These are less commonly employed as cryptanalytic techniques but are nevertheless possible avenues of attack.

Only relatively weak algorithms fail to withstand a ciphertext-only attack. Generally, an encryption algorithm is designed to withstand a known-plaintext attack.

Two more definitions are worthy of note. An encryption scheme is **unconditionally secure** if the ciphertext generated by the scheme does not contain enough information to determine uniquely the corresponding plaintext, no matter how much ciphertext is available. That is, no matter how much time an opponent has, it is impossible for him or her to decrypt the ciphertext simply because the required information is not there. With the exception of a scheme known as the one-time pad (described later in this chapter), there is no encryption algorithm that is unconditionally secure. Therefore, all that the users of an encryption algorithm can strive for is an algorithm that meets one or both of the following criteria:

- The cost of breaking the cipher exceeds the value of the encrypted information.
- The time required to break the cipher exceeds the useful lifetime of the information.

An encryption scheme is said to be **computationally secure** if either of the foregoing two criteria are met. Unfortunately, it is very difficult to estimate the amount of effort required to cryptanalyze ciphertext successfully.

All forms of cryptanalysis for symmetric encryption schemes are designed to exploit the fact that traces of structure or pattern in the plaintext may survive encryption and be discernible in the ciphertext. This will become clear as we examine various symmetric encryption schemes in this chapter. We will see in Part Two that cryptanalysis for public-key schemes proceeds from a fundamentally different premise, namely, that the mathematical properties of the pair of keys may make it possible for one of the two keys to be deduced from the other.

A **brute-force attack** involves trying every possible key until an intelligible translation of the ciphertext into plaintext is obtained. On average, half of all possible keys must be tried to achieve success. That is, if there are X different keys, on average an attacker would discover the actual key after $X/2$ tries. It is important to note that there is more to a brute-force attack than simply running through all possible keys. Unless known plaintext is provided, the analyst must be able to recognize plaintext as plaintext. If the message is just plain text in English, then the result pops out easily, although the task of recognizing English would have to be automated. If the text message has been compressed before encryption, then recognition is more difficult. And if the message is some more general type of data, such as a numerical file, and this has been compressed, the problem becomes even more difficult to automate. Thus, to supplement the brute-force approach, some degree of knowledge about the expected plaintext is needed, and some means of automatically distinguishing plaintext from garble is also needed.

3.2 SUBSTITUTION TECHNIQUES

In this section and the next, we examine a sampling of what might be called classical encryption techniques. A study of these techniques enables us to illustrate the basic approaches to symmetric encryption used today and the types of cryptanalytic attacks that must be anticipated.

The two basic building blocks of all encryption techniques are substitution and transposition. We examine these in the next two sections. Finally, we discuss a system that combines both substitution and transposition.

A substitution technique is one in which the letters of plaintext are replaced by other letters or by numbers or symbols.[1] If the plaintext is viewed as a sequence of bits, then substitution involves replacing plaintext bit patterns with ciphertext bit patterns.

Caesar Cipher

The earliest known, and the simplest, use of a substitution cipher was by Julius Caesar. The Caesar cipher involves replacing each letter of the alphabet with the letter standing three places further down the alphabet. For example,

```
plain:  meet me after the toga party
cipher: PHHW PH DIWHU WKH WRJD SDUWB
```

Note that the alphabet is wrapped around, so that the letter following Z is A. We can define the transformation by listing all possibilities, as follows:

```
plain:  a b c d e f g h i j k l m n o p q r s t u v w x y z
cipher: D E F G H I J K L M N O P Q R S T U V W X Y Z A B C
```

Let us assign a numerical equivalent to each letter:

a	b	c	d	e	f	g	h	i	j	k	l	m
0	1	2	3	4	5	6	7	8	9	10	11	12

n	o	p	q	r	s	t	u	v	w	x	y	z
13	14	15	16	17	18	19	20	21	22	23	24	25

Then the algorithm can be expressed as follows. For each plaintext letter p, substitute the ciphertext letter C:[2]

$$C = \mathrm{E}(3, p) = (p + 3) \bmod 26$$

A shift may be of any amount, so that the general Caesar algorithm is

$$C = \mathrm{E}(k, p) = (p + k) \bmod 26 \tag{3.1}$$

[1]When letters are involved, the following conventions are used in this book. Plaintext is always in lowercase; ciphertext is in uppercase; key values are in italicized lowercase.

[2]We define $a \bmod n$ to be the remainder when a is divided by n. For example, $11 \bmod 7 = 4$. See Chapter 2 for a further discussion of modular arithmetic.

where k takes on a value in the range 1 to 25. The decryption algorithm is simply

$$p = \mathrm{D}(k, C) = (C - k) \bmod 26 \quad \textbf{(3.2)}$$

If it is known that a given ciphertext is a Caesar cipher, then a brute-force cryptanalysis is easily performed: simply try all the 25 possible keys. Figure 3.3 shows the results of applying this strategy to the example ciphertext. In this case, the plaintext leaps out as occupying the third line.

Three important characteristics of this problem enabled us to use a brute-force cryptanalysis:

1. The encryption and decryption algorithms are known.
2. There are only 25 keys to try.
3. The language of the plaintext is known and easily recognizable.

In most networking situations, we can assume that the algorithms are known. What generally makes brute-force cryptanalysis impractical is the use of an algorithm that employs a large number of keys. For example, the triple DES algorithm,

```
            PHHW PH DIWHU WKH WRJD SDUWB
KEY
      1     oggv og chvgt vjg vqic rctva
      2     nffu nf bgufs uif uphb qbsuz
      3     meet me after the toga party
      4     ldds ld zesdq sgd snfz ozqsx
      5     kccr kc ydrcp rfc rmey nyprw
      6     jbbq jb xcqbo qeb qldx mxoqv
      7     iaap ia wbpan pda pkcw lwnpu
      8     hzzo hz vaozm ocz ojbv kvmot
      9     gyyn gy uznyl nby niau julns
     10     fxxm fx tymxk max mhzt itkmr
     11     ewwl ew sxlwj lzw lgys hsjlq
     12     dvvk dv rwkvi kyv kfxr grikp
     13     cuuj cu qvjuh jxu jewq fqhjo
     14     btti bt puitg iwt idvp epgin
     15     assh as othsf hvs hcuo dofhm
     16     zrrg zr nsgre gur gbtn cnegl
     17     yqqf yq mrfqd ftq fasm bmdfk
     18     xppe xp lqepc esp ezrl alcej
     19     wood wo kpdob dro dyqk zkbdi
     20     vnnc vn jocna cqn cxpj yjach
     21     ummb um inbmz bpm bwoi xizbg
     22     tlla tl hmaly aol avnh whyaf
     23     skkz sk glzkx znk zumg vgxze
     24     rjjy rj fkyjw ymj ytlf ufwyd
     25     qiix qi ejxiv xli xske tevxc
```

Figure 3.3 Brute-Force Cryptanalysis of Caesar Cipher

```
~+Wµ"– Ω-O)≤4{∞‡¸ ë~Ω%ràu·¯í ◊¯Z-
Ú≠2Ò#Åæ∂ œ«q7¸Ωn·®3N◊Ú Œz'Y-ƒ∞Í[±Û_ èΩ,<NO¬±«ˇxã  Åä£èü3Å
x}ö§kºÂ
_yÍ ^ΔÉ] ¸¤ J/˚iTê&ı 'c<uΩ-
 ÄD(G WÄC~y_ïõÄW PÔı«ÎÜ†ç],¤¡ˇÌ^üÑπˇ≈ˇLˇ9Ogflˇ&Œ≤ ¬≤ ØÔ§˝:
 ˇŒ!SGqèvo^ ú\¸S>h<-*6ø‡%x´˝|fiÓ#≈˜my‰ˇ≥ñP‹,ƒi Áj  Å◊¿˝Zù-
Ω¨Õ¯6Œÿ{% „ΩÊó ¸ï π÷Áî˚úO2çSÿ´O-
2Äflßi /@^˝∏Kºª PŒπ¸úé^´3∑˘ö˘ÔZÌ"Y¬ŸΩœY› Ω+eô/˙‹K£¿*÷˜"≤û˜
B ZøK˜Qßÿüƒ¸!ÒflÎzsS/]>ÈQ ü
```

Figure 3.4 Sample of Compressed Text

examined in Chapter 7, makes use of a 168-bit key, giving a key space of 2^{168} or greater than 3.7×10^{50} possible keys.

The third characteristic is also significant. If the language of the plaintext is unknown, then plaintext output may not be recognizable. Furthermore, the input may be abbreviated or compressed in some fashion, again making recognition difficult. For example, Figure 3.4 shows a portion of a text file compressed using an algorithm called ZIP. If this file is then encrypted with a simple substitution cipher (expanded to include more than just 26 alphabetic characters), then the plaintext may not be recognized when it is uncovered in the brute-force cryptanalysis.

Monoalphabetic Ciphers

With only 25 possible keys, the Caesar cipher is far from secure. A dramatic increase in the key space can be achieved by allowing an arbitrary substitution. Before proceeding, we define the term *permutation*. A **permutation** of a finite set of elements *S* is an ordered sequence of all the elements of *S*, with each element appearing exactly once. For example, if $S = \{a, b, c\}$, there are six permutations of *S*:

abc, acb, bac, bca, cab, cba

In general, there are $n!$ permutations of a set of n elements, because the first element can be chosen in one of n ways, the second in $n - 1$ ways, the third in $n - 2$ ways, and so on.

Recall the assignment for the Caesar cipher:

```
plain:  a b c d e f g h i j k l m n o p q r s t u v w x y z
cipher: D E F G H I J K L M N O P Q R S T U V W X Y Z A B C
```

If, instead, the "cipher" line can be any permutation of the 26 alphabetic characters, then there are 26! or greater than 4×10^{26} possible keys. This is 10 orders of magnitude greater than the key space for DES and would seem to eliminate brute-force techniques for cryptanalysis. Such an approach is referred to as a **monoalphabetic substitution cipher**, because a single cipher alphabet (mapping from plain alphabet to cipher alphabet) is used per message.

There is, however, another line of attack. If the cryptanalyst knows the nature of the plaintext (e.g., noncompressed English text), then the analyst can exploit the regularities of the language. To see how such a cryptanalysis might proceed, we give a partial example here that is adapted from one in [SINK09]. The ciphertext to be solved is

```
UZQSOVUOHXMOPVGPOZPEVSGZWSZOPFPESXUDBMETSXAIZ
VUEPHZHMDZSHZOWSFPAPPDTSVPQUZWYMXUZUHSX
EPYEPOPDZSZUFPOMBZWPFUPZHMDJUDTMOHMQ
```

As a first step, the relative frequency of the letters can be determined and compared to a standard frequency distribution for English, such as is shown in Figure 3.5 (based on [LEWA00]). If the message were long enough, this technique alone might be sufficient, but because this is a relatively short message, we cannot expect an exact match. In any case, the relative frequencies of the letters in the ciphertext (in percentages) are as follows:

P 13.33	H 5.83	F 3.33	B 1.67	C 0.00
Z 11.67	D 5.00	W 3.33	G 1.67	K 0.00
S 8.33	E 5.00	Q 2.50	Y 1.67	L 0.00
U 8.33	V 4.17	T 2.50	I 0.83	N 0.00
O 7.50	X 4.17	A 1.67	J 0.83	R 0.00
M 6.67				

Comparing this breakdown with Figure 3.5, it seems likely that cipher letters P and Z are the equivalents of plain letters e and t, but it is not certain which is which. The letters S, U, O, M, and H are all of relatively high frequency and probably

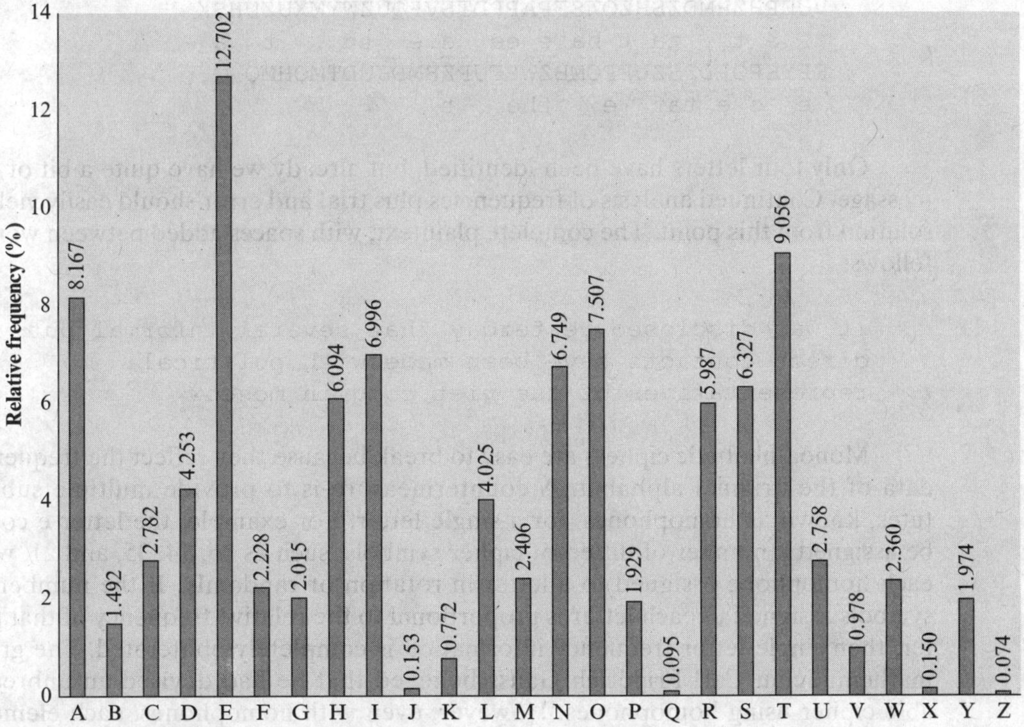

Figure 3.5 Relative Frequency of Letters in English Text

correspond to plain letters from the set {a, h, i, n, o, r, s}. The letters with the lowest frequencies (namely, A, B, G, Y, I, J) are likely included in the set {b, j, k, q, v, x, z}.

There are a number of ways to proceed at this point. We could make some tentative assignments and start to fill in the plaintext to see if it looks like a reasonable "skeleton" of a message. A more systematic approach is to look for other regularities. For example, certain words may be known to be in the text. Or we could look for repeating sequences of cipher letters and try to deduce their plaintext equivalents.

A powerful tool is to look at the frequency of two-letter combinations, known as **digrams**. A table similar to Figure 3.5 could be drawn up showing the relative frequency of digrams. The most common such digram is th. In our ciphertext, the most common digram is ZW, which appears three times. So we make the correspondence of Z with t and W with h. Then, by our earlier hypothesis, we can equate P with e. Now notice that the sequence ZWP appears in the ciphertext, and we can translate that sequence as "the." This is the most frequent trigram (three-letter combination) in English, which seems to indicate that we are on the right track.

Next, notice the sequence ZWSZ in the first line. We do not know that these four letters form a complete word, but if they do, it is of the form th_t. If so, S equates with a.

So far, then, we have

```
UZQSOVUOHXMOPVGPOZPEVSGZWSZOPFPESXUDBMETSXAIZ
 t a        e  e te  a that e e a       a
VUEPHZHMDZSHZOWSFPAPPDTSVPQUZWYMXUZUHSX
   e t   ta t ha e ee  a e  th    t  a
EPYEPOPDZSZUFPOMBZWPFUPZHMDJUDTMOHMQ
 e  e e tat  e   the   t
```

Only four letters have been identified, but already we have quite a bit of the message. Continued analysis of frequencies plus trial and error should easily yield a solution from this point. The complete plaintext, with spaces added between words, follows:

```
it was disclosed yesterday that several informal but
direct contacts have been made with political
representatives of the viet cong in moscow
```

Monoalphabetic ciphers are easy to break because they reflect the frequency data of the original alphabet. A countermeasure is to provide multiple substitutes, known as homophones, for a single letter. For example, the letter e could be assigned a number of different cipher symbols, such as 16, 74, 35, and 21, with each homophone assigned to a letter in rotation or randomly. If the number of symbols assigned to each letter is proportional to the relative frequency of that letter, then single-letter frequency information is completely obliterated. The great mathematician Carl Friedrich Gauss believed that he had devised an unbreakable cipher using homophones. However, even with homophones, each element of plaintext affects only one element of ciphertext, and multiple-letter patterns (e.g., digram frequencies) still survive in the ciphertext, making cryptanalysis relatively straightforward.

Two principal methods are used in substitution ciphers to lessen the extent to which the structure of the plaintext survives in the ciphertext: One approach is to encrypt multiple letters of plaintext, and the other is to use multiple cipher alphabets. We briefly examine each.

Playfair Cipher

The best-known multiple-letter encryption cipher is the Playfair, which treats digrams in the plaintext as single units and translates these units into ciphertext digrams.[3]

The Playfair algorithm is based on the use of a 5×5 matrix of letters constructed using a keyword. Here is an example, solved by Lord Peter Wimsey in Dorothy Sayers's *Have His Carcase*:[4]

M	O	N	A	R
C	H	Y	B	D
E	F	G	I/J	K
L	P	Q	S	T
U	V	W	X	Z

In this case, the keyword is *monarchy*. The matrix is constructed by filling in the letters of the keyword (minus duplicates) from left to right and from top to bottom, and then filling in the remainder of the matrix with the remaining letters in alphabetic order. The letters I and J count as one letter. Plaintext is encrypted two letters at a time, according to the following rules:

1. Repeating plaintext letters that are in the same pair are separated with a filler letter, such as x, so that balloon would be treated as ba lx lo on.
2. Two plaintext letters that fall in the same row of the matrix are each replaced by the letter to the right, with the first element of the row circularly following the last. For example, ar is encrypted as RM.
3. Two plaintext letters that fall in the same column are each replaced by the letter beneath, with the top element of the column circularly following the last. For example, mu is encrypted as CM.
4. Otherwise, each plaintext letter in a pair is replaced by the letter that lies in its own row and the column occupied by the other plaintext letter. Thus, hs becomes BP and ea becomes IM (or JM, as the encipherer wishes).

The Playfair cipher is a great advance over simple monoalphabetic ciphers. For one thing, whereas there are only 26 letters, there are $26 \times 26 = 676$ digrams,

---

[3]This cipher was actually invented by British scientist Sir Charles Wheatstone in 1854, but it bears the name of his friend Baron Playfair of St. Andrews, who championed the cipher at the British foreign office.

[4]The book provides an absorbing account of a probable-word attack.

so that identification of individual digrams is more difficult. Furthermore, the relative frequencies of individual letters exhibit a much greater range than that of digrams, making frequency analysis much more difficult. For these reasons, the Playfair cipher was for a long time considered unbreakable. It was used as the standard field system by the British Army in World War I and still enjoyed considerable use by the U.S. Army and other Allied forces during World War II.

Despite this level of confidence in its security, the Playfair cipher is relatively easy to break, because it still leaves much of the structure of the plaintext language intact. A few hundred letters of ciphertext are generally sufficient.

One way of revealing the effectiveness of the Playfair and other ciphers is shown in Figure 3.6. The line labeled *plaintext* plots a typical frequency distribution of the 26 alphabetic characters (no distinction between upper and lower case) in ordinary text. This is also the frequency distribution of any monoalphabetic substitution cipher, because the frequency values for individual letters are the same, just with different letters substituted for the original letters. The plot is developed in the following way: The number of occurrences of each letter in the text is counted and divided by the number of occurrences of the most frequently used letter. Using the results of Figure 3.5, we see that e is the most frequently used letter. As a result, e has a relative frequency of 1, t of 9.056/12.702 $\approx$ 0.72, and so on. The points on the horizontal axis correspond to the letters in order of decreasing frequency.

Figure 3.6 also shows the frequency distribution that results when the text is encrypted using the Playfair cipher. To normalize the plot, the number of occurrences of each letter in the ciphertext was again divided by the number of occurrences of e in the plaintext. The resulting plot therefore shows the extent to which the frequency distribution of letters, which makes it trivial to solve substitution

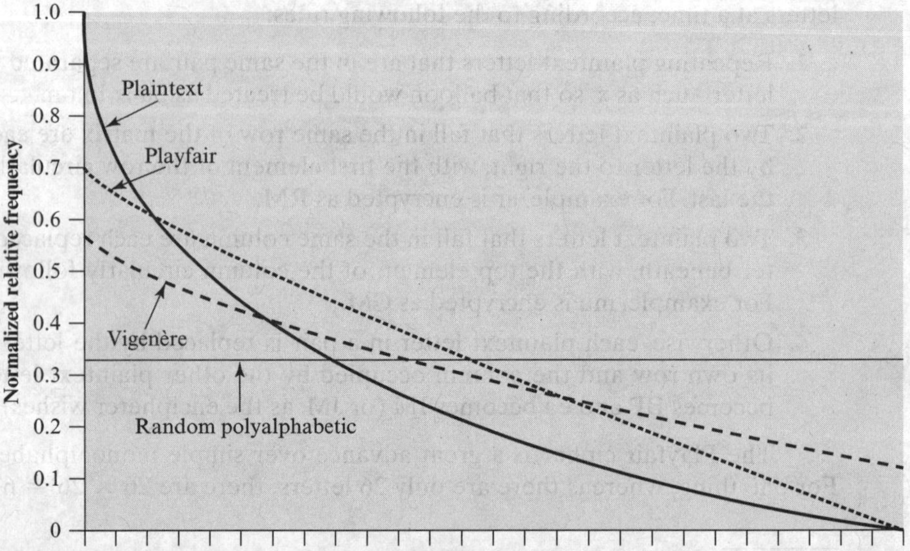

Figure 3.6 Relative Frequency of Occurrence of Letters

ciphers, is masked by encryption. If the frequency distribution information were totally concealed in the encryption process, the ciphertext plot of frequencies would be flat, and cryptanalysis using ciphertext only would be effectively impossible. As the figure shows, the Playfair cipher has a flatter distribution than does plaintext, but nevertheless, it reveals plenty of structure for a cryptanalyst to work with. The plot also shows the Vigenère cipher, discussed subsequently. The Hill and Vigenère curves on the plot are based on results reported in [SIMM93].

Hill Cipher[5]

Another interesting multiletter cipher is the Hill cipher, developed by the mathematician Lester Hill in 1929.

CONCEPTS FROM LINEAR ALGEBRA Before describing the Hill cipher, let us briefly review some terminology from linear algebra. In this discussion, we are concerned with matrix arithmetic modulo 26. For the reader who needs a refresher on matrix multiplication and inversion, see Appendix E.

We define the inverse $\mathbf{M}^{-1}$ of a square matrix $\mathbf{M}$ by the equation $\mathbf{M}(\mathbf{M}^{-1}) = \mathbf{M}^{-1}\mathbf{M} = \mathbf{I}$, where $\mathbf{I}$ is the identity matrix. $\mathbf{I}$ is a square matrix that is all zeros except for ones along the main diagonal from upper left to lower right. The inverse of a matrix does not always exist, but when it does, it satisfies the preceding equation. For example,

$$\mathbf{A} = \begin{pmatrix} 5 & 8 \\ 17 & 3 \end{pmatrix} \qquad \mathbf{A}^{-1} \bmod 26 = \begin{pmatrix} 9 & 2 \\ 1 & 15 \end{pmatrix}$$

$$\mathbf{AA}^{-1} = \begin{pmatrix} (5 \times 9) + (8 \times 1) & (5 \times 2) + (8 \times 15) \\ (17 \times 9) + (3 \times 1) & (17 \times 2) + (3 \times 15) \end{pmatrix}$$

$$= \begin{pmatrix} 53 & 130 \\ 156 & 79 \end{pmatrix} \bmod 26 = \begin{pmatrix} 1 & 0 \\ 0 & 1 \end{pmatrix}$$

To explain how the inverse of a matrix is computed, we begin with the concept of determinant. For any square matrix ($m \times m$), the **determinant** equals the sum of all the products that can be formed by taking exactly one element from each row and exactly one element from each column, with certain of the product terms preceded by a minus sign. For a 2×2 matrix,

$$\begin{pmatrix} k_{11} & k_{12} \\ k_{21} & k_{22} \end{pmatrix}$$

the determinant is $k_{11}k_{22} - k_{12}k_{21}$. For a 3×3 matrix, the value of the determinant is $k_{11}k_{22}k_{33} + k_{21}k_{32}k_{13} + k_{31}k_{12}k_{23} - k_{31}k_{22}k_{13} - k_{21}k_{12}k_{33} - k_{11}k_{32}k_{23}$. If a square

[5]This cipher is somewhat more difficult to understand than the others in this chapter, but it illustrates an important point about cryptanalysis that will be useful later on. This subsection can be skipped on a first reading.

matrix **A** has a nonzero determinant, then the inverse of the matrix is computed as $[\mathbf{A}^{-1}]_{ij} = (\det \mathbf{A})^{-1}(-1)^{i+j}(\mathrm{D}_{ji})$, where (D_{ji}) is the subdeterminant formed by deleting the jth row and the ith column of **A**, det(**A**) is the determinant of **A**, and $(\det \mathbf{A})^{-1}$ is the multiplicative inverse of (det **A**) mod 26.

Continuing our example,

$$\det\begin{pmatrix} 5 & 8 \\ 17 & 3 \end{pmatrix} = (5 \times 3) - (8 \times 17) = -121 \bmod 26 = 9$$

We can show that $9^{-1} \bmod 26 = 3$, because $9 \times 3 = 27 \bmod 26 = 1$ (see Chapter 2 or Appendix E). Therefore, we compute the inverse of **A** as

$$\mathbf{A} = \begin{pmatrix} 5 & 8 \\ 17 & 3 \end{pmatrix}$$

$$\mathbf{A}^{-1} \bmod 26 = 3\begin{pmatrix} 3 & -8 \\ -17 & 5 \end{pmatrix} = 3\begin{pmatrix} 3 & 18 \\ 9 & 5 \end{pmatrix} = \begin{pmatrix} 9 & 54 \\ 27 & 15 \end{pmatrix} = \begin{pmatrix} 9 & 2 \\ 1 & 15 \end{pmatrix}$$

The Hill Algorithm This encryption algorithm takes m successive plaintext letters and substitutes for them m ciphertext letters. The substitution is determined by m linear equations in which each character is assigned a numerical value ($a = 0, b = 1, \ldots, z = 25$). For $m = 3$, the system can be described as

$$c_1 = (k_{11}p_1 + k_{21}p_2 + k_{31}p_3) \bmod 26$$
$$c_2 = (k_{12}p_1 + k_{22}p_2 + k_{32}p_3) \bmod 26$$
$$c_3 = (k_{13}p_1 + k_{23}p_2 + k_{33}p_3) \bmod 26$$

This can be expressed in terms of row vectors and matrices:[6]

$$(c_1\ c_2\ c_3) = (p_1\ p_2\ p_3)\begin{pmatrix} k_{11} & k_{12} & k_{13} \\ k_{21} & k_{22} & k_{23} \\ k_{31} & k_{32} & k_{33} \end{pmatrix} \bmod 26$$

or

$$\mathbf{C} = \mathbf{PK} \bmod 26$$

where **C** and **P** are row vectors of length 3 representing the plaintext and ciphertext, and **K** is a 3×3 matrix representing the encryption key. Operations are performed mod 26.

[6]Some cryptography books express the plaintext and ciphertext as column vectors, so that the column vector is placed after the matrix rather than the row vector placed before the matrix. Sage uses row vectors, so we adopt that convention.

For example, consider the plaintext "paymoremoney" and use the encryption key

$$\mathbf{K} = \begin{pmatrix} 17 & 17 & 5 \\ 21 & 18 & 21 \\ 2 & 2 & 19 \end{pmatrix}$$

The first three letters of the plaintext are represented by the vector (15 0 24). Then (15 0 24)**K** = (303 303 531) mod 26 = (17 17 11) = RRL. Continuing in this fashion, the ciphertext for the entire plaintext is RRLMWBKASPDH.

Decryption requires using the inverse of the matrix **K**. We can compute det **K** = 23, and therefore, $(\det \mathbf{K})^{-1}$ mod 26 = 17. We can then compute the inverse as[7]

$$\mathbf{K}^{-1} = \begin{pmatrix} 4 & 9 & 15 \\ 15 & 17 & 6 \\ 24 & 0 & 17 \end{pmatrix}$$

This is demonstrated as

$$\begin{pmatrix} 17 & 17 & 5 \\ 21 & 18 & 21 \\ 2 & 2 & 19 \end{pmatrix}\begin{pmatrix} 4 & 9 & 15 \\ 15 & 17 & 6 \\ 24 & 0 & 17 \end{pmatrix} = \begin{pmatrix} 443 & 442 & 442 \\ 858 & 495 & 780 \\ 494 & 52 & 365 \end{pmatrix} \bmod 26 = \begin{pmatrix} 1 & 0 & 0 \\ 0 & 1 & 0 \\ 0 & 0 & 1 \end{pmatrix}$$

It is easily seen that if the matrix $\mathbf{K}^{-1}$ is applied to the ciphertext, then the plaintext is recovered.

In general terms, the Hill system can be expressed as

$$\mathbf{C} = \mathrm{E}(\mathbf{K}, \mathbf{P}) = \mathbf{PK} \bmod 26$$

$$\mathbf{P} = \mathrm{D}(\mathbf{K}, \mathbf{C}) = \mathbf{CK}^{-1} \bmod 26 = \mathbf{PKK}^{-1} = \mathbf{P}$$

As with Playfair, the strength of the Hill cipher is that it completely hides single-letter frequencies. Indeed, with Hill, the use of a larger matrix hides more frequency information. Thus, a 3 × 3 Hill cipher hides not only single-letter but also two-letter frequency information.

Although the Hill cipher is strong against a ciphertext-only attack, it is easily broken with a known plaintext attack. For an $m \times m$ Hill cipher, suppose we have m plaintext–ciphertext pairs, each of length m. We label the pairs $\mathbf{P}_j = (p_{1j}p_{1j} \ldots p_{mj})$ and $\mathbf{C}_j = (c_{1j}c_{1j} \ldots c_{mj})$ such that $\mathbf{C}_j = \mathbf{P}_j\mathbf{K}$ for $1 \le j \le m$ and for some unknown key matrix **K**. Now define two $m \times m$ matrices $\mathbf{X} = (p_{ij})$ and $\mathbf{Y} = (c_{ij})$. Then we can form the matrix equation $\mathbf{Y} = \mathbf{XK}$. If **X** has an inverse, then we can determine $\mathbf{K} = \mathbf{X}^{-1}\mathbf{Y}$. If **X** is not invertible, then a new version of **X** can be formed with additional plaintext–ciphertext pairs until an invertible **X** is obtained.

Consider this example. Suppose that the plaintext "hillcipher" is encrypted using a 2 × 2 Hill cipher to yield the ciphertext HCRZSSXNSP. Thus, we know that (7 8)**K** mod 26 = (7 2); (11 11)**K** mod 26 = (17 25); and so on. Using the first two plaintext-ciphertext pairs, we have

[7]The calculations for this example are provided in detail in Appendix E.

$$\begin{pmatrix} 7 & 2 \\ 17 & 25 \end{pmatrix} = \begin{pmatrix} 7 & 8 \\ 11 & 11 \end{pmatrix} \mathbf{K} \bmod 26$$

The inverse of **X** can be computed:

$$\begin{pmatrix} 7 & 8 \\ 11 & 11 \end{pmatrix}^{-1} = \begin{pmatrix} 25 & 22 \\ 1 & 23 \end{pmatrix}$$

so

$$\mathbf{K} = \begin{pmatrix} 25 & 22 \\ 1 & 23 \end{pmatrix} \begin{pmatrix} 7 & 2 \\ 17 & 25 \end{pmatrix} = \begin{pmatrix} 549 & 600 \\ 398 & 577 \end{pmatrix} \bmod 26 = \begin{pmatrix} 3 & 2 \\ 8 & 5 \end{pmatrix}$$

This result is verified by testing the remaining plaintext–ciphertext pairs.

Polyalphabetic Ciphers

Another way to improve on the simple monoalphabetic technique is to use different monoalphabetic substitutions as one proceeds through the plaintext message. The general name for this approach is **polyalphabetic substitution cipher**. All these techniques have the following features in common:

1. A set of related monoalphabetic substitution rules is used.
2. A key determines which particular rule is chosen for a given transformation.

VIGENÈRE CIPHER The best known, and one of the simplest, polyalphabetic ciphers is the Vigenère cipher. In this scheme, the set of related monoalphabetic substitution rules consists of the 26 Caesar ciphers with shifts of 0 through 25. Each cipher is denoted by a key letter, which is the ciphertext letter that substitutes for the plaintext letter a. Thus, a Caesar cipher with a shift of 3 is denoted by the key value 3.[8]

We can express the Vigenère cipher in the following manner. Assume a sequence of plaintext letters $P = p_0, p_1, p_2, \ldots, p_{n-1}$ and a key consisting of the sequence of letters $K = k_0, k_1, k_2, \ldots, k_{m-1}$, where typically $m < n$. The sequence of ciphertext letters $C = C_0, C_1, C_2, \ldots, C_{n-1}$ is calculated as follows:

$$\begin{aligned} C &= C_0, C_1, C_2, \ldots, C_{n-1} = \mathrm{E}(K, P) = \mathrm{E}[(k_0, k_1, k_2, \ldots, k_{m-1}), (p_0, p_1, p_2, \ldots, p_{n-1})] \\ &= (p_0 + k_0) \bmod 26, (p_1 + k_1) \bmod 26, \ldots, (p_{m-1} + k_{m-1}) \bmod 26, \\ &\quad (p_m + k_0) \bmod 26, (p_{m+1} + k_1) \bmod 26, \ldots, (p_{2m-1} + k_{m-1}) \bmod 26, \ldots \end{aligned}$$

Thus, the first letter of the key is added to the first letter of the plaintext, mod 26, the second letters are added, and so on through the first m letters of the plaintext. For the next m letters of the plaintext, the key letters are repeated. This process

[8]To aid in understanding this scheme and also to aid in it use, a matrix known as the Vigenère tableau is often used. This tableau is discussed in a document at box.com/Crypto7e.

continues until all of the plaintext sequence is encrypted. A general equation of the encryption process is

$$C_i = (p_i + k_{i \bmod m}) \bmod 26 \tag{3.3}$$

Compare this with Equation (3.1) for the Caesar cipher. In essence, each plaintext character is encrypted with a different Caesar cipher, depending on the corresponding key character. Similarly, decryption is a generalization of Equation (3.2):

$$p_i = (C_i - k_{i \bmod m}) \bmod 26 \tag{3.4}$$

To encrypt a message, a key is needed that is as long as the message. Usually, the key is a repeating keyword. For example, if the keyword is *deceptive*, the message "we are discovered save yourself" is encrypted as

```
key:         deceptivedeceptivedeceptive
plaintext:   wearediscoveredsaveyourself
ciphertext:  ZICVTWQNGRZGVTWAVZHCQYGLMGJ
```

Expressed numerically, we have the following result.

key	3	4	2	4	15	19	8	21	4	3	4	2	4	15
plaintext	22	4	0	17	4	3	8	18	2	14	21	4	17	4
ciphertext	25	8	2	21	19	22	16	13	6	17	25	6	21	19

key	19	8	21	4	3	4	2	4	15	19	8	21	4
plaintext	3	18	0	21	4	24	14	20	17	18	4	11	5
ciphertext	22	0	21	25	7	2	16	24	6	11	12	6	9

The strength of this cipher is that there are multiple ciphertext letters for each plaintext letter, one for each unique letter of the keyword. Thus, the letter frequency information is obscured. However, not all knowledge of the plaintext structure is lost. For example, Figure 3.6 shows the frequency distribution for a Vigenère cipher with a keyword of length 9. An improvement is achieved over the Playfair cipher, but considerable frequency information remains.

It is instructive to sketch a method of breaking this cipher, because the method reveals some of the mathematical principles that apply in cryptanalysis.

First, suppose that the opponent believes that the ciphertext was encrypted using either monoalphabetic substitution or a Vigenère cipher. A simple test can be made to make a determination. If a monoalphabetic substitution is used, then the statistical properties of the ciphertext should be the same as that of the language of the plaintext. Thus, referring to Figure 3.5, there should be one cipher letter with a relative frequency of occurrence of about 12.7%, one with about 9.06%, and so on. If only a single message is available for analysis, we would not expect an exact match of this small sample with the statistical profile of the plaintext language. Nevertheless, if the correspondence is close, we can assume a monoalphabetic substitution.

If, on the other hand, a Vigenère cipher is suspected, then progress depends on determining the length of the keyword, as will be seen in a moment. For now, let us concentrate on how the keyword length can be determined. The important insight that leads to a solution is the following: If two identical sequences of plaintext letters occur at a distance that is an integer multiple of the keyword length, they will generate identical ciphertext sequences. In the foregoing example, two instances of the sequence "red" are separated by nine character positions. Consequently, in both cases, r is encrypted using key letter *e*, e is encrypted using key letter *p*, and d is encrypted using key letter *t*. Thus, in both cases, the ciphertext sequence is VTW. We indicate this above by underlining the relevant ciphertext letters and shading the relevant ciphertext numbers.

An analyst looking at only the ciphertext would detect the repeated sequences VTW at a displacement of 9 and make the assumption that the keyword is either three or nine letters in length. The appearance of VTW twice could be by chance and may not reflect identical plaintext letters encrypted with identical key letters. However, if the message is long enough, there will be a number of such repeated ciphertext sequences. By looking for common factors in the displacements of the various sequences, the analyst should be able to make a good guess of the keyword length.

Solution of the cipher now depends on an important insight. If the keyword length is *m*, then the cipher, in effect, consists of *m* monoalphabetic substitution ciphers. For example, with the keyword DECEPTIVE, the letters in positions 1, 10, 19, and so on are all encrypted with the same monoalphabetic cipher. Thus, we can use the known frequency characteristics of the plaintext language to attack each of the monoalphabetic ciphers separately.

The periodic nature of the keyword can be eliminated by using a nonrepeating keyword that is as long as the message itself. Vigenère proposed what is referred to as an **autokey system**, in which a keyword is concatenated with the plaintext itself to provide a running key. For our example,

```
key:          deceptivewearediscoveredsav
plaintext:    wearediscoveredsaveyourself
ciphertext:   ZICVTWQNGKZEIIGASXSTSLVVWLA
```

Even this scheme is vulnerable to cryptanalysis. Because the key and the plaintext share the same frequency distribution of letters, a statistical technique can be applied. For example, e enciphered by *e*, by Figure 3.5, can be expected to occur with a frequency of $(0.127)^2 \approx 0.016$, whereas t enciphered by *t* would occur only about half as often. These regularities can be exploited to achieve successful cryptanalysis.[9]

VERNAM CIPHER The ultimate defense against such a cryptanalysis is to choose a keyword that is as long as the plaintext and has no statistical relationship to it. Such a system was introduced by an AT&T engineer named Gilbert Vernam in 1918.

---

[9]Although the techniques for breaking a Vigenère cipher are by no means complex, a 1917 issue of *Scientific American* characterized this system as "impossible of translation." This is a point worth remembering when similar claims are made for modern algorithms.

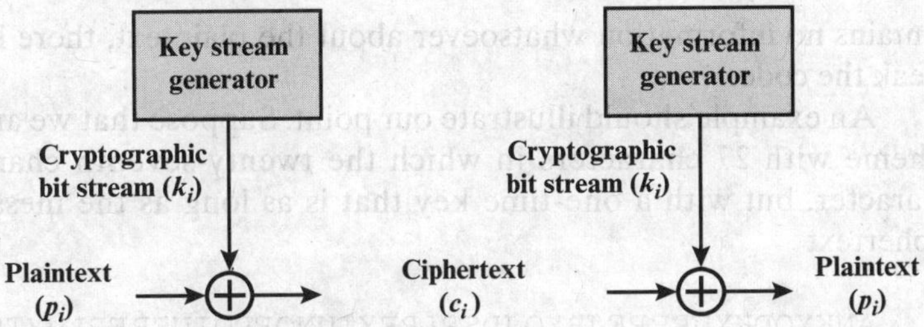

Figure 3.7 Vernam Cipher

His system works on binary data (bits) rather than letters. The system can be expressed succinctly as follows (Figure 3.7):

$$c_i = p_i \oplus k_i$$

where

p_i = ith binary digit of plaintext
k_i = ith binary digit of key
c_i = ith binary digit of ciphertext
$\oplus$ = exclusive-or (XOR) operation

Compare this with Equation (3.3) for the Vigenère cipher.

Thus, the ciphertext is generated by performing the bitwise XOR of the plaintext and the key. Because of the properties of the XOR, decryption simply involves the same bitwise operation:

$$p_i = c_i \oplus k_i$$

which compares with Equation (3.4).

The essence of this technique is the means of construction of the key. Vernam proposed the use of a running loop of tape that eventually repeated the key, so that in fact the system worked with a very long but repeating keyword. Although such a scheme, with a long key, presents formidable cryptanalytic difficulties, it can be broken with sufficient ciphertext, the use of known or probable plaintext sequences, or both.

One-Time Pad

An Army Signal Corp officer, Joseph Mauborgne, proposed an improvement to the Vernam cipher that yields the ultimate in security. Mauborgne suggested using a random key that is as long as the message, so that the key need not be repeated. In addition, the key is to be used to encrypt and decrypt a single message, and then is discarded. Each new message requires a new key of the same length as the new message. Such a scheme, known as a **one-time pad**, is unbreakable. It produces random output that bears no statistical relationship to the plaintext. Because the ciphertext contains no information whatsoever about the plaintext, there is simply no way to break the code.

An example should illustrate our point. Suppose that we are using a Vigenère scheme with 27 characters in which the twenty-seventh character is the space character, but with a one-time key that is as long as the message. Consider the ciphertext

```
ANKYODKYUREPFJBYOJDSPLREYIUNOFDOIUERFPLUYTS
```

We now show two different decryptions using two different keys:

```
ciphertext: ANKYODKYUREPFJBYOJDSPLREYIUNOFDOIUERFPLUYTS
key:        pxlmvmsydofuyrvzwc tnlebnecvgdupahfzzlmnyih
plaintext:  mr mustard with the candlestick in the hall

ciphertext: ANKYODKYUREPFJBYOJDSPLREYIUNOFDOIUERFPLUYTS
key:        pftgpmiydgaxgoufhklllmhsqdqogtewbqfgyovuhwt
plaintext:  miss scarlet with the knife in the library
```

Suppose that a cryptanalyst had managed to find these two keys. Two plausible plaintexts are produced. How is the cryptanalyst to decide which is the correct decryption (i.e., which is the correct key)? If the actual key were produced in a truly random fashion, then the cryptanalyst cannot say that one of these two keys is more likely than the other. Thus, there is no way to decide which key is correct and therefore which plaintext is correct.

In fact, given any plaintext of equal length to the ciphertext, there is a key that produces that plaintext. Therefore, if you did an exhaustive search of all possible keys, you would end up with many legible plaintexts, with no way of knowing which was the intended plaintext. Therefore, the code is unbreakable.

The security of the one-time pad is entirely due to the randomness of the key. If the stream of characters that constitute the key is truly random, then the stream of characters that constitute the ciphertext will be truly random. Thus, there are no patterns or regularities that a cryptanalyst can use to attack the ciphertext.

In theory, we need look no further for a cipher. The one-time pad offers complete security but, in practice, has two fundamental difficulties:

1. There is the practical problem of making large quantities of random keys. Any heavily used system might require millions of random characters on a regular basis. Supplying truly random characters in this volume is a significant task.
2. Even more daunting is the problem of key distribution and protection. For every message to be sent, a key of equal length is needed by both sender and receiver. Thus, a mammoth key distribution problem exists.

Because of these difficulties, the one-time pad is of limited utility and is useful primarily for low-bandwidth channels requiring very high security.

The one-time pad is the only cryptosystem that exhibits what is referred to as *perfect secrecy*. This concept is explored in Appendix F.

3.3 TRANSPOSITION TECHNIQUES

All the techniques examined so far involve the substitution of a ciphertext symbol for a plaintext symbol. A very different kind of mapping is achieved by performing some sort of permutation on the plaintext letters. This technique is referred to as a transposition cipher.

The simplest such cipher is the **rail fence** technique, in which the plaintext is written down as a sequence of diagonals and then read off as a sequence of rows. For example, to encipher the message "meet me after the toga party" with a rail fence of depth 2, we write the following:

```
m e m a t r h t g p r y
 e t e f e t e o a a t
```

The encrypted message is

```
MEMATRHTGPRYETEFETEOAAT
```

This sort of thing would be trivial to cryptanalyze. A more complex scheme is to write the message in a rectangle, row by row, and read the message off, column by column, but permute the order of the columns. The order of the columns then becomes the key to the algorithm. For example,

```
Key:          4 3 1 2 5 6 7
Plaintext:    a t t a c k p
              o s t p o n e
              d u n t i l t
              w o a m x y z
Ciphertext:   TTNAAPTMTSUOAODWCOIXKNLYPETZ
```

Thus, in this example, the key is 4312567. To encrypt, start with the column that is labeled 1, in this case column 3. Write down all the letters in that column. Proceed to column 4, which is labeled 2, then column 2, then column 1, then columns 5, 6, and 7.

A pure transposition cipher is easily recognized because it has the same letter frequencies as the original plaintext. For the type of columnar transposition just shown, cryptanalysis is fairly straightforward and involves laying out the ciphertext in a matrix and playing around with column positions. Digram and trigram frequency tables can be useful.

The transposition cipher can be made significantly more secure by performing more than one stage of transposition. The result is a more complex permutation that is not easily reconstructed. Thus, if the foregoing message is reencrypted using the same algorithm,

```
Key:      4 3 1 2 5 6 7
Input:    t t n a a p t
          m t s u o a o
          d w c o i x k
          n l y p e t z
Output:   NSCYAUOPTTWLTMDNAOIEPAXTTOKZ
```

To visualize the result of this double transposition, designate the letters in the original plaintext message by the numbers designating their position. Thus, with 28 letters in the message, the original sequence of letters is

```
01 02 03 04 05 06 07 08 09 10 11 12 13 14
15 16 17 18 19 20 21 22 23 24 25 26 27 28
```

After the first transposition, we have

```
03 10 17 24 04 11 18 25 02 09 16 23 01 08
15 22 05 12 19 26 06 13 20 27 07 14 21 28
```

which has a somewhat regular structure. But after the second transposition, we have

```
17 09 05 27 24 16 12 07 10 02 22 20 03 25
15 13 04 23 19 14 11 01 26 21 18 08 06 28
```

This is a much less structured permutation and is much more difficult to cryptanalyze.

3.4 ROTOR MACHINES

The example just given suggests that multiple stages of encryption can produce an algorithm that is significantly more difficult to cryptanalyze. This is as true of substitution ciphers as it is of transposition ciphers. Before the introduction of DES, the most important application of the principle of multiple stages of encryption was a class of systems known as rotor machines.[10]

The basic principle of the rotor machine is illustrated in Figure 3.8. The machine consists of a set of independently rotating cylinders through which electrical pulses can flow. Each cylinder has 26 input pins and 26 output pins, with internal wiring that connects each input pin to a unique output pin. For simplicity, only three of the internal connections in each cylinder are shown.

If we associate each input and output pin with a letter of the alphabet, then a single cylinder defines a monoalphabetic substitution. For example, in Figure 3.8, if an operator depresses the key for the letter A, an electric signal is applied to

[10]Machines based on the rotor principle were used by both Germany (Enigma) and Japan (Purple) in World War II. The breaking of both codes by the Allies was a significant factor in the war's outcome.

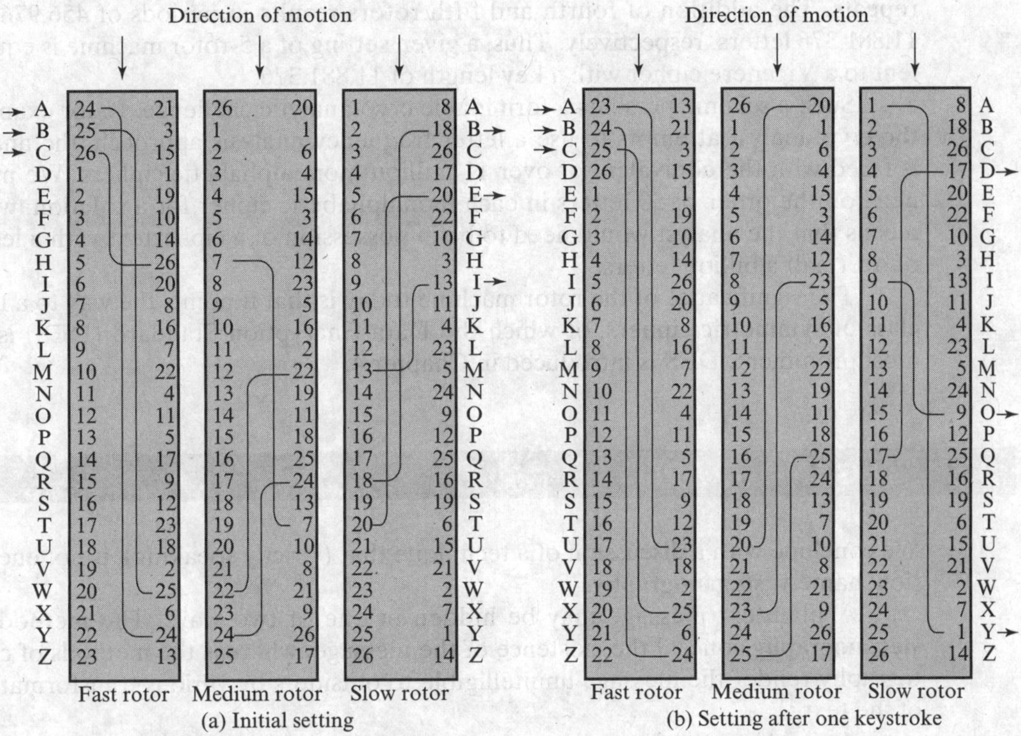

Figure 3.8 Three-Rotor Machine with Wiring Represented by Numbered Contacts

the first pin of the first cylinder and flows through the internal connection to the twenty-fifth output pin.

Consider a machine with a single cylinder. After each input key is depressed, the cylinder rotates one position, so that the internal connections are shifted accordingly. Thus, a different monoalphabetic substitution cipher is defined. After 26 letters of plaintext, the cylinder would be back to the initial position. Thus, we have a polyalphabetic substitution algorithm with a period of 26.

A single-cylinder system is trivial and does not present a formidable cryptanalytic task. The power of the rotor machine is in the use of multiple cylinders, in which the output pins of one cylinder are connected to the input pins of the next. Figure 3.8 shows a three-cylinder system. The left half of the figure shows a position in which the input from the operator to the first pin (plaintext letter a) is routed through the three cylinders to appear at the output of the second pin (ciphertext letter B).

With multiple cylinders, the one closest to the operator input rotates one pin position with each keystroke. The right half of Figure 3.8 shows the system's configuration after a single keystroke. For every complete rotation of the inner cylinder, the middle cylinder rotates one pin position. Finally, for every complete rotation of the middle cylinder, the outer cylinder rotates one pin position. This is the same type of operation seen with an odometer. The result is that there are $26 \times 26 \times 26 = 17{,}576$ different substitution alphabets used before the system repeats. The addition of fourth and fifth rotors results in periods of 456,976 and 11,881,376 letters, respectively. Thus, a given setting of a 5-rotor machine is equivalent to a Vigenère cipher with a key length of 11,881,376.

Such a scheme presents a formidable cryptanalytic challenge. If, for example, the cryptanalyst attempts to use a letter frequency analysis approach, the analyst is faced with the equivalent of over 11 million monoalphabetic ciphers. We might need on the order of 50 letters in each monalphabetic cipher for a solution, which means that the analyst would need to be in possession of a ciphertext with a length of over half a billion letters.

The significance of the rotor machine today is that it points the way to a large class of symmetric ciphers, of which the Data Encryption Standard (DES) is the most prominent. DES is introduced in Chapter 4.

3.5 STEGANOGRAPHY

We conclude with a discussion of a technique that (strictly speaking), is not encryption, namely, **steganography**.

A plaintext message may be hidden in one of two ways. The methods of **steganography** conceal the existence of the message, whereas the methods of cryptography render the message unintelligible to outsiders by various transformations of the text.[11]

A simple form of steganography, but one that is time-consuming to construct, is one in which an arrangement of words or letters within an apparently innocuous text spells out the real message. For example, the sequence of first letters of each word of the overall message spells out the hidden message. Figure 3.9 shows an example in which a subset of the words of the overall message is used to convey the hidden message. See if you can decipher this; it's not too hard.

Various other techniques have been used historically; some examples are the following [MYER91]:

- **Character marking:** Selected letters of printed or typewritten text are overwritten in pencil. The marks are ordinarily not visible unless the paper is held at an angle to bright light.
- **Invisible ink:** A number of substances can be used for writing but leave no visible trace until heat or some chemical is applied to the paper.
- **Pin punctures:** Small pin punctures on selected letters are ordinarily not visible unless the paper is held up in front of a light.
- **Typewriter correction ribbon:** Used between lines typed with a black ribbon, the results of typing with the correction tape are visible only under a strong light.

[11] *Steganography* was an obsolete word that was revived by David Kahn and given the meaning it has today [KAHN96].

3rd March

Dear George,

Greetings to all at Oxford. Many thanks for your
letter and for the Summer examination package.
All Entry Forms and Fees Forms should be ready
for final despatch to the Syndicate by Friday
20th or at the very latest, I'm told. by the 21st.
Admin has improved here, though there's room
for improvement still; just give us all two or three
more years and we'll really show you! Please
don't let these wretched 16+ proposals destroy
your basic O and A pattern. Certainly this
sort of change, if implemented immediately,
would bring chaos.

Sincerely yours.

Figure 3.9 A Puzzle for Inspector Morse
(*From* The Silent World of Nicholas Quinn, *by Colin Dexter*)

Although these techniques may seem archaic, they have contemporary equivalents. [WAYN09] proposes hiding a message by using the least significant bits of frames on a CD. For example, the Kodak Photo CD format's maximum resolution is 3096 × 6144 pixels, with each pixel containing 24 bits of RGB color information. The least significant bit of each 24-bit pixel can be changed without greatly affecting the quality of the image. The result is that you can hide a 130-kB message in a single digital snapshot. There are now a number of software packages available that take this type of approach to steganography.

Steganography has a number of drawbacks when compared to encryption. It requires a lot of overhead to hide a relatively few bits of information, although using a scheme like that proposed in the preceding paragraph may make it more effective. Also, once the system is discovered, it becomes virtually worthless. This problem, too, can be overcome if the insertion method depends on some sort of key (e.g., see Problem 3.22). Alternatively, a message can be first encrypted and then hidden using steganography.

The advantage of steganography is that it can be employed by parties who have something to lose should the fact of their secret communication (not necessarily the content) be discovered. Encryption flags traffic as important or secret or may identify the sender or receiver as someone with something to hide.

3.6 KEY TERMS, REVIEW QUESTIONS, AND PROBLEMS

Key Terms

block cipher	cryptology	Playfair cipher
brute-force attack	deciphering	polyalphabetic cipher
Caesar cipher	decryption	rail fence cipher
cipher	digram	single-key encryption
ciphertext	enciphering	steganography
computationally secure	encryption	stream cipher
conventional encryption	Hill cipher	symmetric encryption
cryptanalysis	monoalphabetic cipher	transposition cipher
cryptographic system	one-time pad	unconditionally secure
cryptography	plaintext	Vigenère cipher

Review Questions

3.1 Name the five essential ingredients of a symmetric cipher model.

3.2 What are the two basic functions used in encryption algorithms?

3.3 How many keys are used for two people to communication using encryption?

3.4 What is the difference between a block cipher and a stream cipher?

3.5 What are the two general approaches to attacking a cipher?

3.6 List and briefly define types of cryptanalytic attacks based on what is known to the attacker.

3.7 When is an encryption scheme said to be unconditionally secure?

3.8 Why is the Caesar cipher substitution technique vulnerable to a brute-force cryptanalysis?

3.9 How much key space is available when a monoalphabetic substitution cipher is used to replace plaintext with ciphertext?

3.10 What is the drawback of a Playfair cipher?

3.11 What is the difference between a monoalphabetic cipher and a polyalphabetic cipher?

3.12 How does the use of random key in one-time pad provide security?

3.13 What is a transposition cipher?

3.14 How is steganography different from cryptography?

Problems

3.1 A generalization of the Caesar cipher, known as the affine Caesar cipher, has the following form: For each plaintext letter p, substitute the ciphertext letter C:

$$C = \mathrm{E}([a, b], p) = (ap + b) \bmod 26$$

A basic requirement of any encryption algorithm is that it be one-to-one. That is, if $p \neq q$, then $\mathrm{E}(k, p) \neq \mathrm{E}(k, q)$. Otherwise, decryption is impossible, because more than one plaintext character maps into the same ciphertext character. The affine Caesar cipher is not one-to-one for all values of a. For example, for $a = 2$ and $b = 3$, then $\mathrm{E}([a, b], 0) = \mathrm{E}([a, b], 13) = 3$.

a. Are there any limitations on the value of b? Explain why or why not.
b. Determine which values of a are not allowed.

c. Provide a general statement of which values of *a* are and are not allowed. Justify your statement.

3.2 How many one-to-one affine Caesar ciphers are there?

3.3 A ciphertext has been generated with an affine cipher. The most frequent letter of the ciphertext is "B", and the second most frequent letter of the ciphertext is "U". Break this code.

3.4 The following ciphertext was generated using a simple substitution algorithm.

```
hzsrnqc klyy wqc flo mflwf ol zqdn nsoznj wskn lj xzsrbjnf,
wzsxz gqv zqhhnf ol ozn glco zlfnco hnlhrn; nsoznj jnrqosdnc
lj fnqj kjsnfbc, wzsxz sc xnjoqsfrv gljn efeceqr. zn rsdnb
qrlfn sf zsc zlecn sf cqdsrrn jlw, wzsoznj flfn hnfnojqonb.
q csfyrn blgncosx cekksxnb ol cnjdn zsg. zn pjnqmkqconb qfb
bsfnb qo ozn xrep, qo zlejc gqozngqosxqrrv ksanb, sf ozn cqgn
jllg, qo ozn cqgn oqprn, fndnj oqmsfy zsc gnqrc wsoz loznj
gngpnjc, gexz rncc pjsfysfy q yenco wsoz zsg; qfb wnfo zlgn
qo naqxorv gsbfsyzo, lfrv ol jnosjn qo lfxn ol pnb. zn fndnj
ecnb ozn xlcv xzqgpnjc wzsxz ozn jnkljg hjldsbnc klj soc
kqdlejnb gngpnjc. zn hqccnb onf zlejc leo lk ozn ownfov-klej
sf cqdsrrn jlw, nsoznj sf crnnhsfy lj gqmsfy zsc olsrno.
```

Decrypt this message.

Hints:

1. As you know, the most frequently occurring letter in English is e. Therefore, the first or second (or perhaps third?) most common character in the message is likely to stand for e. Also, e is often seen in pairs (e.g., meet, fleet, speed, seen, been, agree, etc.). Try to find a character in the ciphertext that decodes to e.
2. The most common word in English is "the." Use this fact to guess the characters that stand for t and h.
3. Decipher the rest of the message by deducing additional words.

Warning: The resulting message is in English but may not make much sense on a first reading.

3.5 One way to solve the key distribution problem is to use a line from a book that both the sender and the receiver possess. Typically, at least in spy novels, the first sentence of a book serves as the key. The particular scheme discussed in this problem is from one of the best suspense novels involving secret codes, *Talking to Strange Men*, by Ruth Rendell. Work this problem without consulting that book!

Consider the following message:

SIDKHKDM AF HCRKIABIE SHIMC KD LFEAILA

This ciphertext was produced using the first sentence of *The Other Side of Silence* (a book about the spy Kim Philby):

> The snow lay thick on the steps and the snowflakes driven by the wind looked black in the headlights of the cars.

A simple substitution cipher was used.

a. What is the encryption algorithm?
b. How secure is it?
c. To make the key distribution problem simple, both parties can agree to use the first or last sentence of a book as the key. To change the key, they simply need to agree on a new book. The use of the first sentence would be preferable to the use of the last. Why?

3.6 In one of his cases, Sherlock Holmes was confronted with the following message.

534 C2 13 127 36 31 4 17 21 41
DOUGLAS 109 293 5 37 BIRLSTONE
26 BIRLSTONE 9 127 171

Although Watson was puzzled, Holmes was able immediately to deduce the type of cipher. Can you?

3.7 This problem uses a real-world example, from an old U.S. Special Forces manual (public domain). The document, filename *SpecialForces.pdf,* is available at box.com/Crypto7e.

a. Using the two keys (memory words) *cryptographic* and *network security*, encrypt the following message:

Be at the third pillar from the left outside the lyceum theatre tonight at seven. If you are distrustful bring two friends.

Make reasonable assumptions about how to treat redundant letters and excess letters in the memory words and how to treat spaces and punctuation. Indicate what your assumptions are. *Note:* The message is from the Sherlock Holmes novel, *The Sign of Four*.

b. Decrypt the ciphertext. Show your work.

c. Comment on when it would be appropriate to use this technique and what its advantages are.

3.8 A disadvantage of the general monoalphabetic cipher is that both sender and receiver must commit the permuted cipher sequence to memory. A common technique for avoiding this is to use a keyword from which the cipher sequence can be generated. For example, using the keyword CIPHER, write out the keyword followed by unused letters in normal order and match this against the plaintext letters:

```
plain:  a b c d e f g h i j k l m n o p q r s t u v w x y z
cipher: C I P H E R A B D F G J K L M N O Q S T U V W X Y Z
```

If it is felt that this process does not produce sufficient mixing, write the remaining letters on successive lines and then generate the sequence by reading down the columns:

```
C I P H E R
A B D F G J
K L M N O Q
S T U V W X
Y Z
```

This yields the sequence:

```
C A K S Y I B L T Z P D M U H F N V E G O W R J Q X
```

Such a system is used in the example in Section 3.2 (the one that begins "it was disclosed yesterday"). Determine the keyword.

3.9 When the PT-109 American patrol boat, under the command of Lieutenant John F. Kennedy, was sunk by a Japanese destroyer, a message was received at an Australian wireless station in Playfair code:

```
KXJEY UREBE ZWEHE WRYTU HEYFS
KREHE GOYFI WTTTU OLKSY CAJPO
BOTEI ZONTX BYBNT GONEY CUZWR
GDSON SXBOU YWRHE BAAHY USEDQ
```

The key used was *royal new zealand navy*. Decrypt the message. Translate TT into tt.

3.10 **a.** Construct a Playfair matrix with the key *decryption*.
b. Construct a Playfair matrix with the key *largest*. Make a reasonable assumption about how to treat redundant letters in the key.

3.11 **a.** Using this Playfair matrix:

H	A	B	F	G
S	J/K	L	M	Q
Z	U	V	W	X
Y	D	E	C	R
N	P	T	I	O

Encrypt this message:

I only regret that I have but one life to give for my country.

Note: This message is by Nathan Hale, a soldier in the American Revolutionary War.
b. Repeat part (a) using the Playfair matrix from Problem 3.10a.
c. How do you account for the results of this problem? Can you generalize your conclusion?

3.12 **a.** How many possible keys does the Playfair cipher have? Ignore the fact that some keys might produce identical encryption results. Express your answer as an approximate power of 2.
b. Now take into account the fact that some Playfair keys produce the same encryption results. How many effectively unique keys does the Playfair cipher have?

3.13 What substitution system results when we use a 1×25 Playfair matrix?

3.14 **a.** Encrypt the message "Let us meet at our usual place" using the Hill cipher with the key $\begin{pmatrix} 9 & 4 \\ 5 & 7 \end{pmatrix}$. Show your calculations and the result.
b. Show the calculations for the corresponding decryption of the ciphertext to recover the original plaintext.

3.15 We have shown that the Hill cipher succumbs to a known plaintext attack if sufficient plaintext–ciphertext pairs are provided. It is even easier to solve the Hill cipher if a chosen plaintext attack can be mounted. Describe such an attack.

3.16 It can be shown that the Hill cipher with the matrix $\begin{pmatrix} a & b \\ c & d \end{pmatrix}$ requires that $(ad - bc)$ is relatively prime to 26; that is, the only common positive integer factor of $(ad - bc)$ and 26 is 1. Thus, if $(ad - bc) = 13$ or is even, the matrix is not allowed. Determine the number of different (good) keys there are for a 2×2 Hill cipher without counting them one by one, using the following steps:
a. Find the number of matrices whose determinant is even because one or both rows are even. (A row is "even" if both entries in the row are even.)
b. Find the number of matrices whose determinant is even because one or both columns are even. (A column is "even" if both entries in the column are even.)
c. Find the number of matrices whose determinant is even because all of the entries are odd.
d. Taking into account overlaps, find the total number of matrices whose determinant is even.
e. Find the number of matrices whose determinant is a multiple of 13 because the first column is a multiple of 13.

f. Find the number of matrices whose determinant is a multiple of 13 where the first column is not a multiple of 13 but the second column is a multiple of the first modulo 13.

g. Find the total number of matrices whose determinant is a multiple of 13.

h. Find the number of matrices whose determinant is a multiple of 26 because they fit cases parts (a) and (e), (b) and (e), (c) and (e), (a) and (f), and so on.

i. Find the total number of matrices whose determinant is neither a multiple of 2 nor a multiple of 13.

3.17 Calculate the determinant mod 26 of

a. $\begin{pmatrix} 19 & 8 \\ 21 & 9 \end{pmatrix}$ **b.** $\begin{pmatrix} 6 & 24 & 1 \\ 13 & 16 & 10 \\ 20 & 17 & 15 \end{pmatrix}$

3.18 Determine the inverse mod 26 of

a. $\begin{pmatrix} 2 & 3 \\ 1 & 22 \end{pmatrix}$ **b.** $\begin{pmatrix} 6 & 24 & 1 \\ 13 & 16 & 10 \\ 20 & 17 & 15 \end{pmatrix}$

3.19 Using the Vigenère cipher, encrypt the word "encryption" using the word "leg".

3.20 This problem explores the use of a one-time pad version of the Vigenère cipher. In this scheme, the key is a stream of random numbers between 0 and 26. For example, if the key is 3 19 5 …, then the first letter of plaintext is encrypted with a shift of 3 letters, the second with a shift of 19 letters, the third with a shift of 5 letters, and so on.

a. Encrypt the plaintext sendmoremoney with the key stream

`8 12 1 7 23 15 21 14 11 19 2 0 9`

b. Using the ciphertext produced in part (a), find a key so that the cipher text decrypts to the plaintext cashnotneeded.

3.21 What is the message embedded in Figure 3.9?

3.22 In one of Dorothy Sayers's mysteries, Lord Peter is confronted with the message shown in Figure 3.10. He also discovers the key to the message, which is a sequence of integers:

```
787656543432112343456567878878765654
3432112343456567878878765654433211234
```

a. Decrypt the message. *Hint:* What is the largest integer value?

b. If the algorithm is known but not the key, how secure is the scheme?

c. If the key is known but not the algorithm, how secure is the scheme?

> *I thought to see the fairies in the fields, but I saw only the evil elephants with their black backs. Woe! how that sight awed me! The elves danced all around and about while I heard voices calling clearly. Ah! how I tried to see—throw off the ugly cloud—but no blind eye of a mortal was permitted to spy them. So then came minstrels, having gold trumpets, harps and drums. These played very loudly beside me, breaking that spell. So the dream vanished, whereat I thanked Heaven. I shed many tears before the thin moon rose up, frail and faint as a sickle of straw. Now though the Enchanter gnash his teeth vainly, yet shall he return as the Spring returns. Oh, wretched man! Hell gapes, Erebus now lies open. The mouths of Death wait on thy end.*

Figure 3.10 A Puzzle for Lord Peter

Programming Problems

3.23 Write a program that can encrypt and decrypt using the general Caesar cipher, also known as an additive cipher.

3.24 Write a program that can encrypt and decrypt using the affine cipher described in Problem 3.1.

3.25 Write a program that can perform a letter frequency attack on an additive cipher without human intervention. Your software should produce possible plaintexts in rough order of likelihood. It would be good if your user interface allowed the user to specify "give me the top 10 possible plaintexts."

3.26 Write a program that can perform a letter frequency attack on any monoalphabetic substitution cipher without human intervention. Your software should produce possible plaintexts in rough order of likelihood. It would be good if your user interface allowed the user to specify "give me the top 10 possible plaintexts."

3.27 Create software that can encrypt and decrypt using a 2×2 Hill cipher.

3.28 Create software that can perform a fast known plaintext attack on a Hill cipher, given the dimension m. How fast are your algorithms, as a function of m?

CHAPTER 4

BLOCK CIPHERS AND THE DATA ENCRYPTION STANDARD

LEARNING OBJECTIVES

After studying this chapter, you should be able to

- Understand the distinction between stream ciphers and block ciphers.
- Present an overview of the Feistel cipher and explain how decryption is the inverse of encryption.
- Present an overview of Data Encryption Standard (DES).
- Explain the concept of the avalanche effect.
- Discuss the cryptographic strength of DES.
- Summarize the principal block cipher design principles.

The objective of this chapter is to illustrate the principles of modern symmetric ciphers. For this purpose, we focus on the most widely used symmetric cipher: the Data Encryption Standard (DES). Although numerous symmetric ciphers have been developed since the introduction of DES, and although it is destined to be replaced by the Advanced Encryption Standard (AES), DES remains the most important such algorithm. Furthermore, a detailed study of DES provides an understanding of the principles used in other symmetric ciphers.

This chapter begins with a discussion of the general principles of symmetric block ciphers, which are the principal type of symmetric ciphers studied in this book. The other form of symmetric ciphers, stream ciphers, are discussed in Chapter 8. Next, we cover full DES. Following this look at a specific algorithm, we return to a more general discussion of block cipher design.

Compared to public-key ciphers, such as RSA, the structure of DES and most symmetric ciphers is very complex and cannot be explained as easily as RSA and similar algorithms. Accordingly, the reader may wish to begin with a simplified version of DES, which is described in Appendix G. This version allows the reader to perform encryption and decryption by hand and gain a good understanding of the working of the algorithm details. Classroom experience indicates that a study of this simplified version enhances understanding of DES.[1]

4.1 TRADITIONAL BLOCK CIPHER STRUCTURE

Several important symmetric block encryption algorithms in current use are based on a structure referred to as a Feistel block cipher [FEIS73]. For that reason, it is important to examine the design principles of the Feistel cipher. We begin with a comparison of stream ciphers and block ciphers. Then we discuss the motivation for the Feistel block cipher structure. Finally, we discuss some of its implications.

---

[1]However, you may safely skip Appendix G, at least on a first reading. If you get lost or bogged down in the details of DES, then you can go back and start with simplified DES.

Stream Ciphers and Block Ciphers

A **stream cipher** is one that encrypts a digital data stream one bit or one byte at a time. Examples of classical stream ciphers are the autokeyed Vigenère cipher and the Vernam cipher. In the ideal case, a one-time pad version of the Vernam cipher would be used (Figure 3.7), in which the keystream (k_i) is as long as the plaintext bit stream (p_i). If the cryptographic keystream is random, then this cipher is unbreakable by any means other than acquiring the keystream. However, the keystream must be provided to both users in advance via some independent and secure channel. This introduces insurmountable logistical problems if the intended data traffic is very large.

Accordingly, for practical reasons, the bit-stream generator must be implemented as an algorithmic procedure, so that the cryptographic bit stream can be produced by both users. In this approach (Figure 4.1a), the bit-stream generator is a key-controlled algorithm and must produce a bit stream that is cryptographically strong. That is, it must be computationally impractical to predict future portions of the bit stream based on previous portions of the bit stream. The two users need only share the generating key, and each can produce the keystream.

A **block cipher** is one in which a block of plaintext is treated as a whole and used to produce a ciphertext block of equal length. Typically, a block size of 64 or

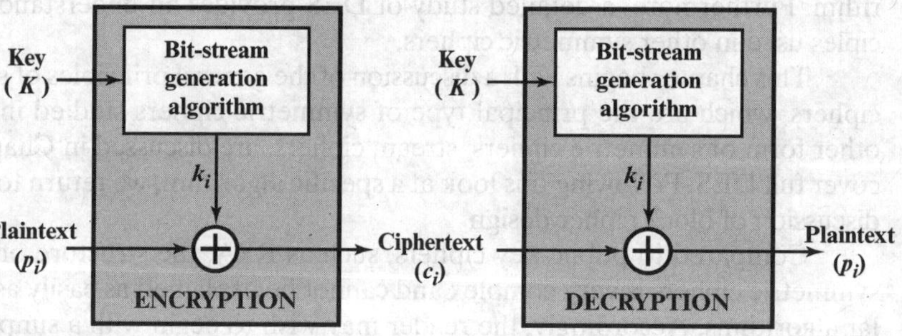

(a) Stream cipher using algorithmic bit-stream generator

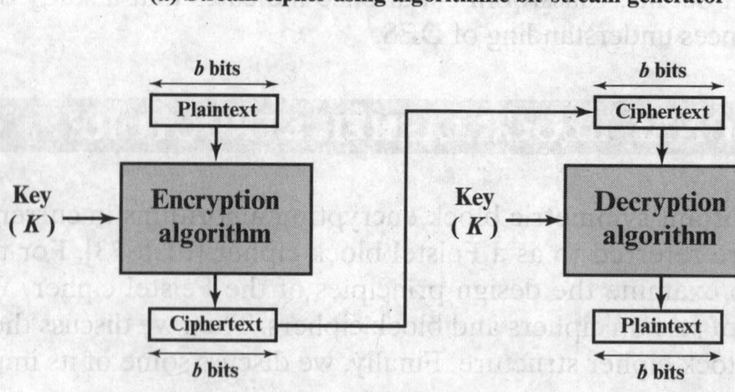

(b) Block cipher

Figure 4.1 Stream Cipher and Block Cipher

128 bits is used. As with a stream cipher, the two users share a symmetric encryption key (Figure 4.1b). Using some of the modes of operation explained in Chapter 7, a block cipher can be used to achieve the same effect as a stream cipher.

Far more effort has gone into analyzing block ciphers. In general, they seem applicable to a broader range of applications than stream ciphers. The vast majority of network-based symmetric cryptographic applications make use of block ciphers. Accordingly, the concern in this chapter, and in our discussions throughout the book of symmetric encryption, will primarily focus on block ciphers.

Motivation for the Feistel Cipher Structure

A block cipher operates on a plaintext block of n bits to produce a ciphertext block of n bits. There are 2^n possible different plaintext blocks and, for the encryption to be reversible (i.e., for decryption to be possible), each must produce a unique ciphertext block. Such a transformation is called reversible, or nonsingular. The following examples illustrate nonsingular and singular transformations for $n = 2$.

Reversible Mapping

Plaintext	Ciphertext
00	11
01	10
10	00
11	01

Irreversible Mapping

Plaintext	Ciphertext
00	11
01	10
10	01
11	01

In the latter case, a ciphertext of 01 could have been produced by one of two plaintext blocks. So if we limit ourselves to reversible mappings, the number of different transformations is $2^n!$.[2]

Figure 4.2 illustrates the logic of a general substitution cipher for $n = 4$. A 4-bit input produces one of 16 possible input states, which is mapped by the substitution cipher into a unique one of 16 possible output states, each of which is represented by 4 ciphertext bits. The encryption and decryption mappings can be defined by a tabulation, as shown in Table 4.1. This is the most general form of block cipher and can be used to define any reversible mapping between plaintext and ciphertext. Feistel refers to this as the *ideal block cipher*, because it allows for the maximum number of possible encryption mappings from the plaintext block [FEIS75].

But there is a practical problem with the ideal block cipher. If a small block size, such as $n = 4$, is used, then the system is equivalent to a classical substitution cipher. Such systems, as we have seen, are vulnerable to a statistical analysis of the plaintext. This weakness is not inherent in the use of a substitution cipher but rather results from the use of a small block size. If n is sufficiently large and an arbitrary reversible substitution between plaintext and ciphertext is allowed, then the statistical characteristics of the source plaintext are masked to such an extent that this type of cryptanalysis is infeasible.

---

[2] The reasoning is as follows: For the first plaintext, we can choose any of 2^n ciphertext blocks. For the second plaintext, we choose from among $2^n - 1$ remaining ciphertext blocks, and so on.

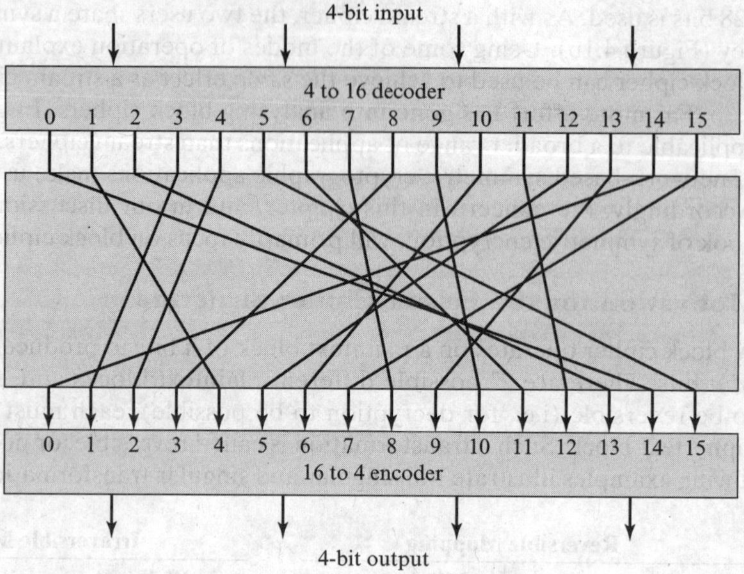

Figure 4.2 General *n*-bit-*n*-bit Block Substitution (shown with $n = 4$)

An arbitrary reversible substitution cipher (the ideal block cipher) for a large block size is not practical, however, from an implementation and performance point of view. For such a transformation, the mapping itself constitutes the key. Consider again Table 4.1, which defines one particular reversible mapping from

Table 4.1 Encryption and Decryption Tables for Substitution Cipher of Figure 4.2

Plaintext	Ciphertext
0000	1110
0001	0100
0010	1101
0011	0001
0100	0010
0101	1111
0110	1011
0111	1000
1000	0011
1001	1010
1010	0110
1011	1100
1100	0101
1101	1001
1110	0000
1111	0111

Ciphertext	Plaintext
0000	1110
0001	0011
0010	0100
0011	1000
0100	0001
0101	1100
0110	1010
0111	1111
1000	0111
1001	1101
1010	1001
1011	0110
1100	1011
1101	0010
1110	0000
1111	0101

plaintext to ciphertext for $n = 4$. The mapping can be defined by the entries in the second column, which show the value of the ciphertext for each plaintext block. This, in essence, is the key that determines the specific mapping from among all possible mappings. In this case, using this straightforward method of defining the key, the required key length is (4 bits) $\times$ (16 rows) = 64 bits. In general, for an n-bit ideal block cipher, the length of the key defined in this fashion is $n \times 2^n$ bits. For a 64-bit block, which is a desirable length to thwart statistical attacks, the required key length is $64 \times 2^{64} = 2^{70} \approx 10^{21}$ bits.

In considering these difficulties, Feistel points out that what is needed is an approximation to the ideal block cipher system for large n, built up out of components that are easily realizable [FEIS75]. But before turning to Feistel's approach, let us make one other observation. We could use the general block substitution cipher but, to make its implementation tractable, confine ourselves to a subset of the $2^n!$ possible reversible mappings. For example, suppose we define the mapping in terms of a set of linear equations. In the case of $n = 4$, we have

$$y_1 = k_{11}x_1 + k_{12}x_2 + k_{13}x_3 + k_{14}x_4$$

$$y_2 = k_{21}x_1 + k_{22}x_2 + k_{23}x_3 + k_{24}x_4$$

$$y_3 = k_{31}x_1 + k_{32}x_2 + k_{33}x_3 + k_{34}x_4$$

$$y_4 = k_{41}x_1 + k_{42}x_2 + k_{43}x_3 + k_{44}x_4$$

where the x_i are the four binary digits of the plaintext block, the y_i are the four binary digits of the ciphertext block, the k_{ij} are the binary coefficients, and arithmetic is mod 2. The key size is just n^2, in this case 16 bits. The danger with this kind of formulation is that it may be vulnerable to cryptanalysis by an attacker that is aware of the structure of the algorithm. In this example, what we have is essentially the Hill cipher discussed in Chapter 3, applied to binary data rather than characters. As we saw in Chapter 3, a simple linear system such as this is quite vulnerable.

The Feistel Cipher

Feistel proposed [FEIS73] that we can approximate the ideal block cipher by utilizing the concept of a product cipher, which is the execution of two or more simple ciphers in sequence in such a way that the final result or product is cryptographically stronger than any of the component ciphers. The essence of the approach is to develop a block cipher with a key length of k bits and a block length of n bits, allowing a total of 2^k possible transformations, rather than the $2^n!$ transformations available with the ideal block cipher.

In particular, Feistel proposed the use of a cipher that alternates substitutions and permutations, where these terms are defined as follows:

- **Substitution:** Each plaintext element or group of elements is uniquely replaced by a corresponding ciphertext element or group of elements.
- **Permutation:** A sequence of plaintext elements is replaced by a permutation of that sequence. That is, no elements are added or deleted or replaced in the sequence, rather the order in which the elements appear in the sequence is changed.

In fact, Feistel's is a practical application of a proposal by Claude Shannon to develop a product cipher that alternates *confusion* and *diffusion* functions [SHAN49].[3] We look next at these concepts of diffusion and confusion and then present the Feistel cipher. But first, it is worth commenting on this remarkable fact: The Feistel cipher structure, which dates back over a quarter century and which, in turn, is based on Shannon's proposal of 1945, is the structure used by a number of significant symmetric block ciphers currently in use. In particular, the Feistel structure is used for Triple Data Encryption Algorithm (TDEA), which is one of the two encryption algorithms (along with AES), approved for general use by the National Institute of Standards and Technology (NIST). The Feistel structure is also used for several schemes for format-preserving encryption, which have recently come into prominence. In addition, the Camellia block cipher is a Feistel structure; it is one of the possible symmetric ciphers in TLS and a number of other Internet security protocols. Both TDEA and format-preserving encryption are covered in Chapter 7.

Diffusion and Confusion The terms *diffusion* and *confusion* were introduced by Claude Shannon to capture the two basic building blocks for any cryptographic system [SHAN49]. Shannon's concern was to thwart cryptanalysis based on statistical analysis. The reasoning is as follows. Assume the attacker has some knowledge of the statistical characteristics of the plaintext. For example, in a human-readable message in some language, the frequency distribution of the various letters may be known. Or there may be words or phrases likely to appear in the message (probable words). If these statistics are in any way reflected in the ciphertext, the cryptanalyst may be able to deduce the encryption key, part of the key, or at least a set of keys likely to contain the exact key. In what Shannon refers to as a strongly ideal cipher, all statistics of the ciphertext are independent of the particular key used. The arbitrary substitution cipher that we discussed previously (Figure 4.2) is such a cipher, but as we have seen, it is impractical.[4]

Other than recourse to ideal systems, Shannon suggests two methods for frustrating statistical cryptanalysis: diffusion and confusion. In **diffusion**, the statistical structure of the plaintext is dissipated into long-range statistics of the ciphertext. This is achieved by having each plaintext digit affect the value of many ciphertext digits; generally, this is equivalent to having each ciphertext digit be affected by many plaintext digits. An example of diffusion is to encrypt a message $M = m_1, m_2, m_3, \ldots$ of characters with an averaging operation:

$$y_n = \left(\sum_{i=1}^{k} m_{n+i} \right) \bmod 26$$

[3]The paper is available at box.com/Crypto7e. Shannon's 1949 paper appeared originally as a classified report in 1945. Shannon enjoys an amazing and unique position in the history of computer and information science. He not only developed the seminal ideas of modern cryptography but is also responsible for inventing the discipline of information theory. Based on his work in information theory, he developed a formula for the capacity of a data communications channel, which is still used today. In addition, he founded another discipline, the application of Boolean algebra to the study of digital circuits; this last he managed to toss off as a master's thesis.

[4]Appendix F expands on Shannon's concepts concerning measures of secrecy and the security of cryptographic algorithms.

adding k successive letters to get a ciphertext letter y_n. One can show that the statistical structure of the plaintext has been dissipated. Thus, the letter frequencies in the ciphertext will be more nearly equal than in the plaintext; the digram frequencies will also be more nearly equal, and so on. In a binary block cipher, diffusion can be achieved by repeatedly performing some permutation on the data followed by applying a function to that permutation; the effect is that bits from different positions in the original plaintext contribute to a single bit of ciphertext.[5]

Every block cipher involves a transformation of a block of plaintext into a block of ciphertext, where the transformation depends on the key. The mechanism of diffusion seeks to make the statistical relationship between the plaintext and ciphertext as complex as possible in order to thwart attempts to deduce the key. On the other hand, **confusion** seeks to make the relationship between the statistics of the ciphertext and the value of the encryption key as complex as possible, again to thwart attempts to discover the key. Thus, even if the attacker can get some handle on the statistics of the ciphertext, the way in which the key was used to produce that ciphertext is so complex as to make it difficult to deduce the key. This is achieved by the use of a complex substitution algorithm. In contrast, a simple linear substitution function would add little confusion.

As [ROBS95b] points out, so successful are diffusion and confusion in capturing the essence of the desired attributes of a block cipher that they have become the cornerstone of modern block cipher design.

Feistel Cipher Structure The left-hand side of Figure 4.3 depicts the encryption structure proposed by Feistel. The inputs to the encryption algorithm are a plaintext block of length $2w$ bits and a key K. The plaintext block is divided into two halves, LE_0 and RE_0. The two halves of the data pass through n rounds of processing and then combine to produce the ciphertext block. Each round i has as inputs LE_{i-1} and RE_{i-1} derived from the previous round, as well as a subkey K_i derived from the overall K. In general, the subkeys K_i are different from K and from each other. In Figure 4.3, 16 rounds are used, although any number of rounds could be implemented.

All rounds have the same structure. A **substitution** is performed on the left half of the data. This is done by applying a *round function* F to the right half of the data and then taking the exclusive-OR of the output of that function and the left half of the data. The round function has the same general structure for each round but is parameterized by the round subkey K_i. Another way to express this is to say that F is a function of right-half block of w bits and a subkey of y bits, which produces an output value of length w bits: $F(RE_i, K_{i+1})$. Following this substitution, a **permutation** is performed that consists of the interchange of the two halves of the data.[6] This structure is a particular form of the substitution-permutation network (SPN) proposed by Shannon.

---

[5]Some books on cryptography equate permutation with diffusion. This is incorrect. Permutation, *by itself*, does not change the statistics of the plaintext at the level of individual letters or permuted blocks. For example, in DES, the permutation swaps two 32-bit blocks, so statistics of strings of 32 bits or less are preserved.

[6]The final round is followed by an interchange that undoes the interchange that is part of the final round. One could simply leave both interchanges out of the diagram, at the sacrifice of some consistency of presentation. In any case, the effective lack of a swap in the final round is done to simplify the implementation of the decryption process, as we shall see.

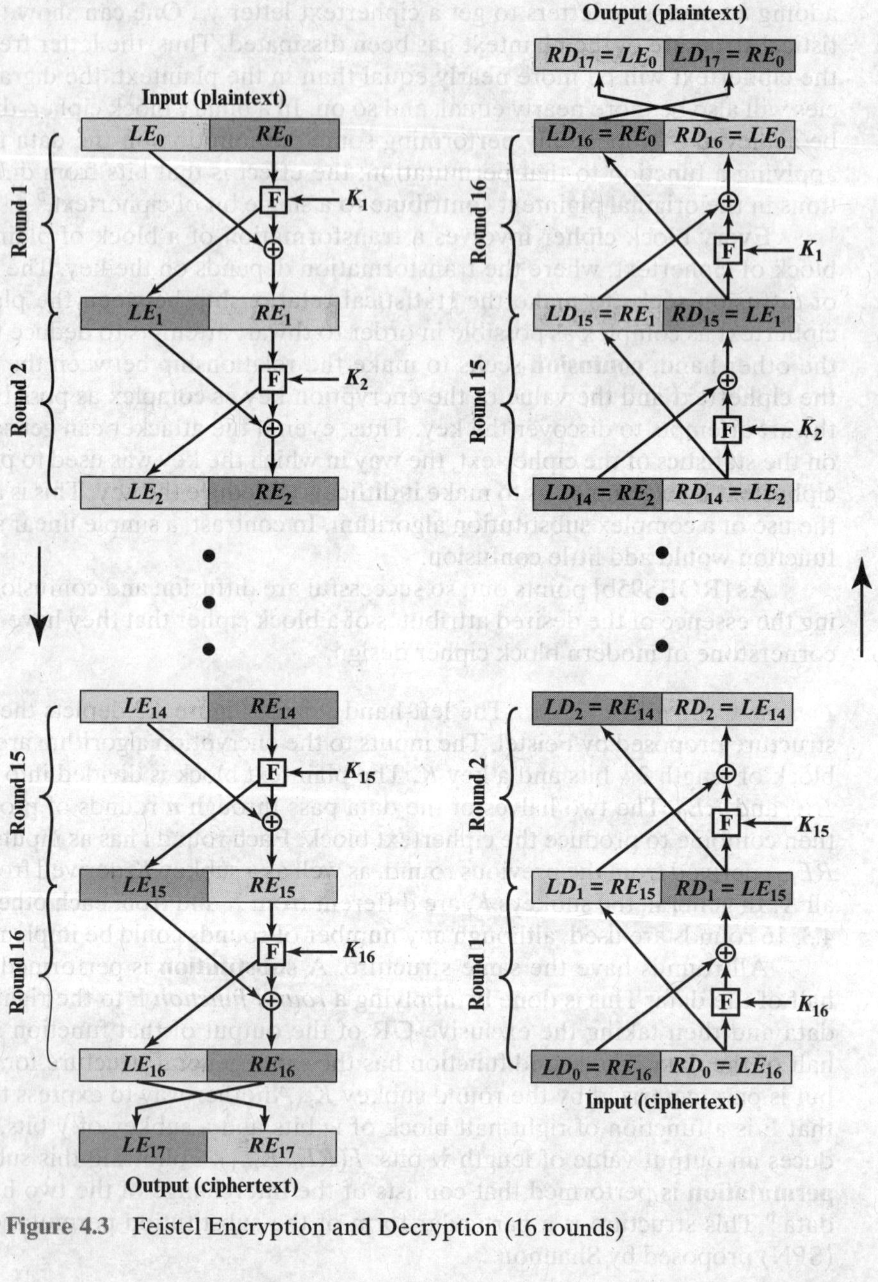

Figure 4.3 Feistel Encryption and Decryption (16 rounds)

The exact realization of a Feistel network depends on the choice of the following parameters and design features:

- **Block size:** Larger block sizes mean greater security (all other things being equal) but reduced encryption/decryption speed for a given algorithm. The greater security is achieved by greater diffusion. Traditionally, a block size of 64 bits has been considered a reasonable tradeoff and was nearly universal in block cipher design. However, the new AES uses a 128-bit block size.

- **Key size:** Larger key size means greater security but may decrease encryption/decryption speed. The greater security is achieved by greater resistance to brute-force attacks and greater confusion. Key sizes of 64 bits or less are now widely considered to be inadequate, and 128 bits has become a common size.
- **Number of rounds:** The essence of the Feistel cipher is that a single round offers inadequate security but that multiple rounds offer increasing security. A typical size is 16 rounds.
- **Subkey generation algorithm:** Greater complexity in this algorithm should lead to greater difficulty of cryptanalysis.
- **Round function F:** Again, greater complexity generally means greater resistance to cryptanalysis.

There are two other considerations in the design of a Feistel cipher:

- **Fast software encryption/decryption:** In many cases, encryption is embedded in applications or utility functions in such a way as to preclude a hardware implementation. Accordingly, the speed of execution of the algorithm becomes a concern.
- **Ease of analysis:** Although we would like to make our algorithm as difficult as possible to cryptanalyze, there is great benefit in making the algorithm easy to analyze. That is, if the algorithm can be concisely and clearly explained, it is easier to analyze that algorithm for cryptanalytic vulnerabilities and therefore develop a higher level of assurance as to its strength. DES, for example, does not have an easily analyzed functionality.

FEISTEL DECRYPTION ALGORITHM The process of decryption with a Feistel cipher is essentially the same as the encryption process. The rule is as follows: Use the ciphertext as input to the algorithm, but use the subkeys K_i in reverse order. That is, use K_n in the first round, K_{n-1} in the second round, and so on, until K_1 is used in the last round. This is a nice feature, because it means we need not implement two different algorithms; one for encryption and one for decryption.

To see that the same algorithm with a reversed key order produces the correct result, Figure 4.3 shows the encryption process going down the left-hand side and the decryption process going up the right-hand side for a 16-round algorithm. For clarity, we use the notation LE_i and RE_i for data traveling through the encryption algorithm and LD_i and RD_i for data traveling through the decryption algorithm. The diagram indicates that, at every round, the intermediate value of the decryption process is equal to the corresponding value of the encryption process with the two halves of the value swapped. To put this another way, let the output of the ith encryption round be $LE_i \| RE_i$ (LE_i concatenated with RE_i). Then the corresponding output of the $(16 - i)$th decryption round is $RE_i \| LE_i$ or, equivalently, $LD_{16-i} \| RD_{16-i}$.

Let us walk through Figure 4.3 to demonstrate the validity of the preceding assertions. After the last iteration of the encryption process, the two halves of the output are swapped, so that the ciphertext is $RE_{16} \| LE_{16}$. The output of that round is the ciphertext. Now take that ciphertext and use it as input to the same algorithm. The input to the first round is $RE_{16} \| LE_{16}$, which is equal to the 32-bit swap of the output of the sixteenth round of the encryption process.

Now we would like to show that the output of the first round of the decryption process is equal to a 32-bit swap of the input to the sixteenth round of the encryption process. First, consider the encryption process. We see that

$$LE_{16} = RE_{15}$$
$$RE_{16} = LE_{15} \oplus \mathrm{F}(RE_{15}, K_{16})$$

On the decryption side,

$$\begin{aligned} LD_1 &= RD_0 = LE_{16} = RE_{15} \\ RD_1 &= LD_0 \oplus \mathrm{F}(RD_0, K_{16}) \\ &= RE_{16} \oplus \mathrm{F}(RE_{15}, K_{16}) \\ &= [LE_{15} \oplus \mathrm{F}(RE_{15}, K_{16})] \oplus \mathrm{F}(RE_{15}, K_{16}) \end{aligned}$$

The XOR has the following properties:

$$[A \oplus B] \oplus C = A \oplus [B \oplus C]$$
$$D \oplus D = 0$$
$$E \oplus 0 = E$$

Thus, we have $LD_1 = RE_{15}$ and $RD_1 = LE_{15}$. Therefore, the output of the first round of the decryption process is $RE_{15} \| LE_{15}$, which is the 32-bit swap of the input to the sixteenth round of the encryption. This correspondence holds all the way through the 16 iterations, as is easily shown. We can cast this process in general terms. For the ith iteration of the encryption algorithm,

$$LE_i = RE_{i-1}$$
$$RE_i = LE_{i-1} \oplus \mathrm{F}(RE_{i-1}, K_i)$$

Rearranging terms:

$$RE_{i-1} = LE_i$$
$$LE_{i-1} = RE_i \oplus \mathrm{F}(RE_{i-1}, K_i) = RE_i \oplus \mathrm{F}(LE_i, K_i)$$

Thus, we have described the inputs to the ith iteration as a function of the outputs, and these equations confirm the assignments shown in the right-hand side of Figure 4.3.

Finally, we see that the output of the last round of the decryption process is $RE_0 \| LE_0$. A 32-bit swap recovers the original plaintext, demonstrating the validity of the Feistel decryption process.

Note that the derivation does not require that F be a reversible function. To see this, take a limiting case in which F produces a constant output (e.g., all ones) regardless of the values of its two arguments. The equations still hold.

To help clarify the preceding concepts, let us look at a specific example (Figure 4.4 and focus on the fifteenth round of encryption, corresponding to the second round of decryption. Suppose that the blocks at each stage are 32 bits (two 16-bit halves) and that the key size is 24 bits. Suppose that at the end of encryption round fourteen, the value of the intermediate block (in hexadecimal) is DE7F03A6. Then LE_{14} = DE7F and RE_{14} = 03A6. Also assume that the value of K_{15} is 12DE52. After round 15, we have LE_{15} = 03A6 and RE_{15} = F(03A6, 12DE52) $\oplus$ DE7F.

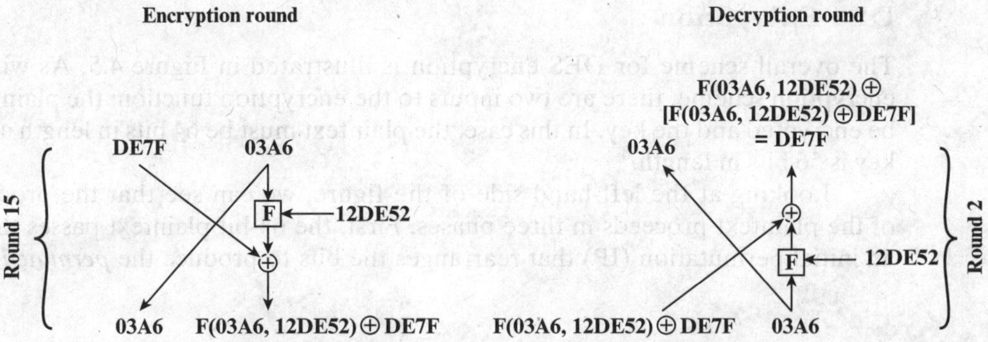

Figure 4.4 Feistel Example

Now let's look at the decryption. We assume that $LD_1 = RE_{15}$ and $RD_1 = LE_{15}$, as shown in Figure 4.3, and we want to demonstrate that $LD_2 = RE_{14}$ and $RD_2 = LE_{14}$. So, we start with $LD_1 = \text{F}(03\text{A}6, 12\text{DE}52) \oplus \text{DE}7\text{F}$ and $RD_1 = 03\text{A}6$. Then, from Figure 4.3, $LD_2 = 03\text{A}6 = RE_{14}$ and $RD_2 = \text{F}(03\text{A}6, 12\text{DE}52) \oplus [\text{F}(03\text{A}6, 12\text{DE}52) \oplus \text{DE}7\text{F}] = \text{DE}7\text{F} = \text{LE}14$.

4.2 THE DATA ENCRYPTION STANDARD

Until the introduction of the Advanced Encryption Standard (AES) in 2001, the Data Encryption Standard (DES) was the most widely used encryption scheme. DES was issued in 1977 by the National Bureau of Standards, now the National Institute of Standards and Technology (NIST), as Federal Information Processing Standard 46 (FIPS PUB 46). The algorithm itself is referred to as the Data Encryption Algorithm (DEA).[7] For DEA, data are encrypted in 64-bit blocks using a 56-bit key. The algorithm transforms 64-bit input in a series of steps into a 64-bit output. The same steps, with the same key, are used to reverse the encryption.

Over the years, DES became the dominant symmetric encryption algorithm, especially in financial applications. In 1994, NIST reaffirmed DES for federal use for another five years; NIST recommended the use of DES for applications other than the protection of classified information. In 1999, NIST issued a new version of its standard (FIPS PUB 46-3) that indicated that DES should be used only for legacy systems and that triple DES (which in essence involves repeating the DES algorithm three times on the plaintext using two or three different keys to produce the ciphertext) be used. We study triple DES in Chapter 7. Because the underlying encryption and decryption algorithms are the same for DES and triple DES, it remains important to understand the DES cipher. This section provides an overview.For the interested reader, Appendix S provides further detail.

---

[7]The terminology is a bit confusing. Until recently, the terms *DES* and *DEA* could be used interchangeably. However, the most recent edition of the DES document includes a specification of the DEA described here plus the triple DEA (TDEA) described in Chapter 7. Both DEA and TDEA are part of the Data Encryption Standard. Further, until the recent adoption of the official term *TDEA*, the triple DEA algorithm was typically referred to as *triple DES* and written as 3DES. For the sake of convenience, we will use the term 3DES.

DES Encryption

The overall scheme for DES encryption is illustrated in Figure 4.5. As with any encryption scheme, there are two inputs to the encryption function: the plaintext to be encrypted and the key. In this case, the plaintext must be 64 bits in length and the key is 56 bits in length.[8]

Looking at the left-hand side of the figure, we can see that the processing of the plaintext proceeds in three phases. First, the 64-bit plaintext passes through an initial permutation (IP) that rearranges the bits to produce the *permuted input*.

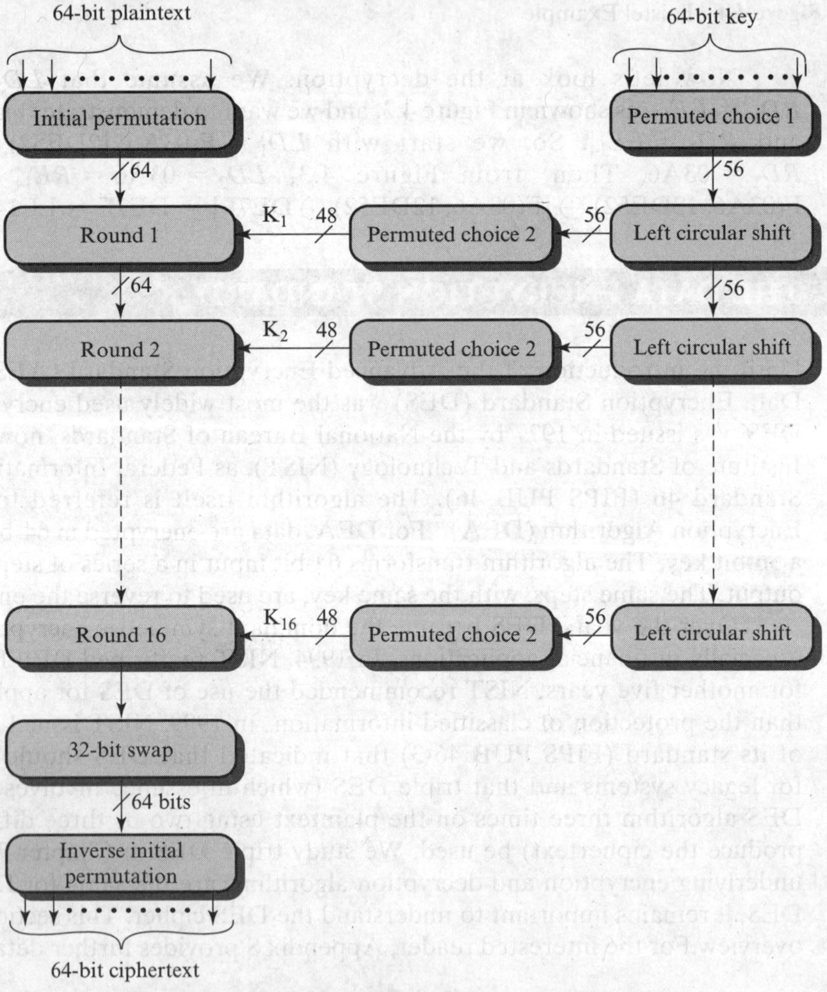

Figure 4.5 General Depiction of DES Encryption Algorithm

[8]Actually, the function expects a 64-bit key as input. However, only 56 of these bits are ever used; the other 8 bits can be used as parity bits or simply set arbitrarily.

This is followed by a phase consisting of sixteen rounds of the same function, which involves both permutation and substitution functions. The output of the last (sixteenth) round consists of 64 bits that are a function of the input plaintext and the key. The left and right halves of the output are swapped to produce the preoutput. Finally, the preoutput is passed through a permutation [IP^{-1}] that is the inverse of the initial permutation function, to produce the 64-bit ciphertext. With the exception of the initial and final permutations, DES has the exact structure of a Feistel cipher, as shown in Figure 4.3.

The right-hand portion of Figure 4.5 shows the way in which the 56-bit key is used. Initially, the key is passed through a permutation function. Then, for each of the sixteen rounds, a *subkey* (K_i) is produced by the combination of a left circular shift and a permutation. The permutation function is the same for each round, but a different subkey is produced because of the repeated shifts of the key bits.

DES Decryption

As with any Feistel cipher, decryption uses the same algorithm as encryption, except that the application of the subkeys is reversed. Additionally, the initial and final permutations are reversed.

4.3 A DES EXAMPLE

We now work through an example and consider some of its implications. Although you are not expected to duplicate the example by hand, you will find it informative to study the hex patterns that occur from one step to the next.

For this example, the plaintext is a hexadecimal palindrome. The plaintext, key, and resulting ciphertext are as follows:

Plaintext:	`02468aceeca86420`
Key:	`0f1571c947d9e859`
Ciphertext:	`da02ce3a89ecac3b`

Results

Table 4.2 shows the progression of the algorithm. The first row shows the 32-bit values of the left and right halves of data after the initial permutation. The next 16 rows show the results after each round. Also shown is the value of the 48-bit subkey generated for each round. Note that $L_i = R_{i-1}$. The final row shows the left- and right-hand values after the inverse initial permutation. These two values combined form the ciphertext.

The Avalanche Effect

A desirable property of any encryption algorithm is that a small change in either the plaintext or the key should produce a significant change in the ciphertext. In particular, a change in one bit of the plaintext or one bit of the key should produce

Table 4.2 DES Example

Round	K_i	L_i	R_i
IP		5a005a00	3cf03c0f
1	1e030f03080d2930	3cf03c0f	bad22845
2	0a31293432242318	bad22845	99e9b723
3	23072318201d0c1d	99e9b723	0bae3b9e
4	05261d3824311a20	0bae3b9e	42415649
5	3325340136002c25	42415649	18b3fa41
6	123a2d0d04262a1c	18b3fa41	9616fe23
7	021f120b1c130611	9616fe23	67117cf2
8	1c10372a2832002b	67117cf2	c11bfc09
9	04292a380c341f03	c11bfc09	887fbc6c
10	2703212607280403	887fbc6c	600f7e8b
11	2826390c31261504	600f7e8b	f596506e
12	12071c241a0a0f08	f596506e	738538b8
13	300935393c0d100b	738538b8	c6a62c4e
14	311e09231321182a	c6a62c4e	56b0bd75
15	283d3e0227072528	56b0bd75	75e8fd8f
16	2921080b13143025	75e8fd8f	25896490
IP^{-1}		da02ce3a	89ecac3b

Note: DES subkeys are shown as eight 6-bit values in hex format

a change in many bits of the ciphertext. This is referred to as the avalanche effect. If the change were small, this might provide a way to reduce the size of the plaintext or key space to be searched.

Using the example from Table 4.2, Table 4.3 shows the result when the fourth bit of the plaintext is changed, so that the plaintext is **12468aceeca86420**. The second column of the table shows the intermediate 64-bit values at the end of each round for the two plaintexts. The third column shows the number of bits that differ between the two intermediate values. The table shows that, after just three rounds, 18 bits differ between the two blocks. On completion, the two ciphertexts differ in 32 bit positions.

Table 4.4 shows a similar test using the original plaintext of with two keys that differ in only the fourth bit position: the original key, **0f1571c947d9e859**, and the altered key, **1f1571c947d9e859**. Again, the results show that about half of the bits in the ciphertext differ and that the avalanche effect is pronounced after just a few rounds.

Table 4.3 Avalanche Effect in DES: Change in Plaintext

Round		δ	Round		δ
	02468aceeca86420 12468aceeca86420	1	9	c11bfc09887fbc6c 99f911532eed7d94	32
1	3cf03c0fbad22845 3cf03c0fbad32845	1	10	887fbc6c600f7e8b 2eed7d94d0f23094	34
2	bad2284599e9b723 bad3284539a9b7a3	5	11	600f7e8bf596506e d0f23094455da9c4	37
3	99e9b7230bae3b9e 39a9b7a3171cb8b3	18	12	f596506e738538b8 455da9c47f6e3cf3	31
4	0bae3b9e42415649 171cb8b3ccaca55e	34	13	738538b8c6a62c4e 7f6e3cf34bc1a8d9	29
5	4241564918b3fa41 ccaca55ed16c3653	37	14	c6a62c4e56b0bd75 4bc1a8d91e07d409	33
6	18b3fa419616fe23 d16c3653cf402c68	33	15	56b0bd7575e8fd8f 1e07d4091ce2e6dc	31
7	9616fe2367117cf2 cf402c682b2cefbc	32	16	75e8fd8f25896490 1ce2e6dc365e5f59	32
8	67117cf2c11bfc09 2b2cefbc99f91153	33	IP^{-1}	da02ce3a89ecac3b 057cde97d7683f2a	32

Table 4.4 Avalanche Effect in DES: Change in Key

Round		δ	Round		δ
	02468aceeca86420 02468aceeca86420	0	9	c11bfc09887fbc6c 548f1de471f64dfd	34
1	3cf03c0fbad22845 3cf03c0f9ad628c5	3	10	887fbc6c600f7e8b 71f64dfd4279876c	36
2	bad2284599e9b723 9ad628c59939136b	11	11	600f7e8bf596506e 4279876c399fdc0d	32
3	99e9b7230bae3b9e 9939136b768067b7	25	12	f596506e738538b8 399fdc0d6d208dbb	28
4	0bae3b9e42415649 768067b75a8807c5	29	13	738538b8c6a62c4e 6d208dbbb9bdeeaa	33
5	4241564918b3fa41 5a8807c5488dbe94	26	14	c6a62c4e56b0bd75 b9bdeeaad2c3a56f	30
6	18b3fa419616fe23 488dbe94aba7fe53	26	15	56b0bd7575e8fd8f d2c3a56f2765c1fb	27
7	9616fe2367117cf2 aba7fe53177d21e4	27	16	75e8fd8f25896490 2765c1fb01263dc4	30
8	67117cf2c11bfc09 177d21e4548f1de4	32	IP^{-1}	da02ce3a89ecac3b ee92b50606b62b0b	30

4.4 THE STRENGTH OF DES

Since its adoption as a federal standard, there have been lingering concerns about the level of security provided by DES. These concerns, by and large, fall into two areas: key size and the nature of the algorithm.

The Use of 56-Bit Keys

With a key length of 56 bits, there are 2^{56} possible keys, which is approximately 7.2×10^{16} keys. Thus, on the face of it, a brute-force attack appears impractical. Assuming that, on average, half the key space has to be searched, a single machine performing one DES encryption per microsecond would take more than a thousand years to break the cipher.

However, the assumption of one encryption per microsecond is overly conservative. As far back as 1977, Diffie and Hellman postulated that the technology existed to build a parallel machine with 1 million encryption devices, each of which could perform one encryption per microsecond [DIFF77]. This would bring the average search time down to about 10 hours. The authors estimated that the cost would be about $20 million in 1977 dollars.

With current technology, it is not even necessary to use special, purpose-built hardware. Rather, the speed of commercial, off-the-shelf processors threaten the security of DES. A recent paper from Seagate Technology [SEAG08] suggests that a rate of 1 billion (10^9) key combinations per second is reasonable for today's multicore computers. Recent offerings confirm this. Both Intel and AMD now offer hardware-based instructions to accelerate the use of AES. Tests run on a contemporary multicore Intel machine resulted in an encryption rate of about half a billion encryptions per second [BASU12]. Another recent analysis suggests that with contemporary supercomputer technology, a rate of 10^{13} encryptions per second is reasonable [AROR12].

With these results in mind, Table 4.5 shows how much time is required for a brute-force attack for various key sizes. As can be seen, a single PC can break DES in about a year; if multiple PCs work in parallel, the time is drastically shortened. And today's supercomputers should be able to find a key in about an hour. Key sizes of 128 bits or greater are effectively unbreakable using simply a brute-force approach. Even if we managed to speed up the attacking system by a factor of 1 trillion (10^{12}), it would still take over 100,000 years to break a code using a 128-bit key.

Fortunately, there are a number of alternatives to DES, the most important of which are AES and triple DES, discussed in Chapters 6 and 7, respectively.

The Nature of the DES Algorithm

Another concern is the possibility that cryptanalysis is possible by exploiting the characteristics of the DES algorithm. The focus of concern has been on the eight substitution tables, or S-boxes, that are used in each iteration (described in Appendix S). Because the design criteria for these boxes, and indeed for the entire algorithm, were not made public, there is a suspicion that the boxes were constructed in such a way that cryptanalysis is possible for an opponent who knows

Table 4.5 Average Time Required for Exhaustive Key Search

Key Size (bits)	Cipher	Number of Alternative Keys	Time Required at 10^9 Decryptions/s	Time Required at 10^{13} Decryptions/s
56	DES	$2^{56} \approx 7.2 \times 10^{16}$	2^{55} ns = 1.125 years	1 hour
128	AES	$2^{128} \approx 3.4 \times 10^{38}$	2^{127} ns = 5.3×10^{21} years	5.3×10^{17} years
168	Triple DES	$2^{168} \approx 3.7 \times 10^{50}$	2^{167} ns = 5.8×10^{33} years	5.8×10^{29} years
192	AES	$2^{192} \approx 6.3 \times 10^{57}$	2^{191} ns = 9.8×10^{40} years	9.8×10^{36} years
256	AES	$2^{256} \approx 1.2 \times 10^{77}$	2^{255} ns = 1.8×10^{60} years	1.8×10^{56} years
26 characters (permutation)	Monoalphabetic	$2! = 4 \times 10^{26}$	2×10^{26} ns = 6.3×10^{9} years	6.3×10^{6} years

the weaknesses in the S-boxes. This assertion is tantalizing, and over the years a number of regularities and unexpected behaviors of the S-boxes have been discovered. Despite this, no one has so far succeeded in discovering the supposed fatal weaknesses in the S-boxes.[9]

Timing Attacks

We discuss timing attacks in more detail in Part Two, as they relate to public-key algorithms. However, the issue may also be relevant for symmetric ciphers. In essence, a timing attack is one in which information about the key or the plaintext is obtained by observing how long it takes a given implementation to perform decryptions on various ciphertexts. A timing attack exploits the fact that an encryption or decryption algorithm often takes slightly different amounts of time on different inputs. [HEVI99] reports on an approach that yields the Hamming weight (number of bits equal to one) of the secret key. This is a long way from knowing the actual key, but it is an intriguing first step. The authors conclude that DES appears to be fairly resistant to a successful timing attack but suggest some avenues to explore. Although this is an interesting line of attack, it so far appears unlikely that this technique will ever be successful against DES or more powerful symmetric ciphers such as triple DES and AES.

4.5 BLOCK CIPHER DESIGN PRINCIPLES

Although much progress has been made in designing block ciphers that are cryptographically strong, the basic principles have not changed all that much since the work of Feistel and the DES design team in the early 1970s. In this section we look at three critical aspects of block cipher design: the number of rounds, design of the function F, and key scheduling.

[9]At least, no one has publicly acknowledged such a discovery.

Number of Rounds

The cryptographic strength of a Feistel cipher derives from three aspects of the design: the number of rounds, the function F, and the key schedule algorithm. Let us look first at the choice of the number of rounds.

The greater the number of rounds, the more difficult it is to perform cryptanalysis, even for a relatively weak F. In general, the criterion should be that the number of rounds is chosen so that known cryptanalytic efforts require greater effort than a simple brute-force key search attack. This criterion was certainly used in the design of DES. Schneier [SCHN96] observes that for 16-round DES, a differential cryptanalysis attack is slightly less efficient than brute force: The differential cryptanalysis attack requires $2^{55.1}$ operations,[10] whereas brute force requires 2^{55}. If DES had 15 or fewer rounds, differential cryptanalysis would require less effort than a brute-force key search.

This criterion is attractive, because it makes it easy to judge the strength of an algorithm and to compare different algorithms. In the absence of a cryptanalytic breakthrough, the strength of any algorithm that satisfies the criterion can be judged solely on key length.

Design of Function F

The heart of a Feistel block cipher is the function F, which provides the element of confusion in a Feistel cipher. Thus, it must be difficult to "unscramble" the substitution performed by F. One obvious criterion is that F be nonlinear, as we discussed previously. The more nonlinear F, the more difficult any type of cryptanalysis will be. There are several measures of nonlinearity, which are beyond the scope of this book. In rough terms, the more difficult it is to approximate F by a set of linear equations, the more nonlinear F is.

Several other criteria should be considered in designing F. We would like the algorithm to have good avalanche properties. Recall that, in general, this means that a change in one bit of the input should produce a change in many bits of the output. A more stringent version of this is the **strict avalanche criterion (SAC)** [WEBS86], which states that any output bit j of an S-box (see Appendix S for a discussion of S-boxes) should change with probability 1/2 when any single input bit i is inverted for all i, j. Although SAC is expressed in terms of S-boxes, a similar criterion could be applied to F as a whole. This is important when considering designs that do not include S-boxes.

Another criterion proposed in [WEBS86] is the **bit independence criterion (BIC)**, which states that output bits j and k should change independently when any single input bit i is inverted for all i, j, and k. The SAC and BIC criteria appear to strengthen the effectiveness of the confusion function.

---

[10]Differential cryptanalysis of DES requires 2^{47} *chosen* plaintext. If all you have to work with is known plaintext, then you must sort through a large quantity of known plaintext–ciphertext pairs looking for the useful ones. This brings the level of effort up to $2^{55.1}$.

Key Schedule Algorithm

With any Feistel block cipher, the key is used to generate one subkey for each round. In general, we would like to select subkeys to maximize the difficulty of deducing individual subkeys and the difficulty of working back to the main key. No general principles for this have yet been promulgated.

Adams suggests [ADAM94] that, at minimum, the key schedule should guarantee key/ciphertext Strict Avalanche Criterion and Bit Independence Criterion.

4.6 KEY TERMS, REVIEW QUESTIONS, AND PROBLEMS

Key Terms

avalanche effect	Feistel cipher	round
block cipher	irreversible mapping	round function
confusion	key	subkey
Data Encryption Standard (DES)	permutation	substitution
	product cipher	
diffusion	reversible mapping	

Review Questions

4.1 Briefly define a nonsingular transformation.

4.2 What is a product cipher?

4.3 Why is it not practical to use an arbitrary reversible substitution cipher of the kind shown in Table 4.1?

4.4 Briefly define the terms substitution and permutation.

4.5 What are the two methods suggested by Claude Shannon to frustrate statistical cryptanalysis?

4.6 Which parameters and design choices determine the actual algorithm of a Feistel cipher?

4.7 Define the avalanche effect.

Problems

4.1 **a.** In Section 4.1, under the subsection on the motivation for the Feistel cipher structure, it was stated that, for a block of n bits, the number of different reversible mappings for the ideal block cipher is $2^n!$. Justify.

b. In that same discussion, it was stated that for the ideal block cipher, which allows all possible reversible mappings, the size of the key is $n \times 2^n$ bits. But, if there are $2^n!$ possible mappings, it should take $\log_2 2^n!$ bits to discriminate among the different mappings, and so the key length should be $\log_2 2^n!$. However, $\log_2 2^n! < n \times 2^n$. Explain the discrepancy.

4.2 Consider a Feistel cipher composed of sixteen rounds with a block length of 128 bits and a key length of 128 bits. Suppose that, for a given k, the key scheduling algorithm determines values for the first eight round keys, $k_1, k_2, \ldots k_8$, and then sets

$$k_9 = k_8, k_{10} = k_7, k_{11} = k_6, \ldots, k_{16} = k_1$$

Suppose you have a ciphertext c. Explain how, with access to an encryption oracle, you can decrypt c and determine m using just a single oracle query. This shows that such a cipher is vulnerable to a chosen plaintext attack. (An encryption oracle can be thought of as a device that, when given a plaintext, returns the corresponding ciphertext. The internal details of the device are not known to you and you cannot break open the device. You can only gain information from the oracle by making queries to it and observing its responses.)

4.3 Let π be a permutation of the integers $0, 1, 2, \ldots, (2^n - 1)$, such that $\pi(m)$ gives the permuted value of m, $0 \leq m < 2^n$. Put another way, π maps the set of n-bit integers into itself and no two integers map into the same integer. DES is such a permutation for 64-bit integers. We say that π has a fixed point at m if $\pi(m) = m$. That is, if π is an encryption mapping, then a fixed point corresponds to a message that encrypts to itself. We are interested in the number of fixed points in a randomly chosen permutation π. Show the somewhat unexpected result that the number of fixed points for π is 1 on an average, and this number is independent of the size of the permutation.

4.4 Consider a block encryption algorithm that encrypts blocks of length n, and let $N = 2^n$. Say we have t plaintext–ciphertext pairs P_i, $C_i = \mathrm{E}(K, P_i)$, where we assume that the key K selects one of the $N!$ possible mappings. Imagine that we wish to find K by exhaustive search. We could generate key K' and test whether $C_i = \mathrm{E}(K', P_i)$ for $1 \leq i \leq t$. If K' encrypts each P_i to its proper C_i, then we have evidence that $K = K'$. However, it may be the case that the mappings $\mathrm{E}(K, \cdot)$ and $\mathrm{E}(K', \cdot)$ exactly agree on the t plaintext–cipher text pairs P_i, C_i and agree on no other pairs.

a. What is the probability that $\mathrm{E}(K, \cdot)$ and $\mathrm{E}(K', \cdot)$ are in fact distinct mappings?

b. What is the probability that $\mathrm{E}(K, \cdot)$ and $\mathrm{E}(K', \cdot)$ agree on another t' plaintext–ciphertext pairs where $0 \leq t' \leq N - t$?

4.5 For any block cipher, the fact that it is a nonlinear function is crucial to its security. To see this, suppose that we have a linear block cipher EL that encrypts 256-bit blocks of plaintext into 256-bit blocks of ciphertext. Let $\mathrm{EL}(k, m)$ denote the encryption of a 256-bit message m under a key k (the actual bit length of k is irrelevant). Thus,

$$\mathrm{EL}(k, [m_1 \oplus m_2]) = \mathrm{EL}(k, m_1) \oplus \mathrm{EL}(k, m_2) \text{ for all 128-bit patterns } m_1, m_2.$$

Describe how, with 256 chosen ciphertexts, an adversary can decrypt any ciphertext without knowledge of the secret key k. (A "chosen ciphertext" means that an adversary has the ability to choose a ciphertext and then obtain its decryption. Here, you have 256 plaintext/ciphertext pairs to work with and you have the ability to choose the value of the ciphertexts.)

4.6 Suppose the DES F function mapped every 32-bit input R, regardless of the value of the input K, to;

a. 32-bit string of ones

b. bitwise complement of R

Then

1. What function would DES then compute?

2. What would the decryption look like?

Hint: Use the following properties of the XOR operation:

$$(A \oplus B) \oplus C = A \oplus (B \oplus C)$$
$$(A \oplus A) = 0$$
$$(A \oplus 0) = A$$
$$A \oplus 1 = \text{bitwise complement of } A$$

where

A, B, C are n-bit strings of bits
0 is an n-bit string of zeros
1 is an n-bit string of one

4.7 Show that DES decryption is, in fact, the inverse of DES encryption.

4.8 The 32-bit swap after the sixteenth iteration of the DES algorithm is needed to make the encryption process invertible by simply running the ciphertext back through the algorithm with the key order reversed. This was demonstrated in the preceding problem. However, it still may not be entirely clear why the 32-bit swap is needed. To demonstrate why, solve the following exercises. First, some notation:

$A\|B$ = the concatenation of the bit strings A and B

$T_i(R\|L)$ = the transformation defined by the ith iteration of the encryption algorithm for $1 \leq I \leq 16$

$TD_i(R\|L)$ = the transformation defined by the ith iteration of the decryption algorithm for $1 \leq I \leq 16$

$T_{17}(R\|L) = L\|R$, where this transformation occurs after the sixteenth iteration of the encryption algorithm

a. Show that the composition $TD_1(IP(IP^{-1}(T_{17}(T_{16}(L_{15}\|R_{15})))))$ is equivalent to the transformation that interchanges the 32-bit halves, L_{15} and R_{15}. That is, show that

$$TD_1(IP(IP^{-1}(T_{17}(T_{16}(L_{15}\|R_{15}))))) = R_{15}\|L_{15}$$

b. Now suppose that we did away with the final 32-bit swap in the encryption algorithm. Then we would want the following equality to hold:

$$TD_1(\text{IP}(IP^{-1}(T_{16}(L_{15}\|R_{15})))) = L_{15}\|R_{15}$$

Does it?

***Note:* The following problems refer to details of DES that are described in Appendix S.**

4.9 Consider the substitution defined by row 1 of S-box S_1 in Table S.2. Show a block diagram similar to Figure 4.2 that corresponds to this substitution.

4.10 Compute the bits number 1, 16, 33, and 48 at the output of the first round of the DES decryption, assuming that the ciphertext block is composed of all ones and the external key is composed of all ones.

4.11 This problem provides a numerical example of encryption using a one-round version of DES. We start with the same bit pattern for the key K and the plaintext, namely:

Hexadecimal notation:	0 1 2 3 4 5 6 7 8 9 A B C D E F
Binary notation:	0000 0001 0010 0011 0100 0101 0110 0111
	1000 1001 1010 1011 1100 1101 1110 1111

a. Derive K_1, the first-round subkey.
b. Derive L_0, R_0.
c. Expand R_0 to get E[R_0], where E[·] is the expansion function of Table S.1.
d. Calculate $A = \text{E}[R_0] \oplus K_1$.
e. Group the 48-bit result of (d) into sets of 6 bits and evaluate the corresponding S-box substitutions.
f. Concatenate the results of (e) to get a 32-bit result, B.

g. Apply the permutation to get P(B).
h. Calculate $R_1 = \text{P}(B) \oplus L_0$.
i. Write down the ciphertext.

4.12 Show that in DES the first 24 bits of each subkey come from the same subset of 28 bits of the initial key and that the second 24 bits of each subkey come from a disjoint subset of 28 bits of the initial key.

4.13 When using the DES algorithm for decryption, the 16 keys ($K_1, K_2, \ldots, K_{16}$) are used in reverse order. Therefore, the right-hand side of Figure S.1 is not valid for decryption. Design a key-generation scheme with the appropriate shift schedule (analogous to Table S.3d) for the decryption process.

4.14 a. Let X' be the bitwise complement of X. Prove that if the complement of the plaintext block is taken and the complement of an encryption key is taken, then the result of DES encryption with these values is the complement of the original ciphertext. That is,

$$\begin{aligned} \text{If} \quad Y &= \text{E}(K, X) \\ \text{Then} \quad Y' &= \text{E}(K', X') \end{aligned}$$

Hint: Begin by showing that for any two bit strings of equal length, A and B, $(A \oplus B)' = A' \oplus B$.

b. It has been said that a brute-force attack on DES requires searching a key space of 2^{56} keys. Does the result of part (a) change that?

4.15 a. What is a weak key in DES? Why should the use of weak keys be avoided?
b. Write a short note on semi weak keys in DES.

***Note:* The following problems refer to simplified DES, described in Appendix G.**

4.16 Refer to Figure G.3, which explains encryption function for S-DES.
a. How important is the initial permutation IP?
b. How important is the SW function in the middle?

4.17 The equations for the variables q and r for S-DES are defined in the section on S-DES analysis. Provide the equations for s and t.

4.18 Using S-DES, decrypt the string `01000110` using the key `1010000010` by hand. Show intermediate results after each function (IP, F_K, SW, F_K, IP^{-1}). Then decode the first 4 bits of the plaintext string to a letter and the second 4 bits to another letter where we encode A through P in base 2 (i.e., A = 0000, B = 0001, . . . , P = 1111). *Hint:* As a midway check, after the xoring with K2, the string should be `11000001`.

Programming Problems

4.19 Create software that can encrypt and decrypt using a general substitution block cipher.

4.20 Create software that can encrypt and decrypt using S-DES. Test data: use plaintext, ciphertext, and key of Problem 4.18.

CHAPTER 5

Finite Fields

LEARNING OBJECTIVES

After studying this chapter, you should be able to:

- Distinguish among groups, rings, and fields.
- Define finite fields of the form GF(p).
- Explain the differences among ordinary polynomial arithmetic, polynomial arithmetic with coefficients in Z_p, and modular polynomial arithmetic in GF(2^n).
- Define finite fields of the form GF(2^n).
- Explain the two different uses of the mod operator.

Finite fields have become increasingly important in cryptography. A number of cryptographic algorithms rely heavily on properties of finite fields, notably the Advanced Encryption Standard (AES) and elliptic curve cryptography. Other examples include the message authentication code CMAC and the authenticated encryption scheme GCM.

This chapter provides the reader with sufficient background on the concepts of finite fields to be able to understand the design of AES and other cryptographic algorithms that use finite fields. Because students unfamiliar with abstract algebra may find the concepts behind finite fields somewhat difficult to grasp, we approach the topic in a way designed to enhance understanding. Our plan of attack is as follows:

1. Fields are a subset of a larger class of algebraic structures called rings, which are in turn a subset of the larger class of groups. In fact, as shown in Figure 5.1, both groups and rings can be further differentiated. Groups are defined by a simple set of properties and are easily understood. Each successive subset (abelian group, ring, commutative ring, and so on) adds additional properties and is thus more complex. Sections 5.1 through 5.3 will examine groups, rings, and fields, successively.
2. Finite fields are a subset of fields, consisting of those fields with a finite number of elements. These are the class of fields that are found in cryptographic algorithms. With the concepts of fields in hand, we turn in Section 5.4 to a specific class of finite fields, namely those with p elements, where p is prime. Certain asymmetric cryptographic algorithms make use of such fields.
3. A more important class of finite fields, for cryptography, comprises those with 2^n elements depicted as fields of the form GF(2^n). These are used in a wide variety of cryptographic algorithms. However, before discussing these fields, we need to analyze the topic of polynomial arithmetic, which is done in Section 5.5.
4. With all of this preliminary work done, we are able at last, in Section 5.6, to discuss finite fields of the form GF(2^n).

Before proceeding, the reader may wish to review Sections 2.1 through 2.3, which cover relevant topics in number theory.

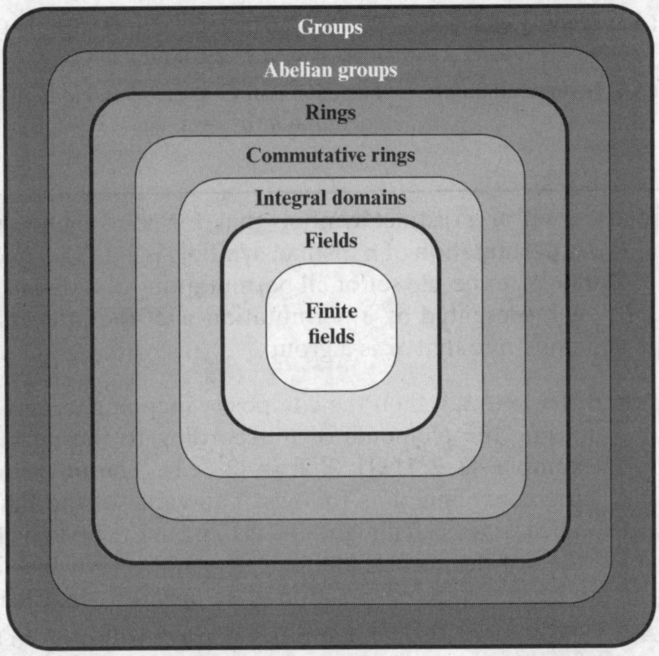

Figure 5.1 Groups, Rings, and Fields

5.1 GROUPS

Groups, rings, and fields are the fundamental elements of a branch of mathematics known as abstract algebra, or modern algebra. In abstract algebra, we are concerned with sets on whose elements we can operate algebraically; that is, we can combine two elements of the set, perhaps in several ways, to obtain a third element of the set. These operations are subject to specific rules, which define the nature of the set. By convention, the notation for the two principal classes of operations on set elements is usually the same as the notation for addition and multiplication on ordinary numbers. However, it is important to note that, in abstract algebra, we are not limited to ordinary arithmetical operations. All this should become clear as we proceed.

Groups

A **group** G, sometimes denoted by $\{G, \cdot\}$, is a set of elements with a binary operation denoted by $\cdot$ that associates to each ordered pair (a, b) of elements in G an element $(a \cdot b)$ in G, such that the following axioms are obeyed:[1]

(A1) Closure: If a and b belong to G, then $a \cdot b$ is also in G.

(A2) Associative: $a \cdot (b \cdot c) = (a \cdot b) \cdot c$ for all a, b, c in G.

[1] The operator $\cdot$ is generic and can refer to addition, multiplication, or some other mathematical operation.

(A3) Identity element: There is an element e in G such that $a \cdot e = e \cdot a = a$ for all a in G.

(A4) Inverse element: For each a in G, there is an element a' in G such that $a \cdot a' = a' \cdot a = e$.

Let N_n denote a set of n distinct symbols that, for convenience, we represent as $\{1, 2, \ldots, n\}$. A **permutation** of n distinct symbols is a one-to-one mapping from N_n to N_n.[2] Define S_n to be the set of all permutations of n distinct symbols. Each element of S_n is represented by a permutation π of the integers in $1, 2, \ldots, n$. It is easy to demonstrate that S_n is a group:

A1: If $(\pi, \rho \in S_n)$, then the composite mapping $\pi \cdot \rho$ is formed by permuting the elements of ρ according to the permutation π. For example, $\{3, 2, 1\} \cdot \{1, 3, 2\} = \{2, 3, 1\}$. The notation for this mapping is explained as follows: The value of the first element of π indicates which element of ρ is to be in the first position in $\pi \cdot \rho$; the value of the second element of π indicates which element of ρ is to be in the second position in $\pi \cdot \rho$; and so on. Clearly, $\pi \cdot \rho \in S_n$.

A2: The composition of mappings is also easily seen to be associative.

A3: The identity mapping is the permutation that does not alter the order of the n elements. For S_n, the identity element is $\{1, 2, \ldots, n\}$.

A4: For any $\pi \in S_n$, the mapping that undoes the permutation defined by π is the inverse element for π. There will always be such an inverse. For example $\{2, 3, 1\} \cdot \{3, 1, 2\} = \{1, 2, 3\}$.

If a group has a finite number of elements, it is referred to as a **finite group**, and the **order** of the group is equal to the number of elements in the group. Otherwise, the group is an **infinite group**.

Abelian Group

A group is said to be **abelian** if it satisfies the following additional condition:

(A5) Commutative: $a \cdot b = b \cdot a$ for all a, b in G.

The set of integers (positive, negative, and 0) under addition is an abelian group. The set of nonzero real numbers under multiplication is an abelian group. The set S_n from the preceding example is a group but not an abelian group for $n > 2$.

[2]This is equivalent to the definition of permutation in Chapter 2, which stated that a permutation of a finite set of elements S is an ordered sequence of all the elements of S, with each element appearing exactly once.

When the group operation is addition, the identity element is 0; the inverse element of a is $-a$; and subtraction is defined with the following rule: $a - b = a + (-b)$.

Cyclic Group

We define exponentiation within a group as a repeated application of the group operator, so that $a^3 = a \cdot a \cdot a$. Furthermore, we define $a^0 = \mathrm{e}$ as the identity element, and $a^{-n} = (a')^n$, where a' is the inverse element of a within the group. A group G is **cyclic** if every element of G is a power a^k (k is an integer) of a fixed element $a \in G$. The element a is said to **generate** the group G or to be a **generator** of G. A cyclic group is always abelian and may be finite or infinite.

> The additive group of integers is an infinite cyclic group generated by the element 1. In this case, powers are interpreted additively, so that n is the nth power of 1.

5.2 RINGS

A **ring** R, sometimes denoted by $\{R, +, \times\}$, is a set of elements with two binary operations, called *addition* and *multiplication*,[3] such that for all a, b, c in R the following axioms are obeyed.

(A1–A5) R is an abelian group with respect to addition; that is, R satisfies axioms A1 through A5. For the case of an additive group, we denote the identity element as 0 and the inverse of a as $-a$.

(M1) Closure under multiplication: If a and b belong to R, then ab is also in R.

(M2) Associativity of multiplication: $a(bc) = (ab)c$ for all a, b, c in R.

(M3) Distributive laws: $a(b + c) = ab + ac$ for all a, b, c in R.
$(a + b)c = ac + bc$ for all a, b, c in R.

In essence, a ring is a set of elements in which we can do addition, subtraction $[a - b = a + (-b)]$, and multiplication without leaving the set.

> With respect to addition and multiplication, the set of all n-square matrices over the real numbers is a ring.

A ring is said to be **commutative** if it satisfies the following additional condition:

(M4) Commutativity of multiplication: $ab = ba$ for all a, b in R.

---

[3]Generally, we do not use the multiplication symbol, $\times$, but denote multiplication by the concatenation of two elements.

Let S be the set of even integers (positive, negative, and 0) under the usual operations of addition and multiplication. S is a commutative ring. The set of all n-square matrices defined in the preceding example is not a commutative ring.

The set Z_n of integers $\{0, 1, \ldots, n - 1\}$, together with the arithmetic operations modulo n, is a commutative ring (Table 4.3).

Next, we define an **integral domain**, which is a commutative ring that obeys the following axioms.

(M5) Multiplicative identity: There is an element 1 in R such that $a1 = 1a = a$ for all a in R.

(M6) No zero divisors: If a, b in R and $ab = 0$, then either $a = 0$ or $b = 0$.

Let S be the set of integers (positive, negative, and 0) under the usual operations of addition and multiplication. S is an integral domain.

5.3 FIELDS

A **field** F, sometimes denoted by $\{F, +, \times\}$, is a set of elements with two binary operations, called *addition* and *multiplication*, such that for all a, b, c in F the following axioms are obeyed.

(A1–M6) F is an integral domain; that is, F satisfies axioms A1 through A5 and M1 through M6.

(M7) Multiplicative inverse: For each a in F, except 0, there is an element a^{-1} in F such that $aa^{-1} = (a^{-1})a = 1$.

In essence, a field is a set of elements in which we can do addition, subtraction, multiplication, and division without leaving the set. Division is defined with the following rule: $a/b = a(b^{-1})$.

Familiar examples of fields are the rational numbers, the real numbers, and the complex numbers. Note that the set of all integers is not a field, because not every element of the set has a multiplicative inverse; in fact, only the elements 1 and −1 have multiplicative inverses in the integers.

In gaining insight into fields, the following alternate characterization may be useful. A **field** F, denoted by $\{F, +\}$, is a set of elements with two binary operations, called *addition* and *multiplication*, such that the following conditions hold:

1. F forms an abelian group with respect to addition.
2. The nonzero elements of F form an abelian group with respect to multiplication.

3. The distributive law holds. That is, for all a, b, c in F,

$$a(b + c) = ab + ac.$$

$$(a + b)c = ac + bc$$

4. Figure 5.2 summarizes the axioms that define groups, rings, and fields.

5.4 FINITE FIELDS OF THE FORM GF(p)

In Section 5.3, we defined a field as a set that obeys all of the axioms of Figure 5.2 and gave some examples of infinite fields. Infinite fields are not of particular interest in the context of cryptography. However, in addition to infinite fields, there are two types of finite fields, as illustrated in Figure 5.3. Finite fields play a crucial role in many cryptographic algorithms.

It can be shown that the order of a finite field (number of elements in the field) must be a power of a prime p^n, where n is a positive integer. The finite field of order p^n is generally written GF(p^n); GF stands for Galois field, in honor of the mathematician who first studied finite fields. Two special cases are of interest for our purposes. For $n = 1$, we have the finite field GF(p); this finite field has a different structure than that for finite fields with $n > 1$ and is studied in this section. For finite fields of the form GF(p^n), GF(2^n) fields are of particular cryptographic interest, and these are covered in Section 5.6.

Finite Fields of Order p

For a given prime, p, we define the finite field of order p, GF(p), as the set Z_p of integers $\{0, 1, \ldots, p - 1\}$ together with the arithmetic operations modulo p. Note therefore that we are using ordinary modular arithmetic to define the operations over these fields.

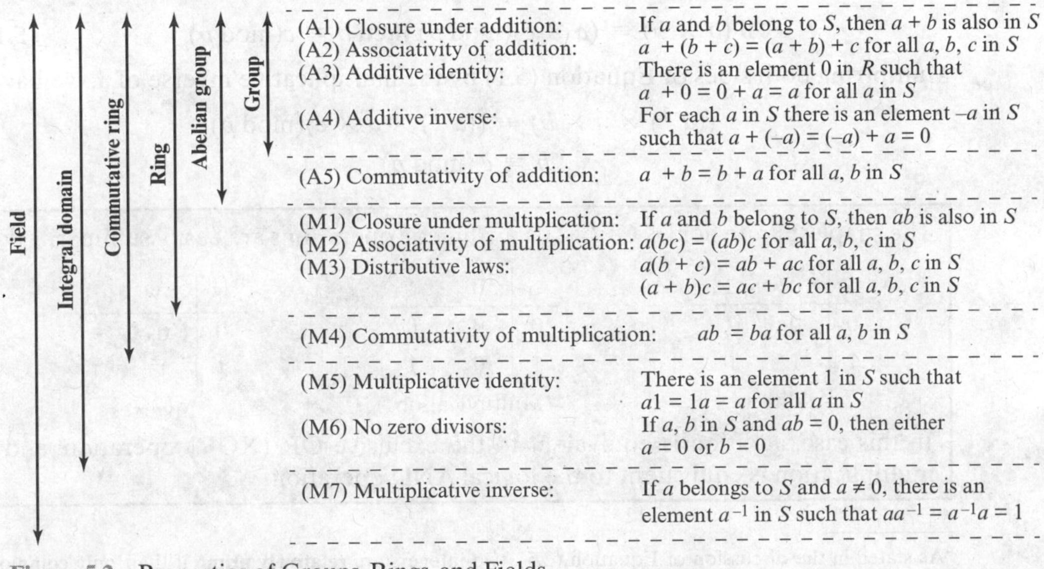

Figure 5.2 Properties of Groups, Rings, and Fields

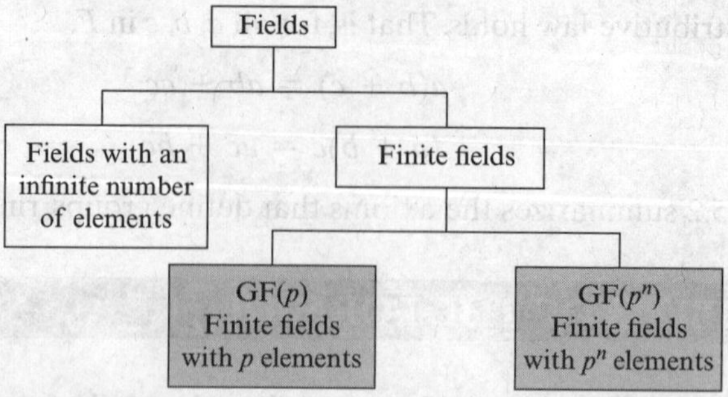

Figure 5.3 Types of Fields

Recall that we showed in Section 5.2 that the set Z_n of integers $\{0, 1, \ldots, n - 1\}$, together with the arithmetic operations modulo n, is a commutative ring (Table 2.5). We further observed that any integer in Z_n has a multiplicative inverse if and only if that integer is relatively prime to n [see discussion of Equation (2.5)].[4] If n is prime, then all of the nonzero integers in Z_n are relatively prime to n, and therefore there exists a multiplicative inverse for all of the nonzero integers in Z_n. Thus, for Z_p we can add the following properties to those listed in Table 5.2:

Multiplicative inverse (w^{-1})	For each $w \in Z_p$, $w \neq 0$, there exists a $z \in Z_p$ such that $w \times z \equiv 1 \pmod p$

Because w is relatively prime to p, if we multiply all the elements of Z_p by w, the resulting residues are all of the elements of Z_p permuted. Thus, exactly one of the residues has the value 1. Therefore, there is some integer in Z_p that, when multiplied by w, yields the residue 1. That integer is the multiplicative inverse of w, designated w^{-1}. Therefore, Z_p is in fact a finite field. Furthermore, Equation (2.5) is consistent with the existence of a multiplicative inverse and can be rewritten without the condition:

$$\textbf{if } (a \times b) \equiv (a \times c) \pmod p \textbf{ then } b \equiv c \pmod p \qquad \textbf{(5.1)}$$

Multiplying both sides of Equation (5.1) by the multiplicative inverse of a, we have

$$((a^{-1}) \times a \times b) \equiv ((a^{-1}) \times a \times c) \pmod p$$
$$b \equiv c \pmod p$$

The simplest finite field is GF(2). Its arithmetic operations are easily summarized:

+	0	1
0	0	1
1	1	0

Addition

×	0	1
0	0	0
1	0	1

Multiplication

w	$-w$	w^{-1}
0	0	–
1	1	1

Inverses

In this case, addition is equivalent to the exclusive-OR (XOR) operation, and multiplication is equivalent to the logical AND operation.

[4]As stated in the discussion of Equation (2.5), two integers are **relatively prime** if their only common positive integer factor is 1.

The right-hand side of Table 5.1 shows arithmetic operations in GF(7). This is a field of order 7 using modular arithmetic modulo 7. As can be seen, it satisfies all of the properties required of a field (Figure 5.2). Compare with the left-hand side of Table 5.1, which reproduces Table 2.2. In the latter case, we see that the set Z_8, using modular arithmetic modulo 8, is not a field. Later in this chapter, we show how to define addition and multiplication operations on Z_8 in such a way as to form a finite field.

Finding the Multiplicative Inverse in GF(p)

It is easy to find the multiplicative inverse of an element in GF(p) for small values of p. You simply construct a multiplication table, such as shown in Table 5.1e, and the desired result can be read directly. However, for large values of p, this approach is not practical.

If a and b are relatively prime, then b has a multiplicative inverse modulo a. That is, if $\gcd(a, b) = 1$, then b has a multiplicative inverse modulo a. That is, for positive integer $b < a$, there exists a $b^{-1} < a$ such that $bb^{-1} = 1 \bmod a$. If a is a prime number and $b < a$, then clearly a and b are relatively prime and have a greatest common divisor of 1. We now show that we can easily compute b^{-1} using the extended Euclidean algorithm.

We repeat here Equation (2.7), which we showed can be solved with the extended Euclidean algorithm:

$$ax + by = d = \gcd(a, b)$$

Now, if $\gcd(a, b) = 1$, then we have $ax + by = 1$. Using the basic equalities of modular arithmetic, defined in Section 2.3, we can say

$$[(ax \bmod a) + (by \bmod a)] \bmod a = 1 \bmod a$$
$$0 + (by \bmod a) = 1$$

But if $by \bmod a = 1$, then $y = b^{-1}$. Thus, applying the extended Euclidean algorithm to Equation (2.7) yields the value of the multiplicative inverse of b if $\gcd(a, b) = 1$.

Consider the example that was shown in Table 2.4. Here we have $a = 1759$, which is a prime number, and $b = 550$. The solution of the equation $1759x + 550y = d$ yields a value of $y = 355$. Thus, $b^{-1} = 355$. To verify, we calculate $550 \times 355 \bmod 1759 = 195250 \bmod 1759 = 1$.

More generally, the extended Euclidean algorithm can be used to find a multiplicative inverse in Z_n for any n. If we apply the extended Euclidean algorithm to the equation $nx + by = d$, and the algorithm yields $d = 1$, then $y = b^{-1}$ in Z_n.

Table 5.1 Arithmetic Modulo 8 and Modulo 7

+	0	1	2	3	4	5	6	7
0	0	1	2	3	4	5	6	7
1	1	2	3	4	5	6	7	0
2	2	3	4	5	6	7	0	1
3	3	4	5	6	7	0	1	2
4	4	5	6	7	0	1	2	3
5	5	6	7	0	1	2	3	4
6	6	7	0	1	2	3	4	5
7	7	0	1	2	3	4	5	6

(a) Addition modulo 8

+	0	1	2	3	4	5	6
0	0	1	2	3	4	5	6
1	1	2	3	4	5	6	0
2	2	3	4	5	6	0	1
3	3	4	5	6	0	1	2
4	4	5	6	0	1	2	3
5	5	6	0	1	2	3	4
6	6	0	1	2	3	4	5

(d) Addition modulo 7

×	0	1	2	3	4	5	6	7
0	0	0	0	0	0	0	0	0
1	0	1	2	3	4	5	6	7
2	0	2	4	6	0	2	4	6
3	0	3	6	1	4	7	2	5
4	0	4	0	4	0	4	0	4
5	0	5	2	7	4	1	6	3
6	0	6	4	2	0	6	4	2
7	0	7	6	5	4	3	2	1

(b) Multiplication modulo 8

×	0	1	2	3	4	5	6
0	0	0	0	0	0	0	0
1	0	1	2	3	4	5	6
2	0	2	4	6	1	3	5
3	0	3	6	2	5	1	4
4	0	4	1	5	2	6	3
5	0	5	3	1	6	4	2
6	0	6	5	4	3	2	1

(e) Multiplication modulo 7

w	0	1	2	3	4	5	6	7
$-w$	0	7	6	5	4	3	2	1
w^{-1}	—	1	—	3	—	5	—	7

(c) Additive and multiplicative inverses modulo 8

w	0	1	2	3	4	5	6
$-w$	0	6	5	4	3	2	1
w^{-1}	—	1	4	5	2	3	6

(f) Additive and multiplicative inverses modulo 7

Summary

In this section, we have shown how to construct a finite field of order p, where p is prime. Specifically, we defined GF(p) with the following properties.

1. GF(p) consists of p elements.
2. The binary operations + and × are defined over the set. The operations of addition, subtraction, multiplication, and division can be performed without leaving the set. Each element of the set other than 0 has a multiplicative inverse, and division is performed by multiplication by the multiplicative inverse.

We have shown that the elements of GF(p) are the integers $\{0, 1, \ldots, p - 1\}$ and that the arithmetic operations are addition and multiplication mod p.

5.5 POLYNOMIAL ARITHMETIC

Before continuing our discussion of finite fields, we need to introduce the interesting subject of polynomial arithmetic. We are concerned with polynomials in a single variable x, and we can distinguish three classes of polynomial arithmetic (Figure 5.4).

- Ordinary polynomial arithmetic, using the basic rules of algebra.
- Polynomial arithmetic in which the arithmetic on the coefficients is performed modulo p; that is, the coefficients are in GF(p).
- Polynomial arithmetic in which the coefficients are in GF(p), and the polynomials are defined modulo a polynomial $m(x)$ whose highest power is some integer n.

This section examines the first two classes, and the next section covers the last class.

Ordinary Polynomial Arithmetic

A **polynomial** of degree n (integer $n \geq 0$) is an expression of the form

$$f(x) = a_n x^n + a_{n-1}x^{n-1} + \cdots + a_1 x + a_0 = \sum_{i=0}^{n} a_i x^i$$

where the a_i are elements of some designated set of numbers S, called the **coefficient set**, and $a_n \neq 0$. We say that such polynomials are defined over the coefficient set S.

A zero-degree polynomial is called a **constant polynomial** and is simply an element of the set of coefficients. An nth-degree polynomial is said to be a **monic polynomial** if $a_n = 1$.

In the context of abstract algebra, we are usually not interested in evaluating a polynomial for a particular value of x [e.g., $f(7)$]. To emphasize this point, the variable x is sometimes referred to as the **indeterminate**.

Polynomial arithmetic includes the operations of addition, subtraction, and multiplication. These operations are defined in a natural way as though the variable

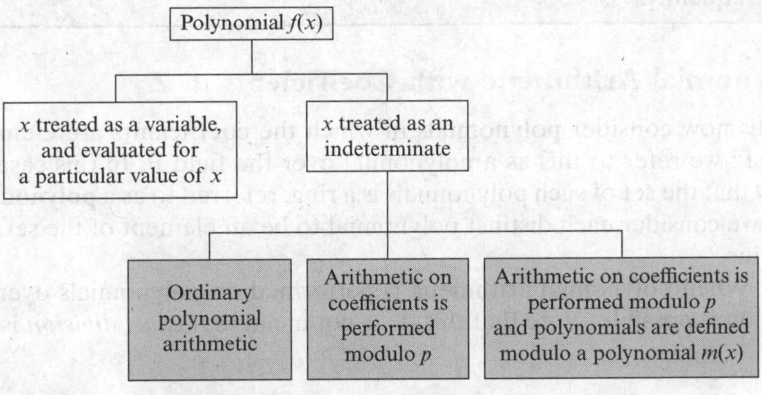

Figure 5.4 Treatment of Polynomials

x was an element of S. Division is similarly defined, but requires that S be a field. Examples of fields include the real numbers, rational numbers, and Z_p for p prime. Note that the set of all integers is not a field and does not support polynomial division.

Addition and subtraction are performed by adding or subtracting corresponding coefficients. Thus, if

$$f(x) = \sum_{i=0}^{n} a_i x^i; \quad g(x) = \sum_{i=0}^{m} b_i x^i; \quad n \geq m$$

then addition is defined as

$$f(x) + g(x) = \sum_{i=0}^{m} (a_i + b_i)x^i + \sum_{i=m+1}^{n} a_i x^i$$

and multiplication is defined as

$$f(x) \times g(x) = \sum_{i=0}^{n+m} c_i x^i$$

where

$$c_k = a_0 b_k + a_1 b_{k-1} + \cdots + a_{k-1} b_1 + a_k b_0$$

In the last formula, we treat a_i as zero for $i > n$ and b_i as zero for $i > m$. Note that the degree of the product is equal to the sum of the degrees of the two polynomials.

As an example, let $f(x) = x^3 + x^2 + 2$ and $g(x) = x^2 - x + 1$, where S is the set of integers. Then

$$f(x) + g(x) = x^3 + 2x^2 - x + 3$$
$$f(x) - g(x) = x^3 + x + 1$$
$$f(x) \times g(x) = x^5 + 3x^2 - 2x + 2$$

Figures 5.5a through 5.5c show the manual calculations. We comment on division subsequently.

Polynomial Arithmetic with Coefficients in Z_p

Let us now consider polynomials in which the coefficients are elements of some field F; we refer to this as a polynomial over the field F. In this case, it is easy to show that the set of such polynomials is a ring, referred to as a **polynomial ring**. That is, if we consider each distinct polynomial to be an element of the set, then that set is a ring.[5]

When polynomial arithmetic is performed on polynomials over a field, then division is possible. Note that this does not mean that *exact division* is possible. Let

---

[5] In fact, the set of polynomials whose coefficients are elements of a commutative ring forms a polynomial ring, but that is of no interest in the present context.

$$
\begin{array}{r}
x^3 + x^2 \qquad\quad + 2 \\
+ \ (x^2 - x + 1) \\
\hline
x^3 + 2x^2 - x + 3
\end{array}
$$

(a) Addition

$$
\begin{array}{r}
x^3 + x^2 \qquad\quad + 2 \\
- \ (x^2 - x + 1) \\
\hline
x^3 \qquad\quad + x + 1
\end{array}
$$

(b) Subtraction

$$
\begin{array}{r}
x^3 + x^2 \qquad\quad + 2 \\
\times \ (x^2 - x + 1) \\
\hline
x^3 + x^2 \qquad\quad + 2 \\
- x^4 - x^3 \qquad - 2x \quad \\
x^5 + x^4 \qquad +2x^2 \qquad\qquad \\
\hline
x^5 \qquad +3x^2 - 2x + 2
\end{array}
$$

(c) Multiplication

$$
\begin{array}{r}
x + 2 \qquad\qquad \\
x^2 - x + 1 \ \big) \ \overline{x^3 + x^2 \qquad + 2} \\
x^3 - x^2 + x \quad \\
\hline
2x^2 - x + 2 \\
2x^2 - 2x + 2 \\
\hline
x \quad
\end{array}
$$

(d) Division

Figure 5.5 Examples of Polynomial Arithmetic

us clarify this distinction. Within a field, given two elements a and b, the quotient a/b is also an element of the field. However, given a ring R that is not a field, in general, division will result in both a quotient and a remainder; this is not exact division.

> Consider the division 5/3 within a set S. If S is the set of rational numbers, which is a field, then the result is simply expressed as 5/3 and is an element of S. Now suppose that S is the field Z_7. In this case, we calculate (using Table 5.1f)
>
> $$5/3 = (5 \times 3^{-1}) \bmod 7 = (5 \times 5) \bmod 7 = 4$$
>
> which is an exact solution. Finally, suppose that S is the set of integers, which is a ring but not a field. Then 5/3 produces a quotient of 1 and a remainder of 2:
>
> $$5/3 = 1 + 2/3$$
> $$5 = 1 \times 3 + 2$$
>
> Thus, division is not exact over the set of integers.

Now, if we attempt to perform polynomial division over a coefficient set that is not a field, we find that division is not always defined.

> If the coefficient set is the integers, then $(5x^2)/(3x)$ does not have a solution, because it would require a coefficient with a value of 5/3, which is not in the coefficient set. Suppose that we perform the same polynomial division over Z_7. Then we have $(5x^2)/(3x) = 4x$, which is a valid polynomial over Z_7.

However, as we demonstrate presently, even if the coefficient set is a field, polynomial division is not necessarily exact. In general, division will produce a quotient and a remainder. We can restate the division algorithm of Equation (2.1) for polynomials over a field as follows. Given polynomials $f(x)$ of degree n and $g(x)$

of degree (m), $(n \geq m)$, if we divide $f(x)$ by $g(x)$, we get a quotient $q(x)$ and a remainder $r(x)$ that obey the relationship

$$f(x) = q(x)g(x) + r(x) \tag{5.2}$$

with polynomial degrees:

Degree $f(x) = n$
Degree $g(x) = m$
Degree $q(x) = n - m$
Degree $r(x) \leq m - 1$

With the understanding that remainders are allowed, we can say that polynomial division is possible if the coefficient set is a field. One common technique used for polynomial division is polynomial long division, similar to long division for integers. Examples of this are shown subsequently.

In an analogy to integer arithmetic, we can write $f(x)$ mod $g(x)$ for the remainder $r(x)$ in Equation (5.2). That is, $r(x) = f(x) \bmod g(x)$. If there is no remainder [i.e., $r(x) = 0$], then we can say $g(x)$ **divides** $f(x)$, written as $g(x)|f(x)$. Equivalently, we can say that $g(x)$ is a **factor** of $f(x)$ or $g(x)$ is a **divisor** of $f(x)$.

For the preceding example [$f(x) = x^3 + x^2 + 2$ and $g(x) = x^2 - x + 1$], $f(x)/g(x)$ produces a quotient of $q(x) = x + 2$ and a remainder $r(x) = x$, as shown in Figure 5.5d. This is easily verified by noting that

$$q(x)g(x) + r(x) = (x + 2)(x^2 - x + 1) + x = (x^3 + x^2 - x + 2) + x$$
$$= x^3 + x^2 + 2 = f(x)$$

For our purposes, polynomials over GF(2) are of most interest. Recall from Section 5.4 that in GF(2), addition is equivalent to the XOR operation, and multiplication is equivalent to the logical AND operation. Further, addition and subtraction are equivalent mod 2:

$$1 + 1 = 1 - 1 = 0$$
$$1 + 0 = 1 - 0 = 1$$
$$0 + 1 = 0 - 1 = 1$$

Figure 5.6 shows an example of polynomial arithmetic over GF(2). For $f(x) = (x^7 + x^5 + x^4 + x^3 + x + 1)$ and $g(x) = (x^3 + x + 1)$, the figure shows $f(x) + g(x)$; $f(x) - g(x)$; $f(x) \times g(x)$; and $f(x)/g(x)$. Note that $g(x)|f(x)$.

A polynomial $f(x)$ over a field F is called **irreducible** if and only if $f(x)$ cannot be expressed as a product of two polynomials, both over F, and both of degree lower than that of $f(x)$. By analogy to integers, an irreducible polynomial is also called a **prime polynomial**.

The polynomial[6] $f(x) = x^4 + 1$ over GF(2) is reducible, because

$$x^4 + 1 = (x + 1)(x^3 + x^2 + x + 1).$$

[6]In the reminder of this chapter, unless otherwise noted, all examples are of polynomials over GF(2).

Consider the polynomial $f(x) = x^3 + x + 1$. It is clear by inspection that x is not a factor of $f(x)$. We easily show that $x + 1$ is not a factor of $f(x)$:

$$
\begin{array}{r l}
 & x^2 + x \\
x + 1 \,\big) & x^3 \qquad + x + 1 \\
 & \underline{x^3 + x^2} \\
 & \quad x^2 + x \\
 & \quad \underline{x^2 + x} \\
 & \qquad\qquad 1
\end{array}
$$

Thus, $f(x)$ has no factors of degree 1. But it is clear by inspection that if $f(x)$ is reducible, it must have one factor of degree 2 and one factor of degree 1. Therefore, $f(x)$ is irreducible.

$$
\begin{array}{r}
x^7 \quad + x^5 + x^4 + x^3 \quad + x + 1 \\
+ (x^3 \quad + x + 1) \\
\hline
x^7 \quad + x^5 + x^4 \qquad\qquad\qquad
\end{array}
$$

(a) Addition

$$
\begin{array}{r}
x^7 \quad + x^5 + x^4 + x^3 \quad + x + 1 \\
- (x^3 \quad + x + 1) \\
\hline
x^7 \quad + x^5 + x^4 \qquad\qquad\qquad
\end{array}
$$

(b) Subtraction

$$
\begin{array}{r}
x^7 \quad + x^5 + x^4 + x^3 \quad + x + 1 \\
\times (x^3 \quad + x + 1) \\
\hline
x^7 \quad + x^5 + x^4 + x^3 \quad + x + 1 \\
x^8 \quad + x^6 + x^5 + x^4 \quad + x^2 + x \qquad \\
x^{10} \quad + x^8 + x^7 + x^6 \quad + x^4 + x^3 \qquad\qquad\qquad \\
\hline
x^{10} \qquad\qquad\qquad + x^4 \qquad + x^2 \qquad + 1
\end{array}
$$

(c) Multiplication

$$
\begin{array}{r l}
 & x^4 + 1 \\
x^3 + x + 1 \,\big) & x^7 \quad + x^5 + x^4 + x^3 \quad + x + 1 \\
 & \underline{x^7 \quad + x^5 + x^4} \\
 & \qquad\qquad\qquad x^3 \quad + x + 1 \\
 & \qquad\qquad\qquad \underline{x^3 \quad + x + 1}
\end{array}
$$

(d) Division

Figure 5.6 Examples of Polynomial Arithmetic over GF(2)

Finding the Greatest Common Divisor

We can extend the analogy between polynomial arithmetic over a field and integer arithmetic by defining the greatest common divisor as follows. The polynomial $c(x)$ is said to be the greatest common divisor of $a(x)$ and $b(x)$ if the following are true.

1. $c(x)$ divides both $a(x)$ and $b(x)$.
2. Any divisor of $a(x)$ and $b(x)$ is a divisor of $c(x)$.

An equivalent definition is the following: $\gcd[a(x), b(x)]$ is the polynomial of maximum degree that divides both $a(x)$ and $b(x)$.

We can adapt the Euclidean algorithm to compute the greatest common divisor of two polynomials. Recall Equation (2.6), from Chapter 2, which is the basis of the Euclidean algorithm: $\gcd(a, b) = \gcd(b, a \bmod b)$. This equality can be rewritten as the following equation:

$$\gcd[a(x), b(x)] = \gcd[b(x), a(x) \bmod b(x)] \tag{5.3}$$

Equation (5.3) can be used repetitively to determine the greatest common divisor. Compare the following scheme to the definition of the Euclidean algorithm for integers.

Euclidean Algorithm for Polynomials	
Calculate	**Which satisfies**
$r_1(x) = a(x) \bmod b(x)$	$a(x) = q_1(x)b(x) + r_1(x)$
$r_2(x) = b(x) \bmod r_1(x)$	$b(x) = q_2(x)r_1(x) + r_2(x)$
$r_3(x) = r_1(x) \bmod r_2(x)$	$r_1(x) = q_3(x)r_2(x) + r_3(x)$
• • •	• • •
$r_n(x) = r_{n-2}(x) \bmod r_{n-1}(x)$	$r_{n-2}(x) = q_n(x)r_{n-1}(x) + r_n(x)$
$r_{n+1}(x) = r_{n-1}(x) \bmod r_n(x) = 0$	$r_{n-1}(x) = q_{n+1}(x)r_n(x) + 0$ $d(x) = \gcd(a(x), b(x)) = r_n(x)$

At each iteration, we have $d(x) = \gcd(r_{i+1}(x), r_i(x))$ until finally $d(x) = \gcd(r_n(x), 0) = r_n(x)$. Thus, we can find the greatest common divisor of two integers by repetitive application of the division algorithm. This is the Euclidean algorithm for polynomials. The algorithm assumes that the degree of $a(x)$ is greater than the degree of $b(x)$.

Find $\gcd[a(x), b(x)]$ for $a(x) = x^6 + x^5 + x^4 + x^3 + x^2 + x + 1$ and $b(x) = x^4 + x^2 + x + 1$. First, we divide $a(x)$ by $b(x)$:

$$\begin{array}{r l}
 & x^2 + x \\
x^4 + x^2 + x + 1 \,/ & x^6 + x^5 + x^4 + x^3 + x^2 + x + 1 \\
 & x^6 + x^4 + x^3 + x^2 \\
\hline
 & x^5 + x + 1 \\
 & x^5 + x^3 + x^2 + x \\
\hline
 & x^3 + x^2 + 1
\end{array}$$

This yields $r_1(x) = x^3 + x^2 + 1$ and $q_1(x) = x^2 + x$.

Then, we divide $b(x)$ by $r_1(x)$.

$$\begin{array}{r}
x + 1 \\
x^3 + x^2 + 1 \overline{\big)\, x^4 + x^2 + x + 1}\\
\underline{x^4 + x^3 + x }\\
x^3 + x^2 + 1\\
\underline{x^3 + x^2 + 1}
\end{array}$$

This yields $r_2(x) = 0$ and $q_2(x) = x + 1$.

Therefore, $\gcd[a(x), b(x)] = r_1(x) = x^3 + x^2 + 1$.

Summary

We began this section with a discussion of arithmetic with ordinary polynomials. In ordinary polynomial arithmetic, the variable is not evaluated; that is, we do not plug a value in for the variable of the polynomials. Instead, arithmetic operations are performed on polynomials (addition, subtraction, multiplication, division) using the ordinary rules of algebra. Polynomial division is not allowed unless the coefficients are elements of a field.

Next, we discussed polynomial arithmetic in which the coefficients are elements of GF(p). In this case, polynomial addition, subtraction, multiplication, and division are allowed. However, division is not exact; that is, in general division results in a quotient and a remainder.

Finally, we showed that the Euclidean algorithm can be extended to find the greatest common divisor of two polynomials whose coefficients are elements of a field.

All of the material in this section provides a foundation for the following section, in which polynomials are used to define finite fields of order p^n.

5.6 FINITE FIELDS OF THE FORM GF(2^n)

Earlier in this chapter, we mentioned that the order of a finite field must be of the form p^n, where p is a prime and n is a positive integer. In Section 5.4, we looked at the special case of finite fields with order p. We found that, using modular arithmetic in Z_p, all of the axioms for a field (Figure 5.2) are satisfied. For polynomials over p^n, with $n > 1$, operations modulo p^n do not produce a field. In this section, we show what structure satisfies the axioms for a field in a set with p^n elements and concentrate on GF(2^n).

Motivation

Virtually all encryption algorithms, both symmetric and asymmetric, involve arithmetic operations on integers. If one of the operations that is used in the algorithm is division, then we need to work in arithmetic defined over a field. For convenience and for implementation efficiency, we would also like to work with integers that fit exactly into a given number of bits with no wasted bit patterns. That is, we wish to work with integers in the range 0 through $2^n - 1$, which fit into an n-bit word.

> Suppose we wish to define a conventional encryption algorithm that operates on data 8 bits at a time, and we wish to perform division. With 8 bits, we can represent integers in the range 0 through 255. However, 256 is not a prime number, so that if arithmetic is performed in Z_{256} (arithmetic modulo 256), this set of integers will not be a field. The closest prime number less than 256 is 251. Thus, the set Z_{251}, using arithmetic modulo 251, is a field. However, in this case the 8-bit patterns representing the integers 251 through 255 would not be used, resulting in inefficient use of storage.

As the preceding example points out, if all arithmetic operations are to be used and we wish to represent a full range of integers in n bits, then arithmetic modulo 2^n will not work. Equivalently, the set of integers modulo 2^n for $n > 1$, is not a field. Furthermore, even if the encryption algorithm uses only addition and multiplication, but not division, the use of the set Z_{2^n} is questionable, as the following example illustrates.

> Suppose we wish to use 3-bit blocks in our encryption algorithm and use only the operations of addition and multiplication. Then arithmetic modulo 8 is well defined, as shown in Table 5.1. However, note that in the multiplication table, the nonzero integers do not appear an equal number of times. For example, there are only four occurrences of 3, but twelve occurrences of 4. On the other hand, as was mentioned, there are finite fields of the form GF(2^n), so there is in particular a finite field of order $2^3 = 8$. Arithmetic for this field is shown in Table 5.2. In this case, the number of occurrences of the nonzero integers is uniform for multiplication. To summarize,

Integer	1	2	3	4	5	6	7
Occurrences in Z_8	4	8	4	12	4	8	4
Occurrences in GF(2^3)	7	7	7	7	7	7	7

> For the moment, let us set aside the question of how the matrices of Table 5.2 were constructed and instead make some observations.
>
> 1. The addition and multiplication tables are symmetric about the main diagonal, in conformance to the commutative property of addition and multiplication. This property is also exhibited in Table 5.1, which uses mod 8 arithmetic.
> 2. All the nonzero elements defined by Table 5.2 have a multiplicative inverse, unlike the case with Table 5.1.
> 3. The scheme defined by Table 5.2 satisfies all the requirements for a finite field. Thus, we can refer to this scheme as GF(2^3).
> 4. For convenience, we show the 3-bit assignment used for each of the elements of GF(2^3).

Intuitively, it would seem that an algorithm that maps the integers unevenly onto themselves might be cryptographically weaker than one that provides a uniform mapping. That is, a cryptanalytic technique might be able to exploit the fact that some integers occur more frequently and some less frequently in the ciphertext. Thus, the finite fields of the form GF(2^n) are attractive for cryptographic algorithms.

To summarize, we are looking for a set consisting of 2^n elements, together with a definition of addition and multiplication over the set that define a field. We can assign a unique integer in the range 0 through $2^n - 1$ to each element of the set. Keep in mind that we will not use modular arithmetic, as we have seen that this does not result in a field. Instead, we will show how polynomial arithmetic provides a means for constructing the desired field.

Modular Polynomial Arithmetic

Consider the set S of all polynomials of degree $n - 1$ or less over the field Z_p. Thus, each polynomial has the form

$$f(x) = a_{n-1}x^{n-1} + a_{n-2}x^{n-2} + \cdots + a_1x + a_0 = \sum_{i=0}^{n-1} a_i x^i$$

Table 5.2 Arithmetic in GF(2^3)

		000	001	010	011	100	101	110	111
	+	0	1	2	3	4	5	6	7
000	0	0	1	2	3	4	5	6	7
001	1	1	0	3	2	5	4	7	6
010	2	2	3	0	1	6	7	4	5
011	3	3	2	1	0	7	6	5	4
100	4	4	5	6	7	0	1	2	3
101	5	5	4	7	6	1	0	3	2
110	6	6	7	4	5	2	3	0	1
111	7	7	6	5	4	3	2	1	0

(a) Addition

		000	001	010	011	100	101	110	111
	×	0	1	2	3	4	5	6	7
000	0	0	0	0	0	0	0	0	0
001	1	0	1	2	3	4	5	6	7
010	2	0	2	4	6	3	1	7	5
011	3	0	3	6	5	7	4	1	2
100	4	0	4	3	7	6	2	5	1
101	5	0	5	1	4	2	7	3	6
110	6	0	6	7	1	5	3	2	4
111	7	0	7	5	2	1	6	4	3

(b) Multiplication

w	$-w$	w^{-1}
0	0	–
1	1	1
2	2	5
3	3	6
4	4	7
5	5	2
6	6	3
7	7	4

(c) Additive and multiplicative inverses

where each a_i takes on a value in the set $\{0, 1, \ldots, p - 1\}$. There are a total of p^n different polynomials in S.

> For $p = 3$ and $n = 2$, the $3^2 = 9$ polynomials in the set are
>
> $$0, 1, 2, x, x + 1, x + 2, 2x, 2x + 1, 2x + 2$$
>
> For $p = 2$ and $n = 3$, the $2^3 = 8$ polynomials in the set are
>
> $$0, 1, x, x + 1, x^2, x^2 + 1, x^2 + x, x^2 + x + 1$$

With the appropriate definition of arithmetic operations, each such set S is a finite field. The definition consists of the following elements.

1. Arithmetic follows the ordinary rules of polynomial arithmetic using the basic rules of algebra, with the following two refinements.
2. Arithmetic on the coefficients is performed modulo p. That is, we use the rules of arithmetic for the finite field Z_p.
3. If multiplication results in a polynomial of degree greater than $n - 1$, then the polynomial is reduced modulo some irreducible polynomial $m(x)$ of degree n. That is, we divide by $m(x)$ and keep the remainder. For a polynomial $f(x)$, the remainder is expressed as $r(x) = f(x) \bmod m(x)$.

> The Advanced Encryption Standard (AES) uses arithmetic in the finite field GF(2^8), with the irreducible polynomial $m(x) = x^8 + x^4 + x^3 + x + 1$. Consider the two polynomials $f(x) = x^6 + x^4 + x^2 + x + 1$ and $g(x) = x^7 + x + 1$. Then
>
> $$\begin{aligned} f(x) + g(x) &= x^6 + x^4 + x^2 + x + 1 + x^7 + x + 1 \\ &= x^7 + x^6 + x^4 + x^2 \end{aligned}$$
>
> $$\begin{aligned} f(x) \times g(x) &= x^{13} + x^{11} + x^9 + x^8 + x^7 \\ &\quad + x^7 + x^5 + x^3 + x^2 + x \\ &\quad + x^6 + x^4 + x^2 + x + 1 \\ &= x^{13} + x^{11} + x^9 + x^8 + x^6 + x^5 + x^4 + x^3 + 1 \end{aligned}$$
>
> $$\begin{array}{r} x^5 + x^3 \qquad\qquad\qquad\qquad\qquad\qquad\qquad\qquad \\ x^8 + x^4 + x^3 + x + 1 \,\big)\, \overline{x^{13} + x^{11} + x^9 + x^8 \qquad + x^6 + x^5 + x^4 + x^3 + 1} \\ \underline{x^{13} \qquad + x^9 + x^8 \qquad + x^6 + x^5} \qquad\qquad\qquad \\ x^{11} \qquad\qquad\qquad\qquad\qquad + x^4 + x^3 \qquad \\ \underline{x^{11} \qquad\qquad + x^7 + x^6 \qquad + x^4 + x^3} \qquad \\ x^7 + x^6 \qquad\qquad\qquad + 1 \end{array}$$
>
> Therefore, $f(x) \times g(x) \bmod m(x) = x^7 + x^6 + 1$.

As with ordinary modular arithmetic, we have the notion of a set of residues in modular polynomial arithmetic. The set of residues modulo $m(x)$, an nth-degree polynomial, consists of p^n elements. Each of these elements is represented by one of the p^n polynomials of degree $m < n$.

The residue class $[x + 1]$, (mod $m(x)$), consists of all polynomials $a(x)$ such that $a(x) \equiv (x + 1)(\text{mod } m(x))$. Equivalently, the residue class $[x + 1]$ consists of all polynomials $a(x)$ that satisfy the equality $a(x) \text{ mod } m(x) = x + 1$.

It can be shown that the set of all polynomials modulo an irreducible nth-degree polynomial $m(x)$ satisfies the axioms in Figure 5.2, and thus forms a finite field. Furthermore, all finite fields of a given order are isomorphic; that is, any two finite-field structures of a given order have the same structure, but the representation or labels of the elements may be different.

To construct the finite field GF(2^3), we need to choose an irreducible polynomial of degree 3. There are only two such polynomials: $(x^3 + x^2 + 1)$ and $(x^3 + x + 1)$. Using the latter, Table 5.3 shows the addition and multiplication tables for GF(2^3). Note that this set of tables has the identical structure to those of Table 5.2. Thus, we have succeeded in finding a way to define a field of order 2^3.

We can now read additions and multiplications from the table easily. For example, consider binary $100 + 010 = 110$. This is equivalent to $x^2 + x$. Also consider $100 \times 010 = 011$, which is equivalent to $x^2 \times x = x^3$ and reduces to $x + 1$. That is, $x^3 \text{ mod } (x^3 + x + 1) = x + 1$, which is equivalent to 011.

Finding the Multiplicative Inverse

Just as the Euclidean algorithm can be adapted to find the greatest common divisor of two polynomials, the extended Euclidean algorithm can be adapted to find the multiplicative inverse of a polynomial. Specifically, the algorithm will find the multiplicative inverse of $b(x)$ modulo $a(x)$ if the degree of $b(x)$ is less than the degree of $a(x)$ and $\text{gcd}[a(x), b(x)] = 1$. If $a(x)$ is an irreducible polynomial, then it has no factor other than itself or 1, so that $\text{gcd}[a(x), b(x)] = 1$. The algorithm can be characterized in the same way as we did for the extended Euclidean algorithm for integers. Given polynomials $a(x)$ and $b(x)$ with the degree of $a(x)$ greater than the degree of $b(x)$, we wish to solve the following equation for the values $v(x)$, $w(x)$, and $d(x)$, where $d(x) = \text{gcd}[a(x), b(x)]$:

$$a(x)v(x) + b(x)w(x) = d(x)$$

If $d(x) = 1$, then $w(x)$ is the multiplicative inverse of $b(x)$ modulo $a(x)$. The calculations are as follows.

Table 5.3 Polynomial Arithmetic Modulo $(x^3 + x + 1)$

		000	001	010	011	100	101	110	111
	+	0	1	x	$x + 1$	x^2	$x^2 + 1$	$x^2 + x$	$x^2 + x + 1$
000	0	0	1	x	$x + 1$	x^2	$x^2 + 1$	$x^2 + x$	$x^2 + x + 1$
001	1	1	0	$x + 1$	x	$x^2 + 1$	x^2	$x^2 + x + 1$	$x^2 + x$
010	x	x	$x + 1$	0	1	$x^2 + x$	$x^2 + x + 1$	x^2	$x^2 + 1$
011	$x + 1$	$x + 1$	x	1	0	$x^2 + x + 1$	$x^2 + x$	$x^2 + 1$	x^2
100	x^2	x^2	$x^2 + 1$	$x^2 + x$	$x^2 + x + 1$	0	1	x	$x + 1$
101	$x^2 + 1$	$x^2 + 1$	x^2	$x^2 + x + 1$	$x^2 + x$	1	0	$x + 1$	x
110	$x^2 + x$	$x^2 + x$	$x^2 + x + 1$	x^2	$x^2 + 1$	x	$x + 1$	0	1
111	$x^2 + x + 1$	$x^2 + x + 1$	$x^2 + x$	$x^2 + 1$	x^2	$x + 1$	x	1	0

(a) Addition

		000	001	010	011	100	101	110	111
	×	0	1	x	$x + 1$	x^2	$x^2 + 1$	$x^2 + x$	$x^2 + x + 1$
000	0	0	0	0	0	0	0	0	0
001	1	0	1	x	$x + 1$	x^2	$x^2 + 1$	$x^2 + x$	$x^2 + x + 1$
010	x	0	x	x^2	$x^2 + x$	$x + 1$	1	$x^2 + x + 1$	$x^2 + 1$
011	$x + 1$	0	$x + 1$	$x^2 + x$	$x^2 + 1$	$x^2 + x + 1$	x^2	1	x
100	x^2	0	x^2	$x + 1$	$x^2 + x + 1$	$x^2 + x$	x	$x^2 + 1$	1
101	$x^2 + 1$	0	$x^2 + 1$	1	x^2	x	$x^2 + x + 1$	$x + 1$	$x^2 + x$
110	$x^2 + x$	0	$x^2 + x$	$x^2 + x + 1$	1	$x^2 + 1$	$x + 1$	x	x^2
111	$x^2 + x + 1$	0	$x^2 + x + 1$	$x^2 + 1$	x	1	$x^2 + 1$	x^2	$x + 1$

(b) Multiplication

Extended Euclidean Algorithm for Polynomials			
Calculate	**Which satisfies**	**Calculate**	**Which satisfies**
$r_{-1}(x) = a(x)$		$v_{-1}(x) = 1; w_{-1}(x) = 0$	$a(x) = a(x)v_{-1}(x) + bw_{-1}(x)$
$r_0(x) = b(x)$		$v_0(x) = 0; w_0(x) = 1$	$b(x) = a(x)v_0(x) + b(x)w_0(x)$
$r_1(x) = a(x) \bmod b(x)$ $q_1(x) =$ quotient of $a(x)/b(x)$	$a(x) = q_1(x)b(x) + r_1(x)$	$v_1(x) = v_{-1}(x) - q_1(x)v_0(x) = 1$ $w_1(x) = w_{-1}(x) - q_1(x)w_0(x) = -q_1(x)$	$r_1(x) = a(x)v_1(x) + b(x)w_1(x)$
$r_2(x) = b(x) \bmod r_1(x)$ $q_2(x) =$ quotient of $b(x)/r_1(x)$	$b(x) = q_2(x)r_1(x) + r_2(x)$	$v_2(x) = v_0(x) - q_2(x)v_1(x)$ $w_2(x) = w_0(x) - q_2(x)w_1(x)$	$r_2(x) = a(x)v_2(x) + b(x)w_2(x)$
$r_3(x) = r_1(x) \bmod r_2(x)$ $q_3(x) =$ quotient of $r_1(x)/r_2(x)$	$r_1(x) = q_3(x)r_2(x) + r_3(x)$	$v_3(x) = v_1(x) - q_3(x)v_2(x)$ $w_3(x) = w_1(x) - q_3(x)w_2(x)$	$r_3(x) = a(x)v_3(x) + b(x)w_3(x)$
⋮	⋮	⋮	⋮
$r_n(x) = r_{n-2}(x) \bmod r_{n-1}(x)$ $q_n(x) =$ quotient of $r_{n-2}(x)/r_{n-2}(x)$	$r_{n-2}(x) = q_n(x)r_{n-1}(x) + r_n(x)$	$v_n(x) = v_{n-2}(x) - q_n(x)v_{n-1}(x)$ $w_n(x) = w_{n-2}(x) - q_n(x)w_{n-1}(x)$	$r_n(x) = a(x)v_n(x) + b(x)w_n(x)$
$r_{n+1}(x) = r_{n-1}(x) \bmod r_n(x) = 0$ $q_{n+1}(x) =$ quotient of $r_{n-1}(x)/r_n(x)$	$r_{n-1}(x) = q_{n+1}(x)r_n(x) + 0$		$d(x) = \gcd(a(x), b(x)) = r_n(x)$ $v(x) = v_n(x); w(x) = w_n(x)$

Table 5.4 shows the calculation of the multiplicative inverse of $(x^7 + x + 1) \bmod (x^8 + x^4 + x^3 + x + 1)$. The result is that $(x^7 + x + 1)^{-1} = (x^7)$. That is, $(x^7 + x + 1)(x^7) \equiv 1(\bmod (x^8 + x^4 + x^3 + x + 1))$.

Computational Considerations

A polynomial $f(x)$ in GF(2^n)

$$f(x) = a_{n-1}x^{n-1} + a_{n-2}x^{n-2} + \cdots + a_1x + a_0 = \sum_{i=0}^{n-1} a_i x^i$$

can be uniquely represented by the sequence of its n binary coefficients $(a_{n-1}, a_{n-2}, \ldots, a_0)$. Thus, every polynomial in GF(2^n) can be represented by an n-bit number.

Table 5.4 Extended Euclid $[(x^8 + x^4 + x^3 + x + 1), (x^7 + x + 1)]$

Initialization	$a(x) = x^8 + x^4 + x^3 + x + 1; v_{-1}(x) = 1; w_{-1}(x) = 0$ $b(x) = x^7 + x + 1; v_0(x) = 0; w_0(x) = 1$
Iteration 1	$q_1(x) = x; r_1(x) = x^4 + x^3 + x^2 + 1$ $v_1(x) = 1; w_1(x) = x$
Iteration 2	$q_2(x) = x^3 + x^2 + 1; r_2(x) = x$ $v_2(x) = x^3 + x^2 + 1; w_2(x) = x^4 + x^3 + x + 1$
Iteration 3	$q_3(x) = x^3 + x^2 + x; r_3(x) = 1$ $v_3(x) = x^6 + x^2 + x + 1; w_3(x) = x^7$
Iteration 4	$q_4(x) = x; r_4(x) = 0$ $v_4(x) = x^7 + x + 1; w_4(x) = x^8 + x^4 + x^3 + x + 1$
Result	$d(x) = r_3(x) = \gcd(a(x), b(x)) = 1$ $w(x) = w_3(x) = (x^7 + x + 1)^{-1} \bmod (x^8 + x^4 + x^3 + x + 1) = x^7$

Tables 5.2 and 5.3 show the addition and multiplication tables for $GF(2^3)$ modulo $m(x) = (x^3 + x + 1)$. Table 5.2 uses the binary representation, and Table 5.3 uses the polynomial representation.

Addition We have seen that addition of polynomials is performed by adding corresponding coefficients, and, in the case of polynomials over Z_2, addition is just the XOR operation. So, addition of two polynomials in $GF(2^n)$ corresponds to a bitwise XOR operation.

Consider the two polynomials in $GF(2^8)$ from our earlier example:

$$f(x) = x^6 + x^4 + x^2 + x + 1 \text{ and } g(x) = x^7 + x + 1.$$

$(x^6 + x^4 + x^2 + x + 1) + (x^7 + x + 1)$	$= x^7 + x^6 + x^4 + x^2$	(polynomial notation)
$(01010111) \oplus (10000011)$	$= (11010100)$	(binary notation)
$\{57\} \oplus \{83\}$	$= \{D4\}$	(hexadecimal notation)[7]

Multiplication There is no simple XOR operation that will accomplish multiplication in $GF(2^n)$. However, a reasonably straightforward, easily implemented technique is available. We will discuss the technique with reference to $GF(2^8)$ using $m(x) = x^8 + x^4 + x^3 + x + 1$, which is the finite field used in AES. The technique readily generalizes to $GF(2^n)$.

The technique is based on the observation that

$$x^8 \bmod m(x) = [m(x) - x^8] = (x^4 + x^3 + x + 1) \quad \textbf{(5.4)}$$

[7]A basic refresher on number systems (decimal, binary, hexadecimal) can be found at the Computer Science Student Resource Site at WilliamStallings.com/StudentSupport.html. Here each of two groups of 4 bits in a byte is denoted by a single hexadecimal character, and the two characters are enclosed in brackets.

A moment's thought should convince you that Equation (5.4) is true; if you are not sure, divide it out. In general, in GF(2^n) with an nth-degree polynomial $p(x)$, we have $x^n \bmod p(x) = [p(x) - x^n]$.

Now, consider a polynomial in GF(2^8), which has the form $f(x) = b_7x^7 + b_6x^6 + b_5x^5 + b_4x^4 + b_3x^3 + b_2x^2 + b_1x + b_0$. If we multiply by x, we have

$$x \times f(x) = (b_7x^8 + b_6x^7 + b_5x^6 + b_4x^5 + b_3x^4 + b_2x^3 + b_1x^2 + b_0x) \bmod m(x) \quad \textbf{(5.5)}$$

If $b_7 = 0$, then the result is a polynomial of degree less than 8, which is already in reduced form, and no further computation is necessary. If $b_7 = 1$, then reduction modulo $m(x)$ is achieved using Equation (5.4):

$$x \times f(x) = (b_6x^7 + b_5x^6 + b_4x^5 + b_3x^4 + b_2x^3 + b_1x^2 + b_0x) + (x^4 + x^3 + x + 1)$$

It follows that multiplication by x (i.e., 00000010) can be implemented as a 1-bit left shift followed by a conditional bitwise XOR with (00011011), which represents $(x^4 + x^3 + x + 1)$. To summarize,

$$x \times f(x) = \begin{cases} (b_6b_5b_4b_3b_2b_1b_00) & \text{if } b_7 = 0 \\ (b_6b_5b_4b_3b_2b_1b_00) \oplus (00011011) & \text{if } b_7 = 1 \end{cases} \quad \textbf{(5.6)}$$

Multiplication by a higher power of x can be achieved by repeated application of Equation (5.6). By adding intermediate results, multiplication by any constant in GF(2^8) can be achieved.

In an earlier example, we showed that for $f(x) = x^6 + x^4 + x^2 + x + 1$, $g(x) = x^7 + x + 1$, and $m(x) = x^8 + x^4 + x^3 + x + 1$, we have $f(x) \times g(x) \bmod m(x) = x^7 + x^6 + 1$. Redoing this in binary arithmetic, we need to compute (01010111) × (10000011). First, we determine the results of multiplication by powers of x:

$$\begin{aligned}
(01010111) \times (00000010) &= (10101110) \\
(01010111) \times (00000100) &= (01011100) \oplus (00011011) = (01000111) \\
(01010111) \times (00001000) &= (10001110) \\
(01010111) \times (00010000) &= (00011100) \oplus (00011011) = (00000111) \\
(01010111) \times (00100000) &= (00001110) \\
(01010111) \times (01000000) &= (00011100) \\
(01010111) \times (10000000) &= (00111000)
\end{aligned}$$

So,

$$\begin{aligned}
(01010111) \times (10000011) &= (01010111) \times [(00000001) \oplus (00000010) \oplus (10000000)] \\
&= (01010111) \oplus (10101110) \oplus (00111000) = (11000001)
\end{aligned}$$

which is equivalent to $x^7 + x^6 + 1$.

Using a Generator

An equivalent technique for defining a finite field of the form GF(2^n), using the same irreducible polynomial, is sometimes more convenient. To begin, we need two definitions: A **generator** g of a finite field F of order q (contains q elements) is an element whose first $q - 1$ powers generate all the nonzero elements of F. That is, the elements of F consist of $0, g^0, g^1, \ldots, g^{q-2}$. Consider a field F defined by a polynomial $f(x)$. An element b contained in F is called a **root** of the polynomial if $f(b) = 0$. Finally, it can be shown that a root g of an irreducible polynomial is a generator of the finite field defined on that polynomial.

Let us consider the finite field GF(2^3), defined over the irreducible polynomial $x^3 + x + 1$, discussed previously. Thus, the generator g must satisfy $f(g) = g^3 + g + 1 = 0$. Keep in mind, as discussed previously, that we need not find a numerical solution to this equality. Rather, we deal with polynomial arithmetic in which arithmetic on the coefficients is performed modulo 2. Therefore, the solution to the preceding equality is $g^3 = -g - 1 = g + 1$. We now show that g in fact generates all of the polynomials of degree less than 3. We have the following.

$$g^4 = g(g^3) = g(g + 1) = g^2 + g$$
$$g^5 = g(g^4) = g(g^2 + g) = g^3 + g^2 = g^2 + g + 1$$
$$g^6 = g(g^5) = g(g^2 + g + 1) = g^3 + g^2 + g = g^2 + g + g + 1 = g^2 + 1$$
$$g^7 = g(g^6) = g(g^2 + 1) = g^3 + g = g + g + 1 = 1 = g^0$$

We see that the powers of g generate all the nonzero polynomials in GF(2^3). Also, it should be clear that $g^k = g^{k \bmod 7}$ for any integer k. Table 5.5 shows the power representation, as well as the polynomial and binary representations.

Table 5.5 Generator for $GF(2^3)$ using $x^3 + x + 1$

Power Representation	Polynomial Representation	Binary Representation	Decimal (Hex) Representation
0	0	000	0
$g^0(= g^7)$	1	001	1
g^1	g	010	2
g^2	g^2	100	4
g^3	$g + 1$	011	3
g^4	$g^2 + g$	110	6
g^5	$g^2 + g + 1$	111	7
g^6	$g^2 + 1$	101	5

This power representation makes multiplication easy. To multiply in the power notation, add exponents modulo 7. For example, $g^4 \times g^6 = g^{(10 \bmod 7)} = g^3 = g + 1$. The same result is achieved using polynomial arithmetic: We have $g^4 = g^2 + g$ and $g^6 = g^2 + 1$. Then, $(g^2 + g) \times (g^2 + 1) = g^4 + g^3 + g^2 + g$. Next, we need to determine $(g^4 + g^3 + g^2 + 1) \bmod (g^3 + g + 1)$ by division:

$$
\begin{array}{r l}
 & \quad g \;\; + 1 \\
\cline{2-2}
g^3 + g + 1 \big) & g^4 + g^3 + g^2 + g \\
 & \underline{g^4 + \; g^2 + g} \\
 & \quad g^3 \\
 & \quad \underline{g^3 + \; g + 1} \\
 & \qquad\qquad\quad g + 1
\end{array}
$$

We get a result of $g + 1$, which agrees with the result obtained using the power representation.

Table 5.6 shows the addition and multiplication tables for GF(2^3) using the power representation. Note that this yields the identical results to the polynomial representation (Table 5.3) with some of the rows and columns interchanged.

In general, for GF(2^n) with irreducible polynomial $f(x)$, determine $g^n = f(g) - g^n$. Then calculate all of the powers of g from g^{n+1} through g^{2^n-2}. The elements of the field correspond to the powers of g from g^0 through g^{2^n-2} plus the value 0. For multiplication of two elements in the field, use the equality $g^k = g^{k \bmod (2^n-1)}$ for any integer k.

Summary

In this section, we have shown how to construct a finite field of order 2^n. Specifically, we defined GF(2^n) with the following properties.

1. GF(2^n) consists of 2^n elements.
2. The binary operations + and $\times$ are defined over the set. The operations of addition, subtraction, multiplication, and division can be performed without leaving the set. Each element of the set other than 0 has a multiplicative inverse.

We have shown that the elements of GF(2^n) can be defined as the set of all polynomials of degree $n - 1$ or less with binary coefficients. Each such polynomial can be represented by a unique n-bit value. Arithmetic is defined as polynomial arithmetic modulo some irreducible polynomial of degree n. We have also seen that an equivalent definition of a finite field GF(2^n) makes use of a generator and that arithmetic is defined using powers of the generator.

Table 5.6 GF(2^3) Arithmetic Using Generator for the Polynomial ($x^3 + x + 1$)

		000	001	010	100	011	110	111	101
	+	0	1	G	g^2	g^3	g^4	g^5	g^6
000	0	0	1	G	g^2	$g + 1$	$g^2 + g$	$g^2 + g + 1$	$g^2 + 1$
001	1	1	0	$g + 1$	$g^2 + 1$	g	$g^2 + g + 1$	$g^2 + g$	g^2
010	g	g	$g + 1$	0	$g^2 + g$	1	g^2	$g^2 + 1$	$g^2 + g + 1$
100	g^2	g^2	$g^2 + 1$	$g^2 + g$	0	$g^2 + g + 1$	g	$g + 1$	1
011	g^3	$g + 1$	g	1	$g^2 + g + 1$	0	$g^2 + 1$	g^2	$g^2 + g$
110	g^4	$g^2 + g$	$g^2 + g + 1$	g^2	g	$g^2 + 1$	0	1	$g + 1$
111	g^5	$g^2 + g + 1$	$g^2 + g$	$g^2 + 1$	$g + 1$	g^2	1	0	g
101	g^6	$g^2 + 1$	g^2	$g^2 + g + 1$	1	$g^2 + g$	$g + 1$	g	0

(a) Addition

		000	001	010	100	011	110	111	101
	×	0	1	G	g^2	g^3	g^4	g^5	g^6
000	0	0	0	0	0	0	0	0	0
001	1	0	1	G	g^2	$g + 1$	$g^2 + g$	$g^2 + g + 1$	$g^2 + 1$
010	g	0	g	g^2	$g + 1$	$g^2 + g$	$g^2 + g + 1$	$g^2 + 1$	1
100	g^2	0	g^2	$g + 1$	$g^2 + g$	$g^2 + g + 1$	$g^2 + 1$	1	g
011	g^3	0	$g + 1$	$g^2 + g$	$g^2 + g + 1$	$g^2 + 1$	1	g	g^2
110	g^4	0	$g^2 + g$	$g^2 + g + 1$	$g^2 + 1$	1	g	g^2	$g + 1$
111	g^5	0	$g^2 + g + 1$	$g^2 + 1$	1	g	g^2	$g + 1$	$g^2 + g$
101	g^6	0	$g^2 + 1$	1	g	g^2	$g + 1$	$g^2 + g$	$g^2 + g + 1$

(b) Multiplication

5.7 KEY TERMS, REVIEW QUESTIONS, AND PROBLEMS

Key Terms

abelian group	greatest common divisor	order
associative	group	polynomial
coefficient set	identity element	polynomial arithmetic
commutative	infinite field	polynomial ring
commutative ring	infinite group	prime number
cyclic group	integral domain	prime polynomial
divisor	inverse element	relatively prime
Euclidean algorithm	irreducible polynomial	residue
field	modular arithmetic	ring
finite field	modular polynomial arithmetic	
finite group	monic polynomial	
generator		

Review Questions

5.1 When is a group said to be abelian?
5.2 Briefly define a ring.
5.3 Briefly define a field.
5.4 List three classes of polynomial arithmetic.

Problems

5.1 For the group S_n of all permutations of n distinct symbols,
  a. what is the number of elements in S_n?
  b. show that S_n is not abelian for $n > 2$.

5.2 Does the set of residue classes (mod3) form a group
  a. with respect to modular addition?
  b. with respect to modular multiplication?

5.3 Let $S = \{a, b\}$. The addition and multiplication on the set S is defined in the following tables:

+	a	b
a	a	b
b	b	a

×	a	b
a	a	a
b	a	b

Is S a ring? Justify your answer.

5.4 Develop a set of tables similar to Table 5.1 for GF(5).

5.5 Demonstrate that the set of polynomials whose coefficients form a field is a ring.

5.6 Demonstrate whether each of these statements is true or false for polynomials over a field.

a. The product of monic polynomials is monic.
b. The product of polynomials of degrees m and n has degree $m + n$.
c. The sum of polynomials of degrees m and n has degree max $[m, n]$.

5.7 For polynomial arithmetic with coefficients in Z_{10}, perform the following calculations.
a. $(7x + 2) - (x^2 + 5)$
b. $(6x^2 + x + 3)(5x^2 + 2)$

5.8 Determine which of the following polynomials are reducible over GF(2).
a. $x^3 + 1$
b. $x^3 + x^2 + 1$
c. $x^4 + x + 1$

5.9 Determine the gcd of the following pairs of polynomials.
a. $x^3 + x + 1$ and $x^2 + x + 1$ over GF(2)
b. $(x^3 + x + 1)$ and $(x^2 + 1)$ over GF(3)
c. $x^5 + x^4 + x^3 + x^2 + x + 1$ and $x^3 + x^2 + x + 1$ over GF(5)
d. $(x^4 + 8x^3 + 7x + 8)$ and $(2x^3 + 9x^2 + 10x + 1)$ over GF(11)

5.10 Develop a set of tables similar to Table 5.3 for GF(3) with $m(x) = x^2 + x + 1$.

5.11 Determine the multiplicative inverse of $x^2 + 1$ in $GF(2^3)$ with $m(x) = x^3 + x - 1$.

5.12 Develop a table similar to Table 5.5 for $GF(2^4)$ with $m(x) = x^4 + x + 1$.

Programming Problems

5.13 Write a simple four-function calculator in $GF(2^4)$. You may use table lookups for the multiplicative inverses.

5.14 Write a simple four-function calculator in $GF(2^8)$. You should compute the multiplicative inverses on the fly.

CHAPTER 6

ADVANCED ENCRYPTION STANDARD

LEARNING OBJECTIVES

After studying this chapter, you should be able to:

- Present an overview of the general structure of Advanced Encryption Standard (AES).
- Understand the four transformations used in AES.
- Explain the AES key expansion algorithm.
- Understand the use of polynomials with coefficients in $GF(2^8)$.

The Advanced Encryption Standard (AES) was published by the National Institute of Standards and Technology (NIST) in 2001. AES is a symmetric block cipher that is intended to replace DES as the approved standard for a wide range of applications. Compared to public-key ciphers such as RSA, the structure of AES and most symmetric ciphers is quite complex and cannot be explained as easily as many other cryptographic algorithms. Accordingly, the reader may wish to begin with a simplified version of AES, which is described in Appendix I. This version allows the reader to perform encryption and decryption by hand and gain a good understanding of the working of the algorithm details. Classroom experience indicates that a study of this simplified version enhances understanding of AES.[1] One possible approach is to read the chapter first, then carefully read Appendix I, and then re-read the main body of the chapter.

Appendix H looks at the evaluation criteria used by NIST to select from among the candidates for AES, plus the rationale for picking Rijndael, which was the winning candidate. This material is useful in understanding not just the AES design but also the criteria by which to judge any symmetric encryption algorithm.

6.1 FINITE FIELD ARITHMETIC

In AES, all operations are performed on 8-bit bytes. In particular, the arithmetic operations of addition, multiplication, and division are performed over the finite field $GF(2^8)$. Section 5.6 discusses such operations in some detail. For the reader who has not studied Chapter 5, and as a quick review for those who have, this section summarizes the important concepts.

In essence, a field is a set in which we can do addition, subtraction, multiplication, and division without leaving the set. Division is defined with the following rule: $a/b = a(b^{-1})$. An example of a finite field (one with a finite number of elements) is the set Z_p consisting of all the integers $\{0, 1, \ldots, p - 1\}$, where p is a prime number and in which arithmetic is carried out modulo p.

[1]However, you may safely skip Appendix I, at least on a first reading. If you get lost or bogged down in the details of AES, then you can go back and start with simplified AES.

Virtually all encryption algorithms, both conventional and public-key, involve arithmetic operations on integers. If one of the operations used in the algorithm is division, then we need to work in arithmetic defined over a field; this is because division requires that each nonzero element have a multiplicative inverse. For convenience and for implementation efficiency, we would also like to work with integers that fit exactly into a given number of bits, with no wasted bit patterns. That is, we wish to work with integers in the range 0 through $2^n - 1$, which fit into an n-bit word. Unfortunately, the set of such integers, Z_{2^n}, using modular arithmetic, is not a field. For example, the integer 2 has no multiplicative inverse in Z_{2^n}, that is, there is no integer b, such that $2b \bmod 2^n = 1$.

There is a way of defining a finite field containing 2^n elements; such a field is referred to as GF(2^n). Consider the set, S, of all polynomials of degree $n - 1$ or less with binary coefficients. Thus, each polynomial has the form

$$f(x) = a_{n-1}x^{n-1} + a_{n-2}x^{n-2} + \cdots + a_1x + a_0 = \sum_{i=0}^{n-1} a_i x^i$$

where each a_i takes on the value 0 or 1. There are a total of 2^n different polynomials in S. For $n = 3$, the $2^3 = 8$ polynomials in the set are

$$\begin{array}{llll} 0 & x & x^2 & x^2 + x \\ 1 & x + 1 & x^2 + 1 & x^2 + x + 1 \end{array}$$

With the appropriate definition of arithmetic operations, each such set S is a finite field. The definition consists of the following elements.

1. Arithmetic follows the ordinary rules of polynomial arithmetic using the basic rules of algebra with the following two refinements.
2. Arithmetic on the coefficients is performed modulo 2. This is the same as the XOR operation.
3. If multiplication results in a polynomial of degree greater than $n - 1$, then the polynomial is reduced modulo some irreducible polynomial $m(x)$ of degree n. That is, we divide by $m(x)$ and keep the remainder. For a polynomial $f(x)$, the remainder is expressed as $r(x) = f(x) \bmod m(x)$. A polynomial $m(x)$ is called **irreducible** if and only if $m(x)$ cannot be expressed as a product of two polynomials, both of degree lower than that of $m(x)$.

For example, to construct the finite field GF(2^3), we need to choose an irreducible polynomial of degree 3. There are only two such polynomials: $(x^3 + x^2 + 1)$ and $(x^3 + x + 1)$. Addition is equivalent to taking the XOR of like terms. Thus, $(x + 1) + x = 1$.

A polynomial in GF(2^n) can be uniquely represented by its n binary coefficients $(a_{n-1}a_{n-2} \ldots a_0)$. Therefore, every polynomial in GF(2^n) can be represented by an n-bit number. Addition is performed by taking the bitwise XOR of the two n-bit elements. There is no simple XOR operation that will accomplish multiplication in GF(2^n). However, a reasonably straightforward, easily implemented, technique is available. In essence, it can be shown that multiplication of a number in GF(2^n) by

2 consists of a left shift followed by a conditional XOR with a constant. Multiplication by larger numbers can be achieved by repeated application of this rule.

For example, AES uses arithmetic in the finite field $GF(2^8)$ with the irreducible polynomial $m(x) = x^8 + x^4 + x^3 + x + 1$. Consider two elements $A = (a_7a_6 \dots a_1a_0)$ and $B = (b_7b_6 \dots b_1b_0)$. The sum $A + B = (c_7c_6 \dots c_1c_0)$, where $c_i = a_i \oplus b_i$. The multiplication $\{02\} \cdot A$ equals $(a_6 \dots a_1a_00)$ if $a_7 = 0$ and equals $(a_6 \dots a_1a_00) \oplus (00011011)$ if $a_7 = 1$.[2]

To summarize, AES operates on 8-bit bytes. Addition of two bytes is defined as the bitwise XOR operation. Multiplication of two bytes is defined as multiplication in the finite field $GF(2^8)$, with the irreducible polynomial[3] $m(x) = x^8 + x^4 + x^3 + x + 1$. The developers of Rijndael give as their motivation for selecting this one of the 30 possible irreducible polynomials of degree 8 that it is the first one on the list given in [LIDL94].

6.2 AES STRUCTURE

General Structure

Figure 6.1 shows the overall structure of the AES encryption process. The cipher takes a plaintext block size of 128 bits, or 16 bytes. The key length can be 16, 24, or 32 bytes (128, 192, or 256 bits). The algorithm is referred to as AES-128, AES-192, or AES-256, depending on the key length.

The input to the encryption and decryption algorithms is a single 128-bit block. In FIPS PUB 197, this block is depicted as a 4×4 square matrix of bytes. This block is copied into the **State** array, which is modified at each stage of encryption or decryption. After the final stage, **State** is copied to an output matrix. These operations are depicted in Figure 6.2a. Similarly, the key is depicted as a square matrix of bytes. This key is then expanded into an array of key schedule words. Figure 6.2b shows the expansion for the 128-bit key. Each word is four bytes, and the total key schedule is 44 words for the 128-bit key. Note that the ordering of bytes within a matrix is by column. So, for example, the first four bytes of a 128-bit plaintext input to the encryption cipher occupy the first column of the **in** matrix, the second four bytes occupy the second column, and so on. Similarly, the first four bytes of the expanded key, which form a word, occupy the first column of the **w** matrix.

The cipher consists of N rounds, where the number of rounds depends on the key length: 10 rounds for a 16-byte key, 12 rounds for a 24-byte key, and 14 rounds for a 32-byte key (Table 6.1). The first $N - 1$ rounds consist of four distinct transformation functions: SubBytes, ShiftRows, MixColumns, and AddRoundKey, which are described subsequently. The final round contains only three transformations, and there is a initial single transformation (AddRoundKey) before the first round, which can be considered Round 0. Each transformation takes one or more

[2]In FIPS PUB 197, a hexadecimal number is indicated by enclosing it in curly brackets. We use that convention in this chapter.

[3]In the remainder of this discussion, references to $GF(2^8)$ refer to the finite field defined with this polynomial.

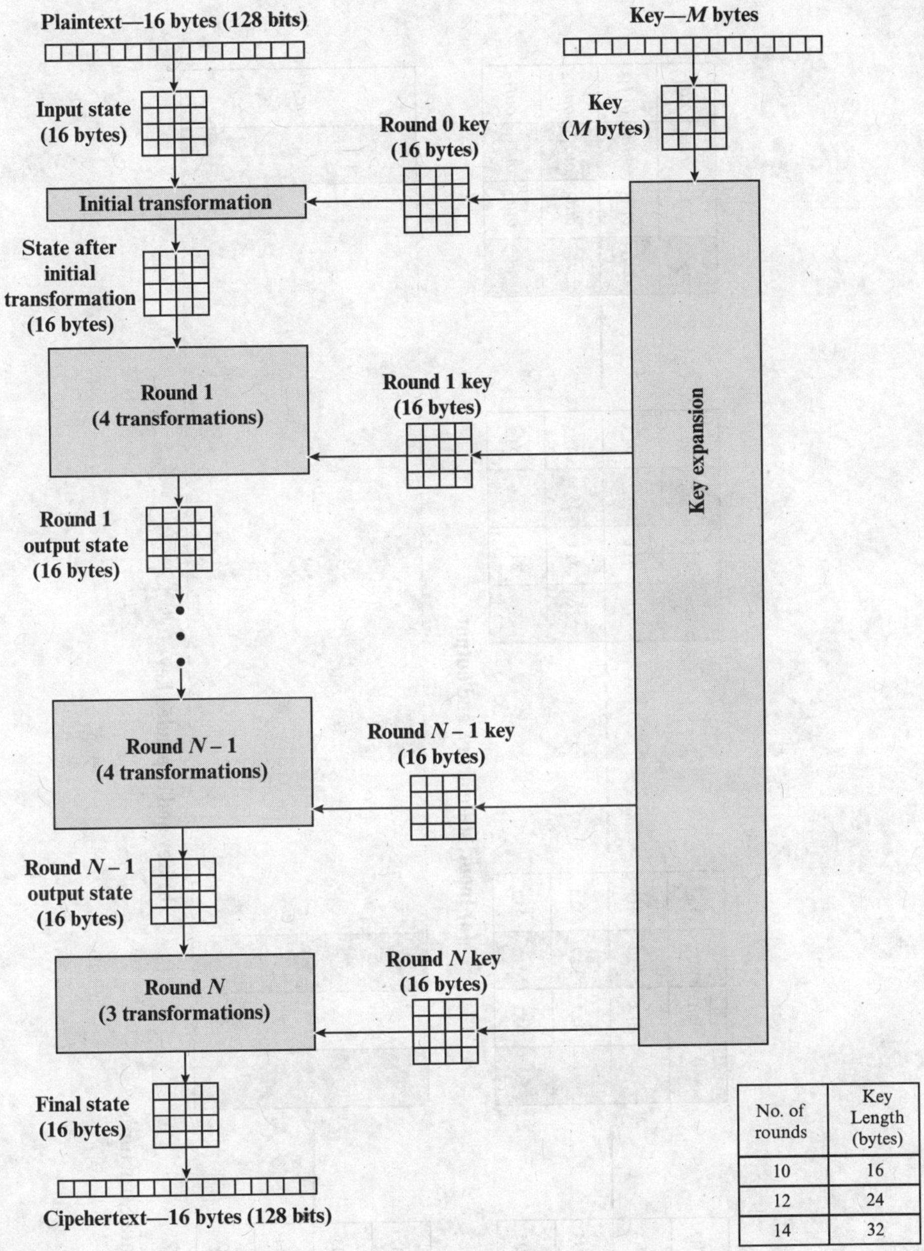

Figure 6.1 AES Encryption Process

4×4 matrices as input and produces a 4×4 matrix as output. Figure 6.1 shows that the output of each round is a 4×4 matrix, with the output of the final round being the ciphertext. Also, the key expansion function generates $N + 1$ round keys, each of which is a distinct 4×4 matrix. Each round key serves as one of the inputs to the AddRoundKey transformation in each round.

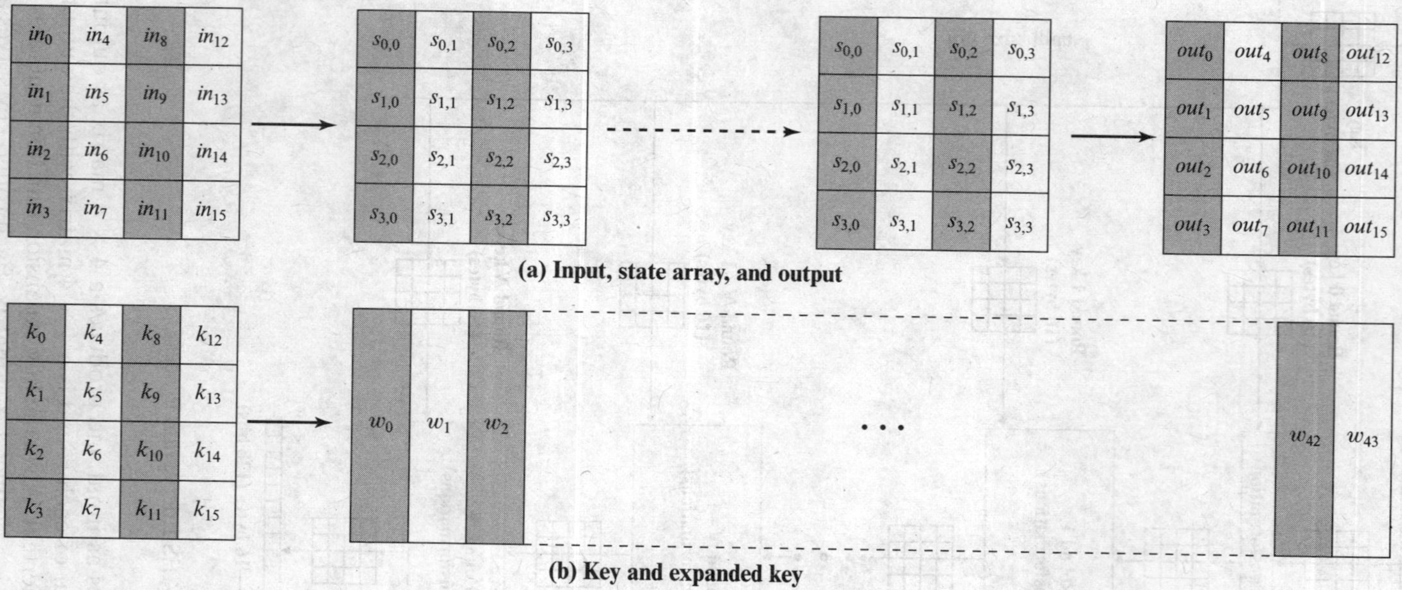

Figure 6.2 AES Data Structures

Table 6.1 AES Parameters

Key Size (words/bytes/bits)	4/16/128	6/24/192	8/32/256
Plaintext Block Size (words/bytes/bits)	4/16/128	4/16/128	4/16/128
Number of Rounds	10	12	14
Round Key Size (words/bytes/bits)	4/16/128	4/16/128	4/16/128
Expanded Key Size (words/bytes)	44/176	52/208	60/240

Detailed Structure

Figure 6.3 shows the AES cipher in more detail, indicating the sequence of transformations in each round and showing the corresponding decryption function. As was done in Chapter 4, we show encryption proceeding down the page and decryption proceeding up the page.

Before delving into details, we can make several comments about the overall AES structure.

1. One noteworthy feature of this structure is that it is not a Feistel structure. Recall that, in the classic Feistel structure, half of the data block is used to modify the other half of the data block and then the halves are swapped. AES instead processes the entire data block as a single matrix during each round using substitutions and permutation.
2. The key that is provided as input is expanded into an array of forty-four 32-bit words, $\mathbf{w}[i]$. Four distinct words (128 bits) serve as a round key for each round; these are indicated in Figure 6.3.
3. Four different stages are used, one of permutation and three of substitution:
   - **Substitute bytes:** Uses an S-box to perform a byte-by-byte substitution of the block.
   - **ShiftRows:** A simple permutation.
   - **MixColumns:** A substitution that makes use of arithmetic over GF(2^8).
   - **AddRoundKey:** A simple bitwise XOR of the current block with a portion of the expanded key.
4. The structure is quite simple. For both encryption and decryption, the cipher begins with an AddRoundKey stage, followed by nine rounds that each includes all four stages, followed by a tenth round of three stages. Figure 6.4 depicts the structure of a full encryption round.
5. Only the AddRoundKey stage makes use of the key. For this reason, the cipher begins and ends with an AddRoundKey stage. Any other stage, applied at the beginning or end, is reversible without knowledge of the key and so would add no security.
6. The AddRoundKey stage is, in effect, a form of Vernam cipher and by itself would not be formidable. The other three stages together provide confusion, diffusion, and nonlinearity, but by themselves would provide no security because they do not use the key. We can view the cipher as alternating operations of XOR encryption (AddRoundKey) of a block, followed by scrambling of the

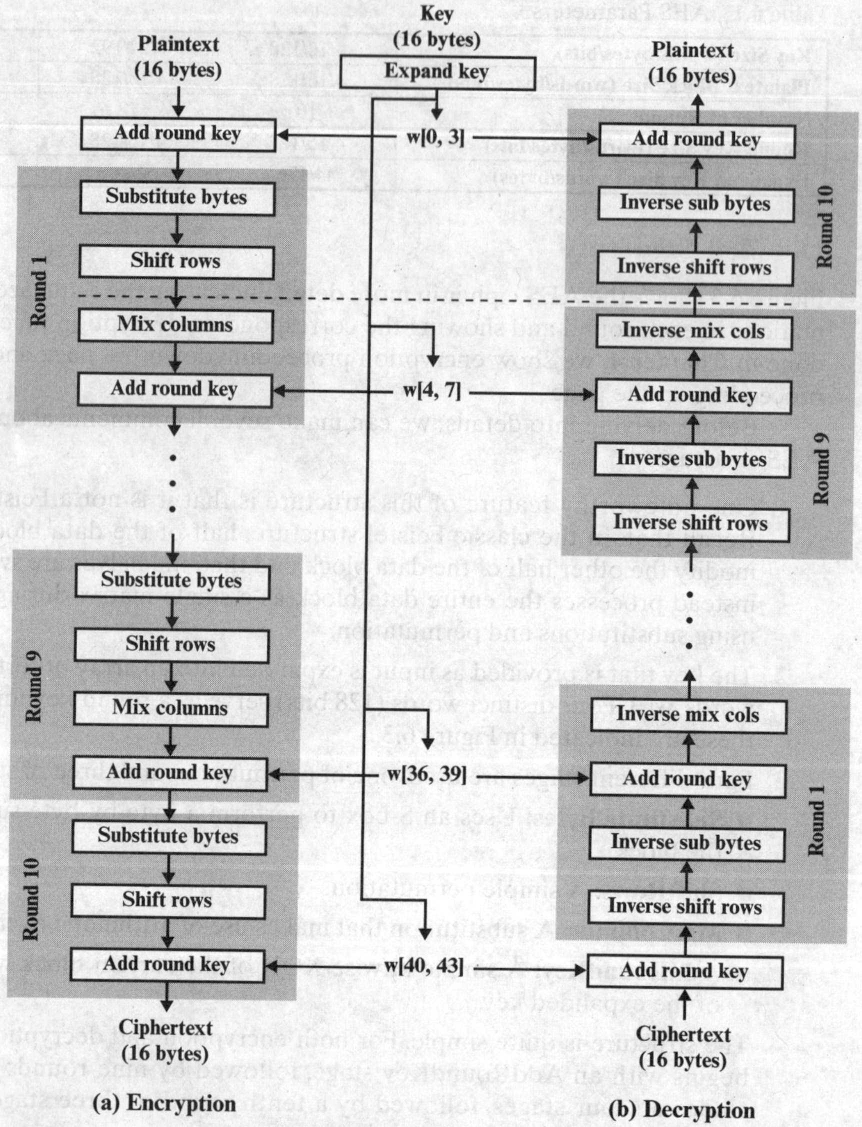

Figure 6.3 AES Encryption and Decryption

block (the other three stages), followed by XOR encryption, and so on. This scheme is both efficient and highly secure.

7. Each stage is easily reversible. For the Substitute Byte, ShiftRows, and MixColumns stages, an inverse function is used in the decryption algorithm. For the AddRoundKey stage, the inverse is achieved by XORing the same round key to the block, using the result that $A \oplus B \oplus B = A$.
8. As with most block ciphers, the decryption algorithm makes use of the expanded key in reverse order. However, the decryption algorithm is not

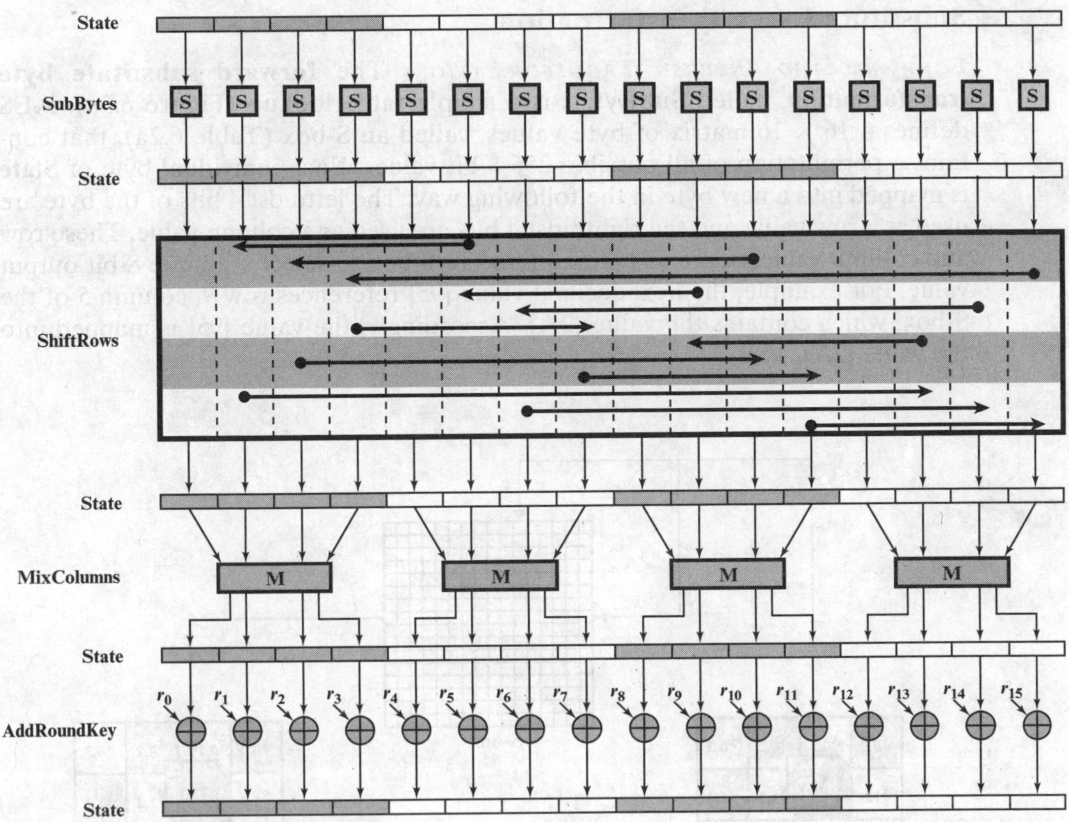

Figure 6.4 AES Encryption Round

identical to the encryption algorithm. This is a consequence of the particular structure of AES.

9. Once it is established that all four stages are reversible, it is easy to verify that decryption does recover the plaintext. Figure 6.3 lays out encryption and decryption going in opposite vertical directions. At each horizontal point (e.g., the dashed line in the figure), **State** is the same for both encryption and decryption.
10. The final round of both encryption and decryption consists of only three stages. Again, this is a consequence of the particular structure of AES and is required to make the cipher reversible.

6.3 AES TRANSFORMATION FUNCTIONS

We now turn to a discussion of each of the four transformations used in AES. For each stage, we describe the forward (encryption) algorithm, the inverse (decryption) algorithm, and the rationale for the stage.

Substitute Bytes Transformation

Forward and Inverse Transformations The **forward substitute byte transformation**, called SubBytes, is a simple table lookup (Figure 6.5a). AES defines a 16 × 16 matrix of byte values, called an S-box (Table 6.2a), that contains a permutation of all possible 256 8-bit values. Each individual byte of **State** is mapped into a new byte in the following way: The leftmost 4 bits of the byte are used as a row value and the rightmost 4 bits are used as a column value. These row and column values serve as indexes into the S-box to select a unique 8-bit output value. For example, the hexadecimal value {95} references row 9, column 5 of the S-box, which contains the value {2A}. Accordingly, the value {95} is mapped into the value {2A}.

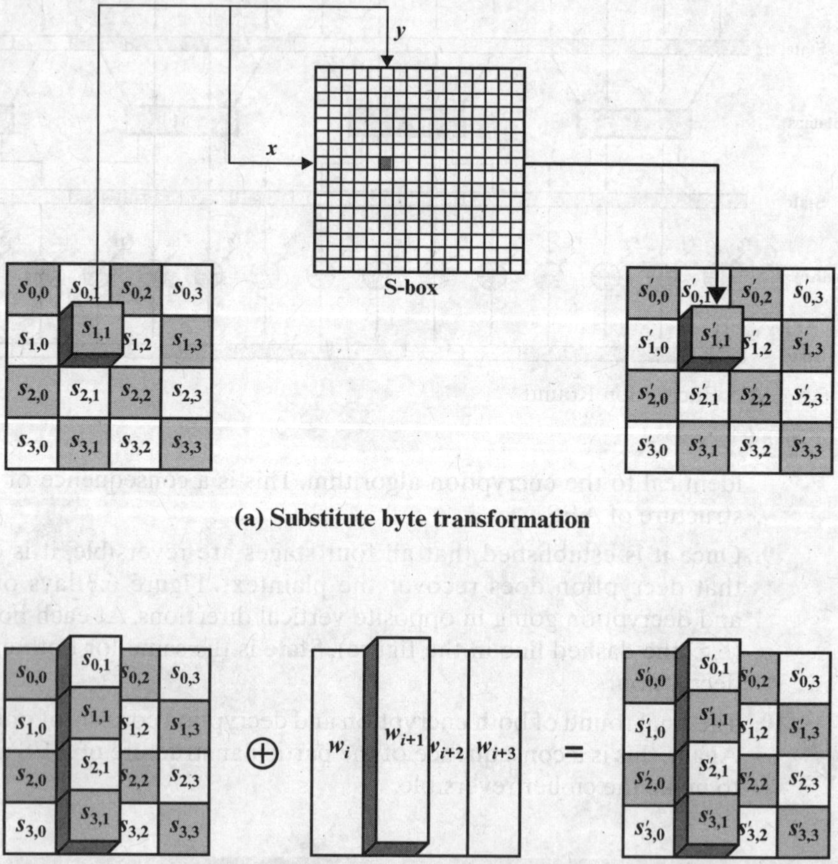

(a) Substitute byte transformation

(b) Add round key transformation

Figure 6.5 AES Byte-Level Operations

Table 6.2 AES S-Boxes

x \ *y*	0	1	2	3	4	5	6	7	8	9	A	B	C	D	E	F
0	63	7C	77	7B	F2	6B	6F	C5	30	01	67	2B	FE	D7	AB	76
1	CA	82	C9	7D	FA	59	47	F0	AD	D4	A2	AF	9C	A4	72	C0
2	B7	FD	93	26	36	3F	F7	CC	34	A5	E5	F1	71	D8	31	15
3	04	C7	23	C3	18	96	05	9A	07	12	80	E2	EB	27	B2	75
4	09	83	2C	1A	1B	6E	5A	A0	52	3B	D6	B3	29	E3	2F	84
5	53	D1	00	ED	20	FC	B1	5B	6A	CB	BE	39	4A	4C	58	CF
6	D0	EF	AA	FB	43	4D	33	85	45	F9	02	7F	50	3C	9F	A8
7	51	A3	40	8F	92	9D	38	F5	BC	B6	DA	21	10	FF	F3	D2
8	CD	0C	13	EC	5F	97	44	17	C4	A7	7E	3D	64	5D	19	73
9	60	81	4F	DC	22	2A	90	88	46	EE	B8	14	DE	5E	0B	DB
A	E0	32	3A	0A	49	06	24	5C	C2	D3	AC	62	91	95	E4	79
B	E7	C8	37	6D	8D	D5	4E	A9	6C	56	F4	EA	65	7A	AE	08
C	BA	78	25	2E	1C	A6	B4	C6	E8	DD	74	1F	4B	BD	8B	8A
D	70	3E	B5	66	48	03	F6	0E	61	35	57	B9	86	C1	1D	9E
E	E1	F8	98	11	69	D9	8E	94	9B	1E	87	E9	CE	55	28	DF
F	8C	A1	89	0D	BF	E6	42	68	41	99	2D	0F	B0	54	BB	16

(a) S-box

x \ *y*	0	1	2	3	4	5	6	7	8	9	A	B	C	D	E	F
0	52	09	6A	D5	30	36	A5	38	BF	40	A3	9E	81	F3	D7	FB
1	7C	E3	39	82	9B	2F	FF	87	34	8E	43	44	C4	DE	E9	CB
2	54	7B	94	32	A6	C2	23	3D	EE	4C	95	0B	42	FA	C3	4E
3	08	2E	A1	66	28	D9	24	B2	76	5B	A2	49	6D	8B	D1	25
4	72	F8	F6	64	86	68	98	16	D4	A4	5C	CC	5D	65	B6	92
5	6C	70	48	50	FD	ED	B9	DA	5E	15	46	57	A7	8D	9D	84
6	90	D8	AB	00	8C	BC	D3	0A	F7	E4	58	05	B8	B3	45	06
7	D0	2C	1E	8F	CA	3F	0F	02	C1	AF	BD	03	01	13	8A	6B
8	3A	91	11	41	4F	67	DC	EA	97	F2	CF	CE	F0	B4	E6	73
9	96	AC	74	22	E7	AD	35	85	E2	F9	37	E8	1C	75	DF	6E
A	47	F1	1A	71	1D	29	C5	89	6F	B7	62	0E	AA	18	BE	1B
B	FC	56	3E	4B	C6	D2	79	20	9A	DB	C0	FE	78	CD	5A	F4
C	1F	DD	A8	33	88	07	C7	31	B1	12	10	59	27	80	EC	5F
D	60	51	7F	A9	19	B5	4A	0D	2D	E5	7A	9F	93	C9	9C	EF
E	A0	E0	3B	4D	AE	2A	F5	B0	C8	EB	BB	3C	83	53	99	61
F	17	2B	04	7E	BA	77	D6	26	E1	69	14	63	55	21	0C	7D

(b) Inverse S-box

Here is an example of the SubBytes transformation:

EA	04	65	85
83	45	5D	96
5C	33	98	B0
F0	2D	AD	C5

→

87	F2	4D	97
EC	6E	4C	90
4A	C3	46	E7
8C	D8	95	A6

The S-box is constructed in the following fashion (Figure 6.6a).

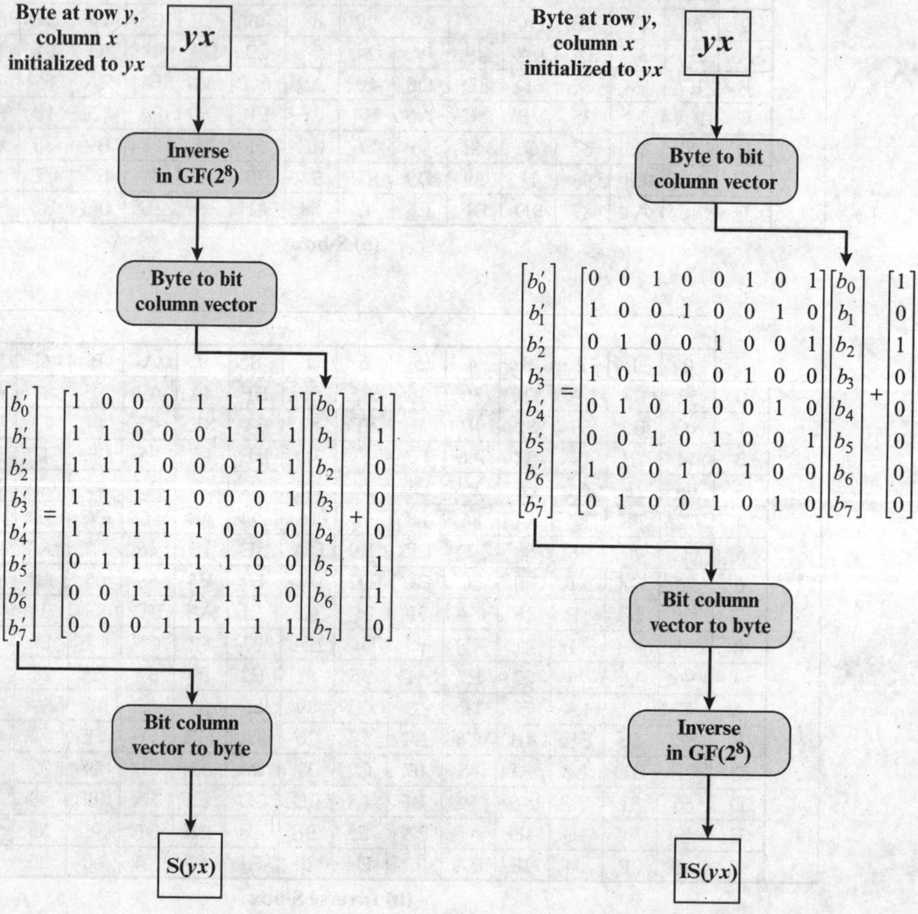

(a) Calculation of byte at row y, column x of S-box

(a) Calculation of byte at row y, column x of IS-box

Figure 6.6 Constuction of S-Box and IS-Box

1. Initialize the S-box with the byte values in ascending sequence row by row. The first row contains {00}, {01}, {02}, . . . , {0F}; the second row contains {10}, {11}, etc.; and so on. Thus, the value of the byte at row *y*, column *x* is {*yx*}.
2. Map each byte in the S-box to its multiplicative inverse in the finite field GF(2^8); the value {00} is mapped to itself.
3. Consider that each byte in the S-box consists of 8 bits labeled ($b_7, b_6, b_5, b_4, b_3, b_2, b_1, b_0$). Apply the following transformation to each bit of each byte in the S-box:

$$b_i' = b_i \oplus b_{(i+4) \bmod 8} \oplus b_{(i+5) \bmod 8} \oplus b_{(i+6) \bmod 8} \oplus b_{(i+7) \bmod 8} \oplus c_i \quad \textbf{(6.1)}$$

where c_i is the ith bit of byte c with the value {63}; that is, $(c_7c_6c_5c_4c_3c_2c_1c_0) = (01100011)$. The prime (′) indicates that the variable is to be updated by the value on the right. The AES standard depicts this transformation in matrix form as follows.

$$\begin{bmatrix} b_0' \\ b_1' \\ b_2' \\ b_3' \\ b_4' \\ b_5' \\ b_6' \\ b_7' \end{bmatrix} = \begin{bmatrix} 1 & 0 & 0 & 0 & 1 & 1 & 1 & 1 \\ 1 & 1 & 0 & 0 & 0 & 1 & 1 & 1 \\ 1 & 1 & 1 & 0 & 0 & 0 & 1 & 1 \\ 1 & 1 & 1 & 1 & 0 & 0 & 0 & 1 \\ 1 & 1 & 1 & 1 & 1 & 0 & 0 & 0 \\ 0 & 1 & 1 & 1 & 1 & 1 & 0 & 0 \\ 0 & 0 & 1 & 1 & 1 & 1 & 1 & 0 \\ 0 & 0 & 0 & 1 & 1 & 1 & 1 & 1 \end{bmatrix} \begin{bmatrix} b_0 \\ b_1 \\ b_2 \\ b_3 \\ b_4 \\ b_5 \\ b_6 \\ b_7 \end{bmatrix} + \begin{bmatrix} 1 \\ 1 \\ 0 \\ 0 \\ 0 \\ 1 \\ 1 \\ 0 \end{bmatrix} \quad \textbf{(6.2)}$$

Equation (6.2) has to be interpreted carefully. In ordinary matrix multiplication,[4] each element in the product matrix is the sum of products of the elements of one row and one column. In this case, each element in the product matrix is the bitwise XOR of products of elements of one row and one column. Furthermore, the final addition shown in Equation (6.2) is a bitwise XOR. Recall from Section 5.6 that the bitwise XOR is addition in GF(2^8).

As an example, consider the input value {95}. The multiplicative inverse in GF(2^8) is $\{95\}^{-1} = \{8A\}$, which is 10001010 in binary. Using Equation (6.2),

$$\begin{bmatrix} 1 & 0 & 0 & 0 & 1 & 1 & 1 & 1 \\ 1 & 1 & 0 & 0 & 0 & 1 & 1 & 1 \\ 1 & 1 & 1 & 0 & 0 & 0 & 1 & 1 \\ 1 & 1 & 1 & 1 & 0 & 0 & 0 & 1 \\ 1 & 1 & 1 & 1 & 1 & 0 & 0 & 0 \\ 0 & 1 & 1 & 1 & 1 & 1 & 0 & 0 \\ 0 & 0 & 1 & 1 & 1 & 1 & 1 & 0 \\ 0 & 0 & 0 & 1 & 1 & 1 & 1 & 1 \end{bmatrix} \begin{bmatrix} 0 \\ 1 \\ 0 \\ 1 \\ 0 \\ 0 \\ 0 \\ 1 \end{bmatrix} \oplus \begin{bmatrix} 1 \\ 1 \\ 0 \\ 0 \\ 0 \\ 1 \\ 1 \\ 0 \end{bmatrix} = \begin{bmatrix} 1 \\ 0 \\ 0 \\ 1 \\ 0 \\ 0 \\ 1 \\ 0 \end{bmatrix} \oplus \begin{bmatrix} 1 \\ 1 \\ 0 \\ 0 \\ 0 \\ 1 \\ 1 \\ 0 \end{bmatrix} = \begin{bmatrix} 0 \\ 1 \\ 0 \\ 1 \\ 0 \\ 1 \\ 0 \\ 0 \end{bmatrix}$$

[4]For a brief review of the rules of matrix and vector multiplication, refer to Appendix E.

The result is {2A}, which should appear in row {09} column {05} of the S-box. This is verified by checking Table 6.2a.

The **inverse substitute byte transformation**, called InvSubBytes, makes use of the inverse S-box shown in Table 6.2b. Note, for example, that the input {2A} produces the output {95}, and the input {95} to the S-box produces {2A}. The inverse S-box is constructed (Figure 6.6b) by applying the inverse of the transformation in Equation (6.1) followed by taking the multiplicative inverse in GF(2^8). The inverse transformation is

$$b'_i = b_{(i+2) \bmod 8} \oplus b_{(i+5) \bmod 8} \oplus b_{(i+7) \bmod 8} \oplus d_i$$

where byte d = {05}, or 00000101. We can depict this transformation as follows.

$$\begin{bmatrix} b'_0 \\ b'_1 \\ b'_2 \\ b'_3 \\ b'_4 \\ b'_5 \\ b'_6 \\ b'_7 \end{bmatrix} = \begin{bmatrix} 0 & 0 & 1 & 0 & 0 & 1 & 0 & 1 \\ 1 & 0 & 0 & 1 & 0 & 0 & 1 & 0 \\ 0 & 1 & 0 & 0 & 1 & 0 & 0 & 1 \\ 1 & 0 & 1 & 0 & 0 & 1 & 0 & 0 \\ 0 & 1 & 0 & 1 & 0 & 0 & 1 & 0 \\ 0 & 0 & 1 & 0 & 1 & 0 & 0 & 1 \\ 1 & 0 & 0 & 1 & 0 & 1 & 0 & 0 \\ 0 & 1 & 0 & 0 & 1 & 0 & 1 & 0 \end{bmatrix} \begin{bmatrix} b_0 \\ b_1 \\ b_2 \\ b_3 \\ b_4 \\ b_5 \\ b_6 \\ b_7 \end{bmatrix} + \begin{bmatrix} 1 \\ 0 \\ 1 \\ 0 \\ 0 \\ 0 \\ 0 \\ 0 \end{bmatrix}$$

To see that InvSubBytes is the inverse of SubBytes, label the matrices in SubBytes and InvSubBytes as **X** and **Y**, respectively, and the vector versions of constants c and d as **C** and **D**, respectively. For some 8-bit vector **B**, Equation (6.2) becomes $\mathbf{B'} = \mathbf{XB} \oplus \mathbf{C}$. We need to show that $\mathbf{Y(XB} \oplus \mathbf{C)} \oplus \mathbf{D} = \mathbf{B}$. To multiply out, we must show $\mathbf{YXB} \oplus \mathbf{YC} \oplus \mathbf{D} = \mathbf{B}$. This becomes

$$\begin{bmatrix} 0 & 0 & 1 & 0 & 0 & 1 & 0 & 1 \\ 1 & 0 & 0 & 1 & 0 & 0 & 1 & 0 \\ 0 & 1 & 0 & 0 & 1 & 0 & 0 & 1 \\ 1 & 0 & 1 & 0 & 0 & 1 & 0 & 0 \\ 0 & 1 & 0 & 1 & 0 & 0 & 1 & 0 \\ 0 & 0 & 1 & 0 & 1 & 0 & 0 & 1 \\ 1 & 0 & 0 & 1 & 0 & 1 & 0 & 0 \\ 0 & 1 & 0 & 0 & 1 & 0 & 1 & 0 \end{bmatrix} \begin{bmatrix} 1 & 0 & 0 & 0 & 1 & 1 & 1 & 1 \\ 1 & 1 & 0 & 0 & 0 & 1 & 1 & 1 \\ 1 & 1 & 1 & 0 & 0 & 0 & 1 & 1 \\ 1 & 1 & 1 & 1 & 0 & 0 & 0 & 1 \\ 1 & 1 & 1 & 1 & 1 & 0 & 0 & 0 \\ 0 & 1 & 1 & 1 & 1 & 1 & 0 & 0 \\ 0 & 0 & 1 & 1 & 1 & 1 & 1 & 0 \\ 0 & 0 & 0 & 1 & 1 & 1 & 1 & 1 \end{bmatrix} \begin{bmatrix} b_0 \\ b_1 \\ b_2 \\ b_3 \\ b_4 \\ b_5 \\ b_6 \\ b_7 \end{bmatrix} \oplus$$

$$\begin{bmatrix} 0 & 0 & 1 & 0 & 0 & 1 & 0 & 1 \\ 1 & 0 & 0 & 1 & 0 & 0 & 1 & 0 \\ 0 & 1 & 0 & 0 & 1 & 0 & 0 & 1 \\ 1 & 0 & 1 & 0 & 0 & 1 & 0 & 0 \\ 0 & 1 & 0 & 1 & 0 & 0 & 1 & 0 \\ 0 & 0 & 1 & 0 & 1 & 0 & 0 & 1 \\ 1 & 0 & 0 & 1 & 0 & 1 & 0 & 0 \\ 0 & 1 & 0 & 0 & 1 & 0 & 1 & 0 \end{bmatrix} \begin{bmatrix} 1 \\ 1 \\ 0 \\ 0 \\ 0 \\ 1 \\ 1 \\ 0 \end{bmatrix} \oplus \begin{bmatrix} 1 \\ 0 \\ 1 \\ 0 \\ 0 \\ 0 \\ 0 \\ 0 \end{bmatrix} =$$

$$\begin{bmatrix} 1 & 0 & 0 & 0 & 0 & 0 & 0 & 0 \\ 0 & 1 & 0 & 0 & 0 & 0 & 0 & 0 \\ 0 & 0 & 1 & 0 & 0 & 0 & 0 & 0 \\ 0 & 0 & 0 & 1 & 0 & 0 & 0 & 0 \\ 0 & 0 & 0 & 0 & 1 & 0 & 0 & 0 \\ 0 & 0 & 0 & 0 & 0 & 1 & 0 & 0 \\ 0 & 0 & 0 & 0 & 0 & 0 & 1 & 0 \\ 0 & 0 & 0 & 0 & 0 & 0 & 0 & 1 \end{bmatrix} \begin{bmatrix} b_0 \\ b_1 \\ b_2 \\ b_3 \\ b_4 \\ b_5 \\ b_6 \\ b_7 \end{bmatrix} \oplus \begin{bmatrix} 1 \\ 0 \\ 1 \\ 0 \\ 0 \\ 0 \\ 0 \\ 0 \end{bmatrix} \oplus \begin{bmatrix} 1 \\ 0 \\ 1 \\ 0 \\ 0 \\ 0 \\ 0 \\ 0 \end{bmatrix} = \begin{bmatrix} b_0 \\ b_1 \\ b_2 \\ b_3 \\ b_4 \\ b_5 \\ b_6 \\ b_7 \end{bmatrix}$$

We have demonstrated that **YX** equals the identity matrix, and the **YC** = **D**, so that **YC** $\oplus$ **D** equals the null vector.

RATIONALE The S-box is designed to be resistant to known cryptanalytic attacks. Specifically, the Rijndael developers sought a design that has a low correlation between input bits and output bits and the property that the output is not a linear mathematical function of the input [DAEM01]. The nonlinearity is due to the use of the multiplicative inverse. In addition, the constant in Equation (6.1) was chosen so that the S-box has no fixed points [S-box(a) = a] and no "opposite fixed points" [S-box(a) = $\bar{a}$], where $\bar{a}$ is the bitwise complement of a.

Of course, the S-box must be invertible, that is, IS-box[S-box(a)] = a. However, the S-box does not self-inverse in the sense that it is not true that S-box(a) = IS-box(a). For example, S-box({95}) = {2A}, but IS-box({95}) = {AD}.

ShiftRows Transformation

FORWARD AND INVERSE TRANSFORMATIONS The **forward shift row transformation**, called ShiftRows, is depicted in Figure 6.7a. The first row of **State** is not altered. For the second row, a 1-byte circular left shift is performed. For the third row, a 2-byte circular left shift is performed. For the fourth row, a 3-byte circular left shift is performed. The following is an example of ShiftRows.

87	F2	4D	97		87	F2	4D	97
EC	6E	4C	90		6E	4C	90	EC
4A	C3	46	E7	→	46	E7	4A	C3
8C	D8	95	A6		A6	8C	D8	95

The **inverse shift row transformation**, called InvShiftRows, performs the circular shifts in the opposite direction for each of the last three rows, with a 1-byte circular right shift for the second row, and so on.

RATIONALE The shift row transformation is more substantial than it may first appear. This is because the **State**, as well as the cipher input and output, is treated as an array of four 4-byte columns. Thus, on encryption, the first 4 bytes of the plaintext are copied to the first column of **State**, and so on. Furthermore, as will be seen, the round key is applied to **State** column by column. Thus, a row shift moves an individual byte from one column to another, which is a linear

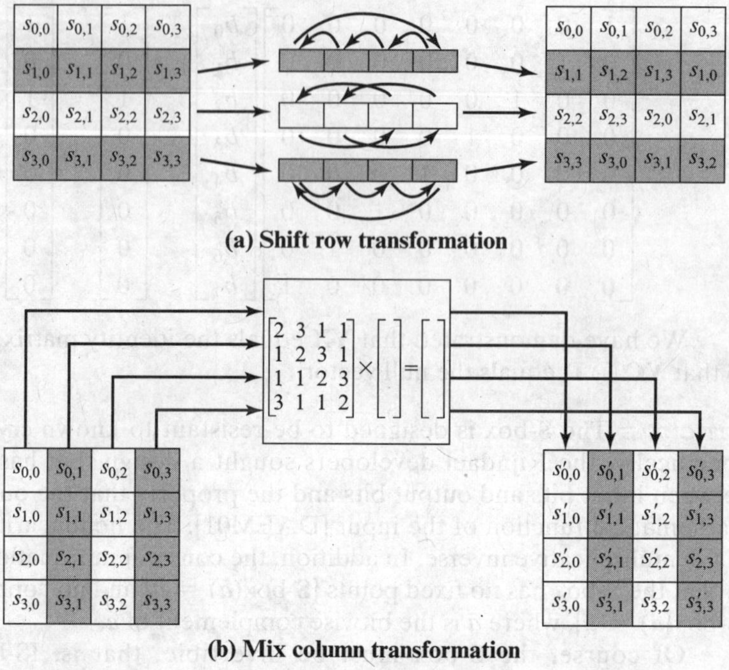

Figure 6.7 AES Row and Column Operations

distance of a multiple of 4 bytes. Also note that the transformation ensures that the 4 bytes of one column are spread out to four different columns. Figure 6.4 illustrates the effect.

MixColumns Transformation

Forward and Inverse Transformations The **forward mix column transformation**, called MixColumns, operates on each column individually. Each byte of a column is mapped into a new value that is a function of all four bytes in that column. The transformation can be defined by the following matrix multiplication on **State** (Figure 6.7b):

$$\begin{bmatrix} 02 & 03 & 01 & 01 \\ 01 & 02 & 03 & 01 \\ 01 & 01 & 02 & 03 \\ 03 & 01 & 01 & 02 \end{bmatrix} \begin{bmatrix} s_{0,0} & s_{0,1} & s_{0,2} & s_{0,3} \\ s_{1,0} & s_{1,1} & s_{1,2} & s_{1,3} \\ s_{2,0} & s_{2,1} & s_{2,2} & s_{2,3} \\ s_{3,0} & s_{3,1} & s_{3,2} & s_{3,3} \end{bmatrix} = \begin{bmatrix} s'_{0,0} & s'_{0,1} & s'_{0,2} & s'_{0,3} \\ s'_{1,0} & s'_{1,1} & s'_{1,2} & s'_{1,3} \\ s'_{2,0} & s'_{2,1} & s'_{2,2} & s'_{2,3} \\ s'_{3,0} & s'_{3,1} & s'_{3,2} & s'_{3,3} \end{bmatrix} \quad \textbf{(6.3)}$$

Each element in the product matrix is the sum of products of elements of one row and one column. In this case, the individual additions and multiplications[5] are

[5]We follow the convention of FIPS PUB 197 and use the symbol $\cdot$ to indicate multiplication over the finite field GF(2^8) and $\oplus$ to indicate bitwise XOR, which corresponds to addition in GF(2^8).

performed in GF(2^8). The MixColumns transformation on a single column of **State** can be expressed as

$$\begin{aligned} s'_{0,j} &= (2 \cdot s_{0,j}) \oplus (3 \cdot s_{1,j}) \oplus s_{2,j} \oplus s_{3,j} \\ s'_{1,j} &= s_{0,j} \oplus (2 \cdot s_{1,j}) \oplus (3 \cdot s_{2,j}) \oplus s_{3,j} \\ s'_{2,j} &= s_{0,j} \oplus s_{1,j} \oplus (2 \cdot s_{2,j}) \oplus (3 \cdot s_{3,j}) \\ s'_{3,j} &= (3 \cdot s_{0,j}) \oplus s_{1,j} \oplus s_{2,j} \oplus (2 \cdot s_{3,j}) \end{aligned} \tag{6.4}$$

The following is an example of MixColumns:

87	F2	4D	97		47	40	A3	4C
6E	4C	90	EC		37	D4	70	9F
46	E7	4A	C3	→	94	E4	3A	42
A6	8C	D8	95		ED	A5	A6	BC

Let us verify the first column of this example. Recall from Section 5.6 that, in GF(2^8), addition is the bitwise XOR operation and that multiplication can be performed according to the rule established in Equation (4.14). In particular, multiplication of a value by x (i.e., by {02}) can be implemented as a 1-bit left shift followed by a conditional bitwise XOR with (0001 1011) if the leftmost bit of the original value (prior to the shift) is 1. Thus, to verify the MixColumns transformation on the first column, we need to show that

$$\begin{aligned} &(\{02\} \cdot \{87\}) \oplus (\{03\} \cdot \{6E\}) \oplus \{46\} \oplus \{A6\} = \{47\} \\ &\{87\} \oplus (\{02\} \cdot \{6E\}) \oplus (\{03\} \cdot \{46\}) \oplus \{A6\} = \{37\} \\ &\{87\} \oplus \{6E\} \oplus (\{02\} \cdot \{46\}) \oplus (\{03\} \cdot \{A6\}) = \{94\} \\ &(\{03\} \cdot \{87\}) \oplus \{6E\} \oplus \{46\} \oplus (\{02\} \cdot \{A6\}) = \{ED\} \end{aligned}$$

For the first equation, we have $\{02\} \cdot \{87\} = (0000\ 1110) \oplus (0001\ 1011) = (0001\ 0101)$ and $\{03\} \cdot \{6E\} = \{6E\} \oplus (\{02\} \cdot \{6E\}) = (0110\ 1110) \oplus (1101\ 1100) = (1011\ 0010)$. Then,

$$\begin{aligned} \{02\} \cdot \{87\} &= 0001\ 0101 \\ \{03\} \cdot \{6E\} &= 1011\ 0010 \\ \{46\} &= 0100\ 0110 \\ \{A6\} &= \underline{1010\ 0110} \\ & \ 0100\ 0111 = \{47\} \end{aligned}$$

The other equations can be similarly verified.

The **inverse mix column transformation**, called InvMixColumns, is defined by the following matrix multiplication:

$$\begin{bmatrix} 0E & 0B & 0D & 09 \\ 09 & 0E & 0B & 0D \\ 0D & 09 & 0E & 0B \\ 0B & 0D & 09 & 0E \end{bmatrix} \begin{bmatrix} s_{0,0} & s_{0,1} & s_{0,2} & s_{0,3} \\ s_{1,0} & s_{1,1} & s_{1,2} & s_{1,3} \\ s_{2,0} & s_{2,1} & s_{2,2} & s_{2,3} \\ s_{3,0} & s_{3,1} & s_{3,2} & s_{3,3} \end{bmatrix} = \begin{bmatrix} s'_{0,0} & s'_{0,1} & s'_{0,2} & s'_{0,3} \\ s'_{1,0} & s'_{1,1} & s'_{1,2} & s'_{1,3} \\ s'_{2,0} & s'_{2,1} & s'_{2,2} & s'_{2,3} \\ s'_{3,0} & s'_{3,1} & s'_{3,2} & s'_{3,3} \end{bmatrix} \tag{6.5}$$

It is not immediately clear that Equation (6.5) is the **inverse** of Equation (6.3). We need to show

$$\begin{bmatrix} 0E & 0B & 0D & 09 \\ 09 & 0E & 0B & 0D \\ 0D & 09 & 0E & 0B \\ 0B & 0D & 09 & 0E \end{bmatrix} \begin{bmatrix} 02 & 03 & 01 & 01 \\ 01 & 02 & 03 & 01 \\ 01 & 01 & 02 & 03 \\ 03 & 01 & 01 & 02 \end{bmatrix} \begin{bmatrix} s_{0,0} & s_{0,1} & s_{0,2} & s_{0,3} \\ s_{1,0} & s_{1,1} & s_{1,2} & s_{1,3} \\ s_{2,0} & s_{2,1} & s_{2,2} & s_{2,3} \\ s_{3,0} & s_{3,1} & s_{3,2} & s_{3,3} \end{bmatrix} = \begin{bmatrix} s_{0,0} & s_{0,1} & s_{0,2} & s_{0,3} \\ s_{1,0} & s_{1,1} & s_{1,2} & s_{1,3} \\ s_{2,0} & s_{2,1} & s_{2,2} & s_{2,3} \\ s_{0,3} & s_{3,1} & s_{3,2} & s_{3,3} \end{bmatrix}$$

which is equivalent to showing

$$\begin{bmatrix} 0E & 0B & 0D & 09 \\ 09 & 0E & 0B & 0D \\ 0D & 09 & 0E & 0B \\ 0B & 0D & 09 & 0E \end{bmatrix} \begin{bmatrix} 02 & 03 & 01 & 01 \\ 01 & 02 & 03 & 01 \\ 01 & 01 & 02 & 03 \\ 03 & 01 & 01 & 02 \end{bmatrix} = \begin{bmatrix} 1 & 0 & 0 & 0 \\ 0 & 1 & 0 & 0 \\ 0 & 0 & 1 & 0 \\ 0 & 0 & 0 & 1 \end{bmatrix} \quad \textbf{(6.6)}$$

That is, the inverse transformation matrix times the forward transformation matrix equals the identity matrix. To verify the first column of Equation (6.6), we need to show

$$\begin{aligned} (\{0E\} \cdot \{02\}) \oplus \{0B\} \oplus \{0D\} \oplus (\{09\} \cdot \{03\}) &= \{01\} \\ (\{09\} \cdot \{02\}) \oplus \{0E\} \oplus \{0B\} \oplus (\{0D\} \cdot \{03\}) &= \{00\} \\ (\{0D\} \cdot \{02\}) \oplus \{09\} \oplus \{0E\} \oplus (\{0B\} \cdot \{03\}) &= \{00\} \\ (\{0B\} \cdot \{02\}) \oplus \{0D\} \oplus \{09\} \oplus (\{0E\} \cdot \{03\}) &= \{00\} \end{aligned}$$

For the first equation, we have $\{0E\} \cdot \{02\} = 00011100$ and $\{09\} \cdot \{03\} = \{09\} \oplus (\{09\} \cdot \{02\}) = 00001001 \oplus 00010010 = 00011011$. Then

$$\begin{aligned} \{0E\} \cdot \{02\} &= 00011100 \\ \{0B\} &= 00001011 \\ \{0D\} &= 00001101 \\ \{09\} \cdot \{03\} &= \underline{00011011} \\ & 00000001 \end{aligned}$$

The other equations can be similarly verified.

The AES document describes another way of characterizing the MixColumns transformation, which is in terms of polynomial arithmetic. In the standard, MixColumns is defined by considering each column of **State** to be a four-term polynomial with coefficients in $GF(2^8)$. Each column is multiplied modulo $(x^4 + 1)$ by the fixed polynomial $a(x)$, given by

$$a(x) = \{03\}x^3 + \{01\}x^2 + \{01\}x + \{02\} \quad \textbf{(6.7)}$$

Appendix 5A demonstrates that multiplication of each column of **State** by $a(x)$ can be written as the matrix multiplication of Equation (6.3). Similarly, it can be seen that the transformation in Equation (6.5) corresponds to treating each column as a four-term polynomial and multiplying each column by $b(x)$, given by

$$b(x) = \{0B\}x^3 + \{0D\}x^2 + \{09\}x + \{0E\} \quad (6.8)$$

It readily can be shown that $b(x) = a^{-1}(x) \bmod (x^4 + 1)$.

Rationale The coefficients of the matrix in Equation (6.3) are based on a linear code with maximal distance between code words, which ensures a good mixing among the bytes of each column. The mix column transformation combined with the shift row transformation ensures that after a few rounds all output bits depend on all input bits. See [DAEM99] for a discussion.

In addition, the choice of coefficients in MixColumns, which are all {01}, {02}, or {03}, was influenced by implementation considerations. As was discussed, multiplication by these coefficients involves at most a shift and an XOR. The coefficients in InvMixColumns are more formidable to implement. However, encryption was deemed more important than decryption for two reasons:

1. For the CFB and OFB cipher modes (Figures 7.5 and 7.6; described in Chapter 7), only encryption is used.
2. As with any block cipher, AES can be used to construct a message authentication code (Chapter 13), and for this, only encryption is used.

AddRoundKey Transformation

Forward and Inverse Transformations In the **forward add round key transformation**, called AddRoundKey, the 128 bits of **State** are bitwise XORed with the 128 bits of the round key. As shown in Figure 6.5b, the operation is viewed as a columnwise operation between the 4 bytes of a **State** column and one word of the round key; it can also be viewed as a byte-level operation. The following is an example of AddRoundKey:

47	40	A3	4C		AC	19	28	57		EB	59	8B	1B
37	D4	70	9F		77	FA	D1	5C		40	2E	A1	C3
94	E4	3A	42	⊕	66	DC	29	00	=	F2	38	13	42
ED	A5	A6	BC		F3	21	41	6A		1E	84	E7	D6

The first matrix is **State**, and the second matrix is the round key.

The **inverse add round key transformation** is identical to the forward add round key transformation, because the XOR operation is its own inverse.

Rationale The add round key transformation is as simple as possible and affects every bit of **State**. The complexity of the round key expansion, plus the complexity of the other stages of AES, ensure security.

Figure 6.8 is another view of a single round of AES, emphasizing the mechanisms and inputs of each transformation.

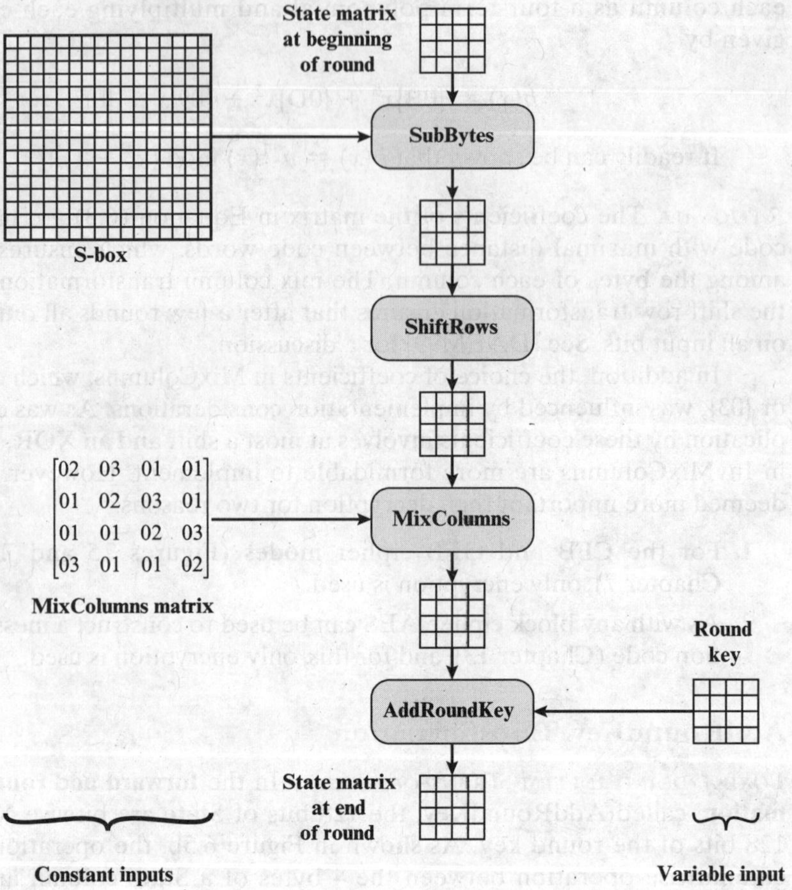

Figure 6.8 Inputs for Single AES Round

6.4 AES KEY EXPANSION

Key Expansion Algorithm

The AES key expansion algorithm takes as input a four-word (16-byte) key and produces a linear array of 44 words (176 bytes). This is sufficient to provide a four-word round key for the initial AddRoundKey stage and each of the 10 rounds of the cipher. The pseudocode on the next page describes the expansion.

The key is copied into the first four words of the expanded key. The remainder of the expanded key is filled in four words at a time. Each added word **w**[i] depends on the immediately preceding word, **w**[i − 1], and the word four positions back, **w**[i − 4]. In three out of four cases, a simple XOR is used. For a word whose position in the **w** array is a multiple of 4, a more complex function is used. Figure 6.9 illustrates the generation of the expanded key, using the symbol g to represent that complex function. The function g consists of the following subfunctions.

```
KeyExpansion (byte key[16], word w[44])
{
    word temp
    for (i = 0; i < 4; i++) w[i] = (key[4*i], key[4*i+1],
                                    key[4*i+2],
                                    key[4*i+3]);

    for (i = 4; i < 44; i++)
    {
    temp = w[i - 1];
    if (i mod 4 = 0) temp = SubWord (RotWord (temp))
                              ⊕ Rcon[i/4];
    w[i] = w[i-4] ⊕ temp
    }
}
```

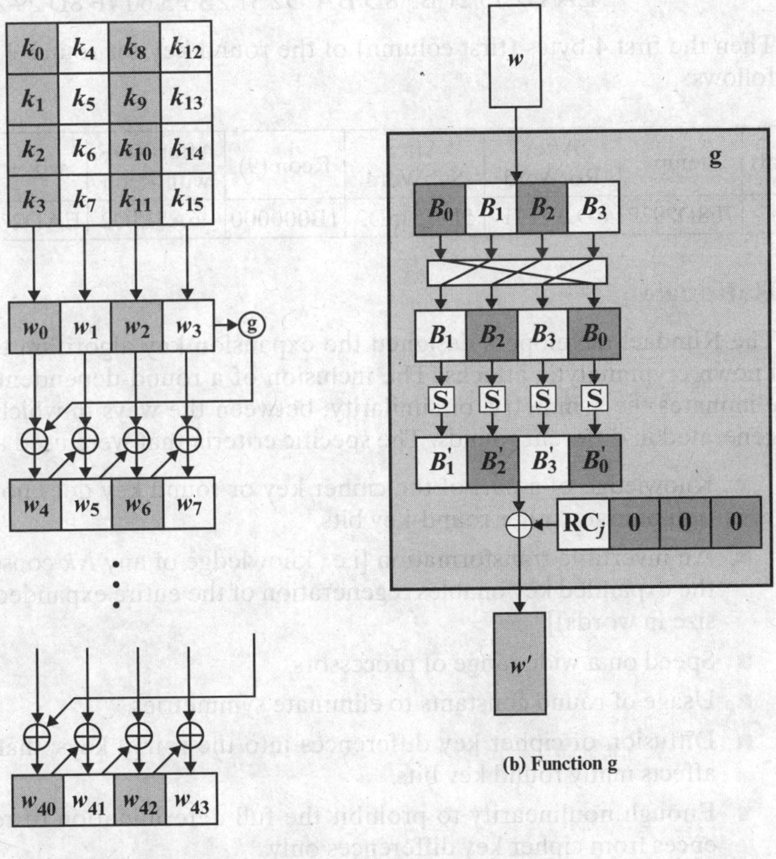

(b) Function g

(a) Overall algorithm

Figure 6.9 AES Key Expansion

1. RotWord performs a one-byte circular left shift on a word. This means that an input word [B_0, B_1, B_2, B_3] is transformed into [B_1, B_2, B_3, B_0].
2. SubWord performs a byte substitution on each byte of its input word, using the S-box (Table 6.2a).
3. The result of steps 1 and 2 is XORed with a round constant, Rcon[j].

The round constant is a word in which the three rightmost bytes are always 0. Thus, the effect of an XOR of a word with Rcon is to only perform an XOR on the leftmost byte of the word. The round constant is different for each round and is defined as Rcon[j] = (RC[j], 0, 0, 0), with RC[1] = 1, RC[j] = 2 · RC[j − 1] and with multiplication defined over the field GF(2^8). The values of RC[j] in hexadecimal are

j	1	2	3	4	5	6	7	8	9	10
RC[j]	01	02	04	08	10	20	40	80	1B	36

For example, suppose that the round key for round 8 is

EA D2 73 21 B5 8D BA D2 31 2B F5 60 7F 8D 29 2F

Then the first 4 bytes (first column) of the round key for round 9 are calculated as follows:

i (decimal)	temp	After RotWord	After SubWord	Rcon (9)	After XOR with Rcon	w[i − 4]	w[i] = temp ⊕ w[i − 4]
36	7F8D292F	8D292F7F	5DA515D2	1B000000	46A515D2	EAD27321	AC7766F3

Rationale

The Rijndael developers designed the expansion key algorithm to be resistant to known cryptanalytic attacks. The inclusion of a round-dependent round constant eliminates the symmetry, or similarity, between the ways in which round keys are generated in different rounds. The specific criteria that were used are [DAEM99]

- Knowledge of a part of the cipher key or round key does not enable calculation of many other round-key bits.
- An invertible transformation [i.e., knowledge of any *Nk* consecutive words of the expanded key enables regeneration of the entire expanded key (*Nk* = key size in words)].
- Speed on a wide range of processors.
- Usage of round constants to eliminate symmetries.
- Diffusion of cipher key differences into the round keys; that is, each key bit affects many round key bits.
- Enough nonlinearity to prohibit the full determination of round key differences from cipher key differences only.
- Simplicity of description.

The authors do not quantify the first point on the preceding list, but the idea is that if you know less than *Nk* consecutive words of either the cipher key or one of the round keys, then it is difficult to reconstruct the remaining unknown bits. The fewer bits one knows, the more difficult it is to do the reconstruction or to determine other bits in the key expansion.

6.5 AN AES EXAMPLE

We now work through an example and consider some of its implications. Although you are not expected to duplicate the example by hand, you will find it informative to study the hex patterns that occur from one step to the next.

For this example, the plaintext is a hexadecimal palindrome. The plaintext, key, and resulting ciphertext are

Plaintext:	**0123456789abcdeffedcba9876543210**
Key:	**0f1571c947d9e8590cb7add6af7f6798**
Ciphertext:	**ff0b844a0853bf7c6934ab4364148fb9**

Results

Table 6.3 shows the expansion of the 16-byte key into 10 round keys. As previously explained, this process is performed word by word, with each four-byte word occupying one column of the word round-key matrix. The left-hand column shows

Table 6.3 Key Expansion for AES Example

Key Words	Auxiliary Function
w0 = 0f 15 71 c9 w1 = 47 d9 e8 59 w2 = 0c b7 ad d6 w3 = af 7f 67 98	RotWord (w3) = 7f 67 98 af = x1 SubWord (x1) = d2 85 46 79 = y1 Rcon (1) = 01 00 00 00 y1 ⊕ Rcon (1) = d3 85 46 79 = z1
w4 = w0 ⊕ z1 = dc 90 37 b0 w5 = w4 ⊕ w1 = 9b 49 df e9 w6 = w5 ⊕ w2 = 97 fe 72 3f w7 = w6 ⊕ w3 = 38 81 15 a7	RotWord (w7) = 81 15 a7 38 = x2 SubWord (x2) = 0c 59 5c 07 = y2 Rcon (2) = 02 00 00 00 y2 ⊕ Rcon (2) = 0e 59 5c 07 = z2
w8 = w4 ⊕ z2 = d2 c9 6b b7 w9 = w8 ⊕ w5 = 49 80 b4 5e w10 = w9 ⊕ w6 = de 7e c6 61 w11 = w10 ⊕ w7 = e6 ff d3 c6	RotWord (w11) = ff d3 c6 e6 = x3 SubWord (x3) = 16 66 b4 83 = y3 Rcon (3) = 04 00 00 00 y3 ⊕ Rcon (3) = 12 66 b4 8e = z3
w12 = w8 ⊕ z3 = c0 af df 39 w13 = w12 ⊕ w9 = 89 2f 6b 67 w14 = w13 ⊕ w10 = 57 51 ad 06 w15 = w14 ⊕ w11 = b1 ae 7e c0	RotWord (w15) = ae 7e c0 b1 = x4 SubWord (x4) = e4 f3 ba c8 = y4 Rcon (4) = 08 00 00 00 y4 ⊕ Rcon (4) = ec f3 ba c8 = 4

(Continued)

Table 6.3 Continued

Key Words	Auxiliary Function
w16 = w12 ⊕ z4 = 2c 5c 65 f1 w17 = w16 ⊕ w13 = a5 73 0e 96 w18 = w17 ⊕ w14 = f2 22 a3 90 w19 = w18 ⊕ w15 = 43 8c dd 50	RotWord (w19) = 8c dd 50 43 = x5 SubWord (x5) = 64 c1 53 1a = y5 Rcon(5) = 10 00 00 00 y5 ⊕ Rcon (5) = 74 c1 53 1a = z5
w20 = w16 ⊕ z5 = 58 9d 36 eb w21 = w20 ⊕ w17 = fd ee 38 7d w22 = w21 ⊕ w18 = 0f cc 9b ed w23 = w22 ⊕ w19 = 4c 40 46 bd	RotWord (w23) = 40 46 bd 4c = x6 SubWord (x6) = 09 5a 7a 29 = y6 Rcon(6) = 20 00 00 00 y6 ⊕ Rcon(6) = 29 5a 7a 29 = z6
w24 = w20 ⊕ z6 = 71 c7 4c c2 w25 = w24 ⊕ w21 = 8c 29 74 bf w26 = w25 ⊕ w22 = 83 e5 ef 52 w27 = w26 ⊕ w23 = cf a5 a9 ef	RotWord (w27) = a5 a9 ef cf = x7 SubWord (x7) = 06 d3 bf 8a = y7 Rcon (7) = 40 00 00 00 y7 ⊕ Rcon(7) = 46 d3 df 8a = z7
w28 = w24 ⊕ z7 = 37 14 93 48 w29 = w28 ⊕ w25 = bb 3d e7 f7 w30 = w29 ⊕ w26 = 38 d8 08 a5 w31 = w30 ⊕ w27 = f7 7d a1 4a	RotWord (w31) = 7d a1 4a f7 = x8 SubWord (x8) = ff 32 d6 68 = y8 Rcon (8) = 80 00 00 00 y8 ⊕ Rcon(8) = 7f 32 d6 68 = z8
w32 = w28 ⊕ z8 = 48 26 45 20 w33 = w32 ⊕ w29 = f3 1b a2 d7 w34 = w33 ⊕ w30 = cb c3 aa 72 w35 = w34 ⊕ w32 = 3c be 0b 3	RotWord (w35) = be 0b 38 3c = x9 SubWord (x9) = ae 2b 07 eb = y9 Rcon (9) = 1B 00 00 00 y9 ⊕ Rcon (9) = b5 2b 07 eb = z9
w36 = w32 ⊕ z9 = fd 0d 42 cb w37 = w36 ⊕ w33 = 0e 16 e0 1c w38 = w37 ⊕ w34 = c5 d5 4a 6e w39 = w38 ⊕ w35 = f9 6b 41 56	RotWord (w39) = 6b 41 56 f9 = x10 SubWord (x10) = 7f 83 b1 99 = y10 Rcon (10) = 36 00 00 00 y10 ⊕ Rcon (10) = 49 83 b1 99 = z10
w40 = w36 ⊕ z10 = b4 8e f3 52 w41 = w40 ⊕ w37 = ba 98 13 4e w42 = w41 ⊕ w38 = 7f 4d 59 20 w43 = w42 ⊕ w39 = 86 26 18 76	

the four round-key words generated for each round. The right-hand column shows the steps used to generate the auxiliary word used in key expansion. We begin, of course, with the key itself serving as the round key for round 0.

Next, Table 6.4 shows the progression of **State** through the AES encryption process. The first column shows the value of **State** at the start of a round. For the first row, **State** is just the matrix arrangement of the plaintext. The second, third, and fourth columns show the value of **State** for that round after the SubBytes, ShiftRows, and MixColumns transformations, respectively. The fifth column shows the round key. You can verify that these round keys equate with those shown in Table 6.3. The first column shows the value of **State** resulting from the bitwise XOR of **State** after the preceding MixColumns with the round key for the preceding round.

Avalanche Effect

If a small change in the key or plaintext were to produce a corresponding small change in the ciphertext, this might be used to effectively reduce the size of the

Table 6.4 AES Example

Start of Round	After SubBytes	After ShiftRows	After MixColumns	Round Key
01 89 fe 76 23 ab dc 54 45 cd ba 32 67 ef 98 10				0f 47 0c af 15 d9 b7 7f 71 e8 ad 67 c9 59 d6 98
0e ce f2 d9 36 72 6b 2b 34 25 17 55 ae b6 4e 88	ab 8b 89 35 05 40 7f f1 18 3f f0 fc e4 4e 2f c4	ab 8b 89 35 40 7f f1 05 f0 fc 18 3f c4 e4 4e 2f	b9 94 57 75 e4 8e 16 51 47 20 9a 3f c5 d6 f5 3b	dc 9b 97 38 90 49 fe 81 37 df 72 15 b0 e9 3f a7
65 0f c0 4d 74 c7 e8 d0 70 ff e8 2a 75 3f ca 9c	4d 76 ba e3 92 c6 9b 70 51 16 9b e5 9d 75 74 de	4d 76 ba e3 c6 9b 70 92 9b e5 51 16 de 9d 75 74	8e 22 db 12 b2 f2 dc 92 df 80 f7 c1 2d c5 1e 52	d2 49 de e6 c9 80 7e ff 6b b4 c6 d3 b7 5e 61 c6
5c 6b 05 f4 7b 72 a2 6d b4 34 31 12 9a 9b 7f 94	4a 7f 6b bf 21 40 3a 3c 8d 18 c7 c9 b8 14 d2 22	4a 7f 6b bf 40 3a 3c 21 c7 c9 8d 18 22 b8 14 d2	b1 c1 0b cc ba f3 8b 07 f9 1f 6a c3 1d 19 24 5c	c0 89 57 b1 af 2f 51 ae df 6b ad 7e 39 67 06 c0
71 48 5c 7d 15 dc da a9 26 74 c7 bd 24 7e 22 9c	a3 52 4a ff 59 86 57 d3 f7 92 c6 7a 36 f3 93 de	a3 52 4a ff 86 57 d3 59 c6 7a f7 92 de 36 f3 93	d4 11 fe 0f 3b 44 06 73 cb ab 62 37 19 b7 07 ec	2c a5 f2 43 5c 73 22 8c 65 0e a3 dd f1 96 90 50
f8 b4 0c 4c 67 37 24 ff ae a5 c1 ea e8 21 97 bc	41 8d fe 29 85 9a 36 16 e4 06 78 87 9b fd 88 65	41 8d fe 29 9a 36 16 85 78 87 e4 06 65 9b fd 88	2a 47 c4 48 83 e8 18 ba 84 18 27 23 eb 10 0a f3	58 fd 0f 4c 9d ee cc 40 36 38 9b 46 eb 7d ed bd
72 ba cb 04 1e 06 d4 fa b2 20 bc 65 00 6d e7 4e	40 f4 1f f2 72 6f 48 2d 37 b7 65 4d 63 3c 94 2f	40 f4 1f f2 6f 48 2d 72 65 4d 37 b7 2f 63 3c 94	7b 05 42 4a 1e d0 20 40 94 83 18 52 94 c4 43 fb	71 8c 83 cf c7 29 e5 a5 4c 74 ef a9 c2 bf 52 ef
0a 89 c1 85 d9 f9 c5 e5 d8 f7 f7 fb 56 7b 11 14	67 a7 78 97 35 99 a6 d9 61 68 68 0f b1 21 82 fa	67 a7 78 97 99 a6 d9 35 68 0f 61 68 fa b1 21 82	ec 1a c0 80 0c 50 53 c7 3b d7 00 ef b7 22 72 e0	37 bb 38 f7 14 3d d8 7d 93 e7 08 a1 48 f7 a5 4a
db a1 f8 77 18 6d 8b ba a8 30 08 4e ff d5 d7 aa	b9 32 41 f5 ad 3c 3d f4 c2 04 30 2f 16 03 0e ac	b9 32 41 f5 3c 3d f4 ad 30 2f c2 04 ac 16 03 0e	b1 1a 44 17 3d 2f ec b6 0a 6b 2f 42 9f 68 f3 b1	48 f3 cb 3c 26 1b c3 be 45 a2 aa 0b 20 d7 72 38
f9 e9 8f 2b 1b 34 2f 08 4f c9 85 49 bf bf 81 89	99 1e 73 f1 af 18 15 30 84 dd 97 3b 08 08 0c a7	99 1e 73 f1 18 15 30 af 97 3b 84 dd a7 08 08 0c	31 30 3a c2 ac 71 8c c4 46 65 48 eb 6a 1c 31 62	fd 0e c5 f9 0d 16 d5 6b 42 e0 4a 41 cb 1c 6e 56
cc 3e ff 3b a1 67 59 af 04 85 02 aa a1 00 5f 34	4b b2 16 e2 32 85 cb 79 f2 97 77 ac 32 63 cf 18	4b b2 16 e2 85 cb 79 32 77 ac f2 97 18 32 63 cf		b4 ba 7f 86 8e 98 4d 26 f3 13 59 18 52 4e 20 76
ff 08 69 64 0b 53 34 14 84 bf ab 8f 4a 7c 43 b9				

Table 6.5 Avalanche Effect in AES: Change in Plaintext

Round		Number of Bits that Differ
	0123456789abcdeffedcba9876543210 0023456789abcdeffedcba9876543210	1
0	0e3634aece7225b6f26b174ed92b5588 0f3634aece7225b6f26b174ed92b5588	1
1	657470750fc7ff3fc0e8e8ca4dd02a9c c4a9ad090fc7ff3fc0e8e8ca4dd02a9c	20
2	5c7bb49a6b72349b05a2317ff46d1294 fe2ae569f7ee8bb8c1f5a2bb37ef53d5	58
3	7115262448dc747e5cdac7227da9bd9c ec093dfb7c45343d689017507d485e62	59
4	f867aee8b437a5210c24c1974cffeabc 43efdb697244df808e8d9364ee0ae6f5	61
5	721eb200ba06206dcbd4bce704fa654e 7b28a5d5ed643287e006c099bb375302	68
6	0ad9d85689f9f77bc1c5f71185e5fb14 3bc2d8b6798d8ac4fe36a1d891ac181a	64
7	db18a8ffa16d30d5f88b08d777ba4eaa 9fb8b5452023c70280e5c4bb9e555a4b	67
8	f91b4fbfe934c9bf8f2f85812b084989 20264e1126b219aef7feb3f9b2d6de40	65
9	cca104a13e678500ff59025f3bafaa34 b56a0341b2290ba7dfdfbddcd8578205	61
10	ff0b844a0853bf7c6934ab4364148fb9 612b89398d0600cde116227ce72433f0	58

plaintext (or key) space to be searched. What is desired is the avalanche effect, in which a small change in plaintext or key produces a large change in the ciphertext.

Using the example from Table 6.4, Table 6.5 shows the result when the eighth bit of the plaintext is changed. The second column of the table shows the value of the **State** matrix at the end of each round for the two plaintexts. Note that after just one round, 20 bits of the **State** vector differ. After two rounds, close to half the bits differ. This magnitude of difference propagates through the remaining rounds. A bit difference in approximately half the positions in the most desirable outcome. Clearly, if almost all the bits are changed, this would be logically equivalent to almost none of the bits being changed. Put another way, if we select two plaintexts at random, we would expect the two plaintexts to differ in about half of the bit positions and the two ciphertexts to also differ in about half the positions.

Table 6.6 shows the change in **State** matrix values when the same plaintext is used and the two keys differ in the eighth bit. That is, for the second case, the key is `0e1571c947d9e8590cb7add6af7f6798`. Again, one round produces a significant change, and the magnitude of change after all subsequent rounds is roughly half the bits. Thus, based on this example, AES exhibits a very strong avalanche effect.

Table 6.6 Avalanche Effect in AES: Change in Key

Round		Number of Bits that Differ
	0123456789abcdeffedcba9876543210 0123456789abcdeffedcba9876543210	0
0	0e3634aece7225b6f26b174ed92b5588 0f3634aece7225b6f26b174ed92b5588	1
1	657470750fc7ff3fc0e8e8ca4dd02a9c c5a9ad090ec7ff3fc1e8e8ca4cd02a9c	22
2	5c7bb49a6b72349b05a2317ff46d1294 90905fa9563356d15f3760f3b8259985	58
3	7115262448dc747e5cdac7227da9bd9c 18aeb7aa794b3b66629448d575c7cebf	67
4	f867aee8b437a5210c24c1974cffeabc f81015f993c978a876ae017cb49e7eec	63
5	721eb200ba06206dcbd4bce704fa654e 5955c91b4e769f3cb4a94768e98d5267	81
6	0ad9d85689f9f77bc1c5f71185e5fb14 dc60a24d137662181e45b8d3726b2920	70
7	db18a8ffa16d30d5f88b08d777ba4eaa fe8343b8f88bef66cab7e977d005a03c	74
8	f91b4fbfe934c9bf8f2f85812b084989 da7dad581d1725c5b72fa0f9d9d1366a	67
9	cca104a13e678500ff59025f3bafaa34 0ccb4c66bbfd912f4b511d72996345e0	59
10	ff0b844a0853bf7c6934ab4364148fb9 fc8923ee501a7d207ab670686839996b	53

Note that this avalanche effect is stronger than that for DES (Table 4.2), which requires three rounds to reach a point at which approximately half the bits are changed, both for a bit change in the plaintext and a bit change in the key.

6.6 AES IMPLEMENTATION

Equivalent Inverse Cipher

As was mentioned, the AES decryption cipher is not identical to the encryption cipher (Figure 6.3). That is, the sequence of transformations for decryption differs from that for encryption, although the form of the key schedules for encryption and decryption is the same. This has the disadvantage that two separate software or firmware modules are needed for applications that require both encryption and decryption. There is, however, an equivalent version of the decryption algorithm that has the same structure as the encryption algorithm. The equivalent version has the same sequence of transformations as the encryption algorithm (with transformations replaced by their inverses). To achieve this equivalence, a change in key schedule is needed.

Two separate changes are needed to bring the decryption structure in line with the encryption structure. As illustrated in Figure 6.3, an encryption round has the structure SubBytes, ShiftRows, MixColumns, AddRoundKey. The standard decryption round has the structure InvShiftRows, InvSubBytes, AddRoundKey, InvMixColumns. Thus, the first two stages of the decryption round need to be interchanged, and the second two stages of the decryption round need to be interchanged.

INTERCHANGING INVSHIFTROWS AND INVSUBBYTES InvShiftRows affects the sequence of bytes in **State** but does not alter byte contents and does not depend on byte contents to perform its transformation. InvSubBytes affects the contents of bytes in **State** but does not alter byte sequence and does not depend on byte sequence to perform its transformation. Thus, these two operations commute and can be interchanged. For a given **State** S_i,

$$\text{InvShiftRows}\,[\text{InvSubBytes}\,(S_i)] = \text{InvSubBytes}\,[\text{InvShiftRows}\,(S_i)]$$

INTERCHANGING ADDROUNDKEY AND INVMIXCOLUMNS The transformations AddRoundKey and InvMixColumns do not alter the sequence of bytes in **State**. If we view the key as a sequence of words, then both AddRoundKey and InvMixColumns operate on **State** one column at a time. These two operations are linear with respect to the column input. That is, for a given **State** S_i and a given round key w_j,

$$\text{InvMixColumns}\,(S_i \oplus w_j) = [\text{InvMixColumns}\,(S_i)] \oplus [\text{InvMixColumns}\,(w_j)]$$

To see this, suppose that the first column of **State** S_i is the sequence (y_0, y_1, y_2, y_3) and the first column of the round key w_j is (k_0, k_1, k_2, k_3). Then we need to show

$$\begin{bmatrix} 0E & 0B & 0D & 09 \\ 09 & 0E & 0B & 0D \\ 0D & 09 & 0E & 0B \\ 0B & 0D & 09 & 0E \end{bmatrix} \begin{bmatrix} y_0 \oplus k_0 \\ y_1 \oplus k_1 \\ y_2 \oplus k_2 \\ y_3 \oplus k_3 \end{bmatrix} = \begin{bmatrix} 0E & 0B & 0D & 09 \\ 09 & 0E & 0B & 0D \\ 0D & 09 & 0E & 0B \\ 0B & 0D & 09 & 0E \end{bmatrix} \begin{bmatrix} y_0 \\ y_1 \\ y_2 \\ y_3 \end{bmatrix} \oplus \begin{bmatrix} 0E & 0B & 0D & 09 \\ 09 & 0E & 0B & 0D \\ 0D & 09 & 0E & 0B \\ 0B & 0D & 09 & 0E \end{bmatrix} \begin{bmatrix} k_0 \\ k_1 \\ k_2 \\ k_3 \end{bmatrix}$$

Let us demonstrate that for the first column entry. We need to show

$$\begin{aligned} &[\{0E\} \cdot (y_0 \oplus k_0)] \oplus [\{0B\} \cdot (y_1 \oplus k_1)] \oplus [\{0D\} \cdot (y_2 \oplus k_2)] \oplus [\{09\} \cdot (y_3 \oplus k_3)] \\ &= [\{0E\} \cdot y_0] \oplus [\{0B\} \cdot y_1] \oplus [\{0D\} \cdot y_2] \oplus [\{09\} \cdot y_3] \oplus \\ &\quad [\{0E\} \cdot k_0] \oplus [\{0B\} \cdot k_1] \oplus [\{0D\} \cdot k_2] \oplus [\{09\} \cdot k_3] \end{aligned}$$

This equation is valid by inspection. Thus, we can interchange AddRoundKey and InvMixColumns, provided that we first apply InvMixColumns to the round key. Note that we do not need to apply InvMixColumns to the round key for the input to the first AddRoundKey transformation (preceding the first round) nor to the last AddRoundKey transformation (in round 10). This is because these two AddRoundKey transformations are not interchanged with InvMixColumns to produce the equivalent decryption algorithm.

Figure 6.10 illustrates the equivalent decryption algorithm.

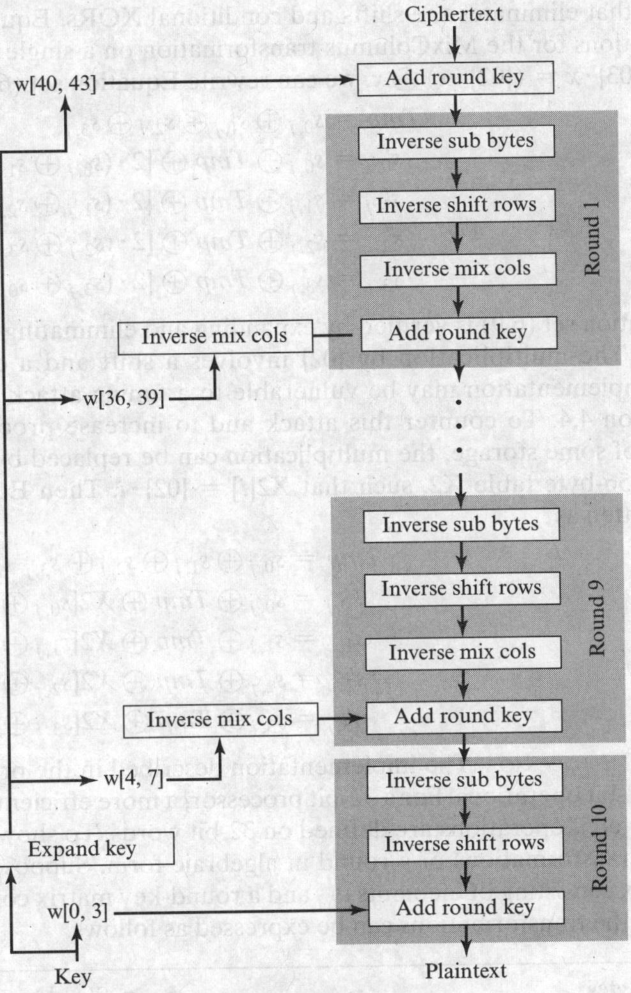

Figure 6.10 Equivalent Inverse Cipher

Implementation Aspects

The Rijndael proposal [DAEM99] provides some suggestions for efficient implementation on 8-bit processors, typical for current smart cards, and on 32-bit processors, typical for PCs.

8-Bit Processor AES can be implemented very efficiently on an 8-bit processor. AddRoundKey is a bytewise XOR operation. ShiftRows is a simple byte-shifting operation. SubBytes operates at the byte level and only requires a table of 256 bytes.

The transformation MixColumns requires matrix multiplication in the field $GF(2^8)$, which means that all operations are carried out on bytes. MixColumns only requires multiplication by {02} and {03}, which, as we have seen, involved simple shifts, conditional XORs, and XORs. This can be implemented in a more efficient way that eliminates the shifts and conditional XORs. Equation set (6.4) shows the equations for the MixColumns transformation on a single column. Using the identity $\{03\} \cdot x = (\{02\} \cdot x) \oplus x$, we can rewrite Equation set (6.4) as follows.

$$\begin{aligned} Tmp &= s_{0,j} \oplus s_{1,j} \oplus s_{2,j} \oplus s_{3,j} \\ s'_{0,j} &= s_{0,j} \oplus Tmp \oplus [2 \cdot (s_{0,j} \oplus s_{1,j})] \\ s'_{1,j} &= s_{1,j} \oplus Tmp \oplus [2 \cdot (s_{1,j} \oplus s_{2,j})] \\ s'_{2,j} &= s_{2,j} \oplus Tmp \oplus [2 \cdot (s_{2,j} \oplus s_{3,j})] \\ s'_{3,j} &= s_{3,j} \oplus Tmp \oplus [2 \cdot (s_{3,j} \oplus s_{0,j})] \end{aligned} \tag{6.9}$$

Equation set (6.9) is verified by expanding and eliminating terms.

The multiplication by {02} involves a shift and a conditional XOR. Such an implementation may be vulnerable to a timing attack of the sort described in Section 4.4. To counter this attack and to increase processing efficiency at the cost of some storage, the multiplication can be replaced by a table lookup. Define the 256-byte table X2, such that $X2[i] = \{02\} \cdot i$. Then Equation set (6.9) can be rewritten as

$$\begin{aligned} Tmp &= s_{0,j} \oplus s_{1,j} \oplus s_{2,j} \oplus s_{3,j} \\ s'_{0,j} &= s_{0,j} \oplus Tmp \oplus X2[s_{0,j} \oplus s_{1,j}] \\ s'_{1,c} &= s_{1,j} \oplus Tmp \oplus X2[s_{1,j} \oplus s_{2,j}] \\ s'_{2,c} &= s_{2,j} \oplus Tmp \oplus X2[s_{2,j} \oplus s_{3,j}] \\ s'_{3,j} &= s_{3,j} \oplus Tmp \oplus X2[s_{3,j} \oplus s_{0,j}] \end{aligned}$$

32-Bit Processor The implementation described in the preceding subsection uses only 8-bit operations. For a 32-bit processor, a more efficient implementation can be achieved if operations are defined on 32-bit words. To show this, we first define the four transformations of a round in algebraic form. Suppose we begin with a **State** matrix consisting of elements $a_{i,j}$ and a round-key matrix consisting of elements $k_{i,j}$. Then the transformations can be expressed as follows.

SubBytes	$b_{i,j} = S[a_{i,j}]$
ShiftRows	$\begin{bmatrix} c_{0,j} \\ c_{1,j} \\ c_{2,j} \\ c_{3,j} \end{bmatrix} = \begin{bmatrix} b_{0,j} \\ b_{1,j-1} \\ b_{2,j-2} \\ b_{3,j-3} \end{bmatrix}$
MixColumns	$\begin{bmatrix} d_{0,j} \\ d_{1,j} \\ d_{2,j} \\ d_{3,j} \end{bmatrix} = \begin{bmatrix} 02 & 03 & 01 & 01 \\ 01 & 02 & 03 & 01 \\ 01 & 01 & 02 & 03 \\ 03 & 01 & 01 & 02 \end{bmatrix} \begin{bmatrix} c_{0,j} \\ c_{1,j} \\ c_{2,j} \\ c_{3,j} \end{bmatrix}$
AddRoundKey	$\begin{bmatrix} e_{0,j} \\ e_{1,j} \\ e_{2,j} \\ e_{3,j} \end{bmatrix} = \begin{bmatrix} d_{0,j} \\ d_{1,j} \\ d_{2,j} \\ d_{3,j} \end{bmatrix} \oplus \begin{bmatrix} k_{0,j} \\ k_{1,j} \\ k_{2,j} \\ k_{3,j} \end{bmatrix}$

In the ShiftRows equation, the column indices are taken mod 4. We can combine all of these expressions into a single equation:

$$\begin{bmatrix} e_{0,j} \\ e_{1,j} \\ e_{2,j} \\ e_{3,j} \end{bmatrix} = \begin{bmatrix} 02 & 03 & 01 & 01 \\ 01 & 02 & 03 & 01 \\ 01 & 01 & 02 & 03 \\ 03 & 01 & 01 & 02 \end{bmatrix} \begin{bmatrix} \mathrm{S}[a_{0,j}] \\ \mathrm{S}[a_{1,j-1}] \\ \mathrm{S}[a_{2,j-2}] \\ \mathrm{S}[a_{3,j-3}] \end{bmatrix} \oplus \begin{bmatrix} k_{0,j} \\ k_{1,j} \\ k_{2,j} \\ k_{3,j} \end{bmatrix}$$

$$= \left(\begin{bmatrix} 02 \\ 01 \\ 01 \\ 03 \end{bmatrix} \cdot \mathrm{S}[a_{0,j}] \right) \oplus \left(\begin{bmatrix} 03 \\ 02 \\ 01 \\ 01 \end{bmatrix} \cdot \mathrm{S}[a_{1,j-1}] \right) \oplus \left(\begin{bmatrix} 01 \\ 03 \\ 02 \\ 01 \end{bmatrix} \cdot \mathrm{S}[a_{2,j-2}] \right)$$

$$\oplus \left(\begin{bmatrix} 01 \\ 01 \\ 03 \\ 02 \end{bmatrix} \cdot \mathrm{S}[a_{3,j-3}] \right) \oplus \begin{bmatrix} k_{0,j} \\ k_{1,j} \\ k_{2,j} \\ k_{3,j} \end{bmatrix}$$

In the second equation, we are expressing the matrix multiplication as a linear combination of vectors. We define four 256-word (1024-byte) tables as follows.

$T_0[x] = \left(\begin{bmatrix} 02 \\ 01 \\ 01 \\ 03 \end{bmatrix} \cdot \mathrm{S}[x] \right)$	$T_1[x] = \left(\begin{bmatrix} 03 \\ 02 \\ 01 \\ 01 \end{bmatrix} \cdot \mathrm{S}[x] \right)$	$T_2[x] = \left(\begin{bmatrix} 01 \\ 03 \\ 02 \\ 01 \end{bmatrix} \cdot \mathrm{S}[x] \right)$	$T_3[x] = \left(\begin{bmatrix} 01 \\ 01 \\ 03 \\ 02 \end{bmatrix} \cdot \mathrm{S}[x] \right)$

Thus, each table takes as input a byte value and produces a column vector (a 32-bit word) that is a function of the S-box entry for that byte value. These tables can be calculated in advance.

We can define a round function operating on a column in the following fashion.

$$\begin{bmatrix} s'_{0,j} \\ s'_{1,j} \\ s'_{2,j} \\ s'_{3,j} \end{bmatrix} = T_0[s_{0,j}] \oplus T_1[s_{1,j-1}] \oplus T_2[s_{2,j-2}] \oplus T_3[s_{3,j-3}] \oplus \begin{bmatrix} k_{0,j} \\ k_{1,j} \\ k_{2,j} \\ k_{3,j} \end{bmatrix}$$

As a result, an implementation based on the preceding equation requires only four table lookups and four XORs per column per round, plus 4 Kbytes to store the table. The developers of Rijndael believe that this compact, efficient implementation was probably one of the most important factors in the selection of Rijndael for AES.

6.7 KEY TERMS, REVIEW QUESTIONS, AND PROBLEMS

Key Terms

Advanced Encryption Standard (AES) avalanche effect field	finite field irreducible polynomial key expansion	National Institute of Standards and Technology (NIST) Rijndael S-box

Review Questions

6.1 What was the original set of criteria used by NIST to evaluate candidate AES ciphers?
6.2 What was the final set of criteria used by NIST to evaluate candidate AES ciphers?
6.3 List and briefly define the four stages used in AES.
6.4 What is the purpose of the **State** array?
6.5 How is the S-box constructed?
6.6 Briefly describe SubBytes.
6.7 Briefly describe InvShiftRows.
6.8 How many bytes in **State** are affected by ShiftRows?
6.9 Briefly describe MixColumns.
6.10 How is the inverse add round key transformation identical to the forward add round key transformation?
6.11 Briefly describe the key expansion algorithm.
6.12 What is the difference between SubBytes and SubWord?
6.13 What is the difference between ShiftRows and RotWord?
6.14 What is the need of the equivalent inverse cipher?

Problems

6.1 In the discussion of MixColumns and InvMixColumns, it was stated that

$$b(x) = a^{-1}(x) \bmod (x^4 + 1)$$

where $a(x) = \{03\}x^3 + \{01\}x^2 + \{01\}x + \{02\}$ and $b(x) = \{0B\}x^3 + \{0D\}x^2 + \{09\}x + \{0E.\}$ Show that this is true.

6.2 a. What is $\{01\}^{-1}$ in GF(2^8)?
b. Verify the entry for {01} in the S-box.

6.3 Show the first eight words of the key expansion for a 128-bit key of all ones.

6.4 Given the plaintext {000102030405060708090A0B0C0D0E0F} and the key {01010101010101010101010101010101}:
a. Show the original contents of State, displayed as a 4 × 4 matrix.
b. Show the value of State after initial AddRoundKey.
c. Show the value of State after SubBytes.
d. Show the value of State after ShiftRows.
e. Show the value of State after MixColumns.

6.5 Verify Equation (6.11) in Appendix 6A. That is, show that $x^i \bmod (x^4 + 1) = x^{i \bmod 4}$.

6.6 Compare AES to DES. For each of the following elements of DES, indicate the comparable element in AES or explain why it is not needed in AES.

a. XOR of subkey material with the input to the f function
b. XOR of the f function output with the left half of the block
c. f function
d. permutation P
e. swapping of halves of the block

6.7 In the subsection on implementation aspects, it is mentioned that the use of tables helps thwart timing attacks. Suggest an alternative technique.

6.8 In the subsection on implementation aspects, a single algebraic equation is developed that describes the four stages of a typical round of the encryption algorithm. Provide the equivalent equation for the tenth round.

6.9 Compute the output of the MixColumns transformation for the following sequence of input bytes "67 89 AB CD". Apply the InvMixColumns transformation to the obtained result to verify your calculations. Change the first byte of the input from "67" to "77" perform the MixColumns transformation again for the new input, and determine how many bits have changed in the output.
Note: You can perform all calculations by hand or write a program supporting these computations. If you choose to write a program, it should be written entirely by you; no use of libraries or public domain source code is allowed in this assignment.

6.10 Use the key 1010 0111 0011 1011 to encrypt the plaintext "ok" as expressed in ASCII as 0110 1111 0110 1011. The designers of S-AES got the ciphertext 0000 0111 0011 1000. Do you?

6.11 Show that the matrix given here, with entries in GF(2^4), is the inverse of the matrix used in the MixColumns step of S-AES.

$$\begin{pmatrix} x^3 + 1 & x \\ x & x^3 + 1 \end{pmatrix}$$

6.12 Carefully write up a complete decryption of the ciphertext 0011 1110 1111 1011 using the key 1010 1001 1100 0011 and the S-AES algorithm. You should get the plaintext we started with in Problem 6.10. Note that the inverse of the S-boxes can be done with a reverse table lookup. The inverse of the MixColumns step is given by the matrix in the previous problem.

6.13 Demonstrate that Equation (6.9) is equivalent to Equation (6.4).

Programming Problems

6.14 Create software that can encrypt and decrypt using S-AES. *Test data*: A binary plaintext of 0110 1111 0110 1011 encrypted with a binary key of 1010 0111 0011 1011 should give a binary ciphertext of 0000 0111 0011 1000. Decryption should work correspondingly.

6.15 Implement a differential cryptanalysis attack on 1-round S-AES.

APPENDIX 6A POLYNOMIALS WITH COEFFICIENTS IN GF(2^8)

In Section 5.5, we discussed polynomial arithmetic in which the coefficients are in Z_p and the polynomials are defined modulo a polynomial $m(x)$ whose highest power is some integer n. In this case, addition and multiplication of coefficients occurred within the field Z_p; that is, addition and multiplication were performed modulo p.

The AES document defines polynomial arithmetic for polynomials of degree 3 or less with coefficients in GF(2^8). The following rules apply.

1. Addition is performed by adding corresponding coefficients in GF(2^8). As was pointed out Section 5.4, if we treat the elements of GF(2^8) as 8-bit strings, then addition is equivalent to the XOR operation. So, if we have

$$a(x) = a_3x^3 + a_2x^2 + a_1x + a_0 \tag{6.10}$$

and

$$b(x) = b_3x^3 + b_2x^2 + b_1x + b_0 \tag{6.11}$$

then

$$a(x) + b(x) = (a_3 \oplus b_3)x^3 + (a_2 \oplus b_2)x^2 + (a_1 \oplus b_1)x + (a_0 \oplus b_0)$$

2. Multiplication is performed as in ordinary polynomial multiplication with two refinements:

   a. Coefficients are multiplied in GF(2^8).

   b. The resulting polynomial is reduced mod $(x^4 + 1)$.

We need to keep straight which polynomial we are talking about. Recall from Section 5.6 that each element of GF(2^8) is a polynomial of degree 7 or less with binary coefficients, and multiplication is carried out modulo a polynomial of degree 8. Equivalently, each element of GF(2^8) can be viewed as an 8-bit byte whose bit values correspond to the binary coefficients of the corresponding polynomial. For the sets defined in this section, we are defining a polynomial ring in which each element of this ring is a polynomial of degree 3 or less with coefficients in GF(2^8), and multiplication is carried out modulo a polynomial of degree 4. Equivalently, each element of this ring can be viewed as a 4-byte word whose byte values are elements of GF(2^8) that correspond to the 8-bit coefficients of the corresponding polynomial.

We denote the modular product of $a(x)$ and $b(x)$ by $a(x) \oplus b(x)$. To compute $d(x) = a(x) \oplus b(x)$, the first step is to perform a multiplication without the modulo operation and to collect coefficients of like powers. Let us express this as $c(x) = a(x) \times b(x)$. Then

$$c(x) = c_6x^6 + c_5x^5 + c_4x^4 + c_3x^3 + c_2x^2 + c_1x + c_0 \tag{6.12}$$

where

$$c_0 = a_0 \cdot b_0 \qquad c_4 = (a_3 \cdot b_1) \oplus (a_2 \cdot b_2) \oplus (a_1 \cdot b_3)$$
$$c_1 = (a_1 \cdot b_0) \oplus (a_0 \cdot b_1) \qquad c_5 = (a_3 \cdot b_2) \oplus (a_2 \cdot b_3)$$
$$c_2 = (a_2 \cdot b_0) \oplus (a_1 \cdot b_1) \oplus (a_0 \cdot b_2) \qquad c_6 = a_3 \cdot b_3$$
$$c_3 = (a_3 \cdot b_0) \oplus (a_2 \cdot b_1) \oplus (a_1 \cdot b_2) \oplus (a_0 \cdot b_3)$$

The final step is to perform the modulo operation

$$d(x) = c(x) \bmod (x^4 + 1)$$

That is, $d(x)$ must satisfy the equation

$$c(x) = [(x^4 + 1) \times q(x)] \oplus d(x)$$

such that the degree of $d(x)$ is 3 or less.

A practical technique for performing multiplication over this polynomial ring is based on the observation that

$$x^i \bmod (x^4 + 1) = x^{i \bmod 4} \tag{6.13}$$

If we now combine Equations (6.12) and (6.13), we end up with

$$\begin{aligned} d(x) &= c(x) \bmod (x^4 + 1) \\ &= [c_6x^6 + c_5x^5 + c_4x^4 + c_3x^3 + c_2x^2 + c_1x + c_0] \bmod (x^4 + 1) \\ &= c_3x^3 + (c_2 \oplus c_6)x^2 + (c_1 \oplus c_5)x + (c_0 \oplus c_4) \end{aligned}$$

Expanding the c_i coefficients, we have the following equations for the coefficients of $d(x)$.

$$\begin{aligned} d_0 &= (a_0 \cdot b_0) \oplus (a_3 \cdot b_1) \oplus (a_2 \cdot b_2) \oplus (a_1 \cdot b_3) \\ d_1 &= (a_1 \cdot b_0) \oplus (a_0 \cdot b_1) \oplus (a_3 \cdot b_2) \oplus (a_2 \cdot b_3) \\ d_2 &= (a_2 \cdot b_0) \oplus (a_1 \cdot b_1) \oplus (a_0 \cdot b_2) \oplus (a_3 \cdot b_3) \\ d_3 &= (a_3 \cdot b_0) \oplus (a_2 \cdot b_1) \oplus (a_1 \cdot b_2) \oplus (a_0 \cdot b_3) \end{aligned}$$

This can be written in matrix form:

$$\begin{bmatrix} d_0 \\ d_1 \\ d_2 \\ d_3 \end{bmatrix} = \begin{bmatrix} a_0 & a_3 & a_2 & a_1 \\ a_1 & a_0 & a_3 & a_2 \\ a_2 & a_1 & a_0 & a_3 \\ a_3 & a_2 & a_1 & a_0 \end{bmatrix} \begin{bmatrix} b_0 \\ b_1 \\ b_2 \\ b_3 \end{bmatrix} \tag{6.14}$$

MixColumns Transformation

In the discussion of MixColumns, it was stated that there were two equivalent ways of defining the transformation. The first is the matrix multiplication shown in Equation (6.3), which is repeated here:

$$\begin{bmatrix} 02 & 03 & 01 & 01 \\ 01 & 02 & 03 & 01 \\ 01 & 01 & 02 & 03 \\ 03 & 01 & 01 & 02 \end{bmatrix} \begin{bmatrix} s_{0,0} & s_{0,1} & s_{0,2} & s_{0,3} \\ s_{1,0} & s_{1,1} & s_{1,2} & s_{1,3} \\ s_{2,0} & s_{2,1} & s_{2,2} & s_{2,3} \\ s_{3,0} & s_{3,1} & s_{3,2} & s_{3,3} \end{bmatrix} = \begin{bmatrix} s'_{0,0} & s'_{0,1} & s'_{0,2} & s'_{0,3} \\ s'_{1,0} & s'_{1,1} & s'_{1,2} & s'_{1,3} \\ s'_{2,0} & s'_{2,1} & s'_{2,2} & s'_{2,3} \\ s'_{3,0} & s'_{3,1} & s'_{3,2} & s'_{3,3} \end{bmatrix}$$

The second method is to treat each column of **State** as a four-term polynomial with coefficients in GF(2^8). Each column is multiplied modulo $(x^4 + 1)$ by the fixed polynomial $a(x)$, given by

$$a(x) = \{03\}x^3 + \{01\}x^2 + \{01\}x + \{02\}$$

From Equation (6.10), we have $a_3 = \{03\}$; $a_2 = \{01\}$; $a_1 = \{01\}$; and $a_0 = \{02\}$. For the jth column of **State**, we have the polynomial $\text{col}_j(x) = s_{3,j}x^3 + s_{2,j}x^2 + s_{1,j}x + s_{0,j}$. Substituting into Equation (6.14), we can express $d(x) = a(x) \times \text{col}_j(x)$ as

$$\begin{bmatrix} d_0 \\ d_1 \\ d_2 \\ d_3 \end{bmatrix} = \begin{bmatrix} a_0 & a_3 & a_2 & a_1 \\ a_1 & a_0 & a_3 & a_2 \\ a_2 & a_1 & a_0 & a_3 \\ a_3 & a_2 & a_1 & a_0 \end{bmatrix} \begin{bmatrix} s_{0,j} \\ s_{1,j} \\ s_{2,j} \\ s_{3,j} \end{bmatrix} = \begin{bmatrix} 02 & 03 & 01 & 01 \\ 01 & 02 & 03 & 01 \\ 01 & 01 & 02 & 03 \\ 03 & 01 & 01 & 02 \end{bmatrix} \begin{bmatrix} s_{0,j} \\ s_{1,j} \\ s_{2,j} \\ s_{3,j} \end{bmatrix}$$

which is equivalent to Equation (6.3).

Multiplication by x

Consider the multiplication of a polynomial in the ring by x: $c(x) = x \oplus b(x)$. We have

$$\begin{aligned} c(x) = x \oplus b(x) &= [x \times (b_3x^3 + b_2x^2 + b_1x + b_0] \bmod (x^4 + 1) \\ &= (b_3x^4 + b_2x^3 + b_1x^2 + b_0x) \bmod (x^4 + 1) \\ &= b_2x^3 + b_1x^2 + b_0x + b_3 \end{aligned}$$

Thus, multiplication by x corresponds to a 1-byte circular left shift of the 4 bytes in the word representing the polynomial. If we represent the polynomial as a 4-byte column vector, then we have

$$\begin{bmatrix} c_0 \\ c_1 \\ c_2 \\ c_3 \end{bmatrix} = \begin{bmatrix} 00 & 00 & 00 & 01 \\ 01 & 00 & 00 & 00 \\ 00 & 01 & 00 & 00 \\ 00 & 00 & 01 & 00 \end{bmatrix} \begin{bmatrix} b_0 \\ b_1 \\ b_2 \\ b_3 \end{bmatrix}$$

CHAPTER 7

Block Cipher Operation

LEARNING OBJECTIVES

After studying this chapter, you should be able to:

- Analyze the security of multiple encryption schemes.
- Explain the meet-in-the-middle attack.
- Compare and contrast ECB, CBC, CFB, OFB, and counter modes of operation.
- Present an overview of the XTS-AES mode of operation.

This chapter continues our discussion of symmetric ciphers. We begin with the topic of multiple encryption, looking in particular at the most widely used multiple-encryption scheme: triple DES.

The chapter next turns to the subject of block cipher modes of operation. We find that there are a number of different ways to apply a block cipher to plaintext, each with its own advantages and particular applications.

7.1 MULTIPLE ENCRYPTION AND TRIPLE DES

Because of its vulnerability to brute-force attack, DES, once the most widely used symmetric cipher, has been largely replaced by stronger encryption schemes. Two approaches have been taken. One approach is to design a completely new algorithm that is resistant to both cryptanalytic and brute-force attacks, of which AES is a prime example. Another alternative, which preserves the existing investment in software and equipment, is to use multiple encryption with DES and multiple keys. We begin by examining the simplest example of this second alternative. We then look at the widely accepted triple DES (3DES) algorithm.

Double DES

The simplest form of multiple encryption has two encryption stages and two keys (Figure 7.1a). Given a plaintext P and two encryption keys K_1 and K_2, ciphertext C is generated as

$$C = \mathrm{E}(K_2, \mathrm{E}(K_1, P))$$

Decryption requires that the keys be applied in reverse order:

$$P = \mathrm{D}(K_1, \mathrm{D}(K_2, C))$$

For DES, this scheme apparently involves a key length of $56 \times 2 = 112$ bits, and should result in a dramatic increase in cryptographic strength. But we need to examine the algorithm more closely.

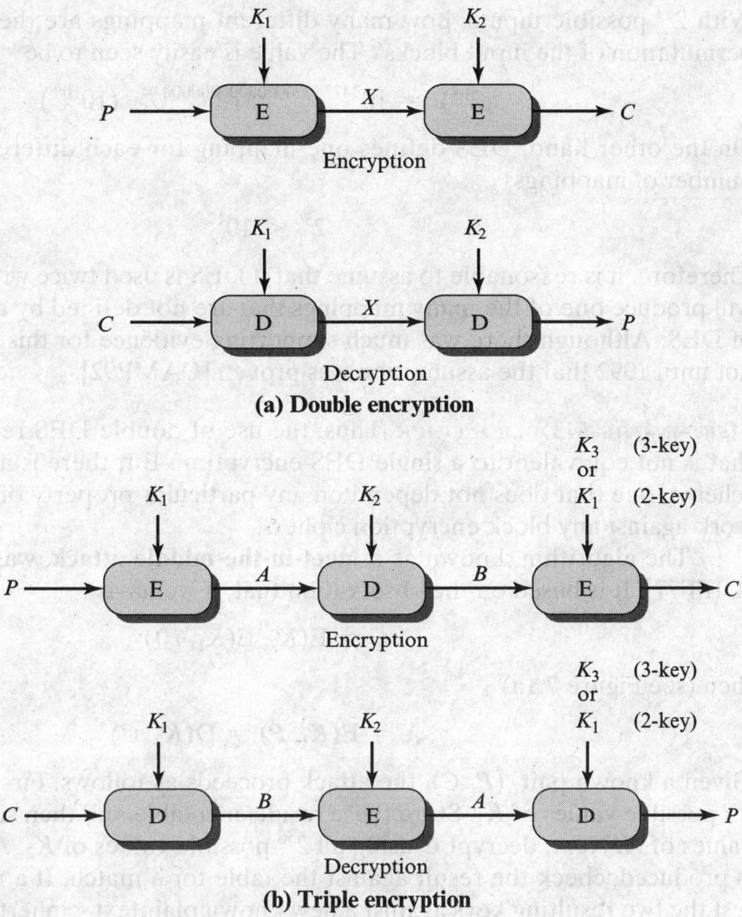

Figure 7.1 Multiple Encryption

REDUCTION TO A SINGLE STAGE Suppose it were true for DES, for all 56-bit key values, that given any two keys K_1 and K_2, it would be possible to find a key K_3 such that

$$E(K_2, E(K_1, P)) = E(K_3, P) \quad (7.1)$$

If this were the case, then double encryption, and indeed any number of stages of multiple encryption with DES, would be useless because the result would be equivalent to a single encryption with a single 56-bit key.

On the face of it, it does not appear that Equation (7.1) is likely to hold. Consider that encryption with DES is a mapping of 64-bit blocks to 64-bit blocks. In fact, the mapping can be viewed as a permutation. That is, if we consider all 2^{64} possible input blocks, DES encryption with a specific key will map each block into a unique 64-bit block. Otherwise, if, say, two given input blocks mapped to the same output block, then decryption to recover the original plaintext would be impossible.

With 2^{64} possible inputs, how many different mappings are there that generate a permutation of the input blocks? The value is easily seen to be

$$(2^{64})! = 10^{347380000000000000000} > (10^{10^{20}})$$

On the other hand, DES defines one mapping for each different key, for a total number of mappings:

$$2^{56} < 10^{17}$$

Therefore, it is reasonable to assume that if DES is used twice with different keys, it will produce one of the many mappings that are not defined by a single application of DES. Although there was much supporting evidence for this assumption, it was not until 1992 that the assumption was proven [CAMP92].

MEET-IN-THE-MIDDLE ATTACK Thus, the use of double DES results in a mapping that is not equivalent to a single DES encryption. But there is a way to attack this scheme, one that does not depend on any particular property of DES but that will work against any block encryption cipher.

The algorithm, known as a **meet-in-the-middle attack**, was first described in [DIFF77]. It is based on the observation that, if we have

$$C = \mathrm{E}(K_2, \mathrm{E}(K_1, P))$$

then (see Figure 7.1a)

$$X = \mathrm{E}(K_1, P) = \mathrm{D}(K_2, C)$$

Given a known pair, (P, C), the attack proceeds as follows. First, encrypt P for all 2^{56} possible values of K_1. Store these results in a table and then sort the table by the values of X. Next, decrypt C using all 2^{56} possible values of K_2. As each decryption is produced, check the result against the table for a match. If a match occurs, then test the two resulting keys against a new known plaintext–ciphertext pair. If the two keys produce the correct ciphertext, accept them as the correct keys.

For any given plaintext P, there are 2^{64} possible ciphertext values that could be produced by double DES. Double DES uses, in effect, a 112-bit key, so that there are 2^{112} possible keys. Therefore, for a given plaintext P, the maximum number of different 112-bit keys that could produce a given ciphertext C is $2^{112}/2^{64} = 2^{48}$. Thus, the foregoing procedure can produce about 2^{48} false alarms on the first (P, C) pair. A similar argument indicates that with an additional 64 bits of known plaintext and ciphertext, the false alarm rate is reduced to $2^{48-64} = 2^{-16}$. Put another way, if the meet-in-the-middle attack is performed on two blocks of known plaintext–ciphertext, the probability that the correct keys are determined is $1 - 2^{-16}$. The result is that a known plaintext attack will succeed against double DES, which has a key size of 112 bits, with an effort on the order of 2^{56}, which is not much more than the 2^{55} required for single DES.

Triple DES with Two Keys

An obvious counter to the meet-in-the-middle attack is to use three stages of encryption with three different keys. Using DES as the underlying algorithm, this approach is commonly referred to as 3DES, or Triple Data Encryption

Algorithm (TDEA). As shown in Figure 7.1b, there are two versions of 3DES; one using two keys and one using three keys. NIST SP 800-67 (*Recommendation for the Triple Data Encryption Block Cipher,* January 2012) defines the two-key and three-key versions. We look first at the strength of the two-key version and then examine the three-key version.

Two-key triple encryption was first proposed by Tuchman [TUCH79]. The function follows an encrypt-decrypt-encrypt (EDE) sequence (Figure 7.1b):

$$C = \mathrm{E}(K_1, \mathrm{D}(K_2, \mathrm{E}(K_1, P)))$$
$$P = \mathrm{D}(K_1, \mathrm{E}(K_2, \mathrm{D}(K_1, C)))$$

There is no cryptographic significance to the use of decryption for the second stage. Its only advantage is that it allows users of 3DES to decrypt data encrypted by users of the older single DES:

$$C = \mathrm{E}(K_1, \mathrm{D}(K_1, \mathrm{E}(K_1, P))) = \mathrm{E}(K_1, P)$$
$$P = \mathrm{D}(K_1, \mathrm{E}(K_1, \mathrm{D}(K_1, C))) = \mathrm{D}(K_1, C)$$

3DES with two keys is a relatively popular alternative to DES and has been adopted for use in the key management standards ANSI X9.17 and ISO 8732.[1]

Currently, there are no practical cryptanalytic attacks on 3DES. Coppersmith [COPP94] notes that the cost of a brute-force key search on 3DES is on the order of $2^{112} \approx (5 \times 10^{33})$ and estimates that the cost of differential cryptanalysis suffers an exponential growth, compared to single DES, exceeding 10^{52}.

It is worth looking at several proposed attacks on 3DES that, although not practical, give a flavor for the types of attacks that have been considered and that could form the basis for more successful future attacks.

The first serious proposal came from Merkle and Hellman [MERK81]. Their plan involves finding plaintext values that produce a first intermediate value of $A = 0$ (Figure 7.1b) and then using the meet-in-the-middle attack to determine the two keys. The level of effort is 2^{56}, but the technique requires 2^{56} chosen plaintext–ciphertext pairs, which is a number unlikely to be provided by the holder of the keys.

A known-plaintext attack is outlined in [VANO90]. This method is an improvement over the chosen-plaintext approach but requires more effort. The attack is based on the observation that if we know A and C (Figure 7.1b), then the problem reduces to that of an attack on double DES. Of course, the attacker does not know A, even if P and C are known, as long as the two keys are unknown. However, the attacker can choose a potential value of A and then try to find a known (P, C) pair that produces A. The attack proceeds as follows.

1. Obtain n (P, C) pairs. This is the known plaintext. Place these in a table (Table 1) sorted on the values of P (Figure 7.2b).

[1]American National Standards Institute (ANSI): *Financial Institution Key Management (Wholesale)*. From its title, X9.17 appears to be a somewhat obscure standard. Yet a number of techniques specified in this standard have been adopted for use in other standards and applications, as we shall see throughout this book.

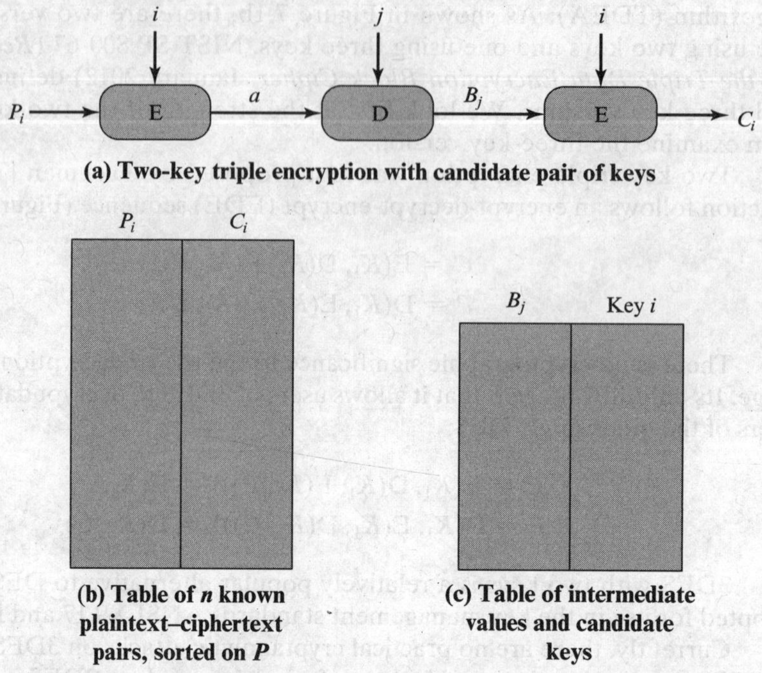

Figure 7.2 Known-Plaintext Attack on Triple DES

2. Pick an arbitrary value a for A, and create a second table (Figure 7.2c) with entries defined in the following fashion. For each of the 2^{56} possible keys $K_1 = i$, calculate the plaintext value P_i such that

$$P_i = D(i, a)$$

For each P_i that matches an entry in Table 1, create an entry in Table 2 consisting of the K_1 value and the value of B that is produced for the (P, C) pair from Table 1, assuming that value of K_1:

$$B = D(i, C)$$

At the end of this step, sort Table 2 on the values of B.

3. We now have a number of candidate values of K_1 in Table 2 and are in a position to search for a value of K_2. For each of the 2^{56} possible keys $K_2 = j$, calculate the second intermediate value for our chosen value of a:

$$B_j = D(j, a)$$

At each step, look up B_j in Table 2. If there is a match, then the corresponding key i from Table 2 plus this value of j are candidate values for the unknown keys (K_1, K_2). Why? Because we have found a pair of keys (i, j) that produce a known (P, C) pair (Figure 7.2a).

4. Test each candidate pair of keys (i, j) on a few other plaintext–ciphertext pairs. If a pair of keys produces the desired ciphertext, the task is complete. If no pair succeeds, repeat from step 1 with a new value of a.

For a given known (P, C), the probability of selecting the unique value of a that leads to success is $1/2^{64}$. Thus, given n (P, C) pairs, the probability of success for a single selected value of a is $n/2^{64}$. A basic result from probability theory is that the expected number of draws required to draw one red ball out of a bin containing n red balls and $N - n$ green balls is $(N + 1)/(n + 1)$ if the balls are not replaced. So the expected number of values of a that must be tried is, for large n,

$$\frac{2^{64} + 1}{n + 1} \approx \frac{2^{64}}{n}$$

Thus, the expected running time of the attack is on the order of

$$(2^{56})\frac{2^{64}}{n} = 2^{120-\log_2 n}$$

Triple DES with Three Keys

Although the attacks just described appear impractical, anyone using two-key 3DES may feel some concern. Thus, many researchers now feel that three-key 3DES is the preferred alternative (e.g., [KALI96a]). In SP 800-57, Part 1 (*Recommendation for Key Management—Part 1: General,* July 2012) NIST recommends that 2-key 3DES be retired as soon as practical and replaced with 3-key 3DES.

Three-key 3DES is defined as

$$C = E(K_3, D(K_2, E(K_1, P)))$$

Backward compatibility with DES is provided by putting $K_3 = K_2$ or $K_1 = K_2$. One might expect that 3TDEA would provide $56 \cdot 3 = 168$ bits of strength. However, there is an attack on 3TDEA that reduces the strength to the work that would be involved in exhausting a 112-bit key [MERK81].

A number of Internet-based applications have adopted three-key 3DES, including PGP and S/MIME, both discussed in Chapter 19.

7.2 ELECTRONIC CODEBOOK

A block cipher takes a fixed-length block of text of length b bits and a key as input and produces a b-bit block of ciphertext. If the amount of plaintext to be encrypted is greater than b bits, then the block cipher can still be used by breaking the plaintext up into b-bit blocks. When multiple blocks of plaintext are encrypted using the same key, a number of security issues arise. To apply a block cipher in a variety of applications, five *modes of operation* have been defined by NIST (SP 800-38A). In essence, a mode of operation is a technique for enhancing the effect of a cryptographic algorithm or adapting the algorithm for an application, such as applying a block cipher to a sequence of data blocks or a data stream. The five modes are intended to cover a wide variety of applications of encryption for which a block cipher could be used. These modes are intended for use with any symmetric block cipher, including triple DES and AES. The modes are summarized in Table 7.1 and described in this and the following sections.

Table 7.1 Block Cipher Modes of Operation

Mode	Description	Typical Application
Electronic Codebook (ECB)	Each block of plaintext bits is encoded independently using the same key.	• Secure transmission of single values (e.g., an encryption key)
Cipher Block Chaining (CBC)	The input to the encryption algorithm is the XOR of the next block of plaintext and the preceding block of ciphertext.	• General-purpose block-oriented transmission • Authentication
Cipher Feedback (CFB)	Input is processed *s* bits at a time. Preceding ciphertext is used as input to the encryption algorithm to produce pseudorandom output, which is XORed with plaintext to produce next unit of ciphertext.	• General-purpose stream-oriented transmission • Authentication
Output Feedback (OFB)	Similar to CFB, except that the input to the encryption algorithm is the preceding encryption output, and full blocks are used.	• Stream-oriented transmission over noisy channel (e.g., satellite communication)
Counter (CTR)	Each block of plaintext is XORed with an encrypted counter. The counter is incremented for each subsequent block.	• General-purpose block-oriented transmission • Useful for high-speed requirements

The simplest mode is the **electronic codebook (ECB)** mode, in which plaintext is handled one block at a time and each block of plaintext is encrypted using the same key (Figure 7.3). The term *codebook* is used because, for a given key, there is a unique ciphertext for every *b*-bit block of plaintext. Therefore, we can imagine a gigantic codebook in which there is an entry for every possible *b*-bit plaintext pattern showing its corresponding ciphertext.

For a message longer than *b* bits, the procedure is simply to break the message into *b*-bit blocks, padding the last block if necessary. Decryption is performed one block at a time, always using the same key. In Figure 7.3, the plaintext (padded as necessary) consists of a sequence of *b*-bit blocks, $P_1, P_2, \ldots, P_N$; the corresponding sequence of ciphertext blocks is $C_1, C_2, \ldots, C_N$. We can define ECB mode as follows.

ECB	$C_j = E(K, P_j)$	$j = 1, \ldots, N$	$P_j = D(K, C_j)$	$j = 1, \ldots, N$

The ECB mode should be used only to secure messages shorter than a single block of underlying cipher (i.e., 64 bits for 3DES and 128 bits for AES), such as to encrypt a secret key. Because in most of the cases messages are longer than the encryption block mode, this mode has a minimum practical value.

The most significant characteristic of ECB is that if the same *b*-bit block of plaintext appears more than once in the message, it always produces the same ciphertext.

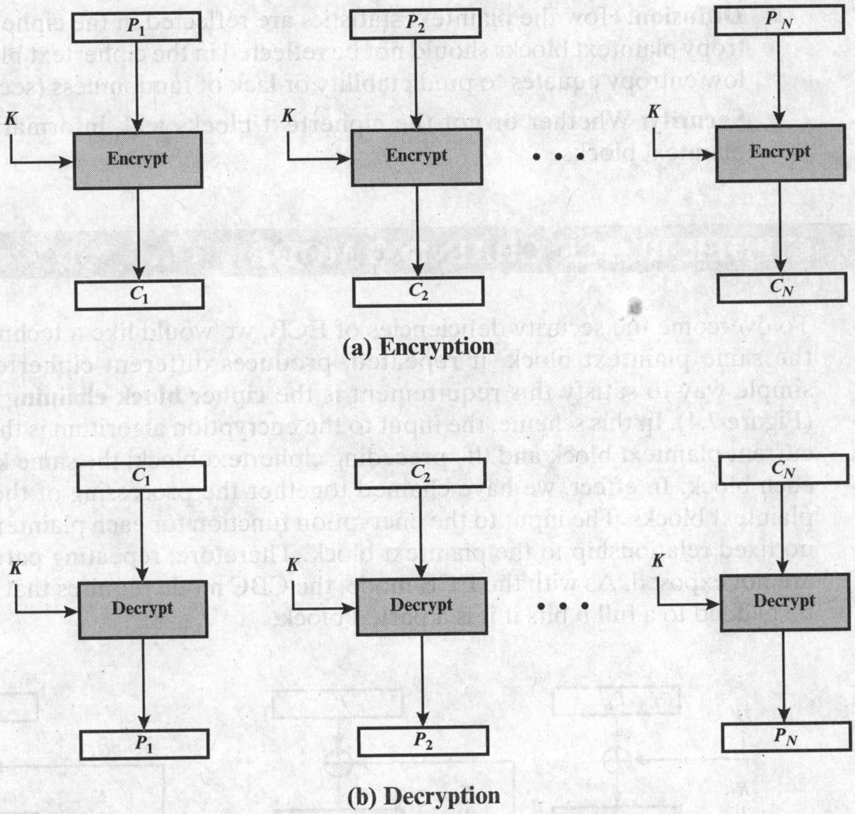

Figure 7.3 Electronic Codebook (ECB) Mode

For lengthy messages, the ECB mode may not be secure. If the message is highly structured, it may be possible for a cryptanalyst to exploit these regularities. For example, if it is known that the message always starts out with certain predefined fields, then the cryptanalyst may have a number of known plaintext–ciphertext pairs to work with. If the message has repetitive elements with a period of repetition a multiple of b bits, then these elements can be identified by the analyst. This may help in the analysis or may provide an opportunity for substituting or rearranging blocks.

We now turn to more complex modes of operation. [KNUD00] lists the following criteria and properties for evaluating and constructing block cipher modes of operation that are superior to ECB:

- **Overhead:** The additional operations for the encryption and decryption operation when compared to encrypting and decrypting in the ECB mode.
- **Error recovery:** The property that an error in the ith ciphertext block is inherited by only a few plaintext blocks after which the mode resynchronizes.
- **Error propagation:** The property that an error in the ith ciphertext block is inherited by the ith and all subsequent plaintext blocks. What is meant here is a bit error that occurs in the transmission of a ciphertext block, not a computational error in the encryption of a plaintext block.

- **Diffusion:** How the plaintext statistics are reflected in the ciphertext. Low entropy plaintext blocks should not be reflected in the ciphertext blocks. Roughly, low entropy equates to predictability or lack of randomness (see Appendix F).
- **Security:** Whether or not the ciphertext blocks leak information about the plaintext blocks.

7.3 CIPHER BLOCK CHAINING MODE

To overcome the security deficiencies of ECB, we would like a technique in which the same plaintext block, if repeated, produces different ciphertext blocks. A simple way to satisfy this requirement is the **cipher block chaining (CBC)** mode (Figure 7.4). In this scheme, the input to the encryption algorithm is the XOR of the current plaintext block and the preceding ciphertext block; the same key is used for each block. In effect, we have chained together the processing of the sequence of plaintext blocks. The input to the encryption function for each plaintext block bears no fixed relationship to the plaintext block. Therefore, repeating patterns of b bits are not exposed. As with the ECB mode, the CBC mode requires that the last block be padded to a full b bits if it is a partial block.

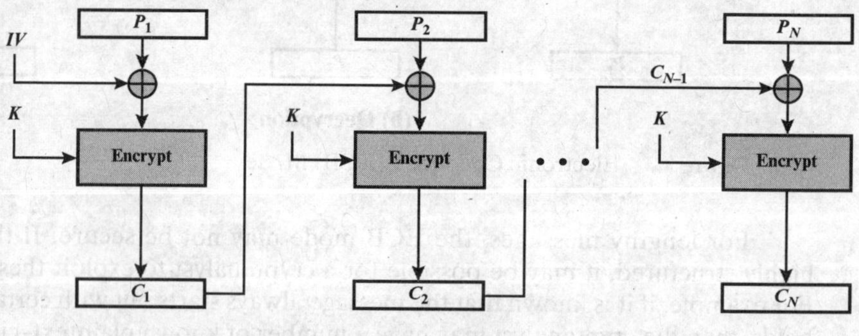

(a) Encryption

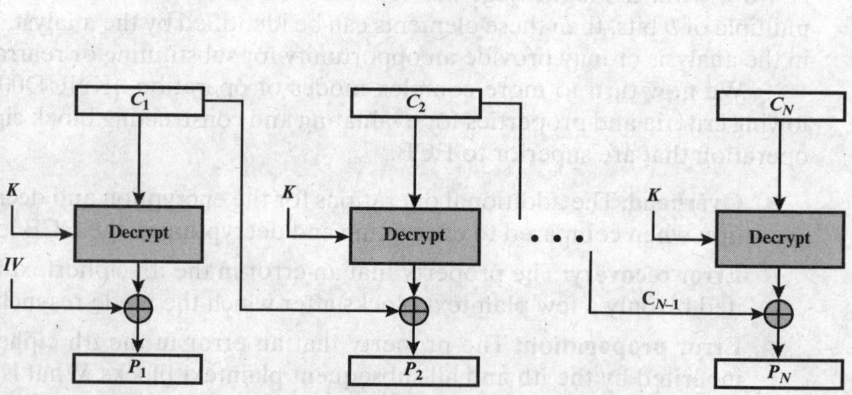

(b) Decryption

Figure 7.4 Cipher Block Chaining (CBC) Mode

For decryption, each cipher block is passed through the decryption algorithm. The result is XORed with the preceding ciphertext block to produce the plaintext block. To see that this works, we can write

$$C_j = E(K, [C_{j-1} \oplus P_j])$$

Then

$$D(K, C_j) = D(K, E(K, [C_{j-1} \oplus P_j]))$$
$$D(K, C_j) = C_{j-1} \oplus P_j$$
$$C_{j-1} \oplus D(K, C_j) = C_{j-1} \oplus C_{j-1} \oplus P_j = P_j$$

To produce the first block of ciphertext, an initialization vector (IV) is XORed with the first block of plaintext. On decryption, the IV is XORed with the output of the decryption algorithm to recover the first block of plaintext. The IV is a data block that is the same size as the cipher block. We can define CBC mode as

CBC	$C_1 = E(K, [P_1 \oplus IV])$ $C_j = E(K, [P_j \oplus C_{j-1}])j = 2, \ldots, N$	$P_1 = D(K, C_1) \oplus IV$ $P_j = D(K, C_j) \oplus C_{j-1} j = 2, \ldots, N$

The IV must be known to both the sender and receiver but be unpredictable by a third party. In particular, for any given plaintext, it must not be possible to predict the IV that will be associated to the plaintext in advance of the generation of the IV. For maximum security, the IV should be protected against unauthorized changes. This could be done by sending the IV using ECB encryption. One reason for protecting the IV is as follows: If an opponent is able to fool the receiver into using a different value for IV, then the opponent is able to invert selected bits in the first block of plaintext. To see this, consider

$$C_1 = E(K, [IV \oplus P_1])$$
$$P_1 = IV \oplus D(K, C_1)$$

Now use the notation that $X[i]$ denotes the ith bit of the b-bit quantity X. Then

$$P_1[i] = IV[i] \oplus D(K, C_1)[i]$$

Then, using the properties of XOR, we can state

$$P_1[i]' = IV[i]' \oplus D(K, C_1)[i]$$

where the prime notation denotes bit complementation. This means that if an opponent can predictably change bits in IV, the corresponding bits of the received value of P_1 can be changed.

For other possible attacks based on prior knowledge of IV, see [VOYD83].

So long as it is unpredictable, the specific choice of IV is unimportant. SP 800-38A recommends two possible methods: The first method is to apply the encryption function, under the same key that is used for the encryption of the plaintext, to a **nonce**.[2] The nonce must be a data block that is unique to each

---

[2]NIST SP 800-90 (*Recommendation for Random Number Generation Using Deterministic Random Bit Generators*) defines nonce as follows: A time-varying value that has at most a negligible chance of repeating, for example, a random value that is generated anew for each use, a timestamp, a sequence number, or some combination of these.

execution of the encryption operation. For example, the nonce may be a counter, a timestamp, or a message number. The second method is to generate a random data block using a random number generator.

In conclusion, because of the chaining mechanism of CBC, it is an appropriate mode for encrypting messages of length greater than b bits.

In addition to its use to achieve confidentiality, the CBC mode can be used for authentication. This use is described in Chapter 12.

7.4 CIPHER FEEDBACK MODE

For AES, DES, or any block cipher, encryption is performed on a block of b bits. In the case of DES, $b = 64$ and in the case of AES, $b = 128$. However, it is possible to convert a block cipher into a stream cipher, using one of the three modes to be discussed in this and the next two sections: **cipher feedback (CFB)** mode, **output feedback (OFB)** mode, and **counter (CTR)** mode. A stream cipher eliminates the need to pad a message to be an integral number of blocks. It also can operate in real time. Thus, if a character stream is being transmitted, each character can be encrypted and transmitted immediately using a character-oriented stream cipher.

One desirable property of a stream cipher is that the ciphertext be of the same length as the plaintext. Thus, if 8-bit characters are being transmitted, each character should be encrypted to produce a ciphertext output of 8 bits. If more than 8 bits are produced, transmission capacity is wasted.

Figure 7.5 depicts the CFB scheme. In the figure, it is assumed that the unit of transmission is s bits; a common value is $s = 8$. As with CBC, the units of plaintext are chained together, so that the ciphertext of any plaintext unit is a function of all the preceding plaintext. In this case, rather than blocks of b bits, the plaintext is divided into *segments* of s bits.

First, consider encryption. The input to the encryption function is a b-bit shift register that is initially set to some initialization vector (IV). The leftmost (most significant) s bits of the output of the encryption function are XORed with the first segment of plaintext P_1 to produce the first unit of ciphertext C_1, which is then transmitted. In addition, the contents of the shift register are shifted left by s bits, and C_1 is placed in the rightmost (least significant) s bits of the shift register. This process continues until all plaintext units have been encrypted.

For decryption, the same scheme is used, except that the received ciphertext unit is XORed with the output of the encryption function to produce the plaintext unit. Note that it is the *encryption* function that is used, not the decryption function. This is easily explained. Let $\text{MSB}_s(X)$ be defined as the most significant s bits of X. Then

$$C_1 = P_1 \oplus \text{MSB}_s[\text{E}(K, \text{IV})]$$

Therefore, by rearranging terms:

$$P_1 = C_1 \oplus \text{MSB}_s[\text{E}(K, \text{IV})]$$

The same reasoning holds for subsequent steps in the process.

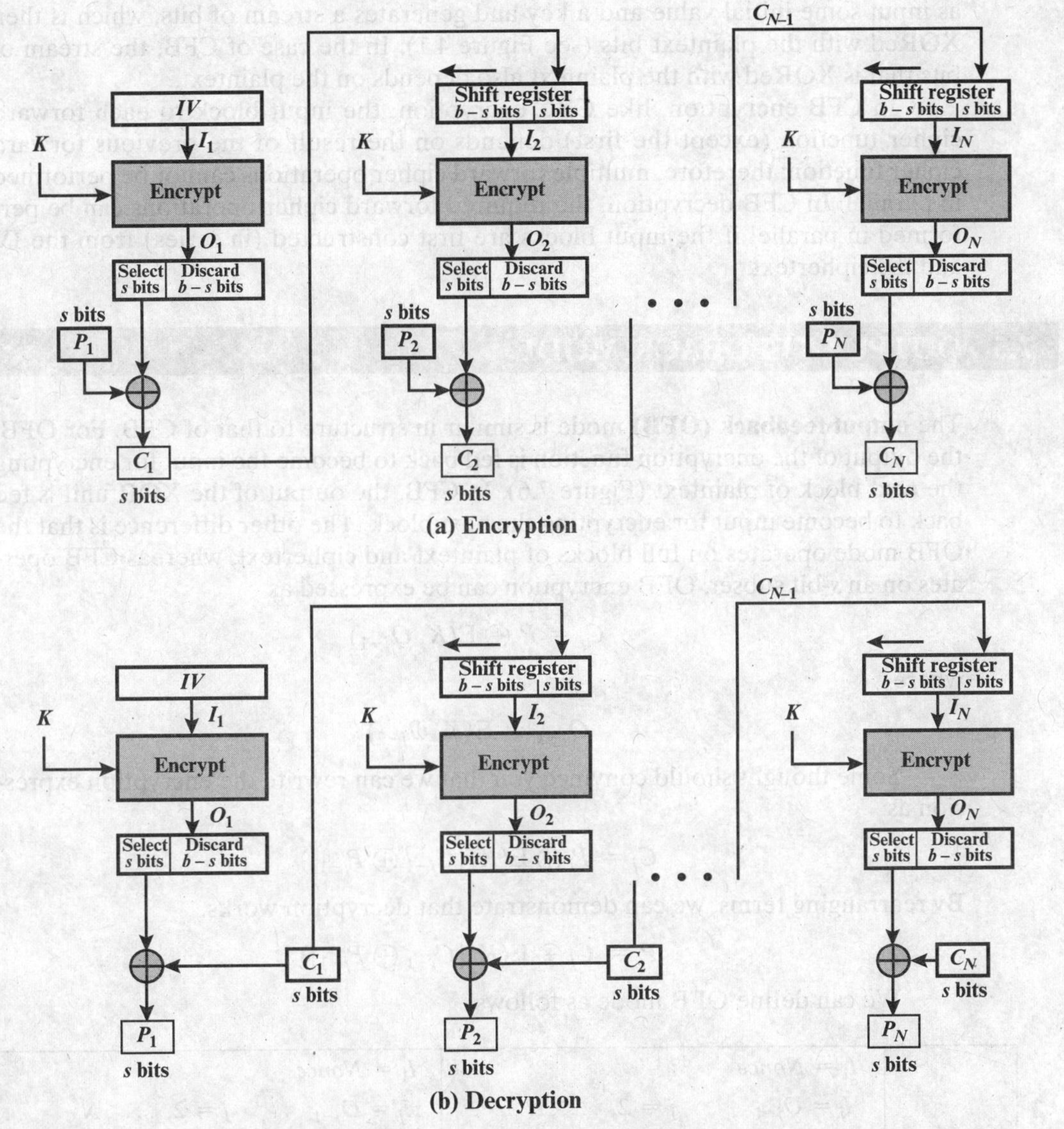

Figure 7.5 *s*-bit Cipher Feedback (CFB) Mode

We can define CFB mode as follows.

CFB	$I_1 = IV$ $I_j = \text{LSB}_{b-s}(I_{j-1}) \| C_{j-1} \quad j = 2, \ldots, N$ $O_j = \text{E}(K, I_j) \quad j = 1, \ldots, N$ $C_j = P_j \oplus \text{MSB}_s(O_j) \quad j = 1, \ldots, N$	$I_1 = IV$ $I_j = \text{LSB}_{b-s}(I_{j-1}) \| C_{j-1} \quad j = 2, \ldots, N$ $O_j = \text{E}(K, I_j) \quad j = 1, \ldots, N$ $P_j = C_j \oplus \text{MSB}_s(O_j) \quad j = 1, \ldots, N$

Although CFB can be viewed as a stream cipher, it does not conform to the typical construction of a stream cipher. In a typical stream cipher, the cipher takes as input some initial value and a key and generates a stream of bits, which is then XORed with the plaintext bits (see Figure 4.1). In the case of CFB, the stream of bits that is XORed with the plaintext also depends on the plaintext.

In CFB encryption, like CBC encryption, the input block to each forward cipher function (except the first) depends on the result of the previous forward cipher function; therefore, multiple forward cipher operations cannot be performed in parallel. In CFB decryption, the required forward cipher operations can be performed in parallel if the input blocks are first constructed (in series) from the IV and the ciphertext.

7.5 OUTPUT FEEDBACK MODE

The **output feedback (OFB)** mode is similar in structure to that of CFB. For OFB, the output of the encryption function is fed back to become the input for encrypting the next block of plaintext (Figure 7.6). In CFB, the output of the XOR unit is fed back to become input for encrypting the next block. The other difference is that the OFB mode operates on full blocks of plaintext and ciphertext, whereas CFB operates on an s-bit subset. OFB encryption can be expressed as

$$C_j = P_j \oplus \mathrm{E}(K, O_{j-1})$$

where

$$O_{j-1} = \mathrm{E}(K, O_{j-2})$$

Some thought should convince you that we can rewrite the encryption expression as:

$$C_j = P_j \oplus \mathrm{E}(K, [C_{j-1} \oplus P_{j-1}])$$

By rearranging terms, we can demonstrate that decryption works.

$$P_j = C_j \oplus \mathrm{E}(K, [C_{j-1} \oplus P_{j-1}])$$

We can define OFB mode as follows.

OFB	$I_1 = Nonce$		$I_1 = Nonce$	
	$I_j = O_{j-1}$	$j = 2, \ldots, N$	$I_j = O_{j-1}$	$j = 2, \ldots, N$
	$O_j = \mathrm{E}(K, I_j)$	$j = 1, \ldots, N$	$O_j = \mathrm{E}(K, I_j)$	$j = 1, \ldots, N$
	$C_j = P_j \oplus O_j$	$j = 1, \ldots, N - 1$	$P_j = C_j \oplus O_j$	$j = 1, \ldots, N - 1$
	$C_N^* = P_N^* \oplus \mathrm{MSB}_u(O_N)$		$P_N^* = C_N^* \oplus \mathrm{MSB}_u(O_N)$	

Let the size of a block be b. If the last block of plaintext contains u bits (indicated by *), with $u < b$, the most significant u bits of the last output block O_N are used for the XOR operation; the remaining $b - u$ bits of the last output block are discarded.

As with CBC and CFB, the OFB mode requires an initialization vector. In the case of OFB, the IV must be a nonce; that is, the IV must be unique to each execution of the encryption operation. The reason for this is that the sequence of

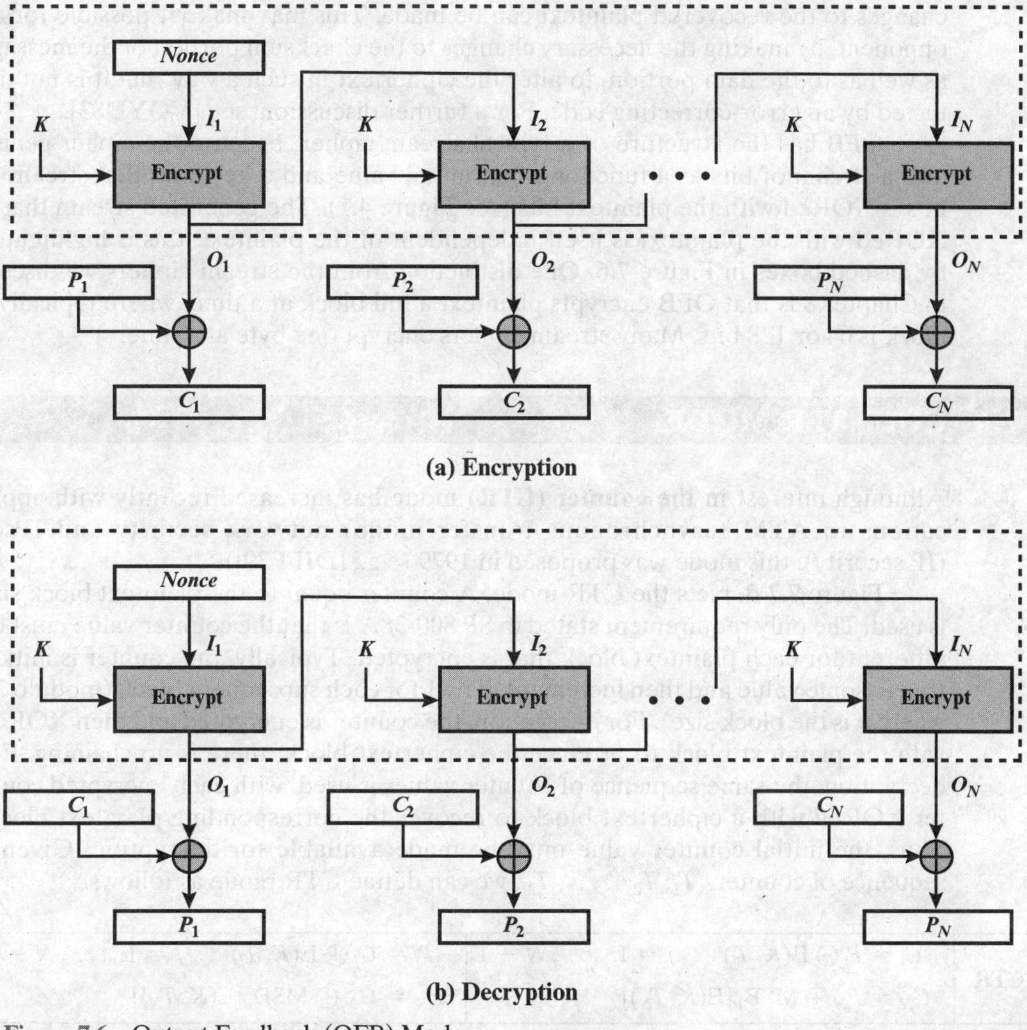

Figure 7.6 Output Feedback (OFB) Mode

encryption output blocks, O_i, depends only on the key and the IV and does not depend on the plaintext. Therefore, for a given key and IV, the stream of output bits used to XOR with the stream of plaintext bits is fixed. If two different messages had an identical block of plaintext in the identical position, then an attacker would be able to determine that portion of the O_i stream.

One advantage of the OFB method is that bit errors in transmission do not propagate. For example, if a bit error occurs in C_1, only the recovered value of P_1 is affected; subsequent plaintext units are not corrupted. With CFB, C_1 also serves as input to the shift register and therefore causes additional corruption downstream.

The disadvantage of OFB is that it is more vulnerable to a message stream modification attack than is CFB. Consider that complementing a bit in the ciphertext complements the corresponding bit in the recovered plaintext. Thus, controlled changes to the recovered plaintext can be made. This may make it possible for an opponent, by making the necessary changes to the checksum portion of the message as well as to the data portion, to alter the ciphertext in such a way that it is not detected by an error-correcting code. For a further discussion, see [VOYD83].

OFB has the structure of a typical stream cipher, because the cipher generates a stream of bits as a function of an initial value and a key, and that stream of bits is XORed with the plaintext bits (see Figure 4.1). The generated stream that is XORed with the plaintext is itself independent of the plaintext; this is highlighted by dashed boxes in Figure 7.6. One distinction from the stream ciphers we discuss in Chapter 8 is that OFB encrypts plaintext a full block at a time, where typically a block is 64 or 128 bits. Many stream ciphers encrypt one byte at a time.

7.6 COUNTER MODE

Although interest in the **counter (CTR)** mode has increased recently with applications to ATM (asynchronous transfer mode) network security and IPsec (IP security), this mode was proposed in 1979 (e.g., [DIFF79]).

Figure 7.7 depicts the CTR mode. A counter equal to the plaintext block size is used. The only requirement stated in SP 800-38A is that the counter value must be different for each plaintext block that is encrypted. Typically, the counter is initialized to some value and then incremented by 1 for each subsequent block (modulo 2^b, where b is the block size). For encryption, the counter is encrypted and then XORed with the plaintext block to produce the ciphertext block; there is no chaining. For decryption, the same sequence of counter values is used, with each encrypted counter XORed with a ciphertext block to recover the corresponding plaintext block. Thus, the initial counter value must be made available for decryption. Given a sequence of counters $T_1, T_2, \ldots, T_N$, we can define CTR mode as follows.

CTR	$C_j = P_j \oplus \mathrm{E}(K, T_j) \quad j = 1, \ldots, N-1$ $C_N^* = P_N^* \oplus \mathrm{MSB}_u[\mathrm{E}(K, T_N)]$	$P_j = C_j \oplus \mathrm{E}(K, T_j) \quad j = 1, \ldots, N-1$ $P_N^* = C_N^* \oplus \mathrm{MSB}_u[\mathrm{E}(K, T_N)]$

For the last plaintext block, which may be a partial block of u bits, the most significant u bits of the last output block are used for the XOR operation; the remaining $b - u$ bits are discarded. Unlike the ECB, CBC, and CFB modes, we do not need to use padding because of the structure of the CTR mode.

As with the OFB mode, the initial counter value must be a nonce; that is, T_1 must be different for all of the messages encrypted using the same key. Further, all T_i values across all messages must be unique. If, contrary to this requirement, a counter value is used multiple times, then the confidentiality of all of the plaintext blocks corresponding to that counter value may be compromised. In particular, if any plaintext block that is encrypted using a given counter value is known, then the output of the encryption function can be determined easily from the associated ciphertext block. This output allows any other plaintext blocks that are encrypted using the same counter value to be easily recovered from their associated ciphertext blocks.

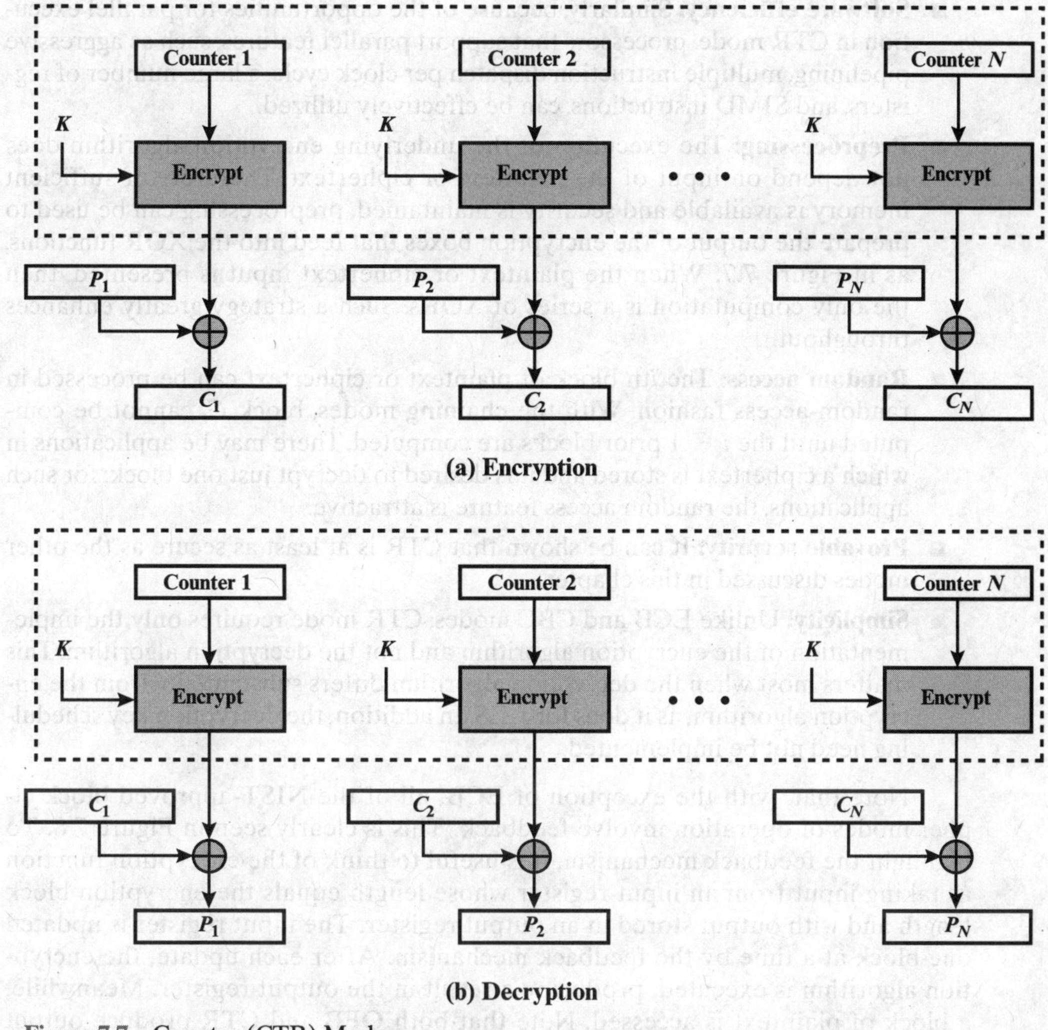

Figure 7.7 Counter (CTR) Mode

One way to ensure the uniqueness of counter values is to continue to increment the counter value by 1 across messages. That is, the first counter value of the each message is one more than the last counter value of the preceding message. [LIPM00] lists the following advantages of CTR mode.

- **Hardware efficiency:** Unlike the three chaining modes, encryption (or decryption) in CTR mode can be done in parallel on multiple blocks of plaintext or ciphertext. For the chaining modes, the algorithm must complete the computation on one block before beginning on the next block. This limits the maximum throughput of the algorithm to the reciprocal of the time for one execution of block encryption or decryption. In CTR mode, the throughput is only limited by the amount of parallelism that is achieved.

- **Software efficiency:** Similarly, because of the opportunities for parallel execution in CTR mode, processors that support parallel features, such as aggressive pipelining, multiple instruction dispatch per clock cycle, a large number of registers, and SIMD instructions, can be effectively utilized.
- **Preprocessing:** The execution of the underlying encryption algorithm does not depend on input of the plaintext or ciphertext. Therefore, if sufficient memory is available and security is maintained, preprocessing can be used to prepare the output of the encryption boxes that feed into the XOR functions, as in Figure 7.7. When the plaintext or ciphertext input is presented, then the only computation is a series of XORs. Such a strategy greatly enhances throughput.
- **Random access:** The *i*th block of plaintext or ciphertext can be processed in random-access fashion. With the chaining modes, block C_i cannot be computed until the $i - 1$ prior blocks are computed. There may be applications in which a ciphertext is stored and it is desired to decrypt just one block; for such applications, the random access feature is attractive.
- **Provable security:** It can be shown that CTR is at least as secure as the other modes discussed in this chapter.
- **Simplicity:** Unlike ECB and CBC modes, CTR mode requires only the implementation of the encryption algorithm and not the decryption algorithm. This matters most when the decryption algorithm differs substantially from the encryption algorithm, as it does for AES. In addition, the decryption key scheduling need not be implemented.

Note that, with the exception of ECB, all of the NIST-approved block cipher modes of operation involve feedback. This is clearly seen in Figure 7.8. To highlight the feedback mechanism, it is useful to think of the encryption function as taking input from an input register whose length equals the encryption block length and with output stored in an output register. The input register is updated one block at a time by the feedback mechanism. After each update, the encryption algorithm is executed, producing a result in the output register. Meanwhile, a block of plaintext is accessed. Note that both OFB and CTR produce output that is independent of both the plaintext and the ciphertext. Thus, they are natural candidates for stream ciphers that encrypt plaintext by XOR one full block at a time.

7.7 XTS-AES MODE FOR BLOCK-ORIENTED STORAGE DEVICES

In 2010, NIST approved an additional block cipher mode of operation, XTS-AES. This mode is also an IEEE standard, IEEE Std 1619-2007, which was developed by the IEEE Security in Storage Working Group (P1619). The standard describes a method of encryption for data stored in sector-based devices where the threat model includes possible access to stored data by the adversary. The standard has received widespread industry support.

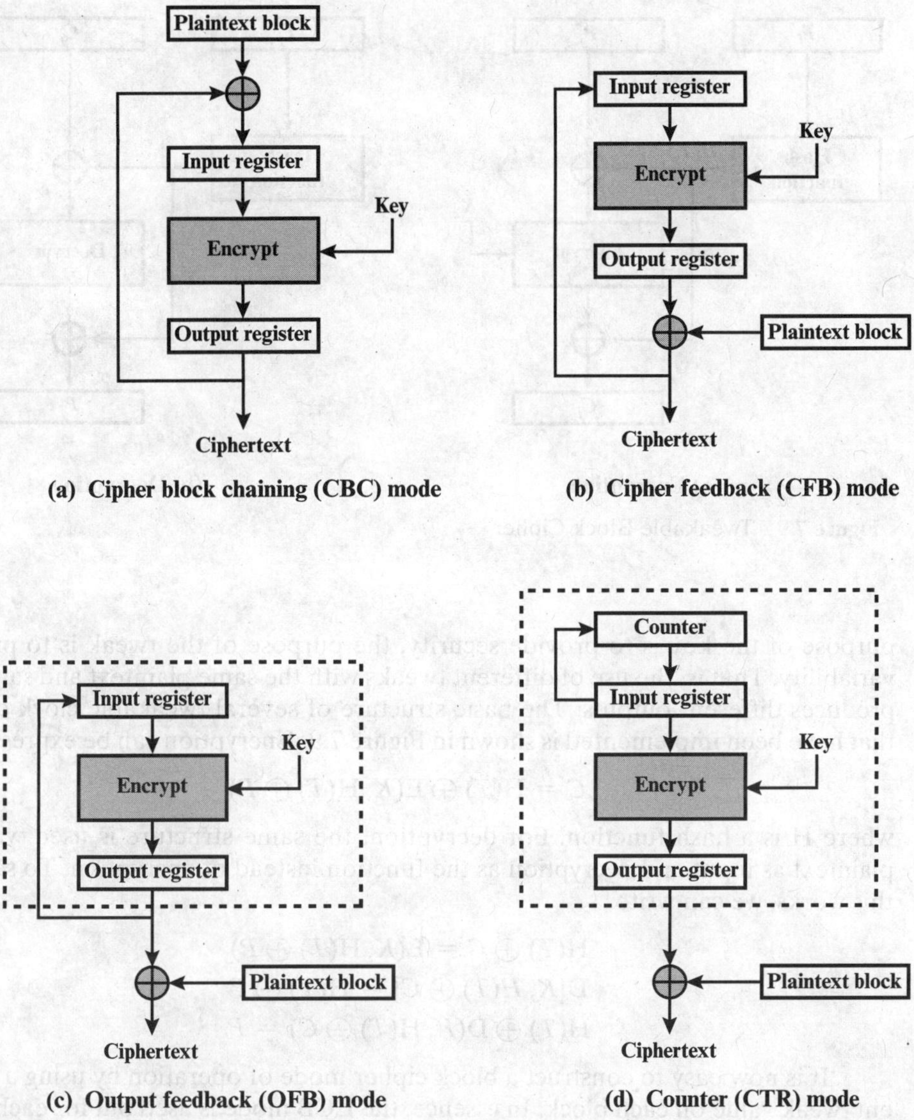

Figure 7.8 Feedback Characteristic of Modes of Operation

Tweakable Block Ciphers

The XTS-AES mode is based on the concept of a **tweakable block cipher**, introduced in [LISK02], which functions in much the same manner as a salt used with passwords, as described in Chapter 22. The form of this concept used in XTS-AES was first described in [ROGA04].

Before examining XTS-AES, let us consider the general structure of a tweakable block cipher. A tweakable block cipher is one that has three inputs: a plaintext P, a symmetric key K, and a tweak T; and produces a ciphertext output C. We can write this as $C = \mathrm{E}(K, T, P)$. The tweak need not be kept secret. Whereas the

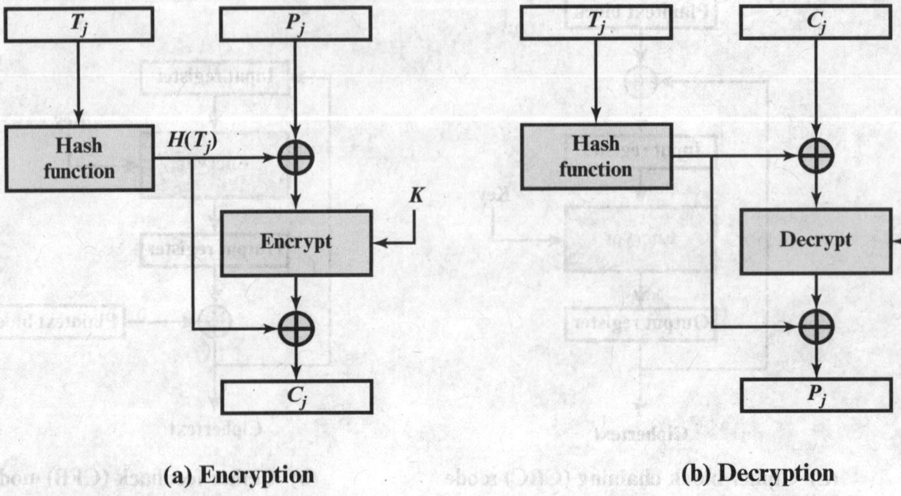

Figure 7.9 Tweakable Block Cipher

purpose of the key is to provide security, the purpose of the tweak is to provide variability. That is, the use of different tweaks with the same plaintext and same key produces different outputs. The basic structure of several tweakable clock ciphers that have been implemented is shown in Figure 7.9. Encryption can be expressed as:

$$C = \mathrm{H}(T) \oplus \mathrm{E}(K, \mathrm{H}(T) \oplus P)$$

where H is a hash function. For decryption, the same structure is used with the plaintext as input and decryption as the function instead of encryption. To see that this works, we can write

$$\mathrm{H}(T) \oplus C = \mathrm{E}(K, \mathrm{H}(T) \oplus P)$$
$$\mathrm{D}[K, H(T) \oplus C] = \mathrm{H}(T) \oplus P$$
$$\mathrm{H}(T) \oplus \mathrm{D}(K, \mathrm{H}(T) \oplus C) = P$$

It is now easy to construct a block cipher mode of operation by using a different tweak value on each block. In essence, the ECB mode is used but for each block the tweak is changed. This overcomes the principal security weakness of ECB, which is that two encryptions of the same block yield the same ciphertext.

Storage Encryption Requirements

The requirements for encrypting stored data, also referred to as "data at rest" differ somewhat from those for transmitted data. The P1619 standard was designed to have the following characteristics:

1. The ciphertext is freely available for an attacker. Among the circumstances that lead to this situation:
   a. A group of users has authorized access to a database. Some of the records in the database are encrypted so that only specific users can successfully read/

write them. Other users can retrieve an encrypted record but are unable to read it without the key.

   b. An unauthorized user manages to gain access to encrypted records.
   c. A data disk or laptop is stolen, giving the adversary access to the encrypted data.

2. The data layout is not changed on the storage medium and in transit. The encrypted data must be the same size as the plaintext data.
3. Data are accessed in fixed sized blocks, independently from each other. That is, an authorized user may access one or more blocks in any order.
4. Encryption is performed in 16-byte blocks, independently from other blocks (except the last two plaintext blocks of a sector, if its size is not a multiple of 16 bytes).
5. There are no other metadata used, except the location of the data blocks within the whole data set.
6. The same plaintext is encrypted to different ciphertexts at different locations, but always to the same ciphertext when written to the same location again.
7. A standard conformant device can be constructed for decryption of data encrypted by another standard conformant device.

The P1619 group considered some of the existing modes of operation for use with stored data. For CTR mode, an adversary with write access to the encrypted media can flip any bit of the plaintext simply by flipping the corresponding ciphertext bit.

Next, consider requirement 6 and the use of CBC. To enforce the requirement that the same plaintext encrypts to different ciphertext in different locations, the IV could be derived from the sector number. Each sector contains multiple blocks. An adversary with read/write access to the encrypted disk can copy a ciphertext sector from one position to another, and an application reading the sector off the new location will still get the same plaintext sector (except perhaps the first 128 bits). For example, this means that an adversary that is allowed to read a sector from the second position but not the first can find the content of the sector in the first position by manipulating the ciphertext. Another weakness is that an adversary can flip any bit of the plaintext by flipping the corresponding ciphertext bit of the previous block, with the side-effect of "randomizing" the previous block.

Operation on a Single Block

Figure 7.10 shows the encryption and decryption of a single block. The operation involves two instances of the AES algorithm with two keys. The following parameters are associated with the algorithm.

Key	The 256 or 512 bit XTS-AES key; this is parsed as a concatenation of two fields of equal size called Key_1 and Key_2, such that $Key = Key_1 \| Key_2$.
P_j	The *j*th block of plaintext. All blocks except possibly the final block have a length of 128 bits. A plaintext data unit, typically a disk sector, consists of a sequence of plaintext blocks $P_1, P_2, \ldots, P_m$.
C_j	The *j*th block of ciphertext. All blocks except possibly the final block have a length of 128 bits.

j	The sequential number of the 128-bit block inside the data unit.
i	The value of the 128-bit tweak. Each data unit (sector) is assigned a tweak value that is a nonnegative integer. The tweak values are assigned consecutively, starting from an arbitrary nonnegative integer.
α	A primitive element of GF(2^{128}) that corresponds to polynomial x (i.e., $0000 \ldots 010_2$).
α^j	α multiplied by itself j times, in GF(2^{128}).
$\oplus$	Bitwise XOR.
$\otimes$	Modular multiplication of two polynomials with binary coefficients modulo $x^{128} + x^7 + x^2 + x + 1$. Thus, this is multiplication in GF(2^{128}).

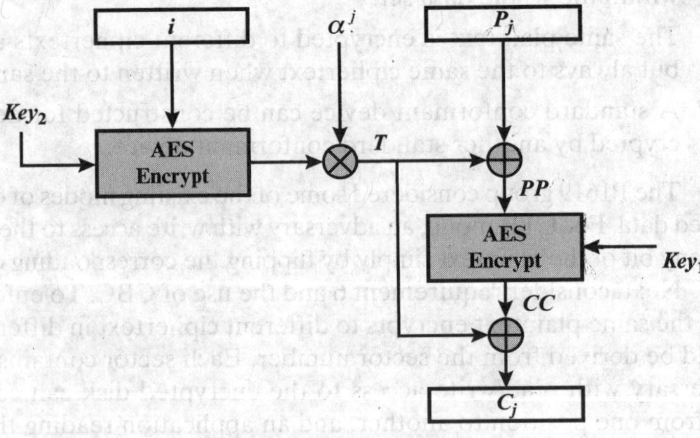

(a) Encryption

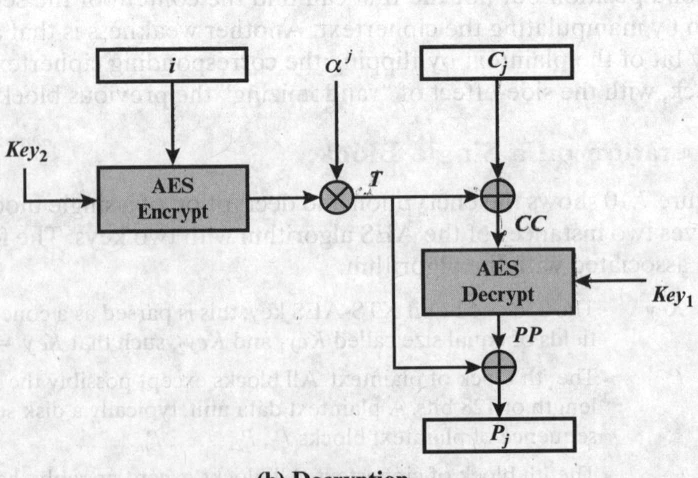

(b) Decryption

Figure 7.10 XTS-AES Operation on Single Block

In essence, the parameter j functions much like the counter in CTR mode. It assures that if the same plaintext block appears at two different positions within a data unit, it will encrypt to two different ciphertext blocks. The parameter i functions much like a nonce at the data unit level. It assures that, if the same plaintext block appears at the same position in two different data units, it will encrypt to two different ciphertext blocks. More generally, it assures that the same plaintext data unit will encrypt to two different ciphertext data units for two different data unit positions.

The encryption and decryption of a single block can be described as

XTS-AES block operation	$T = \mathrm{E}(K_2, i) \otimes \alpha^j$ $PP = P \oplus T$ $CC = \mathrm{E}(K_1, PP)$ $C = CC \oplus T$	$T = \mathrm{E}(K_2, i) \otimes \alpha^j$ $CC = C \oplus T$ $PP = \mathrm{D}(K_1, \mathrm{CC})$ $P = PP \oplus T$

To see that decryption recovers the plaintext, let us expand the last line of both encryption and decryption. For encryption, we have

$$C = CC \oplus T = \mathrm{E}(K_1, \mathrm{PP}) \oplus T = \mathrm{E}(K_1, P \oplus T) \oplus T$$

and for decryption, we have

$$P = PP \oplus T = \mathrm{D}(K_1, CC) \oplus T = \mathrm{D}(K_1, C \oplus T) \oplus T$$

Now, we substitute for C:

$$\begin{aligned} P &= \mathrm{D}(K_1, C \oplus T) \oplus T \\ &= \mathrm{D}(K_1, [E(K_1, P \oplus T) \oplus T] \oplus T) \oplus T \\ &= \mathrm{D}(K_1, E(K_1, P \oplus T)) \oplus T \\ &= (P \oplus T) \oplus T = P \end{aligned}$$

Operation on a Sector

The plaintext of a sector or data unit is organized into blocks of 128 bits. Blocks are labeled $P_0, P_1, \ldots, P_m$. The last block my be null or may contain from 1 to 127 bits. In other words, the input to the XTS-AES algorithm consists of m 128-bit blocks and possibly a final partial block.

For encryption and decryption, each block is treated independently and encrypted/decrypted as shown in Figure 7.10. The only exception occurs when the last block has less than 128 bits. In that case, the last two blocks are encrypted/decrypted using a **ciphertext-stealing** technique instead of padding. Figure 7.11 shows the scheme. P_{m-1} is the last full plaintext block, and P_m is the final plaintext block, which contains s bits with $1 \leq s \leq 127$. C_{m-1} is the last full ciphertext block, and C_m is the final ciphertext block, which contains s bits. This technique is commonly called ciphertext stealing because the processing of the last block "steals" a temporary ciphertext of the penultimate block to complete the cipher block.

Let us label the block encryption and decryption algorithms of Figure 7.10 as

Block encryption: XTS-AES-blockEnc(K, P_j, i, j)
Block decryption: XTS-AES-blockDec(K, C_j, i, j)

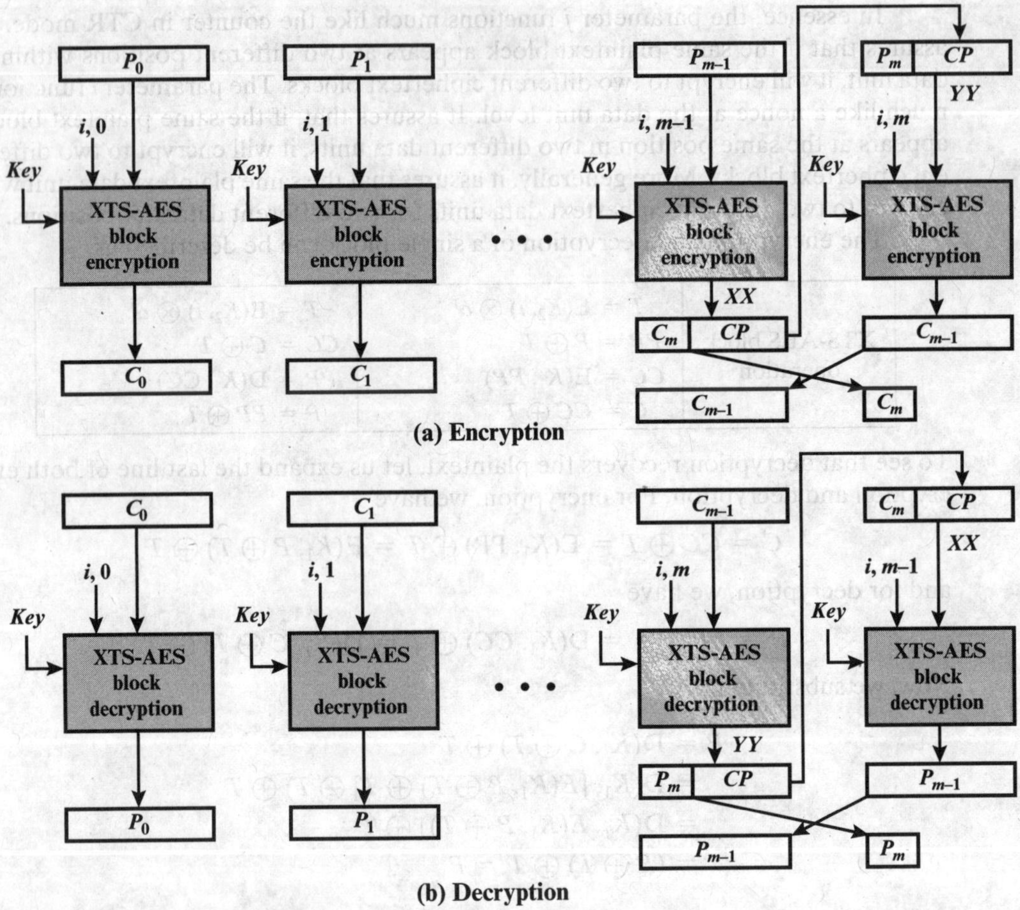

Figure 7.11 XTS-AES Mode

Then, XTS-AES mode is defined as follows:

XTS-AES mode with null final block	$C_j = \text{XTS-AES-blockEnc}(K, P_j, i, j) \quad j = 0, \ldots, m-1$
	$P_j = \text{XTS-AES-blockEnc}(K, C_j, i, j) \quad j = 0, \ldots, m-1$
XTS-AES mode with final block containing s bits	$C_j = \text{XTS-AES-blockEnc}(K, P_j, i, j)\ j = 0, \ldots, m-2$ $XX = \text{XTS-AES-blockEnc}(K, P_{m-1}, i, m-1)$ $CP = \text{LSB}_{128-s}(XX)$ $YY = P_m \Vert CP$ $C_{m-1} = \text{XTS-AES-blockEnc}(K, YY, i, m)$ $C_m = \text{MSB}_s(XX)$
	$P_j = \text{XTS-AES-blockDec}(K, C_j, i, j)\ j = 0, \ldots, m-2$ $YY = \text{XTS-AES-blockDec}(K, C_{m-1}, i, m-1)$ $CP = \text{LSB}_{128-s}(YY)$ $XX = C_m \Vert \text{CP}$ $P_{m-1} = \text{XTS-AES-blockDec}(K, XX, i, m)$ $P_m = \text{MSB}_s(YY)$

As can be seen, XTS-AES mode, like CTR mode, is suitable for parallel operation. Because there is no chaining, multiple blocks can be encrypted or decrypted simultaneously. Unlike CTR mode, XTS-AES mode includes a nonce (the parameter *i*) as well as a counter (parameter *j*).

7.8 FORMAT-PRESERVING ENCRYPTION

Format-preserving encryption (FPE) refers to any encryption technique that takes a plaintext in a given format and produces a ciphertext in the same format. For example, credit cards consist of 16 decimal digits. An FPE that can accept this type of input would produce a ciphertext output of 16 decimal digits. Note that the ciphertext need not be, and in fact is unlikely to be, a valid credit card number. But it will have the same format and can be stored in the same way as credit card number plaintext.

A simple encryption algorithm is not format preserving, with the exception that it preserves the format of binary strings. For example, Table 7.2 shows three types of plaintext for which it might be desired to perform FPE. The third row shows examples of what might be generated by an FPE algorithm. The fourth row shows (in hexadecimal) what is produced by AES with a given key.

Motivation

FPE facilitates the retrofitting of encryption technology to legacy applications, where a conventional encryption mode might not be feasible because it would disrupt data fields/pathways. FPE has emerged as a useful cryptographic tool, whose applications include financial-information security, data sanitization, and transparent encryption of fields in legacy databases.

The principal benefit of FPE is that it enables protection of particular data elements in a legacy database that did not provide encryption of those data elements, while still enabling workflows that were in place before FPE was in use. With FPE, as opposed to ordinary AES encryption or TDEA encryption, no database schema changes and minimal application changes are required. Only applications that need to see the plaintext of a data element need to be modified and generally these modifications will be minimal.

Some examples of legacy applications where FPE is desirable:

- COBOL data-processing applications: Any changes in the structure of a record requires corresponding changes in all code that references that record structure. Typical code sizes involve hundreds of modules, each containing around 5,000–10,000 lines on average.

Table 7.2 Comparison of Format-Preserving Encryption and AES

	Credit Card	Tax ID	Bank Account Number
Plaintext	8123 4512 3456 6780	219-09-9999	800N2982K-22
FPE	8123 4521 7292 6780	078-05-1120	709G9242H-35
AES (hex)	af411326466add24 c86abd8aa525db7a	7b9af4f3f218ab25 07c7376869313afa	9720ec7f793096ff d37141242e1c51bd

- Database applications: Fields that are specified to take only character strings cannot be used to store conventionally encrypted binary ciphertext. Base64 encoding of such binary ciphertext is not always feasible without increase in data lengths, requiring augmentation of corresponding field lengths.
- FPE-encrypted characters can be significantly compressed for efficient transmission. This cannot be said about AES-encrypted binary ciphertext.

Difficulties in Designing an FPE

A general-purpose standardized FPE should meet a number of requirements:

1. The ciphertext is of the same length and format as the plaintext.
2. It should be adaptable to work with a variety of character and number types. Examples include decimal digits, lowercase alphabetic characters, and the full character set of a standard keyboard or international keyboard.
3. It should work with variable plaintext lengths.
4. Security strength should be comparable to that achieved with AES.
5. Security should be strong even for very small plaintext lengths.

Meeting the first requirement is not at all straightforward. As illustrated in Table 7.2, a straightforward encryption with AES yields a 128-bit binary block that does not resemble the required format. Also, a standard symmetric block cipher is not easily adaptable to produce an FPE.

Consider a simple example. Assume that we want an algorithm that can encrypt decimal digit strings of maximum length of 32 digits. The input to the algorithm can be stored in 16 bytes (128 bits) by encoding each digit as four bits and using the corresponding binary value for each digit (e.g., 6 is encoded as 0101). Next, we use AES to encrypt the 128-bit block, in the following fashion:

1. The plaintext input X is represented by the string of 4-bit decimal digits $X[1] \ldots X[16]$. If the plaintext is less than 16 digits long, it is padded out to the left (most significant) with zeros.
2. Treating X as a 128-bit binary string and using key K, form ciphertext $Y = \text{AES}_K(X)$.
3. Treat Y as a string of length 16 of 4-bit elements.
4. Some of the entries in Y may have values greater than 9 (e.g., 1100). To generate ciphertext Z in the required format, calculate

$$Z[i] = Y[i] \bmod 10, \qquad 1 \leq i \leq 16$$

This generates a ciphertext of 16 decimal digits, which conforms to the desired format. However, this algorithm does not meet the basic requirement of any encryption algorithm of reversibility. It is impossible to decrypt Z to recover the original plaintext X because the operation is one-way; that is, it is a many-to-one function. For example, $12 \bmod 10 = 2 \bmod 10 = 2$. Thus, we need to design a reversible function that is both a secure encryption algorithm and format preserving.

A second difficulty in designing an FPE is that some of the input strings are quite short. For example, consider the 16-digit credit card number (CCN). The first six digits provide the issuer identification number (IIN), which identifies the institution that issued the card. The final digit is a check digit to catch typographical errors or other mistakes. The remaining nine digits are the user's account number. However, a number of applications require that the last four digits be in the clear (the check digit plus three account digits) for applications such as credit card receipts, which leaves only six digits for encryption. Now suppose that an adversary is able to obtain a number of plaintext/ciphertext pairs. Each such pair corresponds to not just one CCN, but multiple CCNs that have the same middle six digits. In a large database of credit card numbers, there may be multiple card numbers with the same middle six digits. An adversary may be able to assemble a large dictionary mapping known as six-digit plaintexts to their corresponding ciphertexts. This could be used to decrypt unknown ciphertexts from the database. As pointed out in [BELL10a], in a database of 100 million entries, on average about 100 CCNs will share any given middle-six digits. Thus, if the adversary has learned k CCNs and gains access to such a database, the adversary can decrypt approximately $100k$ CCNs.

The solution to this second difficulty is to use a tweakable block cipher; this concept is described in Section 7.7. For example, the tweak for CCNs could be the first two and last four digits of the CCN. Prior to encryption, the tweak is added, digit-by-digit mod 10, to the middle six-digit plaintext, and the result is then encrypted. Two different CCNs with identical middle six digits will yield different tweaked inputs and therefore different ciphertexts. Consider the following:

CCN	Tweak	Plaintext	Plaintext + Tweak
4012 8812 3456 1884	401884	123456	524230
5105 1012 3456 6782	516782	123456	639138

Two CCNs with the same middle six digits have different tweaks and therefore different values to the middle six digits after the tweak is added.

Feistel Structure for Format-Preserving Encryption

As the preceding discussion shows, the challenge with FPE is to design an algorithm for scrambling the plaintext that is secure, preserves format, and is reversible. A number of approaches have been proposed in recent years [ROGA10, BELL09] for FPE algorithms. The majority of these proposals use a Feistel structure. Although IBM introduced this structure with their Lucifer cipher [SMIT71] almost half a century ago, it remains a powerful basis for implementing ciphers.

This section provides a general description of how the Feistel structure can be used to implement an FPE. In the following section, we look at three specific Feistel-based algorithms that are in the process of receiving NIST approval.

Encryption and Decryption Figure 7.12 shows the Feistel structure used in all of the NIST algorithms, with encryption shown on the left-hand side and decryption on the right-hand side. The structure in Figure 7.12 is the same as that shown in

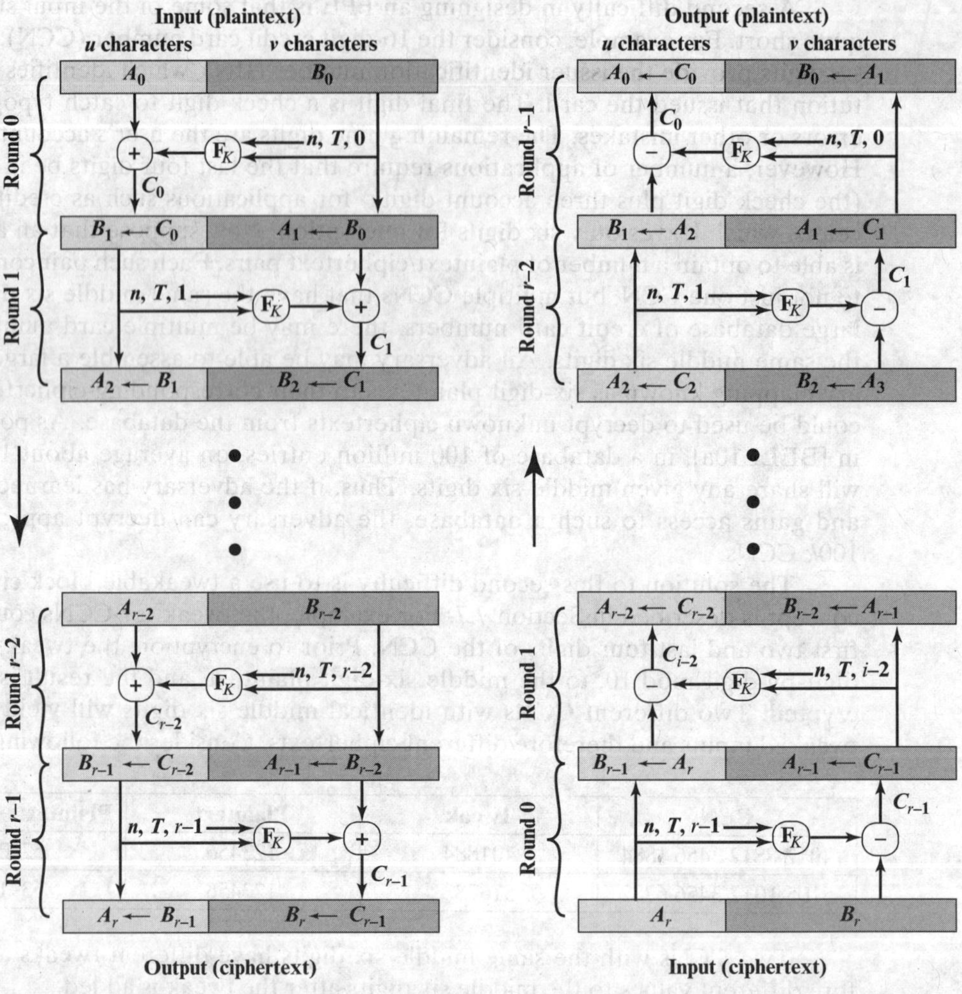

(a) Encryption

(b) Decryption

Figure 7.12 Feistel Structure for Format-Preserving Encryption

Figure 4.3 but, to simplify the presentation, it is untwisted, not illustrating the swap that occurs at the end of each round.

The input to the encryption algorithm is a plaintext character string of $n = u + v$ characters. If n is even, then $u = v$, otherwise u and v differ by 1. The two parts of the string pass through an even number of rounds of processing to produce a ciphertext block of n characters and the same format as the plaintext. Each round i has inputs A_i and B_i, derived from the preceding round (or plaintext for round 0).

All rounds have the same structure. On even-numbered rounds, a substitution is performed on the left part (length u) of the data, A_i. This is done by applying the round function F_K to the right part (length v) of the data, B_i, and then performing a modular addition of the output of F_K with A_i. The modular addition function and the selection of modulus are described subsequently. On odd-numbered rounds, the substitution is done on the right part of the data. F_K is a one-way function that converts the input into a binary string, performs a scrambling transformation on the string, and then converts the result back into a character string of suitable format and length. The function has as parameters the secret key K, the plaintext length n, a tweak T, and the round number i.

Note that on even-numbered rounds, F_K has an input of v characters, and that the modular addition produces a result of u characters, whereas on odd-numbered rounds, F_K has an input of u characters, and that the modular addition produces a result of v characters. The total number of rounds is even, so that the output consists of an A portion of length u concatenated with a B portion of length v, matching the partition of the plaintext.

The process of decryption is essentially the same as the encryption process. The differences are: (1) the addition function is replaced by a subtraction function that is its inverse; and (2) the order of the round indices is reversed.

To demonstrate that the decryption produces the correct result, Figure 7.12b shows the encryption process going down the left-hand side and the decryption process going up the right-hand side. The diagram indicates that, at every round, the intermediate value of the decryption process is equal to the corresponding value of the encryption process. We can walk through the figure to validate this, starting at the bottom. The ciphertext is produced at the end of round $r - 1$ as a string of the form $A_r \| B_r$, with A_r and B_r having string lengths u and v, respectively. Encryption round $r - 1$ can be described with the following equations:

$$A_r = B_{r-1}$$
$$B_r = A_{r-1} + F_K[B_{r-1}]$$

Because we define the subtraction function to be the inverse of the addition function, these equations can be rewritten:

$$B_{r-1} = A_r$$
$$A_{r-1} = B_r - F_K[B_{r-1}]$$

It can be seen that the last two equations describe the action of round 0 of the decryption function, so that the output of round 0 of decryption equals the input of round $r - 1$ of encryption. This correspondence holds all the way through the r iterations, as is easily shown.

Note that the derivation does not require that F be a reversible function. To see this, take a limiting case in which F produces a constant output (e.g., all ones) regardless of the values of its input. The equations still hold.

Character Strings The NIST algorithms, and the other FPE algorithms that have been proposed, are used with plaintext consisting of a string of elements, called characters. Specifically, a finite set of two or more symbols is called an *alphabet*, and the elements of an alphabet are called *characters*. A *character string* is a finite sequence of characters from an alphabet. Individual characters may repeat in the string. The number of different characters in an alphabet is called the *base*, also referred to as the *radix* of the alphabet. For example, the lowercase English alphabet a, b, c, . . . has a radix, or base, of 26. For purposes of encryption and decryption, the plaintext alphabet must be converted to numerals, where a *numeral* is a nonnegative integer that is less than the base. For example, for the lowercase alphabet, the assignment could be characters a, b, c, . . . , z map into 0, 1, 2, . . . , 25.

A limitation of this approach is that all of the elements in a plaintext format must have the same radix. So, for example, an identification number that consists of an alphabetic character followed by nine numeric digits cannot be handled in format-preserving fashion by the FPEs that have been implemented so far.

The NIST document defines notation for specifying these conversions (Table 7.3a). To begin, it is assumed that the character string is represented by a numeral string. To convert a numeral string X into a number x, the function $\text{NUM}_{radix}(X)$ is used. Viewing X as the string $X[1] \ldots X[m]$ with the most significant numeral first, the function is defined as

$$\text{NUM}_{radix}(X) = \sum_{i=1}^{m} X[i]\, radix^{m-i} = \sum_{i=0}^{m-1} X[m-i]\, radix^{i}$$

Observe that $0 \le \text{NUM}_{radix}(X) < radix^m$ and that $0 \le X[i] < radix$.

Table 7.3 Notation and Parameters Used in FPE Algorithms

$[x]^s$	Converts an integer into a byte string; it is the string of s bytes that encodes the number x, with $0 \le x < 2^{8s}$. The equivalent notation is $\text{STR}_2^{8s}(x)$.
LEN(X)	Length of the character string X.
$\text{NUM}_{radix}(X)$	Converts strings to numbers. The number that the numeral string X represents in base *radix*, with the most significant character first. In other words, it is the nonnegative integer less than $radix^{\text{LEN}(X)}$ whose most-significant-character-first representation in base *radix* is X.
$\text{PRF}_K(X)$	A pseudorandom function that produces a 128-bit output with X as the input, using encryption key K.
$\text{STR}^m_{radix}(x)$	Given a nonnegative integer x less than $radix^m$, this function produces a representation of x as a string of m characters in base *radix*, with the most significant character first.
$[i \,..\, j]$	The set of integers between two integers i and j, including i and j.
$X[i \,..\, j]$	The substring of characters of a string X from $X[i]$ to $X[j]$, including $X[i]$ and $X[j]$.
REV(X)	Given a bit string, X, the string that consists of the bits of X in reverse order.

(a) Notation

radix	The base, or number of characters, in a given plaintext alphabet.
tweak	Input parameter to the encryption and decryption functions whose confidentiality is not protected by the mode.
tweakradix	The base for tweak strings
minlen	Minimum message length, in characters.
maxlen	Maximum message length, in characters.
maxTlen	Maximum tweak length

(b) Parameters

For example, consider the string zaby in radix 26, which converts to the numeral string 25 0 1 24. This converts to the number $x = (25 \times 26^3) + (1 \times 26^1) + 24 = 439450$. To go in the opposite direction and convert from a number $x < radix^m$ to a numeral string X of length m, the function $\text{STR}^m_{radix}(x)$ is used:

$$\text{STR}^m_{radix}(x) = X[1] \ldots X[m], \text{ where}$$

$$X[i] = \left\lfloor \frac{x}{radix^{m-i}} \right\rfloor \text{mod } radix, \quad i = 1, \ldots, m$$

With the mapping of characters to numerals and the use of the NUM function, a plaintext character string can be mapped to a number and stored as an unsigned integer. We would like to treat this unsigned integer as a bit string that can be input to a bit-scrambling algorithm in F_K. However, different platforms store unsigned integers differently, some in little-endian and some in big-endian fashion. So one more step is needed. By the definition of the STR function, $\text{STR}^{8s}_2(x)$ will generate a bit string of length $8s$, equivalently a byte string of length s, which is a binary integer with the most significant bit first, regardless of how x is stored as an unsigned integer. For convenience the following notation is used: $[x]^s = \text{STR}^{8s}_2(x)$. Thus, $[\text{NUM}_{radix}(X)]^s$ will convert the character string X into an unsigned integer and then convert that to a byte string of length s bytes with the most significant bit first.

Continuing, the preceding example should help clarify the issues involved.

Character string	**"zaby"**
Numeral string X representation of character string	25 0 1 24
Convert X to number $x = \text{NUM}_{26}(X)$	decimal: 439450 hex: 6B49A binary: 1101011010010011010
x stored on big-endian byte order machine as a 32-bit unsigned integer	hex: 00 06 B4 9A binary: 00000000000001101011010010011010
x stored on little-endian byte order machine as a 32-bit unsigned integer	hex: 9A B4 06 00 binary: 10011010101101000000011000000000
Convert x, regardless of endian format, to a bit string of length 32 bits (4 bytes), expressed as $[x]^4$	00000000000001101011010010011010

The Function F_K We can now define in general terms the function F_K. The core of F_K is some type of randomizing function whose input and output are bit strings. For convenience, the strings should be multiples of 8 bits, forming byte strings. Define m to be u for even rounds and v for odd rounds; this specifies the desired output character string length. Define b to be the number of bytes needed to store the number representing a character string of m bytes. Then the round, including F_K, consists of the following general steps (A and B refer to A_i and B_i for round i):

1. $Q \leftarrow [\text{NUM}_{radix}(B)]^b$	Converts numeral string X into byte string Q of length b bytes.
2. $Y \leftarrow \text{RAN}[Q]$	A pseudorandom function PRNF that produces a pseudorandom byte string Y as a function of the bits of Q.
3. $y \leftarrow \text{NUM}_2(Y)$	Converts Y into unsigned integer.
4. $c \leftarrow (\text{NUM}_{radix}(A) + y) \bmod radix^m$	Converts numeral string A into an integer and adds to y, modulo $radix^m$.
5. $C \leftarrow \text{STR}^m_{radix}(c)$	Converts c into a numeral string C of length m.
6. $A \leftarrow B$; $B \leftarrow C$	Completes the round by placing the unchanged value of B from the preceding round into A, and placing C into B.

Steps 1 through 3 constitute the round function F_K. Step 3 is presented with Y, which is an unstructured bit string. Because different platforms may store unsigned integers using different word lengths and endian conventions, it is necessary to perform $\text{NUM}_2(Y)$ to get an unsigned integer y. The stored bit sequence for y may or may not be identical to the bit sequence for Y.

As mentioned, the pseudorandom function in step 2 need not be reversible. Its purpose is to provide a randomized, scrambled bit string. For DES, this is achieved by using fixed S-boxes, as described in Appendix S. Virtually all FPE schemes that use the Feistel structure use AES as the basis for the scrambling function to achieve stronger security.

Relationship Between Radix, Message Length, and Bit Length Consider a numeral string X of length len and base $radix$. If we convert this to a number $x = \text{NUM}_{radix}(X)$, then the maximum value of x is $radix^{len} - 1$. The number of bits needed to encode x is

$$bitlen = \lceil \text{LOG}_2(radix^{len}) \rceil = \lceil len\text{LOG}_2(radix) \rceil$$

Observe that an increase in either $radix$ or len increases $bitlen$. Often, we want to limit the value of $bitlen$ to some fixed upper limit, for example, 128 bits, which is the size of the input to AES encryption. We also want the FPE to handle a variety of radix values. The typical FPE, and all of those discussed subsequently, allow a given range of radix values and then define a maximum character string length in order to provide the algorithm with a fixed value of $bitlen$. Let the range of radix values be from 2 to $maxradix$, and the maximum allowable character string value be $maxlen$. Then the following relationship holds:

$$maxlen \leq \lfloor bitlen/\text{LOG}_2(radix) \rfloor, \text{ or equivalently}$$
$$maxlen \leq \lfloor bitlen \times \text{LOG}_{radix}(2) \rfloor$$

For example, for a radix of 10, $maxlen \leq \lfloor 0.3 \times bitlen \rfloor$; for a radix of 26, $maxlen \leq \lfloor 0.21 \times bitlen \rfloor$. The larger the radix, the smaller the maximum character length for a given bit length.

NIST Methods for Format-Preserving Encryption

In 2013, NIST issued SP 800-38G: *Recommendation for Block Cipher Modes of Operation: Methods for Format-Preserving Encryption*. This Recommendation specifies three methods for format-preserving encryption, called FF1, FF2, and FF3. The three methods all use the Feistel structure shown in Figure 7.12. They employ somewhat different round functions F_K, which are built using AES. Important differences are the following:

- FF1 supports the greatest range of lengths for the plaintext character string and the tweak. To achieve this, the round function uses a cipher-block-chaining (CBC) style of encryption, whereas FF2 and FF3 employ simple electronic codebook (ECB) encryption.
- FF2 uses a subkey generated from the encryption key and the tweak, whereas FF1 and FF3 use the encryption key directly. The use of a subkey may help protect the original key from side-channel analysis, which is an attack based on information gained from the physical implementation of a cryptosystem, rather than brute force or cryptanalysis. Examples of such attacks are attempts to deduce key bits based on power consumption or execution time.
- FF3 offers the lowest round count, eight, compared to ten for FF1 and FF2, and is the least flexible in the tweaks that it supports.

Algorithm FF1 Algorithm FF1 was submitted to NIST as a proposed FPE mode [BELL10a, BELL10b] with the name FFX[Radix]. FF1 uses a pseudorandom function $PRF_K(X)$ that produces a 128-bit output with inputs X that is a multiple of 128 bits and encryption key K (Figure 7.13). In essence, $PRF_K(X)$ use CBC encryption (Figure 7.4) with X as the plaintext input, encryption key K, and an initial vector (IV) of all zeros. The output is the last block of ciphertext produced. This is also

Prerequisites:
Approved, 128-bit block cipher, CIPH;
Key, K, for the block cipher;

Input:
Nonempty bit string, X, such that LEN(X) is a multiple of 128.

Output:
128-bit block, Y

Steps:
1. Let m = LEN(X)/128.
2. Partition X into m 128-bit blocks $X_1, \ldots, X_m$, so that $X = X_1 \| \ldots \| X_m$
3. Let $Y_0 = [0]^{16}$
4. For j from 1 to m:
4.i let $Y_j = \text{CIPH}_K(Y_{j-1} \oplus X_j)$.
6. Return Y_m.

Figure 7.13 Algorithm PRF(X)

equivalent to the message authentication code known as CBC-MAC, or CMAC, described in Chapter 12.

The FF1 encryption algorithm is illustrated in Figure 7.14. The shaded lines correspond to the function F_K. The algorithm has 10 rounds and the following parameters (Table 7.3b):

- $radix \in [2 .. 2^{16}]$
- $radix^{minlen} \geq 100$
- $minlen \geq 2$
- $maxlen < 2^{32}$. For the maximum radix value of 2^{16}, the maximum bit length to store the integer value of X is 16×2^{32} bits; for the minimum radix value of 2, the maximum bit length to store the integer value of X is 2^{32} bits.
- $maxTlen < 2^{32}$

The inputs to the encryption algorithm are a character string X of length n and a tweak T of length t. The tweak is optional in that it may be the empty string.

Prerequisites:

Approved, 128-bit block cipher, CIPH;
Key, K, for the block cipher;
Base, *radix*, for the character alphabet;
Range of supported message lengths, [minlen .. maxlen];
Maximum byte length for tweaks, maxTlen.

Inputs:

Character string, X, in base *radix* of length n such that $n \in$ [minlen .. maxlen];
Tweak T, a byte string of byte length t, such that $t \in$ [0 .. maxTlen].

Output:

Character string, Y, such that LEN(Y) = n.

Steps:

1. Let $u = \lfloor n/2 \rfloor$; $v = n - u$.
2. Let $A = X[1 .. u]$; $B = X[u + 1 .. n]$.
3. Let $b = \lceil \lceil v \, \text{LOG}_2(radix) \rceil / 8 \rceil$; $d = 4 \lceil b/4 \rceil + 4$
4. Let $P = [1]^1 \| [2]^1 \| [1]^1 \| [radix]^3 \| [10]^1 \| [u \bmod 256]^1 \| [n]^4 \| [t]^4$.
5. For i from 0 to 9:
   i. Let $Q = T \| [0]^{(-t-b-1) \bmod 16} \| [i]^1 \| [\text{NUM}_{radix}(B)]^b$.
   ii. Let $R = \text{PRF}_K(P \| Q)$.
   iii. Let S be the first d bytes of the following string of $\lceil d/16 \rceil$ 128-bit blocks:
   $R \| \text{CIPH}_K(R \oplus [1]^{16}) \| \text{CIPH}_K(R \oplus [2]^{16}) \| \ldots \| \text{CIPH}_K(R \oplus [\lceil d/16 \rceil - 1]^{16})$.
   iv. Let $y = \text{NUM}_2(S)$.
   v. If i is even, let $m = u$; else, let $m = v$.
   vi. Let $c = (\text{NUM}_{radix}(A) + y) \bmod radix^m$.
   vii. Let $C = \text{STR}^m_{radix}(c)$.
   viii. Let $A = B$.
   ix. Let $B = C$.
6. Return $Y = A \| B$.

Figure 7.14 Algorithm FF1 (FFX[Radix])

The output is the encrypted character string Y of length n. What follows is a step-by-step description of the algorithm.

1., 2. The input X is split into two substrings A and B. If n is even, A and B are of equal length. Otherwise, B is one character longer than A.

3. The expression $\lceil v \text{ LOG}_2(\text{radix}) \rceil$ equals the number of bits needed to encode B, which is v characters long. Encoding B as a byte string, b is the number of bytes in the encoding. The definition of d ensures that the output of the Feistel round function is at least 4 bytes longer than this encoding of B, which minimizes any bias in the modular reduction in step 5.vi, as explained subsequently.

4. P is a 128-bit (16-byte) block that is a function of *radix*, u, n, and t. It serves as the first block of plaintext input to the CBC encryption mode used in 5.ii, and is intended to increase security.

5. The loop through the 10 rounds of encryption.

5.i The tweak, T, the substring, B, and the round number, i, are encoded as a binary string, Q, which is one or more 128-bit blocks in length. To understand this step, first note that the value $\text{NUM}_{radix}(B)$ produces a numeral string that represents B in base *radix*. How this numeral string is formatted and stored is outside the scope of the standard. Then, the value $[\text{NUM}_{radix}(B)]^b$ produces the representation of the numerical value of B as a binary number in a string of b bytes. We also have the length of T is t bytes, and the round number is stored in a single byte. This yields a length of $(t + b + 1)$ bytes. This is padded out with $z = (-t - b - 1)$ mod 16 bytes. From the rules of modular arithmetic, we know that $(z + t + b + 1) \bmod 16 = 0$. Thus the length of Q is one or more 128-bit blocks.

5.ii The concatenation of P and Q is input to the pseudorandom function PRF to produce a 128-bit output R. This function is the pseudorandom core of the Feistel round function. It scrambles the bits of B_i (Figure 7.12).

5.iii This step either truncates or expands R to a byte string S of length d bytes. That is, if $d \leq 16$ bytes, then R is the first d bytes of R. Otherwise the 16-byte R is concatenated with successive encryptions of R XORed with successive constants to produce the shortest string of 16-byte blocks whose length is greater than or equal to d bytes.

5.iv This step begins the process of converting the results of the scrambling of B_i into a form suitable for combining with A_i. In this step, the d-byte string S is converted into a numeral string in base 2 that represents S. That is, S is represented as a binary string y.

5.v This step determines the length m of the character string output that is required to match the length of the B portion of the round output. For even-numbered rounds, the length is u characters, and for odd-numbered rounds it is v characters, as shown in Figure 7.12.

5.vi The numerical values of A and y are added modulo $radix^m$. This truncates the value of the sum to a value c that can be stored in m characters.

5.vii This step converts the c into the proper representation C as a string of m characters.

5.viii, 5.ix These steps complete the round by placing the unchanged value of B from the preceding round into A, and placing C into B.

6. After the final round, the result is returned as the concatenation of A and B.

It may be worthwhile to clarify the various uses of the NUM function in FF1. NUM converts strings with a given radix into integers. In step 5.i, B is a character string in base radix, so $NUM_{radix}(B)$ converts this into an integer, which is stored as a byte string, suitable for encryption in step 5.ii. For step 5.iv, S is a byte string output of an encryption function, which can be viewed a bit string, so $NUM_2(S)$ converts this into an integer.

Finally, a brief explanation of the variable d is in order, which is best explained by example. Let $radix = 26$ and $v = 30$ characters. Then $b = 18$ bytes, and $d = 24$ bytes. Step 5.ii produces an output R of 16 bytes. We desire a scrambled output of b bytes to match the input, and so R needs to be padded out. Rather than padding with a constant value such as all zeros, step 5.iii pads out with random bits. The result, in step 5.iv is a number greater than $radix^m$ of fully randomized bits. The use of randomized padding avoids a potential security risk of using a fixed padding.

Algorithm FF2 Algorithm FF2 was submitted to NIST as a proposed FPE mode with the name VAES3 [VANC11]. The encryption algorithm is defined in Figure 7.15. The shaded lines correspond to the function F_K. The algorithm has the following parameters:

- $radix \in [2 .. 2^8]$
- $tweakradix \in [2 .. 2^8]$
- $radix^{minlen} \geq 100$
- $minlen \geq 2$
- $maxlen \leq 2\lfloor 120/LOG_2(radix) \rfloor$ if $radix$ is a power of 2. For the maximum radix value of 2^8, $maxlen \leq 30$; for the minimum radix value of 2, $maxlen \leq 240$. In both cases, the maximum bit length to store the integer value of X is 240 bits, or 30 bytes.
- $maxlen \leq 2\lfloor 98/LOG_2(radix) \rfloor$ if $radix$ is a not a power of 2. For the maximum radix value of 255, $maxlen \leq 24$; for the minimum radix value of 3, $maxlen \leq 124$.
- $maxTlen \leq \lfloor 104/LOG_2(tweakradix) \rfloor$. For the maximum $tweakradix$ value of 2^8, $maxTlen \leq 13$.

For FF2, the plaintext character alphabet and that of the tweak may be different.

The first two steps of FF2 are the same as FF1, setting values for v, u, A, and B. FF2 proceeds with the following steps:

3. P is a 128-bit (16-byte) block. If there is a tweak, then P is a function of $radix$, t, n, and the 13-byte numerical value of the tweak. If there is no tweak ($t = 0$), then P is a function of $radix$ and n. P is used to form an encryption key in step 4.

Approved, 128-bit block cipher, CIPH;
Key, K, for the block cipher;
Base, *tweakradix*, for the tweak character alphabet;
Range of supported message lengths, [*minlen* .. *maxlen*];
Maximum supported tweak length, *maxTlen*.

Inputs:
Numeral string, X, in base *radix*, of length n such that $n \in [minlen .. maxlen]$;
Tweak numeral string, T, in base *tweakradix*, of length t such that $t \in [0 .. maxTlen]$.

Output:
Numeral string, Y, such that $\text{LEN}(Y) = n$.

Steps:
1. Let $u = \lfloor n/2 \rfloor$; $v = n - u$.
2. Let $A = X[1 .. u]$; $B = X[u + 1 .. n]$.
3. If $t > 0$, $P = [radix]^1 \| [t]^1 \| [n]^1 \| [\text{NUM}_{tweakradix}(T)]^{13}$; else $P = [radix]^1 \| [0]^1 \| [n]^1 \| [0]^{13}$.
4. Let $J = \text{CIPH}_K(P)$.
5. For i from 0 to 9:

   i. Let $Q \leftarrow [i]^1 \| [\text{NUM}_{radix}(B)]^{15}$
   ii. Let $Y \leftarrow \text{CIPH}_J(Q)$.
   iii. Let $y \leftarrow \text{NUM}_2(Y)$.
   iv. If i is even, let $m = u$; else, let $m = v$.
   v. Let $c = (\text{NUM}_{radix}(A) + y) \bmod radix^m$.
   vi. Let $C = \text{STR}^m_{radix}(c)$.
   vii. Let $A = B$.
   viii. Let $B = C$.
6. Return $Y = A \| B$.

Figure 7.15 Algorithm FF2 (VAES3)

4. J is the encryption of P using the input key K.

5. The loop through the 10 rounds of encryption.

5.i B is converted into a 15-byte number, prepended by the round number to form a 16-byte block Q.

5.ii Q is encrypted using the encryption key J to yield Y.

The remaining steps are the same as for FF1. The essential difference is in the way in which all of the parameters are incorporated into the encryption that takes place in the block F_K. In both cases, the encryption is not simply an encryption of B using key K. For FF1, B is combined with the tweak, the round number, t, n, u, and *radix* to form a string of multiple 16-byte blocks. Then CBC encryption is used with K to produce a 16-byte output. For FF2, all of the parameters besides B are combined to form a 16-byte block, which is then encrypted with K to form the key value J. J is then used as the key for the one-block encryption of B.

The structure of FF2 explains the maximum length restrictions. In step 3, P incorporates the radix, tweak length, the numeral string length, and the tweak into the calculation. As input to AES, P is restricted to 16 bytes. With a maximum radix value of 2^8, the radix value can be stored in one byte (byte value 0 corresponds to 256). The string length n and tweak length t each easily fits into one byte. This leaves a restriction that the value of the tweak should be stored in at most 13 bytes, or 104 bits. The number of bits to store the tweak is $\text{LOG}_2(\textit{tweakradix}^{Tlen})$. This leads to the restriction $\textit{maxTlen} \geq \lfloor 104/\text{LOG}_2(\textit{tweakradix}) \rfloor$. Similarly step 5i incorporates B and the round number into a 16-byte input to AES, leaving 15 bytes to encode B, or 120 bits, so that the length must be less than or equal to $\lfloor 120/\text{LOG}_2(\textit{radix}) \rfloor$. The parameter *maxlen* refers to the entire block, consisting of partitions A and B, thus $\textit{maxlen} \geq 2\lfloor 120/\text{LOG}_2(\textit{radix}) \rfloor$.

There is a further restriction on *maxlen* for a radix that is not a power of 2. As explained in [VANC11], when the radix is not a power of 2, modular arithmetic causes the value (y mod $\textit{radix}^m$) to not have uniform distribution in the output space, which can result in a cryptographic weakness.

ALGORITHM FF3 Algorithm FF3 was submitted to NIST as a proposed FPE mode with the name BPS-BC [BRIE10]. The encryption algorithm is illustrated in Figure 7.16. The shaded lines correspond to the function F_K. The algorithm has the following parameters:

- $\textit{radix} \in [2 .. 2^{16}]$
- $\textit{radix}^{minlen} \geq 100$
- $\textit{minlen} \geq 2$

Approved, 128-bit block cipher, CIPH;
Key, K, for the block cipher;
Base, *radix*, for the character alphabet such that $\textit{radix} \in [2..2^{16}]$;
Range of supported message lengths, [*minlen* .. *maxlen*], such that $\textit{minlen} \geq 2$ and $\textit{maxlen} \leq 2\lfloor \log_{radix}(2^{96}) \rfloor$.

Inputs:
Numeral string, X, in base *radix* of length n such that $n \in$ [minlen .. maxlen];
Tweak bit string, T, such that LEN(T) = 64.

Output:
Numeral string, Y, such that LEN(Y) = n.

Steps:

1. Let $u = \lceil n/2 \rceil$; $v = n - u$.
2. Let $A = X[1 .. u]$; $B = X[u + 1 .. n]$.
3. Let $T_L = T[0 .. 31]$ and $T_R = T[32 .. 63]$.
4. For i from 0 to 7:
   i. If i is even, let $m = u$ and $W = T_R$, else let $m = v$ and $W = T_L$.
   ii. Let $P = \text{REV}([\text{NUM}_{radix}(\text{REV}(B))]^{12}) \| [W \oplus \text{REV}([i]^4])$.
   iii. Let $Y = \text{CIPH}_K(P)$.
   iv. Let $y = \text{NUM}_2(\text{REV}(Y))$.
   v. Let $c = (\text{NUM}_{radix}(\text{REV}(A)) + y) \bmod \textit{radix}^m$.
   vi. Let $C = \text{REV}(\text{STR}^m_{radix}(c))$.
   vii. Let $A = B$.
   viii. Let $B = C$.
5. Return $A \| B$.

Figure 7.16 Algorithm FF3 (BPS-BC)

- $maxlen \leq 2\lfloor \text{LOG}_{radix}(2^{96}) \rfloor$. For the maximum radix value of 2^{16}, $maxlen \leq 12$; for the minimum radix value of 2, $maxlen \leq 192$. In both cases, the maximum bit length to store the integer value of X is 192 bits, or 24 bytes.
- Tweak length = 64 bits

FF3 proceeds with the following steps:

1., 2. The input X is split into two substrings A and B. If n is even, A and B are of equal length. Otherwise, A is one character longer than B, in contrast to FF1 and FF2, where B is one character longer than A.

3. The tweak is partitioned into a 32-bit left tweak T_L and a 32-bit right tweak T_R.

4. The loop through the 8 rounds of encryption.

4.i As in FF1 and FF2, this step determines the length m of the character string output that is required to match the length of the B portion of the round output. The step also determines whether T_L or T_R will be used as W in step 4ii.

4.ii The bits of B are reversed, then $\text{NUM}_{radix}(B)$ produces a 12-byte numeral string in base *radix*; the results are again reversed. A 32-bit encoding of the round number i is stored in a 4-byte unit, which is reversed and then XORed with W. P is formed by concatenating these two results to form a 16-byte block.

4.iii P is encrypted using the encryption key K to yield Y.

4.iv This is similar to step 5.iv in FF1, except that Y is reversed before converting it into a numeral string in base 2.

4.v The numerical values of the reverse of A and y are added modulo $radix^m$. This truncates the value of the sum to a value c that can be stored in m characters.

4.vi This step converts c to a numeral string C.

The remaining steps are the same as for FF1.

7.9 KEY TERMS, REVIEW QUESTIONS, AND PROBLEMS

Key Terms

block cipher modes of operation	ciphertext stealing	output feedback mode (OFB)
cipher block chaining mode (CBC)	counter mode (CTR)	Triple DES (3DES)
cipher feedback mode (CFB)	electronic codebook mode (ECB)	tweakable block cipher
	meet-in-the-middle attack	XTS-AES mode
	nonce	

Review Questions

7.1 Why is the second stage of triple DES a decryption rather than an encryption?

7.2 What is a meet-in-the-middle attack?

7.3 How many keys are used in triple encryption?

7.4 List the applications of encryption for different block cipher modes of operation.

7.5 Why do some block cipher modes of operation only use encryption while others use both encryption and decryption?

Problems

7.1 You want to build a hardware device to do block encryption in the cipher block chaining (CBC) mode using an algorithm stronger than DES. 3DES is a good candidate. Figure 7.17 shows two possibilities, both of which follow from the definition of CBC. Which of the two would you choose:

a. For security?

b. For performance?

7.2 Can you suggest a security improvement to either option in Figure 7.17, using only three DES chips and some number of XOR functions? Assume you are still limited to two keys.

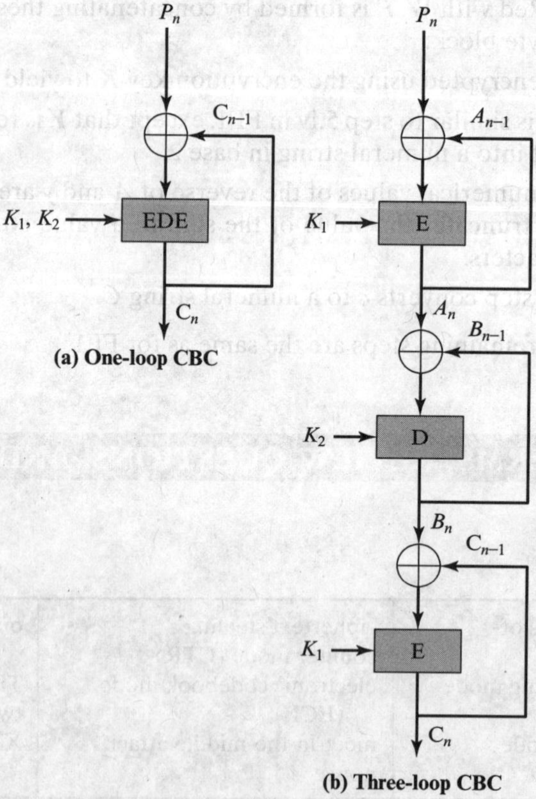

Figure 7.17 Use of Triple DES in CBC Mode

7.3 The Merkle–Hellman attack on 3DES begins by assuming a value of $A = 0$ (Figure 7.1b). Then, for each of the 2^{56} possible values of K_1, the plaintext P that produces $A = 0$ is determined. Describe the rest of the algorithm.

7.4 With the ECB mode, if there is an error in a block of the transmitted ciphertext, only the corresponding plaintext block is affected. However, in the CBC mode, this error propagates. For example, an error in the transmitted C_1 (Figure 7.4) obviously corrupts P_1 and P_2.

a. Are any blocks beyond P_2 affected?

b. Suppose that there is a bit error in the source version of P_1. Through how many ciphertext blocks is this error propagated? What is the effect at the receiver?

7.5 Explain the encryption and decryption operations of CBC mode.

7.6 CBC-Pad is a block cipher mode of operation used in the RC5 block cipher, but it could be used in any block cipher. CBC-Pad handles plaintext of any length. The ciphertext is longer then the plaintext by at most the size of a single block. Padding is used to assure that the plaintext input is a multiple of the block length. It is assumed that the original plaintext is an integer number of bytes. This plaintext is padded at the end by from 1 to *bb* bytes, where *bb* equals the block size in bytes. The pad bytes are all the same and set to a byte that represents the number of bytes of padding. For example, if there are 8 bytes of padding, each byte has the bit pattern 00001000. Why not allow zero bytes of padding? That is, if the original plaintext is an integer multiple of the block size, why not refrain from padding?

7.7 For the ECB, CBC, and CFB modes, the plaintext must be a sequence of one or more complete data blocks (or, for CFB mode, data segments). In other words, for these three modes, the total number of bits in the plaintext must be a positive multiple of the block (or segment) size. One common method of padding, if needed, consists of a 1 bit followed by as few zero bits, possibly none, as are necessary to complete the final block. It is considered good practice for the sender to pad every message, including messages in which the final message block is already complete. What is the motivation for including a padding block when padding is not needed?

7.8 What are the advantages of a stream cipher? Mention the desirable property of a stream cipher.

7.9 Mention the advantage and disadvantage of OFB mode.

7.10 Discuss the hardware and software efficiency of CTR mode. Why, CTR mode is simpler than ECB and CBC modes?

7.11 Padding may not always be appropriate. For example, one might wish to store the encrypted data in the same memory buffer that originally contained the plaintext. In that case, the ciphertext must be the same length as the original plaintext. We saw the use of ciphertext stealing in the case of XTS-AES to deal with partial blocks. Figure 7.18a shows the use of ciphertext stealing to modify CBC mode, called CBC-CTS.

a. Explain how it works.

b. Describe how to decrypt C_{n-1} and C_n.

7.12 Figure 7.18b shows an alternative to CBC-CTS for producing ciphertext of equal length to the plaintext when the plaintext is not an integer multiple of the block size.

a. Explain the algorithm.

b. Explain why CBC-CTS is preferable to this approach illustrated in Figure 7.18b.

7.13 Draw a figure similar to those of Figure 7.8 for XTS-AES mode.

7.14 Work out the following problems from first principles without converting to binary and counting the bits. Then compare with the formulae presented for encoding a character string into an integer, and vice-versa, in the specified radix. (*Hint:* Consider the next-lower and next-higher power of two for each integer.)

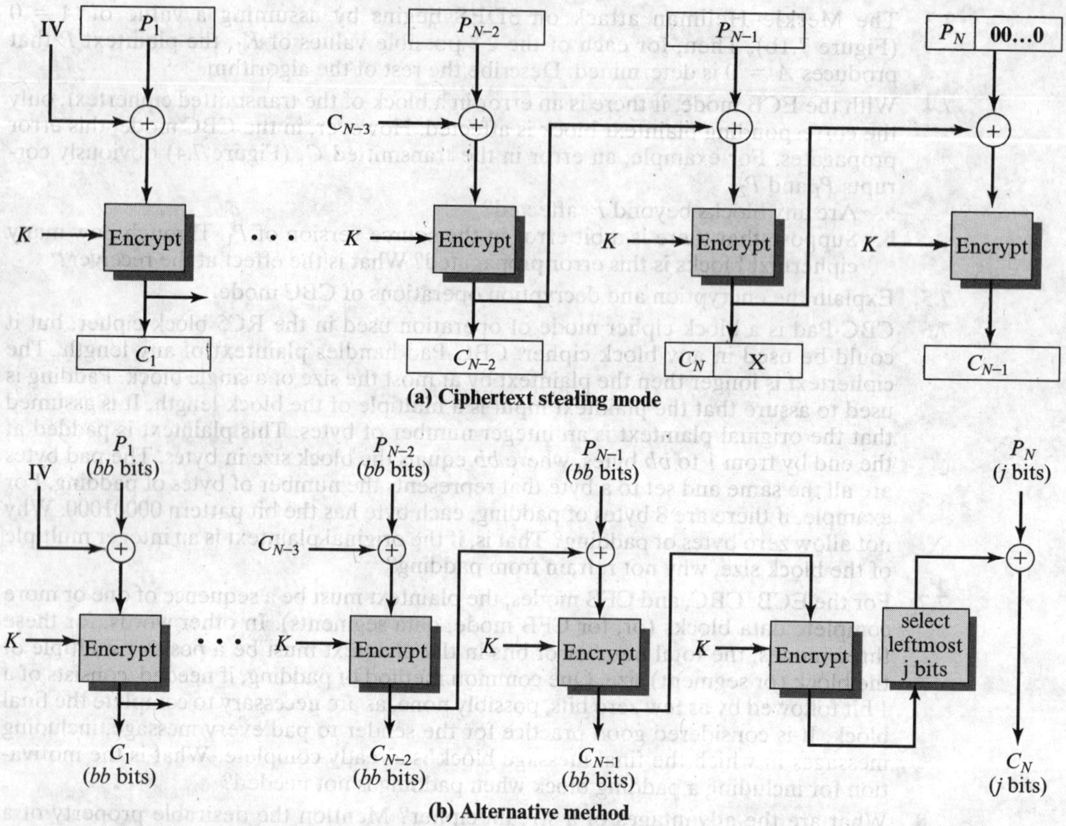

Figure 7.18 Block Cipher Modes for Plaintext not a Multiple of Block Size

a. How many bits are exactly required to encode the following integers? (The number shown as an integer's subscript refers to the radix of that integer.)

i. 2047_{10}
ii. 2048_{10}
iii. 32767_{10}
iv. 32768_{10}
v. 32767_{16}
vi. 32768_{16}
vii. $537F_{16}$
viii. 29431_{10}

b. Exactly how many bytes are required to represent the numbers in (a) above?

7.15 **a.** In radix-26, write down the numeral string X for each of the following character strings, followed by the number of "digits" (i.e., the length of the numeral string) in each case.

i. "hex"
ii. "cipher"
iii. "not"
iv. "symbol"

b. For each case of problem (a), determine the number $x = NUM_{26}(X)$
c. Determine the byte form $[x]$ for each number x computed in problem (b).
d. What is the smallest power of the radix (26) that is greater than each of the numerical strings determined in (b)?
e. Is it related to the length of the numeral string in each case, in problem (a)? If so, what is this relationship?

7.16 Refer to algorithms FF1 and FF2.
a. For step 1, for each algorithm, $u \leftarrow \lfloor n/2 \rfloor$ and $v \leftarrow \lceil n - u \rceil$. Show that for any three integers x, y, and n:
if $x = \lfloor n/2 \rfloor$ and $y = \lceil n - x \rceil$, then:
i. Either $x = n/2$, or $x = (n - 1)/2$.
ii. Either $y = n/2$, or $y = (n + 1)/2$.
iii. $x \leq y$. (Under what condition is $x = y$?)
b. What is the significance of result in the previous sub-problem (iii), in terms of the lengths u and v of the left and right half-strings, respectively?

7.17 In step 3 of Algorithm FF1, what do b and d represent? What is the unit of measurement (bits, bytes, digits, characters) of each of these quantities?

7.18 In the inputs to algorithms FF1, FF2, and FF3, why are the specified radix ranges important? For example, why should $radix \in [0..2^8]$ for Algorithm FF2, or $radix \in [2..2^{16}]$ in the case of Algorithm FF3?

Programming Problems

7.19 Create software that can encrypt and decrypt in cipher block chaining mode using one of the following ciphers: affine modulo 256, Hill modulo 256, S-DES, DES.
Test data for S-DES using a binary initialization vector of 1010 1010. A binary plaintext of 0000 0001 0010 0011 encrypted with a binary key of 01111 11101 should give a binary plaintext of 1111 0100 0000 1011. Decryption should work correspondingly.

7.20 Create software that can encrypt and decrypt in 4-bit cipher feedback mode using one of the following ciphers: additive modulo 256, affine modulo 256, S-DES;

or

8-bit cipher feedback mode using one of the following ciphers: 2×2 Hill modulo 256.
Test data for S-DES using a binary initialization vector of 1010 1011. A binary plaintext of 0001 0010 0011 0100 encrypted with a binary key of 01111 11101 should give a binary plaintext of 1110 1100 1111 1010. Decryption should work correspondingly.

7.21 Create software that can encrypt and decrypt in counter mode using one of the following ciphers: affine modulo 256, Hill modulo 256, S-DES.
Test data for S-DES using a counter starting at 0000 0000. A binary plaintext of 0000 0001 0000 0010 0000 0100 encrypted with a binary key of 01111 11101 should give a binary plaintext of 0011 1000 0100 1111 0011 0010. Decryption should work correspondingly.

7.22 Implement a differential cryptanalysis attack on 3-round S-DES.

CHAPTER 8

RANDOM BIT GENERATION AND STREAM CIPHERS

LEARNING OBJECTIVES

After studying this chapter, you should be able to:

- Explain the concepts of randomness and unpredictability with respect to random numbers.
- Understand the differences among true random number generators, pseudorandom number generators, and pseudorandom functions.
- Present an overview of requirements for pseudorandom number generators.
- Explain how a block cipher can be used to construct a pseudorandom number generator.
- Present an overview of stream ciphers and RC4.
- Explain the significance of skew.

An important cryptographic function is the generation of random bit streams. Random bits streams are used in a wide variety of contexts, including key generation and encryption. In essence, there are two fundamentally different strategies for generating random bits or random numbers. One strategy, which until recently dominated in cryptographic applications, computes bits deterministically using an algorithm. This class of random bit generators is known as pseudorandom number generators (PRNGs) or deterministic random bit generators (DRBGs). The other strategy is to produce bits non-deterministically using some physical source that produces some sort of random output. This latter class of random bit generators is known as true random number generators (TRNGs) or non-deterministic random bit generators (NRBGs).

The chapter begins with an analysis of the basic principles of PRNGs. Next, we look at some common PRNGs, including PRNGs based on the use of a symmetric block cipher. The chapter then moves on to the topic of symmetric stream ciphers, which are based on the use of a PRNG. The chapter next examines the most important stream cipher, RC4.

The remainder of the chapter is devoted to TRNGs. We look first at the basic principles and structure of TRNGs, and then examine a specific product, the Intel Digital Random Number Generator.

Throughout this chapter, reference is made to four important NIST documents:

- SP 800-90A (*Recommendation for Random Number Generation Using Deterministic Random Bit Generators,* January 2012) covers DRNGs.
- SP 800-90B (*Recommendation for the Entropy Sources Used for Random Bit Generation,* August 2012) covers criteria for entropy sources (ES), the devices from which we get unpredictable randomness and NRNGs.
- SP 800-90C (*Recommendation for Random Bit Generator (RBG) Constructions,* August 2012) discusses how to combine the entropy sources in 90B with the DRNG's from 90A to provide large quantities of unpredictable bits for cryptographic applications.

- SP 800-22 (*A Statistical Test Suite for Random and Pseudorandom Number Generators for Cryptographic Applications,* April 2010) discusses the selection and testing of NRBGs and DRBGs.

These specifications have heavily influenced the implementation of random bit generators in industry both in the U.S. and worldwide.

8.1 PRINCIPLES OF PSEUDORANDOM NUMBER GENERATION

Random numbers play an important role in the use of encryption for various network security applications. In this section, we provide a brief overview of the use of random numbers in cryptography and network security and then focus on the principles of pseudorandom number generation.

The Use of Random Numbers

A number of network security algorithms and protocols based on cryptography make use of random binary numbers. For example,

- Key distribution and reciprocal (mutual) authentication schemes, such as those discussed in Chapters 14 and 15. In such schemes, two communicating parties cooperate by exchanging messages to distribute keys and/or authenticate each other. In many cases, nonces are used for handshaking to prevent replay attacks. The use of random numbers for the nonces frustrates an opponent's efforts to determine or guess the nonce, in order to repeat an obsolete transaction.
- Session key generation. We will see a number of protocols in this book where a secret key for symmetric encryption is generated for use for a particular transaction (or session) and is valid for a short period of time. This key is generally called a session key.
- Generation of keys for the RSA public-key encryption algorithm (described in Chapter 9).
- Generation of a bit stream for symmetric stream encryption (described in this chapter).

These applications give rise to two distinct and not necessarily compatible requirements for a sequence of random numbers: randomness and unpredictability.

RANDOMNESS Traditionally, the concern in the generation of a sequence of allegedly random numbers has been that the sequence of numbers be random in some well-defined statistical sense. The following two criteria are used to validate that a sequence of numbers is random:

- **Uniform distribution:** The distribution of bits in the sequence should be uniform; that is, the frequency of occurrence of ones and zeros should be approximately equal.
- **Independence:** No one subsequence in the sequence can be inferred from the others.

Although there are well-defined tests for determining that a sequence of bits matches a particular distribution, such as the uniform distribution, there is no such test to "prove" independence. Rather, a number of tests can be applied to demonstrate if a sequence does not exhibit independence. The general strategy is to apply a number of such tests until the confidence that independence exists is sufficiently strong. That is, if each of a number of tests fails to show that a sequence of bits is not independent, then we can have a high level of confidence that the sequence is in fact independent.

In the context of our discussion, the use of a sequence of numbers that appear statistically random often occurs in the design of algorithms related to cryptography. For example, a fundamental requirement of the RSA public-key encryption scheme discussed in Chapter 9 is the ability to generate prime numbers. In general, it is difficult to determine if a given large number N is prime. A brute-force approach would be to divide N by every odd integer less than $\sqrt{N}$. If N is on the order, say, of 10^{150}, which is a not uncommon occurrence in public-key cryptography, such a brute-force approach is beyond the reach of human analysts and their computers. However, a number of effective algorithms exist that test the primality of a number by using a sequence of randomly chosen integers as input to relatively simple computations. If the sequence is sufficiently long (but far, far less than $\sqrt{10^{150}}$), the primality of a number can be determined with near certainty. This type of approach, known as randomization, crops up frequently in the design of algorithms. In essence, if a problem is too hard or time-consuming to solve exactly, a simpler, shorter approach based on randomization is used to provide an answer with any desired level of confidence.

UNPREDICTABILITY In applications such as reciprocal authentication, session key generation, and stream ciphers, the requirement is not just that the sequence of numbers be statistically random but that the successive members of the sequence are unpredictable. With "true" random sequences, each number is statistically independent of other numbers in the sequence and therefore unpredictable. Although true random numbers are used in some applications, they have their limitations, such as inefficiency, as is discussed shortly. Thus, it is more common to implement algorithms that generate sequences of numbers that appear to be random. In this latter case, care must be taken that an opponent not be able to predict future elements of the sequence on the basis of earlier elements.

TRNGs, PRNGs, and PRFs

Cryptographic applications typically make use of algorithmic techniques for random number generation. These algorithms are deterministic and therefore produce sequences of numbers that are not statistically random. However, if the algorithm is good, the resulting sequences will pass many tests of randomness. Such numbers are referred to as **pseudorandom numbers**.

You may be somewhat uneasy about the concept of using numbers generated by a deterministic algorithm as if they were random numbers. Despite what might be called philosophical objections to such a practice, it generally works. That is, under most circumstances, pseudorandom numbers will perform as well as if they were random for a given use. The phrase "as well as" is unfortunately subjective, but the

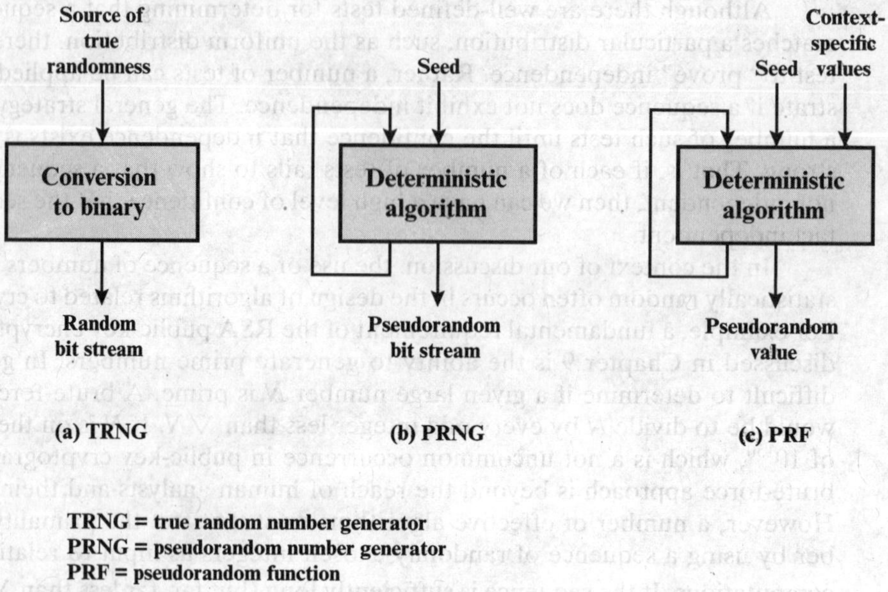

Figure 8.1 Random and Pseudorandom Number Generators

use of pseudorandom numbers is widely accepted. The same principle applies in statistical applications, in which a statistician takes a sample of a population and assumes that the results will be approximately the same as if the whole population were measured.

Figure 8.1 contrasts a **true random number generator (TRNG)** with two forms of pseudorandom number generators. A TRNG takes as input a source that is effectively random; the source is often referred to as an **entropy source**. We discuss such sources in Section 8.6. In essence, the entropy source is drawn from the physical environment of the computer and could include things such as keystroke timing patterns, disk electrical activity, mouse movements, and instantaneous values of the system clock. The source, or combination of sources, serve as input to an algorithm that produces random binary output. The TRNG may simply involve conversion of an analog source to a binary output. The TRNG may involve additional processing to overcome any bias in the source; this is discussed in Section 8.6.

In contrast, a PRNG takes as input a fixed value, called the **seed**, and produces a sequence of output bits using a deterministic algorithm. Quite often, the seed is generated by a TRNG. Typically, as shown, there is some feedback path by which some of the results of the algorithm are fed back as input as additional output bits are produced. The important thing to note is that the output bit stream is determined solely by the input value or values, so that an adversary who knows the algorithm and the seed can reproduce the entire bit stream.

Figure 8.1 shows two different forms of PRNGs, based on application.

- **Pseudorandom number generator:** An algorithm that is used to produce an open-ended sequence of bits is referred to as a PRNG. A common application for an open-ended sequence of bits is as input to a symmetric stream cipher, as discussed in Section 8.4. Also, see Figure 4.1a.

- **Pseudorandom function (PRF):** A PRF is used to produce a pseudorandom string of bits of some fixed length. Examples are symmetric encryption keys and nonces. Typically, the PRF takes as input a seed plus some context specific values, such as a user ID or an application ID. A number of examples of PRFs will be seen throughout this book, notably in Chapters 17 and 18.

Other than the number of bits produced, there is no difference between a PRNG and a PRF. The same algorithms can be used in both applications. Both require a seed and both must exhibit randomness and unpredictability. Further, a PRNG application may also employ context-specific input. In what follows, we make no distinction between these two applications.

PRNG Requirements

When a PRNG or PRF is used for a cryptographic application, then the basic requirement is that an adversary who does not know the seed is unable to determine the pseudorandom string. For example, if the pseudorandom bit stream is used in a stream cipher, then knowledge of the pseudorandom bit stream would enable the adversary to recover the plaintext from the ciphertext. Similarly, we wish to protect the output value of a PRF. In this latter case, consider the following scenario. A 128-bit seed, together with some context-specific values, are used to generate a 128-bit secret key that is subsequently used for symmetric encryption. Under normal circumstances, a 128-bit key is safe from a brute-force attack. However, if the PRF does not generate effectively random 128-bit output values, it may be possible for an adversary to narrow the possibilities and successfully use a brute force attack.

This general requirement for secrecy of the output of a PRNG or PRF leads to specific requirements in the areas of randomness, unpredictability, and the characteristics of the seed. We now look at these in turn.

RANDOMNESS In terms of randomness, the requirement for a PRNG is that the generated bit stream appear random even though it is deterministic. There is no single test that can determine if a PRNG generates numbers that have the characteristic of randomness. The best that can be done is to apply a sequence of tests to the PRNG. If the PRNG exhibits randomness on the basis of multiple tests, then it can be assumed to satisfy the randomness requirement. NIST SP 800-22 specifies that the tests should seek to establish the following three characteristics.

- **Uniformity:** At any point in the generation of a sequence of random or pseudorandom bits, the occurrence of a zero or one is equally likely, that is, the probability of each is exactly 1/2. The expected number of zeros (or ones) is $n/2$, where $n =$ the sequence length.
- **Scalability:** Any test applicable to a sequence can also be applied to subsequences extracted at random. If a sequence is random, then any such extracted subsequence should also be random. Hence, any extracted subsequence should pass any test for randomness.
- **Consistency:** The behavior of a generator must be consistent across starting values (seeds). It is inadequate to test a PRNG based on the output from a single seed or a TRNG on the basis of an output produced from a single physical output.

SP 800-22 lists 15 separate tests of randomness. An understanding of these tests requires a basic knowledge of statistical analysis, so we don't attempt a technical description here. Instead, to give some flavor for the tests, we list three of the tests and the purpose of each test, as follows.

- **Frequency test:** This is the most basic test and must be included in any test suite. The purpose of this test is to determine whether the number of ones and zeros in a sequence is approximately the same as would be expected for a truly random sequence.
- **Runs test:** The focus of this test is the total number of runs in the sequence, where a run is an uninterrupted sequence of identical bits bounded before and after with a bit of the opposite value. The purpose of the runs test is to determine whether the number of runs of ones and zeros of various lengths is as expected for a random sequence.
- **Maurer's universal statistical test:** The focus of this test is the number of bits between matching patterns (a measure that is related to the length of a compressed sequence). The purpose of the test is to detect whether or not the sequence can be significantly compressed without loss of information. A significantly compressible sequence is considered to be non-random.

UNPREDICTABILITY A stream of pseudorandom numbers should exhibit two forms of unpredictability:

- **Forward unpredictability:** If the seed is unknown, the next output bit in the sequence should be unpredictable in spite of any knowledge of previous bits in the sequence.
- **Backward unpredictability:** It should also not be feasible to determine the seed from knowledge of any generated values. No correlation between a seed and any value generated from that seed should be evident; each element of the sequence should appear to be the outcome of an independent random event whose probability is 1/2.

The same set of tests for randomness also provide a test of unpredictability. If the generated bit stream appears random, then it is not possible to predict some bit or bit sequence from knowledge of any previous bits. Similarly, if the bit sequence appears random, then there is no feasible way to deduce the seed based on the bit sequence. That is, a random sequence will have no correlation with a fixed value (the seed).

SEED REQUIREMENTS For cryptographic applications, the seed that serves as input to the PRNG must be secure. Because the PRNG is a deterministic algorithm, if the adversary can deduce the seed, then the output can also be determined. Therefore, the seed must be unpredictable. In fact, the seed itself must be a random or pseudorandom number.

Typically, the seed is generated by a TRNG, as shown in Figure 8.2. This is the scheme recommended by SP 800-90A. The reader may wonder, if a TRNG is available, why it is necessary to use a PRNG. If the application is a stream cipher, then a TRNG is not practical. The sender would need to generate a keystream of

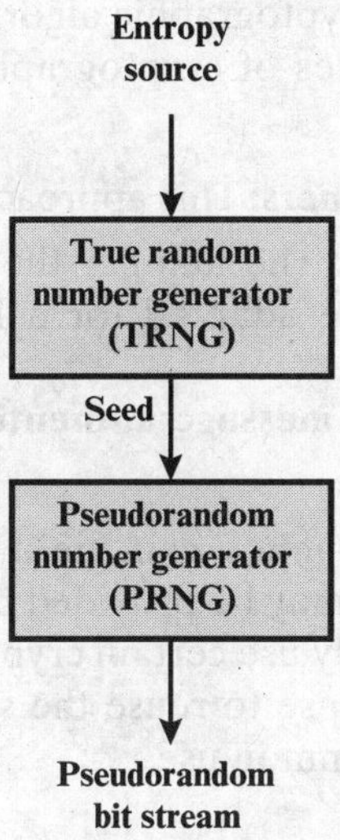

Figure 8.2 Generation of Seed Input to PRNG

bits as long as the plaintext and then transmit the keystream and the ciphertext securely to the receiver. If a PRNG is used, the sender need only find a way to deliver the stream cipher key, which is typically 54 or 128 bits, to the receiver in a secure fashion.

Even in the case of a PRF application, in which only a limited number of bits is generated, it is generally desirable to use a TRNG to provide the seed to the PRF and use the PRF output rather than use the TRNG directly. As is explained in Section 8.6, a TRNG may produce a binary string with some bias. The PRF would have the effect of conditioning the output of the TRNG so as to eliminate that bias.

Finally, the mechanism used to generate true random numbers may not be able to generate bits at a rate sufficient to keep up with the application requiring the random bits.

Algorithm Design

Cryptographic PRNGs have been the subject of much research over the years, and a wide variety of algorithms have been developed. These fall roughly into two categories.

- **Purpose-built algorithms:** These are algorithms designed specifically and solely for the purpose of generating pseudorandom bit streams. Some of these algorithms are used for a variety of PRNG applications; several of these are described in the next section. Others are designed specifically for use in a stream cipher. The most important example of the latter is RC4, described in Section 8.5.
- **Algorithms based on existing cryptographic algorithms:** Cryptographic algorithms have the effect of randomizing input data. Indeed, this is a requirement of such algorithms. For example, if a symmetric block cipher produced ciphertext that had certain regular patterns in it, it would aid in the process of

cryptanalysis. Thus, cryptographic algorithms can serve as the core of PRNGs. Three broad categories of cryptographic algorithms are commonly used to create PRNGs:

–**Symmetric block ciphers:** This approach is discussed in Section 8.3.

–**Asymmetric ciphers:** The number theoretic concepts used for an asymmetric cipher can also be adapted for a PRNG; this approach is examined in Chapter 10.

–**Hash functions and message authentication codes:** This approach is examined in Chapter 12.

Any of these approaches can yield a cryptographically strong PRNG. A purpose-built algorithm may be provided by an operating system for general use. For applications that already use certain cryptographic algorithms for encryption or authentication, it makes sense to reuse the same code for the PRNG. Thus, all of these approaches are in common use.

8.2 PSEUDORANDOM NUMBER GENERATORS

In this section, we look at two types of algorithms for PRNGs.

Linear Congruential Generators

A widely used technique for pseudorandom number generation is an algorithm first proposed by Lehmer [LEHM51], which is known as the linear congruential method. The algorithm is parameterized with four numbers, as follows:

m	the modulus	$m > 0$
a	the multiplier	$0 < a < m$
c	the increment	$0 \leq c < m$
X_0	the starting value, or seed	$0 \leq X_0 < m$

The sequence of random numbers $\{X_n\}$ is obtained via the following iterative equation:

$$X_{n+1} = (aX_n + c) \bmod m$$

If m, a, c, and X_0 are integers, then this technique will produce a sequence of integers with each integer in the range $0 \leq X_n < m$.

The selection of values for a, c, and m is critical in developing a good random number generator. For example, consider $a = c = 1$. The sequence produced is obviously not satisfactory. Now consider the values $a = 7, c = 0, m = 32$, and $X_0 = 1$. This generates the sequence {7, 17, 23, 1, 7, etc.}, which is also clearly unsatisfactory. Of the 32 possible values, only four are used; thus, the sequence is said to have a period of 4. If, instead, we change the value of a to 5, then the sequence is {5, 25, 29, 17, 21, 9, 13, 1, 5, etc. }, which increases the period to 8.

We would like m to be very large, so that there is the potential for producing a long series of distinct random numbers. A common criterion is that m be nearly equal to the maximum representable nonnegative integer for a given computer. Thus, a value of m near to or equal to 2^{31} is typically chosen.

[PARK88] proposes three tests to be used in evaluating a random number generator:

T_1: The function should be a full-period generating function. That is, the function should generate all the numbers from 0 through $m - 1$ before repeating.

T_2: The generated sequence should appear random.

T_3: The function should implement efficiently with 32-bit arithmetic.

With appropriate values of a, c, and m, these three tests can be passed. With respect to T_1, it can be shown that if m is prime and $c = 0$, then for certain values of a the period of the generating function is $m - 1$, with only the value 0 missing. For 32-bit arithmetic, a convenient prime value of m is $2^{31} - 1$. Thus, the generating function becomes

$$X_{n+1} = (aX_n) \bmod (2^{31} - 1)$$

Of the more than 2 billion possible choices for a, only a handful of multipliers pass all three tests. One such value is $a = 7^5 = 16807$, which was originally selected for use in the IBM 360 family of computers [LEWI69]. This generator is widely used and has been subjected to a more thorough testing than any other PRNG. It is frequently recommended for statistical and simulation work (e.g., [JAIN91]).

The strength of the linear congruential algorithm is that if the multiplier and modulus are properly chosen, the resulting sequence of numbers will be statistically indistinguishable from a sequence drawn at random (but without replacement) from the set $1, 2, \ldots, m - 1$. But there is nothing random at all about the algorithm, apart from the choice of the initial value X_0. Once that value is chosen, the remaining numbers in the sequence follow deterministically. This has implications for cryptanalysis.

If an opponent knows that the linear congruential algorithm is being used and if the parameters are known (e.g., $a = 7^5$, $c = 0$, $m = 2^{31} - 1$), then once a single number is discovered, all subsequent numbers are known. Even if the opponent knows only that a linear congruential algorithm is being used, knowledge of a small part of the sequence is sufficient to determine the parameters of the algorithm. Suppose that the opponent is able to determine values for X_0, X_1, X_2, and X_3. Then

$$X_1 = (aX_0 + c) \bmod m$$
$$X_2 = (aX_1 + c) \bmod m$$
$$X_3 = (aX_2 + c) \bmod m$$

These equations can be solved for a, c, and m.

Thus, although it is nice to be able to use a good PRNG, it is desirable to make the actual sequence used nonreproducible, so that knowledge of part of the sequence on the part of an opponent is insufficient to determine future elements of the sequence. This goal can be achieved in a number of ways. For example, [BRIG79] suggests using an internal system clock to modify the random number stream. One way to use the clock would be to restart the sequence after every N numbers using the current clock value (mod m) as the new seed. Another way would be simply to add the current clock value to each random number (mod m).

Blum Blum Shub Generator

A popular approach to generating secure pseudorandom numbers is known as the Blum Blum Shub (BBS) generator (see Figure 8.3), named for its developers [BLUM86]. It has perhaps the strongest public proof of its cryptographic strength of any purpose-built algorithm. The procedure is as follows. First, choose two large prime numbers, p and q, that both have a remainder of 3 when divided by 4. That is,

$$p \equiv q \equiv 3 (\text{mod } 4)$$

This notation, explained more fully in Chapter 4, simply means that (p mod 4) = (q mod 4) = 3. For example, the prime numbers 7 and 11 satisfy $7 \equiv 11 \equiv 3 (\text{mod } 4)$. Let $n = p \times q$. Next, choose a random number s, such that s is relatively prime to n; this is equivalent to saying that neither p nor q is a factor of s. Then the BBS generator produces a sequence of bits B_i according to the following algorithm:

$$\begin{aligned} X_0 &= s^2 \bmod n \\ \textbf{for } i &= 1 \textbf{ to } \infty \\ X_i &= (X_{i-1})^2 \bmod n \\ B_i &= X_i \bmod 2 \end{aligned}$$

Thus, the least significant bit is taken at each iteration. Table 8.1 shows an example of BBS operation. Here, $n = 192649 = 383 \times 503$, and the seed $s = 101355$.

The BBS is referred to as a **cryptographically secure pseudorandom bit generator (CSPRBG)**. A CSPRBG is defined as one that passes the *next-bit test*, which, in turn, is defined as follows [MENE97]: A pseudorandom bit generator is said to pass the next-bit test if there is not a polynomial-time algorithm[1] that, on input of the first k bits of an output sequence, can predict the $(k + 1)$st bit with probability significantly greater than 1/2. In other words, given the first k bits of the

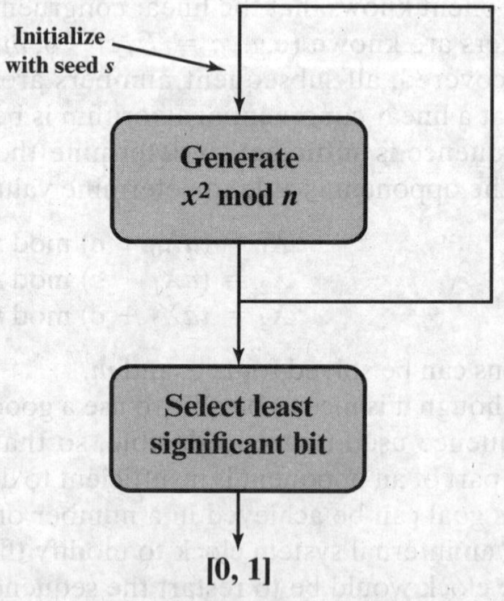

Figure 8.3 Blum Blum Shub Block Diagram

[1] A polynomial-time algorithm of order k is one whose running time is bounded by a polynomial of order k.

Table 8.1 Example Operation of BBS Generator

i	X_i	B_i
0	20749	
1	143135	1
2	177671	1
3	97048	0
4	89992	0
5	174051	1
6	80649	1
7	45663	1
8	69442	0
9	186894	0
10	177046	0
11	137922	0
12	123175	1
13	8630	0
14	114386	0
15	14863	1
16	133015	1
17	106065	1
18	45870	0
19	137171	1
20	48060	0

sequence, there is not a practical algorithm that can even allow you to state that the next bit will be 1 (or 0) with probability greater than 1/2. For all practical purposes, the sequence is unpredictable. The security of BBS is based on the difficulty of factoring n. That is, given n, we need to determine its two prime factors p and q.

8.3 PSEUDORANDOM NUMBER GENERATION USING A BLOCK CIPHER

A popular approach to PRNG construction is to use a symmetric block cipher as the heart of the PRNG mechanism. For any block of plaintext, a symmetric block cipher produces an output block that is apparently random. That is, there are no patterns or regularities in the ciphertext that provide information that can be used to deduce the plaintext. Thus, a symmetric block cipher is a good candidate for building a pseudorandom number generator.

If an established, standardized block cipher is used, such as DES or AES, then the security characteristics of the PRNG can be established. Further, many applications already make use of DES or AES, so the inclusion of the block cipher as part of the PRNG algorithm is straightforward.

PRNG Using Block Cipher Modes of Operation

Two approaches that use a block cipher to build a PNRG have gained widespread acceptance: the CTR mode and the OFB mode. The CTR mode is recommended in NIST SP 800-90A, in the ANSI standard X9.82 (*Random Number Generation*), and in RFC 4086 (*Randomness Requirements for Security,* June 2005). The OFB mode is recommended in X9.82 and RFC 4086.

Figure 8.4 illustrates the two methods. In each case, the seed consists of two parts: the encryption key value and a value V that will be updated after each block of pseudorandom numbers is generated. Thus, for AES-128, the seed consists of a 128-bit key and a 128-bit V value. In the CTR case, the value of V is incremented

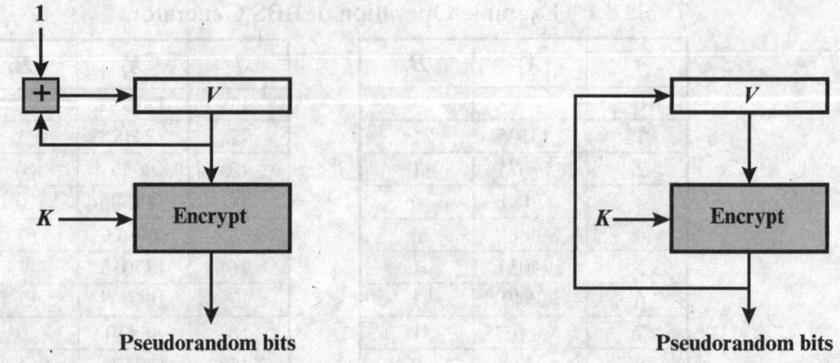

(a) CTR mode **(b) OFB mode**

Figure 8.4 PRNG Mechanisms Based on Block Ciphers

by 1 after each encryption. In the case of OFB, the value of V is updated to equal the value of the preceding PRNG block. In both cases, pseudorandom bits are produced one block at a time (e.g., for AES, PRNG bits are generated 128 bits at a time).

The CTR algorithm for PRNG, called CTR_DRBG, can be summarized as follows.

```
while (len (temp) < requested_number_of_bits) do
    V = (V + 1) mod 2^128
    output_block = E(Key, V)
    temp = temp || output_block
```

The OFB algorithm can be summarized as follows.

```
while (len (temp) < requested_number_of_bits) do
    V = E(Key, V)
    temp = temp || V
```

To get some idea of the performance of these two PRNGs, consider the following short experiment. A random bit sequence of 256 bits was obtained from random.org, which uses three radios tuned between stations to pick up atmospheric noise. These 256 bits form the seed, allocated as

Key:	cfb0ef3108d49cc4562d5810b0a9af60
V:	4c89af496176b728ed1e2ea8ba27f5a4

The total number of one bits in the 256-bit seed is 124, or a fraction of 0.48, which is reassuringly close to the ideal of 0.5.

For the OFB PRNG, Table 8.2 shows the first eight output blocks (1024 bits) with two rough measures of security. The second column shows the fraction of one bits in each 128-bit block. This corresponds to one of the NIST tests. The results indicate that the output is split roughly equally between zero and one bits. The third column shows the fraction of bits that match between adjacent blocks. If this

Table 8.2 Example Results for PRNG Using OFB

Output Block	Fraction of One Bits	Fraction of Bits that Match with Preceding Block
1786f4c7ff6e291dbdfdd90ec3453176	0.57	—
5e17b22b14677a4d66890f87565eae64	0.51	0.52
fd18284ac82251dfb3aa62c326cd46cc	0.47	0.54
c8e545198a758ef5dd86b41946389bd5	0.50	0.44
fe7bae0e23019542962e2c52d215a2e3	0.47	0.48
14fdf5ec99469598ae0379472803accd	0.49	0.52
6aeca972e5a3ef17bd1a1b775fc8b929	0.57	0.48
f7e97badf359d128f00d9b4ae323db64	0.55	0.45

Table 8.3 Example Results for PRNG Using CTR

Output Block	Fraction of One Bits	Fraction of Bits that Match with Preceding Block
1786f4c7ff6e291dbdfdd90ec3453176	0.57	—
60809669a3e092a01b463472fdcae420	0.41	0.41
d4e6e170b46b0573eedf88ee39bff33d	0.59	0.45
5f8fcfc5deca18ea246785d7fadc76f8	0.59	0.52
90e63ed27bb07868c753545bdd57ee28	0.53	0.52
0125856fdf4a17f747c7833695c52235	0.50	0.47
f4be2d179b0f2548fd748c8fc7c81990	0.51	0.48
1151fc48f90eebac658a3911515c3c66	0.47	0.45

number differs substantially from 0.5, that suggests a correlation between blocks, which could be a security weakness. The results suggest no correlation.

Table 8.3 shows the results using the same key and V values for CTR mode. Again, the results are favorable.

ANSI X9.17 PRNG

One of the strongest (cryptographically speaking) PRNGs is specified in ANSI X9.17. A number of applications employ this technique, including financial security applications and PGP (the latter described in Chapter 19).

Figure 8.5 illustrates the algorithm, which makes use of triple DES for encryption. The ingredients are as follows.

- **Input:** Two pseudorandom inputs drive the generator. One is a 64-bit representation of the current date and time, which is updated on each number generation. The other is a 64-bit seed value; this is initialized to some arbitrary value and is updated during the generation process.
- **Keys:** The generator makes use of three triple DES encryption modules. All three make use of the same pair of 56-bit keys, which must be kept secret and are used only for pseudorandom number generation.

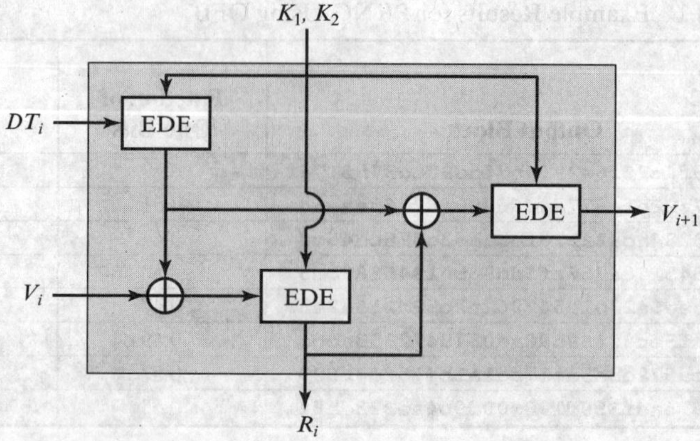

Figure 8.5 ANSI X9.17 Pseudorandom Number Generator

- **Output:** The output consists of a 64-bit pseudorandom number and a 64-bit seed value.

  Let us define the following quantities.

DT_i	Date/time value at the beginning of *i*th generation stage
V_i	Seed value at the beginning of *i*th generation stage
R_i	Pseudorandom number produced by the *i*th generation stage
K_1, K_2	DES keys used for each stage

Then

$$R_i = \text{EDE}([K_1, K_2], [V_i \oplus \text{EDE}([K_1, K_2], DT_i)])$$
$$V_{i+1} = \text{EDE}([K_1, K_2], [R_i \oplus \text{EDE}([K_1, K_2], DT_i)])$$

where EDE($[K_1, K_2]$, X) refers to the sequence encrypt-decrypt-encrypt using two-key triple DES to encrypt X.

Several factors contribute to the cryptographic strength of this method. The technique involves a 112-bit key and three EDE encryptions for a total of nine DES encryptions. The scheme is driven by two independent inputs, the date and time value, and a seed produced by the generator that is distinct from the pseudorandom number produced by the generator. Thus, the amount of material that must be compromised by an opponent appears to be overwhelming. Even if a pseudorandom number R_i were compromised, it would be impossible to deduce the V_{i+1} from the R_i, because an additional EDE operation is used to produce the V_{i+1}.

NIST CTR_DRBG

We now look more closely at the details of the PRNG defined in NIST SP 800-90A based on the CTR mode of operation. The PRNG is referred to as CTRDRBG (counter mode–deterministic random bit generator). CTR_DRBG is widely implemented and is part of the hardware random number generator implemented on all recent Intel processor chips (discussed in Section 8.6).

The DRBG assumes that an entropy source is available to provide random bits. Typically, the entropy source will be a TRNG based on some physical source. Other sources are possible if they meet the required entropy measure of the application. Entropy is an information theoretic concept that measures unpredictability, or randomness; see Appendix F for details. The encryption algorithm used in the DRBG may be 3DES with three keys or AES with a key size of 128, 192, or 256 bits.

Four parameters are associated with the algorithm:

- **Output block length** (*outlen*): Length of the output block of the encryption algorithm.
- **Key length** (*keylen*): Length of the encryption key.
- **Seed length** (*seedlen*): The seed is a string of bits that is used as input to a DRBG mechanism. The seed will determine a portion of the internal state of the DRBG, and its entropy must be sufficient to support the security strength of the DRBG. $seedlen = outlen + keylen$.
- **Reseed interval** (*reseed_interval*): Length of the encryption key. It is the maximum number of output blocks generated before updating the algorithm with a new seed.

Table 8.4 lists the values specified in SP 800-90A for these parameters.

INITIALIZE Figure 8.6 shows the two principal functions that comprise CTR_DRBG. We first consider how CTR_DRBG is initialized, using the initialize and update function (Figure 8.6a). Recall that the CTR block cipher mode requires both an encryption key *K* and an initial counter value, referred to in SP 800-90A as the counter *V*. The combination of *K* and *V* is referred to as the *seed*. To start the DRGB operation, initial values for *K* and *V* are needed, and can be chosen arbitrarily. As an example, the Intel Digital Random Number Generator, discussed in Section 8.6, uses the values $K = 0$ and $V = 0$. These values are used as parameters for the CTR mode of operation to produce at least *seedlen* bits. In addition, exactly *seedlen* bits must be supplied from what is referred to as an *entropy source*. Typically, the entropy source would be some form of TRNG.

With these inputs, the CTR mode of encryption is iterated to produce a sequence of output blocks, with *V* incremented by 1 after each encryption. The process continues until at least *seedlen* bits have been generated. The leftmost *seedlen* bits of output are then XORed with the *seedlen* entropy bits to produce a new seed. In turn, the leftmost *keylen* bits of the seed form the new key and the rightmost *outlen* bits of the seed form the new counter value *V*.

Table 8.4 CTR_DRBG Parameters

	3DES	AES-128	AES-192	AES-256
outlen	64	128	128	128
keylen	168	128	192	256
seedlen	232	256	320	384
reseed_interval	$\leq 2^{32}$	$\leq 2^{48}$	$\leq 2^{48}$	$\leq 2^{48}$

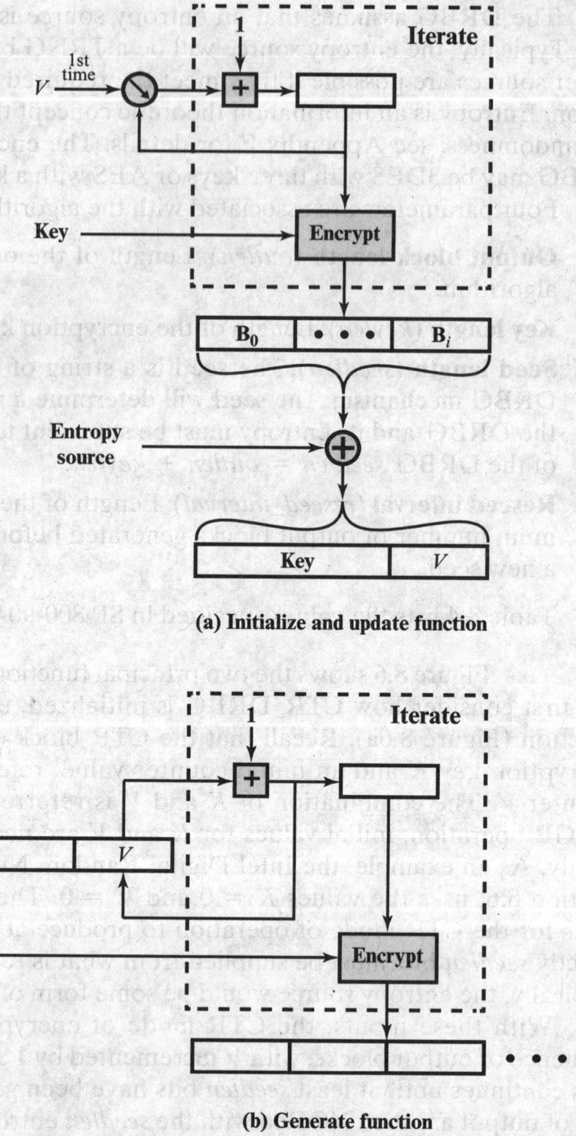

Figure 8.6 CTR_DRBG Functions

Generate Once values of Key and V are obtained, the DRBG enters the generate phase and is able to generate pseudorandom bits, one output block at a time (Figure 8.6b). The encryption function is iterated to generate the number of pseudorandom bits desired. Each iteration uses the same encryption key. The counter value V is incremented by 1 for each iteration.

Update To enhance security, the number of bits generated by any PRNG should be limited. CTR_DRGB uses the parameter *reseed_interval* to set that limit. During the generate phase, a reseed counter is initialized to 1 and then incremented with each iteration (each production of an output block). When the reseed counter reaches *reseed_interval*, the update function is invoked (Figure 8.6a). The update function is the same as the initialize function. In the update case, the Key and *V* values last used by the generate function serve as the input parameters to the update function. The update function takes *seedlen* new bits from an entropy source and produces a new seed (Key, *V*). The generate function can then resume production of pseudorandom bits. Note that the result of the update function is to change both the Key and *V* values used by the generate function.

8.4 STREAM CIPHERS

A typical stream cipher encrypts plaintext one byte at a time, although a stream cipher may be designed to operate on one bit at a time or on units larger than a byte at a time. Figure 8.7 is a representative diagram of stream cipher structure. In this structure, a key is input to a pseudorandom bit generator that produces a stream of 8-bit numbers that are apparently random. The output of the generator, called a **keystream**, is combined one byte at a time with the plaintext stream using the bitwise exclusive-OR (XOR) operation. For example, if the next byte generated by the generator is 01101100 and the next plaintext byte is 11001100, then the resulting ciphertext byte is

```
  11001100 plaintext
⊕ 01101100 key stream
  10100000 ciphertext
```

Decryption requires the use of the same pseudorandom sequence:

```
  10100000 ciphertext
⊕ 01101100 key stream
  11001100 plaintext
```

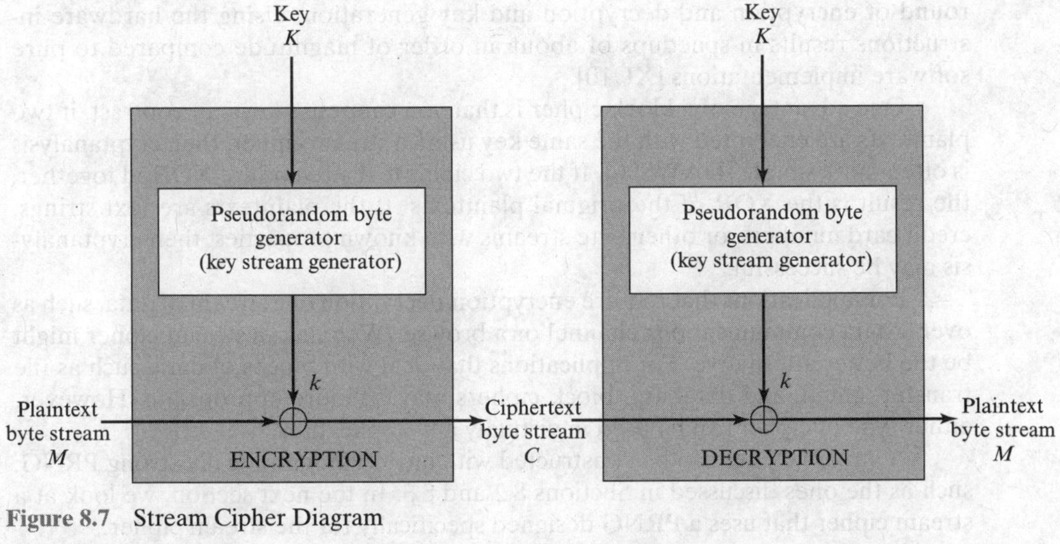

Figure 8.7 Stream Cipher Diagram

The stream cipher is similar to the one-time pad discussed in Chapter 3. The difference is that a one-time pad uses a genuine random number stream, whereas a stream cipher uses a pseudorandom number stream.

[KUMA97] lists the following important design considerations for a stream cipher.

1. The encryption sequence should have a large period. A pseudorandom number generator uses a function that produces a deterministic stream of bits that eventually repeats. The longer the period of repeat the more difficult it will be to do cryptanalysis. This is essentially the same consideration that was discussed with reference to the Vigenère cipher, namely that the longer the keyword the more difficult the cryptanalysis.
2. The keystream should approximate the properties of a true random number stream as close as possible. For example, there should be an approximately equal number of 1s and 0s. If the keystream is treated as a stream of bytes, then all of the 256 possible byte values should appear approximately equally often. The more random-appearing the keystream is, the more randomized the ciphertext is, making cryptanalysis more difficult.
3. Note from Figure 8.7 that the output of the pseudorandom number generator is conditioned on the value of the input key. To guard against brute-force attacks, the key needs to be sufficiently long. The same considerations that apply to block ciphers are valid here. Thus, with current technology, a key length of at least 128 bits is desirable.

With a properly designed pseudorandom number generator, a stream cipher can be as secure as a block cipher of comparable key length. A potential advantage of a stream cipher is that stream ciphers that do not use block ciphers as a building block are typically faster and use far less code than do block ciphers. The example in this chapter, RC4, can be implemented in just a few lines of code. In recent years, this advantage has diminished with the introduction of AES, which is quite efficient in software. Furthermore, hardware acceleration techniques are now available for AES. For example, the Intel AES Instruction Set has machine instructions for one round of encryption and decryption and key generation. Using the hardware instructions results in speedups of about an order of magnitude compared to pure software implementations [XU10].

One advantage of a block cipher is that you can reuse keys. In contrast, if two plaintexts are encrypted with the same key using a stream cipher, then cryptanalysis is often quite simple [DAWS96]. If the two ciphertext streams are XORed together, the result is the XOR of the original plaintexts. If the plaintexts are text strings, credit card numbers, or other byte streams with known properties, then cryptanalysis may be successful.

For applications that require encryption/decryption of a stream of data, such as over a data communications channel or a browser/Web link, a stream cipher might be the better alternative. For applications that deal with blocks of data, such as file transfer, email, and database, block ciphers may be more appropriate. However, either type of cipher can be used in virtually any application.

A stream cipher can be constructed with any cryptographically strong PRNG, such as the ones discussed in Sections 8.2 and 8.3. In the next section, we look at a stream cipher that uses a PRNG designed specifically for the stream cipher.

8.5 RC4

RC4 is a stream cipher designed in 1987 by Ron Rivest for RSA Security. It is a variable key size stream cipher with byte-oriented operations. The algorithm is based on the use of a random permutation. Analysis shows that the period of the cipher is overwhelmingly likely to be greater than 10^{100} [ROBS95a]. Eight to sixteen machine operations are required per output byte, and the cipher can be expected to run very quickly in software. RC4 is used in the WiFi Protected Access (WPA) protocol that are part of the IEEE 802.11 wireless LAN standard. It is optional for use in Secure Shell (SSH) and Kerberos. RC4 was kept as a trade secret by RSA Security. In September 1994, the RC4 algorithm was anonymously posted on the Internet on the Cypherpunks anonymous remailers list.

The RC4 algorithm is remarkably simple and quite easy to explain. A variable-length key of from 1 to 256 bytes (8 to 2048 bits) is used to initialize a 256-byte state vector S, with elements S[0],S[1], . . . ,S[255]. At all times, S contains a permutation of all 8-bit numbers from 0 through 255. For encryption and decryption, a byte *k* (see Figure 8.7) is generated from S by selecting one of the 255 entries in a systematic fashion. As each value of *k* is generated, the entries in S are once again permuted.

Initialization of S

To begin, the entries of S are set equal to the values from 0 through 255 in ascending order; that is, S[0] = 0, S[1] = 1, . . . , S[255] = 255. A temporary vector, T, is also created. If the length of the key K is 256 bytes, then K is transferred to T. Otherwise, for a key of length *keylen* bytes, the first *keylen* elements of T are copied from K, and then K is repeated as many times as necessary to fill out T. These preliminary operations can be summarized as

```
/* Initialization */
for i = 0 to 255 do
 S[i] = i;
 T[i] = K[i mod keylen];
```

Next we use T to produce the initial permutation of S. This involves starting with S[0] and going through to S[255], and for each S[i], swapping S[i] with another byte in S according to a scheme dictated by T[i]:

```
/* Initial Permutation of S */
j = 0;
for i = 0 to 255 do
    j = (j + S[i] + T[i]) mod 256;
    Swap (S[i], S[j]);
```

Because the only operation on S is a swap, the only effect is a permutation. S still contains all the numbers from 0 through 255.

Stream Generation

Once the S vector is initialized, the input key is no longer used. Stream generation involves cycling through all the elements of S[i], and for each S[i], swapping S[i] with another byte in S according to a scheme dictated by the current configuration of S. After S[255] is reached, the process continues, starting over again at S[0]:

```
/* Stream Generation */
i, j = 0;
while (true)
   i = (i + 1) mod 256;
   j = (j + S[i]) mod 256;
   Swap (S[i], S[j]);
   t = (S[i] + S[j]) mod 256;
   k = S[t];
```

To encrypt, XOR the value k with the next byte of plaintext. To decrypt, XOR the value *k* with the next byte of ciphertext.

Figure 8.8 illustrates the RC4 logic.

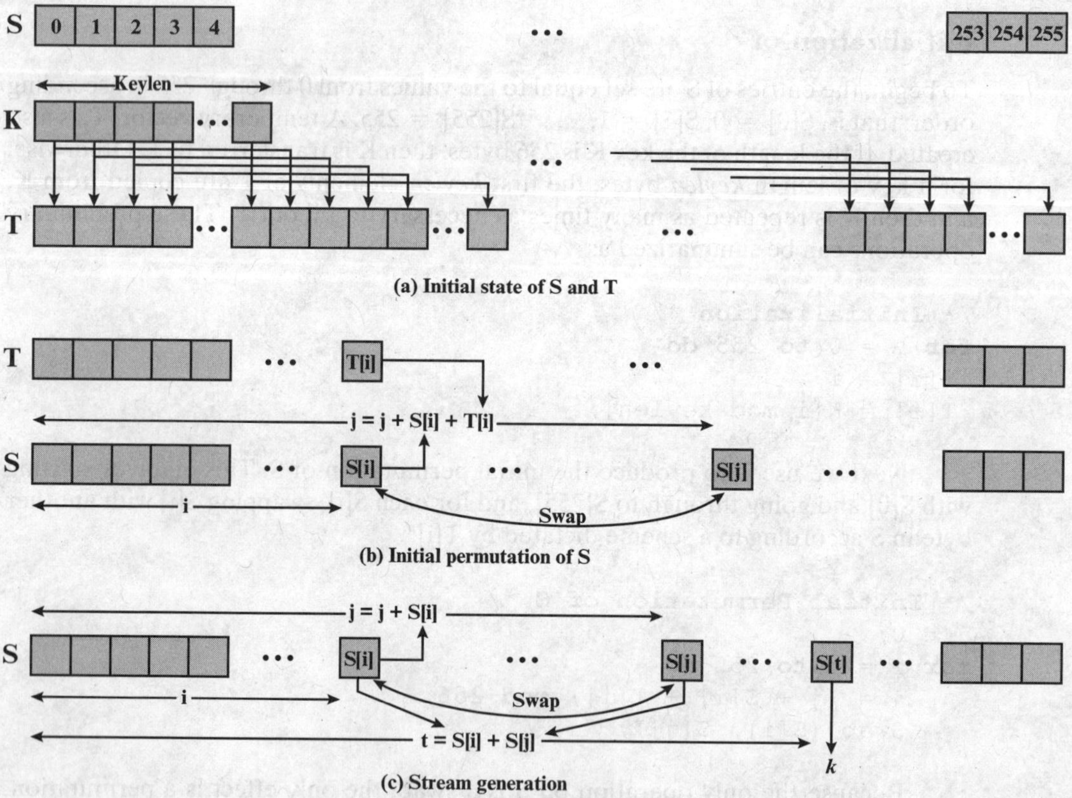

Figure 8.8 RC4

Strength of RC4

A number of papers have been published analyzing methods of attacking RC4 (e.g., [KNUD98], [FLUH00], [MANT01]). None of these approaches is practical against RC4 with a reasonable key length, such as 128 bits. A more serious problem is reported in [FLUH01]. The authors demonstrate that the WEP protocol, intended to provide confidentiality on 802.11 wireless LAN networks, is vulnerable to a particular attack approach. In essence, the problem is not with RC4 itself but the way in which keys are generated for use as input to RC4. This particular problem does not appear to be relevant to other applications using RC4 and can be remedied in WEP by changing the way in which keys are generated. This problem points out the difficulty in designing a secure system that involves both cryptographic functions and protocols that make use of them.

More recently, [PAUL07] revealed a more fundamental vulnerability in the RC4 key scheduling algorithm that reduces the amount of effort to discover the key. Recent cryptanalysis results [ALFA13] exploit biases in the RC4 keystream to recover repeatedly encrypted plaintexts. As a result of the discovered weaknesses, particularly those reported in [ALFA13], the IETF issued RFC 7465 prohibiting the use of RC4 in TLS (*Prohibiting RC4 Cipher Suites*, February 2015). In its latest TLS guidelines, NIST also prohibited the use of RC4 for government use (SP 800-52, *Guidelines for the Selection, Configuration, and Use of Transport Layer Security (TLS) Implementations,* September 2013).

8.6 TRUE RANDOM NUMBER GENERATORS

Entropy Sources

A true random number generator (TRNG) uses a nondeterministic source to produce randomness. Most operate by measuring unpredictable natural processes, such as pulse detectors of ionizing radiation events, gas discharge tubes, and leaky capacitors. Intel has developed a commercially available chip that samples thermal noise by sampling the output of a coupled pair of inverters. LavaRnd is an open source project for creating truly random numbers using inexpensive cameras, open source code, and inexpensive hardware. The system uses a saturated CCD in a light-tight can as a chaotic source to produce the seed. Software processes the result into truly random numbers in a variety of formats.

RFC 4086 lists the following possible sources of randomness that, with care, easily can be used on a computer to generate true random sequences.

- **Sound/video input:** Many computers are built with inputs that digitize some real-world analog source, such as sound from a microphone or video input from a camera. The "input" from a sound digitizer with no source plugged in or from a camera with the lens cap on is essentially thermal noise. If the system has enough gain to detect anything, such input can provide reasonably high quality random bits.
- **Disk drives:** Disk drives have small random fluctuations in their rotational speed due to chaotic air turbulence [JAKO98]. The addition of low-level disk seek-time instrumentation produces a series of measurements that contain this

randomness. Such data is usually highly correlated, so significant processing is needed. Nevertheless, experimentation a decade ago showed that, with such processing, even slow disk drives on the slower computers of that day could easily produce 100 bits a minute or more of excellent random data.

There is also an online service (random.org), which can deliver random sequences securely over the Internet.

Comparison of PRNGs and TRNGs

Table 8.5 summarizes the principal differences between PRNGs and TRNGs. PRNGs are efficient, meaning they can produce many numbers in a short time, and deterministic, meaning that a given sequence of numbers can be reproduced at a later date if the starting point in the sequence is known. Efficiency is a nice characteristic if your application needs many numbers, and determinism is handy if you need to replay the same sequence of numbers again at a later stage. PRNGs are typically also periodic, which means that the sequence will eventually repeat itself. While periodicity is hardly ever a desirable characteristic, modern PRNGs have a period that is so long that it can be ignored for most practical purposes.

TRNGs are generally rather inefficient compared to PRNGs, taking considerably longer time to produce numbers. This presents a difficulty in many applications. For example, cryptography system in banking or national security might need to generate millions of random bits per second. TRNGs are also nondeterministic, meaning that a given sequence of numbers cannot be reproduced, although the same sequence may of course occur several times by chance. TRNGs have no period.

Conditioning[2]

A TRNG may produce an output that is biased in some way, such as having more ones than zeros or vice versa. More generally, NIST SP 800-90B defines a random process as **biased** with respect to an assumed discrete set of potential outcomes (i.e., possible output values) if some of those outcomes have a greater probability of occurring than do others. For example, a physical source such as electronic noise may contain a superposition of regular structures, such as waves or other periodic phenomena, which may appear to be random, yet are determined to be non-random using statistical tests.

Table 8.5 Comparison of PRNGs and TRNGs

	Pseudorandom Number Generators	True Random Number Generators
Efficiency	Very efficient	Generally inefficient
Determinism	Deterministic	Nondeterministic
Periodicity	Periodic	Aperiodic

[2] The reader unfamiliar with the concepts of entropy and min-entropy should read Appendix F before proceeding.

In addition to bias, another concept used by SP 800-98B is that of **entropy rate**. SP 800-90B defines entropy rate as the rate at which a digitized noise source (or entropy source) provides entropy; it is computed as the assessed amount of entropy provided by a bit string output from the source, divided by the total number of bits in the bit string (yielding assessed bits of entropy per output bit). This will be a value between 0 (no entropy) and 1 (full entropy). Entropy rate is a measure of the randomness or unpredictability of a bit string. Another way of expressing it is that the entropy rate is k/n for a random source of length n bits and min-entropy k. Min-entropy is a measure of the number of random bits and is explained in Appendix F. In essence, a block of bits or a bit stream that is unbiased, and in which each bit and each group of bits is independent of all other bits and groups of bits will have an entropy rate of 1.

For hardware sources of random bits, the recommended approach is to assume that there may be bias and/or an entropy rate of less than 1 and to apply techniques to further "randomize" the bits. Various methods of modifying a bit stream for this purpose have been developed. These are referred to as **conditioning algorithms** or **deskewing algorithms**.

Typically, conditioning is done by using a cryptographic algorithm to "scramble" the random bits so as to eliminate bias and increase entropy. The two most common approaches are the use of a hash function or a symmetric block cipher.

Hash Function As we describe in Chapter 11, a hash function produces an n-bit output from an input of arbitrary length. A simple way to use a hash function for conditioning is as follows. Blocks of m input bits, with $m \geq n$, are passed through the hash function and the n output bits are used as random bits. To generate a stream of random bits, successive input blocks pass through the hash function to produce successive hashed output blocks.

Operating systems typically provide a built-in mechanism for generating random numbers. For example, Linux uses four entropy sources: mouse and keyboard activity, disk I/O operations, and specific interrupts. Bits are generated from these four sources and combined in a pooled buffer. When random bits are needed, the appropriate number of bits are read from the buffer and passed through the SHA-1 hash function [GUTT06].

A more complex approach is the hash derivation function specified in SP800-90A. Hash_df can be defined as follows:

Parameters:

input_string: The string to be hashed.

outlen: Output length.

no_of_bits_to_return: The number of bits to be returned by Hash_df. The maximum length (*max_number_of_bits*) is implementation dependent, but shall be less than or equal to (255 × *outlen*). *no_of_bits_to_return* is represented as a 32-bit integer.

requested_bits: The result of performing the Hash_df.

Hash_df Process:

1. *temp* = the Null string
2. $len = \left\lceil \frac{no\_of\_bits\_to\_return}{outlen} \right\rceil$
3. *counter* = 0x01 Comment: An 8-bit binary value representing the integer "1".
4. For *i* = 1 to *len* do Comment: In 4.1, *no_of_bits_to_return* is used as a 32-bit string.

   4.1. *temp* = *temp* || **Hash** (*counter* || *no_of_bits_to_return* || *input_string*).

   4.2. *counter* = *counter* + 1.
5. *requested_bits* = **leftmost** (*temp, no_of_bits_to_return*).
6. Return (**SUCCESS**, *requested_bits*).

This algorithm takes an input block of bits of arbitrary length and returns the requested number of bits, which may be up to 255 times as long as the hash output length.

The reader may be uneasy that the output consists of hashed blocks in which the input to the hash function for each block is the same input string and differs only by the value of the counter. However, cryptographically strong hash functions, such as the SHA family, provide excellent diffusion (as defined in Chapter 4) so that change in the counter value results in dramatically different outputs.

Block Cipher Instead of a hash function, a block cipher such as AES can be used to scramble the TRNG bits. Using AES, a simple approach would be to take 128-bit blocks of TRNG bits and encrypt each block with AES and some arbitrary key. SP 800-90B outlines an approach similar to the hash_df function described previously. The Intel implementation discussed subsequently provides an example of using AES for conditioning.

Health Testing

Figure 8.9 provides a general model for a nondeterministic random bit generator. A hardware noise source produces a true random output. This is digitized to produce true, or nondeterministic, source of bits. This bit source then passes through a conditioning module to mitigate bias and maximize entropy.

Figure 8.9 also shows a health-testing module, which is used on the outputs of both the digitizer and conditioner. In essence, health testing is used to validate that the noise source is working as expected and that the conditioning module is produced output with the desired characteristics. Both forms of health testing are recommended by SP 800-90B.

Health Tests on the Noise Source The nature of the health testing of the noise source depends strongly on the technology used to produce noise. In general, we can assume that the digitized output of the noise source will exhibit some bias. Thus, the traditional statistical tests, such as those defined in SP 800-22 and discussed in Section 8.1, are not useful for monitoring the noise source, because the noise source

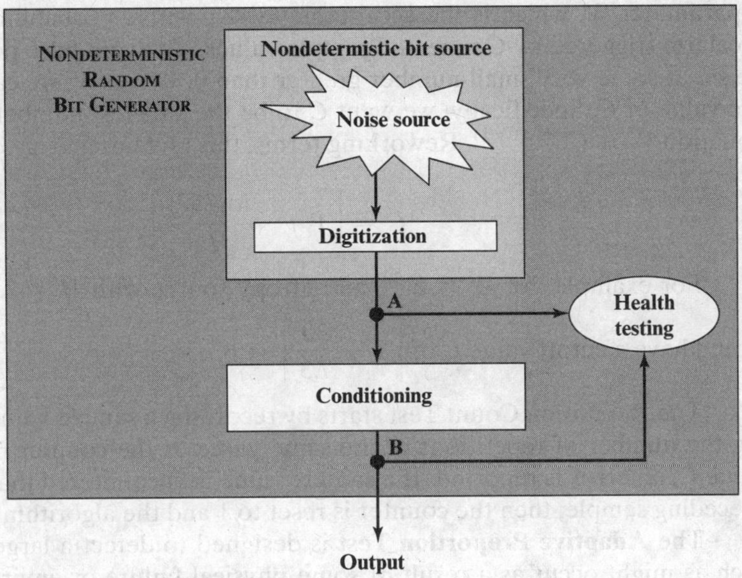

Figure 8.9 NRBG Model

is likely to always fail. Rather, the tests on the noise source need to be tailored to the expected statistical behavior of the correctly operating noise source. The goal is not to determine if the source is unbiased, which it isn't, but if it is operating as expected.

SP 800-90B specifies that continuous tests be done on digitized samples obtained from the noise source (point A in Figure 8.9). The purpose is to test for variability. More specifically, the purpose is to determine if the noise source is producing at the expected entropy rate. SP 800-909B mandates the use of two tests: the Repetition Count Test and the Adaptive Proportion Test.

The **Repetition Count Test** is designed to quickly detect a catastrophic failure that causes the noise source to become "stuck" on a single output value for a long time. For this test, it is assumed that a given noise source is assessed to have a given min-entropy value of H. The entropy is expressed as the amount of entropy per sample, where a sample could be a single bit or some block of bits of length n. With an assessed value of H, it is straightforward to calculate the probability that a sequence of C consecutive samples will yield identical sample values. For example, a noise source with one bit of min-entropy per sample has no more than a 1/2 probability of repeating some sample value twice in a row, no more than 1/4 probability of repeating some sample value three times in a row, and in general, no more than $(1/2)^{C-1}$ probability of repeating some sample value C times in a row. To generalize, for a noise source with H bits of min-entropy per sample, we have:

$$\Pr[C \text{ identical samples in a row}] \leq (2^{-H})^{(C-1)}$$

The Repetition Count Test involves looking for consecutive identical samples. If the count reaches some cutoff value C, then an error condition is raised. To determine the value of C used in the test, the test must be configured with a parameter W, which is the acceptable false-positive probability associated with an alarm triggered by C repeated sample values. To avoid false positives, W should be set at some very small number greater than 0. Given W, we can now determine the value of C. Specifically, we want C to be the smallest number that satisfies the equation $W \leq (2^{-H})^{(C-1)}$. Reworking terms, this gives us a value of:

$$C = \left\lceil 1 + \frac{-\log(W)}{H} \right\rceil$$

For example, for $W = 2^{-30}$, an entropy source with $H = 7.3$ bits per sample would have a cutoff value C of $\left\lceil 1 + \frac{30}{7.3} \right\rceil = 6$.

The Repetition Count Test starts by recording a sample value and then counting the number of repetitions of the same value. If the counter reaches the cutoff value C, an error is reported. If a sample value is encountered that differs from the preceding sample, then the counter is reset to 1 and the algorithm starts over.

The **Adaptive Proportion Test** is designed to detect a large loss of entropy, such as might occur as a result of some physical failure or environmental change affecting the noise source. The test continuously measures the local frequency of occurrence of some sample value in a sequence of noise source samples to determine if the sample occurs too frequently.

The test starts by recording a sample value and then observes N successive sample values. If the initial sample value is observed at least C times, then an error condition is reported. SP 800-90B recommends that a probability of a false positive of $W = 2^{-30}$ be used for the test and provides guidance on the selection of values for N and C.

Health Tests on the Conditioning Function SP 800-90B specifies that health tests should also be applied to the output of the conditioning component (point B in Figure 8.9), but does not indicate which tests to use. The purpose of the health tests on the conditioning component is to assure that the output behaves as a true random bit stream. Thus, it is reasonable to use the tests for randomness defined in SP 800-22, and described in Section 8.1.

Intel Digital Random Number Generator

As was mentioned, TRNGs have traditionally been used only for key generation and other applications where only a small number of random bits were required. This is because TRNGs have generally been inefficient, with a low bit rate of random bit production.

The first commercially available TRNG that achieves bit production rates comparable with that of PRNGs is the Intel digital random number generator (DRNG) [TAYL11, MECH14], offered on new multicore chips since May 2012.[3]

[3]It is unfortunate that Intel chose the acronym DRNG for an NRBG. It confuses with DRBG, which is a pseudorandom number bit generator.

Two notable aspects of the DRNG:

1. It is implemented entirely in hardware. This provides greater security than a facility that includes a software component. A hardware-only implementation should also be able to achieve greater computation speed than a software module.
2. The entire DRNG is on the same multicore chip as the processors. This eliminates the I/O delays found in other hardware random number generators.

DRNG Hardware Architecture Figure 8.10 shows the overall structure of the DRNG. The first stage of the DRNG generates random numbers from thermal noise. The heart of the stage consists of two inverters (NOT gates), with the output of each inverter connected to the input of the other. Such an arrangement has two stable states, with one inverter having an output of logical 1 and the other having an output of logical 0. The circuit is then configured so that both inverters are forced to have the same indeterminate state (both inputs and both outputs at logical 1) by clock pulses. Random thermal noise within the inverters soon jostles the two inverters into a mutually stable state. Additional circuitry is intended to compensate for any biases or correlations. This stage is capable, with current hardware, of generating random bits at a rate of 4 Gbps.

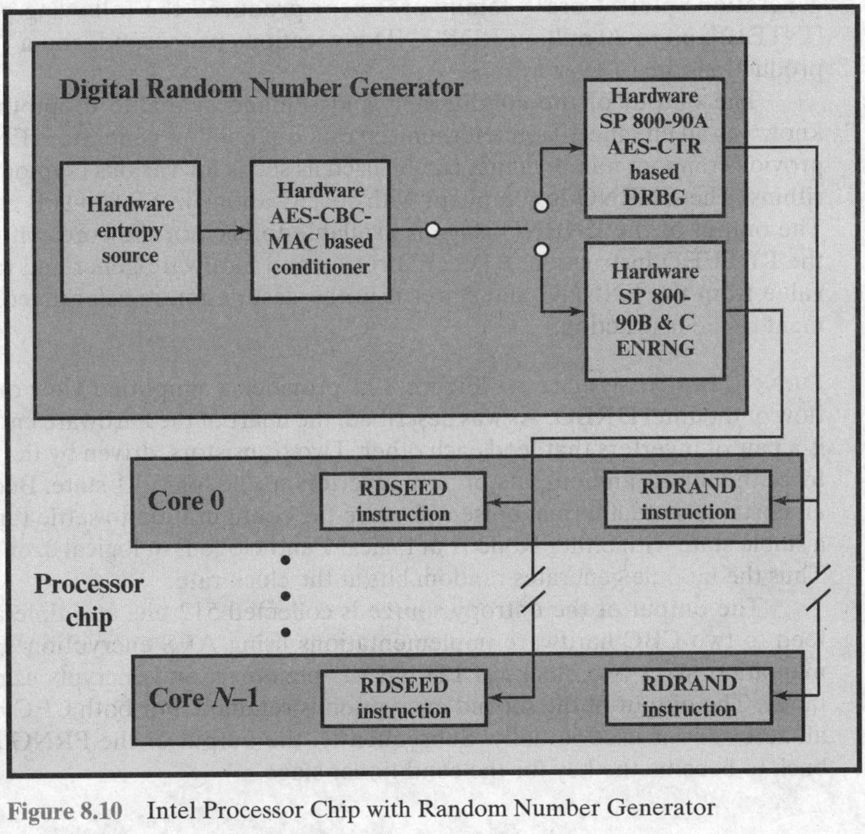

Figure 8.10 Intel Processor Chip with Random Number Generator

The output of the first stage is generated 512 bits at a time. To assure that the bit stream does not have skew or bias, a conditioner randomizes its input using a cryptographic function. In this case, the function is referred to as CBC-MAC or CMAC, as specified in NIST SP 800-38B. In essence, CMAC encrypts its input using the cipher block chaining (CBC) mode (Figure 8.4) and outputs the final block. We examine CMAC in detail in Chapter 12. The output of this stage is generated 256 bits at a time and is intended to exhibit true randomness with no skew or bias.

While the hardware's circuitry generates random numbers from thermal noise much more quickly than its predecessors, it is still not fast enough for some of today's computing requirements. To enable the DRNG to generate random numbers as quickly as a software DRBG, and also maintain the high quality of the random numbers, a third stage is added. This stage uses the 256-bit random numbers to seed a cryptographically secure DRBG that creates 128-bit numbers. From one 256-bit seed, the DRBG can output many pseudorandom numbers, exceeding the 3-Gbps rate of the entropy source. An upper bound of 511 128-bit samples can be generated per seed. The algorithm used for this stage is CTR_DRBG, described in Section 8.3.

The output of the PRNG stage is available to each of the cores on the chip via the RDRAND instruction. RDRAND retrieves a 16-, 32-, or 64-bit random value and makes it available in a software-accessible register.

Preliminary data from a pre-production sample on a system with a third generation Intel® Core™ family processor produced the following performance [INTE12]: up to 70 million RDRAND invocations per second, and a random data production rate of over 4 Gbps.

The output of the conditioner is also made available to another module, known as an enhanced nondeterministic random number generator (ENRNG) that provides random numbers that can be used as seeds for various cryptographic algorithms. The ENRNG is compliant with specifications in SP 800-90B and 900-90C. The output of the ENRNG stage is available to each of the cores on the chip via the RDSEED instruction. RDSEED retrieves a hardware-generated random seed value from the ENRNG and stores it in the destination register given as an argument to the instruction.

DRNG Logical Structure Figure 8.11 provides a simplified view of the logical flow of the Intel DRBG. As was described, the heart of the hardware entropy source is a pair of inverters that feed each other. Two transistors, driven by the same clock, force the inputs and outputs of both inverters to the logical 1 state. Because this is an unstable state, thermal noise will cause the configuration to settle randomly into a stable state with either Node A at logical 1 and Node B at logical 0, or the reverse. Thus the module generates random bits at the clock rate.

The output of the entropy source is collected 512 bits at a time and used to feed to two CBC hardware implementations using AES encryption. Each implementation takes two blocks of 128 bits of "plaintext" and encrypts using the CBC mode. The output of the second encryption is retained. For both CBC modules, an all-zeros key is used initially. Subsequently, the output of the PRNG stage is fed back to become the key for the conditioner stage.

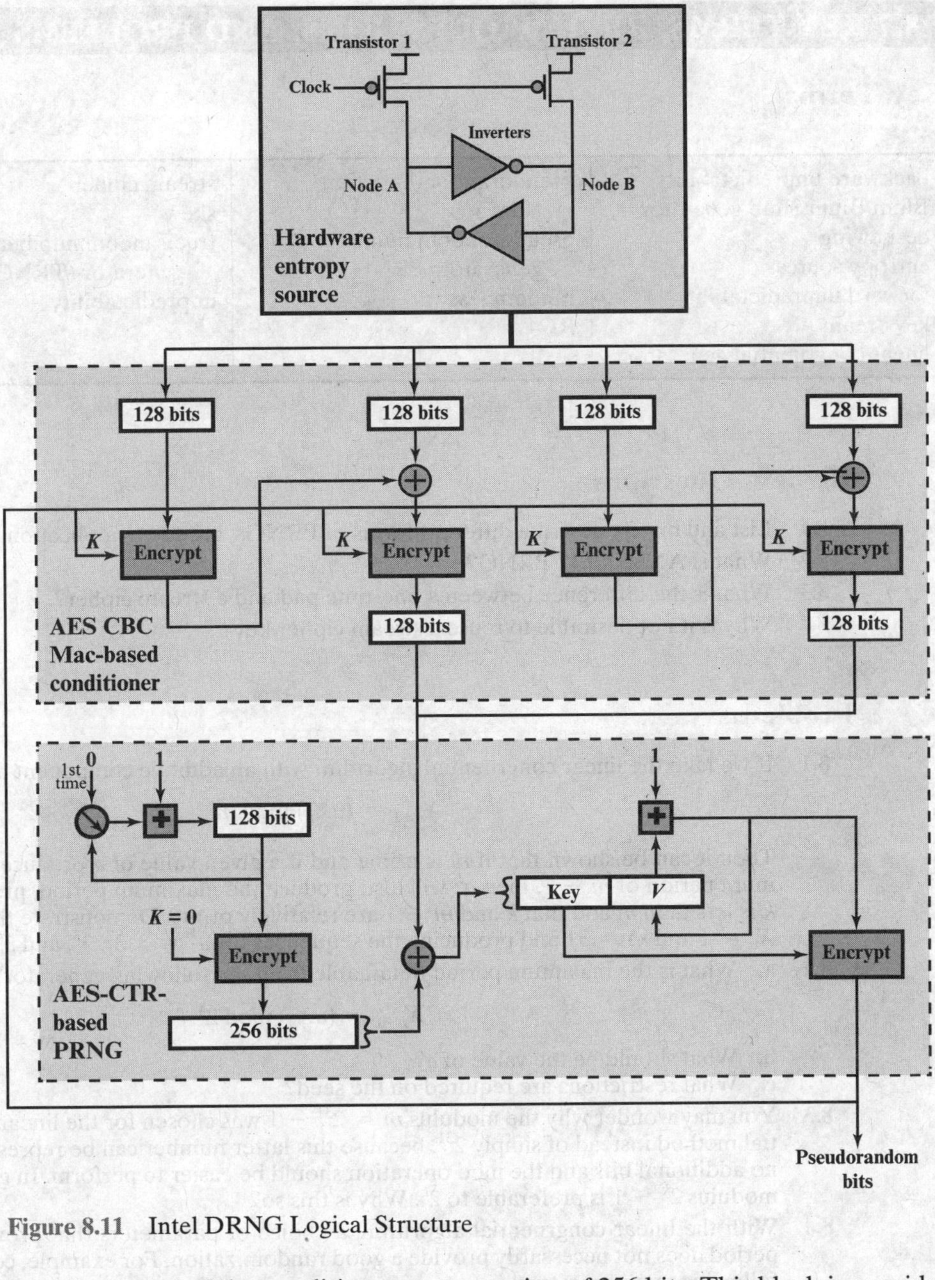

Figure 8.11 Intel DRNG Logical Structure

The output of the conditioner stage consists of 256 bits. This block is provided as input to the update function of the DRGB stage. The update function is initialized with the all-zeros key and the counter value 0. The function is iterated twice to produce a 256-block, which is then XORed with the input from the conditioner stage. The results are used as the 128-bit key and the 128-bit seed for the generate function. The generate function produces pseudorandom bits in 128-bit blocks.

8.7 KEY TERMS, REVIEW QUESTIONS, AND PROBLEMS

Key Terms

backward unpredictability Blum Blum Shub generator deskewing entropy source forward unpredictability keystream linear congruential generator	pseudorandom function (PRF) pseudorandom number generator (PRNG) randomness RC4 seed	stream cipher skew true random number generator (TRNG) unpredictability

Review Questions

8.1 List and briefly describe different forms of PRNGs, based on application.

8.2 What is ANSI X9.17 PRNG?

8.3 What is the difference between a one-time pad and a stream cipher?

8.4 Why is it not desirable to reuse a stream cipher key?

Problems

8.1 If we take the linear congruential algorithm with an additive component of 0,

$$X_{n+1} = (aX_n) \bmod m$$

Then it can be shown that if m is prime and if a given value of a produces the maximum period of $m - 1$, then a^k will also produce the maximum period, provided that k is less than m and that k and $m - 1$ are relatively prime. Demonstrate this by using $X_0 = 1$ and $m = 31$ and producing the sequences for $a^k = 3, 3^2, 3^3$, and 3^4.

8.2 **a.** What is the maximum period obtainable from the following generator?

$$X_{n+1} = (aX_n) \bmod 2^4$$

b. What should be the value of a?

c. What restrictions are required on the seed?

8.3 You may wonder why the modulus $m = 2^{31} - 1$ was chosen for the linear congruential method instead of simply 2^{31}, because this latter number can be represented with no additional bits and the mod operation should be easier to perform. In general, the modulus $2^k - 1$ is preferable to 2^k. Why is this so?

8.4 With the linear congruential algorithm, a choice of parameters that provides a full period does not necessarily provide a good randomization. For example, consider the following two generators:

$$X_{n+1} = (6X_n) \bmod 13$$
$$X_{n+1} = (7X_n) \bmod 13$$

Write out the two sequences to show that both are full period. Which one appears more random to you?

8.5 In any use of pseudorandom numbers, whether for encryption, simulation, or statistical design, it is dangerous to trust blindly the random number generator that happens to be available in your computer's system library. [PARK88] found that many contemporary textbooks and programming packages make use of flawed algorithms for pseudorandom number generation. This exercise will enable you to test your system.

The test is based on a theorem attributed to Ernesto Cesaro (see [KNUT98] for a proof), which states the following: Given two randomly chosen integers, x and y, the probability that $\gcd(x, y) = 1$ is $6/\pi^2$. Use this theorem in a program to determine statistically the value of π. The main program should call three subprograms: the random number generator from the system library to generate the random integers; a subprogram to calculate the greatest common divisor of two integers using Euclid's Algorithm; and a subprogram that calculates square roots. If these latter two programs are not available, you will have to write them as well. The main program should loop through a large number of random numbers to give an estimate of the aforementioned probability. From this, it is a simple matter to solve for your estimate of π.

If the result is close to 3.14, congratulations! If not, then the result is probably low, usually a value of around 2.7. Why would such an inferior result be obtained?

8.6 What RC4 key value will leave S unchanged during initialization? That is, after the initial permutation of S, the entries of S will be equal to the values from 0 through 255 in ascending order.

8.7 RC4 has a secret internal state which is a permutation of all the possible values of the vector S and the two indices i and j.

a. Using a straightforward scheme to store the internal state, how many bits are used?

b. Suppose we think of it from the point of view of how much information is represented by the state. In that case, we need to determine how may different states there are, then take the log to base 2 to find out how many bits of information this represents. Using this approach, how many bits would be needed to represent the state?

8.8 Alice and Bob agree to communicate privately via email using a scheme based on RC4, but want to avoid using a new secret key for each transmission. Alice and Bob privately agree on a 128-bit key k. To encrypt a message m, consisting of a string of bits, the following procedure is used.

1. Choose a random 80-bit value v
2. Generate the ciphertext $c = \text{RC4}(v \| k) \oplus m$
3. Send the bit string $(v \| c)$

a. Suppose Alice uses this procedure to send a message m to Bob. Describe how Bob can recover the message m from $(v \| c)$ using k.

b. If an adversary observes several values $(v_1 \| c_1), (v_2 \| c_2), \ldots$ transmitted between Alice and Bob, how can he/she determine when the same key stream has been used to encrypt two messages?

c. Approximately how many messages can Alice expect to send before the same key stream will be used twice? Use the result from the birthday paradox described in Appendix U.

d. What does this imply about the lifetime of the key k (i.e., the number of messages that can be encrypted using k)?

8.9 Suppose you have a true random bit generator where each bit in the generated stream has the same probability of being a 0 or 1 as any other bit in the stream and that the bits are not correlated; that is the bits are generated from identical independent distribution. However, the bit stream is biased. The probability of a 1 is $0.5 + \partial$ and the probability of a 0 is $0.5 - \partial$, where $0 < \partial < 0.5$. A simple conditioning algorithm is as follows: Examine the bit stream as a sequence of nonoverlapping pairs. Discard all 00 and 11 pairs. Replace each 01 pair with 0 and each 10 pair with 1.

a. What is the probability of occurrence of each pair in the original sequence?
b. What is the probability of occurrence of 0 and 1 in the modified sequence?
c. What is the expected number of input bits to produce x output bits?
d. Suppose that the algorithm uses overlapping successive bit pairs instead of non-overlapping successive bit pairs. That is, the first output bit is based on input bits 1 and 2, the second output bit is based on input bits 2 and 3, and so on. What can you say about the output bit stream?

8.10 Another approach to conditioning is to consider the bit stream as a sequence of non-overlapping groups of n bits each and output the parity of each group. That is, if a group contains an odd number of ones, the output is 1; otherwise the output is 0.
a. Express this operation in terms of a basic Boolean function.
b. Assume, as in the preceding problem, that the probability of a 1 is $0.5 + \partial$. If each group consists of 2 bits, what is the probability of an output of 1?
c. If each group consists of 4 bits, what is the probability of an output of 1?
d. Generalize the result to find the probability of an output of 1 for input groups of n bits.

8.11 It is important to note that the Repetition Count Test described in Section 8.6 is not a very powerful health test. It is able to detect only catastrophic failures of an entropy source. For example, a noise source evaluated at 8 bits of min-entropy per sample has a cutoff value of 5 repetitions to ensure a false-positive rate of approximately once per four billion samples generated. If that noise source somehow failed to the point that it was providing only 6 bits of min-entropy per sample, how many samples would be expected to be needed before the Repetition Count Test would notice the problem?

PART THREE: ASYMMETRIC CIPHERS

CHAPTER 9

PUBLIC-KEY CRYPTOGRAPHY AND RSA

LEARNING OBJECTIVES

After studying this chapter, you should be able to:

- Present an overview of the basic principles of public-key cryptosystems.
- Explain the two distinct uses of public-key cryptosystems.
- List and explain the requirements for a public-key cryptosystem.
- Present an overview of the RSA algorithm.
- Understand the timing attack.
- Summarize the relevant issues related to the complexity of algorithms.

The development of public-key, or asymmetric, cryptography is the greatest and perhaps the only true revolution in the entire history of cryptography. From its earliest beginnings to modern times, virtually all cryptographic systems have been based on the elementary tools of substitution and permutation. After millennia of working with algorithms that could be calculated by hand, a major advance in symmetric cryptography occurred with the development of the rotor encryption/decryption machine. The electromechanical rotor enabled the development of fiendishly complex cipher systems. With the availability of computers, even more complex systems were devised, the most prominent of which was the Lucifer effort at IBM that culminated in the Data Encryption Standard (DES). But both rotor machines and DES, although representing significant advances, still relied on the bread-and-butter tools of substitution and permutation.

Public-key cryptography provides a radical departure from all that has gone before. For one thing, public-key algorithms are based on mathematical functions rather than on substitution and permutation. More important, public-key cryptography is asymmetric, involving the use of two separate keys, in contrast to symmetric encryption, which uses only one key. The use of two keys has profound consequences in the areas of confidentiality, key distribution, and authentication, as we shall see.

Before proceeding, we should mention several common misconceptions concerning public-key encryption. One such misconception is that public-key encryption is more secure from cryptanalysis than is symmetric encryption. In fact, the security of any encryption scheme depends on the length of the key and the computational work involved in breaking a cipher. There is nothing in principle about either symmetric or public-key encryption that makes one superior to another from the point of view of resisting cryptanalysis.

A second misconception is that public-key encryption is a general-purpose technique that has made symmetric encryption obsolete. On the contrary, because of the computational overhead of current public-key encryption schemes, there seems no foreseeable likelihood that symmetric encryption will be abandoned. As one of the inventors of public-key encryption has put it [DIFF88], "the restriction of public-key cryptography to key management and signature applications is almost universally accepted."

Table 9.1 Terminology Related to Asymmetric Encryption

Asymmetric Keys Two related keys, a public key and a private key, that are used to perform complementary operations, such as encryption and decryption or signature generation and signature verification.
Public Key Certificate A digital document issued and digitally signed by the private key of a Certification Authority that binds the name of a subscriber to a public key. The certificate indicates that the subscriber identified in the certificate has sole control and access to the corresponding private key.
Public Key (Asymmetric) Cryptographic Algorithm A cryptographic algorithm that uses two related keys, a public key and a private key. The two keys have the property that deriving the private key from the public key is computationally infeasible.
Public Key Infrastructure (PKI) A set of policies, processes, server platforms, software and workstations used for the purpose of administering certificates and public-private key pairs, including the ability to issue, maintain, and revoke public key certificates.

Source: *Glossary of Key Information Security Terms*, NIST IR 7298 [KISS06].

Finally, there is a feeling that key distribution is trivial when using public-key encryption, compared to the rather cumbersome handshaking involved with key distribution centers for symmetric encryption. In fact, some form of protocol is needed, generally involving a central agent, and the procedures involved are not simpler nor any more efficient than those required for symmetric encryption (e.g., see analysis in [NEED78]).

This chapter and the next provide an overview of public-key cryptography. First, we look at its conceptual framework. Interestingly, the concept for this technique was developed and published before it was shown to be practical to adopt it. Next, we examine the RSA algorithm, which is the most important encryption/decryption algorithm that has been shown to be feasible for public-key encryption. Other important public-key cryptographic algorithms are covered in Chapter 10.

Much of the theory of public-key cryptosystems is based on number theory. If one is prepared to accept the results given in this chapter, an understanding of number theory is not strictly necessary. However, to gain a full appreciation of public-key algorithms, some understanding of number theory is required. Chapter 2 provides the necessary background in number theory.

Table 9.1 defines some key terms.

9.1 PRINCIPLES OF PUBLIC-KEY CRYPTOSYSTEMS

The concept of public-key cryptography evolved from an attempt to attack two of the most difficult problems associated with symmetric encryption. The first problem is that of key distribution, which is examined in some detail in Chapter 14.

As Chapter 14 discusses, key distribution under symmetric encryption requires either (1) that two communicants already share a key, which somehow has been distributed to them; or (2) the use of a key distribution center. Whitfield Diffie, one of the discoverers of public-key encryption (along with Martin Hellman, both at Stanford University at the time), reasoned that this second requirement negated the very essence of cryptography: the ability to maintain total secrecy over your own communication. As Diffie put it [DIFF88], "what good would it do after all to develop impenetrable cryptosystems, if their users were forced to share their keys with a KDC that could be compromised by either burglary or subpoena?"

The second problem that Diffie pondered, and one that was apparently unrelated to the first, was that of *digital signatures*. If the use of cryptography was to become widespread, not just in military situations but for commercial and private purposes, then electronic messages and documents would need the equivalent of signatures used in paper documents. That is, could a method be devised that would stipulate, to the satisfaction of all parties, that a digital message had been sent by a particular person? This is a somewhat broader requirement than that of authentication, and its characteristics and ramifications are explored in Chapter 13.

Diffie and Hellman achieved an astounding breakthrough in 1976 [DIFF76 a, b] by coming up with a method that addressed both problems and was radically different from all previous approaches to cryptography, going back over four millennia.[1]

In the next subsection, we look at the overall framework for public-key cryptography. Then we examine the requirements for the encryption/decryption algorithm that is at the heart of the scheme.

Public-Key Cryptosystems

Asymmetric algorithms rely on one key for encryption and a different but related key for decryption. These algorithms have the following important characteristic.

- It is computationally infeasible to determine the decryption key given only knowledge of the cryptographic algorithm and the encryption key.

In addition, some algorithms, such as RSA, also exhibit the following characteristic.

- Either of the two related keys can be used for encryption, with the other used for decryption.

A **public-key encryption** scheme has six ingredients (Figure 9.1a; compare with Figure 3.1).

- **Plaintext:** This is the readable message or data that is fed into the algorithm as input.
- **Encryption algorithm:** The encryption algorithm performs various transformations on the plaintext.

[1]Diffie and Hellman first *publicly* introduced the concepts of public-key cryptography in 1976. Hellman credits Merkle with independently discovering the concept at that same time, although Merkle did not publish until 1978 [MERK78]. In fact, the first unclassified document describing public-key distribution and public-key cryptography was a 1974 project proposal by Merkle (http://merkle.com/1974). However, this is not the true beginning. Admiral Bobby Inman, while director of the National Security Agency (NSA), claimed that public-key cryptography had been discovered at NSA in the mid-1960s [SIMM93]. The first *documented* introduction of these concepts came in 1970, from the Communications-Electronics Security Group, Britain's counterpart to NSA, in a classified report by James Ellis [ELLI70]. Ellis referred to the technique as *nonsecret encryption* and describes the discovery in [ELLI99].

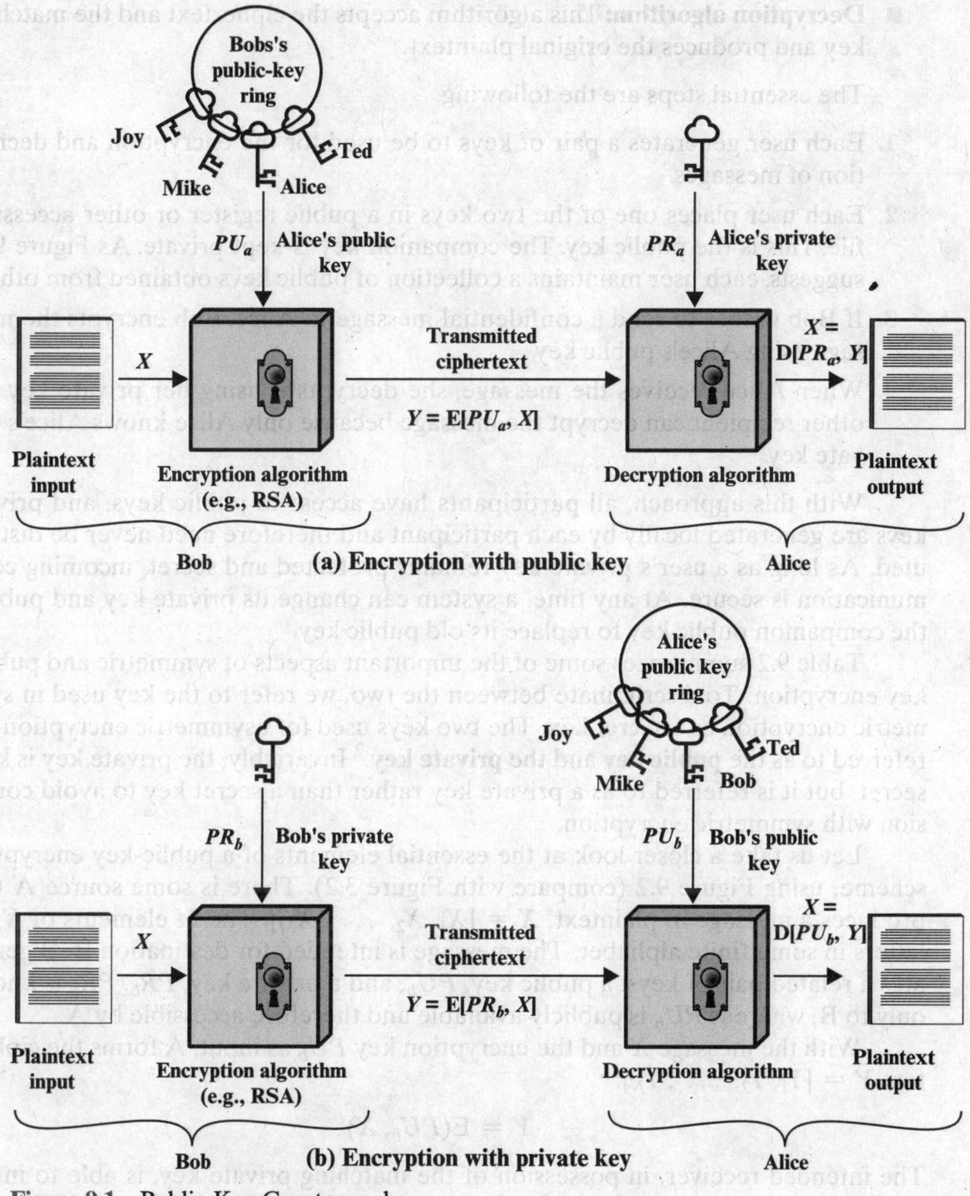

Figure 9.1 Public-Key Cryptography

- **Public and private keys:** This is a pair of keys that have been selected so that if one is used for encryption, the other is used for decryption. The exact transformations performed by the algorithm depend on the public or private key that is provided as input.
- **Ciphertext:** This is the encrypted message produced as output. It depends on the plaintext and the key. For a given message, two different keys will produce two different ciphertexts.

- **Decryption algorithm:** This algorithm accepts the ciphertext and the matching key and produces the original plaintext.

The essential steps are the following.

1. Each user generates a pair of keys to be used for the encryption and decryption of messages.
2. Each user places one of the two keys in a public register or other accessible file. This is the public key. The companion key is kept private. As Figure 9.1a suggests, each user maintains a collection of public keys obtained from others.
3. If Bob wishes to send a confidential message to Alice, Bob encrypts the message using Alice's public key.
4. When Alice receives the message, she decrypts it using her private key. No other recipient can decrypt the message because only Alice knows Alice's private key.

With this approach, all participants have access to public keys, and private keys are generated locally by each participant and therefore need never be distributed. As long as a user's private key remains protected and secret, incoming communication is secure. At any time, a system can change its private key and publish the companion public key to replace its old public key.

Table 9.2 summarizes some of the important aspects of symmetric and public-key encryption. To discriminate between the two, we refer to the key used in symmetric encryption as a **secret key**. The two keys used for asymmetric encryption are referred to as the **public key** and the **private key**.[2] Invariably, the private key is kept secret, but it is referred to as a private key rather than a secret key to avoid confusion with symmetric encryption.

Let us take a closer look at the essential elements of a public-key encryption scheme, using Figure 9.2 (compare with Figure 3.2). There is some source A that produces a message in plaintext, $X = [X_1, X_2, \ldots, X_M]$. The M elements of X are letters in some finite alphabet. The message is intended for destination B. B generates a related pair of keys: a public key, PU_b, and a private key, PR_b. PR_b is known only to B, whereas PU_b is publicly available and therefore accessible by A.

With the message X and the encryption key PU_b as input, A forms the ciphertext $Y = [Y_1, Y_2, \ldots, Y_N]$:

$$Y = \mathrm{E}(PU_b, X)$$

The intended receiver, in possession of the matching private key, is able to invert the transformation:

$$X = \mathrm{D}(PR_b, Y)$$

[2]The following notation is used consistently throughout. A secret key is represented by K_m, where m is some modifier; for example, K_a is a secret key owned by user A. A public key is represented by PU_a, for user A, and the corresponding private key is PR_a. Encryption of plaintext X can be performed with a secret key, a public key, or a private key, denoted by $\mathrm{E}(K_a, X)$, $\mathrm{E}(PU_a, X)$, and $\mathrm{E}(PR_a, X)$, respectively. Similarly, decryption of ciphertext Y can be performed with a secret key, a public key, or a private key, denoted by $\mathrm{D}(K_a, Y)$, $\mathrm{D}(PU_a, Y)$, and $\mathrm{D}(PR_a, Y)$, respectively.

Table 9.2 Conventional and Public-Key Encryption

Conventional Encryption	Public-Key Encryption
Needed to Work: 1. The same algorithm with the same key is used for encryption and decryption. 2. The sender and receiver must share the algorithm and the key. *Needed for Security:* 1. The key must be kept secret. 2. It must be impossible or at least impractical to decipher a message if the key is kept secret. 3. Knowledge of the algorithm plus samples of ciphertext must be insufficient to determine the key.	*Needed to Work:* 1. One algorithm is used for encryption and a related algorithm for decryption with a pair of keys, one for encryption and one for decryption. 2. The sender and receiver must each have one of the matched pair of keys (not the same one). *Needed for Security:* 1. One of the two keys must be kept secret. 2. It must be impossible or at least impractical to decipher a message if one of the keys is kept secret. 3. Knowledge of the algorithm plus one of the keys plus samples of ciphertext must be insufficient to determine the other key.

An adversary, observing Y and having access to PU_b, but not having access to PR_b or X, must attempt to recover X and/or PR_b. It is assumed that the adversary does have knowledge of the encryption (E) and decryption (D) algorithms. If the adversary is interested only in this particular message, then the focus of effort is to recover X by generating a plaintext estimate $\hat{X}$. Often, however, the adversary is interested in being able to read future messages as well, in which case an attempt is made to recover PR_b by generating an estimate $\hat{PR}_b$.

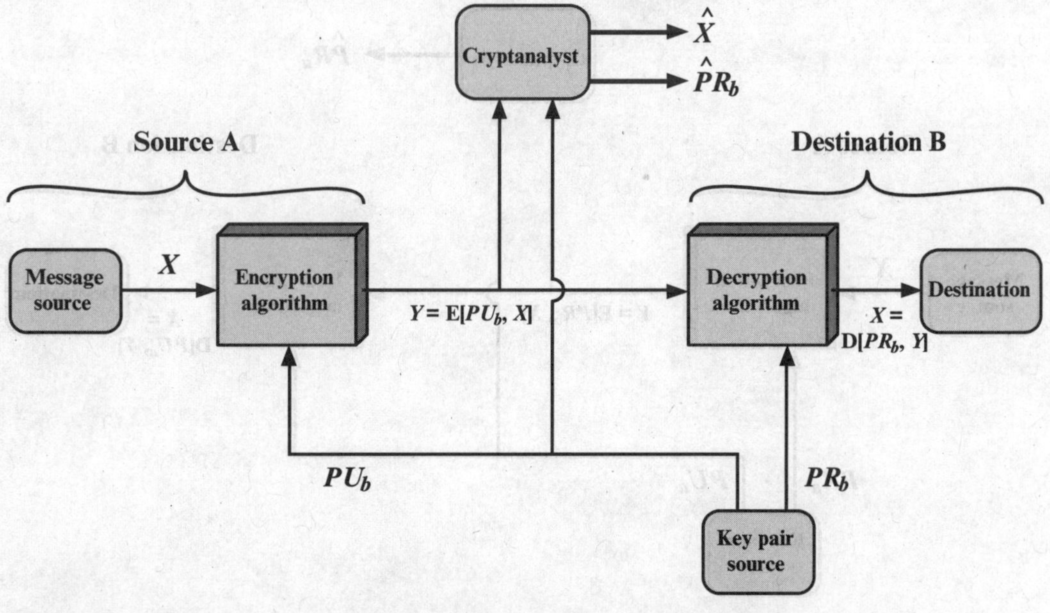

Figure 9.2 Public-Key Cryptosystem: Confidentiality

We mentioned earlier that either of the two related keys can be used for encryption, with the other being used for decryption. This enables a rather different cryptographic scheme to be implemented. Whereas the scheme illustrated in Figure 9.2 provides confidentiality, Figures 9.1b and 9.3 show the use of public-key encryption to provide authentication:

$$Y = E(PR_a, X)$$
$$X = D(PU_a, Y)$$

In this case, A prepares a message to B and encrypts it using A's private key before transmitting it. B can decrypt the message using A's public key. Because the message was encrypted using A's private key, only A could have prepared the message. Therefore, the entire encrypted message serves as a **digital signature**. In addition, it is impossible to alter the message without access to A's private key, so the message is authenticated both in terms of source and in terms of data integrity.

In the preceding scheme, the entire message is encrypted, which, although validating both author and contents, requires a great deal of storage. Each document must be kept in plaintext to be used for practical purposes. A copy also must be stored in ciphertext so that the origin and contents can be verified in case of a dispute. A more efficient way of achieving the same results is to encrypt a small block of bits that is a function of the document. Such a block, called an authenticator, must have the property that it is infeasible to change the document without changing the authenticator. If the authenticator is encrypted with the sender's private key, it serves as a signature that verifies origin, content, and sequencing. Chapter 13 examines this technique in detail.

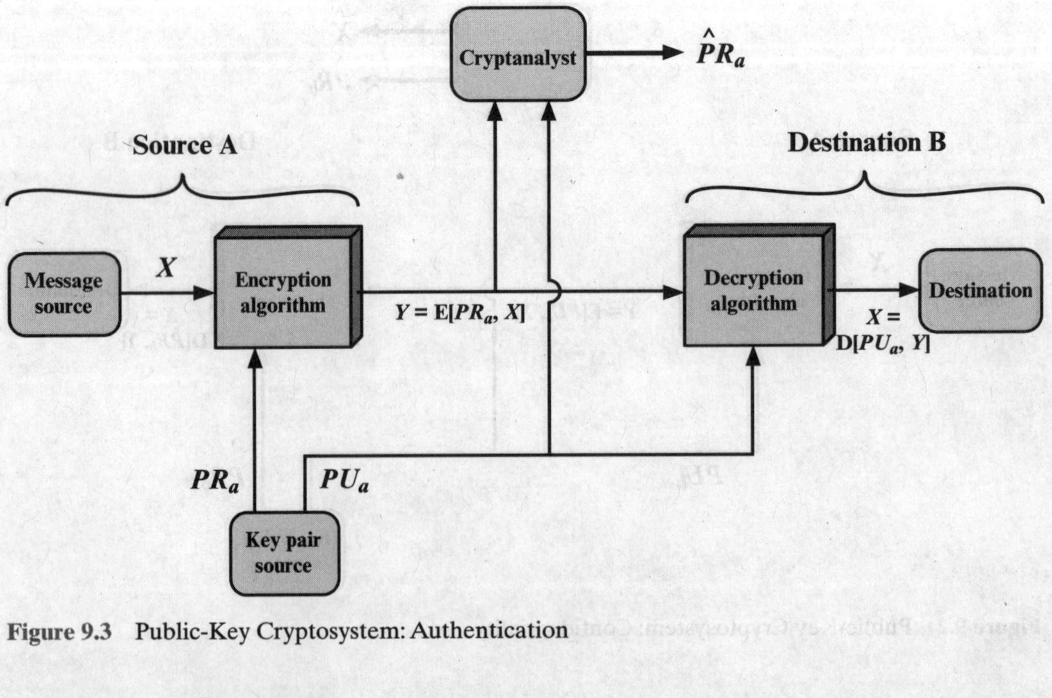

Figure 9.3 Public-Key Cryptosystem: Authentication

It is important to emphasize that the encryption process depicted in Figures 9.1b and 9.3 does not provide confidentiality. That is, the message being sent is safe from alteration but not from eavesdropping. This is obvious in the case of a signature based on a portion of the message, because the rest of the message is transmitted in the clear. Even in the case of complete encryption, as shown in Figure 9.3, there is no protection of confidentiality because any observer can decrypt the message by using the sender's public key.

It is, however, possible to provide both the authentication function and confidentiality by a double use of the public-key scheme (Figure 9.4):

$$Z = E(PU_b, E(PR_a, X))$$
$$X = D(PU_a, D(PR_b, Z))$$

In this case, we begin as before by encrypting a message, using the sender's private key. This provides the digital signature. Next, we encrypt again, using the receiver's public key. The final ciphertext can be decrypted only by the intended receiver, who alone has the matching private key. Thus, confidentiality is provided. The disadvantage of this approach is that the public-key algorithm, which is complex, must be exercised four times rather than two in each communication.

Applications for Public-Key Cryptosystems

Before proceeding, we need to clarify one aspect of public-key cryptosystems that is otherwise likely to lead to confusion. Public-key systems are characterized by the use of a cryptographic algorithm with two keys, one held private and one available publicly. Depending on the application, the sender uses either the sender's private key or the receiver's public key, or both, to perform some type of cryptographic

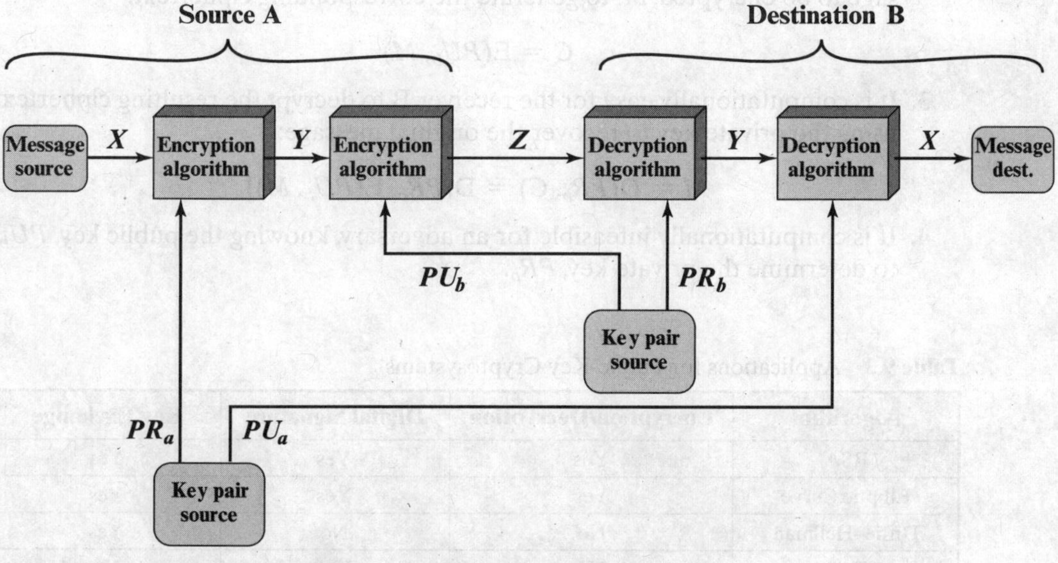

Figure 9.4 Public-Key Cryptosystem: Authentication and Secrecy

function. In broad terms, we can classify the use of **public-key cryptosystems** into three categories

- **Encryption/decryption:** The sender encrypts a message with the recipient's public key, and the recipient decrypts the message with the recipient's private key.
- **Digital signature:** The sender "signs" a message with its private key. Signing is achieved by a cryptographic algorithm applied to the message or to a small block of data that is a function of the message.
- **Key exchange:** Two sides cooperate to exchange a session key, which is a secret key for symmetric encryption generated for use for a particular transaction (or session) and valid for a short period of time. Several different approaches are possible, involving the private key(s) of one or both parties; this is discussed in Chapter 10.

Some algorithms are suitable for all three applications, whereas others can be used only for one or two of these applications. Table 9.3 indicates the applications supported by the algorithms discussed in this book.

Requirements for Public-Key Cryptography

The cryptosystem illustrated in Figures 9.2 through 9.4 depends on a cryptographic algorithm based on two related keys. Diffie and Hellman postulated this system without demonstrating that such algorithms exist. However, they did lay out the conditions that such algorithms must fulfill [DIFF76b].

1. It is computationally easy for a party B to generate a key pair (public key PU_b, private key PR_b).
2. It is computationally easy for a sender A, knowing the public key and the message to be encrypted, M, to generate the corresponding ciphertext:

$$C = E(PU_b, M)$$

3. It is computationally easy for the receiver B to decrypt the resulting ciphertext using the private key to recover the original message:

$$M = D(PR_b, C) = D[PR_b, E(PU_b, M)]$$

4. It is computationally infeasible for an adversary, knowing the public key, PU_b, to determine the private key, PR_b.

Table 9.3 Applications for Public-Key Cryptosystems

Algorithm	Encryption/Decryption	Digital Signature	Key Exchange
RSA	Yes	Yes	Yes
Elliptic Curve	Yes	Yes	Yes
Diffie–Hellman	No	No	Yes
DSS	No	Yes	No

5. It is computationally infeasible for an adversary, knowing the public key, PU_b, and a ciphertext, C, to recover the original message, M.

We can add a sixth requirement that, although useful, is not necessary for all public-key applications:

6. The two keys can be applied in either order:

$$M = \mathrm{D}[PU_b, \mathrm{E}(PR_b, M)] = \mathrm{D}[PR_b, \mathrm{E}(PU_b, M)]$$

These are formidable requirements, as evidenced by the fact that only a few algorithms (RSA, elliptic curve cryptography, Diffie–Hellman, DSS) have received widespread acceptance in the several decades since the concept of public-key cryptography was proposed.

Before elaborating on why the requirements are so formidable, let us first recast them. The requirements boil down to the need for a trap-door one-way function. A **one-way function**[3] is one that maps a domain into a range such that every function value has a unique inverse, with the condition that the calculation of the function is easy, whereas the calculation of the inverse is infeasible:

$$Y = \mathrm{f}(X) \quad \text{easy}$$
$$X = \mathrm{f}^{-1}(Y) \quad \text{infeasible}$$

Generally, *easy* is defined to mean a problem that can be solved in polynomial time as a function of input length. Thus, if the length of the input is n bits, then the time to compute the function is proportional to n^a, where a is a fixed constant. Such algorithms are said to belong to the class **P**. The term *infeasible* is a much fuzzier concept. In general, we can say a problem is infeasible if the effort to solve it grows faster than polynomial time as a function of input size. For example, if the length of the input is n bits and the time to compute the function is proportional to 2^n, the problem is considered infeasible. Unfortunately, it is difficult to determine if a particular algorithm exhibits this complexity. Furthermore, traditional notions of computational complexity focus on the worst-case or average-case complexity of an algorithm. These measures are inadequate for cryptography, which requires that it be infeasible to invert a function for virtually all inputs, not for the worst case or even average case. A brief introduction to some of these concepts is provided in Appendix W.

We now turn to the definition of a **trap-door one-way function**, which is easy to calculate in one direction and infeasible to calculate in the other direction unless certain additional information is known. With the additional information the inverse can be calculated in polynomial time. We can summarize as follows: A trap-door one-way function is a family of invertible functions f_k, such that

$$Y = \mathrm{f}_k(X) \quad \text{easy, if } k \text{ and } X \text{ are known}$$
$$X = \mathrm{f}_k^{-1}(Y) \quad \text{easy, if } k \text{ and } Y \text{ are known}$$
$$X = \mathrm{f}_k^{-1}(Y) \quad \text{infeasible, if } Y \text{ is known but } k \text{ is not known}$$

[3]Not to be confused with a one-way hash function, which takes an arbitrarily large data field as its argument and maps it to a fixed output. Such functions are used for authentication (see Chapter 11).

Thus, the development of a practical public-key scheme depends on discovery of a suitable trap-door one-way function.

Public-Key Cryptanalysis

As with symmetric encryption, a public-key encryption scheme is vulnerable to a brute-force attack. The countermeasure is the same: Use large keys. However, there is a tradeoff to be considered. Public-key systems depend on the use of some sort of invertible mathematical function. The complexity of calculating these functions may not scale linearly with the number of bits in the key but grow more rapidly than that. Thus, the key size must be large enough to make brute-force attack impractical but small enough for practical encryption and decryption. In practice, the key sizes that have been proposed do make brute-force attack impractical but result in encryption/decryption speeds that are too slow for general-purpose use. Instead, as was mentioned earlier, public-key encryption is currently confined to key management and signature applications.

Another form of attack is to find some way to compute the private key given the public key. To date, it has not been mathematically proven that this form of attack is infeasible for a particular public-key algorithm. Thus, any given algorithm, including the widely used RSA algorithm, is suspect. The history of cryptanalysis shows that a problem that seems insoluble from one perspective can be found to have a solution if looked at in an entirely different way.

Finally, there is a form of attack that is peculiar to public-key systems. This is, in essence, a probable-message attack. Suppose, for example, that a message were to be sent that consisted solely of a 56-bit DES key. An adversary could encrypt all possible 56-bit DES keys using the public key and could discover the encrypted key by matching the transmitted ciphertext. Thus, no matter how large the key size of the public-key scheme, the attack is reduced to a brute-force attack on a 56-bit key. This attack can be thwarted by appending some random bits to such simple messages.

9.2 THE RSA ALGORITHM

The pioneering paper by Diffie and Hellman [DIFF76b] introduced a new approach to cryptography and, in effect, challenged cryptologists to come up with a cryptographic algorithm that met the requirements for public-key systems. A number of algorithms have been proposed for public-key cryptography. Some of these, though initially promising, turned out to be breakable.[4]

One of the first successful responses to the challenge was developed in 1977 by Ron Rivest, Adi Shamir, and Len Adleman at MIT and first published in 1978 [RIVE78].[5] The Rivest-Shamir-Adleman (RSA) scheme has since that time reigned supreme as the most widely accepted and implemented general-purpose approach to public-key encryption.

---

[4]The most famous of the fallen contenders is the trapdoor knapsack proposed by Ralph Merkle. We describe this in Appendix J.

[5]Apparently, the first workable public-key system for encryption/decryption was put forward by Clifford Cocks of Britain's CESG in 1973 [COCK73]; Cocks' method is virtually identical to RSA.

The **RSA** scheme is a cipher in which the plaintext and ciphertext are integers between 0 and $n - 1$ for some n. A typical size for n is 1024 bits, or 309 decimal digits. That is, n is less than 2^{1024}. We examine RSA in this section in some detail, beginning with an explanation of the algorithm. Then we examine some of the computational and cryptanalytical implications of RSA.

Description of the Algorithm

RSA makes use of an expression with exponentials. Plaintext is encrypted in blocks, with each block having a binary value less than some number n. That is, the block size must be less than or equal to $\log_2(n) + 1$; in practice, the block size is i bits, where $2^i < n \leq 2^{i+1}$. Encryption and decryption are of the following form, for some plaintext block M and ciphertext block C.

$$C = M^e \bmod n$$
$$M = C^d \bmod n = (M^e)^d \bmod n = M^{ed} \bmod n$$

Both sender and receiver must know the value of n. The sender knows the value of e, and only the receiver knows the value of d. Thus, this is a public-key encryption algorithm with a public key of $PU = \{e, n\}$ and a private key of $PR = \{d, n\}$. For this algorithm to be satisfactory for public-key encryption, the following requirements must be met.

1. It is possible to find values of $e, d,$ and n such that $M^{ed} \bmod n = M$ for all $M < n$.
2. It is relatively easy to calculate $M^e \bmod n$ and $C^d \bmod n$ for all values of $M < n$.
3. It is infeasible to determine d given e and n.

For now, we focus on the first requirement and consider the other questions later. We need to find a relationship of the form

$$M^{ed} \bmod n = M$$

The preceding relationship holds if e and d are multiplicative inverses modulo $\phi(n)$, where $\phi(n)$ is the Euler totient function. It is shown in Chapter 2 that for p, q prime, $\phi(pq) = (p - 1)(q - 1)$. The relationship between e and d can be expressed as

$$ed \bmod \phi(n) = 1 \tag{9.1}$$

This is equivalent to saying

$$ed \equiv 1 \bmod \phi(n)$$
$$d \equiv e^{-1} \bmod \phi(n)$$

That is, e and d are multiplicative inverses mod $\phi(n)$. Note that, according to the rules of modular arithmetic, this is true only if d (and therefore e) is relatively prime to $\phi(n)$. Equivalently, $\gcd(\phi(n), d) = 1$. See Appendix R for a proof that Equation (9.1) satisfies the requirement for RSA.

We are now ready to state the RSA scheme. The ingredients are the following:

p, q, two prime numbers	(private, chosen)
$n = pq$	(public, calculated)
e, with $\gcd(\phi(n), e) = 1; 1 < e < \phi(n)$	(public, chosen)
$d \equiv e^{-1} (\bmod \phi(n))$	(private, calculated)

The private key consists of $\{d, n\}$ and the public key consists of $\{e, n\}$. Suppose that user A has published its public key and that user B wishes to send the message M to A. Then B calculates $C = M^e \bmod n$ and transmits C. On receipt of this ciphertext, user A decrypts by calculating $M = C^d \bmod n$.

Figure 9.5 summarizes the RSA algorithm. It corresponds to Figure 9.1a: Alice generates a public/private key pair; Bob encrypts using Alice's public key; and Alice decrypts using her private key. An example from [SING99] is shown in Figure 9.6. For this example, the keys were generated as follows.

1. Select two prime numbers, $p = 17$ and $q = 11$.
2. Calculate $n = pq = 17 \times 11 = 187$.
3. Calculate $\phi(n) = (p - 1)(q - 1) = 16 \times 10 = 160$.
4. Select e such that e is relatively prime to $\phi(n) = 160$ and less than $\phi(n)$; we choose $e = 7$.
5. Determine d such that $de \equiv 1 \pmod{160}$ and $d < 160$. The correct value is $d = 23$, because $23 \times 7 = 161 = (1 \times 160) + 1$; d can be calculated using the extended Euclid's algorithm (Chapter 2).

The resulting keys are public key $PU = \{7, 187\}$ and private key $PR = \{23, 187\}$. The example shows the use of these keys for a plaintext input of $M = 88$. For encryption, we need to calculate $C = 88^7 \bmod 187$. Exploiting the properties of modular arithmetic, we can do this as follows.

$$88^7 \bmod 187 = [(88^4 \bmod 187) \times (88^2 \bmod 187) \times (88^1 \bmod 187)] \bmod 187$$

$$88^1 \bmod 187 = 88$$

$$88^2 \bmod 187 = 7744 \bmod 187 = 77$$

$$88^4 \bmod 187 = 59{,}969{,}536 \bmod 187 = 132$$

$$88^7 \bmod 187 = (88 \times 77 \times 132) \bmod 187 = 894{,}432 \bmod 187 = 11$$

For decryption, we calculate $M = 11^{23} \bmod 187$:

$$11^{23} \bmod 187 = [(11^1 \bmod 187) \times (11^2 \bmod 187) \times (11^4 \bmod 187) \times (11^8 \bmod 187) \times (11^8 \bmod 187)] \bmod 187$$

$$11^1 \bmod 187 = 11$$

$$11^2 \bmod 187 = 121$$

$$11^4 \bmod 187 = 14{,}641 \bmod 187 = 55$$

$$11^8 \bmod 187 = 214{,}358{,}881 \bmod 187 = 33$$

$$11^{23} \bmod 187 = (11 \times 121 \times 55 \times 33 \times 33) \bmod 187 = 79{,}720{,}245 \bmod 187 = 88$$

We now look at an example from [HELL79], which shows the use of RSA to process multiple blocks of data. In this simple example, the plaintext is an alphanumeric string. Each plaintext symbol is assigned a unique code of two decimal

Key Generation by Alice	
Select p, q	p and q both prime, $p \neq q$
Calculate $n = p \times q$	
Calcuate $\phi(n) = (p - 1)(q - 1)$	
Select integer e	$\gcd(\phi(n), e) = 1; 1 < e < \phi(n)$
Calculate d	$d \equiv e^{-1} \pmod{\phi(n)}$
Public key	$PU = \{e, n\}$
Private key	$PR = \{d, n\}$

Encryption by Bob with Alice's Public Key	
Plaintext:	$M < n$
Ciphertext:	$C = M^e \bmod n$

Decryption by Alice with Alice's Public Key	
Ciphertext:	C
Plaintext:	$M = C^d \bmod n$

Figure 9.5 The RSA Algorithm

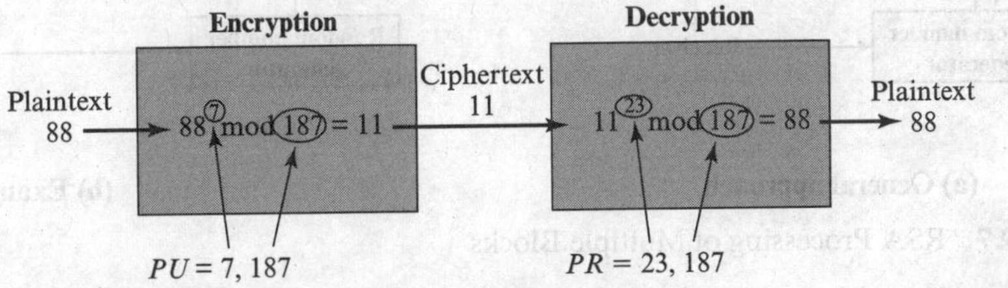

Figure 9.6 Example of RSA Algorithm

digits (e.g., a = 00, A = 26).[6] A plaintext block consists of four decimal digits, or two alphanumeric characters. Figure 9.7a illustrates the sequence of events for the encryption of multiple blocks, and Figure 9.7b gives a specific example. The circled numbers indicate the order in which operations are performed.

Computational Aspects

We now turn to the issue of the complexity of the computation required to use RSA. There are actually two issues to consider: encryption/decryption and key generation. Let us look first at the process of encryption and decryption and then consider key generation.

[6] The complete mapping of alphanumeric characters to decimal digits is at box.com/Crypto7e in the document `RSAexample.pdf`.

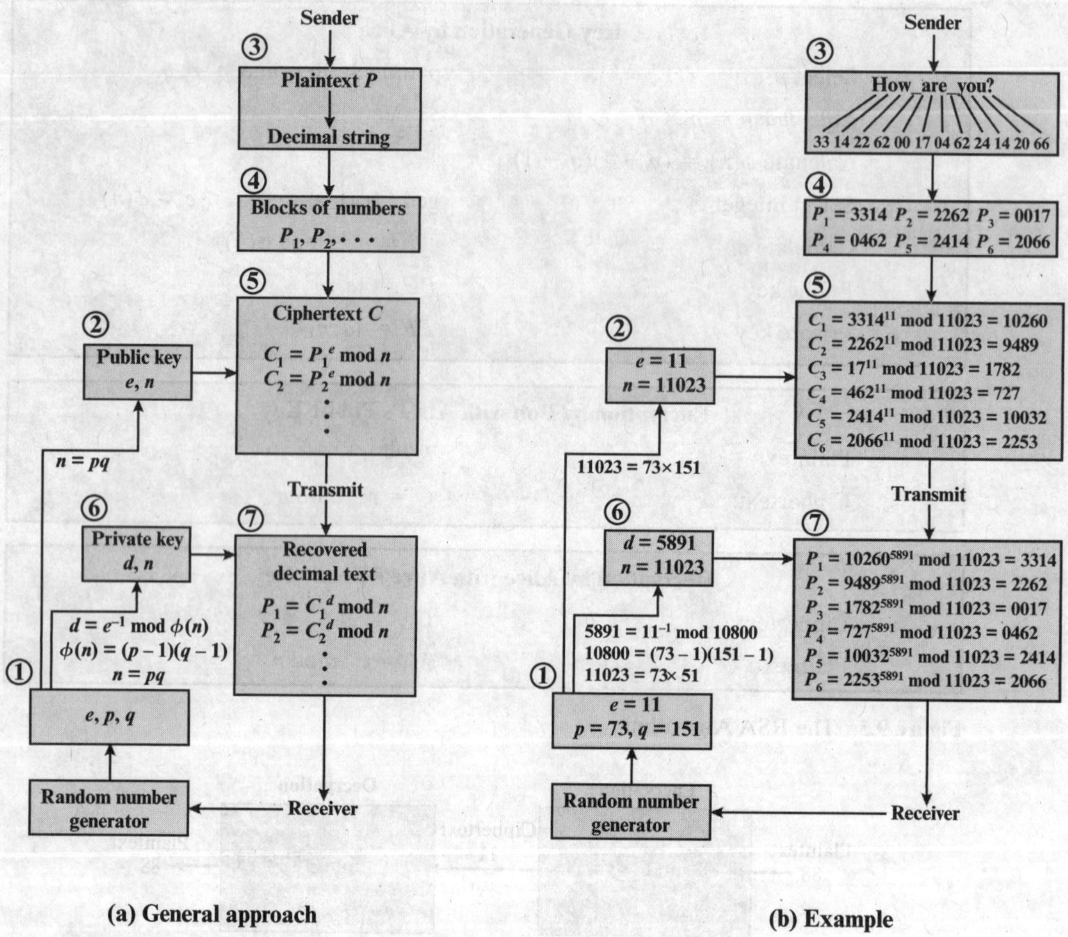

Figure 9.7 RSA Processing of Multiple Blocks

Exponentiation in Modular Arithmetic Both encryption and decryption in RSA involve raising an integer to an integer power, mod n. If the exponentiation is done over the integers and then reduced modulo n, the intermediate values would be gargantuan. Fortunately, as the preceding example shows, we can make use of a property of modular arithmetic:

$$[(a \bmod n) \times (b \bmod n)] \bmod n = (a \times b) \bmod n$$

Thus, we can reduce intermediate results modulo n. This makes the calculation practical.

Another consideration is the efficiency of exponentiation, because with RSA, we are dealing with potentially large exponents. To see how efficiency might be increased, consider that we wish to compute x^{16}. A straightforward approach requires 15 multiplications:

$$x^{16} = x \times x \times x \times x \times x \times x \times x \times x \times x \times x \times x \times x \times x \times x \times x \times x$$

However, we can achieve the same final result with only four multiplications if we repeatedly take the square of each partial result, successively forming (x^2, x^4, x^8, x^{16}). As another example, suppose we wish to calculate $x^{11} \bmod n$ for some integers x and n. Observe that $x^{11} = x^{1+2+8} = (x)(x^2)(x^8)$. In this case, we compute $x \bmod n$, $x^2 \bmod n$, $x^4 \bmod n$, and $x^8 \bmod n$ and then calculate $[(x \bmod n) \times (x^2 \bmod n) \times (x^8 \bmod n)] \bmod n$.

More generally, suppose we wish to find the value $a^b \bmod n$ with a, b, and m positive integers. If we express b as a binary number $b_k b_{k-1} \ldots b_0$, then we have

$$b = \sum_{b_i \neq 0} 2^i$$

Therefore,

$$a^b = a^{\left(\sum\limits_{b_i \neq 0} 2^i\right)} = \prod_{b_i \neq 0} a^{(2^i)}$$

$$a^b \bmod n = \left[\prod_{b_i \neq 0} a^{(2^i)}\right] \bmod n = \left(\prod_{b_i \neq 0}\left[a^{(2^i)} \bmod n\right]\right) \bmod n$$

We can therefore develop the algorithm[7] for computing $a^b \bmod n$, shown in Figure 9.8. Table 9.4 shows an example of the execution of this algorithm. Note that the variable c is not needed; it is included for explanatory purposes. The final value of c is the value of the exponent.

Efficient Operation Using the Public Key To speed up the operation of the RSA algorithm using the public key, a specific choice of e is usually made. The most common choice is 65537 $(2^{16} + 1)$; two other popular choices are 3 and 17. Each of these choices has only two 1 bits, so the number of multiplications required to perform exponentiation is minimized.

```
c ← 0; f ← 1
for i ← k downto 0
    do  c ← 2 × c
        f ← (f × f) mod n
    if  bi = 1
        then c ← c + 1
             f ← (f × a) mod n
return f
```

Note: The integer b is expressed as a binary number $b_k b_{k-1} \ldots b_0$.

Figure 9.8 Algorithm for Computing $a^b \bmod n$

[7]The algorithm has a long history; this particular pseudocode expression is from [CORM09].

Table 9.4 Result of the Fast Modular Exponentiation Algorithm for $a^b \bmod n$, where $a = 7$, $b = 560 = 1000110000$, and $n = 561$

i	9	8	7	6	5	4	3	2	1	0
b_i	1	0	0	0	1	1	0	0	0	0
c	1	2	4	8	17	35	70	140	280	560
f	7	49	157	526	160	241	298	166	67	1

However, with a very small public key, such as $e = 3$, RSA becomes vulnerable to a simple attack. Suppose we have three different RSA users who all use the value $e = 3$ but have unique values of n, namely (n_1, n_2, n_3). If user A sends the same encrypted message M to all three users, then the three ciphertexts are $C_1 = M^3 \bmod n_1$, $C_2 = M^3 \bmod n_2$, and $C_3 = M^3 \bmod n_3$. It is likely that n_1, n_2, and n_3 are pairwise relatively prime. Therefore, one can use the Chinese remainder theorem (CRT) to compute $M^3 \bmod (n_1 n_2 n_3)$. By the rules of the RSA algorithm, M is less than each of the n_i; therefore $M^3 < n_1 n_2 n_3$. Accordingly, the attacker need only compute the cube root of M^3. This attack can be countered by adding a unique pseudorandom bit string as padding to each instance of M to be encrypted. This approach is discussed subsequently.

The reader may have noted that the definition of the RSA algorithm (Figure 9.5) requires that during key generation the user selects a value of e that is relatively prime to $\phi(n)$. Thus, if a value of e is selected first and the primes p and q are generated, it may turn out that $\gcd(\phi(n), e) \neq 1$. In that case, the user must reject the p, q values and generate a new p, q pair.

Efficient Operation Using the Private Key We cannot similarly choose a small constant value of d for efficient operation. A small value of d is vulnerable to a brute-force attack and to other forms of cryptanalysis [WIEN90]. However, there is a way to speed up computation using the CRT. We wish to compute the value $M = C^d \bmod n$. Let us define the following intermediate results:

$$V_p = C^d \bmod p \quad V_q = C^d \bmod q$$

Following the CRT using Equation (8.8), define the quantities

$$X_p = q \times (q^{-1} \bmod p) \quad X_q = p \times (p^{-1} \bmod q)$$

The CRT then shows, using Equation (8.9), that

$$M = (V_p X_p + V_q X_q) \bmod n$$

Furthermore, we can simplify the calculation of V_p and V_q using Fermat's theorem, which states that $a^{p-1} \equiv 1 \pmod p$ if p and a are relatively prime. Some thought should convince you that the following are valid.

$$V_p = C^d \bmod p = C^{d \bmod (p-1)} \bmod p \quad V_q = C^d \bmod q = C^{d \bmod (q-1)} \bmod q$$

The quantities $d \bmod (p - 1)$ and $d \bmod (q - 1)$ can be precalculated. The end result is that the calculation is approximately four times as fast as evaluating $M = C^d \bmod n$ directly [BONE02].

KEY GENERATION Before the application of the public-key cryptosystem, each participant must generate a pair of keys. This involves the following tasks.

- Determining two prime numbers, p and q.
- Selecting either e or d and calculating the other.

First, consider the selection of p and q. Because the value of $n = pq$ will be known to any potential adversary, in order to prevent the discovery of p and q by exhaustive methods, these primes must be chosen from a sufficiently large set (i.e., p and q must be large numbers). On the other hand, the method used for finding large primes must be reasonably efficient.

At present, there are no useful techniques that yield arbitrarily large primes, so some other means of tackling the problem is needed. The procedure that is generally used is to pick at random an odd number of the desired order of magnitude and test whether that number is prime. If not, pick successive random numbers until one is found that tests prime.

A variety of tests for primality have been developed (e.g., see [KNUT98] for a description of a number of such tests). Almost invariably, the tests are probabilistic. That is, the test will merely determine that a given integer is *probably* prime. Despite this lack of certainty, these tests can be run in such a way as to make the probability as close to 1.0 as desired. As an example, one of the more efficient and popular algorithms, the Miller–Rabin algorithm, is described in Chapter 2. With this algorithm and most such algorithms, the procedure for testing whether a given integer n is prime is to perform some calculation that involves n and a randomly chosen integer a. If n "fails" the test, then n is not prime. If n "passes" the test, then n may be prime or nonprime. If n passes many such tests with many different randomly chosen values for a, then we can have high confidence that n is, in fact, prime.

In summary, the procedure for picking a prime number is as follows.

1. Pick an odd integer n at random (e.g., using a pseudorandom number generator).
2. Pick an integer $a < n$ at random.
3. Perform the probabilistic primality test, such as Miller–Rabin, with a as a parameter. If n fails the test, reject the value n and go to step 1.
4. If n has passed a sufficient number of tests, accept n; otherwise, go to step 2.

This is a somewhat tedious procedure. However, remember that this process is performed relatively infrequently: only when a new pair (PU, PR) is needed.

It is worth noting how many numbers are likely to be rejected before a prime number is found. A result from number theory, known as the prime number theorem, states that the primes near N are spaced on the average one every ln (N) integers. Thus, on average, one would have to test on the order of ln(N) integers before a prime is found. Actually, because all even integers can be immediately rejected, the correct figure is ln(N)/2. For example, if a prime on the order of magnitude of 2^{200} were sought, then about $\ln(2^{200})/2 = 70$ trials would be needed to find a prime.

Having determined prime numbers p and q, the process of key generation is completed by selecting a value of e and calculating d or, alternatively, selecting a value of d and calculating e. Assuming the former, then we need to select an e such that $\gcd(\phi(n), e) = 1$ and then calculate $d \equiv e^{-1} \pmod{\phi(n)}$. Fortunately, there is a single algorithm that will, at the same time, calculate the greatest common divisor of two integers and, if the gcd is 1, determine the inverse of one of the integers modulo the other. The algorithm, referred to as the extended Euclid's algorithm, is explained in Chapter 2. Thus, the procedure is to generate a series of random numbers, testing each against $\phi(n)$ until a number relatively prime to $\phi(n)$ is found. Again, we can ask the question: How many random numbers must we test to find a usable number, that is, a number relatively prime to $\phi(n)$? It can be shown easily that the probability that two random numbers are relatively prime is about 0.6; thus, very few tests would be needed to find a suitable integer (see Problem 2.18).

The Security of RSA

Five possible approaches to attacking the RSA algorithm are

- **Brute force:** This involves trying all possible private keys.
- **Mathematical attacks:** There are several approaches, all equivalent in effort to factoring the product of two primes.
- **Timing attacks:** These depend on the running time of the decryption algorithm.
- **Hardware fault-based attack:** This involves inducing hardware faults in the processor that is generating digital signatures.
- **Chosen ciphertext attacks:** This type of attack exploits properties of the RSA algorithm.

The defense against the brute-force approach is the same for RSA as for other cryptosystems, namely, to use a large key space. Thus, the larger the number of bits in d, the better. However, because the calculations involved, both in key generation and in encryption/decryption, are complex, the larger the size of the key, the slower the system will run.

In this subsection, we provide an overview of mathematical and timing attacks.

The Factoring Problem We can identify three approaches to attacking RSA mathematically.

1. Factor n into its two prime factors. This enables calculation of $\phi(n) = (p - 1) \times (q - 1)$, which in turn enables determination of $d \equiv e^{-1} \pmod{\phi(n)}$.
2. Determine $\phi(n)$ directly, without first determining p and q. Again, this enables determination of $d \equiv e^{-1} \pmod{\phi(n)}$.
3. Determine d directly, without first determining $\phi(n)$.

Most discussions of the cryptanalysis of RSA have focused on the task of factoring n into its two prime factors. Determining $\phi(n)$ given n is equivalent to factoring n [RIBE96]. With presently known algorithms, determining d given e and n appears to be at least as time-consuming as the factoring problem [KALI95]. Hence, we can use factoring performance as a benchmark against which to evaluate the security of RSA.

For a large n with large prime factors, factoring is a hard problem, but it is not as hard as it used to be. A striking illustration of this is the following. In 1977, the three inventors of RSA dared *Scientific American* readers to decode a cipher they printed in Martin Gardner's "Mathematical Games" column [GARD77]. They offered a $100 reward for the return of a plaintext sentence, an event they predicted might not occur for some 40 quadrillion years. In April of 1994, a group working over the Internet claimed the prize after only eight months of work [LEUT94]. This challenge used a public key size (length of n) of 129 decimal digits, or around 428 bits. In the meantime, just as they had done for DES, RSA Laboratories had issued challenges for the RSA cipher with key sizes of 100, 110, 120, and so on, digits. The latest challenge to be met is the RSA-768 challenge with a key length of 232 decimal digits, or 768 bits. Table 9.5 shows the results.

A striking fact about the progress reflected in Table 9.5 concerns the method used. Until the mid-1990s, factoring attacks were made using an approach known as the quadratic sieve. The attack on RSA-130 used a newer algorithm, the generalized number field sieve (GNFS), and was able to factor a larger number than RSA-129 at only 20% of the computing effort.

The threat to larger key sizes is twofold: the continuing increase in computing power and the continuing refinement of factoring algorithms. We have seen that the move to a different algorithm resulted in a tremendous speedup. We can expect further refinements in the GNFS, and the use of an even better algorithm is also a possibility. In fact, a related algorithm, the special number field sieve (SNFS),

Table 9.5 Progress in RSA Factorization

Number of Decimal Digits	Number of Bits	Date Achieved
100	332	April 1991
110	365	April 1992
120	398	June 1993
129	428	April 1994
130	431	April 1996
140	465	February 1999
155	512	August 1999
160	530	April 2003
174	576	December 2003
200	663	May 2005
193	640	November 2005
232	768	December 2009

can factor numbers with a specialized form considerably faster than the generalized number field sieve. Figure 9.9 compares the performance of the two algorithms. It is reasonable to expect a breakthrough that would enable a general factoring performance in about the same time as SNFS, or even better [ODLY95]. Thus, we need to be careful in choosing a key size for RSA. The team that produced the 768-bit factorization [KLEI10] observed that factoring a 1024-bit RSA modulus would be about a thousand times harder than factoring a 768-bit modulus, and a 768-bit RSA modulus is several thousands times harder to factor than a 512-bit one. Based on the amount of time between the 512-bit and 768-bit factorization successes, the team felt it to be reasonable to expect that the 1024-bit RSA moduli could be factored well within the next decade by a similar academic effort. Thus, they recommended phasing out usage of 1024-bit RSA within the next few years (from 2010).

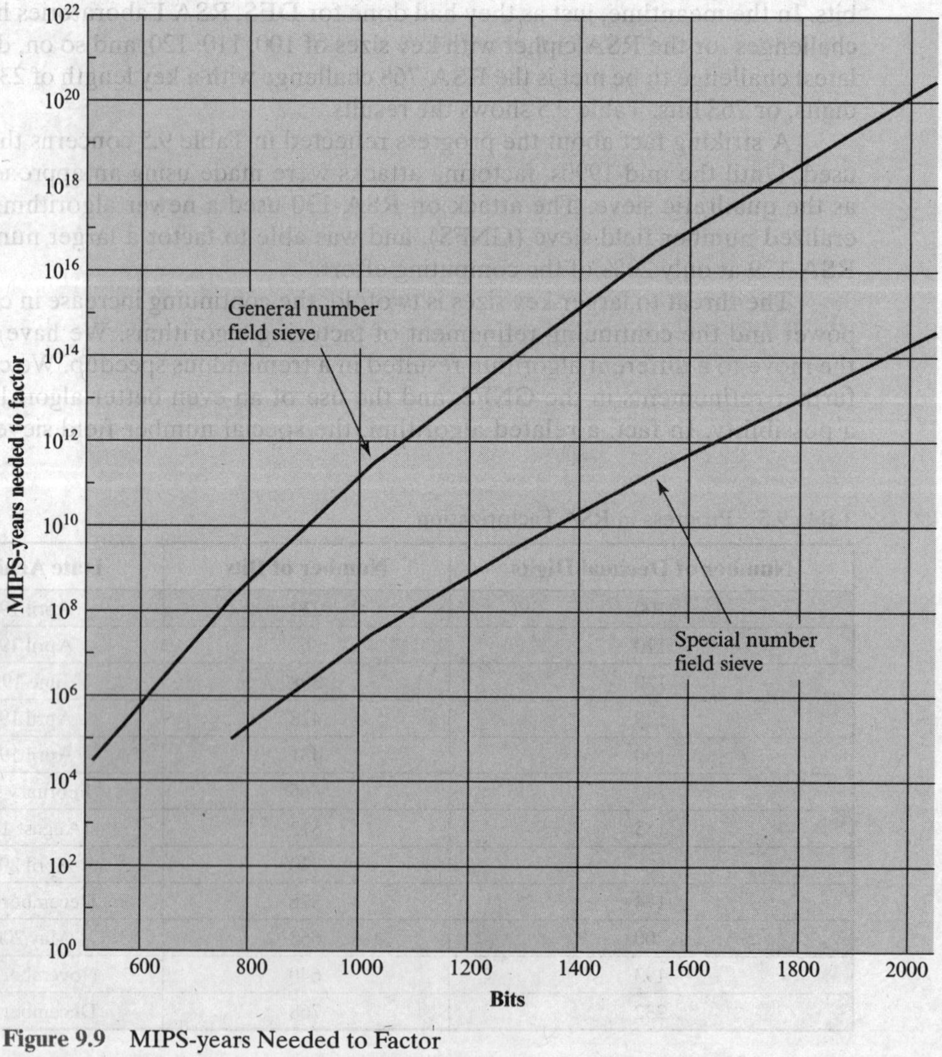

Figure 9.9 MIPS-years Needed to Factor

In addition to specifying the size of n, a number of other constraints have been suggested by researchers. To avoid values of n that may be factored more easily, the algorithm's inventors suggest the following constraints on p and q.

1. p and q should differ in length by only a few digits. Thus, for a 1024-bit key (309 decimal digits), both p and q should be on the order of magnitude of 10^{75} to 10^{100}.
2. Both $(p - 1)$ and $(q - 1)$ should contain a large prime factor.
3. $\gcd(p - 1, q - 1)$ should be small.

In addition, it has been demonstrated that if $e < n$ and $d < n^{1/4}$, then d can be easily determined [WIEN90].

TIMING ATTACKS If one needed yet another lesson about how difficult it is to assess the security of a cryptographic algorithm, the appearance of timing attacks provides a stunning one. Paul Kocher, a cryptographic consultant, demonstrated that a snooper can determine a private key by keeping track of how long a computer takes to decipher messages [KOCH96, KALI96b]. Timing attacks are applicable not just to RSA, but to other public-key cryptography systems. This attack is alarming for two reasons: It comes from a completely unexpected direction, and it is a ciphertext-only attack.

A **timing attack** is somewhat analogous to a burglar guessing the combination of a safe by observing how long it takes for someone to turn the dial from number to number. We can explain the attack using the modular exponentiation algorithm of Figure 9.8, but the attack can be adapted to work with any implementation that does not run in fixed time. In this algorithm, modular exponentiation is accomplished bit by bit, with one modular multiplication performed at each iteration and an additional modular multiplication performed for each 1 bit.

As Kocher points out in his paper, the attack is simplest to understand in an extreme case. Suppose the target system uses a modular multiplication function that is very fast in almost all cases but in a few cases takes much more time than an entire average modular exponentiation. The attack proceeds bit-by-bit starting with the leftmost bit, b_k. Suppose that the first j bits are known (to obtain the entire exponent, start with $j = 0$ and repeat the attack until the entire exponent is known). For a given ciphertext, the attacker can complete the first j iterations of the **for** loop. The operation of the subsequent step depends on the unknown exponent bit. If the bit is set, $d \leftarrow (d \times a) \bmod n$ will be executed. For a few values of a and d, the modular multiplication will be extremely slow, and the attacker knows which these are. Therefore, if the observed time to execute the decryption algorithm is always slow when this particular iteration is slow with a 1 bit, then this bit is assumed to be 1. If a number of observed execution times for the entire algorithm are fast, then this bit is assumed to be 0.

In practice, modular exponentiation implementations do not have such extreme timing variations, in which the execution time of a single iteration can exceed the mean execution time of the entire algorithm. Nevertheless, there is enough variation to make this attack practical. For details, see [KOCH96].

Although the timing attack is a serious threat, there are simple countermeasures that can be used, including the following.

- **Constant exponentiation time:** Ensure that all exponentiations take the same amount of time before returning a result. This is a simple fix but does degrade performance.
- **Random delay:** Better performance could be achieved by adding a random delay to the exponentiation algorithm to confuse the timing attack. Kocher points out that if defenders don't add enough noise, attackers could still succeed by collecting additional measurements to compensate for the random delays.
- **Blinding:** Multiply the ciphertext by a random number before performing exponentiation. This process prevents the attacker from knowing what ciphertext bits are being processed inside the computer and therefore prevents the bit-by-bit analysis essential to the timing attack.

RSA Data Security incorporates a blinding feature into some of its products. The private-key operation $M = C_d \bmod n$ is implemented as follows.

1. Generate a secret random number r between 0 and $n - 1$.
2. Compute $C' = C(r^e) \bmod n$, where e is the public exponent.
3. Compute $M' = (C')^d \bmod n$ with the ordinary RSA implementation.
4. Compute $M = M'r^{-1} \bmod n$. In this equation, r^{-1} is the multiplicative inverse of $r \bmod n$; see Chapter 2 for a discussion of this concept. It can be demonstrated that this is the correct result by observing that $r^{ed} \bmod n = r \bmod n$.

RSA Data Security reports a 2 to 10% performance penalty for blinding.

FAULT-BASED ATTACK Still another unorthodox approach to attacking RSA is reported in [PELL10]. The approach is an attack on a processor that is generating RSA digital signatures. The attack induces faults in the signature computation by reducing the power to the processor. The faults cause the software to produce invalid signatures, which can then be analyzed by the attacker to recover the private key. The authors show how such an analysis can be done and then demonstrate it by extracting a 1024-bit private RSA key in approximately 100 hours, using a commercially available microprocessor.

The attack algorithm involves inducing single-bit errors and observing the results. The details are provided in [PELL10], which also references other proposed hardware fault-based attacks against RSA.

This attack, while worthy of consideration, does not appear to be a serious threat to RSA. It requires that the attacker have physical access to the target machine and that the attacker is able to directly control the input power to the processor. Controlling the input power would for most hardware require more than simply controlling the AC power, but would also involve the power supply control hardware on the chip.

CHOSEN CIPHERTEXT ATTACK AND OPTIMAL ASYMMETRIC ENCRYPTION PADDING The basic RSA algorithm is vulnerable to a **chosen ciphertext attack (CCA)**. CCA is defined as an attack in which the adversary chooses a number of ciphertexts and is then given the corresponding plaintexts, decrypted with the target's private key. Thus, the adversary could select a plaintext, encrypt it with the target's public key, and then be able to get the plaintext back by having it decrypted with the private key. Clearly, this provides the adversary with no new information. Instead, the adversary exploits properties of RSA and selects blocks of data that, when processed using the target's private key, yield information needed for cryptanalysis.

A simple example of a CCA against RSA takes advantage of the following property of RSA:

$$\mathrm{E}(PU, M_1) \times \mathrm{E}(PU, M_2) = \mathrm{E}(PU, [M_1 \times M_2]) \qquad \textbf{(9.2)}$$

We can decrypt $C = M^e \bmod n$ using a CCA as follows.

1. Compute $X = (C \times 2^e) \bmod n$.
2. Submit X as a chosen ciphertext and receive back $Y = X^d \bmod n$.

But now note that

$$\begin{aligned} X &= (C \bmod n) \times (2^e \bmod n) \\ &= (M^e \bmod n) \times (2^e \bmod n) \\ &= (2M)^e \bmod n \end{aligned}$$

Therefore, $Y = (2M) \bmod n$. From this, we can deduce M. To overcome this simple attack, practical RSA-based cryptosystems randomly pad the plaintext prior to encryption. This randomizes the ciphertext so that Equation (9.2) no longer holds. However, more sophisticated CCAs are possible, and a simple padding with a random value has been shown to be insufficient to provide the desired security. To counter such attacks, RSA Security Inc., a leading RSA vendor and former holder of the RSA patent, recommends modifying the plaintext using a procedure known as **optimal asymmetric encryption padding** (OAEP). A full discussion of the threats and OAEP are beyond our scope; see [POIN02] for an introduction and [BELL94] for a thorough analysis. Here, we simply summarize the OAEP procedure.

Figure 9.10 depicts OAEP encryption. As a first step, the message M to be encrypted is padded. A set of optional parameters, P, is passed through a hash function, H.[8] The output is then padded with zeros to get the desired length in the overall data block (DB). Next, a random seed is generated and passed through another hash function, called the mask generating function (MGF). The resulting hash value is bit-by-bit XORed with DB to produce a maskedDB. The maskedDB is in turn passed through the MGF to form a hash that is XORed with the seed to produce the maskedseed. The concatenation of the maskedseed and the maskedDB forms the encoded message EM. Note that the EM includes the padded message, masked by the seed, and the seed, masked by the maskedDB. The EM is then encrypted using RSA.

[8]A hash function maps a variable-length data block or message into a fixed-length value called a hash code. Hash functions are discussed in depth in Chapter 11.

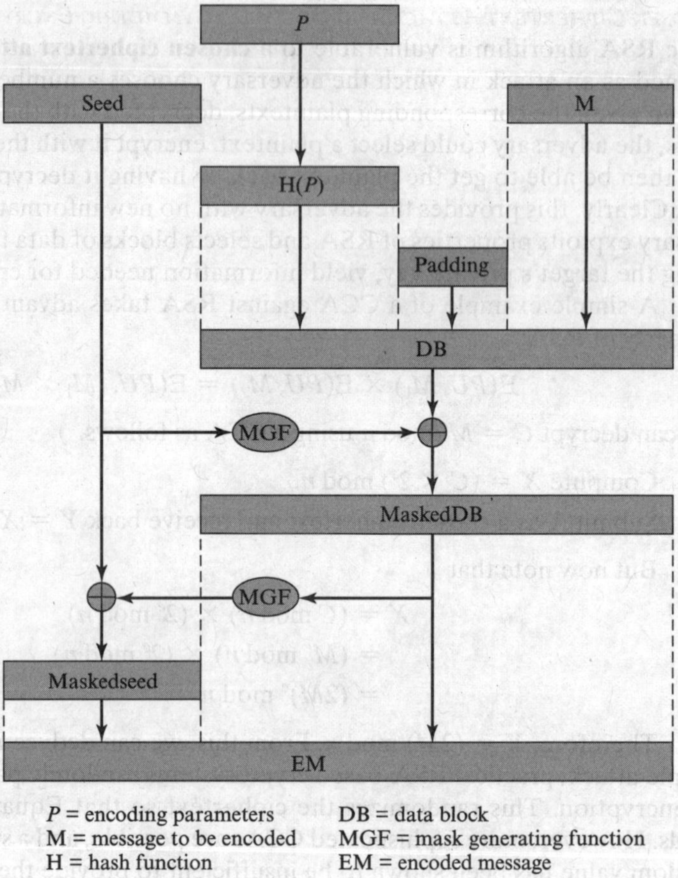

Figure 9.10 Encryption Using Optimal Asymmetric Encryption Padding (OAEP)

9.3 KEY TERMS, REVIEW QUESTIONS, AND PROBLEMS

Key Terms

chosen ciphertext attack (CCA) digital signature key exchange one-way function	optimal asymmetric encryption padding (OAEP) private key public key public-key cryptography	public-key cryptosystems public-key encryption RSA timing attack trap-door one-way function

Review Questions

9.1 What is public key infrastructure?

9.2 What are the roles of the public and private key?

9.3 What are three broad categories of applications of public-key cryptosystems?

9.4 What is a one-way function?
9.5 How can a probable-message attack be used for public-key cryptanalysis?
9.6 Briefly describe the RSA algorithm.
9.7 Describe the countermeasures to be used against the timing attack.

Problems

9.1 Prior to the discovery of any specific public-key schemes, such as RSA, an existence proof was developed whose purpose was to demonstrate that public-key encryption is possible in theory. Consider the functions $f_1(x_1) = z_1$; $f_2(x_2, y_2) = z_2$; $f_3(x_3, y_3) = z_3$, where all values are integers with $1 \leq x_i, y_i, z_i \leq N$. Function f_1 can be represented by a vector M1 of length N, in which the kth entry is the value of $f_1(k)$. Similarly, f_2 and f_3 can be represented by $N \times N$ matrices M2 and M3. The intent is to represent the encryption/decryption process by table lookups for tables with very large values of N. Such tables would be impractically huge but could be constructed in principle. The scheme works as follows: Construct M1 with a random permutation of all integers between 1 and N; that is, each integer appears exactly once in M1. Construct M2 so that each row contains a random permutation of the first N integers. Finally, fill in M3 to satisfy the following condition:

$$f_3(f_2(f_1(k), p), k) = p \qquad \text{for all } k, p \text{ with } 1 \leq k, p, \leq N$$

To summarize,
1. M1 takes an input k and produces an output x.
2. M2 takes inputs x and p giving output z.
3. M3 takes inputs z and k and produces p.

The three tables, once constructed, are made public.

a. It should be clear that it is possible to construct M3 to satisfy the preceding condition. As an example, fill in M3 for the following simple case:

M1 =

4
3
2
5
1

M2 =

3	5	2	4	1
4	2	5	3	1
5	4	3	1	2
1	3	2	5	4
2	1	4	3	5

M3 =

Convention: The ith element of M1 corresponds to $k = i$. The ith row of M2 corresponds to $x = i$; the jth column of M2 corresponds to $p = j$. The ith row of M3 corresponds to $z = i$; the jth column of M3 corresponds to $k = j$.

b. Describe the use of this set of tables to perform encryption and decryption between two users.

c. Argue that this is a secure scheme.

9.2 Perform encryption and decryption using the RSA algorithm, as in Figure 9.5, for the following:

a. $p = 3; q = 11, e = 7; M = 6$
b. $p = 5; q = 11, e = 3; M = 9$
c. $p = 7; q = 11, e = 17; M = 8$
d. $p = 11; q = 13, e = 11; M = 7$
e. $p = 17; q = 31, e = 7; M = 2$

Hint: Decryption is not as hard as you think; use some finesse.

9.3 In a public-key system using RSA, you intercept the ciphertext $C = 10$ sent to a user whose public key is $e = 5, n = 35$. What is the plaintext M?

9.4 In an RSA system, the public key of a given user is $e = 31$, $n = 3599$. What is the private key of this user? *Hint:* First use trial and error to determine p and q; then use the extended Euclidean algorithm to find the multiplicative inverse of 31 modulo $\phi(n)$.

9.5 In using the RSA algorithm, if a small number of repeated encodings give back the plaintext, what is the likely cause?

9.6 Suppose we have a set of blocks encoded with the RSA algorithm and we don't have the private key. Assume $n = pq$, e is the public key. Suppose also someone tells us they know one of the plaintext blocks has a common factor with n. Does this help us in any way?

9.7 In the RSA public-key encryption scheme, each user has a public key, e, and a private key, d. Suppose Bob leaks his private key. Rather than generating a new modulus, he decides to generate a new public and a new private key. Is this safe?

9.8 Suppose Bob uses the RSA cryptosystem with a very large modulus n for which the factorization cannot be found in a reasonable amount of time. Suppose Alice sends a message to Bob by representing each alphabetic character as an integer between 0 and 25 ($A \rightarrow 0, \ldots, Z \rightarrow 25$) and then encrypting each number separately using RSA with large e and large n. Is this method secure? If not, describe the most efficient attack against this encryption method.

9.9 Using a spreadsheet (such as Excel), or a calculator, perform the described below operations. Document results of all intermediate modular multiplications. Determine a number of modular multiplications per each major transformation (such as encryption, decryption, primality testing, etc.).

a. Test all odd numbers in the range from 233 to 241 for primality using the Miller-Rabin test with base 2.

b. Encrypt the message block $M = 2$ using RSA with the following parameters: $e = 23$ and $n = 233 \times 241$.

c. Compute a private key (d, p, q) corresponding to the given above public key (e, n).

d. Perform the decryption of the obtained ciphertext

1. without using the Chinese Remainder Theorem, and

2. using the Chinese Remainder Theorem.

9.10 Assume that you generate an authenticated and encrypted message by first applying the RSA transformation determined by your private key, and then enciphering the message using recipient's public key (note that you do NOT use hash function before the first transformation). Will this scheme work correctly [i.e., give the possibility to reconstruct the original message at the recipient's side, for all possible relations between the sender's modulus n_S and the recipient's modulus n_R ($n_S > n_R$, $n_S < n_R$, $n_S = n_R$)]? Explain your answer. In case your answer is "no," how would you correct this scheme?

9.11 "I want to tell you, Holmes," Dr. Watson's voice was enthusiastic, "that your recent activities in network security have increased my interest in cryptography. And just yesterday I found a way to make one-time pad encryption practical."

"Oh, really?" Holmes' face lost its sleepy look.

"Yes, Holmes. The idea is quite simple. For a given one-way function F, I generate a long pseudorandom sequence of elements by applying F to some standard sequence of arguments. The cryptanalyst is assumed to know F and the general nature of the sequence, which may be as simple as S, S + 1, S + 2, . . . , but not secret S. And due to the one-way nature of F, no one is able to extract S given F(S + i) for some i, thus even if he somehow obtains a certain segment of the sequence, he will not be able to determine the rest."

"I am afraid, Watson, that your proposal isn't without flaws and at least it needs some additional conditions to be satisfied by F. Let's consider, for instance, the RSA encryption function, that is $F(M) = M^K \bmod N$, K is secret. This function is believed to be one-way, but I wouldn't recommend its use, for example, on the sequence $M = 2, 3, 4, 5, 6, \ldots$"

"But why, Holmes?" Dr. Watson apparently didn't understand. "Why do you think that the resulting sequence $2^K \bmod N, 3^K \bmod N, 4^K \bmod N, \ldots$ is not appropriate for one-time pad encryption if K is kept secret?"

"Because it is—at least partially—predictable, dear Watson, even if K is kept secret. You have said that the cryptanalyst is assumed to know F and the general nature of the sequence. Now let's assume that he will obtain somehow a short segment of the output sequence. In crypto circles, this assumption is generally considered to be a viable one. And for this output sequence, knowledge of just the first two elements will allow him to predict quite a lot of the next elements of the sequence, even if not all of them, thus this sequence can't be considered to be cryptographically strong. And with the knowledge of a longer segment he could predict even more of the next elements of the sequence. Look, knowing the general nature of the sequence and its first two elements $2^K \bmod N$ and $3^K \bmod N$, you can easily compute its following elements."

Show how this can be done.

9.12 Show how RSA can be represented by matrices M1, M2, and M3 of Problem 9.1.

9.13 Consider the following scheme:

1. Pick an odd number, E.
2. Pick two prime numbers, P and Q, where $(P-1)(Q-1)-1$ is evenly divisible by E.
3. Multiply P and Q to get N.
4. Calculate $D = \dfrac{(P-1)(Q-1)(E-1)+1}{E}$

Is this scheme equivalent to RSA? Show why or why not.

9.14 Consider the following scheme by which B encrypts a message for A.

1. A chooses two large primes P and Q that are also relatively prime to $(P-1)$ and $(Q-1)$.
2. A publishes $N = PQ$ as its public key.
3. A calculates P' and Q' such that $PP' \equiv 1 \pmod{Q-1}$ and $QQ' \equiv 1 \pmod{P-1}$.
4. B encrypts message M as $C = M^N \bmod N$.
5. A finds M by solving $M \equiv C^{P'} \pmod{Q}$ and $M \equiv C^{Q'} \pmod{P}$.

   a. Explain how this scheme works.
   b. How does it differ from RSA?
   c. Is there any particular advantage to RSA compared to this scheme?
   d. Show how this scheme can be represented by matrices M1, M2, and M3 of Problem 9.1.

9.15 "This is a very interesting case, Watson," Holmes said. "The young man loves a girl, and she loves him too. However, her father is a strange fellow who insists that his would-be son-in-law must design a simple and secure protocol for an appropriate public-key cryptosystem he could use in his company's computer network. The young man came up with the following protocol for communication between two parties. For example, user A wishing to send message M to user B: (messages exchanged are in the format sender's name, text, receiver's name)"

1. A sends B the following block: $(A, \mathrm{E}(PU_b, [M, A]), B)$.
2. B acknowledges receipt by sending to A the following block: $(B, \mathrm{E}(PU_a, [M, B]), A)$.

"You can see that the protocol is really simple. But the girl's father claims that the young man has not satisfied his call for a simple protocol, because the proposal contains a certain redundancy and can be further simplified to the following:"

1. A sends B the block: $(A, \mathrm{E}(PU_b, M), B)$.
2. B acknowledges receipt by sending to A the block: $(B, \mathrm{E}(PU_a, M), A)$.

"On the basis of that, the girl's father refuses to allow his daughter to marry the young man, thus making them both unhappy. The young man was just here to ask me for help."

"Hmm, I don't see how you can help him." Watson was visibly unhappy with the idea that the sympathetic young man has to lose his love.

"Well, I think I could help. You know, Watson, redundancy is sometimes good to ensure the security of protocol. Thus, the simplification the girl's father has proposed could make the new protocol vulnerable to an attack the original protocol was able to resist," mused Holmes. "Yes, it is so, Watson. Look, all an adversary needs is to be one of the users of the network and to be able to intercept messages exchanged between A and B. Being a user of the network, he has his own public encryption key and is able to send his own messages to A or to B and to receive theirs. With the help of the simplified protocol, he could then obtain message M user A has previously sent to B using the following procedure:"

Complete the description.

9.16 Use the fast exponentiation algorithm of Figure 9.8 to determine $5^{596} \bmod 1234$. Show the steps involved in the computation.

9.17 Here is another realization of the fast exponentiation algorithm. Demonstrate that it is equivalent to the one in Figure 9.8.

```
1. f ← 1; T ← a; E ← b
2. if odd(E) then f ← f × T
3. E ← [ E/2 ]
4. T ← T × T
5. if E > 0 then goto 2
6. output f
```

9.18 This problem illustrates a simple application of the chosen ciphertext attack. Bob intercepts a ciphertext C intended for Alice and encrypted with Alice's public key e. Bob wants to obtain the original message $M = C^d \bmod n$. Bob chooses a random value r less than n and computes

$$Z = r^e \bmod n$$
$$X = ZC \bmod n$$
$$t = r^{-1} \bmod n$$

Next, Bob gets Alice to authenticate (sign) X with her private key (as in Figure 9.3), thereby decrypting X. Alice returns $Y = X^d \bmod n$. Show how Bob can use the information now available to him to determine M.

9.19 Show the OAEP decoding operation used for decryption that corresponds to the encoding operation of Figure 9.10.

9.20 Improve on algorithm P1 in Appendix W.

a. Develop an algorithm that requires $2n$ multiplications and $n + 1$ additions. *Hint:* $x^{i+1} = x^i \times x$.

b. Develop an algorithm that requires only $n + 1$ multiplications and $n + 1$ additions. *Hint:* $P(x) = a_0 + x \times q(x)$, where $q(x)$ is a polynomial of degree $(n - 1)$.

Note: The remaining problems concern the knapsack public-key algorithm described in Appendix J.

9.21 What items are in the knapsack in Figure F.1?

9.22 Perform encryption and decryption using the knapsack algorithm for the following:

a. $\mathbf{a}' = (1, 3, 5, 10); w = 7; m = 20; \mathbf{x} = 1101$

b. $\mathbf{a}' = (1, 3, 5, 11, 23, 46, 136, 263); w = 203; m = 491; \mathbf{x} = 11101000$

c. $\mathbf{a}' = (2, 3, 6, 12, 25); w = 46; m = 53; \mathbf{x} = 11101$

d. $\mathbf{a}' = (15, 92, 108, 279, 563, 1172, 2243, 4468); w = 2393; m = 9291; \mathbf{x} = 10110001$

9.23 Why is it a requirement that $m > \sum_{1=1}^{n} a'_i$?

CHAPTER 10

OTHER PUBLIC-KEY CRYPTOSYSTEMS

LEARNING OBJECTIVES

After studying this chapter, you should be able to:

- Define Diffie–Hellman key exchange.
- Understand the man-in-the-middle attack.
- Present an overview of the Elgamal cryptographic system.
- Understand elliptic curve arithmetic.
- Present an overview of elliptic curve cryptography.
- Present two techniques for generating pseudorandom numbers using an asymmetric cipher.

This chapter begins with a description of one of the earliest and simplest PKCS: Diffie–Hellman key exchange. The chapter then looks at another important scheme, the Elgamal PKCS. Next, we look at the increasingly important PKCS known as elliptic curve cryptography. Finally, the use of public-key algorithms for pseudorandom number generation is examined.

10.1 DIFFIE–HELLMAN KEY EXCHANGE

The first published public-key algorithm appeared in the seminal paper by Diffie and Hellman that defined public-key cryptography [DIFF76b] and is generally referred to as Diffie–Hellman key exchange.[1] A number of commercial products employ this key exchange technique.

The purpose of the algorithm is to enable two users to securely exchange a key that can then be used for subsequent symmetric encryption of messages. The algorithm itself is limited to the exchange of secret values.

The Diffie–Hellman algorithm depends for its effectiveness on the difficulty of computing discrete logarithms. Briefly, we can define the discrete logarithm in the following way. Recall from Chapter 2 that a primitive root of a prime number p is one whose powers modulo p generate all the integers from 1 to $p - 1$. That is, if a is a primitive root of the prime number p, then the numbers

$$a \bmod p,\ a^2 \bmod p,\ \ldots,\ a^{p-1} \bmod p$$

are distinct and consist of the integers from 1 through $p - 1$ in some permutation.

For any integer b and a primitive root a of prime number p, we can find a unique exponent i such that

$$b \equiv a^i \pmod{p} \qquad \text{where } 0 \le i \le (p - 1)$$

[1]Williamson of Britain's CESG published the identical scheme a few months earlier in a classified document [WILL76] and claims to have discovered it several years prior to that; see [ELLI99] for a discussion.

The exponent i is referred to as the **discrete logarithm** of b for the base a, mod p. We express this value as $\text{dlog}_{a,p}(b)$. See Chapter 2 for an extended discussion of discrete logarithms.

The Algorithm

Figure 10.1 summarizes the Diffie–Hellman key exchange algorithm. For this scheme, there are two publicly known numbers: a prime number q and an integer α that is a primitive root of q. Suppose the users A and B wish to create a shared key.

User A selects a random integer $X_A < q$ and computes $Y_A = \alpha^{X_A} \bmod q$. Similarly, user B independently selects a random integer $X_B < q$ and computes $Y_B = \alpha^{X_B} \bmod q$. Each side keeps the X value private and makes the Y value available publicly to the other side. Thus, X_A is A's private key and Y_A is A's corresponding public key, and similarly for B. User A computes the key as $K = (Y_B)^{X_A} \bmod q$ and user B computes the key as $K = (Y_A)^{X_B} \bmod q$. These two calculations produce identical results:

Figure 10.1 The Diffie–Hellman Key Exchange

$$
\begin{aligned}
K &= (Y_B)^{X_A} \bmod q \\
&= (\alpha^{X_B} \bmod q)^{X_A} \bmod q \\
&= (\alpha^{X_B})^{X_A} \bmod q && \text{by the rules of modular arithmetic} \\
&= \alpha^{X_B X_A} \bmod q \\
&= (\alpha^{X_A})^{X_B} \bmod q \\
&= (\alpha^{X_A} \bmod q)^{X_B} \bmod q \\
&= (Y_A)^{X_B} \bmod q
\end{aligned}
$$

The result is that the two sides have exchanged a secret value. Typically, this secret value is used as shared symmetric secret key. Now consider an adversary who can observe the key exchange and wishes to determine the secret key K. Because X_A and X_B are private, an adversary only has the following ingredients to work with: q, α, Y_A, and Y_B. Thus, the adversary is forced to take a discrete logarithm to determine the key. For example, to determine the private key of user B, an adversary must compute

$$X_B = \text{dlog}_{\alpha,q}(Y_B)$$

The adversary can then calculate the key K in the same manner as user B calculates it. That is, the adversary can calculate K as

$$K = (Y_A)^{X_B} \bmod q$$

The security of the Diffie–Hellman key exchange lies in the fact that, while it is relatively easy to calculate exponentials modulo a prime, it is very difficult to calculate discrete logarithms. For large primes, the latter task is considered infeasible.

Here is an example. Key exchange is based on the use of the prime number $q = 353$ and a primitive root of 353, in this case $\alpha = 3$. A and B select private keys $X_A = 97$ and $X_B = 233$, respectively. Each computes its public key:

A computes $Y_A = 3^{97} \bmod 353 = 40$.
B computes $Y_B = 3^{233} \bmod 353 = 248$.

After they exchange public keys, each can compute the common secret key:

A computes $K = (Y_B)^{X_A} \bmod 353 = 248^{97} \bmod 353 = 160$.
B computes $K = (Y_A)^{X_B} \bmod 353 = 40^{233} \bmod 353 = 160$.

We assume an attacker would have available the following information:

$$q = 353;\ \alpha = 3;\ Y_A = 40;\ Y_B = 248$$

In this simple example, it would be possible by brute force to determine the secret key 160. In particular, an attacker E can determine the common key by discovering a solution to the equation $3^a \bmod 353 = 40$ or the equation $3^b \bmod 353 = 248$. The brute-force approach is to calculate powers of 3 modulo 353, stopping when the result equals either 40 or 248. The desired answer is reached with the exponent value of 97, which provides $3^{97} \bmod 353 = 40$.

With larger numbers, the problem becomes impractical.

Key Exchange Protocols

Figure 10.1 shows a simple protocol that makes use of the Diffie–Hellman calculation. Suppose that user A wishes to set up a connection with user B and use a secret key to encrypt messages on that connection. User A can generate a one-time private key X_A, calculate Y_A, and send that to user B. User B responds by generating a private value X_B, calculating Y_B, and sending Y_B to user A. Both users can now calculate the key. The necessary public values q and α would need to be known ahead of time. Alternatively, user A could pick values for q and α and include those in the first message.

As an example of another use of the Diffie–Hellman algorithm, suppose that a group of users (e.g., all users on a LAN) each generate a long-lasting private value X_i (for user i) and calculate a public value Y_i. These public values, together with global public values for q and α, are stored in some central directory. At any time, user j can access user i's public value, calculate a secret key, and use that to send an encrypted message to user A. If the central directory is trusted, then this form of communication provides both confidentiality and a degree of authentication. Because only i and j can determine the key, no other user can read the message (confidentiality). Recipient i knows that only user j could have created a message using this key (authentication). However, the technique does not protect against replay attacks.

Man-in-the-Middle Attack

The protocol depicted in Figure 10.1 is insecure against a man-in-the-middle attack. Suppose Alice and Bob wish to exchange keys, and Darth is the adversary. The attack proceeds as follows (Figure 10.2).

1. Darth prepares for the attack by generating two random private keys X_{D1} and X_{D2} and then computing the corresponding public keys Y_{D1} and Y_{D2}.
2. Alice transmits Y_A to Bob.
3. Darth intercepts Y_A and transmits Y_{D1} to Bob. Darth also calculates $K2 = (Y_A)^{X_{D2}} \bmod q$.
4. Bob receives Y_{D1} and calculates $K1 = (Y_{D1})^{X_B} \bmod q$.
5. Bob transmits Y_B to Alice.
6. Darth intercepts Y_B and transmits Y_{D2} to Alice. Darth calculates $K1 = (Y_B)^{X_{D1}} \bmod q$.
7. Alice receives Y_{D2} and calculates $K2 = (Y_{D2})^{X_A} \bmod q$.

At this point, Bob and Alice think that they share a secret key, but instead Bob and Darth share secret key $K1$ and Alice and Darth share secret key $K2$. All future communication between Bob and Alice is compromised in the following way.

1. Alice sends an encrypted message M: E($K2$, M).
2. Darth intercepts the encrypted message and decrypts it to recover M.
3. Darth sends Bob $E(K1, M)$ or E($K1$, M'), where M' is any message. In the first case, Darth simply wants to eavesdrop on the communication without altering it. In the second case, Darth wants to modify the message going to Bob.

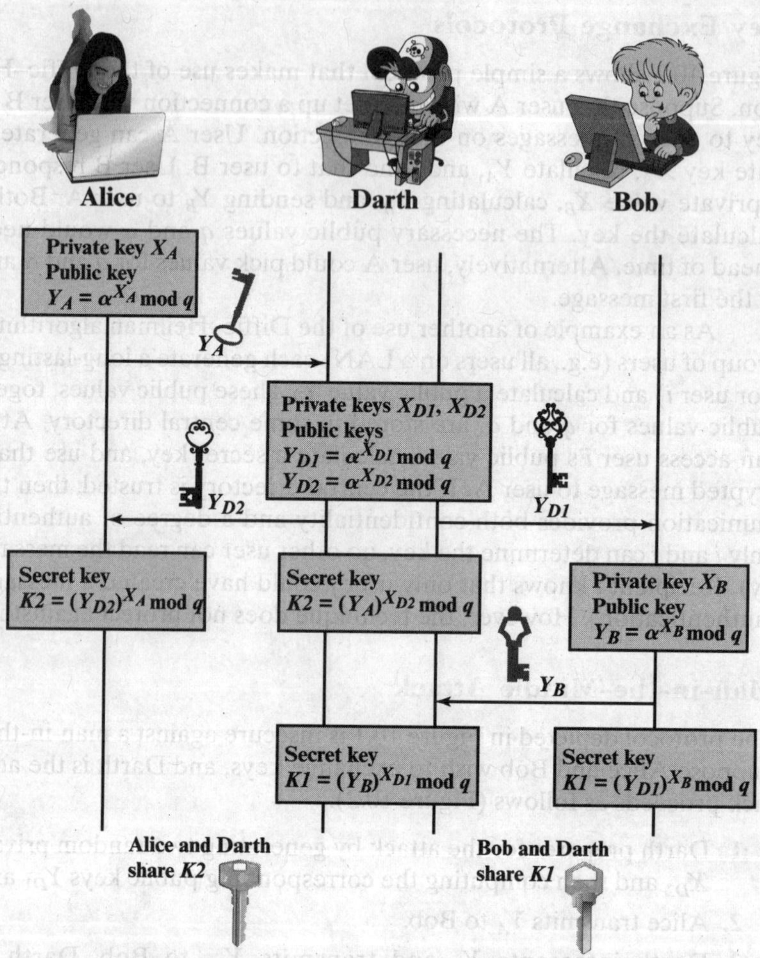

Figure 10.2 Man-in-the-Middle Attack

The key exchange protocol is vulnerable to such an attack because it does not authenticate the participants. This vulnerability can be overcome with the use of digital signatures and public-key certificates; these topics are explored in Chapters 13 and 14.

10.2 ELGAMAL CRYPTOGRAPHIC SYSTEM

In 1984, T. Elgamal announced a public-key scheme based on discrete logarithms, closely related to the Diffie–Hellman technique [ELGA84, ELGA85]. The Elgamal[2] cryptosystem is used in some form in a number of standards including the digital signature standard (DSS), which is covered in Chapter 13, and the S/MIME email standard (Chapter 19).

[2]For no apparent reason, most of the literature uses the term *ElGamal*, although Mr. Elgamal's last name does not have a capital letter G.

As with Diffie–Hellman, the global elements of Elgamal are a prime number q and α, which is a primitive root of q. User A generates a private/public key pair as follows:

1. Generate a random integer X_A, such that $1 < X_A < q - 1$.
2. Compute $Y_A = \alpha^{X_A} \bmod q$.
3. A's private key is X_A and A's public key is $\{q, \alpha, Y_A\}$.

Any user B that has access to A's public key can encrypt a message as follows:

1. Represent the message as an integer M in the range $0 \leq M \leq q - 1$. Longer messages are sent as a sequence of blocks, with each block being an integer less than q.
2. Choose a random integer k such that $1 \leq k \leq q - 1$.
3. Compute a one-time key $K = (Y_A)^k \bmod q$.
4. Encrypt M as the pair of integers (C_1, C_2) where

$$C_1 = \alpha^k \bmod q; \; C_2 = KM \bmod q$$

User A recovers the plaintext as follows:

1. Recover the key by computing $K = (C_1)^{X_A} \bmod q$.
2. Compute $M = (C_2K^{-1}) \bmod q$.

These steps are summarized in Figure 10.3. It corresponds to Figure 9.1a: Alice generates a public/private key pair; Bob encrypts using Alice's public key; and Alice decrypts using her private key.

Let us demonstrate why the Elgamal scheme works. First, we show how K is recovered by the decryption process:

$K = (Y_A)^k \bmod q$	K is defined during the encryption process
$K = (\alpha^{X_A} \bmod q)^k \bmod q$	substitute using $Y_A = \alpha^{X_A} \bmod q$
$K = \alpha^{kX_A} \bmod q$	by the rules of modular arithmetic
$K = (C_1)^{X_A} \bmod q$	substitute using $C_1 = \alpha^k \bmod q$

Next, using K, we recover the plaintext as

$$C_2 = KM \bmod q$$
$$(C_2K^{-1}) \bmod q = KMK^{-1} \bmod q = M \bmod q = M$$

We can restate the Elgamal process as follows, using Figure 10.3.

1. Bob generates a random integer k.
2. Bob generates a one-time key K using Alice's public-key components Y_A, q, and k.
3. Bob encrypts k using the public-key component α, yielding C_1. C_1 provides sufficient information for Alice to recover K.
4. Bob encrypts the plaintext message M using K.
5. Alice recovers K from C_1 using her private key.
6. Alice uses K^{-1} to recover the plaintext message from C_2.

Global Public Elements	
q	prime number
α	$\alpha < q$ and α a primitive root of q

Key Generation by Alice	
Select private X_A	$X_A < q - 1$
Calculate Y_A	$Y_A = \alpha^{X_A} \bmod q$
Public key	$\{q, \alpha, Y_A\}$
Private key	X_A

Encryption by Bob with Alice's Public Key	
Plaintext:	$M < q$
Select random integer k	$k < q$
Calculate K	$K = (Y_A)^k \bmod q$
Calculate C_1	$C_1 = \alpha^k \bmod q$
Calculate C_2	$C_2 = KM \bmod q$
Ciphertext:	(C_1, C_2)

Decryption by Alice with Alice's Private Key	
Ciphertext:	(C_1, C_2)
Calculate K	$K = (C_1)^{X_A} \bmod q$
Plaintext:	$M = (C_2K^{-1}) \bmod q$

Figure 10.3 The Elgamal Cryptosystem

Thus, K functions as a one-time key, used to encrypt and decrypt the message.

For example, let us start with the prime field GF(19); that is, $q = 19$. It has primitive roots {2, 3, 10, 13, 14, 15}, as shown in Table 2.7. We choose $\alpha = 10$.

Alice generates a key pair as follows:

1. Alice chooses $X_A = 5$.
2. Then $Y_A = \alpha^{X_A} \bmod q = \alpha^5 \bmod 19 = 3$ (see Table 2.7).
3. Alice's private key is 5 and Alice's public key is $\{q, \alpha, Y_A\} = \{19, 10, 3\}$.

Suppose Bob wants to send the message with the value $M = 17$. Then:

1. Bob chooses $k = 6$.
2. Then $K = (Y_A)^k \bmod q = 3^6 \bmod 19 = 729 \bmod 19 = 7$.
3. So

$$C_1 = \alpha^k \bmod q = \alpha^6 \bmod 19 = 11$$
$$C_2 = \text{KM} \bmod q = 7 \times 17 \bmod 19 = 119 \bmod 19 = 5$$

4. Bob sends the ciphertext (11, 5).

For decryption:

1. Alice calculates $K = (C_1)^{X_A} \bmod q = 11^5 \bmod 19 = 161051 \bmod 19 = 7$.
2. Then K^{-1} in GF(19) is $7^{-1} \bmod 19 = 11$.
3. Finally, $M = (C_2K^{-1}) \bmod q = 5 \times 11 \bmod 19 = 55 \bmod 19 = 17$.

If a message must be broken up into blocks and sent as a sequence of encrypted blocks, a unique value of k should be used for each block. If k is used for more than one block, knowledge of one block M_1 of the message enables the user to compute other blocks as follows. Let

$$C_{1,1} = \alpha^k \bmod q;\ C_{2,1} = KM_1 \bmod q$$
$$C_{1,2} = \alpha^k \bmod q;\ C_{2,2} = KM_2 \bmod q$$

Then,

$$\frac{C_{2,1}}{C_{2,2}} = \frac{KM_1 \bmod q}{KM_2 \bmod q} = \frac{M_1 \bmod q}{M_2 \bmod q}$$

If M_1 is known, then M_2 is easily computed as

$$M_2 = (C_{2,1})^{-1}\, C_{2,2}\, M_1 \bmod q$$

The security of Elgamal is based on the difficulty of computing discrete logarithms. To recover A's private key, an adversary would have to compute $X_A = \text{dlog}_{\alpha,q}(Y_A)$. Alternatively, to recover the one-time key K, an adversary would have to determine the random number k, and this would require computing the discrete logarithm $k = \text{dlog}_{\alpha,q}(C_1)$. [STIN06] points out that these calculations are regarded as infeasible if p is at least 300 decimal digits and $q - 1$ has at least one "large" prime factor.

10.3 ELLIPTIC CURVE ARITHMETIC

Most of the products and standards that use public-key cryptography for encryption and digital signatures use RSA. As we have seen, the key length for secure RSA use has increased over recent years, and this has put a heavier processing load on applications using RSA. This burden has ramifications, especially for electronic commerce sites that conduct large numbers of secure transactions. A competing system challenges RSA: elliptic curve cryptography (ECC). ECC is showing up in standardization efforts, including the IEEE P1363 Standard for Public-Key Cryptography.

The principal attraction of ECC, compared to RSA, is that it appears to offer equal security for a far smaller key size, thereby reducing processing overhead.

ECC is fundamentally more difficult to explain than either RSA or Diffie–Hellman, and a full mathematical description is beyond the scope of this book. This section and the next give some background on elliptic curves and ECC. We begin with a brief review of the concept of abelian group. Next, we examine the concept of elliptic curves defined over the real numbers. This is followed by a look at elliptic curves defined over finite fields. Finally, we are able to examine elliptic curve ciphers.

The reader may wish to review the material on finite fields in Chapter 5 before proceeding.

Abelian Groups

Recall from Chapter 5 that an **abelian group** G, sometimes denoted by $\{G, \cdot\}$, is a set of elements with a binary operation, denoted by $\cdot$, that associates to each ordered pair (a, b) of elements in G an element $(a \cdot b)$ in G, such that the following axioms are obeyed:[3]

(A1) Closure:	If a and b belong to G, then $a \cdot b$ is also in G.
(A2) Associative:	$a \cdot (b \cdot c) = (a \cdot b) \cdot c$ for all a, b, c in G.
(A3) Identity element:	There is an element e in G such that $a \cdot \text{e} = \text{e} \cdot a = a$ for all a in G.
(A4) Inverse element:	For each a in G there is an element a' in G such that $a \cdot a' = a' \cdot a = \text{e}$.
(A5) Commutative:	$a \cdot b = b \cdot a$ for all a, b in G.

A number of public-key ciphers are based on the use of an abelian group. For example, Diffie–Hellman key exchange involves multiplying pairs of nonzero integers modulo a prime number q. Keys are generated by exponentiation over the group, with exponentiation defined as repeated multiplication. For example, $a^k \bmod q = \underbrace{(a \times a \times \ldots \times a)}_{k \text{ times}} \bmod q$. To attack Diffie–Hellman, the attacker must determine k given a and a^k; this is the discrete logarithm problem.

For elliptic curve cryptography, an operation over elliptic curves, called addition, is used. Multiplication is defined by repeated addition. For example,

$$a \times k = \underbrace{(a + a + \ldots + a)}_{k \text{ times}}$$

where the addition is performed over an elliptic curve. Cryptanalysis involves determining k given a and $(a \times k)$.

[3]The operator $\cdot$ is generic and can refer to addition, multiplication, or some other mathematical operation.

An **elliptic curve** is defined by an equation in two variables with coefficients. For cryptography, the variables and coefficients are restricted to elements in a finite field, which results in the definition of a finite abelian group. Before looking at this, we first look at elliptic curves in which the variables and coefficients are real numbers. This case is perhaps easier to visualize.

Elliptic Curves over Real Numbers

Elliptic curves are not ellipses. They are so named because they are described by cubic equations, similar to those used for calculating the circumference of an ellipse. In general, cubic equations for elliptic curves take the following form, known as a **Weierstrass equation**:

$$y^2 + axy + by = x^3 + cx^2 + dx + e$$

where a, b, c, d, e are real numbers and x and y take on values in the real numbers.[4] For our purpose, it is sufficient to limit ourselves to equations of the form

$$y^2 = x^3 + ax + b \qquad \textbf{(10.1)}$$

Such equations are said to be cubic, or of degree 3, because the highest exponent they contain is a 3. Also included in the definition of an elliptic curve is a single element denoted O and called the *point at infinity* or the *zero point*, which we discuss subsequently. To plot such a curve, we need to compute

$$y = \sqrt{x^3 + ax + b}$$

For given values of a and b, the plot consists of positive and negative values of y for each value of x. Thus, each curve is symmetric about $y = 0$. Figure 10.4 shows two examples of elliptic curves. As you can see, the formula sometimes produces weird-looking curves.

Now, consider the set of points E(a, b) consisting of all of the points (x, y) that satisfy Equation (10.1) together with the element O. Using a different value of the pair (a, b) results in a different set E(a, b). Using this terminology, the two curves in Figure 10.4 depict the sets E(−1, 0) and E(1, 1), respectively.

Geometric Description of Addition It can be shown that a group can be defined based on the set E(a, b) for specific values of a and b in Equation (10.1), provided the following condition is met:

$$4a^3 + 27b^2 \neq 0 \qquad \textbf{(10.2)}$$

To define the group, we must define an operation, called addition and denoted by +, for the set E(a, b), where a and b satisfy Equation (10.2). In geometric terms, the rules for addition can be stated as follows: If three points on an elliptic curve lie on a straight line, their sum is O. From this definition, we can define the rules of addition over an elliptic curve.

[4] Note that x and y are true variables, which take on values. This is in contrast to our discussion of polynomial rings and fields in Chapter 5, where was treated as an indeterminate.

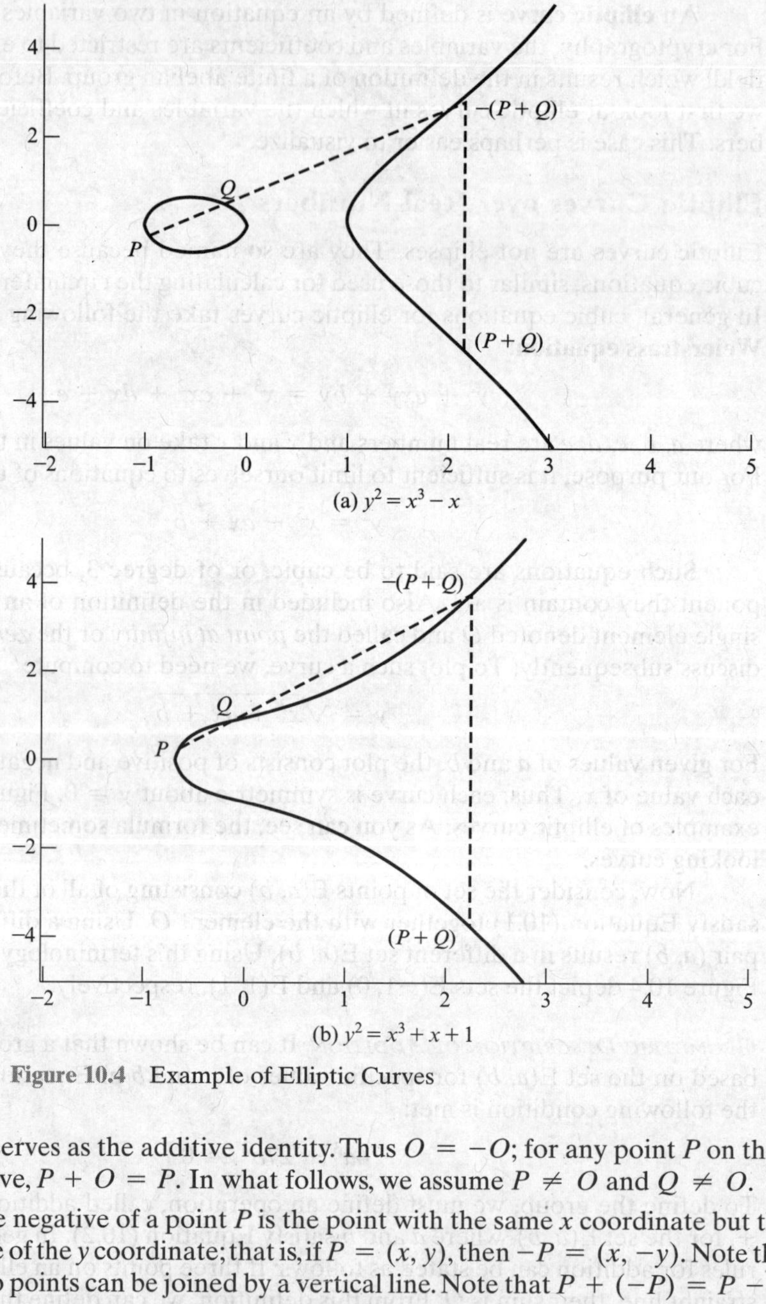

Figure 10.4 Example of Elliptic Curves

1. O serves as the additive identity. Thus $O = -O$; for any point P on the elliptic curve, $P + O = P$. In what follows, we assume $P \neq O$ and $Q \neq O$.
2. The negative of a point P is the point with the same x coordinate but the negative of the y coordinate; that is, if $P = (x, y)$, then $-P = (x, -y)$. Note that these two points can be joined by a vertical line. Note that $P + (-P) = P - P = O$.
3. To add two points P and Q with different x coordinates, draw a straight line between them and find the third point of intersection R. It is easily seen that there is a unique point R that is the point of intersection (unless the line is tangent to the curve at either P or Q, in which case we take $R = P$ or $R = Q$, respectively). To form a group structure, we need to define addition on these three points: $P + Q = -R$. That is, we define $P + Q$ to be the mirror image

(with respect to the x axis) of the third point of intersection. Figure 10.4 illustrates this construction.

4. The geometric interpretation of the preceding item also applies to two points, P and $-P$, with the same x coordinate. The points are joined by a vertical line, which can be viewed as also intersecting the curve at the infinity point. We therefore have $P + (-P) = O$, which is consistent with item (2).
5. To double a point Q, draw the tangent line and find the other point of intersection S. Then $Q + Q = 2Q = -S$.

With the preceding list of rules, it can be shown that the set $E(a, b)$ is an abelian group.

Algebraic Description of Addition In this subsection, we present some results that enable calculation of additions over elliptic curves.[5] For two distinct points, $P = (x_P, y_P)$ and $Q = (x_Q, y_Q)$, that are not negatives of each other, the slope of the line l that joins them is $\Delta = (y_Q - y_P)/(x_Q - x_P)$. There is exactly one other point where l intersects the elliptic curve, and that is the negative of the sum of P and Q. After some algebraic manipulation, we can express the sum $R = P + Q$ as

$$\begin{aligned} x_R &= \Delta^2 - x_P - x_Q \\ y_R &= -y_P + \Delta(x_P - x_R) \end{aligned} \quad \textbf{(10.3)}$$

We also need to be able to add a point to itself: $P + P = 2P = R$. When $y_P \neq 0$, the expressions are

$$\begin{aligned} x_R &= \left(\frac{3x_P^2 + a}{2y_P}\right)^2 - 2x_P \\ y_R &= \left(\frac{3x_P^2 + a}{2y_P}\right)(x_P - x_R) - y_P \end{aligned} \quad \textbf{(10.4)}$$

Elliptic Curves over Z_p

Elliptic curve cryptography makes use of elliptic curves in which the variables and coefficients are all restricted to elements of a finite field. Two families of elliptic curves are used in cryptographic applications: prime curves over Z_p and binary curves over $GF(2^m)$. For a **prime curve** over Z_p, we use a cubic equation in which the variables and coefficients all take on values in the set of integers from 0 through $p - 1$ and in which calculations are performed modulo p. For a **binary curve** defined over $GF(2^m)$, the variables and coefficients all take on values in $GF(2^m)$ and in calculations are performed over $GF(2^m)$. [FERN99] points out that prime curves are best for software applications, because the extended bit-fiddling operations needed by binary curves are not required; and that binary curves are best for hardware applications, where it takes remarkably few logic gates to create a powerful, fast cryptosystem. We examine these two families in this section and the next.

---

[5]For derivations of these results, see [KOBL94] or other mathematical treatments of elliptic curves.

There is no obvious geometric interpretation of elliptic curve arithmetic over finite fields. The algebraic interpretation used for elliptic curve arithmetic over real numbers does readily carry over, and this is the approach we take.

For elliptic curves over Z_p, as with real numbers, we limit ourselves to equations of the form of Equation (10.1), but in this case with coefficients and variables limited to Z_p:

$$y^2 \bmod p = (x^3 + ax + b) \bmod p \tag{10.5}$$

For example, Equation (10.5) is satisfied for $a = 1, b = 1, x = 9, y = 7, p = 23$:

$$7^2 \bmod 23 = (9^3 + 9 + 1) \bmod 23$$
$$49 \bmod 23 = 739 \bmod 23$$
$$3 = 3$$

Now consider the set $E_p(a, b)$ consisting of all pairs of integers (x, y) that satisfy Equation (10.5), together with a point at infinity O. The coefficients a and b and the variables x and y are all elements of Z_p.

For example, let $p = 23$ and consider the elliptic curve $y^2 = x^3 + x + 1$. In this case, $a = b = 1$. Note that this equation is the same as that of Figure 10.4b. The figure shows a continuous curve with all of the real points that satisfy the equation. For the set $E_{23}(1, 1)$, we are only interested in the nonnegative integers in the quadrant from (0, 0) through $(p - 1, p - 1)$ that satisfy the equation mod p. Table 10.1 lists the points (other than O) that are part of $E_{23}(1, 1)$. Figure 10.5 plots the points of $E_{23}(1, 1)$; note that the points, with one exception, are symmetric about $y = 11.5$.

It can be shown that a finite abelian group can be defined based on the set $E_p(a, b)$ provided that $(x^3 + ax + b) \bmod p$ has no repeated factors. This is equivalent to the condition

$$(4a^3 + 27b^2) \bmod p \neq 0 \bmod p \tag{10.6}$$

Note that Equation (10.6) has the same form as Equation (10.2).

The rules for addition over $E_p(a, b)$, correspond to the algebraic technique described for elliptic curves defined over real numbers. For all points $P, Q \in E_p(a, b)$:

Table 10.1 Points (other than O) on the Elliptic Curve $E_{23}(1, 1)$

(0, 1)	(6, 4)	(12, 19)
(0, 22)	(6, 19)	(13, 7)
(1, 7)	(7, 11)	(13, 16)
(1, 16)	(7, 12)	(17, 3)
(3, 10)	(9, 7)	(17, 20)
(3, 13)	(9, 16)	(18, 3)
(4, 0)	(11, 3)	(18, 20)
(5, 4)	(11, 20)	(19, 5)
(5, 19)	(12, 4)	(19, 18)

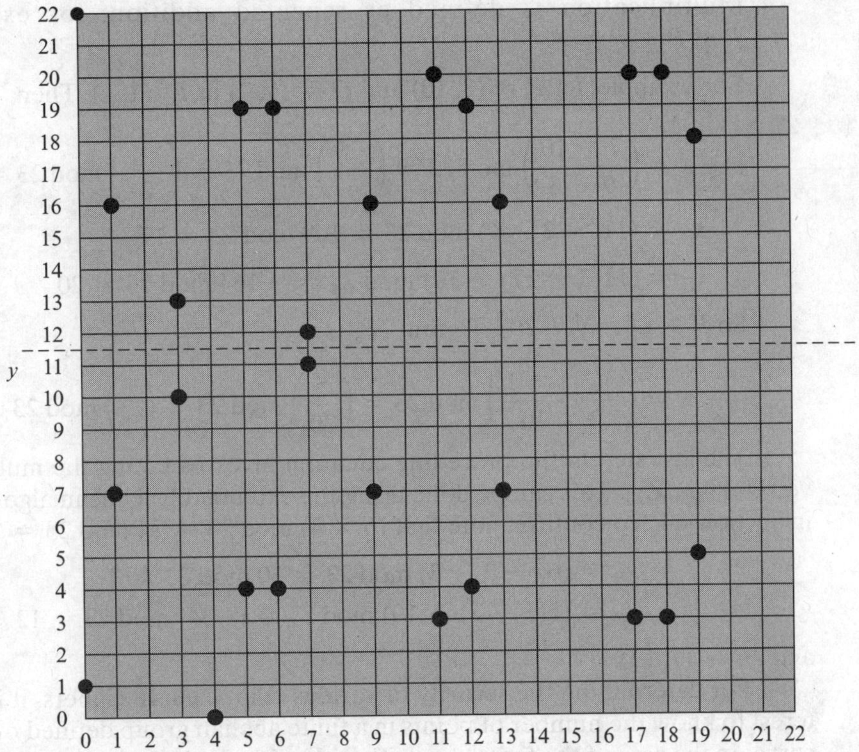

Figure 10.5 The Elliptic Curve $E_{23}(1, 1)$

1. $P + O = P$.
2. If $P = (x_P, y_P)$, then $P + (x_P, -y_P) = O$. The point $(x_P, -y_P)$ is the negative of P, denoted as $-P$. For example, in $E_{23}(1, 1)$, for $P = (13, 7)$, we have $-P = (13, -7)$. But $-7 \bmod 23 = 16$. Therefore, $-P = (13, 16)$, which is also in $E_{23}(1, 1)$.
3. If $P = (x_p, y_p)$ and $Q = (x_Q, y_Q)$ with $P \neq -Q$, then $R = P + Q = (x_R, y_R)$ is determined by the following rules:

$$x_R = (\lambda^2 - x_P - x_Q) \bmod p$$
$$y_R = (\lambda(x_P - x_R) - y_P) \bmod p$$

where

$$\lambda = \begin{cases} \left(\dfrac{y_Q - y_P}{x_Q - x_P}\right) \bmod p & \text{if } P \neq Q \\[2ex] \left(\dfrac{3x_P^2 + a}{2y_P}\right) \bmod p & \text{if } P = Q \end{cases}$$

4. Multiplication is defined as repeated addition; for example, $4P = P + P + P + P$.

For example, let $P = (3, 10)$ and $Q = (9, 7)$ in $E_{23}(1, 1)$. Then

$$\lambda = \left(\frac{7 - 10}{9 - 3}\right) \bmod 23 = \left(\frac{-3}{6}\right) \bmod 23 = \left(\frac{-1}{2}\right) \bmod 23 = 11$$

$$x_R = (11^2 - 3 - 9) \bmod 23 = 109 \bmod 23 = 17$$

$$y_R = (11(3 - 17) - 10) \bmod 23 = -164 \bmod 23 = 20$$

So $P + Q = (17, 20)$. To find $2P$,

$$\lambda = \left(\frac{3(3^2) + 1}{2 \times 10}\right) \bmod 23 = \left(\frac{5}{20}\right) \bmod 23 = \left(\frac{1}{4}\right) \bmod 23 = 6$$

The last step in the preceding equation involves taking the multiplicative inverse of 4 in Z_{23}. This can be done using the extended Euclidean algorithm defined in Section 4.4. To confirm, note that $(6 \times 4) \bmod 23 = 24 \bmod 23 = 1$.

$$x_R = (6^2 - 3 - 3) \bmod 23 = 30 \bmod 23 = 7$$

$$y_R = (6(3 - 7) - 10) \bmod 23 = (-34) \bmod 23 = 12$$

and $2P = (7, 12)$.

For determining the security of various elliptic curve ciphers, it is of some interest to know the number of points in a finite abelian group defined over an elliptic curve. In the case of the finite group $E_P(a, b)$, the number of points N is bounded by

$$p + 1 - 2\sqrt{p} \leq N \leq p + 1 + 2\sqrt{p}$$

Note that the number of points in $E_p(a, b)$ is approximately equal to the number of elements in Z_p, namely p elements.

Elliptic Curves over GF(2^m)

Recall from Chapter 5 that a **finite field** GF(2^m) consists of 2^m elements, together with addition and multiplication operations that can be defined over polynomials. For elliptic curves over GF(2^m), we use a cubic equation in which the variables and coefficients all take on values in GF(2^m) for some number m and in which calculations are performed using the rules of arithmetic in GF(2^m).

Table 10.2 Points (other than O) on the Elliptic Curve $E_{2^4}(g^4, 1)$

$(0, 1)$	(g^5, g^3)	(g^9, g^{13})
$(1, g^6)$	(g^5, g^{11})	(g^{10}, g)
$(1, g^{13})$	(g^6, g^8)	(g^{10}, g^8)
(g^3, g^8)	(g^6, g^{14})	$(g^{12}, 0)$
(g^3, g^{13})	(g^9, g^{10})	(g^{12}, g^{12})

It turns out that the form of cubic equation appropriate for cryptographic applications for elliptic curves is somewhat different for $GF(2^m)$ than for Z_p. The form is

$$y^2 + xy = x^3 + ax^2 + b \quad \textbf{(10.7)}$$

where it is understood that the variables x and y and the coefficients a and b are elements of $GF(2^m)$ and that calculations are performed in $GF(2^m)$.

Now consider the set $E_{2^m}(a, b)$ consisting of all pairs of integers (x, y) that satisfy Equation (10.7), together with a point at infinity O.

For example, let us use the finite field $GF(2^4)$ with the irreducible polynomial $f(x) = x^4 + x + 1$. This yields a generator g that satisfies $f(g) = 0$ with a value of $g^4 = g + 1$, or in binary, $g = 0010$. We can develop the powers of g as follows.

$g^0 = 0001$	$g^4 = 0011$	$g^8 = 0101$	$g^{12} = 1111$
$g^1 = 0010$	$g^5 = 0110$	$g^9 = 1010$	$g^{13} = 1101$
$g^2 = 0100$	$g^6 = 1100$	$g^{10} = 0111$	$g^{14} = 1001$
$g^3 = 1000$	$g^7 = 1011$	$g^{11} = 1110$	$g^{15} = 0001$

For example, $g^5 = (g^4)(g) = (g + 1)(g) = g^2 + g = 0110$.

Now consider the elliptic curve $y^2 + xy = x^3 + g^4x^2 + 1$. In this case, $a = g^4$ and $b = g^0 = 1$. One point that satisfies this equation is (g^5, g^3):

$$(g^3)^2 + (g^5)(g^3) = (g^5)^3 + (g^4)(g^5)^2 + 1$$
$$g^6 + g^8 = g^{15} + g^{14} + 1$$
$$1100 + 0101 = 0001 + 1001 + 0001$$
$$1001 = 1001$$

Table 10.2 lists the points (other than O) that are part of $E_{2^4}(g^4, 1)$. Figure 10.6 plots the points of $E_{2^4}(g^4, 1)$.

It can be shown that a finite abelian group can be defined based on the set $E_{2^m}(a, b)$, provided that $b \neq 0$. The rules for addition can be stated as follows. For all points $P, Q \in E_{2^m}(a, b)$:

1. $P + O = P$.
2. If $P = (x_P, y_P)$, then $P + (x_P, x_P + y_P) = O$. The point $(x_P, x_P + y_P)$ is the negative of P, which is denoted as $-P$.
3. If $P = (x_P, y_P)$ and $Q = (x_Q, y_Q)$ with $P \neq -Q$ and $P \neq Q$, then $R = P + Q = (x_R, y_R)$ is determined by the following rules:

$$x_R = \lambda^2 + \lambda + x_P + x_Q + a$$
$$y_R = \lambda(x_P + x_R) + x_R + y_P$$

where

$$\lambda = \frac{y_Q + y_P}{x_Q + x_P}$$

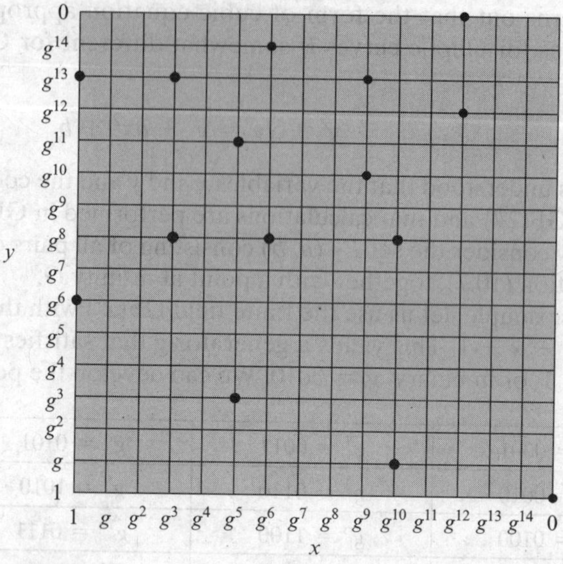

Figure 10.6 The Elliptic Curve $E_{2^4}(g^4, 1)$

4. If $P = (x_P, y_P)$ then $R = 2P = (x_R, y_R)$ is determined by the following rules:

$$x_R = \lambda^2 + \lambda + a$$

$$y_R = x_P^2 + (\lambda + 1)x_R$$

where

$$\lambda = x_P + \frac{y_P}{x_P}$$

10.4 ELLIPTIC CURVE CRYPTOGRAPHY

The addition operation in ECC is the counterpart of modular multiplication in RSA, and multiple addition is the counterpart of modular exponentiation. To form a cryptographic system using elliptic curves, we need to find a "hard problem" corresponding to factoring the product of two primes or taking the discrete logarithm.

Consider the equation $Q = kP$ where $Q, P \in E_P(a, b)$ and $k < p$. It is relatively easy to calculate Q given k and P, but it is hard to determine k given Q and P. This is called the discrete logarithm problem for elliptic curves.

We give an example taken from the Certicom Web site (www.certicom.com). Consider the group $E_{23}(9,17)$. This is the group defined by the equation $y^2 \bmod 23 = (x^3 + 9x + 17) \bmod 23$. What is the discrete logarithm k of $Q = (4, 5)$ to the base $P = (16, 5)$? The brute-force method is to compute multiples of P until Q is found. Thus,

$$P = (16,5); 2P = (20, 20); 3P = (14, 14); 4P = (19, 20); 5P = (13, 10);$$
$$6P = (7, 3); 7P = (8, 7); 8P = (12, 17); 9P = (4, 5)$$

Because $9P = (4, 5) = Q$, the discrete logarithm $Q = (4, 5)$ to the base $P = (16, 5)$ is $k = 9$. In a real application, k would be so large as to make the brute-force approach infeasible.

In the remainder of this section, we show two approaches to ECC that give the flavor of this technique.

Analog of Diffie–Hellman Key Exchange

Key exchange using elliptic curves can be done in the following manner. First pick a large integer q, which is either a prime number p or an integer of the form 2^m, and elliptic curve parameters a and b for Equation (10.5) or Equation (10.7). This defines the elliptic group of points $E_q(a, b)$. Next, pick a *base point* $G = (x_1, y_1)$ in $E_p(a, b)$ whose order is a very large value n. The **order** n of a point G on an elliptic curve is the smallest positive integer n such that $nG = 0$ and G are parameters of the cryptosystem known to all participants.

A key exchange between users A and B can be accomplished as follows (Figure 10.7).

1. A selects an integer n_A less than n. This is A's private key. A then generates a public key $P_A = n_A \times G$; the public key is a point in $E_q(a, b)$.
2. B similarly selects a private key n_B and computes a public key P_B.
3. A generates the secret key $k = n_A \times P_B$. B generates the secret key $k = n_B \times P_A$.

The two calculations in step 3 produce the same result because

$$n_A \times P_B = n_A \times (n_B \times G) = n_B \times (n_A \times G) = n_B \times P_A$$

To break this scheme, an attacker would need to be able to compute k given G and kG, which is assumed to be hard.

As an example,[6] take $p = 211$; $E_p(0, -4)$, which is equivalent to the curve $y^2 = x^3 - 4$; and $G = (2, 2)$. One can calculate that $240G = O$. A's private key is $n_A = 121$, so A's public key is $P_A = 121(2, 2) = (115, 48)$. B's private key is $n_B = 203$, so B's public key is $203(2, 3) = (130, 203)$. The shared secret key is $121(130, 203) = 203(115, 48) = (161, 69)$.

Note that the secret key is a pair of numbers. If this key is to be used as a session key for conventional encryption, then a single number must be generated. We could simply use the x coordinates or some simple function of the x coordinate.

Elliptic Curve Encryption/Decryption

Several approaches to encryption/decryption using elliptic curves have been analyzed in the literature. In this subsection, we look at perhaps the simplest. The first task in this system is to encode the plaintext message m to be sent as an (x, y) point P_m.

[6]Provided by Ed Schaefer of Santa Clara University.

Global Public Elements	
$E_q(a, b)$	elliptic curve with parameters a, b, and q, where q is a prime or an integer of the form 2^m
G	point on elliptic curve whose order is large value n

User A Key Generation	
Select private n_A	$n_A < n$
Calculate public P_A	$P_A = n_A \times G$

User B Key Generation	
Select private n_B	$n_B < n$
Calculate public P_B	$P_B = n_B \times G$

Calculation of Secret Key by User A
$K = n_A \times P_B$

Calculation of Secret Key by User B
$K = n_B \times P_A$

Figure 10.7 ECC Diffie–Hellman Key Exchange

It is the point P_m that will be encrypted as a ciphertext and subsequently decrypted. Note that we cannot simply encode the message as the x or y coordinate of a point, because not all such coordinates are in $E_q(a, b)$; for example, see Table 10.1. Again, there are several approaches to this encoding, which we will not address here, but suffice it to say that there are relatively straightforward techniques that can be used.

As with the key exchange system, an encryption/decryption system requires a point G and an elliptic group $E_q(a, b)$ as parameters. Each user A selects a private key n_A and generates a public key $P_A = n_A \times G$.

To encrypt and send a message P_m to B, A chooses a random positive integer k and produces the ciphertext C_m consisting of the pair of points:

$$C_m = \{kG, P_m + kP_B\}$$

Note that A has used B's public key P_B. To decrypt the ciphertext, B multiplies the first point in the pair by B's private key and subtracts the result from the second point:

$$P_m + kP_B - n_B(kG) = P_m + k(n_BG) - n_B(kG) = P_m$$

Table 10.3 Comparable Key Sizes in Terms of Computational Effort for Cryptanalysis (NIST SP-800-57)

Symmetric Key Algorithms	Diffie–Hellman, Digital Signature Algorithm	RSA (size of n in bits)	ECC (modulus size in bits)
80	$L = 1024$ $N = 160$	1024	160–223
112	$L = 2048$ $N = 224$	2048	224–255
128	$L = 3072$ $N = 256$	3072	256–383
192	$L = 7680$ $N = 384$	7680	384–511
256	$L = 15{,}360$ $N = 512$	15,360	512+

Note: L = size of public key, N = size of private key.

A has masked the message P_m by adding kP_B to it. Nobody but A knows the value of k, so even though P_b is a public key, nobody can remove the mask kP_B. However, A also includes a "clue," which is enough to remove the mask if one knows the private key n_B. For an attacker to recover the message, the attacker would have to compute k given G and kG, which is assumed to be hard.

Let us consider a simple example. The global public elements are $q = 257$; $E_q(a, b) = E_{257}(0, -4)$, which is equivalent to the curve $y^2 = x^3 - 4$; and $G = (2, 2)$. Bob's private key is $n_B = 101$, and his public key is $P_B = n_BG = 101(2, 2) = (197, 167)$. Alice wishes to send a message to Bob that is encoded in the elliptic point $P_m = (112, 26)$. Alice chooses random integer $k = 41$ and computes $kG = 41(2, 2) = (136, 128)$, $kP_B = 41(197, 167) = (68, 84)$ and $P_m + kP_B = (112, 26) + (68, 84) = (246, 174)$. Alice sends the ciphertext $C_m = (C_1, C_2) = \{(136, 128), (246, 174)\}$ to Bob. Bob receives the ciphertext and computes $C_2 - n_BC_1 = (246, 174) - 101(136, 128) = (246, 174) - (68, 84) = (112, 26)$.

Security of Elliptic Curve Cryptography

The security of ECC depends on how difficult it is to determine k given kP and P. This is referred to as the elliptic curve logarithm problem. The fastest known technique for taking the elliptic curve logarithm is known as the Pollard rho method. Table 10.3, from NIST SP 800-57 (*Recommendation for Key Management—Part 1: General*, September 2015), compares various algorithms by showing comparable key sizes in terms of computational effort for cryptanalysis. As can be seen, a considerably smaller key size can be used for ECC compared to RSA.

Based on this analysis, SP 800-57 recommends that at least through 2030, acceptable key lengths are from 3072 to 14,360 bits for RSA and 256 to 512 bits for ECC. Similarly, the European Union Agency for Network and Information Security (ENISA) recommends in their 2014 report (*Algorithms, Key Size and Parameters report—2014*, November 2014) minimum key lengths for future system of 3072 bits and 256 bits for RSA and ECC, respectively.

Analysis indicates that for equal key lengths, the computational effort required for ECC and RSA is comparable [JURI97]. Thus, there is a computational advantage to using ECC with a shorter key length than a comparably secure RSA.

10.5 PSEUDORANDOM NUMBER GENERATION BASED ON AN ASYMMETRIC CIPHER

We noted in Chapter 8 that because a symmetric block cipher produces an apparently random output, it can serve as the basis of a pseudorandom number generator (PRNG). Similarly, an asymmetric encryption algorithm produces apparently random output and can be used to build a PRNG. Because asymmetric algorithms are typically much slower than symmetric algorithms, asymmetric algorithms are not used to generate open-ended PRNG bit streams. Rather, the asymmetric approach is useful for creating a pseudorandom function (PRF) for generating a short pseudorandom bit sequence.

In this section, we examine two PRNG designs based on pseudorandom functions.

PRNG Based on RSA

For a sufficient key length, the RSA algorithm is considered secure and is a good candidate to form the basis of a PRNG. Such a PRNG, known as the Micali–Schnorr PRNG [MICA91], is recommended in the ANSI standard X9.82 (*Random Number Generation*) and in the ISO standard 18031 (*Random Bit Generation*).

The PRNG is illustrated in Figure 10.8. As can be seen, this PRNG has much the same structure as the output feedback (OFB) mode used as a PRNG (see Figure 8.4b and the portion of Figure 7.6a enclosed with a dashed box). In this case, the encryption algorithm is RSA rather than a symmetric block cipher. Also, a portion of the output is fed back to the next iteration of the encryption algorithm and the remainder of the output is used as pseudorandom bits. The motivation for this separation of the output into two distinct parts is so that the pseudorandom bits from one stage do not provide input to the next stage. This separation should contribute to forward unpredictability.

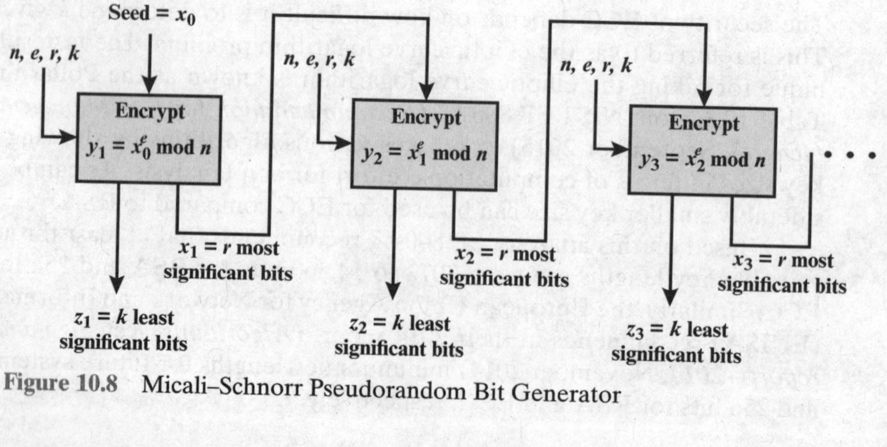

Figure 10.8 Micali–Schnorr Pseudorandom Bit Generator

We can define the PRNG as follows.

Setup Select p, q primes; $n = pq$; $\phi(n) = (p - 1)(q - 1)$. Select e such that $\gcd(e, \phi(n)) = 1$. These are the standard RSA setup selections (see Figure 9.5). In addition, let $N = [\log_2 n] + 1$ (the bitlength of n). Select r, k such that $r + k = N$.

Seed Select a random seed x_0 of bitlength r.

Generate Generate a pseudorandom sequence of length $k \times m$ using the loop
for i **from** 1 to m **do**

$$y_i = x_{i-1}^e \bmod n$$
$$x_i = r \text{ most significant bits of } y_i$$
$$z_i = k \text{ least significant bits of } y_i$$

Output The output sequence is $z_1 \| z_2 \| \ldots \| z_m$.

The parameters n, r, e, and k are selected to satisfy the following six requirements.

1. $n = pq$	n is chosen as the product of two primes to have the cryptographic strength required of RSA.
2. $1 < e < \phi(n)$; $\gcd(e, \phi(n)) = 1$	Ensures that the mapping $s \rightarrow s^e \bmod n$ is 1 to 1.
3. $re \geq 2N$	Ensures that the exponentiation requires a full modular reduction.
4. $r \geq 2 \times strength$	Protects against a cryptographic attacks.
5. k, r are multiples of 8	An implementation convenience.
6. $k \geq 8$; $r + k = N$	All bits are used.

The variable *strength* in requirement 4 is defined in NIST SP 800-90 as follows: A number associated with the amount of work (that is, the number of operations) required to break a cryptographic algorithm or system; a security strength is specified in bits and is a specific value from the set (112, 128, 192, 256) for this Recommendation. The amount of work needed is $2^{strength}$.

There is clearly a tradeoff between r and k. Because RSA is computationally intensive compared to a block cipher, we would like to generate as many pseudorandom bits per iteration as possible and therefore would like a large value of k. However, for cryptographic strength, we would like r to be as large as possible.

For example, if $e = 3$ and $N = 1024$, then we have the inequality $3r > 1024$, yielding a minimum required size for r of 683 bits. For r set to that size, $k = 341$ bits are generated for each exponentiation (each RSA encryption). In this case, each exponentiation requires only one modular squaring of a 683-bit number and one modular multiplication. That is, we need only calculate $(x_i \times (x_i^2 \bmod n)) \bmod n$.

PRNG Based on Elliptic Curve Cryptography

In this subsection, we briefly summarize a technique developed by the U.S. National Security Agency (NSA) known as dual elliptic curve PRNG (DEC PRNG). This technique is recommended in NIST SP 800-90, the ANSI standard X9.82, and the ISO standard 18031. There has been some controversy regarding both the security and efficiency of this algorithm compared to other alternatives (e.g., see [SCHO06], [BROW07]).

[SCHO06] summarizes the algorithm as follows: Let P and Q be two known points on a given elliptic curve. The seed of the DEC PRNG is a random integer $s_0 \in \{0, 1, \ldots, \#E(GF(p)) - 1\}$, where # E(GF(p)) denotes the number of points on the curve. Let x denote a function that gives the x-coordinate of a point of the curve. Let $lsb_i(s)$ denote the i least significant bits of an integer s. The DEC PRNG transforms the seed into the pseudorandom sequence of length $240k$, $k > 0$, as follows:

```
for i = 1 to k do
    Set si ← x(Si-1 P)
    Set ri ← lsb240 (x(si Q))
end for
    Return r1,...,rk
```

Given the security concerns expressed for this PRNG, the only motivation for its use would be that it is used in a system that already implements ECC but does not implement any other symmetric, asymmetric, or hash cryptographic algorithm that could be used to build a PRNG.

10.6 KEY TERMS, REVIEW QUESTIONS, AND PROBLEMS

Key Terms

abelian group	elliptic curve	Micali–Schnorr
binary curve	elliptic curve arithmetic	prime curve
cubic equation	elliptic curve cryptography	primitive root
Diffie–Hellman key exchange	finite field	zero point
discrete logarithm	man-in-the-middle attack	

Review Questions

10.1 Briefly explain Diffie–Hellman key exchange.

10.2 What is the difference between two families of elliptic curves used in cryptographic applications?

10.3 What is the zero point of an elliptic curve?

10.4 What is the sum of three points on an elliptic curve that lie on a straight line?

Problems

10.1 Alice and Bob use the Diffie-Hellman key exchange technique with a common prime $q = 353$ and a primitive root $\alpha = 3$.

a. If Alice has a private key $X_A = 97$, find her public key Y_A.
b. If Bob has a private key $X_B = 233$, find his public key Y_B.
c. What is the shared secret key between Alice and Bob?

10.2 Alice and Bob use the Diffie-Hellman key exchange technique with a common prime $q = 23$ and a primitive root $\alpha = 5$.

a. If Bob has a public key $Y_B = 10$, what is Bob's private key Y_B?
b. If Alice has a public key $Y_A = 8$, what is the shared key K with Bob?
c. Show that 5 is a primitive root of 23.

10.3 In the Diffie–Hellman protocol, each participant selects a secret number x and sends the other participant $\alpha^x \bmod q$ for some public number α. What would happen if the participants sent each other x^α for some public number α instead? Give at least one method Alice and Bob could use to agree on a key. Can Eve break your system without finding the secret numbers? Can Eve find the secret numbers?

10.4 This problem illustrates the point that the Diffie–Hellman protocol is not secure without the step where you take the modulus; i.e. the "Indiscrete Log Problem" is not a hard problem! You are Eve and have captured Alice and Bob and imprisoned them. You overhear the following dialog.

Bob: Oh, let's not bother with the prime in the Diffie–Hellman protocol, it will make things easier.

Alice: Okay, but we still need a base α to raise things to. How about $\alpha = 3$?

Bob: All right, then my result is 27.

Alice: And mine is 243.

What is Bob's private key X_B and Alice's private key X_A? What is their secret combined key? (Don't forget to show your work.)

10.5 Section 10.1 describes a man-in-the-middle attack on the Diffie–Hellman key exchange protocol in which the adversary generates two public–private key pairs for the attack. Could the same attack be accomplished with one pair? Explain.

10.6 Suppose Alice and Bob use an ElGamal scheme with a common prime $q = 71$ and a primitive root $\alpha = 7$.

a. If Bob has public key $Y_B = 3$ and Alice chose the random integer $k = 2$, what is the ciphertext of $M = 30$?
b. If Alice now chooses a different value of k so that the encoding of $M = 30$ is $C = (59, C_2)$, what is the integer C_2?

10.7 Rule (5) for doing arithmetic in elliptic curves over real numbers states that to double a point Q_2, draw the tangent line and find the other point of intersection S. Then $Q + Q = 2Q = -S$. If the tangent line is not vertical, there will be exactly one point of intersection. However, suppose the tangent line is vertical? In that case, what is the value $2Q$? What is the value $3Q$?

10.8 Demonstrate that the two elliptic curves of Figure 10.4 each satisfy the conditions for a group over the real numbers.

10.9 Is (4, 7) a point on the elliptic curve $y^2 = x^3 - 5x + 5$ over real numbers?

10.10 On the elliptic curve over the real numbers $y^2 = x^3 - \frac{17}{12}x + 1$, Let $P = (0,1)$ and $Q = (1.5,1.5)$. Find $P + Q$ and $2P$.

10.11 Does the elliptic curve equation $y^2 = x^3 + 10x + 5$ define a group over Z_{17}?

10.12 Consider the elliptic curve $E_7(2,1)$; that is, the curve is defined by $y^2 = x^3 + 2x + 1$ with a modulus of $p = 7$. Determine all of the points in $E_7(2, 1)$. *Hint:* Start by calculating the right-hand side of the equation for all values of x.

10.13 What are the negatives of the following elliptic curve points over Z_{17}? $P = (5, 8)$; $Q = (3, 0)$; $R = (0, 6)$.

10.14 For $E_{11}(1, 7)$, consider the point $G = (3, 2)$. Compute the multiple of G from $2G$ through $13G$.

10.15 This problem performs elliptic curve encryption/decryption using the scheme outlined in Section 10.4. The cryptosystem parameters are $E_{11}(1, 6)$ and $G = (2, 7)$. B's private key is $n_B = 7$.

  a. Find B's public key P_B.

  b. A wishes to encrypt the message $P_m = (10, 9)$ and chooses the random value $k = 3$. Determine the ciphertext C_m.

  c. Show the calculation by which B recovers P_m from C_m.

10.16 The following is a first attempt at an elliptic curve signature scheme. We have a global elliptic curve, prime p, and "generator" G. Alice picks a private signing key X_A and forms the public verifying key $Y_A = X_AG$. To sign a message M:

- Alice picks a value k.
- Alice sends Bob M, k, and the signature $S = M - kX_AG$.
- Bob verifies that $M = S + kY_A$.

  a. Show that this scheme works. That is, show that the verification process produces an equality if the signature is valid.

  b. Show that the scheme is unacceptable by describing a simple technique for forging a user's signature on an arbitrary message.

10.17 Here is an improved version of the scheme given in the previous problem. As before, we have a global elliptic curve, prime p, and "generator" G. Alice picks a private signing key X_A and forms the public verifying key $Y_A = X_AG$. To sign a message M:

- Bob picks a value k.
- Bob sends Alice $C_1 = kG$.
- Alice sends Bob M and the signature $S = M - X_AC_1$.
- Bob verifies that $M = S + kY_A$.

  a. Show that this scheme works. That is, show that the verification process produces an equality if the signature is valid.

  b. Show that forging a message in this scheme is as hard as breaking (Elgamal) elliptic curve cryptography. (Or find an easier way to forge a message?)

  c. This scheme has an extra "pass" compared to other cryptosystems and signature schemes we have looked at. What are some drawbacks to this?

Part Four: Cryptographic Data Integrity Algorithms

CHAPTER 11

Cryptographic Hash Functions

LEARNING OBJECTIVES

After studying this chapter, you should be able to:

- Summarize the applications of cryptographic hash functions.
- Explain why a hash function used for message authentication needs to be secured.
- Understand the differences among preimage resistant, second preimage resistant, and collision resistant properties.
- Present an overview of the basic structure of cryptographic hash functions.
- Describe how cipher block chaining can be used to construct a hash function.
- Understand the operation of SHA-512.
- Understand the birthday paradox and present an overview of the birthday attack.

A **hash function** H accepts a variable-length block of data M as input and produces a fixed-size hash value $h = \mathrm{H}(M)$. A "good" hash function has the property that the results of applying the function to a large set of inputs will produce outputs that are evenly distributed and apparently random. In general terms, the principal object of a hash function is data integrity. A change to any bit or bits in M results, with high probability, in a change to the hash value.

The kind of hash function needed for security applications is referred to as a **cryptographic hash function**. A cryptographic hash function is an algorithm for which it is computationally infeasible (because no attack is significantly more efficient than brute force) to find either (a) a data object that maps to a pre-specified hash result (the one-way property) or (b) two data objects that map to the same hash result (the collision-free property). Because of these characteristics, hash functions are often used to determine whether or not data has changed.

Figure 11.1 depicts the general operation of a cryptographic hash function. Typically, the input is padded out to an integer multiple of some fixed length (e.g., 1024 bits), and the padding includes the value of the length of the original message in bits. The length field is a security measure to increase the difficulty for an attacker to produce an alternative message with the same hash value, as explained subsequently.

This chapter begins with a discussion of the wide variety of applications for cryptographic hash functions. Next, we look at the security requirements for such functions. Then we look at the use of cipher block chaining to implement a cryptographic hash function. The remainder of the chapter is devoted to the most important and widely used family of cryptographic hash functions, the Secure Hash Algorithm (SHA) family.

Appendix N describes MD5, a well-known cryptographic hash function with similarities to SHA-1.

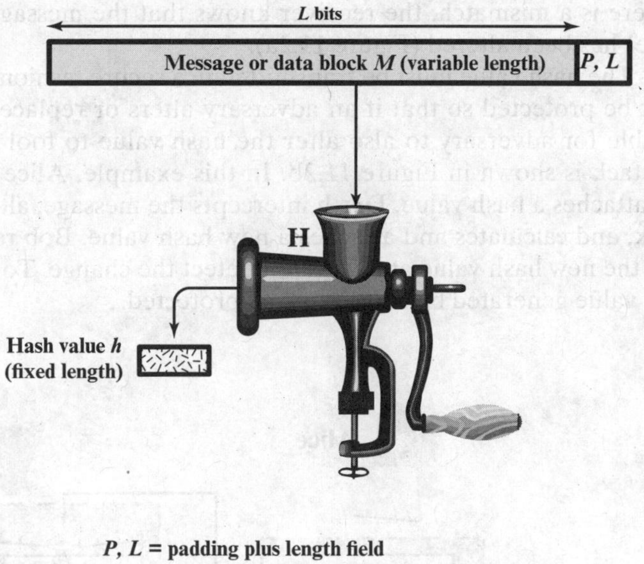

Figure 11.1 Cryptographic Hash Function; $h = \mathrm{H}(M)$

11.1 APPLICATIONS OF CRYPTOGRAPHIC HASH FUNCTIONS

Perhaps the most versatile cryptographic algorithm is the cryptographic hash function. It is used in a wide variety of security applications and Internet protocols. To better understand some of the requirements and security implications for cryptographic hash functions, it is useful to look at the range of applications in which it is employed.

Message Authentication

Message authentication is a mechanism or service used to verify the integrity of a message. Message authentication assures that data received are exactly as sent (i.e., there is no modification, insertion, deletion, or replay). In many cases, there is a requirement that the authentication mechanism assures that purported identity of the sender is valid. When a hash function is used to provide message authentication, the hash function value is often referred to as a **message digest**.[1]

The essence of the use of a hash function for message integrity is as follows. The sender computes a hash value as a function of the bits in the message and transmits both the hash value and the message. The receiver performs the same hash calculation on the message bits and compares this value with the incoming hash value.

[1]The topic of this section is invariably referred to as message authentication. However, the concepts and techniques apply equally to data at rest. For example, authentication techniques can be applied to a file in storage to assure that the file is not tampered with.

If there is a mismatch, the receiver knows that the message (or possibly the hash value) has been altered (Figure 11.2a).

The hash value must be transmitted in a secure fashion. That is, the hash value must be protected so that if an adversary alters or replaces the message, it is not feasible for adversary to also alter the hash value to fool the receiver. This type of attack is shown in Figure 11.2b. In this example, Alice transmits a data block and attaches a hash value. Darth intercepts the message, alters or replaces the data block, and calculates and attaches a new hash value. Bob receives the altered data with the new hash value and does not detect the change. To prevent this attack, the hash value generated by Alice must be protected.

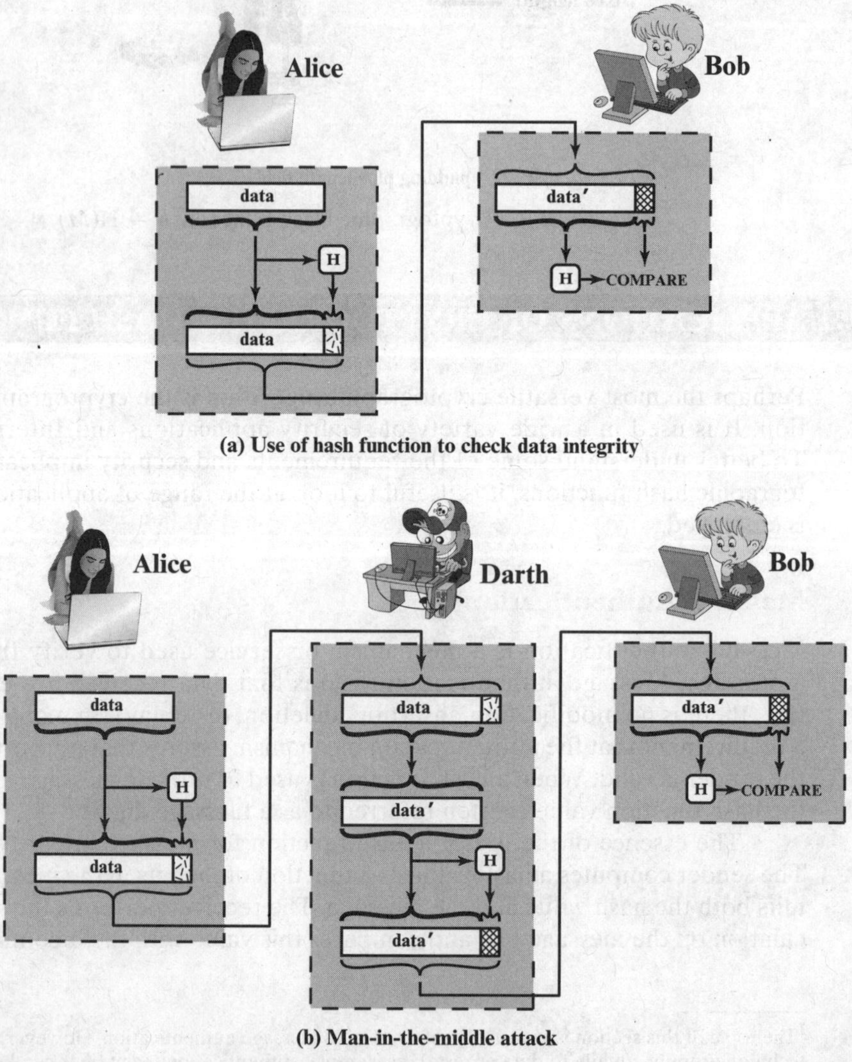

Figure 11.2 Attack Against Hash Function

Figure 11.3 illustrates a variety of ways in which a hash code can be used to provide message authentication, as follows.

a. The message plus concatenated hash code is encrypted using symmetric encryption. Because only A and B share the secret key, the message must have come from A and has not been altered. The hash code provides the structure or redundancy required to achieve authentication. Because encryption is applied to the entire message plus hash code, confidentiality is also provided.

b. Only the hash code is encrypted, using symmetric encryption. This reduces the processing burden for those applications that do not require confidentiality.

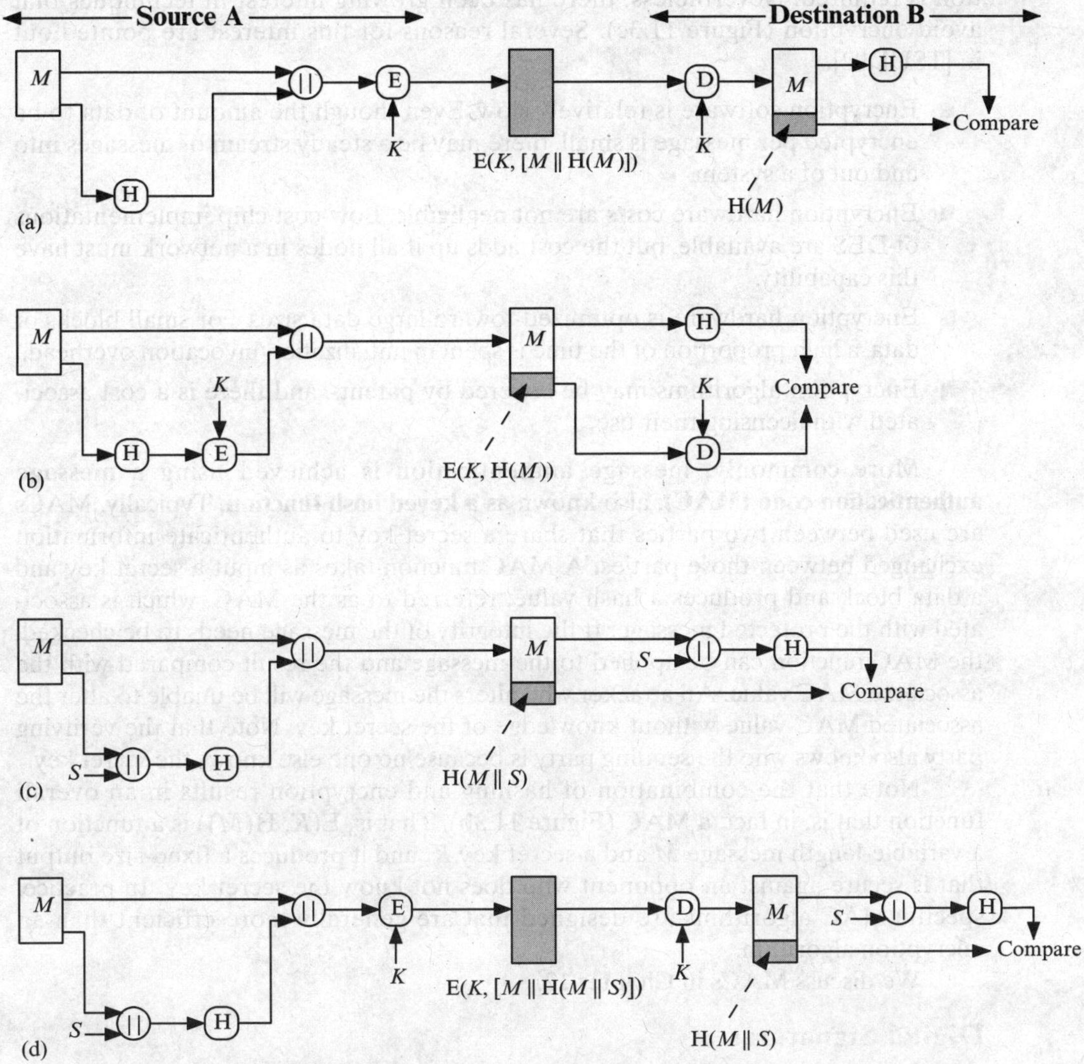

Figure 11.3 Simplified Examples of the Use of a Hash Function for Message Authentication

c. It is possible to use a hash function but no encryption for message authentication. The technique assumes that the two communicating parties share a common secret value S. A computes the hash value over the concatenation of M and S and appends the resulting hash value to M. Because B possesses S, it can recompute the hash value to verify. Because the secret value itself is not sent, an opponent cannot modify an intercepted message and cannot generate a false message.

d. Confidentiality can be added to the approach of method (c) by encrypting the entire message plus the hash code.

When confidentiality is not required, method (b) has an advantage over methods (a) and (d), which encrypts the entire message, in that less computation is required. Nevertheless, there has been growing interest in techniques that avoid encryption (Figure 11.3c). Several reasons for this interest are pointed out in [TSUD92].

- Encryption software is relatively slow. Even though the amount of data to be encrypted per message is small, there may be a steady stream of messages into and out of a system.
- Encryption hardware costs are not negligible. Low-cost chip implementations of DES are available, but the cost adds up if all nodes in a network must have this capability.
- Encryption hardware is optimized toward large data sizes. For small blocks of data, a high proportion of the time is spent in initialization/invocation overhead.
- Encryption algorithms may be covered by patents, and there is a cost associated with licensing their use.

More commonly, message authentication is achieved using a **message authentication code (MAC)**, also known as a **keyed hash function**. Typically, MACs are used between two parties that share a secret key to authenticate information exchanged between those parties. A MAC function takes as input a secret key and a data block and produces a hash value, referred to as the MAC, which is associated with the protected message. If the integrity of the message needs to be checked, the MAC function can be applied to the message and the result compared with the associated MAC value. An attacker who alters the message will be unable to alter the associated MAC value without knowledge of the secret key. Note that the verifying party also knows who the sending party is because no one else knows the secret key.

Note that the combination of hashing and encryption results in an overall function that is, in fact, a MAC (Figure 11.3b). That is, $E(K, H(M))$ is a function of a variable-length message M and a secret key K, and it produces a fixed-size output that is secure against an opponent who does not know the secret key. In practice, specific MAC algorithms are designed that are generally more efficient than an encryption algorithm.

We discuss MACs in Chapter 12.

Digital Signatures

Another important application, which is similar to the message authentication application, is the **digital signature**. The operation of the digital signature is similar to that of the MAC. In the case of the digital signature, the hash value of a message

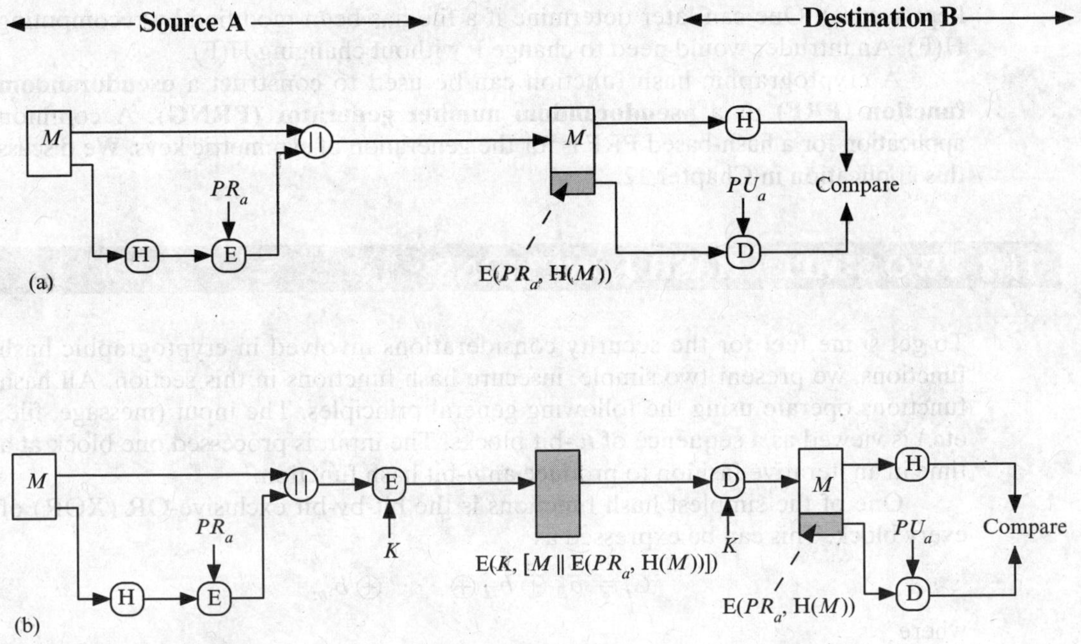

Figure 11.4 Simplified Examples of Digital Signatures

is encrypted with a user's private key. Anyone who knows the user's public key can verify the integrity of the message that is associated with the digital signature. In this case, an attacker who wishes to alter the message would need to know the user's private key. As we shall see in Chapter 14, the implications of digital signatures go beyond just message authentication.

Figure 11.4 illustrates, in a simplified fashion, how a hash code is used to provide a digital signature.

a. The hash code is encrypted, using public-key encryption with the sender's private key. As with Figure 11.3b, this provides authentication. It also provides a digital signature, because only the sender could have produced the encrypted hash code. In fact, this is the essence of the digital signature technique.

b. If confidentiality as well as a digital signature is desired, then the message plus the private-key-encrypted hash code can be encrypted using a symmetric secret key. This is a common technique.

Other Applications

Hash functions are commonly used to create a **one-way password file**. Chapter 21 explains a scheme in which a hash of a password is stored by an operating system rather than the password itself. Thus, the actual password is not retrievable by a hacker who gains access to the password file. In simple terms, when a user enters a password, the hash of that password is compared to the stored hash value for verification. This approach to password protection is used by most operating systems.

Hash functions can be used for **intrusion detection** and **virus detection**. Store H(F) for each file on a system and secure the hash values (e.g., on a CD-R that is kept secure). One can later determine if a file has been modified by recomputing H(F). An intruder would need to change F without changing H(F).

A cryptographic hash function can be used to construct a **pseudorandom function (PRF)** or a **pseudorandom number generator (PRNG)**. A common application for a hash-based PRF is for the generation of symmetric keys. We discuss this application in Chapter 12.

11.2 TWO SIMPLE HASH FUNCTIONS

To get some feel for the security considerations involved in cryptographic hash functions, we present two simple, insecure hash functions in this section. All hash functions operate using the following general principles. The input (message, file, etc.) is viewed as a sequence of n -bit blocks. The input is processed one block at a time in an iterative fashion to produce an n-bit hash function.

One of the simplest hash functions is the bit-by-bit exclusive-OR (XOR) of every block. This can be expressed as

$$C_i = b_{i1} \oplus b_{i2} \oplus \cdots \oplus b_{im}$$

where

C_i = ith bit of the hash code, $1 \leq i \leq$ n

m = number of n-bit blocks in the input

b_{ij} = ith bit in jth block

$\oplus$ = XOR operation

This operation produces a simple parity bit for each bit position and is known as a longitudinal redundancy check. It is reasonably effective for random data as a data integrity check. Each n-bit hash value is equally likely. Thus, the probability that a data error will result in an unchanged hash value is 2^{-n}. With more predictably formatted data, the function is less effective. For example, in most normal text files, the high-order bit of each octet is always zero. So if a 128-bit hash value is used, instead of an effectiveness of 2^{-128}, the hash function on this type of data has an effectiveness of 2^{-112}.

A simple way to improve matters is to perform a one-bit circular shift, or rotation, on the hash value after each block is processed. The procedure can be summarized as follows.

1. Initially set the n-bit hash value to zero.
2. Process each successive n-bit block of data as follows:
   a. Rotate the current hash value to the left by one bit.
   b. XOR the block into the hash value.

This has the effect of "randomizing" the input more completely and overcoming any regularities that appear in the input. Figure 11.5 illustrates these two types of hash functions for 16-bit hash values.

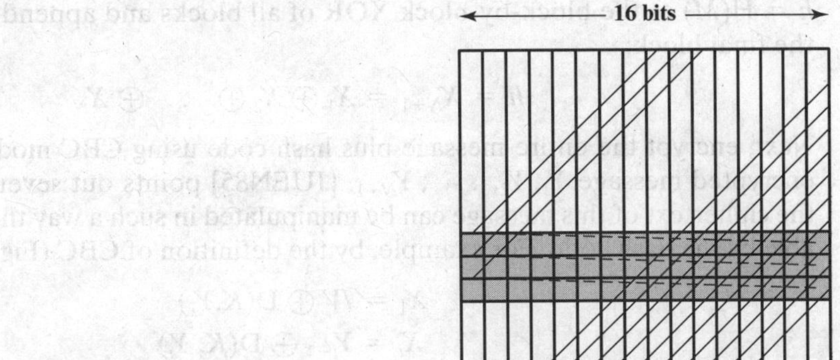

Figure 11.5 Two Simple Hash Functions

Although the second procedure provides a good measure of data integrity, it is virtually useless for data security when an encrypted hash code is used with a plaintext message, as in Figures 11.3b and 11.4a. Given a message, it is an easy matter to produce a new message that yields that hash code: Simply prepare the desired alternate message and then append an n-bit block that forces the new message plus block to yield the desired hash code.

Although a simple XOR or rotated XOR (RXOR) is insufficient if only the hash code is encrypted, you may still feel that such a simple function could be useful when the message together with the hash code is encrypted (Figure 11.3a). But you must be careful. A technique originally proposed by the National Bureau of Standards used the simple XOR applied to 64-bit blocks of the message and then an encryption of the entire message that used the cipher block chaining (CBC) mode. We can define the scheme as follows: Given a message M consisting of a sequence of 64-bit blocks $X_1, X_2, \ldots, X_N$, define the hash code

$h = H(M)$ as the block-by-block XOR of all blocks and append the hash code as the final block:

$$h = X_{N+1} = X_1 \oplus X_2 \oplus \ldots \oplus X_N$$

Next, encrypt the entire message plus hash code using CBC mode to produce the encrypted message $Y_1, Y_2, \ldots, Y_{N+1}$. [JUEN85] points out several ways in which the ciphertext of this message can be manipulated in such a way that it is not detectable by the hash code. For example, by the definition of CBC (Figure 6.4), we have

$$\begin{aligned} X_1 &= IV \oplus D(K, Y_1) \\ X_i &= Y_{i-1} \oplus D(K, Y_i) \\ X_{N+1} &= Y_N \oplus D(K, Y_{N+1}) \end{aligned}$$

But X_{N+1} is the hash code:

$$\begin{aligned} X_{N+1} &= X_1 \oplus X_2 \oplus \ldots \oplus X_N \\ &= [IV \oplus D(K, Y_1)] \oplus [Y_1 \oplus D(K, Y_2)] \oplus \ldots \oplus [Y_{N-1} \oplus D(K, Y_N)] \end{aligned}$$

Because the terms in the preceding equation can be XORed in any order, it follows that the hash code would not change if the ciphertext blocks were permuted.

11.3 REQUIREMENTS AND SECURITY

Before proceeding, we need to define two terms. For a hash value $h = H(x)$, we say that x is the **preimage** of h. That is, x is a data block whose hash value, using the function H, is h. Because H is a many-to-one mapping, for any given hash value h, there will in general be multiple preimages. A **collision** occurs if we have $x \neq y$ and $H(x) = H(y)$. Because we are using hash functions for data integrity, collisions are clearly undesirable.

Let us consider how many preimages are there for a given hash value, which is a measure of the number of potential collisions for a given hash value. Suppose the length of the hash code is n bits, and the function H takes as input messages or data blocks of length b bits with $b > n$. Then, the total number of possible messages is 2^b and the total number of possible hash values is 2^n. On average, each hash value corresponds to 2^{b-n} preimages. If H tends to uniformly distribute hash values then, in fact, each hash value will have close to 2^{b-n} preimages. If we now allow inputs of arbitrary length, not just a fixed length of some number of bits, then the number of preimages per hash value is arbitrarily large. However, the security risks in the use of a hash function are not as severe as they might appear from this analysis. To understand better the security implications of cryptographic hash functions, we need precisely define their security requirements.

Security Requirements for Cryptographic Hash Functions

Table 11.1 lists the generally accepted requirements for a cryptographic hash function. The first three properties are requirements for the practical application of a hash function.

Table 11.1 Requirements for a Cryptographic Hash Function H

Requirement	Description
Variable input size	H can be applied to a block of data of any size.
Fixed output size	H produces a fixed-length output.
Efficiency	$H(x)$ is relatively easy to compute for any given x, making both hardware and software implementations practical.
Preimage resistant (one-way property)	For any given hash value h, it is computationally infeasible to find y such that $H(y) = h$.
Second preimage resistant (weak collision resistant)	For any given block x, it is computationally infeasible to find $y \neq x$ with $H(y) = H(x)$.
Collision resistant (strong collision resistant)	It is computationally infeasible to find any pair (x, y) with $x \neq y$, such that $H(x) = H(y)$.
Pseudorandomness	Output of H meets standard tests for pseudorandomness.

The fourth property, **preimage resistant**, is the one-way property: it is easy to generate a code given a message, but virtually impossible to generate a message given a code. This property is important if the authentication technique involves the use of a secret value (Figure 11.3c). The secret value itself is not sent. However, if the hash function is not one way, an attacker can easily discover the secret value: If the attacker can observe or intercept a transmission, the attacker obtains the message M, and the hash code $h = H(S \| M)$. The attacker then inverts the hash function to obtain $S \| M = H^{-1}(MD_M)$. Because the attacker now has both M and $S_{AB} \| M$, it is a trivial matter to recover S_{AB}.

The fifth property, **second preimage resistant**, guarantees that it is infeasible to find an alternative message with the same hash value as a given message. This prevents forgery when an encrypted hash code is used (Figures 11.3b and 11.4a). If this property were not true, an attacker would be capable of the following sequence: First, observe or intercept a message plus its encrypted hash code; second, generate an unencrypted hash code from the message; third, generate an alternate message with the same hash code.

A hash function that satisfies the first five properties in Table 11.1 is referred to as a weak hash function. If the sixth property, **collision resistant**, is also satisfied, then it is referred to as a strong hash function. A strong hash function protects against an attack in which one party generates a message for another party to sign. For example, suppose Bob writes an IOU message, sends it to Alice, and she signs it. Bob finds two messages with the same hash, one of which requires Alice to pay a small amount and one that requires a large payment. Alice signs the first message, and Bob is then able to claim that the second message is authentic.

Figure 11.6 shows the relationships among the three resistant properties. A function that is collision resistant is also second preimage resistant, but the reverse is not necessarily true. A function can be collision resistant but not preimage resistant and vice versa. A function can be preimage resistant but not second preimage resistant and vice versa. See [MENE97] for a discussion.

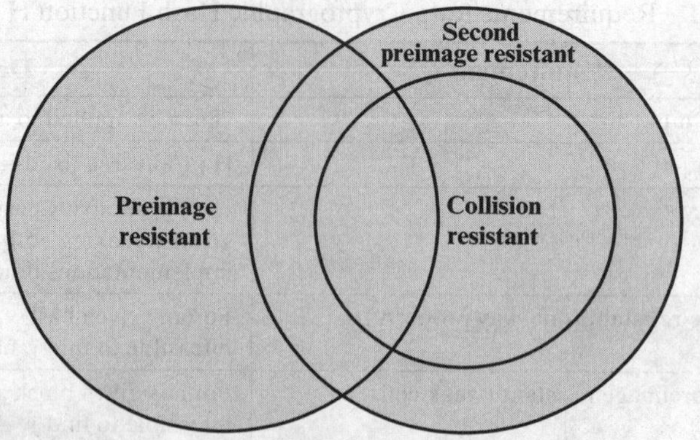

Figure 11.6 Relationship Among Hash Function Properties

Table 11.2 Hash Function Resistance Properties Required for Various Data Integrity Applications

	Preimage Resistant	Second Preimage Resistant	Collision Resistant
Hash + digital signature	yes	yes	yes*
Intrusion detection and virus detection		yes	
Hash + symmetric encryption			
One-way password file	yes		
MAC	yes	yes	yes*

*Resistance required if attacker is able to mount a chosen message attack

Table 11.2 shows the resistant properties required for various hash function applications.

The final requirement in Table 11.1, **pseudorandomness**, has not traditionally been listed as a requirement of cryptographic hash functions but is more or less implied. [JOHN05] points out that cryptographic hash functions are commonly used for key derivation and pseudorandom number generation, and that in message integrity applications, the three resistant properties depend on the output of the hash function appearing to be random. Thus, it makes sense to verify that in fact a given hash function produces pseudorandom output.

Brute-Force Attacks

As with encryption algorithms, there are two categories of attacks on hash functions: brute-force attacks and cryptanalysis. A brute-force attack does not depend on the specific algorithm but depends only on bit length. In the case of a hash function, a brute-force attack depends only on the bit length of the hash value. A cryptanalysis, in contrast, is an attack based on weaknesses in a particular cryptographic algorithm. We look first at brute-force attacks.

PREIMAGE AND SECOND PREIMAGE ATTACKS For a preimage or second preimage attack, an adversary wishes to find a value y such that H(y) is equal to a given hash value h. The brute-force method is to pick values of y at random and try each value until a collision occurs. For an m-bit hash value, the level of effort is proportional to 2^m. Specifically, the adversary would have to try, on average, 2^{m-1} values of y to find one that generates a given hash value h. This result is derived in Appendix U [Equation (U.1)].

COLLISION RESISTANT ATTACKS For a collision resistant attack, an adversary wishes to find two messages or data blocks, x and y, that yield the same hash function: $H(x) = H(y)$. This turns out to require considerably less effort than a preimage or second preimage attack. The effort required is explained by a mathematical result referred to as the **birthday paradox**. In essence, if we choose random variables from a uniform distribution in the range 0 through $N - 1$, then the probability that a repeated element is encountered exceeds 0.5 after $\sqrt{N}$ choices have been made. Thus, for an m-bit hash value, if we pick data blocks at random, we can expect to find two data blocks with the same hash value within $\sqrt{2^m} = 2^{m/2}$ attempts. The mathematical derivation of this result is found in Appendix U.

Yuval proposed the following strategy to exploit the birthday paradox in a collision resistant attack [YUVA79].

1. The source, A, is prepared to sign a legitimate message x by appending the appropriate m-bit hash code and encrypting that hash code with A's private key (Figure 11.4a).
2. The opponent generates $2^{m/2}$ variations x' of x, all of which convey essentially the same meaning, and stores the messages and their hash values.
3. The opponent prepares a fraudulent message y for which A's signature is desired.
4. The opponent generates minor variations y' of y, all of which convey essentially the same meaning. For each y', the opponent computes $H(y')$, checks for matches with any of the $H(x')$ values, and continues until a match is found. That is, the process continues until a y' is generated with a hash value equal to the hash value of one of the x' values.
5. The opponent offers the valid variation to A for signature. This signature can then be attached to the fraudulent variation for transmission to the intended recipient. Because the two variations have the same hash code, they will produce the same signature; the opponent is assured of success even though the encryption key is not known.

Thus, if a 64-bit hash code is used, the level of effort required is only on the order of 2^{32} [see Appendix U, Equation (U.7)].

The generation of many variations that convey the same meaning is not difficult. For example, the opponent could insert a number of "space-space-backspace" character pairs between words throughout the document. Variations could then be generated by substituting "space-backspace-space" in selected instances.

Alternatively, the opponent could simply reword the message but retain the meaning. Figure 11.7 provides an example.

To summarize, for a hash code of length m, the level of effort required, as we have seen, is proportional to the following.

Preimage resistant	2^m
Second preimage resistant	2^m
Collision resistant	$2^{m/2}$

As {the / —} Dean of Blakewell College, I have {had the pleasure of knowing / known} Cherise
Rosetti for the {last / past} four years. She {has been / was} {a tremendous / an outstanding} {asset to / role model in}
{our / the} school. I {would like to take this opportunity to / wholeheartedly} recommend Cherise for your
{school's / —} graduate program. I {am / feel} {confident / certain} {that / —} {she / Cherise} will
{continue to / —} succeed in her studies. {She / Cherise} is a dedicated student and
{thus far her grades / her grades thus far} {have been / are} {exemplary / excellent}. In class,
{she / Cherise} {has proven to be / has been} a take-charge {person / individual} {who is / —} able to
successfully develop plans and implement them.

{She / Cherise} has also assisted {us / —} in our admissions office. {She / Cherise} has
{successfully / —} demonstrated leadership ability by counseling new and prospective students.

{Her / Cherise's} advice has been {a great / of considerable} help to these students, many of whom
have {taken time to share / shared} their comments with me regarding her pleasant and
{encouraging / reassuring} attitude. {For these reasons / It is for these reasons that} I
{highly recommend / offer high recommendations for} Cherise {without reservation / unreservedly}. Her {ambition / drive} and
{abilities / potential} will {truly / surely} be an {asset to / plus for} your {establishment / school}.

Figure 11.7 A Letter in 2^{38} Variations

If collision resistance is required (and this is desirable for a general-purpose secure hash code), then the value $2^{m/2}$ determines the strength of the hash code against brute-force attacks. Van Oorschot and Wiener [VANO94] presented a design for a $10 million collision search machine for MD5, which has a 128-bit hash length, that could find a collision in 24 days. Thus, a 128-bit code may be viewed as inadequate. The next step up, if a hash code is treated as a sequence of 32 bits, is a 160-bit hash length. With a hash length of 160 bits, the same search machine would require over four thousand years to find a collision. With today's technology, the time would be much shorter, so that 160 bits now appears suspect.

Cryptanalysis

As with encryption algorithms, cryptanalytic attacks on hash functions seek to exploit some property of the algorithm to perform some attack other than an exhaustive search. The way to measure the resistance of a hash algorithm to cryptanalysis is to compare its strength to the effort required for a brute-force attack. That is, an ideal hash algorithm will require a cryptanalytic effort greater than or equal to the brute-force effort.

In recent years, there has been considerable effort, and some successes, in developing cryptanalytic attacks on hash functions. To understand these, we need to look at the overall structure of a typical secure hash function, indicated in Figure 11.8. This structure, referred to as an iterated hash function, was proposed by Merkle [MERK79, MERK89] and is the structure of most hash functions in use today, including SHA, which is discussed later in this chapter. The hash function takes an input message and partitions it into L fixed-sized blocks of b bits each. If necessary, the final block is padded to b bits. The final block also includes the value of the total length of the input to the hash function. The inclusion of the length makes the job of the opponent more difficult. Either the opponent must find two messages of equal length that hash to the same value or two messages of differing lengths that, together with their length values, hash to the same value.

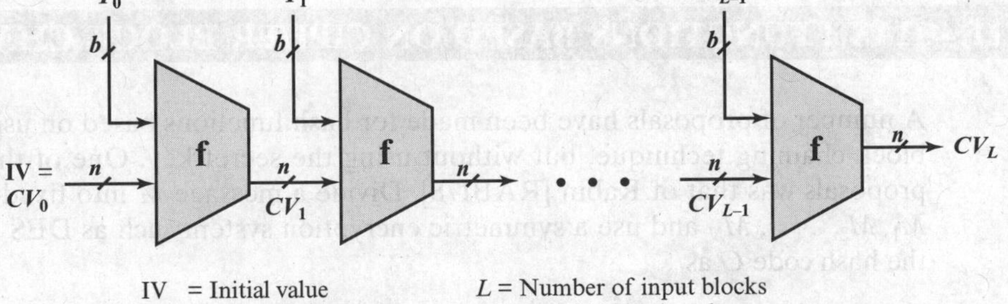

IV = Initial value
CV_i = Chaining variable
Y_i = ith input block
f = Compression algorithm
L = Number of input blocks
n = Length of hash code
b = Length of input block

Figure 11.8 General Structure of Secure Hash Code

The hash algorithm involves repeated use of a **compression function**, f, that takes two inputs (an n-bit input from the previous step, called the *chaining variable*, and a b-bit block) and produces an n-bit output. At the start of hashing, the chaining variable has an initial value that is specified as part of the algorithm. The final value of the chaining variable is the hash value. Often, $b > n$; hence the term *compression*. The hash function can be summarized as

$$CV_0 = IV = \text{initial } n\text{-bit value}$$
$$CV_i = \text{f}(CV_{i-1}, Y_{i-1}) \quad 1 \leq i \leq L$$
$$\text{H}(M) = CV_L$$

where the input to the hash function is a message M consisting of the blocks $Y_0, Y_1, \ldots, Y_{L-1}$.

The motivation for this iterative structure stems from the observation by Merkle [MERK89] and Damgard [DAMG89] that if the length field is included in the input, and if the compression function is collision resistant, then so is the resultant iterated hash function.[2] Therefore, the structure can be used to produce a secure hash function to operate on a message of any length. The problem of designing a secure hash function reduces to that of designing a collision-resistant compression function that operates on inputs of some fixed size.

Cryptanalysis of hash functions focuses on the internal structure of f and is based on attempts to find efficient techniques for producing collisions for a single execution of f. Once that is done, the attack must take into account the fixed value of IV. The attack on f depends on exploiting its internal structure. Typically, as with symmetric block ciphers, f consists of a series of rounds of processing, so that the attack involves analysis of the pattern of bit changes from round to round.

Keep in mind that for any hash function there must exist collisions, because we are mapping a message of length at least equal to twice the block size b (because we must append a length field) into a hash code of length n, where $b \geq n$. What is required is that it is computationally infeasible to find collisions.

The attacks that have been mounted on hash functions are rather complex and beyond our scope here. For the interested reader, [DOBB96] and [BELL97] are recommended.

11.4 HASH FUNCTIONS BASED ON CIPHER BLOCK CHAINING

A number of proposals have been made for hash functions based on using a cipher block chaining technique, but without using the secret key. One of the first such proposals was that of Rabin [RABI78]. Divide a message M into fixed-size blocks $M_1, M_2, \ldots, M_N$ and use a symmetric encryption system such as DES to compute the hash code G as

$$H_0 = \text{initial value}$$
$$H_i = \text{E}(M_i, H_{i-1})$$
$$G = H_N$$

[2] The converse is not necessarily true.

This is similar to the CBC technique, but in this case, there is no secret key. As with any hash code, this scheme is subject to the birthday attack, and if the encryption algorithm is DES and only a 64-bit hash code is produced, then the system is vulnerable.

Furthermore, another version of the birthday attack can be used even if the opponent has access to only one message and its valid signature and cannot obtain multiple signings. Here is the scenario: We assume that the opponent intercepts a message with a signature in the form of an encrypted hash code and that the unencrypted hash code is m bits long.

1. Use the algorithm defined at the beginning of this subsection to calculate the unencrypted hash code G.
2. Construct any desired message in the form $Q_1, Q_2, \ldots, Q_{N-2}$.
3. Compute $H_i = \text{E}(Q_i, H_{i-1})$ for $1 \leq i \leq (N-2)$.
4. Generate $2^{m/2}$ random blocks; for each block X, compute $\text{E}(X, H_{N-2})$. Generate an additional $2^{m/2}$ random blocks; for each block Y, compute $\text{D}(Y, G)$, where D is the decryption function corresponding to E.
5. Based on the birthday paradox, with high probability there will be an X and Y such that $\text{E}(X, H_{N-2}) = \text{D}(Y, G)$.
6. Form the message $Q_1, Q_2, \ldots, Q_{N-2}, X, Y$. This message has the hash code G and therefore can be used with the intercepted encrypted signature.

This form of attack is known as a **meet-in-the-middle-attack**. A number of researchers have proposed refinements intended to strengthen the basic block chaining approach. For example, Davies and Price [DAVI89] describe the variation:

$$H_i = \text{E}(M_i, \text{H}_{i-1}) \oplus H_{i-1}$$

Another variation, proposed in [MEYE88], is

$$H_i = \text{E}(H_{i-1}, M_i) \oplus M_i$$

However, both of these schemes have been shown to be vulnerable to a variety of attacks [MIYA90]. More generally, it can be shown that some form of birthday attack will succeed against any hash scheme involving the use of cipher block chaining without a secret key, provided that either the resulting hash code is small enough (e.g., 64 bits or less) or that a larger hash code can be decomposed into independent subcodes [JUEN87].

Thus, attention has been directed at finding other approaches to hashing. Many of these have also been shown to have weaknesses [MITC92].

11.5 SECURE HASH ALGORITHM (SHA)

In recent years, the most widely used hash function has been the Secure Hash Algorithm (SHA). Indeed, because virtually every other widely used hash function had been found to have substantial cryptanalytic weaknesses, SHA was more or less the last remaining standardized hash algorithm by 2005. SHA was developed

Table 11.3 Comparison of SHA Parameters

Algorithm	Message Size	Block Size	Word Size	Message Digest Size
SHA-1	$< 2^{64}$	512	32	160
SHA-224	$< 2^{64}$	512	32	224
SHA-256	$< 2^{64}$	512	32	256
SHA-384	$< 2^{128}$	1024	64	384
SHA-512	$< 2^{128}$	1024	64	512
SHA-512/224	$< 2^{128}$	1024	64	224
SHA-512/256	$< 2^{128}$	1024	64	256

Note: All sizes are measured in bits.

by the National Institute of Standards and Technology (NIST) and published as a federal information processing standard (FIPS 180) in 1993. When weaknesses were discovered in SHA, now known as **SHA-0**, a revised version was issued as FIPS 180-1 in 1995 and is referred to as **SHA-1**. The actual standards document is entitled "Secure Hash Standard." SHA is based on the hash function MD4, and its design closely models MD4.

SHA-1 produces a hash value of 160 bits. In 2002, NIST produced a revised version of the standard, FIPS 180-2, that defined three new versions of SHA, with hash value lengths of 256, 384, and 512 bits, known as SHA-256, SHA-384, and SHA-512, respectively. Collectively, these hash algorithms are known as **SHA-2**. These new versions have the same underlying structure and use the same types of modular arithmetic and logical binary operations as SHA-1. A revised document was issued as FIP PUB 180-3 in 2008, which added a 224-bit version (Table 11.3). In 2015, NIST issued FIPS 180-4, which added two additional algorithms: SHA-512/224 and SHA-512/256. SHA-1 and SHA-2 are also specified in RFC 6234, which essentially duplicates the material in FIPS 180-3 but adds a C code implementation.

In 2005, NIST announced the intention to phase out approval of SHA-1 and move to a reliance on SHA-2 by 2010. Shortly thereafter, a research team described an attack in which two separate messages could be found that deliver the same SHA-1 hash using 2^{69} operations, far fewer than the 2^{80} operations previously thought needed to find a collision with an SHA-1 hash [WANG05]. This result should hasten the transition to SHA-2.

In this section, we provide a description of SHA-512. The other versions are quite similar.

SHA-512 Logic

The algorithm takes as input a message with a maximum length of less than 2^{128} bits and produces as output a 512-bit message digest. The input is processed in 1024-bit blocks. Figure 11.9 depicts the overall processing of a message to produce a digest.

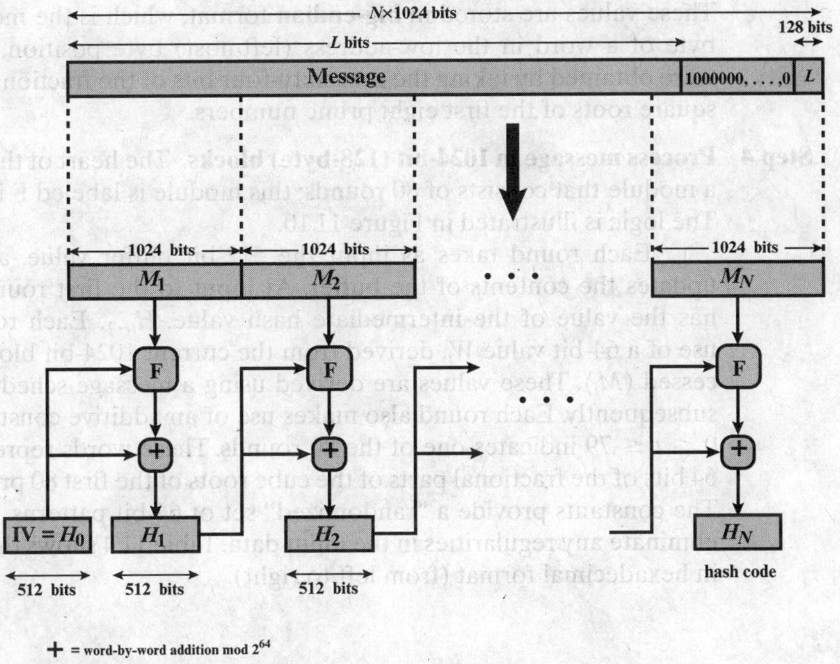

Figure 11.9 Message Digest Generation Using SHA-512

This follows the general structure depicted in Figure 11.8. The processing consists of the following steps.

Step 1 **Append padding bits.** The message is padded so that its length is congruent to 896 modulo 1024 [length ≡ 896(mod 1024)]. Padding is always added, even if the message is already of the desired length. Thus, the number of padding bits is in the range of 1 to 1024. The padding consists of a single 1 bit followed by the necessary number of 0 bits.

Step 2 **Append length.** A block of 128 bits is appended to the message. This block is treated as an unsigned 128-bit integer (most significant byte first) and contains the length of the original message in bits (before the padding).

The outcome of the first two steps yields a message that is an integer multiple of 1024 bits in length. In Figure 11.9, the expanded message is represented as the sequence of 1024-bit blocks $M_1, M_2, \ldots, M_N$, so that the total length of the expanded message is $N \times 1024$ bits.

Step 3 **Initialize hash buffer.** A 512-bit buffer is used to hold intermediate and final results of the hash function. The buffer can be represented as eight 64-bit registers (a, b, c, d, e, f, g, h). These registers are initialized to the following 64-bit integers (hexadecimal values):

```
a = 6A09E667F3BCC908    e = 510E527FADE682D1
b = BB67AE8584CAA73B    f = 9B05688C2B3E6C1F
c = 3C6EF372FE94F82B    g = 1F83D9ABFB41BD6B
d = A54FF53A5F1D36F1    h = 5BE0CD19137E2179
```

These values are stored in **big-endian** format, which is the most significant byte of a word in the low-address (leftmost) byte position. These words were obtained by taking the first sixty-four bits of the fractional parts of the square roots of the first eight prime numbers.

Step 4 **Process message in 1024-bit (128-byte) blocks.** The heart of the algorithm is a module that consists of 80 rounds; this module is labeled F in Figure 11.9. The logic is illustrated in Figure 11.10.

Each round takes as input the 512-bit buffer value, abcdefgh, and updates the contents of the buffer. At input to the first round, the buffer has the value of the intermediate hash value, H_{i-1}. Each round t makes use of a 64-bit value W_t, derived from the current 1024-bit block being processed (M_i). These values are derived using a message schedule described subsequently. Each round also makes use of an additive constant K_t, where $0 \leq t \leq 79$ indicates one of the 80 rounds. These words represent the first 64 bits of the fractional parts of the cube roots of the first 80 prime numbers. The constants provide a "randomized" set of 64-bit patterns, which should eliminate any regularities in the input data. Table 11.4 shows these constants in hexadecimal format (from left to right).

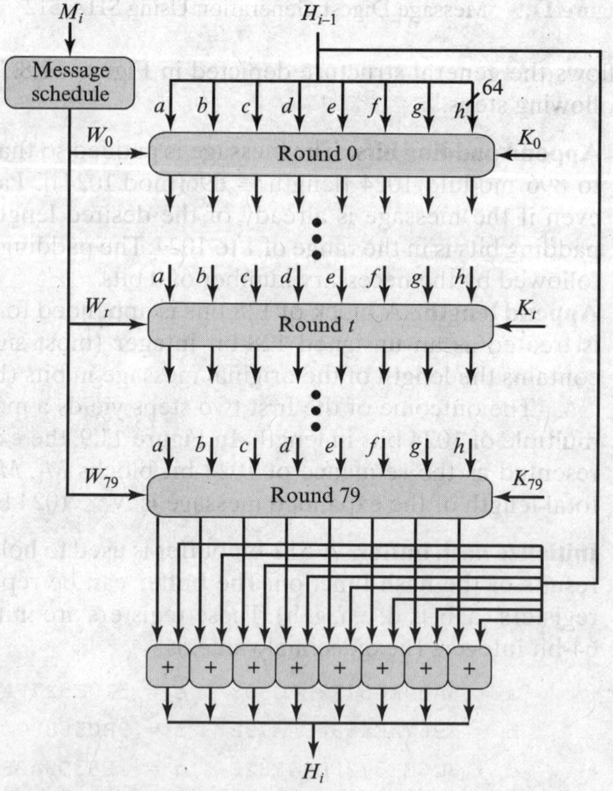

Figure 11.10 SHA-512 Processing of a Single 1024-Bit Block

Table 11.4 SHA-512 Constants

428a2f98d728ae22	7137449123ef65cd	b5c0fbcfec4d3b2f	e9b5dba58189dbbc
3956c25bf348b538	59f111f1b605d019	923f82a4af194f9b	ab1c5ed5da6d8118
d807aa98a3030242	12835b0145706fbe	243185be4ee4b28c	550c7dc3d5ffb4e2
72be5d74f27b896f	80deb1fe3b1696b1	9bdc06a725c71235	c19bf174cf692694
e49b69c19ef14ad2	efbe4786384f25e3	0fc19dc68b8cd5b5	240ca1cc77ac9c65
2de92c6f592b0275	4a7484aa6ea6e483	5cb0a9dcbd41fbd4	76f988da831153b5
983e5152ee66dfab	a831c66d2db43210	b00327c898fb213f	bf597fc7beef0ee4
c6e00bf33da88fc2	d5a79147930aa725	06ca6351e003826f	142929670a0e6e70
27b70a8546d22ffc	2e1b21385c26c926	4d2c6dfc5ac42aed	53380d139d95b3df
650a73548baf63de	766a0abb3c77b2a8	81c2c92e47edaee6	92722c851482353b
a2bfe8a14cf10364	a81a664bbc423001	c24b8b70d0f89791	c76c51a30654be30
d192e819d6ef5218	d69906245565a910	f40e35855771202a	106aa07032bbd1b8
19a4c116b8d2d0c8	1e376c085141ab53	2748774cdf8eeb99	34b0bcb5e19b48a8
391c0cb3c5c95a63	4ed8aa4ae3418acb	5b9cca4f7763e373	682e6ff3d6b2b8a3
748f82ee5defb2fc	78a5636f43172f60	84c87814a1f0ab72	8cc702081a6439ec
90befffa23631e28	a4506cebde82bde9	bef9a3f7b2c67915	c67178f2e372532b
ca273eceea26619c	d186b8c721c0c207	eada7dd6cde0eb1e	f57d4f7fee6ed178
06f067aa72176fba	0a637dc5a2c898a6	113f9804bef90dae	1b710b35131c471b
28db77f523047d84	32caab7b40c72493	3c9ebe0a15c9bebc	431d67c49c100d4c
4cc5d4becb3e42b6	597f299cfc657e2a	5fcb6fab3ad6faec	6c44198c4a475817

The output of the eightieth round is added to the input to the first round (H_{i-1}) to produce H_i. The addition is done independently for each of the eight words in the buffer with each of the corresponding words in H_{i-1}, using addition modulo 2^{64}.

Step 5 Output. After all N 1024-bit blocks have been processed, the output from the Nth stage is the 512-bit message digest.

We can summarize the behavior of SHA-512 as follows:

$$H_0 = \text{IV}$$
$$H_i = \text{SUM}_{64}(H_{i-1}, \text{abcdefgh}_i)$$
$$MD = H_N$$

where

IV = initial value of the abcdefgh buffer, defined in step 3

abcdefgh_i = the output of the last round of processing of the ith message block

N = the number of blocks in the message (including padding and length fields)

SUM_{64} = addition modulo 2^{64} performed separately on each word of the pair of inputs

MD = final message digest value

SHA-512 Round Function

Let us look in more detail at the logic in each of the 80 steps of the processing of one 512-bit block (Figure 11.11). Each round is defined by the following set of equations:

$$T_1 = h + \text{Ch}(e, f, g) + \left(\textstyle\sum_1^{512} e\right) + W_t + K_t$$
$$T_2 = \left(\textstyle\sum_0^{512} a\right) + \text{Maj}(a, b, c)$$
$$h = g$$
$$g = f$$
$$f = e$$
$$e = d + T_1$$
$$d = c$$
$$c = b$$
$$b = a$$
$$a = T_1 + T_2$$

where

t = step number; $0 \le t \le 79$

$\text{Ch}(e, f, g)$ = (e AND f) $\oplus$ (NOT e AND g)
the conditional function: If e then f else g

$\text{Maj}(a, b, c)$ = (a AND b) $\oplus$ (a AND c) $\oplus$ (b AND c)
the function is true only of the majority (two or three) of the arguments are true

$(\Sigma_0^{512} a)$ = $\text{ROTR}^{28}(a) \oplus \text{ROTR}^{34}(a) \oplus \text{ROTR}^{39}(a)$

$(\Sigma_1^{512} e)$ = $\text{ROTR}^{14}(e) \oplus \text{ROTR}^{18}(e) \oplus \text{ROTR}^{41}(e)$

$\text{ROTR}^n(x)$ = circular right shift (rotation) of the 64-bit argument x by n bits

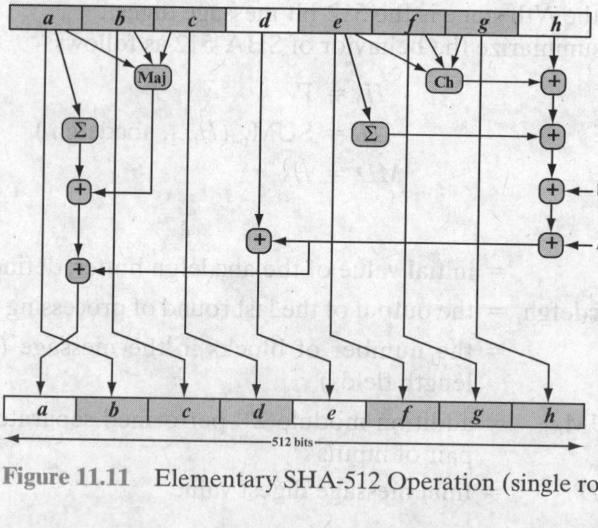

Figure 11.11 Elementary SHA-512 Operation (single round)

W_t = a 64-bit word derived from the current 1024-bit input block
K_t = a 64-bit additive constant
$+$ = addition modulo 2^{64}

Two observations can be made about the round function.

1. Six of the eight words of the output of the round function involve simply permutation (b, c, d, f, g, h) by means of rotation. This is indicated by shading in Figure 11.11.
2. Only two of the output words (a, e) are generated by substitution. Word e is a function of input variables (d, e, f, g, h), as well as the round word W_t and the constant K_t. Word a is a function of all of the input variables except d, as well as the round word W_t and the constant K_t.

It remains to indicate how the 64-bit word values W_t are derived from the 1024-bit message. Figure 11.12 illustrates the mapping. The first 16 values of W_t are taken directly from the 16 words of the current block. The remaining values are defined as

$$W_t = \sigma_1^{512}(W_{t-2}) + W_{t-7} + \sigma_0^{512}(W_{t-15}) + W_{t-16}$$

where

$\sigma_0^{512}(x) = \text{ROTR}^1(x) \oplus \text{ROTR}^8(x) \oplus \text{SHR}^7(x)$
$\sigma_1^{512}(x) = \text{ROTR}^{19}(x) \oplus \text{ROTR}^{61}(x) \oplus \text{SHR}^6(x)$
$\text{ROTR}^n(x)$ = circular right shift (rotation) of the 64-bit argument x by n bits
$\text{SHR}^n(x)$ = right shift of the 64-bit argument x by n bits with padding by zeros on the left
$+$ = addition modulo 2^{64}

Thus, in the first 16 steps of processing, the value of W_t is equal to the corresponding word in the message block. For the remaining 64 steps, the value of W_t consists of the circular left shift by one bit of the XOR of four of the preceding values of W_t, with two of those values subjected to shift and rotate operations.

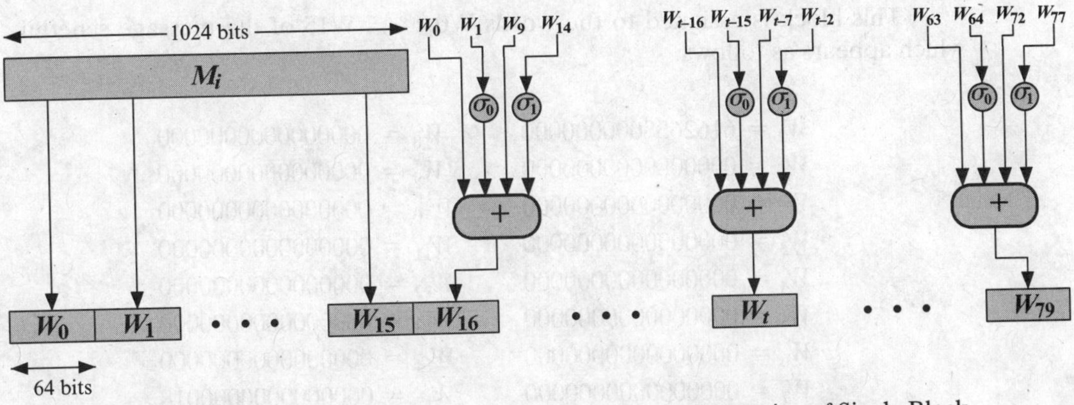

Figure 11.12 Creation of 80-word Input Sequence for SHA-512 Processing of Single Block

This introduces a great deal of redundancy and interdependence into the message blocks that are compressed, which complicates the task of finding a different message block that maps to the same compression function output. Figure 11.13 summarizes the SHA-512 logic.

The SHA-512 algorithm has the property that every bit of the hash code is a function of every bit of the input. The complex repetition of the basic function F produces results that are well mixed; that is, it is unlikely that two messages chosen at random, even if they exhibit similar regularities, will have the same hash code. Unless there is some hidden weakness in SHA-512, which has not so far been published, the difficulty of coming up with two messages having the same message digest is on the order of 2^{256} operations, while the difficulty of finding a message with a given digest is on the order of 2^{512} operations.

Example

We include here an example based on one in FIPS 180. We wish to hash a one-block message consisting of three ASCII characters: "abc," which is equivalent to the following 24-bit binary string:

```
01100001 01100010 01100011
```

Recall from step 1 of the SHA algorithm, that the message is padded to a length congruent to 896 modulo 1024. In this case of a single block, the padding consists of 896 − 24 = 872 bits, consisting of a "1" bit followed by 871 "0" bits. Then a 128-bit length value is appended to the message, which contains the length of the original message in bits (before the padding). The original length is 24 bits, or a hexadecimal value of 18. Putting this all together, the 1024-bit message block, in hexadecimal, is

```
6162638000000000 0000000000000000 0000000000000000 0000000000000000
0000000000000000 0000000000000000 0000000000000000 0000000000000000
0000000000000000 0000000000000000 0000000000000000 0000000000000000
0000000000000000 0000000000000000 0000000000000000 0000000000000018
```

This block is assigned to the words W0, . . . , W15 of the message schedule, which appears as follows.

W_0 = 6162638000000000	W_8 = 0000000000000000
W_1 = 0000000000000000	W_9 = 0000000000000000
W_2 = 0000000000000000	W_{10} = 0000000000000000
W_3 = 0000000000000000	W_{11} = 0000000000000000
W_4 = 0000000000000000	W_{12} = 0000000000000000
W_5 = 0000000000000000	W_{13} = 0000000000000000
W_6 = 0000000000000000	W_{14} = 0000000000000000
W_7 = 0000000000000000	W_{15} = 0000000000000018

The padded message consists blocks $M_1, M_2, \ldots, M_N$. Each message block M_i consists of 16 64-bit words $M_{i,0}, M_{i,1}, \ldots, M_{i,15}$. All addition is performed modulo 2^{64}.

$H_{0,0}$ = 6A09E667F3BCC908 $H_{0,4}$ = 510E527FADE682D1
$H_{0,1}$ = BB67AE8584CAA73B $H_{0,5}$ = 9B05688C2B3E6C1F
$H_{0,2}$ = 3C6EF372FE94F82B $H_{0,6}$ = 1F83D9ABFB41BD6B
$H_{0,3}$ = A54FF53A5F1D36F1 $H_{0,7}$ = 5BE0CD19137E2179

for $i = 1$ to N

1. Prepare the message schedule W
   for $t = 0$ **to** 15
   $W_t = M_{i,t}$
   for $t = 16$ **to** 79
   $W_t = \sigma_1^{512}(W_{t-2}) + W_{t-7} + \sigma_0^{512}(W_{t-15}) + W_{t-16}$
2. Initialize the working variables
   $a = H_{i-1,0}$ $e = H_{i-1,4}$
   $b = H_{i-1,1}$ $f = H_{i-1,5}$
   $c = H_{i-1,2}$ $g = H_{i-1,6}$
   $d = H_{i-1,3}$ $h = H_{i-1,7}$
3. Perform the main hash computation
   for $t = 0$ **to** 79
   $$T_1 = h + \text{Ch}(e, f, g) + \left(\Sigma_1^{512}e\right) + W_t + K_t$$
   $$T_2 = \left(\Sigma_0^{512}a\right) + \text{Maj}(a, b, c)$$
   $h = g$
   $g = f$
   $f = e$
   $e = d + T_1$
   $d = c$
   $c = b$
   $b = a$
   $a = T_1 + T_2$
4. Compute the intermediate hash value
   $H_{i,0} = a + H_{i-1,0}$ $H_{i,4} = e + H_{i-1,4}$
   $H_{i,1} = b + H_{i-1,1}$ $H_{i,5} = f + H_{i-1,5}$
   $H_{i,2} = c + H_{i-1,2}$ $H_{i,6} = g + H_{i-1,6}$
   $H_{i,3} = d + H_{i-1,3}$ $H_{i,7} = h + H_{i-1,7}$

return $\{H_{N,0} \| H_{N,1} \| H_{N,2} \| H_{N,3} \| H_{N,4} \| H_{N,5} \| H_{N,6} \| H_{N,7}\}$

Figure 11.13 SHA-512 Logic

As indicated in Figure 11.13, the eight 64-bit variables, a through h, are initialized to values $H_{0,0}$ through $H_{0,7}$. The following table shows the initial values of these variables and their values after each of the first two rounds.

a	6a09e667f3bcc908	f6afceb8bcfcddf5	1320f8c9fb872cc0
b	bb67ae8584caa73b	6a09e667f3bcc908	f6afceb8bcfcddf5
c	3c6ef372fe94f82b	bb67ae8584caa73b	6a09e667f3bcc908
d	a54ff53a5f1d36f1	3c6ef372fe94f82b	bb67ae8584caa73b
e	510e527fade682d1	58cb02347ab51f91	c3d4ebfd48650ffa
f	9b05688c2b3e6c1f	510e527fade682d1	58cb02347ab51f91
g	1f83d9abfb41bd6b	9b05688c2b3e6c1f	510e527fade682d1
h	5be0cd19137e2179	1f83d9abfb41bd6b	9b05688c2b3e6c1f

Note that in each of the rounds, six of the variables are copied directly from variables from the preceding round.

The process continues through 80 rounds. The output of the final round is

```
73a54f399fa4b1b2 10d9c4c4295599f6 d67806db8b148677 654ef9abec389ca9
d08446aa79693ed7 9bb4d39778c07f9e 25c96a7768fb2aa3 ceb9fc3691ce8326
```

The hash value is then calculated as

$$
\begin{aligned}
H_{1,0} &= \texttt{6a09e667f3bcc908} + \texttt{73a54f399fa4b1b2} = \texttt{ddaf35a193617aba}\\
H_{1,1} &= \texttt{bb67ae8584caa73b} + \texttt{10d9c4c4295599f6} = \texttt{cc417349ae204131}\\
H_{1,2} &= \texttt{3c6ef372fe94f82b} + \texttt{d67806db8b148677} = \texttt{12e6fa4e89a97ea2}\\
H_{1,3} &= \texttt{a54ff53a5f1d36f1} + \texttt{654ef9abec389ca9} = \texttt{0a9eeee64b55d39a}\\
H_{1,4} &= \texttt{510e527fade682d1} + \texttt{d08446aa79693ed7} = \texttt{2192992a274fc1a8}\\
H_{1,5} &= \texttt{9b05688c2b3e6c1f} + \texttt{9bb4d39778c07f9e} = \texttt{36ba3c23a3feebbd}\\
H_{1,6} &= \texttt{1f83d9abfb41bd6b} + \texttt{25c96a7768fb2aa3} = \texttt{454d4423643ce80e}\\
H_{1,7} &= \texttt{5be0cd19137e2179} + \texttt{ceb9fc3691ce8326} = \texttt{2a9ac94fa54ca49f}
\end{aligned}
$$

The resulting 512-bit message digest is

```
ddaf35a193617aba cc417349ae204131 12e6fa4e89a97ea2 0a9eeee64b55d39a
2192992a274fc1a8 36ba3c23a3feebbd 454d4423643ce80e 2a9ac94fa54ca49f
```

Suppose now that we change the input message by one bit, from "abc" to "cbc." Then, the 1024-bit message block is

```
6362638000000000 0000000000000000 0000000000000000 0000000000000000
0000000000000000 0000000000000000 0000000000000000 0000000000000000
0000000000000000 0000000000000000 0000000000000000 0000000000000000
0000000000000000 0000000000000000 0000000000000000 0000000000000018
```

And the resulting 512-bit message digest is

```
531668966ee79b70 0b8e593261101354 4273f7ef7b31f279 2a7ef68d53f93264
319c165ad96d9187 55e6a204c2607e27 6e05cdf993a64c85 ef9e1e125c0f925f
```

The number of bit positions that differ between the two hash values is 253, almost exactly half the bit positions, indicating that SHA-512 has a good avalanche effect.

11.6 SHA-3

As of this writing, the Secure Hash Algorithm (SHA-1) has not yet been "broken." That is, no one has demonstrated a technique for producing collisions in a practical amount of time. However, because SHA-1 is very similar, in structure and in the basic mathematical operations used, to MD5 and SHA-0, both of which have been broken, SHA-1 is considered insecure and has been phased out for SHA-2.

SHA-2, particularly the 512-bit version, would appear to provide unassailable security. However, SHA-2 shares the same structure and mathematical operations as its predecessors, and this is a cause for concern. Because it will take years to find a suitable replacement for SHA-2, should it become vulnerable, NIST decided to begin the process of developing a new hash standard.

Accordingly, NIST announced in 2007 a competition to produce the next generation NIST hash function, to be called SHA-3. The winning design for SHA-3 was announced by NIST in October 2012 and published as FIP 102 in August 2015. SHA-3 is a cryptographic hash function that is intended to complement SHA-2 as the approved standard for a wide range of applications.

Appendix V looks at the evaluation criteria used by NIST to select from among the candidates for AES, plus the rationale for picking Keccak, which was the winning candidate. This material is useful in understanding not just the SHA-3 design but also the criteria by which to judge any cryptographic hash algorithm.

The Sponge Construction

The underlying structure of SHA-3 is a scheme referred to by its designers as a **sponge construction** [BERT07, BERT11]. The sponge construction has the same general structure as other iterated hash functions (Figure 11.8). The sponge function takes an input message and partitions it into fixed-size blocks. Each block is processed in turn with the output of each iteration fed into the next iteration, finally producing an output block.

The sponge function is defined by three parameters:

f = the internal function used to process each input block[3]

r = the size in bits of the input blocks, called the **bitrate**

pad = the padding algorithm

A sponge function allows both variable length input and output, making it a flexible structure that can be used for a hash function (fixed-length output), a pseudorandom number generator (fixed-length input), and other cryptographic functions. Figure 11.14 illustrates this point. An input message of n bits is partitioned into k fixed-size blocks of r bits each. The message is padded to achieve a length that is an integer multiple of r bits. The resulting partition is the sequence of blocks $P_0, P_1, \ldots, P_{k-1}$, with length $k \times r$. For uniformity, padding is always added, so

[3]The Keccak documentation refers to f as a permutation. As we shall see, it involves both permutations and substitutions. We refer to f as the **iteration function**, because it is the function that is executed once for each iteration, that is, once for each block of the message that is processed.

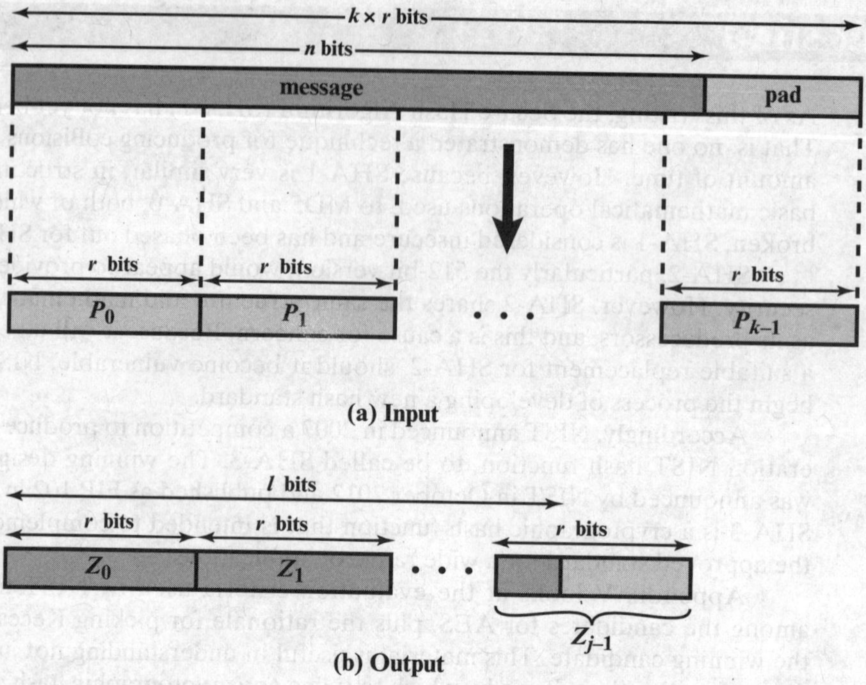

Figure 11.14 Sponge Function Input and Output

that if $n \bmod r = 0$, a padding block of r bits is added. The actual padding algorithm is a parameter of the function. The sponge specification [BERT11] proposes two padding schemes:

- **Simple padding:** Denoted by pad10*, appends a single bit 1 followed by the minimum number of bits 0 such that the length of the result is a multiple of the block length.
- **Multirate padding:** Denoted by pad10*1, appends a single bit 1 followed by the minimum number of bits 0 followed by a single bit 1 such that the length of the result is a multiple of the block length. This is the simplest padding scheme that allows secure use of the same f with different rates r. FIPS 202 uses multirate padding.

After processing all of the blocks, the sponge function generates a sequence of output blocks $Z_0, Z_1, \ldots, Z_{j-1}$. The number of output blocks generated is determined by the number of output bits desired. If the desired output is ℓ bits, then j blocks are produced, such that $(j - 1) \times r < \ell \leq j \times r$.

Figure 11.15 shows the iterated structure of the sponge function. The sponge construction operates on a state variable s of $b = r + c$ bits, which is initialized to all zeros and modified at each iteration. The value r is called the bitrate. This value is the block size used to partition the input message. The term *bitrate* reflects the fact that r is the number of bits processed at each iteration: the larger the value of r, the greater the rate at which message bits are processed by the sponge

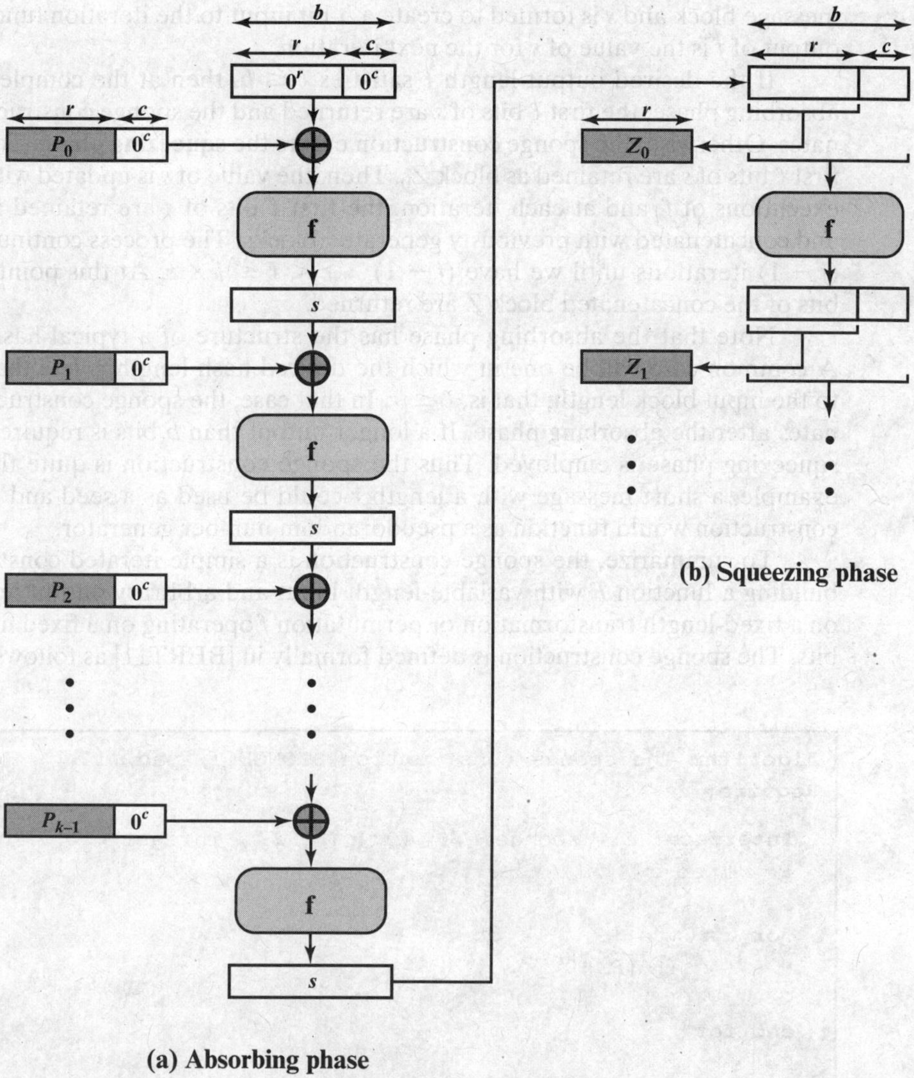

Figure 11.15 Sponge Construction

construction. The value c is referred to as the **capacity**. A discussion of the security implications of the capacity is beyond our scope. In essence, the capacity is a measure of the achievable complexity of the sponge construction and therefore the achievable level of security. A given implementation can trade claimed security for speed by increasing the capacity c and decreasing the bitrate r accordingly, or vice versa. The default values for Keccak are $c = 1024$ bits, $r = 576$ bits, and therefore $b = 1600$ bits.

The sponge construction consists of two phases. The **absorbing phase** proceeds as follows: For each iteration, the input block to be processed is padded with zeroes to extend its length from r bits to b bits. Then, the bitwise XOR of the extended message block and s is formed to create a b-bit input to the iteration function f. The output of f is the value of s for the next iteration.

If the desired output length ℓ satisfies $\ell \leq b$, then at the completion of the absorbing phase, the first ℓ bits of s are returned and the sponge construction terminates. Otherwise, the sponge construction enters the **squeezing phase**. To begin, the first ℓ bits of s are retained as block Z_0. Then, the value of s is updated with repeated executions of f, and at each iteration, the first ℓ bits of s are retained as block Z_i and concatenated with previously generated blocks. The process continues through $(j - 1)$ iterations until we have $(j - 1) \times r < \ell \leq j \times r$. At this point the first ℓ bits of the concatenated block Z are returned.

Note that the absorbing phase has the structure of a typical hash function. A common case will be one in which the desired hash length is less than or equal to the input block length; that is, $\ell \leq r$. In that case, the sponge construction terminates after the absorbing phase. If a longer output than b bits is required, then the squeezing phase is employed. Thus the sponge construction is quite flexible. For example, a short message with a length r could be used as a seed and the sponge construction would function as a pseudorandom number generator.

To summarize, the sponge construction is a simple iterated construction for building a function F with variable-length input and arbitrary output length based on a fixed-length transformation or permutation f operating on a fixed number b of bits. The sponge construction is defined formally in [BERT11] as follows:

```
Algorithm The sponge construction SPONGE[f, pad, r]
Require: r < b

  Interface: Z = sponge(M, ℓ) with M ∈ Z2*, integer ℓ > 0 and Z ∈ Z2^ℓ
  P = M || pad[r](|M|)
  s = 0^b
  for i = 0 to |P|r − 1 do
       s = s ⊕ (Pi || 0^(b−r))
       s = f(s)
  end for
  Z = ⌊s⌋r
  while |Z|r r < ℓ do
     s = f (s)
     Z = Z || ⌊s⌋r
  end while
  return ⌊Z⌋ℓ
```

In the algorithm definition, the following notation is used: $|M|$ is the length in bits of a bit string M. A bit string M can be considered as a sequence of blocks of some fixed length x, where the last block may be shorter. The number of blocks of M is denoted by $|M|_x$. The blocks of M are denoted by M_i and the index ranges from 0 to $|M|_x - 1$. The expression $\lfloor M \rfloor_\ell$ denotes the truncation of M to its first ℓ bits.

Table 11.5 SHA-3 Parameters

Message Digest Size	224	256	384	512
Message Size	no maximum	no maximum	no maximum	no maximum
Block Size (bitrate *r*)	1152	1088	832	576
Word Size	64	64	64	64
Number of Rounds	24	24	24	24
Capacity *c*	448	512	768	1024
Collision Resistance	2^{112}	2^{128}	2^{192}	2^{256}
Second Preimage Resistance	2^{224}	2^{256}	2^{384}	2^{512}

Note: All sizes and security levels—are measured in bits.

SHA-3 makes use of the iteration function f, labeled Keccak-f, which is described in the next section. The overall SHA-3 function is a sponge function expressed as Keccak$[r, c]$ to reflect that SHA-3 has two operational parameters, r, the message block size, and c, the capacity, with the default of $r + c = 1600$ bits. Table 11.5 shows the supported values of r and c. As Table 11.5 shows, the hash function security associated with the sponge construction is a function of the capacity c.

In terms of the sponge algorithm defined above, Keccak$[r, c]$ is defined as

$$\text{Keccak } [r, c] \triangleq \text{SPONGE } [\text{Keccak-}f\,[r + c], \text{pad } 10^*1, r]$$

We now turn to a discussion of the iteration function Keccak-f.

The SHA-3 Iteration Function f

We now examine the iteration function Keccak-f used to process each successive block of the input message. Recall that f takes as input a 1600-bit variable s consisting of r bits, corresponding to the message block size followed by c bits, referred to as the capacity. For internal processing within f, the input state variable s is organized as a $5 \times 5 \times 64$ array a. The 64-bit units are referred to as lanes. For our purposes, we generally use the notation $a[x, y, z]$ to refer to an individual bit with the state array. When we are more concerned with operations that affect entire lanes, we designate the 5×5 matrix as $L[x, y]$, where each entry in L is a 64-bit lane. The use of indices within this matrix is shown in Figure 11.16.[4] Thus, the columns are labeled $x = 0$ through $x = 4$, the rows are labeled $y = 0$ through $y = 4$, and the individual bits within a lane are labeled $z = 0$ through $z = 63$. The mapping between the bits of s and those of a is

$$s[64(5y + x) + z] = a[x, y, z]$$

[4]Note that the first index (x) designates a column and the second index (y) designates a row. This is in conflict with the convention used in most mathematics sources, where the first index designates a row and the second index designates a column (e.g., Knuth, D. *The Art of Computing Programming, Volume 1, Fundamental Algorithms*; and Korn, G., and Korn, T. *Mathematical Handbook for Scientists and Engineers*).

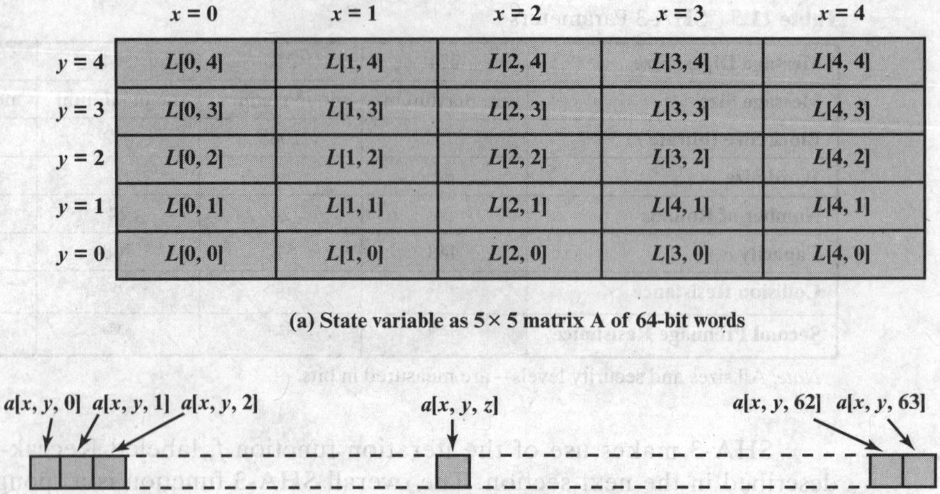

(a) State variable as 5× 5 matrix A of 64-bit words

(b) Bit labeling of 64-bit words

Figure 11.16 SHA-3 State Matrix

We can visualize this with respect to the matrix in Figure 11.16. When treating the state as a matrix of lanes, the first lane in the lower left corner, $L[0, 0]$, corresponds to the first 64 bits of *s*. The lane in the second column, lowest row, $L[1, 0]$, corresponds to the next 64 bits of *s*. Thus, the array *a* is filled with the bits of *s* starting with row $y = 0$ and proceeding row by row.

STRUCTURE OF f The function *f* is executed once for each input block of the message to be hashed. The function takes as input the 1600-bit state variable and converts it into a 5×5 matrix of 64-bit lanes. This matrix then passes through 24 rounds of processing. Each round consists of five steps, and each step updates the state matrix by permutation or substitution operations. As shown in Figure 11.17, the rounds are identical with the exception of the final step in each round, which is modified by a round constant that differs for each round.

The application of the five steps can be expressed as the composition[5] of functions:

$$R = \iota \circ \chi \circ \pi \circ \rho \circ \theta$$

Table 11.6 summarizes the operation of the five steps. The steps have a simple description leading to a specification that is compact and in which no trapdoor can be hidden. The operations on lanes in the specification are limited to bitwise Boolean operations (XOR, AND, NOT) and rotations. There is no need for table lookups, arithmetic operations, or data-dependent rotations. Thus, SHA-3 is easily and efficiently implemented in either hardware or software.

We examine each of the step functions in turn.

[5]If f and g are two functions, then the function F with the equation $y = F(x) = g[f(x)]$ is called the **composition** of f and g and is denoted as $F = g \circ f$.

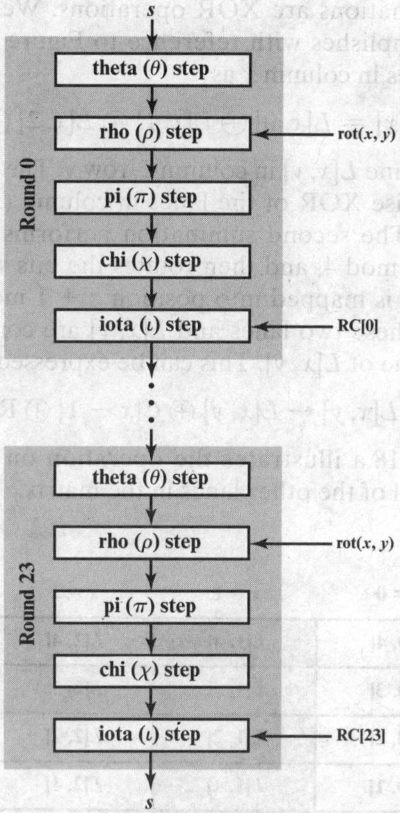

Figure 11.17 SHA-3 Iteration Function *f*

Table 11.6 Step Functions in SHA-3

Function	Type	Description
θ	Substitution	New value of each bit in each word depends on its current value and on one bit in each word of preceding column and one bit of each word in succeeding column.
ρ	Permutation	The bits of each word are permuted using a circular bit shift. $W[0, 0]$ is not affected.
π	Permutation	Words are permuted in the 5×5 matrix. $W[0, 0]$ is not affected.
χ	Substitution	New value of each bit in each word depends on its current value and on one bit in next word in the same row and one bit in the second next word in the same row.
ι	Substitution	$W[0, 0]$ is updated by XOR with a round constant.

THETA STEP FUNCTION The Keccak reference defines the θ function as follows. For bit z in column x, row y,

$$\theta: a[x, y, z] \leftarrow a[x, y, z] \oplus \sum_{y'=0}^{4} a[(x-1), y', z] \oplus \sum_{y'=0}^{4} a[(x+1), y', (z-1)] \quad \textbf{(11.1)}$$

where the summations are XOR operations. We can see more clearly what this operation accomplishes with reference to Figure 11.18a. First, define the bitwise XOR of the lanes in column x as

$$C[x] = L[x, 0] \oplus L[x, 1] \oplus L[x, 2] \oplus L[x, 3] \oplus L[x, 4]$$

Consider lane $L[x, y]$ in column x, row y. The first summation in Equation 11.1 performs a bitwise XOR of the lanes in column $(x - 1)$ mod 4 to form the 64-bit lane $C[x - 1]$. The second summation performs a bitwise XOR of the lanes in column $(x + 1)$ mod 4, and then rotates the bits within the 64-bit lane so that the bit in position z is mapped into position $z + 1$ mod 64. This forms the lane ROT $(C[x + 1], 1)$. These two lanes and $L[x, y]$ are combined by bitwise XOR to form the updated value of $L[x, y]$. This can be expressed as

$$L[x, y] \leftarrow L[x, y] \oplus C[x - 1] \oplus \text{ROT}(C[x + 1], 1)$$

Figure 11.18.a illustrates the operation on $L[3, 2]$. The same operation is performed on all of the other lanes in the matrix.

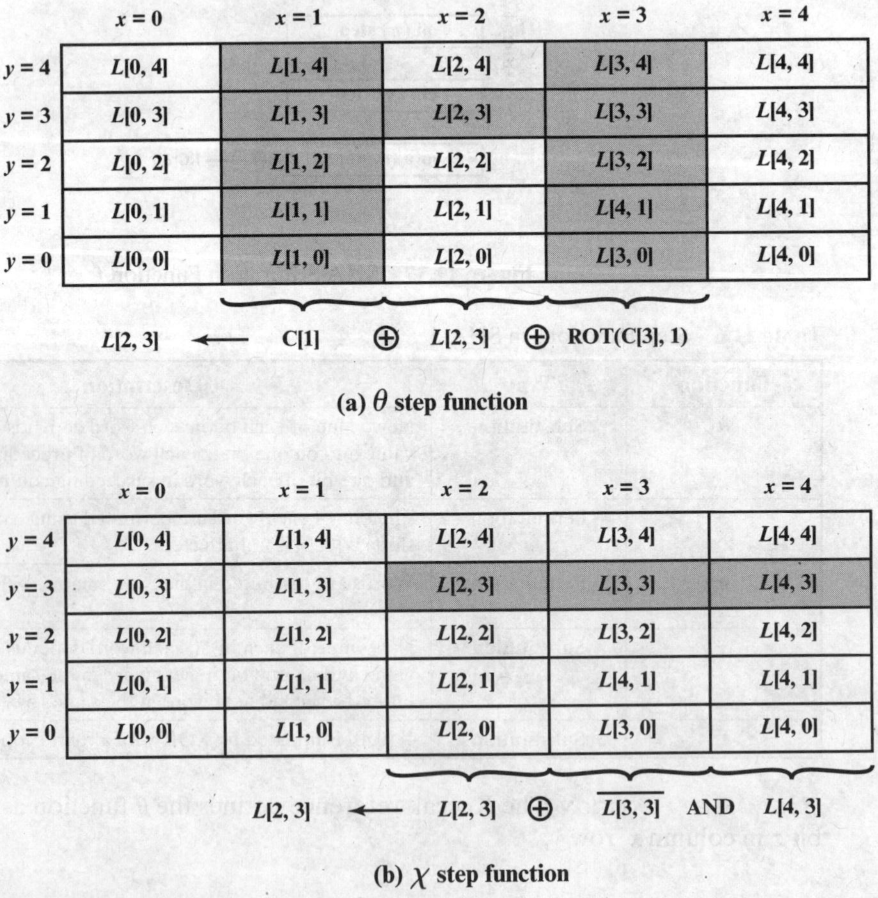

Figure 11.18 Theta and Chi Step Functions

Several observations are in order. Each bit in a lane is updated using the bit itself and one bit in the same bit position from each lane in the preceding column and one bit in the adjacent bit position from each lane in the succeeding column. Thus the updated value of each bit depends on 11 bits. This provides good mixing. Also, the theta step provides good diffusion, as that term was defined in Chapter 4. The designers of Keccak state that the theta step provides a high level of diffusion on average and that without theta, the round function would not provide diffusion of any significance.

RHO STEP FUNCTION The ρ function is defined as follows:

$$\rho: a[x, y, z] \leftarrow a[x, y, z] \quad \text{if } x = y = 0$$

otherwise,

$$\rho: a[x, y, z] \leftarrow a\left[x, y, \left(z - \frac{(t+1)(t+2)}{2}\right)\right] \quad \textbf{(11.2)}$$

with t satisfying $0 \leq t < 24$ and $\begin{pmatrix} 0 & 1 \\ 2 & 3 \end{pmatrix}^t \begin{pmatrix} 1 \\ 0 \end{pmatrix} = \begin{pmatrix} x \\ y \end{pmatrix}$ in $GF(5)^{2 \times 2}$

It is not immediately obvious what this step performs, so let us look at the process in detail.

1. The lane in position $(x, y) = (0, 0)$, that is $L[0, 0]$, is unaffected. For all other words, a circular bit shift within the lane is performed.
2. The variable t, with $0 \leq t < 24$, is used to determine both the amount of the circular bit shift and which lane is assigned which shift value.
3. The 24 individual bit shifts that are performed have the respective values $\frac{(t+1)(t+2)}{2} \bmod 64$.
4. The shift determined by the value of t is performed on the lane in position (x, y) in the 5×5 matrix of lanes. Specifically, for each value of t, the corresponding matrix position is defined by $\begin{pmatrix} x \\ y \end{pmatrix} = \begin{pmatrix} 0 & 1 \\ 2 & 3 \end{pmatrix}^t \begin{pmatrix} 1 \\ 0 \end{pmatrix}$. For example, for $t = 3$, we have

$$\begin{pmatrix} x \\ y \end{pmatrix} = \begin{pmatrix} 0 & 1 \\ 2 & 3 \end{pmatrix}^3 \begin{pmatrix} 1 \\ 0 \end{pmatrix} \bmod 5$$

$$= \begin{pmatrix} 0 & 1 \\ 2 & 3 \end{pmatrix}\begin{pmatrix} 0 & 1 \\ 2 & 3 \end{pmatrix}\begin{pmatrix} 0 & 1 \\ 2 & 3 \end{pmatrix}\begin{pmatrix} 1 \\ 0 \end{pmatrix} \bmod 5$$

$$= \begin{pmatrix} 0 & 1 \\ 2 & 3 \end{pmatrix}\begin{pmatrix} 0 & 1 \\ 2 & 3 \end{pmatrix}\begin{pmatrix} 0 \\ 2 \end{pmatrix} \bmod 5$$

$$= \begin{pmatrix} 0 & 1 \\ 2 & 3 \end{pmatrix}\begin{pmatrix} 2 \\ 6 \end{pmatrix} \bmod 5 = \begin{pmatrix} 0 & 1 \\ 2 & 3 \end{pmatrix}\begin{pmatrix} 2 \\ 1 \end{pmatrix} \bmod 5$$

$$= \begin{pmatrix} 1 \\ 7 \end{pmatrix} \bmod 5 = \begin{pmatrix} 1 \\ 2 \end{pmatrix}$$

Table 11.7 Rotation Values Used in SHA-3

(a) Calculation of values and positions

t	g(t)	g (t) mod 64	x, y	t	g(t)	g (t) mod 64	x, y
0	1	1	1, 0	12	91	27	4, 0
1	3	3	0, 2	13	105	41	0, 3
2	6	6	2, 1	14	120	56	3, 4
3	10	10	1, 2	15	136	8	4, 3
4	15	15	2, 3	16	153	25	3, 2
5	21	21	3, 3	17	171	43	2, 2
6	28	28	3, 0	18	190	62	2, 0
7	36	36	0, 1	19	210	18	0, 4
8	45	45	1, 3	20	231	39	4, 2
9	55	55	3, 1	21	253	61	2, 4
10	66	2	1, 4	22	276	20	4, 1
11	78	14	4, 4	23	300	44	1, 1

Note: $g(t) = (t + 1)(t + 2)/2$

$$\begin{pmatrix} x \\ y \end{pmatrix} = \begin{pmatrix} 0 & 1 \\ 2 & 3 \end{pmatrix}^t \begin{pmatrix} 1 \\ 0 \end{pmatrix} \text{mod } 5$$

(b) Rotation values by word position in matrix

	$x = 0$	$x = 1$	$x = 2$	$x = 3$	$x = 4$
$y = 4$	18	2	61	56	14
$y = 3$	41	45	15	21	8
$y = 2$	3	10	43	25	39
$y = 1$	36	44	6	55	20
$y = 0$	0	1	62	28	27

Table 11.7 shows the calculations that are performed to determine the amount of the bit shift and the location of each bit shift value. Note that all of the rotation amounts are different.

The ρ function thus consists of a simple permutation (circular shift) within each lane. The intent is to provide diffusion within each lane. Without this function, diffusion between lanes would be very slow.

PI STEP FUNCTION The π function is defined as follows:

$$\pi: \quad a[x, y] \leftarrow a[x', y'], \quad with \begin{pmatrix} x \\ y \end{pmatrix} = \begin{pmatrix} 0 & 1 \\ 2 & 3 \end{pmatrix} \begin{pmatrix} x' \\ y' \end{pmatrix} \qquad \textbf{(11.3)}$$

This can be rewritten as $(x, y) \times (y, (2x + 3y))$. Thus, the lanes within the 5×5 matrix are moved so that the new x position equals the old y position and the

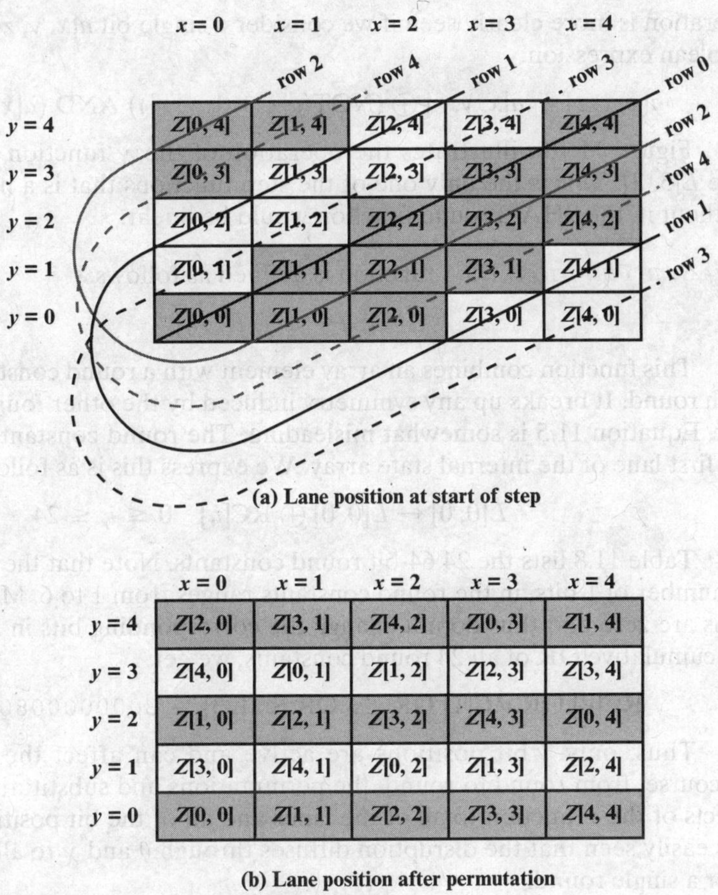

Figure 11.19 Pi Step Function

new y position is determined by $(2x + 3y) \bmod 5$. Figure 11.19 helps in visualizing this permutation. Lanes that are along the same diagonal (increasing in y value, going from left to right) prior to π are arranged on the same row in the matrix after π is executed. Note that the position of $L[0, 0]$ is unchanged.

Thus the π step is a permutation of lanes: The lanes move position within the 5×5 matrix. The ρ step is a permutation of bits: Bits within a lane are rotated. Note that the π step matrix positions are calculated in the same way that, for the ρ step, the one-dimensional sequence of rotation constants is mapped to the lanes of the matrix.

Chi Step Function The χ function is defined as follows:

$$\chi: a[x] \leftarrow a[x] \oplus ((a[x + 1] \oplus 1) \text{ AND } a[x + 2]) \qquad \textbf{(11.4)}$$

This function operates to update each bit based on its current value and the value of the corresponding bit position in the next two lanes in the same row. The operation is more clearly seen if we consider a single bit $a[x, y, z]$ and write out the Boolean expression:

$$a[x, y, z] \leftarrow a[x, y, z] \oplus (\text{NOT}(a[x + 1, y, z])) \text{ AND } (a[x + 2, y, z])$$

Figure 11.18b illustrates the operation of the χ function on the bits of the lane $L[3, 2]$. This is the only one of the step functions that is a nonlinear mapping. Without it, the SHA-3 round function would be linear.

Iota Step Function The ι function is defined as follows:

$$\iota: a \leftarrow a \oplus RC[i_r] \quad \textbf{(11.5)}$$

This function combines an array element with a round constant that differs for each round. It breaks up any symmetry induced by the other four step functions. In fact, Equation 11.5 is somewhat misleading. The round constant is applied only to the first lane of the internal state array. We express this is as follows:

$$L[0, 0] \leftarrow L[0, 0] \oplus \text{RC}[i_r] \quad 0 \le i_r \le 24$$

Table 11.8 lists the 24 64-bit round constants. Note that the Hamming weight, or number of 1 bits, in the round constants ranges from 1 to 6. Most of the bit positions are zero and thus do not change the corresponding bits in $L[0, 0]$. If we take the cumulative OR of all 24 round constants, we get

$$\text{RC}[0] \text{ OR } \text{RC}[1] \text{ OR} \ldots \text{ OR } \text{RC}[23] = \texttt{800000008000808B}$$

Thus, only 7 bit positions are active and can affect the value of $L[0, 0]$. Of course, from round to round, the permutations and substitutions propagate the effects of the ι function to all of the lanes and all of the bit positions in the matrix. It is easily seen that the disruption diffuses through θ and χ to all lanes of the state after a single round.

Table 11.8 Round Constants in SHA-3

Round	Constant (hexadecimal)	Number of 1 bits	Round	Constant (hexadecimal)	Number of 1 bits
0	0000000000000001	1	12	000000008000808B	6
1	0000000000008082	3	13	800000000000008B	5
2	800000000000808A	5	14	8000000000008089	5
3	8000000080008000	3	15	8000000000008003	4
4	000000000000808B	5	16	8000000000008002	3
5	0000000080000001	2	17	8000000000000080	2
6	8000000080008081	5	18	000000000000800A	3
7	8000000000008009	4	19	800000008000000A	4
8	000000000000008A	3	20	8000000080008081	5
9	0000000000000088	2	21	8000000000008080	3
10	0000000080008009	4	22	0000000080000001	2
11	000000008000000A	3	23	8000000080008008	4

11.7 KEY TERMS, REVIEW QUESTIONS, AND PROBLEMS

Key Terms

absorbing phase	Iota step function	Rho step function
big endian	Keccak	second preimage resistant
birthday attack	keyed hash function	SHA-1
birthday paradox	lane	SHA-224
bitrate	little endian	SHA-256
capacity	MD4	SHA-3
Chi step function	MD5	SHA-384
collision resistant	message authentication code (MAC)	SHA-512
compression function	message digest	sponge construction
cryptographic hash function	one-way hash function	squeezing phase
hash code	Pi step function	strong collision resistance
hash function	preimage resistant	Theta step function
hash value		weak collision resistance

Review Questions

11.1 What characteristics are needed in a secure hash function?

11.2 What is the difference between a weak and strong hash function?

11.3 What is the role of a compression function in a hash function?

11.4 What is the size of message, block, word and message digest in different versions of SHA?

11.5 What basic arithmetical and logical functions are used in SHA?

11.6 List the requirements that must be satisfied by any candidate for SHA-3.

11.7 Define the term *sponge construction*.

11.8 Briefly describe the internal structure of the iteration function *f*.

11.9 What is the difference between Rho (ρ) and Pi (π) step function of the iteration function *f*?

Problems

11.1 The high-speed transport protocol XTP (Xpress Transfer Protocol) uses a 32-bit checksum function defined as the concatenation of two 16-bit functions: XOR and RXOR, defined in Section 11.4 as "two simple hash functions" and illustrated in Figure 11.5.

a. Will this checksum detect all errors caused by an odd number of error bits? Explain.

b. Will this checksum detect all errors caused by an even number of error bits? If not, characterize the error patterns that will cause the checksum to fail.

c. Comment on the effectiveness of this function for use as a hash function for authentication.

11.2 **a.** Consider the Davies and Price hash code scheme described in Section 11.4 and assume that DES is used as the encryption algorithm:

$$H_i = H_{i-1} \oplus \mathrm{E}(M_i, \mathrm{H}_{i-1})$$

Recall the complementarity property of DES (Problem 3.14): If $Y = E(K, X)$, then $Y' = E(K', X')$. Use this property to show how a message consisting of blocks $M_1, M_2, \ldots, M_N$ can be altered without altering its hash code.

b. Show that a similar attack will succeed against the scheme proposed in [MEYE88]:

$$H_i = M_i \oplus E(H_{i-1}, M_i)$$

11.3 **a.** Consider the following hash function. Messages are in the form of a sequence of numbers in Z_n, $M = (a_1, a_2, \ldots a_t)$. The hash value h is calculated as $\left(\sum_{i=1}^{t} a_i\right)$ for some predefined value n. Does this hash function satisfy any of the requirements for a hash function listed in Table 11.1? Explain your answer.

b. Repeat part (a) for the hash function $h = \left(\sum_{i=1}^{t} (a_i)^2\right) \bmod n$.

c. Calculate the hash function of part (b) for $M = (189, 632, 900, 722, 349)$ and $n = 989$.

11.4 It is possible to use a hash function to construct a block cipher with a structure similar to DES. Because a hash function is one way and a block cipher must be reversible (to decrypt), how is it possible?

11.5 Now consider the opposite problem: using an encryption algorithm to construct a one-way hash function. Consider using RSA with a known key. Then process a message consisting of a sequence of blocks as follows: Encrypt the first block, XOR the result with the second block and encrypt again, etc. Show that this scheme is not secure by solving the following problem. Given a two-block message B1, B2, and its hash

$$\text{RSAH}(B_1, B_2) = \text{RSA}(\text{RSA}(B1) \oplus B2)$$

Given an arbitrary block C1, choose C2 so that RSAH(C1, C2) = RSAH(B1, B2). Thus, the hash function does not satisfy weak collision resistance.

11.6 Suppose H(m) is a collision-resistant hash function that maps a message of arbitrary bit length into an n-bit hash value. Is it true that, for all messages x, x' with $x \neq x'$, we have $H(x) \neq H(x')$ Explain your answer.

11.7 In Figure 11.12, it is assumed that an array of 80 64-bit words is available to store the values of W_t, so that they can be precomputed at the beginning of the processing of a block. Now assume that space is at a premium. As an alternative, consider the use of a 16-word circular buffer that is initially loaded with W_0 through W_{15}. Design an algorithm that, for each step t, computes the required input value W_t.

11.8 For SHA-512, show the equations for the values of W_{16}, W_{17}, W_{18}, and W_{19}.

11.9 State the value of the padding field in SHA-512 if the length of the message is
a. 5118 bits
b. 5119 bits
c. 5120 bits

11.10 State the value of the length field in SHA-512 if the length of the message is
a. 5118 bits
b. 5119 bits
c. 5120 bits

11.11 Suppose $a_1a_2a_3a_4$ are the 4 bytes in a 32-bit word. Each a_i can be viewed as an integer in the range 0 to 255, represented in binary. In a big-endian architecture, this word represents the integer

$$a_1 2^{24} + a_2 2^{16} + a_3 2^8 + a_4$$

In a little-endian architecture, this word represents the integer

$$a_4 2^{24} + a_3 2^{16} + a_2 2^8 + a_1$$

a. Some hash functions, such as MD5, assume a little-endian architecture. It is important that the message digest be independent of the underlying architecture. Therefore, to perform the modulo 2 addition operation of MD5 or RIPEMD-160 on a big-endian architecture, an adjustment must be made. Suppose $X = x_1\, x_2\, x_3\, x_4$ and $Y = y_1\, y_2\, y_3\, y_4$. Show how the MD5 addition operation $(X + Y)$ would be carried out on a big-endian machine.

b. SHA assumes a big-endian architecture. Show how the operation $(X + Y)$ for SHA would be carried out on a little-endian machine.

11.12 This problem introduces a hash function similar in spirit to SHA that operates on letters instead of binary data. It is called the *toy tetragraph hash* (tth).[6] Given a message consisting of a sequence of letters, tth produces a hash value consisting of four letters. First, tth divides the message into blocks of 16 letters, ignoring spaces, punctuation, and capitalization. If the message length is not divisible by 16, it is padded out with nulls. A four-number running total is maintained that starts out with the value (0, 0, 0, 0); this is input to the compression function for processing the first block. The compression function consists of two rounds.

Round 1 Get the next block of text and arrange it as a row-wise 4 × 4 block of text and convert it to numbers ($A = 0, B = 1$, etc.). For example, for the block ABCDEFGHIJKLMNOP, we have

A	B	C	D
E	F	G	H
I	J	K	L
M	N	O	P

0	1	2	3
4	5	6	7
8	9	10	11
12	13	14	15

Then, add each column mod 26 and add the result to the running total, mod 26. In this example, the running total is (24, 2, 6, 10).

Round 2 Using the matrix from round 1, rotate the first row left by 1, second row left by 2, third row left by 3, and reverse the order of the fourth row.
In our example:

B	C	D	A
G	H	E	F
L	I	J	K
P	O	N	M

1	2	3	0
6	7	4	5
11	8	9	10
15	14	13	12

Now, add each column mod 26 and add the result to the running total. The new running total is (5, 7, 9, 11). This running total is now the input into the first round of the compression function for the next block of text. After the final block is processed, convert the final running total to letters. For example, if the message is ABCDEFGHIJKLMNOP, then the hash is FHJL.

---

[6]I thank William K. Mason, of the magazine staff of *The Cryptogram*, for providing this example.

a. Draw figures comparable to Figures 11.9 and 11.10 to depict the overall tth logic and the compression function logic.

b. Calculate the hash function for the 22-letter message "Practice makes us perfect."

c. To demonstrate the weakness of tth, find a message of length 32-letter to produces the same hash.

11.13 For each of the possible capacity values of SHA-3 (Table 11.5), which lanes in the internal 55 state matrix start out as lanes of all zeros?

11.14 Consider the SHA-3 option with a block size of 1024 bits and assume that each of the lanes in the first message block (P_0) has at least one nonzero bit. To start, all of the lanes in the internal state matrix that correspond to the capacity portion of the initial state are all zeros. Show how long it will take before all of these lanes have at least one nonzero bit. *Note:* Ignore the permutation. That is, keep track of the original zero lanes even after they have changed position in the matrix.

11.15 Consider the state matrix as illustrated in Figure 11.16a. Now rearrange the rows and columns of the matrix so that $L[0, 0]$ is in the center. Specifically, arrange the columns in the left-to-right order ($x = 3, x = 4, x = 0, x = 1, x = 2$) and arrange the rows in the top-to-bottom order ($y = 2, y = 1, y = 0, y = 4, y = 6$). This should give you some insight into the permutation algorithm used for the function and for permuting the rotation constants in the function. Using this rearranged matrix, describe the permutation algorithm.

11.16 The function only affects $L[0, 0]$. Section 11.6 states that the changes to $L[0, 0]$ diffuse through θ and to all lanes of the state after a single round.

a. Show that this is so.

b. How long before all of the bit positions in the matrix are affected by the changes to $L[0, 0]$?

CHAPTER 12

MESSAGE AUTHENTICATION CODES

LEARNING OBJECTIVES

After studying this chapter, you should be able to:

- List and explain the possible attacks that are relevant to message authentication.
- Define the term *message authentication code.*
- List and explain the requirements for a message authentication code.
- Present an overview of HMAC.
- Present an overview of CMAC.
- Explain the concept of authenticated encryption.
- Present an overview of CCM.
- Present an overview of GCM.
- Discuss the concept of key wrapping and explain its use.
- Understand how a hash function or a message authentication code can be used for pseudorandom number generation.

One of the most fascinating and complex areas of cryptography is that of message authentication and the related area of digital signatures. It would be impossible, in anything less than book length, to exhaust all the cryptographic functions and protocols that have been proposed or implemented for message authentication and digital signatures. Instead, the purpose of this chapter and the next is to provide a broad overview of the subject and to develop a systematic means of describing the various approaches.

This chapter begins with an introduction to the requirements for authentication and digital signature and the types of attacks to be countered. Then the basic approaches are surveyed. The remainder of the chapter deals with the fundamental approach to message authentication known as the message authentication code (MAC). Following an overview of this topic, the chapter looks at security considerations for MACs. This is followed by a discussion of specific MACs in two categories: those built from cryptographic hash functions and those built using a block cipher mode of operation. Next, we look at a relatively recent approach known as authenticated encryption. Finally, we look at the use of cryptographic hash functions and MACs for pseudorandom number generation.

12.1 MESSAGE AUTHENTICATION REQUIREMENTS

In the context of communications across a network, the following attacks can be identified.

1. **Disclosure:** Release of message contents to any person or process not possessing the appropriate cryptographic key.

2. **Traffic analysis:** Discovery of the pattern of traffic between parties. In a connection-oriented application, the frequency and duration of connections could be determined. In either a connection-oriented or connectionless environment, the number and length of messages between parties could be determined.
3. **Masquerade:** Insertion of messages into the network from a fraudulent source. This includes the creation of messages by an opponent that are purported to come from an authorized entity. Also included are fraudulent acknowledgments of message receipt or nonreceipt by someone other than the message recipient.
4. **Content modification:** Changes to the contents of a message, including insertion, deletion, transposition, and modification.
5. **Sequence modification:** Any modification to a sequence of messages between parties, including insertion, deletion, and reordering.
6. **Timing modification:** Delay or replay of messages. In a connection-oriented application, an entire session or sequence of messages could be a replay of some previous valid session, or individual messages in the sequence could be delayed or replayed. In a connectionless application, an individual message (e.g., datagram) could be delayed or replayed.
7. **Source repudiation:** Denial of transmission of message by source.
8. **Destination repudiation:** Denial of receipt of message by destination.

Measures to deal with the first two attacks are in the realm of message confidentiality and are dealt with in Part One. Measures to deal with items (3) through (6) in the foregoing list are generally regarded as message authentication. Mechanisms for dealing specifically with item (7) come under the heading of digital signatures. Generally, a digital signature technique will also counter some or all of the attacks listed under items (3) through (6). Dealing with item (8) may require a combination of the use of digital signatures and a protocol designed to counter this attack.

In summary, message authentication is a procedure to verify that received messages come from the alleged source and have not been altered. Message authentication may also verify sequencing and timeliness. A digital signature is an authentication technique that also includes measures to counter repudiation by the source.

12.2 MESSAGE AUTHENTICATION FUNCTIONS

Any message authentication or digital signature mechanism has two levels of functionality. At the lower level, there must be some sort of function that produces an authenticator: a value to be used to authenticate a message. This lower-level function is then used as a primitive in a higher-level authentication protocol that enables a receiver to verify the authenticity of a message.

This section is concerned with the types of functions that may be used to produce an authenticator. These may be grouped into three classes.

- **Hash function:** A function that maps a message of any length into a fixed-length hash value, which serves as the authenticator
- **Message encryption:** The ciphertext of the entire message serves as its authenticator
- **Message authentication code (MAC):** A function of the message and a secret key that produces a fixed-length value that serves as the authenticator

Hash functions, and how they may serve for message authentication, are discussed in Chapter 11. The remainder of this section briefly examines the remaining two topics. The remainder of the chapter elaborates on the topic of MACs.

Message Encryption

Message encryption by itself can provide a measure of authentication. The analysis differs for symmetric and public-key encryption schemes.

Symmetric Encryption Consider the straightforward use of symmetric encryption (Figure 12.1a). A message *M* transmitted from source A to destination B is encrypted using a secret key *K* shared by A and B. If no other party knows the key, then confidentiality is provided: No other party can recover the plaintext of the message.

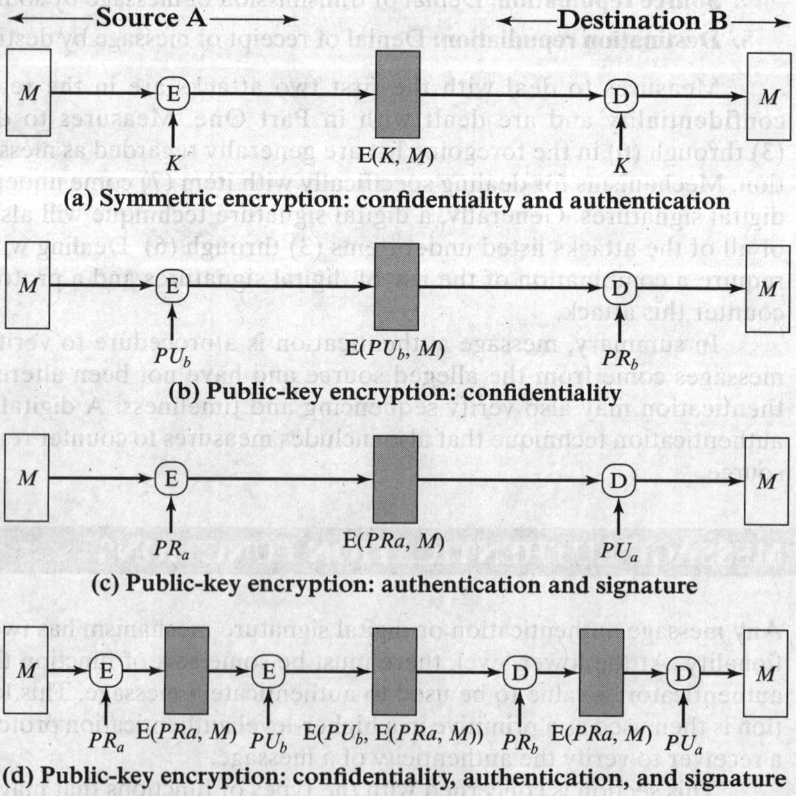

Figure 12.1 Basic Uses of Message Encryption

In addition, B is assured that the message was generated by A. Why? The message must have come from A, because A is the only other party that possesses K and therefore the only other party with the information necessary to construct ciphertext that can be decrypted with K. Furthermore, if M is recovered, B knows that none of the bits of M have been altered, because an opponent that does not know K would not know how to alter bits in the ciphertext to produce the desired changes in the plaintext.

So we may say that symmetric encryption provides authentication as well as confidentiality. However, this flat statement needs to be qualified. Consider exactly what is happening at B. Given a decryption function D and a secret key K, the destination will accept *any* input X and produce output $Y = D(K, X)$. If X is the ciphertext of a legitimate message M produced by the corresponding encryption function, then Y is some plaintext message M. Otherwise, Y will likely be a meaningless sequence of bits. There may need to be some automated means of determining at B whether Y is legitimate plaintext and therefore must have come from A.

The implications of the line of reasoning in the preceding paragraph are profound from the point of view of authentication. Suppose the message M can be any arbitrary bit pattern. In that case, there is no way to determine automatically, at the destination, whether an incoming message is the ciphertext of a legitimate message. This conclusion is incontrovertible: If M can be any bit pattern, then regardless of the value of X, the value $Y = \mathrm{D}(K, X)$ is *some* bit pattern and therefore must be accepted as authentic plaintext.

Thus, in general, we require that only a small subset of all possible bit patterns be considered legitimate plaintext. In that case, any spurious ciphertext is unlikely to produce legitimate plaintext. For example, suppose that only one bit pattern in 10^6 is legitimate plaintext. Then the probability that any randomly chosen bit pattern, treated as ciphertext, will produce a legitimate plaintext message is only 10^{-6}.

For a number of applications and encryption schemes, the desired conditions prevail as a matter of course. For example, suppose that we are transmitting English-language messages using a Caesar cipher with a shift of one (K = 1). A sends the following legitimate ciphertext:

```
nbsftfbupbutboeepftfbupbutboemjuumfmbnctfbujwz
```

B decrypts to produce the following plaintext:

```
mareseatoatsanddoeseatoatsandlittlelambseativy
```

A simple frequency analysis confirms that this message has the profile of ordinary English. On the other hand, if an opponent generates the following random sequence of letters:

```
zuvrsoevgqxlzwigamdvnmhpmccxiuureosfbcebtqxsxq
```

this decrypts to

```
ytuqrndufpwkyvhfzlcumlgolbbwhttqdnreabdaspwrwp
```

which does not fit the profile of ordinary English.

It may be difficult to determine *automatically* if incoming ciphertext decrypts to intelligible plaintext. If the plaintext is, say, a binary object file or digitized X-rays, determination of properly formed and therefore authentic plaintext may be difficult. Thus, an opponent could achieve a certain level of disruption simply by issuing messages with random content purporting to come from a legitimate user.

One solution to this problem is to force the plaintext to have some structure that is easily recognized but that cannot be replicated without recourse to the encryption function. We could, for example, append an error-detecting code, also known as a frame check sequence (FCS) or checksum, to each message before encryption, as illustrated in Figure 12.2a. A prepares a plaintext message M and then provides this as input to a function F that produces an FCS. The FCS is appended to M and the entire block is then encrypted. At the destination, B decrypts the incoming block and treats the results as a message with an appended FCS. B applies the same function F to attempt to reproduce the FCS. If the calculated FCS is equal to the incoming FCS, then the message is considered authentic. It is unlikely that any random sequence of bits would exhibit the desired relationship.

Note that the order in which the FCS and encryption functions are performed is critical. The sequence illustrated in Figure 12.2a is referred to in [DIFF79] as **internal error control**, which the authors contrast with **external error control** (Figure 12.2b). With internal error control, authentication is provided because an opponent would have difficulty generating ciphertext that, when decrypted, would have valid error control bits. If instead the FCS is the outer code, an opponent can construct messages with valid error-control codes. Although the opponent cannot know what the decrypted plaintext will be, he or she can still hope to create confusion and disrupt operations.

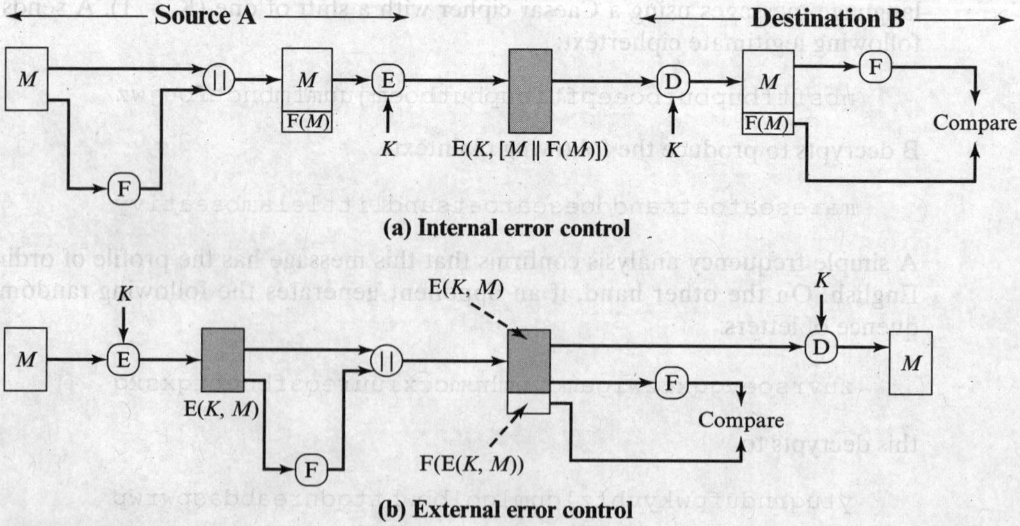

Figure 12.2 Internal and External Error Control

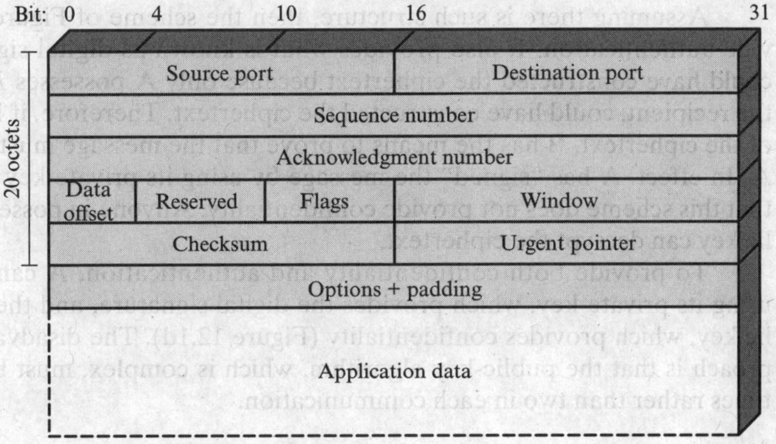

Figure 12.3 TCP Segment

An error-control code is just one example; in fact, any sort of structuring added to the transmitted message serves to strengthen the authentication capability. Such structure is provided by the use of a communications architecture consisting of layered protocols. As an example, consider the structure of messages transmitted using the TCP/IP protocol architecture. Figure 12.3 shows the format of a TCP segment, illustrating the TCP header. Now suppose that each pair of hosts shared a unique secret key, so that all exchanges between a pair of hosts used the same key, regardless of application. Then we could simply encrypt all of the datagram except the IP header. Again, if an opponent substituted some arbitrary bit pattern for the encrypted TCP segment, the resulting plaintext would not include a meaningful header. In this case, the header includes not only a checksum (which covers the header) but also other useful information, such as the sequence number. Because successive TCP segments on a given connection are numbered sequentially, encryption assures that an opponent does not delay, misorder, or delete any segments.

Public-Key Encryption The straightforward use of public-key encryption (Figure 12.1b) provides confidentiality but not authentication. The source (A) uses the public key PU_b of the destination (B) to encrypt M. Because only B has the corresponding private key PR_b, only B can decrypt the message. This scheme provides no authentication, because any opponent could also use B's public key to encrypt a message and claim to be A.

To provide authentication, A uses its private key to encrypt the message, and B uses A's public key to decrypt (Figure 12.1c). This provides authentication using the same type of reasoning as in the symmetric encryption case: The message must have come from A because A is the only party that possesses PR_a and therefore the only party with the information necessary to construct ciphertext that can be decrypted with PU_a. Again, the same reasoning as before applies: There must be some internal structure to the plaintext so that the receiver can distinguish between well-formed plaintext and random bits.

Assuming there is such structure, then the scheme of Figure 12.1c does provide authentication. It also provides what is known as digital signature.[1] Only A could have constructed the ciphertext because only A possesses PR_a. Not even B, the recipient, could have constructed the ciphertext. Therefore, if B is in possession of the ciphertext, B has the means to prove that the message must have come from A. In effect, A has "signed" the message by using its private key to encrypt. Note that this scheme does not provide confidentiality. Anyone in possession of A's public key can decrypt the ciphertext.

To provide both confidentiality and authentication, A can encrypt M first using its private key, which provides the digital signature, and then using B's public key, which provides confidentiality (Figure 12.1d). The disadvantage of this approach is that the public-key algorithm, which is complex, must be exercised four times rather than two in each communication.

Message Authentication Code

An alternative authentication technique involves the use of a secret key to generate a small fixed-size block of data, known as a **cryptographic checksum** or MAC, that is appended to the message. This technique assumes that two communicating parties, say A and B, share a common secret key K. When A has a message to send to B, it calculates the MAC as a function of the message and the key:

$$\text{MAC} = \text{C}(K, M)$$

where

M = input message
C = MAC function
K = shared secret key
MAC = message authentication code

The message plus MAC are transmitted to the intended recipient. The recipient performs the same calculation on the received message, using the same secret key, to generate a new MAC. The received MAC is compared to the calculated MAC (Figure 12.4a). If we assume that only the receiver and the sender know the identity of the secret key, and if the received MAC matches the calculated MAC, then

1. The receiver is assured that the message has not been altered. If an attacker alters the message but does not alter the MAC, then the receiver's calculation of the MAC will differ from the received MAC. Because the attacker is assumed not to know the secret key, the attacker cannot alter the MAC to correspond to the alterations in the message.
2. The receiver is assured that the message is from the alleged sender. Because no one else knows the secret key, no one else could prepare a message with a proper MAC.

[1]This is not the way in which digital signatures are constructed, as we shall see, but the principle is the same.

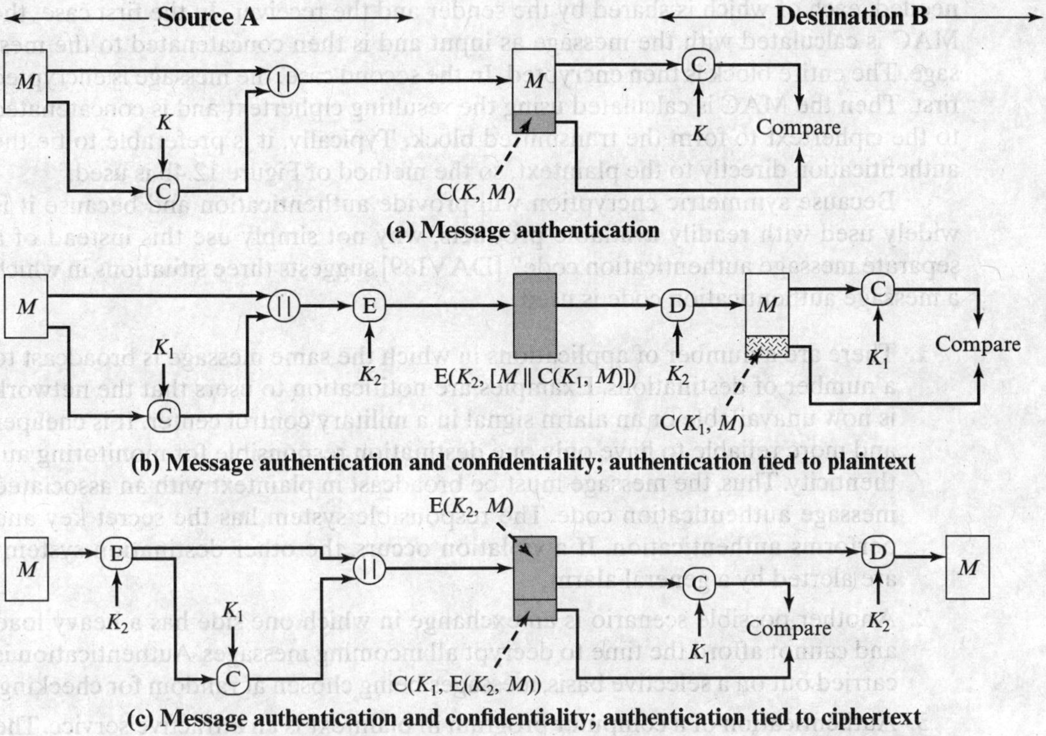

Figure 12.4 Basic Uses of Message Authentication code (MAC)

3. If the message includes a sequence number (such as is used with HDLC, X.25, and TCP), then the receiver can be assured of the proper sequence because an attacker cannot successfully alter the sequence number.

A MAC function is similar to encryption. One difference is that the MAC algorithm need not be reversible, as it must be for decryption. In general, the MAC function is a many-to-one function. The domain of the function consists of messages of some arbitrary length, whereas the range consists of all possible MACs and all possible keys. If an n-bit MAC is used, then there are 2^n possible MACs, whereas there are N possible messages with $N \gg 2^n$. Furthermore, with a k-bit key, there are 2^k possible keys.

For example, suppose that we are using 100-bit messages and a 10-bit MAC. Then, there are a total of 2^{100} different messages but only 2^{10} different MACs. So, on average, each MAC value is generated by a total of $2^{100}/2^{10} = 2^{90}$ different messages. If a 5-bit key is used, then there are $2^5 = 32$ different mappings from the set of messages to the set of MAC values.

It turns out that, because of the mathematical properties of the authentication function, it is less vulnerable to being broken than encryption.

The process depicted in Figure 12.4a provides authentication but not confidentiality, because the message as a whole is transmitted in the clear. Confidentiality can be provided by performing message encryption either after (Figure 12.4b) or before (Figure 12.4c) the MAC algorithm. In both these cases, two separate keys are needed, each of which is shared by the sender and the receiver. In the first case, the MAC is calculated with the message as input and is then concatenated to the message. The entire block is then encrypted. In the second case, the message is encrypted first. Then the MAC is calculated using the resulting ciphertext and is concatenated to the ciphertext to form the transmitted block. Typically, it is preferable to tie the authentication directly to the plaintext, so the method of Figure 12.4b is used.

Because symmetric encryption will provide authentication and because it is widely used with readily available products, why not simply use this instead of a separate message authentication code? [DAVI89] suggests three situations in which a message authentication code is used.

1. There are a number of applications in which the same message is broadcast to a number of destinations. Examples are notification to users that the network is now unavailable or an alarm signal in a military control center. It is cheaper and more reliable to have only one destination responsible for monitoring authenticity. Thus, the message must be broadcast in plaintext with an associated message authentication code. The responsible system has the secret key and performs authentication. If a violation occurs, the other destination systems are alerted by a general alarm.
2. Another possible scenario is an exchange in which one side has a heavy load and cannot afford the time to decrypt all incoming messages. Authentication is carried out on a selective basis, messages being chosen at random for checking.
3. Authentication of a computer program in plaintext is an attractive service. The computer program can be executed without having to decrypt it every time, which would be wasteful of processor resources. However, if a message authentication code were attached to the program, it could be checked whenever assurance was required of the integrity of the program.

Three other rationales may be added.

4. For some applications, it may not be of concern to keep messages secret, but it is important to authenticate messages. An example is the Simple Network Management Protocol Version 3 (SNMPv3), which separates the functions of confidentiality and authentication. For this application, it is usually important for a managed system to authenticate incoming SNMP messages, particularly if the message contains a command to change parameters at the managed system. On the other hand, it may not be necessary to conceal the SNMP traffic.
5. Separation of authentication and confidentiality functions affords architectural flexibility. For example, it may be desired to perform authentication at the application level but to provide confidentiality at a lower level, such as the transport layer.
6. A user may wish to prolong the period of protection beyond the time of reception and yet allow processing of message contents. With message encryption, the protection is lost when the message is decrypted, so the message is protected against fraudulent modifications only in transit but not within the target system.

Finally, note that the MAC does not provide a digital signature, because both sender and receiver share the same key.

12.3 REQUIREMENTS FOR MESSAGE AUTHENTICATION CODES

A MAC, also known as a cryptographic checksum, is generated by a function C of the form

$$T = \text{MAC}(K, M)$$

where M is a variable-length message, K is a secret key shared only by sender and receiver, and MAC(K, M) is the fixed-length authenticator, sometimes called a **tag**. The tag is appended to the message at the source at a time when the message is assumed or known to be correct. The receiver authenticates that message by recomputing the tag.

When an entire message is encrypted for confidentiality, using either symmetric or asymmetric encryption, the security of the scheme generally depends on the bit length of the key. Barring some weakness in the algorithm, the opponent must resort to a brute-force attack using all possible keys. On average, such an attack will require $2^{(k-1)}$ attempts for a k-bit key. In particular, for a ciphertext-only attack, the opponent, given ciphertext C, performs $P_i = \text{D}(K_i, C)$ for all possible key values K_i until a P_i is produced that matches the form of acceptable plaintext.

In the case of a MAC, the considerations are entirely different. In general, the MAC function is a many-to-one function, due to the many-to-one nature of the function. Using brute-force methods, how would an opponent attempt to discover a key? If confidentiality is not employed, the opponent has access to plaintext messages and their associated MACs. Suppose $k > n$; that is, suppose that the key size is greater than the MAC size. Then, given a known M_1 and T_1, with $T_1 = \text{MAC}(K, M_1)$, the cryptanalyst can perform $T_i = \text{MAC}(K_i, M_1)$ for all possible key values k_i. At least one key is guaranteed to produce a match of $T_i = T_1$. Note that a total of 2^k tags will be produced, but there are only $2^n < 2^k$ different tag values. Thus, a number of keys will produce the correct tag and the opponent has no way of knowing which is the correct key. On average, a total of $2^k/2^n = 2^{(k-n)}$ keys will produce a match. Thus, the opponent must iterate the attack.

- **Round 1**

  Given: M_1, $T_1 = \text{MAC}(K, M_1)$

  Compute $T_i = \text{MAC}(K_i, M_1)$ for all 2^k keys

  Number of matches $\approx 2^{(k-n)}$

- **Round 2**

  Given: M_2, $T_2 = \text{MAC}(K, M_2)$

  Compute $T_i = \text{MAC}(K_i, M_2)$ for the $2^{(k-n)}$ keys resulting from Round 1

  Number of matches $\approx 2^{(k-2\times n)}$

And so on. On average, α rounds will be needed $k = \alpha \times n$. For example, if an 80-bit key is used and the tag is 32 bits, then the first round will produce about 2^{48} possible keys. The second round will narrow the possible keys to about 2^{16} possibilities. The third round should produce only a single key, which must be the one used by the sender.

If the key length is less than or equal to the tag length, then it is likely that a first round will produce a single match. It is possible that more than one key will produce such a match, in which case the opponent would need to perform the same test on a new (message, tag) pair.

Thus, a brute-force attempt to discover the authentication key is no less effort and may be more effort than that required to discover a decryption key of the same length. However, other attacks that do not require the discovery of the key are possible.

Consider the following MAC algorithm. Let $M = (X_1 \| X_2 \| \ldots \| X_m)$ be a message that is treated as a concatenation of 64-bit blocks X_i. Then define

$$\Delta(M) = X_1 \oplus X_2 \oplus \cdots \oplus X_m$$
$$\text{MAC}(K, M) = \text{E}(K, \Delta(M))$$

where $\oplus$ is the exclusive-OR (XOR) operation and the encryption algorithm is DES in electronic codebook mode. Thus, the key length is 56 bits, and the tag length is 64 bits. If an opponent observes $\{M \| \text{MAC}(K, M)\}$, a brute-force attempt to determine K will require at least 2^{56} encryptions. But the opponent can attack the system by replacing X_1 through X_{m-1} with any desired values Y_1 through Y_{m-1} and replacing X_m with Y_m, where Y_m is calculated as

$$Y_m = Y_1 \oplus Y_2 \oplus \cdots \oplus Y_{m-1} \oplus \Delta(M)$$

The opponent can now concatenate the new message, which consists of Y_1 through Y_m, using the original tag to form a message that will be accepted as authentic by the receiver. With this tactic, any message of length $64 \times (m - 1)$ bits can be fraudulently inserted.

Thus, in assessing the security of a MAC function, we need to consider the types of attacks that may be mounted against it. With that in mind, let us state the requirements for the function. Assume that an opponent knows the MAC function but does not know K. Then the MAC function should satisfy the following requirements.

1. If an opponent observes M and $\text{MAC}(K, M)$, it should be computationally infeasible for the opponent to construct a message M' such that

$$\text{MAC}(K, M') = \text{MAC}(K, M)$$

2. $\text{MAC}(K, M)$ should be uniformly distributed in the sense that for randomly chosen messages, M and M', the probability that $\text{MAC}(K, M) = \text{MAC}(K, M')$ is 2^{-n}, where n is the number of bits in the tag.

3. Let M' be equal to some known transformation on M. That is, $M' = \text{f}(M)$. For example, f may involve inverting one or more specific bits. In that case,

$$\Pr[\text{MAC}(K, M) = \text{MAC}(K, M')] = 2^{-n}$$

The first requirement speaks to the earlier example, in which an opponent is able to construct a new message to match a given tag, even though the opponent does not know and does not learn the key. The second requirement deals with the need to thwart a brute-force attack based on chosen plaintext. That is, if we assume that the opponent does not know K but does have access to the MAC function and can present messages for MAC generation, then the opponent could try various messages until finding one that matches a given tag. If the MAC function exhibits uniform distribution, then a brute-force method would require, on average, $2^{(n-1)}$ attempts before finding a message that fits a given tag.

The final requirement dictates that the authentication algorithm should not be weaker with respect to certain parts or bits of the message than others. If this were not the case, then an opponent who had M and MAC(K, M) could attempt variations on M at the known "weak spots" with a likelihood of early success at producing a new message that matched the old tags.

12.4 SECURITY OF MACs

Just as with encryption algorithms and hash functions, we can group attacks on MACs into two categories: brute-force attacks and cryptanalysis.

Brute-Force Attacks

A brute-force attack on a MAC is a more difficult undertaking than a brute-force attack on a hash function because it requires known message-tag pairs. Let us see why this is so. To attack a hash code, we can proceed in the following way. Given a fixed message x with n-bit hash code $h = \mathrm{H}(x)$, a brute-force method of finding a collision is to pick a random bit string y and check if $\mathrm{H}(y) = \mathrm{H}(x)$. The attacker can do this repeatedly off line. Whether an off-line attack can be used on a MAC algorithm depends on the relative size of the key and the tag.

To proceed, we need to state the desired security property of a MAC algorithm, which can be expressed as follows.

- **Computation resistance:** Given one or more text-MAC pairs $[x_i, \mathrm{MAC}(K, x_i)]$, it is computationally infeasible to compute any text-MAC pair $[x, \mathrm{MAC}(K, x)]$ for any new input $x \neq x_i$.

In other words, the attacker would like to come up with the valid MAC code for a given message x. There are two lines of attack possible: attack the key space and attack the MAC value. We examine each of these in turn.

If an attacker can determine the MAC key, then it is possible to generate a valid MAC value for any input x. Suppose the key size is k bits and that the attacker has one known text-tag pair. Then the attacker can compute the n-bit tag on the known text for all possible keys. At least one key is guaranteed to produce the correct tag, namely, the valid key that was initially used to produce the known text-tag pair. This phase of the attack takes a level of effort proportional to 2^k (that is, one operation for each of the 2^k possible key values). However, as was described earlier, because the MAC is a many-to-one mapping, there may be other keys that produce the correct value. Thus, if more than one key is found to produce the correct value, additional text-tag pairs must be tested. It can be shown that the level of effort drops off rapidly with each additional text-MAC pair and that the overall level of effort is roughly 2^k [MENE97].

An attacker can also work on the tag without attempting to recover the key. Here, the objective is to generate a valid tag for a given message or to find a message that matches a given tag. In either case, the level of effort is comparable to that for attacking the one-way or weak collision-resistant property of a hash code, or 2^n. In the case of the MAC, the attack cannot be conducted off line without further input; the attacker will require chosen text-tag pairs or knowledge of the key.

To summarize, the level of effort for brute-force attack on a MAC algorithm can be expressed as $\min(2^k, 2^n)$. The assessment of strength is similar to that for symmetric encryption algorithms. It would appear reasonable to require that the key length and tag length satisfy a relationship such as $\min(k, n) \geq N$, where N is perhaps in the range of 128 bits.

Cryptanalysis

As with encryption algorithms and hash functions, cryptanalytic attacks on MAC algorithms seek to exploit some property of the algorithm to perform some attack other than an exhaustive search. The way to measure the resistance of a MAC algorithm to cryptanalysis is to compare its strength to the effort required for a brute-force attack. That is, an ideal MAC algorithm will require a cryptanalytic effort greater than or equal to the brute-force effort.

There is much more variety in the structure of MACs than in hash functions, so it is difficult to generalize about the cryptanalysis of MACs. Furthermore, far less work has been done on developing such attacks. A useful survey of some methods for specific MACs is [PREN96].

12.5 MACs BASED ON HASH FUNCTIONS: HMAC

Later in this chapter, we look at examples of a MAC based on the use of a symmetric block cipher. This has traditionally been the most common approach to constructing a MAC. In recent years, there has been increased interest in developing a MAC derived from a cryptographic hash function. The motivations for this interest are

1. Cryptographic hash functions such as MD5 and SHA generally execute faster in software than symmetric block ciphers such as DES.
2. Library code for cryptographic hash functions is widely available.

With the development of AES and the more widespread availability of code for encryption algorithms, these considerations are less significant, but hash-based MACs continue to be widely used.

A hash function such as SHA was not designed for use as a MAC and cannot be used directly for that purpose, because it does not rely on a secret key. There have been a number of proposals for the incorporation of a secret key into an existing hash algorithm. The approach that has received the most support is HMAC [BELL96a, BELL96b]. HMAC has been issued as RFC 2104, has been chosen as the mandatory-to-implement MAC for IP security, and is used in other Internet protocols, such as SSL. HMAC has also been issued as a NIST standard (FIPS 198).

HMAC Design Objectives

RFC 2104 lists the following design objectives for HMAC.

- To use, without modifications, available hash functions. In particular, to use hash functions that perform well in software and for which code is freely and widely available.
- To allow for easy replaceability of the embedded hash function in case faster or more secure hash functions are found or required.
- To preserve the original performance of the hash function without incurring a significant degradation.
- To use and handle keys in a simple way.
- To have a well understood cryptographic analysis of the strength of the authentication mechanism based on reasonable assumptions about the embedded hash function.

The first two objectives are important to the acceptability of HMAC. HMAC treats the hash function as a "black box." This has two benefits. First, an existing implementation of a hash function can be used as a module in implementing HMAC. In this way, the bulk of the HMAC code is prepackaged and ready to use without modification. Second, if it is ever desired to replace a given hash function in an HMAC implementation, all that is required is to remove the existing hash function module and drop in the new module. This could be done if a faster hash function were desired. More important, if the security of the embedded hash function were compromised, the security of HMAC could be retained simply by replacing the embedded hash function with a more secure one (e.g., replacing SHA-2 with SHA-3).

The last design objective in the preceding list is, in fact, the main advantage of HMAC over other proposed hash-based schemes. HMAC can be proven secure provided that the embedded hash function has some reasonable cryptographic strengths. We return to this point later in this section, but first we examine the structure of HMAC.

HMAC Algorithm

Figure 12.5 illustrates the overall operation of HMAC. Define the following terms.

H = embedded hash function (e.g., MD5, SHA-1, RIPEMD-160)

IV = initial value input to hash function

M = message input to HMAC (including the padding specified in the embedded hash function)

Y_i = i th block of M, $0 \leq i \leq (L - 1)$

L = number of blocks in M

b = number of bits in a block

n = length of hash code produced by embedded hash function

K = secret key; recommended length is $\geq n$; if key length is greater than b, the key is input to the hash function to produce an n-bit key

K^+ = K padded with zeros on the left so that the result is b bits in length

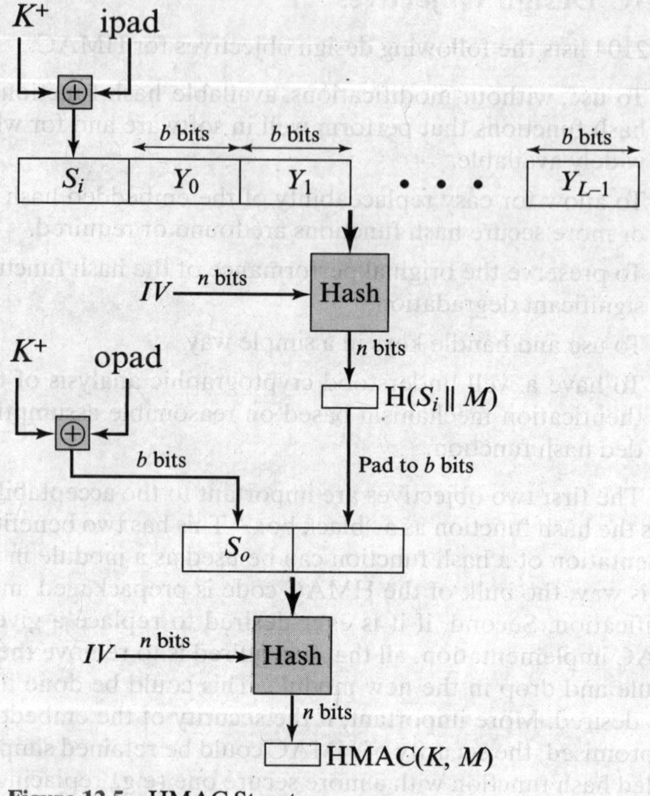

Figure 12.5 HMAC Structure

ipad = 00110110 (36 in hexadecimal) repeated $b/8$ times
opad = 01011100 (5C in hexadecimal) repeated $b/8$ times

Then HMAC can be expressed as

$$\text{HMAC}(K, M) = \text{H}[(K^+ \oplus \text{opad}) \| \text{H}[(K^+ \oplus \text{ipad}) \| M]]$$

We can describe the algorithm as follows.

1. Append zeros to the left end of K to create a b-bit string K^+ (e.g., if K is of length 160 bits and $b = 512$, then K will be appended with 44 zeroes).
2. XOR (bitwise exclusive-OR) K^+ with ipad to produce the b-bit block S_i.
3. Append M to S_i.
4. Apply H to the stream generated in step 3.
5. XOR K^+ with opad to produce the b-bit block S_o.
6. Append the hash result from step 4 to S_o.
7. Apply H to the stream generated in step 6 and output the result.

Note that the XOR with ipad results in flipping one-half of the bits of K. Similarly, the XOR with opad results in flipping one-half of the bits of K, using a different set of bits. In effect, by passing S_i and S_o through the compression function of the hash algorithm, we have pseudorandomly generated two keys from K.

HMAC should execute in approximately the same time as the embedded hash function for long messages. HMAC adds three executions of the hash compression function (for S_i, S_o, and the block produced from the inner hash).

A more efficient implementation is possible, as shown in Figure 12.6. Two quantities are precomputed:

$$f(IV, (K^+ \oplus \text{ipad}))$$
$$f(IV, (K^+ \oplus \text{opad}))$$

where f(cv, block) is the compression function for the hash function, which takes as arguments a chaining variable of n bits and a block of b bits and produces a chaining variable of n bits. These quantities only need to be computed initially and every time the key changes. In effect, the precomputed quantities substitute for the initial value (IV) in the hash function. With this implementation, only one additional instance of the compression function is added to the processing normally produced

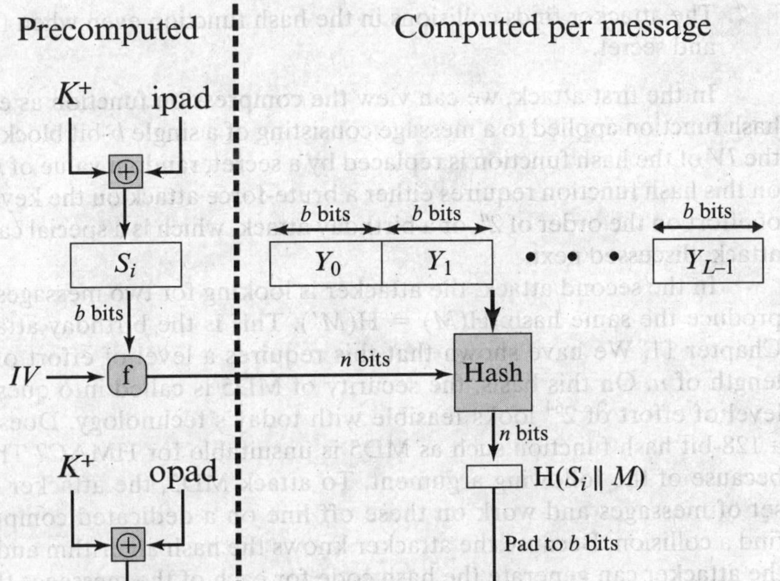

Figure 12.6 Efficient Implementation of HMAC

by the hash function. This more efficient implementation is especially worthwhile if most of the messages for which a MAC is computed are short.

Security of HMAC

The security of any MAC function based on an embedded hash function depends in some way on the cryptographic strength of the underlying hash function. The appeal of HMAC is that its designers have been able to prove an exact relationship between the strength of the embedded hash function and the strength of HMAC.

The security of a MAC function is generally expressed in terms of the probability of successful forgery with a given amount of time spent by the forger and a given number of message-tag pairs created with the same key. In essence, it is proved in [BELL96a] that for a given level of effort (time, message–tag pairs) on messages generated by a legitimate user and seen by the attacker, the probability of successful attack on HMAC is equivalent to one of the following attacks on the embedded hash function.

1. The attacker is able to compute an output of the compression function even with an *IV* that is random, secret, and unknown to the attacker.
2. The attacker finds collisions in the hash function even when the *IV* is random and secret.

In the first attack, we can view the compression function as equivalent to the hash function applied to a message consisting of a single *b*-bit block. For this attack, the *IV* of the hash function is replaced by a secret, random value of *n* bits. An attack on this hash function requires either a brute-force attack on the key, which is a level of effort on the order of 2^n, or a birthday attack, which is a special case of the second attack, discussed next.

In the second attack, the attacker is looking for two messages M and M' that produce the same hash: $H(M) = H(M')$. This is the birthday attack discussed in Chapter 11. We have shown that this requires a level of effort of $2^{n/2}$ for a hash length of n. On this basis, the security of MD5 is called into question, because a level of effort of 2^{64} looks feasible with today's technology. Does this mean that a 128-bit hash function such as MD5 is unsuitable for HMAC? The answer is no, because of the following argument. To attack MD5, the attacker can choose any set of messages and work on these off line on a dedicated computing facility to find a collision. Because the attacker knows the hash algorithm and the default *IV*, the attacker can generate the hash code for each of the messages that the attacker generates. However, when attacking HMAC, the attacker cannot generate message/code pairs off line because the attacker does not know K. Therefore, the attacker must observe a sequence of messages generated by HMAC under the same key and perform the attack on these known messages. For a hash code length of 128 bits, this requires 2^{64} observed blocks (2^{72} bits) generated using the same key. On a 1-Gbps link, one would need to observe a continuous stream of messages with no change in key for about 150,000 years in order to succeed. Thus, if speed is a concern, it is fully acceptable to use MD5 rather than SHA-1 as the embedded hash function for HMAC.

12.6 MACs BASED ON BLOCK CIPHERS: DAA AND CMAC

In this section, we look at two MACs that are based on the use of a block cipher mode of operation. We begin with an older algorithm, the Data Authentication Algorithm (DAA), which is now obsolete. Then we examine CMAC, which is designed to overcome the deficiencies of DAA.

Data Authentication Algorithm

The **Data Authentication Algorithm (DAA)**, based on DES, has been one of the most widely used MACs for a number of years. The algorithm is both a FIPS publication (FIPS PUB 113) and an ANSI standard (X9.17). However, as we discuss subsequently, security weaknesses in this algorithm have been discovered, and it is being replaced by newer and stronger algorithms.

The algorithm can be defined as using the cipher block chaining (CBC) mode of operation of DES (Figure 6.4) with an initialization vector of zero. The data (e.g., message, record, file, or program) to be authenticated are grouped into contiguous 64-bit blocks: $D_1, D_2, \ldots, D_N$. If necessary, the final block is padded on the right with zeroes to form a full 64-bit block. Using the DES encryption algorithm E and a secret key K, a data authentication code (DAC) is calculated as follows (Figure 12.7).

$$\begin{aligned} O_1 &= \mathrm{E}(K, D) \\ O_2 &= \mathrm{E}(K, [D_2 \oplus O_1]) \\ O_3 &= \mathrm{E}(K, [D_3 \oplus O_2]) \\ &\;\;\vdots \\ O_N &= \mathrm{E}(K, [D_N \oplus O_{N-1}]) \end{aligned}$$

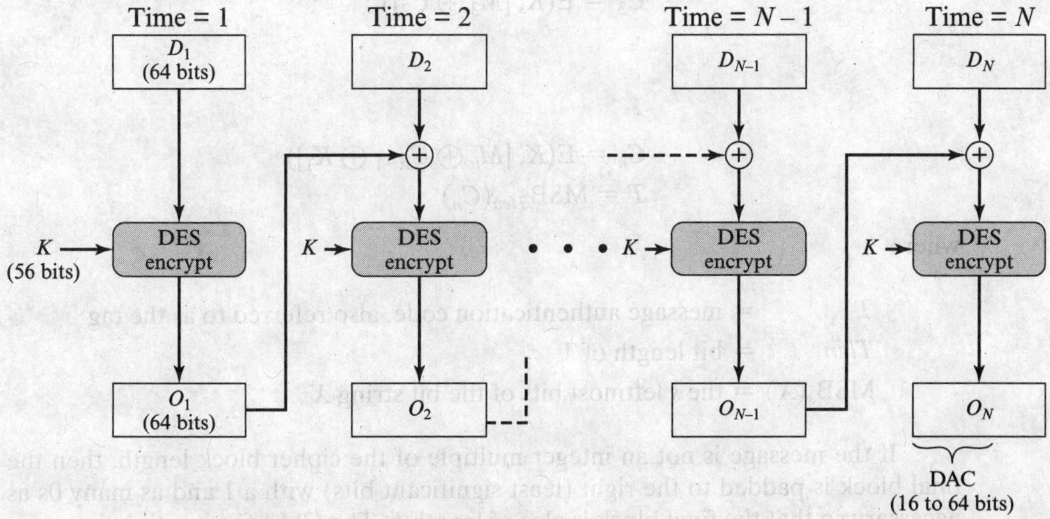

Figure 12.7 Data Authentication Algorithm (FIPS PUB 113)

The DAC consists of either the entire block O_N or the leftmost M bits of the block, with $16 \leq M \leq 64$.

Cipher-Based Message Authentication Code (CMAC)

As was mentioned, DAA has been widely adopted in government and industry. [BELL00] demonstrated that this MAC is secure under a reasonable set of security criteria, with the following restriction. Only messages of one fixed length of mn bits are processed, where n is the cipher block size and m is a fixed positive integer. As a simple example, notice that given the CBC MAC of a one-block message X, say $T = \text{MAC}(K, X)$, the adversary immediately knows the CBC MAC for the two-block message $X \| (X \oplus T)$ since this is once again T.

Black and Rogaway [BLAC00] demonstrated that this limitation could be overcome using three keys: one key K of length k to be used at each step of the cipher block chaining and two keys of length b, where b is the cipher block length. This proposed construction was refined by Iwata and Kurosawa so that the two n-bit keys could be derived from the encryption key, rather than being provided separately [IWAT03]. This refinement, adopted by NIST, is the **Cipher-based Message Authentication Code (CMAC)** mode of operation for use with AES and triple DES. It is specified in NIST Special Publication 800-38B.

First, let us define the operation of CMAC when the message is an integer multiple n of the cipher block length b. For AES, $b = 128$, and for triple DES, $b = 64$. The message is divided into n blocks $(M_1, M_2, \ldots, M_n)$. The algorithm makes use of a k-bit encryption key K and a b-bit constant, K_1. For AES, the key size k is 128, 192, or 256 bits; for triple DES, the key size is 112 or 168 bits. CMAC is calculated as follows (Figure 12.8).

$$
\begin{aligned}
C_1 &= \text{E}(K, M_1) \\
C_2 &= \text{E}(K, [M_2 \oplus C_1]) \\
C_3 &= \text{E}(K, [M_3 \oplus C_2]) \\
&\;\;\vdots \\
C_n &= \text{E}(K, [M_n \oplus C_{n-1} \oplus K_1]) \\
T &= \text{MSB}_{Tlen}(C_n)
\end{aligned}
$$

where

T	=	message authentication code, also referred to as the tag
$Tlen$	=	bit length of T
$\text{MSB}_s(X)$	=	the s leftmost bits of the bit string X

If the message is not an integer multiple of the cipher block length, then the final block is padded to the right (least significant bits) with a 1 and as many 0s as necessary so that the final block is also of length b. The CMAC operation then proceeds as before, except that a different b-bit key K_2 is used instead of K_1.

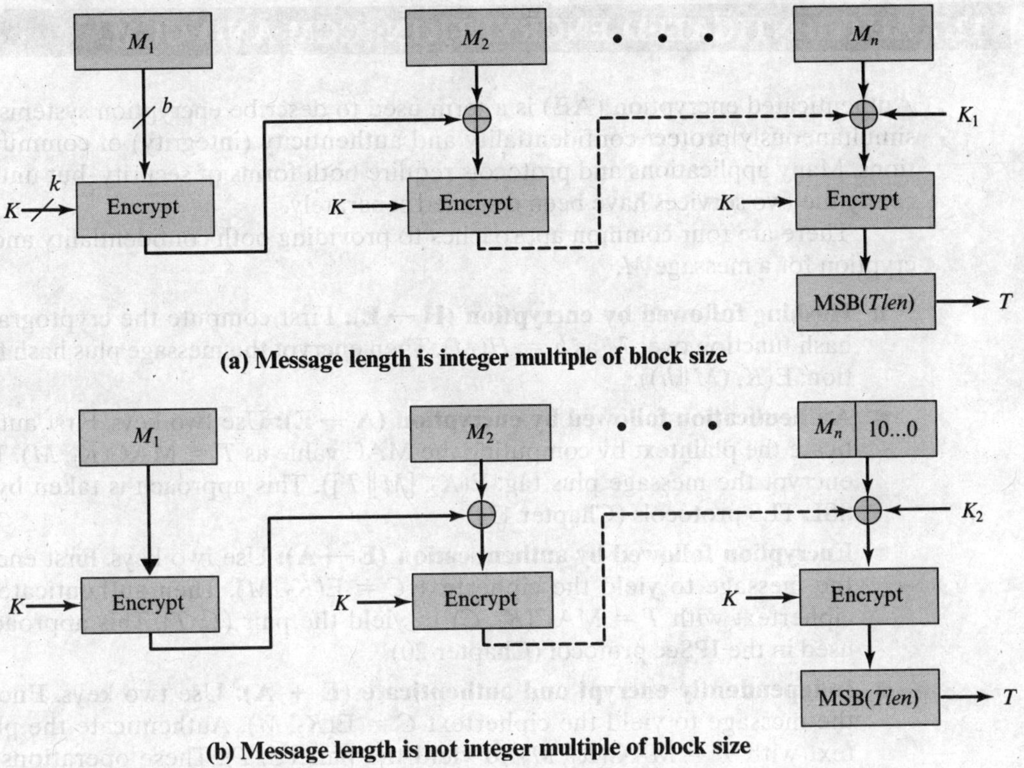

Figure 12.8 Cipher-Based Message Authentication Code (CMAC)

The two b-bit keys are derived from the k-bit encryption key as follows.

$$L = E(K, 0^b)$$
$$K_1 = L \cdot x$$
$$K_2 = L \cdot x^2 = (L \cdot x) \cdot x$$

where multiplication ($\cdot$) is done in the finite field GF(2^b) and x and x^2 are first- and second-order polynomials that are elements of GF(2^b). Thus, the binary representation of x consists of $b - 2$ zeros followed by 10; the binary representation of x^2 consists of $b - 3$ zeros followed by 100. The finite field is defined with respect to an irreducible polynomial that is lexicographically first among all such polynomials with the minimum possible number of nonzero terms. For the two approved block sizes, the polynomials are $x^{64} + x^4 + x^3 + x + 1$ and $x^{128} + x^7 + x^2 + x + 1$.

To generate K_1 and K_2, the block cipher is applied to the block that consists entirely of 0 bits. The first subkey is derived from the resulting ciphertext by a left shift of one bit and, conditionally, by XORing a constant that depends on the block size. The second subkey is derived in the same manner from the first subkey. This property of finite fields of the form GF(2^b) was explained in the discussion of MixColumns in Chapter 6.

12.7 AUTHENTICATED ENCRYPTION: CCM AND GCM

Authenticated encryption (AE) is a term used to describe encryption systems that simultaneously protect confidentiality and authenticity (integrity) of communications. Many applications and protocols require both forms of security, but until recently the two services have been designed separately.

There are four common approaches to providing both confidentiality and encryption for a message M.

- **Hashing followed by encryption (H → E):** First compute the cryptographic hash function over M as $h = H(M)$. Then encrypt the message plus hash function: $E(K, (M \| h))$.
- **Authentication followed by encryption (A → E):** Use two keys. First authenticate the plaintext by computing the MAC value as $T = \text{MAC}(K_1, M)$. Then encrypt the message plus tag: $E(K_2, [M \| T])$. This approach is taken by the SSL/TLS protocols (Chapter 17).
- **Encryption followed by authentication (E → A):** Use two keys. First encrypt the message to yield the ciphertext $C = E(K_2, M)$. Then authenticate the ciphertext with $T = \text{MAC}(K_1, C)$ to yield the pair (C, T). This approach is used in the IPSec protocol (Chapter 20).
- **Independently encrypt and authenticate (E + A).** Use two keys. Encrypt the message to yield the ciphertext $C = E(K_2, M)$. Authenticate the plaintext with $T = \text{MAC}(K_1, M)$ to yield the pair (C, T). These operations can be performed in either order. This approach is used by the SSH protocol (Chapter 17).

Both decryption and verification are straightforward for each approach. For H → E, A → E, and E + A, decrypt first, then verify. For E → A, verify first, then decrypt. There are security vulnerabilities with all of these approaches. The H → E approach is used in the Wired Equivalent Privacy (WEP) protocol to protect WiFi networks. This approach had fundamental weaknesses and led to the replacement of the WEP protocol. [BLAC05] and [BELL00] point out that there are security concerns in each of the three encryption/MAC approaches listed above. Nevertheless, with proper design, any of these approaches can provide a high level of security. This is the goal of the two approaches discussed in this section, both of which have been standardized by NIST.

Counter with Cipher Block Chaining-Message Authentication Code

The CCM mode of operation was standardized by NIST specifically to support the security requirements of IEEE 802.11 WiFi wireless local area networks (Chapter 18), but can be used in any networking application requiring authenticated encryption. CCM is a variation of the encrypt-and-MAC approach to authenticated encryption. It is defined in NIST SP 800-38C.

The key algorithmic ingredients of CCM are the AES encryption algorithm (Chapter 6), the CTR mode of operation (Chapter 7), and the CMAC authentication algorithm (Section 12.6). A single key K is used for both encryption and MAC algorithms. The input to the CCM encryption process consists of three elements.

1. Data that will be both authenticated and encrypted. This is the plaintext message P of data block.
2. Associated data A that will be authenticated but not encrypted. An example is a protocol header that must be transmitted in the clear for proper protocol operation but which needs to be authenticated.
3. A nonce N that is assigned to the payload and the associated data. This is a unique value that is different for every instance during the lifetime of a protocol association and is intended to prevent replay attacks and certain other types of attacks.

Figure 12.9 illustrates the operation of CCM. For authentication, the input includes the nonce, the associated data, and the plaintext. This input is formatted as a sequence of blocks B_0 through B_r. The first block contains the nonce plus some formatting bits that indicate the lengths of the N, A, and P elements. This is followed by zero or more blocks that contain A, followed by zero of more blocks that contain P. The resulting sequence of blocks serves as input to the CMAC algorithm, which produces a MAC value with length *Tlen*, which is less than or equal to the block length (Figure 12.9a).

For encryption, a sequence of counters is generated that must be independent of the nonce. The authentication tag is encrypted in CTR mode using the single counter Ctr_0. The *Tlen* most significant bits of the output are XORed with the tag to produce an encrypted tag. The remaining counters are used for the CTR mode encryption of the plaintext (Figure 7.7). The encrypted plaintext is concatenated with the encrypted tag to form the ciphertext output (Figure 12.9b).

SP 800-38C defines the authentication/encryption process as follows.

1. Apply the formatting function to (N, A, P) to produce the blocks $B_0, B_1, \ldots, B_r$.
2. Set $Y_0 = \mathrm{E}(K, B_0)$.
3. For $i = 1$ to r, do $Y_i = \mathrm{E}(K, (B_i \oplus Y_{i-1}))$.
4. Set $T = \mathrm{MSB}_{Tlen}(Y_r)$.
5. Apply the counter generation function to generate the counter blocks $Ctr_0, Ctr_1, \ldots, Ctr_m$, where $m = \lceil Plen/128 \rceil$.
6. For $j = 0$ to m, do $S_j = \mathrm{E}(K, Ctr_j)$.
7. Set $S = S_1 \| S_2 \| \cdots \| S_m$.
8. Return $C = (P \oplus \mathrm{MSB}_{Plen}(S)) \| (T \oplus \mathrm{MSB}_{Tlen}(S_0))$.

For decryption and verification, the recipient requires the following input: the ciphertext C, the nonce N, the associated data A, the key K, and the initial counter Ctr_0. The steps are as follows.

1. If $Clen \le Tlen$, then return INVALID.
2. Apply the counter generation function to generate the counter blocks $Ctr_0, Ctr_1, \ldots, Ctr_m$, where $m = \lceil Clen/128 \rceil$.
3. For $j = 0$ to m, do $S_j = \mathrm{E}(K, Ctr_j)$.

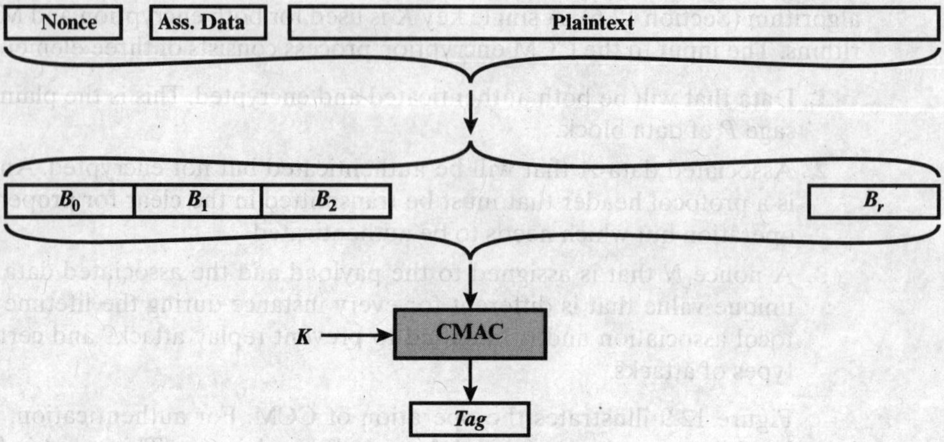

(a) Authentication

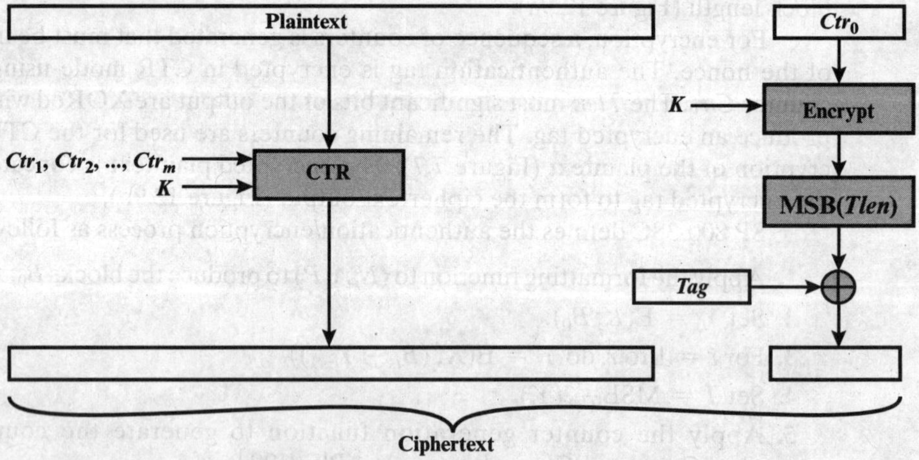

(b) Encryption

Figure 12.9 Counter with Cipher Block Chaining-Message Authentication Code (CCM)

4. Set $S = S_1 \| S_2 \| \cdots \| S_m$.
5. Set $P = \text{MSB}_{Clen-Tlen}(C) \oplus \text{MSB}_{Clen-Tlen}(S)$.
6. Set $T = \text{LSB}_{Tlen}(C) \oplus \text{MSB}_{Tlen}(S_0)$.
7. Apply the formatting function to $N, A, P)$ to produce the blocks $B_0, B_1, \ldots, B_r$.
8. Set $Y_0 = \text{E}(K, B_0)$.
9. For $i = 1$ to r do $Y_i = \text{E}(K, (B_i \oplus Y_{i-1}))$.
10. If $T \neq \text{MSB}_{Tlen}(Y_r)$, then return INVALID, else return P.

CCM is a relatively complex algorithm. Note that it requires two complete passes through the plaintext, once to generate the MAC value, and once for encryption. Further, the details of the specification require a tradeoff between the length of the nonce and the length of the tag, which is an unnecessary restriction. Also note that the encryption key is used twice with the CTR encryption mode: once to generate the tag and once to encrypt the plaintext plus tag. Whether these complexities add to the security of the algorithm is not clear. In any case, two analyses of the algorithm ([JONS02] and [ROGA03]) conclude that CCM provides a high level of security.

Galois/Counter Mode

The GCM mode of operation, standardized by NIST in NIST SP 800-38D, is designed to be parallelizable so that it can provide high throughput with low cost and low latency. In essence, the message is encrypted in variant of CTR mode. The resulting ciphertext is multiplied with key material and message length information over $GF(2^{128})$ to generate the authenticator tag. The standard also specifies a mode of operation that supplies the MAC only, known as GMAC.

The GCM mode makes use of two functions: GHASH, which is a keyed hash function, and GCTR, which is essentially the CTR mode with the counters determined by a simple increment by one operation.

$\text{GHASH}_H(X)$ takes a input the hash key H and a bit string X such that $\text{len}(X) = 128m$ bits for some positive integer m and produces a 128-bit MAC value. The function may be specified as follows (Figure 12.10a).

1. Let $X_1, X_2, \ldots, X_{m-1}, X_m$ denote the unique sequence of blocks such that $X = X_1 \| X_2 \| \cdots \| X_{m-1} \| X_m$.
2. Let Y_0 be a block of 128 zeros, designated as 0^{128}.
3. For $i = 1, \ldots, m$, let $Y_i = (Y_{i-1} \oplus X_i) \cdot H$, where $\cdot$ designates multiplication in $GF(2^{128})$.
4. Return Y_m.

The $\text{GHASH}_H(X)$ function can be expressed as

$$(X_1 \cdot H^m) \oplus (X_2 \cdot H^{m-1}) \oplus \cdots \oplus (X_{m-1} \cdot H^2) \oplus (X_m \cdot H)$$

This formulation has desirable performance implications. If the same hash key is to be used to authenticate multiple messages, then the values $H^2, H^3, \ldots$ can be precalculated one time for use with each message to be authenticated. Then, the blocks of the data to be authenticated $(X_1, X_2, \ldots, X_m)$ can be processed in parallel, because the computations are independent of one another.

$\text{GCTR}_K(ICB, X)$ takes a input a secret key K and a bit string X arbitrary length and returns a ciphertext Y of bit length (X). The function may be specified as follows (Figure 12.10b).

1. If X is the empty string, then return the empty string as Y.
2. Let $n = \lceil (\text{len}(X)/128) \rceil$. That is, n is the smallest integer greater than or equal to $(X)/128$.

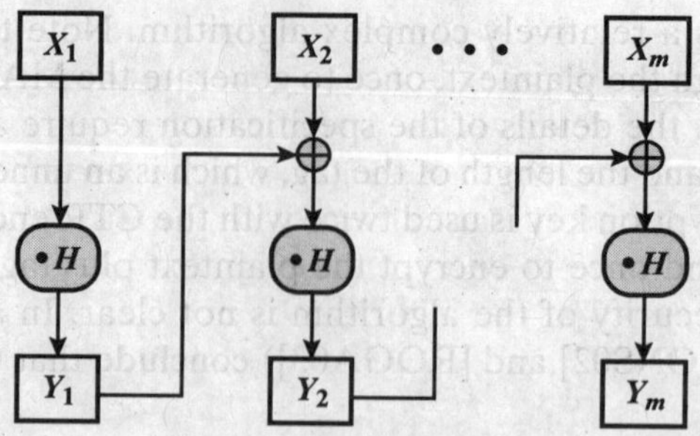

(a) $\text{GHASH}_H(X_1 \| X_2 \| \ldots \| X_m) = Y_m$

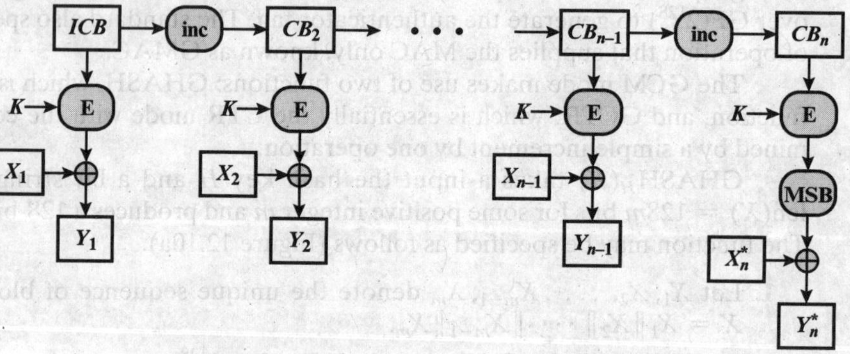

(b) $\text{GCTR}_K(ICB, X_1 \| X_2 \| \ldots \| X_n^*) = Y_1 \| Y_2 \| \ldots \| Y_n^*$

Figure 12.10 GCM Authentication and Encryption Functions

3. Let $X_1, X_2, \ldots, X_{n-1}, X_n^*$ denote the unique sequence of bit strings such that

$$X = X_1 \| X_2 \| \cdots \| X_{n-1} \| X_n^*;$$

$$X_1, X_2, \ldots, X_{n-1} \text{ are complete 128-bit blocks.}$$

4. Let $CB_1 = ICB$.
5. For, $i = 2$ to n let $CB_i = \text{inc}_{32}(CB_{i-1})$, where the $\text{inc}_{32}(S)$ function increments the rightmost 32 bits of S by 1 mod 2^{32}, and the remaining bits are unchanged.
6. For $i = 1$ to $n - 1$, do $Y_i = X_i \oplus \text{E}(K, CB_i)$.
7. Let $Y_n^* = X_n^* \oplus \text{MSB}_{\text{len}(X_n^*)}(\text{E}(K, CB_n))$.
8. Let $Y = Y_1 \| Y_2 \| \ldots \| Y_{n-1} \| Y_n^*$
9. Return Y.

Note that the counter values can be quickly generated and that the encryption operations can be performed in parallel.

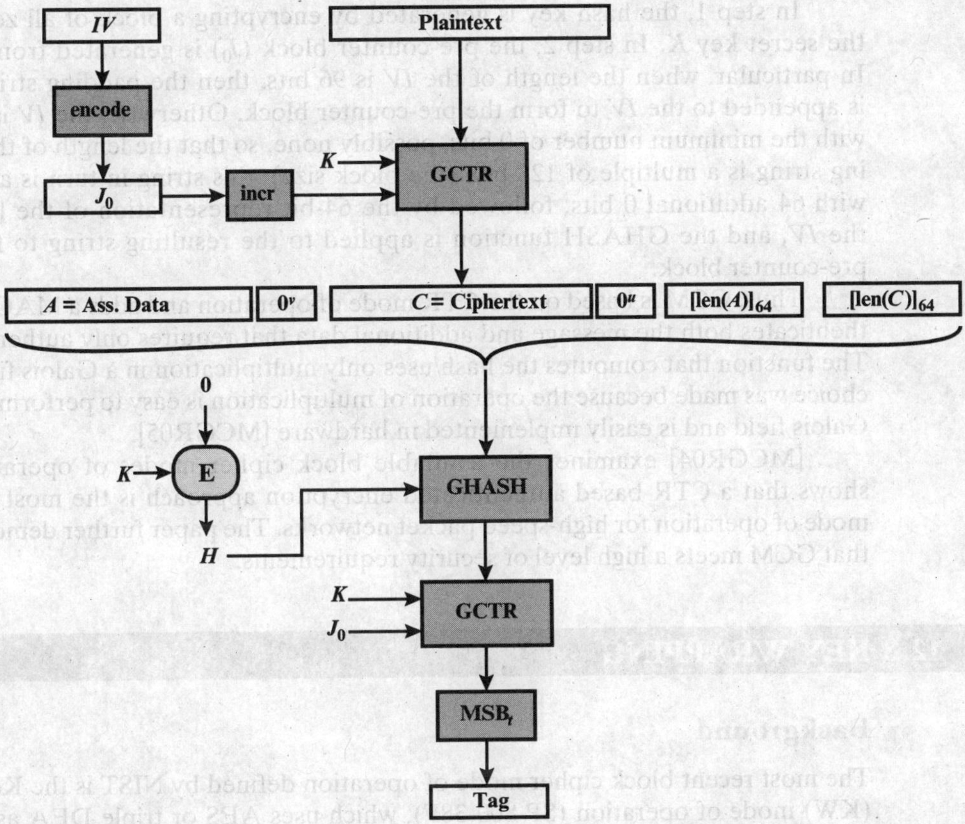

Figure 12.11 Galois Counter–Message Authentication Code (GCM)

We can now define the overall authenticated encryption function (Figure 12.11). The input consists of a secret key K, an initialization vector IV, a plaintext P, and additional authenticated data A. The notation $[x]_s$ means the s-bit binary representation of the nonnegative integer x. The steps are as follows.

1. Let $H = E(K, 0^{128})$.
2. Define a block, J_0, as
   If $\text{len}(IV) = 96$, then let $J_0 = IV \| 0^{31} \| 1$.
   If $\text{len}(IV) \neq 96$, then let $s = 128\lceil \text{len}(IV)/128 \rceil - \text{len}(IV)$, and let
   $J_0 = \text{GHASH}_H(IV \| 0^{s+64} \| [\text{len}(IV)]_{64})$.
3. Let $C = \text{GCTR}_K(\text{inc}_{32}(J_0), P)$.
4. Let $u = 128\lceil \text{len}(C)/128 \rceil - \text{len}(C)$ and let $v = 128\lceil \text{len}(A)/128 \rceil - \text{len}(A)$.
5. Define a block, S, as

$$S = \text{GHASH}_H(A \| 0^v \| C \| 0^u \| [\text{len}(A)]_{64} \| [\text{len}(C)]_{64})$$

6. Let $T = MSB_t(GCTR_K(J_0, S))$, where t is the supported tag length.
7. Return (C, T).

In step 1, the hash key is generated by encrypting a block of all zeros with the secret key K. In step 2, the pre-counter block (J_0) is generated from the IV. In particular, when the length of the IV is 96 bits, then the padding string $0^{31} \| 1$ is appended to the IV to form the pre-counter block. Otherwise, the IV is padded with the minimum number of 0 bits, possibly none, so that the length of the resulting string is a multiple of 128 bits (the block size); this string in turn is appended with 64 additional 0 bits, followed by the 64-bit representation of the length of the IV, and the GHASH function is applied to the resulting string to form the pre-counter block.

Thus, GCM is based on the CTR mode of operation and adds a MAC that authenticates both the message and additional data that requires only authentication. The function that computes the hash uses only multiplication in a Galois field. This choice was made because the operation of multiplication is easy to perform within a Galois field and is easily implemented in hardware [MCGR05].

[MCGR04] examines the available block cipher modes of operation and shows that a CTR-based authenticated encryption approach is the most efficient mode of operation for high-speed packet networks. The paper further demonstrates that GCM meets a high level of security requirements.

12.8 KEY WRAPPING

Background

The most recent block cipher mode of operation defined by NIST is the Key Wrap (KW) mode of operation (SP 800-38F), which uses AES or triple DEA as the underlying encryption algorithm. The AES version is also documented in RFC 3394.

The purpose of key wrapping is to securely exchange a symmetric key to be shared by two parties, using a symmetric key already shared by those parties. The latter key is called a **key encryption key (KEK)**.

Two questions need to be addressed at this point. First, why do we need to use a symmetric key already known to two parties to encrypt a new symmetric key? Such a requirement is found in a number of protocols described in this book, such as the key management portion of IEEE 802.11 and IPsec. Quite often, a protocol calls for a hierarchy of keys, with keys lower on the hierarchy used more frequently, and changed more frequently to thwart attacks. A higher-level key, which is used infrequently and therefore more resistant to cryptanalysis, is used to encrypt a newly created lower-level key so that it can be exchanged between parties that share the higher-level key.

The second question is, why do we need a new mode? The intent of the new mode is to operate on keys whose length is greater than the block size of the encryption algorithm. For example, AES uses a block size of 128 bits but can use a key size of 128, 192, or 256 bits. In the latter two cases, encryption of the key involves multiple blocks. We consider the value of key data to be greater than the value of other data, because the key will be used multiple times, and compromise of the key compromises all of the data encrypted with the key. Therefore, NIST desired a robust encryption mode. KW is robust in the sense that each bit of output can be expected to depend in a nontrivial fashion on each bit of input. This is not the case for any of the other modes of operation that we have described. For example, in all of the modes so far described, the last block of plaintext only influences the last block of ciphertext. Similarly, the first block of ciphertext is derived only from the first block of plaintext.

To achieve this robust operation, KW achieves a considerably lower throughput than the other modes, but the tradeoff may be appropriate for some key management applications. Also, KW is only used for small amounts of plaintext compared to, say, the encryption of a message or a file.

The Key Wrapping Algorithm

The key wrapping algorithm operates on blocks of 64 bits. The input to the algorithm consists of a 64-bit constant, discussed subsequently, and a plaintext key that is divided into blocks of 64 bits. We use the following notation:

$MSB_{64}(W)$	most significant 64 bits of W
$LSB_{64}(W)$	least significant 64 bits of W
W	temporary value; output of encryption function
$\oplus$	bitwise exclusive-OR
$\|$	concatenation
K	key encryption key
n	number of 64-bit key data blocks
s	number of stages in the wrapping process; $s = 6n$
P_i	ith plaintext key data block; $1 \leq i \leq n$
C_i	ith ciphertext data block; $0 \leq i \leq n$
$A(t)$	64-bit integrity check register after encryption stage t; $1 \leq t \leq s$
$A(0)$	initial integrity check value (ICV); in hexadecimal: A6A6A6A6A6A6A6A6
$R(t, i)$	64-bit register i after encryption stage t; $1 \leq t \leq s$; $1 \leq i \leq n$

We now describe the key wrapping algorithm:

Inputs: Plaintext, n 64-bit values $(P_1, P_2, \ldots, P_n)$
Key encryption key, K

Outputs: Ciphertext, $(n + 1)$ 64-bit values $(C_0, C_1, \ldots, C_n)$

1. Initialize variables.

```
A(0) = A6A6A6A6A6A6A6A6
  for i = 1 to n
    R(0, i) = Pi
```

2. Calculate intermediate values.

```
for t = 1 to s
W = E(K, [A(t−1) || R(t−1, 1)])
A(t)  = t ⊕ MSB64(W)
R(t, n)  = LSB64(W)
for i = 1 to n−1
    R(t, i)  = R(t−1, i+1)
```

3. Output results.

```
C0 = A(s)
for i = 1 to n
    Ci = R(s, i)
```

Note that the ciphertext is one block longer than the plaintext key, to accommodate the ICV. Upon unwrapping (decryption), both the 64-bit ICV and the plaintext key are recovered. If the recovered ICV differs from the input value of hexadecimal A6A6A6A6A6A6A6A6, then an error or alteration has been detected and the plaintext key is rejected. Thus, the key wrap algorithm provides not only confidentiality but also data integrity.

Figure 12.12 illustrated the key wrapping algorithm for encrypting a 256-bit key. Each box represents one encryption stage (one value of t). Note that the A output is fed as input to the next stage $(t + 1)$, whereas the R output skips forward n stages $(t + n)$, which in this example is $n = 4$. This arrangement further increases the avalanche effect and the mixing of bits. To achieve this skipping of stages, a sliding buffer is used, so that the R output from stage t is shifted in the buffer one position for each stage, until it becomes the input for stage $t + n$. This might be clearer if we expand the inner **for** loop for a 256-bit key $(n = 4)$. Then the assignments are as follows:

$$R(t, 1) = R(t - 1, 2)$$
$$R(t, 2) = R(t - 1, 3)$$
$$R(t, 3) = R(t - 1, 4)$$

For example, consider that at stage 5, the R output has a value of $R(5, 4) = x$. At stage 6, we execute $R(6, 3) = R(5, 4) = x$. At stage 7, we execute $R(7, 2) = R(6, 3) = x$. At stage 8, we execute $R(8, 1) = R(7, 2) = x$. So, at stage 9, the input value of $R(t - 1, 1)$ is $R(8, 1) = x$.

Figure 12.13 depicts the operation of stage t for a 256-bit key. The dashed feedback lines indicate the assignment of new values to the stage variables.

Key Unwrapping

The key unwrapping algorithm can be defined as follows:

Inputs: Ciphertext, $(n + 1)$ 64-bit values $(C_0, C_1, \ldots, C_n)$
Key encryption key, K

Outputs: Plaintext, n 64-bit values $(P_1, P_2, \ldots, P_n)$, ICV

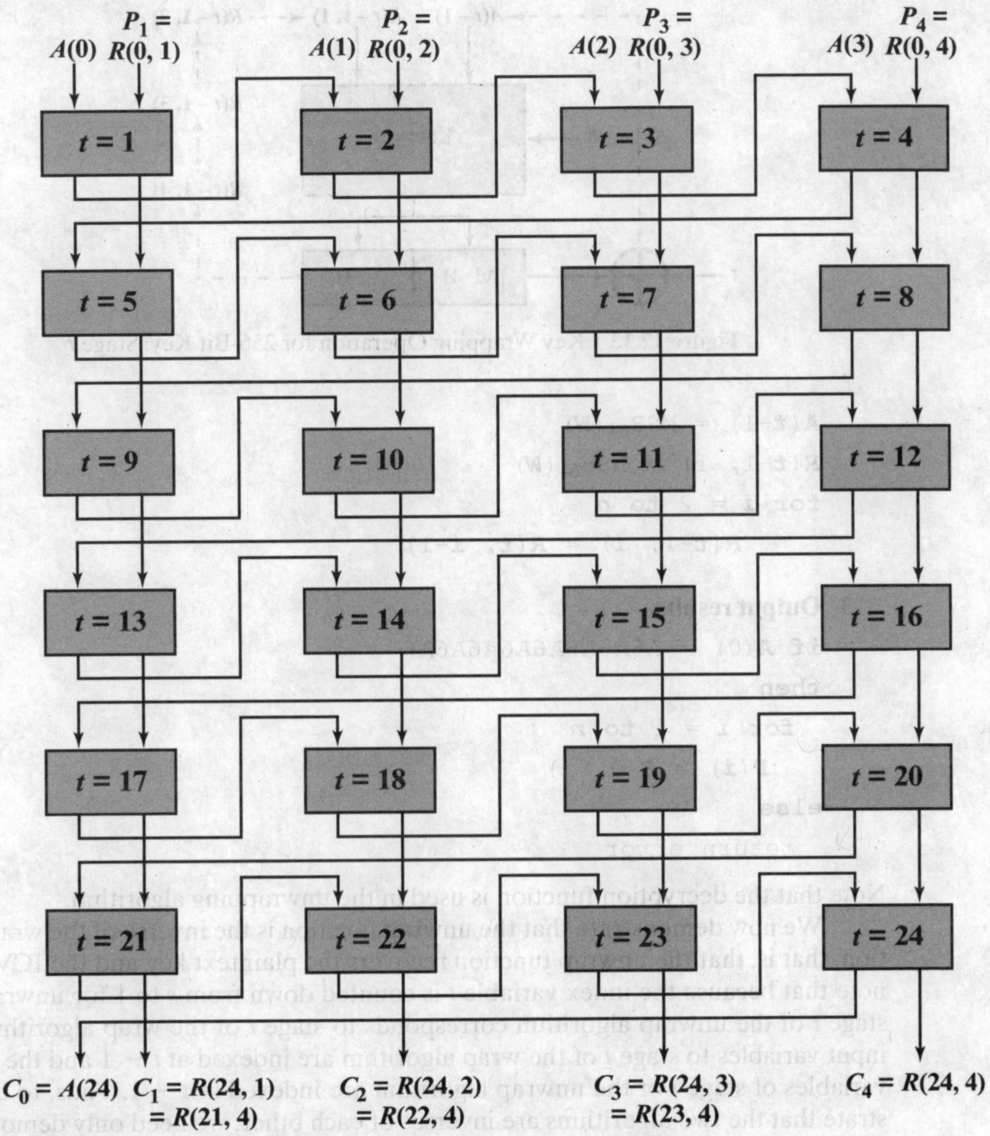

Figure 12.12 Key Wrapping Operation for 256-Bit Key

1. **Initialize variables.**

```
A(s) = C0
for i = 1 to n
R(s, i) = Ci
```

2. **Calculate intermediate values.**

```
for t = s to 1
W = D(K, [(A(t) ⊕ t) ‖ R(t, n)])
```

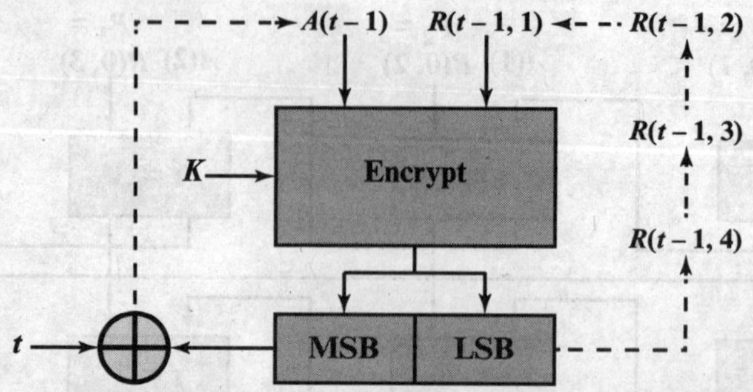

Figure 12.13 Key Wrapping Operation for 256-Bit Key: Stage *t*

```
A(t-1) = MSB64(W)
R(t-1, 1) = LSB64(W)
for i = 2 to n
        R(t-1, i) = R(t, i-1)
```

3. **Output results.**

```
if A(0) = A6A6A6A6A6A6A6A6
then
  for i = 1 to n
    P(i) = R(0, i)
else
  return error
```

Note that the decryption function is used in the unwrapping algorithm.

We now demonstrate that the unwrap function is the inverse of the wrap function, that is, that the unwrap function recovers the plaintext key and the ICV. First, note that because the index variable *t* is counted down from *s* to 1 for unwrapping, stage *t* of the unwrap algorithm corresponds to stage *t* of the wrap algorithm. The input variables to stage *t* of the wrap algorithm are indexed at $t - 1$ and the output variables of stage *t* of the unwrap algorithm are indexed at $t - 1$. Thus, to demonstrate that the two algorithms are inverses of each other, we need only demonstrate that the output variables of stage *t* of the unwrap algorithm are equal to the input variables to stage *t* of the wrap algorithm.

This demonstration is in two parts. First we demonstrate that the calculation of *A* and *R* variables prior to the **for** loop are inverses. To do this, let us simplify the notation a bit. Define the 128-bit value *T* to be the 64-bit value *t* followed by 64 zeros. Then, the first three lines of step 2 of the wrap algorithm can be written as the following single line:

$$A(t) \| R(t, n) = T \oplus \mathrm{E}(K, [A(t-1) \| R(t-1, 1)]) \qquad \textbf{(12.1)}$$

The first three lines of step 2 of the unwrap algorithm can be written as:

$$A(t-1) \| R(t-1, 1) = \mathrm{D}(K, ([A(t) \| R(t, n)] \oplus T)) \qquad \textbf{(12.2)}$$

Expanding the right-hand side by substituting from Equation 12.1,

$$D(K, ([A(t) \| R(t, n)] \oplus T)) = D(K, ([T \oplus E(K, [A(t-1) \| R(t-1, 1)])] \oplus T))$$

Now we recognize that $T \oplus T = 0$ and that for any x, $x \oplus 0 = x$. So,

$$\begin{aligned} D(K, ([A(t) \| R(t, n)] \oplus T)) &= D(K, ([E(K, [A(t-1) \| R(t-1, 1)])) \\ &= A(t-1) \| R(t-1, 1) \end{aligned}$$

The second part of the demonstration is to show that the **for** loops in step 2 of the wrap and unwrap algorithms are inverses. For stage k of the wrap algorithm, the variables $R(t-1, 1)$ through $R(t-1, n)$ are input. $R(t-1, 1)$ is used in the encryption calculation. $R(t-1, 2)$ through $R(t-1, n)$ are mapped, respectively into $R(t, 1)$ through $R(t, n-1)$, and $R(t, n)$ is output from the encryption function. For stage k of the unwrap algorithm, the variables $R(t, 1)$ through $R(t, n)$ are input. $R(t, n)$ is input to the decryption function to produce $R(t-1, 1)$. The remaining variables $R(t-1, 2)$ through $R(t-1, n)$ are generated by the **for** loop, such that they are mapped, respectively, from $R(t, 1)$ through $R(t, n-1)$.

Thus, we have shown that the output variables of stage k of the unwrap algorithm equal the input variables of stage k of the wrap algorithm.

12.9 PSEUDORANDOM NUMBER GENERATION USING HASH FUNCTIONS AND MACs

The essential elements of any pseudorandom number generator (PRNG) are a seed value and a deterministic algorithm for generating a stream of pseudorandom bits. If the algorithm is used as a pseudorandom function (PRF) to produce a required value, such as a session key, then the seed should only be known to the user of the PRF. If the algorithm is used to produce a stream encryption function, then the seed has the role of a secret key that must be known to the sender and the receiver.

We noted in Chapters 8 and 10 that, because an encryption algorithm produces an apparently random output, it can serve as the basis of a (PRNG). Similarly, a hash function or MAC produces apparently random output and can be used to build a PRNG. Both ISO standard 18031 (*Random Bit Generation*) and NIST SP 800-90 (*Recommendation for Random Number Generation Using Deterministic Random Bit Generators*) define an approach for random number generation using a cryptographic hash function. SP 800-90 also defines a random number generator based on HMAC. We look at these two approaches in turn.

PRNG Based on Hash Function

Figure 12.14a shows the basic strategy for a hash-based PRNG specified in SP 800-90 and ISO 18031. The algorithm takes as input:

V = seed

seedlen = bit length of V $\geq K + 64$, where k is a desired security level expressed in bits

n = desired number of output bits

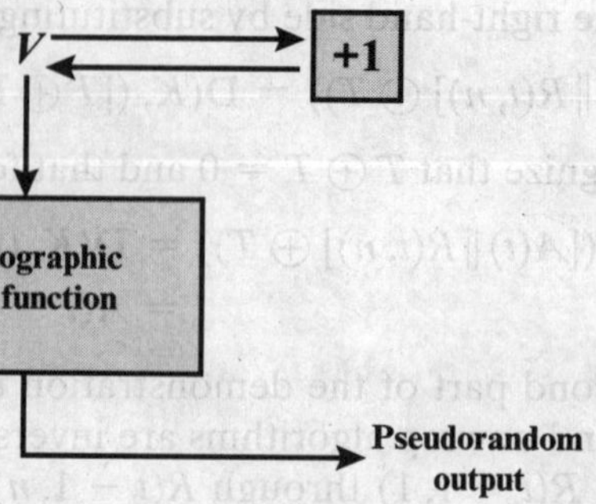

(a) PRNG using cryptographic hash function

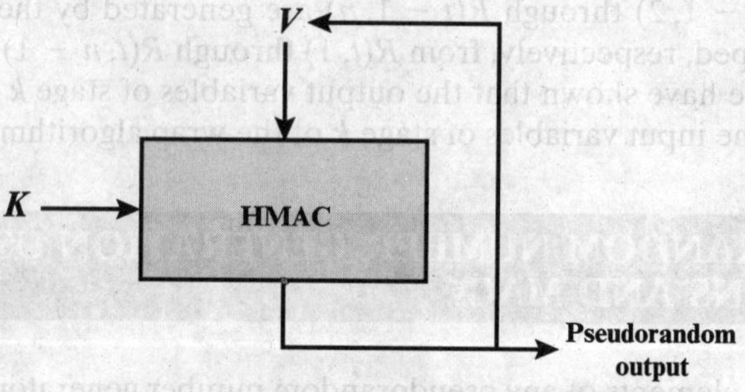

(b) PRNG using HMAC

Figure 12.14 Basic Structure of Hash-Based PRNGs (SP 800-90)

The algorithm uses the cryptographic hash function H with an hash value output of *outlen* bits. The basic operation of the algorithm is

```
m = ⌈n/outlen⌉
data = V
W = the null string
For i = 1 to m
    wi = H (data)
    W = || wi
  data = (data + 1) mod 2^seedlen
Return leftmost n bits of W
```

Thus, the pseudorandom bit stream is $w_1 \| w_2 \| \ldots \| w_m$ with the final block truncated if required.

The SP 800-90 specification also provides for periodically updating V to enhance security. The specification also indicates that there are no known or suspected weaknesses in the hash-based approach for a strong cryptographic hash algorithm, such as SHA-2.

PRNG Based on MAC Function

Although there are no known or suspected weaknesses in the use of a cryptographic hash function for a PRNG in the manner of Figure 12.14a, a higher degree of confidence can be achieved by using a MAC. Almost invariably, HMAC is used for constructing a MAC-based PRNG. This is because HMAC is a widely used standardized MAC function and is implemented in many protocols and applications. As SP 800-90 points out, the disadvantage of this approach compared to the hash-based approach is that the execution time is twice as long, because HMAC involves two executions of the underlying hash function for each output block. The advantage of the HMAC approach is that it provides a greater degree of confidence in its security, compared to a pure hash-based approach.

For the MAC-based approach, there are two inputs: a key K and a seed V. In effect, the combination of K and V form the overall seed for the PRNG specified in SP 800-90. Figure 12.14b shows the basic structure of the PRNG mechanism, and the leftmost column of Figure 12.15 shows the logic. Note that the key remains the same for each block of output, and the data input for each block is equal to the tag output of the previous block. The SP 800-90 specification also provides for periodically updating K and V to enhance security.

It is instructive to compare the SP 800-90 recommendation with the use of HMAC for a PRNG in some applications, and this is shown in Figure 12.15. For the IEEE 802.11i wireless LAN security standard (Chapter 18), the data input consists of the seed concatenated with a counter. The counter is incremented for each block w_i of output. This approach would seem to offer enhanced security compared to the SP 800-90 approach. Consider that for SP 800-90, the data input for output block w_i is just the output w_{i-1} of the previous execution of HMAC. Thus, an opponent who is able to observe the pseudorandom output knows both the input and output of HMAC. Even so, with the assumption that HMAC is secure, knowledge of the input and output should not be sufficient to recover K and hence not sufficient to predict future pseudorandom bits.

The approach taken by the Transport Layer Security protocol (Chapter 17) and the Wireless Transport Layer Security Protocol (Chapter 18) involves invoking HMAC twice for each block of output w_i. As with IEEE 802.11, this is done in such a way that the output does not yield direct information about the input. The double use of HMAC doubles the execution burden and would seem to be security overkill.

NIST SP 800-90	IEEE 802.11i	TLS/WTLS
$m = \lceil n/\text{outlen} \rceil$ $w_0 = V$ $W =$ the null string For $i = 1$ to m $\quad w_i = \text{MAC}(K, w_{i-1})$ $\quad W = W \| w_i$ Return leftmost n bits of W	$m = \lceil n/outlen \rceil$ $W =$ the null string For $i = 1$ to m $\quad w_i = \text{MAC}(K, (V \| i))$ $\quad W = W \| w_i$ Return leftmost n bits of W	$m = \lceil n/outlen \rceil$ $A(0) = V$ $W =$ the null string For $i = 1$ to m $\quad A(i) = \text{MAC}(K, A(i-1))$ $\quad w_i = \text{MAC}(K, (A(i) \| V)$ $\quad W = W \| w_i$ Return leftmost n bits of W

Figure 12.15 Three PRNGs Based on HMAC

12.10 KEY TERMS, REVIEW QUESTIONS, AND PROBLEMS

Key Terms

authenticator Cipher-Based Message Authentication Code (CMAC) CMAC Counter with Cipher Block Chaining-Message Authentication Code (CCM)	cryptographic checksum cryptographic hash function Data Authentication Algorithm (DAA) Galois/Counter Mode (GCM) HMAC	key encryption key Key Wrap mode key wrapping message authentication message authentication code (MAC)

Review Questions

12.1 Define message authentication.

12.2 What two levels of functionality comprise a message authentication or digital signature mechanism?

12.3 What are some approaches to producing message authentication?

12.4 What is the difference between internal and external error control in symmetric encryption?

12.5 What is a message authentication code?

12.6 Why has there been an interest in developing a message authentication code derived from a cryptographic hash function as opposed to one derived from a symmetric cipher?

12.7 In what ways can a hash value be secured so as to provide message authentication?

12.8 Is it necessary to recover the secret key in order to attack a MAC algorithm?

12.9 List and briefly describe the design objectives for HMAC.

Problems

12.1 If F is an error-detection function, either internal or external use (Figure 12.2) will provide error-detection capability. If any bit of the transmitted message is altered, this will be reflected in a mismatch of the received FCS and the calculated FCS, whether the FCS function is performed inside or outside the encryption function. Some codes also provide an error-correction capability. Depending on the nature of the function, if one or a small number of bits is altered in transit, the error-correction code contains sufficient redundant information to determine the errored bit or bits and correct them. Clearly, an error-correction code will provide error correction capability when used external to the encryption function. Will it also provide this capability if used internal to the encryption function?

12.2 The data authentication algorithm, described in Section 12.6, can be defined as using the cipher block chaining (CBC) mode of operation of DES with an initialization vector of zero (Figure 12.7). Show that the same result can be produced using the cipher feedback mode.

12.3 At the beginning of Section 12.6, it was noted that given the CBC MAC of a one-block message X, say $T = \text{MAC}(K, X)$, the adversary immediately knows the CBC MAC for the two-block message $X \| (X \oplus T)$ since this is once again T. Justify this statement.

12.4 In this problem, we demonstrate that for CMAC, a variant that XORs the second key after applying the final encryption doesn't work. Let us consider this for the case of the message being an integer multiple of the block size. Then, the variant can be expressed as $\text{VMAC}(K, M) = \text{CBC}(K, M) \oplus K_1$. Now suppose an adversary is able to ask for the MACs of three messages: the message $\mathbf{0} = 0^n$, where n is the cipher block size; the message $\mathbf{1} = 1^n$; and the message $\mathbf{1} \| \mathbf{0}$. As a result of these three queries, the adversary gets $T_0 = \text{CBC}(K, \mathbf{0}) \oplus K_1$; $T_1 = \text{CBC}(K, \mathbf{1}) \oplus K_1$ and $T_2 = \text{CBC}(K, [CBC(K, 1)]) \oplus K_1$. Show that the adversary can compute the correct MAC for the (unqueried) message $\mathbf{0} \| (T_0 \oplus T_1)$.

12.5 In the discussion of subkey generation in CMAC, it states that the block cipher is applied to the block that consists entirely of 0 bits. The first subkey is derived from the resulting string by a left shift of one bit and, conditionally, by XORing a constant that depends on the block size. The second subkey is derived in the same manner from the first subkey.

a. What constants are needed for block sizes of 64 bits and 128 bits?

b. Explain how the left shift and XOR accomplishes the desired result.

12.6 Section 12.7 described authenticated encryption, a term used to describe encryption systems that simultaneously protect confidentiality and authenticity (integrity) of communications.

a. List and briefly describe the four common approaches to providing both confidentiality and encryption for a message M.

b. In which order are decryption and verification performed in each approach?

12.7 Show that the GHASH function calculates

$$(X_1 \cdot H^m) \oplus (X_2 \cdot H^{m-1}) \oplus \cdots \oplus (X_{m-1} \cdot H^2) \oplus (X_m \cdot H)$$

12.8 Draw a figure similar to Figure 12.11 that shows authenticated decryption.

12.9 Alice want to send a single bit of information (a yes or a no) to Bob by means of a word of length 2. Alice and Bob have four possible keys available to perform message authentication. The following matrix shows the 2-bit word sent for each message under each key:

	Message	
Key	0	1
1	00	11
2	01	10
3	10	01
4	11	00

a. The preceding matrix is in a useful form for Alice. Construct a matrix with the same information that would be more useful for Bob.

b. What is the probability that someone else can successfully impersonate Alice?

c. What is the probability that someone can replace an intercepted message with another message successfully?

12.10 Draw figures similar to Figures 12.12 and 12.13 for the unwrap algorithm.

12.11 Consider the following key wrapping algorithm:

1. Initialize variables.

```
A = A6A6A6A6A6A6A6A6
for i = 1 to n
    R(i) = P_i
```

2. Calculate intermediate values.

```
for j = 0 to 5
    for i = 1 to n
        B = E(K, [A || R(i)])
        t = (n × j) + i
        A = t ⊕ MSB_64(B)
        R(i) = LSB_64(B)
```

3. Output results.

```
C_0 = A
for i = 1 to n
    C_i = R(i)
```

a. Compare this algorithm, functionally, with the algorithm specified in SP 800-38F and described in Section 12.8.

b. Write the corresponding unwrap algorithm.

CHAPTER 13

Digital Signatures

LEARNING OBJECTIVES

After studying this chapter, you should be able to:

- Present an overview of the digital signature process.
- Understand the Elgamal digital signature scheme.
- Understand the Schnorr digital signature scheme.
- Understand the NIST digital signature scheme.
- Compare and contrast the NIST digital signature scheme with the Elgamal and Schnorr digital signature schemes.
- Understand the elliptic curve digital signature scheme.
- Understand the RSA-PSS digital signature scheme.

The most important development from the work on public-key cryptography is the digital signature. The digital signature provides a set of security capabilities that would be difficult to implement in any other way.

Figure 13.1 is a generic model of the process of constructing and using digital signatures. All of the digital signature schemes discussed in this chapter have this structure. Suppose that Bob wants to send a message to Alice. Although it is not important that the message be kept secret, he wants Alice to be certain that the message is indeed from him. For this purpose, Bob uses a secure hash function, such as SHA-512, to generate a hash value for the message. That hash value, together with Bob's private key serves as input to a digital signature generation algorithm, which produces a short block that functions as a **digital signature**. Bob sends the message with the signature attached. When Alice receives the message plus signature, she (1) calculates a hash value for the message; (2) provides the hash value and Bob's public key as inputs to a digital signature verification algorithm. If the algorithm returns the result that the signature is valid, Alice is assured that the message must have been signed by Bob. No one else has Bob's private key and therefore no one else could have created a signature that could be verified for this message with Bob's public key. In addition, it is impossible to alter the message without access to Bob's private key, so the message is authenticated both in terms of source and in terms of data integrity.

We begin this chapter with an overview of digital signatures. We then present the Elgamal and Schnorr digital signature schemes, understanding of which makes it easier to understand the NIST Digital Signature Algorithm (DSA). The chapter then covers the two other important standardized digital signature schemes: the Elliptic Curve Digital Signature Algorithm (ECDSA) and the RSA Probabilistic Signature Scheme (RSA-PSS).

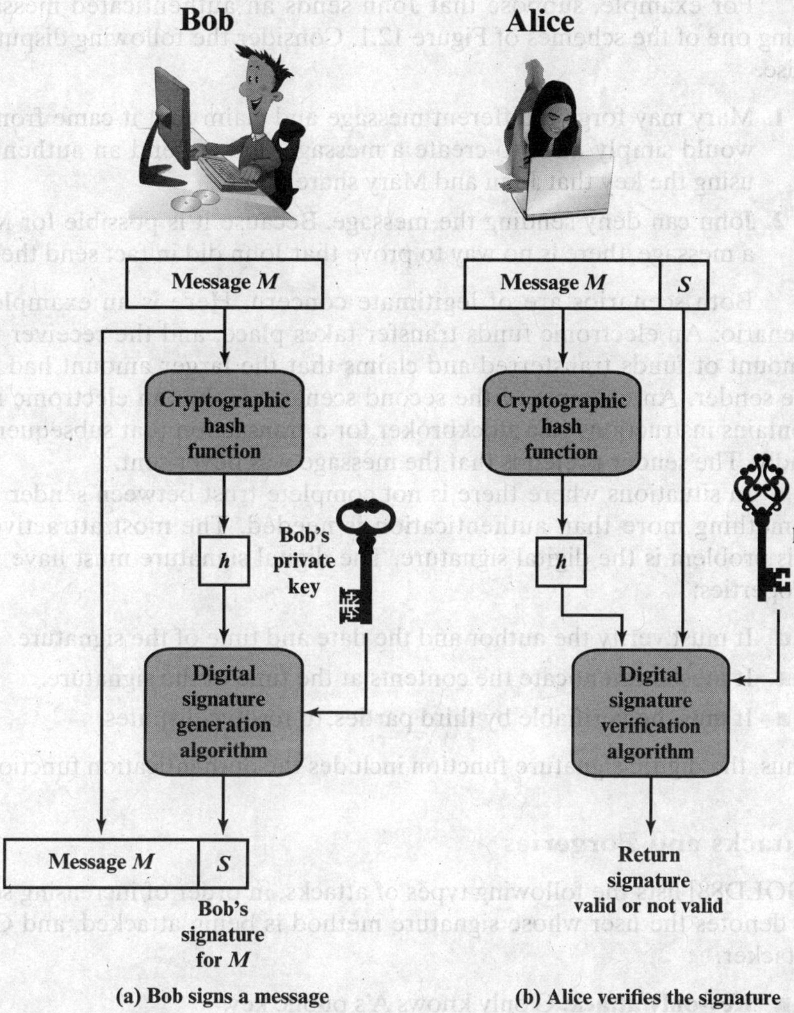

Figure 13.1 Simplified Depiction of Essential Elements of Digital Signature Process

13.1 DIGITAL SIGNATURES

Properties

Message authentication protects two parties who exchange messages from any third party. However, it does not protect the two parties against each other. Several forms of dispute between the two parties are possible.

For example, suppose that John sends an authenticated message to Mary, using one of the schemes of Figure 12.1. Consider the following disputes that could arise.

1. Mary may forge a different message and claim that it came from John. Mary would simply have to create a message and append an authentication code using the key that John and Mary share.
2. John can deny sending the message. Because it is possible for Mary to forge a message, there is no way to prove that John did in fact send the message.

Both scenarios are of legitimate concern. Here is an example of the first scenario: An electronic funds transfer takes place, and the receiver increases the amount of funds transferred and claims that the larger amount had arrived from the sender. An example of the second scenario is that an electronic mail message contains instructions to a stockbroker for a transaction that subsequently turns out badly. The sender pretends that the message was never sent.

In situations where there is not complete trust between sender and receiver, something more than authentication is needed. The most attractive solution to this problem is the digital signature. The digital signature must have the following properties:

- It must verify the author and the date and time of the signature.
- It must authenticate the contents at the time of the signature.
- It must be verifiable by third parties, to resolve disputes.

Thus, the digital signature function includes the authentication function.

Attacks and Forgeries

[GOLD88] lists the following types of attacks, in order of increasing severity. Here A denotes the user whose signature method is being attacked, and C denotes the attacker.

- **Key-only attack:** C only knows A's public key.
- **Known message attack:** C is given access to a set of messages and their signatures.
- **Generic chosen message attack:** C chooses a list of messages before attempting to breaks A's signature scheme, independent of A's public key. C then obtains from A valid signatures for the chosen messages. The attack is generic, because it does not depend on A's public key; the same attack is used against everyone.
- **Directed chosen message attack:** Similar to the generic attack, except that the list of messages to be signed is chosen after C knows A's public key but before any signatures are seen.
- **Adaptive chosen message attack:** C is allowed to use A as an "oracle." This means that C may request from A signatures of messages that depend on previously obtained message-signature pairs.

[GOLD88] then defines success at breaking a signature scheme as an outcome in which C can do any of the following with a non-negligible probability:

- **Total break:** C determines A's private key.
- **Universal forgery:** C finds an efficient signing algorithm that provides an equivalent way of constructing signatures on arbitrary messages.
- **Selective forgery:** C forges a signature for a particular message chosen by C.
- **Existential forgery:** C forges a signature for at least one message. C has no control over the message. Consequently, this forgery may only be a minor nuisance to A.

Digital Signature Requirements

On the basis of the properties and attacks just discussed, we can formulate the following requirements for a digital signature.

- The signature must be a bit pattern that depends on the message being signed.
- The signature must use some information only known to the sender to prevent both forgery and denial.
- It must be relatively easy to produce the digital signature.
- It must be relatively easy to recognize and verify the digital signature.
- It must be computationally infeasible to forge a digital signature, either by constructing a new message for an existing digital signature or by constructing a fraudulent digital signature for a given message.
- It must be practical to retain a copy of the digital signature in storage.

A secure hash function, embedded in a scheme such as that of Figure 13.1, provides a basis for satisfying these requirements. However, care must be taken in the design of the details of the scheme.

Direct Digital Signature

The term **direct digital signature** refers to a digital signature scheme that involves only the communicating parties (source, destination). It is assumed that the destination knows the public key of the source.

Confidentiality can be provided by encrypting the entire message plus signature with a shared secret key (symmetric encryption). Note that it is important to perform the signature function first and then an outer confidentiality function. In case of dispute, some third party must view the message and its signature. If the signature is calculated on an encrypted message, then the third party also needs access to the decryption key to read the original message. However, if the signature is the inner operation, then the recipient can store the plaintext message and its signature for later use in dispute resolution.

The validity of the scheme just described depends on the security of the sender's private key. If a sender later wishes to deny sending a particular message, the sender can claim that the private key was lost or stolen and that someone else forged his or her signature. Administrative controls relating to the security of private keys can be employed to thwart or at least weaken this ploy, but the threat is still there, at least to some degree. One example is to require every signed message to include a **timestamp** (date and time) and to require prompt reporting of compromised keys to a central authority.

Another threat is that a private key might actually be stolen from X at time T. The opponent can then send a message signed with X's signature and stamped with a time before or equal to T.

The universally accepted technique for dealing with these threats is the use of a digital certificate and certificate authorities. We defer a discussion of this topic until Chapter 14, and focus in this chapter on digital signature algorithms.

13.2 ELGAMAL DIGITAL SIGNATURE SCHEME

Before examining the NIST Digital Signature Algorithm, it will be helpful to understand the Elgamal and Schnorr signature schemes. Recall from Chapter 10, that the Elgamal encryption scheme is designed to enable encryption by a user's public key with decryption by the user's private key. The Elgamal signature scheme involves the use of the private key for digital signature generation and the public key for digital signature verification [ELGA84, ELGA85].

Before proceeding, we need a result from number theory. Recall from Chapter 2 that for a prime number q, if α is a primitive root of q, then

$$\alpha, \alpha^2, \ldots, \alpha^{q-1}$$

are distinct (mod q). It can be shown that, if α is a primitive root of q, then

1. For any integer m, $\alpha^m \equiv 1 \pmod{q}$ if and only if $m \equiv 0 \pmod{q-1}$.
2. For any integers, i, j, $\alpha^i \equiv \alpha^j \pmod{q}$ if and only if $i \equiv j \pmod{q-1}$.

As with Elgamal encryption, the global elements of **Elgamal digital signature** are a prime number q and α, which is a primitive root of q. User A generates a private/public key pair as follows.

1. Generate a random integer X_A, such that $1 < X_A < q - 1$.
2. Compute $Y_A = \alpha^{X_A} \bmod q$.
3. A's private key is X_A; A's pubic key is $\{q, \alpha, Y_A\}$.

To sign a message M, user A first computes the hash $m = \mathrm{H}(M)$, such that m is an integer in the range $0 \leq m \leq q - 1$. A then forms a digital signature as follows.

1. Choose a random integer K such that $1 \leq K \leq q - 1$ and $\gcd(K, q - 1) = 1$. That is, K is relatively prime to $q - 1$.
2. Compute $S_1 = \alpha^K \bmod q$. Note that this is the same as the computation of C_1 for Elgamal encryption.
3. Compute $K^{-1} \bmod (q - 1)$. That is, compute the inverse of K modulo $q - 1$.
4. Compute $S_2 = K^{-1}(m - X_A S_1) \bmod (q - 1)$.
5. The signature consists of the pair (S_1, S_2).

Any user B can verify the signature as follows.

1. Compute $V_1 = \alpha^m \bmod q$.
2. Compute $V_2 = (Y_A)^{S_1}(S_1)^{S_2} \bmod q$.

The signature is valid if $V_1 = V_2$. Let us demonstrate that this is so. Assume that the equality is true. Then we have

$\alpha^m \bmod q = (Y_A)^{S_1}(S_1)^{S_2} \bmod q$	assume $V_1 = V_2$
$\alpha^m \bmod q = \alpha^{X_A S_1}\alpha^{K S_2} \bmod q$	substituting for Y_A and S_1
$\alpha^{m - X_A S_1} \bmod q = \alpha^{K S_2} \bmod q$	rearranging terms
$m - X_A S_1 \equiv K S_2 \bmod (q - 1)$	property of primitive roots
$m - X_A S_1 \equiv K K^{-1} (m - X_A S_1) \bmod (q - 1)$	substituting for S_2

For example, let us start with the prime field GF(19); that is, $q = 19$. It has primitive roots {2, 3, 10, 13, 14, 15}, as shown in Table 2.7. We choose $\alpha = 10$.

Alice generates a key pair as follows:

1. Alice chooses $X_A = 16$.
2. Then $Y_A = \alpha^{X_A} \bmod q = \alpha^{16} \bmod 19 = 4$.
3. Alice's private key is 16; Alice's pubic key is $\{q, \alpha, Y_A\} = \{19, 10, 4\}$.

Suppose Alice wants to sign a message with hash value $m = 14$.

1. Alice chooses $K = 5$, which is relatively prime to $q - 1 = 18$.
2. $S_1 = \alpha^K \bmod q = 10^5 \bmod 19 = 3$ (see Table 2.7).
3. $K^{-1} \bmod (q - 1) = 5^{-1} \bmod 18 = 11$.
4. $S_2 = K^{-1}(m - X_A S_1) \bmod (q - 1) = 11(14 - (16)(3)) \bmod 18 = -374 \bmod 18 = 4$.

Bob can verify the signature as follows.

1. $V_1 = \alpha^m \bmod q = 10^{14} \bmod 19 = 16$.
2. $V_2 = (Y_A)^{S_1}(S_1)^{S_2} \bmod q = (4^3)(3^4) \bmod 19 = 5184 \bmod 19 = 16$.

Thus, the signature is valid because $V_1 = V_2$.

13.3 SCHNORR DIGITAL SIGNATURE SCHEME

As with the Elgamal digital signature scheme, the Schnorr signature scheme is based on discrete logarithms [SCHN89, SCHN91]. The Schnorr scheme minimizes the message-dependent amount of computation required to generate a signature. The main work for signature generation does not depend on the message and can be done during the idle time of the processor. The message-dependent part of the signature generation requires multiplying a $2n$-bit integer with an n-bit integer.

The scheme is based on using a prime modulus p, with $p - 1$ having a prime factor q of appropriate size; that is, $p - 1 \equiv 0 \pmod{q}$. Typically, we use $p \approx 2^{1024}$ and $q \approx 2^{160}$. Thus, p is a 1024-bit number, and q is a 160-bit number, which is also the length of the SHA-1 hash value.

The first part of this scheme is the generation of a private/public key pair, which consists of the following steps.

1. Choose primes p and q, such that q is a prime factor of $p - 1$.
2. Choose an integer a, such that $a^q = 1 \bmod p$. The values a, p, and q comprise a global public key that can be common to a group of users.
3. Choose a random integer s with $0 < s < q$. This is the user's private key.
4. Calculate $v = a^{-s} \bmod p$. This is the user's public key.

A user with private key s and public key v generates a signature as follows.

1. Choose a random integer r with $0 < r < q$ and compute $x = a^r \bmod p$. This computation is a preprocessing stage independent of the message M to be signed.
2. Concatenate the message with x and hash the result to compute the value e:
$$e = H(M \| x)$$
3. Compute $y = (r + se) \bmod q$. The signature consists of the pair (e, y).

Any other user can verify the signature as follows.

1. Compute $x' = a^y v^e \bmod p$.
2. Verify that $e = H(M \| x')$.

To see that the verification works, observe that

$$x' \equiv a^y v^e \equiv a^y a^{-se} \equiv a^{y-se} \equiv a^r \equiv x \pmod p$$

Hence, $H(M \| x') = H(M \| x)$.

13.4 NIST DIGITAL SIGNATURE ALGORITHM

The National Institute of Standards and Technology (NIST) has published Federal Information Processing Standard FIPS 186, known as the Digital Signature Algorithm (DSA). The DSA makes use of the Secure Hash Algorithm (SHA) described in Chapter 12. The DSA was originally proposed in 1991 and revised in 1993 in response to public feedback concerning the security of the scheme. There was a further minor revision in 1996. In 2000, an expanded version of the standard was issued as FIPS 186-2, subsequently updated to FIPS 186-3 in 2009, and FIPS 186-4 in 2013. This latest version also incorporates digital signature algorithms based on RSA and on elliptic curve cryptography. In this section, we discuss DSA.

The DSA Approach

The DSA uses an algorithm that is designed to provide only the digital signature function. Unlike RSA, it cannot be used for encryption or key exchange. Nevertheless, it is a public-key technique.

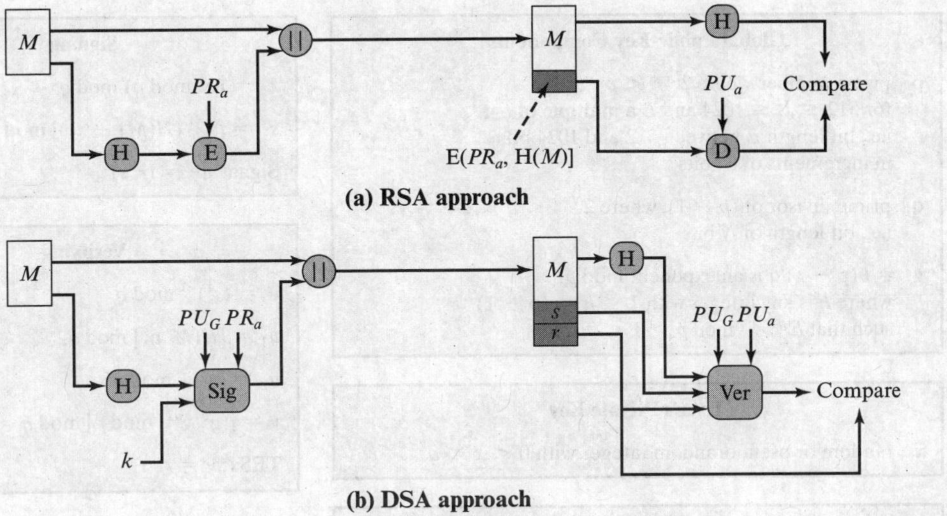

Figure 13.2 Two Approaches to Digital Signatures

Figure 13.2 contrasts the DSA approach for generating digital signatures to that used with RSA. In the RSA approach, the message to be signed is input to a hash function that produces a secure hash code of fixed length. This hash code is then encrypted using the sender's private key to form the signature. Both the message and the signature are then transmitted. The recipient takes the message and produces a hash code. The recipient also decrypts the signature using the sender's public key. If the calculated hash code matches the decrypted signature, the signature is accepted as valid. Because only the sender knows the private key, only the sender could have produced a valid signature.

The DSA approach also makes use of a hash function. The hash code is provided as input to a signature function along with a random number k generated for this particular signature. The signature function also depends on the sender's private key (PR_a) and a set of parameters known to a group of communicating principals. We can consider this set to constitute a global public key (PU_G).[1] The result is a signature consisting of two components, labeled s and r.

At the receiving end, the hash code of the incoming message is generated. The hash code and the signature are inputs to a verification function. The verification function also depends on the global public key as well as the sender's public key (PU_a), which is paired with the sender's private key. The output of the verification function is a value that is equal to the signature component r if the signature is valid. The signature function is such that only the sender, with knowledge of the private key, could have produced the valid signature.

We turn now to the details of the algorithm.

[1]It is also possible to allow these additional parameters to vary with each user so that they are a part of a user's public key. In practice, it is more likely that a global public key will be used that is separate from each user's public key.

Global Public-Key Components

p prime number where $2^{L-1} < p < 2^L$ for $512 \le L \le 1024$ and L a multiple of 64; i.e., bit length L between 512 and 1024 bits in increments of 64 bits

q prime divisor of $(p - 1)$, where $2^{N-1} < q < 2^N$ i.e., bit length of N bits

g $= h(p - 1)/q$ is an exponent mod p, where h is any integer with $1 < h < (p - 1)$ such that $h^{(p-1)/q} \bmod p > 1$

User's Private Key

x random or pseudorandom integer with $0 < x < q$

User's Public Key

$y = g^x \bmod p$

User's Per-Message Secret Number

k random or pseudorandom integer with $0 < k < q$

Signing

$r = (g^k \bmod p) \bmod q$

$s = [k^{-1}(H(M) + xr)] \bmod q$

Signature $= (r, s)$

Verifying

$w = (s')^{-1} \bmod q$

$u_1 = [H(M')w] \bmod q$

$u_2 = (r')w \bmod q$

$v = [(g^{u1} y^{u2}) \bmod p] \bmod q$

TEST: $v = r'$

M = message to be signed

$H(M)$ = hash of M using SHA-1

M', r', s' = received versions of M, r, s

Figure 13.3 The Digital Signature Algorithm (DSA)

The Digital Signature Algorithm

DSA is based on the difficulty of computing discrete logarithms (see Chapter 2) and is based on schemes originally presented by Elgamal [ELGA85] and Schnorr [SCHN91].

Figure 13.3 summarizes the algorithm. There are three parameters that are public and can be common to a group of users. An N-bit prime number q is chosen. Next, a prime number p is selected with a length between 512 and 1024 bits such that q divides $(p - 1)$. Finally, g is chosen to be of the form $h^{(p-1)/q} \bmod p$, where h is an integer between 1 and $(p - 1)$ with the restriction that g must be greater than 1.[2] Thus, the global public-key components of DSA are the same as in the Schnorr signature scheme.

With these parameters in hand, each user selects a private key and generates a public key. The private key x must be a number from 1 to $(q - 1)$ and should be chosen randomly or pseudorandomly. The public key is calculated from the private key as $y = g^x \bmod p$. The calculation of y given x is relatively straightforward. However, given the public key y, it is believed to be computationally infeasible to determine x, which is the discrete logarithm of y to the base g, mod p (see Chapter 2).

[2]In number-theoretic terms, g is of order q mod p; see Chapter 2.

The signature of a message M consists of the pair of numbers r and s, which are functions of the public key components (p, q, g), the user's private key (x), the hash code of the message H(M), and an additional integer k that should be generated randomly or pseudorandomly and be unique for each signing.

Let M, r', and s' be the received versions of M, r, and s, respectively. Verification is performed using the formulas shown in Figure 13.3. The receiver generates a quantity v that is a function of the public key components, the sender's public key, the hash code of the incoming message, and the received versions of r and s. If this quantity matches the r component of the signature, then the signature is validated.

Figure 13.4 depicts the functions of signing and verifying.

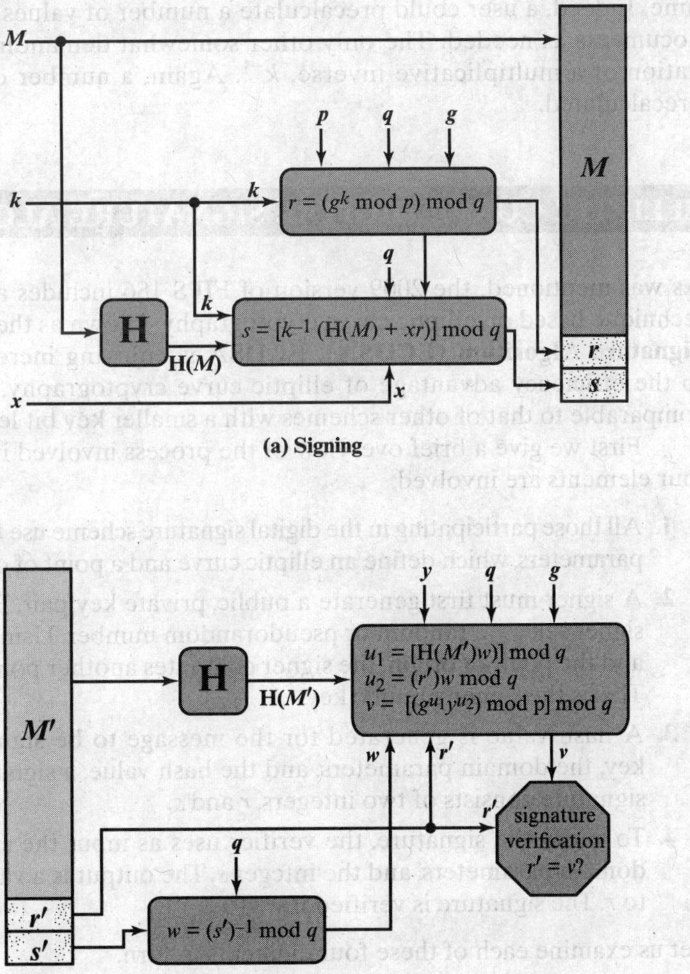

Figure 13.4 DSA Signing and Verifying

The structure of the algorithm, as revealed in Figure 13.4, is quite interesting. Note that the test at the end is on the value r, which does not depend on the message at all. Instead, r is a function of k and the three global public-key components. The multiplicative inverse of k (mod q) is passed to a function that also has as inputs the message hash code and the user's private key. The structure of this function is such that the receiver can recover r using the incoming message and signature, the public key of the user, and the global public key. It is certainly not obvious from Figure 13.3 or Figure 13.4 that such a scheme would work. A proof is provided in Appendix K.

Given the difficulty of taking discrete logarithms, it is infeasible for an opponent to recover k from r or to recover x from s.

Another point worth noting is that the only computationally demanding task in signature generation is the exponential calculation $g^k \bmod p$. Because this value does not depend on the message to be signed, it can be computed ahead of time. Indeed, a user could precalculate a number of values of r to be used to sign documents as needed. The only other somewhat demanding task is the determination of a multiplicative inverse, k^{-1}. Again, a number of these values can be precalculated.

13.5 ELLIPTIC CURVE DIGITAL SIGNATURE ALGORITHM

As was mentioned, the 2009 version of FIPS 186 includes a new digital signature technique based on elliptic curve cryptography, known as the **Elliptic Curve Digital Signature Algorithm (ECDSA)**. ECDSA is enjoying increasing acceptance due to the efficiency advantage of elliptic curve cryptography, which yields security comparable to that of other schemes with a smaller key bit length.

First we give a brief overview of the process involved in ECDSA. In essence, four elements are involved.

1. All those participating in the digital signature scheme use the same global domain parameters, which define an elliptic curve and a point of origin on the curve.
2. A signer must first generate a public, private key pair. For the private key, the signer selects a random or pseudorandom number. Using that random number and the point of origin, the signer computes another point on the elliptic curve. This is the signer's public key.
3. A hash value is generated for the message to be signed. Using the private key, the domain parameters, and the hash value, a signature is generated. The signature consists of two integers, r and s.
4. To verify the signature, the verifier uses as input the signer's public key, the domain parameters, and the integer s. The output is a value v that is compared to r. The signature is verified if $v = r$.

Let us examine each of these four elements in turn.

Global Domain Parameters

Recall from Chapter 10 that two families of elliptic curves are used in cryptographic applications: prime curves over Z_p and binary curves over GF(2^m). For ECDSA, prime curves are used. The global domain parameters for ECDSA are the following:

q	a prime number
a, b	integers that specify the elliptic curve equation defined over Z_q with the equation $y^2 = x^3 + ax + b$
G	a base point represented by $G = (x_g, y_g)$ on the elliptic curve equation
n	order of point G; that is, n is the smallest positive integer such that $nG = O$. This is also the number of points on the curve.

Key Generation

Each signer must generate a pair of keys, one private and one public. The signer, let us call him Bob, generates the two keys using the following steps:

1. Select a random integer d, $d \in [1, n - 1]$
2. Compute $Q = dG$. This is a point in $E_q(a, b)$
3. Bob's public key is Q and private key is d.

Digital Signature Generation and Authentication

With the public domain parameters and a private key in hand, Bob generates a digital signature of 320 bytes for message m using the following steps:

1. Select a random or pseudorandom integer k, $k \in [1, n - 1]$
2. Compute point $P = (x, y) = kG$ and $r = x \bmod n$. If $r = 0$ then goto step 1
3. Compute $t = k^{-1} \bmod n$
4. Compute $e = H(m)$, where H is one of the SHA-2 or SHA-3 hash functions.
5. Compute $s = k^{-1}(e + dr) \bmod n$. If $s = O$ then goto step 1
6. The signature of message m is the pair (r, s).

Alice knows the public domain parameters and Bob's public key. Alice is presented with Bob's message and digital signature and verifies the signature using the following steps:

1. Verify that r and s are integers in the range 1 through $n - 1$
2. Using SHA, compute the 160-bit hash value $e = H(m)$
3. Compute $w = s^{-1} \bmod n$
4. Compute $u_1 = ew$ and $u_2 = rw$
5. Compute the point $X = (x_1, y_1) = u_1G + u_2Q$
6. If $X = O$, reject the signature else compute $v = x_1 \bmod n$
7. Accept Bob's signature if and only if $v = r$

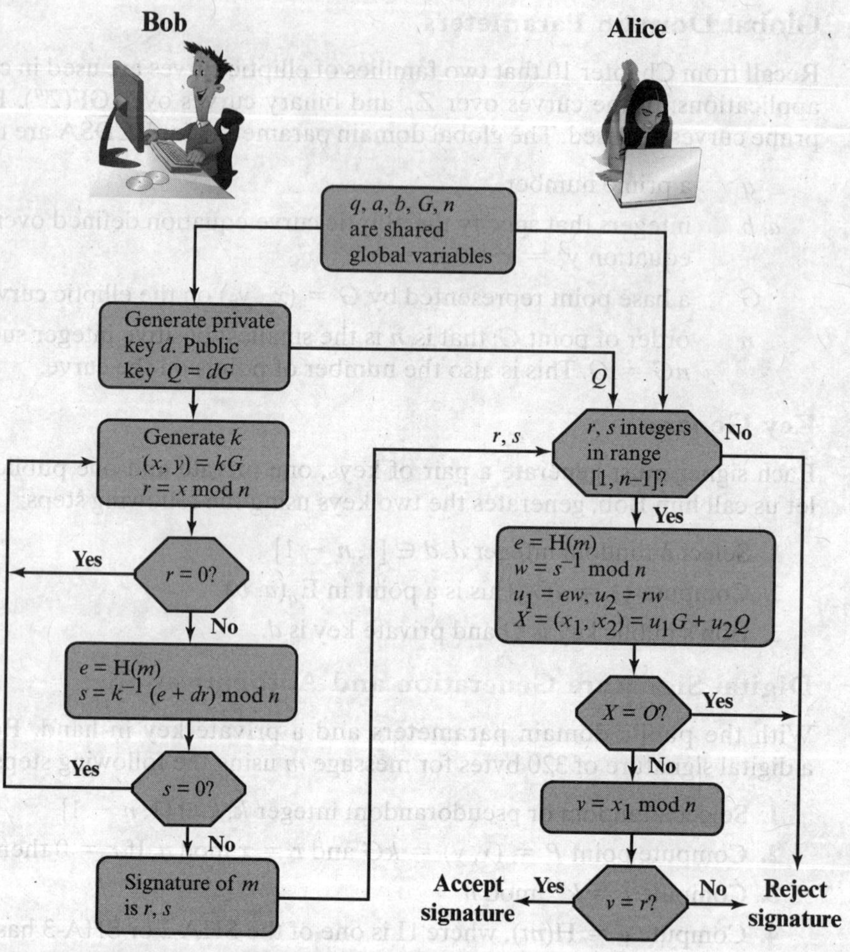

Figure 13.5 ECDSA Signing and Verifying

Figure 13.5 illustrates the signature authentication process. We can verify that this process is valid as follows. If the message received by Alice is in fact signed by Bob, then

$$s = k^{-1}(e + dr) \bmod n$$

Then

$$k = s^{-1}(e + dr) \bmod n$$
$$k = (s^{-1}e + s^{-1}dr) \bmod n$$
$$k = (we + wdr) \bmod n$$
$$k = (u_1 + u_2 d) \bmod n$$

Now consider that

$$u_1G + u_2Q = u_1G + u_2dG = (u_1 + u_2d)G = kG$$

In step 6 of the verification process, we have $v = x_1 \bmod n$, where point $X = (x_1, y_1) = u_1G + u_2Q$. Thus we see that $v = r$ since $r = x \bmod n$ and x is the x coordinate of the point kG and we have already seen that $u_1G + u_2Q = kG$.

13.6 RSA-PSS DIGITAL SIGNATURE ALGORITHM

In addition to the NIST Digital Signature Algorithm and ECDSA, the 2009 version of FIPS 186 also includes several techniques based on RSA, all of which were developed by RSA Laboratories and are in wide use. A worked-out example, using RSA, is available at this book's Web site.

In this section, we discuss the RSA Probabilistic Signature Scheme (RSA-PSS), which is the latest of the RSA schemes and the one that RSA Laboratories recommends as the most secure of the RSA schemes.

Because the RSA-based schemes are widely deployed in many applications, including financial applications, there has been great interest in demonstrating that such schemes are secure. The three main RSA signature schemes differ mainly in the padding format the signature generation operation employs to embed the hash value into a message representative, and in how the signature verification operation determines that the hash value and the message representative are consistent. For all of the schemes developed prior to PSS, it has not been possible to develop a mathematical proof that the signature scheme is as secure as the underlying RSA encryption/decryption primitive [KALI01]. The PSS approach was first proposed by Bellare and Rogaway [BELL96c, BELL98]. This approach, unlike the other RSA-based schemes, introduces a randomization process that enables the security of the method to be shown to be closely related to the security of the RSA algorithm itself. This makes RSA-PSS more desirable as the choice for RSA-based digital signature applications.

Mask Generation Function

Before explaining the RSA-PSS operation, we need to describe the mask generation function (MGF) used as a building block. MGF(X, *maskLen*) is a pseudorandom function that has as input parameters a bit string X of any length and the desired length L in octets of the output. MGFs are typically based on a secure cryptographic hash function such as SHA-1. An MGF based on a hash function is intended to be a cryptographically secure way of generating a message digest, or hash, of variable length based on an underlying cryptographic hash function that produces a fixed-length output.

The MGF function used in the current specification for RSA-PSS is MGF1, with the following parameters:

Options	Hash	hash function with output *hLen* octets
Input	X	octet string to be masked
	maskLen	length in octets of the mask
Output	*mask*	an octet string of length *maskLen*

MGF1 is defined as follows:

1. **Initialize variables.**

```
T = empty string
k = ⌈maskLen/hLen⌉ - 1
```

2. **Calculate intermediate values.**

```
for counter = 0 to k
Represent counter as a 32-bit string C
T = T ‖ Hash(X ‖ C)
```

3. **Output results.**

```
mask = the leading maskLen octets of T
```

In essence, MGF1 does the following. If the length of the desired output is equal to the length of the hash value ($maskLen = hLen$), then the output is the hash of the input value X concatenated with a 32-bit counter value of 0. If *maskLen* is greater than *hLen*, the MGF1 keeps iterating by hashing X concatenated with the counter and appending that to the current string T. So that the output is

$$\text{Hash}(X\|0)\,\|\,\text{Hash}(X\|1)\,\|\,\ldots\,\|\,\text{Hash}(X\|k)$$

This is repeated until the length of T is greater than or equal to *maskLen*, at which point the output is the first *maskLen* octets of T.

The Signing Operation

MESSAGE ENCODING The first stage in generating an RSA-PSS signature of a message M is to generate from M a fixed-length message digest, called an encoded message (*EM*). Figure 13.6 illustrates this process. We define the following parameters and functions:

Options	Hash	hash function with output *hLen* octets. The current preferred alternative is SHA-1, which produces a 20-octet hash value.
	MGF	mask generation function. The current specification calls for MGF1.
	sLen	length in octets of the salt. Typically $sLen = hLen$, which for the current version is 20 octets.
Input	*M*	message to be encoded for signing.
	emBits	This value is one less than the length in bits of the RSA modulus *n*.
Output	*EM*	encoded message. This is the message digest that will be encrypted to form the digital signature.
Parameters	*emLen*	length of *EM* in octets = $\lceil emBits/8 \rceil$.
	padding_1	hexadecimal string 00 00 00 00 00 00 00 00; that is, a string of 64 zero bits.

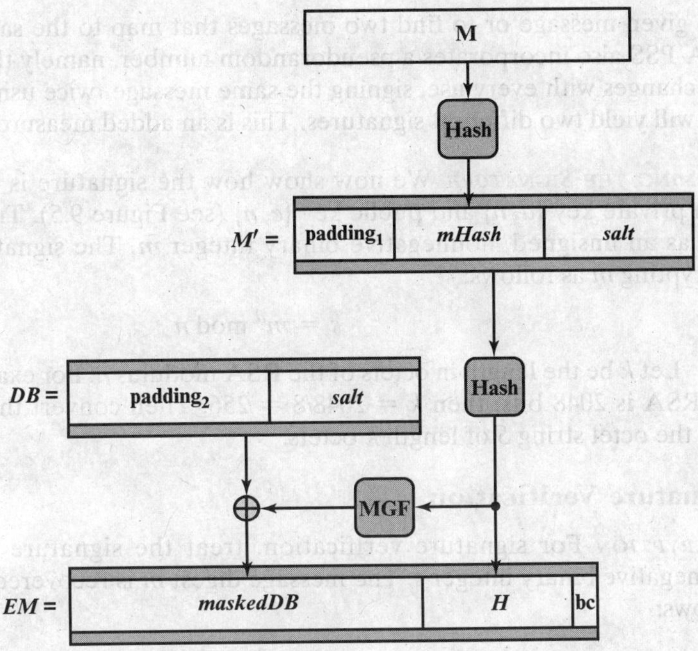

Figure 13.6 RSA-PSS Encoding

padding$_2$	hexadecimal string of 00 octets with a length ($emLen - sLen - hLen - 2$) octets, followed by the hexadecimal octet with value 01.
salt	a pseudorandom number.
bc	the hexadecimal value BC.

The encoding process consists of the following steps.

1. Generate the hash value of M: $mHash = \text{Hash}(M)$
2. Generate a pseudorandom octet string *salt* and form block $M' = \text{padding}_1 \| mHash \| salt$
3. Generate the hash value of M': $H = \text{Hash}(M')$
4. Form data block $DB = \text{padding}_2 \| salt$
5. Calculate the MGF value of H: $dbMask = \text{MGF}(H, emLen - hLen - 1)$
6. Calculate $maskedDB = DB \oplus dbMsk$
7. Set the leftmost $8emLen - emBits$ bits of the leftmost octet in *maskedDB* to 0
8. $EM = maskedDB \| H \| \text{0xbc}$

We make several comments about the complex nature of this message digest algorithm. All of the RSA-based standardized digital signature schemes involve appending one or more constants (e.g., padding$_1$ and padding$_2$) in the process of forming the message digest. The objective is to make it more difficult for an adversary to find another message that maps to the same message digest as a given message or to find two messages that map to the same message digest. RSA-PSS also incorporates a pseudorandom number, namely the salt. Because the salt changes with every use, signing the same message twice using the same private key will yield two different signatures. This is an added measure of security.

Forming the Signature We now show how the signature is formed by a signer with private key $\{d, n\}$ and public key $\{e, n\}$ (see Figure 9.5). Treat the octet string *EM* as an unsigned, nonnegative binary integer m. The signature s is formed by encrypting m as follows:

$$s = m^d \bmod n$$

Let k be the length in octets of the RSA modulus n. For example if the key size for RSA is 2048 bits, then $k = 2048/8 = 256$. Then convert the signature value s into the octet string S of length k octets.

Signature Verification

Decryption For signature verification, treat the signature S as an unsigned, nonnegative binary integer s. The message digest m is recovered by decrypting s as follows:

$$m = s^e \bmod n$$

Then, convert the message representative m to an encoded message *EM* of length $emLen = \lceil (modBits - 1)/8 \rceil$ octets, where *modBits* is the length in bits of the RSA modulus n.

EM Verification *EM* verification can be described as follows:

Options	Hash	hash function with output *hLen* octets.
	MGF	mask generation function.
	sLen	length in octets of the salt.
Input	*M*	message to be verified.
	EM	the octet string representing the decrypted signature, with length $emLen = \lceil emBits/8 \rceil$.
	emBits	This value is one less than the length in bits of the RSA modulus n.
Parameters	padding_1	hexadecimal string 00 00 00 00 00 00 00 00; that is, a string of 64 zero bits.
	padding_2	hexadecimal string of 00 octets with a length $(emLen - sLen - hLen - 2)$ octets, followed by the hexadecimal octet with value 01.

1. Generate the hash value of M: $mHash = \text{Hash}(M)$
2. If $emLen < hLen + sLen + 2$, output "inconsistent" and stop
3. If the rightmost octet of *EM* does not have hexadecimal value BC, output "inconsistent" and stop

4. Let *maskedDB* be the leftmost $emLen - hLen - 1$ octets of *EM*, and let *H* be the next *hLen* octets
5. If the leftmost $8emLen - emBits$ bits of the leftmost octet in *maskedDB* are not all equal to zero, output "inconsistent" and stop
6. Calculate $dbMask = \text{MGF}(H, emLen - hLen - 1)$
7. Calculate $DB = maskedDB \oplus dbMsk$
8. Set the leftmost $8emLen - emBits$ bits of the leftmost octet in *DB* to zero
9. If the leftmost $(emLen - hLen - sLen - 1)$ octets of *DB* are not equal to padding_2, output "inconsistent" and stop
10. Let *salt* be the last *sLen* octets of *DB*
11. Form block $M' = \text{padding}_1 \| mHash \| salt$
12. Generate the hash value of M': $H' = \text{Hash}(M')$
13. If $H = H'$, output "consistent." Otherwise, output "inconsistent"

Figure 13.7 illustrates the process. The shaded boxes labeled *H* and *H'* correspond, respectively, to the value contained in the decrypted signature and the value generated from the message *M* associated with the signature. The remaining three shaded areas contain values generated from the decrypted signature and compared to known constants. We can now see more clearly the different roles played by the constants and the pseudorandom value *salt*, all of which are embedded in the

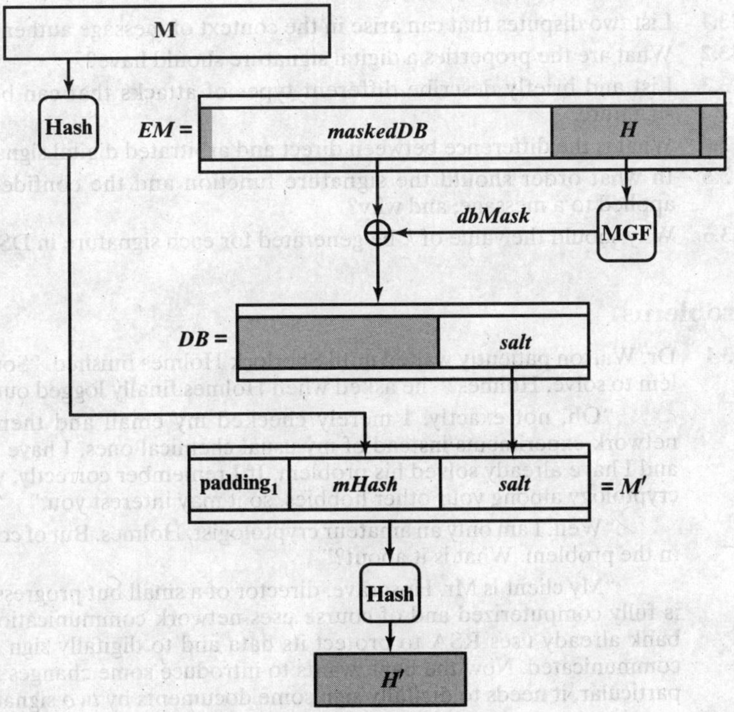

Figure 13.7 RSA-PSS EM Verification

EM generated by the signer. The constants are known to the verifier, so that the computed constants can be compared to the known constants as an additional check that the signature is valid (in addition to comparing H and H'). The salt results in a different signature every time a given message is signed with the same private key. The verifier does not know the value of the salt and does not attempt a comparison. Thus, the salt plays a similar role to the pseudorandom variable k in the NIST DSA and in ECDSA. In both of those schemes, k is a pseudorandom number generated by the signer, resulting in different signatures from multiple signings of the same message with the same private key. A verifier does not and need not know the value of k.

13.7 KEY TERMS, REVIEW QUESTIONS, AND PROBLEMS

Key Terms

digital signature Digital Signature Algorithm (DSA) direct digital signature	Elgamal digital signature Elliptic Curve Digital Signature Algorithm (ECDSA)	Schnorr digital signature timestamp

Review Questions

13.1 List two disputes that can arise in the context of message authentication.

13.2 What are the properties a digital signature should have?

13.3 List and briefly describe different types of attacks that can be made on a digital signature.

13.4 What is the difference between direct and arbitrated digital signature?

13.5 In what order should the signature function and the confidentiality function be applied to a message, and why?

13.6 Why should the value of k be generated for each signature in DSA?

Problems

13.1 Dr. Watson patiently waited until Sherlock Holmes finished. "Some interesting problem to solve, Holmes?" he asked when Holmes finally logged out.

"Oh, not exactly. I merely checked my email and then made a couple of network experiments instead of my usual chemical ones. I have only one client now and I have already solved his problem. If I remember correctly, you once mentioned cryptology among your other hobbies, so it may interest you."

"Well, I am only an amateur cryptologist, Holmes. But of course I am interested in the problem. What is it about?"

"My client is Mr. Hosgrave, director of a small but progressive bank. The bank is fully computerized and of course uses network communications extensively. The bank already uses RSA to protect its data and to digitally sign documents that are communicated. Now the bank wants to introduce some changes in its procedures; in particular, it needs to digitally sign some documents by *two* signatories.

1. The first signatory prepares the document, forms its signature, and passes the document to the second signatory.

2. The second signatory as a first step must verify that the document was really signed by the first signatory. She then incorporates her signature into the document's signature so that the recipient, as well as any member of the public, may verify that the document was indeed signed by both signatories. In addition, only the second signatory has to be able to verify the document's signature after the first step; that is, the recipient (or any member of the public) should be able to verify only the complete document with signatures of both signatories, but not the document in its intermediate form where only one signatory has signed it. Moreover, the bank would like to make use of its existing modules that support RSA-style digital signatures."

"Hm, I understand how RSA can be used to digitally sign documents by *one* signatory, Holmes. I guess you have solved the problem of Mr. Hosgrave by appropriate generalization of RSA digital signatures."

"Exactly, Watson," nodded Sherlock Holmes. "Originally, the RSA digital signature was formed by encrypting the document by the signatory's private decryption key 'd', and the signature could be verified by anyone through its decryption using publicly known encryption key 'e'. One can verify that the signature S was formed by the person who knows d, which is supposed to be the only signatory. Now the problem of Mr. Hosgrave can be solved in the same way by slight generalization of the process, that is ..."

Finish the explanation.

13.2 DSA specifies that if the signature generation process results in a value of $s = 0$, a new value of k should be generated and the signature should be recalculated. Why?

13.3 In DSA explain why the calculation of r is done in modulo p modulo q, but the calculation of s is done only in modulo q?

13.4 The DSA document includes a recommended algorithm for testing a number for primality.

1. **[Choose** w**]** Let w be a random odd integer. Then $(w - 1)$ is even and can be expressed in the form $2^a m$ with m odd. That is, 2^a is the largest power of 2 that divides $(w - 1)$.
2. **[Generate** b**]** Let b be a random integer in the range $1 < b < w$.
3. **[Exponentiate]** Set $j = 0$ and $z = b^m \bmod w$.
4. **[Done?]** If $j = 0$ and $z = 1$, or if $z = w - 1$, then w passes the test and may be prime; go to step 8.
5. **[Terminate?]** If $j > 0$ and $z = 1$, then w is not prime; terminate algorithm for this w.
6. **[Increase** j**]** Set $j = j + 1$. If $j < a$, set $z = z^2 \bmod w$ and go to step 4.
7. **[Terminate]** w is not prime; terminate algorithm for this w.
8. **[Test again?]** If enough random values of b have been tested, then accept w as prime and terminate algorithm; otherwise, go to step 2.

 a. Explain how the algorithm works.
 b. Show that it is equivalent to the Miller–Rabin test described in Chapter 2.

13.5 With DSA, because the value of k is generated for each signature, even if the same message is signed twice on different occasions, the signatures will differ. This is not true of RSA signatures. What is the practical implication of this difference?

13.6 Consider the problem of creating domain parameters for DSA. Suppose we have already found primes p and q such that $q \mid (p - 1)$. Now we need to find $g \in Z_p$ with g of order q mod p. Consider the following two algorithms:

Algorithm 1	Algorithm 2
repeat	**repeat**
select $g \in Z_p$	**select** $h \in Z_p$
$h \leftarrow g^q \bmod p$	$g \leftarrow h^{(p-1)/q} \bmod p$
until $(h = 1$ and $g \neq 1)$	**until** $(g \neq 1)$
return g	**return** g

a. Prove that the value returned by Algorithm 1 has order q.
b. Prove that the value returned by Algorithm 2 has order q.
c. Suppose $p = 40193$ and $q = 157$. How many loop iterations do you expect Algorithm 1 to make before it finds a generator?
d. If p is 1024 bits and q is 160 bits, would you recommend using Algorithm 1 to find g? Explain.
e. Suppose $p = 40193$ and $q = 157$. What is the probability that Algorithm 2 computes a generator in its very first loop iteration? (If it is helpful, you may use the fact that $\sum_{(d|n)}\psi(d) = n$ when answering this question.)

13.7 It is tempting to try to develop a variation on Diffie–Hellman that could be used as a digital signature. Here is one that is simpler than DSA and that does not require a secret random number in addition to the private key.

Public elements:	q	prime number
	α	$\alpha < q$ and α is primitive root of q
Private key:	X	$X < q$
Public key:		$Y = \alpha^X \bmod q \bmod q$

To sign a message M, compute $h = H(M)$, which is the hash code of the message. We require that $\gcd(h, q - 1) = 1$. If not, append the hash to the message and calculate a new hash. Continue this process until a hash code is produced that is relatively prime to $(q - 1)$. Then calculate Z to satisfy $Z \equiv X \times h(\bmod\, q - 1)$. The signature of the message is $\sigma = \alpha^Z$. To verify the signature, a user compute t such that $t \times h = 1 \bmod (q - 1)$ and verifies $Y = \sigma\, t \bmod q$.

a. Show that the scheme is unacceptable by describing a simple technique for forging a user's signature on an arbitrary message.
b. Show that the scheme is unacceptable by describing a simple technique for forging a user's signature on an arbitrary message.

13.8 Assume a technique for a digital signature scheme using a cryptographic one-way hash function (H) as follows. To sign an n-bit message, the sender randomly generates in advance $2n$ 64-bit cryptographic keys:

$$k_1, k_2, \ldots, k_n\ k_1', k_2', \ldots, k_n'$$

which are kept private. The sender generates the following two sets of validation parameters which are made public.

$$v_1, v_2, \ldots, v_n \text{ and } v_1', v_2', \ldots, v_n'$$

where

$$v_i = H(k_i \| 0),\ v_i' = H(k_i' \| 1)$$

The user sends the appropriate k_i or K_i' according to whether M_i is 0 or 1 respectively. For example, if the first 3-bits of the message are 011, then the first three keys of the signature are k_1, k_2', k_3'.

a. How does the receiver validate the message?
b. Is the technique secure?
c. How many times can the same set of secret keys be safely used for different messages?
d. What, if any, practical problems does this scheme present?

Part Five: Mutual Trust

CHAPTER 14

Key Management and Distribution

LEARNING OBJECTIVES

After studying this chapter, you should be able to:

- Discuss the concept of a key hierarchy.
- Understand the issues involved in using asymmetric encryption to distribute symmetric keys.
- Present an overview of approaches to public-key distribution and analyze the risks involved in various approaches.
- List and explain the elements in an X.509 certificate.
- Present an overview of public-key infrastructure concepts.

The topics of cryptographic key management and cryptographic key distribution are complex, involving cryptographic, protocol, and management considerations. The purpose of this chapter is to give the reader a feel for the issues involved and a broad survey of the various aspects of key management and distribution. For more information, the place to start is the three-volume NIST SP 800-57, followed by the recommended readings listed at the end of this chapter.

14.1 SYMMETRIC KEY DISTRIBUTION USING SYMMETRIC ENCRYPTION

For symmetric encryption to work, the two parties to an exchange must share the same key, and that key must be protected from access by others. Furthermore, frequent key changes are usually desirable to limit the amount of data compromised if an attacker learns the key. Therefore, the strength of any cryptographic system rests with the *key distribution technique*, a term that refers to the means of delivering a key to two parties who wish to exchange data without allowing others to see the key. For two parties A and B, key distribution can be achieved in a number of ways, as follows:

1. A can select a key and physically deliver it to B.
2. A third party can select the key and physically deliver it to A and B.
3. If A and B have previously and recently used a key, one party can transmit the new key to the other, encrypted using the old key.
4. If A and B each has an encrypted connection to a third party C, C can deliver a key on the encrypted links to A and B.

Options 1 and 2 call for manual delivery of a key. For link encryption, this is a reasonable requirement, because each link encryption device is going to be exchanging data only with its partner on the other end of the link. However, for **end-to-end encryption** over a network, manual delivery is awkward. In a distributed system, any given host or terminal may need to engage in exchanges with many other

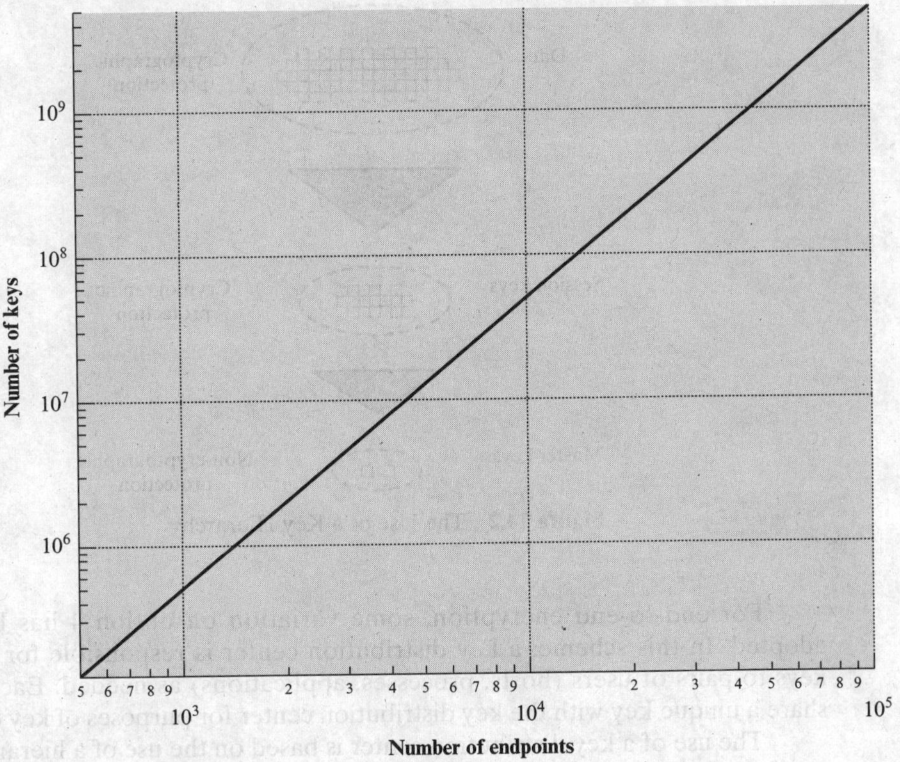

Figure 14.1 Number of Keys Required to Support Arbitrary Connections between Endpoints

hosts and terminals over time. Thus, each device needs a number of keys supplied dynamically. The problem is especially difficult in a wide-area distributed system.

The scale of the problem depends on the number of communicating pairs that must be supported. If end-to-end encryption is done at a network or IP level, then a key is needed for each pair of hosts on the network that wish to communicate. Thus, if there are N hosts, the number of required keys is $[N(N - 1)]/2$. If encryption is done at the application level, then a key is needed for every pair of users or processes that require communication. Thus, a network may have hundreds of hosts but thousands of users and processes. Figure 14.1 illustrates the magnitude of the key distribution task for end-to-end encryption.[1] A network using node-level encryption with 1000 nodes would conceivably need to distribute as many as half a million keys. If that same network supported 10,000 applications, then as many as 50 million keys may be required for application-level encryption.

Returning to our list, option 3 is a possibility for either link encryption or end-to-end encryption, but if an attacker ever succeeds in gaining access to one key, then all subsequent keys will be revealed. Furthermore, the initial distribution of potentially millions of keys still must be made.

[1]Note that this figure uses a log-log scale, so that a linear graph indicates exponential growth. A basic review of log scales is in the math refresher document at the Computer Science Student Resource Site at WilliamStallings.com/StudentSupport.html.

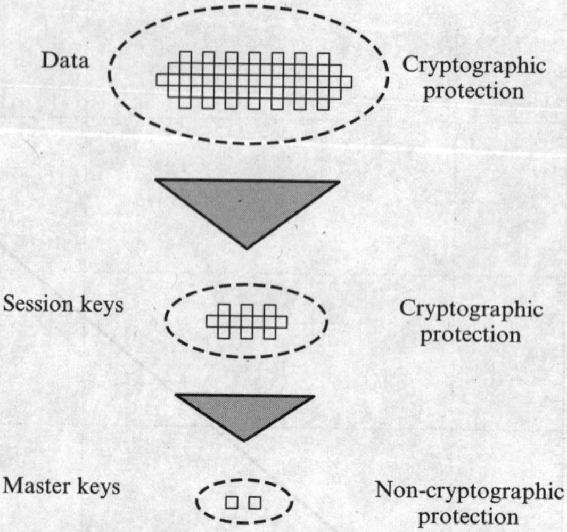

Figure 14.2 The Use of a Key Hierarchy

For end-to-end encryption, some variation on option 4 has been widely adopted. In this scheme, a key distribution center is responsible for distributing keys to pairs of users (hosts, processes, applications) as needed. Each user must share a unique key with the key distribution center for purposes of key distribution.

The use of a key distribution center is based on the use of a hierarchy of keys. At a minimum, two levels of keys are used (Figure 14.2). Communication between end systems is encrypted using a temporary key, often referred to as a **session key**. Typically, the session key is used for the duration of a logical connection, such as a frame relay connection or transport connection, and then discarded. Each session key is obtained from the key distribution center over the same networking facilities used for end-user communication. Accordingly, session keys are transmitted in encrypted form, using a **master key** that is shared by the key distribution center and an end system or user.

For each end system or user, there is a unique master key that it shares with the key distribution center. Of course, these master keys must be securely distributed in some fashion. However, the scale of the problem is vastly reduced. If there are N entities that wish to communicate in pairs, then, as was mentioned, as many as $[N(N - 1)]/2$ session keys are needed at any one time. However, only N master keys are required, one for each entity. Thus, master keys can be distributed in some non-cryptographic way, such as physical delivery.

A Key Distribution Scenario

The key distribution concept can be deployed in a number of ways. A typical scenario is illustrated in Figure 14.3, which is based on a figure in [POPE79]. The scenario assumes that each user shares a unique master key with the key distribution center (KDC).

Let us assume that user A wishes to establish a logical connection with B and requires a one-time session key to protect the data transmitted over the connection.

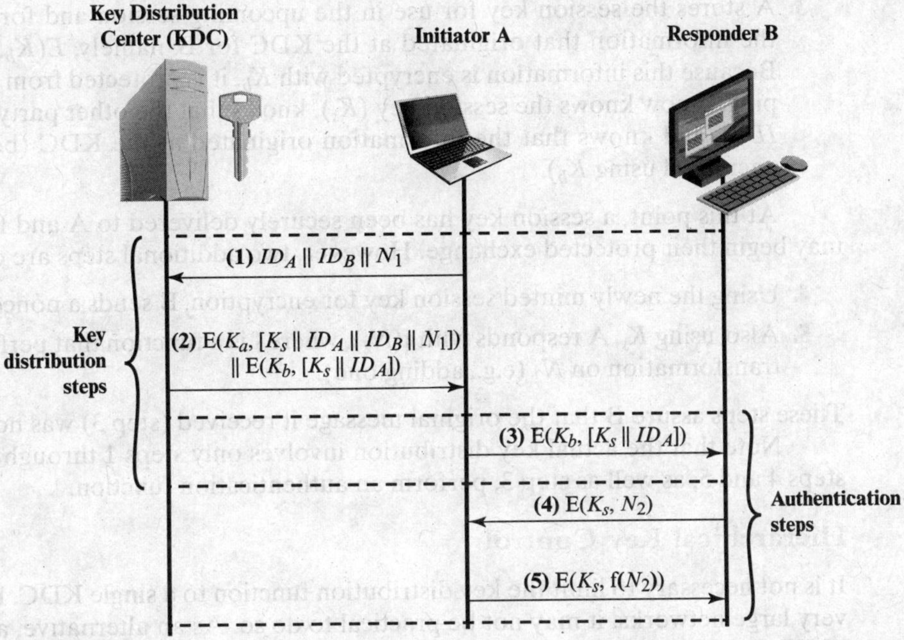

Figure 14.3 Key Distribution Scenario

A has a master key, K_a, known only to itself and the KDC; similarly, B shares the master key K_b with the KDC. The following steps occur.

1. A issues a request to the KDC for a session key to protect a logical connection to B. The message includes the identity of A and B and a unique identifier, N_1, for this transaction, which we refer to as a **nonce**. The nonce may be a timestamp, a counter, or a random number; the minimum requirement is that it differs with each request. Also, to prevent masquerade, it should be difficult for an opponent to guess the nonce. Thus, a random number is a good choice for a nonce.
2. The KDC responds with a message encrypted using K_a. Thus, A is the only one who can successfully read the message, and A knows that it originated at the KDC. The message includes two items intended for A:
   - The one-time session key, K_s, to be used for the session
   - The original request message, including the nonce, to enable A to match this response with the appropriate request

   Thus, A can verify that its original request was not altered before reception by the KDC and, because of the nonce, that this is not a replay of some previous request.

   In addition, the message includes two items intended for B:
   - The one-time session key, K_s, to be used for the session
   - An identifier of A (e.g., its network address), ID_A

   These last two items are encrypted with K_b (the master key that the KDC shares with B). They are to be sent to B to establish the connection and prove A's identity.

3. A stores the session key for use in the upcoming session and forwards to B the information that originated at the KDC for B, namely, $E(K_b,[K_s \| ID_A])$. Because this information is encrypted with K_b, it is protected from eavesdropping. B now knows the session key (K_s), knows that the other party is A (from ID_A), and knows that the information originated at the KDC (because it is encrypted using K_b).

At this point, a session key has been securely delivered to A and B, and they may begin their protected exchange. However, two additional steps are desirable:

4. Using the newly minted session key for encryption, B sends a nonce, N_2, to A.
5. Also, using K_s, A responds with $f(N_2)$, where f is a function that performs some transformation on N_2 (e.g., adding one).

These steps assure B that the original message it received (step 3) was not a replay.

Note that the actual key distribution involves only steps 1 through 3, but that steps 4 and 5, as well as step 3, perform an authentication function.

Hierarchical Key Control

It is not necessary to limit the key distribution function to a single KDC. Indeed, for very large networks, it may not be practical to do so. As an alternative, a hierarchy of KDCs can be established. For example, there can be local KDCs, each responsible for a small domain of the overall internetwork, such as a single LAN or a single building. For communication among entities within the same local domain, the local KDC is responsible for key distribution. If two entities in different domains desire a shared key, then the corresponding local KDCs can communicate through a global KDC. In this case, any one of the three KDCs involved can actually select the key. The hierarchical concept can be extended to three or even more layers, depending on the size of the user population and the geographic scope of the internetwork.

A hierarchical scheme minimizes the effort involved in master key distribution, because most master keys are those shared by a local KDC with its local entities. Furthermore, such a scheme limits the damage of a faulty or subverted KDC to its local area only.

Session Key Lifetime

The more frequently session keys are exchanged, the more secure they are, because the opponent has less ciphertext to work with for any given session key. On the other hand, the distribution of session keys delays the start of any exchange and places a burden on network capacity. A security manager must try to balance these competing considerations in determining the lifetime of a particular session key.

For connection-oriented protocols, one obvious choice is to use the same session key for the length of time that the connection is open, using a new session key for each new session. If a logical connection has a very long lifetime, then it would be prudent to change the session key periodically, perhaps every time the PDU (protocol data unit) sequence number cycles.

For a connectionless protocol, such as a transaction-oriented protocol, there is no explicit connection initiation or termination. Thus, it is not obvious how often one needs to change the session key. The most secure approach is to use a new session key for each exchange. However, this negates one of the principal benefits of connectionless protocols, which is minimum overhead and delay for each transaction. A better strategy is to use a given session key for a certain fixed period only or for a certain number of transactions.

A Transparent Key Control Scheme

The approach suggested in Figure 14.3 has many variations, one of which is described in this subsection. The scheme (Figure 14.4) is useful for providing end-to-end encryption at a network or transport level in a way that is transparent to the end users. The approach assumes that communication makes use of a connection-oriented end-to-end protocol, such as TCP. The noteworthy element of this approach is a session security module (SSM), which may consist of functionality

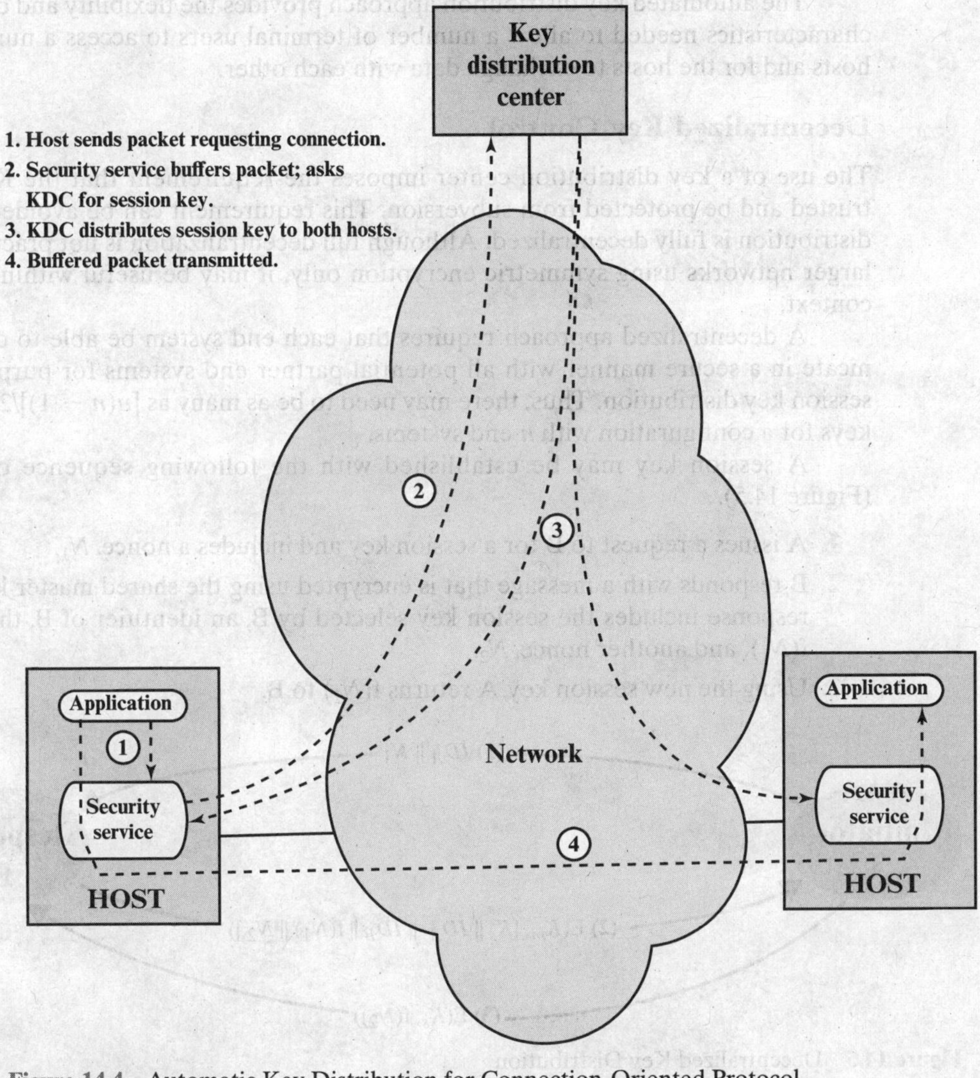

Figure 14.4 Automatic Key Distribution for Connection-Oriented Protocol

at one protocol layer, that performs end-to-end encryption and obtains session keys on behalf of its host or terminal.

The steps involved in establishing a connection are shown in Figure 14.4. When one host wishes to set up a connection to another host, it transmits a connection-request packet (step 1). The SSM saves that packet and applies to the KDC for permission to establish the connection (step 2). The communication between the SSM and the KDC is encrypted using a master key shared only by this SSM and the KDC. If the KDC approves the connection request, it generates the session key and delivers it to the two appropriate SSMs, using a unique permanent key for each SSM (step 3). The requesting SSM can now release the connection request packet, and a connection is set up between the two end systems (step 4). All user data exchanged between the two end systems are encrypted by their respective SSMs using the one-time session key.

The automated key distribution approach provides the flexibility and dynamic characteristics needed to allow a number of terminal users to access a number of hosts and for the hosts to exchange data with each other.

Decentralized Key Control

The use of a key distribution center imposes the requirement that the KDC be trusted and be protected from subversion. This requirement can be avoided if key distribution is fully decentralized. Although full decentralization is not practical for larger networks using symmetric encryption only, it may be useful within a local context.

A decentralized approach requires that each end system be able to communicate in a secure manner with all potential partner end systems for purposes of session key distribution. Thus, there may need to be as many as $[n(n-1)]/2$ master keys for a configuration with n end systems.

A session key may be established with the following sequence of steps (Figure 14.5).

1. A issues a request to B for a session key and includes a nonce, N_1.
2. B responds with a message that is encrypted using the shared master key. The response includes the session key selected by B, an identifier of B, the value $f(N_1)$, and another nonce, N_2.
3. Using the new session key, A returns $f(N_2)$ to B.

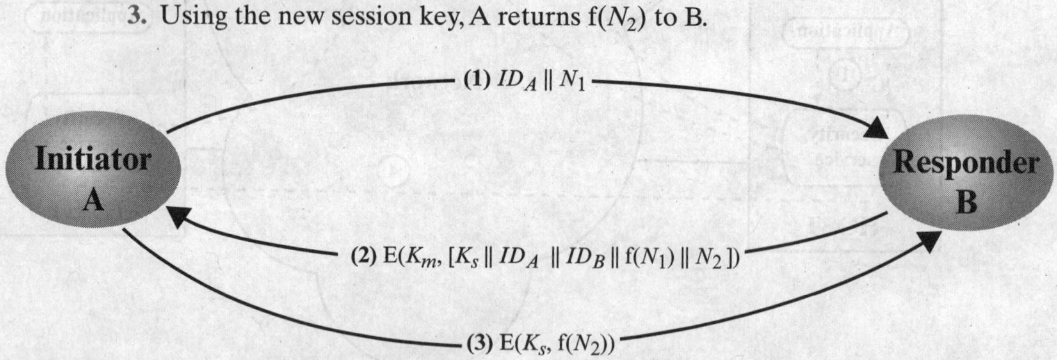

Figure 14.5 Decentralized Key Distribution

Thus, although each node must maintain at most $(n - 1)$ master keys, as many session keys as required may be generated and used. Because the messages transferred using the master key are short, cryptanalysis is difficult. As before, session keys are used for only a limited time to protect them.

Controlling Key Usage

The concept of a key hierarchy and the use of automated key distribution techniques greatly reduce the number of keys that must be manually managed and distributed. It also may be desirable to impose some control on the way in which automatically distributed keys are used. For example, in addition to separating master keys from session keys, we may wish to define different types of session keys on the basis of use, such as

- Data-encrypting key, for general communication across a network
- PIN-encrypting key, for personal identification numbers (PINs) used in electronic funds transfer and point-of-sale applications
- File-encrypting key, for encrypting files stored in publicly accessible locations

To illustrate the value of separating keys by type, consider the risk that a master key is imported as a data-encrypting key into a device. Normally, the master key is physically secured within the cryptographic hardware of the key distribution center and of the end systems. Session keys encrypted with this master key are available to application programs, as are the data encrypted with such session keys. However, if a master key is treated as a session key, it may be possible for an unauthorized application to obtain plaintext of session keys encrypted with that master key.

Thus, it may be desirable to institute controls in systems that limit the ways in which keys are used, based on characteristics associated with those keys. One simple plan is to associate a tag with each key ([JONE82]; see also [DAVI89]). The proposed technique is for use with DES and makes use of the extra 8 bits in each 64-bit DES key. That is, the eight non-key bits ordinarily reserved for parity checking form the key tag. The bits have the following interpretation:

- One bit indicates whether the key is a session key or a master key
- One bit indicates whether the key can be used for encryption
- One bit indicates whether the key can be used for decryption
- The remaining bits are spares for future use.

Because the tag is embedded in the key, it is encrypted along with the key when that key is distributed, thus providing protection. The drawbacks of this scheme are

1. The tag length is limited to 8 bits, limiting its flexibility and functionality.
2. Because the tag is not transmitted in clear form, it can be used only at the point of decryption, limiting the ways in which key use can be controlled.

A more flexible scheme, referred to as the control vector, is described in [MATY91a and b]. In this scheme, each session key has an associated control vector consisting of a number of fields that specify the uses and restrictions for that session key. The length of the control vector may vary.

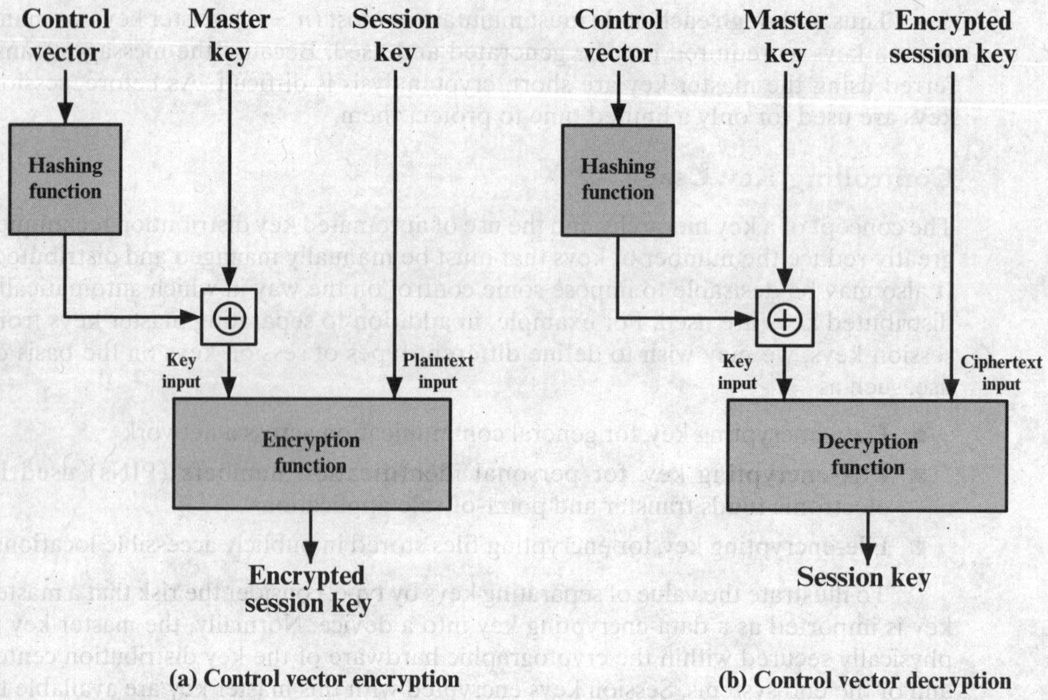

Figure 14.6 Control Vector Encryption and Decryption

The control vector is cryptographically coupled with the key at the time of key generation at the KDC. The coupling and decoupling processes are illustrated in Figure 14.6. As a first step, the control vector is passed through a hash function that produces a value whose length is equal to the encryption key length. Hash functions are discussed in detail in Chapter 11. In essence, a hash function maps values from a larger range into a smaller range with a reasonably uniform spread. Thus, for example, if numbers in the range 1 to 100 are hashed into numbers in the range 1 to 10, approximately 10% of the source values should map into each of the target values.

The hash value is then XORed with the master key to produce an output that is used as the key input for encrypting the session key. Thus,

$$\text{Hash value} = H = \text{h(CV)}$$
$$\text{Key input} = K_m \oplus H$$
$$\text{Ciphertext} = \text{E}([K_m \oplus H], K_s)$$

where K_m is the master key and K_s is the session key. The session key is recovered in plaintext by the reverse operation:

$$\text{D}([K_m \oplus H], \text{E}([K_m \oplus H], K_s))$$

When a session key is delivered to a user from the KDC, it is accompanied by the control vector in clear form. The session key can be recovered only by using both the master key that the user shares with the KDC and the control vector. Thus, the linkage between the session key and its control vector is maintained.

Use of the control vector has two advantages over use of an 8-bit tag. First, there is no restriction on length of the control vector, which enables arbitrarily complex controls to be imposed on key use. Second, the control vector is available in clear form at all stages of operation. Thus, control of key use can be exercised in multiple locations.

14.2 SYMMETRIC KEY DISTRIBUTION USING ASYMMETRIC ENCRYPTION

Because of the inefficiency of public-key cryptosystems, they are almost never used for the direct encryption of sizable blocks of data, but are limited to relatively small blocks. One of the most important uses of a public-key cryptosystem is to encrypt secret keys for distribution. We see many specific examples of this in Part Five. Here, we discuss general principles and typical approaches.

Simple Secret Key Distribution

An extremely simple scheme was put forward by Merkle [MERK79], as illustrated in Figure 14.7. If A wishes to communicate with B, the following procedure is employed:

1. A generates a public/private key pair $\{PU_a, PR_a\}$ and transmits a message to B consisting of PU_a and an identifier of A, ID_A.
2. B generates a secret key, K_s, and transmits it to A, which is encrypted with A's public key.
3. A computes $D(PR_a, E(PU_a, K_s))$ to recover the secret key. Because only A can decrypt the message, only A and B will know the identity of K_s.
4. A discards PU_a and PR_a and B discards PU_a.

A and B can now securely communicate using conventional encryption and the session key K_s. At the completion of the exchange, both A and B discard K_s. Despite its simplicity, this is an attractive protocol. No keys exist before the start of the communication and none exist after the completion of communication. Thus, the risk of compromise of the keys is minimal. At the same time, the communication is secure from eavesdropping.

The protocol depicted in Figure 14.7 is insecure against an adversary who can intercept messages and then either relay the intercepted message or substitute another message (see Figure 1.3c). Such an attack is known as a **man-in-the-middle attack** [RIVE84]. We saw this type of attack in Chapter 10 (Figure 10.2). In the present

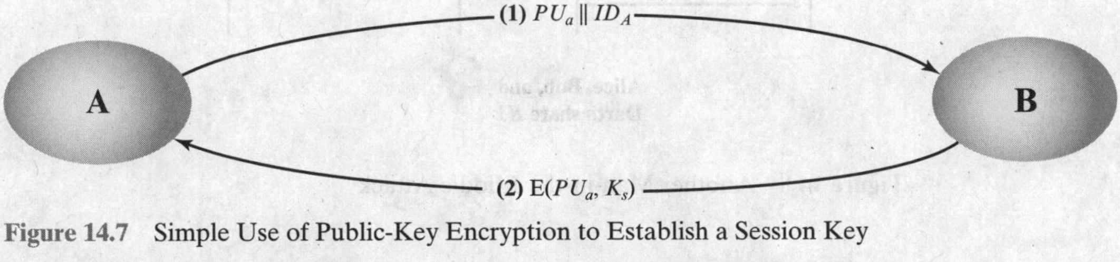

Figure 14.7 Simple Use of Public-Key Encryption to Establish a Session Key

case, if an adversary, D, has control of the intervening communication channel, then D can compromise the communication in the following fashion without being detected (Figure 14.8).

1. A generates a public/private key pair $\{PU_a, PR_a\}$ and transmits a message intended for B consisting of PU_a and an identifier of A, ID_A.
2. D intercepts the message, creates its own public/private key pair $\{PU_d, PR_d\}$ and transmits $PU_d \| ID_A$ to B.
3. B generates a secret key, K_s, and transmits $E(PU_d, K_s)$.
4. D intercepts the message and learns K_s by computing $D(PR_d, E(PU_d, K_s))$.
5. D transmits $E(PU_a, K_s)$ to A.

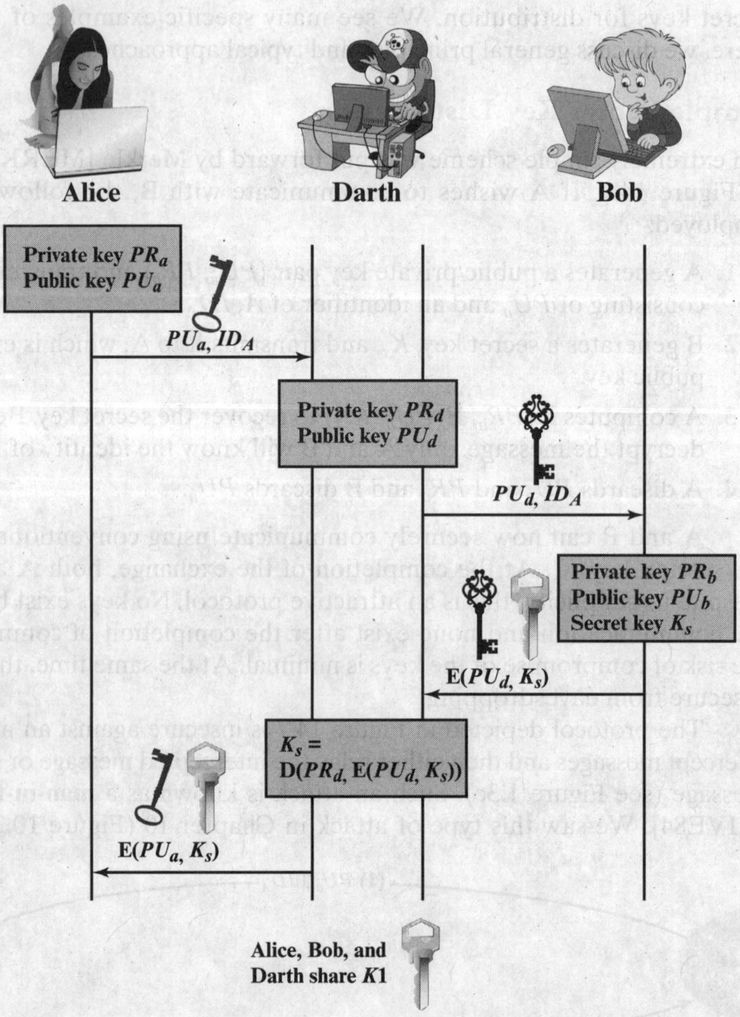

Figure 14.8 Another Man-in-the-Middle Attack

The result is that both A and B know K_s and are unaware that K_s has also been revealed to D. A and B can now exchange messages using K_s. D no longer actively interferes with the communications channel but simply eavesdrops. Knowing K_s, D can decrypt all messages, and both A and B are unaware of the problem. Thus, this simple protocol is only useful in an environment where the only threat is eavesdropping.

Secret Key Distribution with Confidentiality and Authentication

Figure 14.9, based on an approach suggested in [NEED78], provides protection against both active and passive attacks. We begin at a point when it is assumed that A and B have exchanged public keys by one of the schemes described subsequently in this chapter. Then the following steps occur.

1. A uses B's public key to encrypt a message to B containing an identifier of A(ID_A) and a nonce (N_1), which is used to identify this transaction uniquely.
2. B sends a message to A encrypted with PU_a and containing A's nonce (N_1) as well as a new nonce generated by B (N_2). Because only B could have decrypted message (1), the presence of N_1 in message (2) assures A that the correspondent is B.
3. A returns N_2, encrypted using B's public key, to assure B that its correspondent is A.
4. A selects a secret key K_s and sends $M = \mathrm{E}(PU_b, \mathrm{E}(PR_a, K_s))$ to B. Encryption of this message with B's public key ensures that only B can read it; encryption with A's private key ensures that only A could have sent it.
5. B computes $\mathrm{D}(PU_a, \mathrm{D}(PR_b, M))$ to recover the secret key.

The result is that this scheme ensures both confidentiality and authentication in the exchange of a secret key.

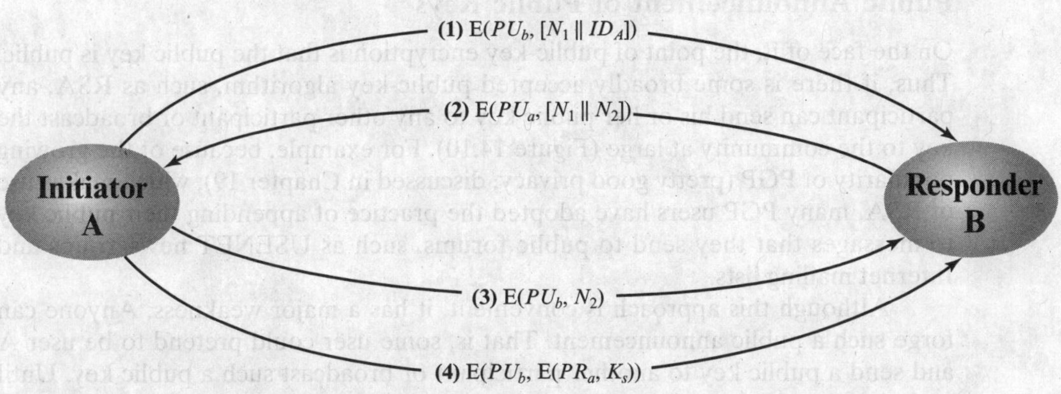

Figure 14.9 Public-Key Distribution of Secret Keys

A Hybrid Scheme

Yet another way to use public-key encryption to distribute secret keys is a hybrid approach in use on IBM mainframes [LE93]. This scheme retains the use of a key distribution center (KDC) that shares a secret master key with each user and distributes secret session keys encrypted with the master key. A public-key scheme is used to distribute the master keys. The following rationale is provided for using this three-level approach:

- **Performance:** There are many applications, especially transaction-oriented applications, in which the session keys change frequently. Distribution of session keys by public-key encryption could degrade overall system performance because of the relatively high computational load of public-key encryption and decryption. With a three-level hierarchy, public-key encryption is used only occasionally to update the master key between a user and the KDC.
- **Backward compatibility:** The hybrid scheme is easily overlaid on an existing KDC scheme with minimal disruption or software changes.

The addition of a public-key layer provides a secure, efficient means of distributing master keys. This is an advantage in a configuration in which a single KDC serves a widely distributed set of users.

14.3 DISTRIBUTION OF PUBLIC KEYS

Several techniques have been proposed for the distribution of public keys. Virtually all these proposals can be grouped into the following general schemes:

- Public announcement
- Publicly available directory
- Public-key authority
- Public-key certificates

Public Announcement of Public Keys

On the face of it, the point of public-key encryption is that the public key is public. Thus, if there is some broadly accepted public-key algorithm, such as RSA, any participant can send his or her public key to any other participant or broadcast the key to the community at large (Figure 14.10). For example, because of the growing popularity of PGP (pretty good privacy, discussed in Chapter 19), which makes use of RSA, many PGP users have adopted the practice of appending their public key to messages that they send to public forums, such as USENET newsgroups and Internet mailing lists.

Although this approach is convenient, it has a major weakness. Anyone can forge such a public announcement. That is, some user could pretend to be user A and send a public key to another participant or broadcast such a public key. Until such time as user A discovers the forgery and alerts other participants, the forger is able to read all encrypted messages intended for A and can use the forged keys for authentication (see Figure 9.3).

Figure 14.10 Uncontrolled Public-Key Distribution

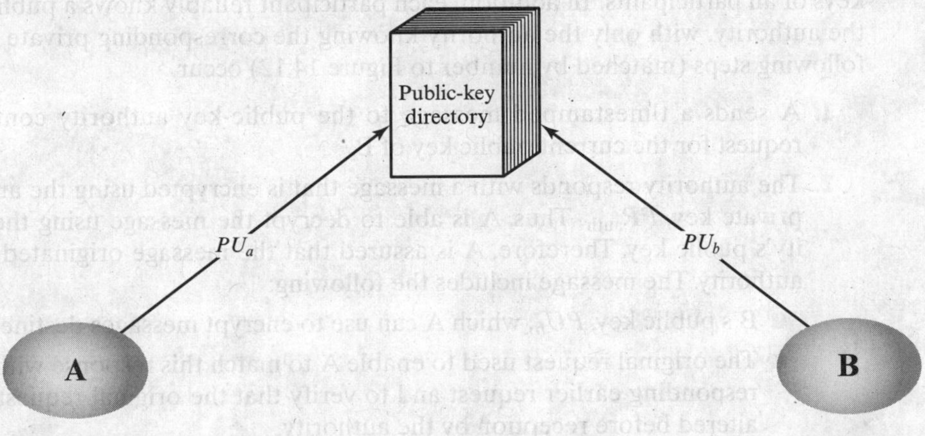

Figure 14.11 Public-Key Publication

Publicly Available Directory

A greater degree of security can be achieved by maintaining a publicly available dynamic directory of public keys. Maintenance and distribution of the public directory would have to be the responsibility of some trusted entity or organization (Figure 14.11). Such a scheme would include the following elements:

1. The authority maintains a directory with a {name, public key} entry for each participant.
2. Each participant registers a public key with the directory authority. Registration would have to be in person or by some form of secure authenticated communication.
3. A participant may replace the existing key with a new one at any time, either because of the desire to replace a public key that has already been used for a large amount of data, or because the corresponding private key has been compromised in some way.
4. Participants could also access the directory electronically. For this purpose, secure, authenticated communication from the authority to the participant is mandatory.

This scheme is clearly more secure than individual public announcements but still has vulnerabilities. If an adversary succeeds in obtaining or computing the private key of the directory authority, the adversary could authoritatively pass out counterfeit public keys and subsequently impersonate any participant and eavesdrop on messages sent to any participant. Another way to achieve the same end is for the adversary to tamper with the records kept by the authority.

Public-Key Authority

Stronger security for public-key distribution can be achieved by providing tighter control over the distribution of public keys from the directory. A typical scenario is illustrated in Figure 14.12, which is based on a figure in [POPE79]. As before, the scenario assumes that a central authority maintains a dynamic directory of public keys of all participants. In addition, each participant reliably knows a public key for the authority, with only the authority knowing the corresponding private key. The following steps (matched by number to Figure 14.12) occur.

1. A sends a timestamped message to the public-key authority containing a request for the current public key of B.
2. The authority responds with a message that is encrypted using the authority's private key, PR_{auth}. Thus, A is able to decrypt the message using the authority's public key. Therefore, A is assured that the message originated with the authority. The message includes the following:
   - B's public key, PU_b, which A can use to encrypt messages destined for B
   - The original request used to enable A to match this response with the corresponding earlier request and to verify that the original request was not altered before reception by the authority
   - The original timestamp given so A can determine that this is not an old message from the authority containing a key other than B's current public key
3. A stores B's public key and also uses it to encrypt a message to B containing an identifier of A (ID_A) and a nonce (N_1), which is used to identify this transaction uniquely.

4, 5. B retrieves A's public key from the authority in the same manner as A retrieved B's public key.

At this point, public keys have been securely delivered to A and B, and they may begin their protected exchange. However, two additional steps are desirable:

6. B sends a message to A encrypted with PU_a and containing A's nonce (N_1) as well as a new nonce generated by B (N_2). Because only B could have decrypted message (3), the presence of N_1 in message (6) assures A that the correspondent is B.
7. A returns N_2, which is encrypted using B's public key, to assure B that its correspondent is A.

Thus, a total of seven messages are required. However, the initial five messages need be used only infrequently because both A and B can save the other's public key for future use—a technique known as caching. Periodically, a user should request fresh copies of the public keys of its correspondents to ensure currency.

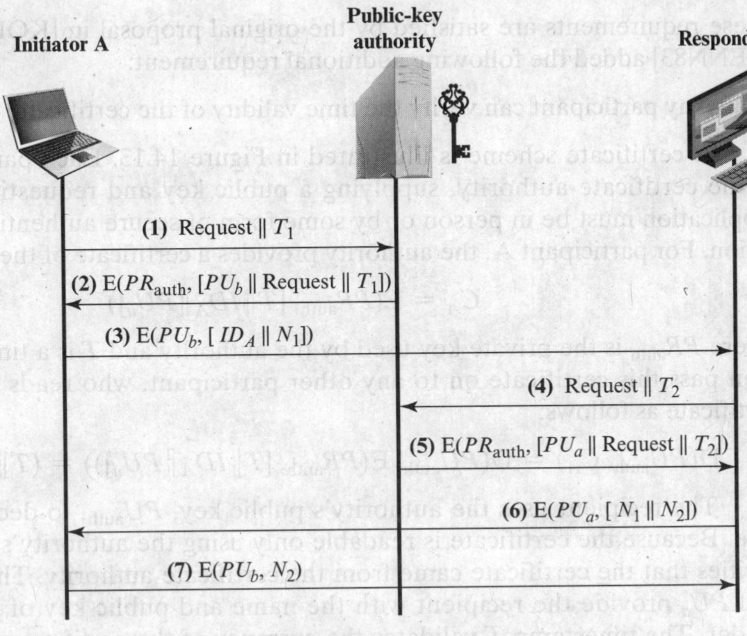

Figure 14.12 Public-Key Distribution Scenario

Public-Key Certificates

The scenario of Figure 14.12 is attractive, yet it has some drawbacks. The public-key authority could be somewhat of a bottleneck in the system, for a user must appeal to the authority for a public key for every other user that it wishes to contact. As before, the directory of names and public keys maintained by the authority is vulnerable to tampering.

An alternative approach, first suggested by Kohnfelder [KOHN78], is to use **certificates** that can be used by participants to exchange keys without contacting a public-key authority, in a way that is as reliable as if the keys were obtained directly from a public-key authority. In essence, a certificate consists of a public key, an identifier of the key owner, and the whole block signed by a trusted third party. Typically, the third party is a certificate authority, such as a government agency or a financial institution, that is trusted by the user community. A user can present his or her public key to the authority in a secure manner and obtain a certificate. The user can then publish the certificate. Anyone needing this user's public key can obtain the certificate and verify that it is valid by way of the attached trusted signature. A participant can also convey its key information to another by transmitting its certificate. Other participants can verify that the certificate was created by the authority. We can place the following requirements on this scheme:

1. Any participant can read a certificate to determine the name and public key of the certificate's owner.
2. Any participant can verify that the certificate originated from the certificate authority and is not counterfeit.
3. Only the certificate authority can create and update certificates.

These requirements are satisfied by the original proposal in [KOHN78]. Denning [DENN83] added the following additional requirement:

4. Any participant can verify the time validity of the certificate.

A certificate scheme is illustrated in Figure 14.13. Each participant applies to the certificate authority, supplying a public key and requesting a certificate. Application must be in person or by some form of secure authenticated communication. For participant A, the authority provides a certificate of the form

$$C_A = \mathrm{E}(PR_{\mathrm{auth}}, [T \| ID_A \| PU_a])$$

where PR_{auth} is the private key used by the authority and T is a timestamp. A may then pass this certificate on to any other participant, who reads and verifies the certificate as follows:

$$\mathrm{D}(PU_{\mathrm{auth}}, C_A) = \mathrm{D}(PU_{\mathrm{auth}}, \mathrm{E}(PR_{\mathrm{auth}}, [T \| ID_A \| PU_a])) = (T \| ID_A \| PU_a)$$

The recipient uses the authority's public key, PU_{auth}, to decrypt the certificate. Because the certificate is readable only using the authority's public key, this verifies that the certificate came from the certificate authority. The elements ID_A and PU_a provide the recipient with the name and public key of the certificate's holder. The timestamp T validates the currency of the certificate. The timestamp

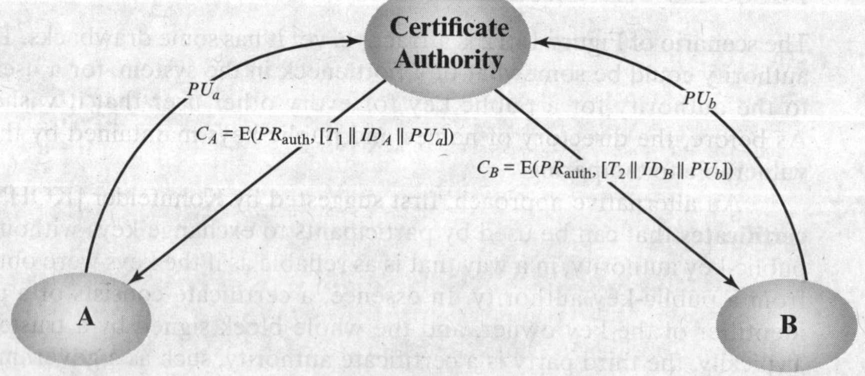

(a) Obtaining certificates from CA

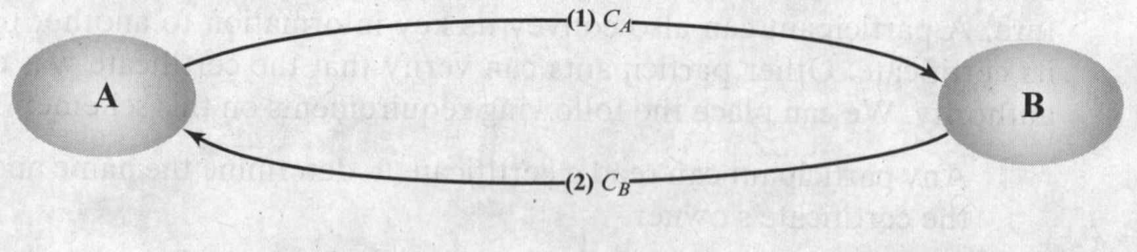

(b) Exchanging certificates

Figure 14.13 Exchange of Public-Key Certificates

counters the following scenario. A's private key is learned by an adversary. A generates a new private/public key pair and applies to the certificate authority for a new certificate. Meanwhile, the adversary replays the old certificate to B. If B then encrypts messages using the compromised old public key, the adversary can read those messages.

In this context, the compromise of a private key is comparable to the loss of a credit card. The owner cancels the credit card number but is at risk until all possible communicants are aware that the old credit card is obsolete. Thus, the timestamp serves as something like an expiration date. If a certificate is sufficiently old, it is assumed to be expired.

One scheme has become universally accepted for formatting public-key certificates: the X.509 standard. X.509 certificates are used in most network security applications, including IP security, transport layer security (TLS), and S/MIME, all of which are discussed in Part Five. X.509 is examined in detail in the next section.

14.4 X.509 CERTIFICATES

ITU-T recommendation X.509 is part of the X.500 series of recommendations that define a directory service. The directory is, in effect, a server or distributed set of servers that maintains a database of information about users. The information includes a mapping from user name to network address, as well as other attributes and information about the users.

X.509 defines a framework for the provision of authentication services by the X.500 directory to its users. The directory may serve as a repository of public-key certificates of the type discussed in Section 14.3. Each certificate contains the public key of a user and is signed with the private key of a trusted certification authority. In addition, X.509 defines alternative authentication protocols based on the use of public-key certificates.

X.509 is an important standard because the certificate structure and authentication protocols defined in X.509 are used in a variety of contexts. For example, the X.509 certificate format is used in S/MIME (Chapter 19), IP Security (Chapter 20), and SSL/TLS (Chapter 17).

X.509 was initially issued in 1988. The standard was subsequently revised in 1993 to address some of the security concerns documented in [IANS90] and [MITC90]. The standard is currently at version 7, issued in 2012.

X.509 is based on the use of public-key cryptography and digital signatures. The standard does not dictate the use of a specific digital signature algorithm nor a specific hash function. Figure 14.14 illustrates the overall X.509 scheme for generation of a public-key certificate. The certificate for Bob's public key includes unique identifying information for Bob, Bob's public key, and identifying information about the CA, plus other information as explained subsequently. This information is then signed by computing a hash value of the information and generating a digital signature using the hash value and the CA's private key. X.509 indicates that the signature is formed by encrypting the hash value. This suggests the use of one of the RSA schemes discussed in Section 13.6. However, the current version of X.509 does

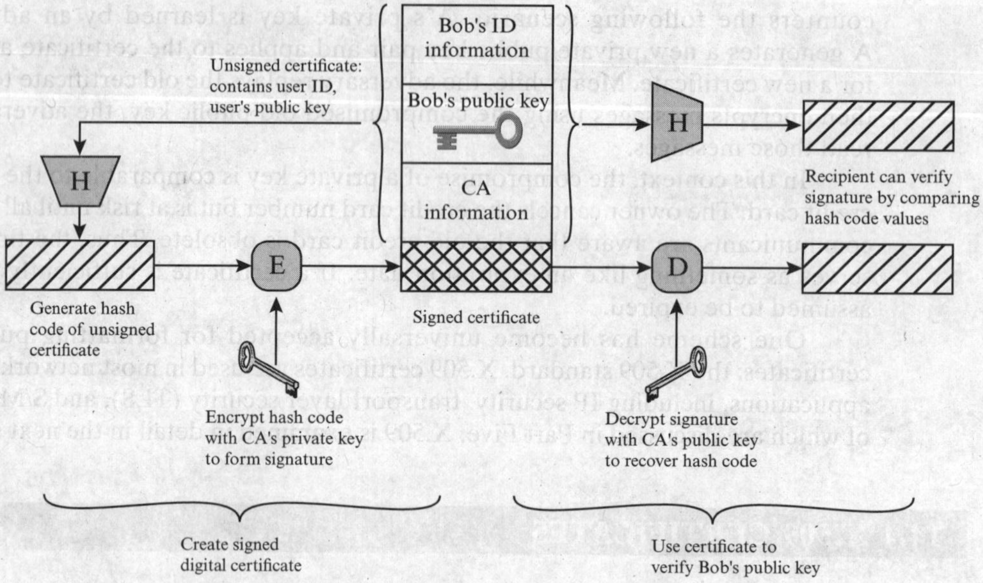

Figure 14.14 X.509 Public-Key Certificate Use

not dictate a specific digital signature algorithm. If the NIST DSA (Section 13.4) or the ECDSA (Section 13.5) scheme is used, then the hash value is not encrypted but serves as input to a digital signature generation algorithm.

Certificates

The heart of the X.509 scheme is the public-key certificate associated with each user. These user certificates are assumed to be created by some trusted certification authority (CA) and placed in the directory by the CA or by the user. The directory server itself is not responsible for the creation of public keys or for the certification function; it merely provides an easily accessible location for users to obtain certificates.

Figure 14.15a shows the general format of a certificate, which includes the following elements.

- **Version:** Differentiates among successive versions of the certificate format; the default is version 1. If the *issuer unique identifier* or *subject unique identifier* are present, the value must be version 2. If one or more extensions are present, the version must be version 3. Although the X.509 specification is currently at version 7, no changes have been made to the fields that make up the certificate since version 3.
- **Serial number:** An integer value unique within the issuing CA that is unambiguously associated with this certificate.
- **Signature algorithm identifier:** The algorithm used to sign the certificate together with any associated parameters. Because this information is repeated in the signature field at the end of the certificate, this field has little, if any, utility.

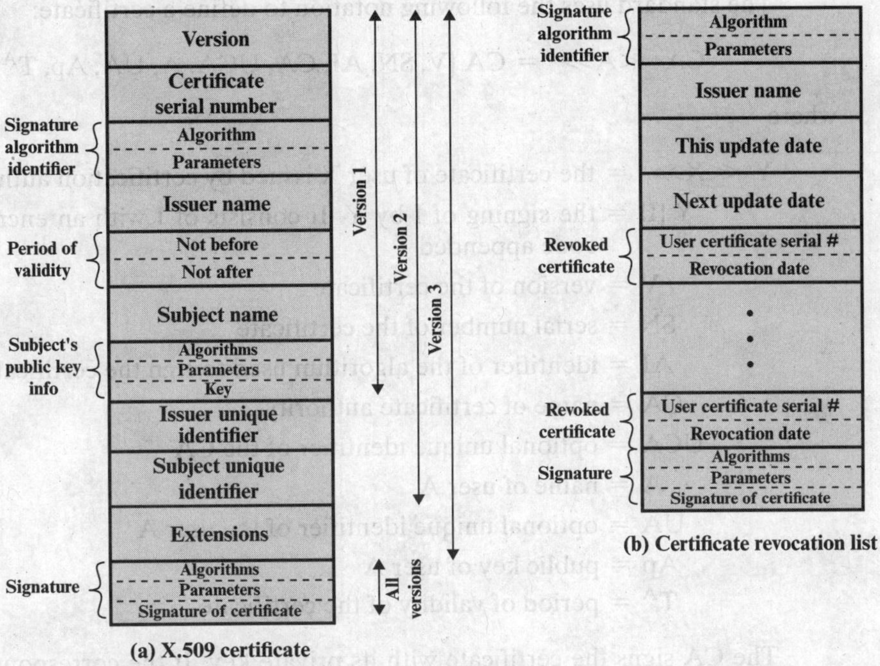

Figure 14.15 X.509 Formats

- **Issuer name:** X.500 name of the CA that created and signed this certificate.
- **Period of validity:** Consists of two dates: the first and last on which the certificate is valid.
- **Subject name:** The name of the user to whom this certificate refers. That is, this certificate certifies the public key of the subject who holds the corresponding private key.
- **Subject's public-key information:** The public key of the subject, plus an identifier of the algorithm for which this key is to be used, together with any associated parameters.
- **Issuer unique identifier:** An optional-bit string field used to identify uniquely the issuing CA in the event the X.500 name has been reused for different entities.
- **Subject unique identifier:** An optional-bit string field used to identify uniquely the subject in the event the X.500 name has been reused for different entities.
- **Extensions:** A set of one or more extension fields. Extensions were added in version 3 and are discussed later in this section.
- **Signature:** Covers all of the other fields of the certificate. One component of this field is the digital signature applied to the other fields of the certificate. This field includes the signature algorithm identifier.

The unique identifier fields were added in version 2 to handle the possible reuse of subject and/or issuer names over time. These fields are rarely used.

The standard uses the following notation to define a certificate:

$$CA \ll A \gg = CA \{V, SN, AI, CA, UCA, A, UA, Ap, T^A\}$$

where

- $Y \ll X \gg$ = the certificate of user X issued by certification authority Y
- $Y \{I\}$ = the signing of I by Y. It consists of I with an encrypted hash code appended
- V = version of the certificate
- SN = serial number of the certificate
- AI = identifier of the algorithm used to sign the certificate
- CA = name of certificate authority
- UCA = optional unique identifier of the CA
- A = name of user A
- UA = optional unique identifier of the user A
- Ap = public key of user A
- T^A = period of validity of the certificate

The CA signs the certificate with its private key. If the corresponding public key is known to a user, then that user can verify that a certificate signed by the CA is valid. This is the typical digital signature approach illustrated in Figure 13.2.

OBTAINING A USER'S CERTIFICATE User certificates generated by a CA have the following characteristics:

- Any user with access to the public key of the CA can verify the user public key that was certified.
- No party other than the certification authority can modify the certificate without this being detected.

Because certificates are unforgeable, they can be placed in a directory without the need for the directory to make special efforts to protect them.

If all users subscribe to the same CA, then there is a common trust of that CA. All user certificates can be placed in the directory for access by all users. In addition, a user can transmit his or her certificate directly to other users. In either case, once B is in possession of A's certificate, B has confidence that messages it encrypts with A's public key will be secure from eavesdropping and that messages signed with A's private key are unforgeable.

If there is a large community of users, it may not be practical for all users to subscribe to the same CA. Because it is the CA that signs certificates, each participating user must have a copy of the CA's own public key to verify signatures. This public key must be provided to each user in an absolutely secure (with respect to integrity and authenticity) way so that the user has confidence in the associated certificates. Thus, with many users, it may be more practical for there to be a number of CAs, each of which securely provides its public key to some fraction of the users.

Now suppose that A has obtained a certificate from certification authority X_1 and B has obtained a certificate from CA X_2. If A does not securely know the public key of X_2, then B's certificate, issued by X_2, is useless to A. A can read B's certificate, but A cannot verify the signature. However, if the two CAs have securely exchanged their own public keys, the following procedure will enable A to obtain B's public key.

Step 1 A obtains from the directory the certificate of X_2 signed by X_1. Because A securely knows X_1's public key, A can obtain X_2's public key from its certificate and verify it by means of X_1's signature on the certificate.

Step 2 A then goes back to the directory and obtains the certificate of B signed by X_2. Because A now has a trusted copy of X_2's public key, A can verify the signature and securely obtain B's public key.

A has used a chain of certificates to obtain B's public key. In the notation of X.509, this chain is expressed as

$$X_1 \ll X_2 \gg X_2 \ll B \gg$$

In the same fashion, B can obtain A's public key with the reverse chain:

$$X_2 \ll X_1 \gg X_1 \ll A \gg$$

This scheme need not be limited to a chain of two certificates. An arbitrarily long path of CAs can be followed to produce a chain. A chain with N elements would be expressed as

$$X_1 \ll X_2 \gg X_2 \ll X_3 \gg \ \ldots\ X_N \ll B \gg$$

In this case, each pair of CAs in the chain (X_i, X_{i+1}) must have created certificates for each other.

All these certificates of CAs by CAs need to appear in the directory, and the user needs to know how they are linked to follow a path to another user's public-key certificate. X.509 suggests that CAs be arranged in a hierarchy so that navigation is straightforward.

Figure 14.16, taken from X.509, is an example of such a hierarchy. The connected circles indicate the hierarchical relationship among the CAs; the associated boxes indicate certificates maintained in the directory for each CA entry. The directory entry for each CA includes two types of certificates:

- **Forward certificates:** Certificates of X generated by other CAs
- **Reverse certificates:** Certificates generated by X that are the certificates of other CAs

In this example, user A can acquire the following certificates from the directory to establish a certification path to B:

$$X \ll W \gg W \ll V \gg V \ll Y \gg Y \ll Z \gg Z \ll B \gg$$

When A has obtained these certificates, it can unwrap the certification path in sequence to recover a trusted copy of B's public key. Using this public key, A can send encrypted messages to B. If A wishes to receive encrypted messages back

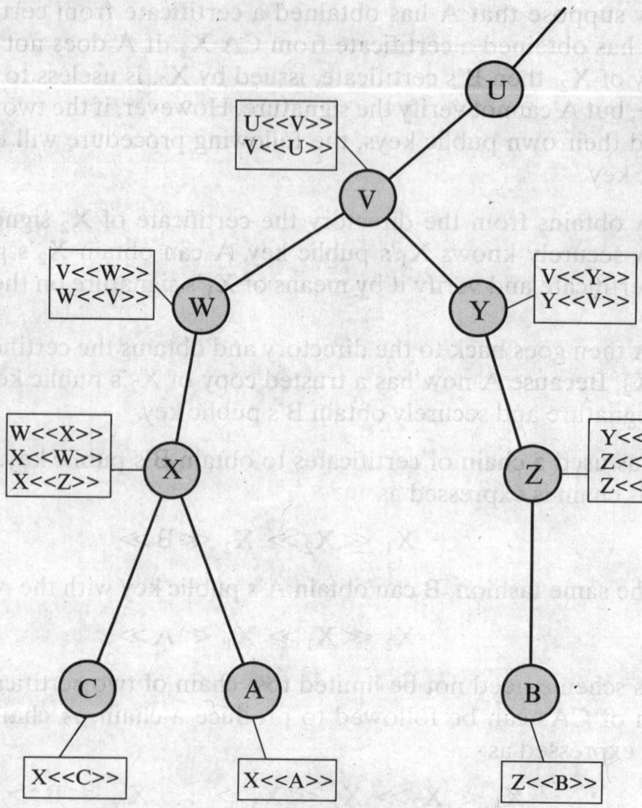

Figure 14.16 X.509 Hierarchy: A Hypothetical Example

from B, or to sign messages sent to B, then B will require A's public key, which can be obtained from the following certification path:

$$Z \ll Y \gg \; Y \ll V \gg \; V \ll W \gg \; W \ll X \gg \; X \ll A \gg$$

B can obtain this set of certificates from the directory, or A can provide them as part of its initial message to B.

Revocation of Certificates Recall from Figure 14.15 that each certificate includes a period of validity, much like a credit card. Typically, a new certificate is issued just before the expiration of the old one. In addition, it may be desirable on occasion to revoke a certificate before it expires, for one of the following reasons.

1. The user's private key is assumed to be compromised.
2. The user is no longer certified by this CA. Reasons for this include that the subject's name has changed, the certificate is superseded, or the certificate was not issued in conformance with the CA's policies.
3. The CA's certificate is assumed to be compromised.

Each CA must maintain a list consisting of all revoked but not expired certificates issued by that CA, including both those issued to users and to other CAs. These lists should also be posted on the directory.

Each certificate revocation list (CRL) posted to the directory is signed by the issuer and includes (Figure 14.15b) the issuer's name, the date the list was created, the date the next CRL is scheduled to be issued, and an entry for each revoked certificate. Each entry consists of the serial number of a certificate and revocation date for that certificate. Because serial numbers are unique within a CA, the serial number is sufficient to identify the certificate.

When a user receives a certificate in a message, the user must determine whether the certificate has been revoked. The user could check the directory each time a certificate is received. To avoid the delays (and possible costs) associated with directory searches, it is likely that the user would maintain a local cache of certificates and lists of revoked certificates.

X.509 Version 3

The X.509 version 2 format does not convey all of the information that recent design and implementation experience has shown to be needed. [FORD95] lists the following requirements not satisfied by version 2.

1. The subject field is inadequate to convey the identity of a key owner to a public-key user. X.509 names may be relatively short and lacking in obvious identification details that may be needed by the user.
2. The subject field is also inadequate for many applications, which typically recognize entities by an Internet email address, a URL, or some other Internet-related identification.
3. There is a need to indicate security policy information. This enables a security application or function, such as IPSec, to relate an X.509 certificate to a given policy.
4. There is a need to limit the damage that can result from a faulty or malicious CA by setting constraints on the applicability of a particular certificate.
5. It is important to be able to identify different keys used by the same owner at different times. This feature supports key lifecycle management: in particular, the ability to update key pairs for users and CAs on a regular basis or under exceptional circumstances.

Rather than continue to add fields to a fixed format, standards developers felt that a more flexible approach was needed. Thus, version 3 includes a number of optional extensions that may be added to the version 2 format. Each extension consists of an extension identifier, a criticality indicator, and an extension value. The criticality indicator indicates whether an extension can be safely ignored. If the indicator has a value of TRUE and an implementation does not recognize the extension, it must treat the certificate as invalid.

The certificate extensions fall into three main categories: key and policy information, subject and issuer attributes, and certification path constraints.

Key and Policy Information These extensions convey additional information about the subject and issuer keys, plus indicators of certificate policy. A certificate policy is a named set of rules that indicates the applicability of a certificate to a particular community and/or class of application with common security requirements. For example, a policy might be applicable to the authentication of electronic data interchange (EDI) transactions for the trading of goods within a given price range.

This area includes:

- **Authority key identifier:** Identifies the public key to be used to verify the signature on this certificate or CRL. Enables distinct keys of the same CA to be differentiated. One use of this field is to handle CA key pair updating.
- **Subject key identifier:** Identifies the public key being certified. Useful for subject key pair updating. Also, a subject may have multiple key pairs and, correspondingly, different certificates for different purposes (e.g., digital signature and encryption key agreement).
- **Key usage:** Indicates a restriction imposed as to the purposes for which, and the policies under which, the certified public key may be used. May indicate one or more of the following: digital signature, nonrepudiation, key encryption, data encryption, key agreement, CA signature verification on certificates, CA signature verification on CRLs.
- **Private-key usage period:** Indicates the period of use of the private key corresponding to the public key. Typically, the private key is used over a different period from the validity of the public key. For example, with digital signature keys, the usage period for the signing private key is typically shorter than that for the verifying public key.
- **Certificate policies:** Certificates may be used in environments where multiple policies apply. This extension lists policies that the certificate is recognized as supporting, together with optional qualifier information.
- **Policy mappings:** Used only in certificates for CAs issued by other CAs. Policy mappings allow an issuing CA to indicate that one or more of that issuer's policies can be considered equivalent to another policy used in the subject CA's domain.

Certificate Subject and Issuer Attributes These extensions support alternative names, in alternative formats, for a certificate subject or certificate issuer and can convey additional information about the certificate subject to increase a certificate user's confidence that the certificate subject is a particular person or entity. For example, information such as postal address, position within a corporation, or picture image may be required.

The extension fields in this area include:

- **Subject alternative name:** Contains one or more alternative names, using any of a variety of forms. This field is important for supporting certain applications, such as electronic mail, EDI, and IPSec, which may employ their own name forms.
- **Issuer alternative name:** Contains one or more alternative names, using any of a variety of forms.
- **Subject directory attributes:** Conveys any desired X.500 directory attribute values for the subject of this certificate.

Certification Path Constraints These extensions allow constraint specifications to be included in certificates issued for CAs by other CAs. The constraints may restrict the types of certificates that can be issued by the subject CA or that may occur subsequently in a certification chain.

The extension fields in this area include:

- **Basic constraints:** Indicates if the subject may act as a CA. If so, a certification path length constraint may be specified.
- **Name constraints:** Indicates a name space within which all subject names in subsequent certificates in a certification path must be located.
- **Policy constraints:** Specifies constraints that may require explicit certificate policy identification or inhibit policy mapping for the remainder of the certification path.

14.5 PUBLIC-KEY INFRASTRUCTURE

RFC 4949 (*Internet Security Glossary*) defines public-key infrastructure (PKI) as the set of hardware, software, people, policies, and procedures needed to create, manage, store, distribute, and revoke digital certificates based on asymmetric cryptography. The principal objective for developing a PKI is to enable secure, convenient, and efficient acquisition of public keys. The Internet Engineering Task Force (IETF) Public Key Infrastructure X.509 (PKIX) working group has been the driving force behind setting up a formal (and generic) model based on X.509 that is suitable for deploying a certificate-based architecture on the Internet. This section describes the PKIX model.

Figure 14.17 shows the interrelationship among the key elements of the PKIX model. These elements are

- **End entity:** A generic term used to denote end users, devices (e.g., servers, routers), or any other entity that can be identified in the subject field of a public-key certificate. End entities typically consume and/or support PKI-related services.
- **Certification authority (CA):** The issuer of certificates and (usually) certificate revocation lists (CRLs). It may also support a variety of administrative functions, although these are often delegated to one or more Registration Authorities.
- **Registration authority (RA):** An optional component that can assume a number of administrative functions from the CA. The RA is often associated with the end entity registration process but can assist in a number of other areas as well.
- **CRL issuer:** An optional component that a CA can delegate to publish CRLs.
- **Repository:** A generic term used to denote any method for storing certificates and CRLs so that they can be retrieved by end entities.

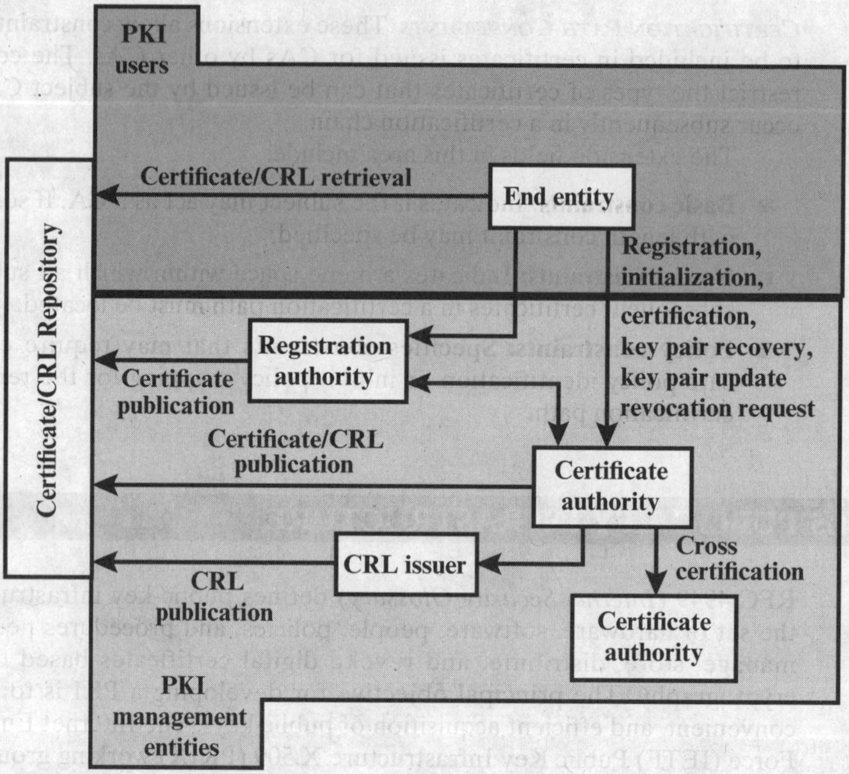

Figure 14.17 PKIX Architectural Model

PKIX Management Functions

PKIX identifies a number of management functions that potentially need to be supported by management protocols. These are indicated in Figure 14.17 and include the following:

- **Registration:** This is the process whereby a user first makes itself known to a CA (directly or through an RA), prior to that CA issuing a certificate or certificates for that user. Registration begins the process of enrolling in a PKI. Registration usually involves some offline or online procedure for mutual authentication. Typically, the end entity is issued one or more shared secret keys used for subsequent authentication.
- **Initialization:** Before a client system can operate securely, it is necessary to install key materials that have the appropriate relationship with keys stored elsewhere in the infrastructure. For example, the client needs to be securely initialized with the public key and other assured information of the trusted CA(s), to be used in validating certificate paths.
- **Certification:** This is the process in which a CA issues a certificate for a user's public key, returns that certificate to the user's client system, and/or posts that certificate in a repository.
- **Key pair recovery:** Key pairs can be used to support digital signature creation and verification, encryption and decryption, or both. When a key pair is used for

encryption/decryption, it is important to provide a mechanism to recover the necessary decryption keys when normal access to the keying material is no longer possible, otherwise it will not be possible to recover the encrypted data. Loss of access to the decryption key can result from forgotten passwords/PINs, corrupted disk drives, damage to hardware tokens, and so on. Key pair recovery allows end entities to restore their encryption/decryption key pair from an authorized key backup facility (typically, the CA that issued the end entity's certificate).

- **Key pair update:** All key pairs need to be updated regularly (i.e., replaced with a new key pair) and new certificates issued. Update is required when the certificate lifetime expires and as a result of certificate revocation.
- **Revocation request:** An authorized person advises a CA of an abnormal situation requiring certificate revocation. Reasons for revocation include private-key compromise, change in affiliation, and name change.
- **Cross certification:** Two CAs exchange information used in establishing a cross-certificate. A cross-certificate is a certificate issued by one CA to another CA that contains a CA signature key used for issuing certificates.

PKIX Management Protocols

The PKIX working group has defines two alternative management protocols between PKIX entities that support the management functions listed in the preceding subsection. RFC 2510 defines the certificate management protocols (CMP). Within CMP, each of the management functions is explicitly identified by specific protocol exchanges. CMP is designed to be a flexible protocol able to accommodate a variety of technical, operational, and business models.

RFC 2797 defines certificate management messages over CMS (CMC), where CMS refers to RFC 2630, cryptographic message syntax. CMC is built on earlier work and is intended to leverage existing implementations. Although all of the PKIX functions are supported, the functions do not all map into specific protocol exchanges.

14.6 KEY TERMS, REVIEW QUESTIONS, AND PROBLEMS

Key Terms

end-to-end encryption key distribution key distribution center (KDC) key management	man-in-the-middle attack master key nonce public-key certificate	public-key directory X.509 certificate

Review Questions

14.1 List the ways in which secret keys can be distributed to two communicating parties.

14.2 What is the major issue in end to end key distribution? How does the key hierarchy concept address that issue?

14.3 What is a nonce?

14.4 What is a key distribution center?

14.5 Mention the advantage of simple secret key distribution scheme using public key encryption.

14.6 List four general categories of schemes for the distribution of public keys.
14.7 What are the elements included in public key directory based system?
14.8 What is a public-key certificate?
14.9 What is the need of timestamp in a public key certificate?
14.10 What is the purpose of the X.509 standard?
14.11 What is a chain of certificates?
14.12 Why is it sometimes desirable to revoke an X.509 certificate before it expires?

Problems

14.1 One local area network vendor provides a key distribution facility, as illustrated in Figure 14.18.
   a. Describe the scheme.
   b. Compare this scheme to that of Figure 14.3. What are the pros and cons?

14.2 "We are under great pressure, Holmes." Detective Lestrade looked nervous. "We have learned that copies of sensitive government documents are stored in computers of one foreign embassy here in London. Normally these documents exist in electronic form only on a selected few government computers that satisfy the most stringent security requirements. However, sometimes they must be sent through the network connecting all government computers. But all messages in this network are encrypted using a top-secret encryption algorithm certified by our best crypto experts. Even the NSA and the KGB are unable to break it. And now these documents have appeared in hands of diplomats of a small, otherwise insignificant, country. And we have no idea how it could happen."

"But you do have some suspicion who did it, do you?" asked Holmes.

"Yes, we did some routine investigation. There is a man who has legal access to one of the government computers and has frequent contacts with diplomats from the embassy. But the computer he has access to is not one of the trusted ones where these documents are normally stored. He is the suspect, but we have no idea how he could obtain copies of the documents. Even if he could obtain a copy of an encrypted document, he couldn't decrypt it."

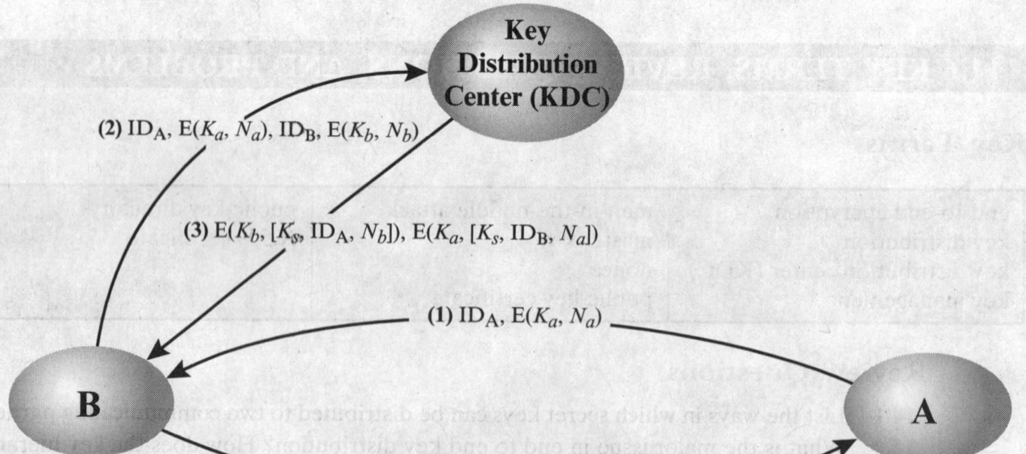

Figure 14.18 Figure for Problem 14.1

"Hmm, please describe the communication protocol used on the network." Holmes opened his eyes, thus proving that he had followed Lestrade's talk with an attention that contrasted with his sleepy look.

"Well, the protocol is as follows. Each node N of the network has been assigned a unique secret key K_n. This key is used to secure communication between the node and a trusted server. That is, all the keys are stored also on the server. User A, wishing to send a secret message M to user B, initiates the following protocol:

1. A generates a random number R and sends to the server his name A, destination B, and $E(K_a, R)$.
2. Server responds by sending $E(K_b, R)$ to A.
3. A sends $E(R, M)$ together with $E(K_b, R)$ to B.
4. B knows K_b, thus decrypts $E(K_b, R)$, to get R and will subsequently use R to decrypt $E(R, M)$ to get M.

You see that a random key is generated every time a message has to be sent. I admit the man could intercept messages sent between the top-secret trusted nodes, but I see no way he could decrypt them."

"Well, I think you have your man, Lestrade. The protocol isn't secure because the server doesn't authenticate users who send him a request. Apparently designers of the protocol have believed that sending $E(K_x, R)$ implicitly authenticates user X as the sender, as only X (and the server) knows K_x. But you know that $E(K_x, R)$ can be intercepted and later replayed. Once you understand where the hole is, you will be able to obtain enough evidence by monitoring the man's use of the computer he has access to. Most likely he works as follows. After intercepting $E(K_a, R)$ and $E(R, M)$ (see steps 1 and 3 of the protocol), the man, let's denote him as Z, will continue by pretending to be A and . . .

Finish the sentence for Holmes.

14.3 The 1988 version of X.509 lists properties that RSA keys must satisfy to be secure given current knowledge about the difficulty of factoring large numbers. The discussion concludes with a constraint on the public exponent and the modulus n:

> It must be ensured that $e > \log_2(n)$ to prevent attack by taking the eth root mod n to disclose the plaintext.

Although the constraint is correct, the reason given for requiring it is incorrect. What is wrong with the reason given and what is the correct reason?

14.4 The heart of the X.509 scheme is the public-key certificate associated with each user. These user certificates are assumed to be created by some trusted certification authority (CA) and placed in the directory by the CA or by the user. Discuss the general format of the certificate.

14.5 NIST defines the term cryptoperiod as the time span during which a specific key is authorized for use or in which the keys for a given system or application may remain in effect. One document on key management uses the following time diagram for a shared secret key.

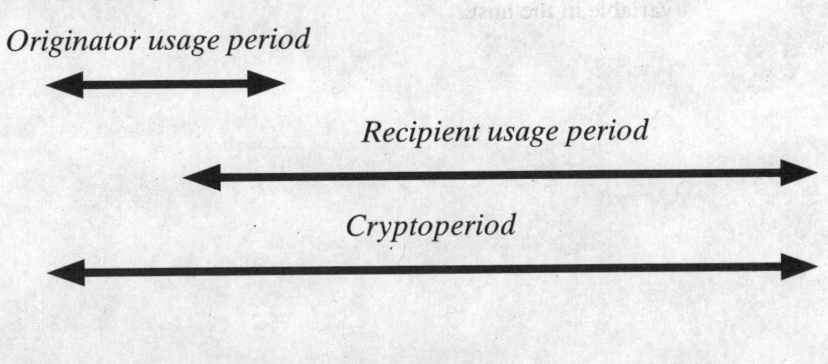

Explain the overlap by giving an example application in which the originator's usage period for the shared secret key begins before the recipient's usage period and also ends before the recipients usage period.

14.6 Consider the following protocol, designed to let A and B decide on a fresh, shared session key K'_{AB}. We assume that they already share a long-term key K_{AB}.

1. $A \rightarrow B$: A, N_A.
2. $B \rightarrow A$: $E(K_{AB}, [N_A, K'_{AB}])$
3. $A \rightarrow B$: $E(K'_{AB}, N_A)$

a. We first try to understand the protocol designer's reasoning:
– Why would A and B believe after the protocol ran that they share K'_{AB} with the other party?
– Why would they believe that this shared key is fresh?
In both cases, you should explain both the reasons of both A and B, so your answer should complete the sentences
A believes that she shares K'_{AB} with B since . . .
B believes that he shares K'_{AB} with A since . . .
A believes that K'_{AB} is fresh since . . .
B believes that K'_{AB} is fresh since . . .

b. Assume now that A starts a run of this protocol with B. However, the connection is intercepted by the adversary C. Show how C can start a new run of the protocol using reflection, causing A to believe that she has agreed on a fresh key with B (in spite of the fact that she has only been communicating with C). Thus, in particular, the belief in (a) is false.

c. Propose a modification of the protocol that prevents this attack.

14.7 What are the core components of a PKI? Briefly describe each component.

14.8 Explain the problems with key management and how it affects symmetric cryptography.

Note: The remaining problems deal with the a cryptographic product developed by IBM, which is briefly described in a document at box.com/Crypto7e (IBMCrypto.pdf). Try these problems after reviewing the document.

14.9 What is the effect of adding the instruction EMKi

$$EMK_i: X \rightarrow E(KMH_i, X) \; i = 0, 1$$

14.10 Suppose *N* different systems use the IBM Cryptographic Subsystem with host master keys KMH[*i*](i = 1, 2, . . . *N*). Devise a method for communicating between systems without requiring the system to either share a common host master key or to divulge their individual host master keys. *Hint*: Each system needs three variants of its host master key.

14.11 The principal objective of the IBM Cryptographic Subsystem is to protect transmissions between a terminal and the processing system. Devise a procedure, perhaps adding instructions, which will allow the processor to generate a session key KS and distribute it to Terminal i and Terminal *j* without having to store a key-equivalent variable in the host.

CHAPTER 15

User Authentication

LEARNING OBJECTIVES

After studying this chapter, you should be able to:

- Understand the distinction between identification and verification.
- Present an overview of techniques for remote user authentication using symmetric encryption.
- Give a presentation on Kerberos.
- Explain the differences between versions 4 and 5 of Kerberos.
- Describe the use of Kerberos in multiple realms.
- Present an overview of techniques for remote user authentication using asymmetric encryption.
- Understand the need for a federated identity management system.
- Explain the use of PIV mechanisms as part of a user authentication system.

This chapter examines some of the authentication functions that have been developed to support network-based user authentication. The chapter begins with an introduction to some of the concepts and key considerations for user authentication over a network or the Internet. The next section examines user-authentication protocols that rely on symmetric encryption. This is followed by a section on one of the earliest and also one of the most widely used authentication services: Kerberos. Next, the chapter looks at user-authentication protocols that rely on asymmetric encryption. This is followed by a discussion of the X.509 user-authentication protocol. Finally, the concept of federated identity is introduced.

15.1 REMOTE USER-AUTHENTICATION PRINCIPLES

In most computer security contexts, user authentication is the fundamental building block and the primary line of defense. User authentication is the basis for most types of access control and for user accountability. RFC 4949 (*Internet Security Glossary*) defines user authentication as the process of verifying an identity claimed by or for a system entity. This process consists of two steps:

- **Identification step:** Presenting an identifier to the security system. (Identifiers should be assigned carefully, because authenticated identities are the basis for other security services, such as access control service.)
- **Verification step:** Presenting or generating authentication information that corroborates the binding between the entity and the identifier.

For example, user Alice Toklas could have the user identifier ABTOKLAS. This information needs to be stored on any server or computer system that Alice wishes to use and could be known to system administrators and other users.

A typical item of authentication information associated with this user ID is a password, which is kept secret (known only to Alice and to the system). If no one is able to obtain or guess Alice's password, then the combination of Alice's user ID and password enables administrators to set up Alice's access permissions and audit her activity. Because Alice's ID is not secret, system users can send her email, but because her password is secret, no one can pretend to be Alice.

In essence, identification is the means by which a user provides a claimed identity to the system; user authentication is the means of establishing the validity of the claim. Note that user authentication is distinct from message authentication. As defined in Chapter 12, message authentication is a procedure that allows communicating parties to verify that the contents of a received message have not been altered and that the source is authentic. This chapter is concerned solely with user authentication.

The NIST Model for Electronic User Authentication

NIST SP 800-63-2 (*Electronic Authentication Guideline,* August 2013) defines electronic user authentication as the process of establishing confidence in user identities that are presented electronically to an information system. Systems can use the authenticated identity to determine if the authenticated individual is authorized to perform particular functions, such as database transactions or access to system resources. In many cases, the authentication and transaction or other authorized function takes place across an open network such as the Internet. Equally authentication and subsequent authorization can take place locally, such as across a local area network.

SP 800-63-2 defines a general model for user authentication that involves a number of entities and procedures. We discuss this model with reference to Figure 15.1.

The initial requirement for performing user authentication is that the user must be registered with the system. The following is a typical sequence for registration. An applicant applies to a **registration authority (RA)** to become a **subscriber**

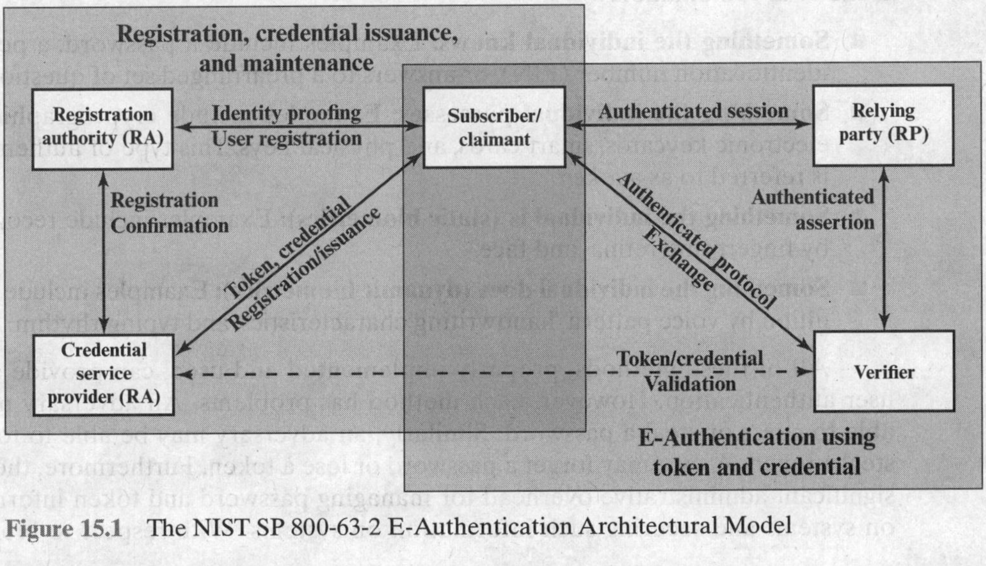

Figure 15.1 The NIST SP 800-63-2 E-Authentication Architectural Model

of a **credential service provider (CSP)**. In this model, the RA is a trusted entity that establishes and vouches for the identity of an applicant to a CSP. The CSP then engages in an exchange with the subscriber. Depending on the details of the overall authentication system, the CSP issues some sort of electronic credential to the subscriber. The **credential** is a data structure that authoritatively binds an identity and additional attributes to a token possessed by a subscriber, and can be verified when presented to the verifier in an authentication transaction. The token could be an encryption key or an encrypted password that identifies the subscriber. The token may be issued by the CSP, generated directly by the subscriber, or provided by a third party. The token and credential may be used in subsequent authentication events.

Once a user is registered as a subscriber, the actual authentication process can take place between the subscriber and one or more systems that perform authentication and, subsequently, authorization. The party to be authenticated is called a **claimant** and the party verifying that identity is called a **verifier**. When a claimant successfully demonstrates possession and control of a token to a verifier through an authentication protocol, the verifier can verify that the claimant is the subscriber named in the corresponding credential. The verifier passes on an assertion about the identity of the subscriber to the **relying party (RP)**. That assertion includes identity information about a subscriber, such as the subscriber name, an identifier assigned at registration, or other subscriber attributes that were verified in the registration process. The RP can use the authenticated information provided by the verifier to make access control or authorization decisions.

An implemented system for authentication will differ from or be more complex than this simplified model, but the model illustrates the key roles and functions needed for a secure authentication system.

Means of Authentication

There are four general means of authenticating a user's identity, which can be used alone or in combination:

- **Something the individual knows:** Examples include a password, a personal identification number (PIN), or answers to a prearranged set of questions.
- **Something the individual possesses:** Examples include cryptographic keys, electronic keycards, smart cards, and physical keys. This type of authenticator is referred to as a *token*.
- **Something the individual is (static biometrics):** Examples include recognition by fingerprint, retina, and face.
- **Something the individual does (dynamic biometrics):** Examples include recognition by voice pattern, handwriting characteristics, and typing rhythm.

All of these methods, properly implemented and used, can provide secure user authentication. However, each method has problems. An adversary may be able to guess or steal a password. Similarly, an adversary may be able to forge or steal a token. A user may forget a password or lose a token. Furthermore, there is a significant administrative overhead for managing password and token information on systems and securing such information on systems. With respect to biometric authenticators, there are a variety of problems, including dealing with false positives and false negatives, user acceptance, cost, and convenience. For network-based user authentication, the most important methods involve cryptographic keys and something the individual knows, such as a password.

Mutual Authentication

An important application area is that of mutual authentication protocols. Such protocols enable communicating parties to satisfy themselves mutually about each other's identity and to exchange session keys. This topic was examined in Chapter 14. There, the focus was key distribution. We return to this topic here to consider the wider implications of authentication.

Central to the problem of authenticated key exchange are two issues: confidentiality and timeliness. To prevent masquerade and to prevent compromise of session keys, essential identification and session-key information must be communicated in encrypted form. This requires the prior existence of secret or public keys that can be used for this purpose. The second issue, timeliness, is important because of the threat of message replays. Such replays, at worst, could allow an opponent to compromise a session key or successfully impersonate another party. At minimum, a successful replay can disrupt operations by presenting parties with messages that appear genuine but are not.

[GONG93] lists the following examples of **replay attacks**:

1. The simplest replay attack is one in which the opponent simply copies a message and replays it later.
2. An opponent can replay a timestamped message within the valid time window. If both the original and the replay arrive within then time window, this incident can be logged.
3. As with example (2), an opponent can replay a timestamped message within the valid time window, but in addition, the opponent suppresses the original message. Thus, the repetition cannot be detected.
4. Another attack involves a backward replay without modification. This is a replay back to the message sender. This attack is possible if symmetric encryption is used and the sender cannot easily recognize the difference between messages sent and messages received on the basis of content.

One approach to coping with replay attacks is to attach a sequence number to each message used in an authentication exchange. A new message is accepted only if its sequence number is in the proper order. The difficulty with this approach is that it requires each party to keep track of the last sequence number for each claimant it has dealt with. Because of this overhead, sequence numbers are generally not used for authentication and key exchange. Instead, one of the following two general approaches is used:

- **Timestamps:** Party A accepts a message as fresh only if the message contains a **timestamp** that, in A's judgment, is close enough to A's knowledge of current time. This approach requires that clocks among the various participants be synchronized.

- **Challenge/response:** Party A, expecting a fresh message from B, first sends B a **nonce** (challenge) and requires that the subsequent message (response) received from B contain the correct nonce value.

It can be argued (e.g., [LAM92a]) that the timestamp approach should not be used for connection-oriented applications because of the inherent difficulties with this technique. First, some sort of protocol is needed to maintain synchronization among the various processor clocks. This protocol must be both fault tolerant, to cope with network errors, and secure, to cope with hostile attacks. Second, the opportunity for a successful attack will arise if there is a temporary loss of synchronization resulting from a fault in the clock mechanism of one of the parties. Finally, because of the variable and unpredictable nature of network delays, distributed clocks cannot be expected to maintain precise synchronization. Therefore, any timestamp-based procedure must allow for a window of time sufficiently large to accommodate network delays yet sufficiently small to minimize the opportunity for attack.

On the other hand, the challenge-response approach is unsuitable for a connectionless type of application, because it requires the overhead of a handshake before any connectionless transmission, effectively negating the chief characteristic of a connectionless transaction. For such applications, reliance on some sort of secure time server and a consistent attempt by each party to keep its clocks in synchronization may be the best approach (e.g., [LAM92b]).

One-Way Authentication

One application for which encryption is growing in popularity is electronic mail (email). The very nature of electronic mail, and its chief benefit, is that it is not necessary for the sender and receiver to be online at the same time. Instead, the email message is forwarded to the receiver's electronic mailbox, where it is buffered until the receiver is available to read it.

The "envelope" or header of the email message must be in the clear, so that the message can be handled by the store-and-forward email protocol, such as the Simple Mail Transfer Protocol (SMTP) or X.400. However, it is often desirable that the mail-handling protocol not require access to the plaintext form of the message, because that would require trusting the mail-handling mechanism. Accordingly, the email message should be encrypted such that the mail-handling system is not in possession of the decryption key.

A second requirement is that of **authentication**. Typically, the recipient wants some assurance that the message is from the alleged sender.

15.2 REMOTE USER-AUTHENTICATION USING SYMMETRIC ENCRYPTION

Mutual Authentication

As was discussed in Chapter 14, a two-level hierarchy of symmetric encryption keys can be used to provide confidentiality for communication in a distributed environment. In general, this strategy involves the use of a trusted key distribution center

(KDC). Each party in the network shares a secret key, known as a master key, with the KDC. The KDC is responsible for generating keys to be used for a short time over a connection between two parties, known as session keys, and for distributing those keys using the master keys to protect the distribution. This approach is quite common. As an example, we look at the Kerberos system in Section 15.3. The discussion in this subsection is relevant to an understanding of the Kerberos mechanisms.

Figure 14.3 illustrates a proposal initially put forth by Needham and Schroeder [NEED78] for secret key distribution using a KDC that, as was mentioned in Chapter 14, includes authentication features. The protocol can be summarized as follows.[1]

1. A → KDC: $ID_A \| ID_B \| N_1$
2. KDC → A: $\mathrm{E}(K_a, [K_s \| ID_B \| N_1 \| \mathrm{E}(K_b, [K_s \| ID_A])])$
3. A → B: $\mathrm{E}(K_b, [K_s \| ID_A])$
4. B → A: $\mathrm{E}(K_s, N_2)$
5. A → B: $\mathrm{E}(K_s, \mathrm{f}(N_2))$ where f() is a generic function that modifies the value of the nonce.

Secret keys K_a and K_b are shared between A and the KDC and B and the KDC, respectively. The purpose of the protocol is to distribute securely a session key K_s to A and B. Entity A securely acquires a new session key in step 2. The message in step 3 can be decrypted, and hence understood, only by B. Step 4 reflects B's knowledge of K_s, and step 5 assures B of A's knowledge of K_s and assures B that this is a fresh message because of the use of the nonce N_2. Recall from our discussion in Chapter 14 that the purpose of steps 4 and 5 is to prevent a certain type of replay attack. In particular, if an opponent is able to capture the message in step 3 and replay it, this might in some fashion disrupt operations at B.

Despite the handshake of steps 4 and 5, the protocol is still vulnerable to a form of replay attack. Suppose that an opponent, X, has been able to compromise an old session key. Admittedly, this is a much more unlikely occurrence than that an opponent has simply observed and recorded step 3. Nevertheless, it is a potential security risk. X can impersonate A and trick B into using the old key by simply replaying step 3. Unless B remembers indefinitely all previous session keys used with A, B will be unable to determine that this is a replay. If X can intercept the handshake message in step 4, then it can impersonate A's response in step 5. From this point on, X can send bogus messages to B that appear to B to come from A using an authenticated session key.

Denning [DENN81, DENN82] proposes to overcome this weakness by a modification to the Needham/Schroeder protocol that includes the addition of a timestamp to steps 2 and 3. Her proposal assumes that the master keys, K_a and K_b, are secure, and it consists of the following steps.

[1]The portion to the left of the colon indicates the sender and the receiver; the portion to the right indicates the contents of the message; the symbol $\|$ indicates concatenation.

1. A → KDC: $ID_A \| ID_B$
2. KDC → A: $E(K_a, [K_s \| ID_B \| T \| E(K_b, [K_s \| ID_A \| T])])$
3. A → B: $E(K_b, [K_s \| ID_A \| T])$
4. B → A: $E(K_s, N_1)$
5. A → B: $E(K_s, f(N_1))$

T is a timestamp that assures A and B that the session key has only just been generated. Thus, both A and B know that the key distribution is a fresh exchange. A and B can verify timeliness by checking that

$$|\text{Clock} - T| < \Delta t_1 + \Delta t_2$$

where Δt_1 is the estimated normal discrepancy between the KDC's clock and the local clock (at A or B) and Δt_2 is the expected network delay time. Each node can set its clock against some standard reference source. Because the timestamp T is encrypted using the secure master keys, an opponent, even with knowledge of an old session key, cannot succeed because a replay of step 3 will be detected by B as untimely.

A final point: Steps 4 and 5 were not included in the original presentation [DENN81] but were added later [DENN82]. These steps confirm the receipt of the session key at B.

The Denning protocol seems to provide an increased degree of security compared to the Needham/Schroeder protocol. However, a new concern is raised: namely, that this new scheme requires reliance on clocks that are synchronized throughout the network. [GONG92] points out a risk involved. The risk is based on the fact that the distributed clocks can become unsynchronized as a result of sabotage on or faults in the clocks or the synchronization mechanism.[2] The problem occurs when a sender's clock is ahead of the intended recipient's clock. In this case, an opponent can intercept a message from the sender and replay it later when the timestamp in the message becomes current at the recipient's site. This replay could cause unexpected results. Gong refers to such attacks as **suppress-replay attacks**.

One way to counter suppress-replay attacks is to enforce the requirement that parties regularly check their clocks against the KDC's clock. The other alternative, which avoids the need for clock synchronization, is to rely on handshaking protocols using nonces. This latter alternative is not vulnerable to a suppress-replay attack, because the nonces the recipient will choose in the future are unpredictable to the sender. The Needham/Schroeder protocol relies on nonces only but, as we have seen, has other vulnerabilities.

In [KEHN92], an attempt is made to respond to the concerns about suppress-replay attacks and at the same time fix the problems in the Needham/Schroeder protocol. Subsequently, an inconsistency in this latter protocol was noted and an improved strategy was presented in [NEUM93a].[3] The protocol is

[2]Such things can and do happen. In recent years, flawed chips were used in a number of computers and other electronic systems to track the time and date. The chips had a tendency to skip forward one day. [NEUM90]

[3]It really is hard to get these things right.

1. A → B: $ID_A \| N_a$
2. B → KDC: $ID_B \| N_b \| E(K_b, [ID_A \| N_a \| T_b])$
3. KDC → A: $E(K_a, [ID_B \| N_a \| K_s \| T_b]) \| E(K_b, [ID_A \| K_s \| T_b]) \| N_b$
4. A → B: $E(K_b, [ID_A \| K_s \| T_b]) \| E(K_s, N_b)$

Let us follow this exchange step by step.

1. A initiates the authentication exchange by generating a nonce, N_a, and sending that plus its identifier to B in plaintext. This nonce will be returned to A in an encrypted message that includes the session key, assuring A of its timeliness.
2. B alerts the KDC that a session key is needed. Its message to the KDC includes its identifier and a nonce, N_b. This nonce will be returned to B in an encrypted message that includes the session key, assuring B of its timeliness. B's message to the KDC also includes a block encrypted with the secret key shared by B and the KDC. This block is used to instruct the KDC to issue credentials to A; the block specifies the intended recipient of the credentials, a suggested expiration time for the credentials, and the nonce received from A.
3. The KDC passes on to A B's nonce and a block encrypted with the secret key that B shares with the KDC. The block serves as a "ticket" that can be used by A for subsequent authentications, as will be seen. The KDC also sends to A a block encrypted with the secret key shared by A and the KDC. This block verifies that B has received A's initial message (ID_B) and that this is a timely message and not a replay (N_a), and it provides A with a session key (K_s) and the time limit on its use (T_b).
4. A transmits the ticket to B, together with the B's nonce, the latter encrypted with the session key. The ticket provides B with the secret key that is used to decrypt $E(K_s, N_b)$ to recover the nonce. The fact that B's nonce is encrypted with the session key authenticates that the message came from A and is not a replay.

This protocol provides an effective, secure means for A and B to establish a session with a secure session key. Furthermore, the protocol leaves A in possession of a key that can be used for subsequent authentication to B, avoiding the need to contact the authentication server repeatedly. Suppose that A and B establish a session using the aforementioned protocol and then conclude that session. Subsequently, but within the time limit established by the protocol, A desires a new session with B. The following protocol ensues:

1. A → B: $E(K_b, [ID_A \| K_s \| T_b]) \| N'_a$
2. B → A: $N'_b \| E(K_s, N'_a)$
3. A → B: $E(K_s, N'_b)$

When B receives the message in step 1, it verifies that the ticket has not expired. The newly generated nonces N'_a and N'_b assure each party that there is no replay attack.

In all the foregoing, the time specified in T_b is a time relative to B's clock. Thus, this timestamp does not require synchronized clocks, because B checks only self-generated timestamps.

One-Way Authentication

Using symmetric encryption, the decentralized key distribution scenario illustrated in Figure 14.5 is impractical. This scheme requires the sender to issue a request to the intended recipient, await a response that includes a session key, and only then send the message.

With some refinement, the KDC strategy illustrated in Figure 14.3 is a candidate for encrypted electronic mail. Because we wish to avoid requiring that the recipient (B) be on line at the same time as the sender (A), steps 4 and 5 must be eliminated. For a message with content M, the sequence is as follows:

1. A → KDC: $ID_A \| ID_B \| N_1$
2. KDC → A: $E(K_a, [K_s \| ID_B \| N_1 \| E(K_b, [K_s \| ID_A])])$
3. A → B: $E(K_b, [K_s \| ID_A]) \| E(K_s, M)$

This approach guarantees that only the intended recipient of a message will be able to read it. It also provides a level of authentication that the sender is A. As specified, the protocol does not protect against replays. Some measure of defense could be provided by including a timestamp with the message. However, because of the potential delays in the email process, such timestamps may have limited usefulness.

15.3 KERBEROS

Kerberos[4] is an authentication service developed as part of Project Athena at MIT. The problem that Kerberos addresses is this: Assume an open distributed environment in which users at workstations wish to access services on servers distributed throughout the network. We would like for servers to be able to restrict access to authorized users and to be able to authenticate requests for service. In this environment, a workstation cannot be trusted to identify its users correctly to network services. In particular, the following three threats exist:

1. A user may gain access to a particular workstation and pretend to be another user operating from that workstation.
2. A user may alter the network address of a workstation so that the requests sent from the altered workstation appear to come from the impersonated workstation.
3. A user may eavesdrop on exchanges and use a replay attack to gain entrance to a server or to disrupt operations.

In any of these cases, an unauthorized user may be able to gain access to services and data that he or she is not authorized to access. Rather than building in elaborate

[4]"In Greek mythology, a many headed dog, commonly three, perhaps with a serpent's tail, the guardian of the entrance of Hades." From *Dictionary of Subjects and Symbols in Art*, by James Hall, Harper & Row, 1979. Just as the Greek Kerberos has three heads, the modern Kerberos was intended to have three components to guard a network's gate: authentication, accounting, and audit. The last two heads were never implemented.

authentication protocols at each server, Kerberos provides a centralized authentication server whose function is to authenticate users to servers and servers to users. Unlike most other authentication schemes described in this book, Kerberos relies exclusively on symmetric encryption, making no use of public-key encryption.

Two versions of Kerberos are in common use. Version 4 [MILL88, STEI88] implementations still exist. Version 5 [KOHL94] corrects some of the security deficiencies of version 4 and has been issued as a proposed Internet Standard (RFC 4120 and RFC 4121).[5]

We begin this section with a brief discussion of the motivation for the Kerberos approach. Then, because of the complexity of Kerberos, it is best to start with a description of the authentication protocol used in version 4. This enables us to see the essence of the Kerberos strategy without considering some of the details required to handle subtle security threats. Finally, we examine version 5.

Motivation

If a set of users is provided with dedicated personal computers that have no network connections, then a user's resources and files can be protected by physically securing each personal computer. When these users instead are served by a centralized time-sharing system, the time-sharing operating system must provide the security. The operating system can enforce access-control policies based on user identity and use the logon procedure to identify users.

Today, neither of these scenarios is typical. More common is a distributed architecture consisting of dedicated user workstations (clients) and distributed or centralized servers. In this environment, three approaches to security can be envisioned.

1. Rely on each individual client workstation to assure the identity of its user or users and rely on each server to enforce a security policy based on user identification (ID).
2. Require that client systems authenticate themselves to servers, but trust the client system concerning the identity of its user.
3. Require the user to prove his or her identity for each service invoked. Also require that servers prove their identity to clients.

In a small, closed environment in which all systems are owned and operated by a single organization, the first or perhaps the second strategy may suffice.[6] But in a more open environment in which network connections to other machines are supported, the third approach is needed to protect user information and resources housed at the server. Kerberos supports this third approach. Kerberos assumes a distributed client/server architecture and employs one or more Kerberos servers to provide an authentication service.

[5] Versions 1 through 3 were internal development versions. Version 4 is the "original" Kerberos.

[6] However, even a closed environment faces the threat of attack by a disgruntled employee.

The first published report on Kerberos [STEI88] listed the following requirements.

- **Secure:** A network eavesdropper should not be able to obtain the necessary information to impersonate a user. More generally, Kerberos should be strong enough that a potential opponent does not find it to be the weak link.
- **Reliable:** For all services that rely on Kerberos for access control, lack of availability of the Kerberos service means lack of availability of the supported services. Hence, Kerberos should be highly reliable and should employ a distributed server architecture with one system able to back up another.
- **Transparent:** Ideally, the user should not be aware that authentication is taking place beyond the requirement to enter a password.
- **Scalable:** The system should be capable of supporting large numbers of clients and servers. This suggests a modular, distributed architecture.

To support these requirements, the overall scheme of Kerberos is that of a trusted third-party authentication service that uses a protocol based on that proposed by Needham and Schroeder [NEED78], which was discussed in Section 15.2. It is trusted in the sense that clients and servers trust Kerberos to mediate their mutual authentication. Assuming the Kerberos protocol is well designed, then the authentication service is secure if the Kerberos server itself is secure.[7]

Kerberos Version 4

Version 4 of Kerberos makes use of DES, in a rather elaborate protocol, to provide the authentication service. Viewing the protocol as a whole, it is difficult to see the need for the many elements contained therein. Therefore, we adopt a strategy used by Bill Bryant of Project Athena [BRYA88] and build up to the full protocol by looking first at several hypothetical dialogues. Each successive dialogue adds additional complexity to counter security vulnerabilities revealed in the preceding dialogue.

After examining the protocol, we look at some other aspects of version 4.

A Simple Authentication Dialogue In an unprotected network environment, any client can apply to any server for service. The obvious security risk is that of impersonation. An opponent can pretend to be another client and obtain unauthorized privileges on server machines. To counter this threat, servers must be able to confirm the identities of clients who request service. Each server can be required to undertake this task for each client/server interaction, but in an open environment, this places a substantial burden on each server.

[7]Remember that the security of the Kerberos server should not automatically be assumed but must be guarded carefully (e.g., in a locked room). It is well to remember the fate of the Greek Kerberos, whom Hercules was ordered by Eurystheus to capture as his Twelfth Labor: "Hercules found the great dog on its chain and seized it by the throat. At once the three heads tried to attack, and Kerberos lashed about with his powerful tail. Hercules hung on grimly, and Kerberos relaxed into unconsciousness. Eurystheus may have been surprised to see Hercules alive—when he saw the three slavering heads and the huge dog they belonged to he was frightened out of his wits, and leapt back into the safety of his great bronze jar." From *The Hamlyn Concise Dictionary of Greek and Roman Mythology*, by Michael Stapleton, Hamlyn, 1982.

An alternative is to use an authentication server (AS) that knows the passwords of all users and stores these in a centralized database. In addition, the AS shares a unique secret key with each server. These keys have been distributed physically or in some other secure manner. Consider the following hypothetical dialogue:

$$\textbf{(1)}\ C \rightarrow AS: \quad ID_C \| P_C \| ID_V$$

$$\textbf{(2)}\ AS \rightarrow C: \quad Ticket$$

$$\textbf{(3)}\ C \rightarrow V: \quad ID_C \| Ticket$$

$$Ticket = E(K_v, [ID_C \| AD_C \| ID_V])$$

where

C = client

AS = authentication server

V = server

ID_C = identifier of user on C

ID_V = identifier of V

P_C = password of user on C

AD_C = network address of C

K_v = secret encryption key shared by AS and V

In this scenario, the user logs on to a workstation and requests access to server V. The client module C in the user's workstation requests the user's password and then sends a message to the AS that includes the user's ID, the server's ID, and the user's password. The AS checks its database to see if the user has supplied the proper password for this user ID and whether this user is permitted access to server V. If both tests are passed, the AS accepts the user as authentic and must now convince the server that this user is authentic. To do so, the AS creates a **ticket** that contains the user's ID and network address and the server's ID. This ticket is encrypted using the secret key shared by the AS and this server. This ticket is then sent back to C. Because the ticket is encrypted, it cannot be altered by C or by an opponent.

With this ticket, C can now apply to V for service. C sends a message to V containing C's ID and the ticket. V decrypts the ticket and verifies that the user ID in the ticket is the same as the unencrypted user ID in the message. If these two match, the server considers the user authenticated and grants the requested service.

Each of the ingredients of message (3) is significant. The ticket is encrypted to prevent alteration or forgery. The server's ID (ID_V) is included in the ticket so that the server can verify that it has decrypted the ticket properly. ID_C is included in the ticket to indicate that this ticket has been issued on behalf of C. Finally, AD_C serves to counter the following threat. An opponent could capture the ticket transmitted in message (2), then use the name ID_C and transmit a message of form (3) from another workstation. The server would receive a valid ticket that matches the user ID and grant access to the user on that other workstation. To prevent this attack, the AS includes in the ticket the network address from which the original request came. Now the ticket is valid only if it is transmitted from the same workstation that initially requested the ticket.

A More Secure Authentication Dialogue Although the foregoing scenario solves some of the problems of authentication in an open network environment, problems remain. Two in particular stand out. First, we would like to minimize the number of times that a user has to enter a password. Suppose each ticket can be used only once. If user C logs on to a workstation in the morning and wishes to check his or her mail at a mail server, C must supply a password to get a ticket for the mail server. If C wishes to check the mail several times during the day, each attempt requires reentering the password. We can improve matters by saying that tickets are reusable. For a single logon session, the workstation can store the mail server ticket after it is received and use it on behalf of the user for multiple accesses to the mail server.

However, under this scheme, it remains the case that a user would need a new ticket for every different service. If a user wished to access a print server, a mail server, a file server, and so on, the first instance of each access would require a new ticket and hence require the user to enter the password.

The second problem is that the earlier scenario involved a plaintext transmission of the password [message (1)]. An eavesdropper could capture the password and use any service accessible to the victim.

To solve these additional problems, we introduce a scheme for avoiding plaintext passwords and a new server, known as the **ticket-granting server (TGS)**. The new (but still hypothetical) scenario is as follows.

Once per user logon session:

(1) $C \rightarrow AS$: $ID_C \| ID_{tgs}$

(2) $AS \rightarrow C$: $E(K_c, Ticket_{tgs})$

Once per type of service:

(3) $C \rightarrow TGS$: $ID_C \| ID_V \| Ticket_{tgs}$

(4) $TGS \rightarrow C$: $Ticket_v$

Once per service session:

(5) $C \rightarrow V$: $ID_C \| Ticket_v$

$$Ticket_{tgs} = E(K_{tgs}, [ID_C \| AD_C \| ID_{tgs} \| TS_1 \| Lifetime_1])$$

$$Ticket_v = E(K_v, [ID_C \| AD_C \| ID_v \| TS_2 \| Lifetime_2])$$

The new service, TGS, issues tickets to users who have been authenticated to AS. Thus, the user first requests a ticket-granting ticket ($Ticket_{tgs}$) from the AS. The client module in the user workstation saves this ticket. Each time the user requires access to a new service, the client applies to the TGS, using the ticket to authenticate itself. The TGS then grants a ticket for the particular service. The client saves each service-granting ticket and uses it to authenticate its user to a server each time a particular service is requested. Let us look at the details of this scheme:

1. The client requests a ticket-granting ticket on behalf of the user by sending its user's ID to the AS, together with the TGS ID, indicating a request to use the TGS service.

2. The AS responds with a ticket that is encrypted with a key that is derived from the user's password (K_c), which is already stored at the AS. When this response arrives at the client, the client prompts the user for his or her password, generates the key, and attempts to decrypt the incoming message. If the correct password is supplied, the ticket is successfully recovered.

Because only the correct user should know the password, only the correct user can recover the ticket. Thus, we have used the password to obtain credentials from Kerberos without having to transmit the password in plaintext. The ticket itself consists of the ID and network address of the user, and the ID of the TGS. This corresponds to the first scenario. The idea is that the client can use this ticket to request multiple service-granting tickets. So the ticket-granting ticket is to be reusable. However, we do not wish an opponent to be able to capture the ticket and use it. Consider the following scenario: An opponent captures the login ticket and waits until the user has logged off his or her workstation. Then the opponent either gains access to that workstation or configures his workstation with the same network address as that of the victim. The opponent would be able to reuse the ticket to spoof the TGS. To counter this, the ticket includes a timestamp, indicating the date and time at which the ticket was issued, and a lifetime, indicating the length of time for which the ticket is valid (e.g., eight hours). Thus, the client now has a reusable ticket and need not bother the user for a password for each new service request. Finally, note that the ticket-granting ticket is encrypted with a secret key known only to the AS and the TGS. This prevents alteration of the ticket. The ticket is reencrypted with a key based on the user's password. This assures that the ticket can be recovered only by the correct user, providing the authentication.

Now that the client has a ticket-granting ticket, access to any server can be obtained with steps 3 and 4.

3. The client requests a service-granting ticket on behalf of the user. For this purpose, the client transmits a message to the TGS containing the user's ID, the ID of the desired service, and the ticket-granting ticket.
4. The TGS decrypts the incoming ticket using a key shared only by the AS and the TGS (K_{tgs}) and verifies the success of the decryption by the presence of its ID. It checks to make sure that the lifetime has not expired. Then it compares the user ID and network address with the incoming information to authenticate the user. If the user is permitted access to the server V, the TGS issues a ticket to grant access to the requested service.

The service-granting ticket has the same structure as the ticket-granting ticket. Indeed, because the TGS is a server, we would expect that the same elements are needed to authenticate a client to the TGS and to authenticate a client to an application server. Again, the ticket contains a timestamp and lifetime. If the user wants access to the same service at a later time, the client can simply use the previously acquired service-granting ticket and need not bother the user for a password. Note that the ticket is encrypted with a secret key (K_v) known only to the TGS and the server, preventing alteration.

Finally, with a particular service-granting ticket, the client can gain access to the corresponding service with step 5.

5. The client requests access to a service on behalf of the user. For this purpose, the client transmits a message to the server containing the user's ID and the service-granting ticket. The server authenticates by using the contents of the ticket.

This new scenario satisfies the two requirements of only one password query per user session and protection of the user password.

The Version 4 Authentication Dialogue Although the foregoing scenario enhances security compared to the first attempt, two additional problems remain. The heart of the first problem is the lifetime associated with the ticket-granting ticket. If this lifetime is very short (e.g., minutes), then the user will be repeatedly asked for a password. If the lifetime is long (e.g., hours), then an opponent has a greater opportunity for replay. An opponent could eavesdrop on the network and capture a copy of the ticket-granting ticket and then wait for the legitimate user to log out. Then the opponent could forge the legitimate user's network address and send the message of step (3) to the TGS. This would give the opponent unlimited access to the resources and files available to the legitimate user.

Similarly, if an opponent captures a service-granting ticket and uses it before it expires, the opponent has access to the corresponding service.

Thus, we arrive at an additional requirement. A network service (the TGS or an application service) must be able to prove that the person using a ticket is the same person to whom that ticket was issued.

The second problem is that there may be a requirement for servers to authenticate themselves to users. Without such authentication, an opponent could sabotage the configuration so that messages to a server were directed to another location. The false server would then be in a position to act as a real server and capture any information from the user and deny the true service to the user.

We examine these problems in turn and refer to Table 15.1, which shows the actual Kerberos protocol. Figure 15.2 provides a simplified overview.

Table 15.1 Summary of Kerberos Version 4 Message Exchanges

(1) C → AS $ID_c \| ID_{tgs} \| TS_1$

(2) AS → C $E(K_c, [K_{c,tgs} \| ID_{tgs} \| TS_2 \| Lifetime_2 \| Ticket_{tgs}])$

$$Ticket_{tgs} = E(K_{tgs}, [K_{c,tgs} \| ID_C \| AD_C \| ID_{tgs} \| TS_2 \| Lifetime_2])$$

(a) Authentication Service Exchange to obtain ticket-granting ticket

(3) C → TGS $ID_v \| Ticket_{tgs} \| Authenticator_c$

(4) TGS → C $E(K_{c,tgs}, [K_{c,v} \| ID_v \| TS_4 \| Ticket_v])$

$$Ticket_{tgs} = E(K_{tgs}, [K_{c,tgs} \| ID_C \| AD_C \| ID_{tgs} \| TS_2 \| Lifetime_2])$$

$$Ticket_v = E(K_v, [K_{c,v} \| ID_C \| AD_C \| ID_v \| TS_4 \| Lifetime_4])$$

$$Authenticator_c = E(K_{c,tgs}, [ID_C \| AD_C \| TS_3])$$

(b) Ticket-Granting Service Exchange to obtain service-granting ticket

(5) C → V $Ticket_v \| Authenticator_c$

(6) V → C $E(K_{c,v}, [TS_5 + 1])$ (for mutual authentication)

$$Ticket_v = E(K_v, [K_{c,v} \| ID_C \| AD_C \| ID_v \| TS_4 \| Lifetime_4])$$

$$Authenticator_c = E(K_{c,v}, [ID_C \| AD_C \| TS_5])$$

(c) Client/Server Authentication Exchange to obtain service

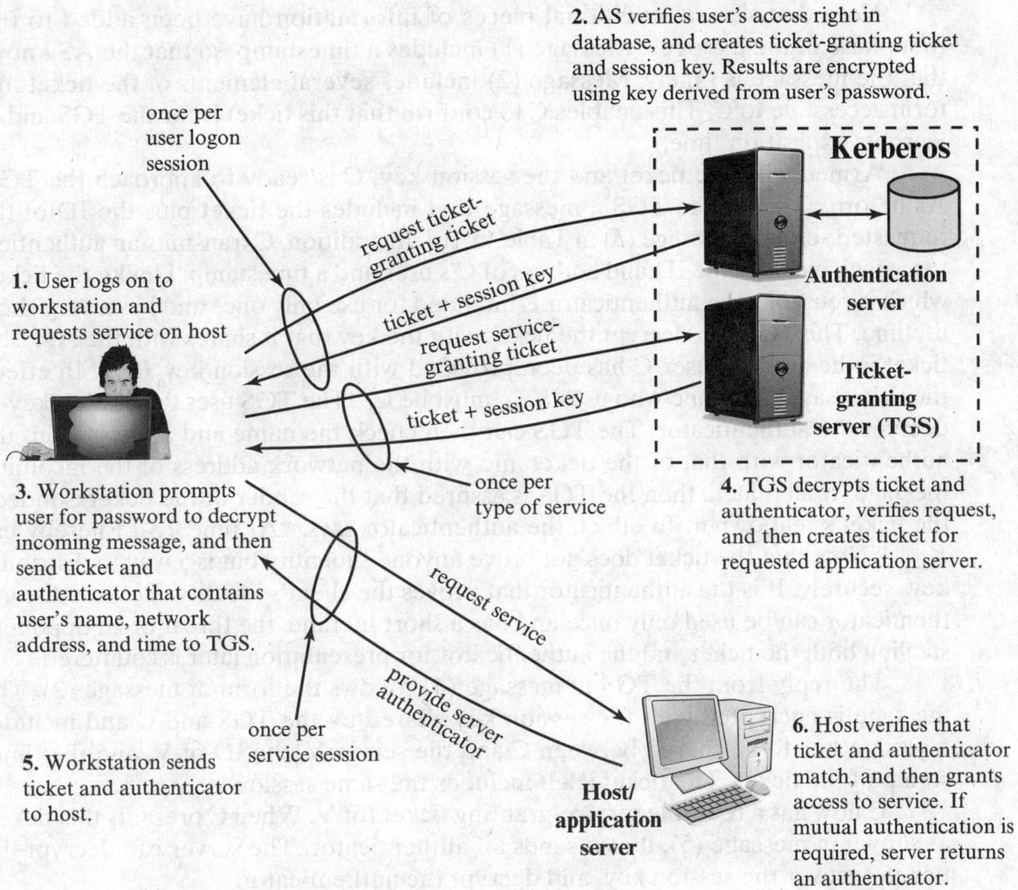

Figure 15.2 Overview of Kerberos

First, consider the problem of captured ticket-granting tickets and the need to determine that the ticket presenter is the same as the client for whom the ticket was issued. The threat is that an opponent will steal the ticket and use it before it expires. To get around this problem, let us have the AS provide both the client and the TGS with a secret piece of information in a secure manner. Then the client can prove its identity to the TGS by revealing the secret information—again in a secure manner. An efficient way of accomplishing this is to use an encryption key as the secure information; this is referred to as a session key in Kerberos.

Table 15.1a shows the technique for distributing the session key. As before, the client sends a message to the AS requesting access to the TGS. The AS responds with a message, encrypted with a key derived from the user's password (K_c), that contains the ticket. The encrypted message also contains a copy of the session key, $K_{c,tgs}$, where the subscripts indicate that this is a session key for C and TGS. Because this session key is inside the message encrypted with K_c, only the user's client can read it. The same session key is included in the ticket, which can be read only by the TGS. Thus, the session key has been securely delivered to both C and the TGS.

Note that several additional pieces of information have been added to this first phase of the dialogue. Message (1) includes a timestamp, so that the AS knows that the message is timely. Message (2) includes several elements of the ticket in a form accessible to C. This enables C to confirm that this ticket is for the TGS and to learn its expiration time.

Armed with the ticket and the session key, C is ready to approach the TGS. As before, C sends the TGS a message that includes the ticket plus the ID of the requested service [message (3) in Table 15.1b]. In addition, C transmits an authenticator, which includes the ID and address of C's user and a timestamp. Unlike the ticket, which is reusable, the authenticator is intended for use only once and has a very short lifetime. The TGS can decrypt the ticket with the key that it shares with the AS. This ticket indicates that user C has been provided with the session key $K_{c,tgs}$. In effect, the ticket says, "Anyone who uses $K_{c,tgs}$ must be C." The TGS uses the session key to decrypt the authenticator. The TGS can then check the name and address from the authenticator with that of the ticket and with the network address of the incoming message. If all match, then the TGS is assured that the sender of the ticket is indeed the ticket's real owner. In effect, the authenticator says, "At time TS_3, I hereby use $K_{c,tgs}$." Note that the ticket does not prove anyone's identity but is a way to distribute keys securely. It is the authenticator that proves the client's identity. Because the authenticator can be used only once and has a short lifetime, the threat of an opponent stealing both the ticket and the authenticator for presentation later is countered.

The reply from the TGS in message (4) follows the form of message (2). The message is encrypted with the session key shared by the TGS and C and includes a session key to be shared between C and the server V, the ID of V, and the timestamp of the ticket. The ticket itself includes the same session key.

C now has a reusable service-granting ticket for V. When C presents this ticket, as shown in message (5), it also sends an authenticator. The server can decrypt the ticket, recover the session key, and decrypt the authenticator.

If mutual authentication is required, the server can reply as shown in message (6) of Table 15.1. The server returns the value of the timestamp from the authenticator, incremented by 1, and encrypted in the session key. C can decrypt this message to recover the incremented timestamp. Because the message was encrypted by the session key, C is assured that it could have been created only by V. The contents of the message assure C that this is not a replay of an old reply.

Finally, at the conclusion of this process, the client and server share a secret key. This key can be used to encrypt future messages between the two or to exchange a new random session key for that purpose.

Figure 15.3 illustrates the Kerberos exchanges among the parties. Table 15.2 summarizes the justification for each of the elements in the Kerberos protocol.

Kerberos Realms and Multiple Kerberi A full-service Kerberos environment consisting of a Kerberos server, a number of clients, and a number of application servers requires the following:

1. The Kerberos server must have the user ID and hashed passwords of all participating users in its database. All users are registered with the Kerberos server.
2. The Kerberos server must share a secret key with each server. All servers are registered with the Kerberos server.

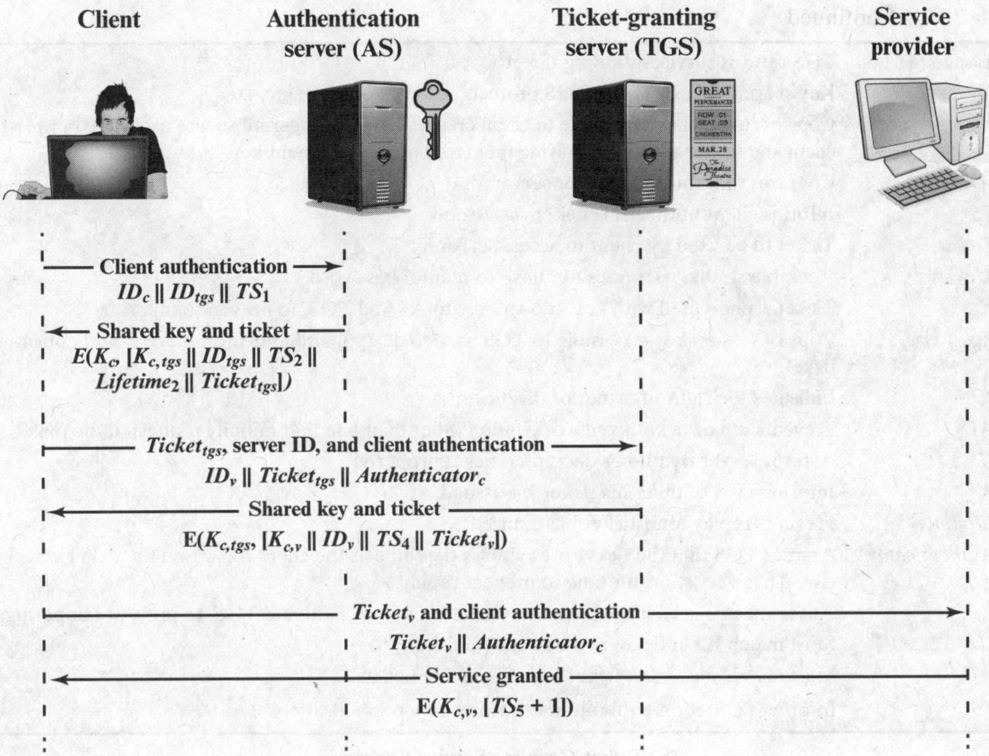

Figure 15.3 Kerberos Exchanges

Table 15.2 Rationale for the Elements of the Kerberos Version 4 Protocol

Message (1)	Client requests ticket-granting ticket.
ID_C	Tells AS identity of user from this client.
ID_{tgs}	Tells AS that user requests access to TGS.
TS_1	Allows AS to verify that client's clock is synchronized with that of AS.
Message (2)	AS returns ticket-granting ticket.
K_c	Encryption is based on user's password, enabling AS and client to verify password, and protecting contents of message (2).
$K_{c,\,tgs}$	Copy of session key accessible to client created by AS to permit secure exchange between client and TGS without requiring them to share a permanent key.
ID_{tgs}	Confirms that this ticket is for the TGS.
TS_2	Informs client of time this ticket was issued.
$Lifetime_2$	Informs client of the lifetime of this ticket.
$Ticket_{tgs}$	Ticket to be used by client to access TGS.

(a) Authentication Service Exchange

Message (3)	Client requests service-granting ticket.
ID_V	Tells TGS that user requests access to server V.
$Ticket_{tgs}$	Assures TGS that this user has been authenticated by AS.
$Authenticator_c$	Generated by client to validate ticket.

(Continued)

Table 15.2 Continued

Message (4)	TGS returns service-granting ticket.
$K_{c,tgs}$	Key shared only by C and TGS protects contents of message (4).
$K_{c,v}$	Copy of session key accessible to client created by TGS to permit secure exchange between client and server without requiring them to share a permanent key.
ID_V	Confirms that this ticket is for server V.
TS_4	Informs client of time this ticket was issued.
$Ticket_V$	Ticket to be used by client to access server V.
$Ticket_{tgs}$	Reusable so that user does not have to reenter password.
K_{tgs}	Ticket is encrypted with key known only to AS and TGS, to prevent tampering.
$K_{c,tgs}$	Copy of session key accessible to TGS used to decrypt authenticator, thereby authenticating ticket.
ID_C	Indicates the rightful owner of this ticket.
AD_C	Prevents use of ticket from workstation other than one that initially requested the ticket.
ID_{tgs}	Assures server that it has decrypted ticket properly.
TS_2	Informs TGS of time this ticket was issued.
$Lifetime_2$	Prevents replay after ticket has expired.
$Authenticator_c$	Assures TGS that the ticket presenter is the same as the client for whom the ticket was issued has very short lifetime to prevent replay.
$K_{c,tgs}$	Authenticator is encrypted with key known only to client and TGS, to prevent tampering.
ID_C	Must match ID in ticket to authenticate ticket.
AD_C	Must match address in ticket to authenticate ticket.
TS_3	Informs TGS of time this authenticator was generated.

(b) Ticket-Granting Service Exchange

Message (5)	Client requests service.
$Ticket_V$	Assures server that this user has been authenticated by AS.
$Authenticator_c$	Generated by client to validate ticket.
Message (6)	Optional authentication of server to client.
$K_{c,v}$	Assures C that this message is from V.
$TS_5 + 1$	Assures C that this is not a replay of an old reply.
$Ticket_v$	Reusable so that client does not need to request a new ticket from TGS for each access to the same server.
K_v	Ticket is encrypted with key known only to TGS and server, to prevent tampering.
$K_{c,v}$	Copy of session key accessible to client; used to decrypt authenticator, thereby authenticating ticket.
ID_C	Indicates the rightful owner of this ticket.
AD_C	Prevents use of ticket from workstation other than one that initially requested the ticket.
ID_V	Assures server that it has decrypted ticket properly.
TS_4	Informs server of time this ticket was issued.
$Lifetime_4$	Prevents replay after ticket has expired.
$Authenticator_c$	Assures server that the ticket presenter is the same as the client for whom the ticket was issued; has very short lifetime to prevent replay.
$K_{c,v}$	Authenticator is encrypted with key known only to client and server, to prevent tampering.
ID_C	Must match ID in ticket to authenticate ticket.
AD_C	Must match address in ticket to authenticate ticket.
TS_5	Informs server of time this authenticator was generated.

(c) Client/Server Authentication Exchange

Such an environment is referred to as a **Kerberos realm**. The concept of **realm** can be explained as follows. A Kerberos realm is a set of managed nodes that share the same Kerberos database. The Kerberos database resides on the Kerberos master computer system, which should be kept in a physically secure room. A read-only copy of the Kerberos database might also reside on other Kerberos computer systems. However, all changes to the database must be made on the master computer system. Changing or accessing the contents of a Kerberos database requires the Kerberos master password. A related concept is that of a **Kerberos principal**, which is a service or user that is known to the Kerberos system. Each Kerberos principal is identified by its principal name. Principal names consist of three parts: a service or user name, an instance name, and a realm name.

Networks of clients and servers under different administrative organizations typically constitute different realms. That is, it generally is not practical or does not conform to administrative policy to have users and servers in one administrative domain registered with a Kerberos server elsewhere. However, users in one realm may need access to servers in other realms, and some servers may be willing to provide service to users from other realms, provided that those users are authenticated.

Kerberos provides a mechanism for supporting such interrealm authentication. For two realms to support interrealm authentication, a third requirement is added:

3. The Kerberos server in each interoperating realm shares a secret key with the server in the other realm. The two Kerberos servers are registered with each other.

The scheme requires that the Kerberos server in one realm trust the Kerberos server in the other realm to authenticate its users. Furthermore, the participating servers in the second realm must also be willing to trust the Kerberos server in the first realm.

With these ground rules in place, we can describe the mechanism as follows (Figure 15.4): A user wishing service on a server in another realm needs a ticket for that server. The user's client follows the usual procedures to gain access to the local TGS and then requests a ticket-granting ticket for a remote TGS (TGS in another realm). The client can then apply to the remote TGS for a service-granting ticket for the desired server in the realm of the remote TGS.

The details of the exchanges illustrated in Figure 15.4 are as follows (compare Table 15.1).

(1) C → AS: $ID_c \| ID_{tgs} \| TS_1$

(2) AS → C: $E(K_c, [K_{c,tgs} \| ID_{tgs} \| TS_2 \| Lifetime_2 \| Ticket_{tgs}])$

(3) C → TGS: $ID_{tgsrem} \| Ticket_{tgs} \| Authenticator_c$

(4) TGS → C: $E(K_{c,tgs}, [K_{c,tgsrem} \| ID_{tgsrem} \| TS_4 \| Ticket_{tgsrem}])$

(5) C → TGS_{rem}: $ID_{vrem} \| Ticket_{tgsrem} \| Authenticator_c$

(6) TGS_{rem} → C: $E(K_{c,tgsrem}, [K_{c,vrem} \| ID_{vrem} \| TS_6 \| Ticket_{vrem}])$

(7) C → V_{rem}: $Ticket_{vrem} \| Authenticator_c$

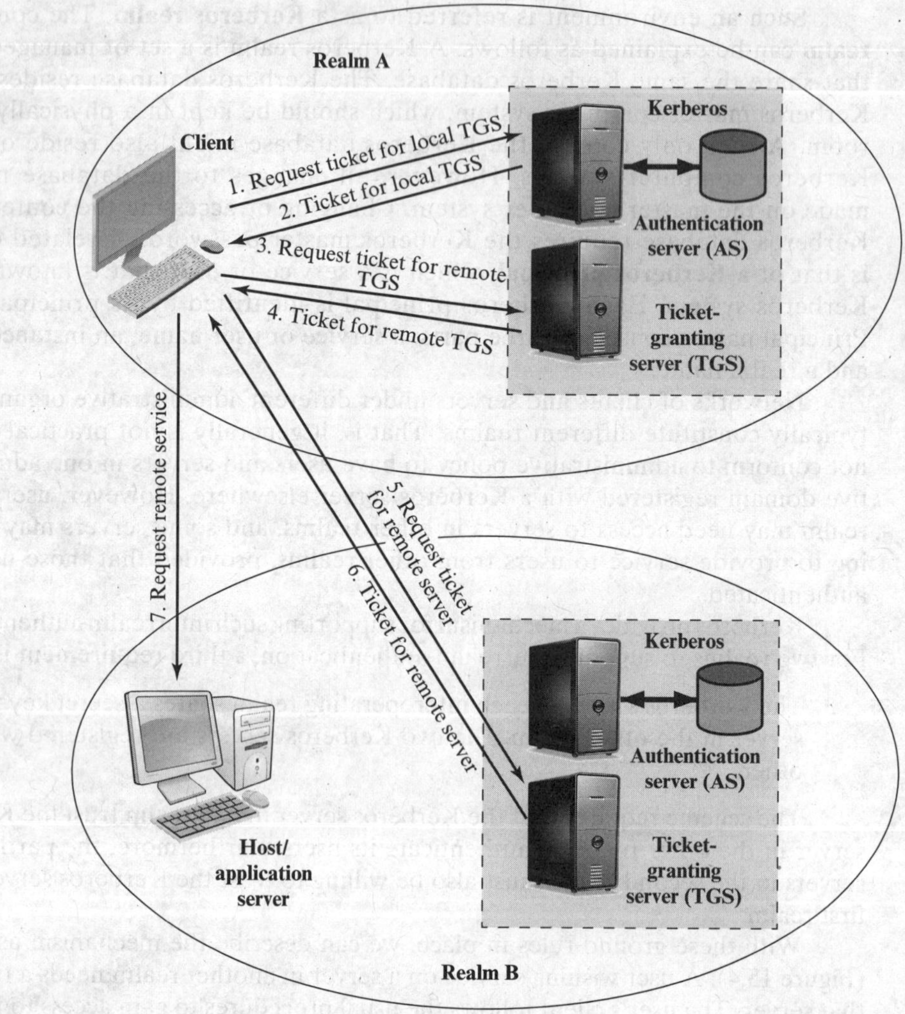

Figure 15.4 Request for Service in Another Realm

The ticket presented to the remote server (V_{rem}) indicates the realm in which the user was originally authenticated. The server chooses whether to honor the remote request.

One problem presented by the foregoing approach is that it does not scale well to many realms. If there are N realms, then there must be $N(N - 1)/2$ secure key exchanges so that each Kerberos realm can interoperate with all other Kerberos realms.

Kerberos Version 5

Kerberos version 5 is specified in RFC 4120 and provides a number of improvements over version 4 [KOHL94]. To begin, we provide an overview of the changes from version 4 to version 5 and then look at the version 5 protocol.

Differences between Versions 4 and 5 Version 5 is intended to address the limitations of version 4 in two areas: environmental shortcomings and technical deficiencies. Let us briefly summarize the improvements in each area.[8]

Kerberos version 4 was developed for use within the Project Athena environment and, accordingly, did not fully address the need to be of general purpose. This led to the following **environmental shortcomings**.

1. **Encryption system dependence:** Version 4 requires the use of DES. Export restriction on DES as well as doubts about the strength of DES were thus of concern. In version 5, ciphertext is tagged with an encryption-type identifier so that any encryption technique may be used. Encryption keys are tagged with a type and a length, allowing the same key to be used in different algorithms and allowing the specification of different variations on a given algorithm.
2. **Internet protocol dependence:** Version 4 requires the use of Internet Protocol (IP) addresses. Other address types, such as the ISO network address, are not accommodated. Version 5 network addresses are tagged with type and length, allowing any network address type to be used.
3. **Message byte ordering:** In version 4, the sender of a message employs a byte ordering of its own choosing and tags the message to indicate least significant byte in lowest address or most significant byte in lowest address. This techniques works but does not follow established conventions. In version 5, all message structures are defined using Abstract Syntax Notation One (ASN.1) and Basic Encoding Rules (BER), which provide an unambiguous byte ordering.
4. **Ticket lifetime:** Lifetime values in version 4 are encoded in an 8-bit quantity in units of five minutes. Thus, the maximum lifetime that can be expressed is $2^8 \times 5 = 1280$ minutes (a little over 21 hours). This may be inadequate for some applications (e.g., a long-running simulation that requires valid Kerberos credentials throughout execution). In version 5, tickets include an explicit start time and end time, allowing tickets with arbitrary lifetimes.
5. **Authentication forwarding:** Version 4 does not allow credentials issued to one client to be forwarded to some other host and used by some other client. This capability would enable a client to access a server and have that server access another server on behalf of the client. For example, a client issues a request to a print server that then accesses the client's file from a file server, using the client's credentials for access. Version 5 provides this capability.
6. **Interrealm authentication:** In version 4, interoperability among N realms requires on the order of N^2 Kerberos-to-Kerberos relationships, as described earlier. Version 5 supports a method that requires fewer relationships, as described shortly.

[8]The following discussion follows the presentation in [KOHL94].

Apart from these environmental limitations, there are **technical deficiencies** in the version 4 protocol itself. Most of these deficiencies were documented in [BELL90], and version 5 attempts to address these. The deficiencies are the following.

1. **Double encryption:** Note in Table 15.1 [messages (2) and (4)] that tickets provided to clients are encrypted twice—once with the secret key of the target server and then again with a secret key known to the client. The second encryption is not necessary and is computationally wasteful.
2. **PCBC encryption:** Encryption in version 4 makes use of a nonstandard mode of DES known as **propagating cipher block chaining (PCBC)**.[9] It has been demonstrated that this mode is vulnerable to an attack involving the interchange of ciphertext blocks [KOHL89]. PCBC was intended to provide an integrity check as part of the encryption operation. Version 5 provides explicit integrity mechanisms, allowing the standard CBC mode to be used for encryption. In particular, a checksum or hash code is attached to the message prior to encryption using CBC.
3. **Session keys:** Each ticket includes a session key that is used by the client to encrypt the authenticator sent to the service associated with that ticket. In addition, the session key may subsequently be used by the client and the server to protect messages passed during that session. However, because the same ticket may be used repeatedly to gain service from a particular server, there is the risk that an opponent will replay messages from an old session to the client or the server. In version 5, it is possible for a client and server to negotiate a subsession key, which is to be used only for that one connection. A new access by the client would result in the use of a new subsession key.
4. **Password attacks:** Both versions are vulnerable to a password attack. The message from the AS to the client includes material encrypted with a key based on the client's password.[10] An opponent can capture this message and attempt to decrypt it by trying various passwords. If the result of a test decryption is of the proper form, then the opponent has discovered the client's password and may subsequently use it to gain authentication credentials from Kerberos. This is the same type of password attack described in Chapter 21, with the same kinds of countermeasures being applicable. Version 5 does provide a mechanism known as preauthentication, which should make password attacks more difficult, but it does not prevent them.

THE VERSION 5 AUTHENTICATION DIALOGUE Table 15.3 summarizes the basic version 5 dialogue. This is best explained by comparison with version 4 (Table 15.1).

First, consider the **authentication service exchange**. Message (1) is a client request for a ticket-granting ticket. As before, it includes the ID of the user and the TGS. The following new elements are added:

---

[9] This is described in Appendix T.

[10] Appendix T describes the mapping of passwords to encryption keys.

Table 15.3 Summary of Kerberos Version 5 Message Exchanges

(1)	**C → AS**	$Options \| ID_c \| Realm_c \| ID_{tgs} \| Times \| Nonce_1$
(2)	**AS → C**	$Realm_C \| ID_C \| Ticket_{tgs} \| E(K_c, [K_{c,tgs} \| Times \| Nonce_1 \| Realm_{tgs} \| ID_{tgs}])$
		$Ticket_{tgs} = E(K_{tgs}, [Flags \| K_{c,tgs} \| Realm_c \| ID_C \| AD_C \| Times])$

(a) Authentication Service Exchange to obtain ticket-granting ticket

(3)	**C → TGS**	$Options \| ID_v \| Times \| Nonce_2 \| Ticket_{tgs} \| Authenticator_c$
(4)	**TGS → C**	$Realm_c \| ID_C \| Ticket_v \| E(K_{c,tgs}, [K_{c,v} \| Times \| Nonce_2 \| Realm_v \| ID_v])$
		$Ticket_{tgs} = E(K_{tgs}, [Flags \| K_{c,tgs} \| Realm_c \| ID_C \| AD_C \| Times])$
		$Ticket_v = E(K_v, [Flags \| K_{c,v} \| Realm_c \| ID_C \| AD_C \| Times])$
		$Authenticator_c = E(K_{c,tgs}, [ID_C \| Realm_c \| TS_1])$

(b) Ticket-Granting Service Exchange to obtain service-granting ticket

(5)	**C → V**	$Options \| Ticket_v \| Authenticator_c$
(6)	**V → C**	$E_{K_{c,v}}[TS_2 \| Subkey \| Seq \#]$
		$Ticket_v = E(K_v, [Flag \| K_{c,v} \| Realm_c \| ID_C \| AD_C \| Times])$
		$Authenticator_c = E(K_{c,v}, [ID_C \| Relam_c \| TS_2 \| Subkey \| Seq \#])$

(c) Client/Server Authentication Exchange to obtain service

- **Realm:** Indicates realm of user
- **Options:** Used to request that certain flags be set in the returned ticket
- **Times:** Used by the client to request the following time settings in the ticket:
  - —**from**: the desired start time for the requested ticket
  - —**till**: the requested expiration time for the requested ticket
  - —**rtime**: requested renew-till time
- **Nonce:** A random value to be repeated in message (2) to assure that the response is fresh and has not been replayed by an opponent

Message (2) returns a ticket-granting ticket, identifying information for the client, and a block encrypted using the encryption key based on the user's password. This block includes the session key to be used between the client and the TGS, times specified in message (1), the nonce from message (1), and TGS identifying information. The ticket itself includes the session key, identifying information for the client, the requested time values, and flags that reflect the status of this ticket and the requested options. These flags introduce significant new functionality to version 5. For now, we defer a discussion of these flags and concentrate on the overall structure of the version 5 protocol.

Let us now compare the **ticket-granting service exchange** for versions 4 and 5. We see that message (3) for both versions includes an authenticator, a ticket, and the name of the requested service. In addition, version 5 includes requested times and options for the ticket and a nonce—all with functions similar to those of message (1). The authenticator itself is essentially the same as the one used in version 4.

Message (4) has the same structure as message (2). It returns a ticket plus information needed by the client, with the information encrypted using the session key now shared by the client and the TGS.

Finally, for the **client/server authentication exchange**, several new features appear in version 5. In message (5), the client may request as an option that mutual authentication is required. The authenticator includes several new fields:

- **Subkey:** The client's choice for an encryption key to be used to protect this specific application session. If this field is omitted, the session key from the ticket ($K_{c,v}$) is used.
- **Sequence number:** An optional field that specifies the starting sequence number to be used by the server for messages sent to the client during this session. Messages may be sequence numbered to detect replays.

If mutual authentication is required, the server responds with message (6). This message includes the timestamp from the authenticator. Note that in version 4, the timestamp was incremented by one. This is not necessary in version 5, because the nature of the format of messages is such that it is not possible for an opponent to create message (6) without knowledge of the appropriate encryption keys. The subkey field, if present, overrides the subkey field, if present, in message (5). The optional sequence number field specifies the starting sequence number to be used by the client.

TICKET FLAGS The flags field included in tickets in version 5 supports expanded functionality compared to that available in version 4. Table 15.4 summarizes the flags that may be included in a ticket.

Table 15.4 Kerberos Version 5 Flags

INITIAL	This ticket was issued using the AS protocol and not issued based on a ticket-granting ticket.
PRE-AUTHENT	During initial authentication, the client was authenticated by the KDC before a ticket was issued.
HW-AUTHENT	The protocol employed for initial authentication required the use of hardware expected to be possessed solely by the named client.
RENEWABLE	Tells TGS that this ticket can be used to obtain a replacement ticket that expires at a later date.
MAY-POSTDATE	Tells TGS that a postdated ticket may be issued based on this ticket-granting ticket.
POSTDATED	Indicates that this ticket has been postdated; the end server can check the authtime field to see when the original authentication occurred.
INVALID	This ticket is invalid and must be validated by the KDC before use.
PROXIABLE	Tells TGS that a new service-granting ticket with a different network address may be issued based on the presented ticket.
PROXY	Indicates that this ticket is a proxy.
FORWARDABLE	Tells TGS that a new ticket-granting ticket with a different network address may be issued based on this ticket-granting ticket.
FORWARDED	Indicates that this ticket has either been forwarded or was issued based on authentication involving a forwarded ticket-granting ticket.

The INITIAL flag indicates that this ticket was issued by the AS, not by the TGS. When a client requests a service-granting ticket from the TGS, it presents a ticket-granting ticket obtained from the AS. In version 4, this was the only way to obtain a service-granting ticket. Version 5 provides the additional capability that the client can get a service-granting ticket directly from the AS. The utility of this is as follows: A server, such as a password-changing server, may wish to know that the client's password was recently tested.

The PRE-AUTHENT flag, if set, indicates that when the AS received the initial request [message (1)], it authenticated the client before issuing a ticket. The exact form of this preauthentication is left unspecified. As an example, the MIT implementation of version 5 has encrypted timestamp preauthentication, enabled by default. When a user wants to get a ticket, it has to send to the AS a preauthentication block containing a random confounder, a version number, and a timestamp all encrypted in the client's password-based key. The AS decrypts the block and will not send a ticket-granting ticket back unless the timestamp in the preauthentication block is within the allowable time skew (time interval to account for clock drift and network delays). Another possibility is the use of a smart card that generates continually changing passwords that are included in the preauthenticated messages. The passwords generated by the card can be based on a user's password but be transformed by the card so that, in effect, arbitrary passwords are used. This prevents an attack based on easily guessed passwords. If a smart card or similar device was used, this is indicated by the HW-AUTHENT flag.

When a ticket has a long lifetime, there is the potential for it to be stolen and used by an opponent for a considerable period. If a short lifetime is used to lessen the threat, then overhead is involved in acquiring new tickets. In the case of a ticket-granting ticket, the client would either have to store the user's secret key, which is clearly risky, or repeatedly ask the user for a password. A compromise scheme is the use of renewable tickets. A ticket with the RENEWABLE flag set includes two expiration times: One for this specific ticket and one that is the latest permissible value for an expiration time. A client can have the ticket renewed by presenting it to the TGS with a requested new expiration time. If the new time is within the limit of the latest permissible value, the TGS can issue a new ticket with a new session time and a later specific expiration time. The advantage of this mechanism is that the TGS may refuse to renew a ticket reported as stolen.

A client may request that the AS provide a ticket-granting ticket with the MAY-POSTDATE flag set. The client can then use this ticket to request a ticket that is flagged as POSTDATED and INVALID from the TGS. Subsequently, the client may submit the postdated ticket for validation. This scheme can be useful for running a long batch job on a server that requires a ticket periodically. The client can obtain a number of tickets for this session at once, with spread out time values. All but the first ticket are initially invalid. When the execution reaches a point in time when a new ticket is required, the client can get the appropriate ticket validated. With this approach, the client does not have to repeatedly use its ticket-granting ticket to obtain a service-granting ticket.

In version 5, it is possible for a server to act as a proxy on behalf of a client, in effect adopting the credentials and privileges of the client to request a service from another server. If a client wishes to use this mechanism, it requests a ticket-granting ticket with the PROXIABLE flag set. When this ticket is presented to the TGS, the TGS is permitted to issue a service-granting ticket with a different network address; this latter ticket will have its PROXY flag set. An application receiving such a ticket may accept it or require additional authentication to provide an audit trail.[11]

The proxy concept is a limited case of the more powerful forwarding procedure. If a ticket is set with the FORWARDABLE flag, a TGS can issue to the requestor a ticket-granting ticket with a different network address and the FORWARDED flag set. This ticket then can be presented to a remote TGS. This capability allows a client to gain access to a server on another realm without requiring that each Kerberos maintain a secret key with Kerberos servers in every other realm. For example, realms could be structured hierarchically. Then a client could walk up the tree to a common node and then back down to reach a target realm. Each step of the walk would involve forwarding a ticket-granting ticket to the next TGS in the path.

15.4 REMOTE USER-AUTHENTICATION USING ASYMMETRIC ENCRYPTION

Mutual Authentication

In Chapter 14, we presented one approach to the use of public-key encryption for the purpose of session-key distribution (Figure 14.9). This protocol assumes that each of the two parties is in possession of the current public key of the other. It may not be practical to require this assumption.

A protocol using timestamps is provided in [DENN81]:

1. A → AS: $ID_A \| ID_B$
2. AS → A: $E(PR_{as}, [ID_A \| PU_a \| T]) \| E(PR_{as}, [ID_B \| PU_b \| T])$
3. A → B: $E(PR_{as}, [ID_A \| PU_a \| T]) \| E(PR_{as}, [ID_B \| PU_b \| T]) \|$ $E(PU_b, E(PR_a, [K_s \| T]))$

In this case, the central system is referred to as an authentication server (AS), because it is not actually responsible for secret-key distribution. Rather, the AS provides public-key certificates. The session key is chosen and encrypted by A; hence, there is no risk of exposure by the AS. The timestamps protect against replays of compromised keys.

This protocol is compact but, as before, requires the synchronization of clocks. Another approach, proposed by Woo and Lam [WOO92a], makes use of nonces. The protocol consists of the following steps.

1. A → KDC: $ID_A \| ID_B$
2. KDC → A: $E(PR_{auth}, [ID_B \| PU_b])$
3. A → B: $E(PU_b, [N_a \| ID_A])$
4. B → KDC: $ID_A \| ID_B \| E(PU_{auth}, N_a)$
5. KDC → B: $E(PR_{auth}, [ID_A \| PU_a]) \| E(PU_b, E(PR_{auth}, [N_a \| K_s \| ID_B]))$

[11] For a discussion of some of the possible uses of the proxy capability, see [NEUM93b].

6. B → A: $E(PU_a, [E(PR_{auth}, [(N_a \| K_s \| ID_B)]) \| N_b])$
7. A → B: $E(K_s, N_b)$

In step 1, A informs the KDC of its intention to establish a secure connection with B. The KDC returns to A a copy of B's public-key certificate (step 2). Using B's public key, A informs B of its desire to communicate and sends a nonce N_a (step 3). In step 4, B asks the KDC for A's public-key certificate and requests a session key; B includes A's nonce so that the KDC can stamp the session key with that nonce. The nonce is protected using the KDC's public key. In step 5, the KDC returns to B a copy of A's public-key certificate, plus the information $\{N_a, K_s, ID_B\}$. This information basically says that K_s is a secret key generated by the KDC on behalf of B and tied to N_a; the binding of K_s and N_a will assure A that K_s is fresh. This triple is encrypted using the KDC's private key to allow B to verify that the triple is in fact from the KDC. It is also encrypted using B's public key so that no other entity may use the triple in an attempt to establish a fraudulent connection with A. In step 6, the triple $\{N_a, K_s, ID_B\}$, still encrypted with the KDC's private key, is relayed to A, together with a nonce N_b generated by B. All the foregoing are encrypted using A's public key. A retrieves the session key K_s, uses it to encrypt N_b, and returns it to B. This last message assures B of A's knowledge of the session key.

This seems to be a secure protocol that takes into account the various attacks. However, the authors themselves spotted a flaw and submitted a revised version of the algorithm in [WOO92b]:

1. A → KDC: $ID_A \| ID_B$
2. KDC → A: $E(PR_{auth}, [ID_B \| PU_b])$
3. A → B: $E(PU_b, [N_a \| ID_A])$
4. B → KDC: $ID_A \| ID_B \| E(PU_{auth}, N_a)$
5. KDC → B: $E(PR_{auth}, [ID_A \| PU_a]) \| E(PU_b, E(PR_{auth}, [N_a \| K_s \| ID_A \| ID_B]))$
6. B → A: $E(PU_a, [N_b \| E(PR_{auth}, [N_a \| K_s \| ID_A \| ID_B])])$
7. A → B: $E(K_s, N_b)$

The identifier of A, ID_A, is added to the set of items encrypted with the KDC's private key in steps 5 and 6. This binds the session key K_s to the identities of the two parties that will be engaged in the session. This inclusion of ID_A accounts for the fact that the nonce value N_a is considered unique only among all nonces generated by A, not among all nonces generated by all parties. Thus, it is the pair $\{ID_A, N_a\}$ that uniquely identifies the connection request of A.

In both this example and the protocols described earlier, protocols that appeared secure were revised after additional analysis. These examples highlight the difficulty of getting things right in the area of authentication.

One-Way Authentication

We have already presented public-key encryption approaches that are suited to electronic mail, including the straightforward encryption of the entire message for confidentiality (Figure 12.1b), authentication (Figure 12.1c), or both (Figure 12.1d). These approaches require that either the sender know the recipient's public key (confidentiality), the recipient know the sender's public key (authentication), or both (confidentiality plus authentication). In addition, the public-key algorithm must be applied once or twice to what may be a long message.

If confidentiality is the primary concern, then the following may be more efficient:

$$A \rightarrow B: \quad E(PU_b, K_s) \| E(K_s, M)$$

In this case, the message is encrypted with a one-time secret key. A also encrypts this one-time key with B's public key. Only B will be able to use the corresponding private key to recover the one-time key and then use that key to decrypt the message. This scheme is more efficient than simply encrypting the entire message with B's public key.

If authentication is the primary concern, then a digital signature may suffice, as was illustrated in Figure 13.2:

$$A \rightarrow B: \quad M \| E(PR_a, H(M))$$

This method guarantees that A cannot later deny having sent the message. However, this technique is open to another kind of fraud. Bob composes a message to his boss Alice that contains an idea that will save the company money. He appends his digital signature and sends it into the email system. Eventually, the message will get delivered to Alice's mailbox. But suppose that Max has heard of Bob's idea and gains access to the mail queue before delivery. He finds Bob's message, strips off his signature, appends his, and requeues the message to be delivered to Alice. Max gets credit for Bob's idea.

To counter such a scheme, both the message and signature can be encrypted with the recipient's public key:

$$A \rightarrow B: \quad E(PU_b, [M \| E(PR_a, H(M))])$$

The latter two schemes require that B know A's public key and be convinced that it is timely. An effective way to provide this assurance is the digital certificate, described in Chapter 14. Now we have

$$A \rightarrow B: \quad M \| E(PR_a, H(M)) \| E(PR_{as}, [T \| ID_A \| PU_a])$$

In addition to the message, A sends B the signature encrypted with A's private key and A's certificate encrypted with the private key of the authentication server. The recipient of the message first uses the certificate to obtain the sender's public key and verify that it is authentic and then uses the public key to verify the message itself. If confidentiality is required, then the entire message can be encrypted with B's public key. Alternatively, the entire message can be encrypted with a one-time secret key; the secret key is also transmitted, encrypted with B's public key. This approach is explored in Chapter 19.

15.5 FEDERATED IDENTITY MANAGEMENT

Federated identity management is a relatively new concept dealing with the use of a common identity management scheme across multiple enterprises and numerous applications and supporting many thousands, even millions, of users. We begin our overview with a discussion of the concept of identity management and then examine federated identity management.

Identity Management

Identity management is a centralized, automated approach to provide enterprise-wide access to resources by employees and other authorized individuals. The focus of identity management is defining an identity for each user (human or process), associating attributes with the identity, and enforcing a means by which a user can verify identity. The central concept of an identity management system is the use of single sign-on (SSO).

SSO enables a user to access all network resources after a single authentication.

Typical services provided by a federated identity management system include the following:

- **Point of contact:** Includes authentication that a user corresponds to the user name provided, and management of user/server sessions.
- **SSO protocol services:** Provides a vendor-neutral security token service for supporting a single sign on to federated services.
- **Trust services:** Federation relationships require a trust relationship-based federation between business partners. A trust relationship is represented by the combination of the security tokens used to exchange information about a user, the cryptographic information used to protect these security tokens, and optionally the identity mapping rules applied to the information contained within this token.
- **Key services:** Management of keys and certificates.
- **Identity services:** services that provide the interface to local data stores, including user registries and databases, for identity-related information management.
- **Authorization:** Granting access to specific services and/or resources based on the authentication.
- **Provisioning:** Includes creating an account in each target system for the user, enrollment or registration of user in accounts, establishment of access rights or credentials to ensure the privacy and integrity of account data.
- **Management:** Services related to runtime configuration and deployment.

Note that Kerberos contains a number of the elements of an identity management system.

Figure 15.5 illustrates entities and data flows in a generic identity management architecture. A **principal** is an identity holder. Typically, this is a human user that seeks access to resources and services on the network. User devices, agent processes, and server systems may also function as principals. Principals authenticate themselves to an **identity provider**. The identity provider associates authentication information with a principal, as well as attributes and one or more identifiers.

Increasingly, digital identities incorporate attributes other than simply an identifier and authentication information (such as passwords and biometric information). An **attribute service** manages the creation and maintenance of such attributes. For example, a user needs to provide a shipping address each time an order is placed at a new Web merchant, and this information needs to be revised when the user moves. Identity management enables the user to provide this information once, so that it is maintained in a single place and released to data consumers in accordance with

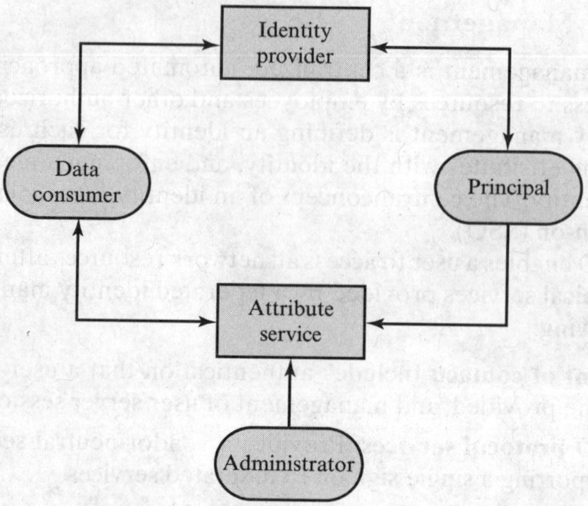

Figure 15.5 Generic Identity Management Architecture

authorization and privacy policies. Users may create some of the attributes to be associated with their digital identity, such as an address. **Administrators** may also assign attributes to users, such as roles, access permissions, and employee information.

Data consumers are entities that obtain and employ data maintained and provided by identity and attribute providers, which are often used to support authorization decisions and to collect audit information. For example, a database server or file server is a data consumer that needs a client's credentials so as to know what access to provide to that client.

Identity Federation

Identity federation is, in essence, an extension of identity management to multiple security domains. Such domains include autonomous internal business units, external business partners, and other third-party applications and services. The goal is to provide the sharing of digital identities so that a user can be authenticated a single time and then access applications and resources across multiple domains. Because these domains are relatively autonomous or independent, no centralized control is possible. Rather, the cooperating organizations must form a federation based on agreed standards and mutual levels of trust to securely share digital identities.

Federated identity management refers to the agreements, standards, and technologies that enable the portability of identities, identity attributes, and entitlements across multiple enterprises and numerous applications and supporting many thousands, even millions, of users. When multiple organizations implement interoperable federated identity schemes, an employee in one organization can use a single sign-on to access services across the federation with trust relationships associated with the identity. For example, an employee may log onto her corporate intranet and be authenticated to perform authorized functions and access authorized services on that intranet. The employee could then access their health benefits from an outside health-care provider without having to reauthenticate.

Beyond SSO, federated identity management provides other capabilities. One is a standardized means of representing attributes. Increasingly, digital identities incorporate attributes other than simply an identifier and authentication information (such as passwords and biometric information). Examples of attributes include account numbers, organizational roles, physical location, and file ownership. A user may have multiple identifiers; for example, each identifier may be associated with a unique role with its own access permissions.

Another key function of federated identity management is identity mapping. Different security domains may represent identities and attributes differently. Further, the amount of information associated with an individual in one domain may be more than is necessary in another domain. The federated identity management protocols map identities and attributes of a user in one domain to the requirements of another domain.

Figure 15.6 illustrates entities and data flows in a generic federated identity management architecture.

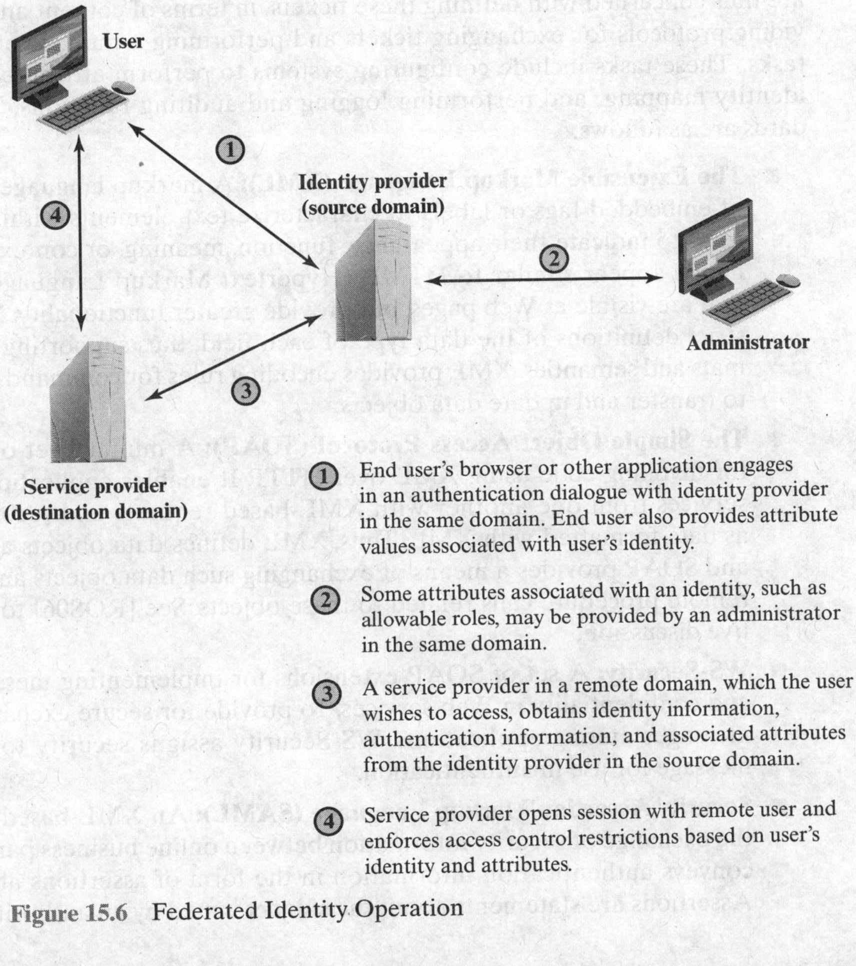

Figure 15.6 Federated Identity Operation

The identity provider acquires attribute information through dialogue and protocol exchanges with users and administrators. For example, a user needs to provide a shipping address each time an order is placed at a new Web merchant, and this information needs to be revised when the user moves. Identity management enables the user to provide this information once, so that it is maintained in a single place and released to data consumers in accordance with authorization and privacy policies.

Service providers are entities that obtain and employ data maintained and provided by identity providers, often to support authorization decisions and to collect audit information. For example, a database server or file server is a data consumer that needs a client's credentials so as to know what access to provide to that client. A service provider can be in the same domain as the user and the identity provider. The power of this approach is for federated identity management, in which the service provider is in a different domain (e.g., a vendor or supplier network).

Standards Federated identity management uses a number of standards as the building blocks for secure identity exchange across different domains or heterogeneous systems. In essence, organizations issue some form of security tickets for their users that can be processed by cooperating partners. Identity federation standards are thus concerned with defining these tickets, in terms of content and format, providing protocols for exchanging tickets and performing a number of management tasks. These tasks include configuring systems to perform attribute transfers and identity mapping, and performing logging and auditing functions. The key standards are as follows:

- **The Extensible Markup Language (XML):** A markup language that uses sets of embedded tags or labels to characterize text elements within a document so as to indicate their appearance, function, meaning, or context. XML documents appear similar to HTML (Hypertext Markup Language) documents that are visible as Web pages, but provide greater functionality. XML includes strict definitions of the data type of each field, thus supporting database formats and semantics. XML provides encoding rules for commands that are used to transfer and update data objects.
- **The Simple Object Access Protocol (SOAP):** A minimal set of conventions for invoking code using XML over HTTP. It enables applications to request services from one another with XML-based requests and receive responses as data formatted with XML. Thus, XML defines data objects and structures, and SOAP provides a means of exchanging such data objects and performing remote procedure calls related to these objects. See [ROS06] for an informative discussion.
- **WS-Security:** A set of SOAP extensions for implementing message integrity and confidentiality in Web services. To provide for secure exchange of SOAP messages among applications, WS-Security assigns security tokens to each message for use in authentication.
- **Security Assertion Markup Language (SAML):** An XML-based language for the exchange of security information between online business partners. SAML conveys authentication information in the form of assertions about subjects. Assertions are statements about the subject issued by an authoritative entity.

The challenge with federated identity management is to integrate multiple technologies, standards, and services to provide a secure, user-friendly utility. The key, as in most areas of security and networking, is the reliance on a few mature standards widely accepted by industry. Federated identity management seems to have reached this level of maturity.

EXAMPLES To get some feel for the functionality of identity federation, we look at three scenarios, taken from [COMP06].

In the first scenario (Figure 15.7a), Workplace.com contracts with Health.com to provide employee health benefits. An employee uses a Web interface to sign on to Workplace.com and goes through an authentication procedure there. This enables the employee to access authorized services and resources at Workplace.com. When the employee clicks on a link to access health benefits, her browser is redirected to Health.com. At the same time, the Workplace.com software passes the user's identifier to Health.com in a secure manner. The two organizations are part of a federation that cooperatively exchanges user identifiers. Health.com maintains user identities

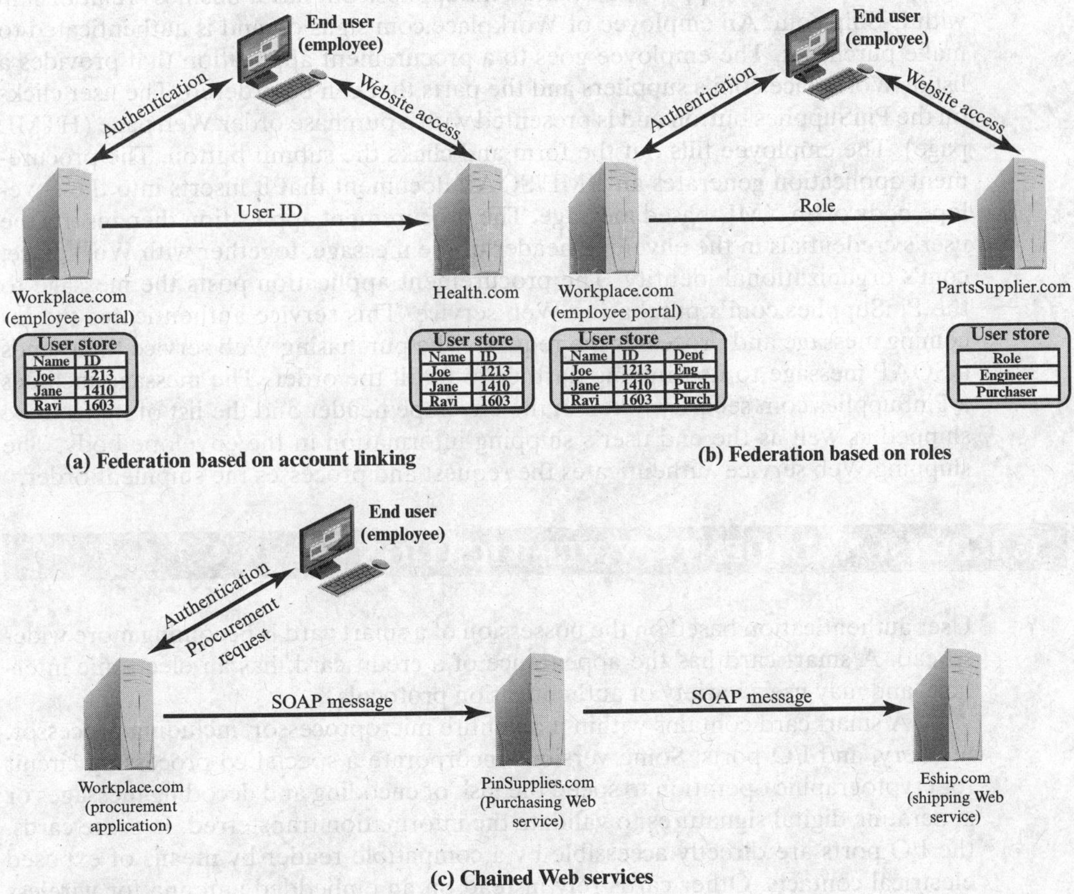

Figure 15.7 Federated Identity Scenarios

for every employee at Workplace.com and associates with each identity health-benefits information and access rights. In this example, the linkage between the two companies is based on account information and user participation is browser based.

Figure 15.7b shows a second type of browser-based scheme. PartsSupplier.com is a regular supplier of parts to Workplace.com. In this case, a role-based access-control (RBAC) scheme is used for access to information. An engineer of Workplace.com authenticates at the employee portal at Workplace.com and clicks on a link to access information at PartsSupplier.com. Because the user is authenticated in the role of an engineer, he is taken to the technical documentation and troubleshooting portion of PartsSupplier.com's Web site without having to sign on. Similarly, an employee in a purchasing role signs on at Workplace.com and is authorized, in that role, to place purchases at PartsSupplier.com without having to authenticate to PartsSupplier.com. For this scenario, PartsSupplier.com does not have identity information for individual employees at Workplace.com. Rather, the linkage between the two federated partners is in terms of roles.

The scenario illustrated in Figure 15.7c can be referred to as document based rather than browser based. In this third example, Workplace.com has a purchasing agreement with PinSupplies.com, and PinSupplies.com has a business relationship with E-Ship.com. An employee of Workplace.com signs on and is authenticated to make purchases. The employee goes to a procurement application that provides a list of Workplace.com's suppliers and the parts that can be ordered. The user clicks on the PinSupplies button and is presented with a purchase order Web page (HTML page). The employee fills out the form and clicks the submit button. The procurement application generates an XML/SOAP document that it inserts into the envelope body of an XML-based message. The procurement application then inserts the user's credentials in the envelope header of the message, together with Workplace.com's organizational identity. The procurement application posts the message to the PinSupplies.com's purchasing Web service. This service authenticates the incoming message and processes the request. The purchasing Web service then sends a SOAP message to its shipping partner to fulfill the order. The message includes a PinSupplies.com security token in the envelope header and the list of items to be shipped as well as the end user's shipping information in the envelope body. The shipping Web service authenticates the request and processes the shipment order.

15.6 PERSONAL IDENTITY VERIFICATION

User authentication based on the possession of a smart card is becoming more widespread. A smart card has the appearance of a credit card, has an electronic interface, and may use a variety of authentication protocols.

A smart card contains within it an entire microprocessor, including processor, memory, and I/O ports. Some versions incorporate a special co-processing circuit for cryptographic operation to speed the task of encoding and decoding messages or generating digital signatures to validate the information transferred. In some cards, the I/O ports are directly accessible by a compatible reader by means of exposed electrical contacts. Other cards rely instead on an embedded antenna for wireless communication with the reader.

A typical smart card includes three types of memory. Read-only memory (ROM) stores data that does not change during the card's life, such as the card number and the cardholder's name. Electrically erasable programmable ROM (EEPROM) holds application data and programs, such as the protocols that the card can execute. It also holds data that may vary with time. For example, in a telephone card, the EEPROM holds the talk time remaining. Random access memory (RAM) holds temporary data generated when applications are executed.

For the practical application of smart card authentication, a wide range of vendors must conform to standards that cover smart card protocols, authentication and access control formats and protocols, database entries, message formats, and so on. An important step in this direction is FIPS 201-2 (*Personal Identity Verification [PIV] of Federal Employees and Contractors*, June 2012). The standard defines a reliable, government-wide PIV system for use in applications such as access to federally controlled facilities and information systems. The standard specifies a PIV system within which common identification credentials can be created and later used to verify a claimed identity. The standard also identifies Federal government-wide requirements for security levels that are dependent on risks to the facility or information being protected. The standard applies to private-sector contractors as well, and serves as a useful guideline for any organization.

PIV System Model

Figure 15.8 illustrates the major components of FIPS 201-2 compliant systems. The PIV front end defines the physical interface to a user who is requesting access to a facility, which could be either physical access to a protected physical area or logical access to an information system. The **PIV front-end subsystem** supports up to three-factor authentication; the number of factors used depends on the level of security required. The front end makes use of a smart card, known as a PIV card, which is a dual-interface contact and contactless card. The card holds a cardholder photograph, X.509 certificates, cryptographic keys, biometric data, and a cardholder unique identifier (CHUID). Certain cardholder information may be read-protected and require a personal identification number (PIN) for read access by the card reader. The biometric reader, in the current version of the standard, is a fingerprint reader or an iris scanner.

The standard defines three assurance levels for verification of the card and the encoded data stored on the card, which in turn leads to verifying the authenticity of the person holding the credential. A level of *some confidence* corresponds to use of the card reader and PIN. A level of *high confidence* adds a biometric comparison of a fingerprint captured and encoded on the card during the card-issuing process and a fingerprint scanned at the physical access point. A *very high confidence* level requires that the process just described is completed at a control point attended by an official observer.

The other major component of the PIV system is the **PIV card issuance and management subsystem**. This subsystem includes the components responsible for identity proofing and registration, card and key issuance and management, and the various repositories and services (e.g., public key infrastructure [PKI] directory, certificate status servers) required as part of the verification infrastructure.

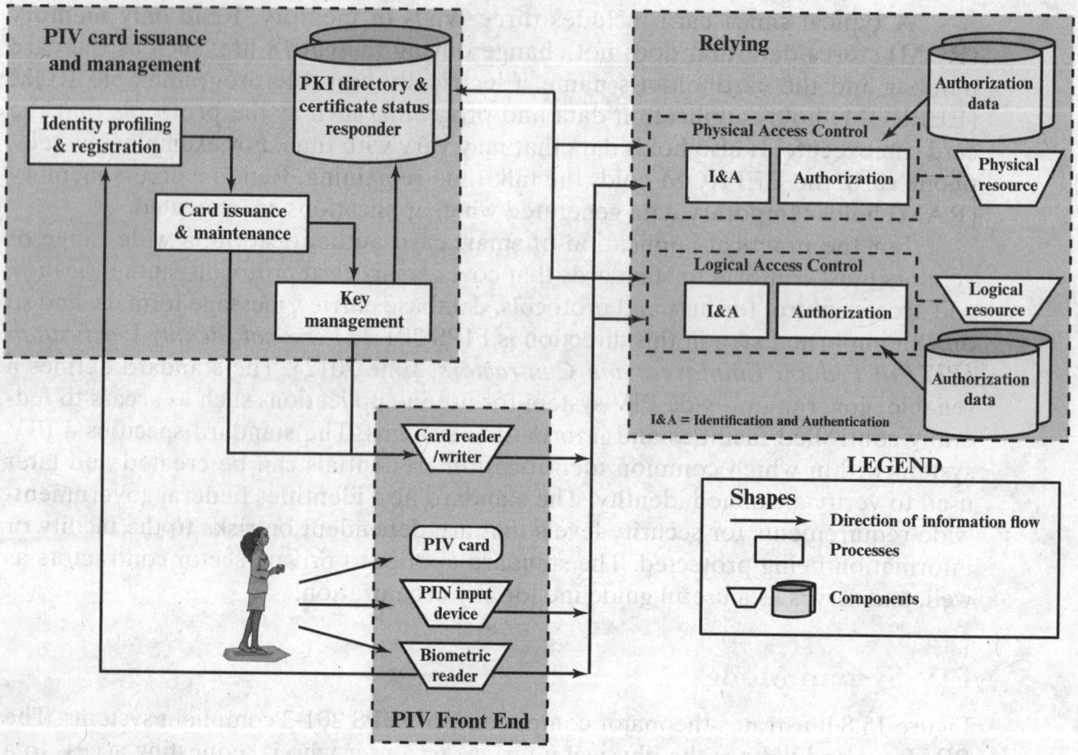

Figure 15.8 FIPS 201 PIV System Model

The PIV system interacts with a **relying subsystem**, which includes components responsible for determining a particular PIV cardholder's access to a physical or logical resource. FIPS 201-2 standardizes data formats and protocols for interaction between the PIV system and the relying system.

Unlike the typical card number/facility code encoded on most access control cards, the FIPS 201 CHUID takes authentication to a new level, through the use of an expiration date (a required CHUID data field) and an optional CHUID digital signature. A digital signature can be checked to ensure that the CHUID recorded on the card was digitally signed by a trusted source and that the CHUID data have not been altered since the card was signed. The CHUID expiration date can be checked to verify that the card has not expired. This is independent from whatever expiration date is associated with cardholder privileges. Reading and verifying the CHUID alone provides only some assurance of identity because it authenticates the card data, not the cardholder. The PIN and biometric factors provide identity verification of the individual.

PIV Documentation

The PIV specification is quite complex, and NIST has issued a number of documents that cover a broad range of PIV topics. These are as follows:

- **FIPS 201-2—Personal Identity Verification (PIV) of Federal Employees and Contractors:** Specifies the physical card characteristics, storage media, and data elements that make up the identity credentials resident on the PIV card.
- **SP 800-73-3—Interfaces for Personal Identity Verification:** Specifies the interfaces and card architecture for storing and retrieving identity credentials from a smart card, and provides guidelines for the use of authentication mechanisms and protocols.
- **SP 800-76-2—Biometric Data Specification for Personal Identity Verification:** Describes technical acquisition and formatting specifications for the biometric credentials of the PIV system.
- **SP 800-78-3—Cryptographic Algorithms and Key Sizes for Personal Identity Verification:** Identifies acceptable symmetric and asymmetric encryption algorithms, digital signature algorithms, and message digest algorithms, and specifies mechanisms to identify the algorithms associated with PIV keys or digital signatures.
- **SP 800-104—A Scheme for PIV Visual Card Topography:** Provides additional recommendations on the PIV card color-coding for designating employee affiliation.
- **SP 800-116—A Recommendation for the Use of PIV Credentials in Physical Access Control Systems (PACS):** Describes a risk-based approach for selecting appropriate PIV authentication mechanisms to manage physical access to Federal government facilities and assets.
- **SP 800-79-1—Guidelines for the Accreditation of Personal Identity Verification Card Issuers:** Provides guidelines for accrediting the reliability of issuers of PIV cards that collect, store, and disseminate personal identity credentials and issue smart cards.
- **SP 800-96—PIV Card to Reader Interoperability Guidelines:** Provides requirements that facilitate interoperability between any card and any reader.

In addition there are other documents that deal with conformance testing and codes for identifiers.

PIV Credentials and Keys

The PIV card contains a number of mandatory and optional data elements that serve as identity credentials with varying levels of strength and assurance. These credentials are used singly or in sets to authenticate the holder of the PIV card to achieve the level of assurance required for a particular activity or transaction. The mandatory data elements are the following:

- **Personal Identification Number (PIN):** Required to activate the card for privileged operation.
- **Cardholder Unique Identifier (CHUID):** Includes the Federal Agency Smart Credential Number (FASC-N) and the Global Unique Identification Number (GUID), which uniquely identify the card and the cardholder.

- **PIV Authentication Key:** Asymmetric key pair and corresponding certificate for user authentication.
- **Two fingerprint templates:** For biometric authentication.
- **Electronic facial image:** For biometric authentication.
- **Asymmetric Card Authentication Key:** Asymmetric key pair and corresponding certificate used for card authentication.

Optional elements include the following:

- **Digital Signature Key:** Asymmetric key pair and corresponding certificate that supports document signing and signing of data elements such as the CHUID.
- **Key Management Key:** Asymmetric key pair and corresponding certificate supporting key establishment and transport.
- **Symmetric Card Authentication Key:** For supporting physical access applications.
- **PIV Card Application Administration Key:** Symmetric key associated with the card management system.
- **One or two iris images:** For biometric authentication.

Table 15.5 lists the algorithm and key size requirements for PIV key types.

Authentication

Using the electronic credentials resident on a PIV card, the card supports the following authentication mechanisms:

- **CHUID:** The cardholder is authenticated using the signed CHUID data element on the card. The PIN is not required. This mechanism is useful in environments where a low level of assurance is acceptable and rapid contactless authentication is necessary.

Table 15.5 PIV Algorithms and Key Sizes

PIV Key Type	Algorithms	Key Sizes (bits)	Application
PIV Authentication Key	RSA	2048	Supports card and cardholder authentication for an interoperable environment
	ECDSA	256	
Card Authentication Key	3TDEA	168	Supports card authentication for physical access
	AES	128, 192, or 256	
	RSA	2048	Supports card authentication for an interoperable environment
	ECDSA	256	
Digital Signature Key	RSA	2048 or 3072	Supports document signing and nonce signing
	ECDSA	256 or 384	
Key Management Key	RSA	2048	Supports key establishment and transport
	ECDH	256 or 384	

- **Card Authentication Key:** The PIV card is authenticated using the Card Authentication Key in a challenge response protocol. The PIN is not required. This mechanism allows contact (via card reader) or contactless (via radio waves) authentication of the PIV card without the holder's active participation, and provides a low level of assurance.
- **BIO:** The cardholder is authenticated by matching his or her fingerprint sample(s) to the signed biometric data element in an environment without a human attendant in view. The PIN is required to activate the card. This mechanism achieves a high level of assurance and requires the cardholder's active participation is submitting the PIN as well as the biometric sample.
- **BIO-A:** The cardholder is authenticated by matching his or her fingerprint sample(s) to the signed biometric data element in an environment with a human attendant in view. The PIN is required to activate the card. This mechanism achieves a very high level of assurance when coupled with full trust validation of the biometric template retrieved from the card, and requires the cardholder's active participation is submitting the PIN as well as the biometric sample.
- **PKI:** The cardholder is authenticated by demonstrating control of the PIV authentication private key in a challenge response protocol that can be validated using the PIV authentication certificate. The PIN is required to activate the card. This mechanism achieves a very high level of identity assurance and requires the cardholder's knowledge of the PIN.

In each of the above use cases, except the symmetric Card Authentication Key use case, the source and the integrity of the corresponding PIV credential are validated by verifying the digital signature on the credential, with the signature being provided by a trusted entity.

A variety of protocols can be constructed for each of these authentication types. SP 800-78-3 gives examples for each type. Figure 15.9 illustrates an authentication scenario that includes the use of the PIV Authentication Key. This scenario provides a high level of assurance. This scenario would be appropriate for authentication of a user who possesses a PIV card and seeks access to a computer resource. The computer, designated *local system* in the figure, includes PIV application software and communicates to the card via an application program interface that enables the use of relatively high-level procedure calls. These high-level commands are converted into PIV commands that are issued to the card through a physical interface via a card reader or via a wireless interface. In either case, SP 800-73 refers to the card command interface as the PIV card edge.

The process begins when the local system detects the card either through an attached card reader or wirelessly. It then selects an application on the card for authentication. The local system then requests the public-key certificate for the card's PIV Authentication Key. If the certificate is valid (i.e., has a valid signature, has not expired or been revoked), authentication continues. Otherwise the card is rejected. The next step is for the local system to request that the cardholder enter the PIN for the card. If the submitted PIN matches the PIN stored on the card, the card returns a positive acknowledgment; otherwise the card returns a failure message.

The local system either continues or rejects the card accordingly. The next phase is a challenge-response protocol. The local system sends a nonce to be signed by the PIV, and the PIV returns the signature. The local system uses the PIV authentication public key to verify the signature. If the signature is valid, the cardholder is accepted as being identified. Otherwise the local system rejects the card.

The scenario of Figure 15.9 accomplishes three types of authentication. The combination of possession of the card and knowledge of the PIN service authenticates the cardholder. The PIV Authentication Key certificate validates the card's credentials. The challenge-response protocol authenticates the card.

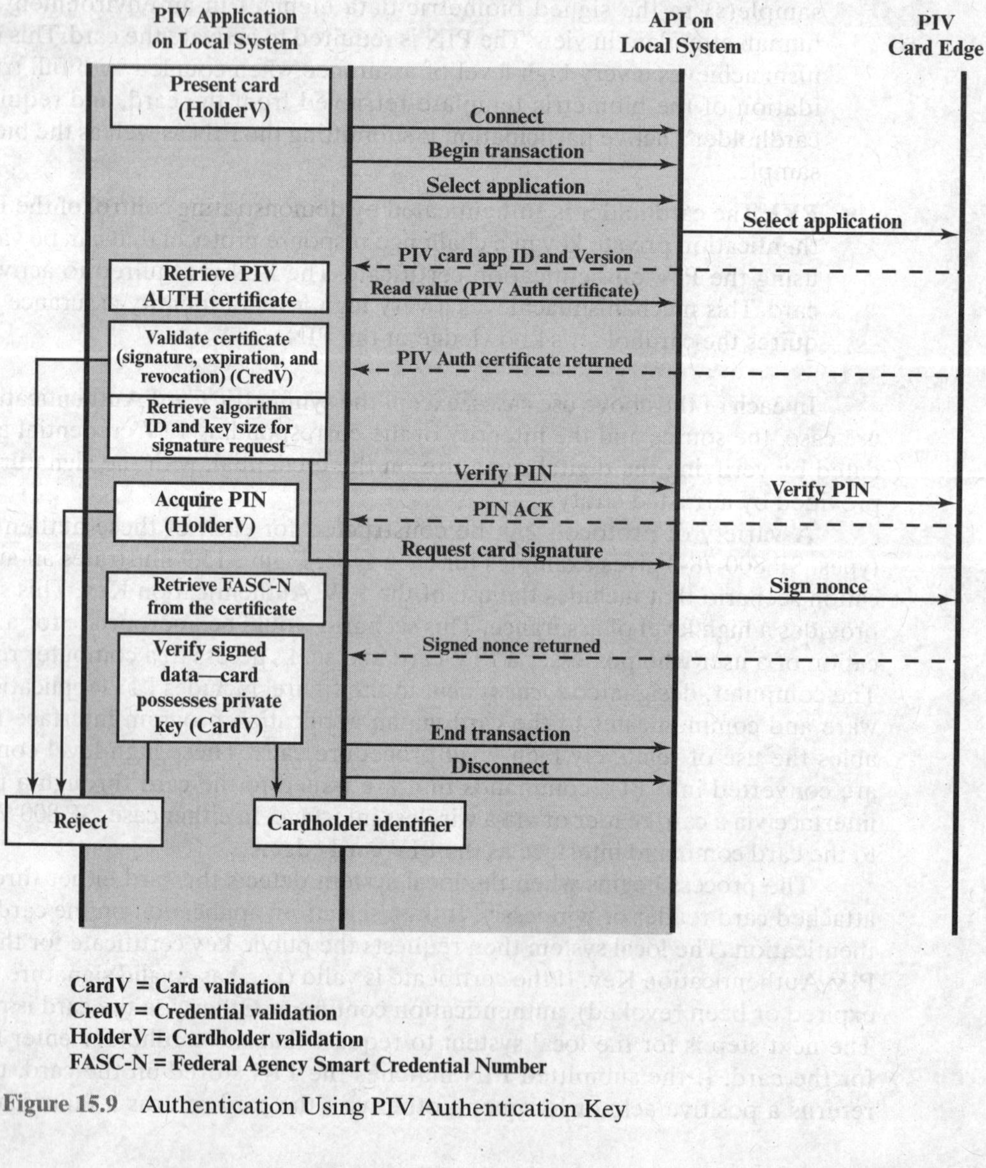

Figure 15.9 Authentication Using PIV Authentication Key

15.7 KEY TERMS, REVIEW QUESTIONS, AND PROBLEMS

Key Terms

authentication	Kerberos	relying party (RP)
authentication server	Kerberos realm	replay attack
claimant	mutual authentication	subscriber
credential	nonce	suppress-replay attack
credential service provider (CSP)	one-way authentication	ticket
federated identity management	personal identity verification (PIV)	ticket-granting server (TGS)
identity management	realm	timestamp
	registration authority (RA)	verifier

Review Questions

15.1 What are the four general means of authentication?
15.2 List few examples of replay attacks.
15.3 What is a suppress-replay attack?
15.4 What problem was Kerberos designed to address?
15.5 What are three threats associated with user authentication over a network or Internet?
15.6 List three approaches to secure user authentication in a distributed environment.
15.7 What four requirements were defined for Kerberos?
15.8 What entities constitute a full-service Kerberos environment?
15.9 In the context of Kerberos, what is a principal?
15.10 What are the optional elements to authenticate a PIV card holder?

Problems

15.1 In Section 15.4, we outlined the public-key scheme proposed in [WOO92a] for the distribution of secret keys. The revised version includes ID_A in steps 5 and 6. What attack, specifically, is countered by this revision?

15.2 The protocol referred to in Problem 15.1 can be reduced from seven steps to five, having the following sequence:

a. $A \rightarrow B$:
b. $A \rightarrow KDC$:
c. $KDC \rightarrow B$:
d. $B \rightarrow A$:
e. $A \rightarrow B$:

Show the message transmitted at each step. *Hint:* The final message in this protocol is the same as the final message in the original protocol.

15.3 Reference the suppress-replay attack described in Section 15.2 to answer the following.

a. Give an example of an attack when a party's clock is ahead of that of the KDC.
b. Give an example of an attack when a party's clock is ahead of that of another party.

15.4 There are three typical ways to use nonces as challenges. Suppose N_a is a nonce generated by A, A and B share key K, and f() is a function (such as an increment). The three usages are

Usage 1	Usage 2	Usage 3
(1) $A \rightarrow B$: N_a	(1) $A \rightarrow B$: $E(K, N_a)$	(1) $A \rightarrow B$: $E(K, N_a)$
(2) $B \rightarrow A$: $E(K, N_a)$	(2) $B \rightarrow A$: N_a	(2) $B \rightarrow A$: $E(K, f(N_a))$

Describe situations for which each usage is appropriate.

15.5 Show that a random error in one block of ciphertext is propagated to all subsequent blocks of plaintext in PCBC mode (See Figure T.2 in Appendix T).

15.6 Suppose that, in PCBC mode, blocks C_i and C_{i+1} are interchanged during transmission. Show that this affects only the decrypted blocks P_i and P_{i+1} but not subsequent blocks.

15.7 In addition to providing a standard for public-key certificate formats, X.509 specifies an authentication protocol. The original version of X.509 contains a security flaw. The essence of the protocol is as follows.

$$A \rightarrow B: \quad A\{t_A, r_A, ID_B\}$$
$$B \rightarrow A: \quad B\{t_B, r_B, ID_A, r_A\}$$
$$A \rightarrow B: \quad A\{r_B\}$$

where t_A and t_B are timestamps, r_A and r_B are nonces and the notation X{Y} indicates that the message Y is transmitted, encrypted, and signed by X.

The text of X.509 states that checking timestamps t_A and t_B is optional for three-way authentication. But consider the following example: Suppose A and B have used the preceding protocol on some previous occasion, and that opponent C has intercepted the preceding three messages. In addition, suppose that timestamps are not used and are all set to 0. Finally, suppose C wishes to impersonate A to B. C initially sends the first captured message to B:

$$C \rightarrow B: \quad A\{0, r_A, ID_B\}$$

B responds, thinking it is talking to A but is actually talking to C:

$$B \rightarrow C: \quad B\{0, r'_B, ID_A, r_A\}$$

C meanwhile causes A to initiate authentication with C by some means. As a result, A sends C the following:

$$A \rightarrow C: \quad A\{0, r'_A, ID_C\}$$

C responds to A using the same nonce provided to C by B:

$$C \rightarrow A: \quad C\{0, r'_B, ID_A, r'_A\}$$

A responds with

$$A \rightarrow C: \quad A\{r'_B\}$$

This is exactly what C needs to convince B that it is talking to A, so C now repeats the incoming message back out to B.

$$C \rightarrow B: \quad A\ \{r'_B\}$$

So B will believe it is talking to A whereas it is actually talking to C. Suggest a simple solution to this problem that does not involve the use of timestamps.

15.8 Consider a one-way authentication technique based on asymmetric encryption:

$$A \rightarrow B: \quad ID_A$$
$$B \rightarrow A: \quad R_1$$
$$A \rightarrow B: \quad E(PR_a, R_1)$$

a. Explain the protocol.
b. What type of attack is this protocol susceptible to?

15.9 Consider a one-way authentication technique based on asymmetric encryption:

$$A \rightarrow B: \quad ID_A$$
$$B \rightarrow A: \quad E(PU_a, R_2)$$
$$A \rightarrow B: \quad R_2$$

a. Explain the protocol.
b. What type of attack is this protocol susceptible to?

15.10 In Kerberos, when Bob receives a Ticket from Alice, how does he know it is genuine?

15.11 In Kerberos, when Bob receives a Ticket from Alice, how does he know it came from Alice?

15.12 In Kerberos, how does Alice know that a reply to an earlier message is from Bob?

15.13 In Kerberos, what does the Ticket contain that allows Alice and Bob to talk securely?

Part Six: Network and Internet Security

CHAPTER 16

Network Access Control and Cloud Security

LEARNING OBJECTIVES

After studying this chapter, you should be able to:

- Discuss the principal elements of a network access control system.
- Discuss the principal network access enforcement methods.
- Present an overview of the Extensible Authentication Protocol.
- Understand the operation and role of the IEEE 802.1X Port-Based Network Access Control mechanism.
- Present an overview of cloud computing concepts.
- Understand the unique security issues related to cloud computing.

This chapter begins our discussion of network security, focusing on two key topics: network access control and cloud security. We begin with an overview of network access control systems, summarizing the principal elements and techniques involved in such a system. Next, we discuss the Extensible Authentication Protocol and IEEE 802.1X, two widely implemented standards that are the foundation of many network access control systems.

The remainder of the chapter deals with cloud security. We begin with an overview of cloud computing, and follow this with a discussion of cloud security issues.

16.1 NETWORK ACCESS CONTROL

Network access control (NAC) is an umbrella term for managing access to a network. NAC authenticates users logging into the network and determines what data they can access and actions they can perform. NAC also examines the health of the user's computer or mobile device (the endpoints).

Elements of a Network Access Control System

NAC systems deal with three categories of components:

- **Access requestor (AR):** The AR is the node that is attempting to access the network and may be any device that is managed by the NAC system, including workstations, servers, printers, cameras, and other IP-enabled devices. ARs are also referred to as **supplicants**, or simply, clients.
- **Policy server:** Based on the AR's posture and an enterprise's defined policy, the policy server determines what access should be granted. The policy server often relies on backend systems, including antivirus, patch management, or a user directory, to help determine the host's condition.

- **Network access server (NAS):** The NAS functions as an access control point for users in remote locations connecting to an enterprise's internal network. Also called a **media gateway**, a **remote access server (RAS)**, or a **policy server**, an NAS may include its own authentication services or rely on a separate authentication service from the policy server.

Figure 16.1 is a generic network access diagram. A variety of different ARs seek access to an enterprise network by applying to some type of NAS. The first step is generally to authenticate the AR. Authentication typically involves some sort of secure protocol and the use of cryptographic keys. Authentication may be performed by the NAS, or the NAS may mediate the authentication process. In the latter case, authentication takes place between the supplicant and an authentication server that is part of the policy server or that is accessed by the policy server.

The authentication process serves a number of purposes. It verifies a supplicant's claimed identity, which enables the policy server to determine what access privileges, if any, the AR may have. The authentication exchange may result in the

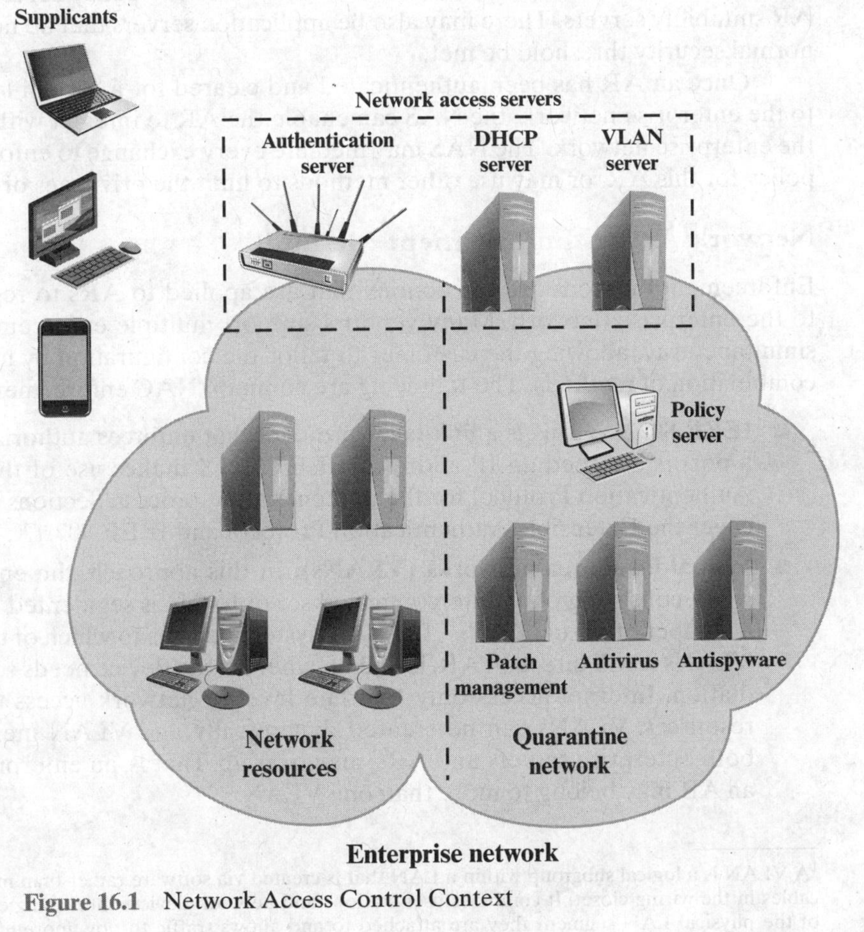

Figure 16.1 Network Access Control Context

establishment of session keys to enable future secure communication between the supplicant and resources on the enterprise network.

Typically, the policy server or a supporting server will perform checks on the AR to determine if it should be permitted interactive remote access connectivity. These checks—sometimes called health, suitability, screening, or assessment checks—require software on the user's system to verify compliance with certain requirements from the organization's secure configuration baseline. For example, the user's antimalware software must be up-to-date, the operating system must be fully patched, and the remote computer must be owned and controlled by the organization. These checks should be performed before granting the AR access to the enterprise network. Based on the results of these checks, the organization can determine whether the remote computer should be permitted to use interactive remote access. If the user has acceptable authorization credentials but the remote computer does not pass the health check, the user and remote computer should be denied network access or have limited access to a quarantine network so that authorized personnel can fix the security deficiencies. Figure 16.1 indicates that the quarantine portion of the enterprise network consists of the policy server and related AR suitability servers. There may also be application servers that do not require the normal security threshold be met.

Once an AR has been authenticated and cleared for a certain level of access to the enterprise network, the NAS can enable the AR to interact with resources in the enterprise network. The NAS may mediate every exchange to enforce a security policy for this AR, or may use other methods to limit the privileges of the AR.

Network Access Enforcement Methods

Enforcement methods are the actions that are applied to ARs to regulate access to the enterprise network. Many vendors support multiple enforcement methods simultaneously, allowing the customer to tailor the configuration by using one or a combination of methods. The following are common NAC enforcement methods.

- **IEEE 802.1X:** This is a link layer protocol that enforces authorization before a port is assigned an IP address. IEEE 802.1X makes use of the Extensible Authentication Protocol for the authentication process. Sections 16.2 and 16.3 cover the Extensible Authentication Protocol and IEEE 802.1X, respectively.
- **Virtual local area networks (VLANs):** In this approach, the enterprise network, consisting of an interconnected set of LANs, is segmented logically into a number of virtual LANs.[1] The NAC system decides to which of the network's VLANs it will direct an AR, based on whether the device needs security remediation, Internet access only, or some level of network access to enterprise resources. VLANs can be created dynamically and VLAN membership, of both enterprise servers and ARs, may overlap. That is, an enterprise server or an AR may belong to more than one VLAN.

---

[1]A VLAN is a logical subgroup within a LAN that is created via software rather than manually moving cables in the wiring closet. It combines user stations and network devices into a single unit regardless of the physical LAN segment they are attached to and allows traffic to flow more efficiently within populations of mutual interest. VLANs are implemented in port-switching hubs and LAN switches.

- **Firewall:** A firewall provides a form of NAC by allowing or denying network traffic between an enterprise host and an external user. Firewalls are discussed in Chapter 23.
- **DHCP management:** The Dynamic Host Configuration Protocol (DHCP) is an Internet protocol that enables dynamic allocation of IP addresses to hosts. A DHCP server intercepts DHCP requests and assigns IP addresses instead. Thus, NAC enforcement occurs at the IP layer based on subnet and IP assignment. A DCHP server is easy to install and configure, but is subject to various forms of IP spoofing, providing limited security.

There are a number of other enforcement methods available from vendors. The ones in the preceding list are perhaps the most common, and IEEE 802.1X is by far the most commonly implemented solution.

16.2 EXTENSIBLE AUTHENTICATION PROTOCOL

The Extensible Authentication Protocol (EAP), defined in RFC 3748, acts as a framework for network access and authentication protocols. EAP provides a set of protocol messages that can encapsulate various authentication methods to be used between a client and an authentication server. EAP can operate over a variety of network and link level facilities, including point-to-point links, LANs, and other networks, and can accommodate the authentication needs of the various links and networks. Figure 16.2 illustrates the protocol layers that form the context for EAP.

Authentication Methods

EAP supports multiple authentication methods. This is what is meant by referring to EAP as *extensible*. EAP provides a generic transport service for the exchange of authentication information between a client system and an authentication server. The basic EAP transport service is extended by using a specific authentication protocol, or method, that is installed in both the EAP client and the authentication server.

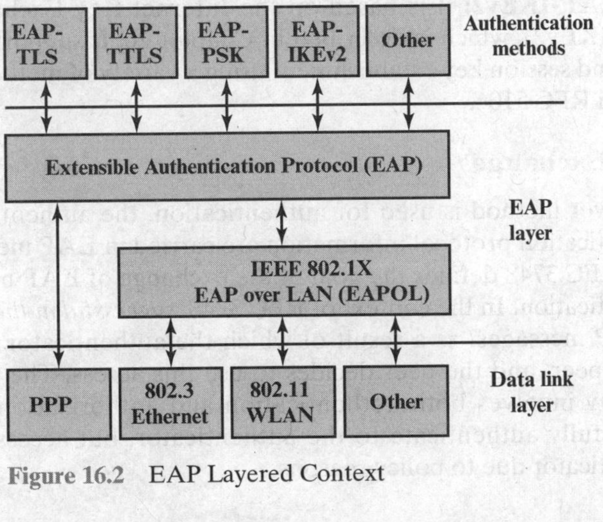

Figure 16.2 EAP Layered Context

Numerous methods have been defined to work over EAP. The following are commonly supported EAP methods:

- **EAP-TLS (EAP Transport Layer Security):** EAP-TLS (RFC 5216) defines how the TLS protocol (described in Chapter 17) can be encapsulated in EAP messages. EAP-TLS uses the handshake protocol in TLS, not its encryption method. Client and server authenticate each other using digital certificates. Client generates a pre-master secret key by encrypting a random number with the server's public key and sends it to the server. Both client and server use the pre-master to generate the same secret key.
- **EAP-TTLS (EAP Tunneled TLS):** EAP-TTLS is like EAP-TLS, except only the server has a certificate to authenticate itself to the client first. As in EAP-TLS, a secure connection (the "tunnel") is established with secret keys, but that connection is used to continue the authentication process by authenticating the client and possibly the server again using any EAP method or legacy method such as PAP (Password Authentication Protocol) and CHAP (Challenge-Handshake Authentication Protocol). EAP-TTLS is defined in RFC 5281.
- **EAP-GPSK (EAP Generalized Pre-Shared Key):** EAP-GPSK, defined in RFC 5433, is an EAP method for mutual authentication and session key derivation using a Pre-Shared Key (PSK). EAP-GPSK specifies an EAP method based on pre-shared keys and employs secret key-based cryptographic algorithms. Hence, this method is efficient in terms of message flows and computational costs, but requires the existence of pre-shared keys between each peer and EAP server. The set up of these pairwise secret keys is part of the peer registration, and thus, must satisfy the system preconditions. It provides a protected communication channel when mutual authentication is successful for both parties to communicate over and is designed for authentication over insecure networks such as IEEE 802.11. EAP-GPSK does not require any public-key cryptography. The EAP method protocol exchange is done in a minimum of four messages.
- **EAP-IKEv2:** It is based on the Internet Key Exchange protocol version 2 (IKEv2), which is described in Chapter 20. It supports mutual authentication and session key establishment using a variety of methods. EAP-TLS is defined in RFC 5106.

EAP Exchanges

Whatever method is used for authentication, the authentication information and authentication protocol information are carried in EAP messages.

RFC 3748 defines the goal of the exchange of EAP messages to be successful authentication. In the context of RFC 3748, *successful authentication* is an exchange of EAP messages, as a result of which the authenticator decides to allow access by the peer, and the peer decides to use this access. The authenticator's decision typically involves both authentication and authorization aspects; the peer may successfully authenticate to the authenticator, but access may be denied by the authenticator due to policy reasons.

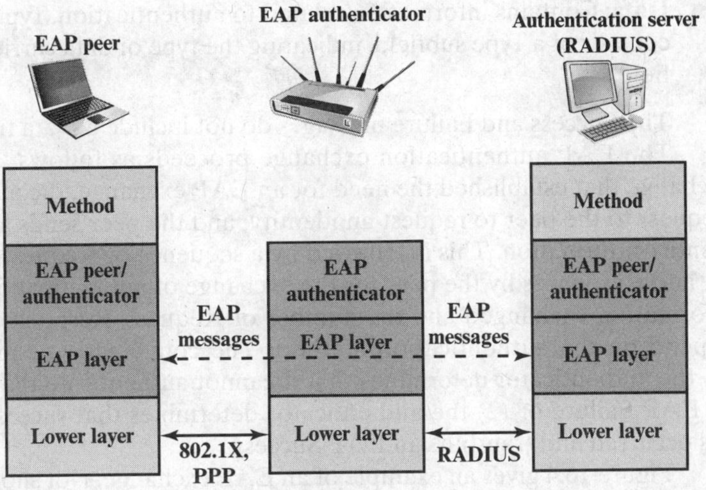

Figure 16.3 EAP Protocol Exchanges

Figure 16.3 indicates a typical arrangement in which EAP is used. The following components are involved:

- **EAP peer:** Client computer that is attempting to access a network.
- **EAP authenticator:** An access point or NAS that requires EAP authentication prior to granting access to a network.
- **Authentication server:** A server computer that negotiates the use of a specific EAP method with an EAP peer, validates the EAP peer's credentials, and authorizes access to the network. Typically, the authentication server is a Remote Authentication Dial-In User Service (RADIUS) server.

The authentication server functions as a backend server that can authenticate peers as a service to a number of EAP authenticators. The EAP authenticator then makes the decision of whether to grant access. This is referred to as the **EAP pass-through mode**. Less commonly, the authenticator takes over the role of the EAP server; that is, only two parties are involved in the EAP execution.

As a first step, a lower-level protocol, such as PPP (point-to-point protocol) or IEEE 802.1X, is used to connect to the EAP authenticator. The software entity in the EAP peer that operates at this level is referred to as the **supplicant**. EAP messages containing the appropriate information for a chosen EAP method are then exchanged between the EAP peer and the authentication server.

EAP messages may include the following fields:

- **Code:** Identifies the Type of EAP message. The codes are Request (1), Response (2), Success (3), and Failure (4).
- **Identifier:** Used to match Responses with Requests.
- **Length:** Indicates the length, in octets, of the EAP message, including the Code, Identifier, Length, and Data fields.

- **Data:** Contains information related to authentication. Typically, the Data field consists of a Type subfield, indicating the type of data carried, and a Type-Data field.

The Success and Failure messages do not include a Data field.

The EAP authentication exchange proceeds as follows. After a lower-level exchange that established the need for an EAP exchange, the authenticator sends a Request to the peer to request an identity, and the peer sends a Response with the identity information. This is followed by a sequence of Requests by the authenticator and Responses by the peer for the exchange of authentication information. The information exchanged and the number of Request–Response exchanges needed depend on the authentication method. The conversation continues until either (1) the authenticator determines that it cannot authenticate the peer and transmits an EAP Failure or (2) the authenticator determines that successful authentication has occurred and transmits an EAP Success.

Figure 16.4 gives an example of an EAP exchange. Not shown in the figure is a message or signal sent from the EAP peer to the authenticator using some protocol other than EAP and requesting an EAP exchange to grant network access. One protocol used for this purpose is IEEE 802.1X, discussed in the next section. The first pair of EAP Request and Response messages is of Type identity, in which the authenticator requests the peer's identity, and the peer returns its claimed identity in the Response message. This Response is passed through the authenticator to the authentication server. Subsequent EAP messages are exchanged between the peer and the authentication server.

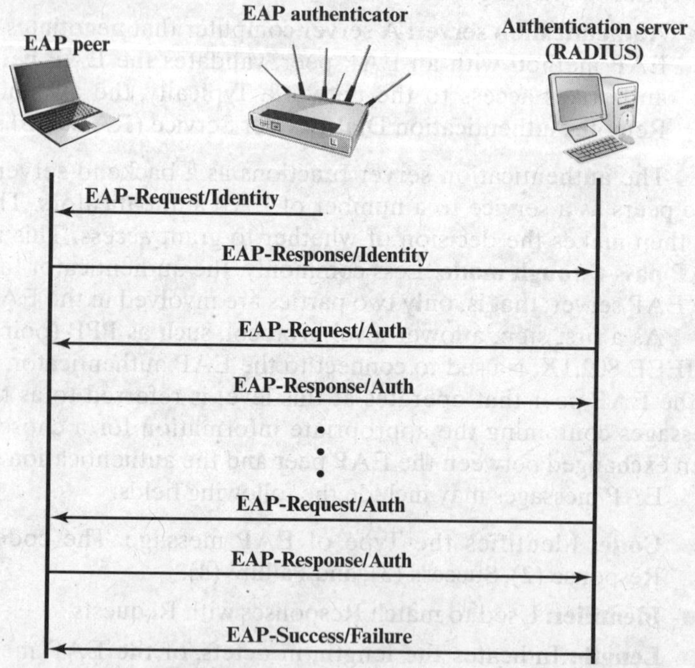

Figure 16.4 EAP Message Flow in Pass-Through Mode

Upon receiving the identity Response message from the peer, the server selects an EAP method and sends the first EAP message with a Type field related to an authentication method. If the peer supports and accepts the selected EAP method, it replies with the corresponding Response message of the same type. Otherwise, the peer sends a NAK, and the EAP server either selects another EAP method or aborts the EAP execution with a failure message. The selected EAP method determines the number of Request/Response pairs. During the exchange the appropriate authentication information, including key material, is exchanged. The exchange ends when the server determines that authentication has succeeded or that no further attempt can be made and authentication has failed.

16.3 IEEE 802.1X PORT-BASED NETWORK ACCESS CONTROL

IEEE 802.1X Port-Based Network Access Control was designed to provide access control functions for LANs. Table 16.1 briefly defines key terms used in the IEEE 802.11 standard. The terms *supplicant*, *network access point*, and *authentication*

Table 16.1 Terminology Related to IEEE 802.1X

Authenticator	An entity at one end of a point-to-point LAN segment that facilities authentication of the entity to the other end of the link.
Authentication exchange	The two-party conversation between systems performing an authentication process.
Authentication process	The cryptographic operations and supporting data frames that perform the actual authentication.
Authentication server (AS)	An entity that provides an authentication service to an authenticator. This service determines, from the credentials provided by supplicant, whether the supplicant is authorized to access the services provided by the system in which the authenticator resides.
Authentication transport	The datagram session that actively transfers the authentication exchange between two systems.
Bridge port	A port of an IEEE 802.1D or 802.1Q bridge.
Edge port	A bridge port attached to a LAN that has no other bridges attached to it.
Network access port	A point of attachment of a system to a LAN. It can be a physical port, such as a single LAN MAC attached to a physical LAN segment, or a logical port, for example, an IEEE 802.11 association between a station and an access point.
Port access entity (PAE)	The protocol entity associated with a port. It can support the protocol functionality associated with the authenticator, the supplicant, or both.
Supplicant	An entity at one end of a point-to-point LAN segment that seeks to be authenticated by an authenticator attached to the other end of that link.

server correspond to the EAP terms *peer*, *authenticator*, and *authentication server*, respectively.

Until the AS authenticates a supplicant (using an authentication protocol), the authenticator only passes control and authentication messages between the supplicant and the AS; the 802.1X control channel is unblocked, but the 802.11 data channel is blocked. Once a supplicant is authenticated and keys are provided, the authenticator can forward data from the supplicant, subject to predefined access control limitations for the supplicant to the network. Under these circumstances, the data channel is unblocked.

As indicated in Figure 16.5, 802.1X uses the concepts of controlled and uncontrolled ports. Ports are logical entities defined within the authenticator and refer to physical network connections. Each logical port is mapped to one of these two types of physical ports. An uncontrolled port allows the exchange of protocol data units (PDUs) between the supplicant and the AS, regardless of the authentication state of the supplicant. A controlled port allows the exchange of PDUs between a supplicant and other systems on the network only if the current state of the supplicant authorizes such an exchange.

The essential element defined in 802.1X is a protocol known as EAPOL (EAP over LAN). EAPOL operates at the network layers and makes use of an IEEE 802 LAN, such as Ethernet or Wi-Fi, at the link level. EAPOL enables a supplicant to communicate with an authenticator and supports the exchange of EAP packets for authentication.

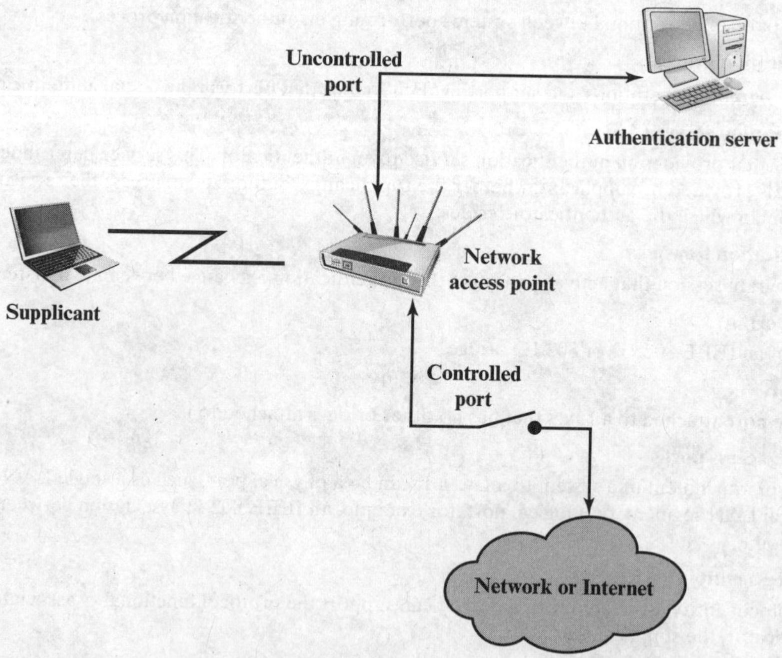

Figure 16.5 802.1X Access Control

Table 16.2 Common EAPOL Frame Types

Frame Type	Definition
EAPOL-EAP	Contains an encapsulated EAP packet.
EAPOL-Start	A supplicant can issue this packet instead of waiting for a challenge from the authenticator.
EAPOL-Logoff	Used to return the state of the port to unauthorized when the supplicant is finished using the network.
EAPOL-Key	Used to exchange cryptographic keying information.

The most common EAPOL packets are listed in Table 16.2. When the supplicant first connects to the LAN, it does not know the MAC address of the authenticator. Actually it doesn't know whether there is an authenticator present at all. By sending an **EAPOL-Start** packet to a special group-multicast address reserved for IEEE 802.1X authenticators, a supplicant can determine whether an authenticator is present and let it know that the supplicant is ready. In many cases, the authenticator will already be notified that a new device has connected from some hardware notification. For example, a hub knows that a cable is plugged in before the device sends any data. In this case the authenticator may preempt the Start message with its own message. In either case the authenticator sends an EAP-Request Identity message encapsulated in an **EAPOL-EAP** packet. The EAPOL-EAP is the EAPOL frame type used for transporting EAP packets.

The authenticator uses the **EAP-Key** packet to send cryptographic keys to the supplicant once it has decided to admit it to the network. The **EAP-Logoff** packet type indicates that the supplicant wishes to be disconnected from the network.

The EAPOL packet format includes the following fields:

- **Protocol version:** version of EAPOL.
- **Packet type:** indicates start, EAP, key, logoff, etc.
- **Packet body length:** If the packet includes a body, this field indicates the body length.
- **Packet body:** The payload for this EAPOL packet. An example is an EAP packet.

Figure 16.6 shows an example of exchange using EAPOL. In Chapter 18, we examine the use of EAP and EAPOL in the context of IEEE 802.11 wireless LAN security.

16.4 CLOUD COMPUTING

There is an increasingly prominent trend in many organizations to move a substantial portion of or even all information technology (IT) operations to an Internet-connected infrastructure known as enterprise cloud computing. This section provides an overview of cloud computing. For a more detailed treatment, see [STAL16].

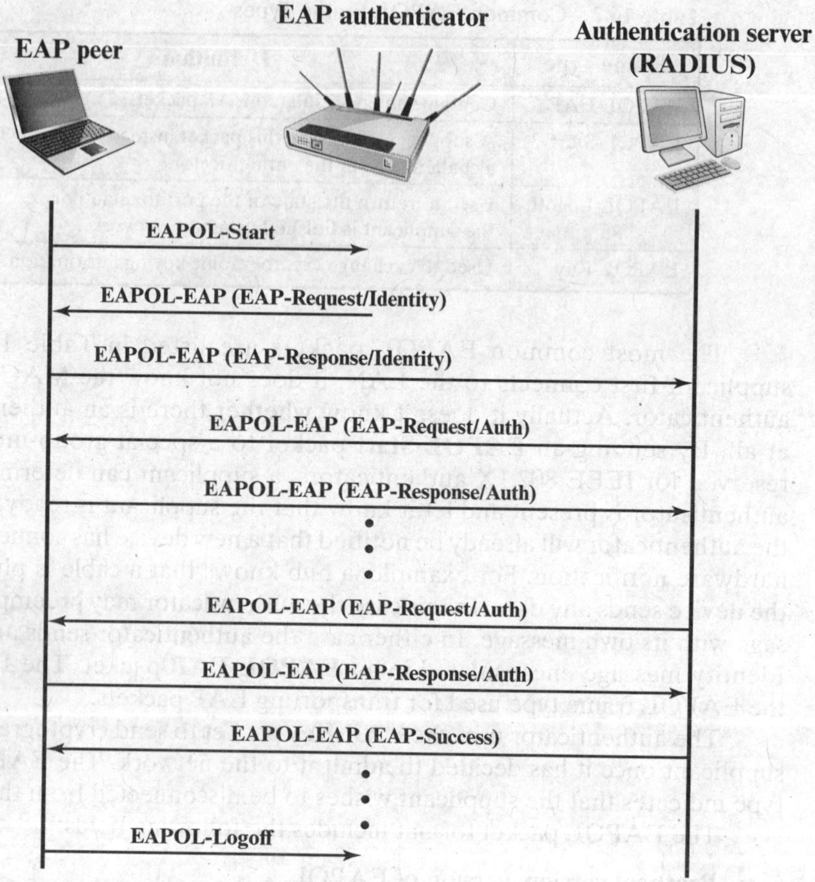

Figure 16.6 Example Timing Diagram for IEEE 802.1X

Cloud Computing Elements

NIST defines cloud computing, in NIST SP-800-145 (*The NIST Definition of Cloud Computing*), as follows:

> **Cloud computing**: A model for enabling ubiquitous, convenient, on-demand network access to a shared pool of configurable computing resources (e.g., networks, servers, storage, applications, and services) that can be rapidly provisioned and released with minimal management effort or service provider interaction. This cloud model promotes availability and is composed of five essential characteristics, three service models, and four deployment models.

The definition refers to various models and characteristics, whose relationship is illustrated in Figure 16.7. The essential characteristics of cloud computing include the following:

- **Broad network access:** Capabilities are available over the network and accessed through standard mechanisms that promote use by heterogeneous thin

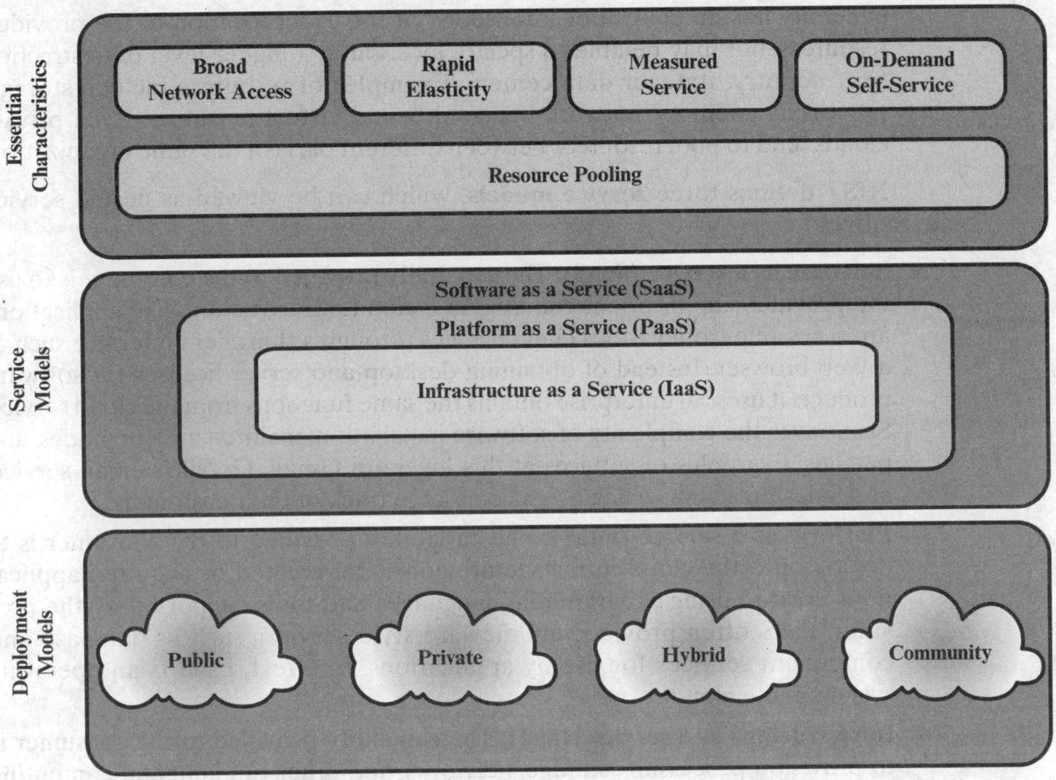

Figure 16.7 Cloud Computing Elements

or thick client platforms (e.g., mobile phones, laptops, and PDAs) as well as other traditional or cloud-based software services.

- **Rapid elasticity:** Cloud computing gives you the ability to expand and reduce resources according to your specific service requirement. For example, you may need a large number of server resources for the duration of a specific task. You can then release these resources upon completion of the task.
- **Measured service:** Cloud systems automatically control and optimize resource use by leveraging a metering capability at some level of abstraction appropriate to the type of service (e.g., storage, processing, bandwidth, and active user accounts). Resource usage can be monitored, controlled, and reported, providing transparency for both the provider and consumer of the utilized service.
- **On-demand self-service:** A consumer can unilaterally provision computing capabilities, such as server time and network storage, as needed automatically without requiring human interaction with each service provider. Because the service is on demand, the resources are not permanent parts of your IT infrastructure.
- **Resource pooling:** The provider's computing resources are pooled to serve multiple consumers using a multi-tenant model, with different physical and virtual resources dynamically assigned and reassigned according to consumer demand. There is a degree of location independence in that the customer

generally has no control or knowledge of the exact location of the provided resources, but may be able to specify location at a higher level of abstraction (e.g., country, state, or data center). Examples of resources include storage, processing, memory, network bandwidth, and virtual machines. Even private clouds tend to pool resources between different parts of the same organization.

NIST defines three **service models**, which can be viewed as nested service alternatives:

- **Software as a service (SaaS):** The capability provided to the consumer is to use the provider's applications running on a cloud infrastructure. The applications are accessible from various client devices through a thin client interface such as a Web browser. Instead of obtaining desktop and server licenses for software products it uses, an enterprise obtains the same functions from the cloud service. SaaS saves the complexity of software installation, maintenance, upgrades, and patches. Examples of services at this level are Gmail, Google's email service, and Salesforce.com, which helps firms keep track of their customers.
- **Platform as a service (PaaS):** The capability provided to the consumer is to deploy onto the cloud infrastructure consumer-created or acquired applications created using programming languages and tools supported by the provider. PaaS often provides middleware-style services such as database and component services for use by applications. In effect, PaaS is an operating system in the cloud.
- **Infrastructure as a service (IaaS):** The capability provided to the consumer is to provision processing, storage, networks, and other fundamental computing resources where the consumer is able to deploy and run arbitrary software, which can include operating systems and applications. IaaS enables customers to combine basic computing services, such as number crunching and data storage, to build highly adaptable computer systems.

NIST defines four **deployment models**:

- **Public cloud:** The cloud infrastructure is made available to the general public or a large industry group and is owned by an organization selling cloud services. The cloud provider is responsible both for the cloud infrastructure and for the control of data and operations within the cloud.
- **Private cloud:** The cloud infrastructure is operated solely for an organization. It may be managed by the organization or a third party and may exist on premise or off premise. The cloud provider (CP) is responsible only for the infrastructure and not for the control.
- **Community cloud:** The cloud infrastructure is shared by several organizations and supports a specific community that has shared concerns (e.g., mission, security requirements, policy, and compliance considerations). It may be managed by the organizations or a third party and may exist on premise or off premise.
- **Hybrid cloud:** The cloud infrastructure is a composition of two or more clouds (private, community, or public) that remain unique entities but are bound together by standardized or proprietary technology that enables data and application portability (e.g., cloud bursting for load balancing between clouds).

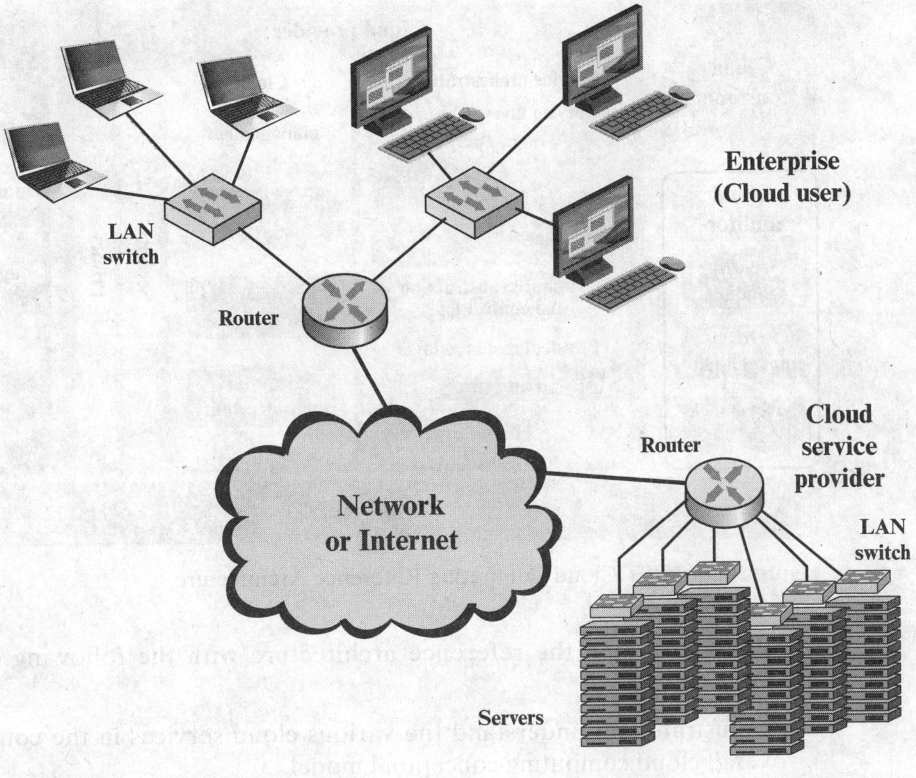

Figure 16.8 Cloud Computing Context

Figure 16.8 illustrates the typical cloud service context. An enterprise maintains workstations within an enterprise LAN or set of LANs, which are connected by a router through a network or the Internet to the cloud service provider. The cloud service provider maintains a massive collection of servers, which it manages with a variety of network management, redundancy, and security tools. In the figure, the cloud infrastructure is shown as a collection of blade servers, which is a common architecture.

Cloud Computing Reference Architecture

NIST SP 500-292 (*NIST Cloud Computing Reference Architecture*) establishes a reference architecture, described as follows:

> The NIST cloud computing reference architecture focuses on the requirements of "what" cloud services provide, not a "how to" design solution and implementation. The reference architecture is intended to facilitate the understanding of the operational intricacies in cloud computing. It does not represent the system architecture of a specific cloud computing system; instead it is a tool for describing, discussing, and developing a system-specific architecture using a common framework of reference.

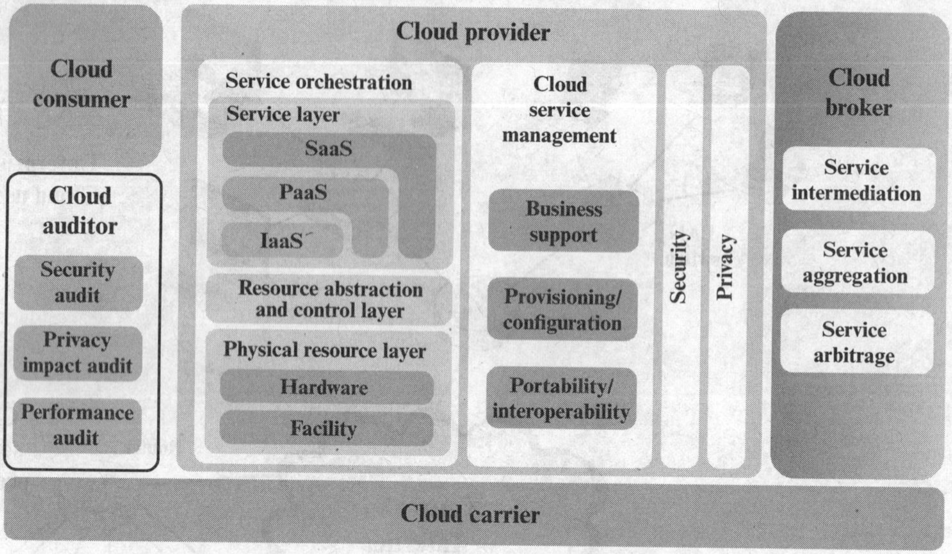

Figure 16.9 NIST Cloud Computing Reference Architecture

NIST developed the reference architecture with the following objectives in mind:

- to illustrate and understand the various cloud services in the context of an overall cloud computing conceptual model
- to provide a technical reference for consumers to understand, discuss, categorize, and compare cloud services
- to facilitate the analysis of candidate standards for security, interoperability, and portability and reference implementations

The reference architecture, depicted in Figure 16.9, defines five major actors in terms of the roles and responsibilities:

- **Cloud consumer:** A person or organization that maintains a business relationship with, and uses service from, cloud providers.
- **Cloud provider:** A person, organization, or entity responsible for making a service available to interested parties.
- **Cloud auditor:** A party that can conduct independent assessment of cloud services, information system operations, performance, and security of the cloud implementation.
- **Cloud broker:** An entity that manages the use, performance, and delivery of cloud services, and negotiates relationships between CPs and cloud consumers.
- **Cloud carrier:** An intermediary that provides connectivity and transport of cloud services from CPs to cloud consumers.

The roles of the cloud consumer and provider have already been discussed. To summarize, a **cloud provider** can provide one or more of the cloud services to meet IT and business requirements of **cloud consumers**. For each of the three service models (SaaS, PaaS, IaaS), the CP provides the storage and processing facilities needed to support that service model, together with a cloud interface for cloud service consumers. For SaaS, the CP deploys, configures, maintains, and updates the operation of the software applications on a cloud infrastructure so that the services are provisioned at the expected service levels to cloud consumers. The consumers of SaaS can be organizations that provide their members with access to software applications, end users who directly use software applications, or software application administrators who configure applications for end users.

For PaaS, the CP manages the computing infrastructure for the platform and runs the cloud software that provides the components of the platform, such as runtime software execution stack, databases, and other middleware components. Cloud consumers of PaaS can employ the tools and execution resources provided by CPs to develop, test, deploy, and manage the applications hosted in a cloud environment.

For IaaS, the CP acquires the physical computing resources underlying the service, including the servers, networks, storage, and hosting infrastructure. The IaaS cloud consumer in turn uses these computing resources, such as a virtual computer, for their fundamental computing needs.

The **cloud carrier** is a networking facility that provides connectivity and transport of cloud services between cloud consumers and CPs. Typically, a CP will set up service level agreements (SLAs) with a cloud carrier to provide services consistent with the level of SLAs offered to cloud consumers, and may require the cloud carrier to provide dedicated and secure connections between cloud consumers and CPs.

A **cloud broker** is useful when cloud services are too complex for a cloud consumer to easily manage. Three areas of support can be offered by a cloud broker:

- **Service intermediation:** These are value-added services, such as identity management, performance reporting, and enhanced security.
- **Service aggregation:** The broker combines multiple cloud services to meet consumer needs not specifically addressed by a single CP, or to optimize performance or minimize cost.
- **Service arbitrage:** This is similar to service aggregation except that the services being aggregated are not fixed. Service arbitrage means a broker has the flexibility to choose services from multiple agencies. The cloud broker, for example, can use a credit-scoring service to measure and select an agency with the best score.

A **cloud auditor** can evaluate the services provided by a CP in terms of security controls, privacy impact, performance, and so on. The auditor is an independent entity that can assure that the CP conforms to a set of standards.

16.5 CLOUD SECURITY RISKS AND COUNTERMEASURES

In general terms, security controls in cloud computing are similar to the security controls in any IT environment. However, because of the operational models and technologies used to enable cloud service, cloud computing may present risks that are specific to the cloud environment. The essential concept in this regard is that the enterprise loses a substantial amount of control over resources, services, and applications but must maintain accountability for security and privacy policies.

The Cloud Security Alliance [CSA10] lists the following as the top cloud-specific security threats, together with suggested countermeasures:

- **Abuse and nefarious use of cloud computing:** For many CPs, it is relatively easy to register and begin using cloud services, some even offering free limited trial periods. This enables attackers to get inside the cloud to conduct various attacks, such as spamming, malicious code attacks, and denial of service. PaaS providers have traditionally suffered most from this kind of attacks; however, recent evidence shows that hackers have begun to target IaaS vendors as well. The burden is on the CP to protect against such attacks, but cloud service clients must monitor activity with respect to their data and resources to detect any malicious behavior.

  Countermeasures include (1) stricter initial registration and validation processes; (2) enhanced credit card fraud monitoring and coordination; (3) comprehensive introspection of customer network traffic; and (4) monitoring public blacklists for one's own network blocks.
- **Insecure interfaces and APIs:** CPs expose a set of software interfaces or APIs that customers use to manage and interact with cloud services. The security and availability of general cloud services are dependent upon the security of these basic APIs. From authentication and access control to encryption and activity monitoring, these interfaces must be designed to protect against both accidental and malicious attempts to circumvent policy.

  Countermeasures include (1) analyzing the security model of CP interfaces; (2) ensuring that strong authentication and access controls are implemented in concert with encrypted transmission; and (3) understanding the dependency chain associated with the API.
- **Malicious insiders:** Under the cloud computing paradigm, an organization relinquishes direct control over many aspects of security and, in doing so, confers an unprecedented level of trust onto the CP. One grave concern is the risk of malicious insider activity. Cloud architectures necessitate certain roles that are extremely high risk. Examples include CP system administrators and managed security service providers.

  Countermeasures include the following: (1) enforce strict supply chain management and conduct a comprehensive supplier assessment; (2) specify human resource requirements as part of legal contract; (3) require transparency into overall information security and management practices, as well as compliance reporting; and (4) determine security breach notification processes.
- **Shared technology issues:** IaaS vendors deliver their services in a scalable way by sharing infrastructure. Often, the underlying components that make up this infrastructure (CPU caches, GPUs, etc.) were not designed to offer strong isolation properties for a multi-tenant architecture. CPs typically approach this risk by the use of isolated virtual machines for individual clients. This approach is still vulnerable to attack, by both insiders and outsiders, and so can only be a part of an overall security strategy.

  Countermeasures include the following: (1) implement security best practices for installation/configuration; (2) monitor environment for unauthorized changes/activity; (3) promote strong authentication and access control for administrative access and operations; (4) enforce SLAs for patching and vulnerability remediation; and (5) conduct vulnerability scanning and configuration audits.

- **Data loss or leakage:** For many clients, the most devastating impact from a security breach is the loss or leakage of data. We address this issue in the next subsection.

  Countermeasures include the following: (1) implement strong API access control; (2) encrypt and protect integrity of data in transit; (3) analyze data protection at both design and run time; and (4) implement strong key generation, storage and management, and destruction practices.

- **Account or service hijacking:** Account or service hijacking, usually with stolen credentials, remains a top threat. With stolen credentials, attackers can often access critical areas of deployed cloud computing services, allowing them to compromise the confidentiality, integrity, and availability of those services.

  Countermeasures include the following: (1) prohibit the sharing of account credentials between users and services; (2) leverage strong two-factor authentication techniques where possible; (3) employ proactive monitoring to detect unauthorized activity; and (4) understand CP security policies and SLAs.

- **Unknown risk profile:** In using cloud infrastructures, the client necessarily cedes control to the CP on a number of issues that may affect security. Thus the client must pay attention to and clearly define the roles and responsibilities involved for managing risks. For example, employees may deploy applications and data resources at the CP without observing the normal policies and procedures for privacy, security, and oversight.

  Countermeasures include (1) disclosure of applicable logs and data; (2) partial/full disclosure of infrastructure details (e.g., patch levels and firewalls); and (3) monitoring and alerting on necessary information.

Similar lists have been developed by the European Network and Information Security Agency [ENIS09] and NIST [JANS11].

16.6 DATA PROTECTION IN THE CLOUD

As can be seen from the previous section, there are numerous aspects to cloud security and numerous approaches to providing cloud security measures. A further example is seen in the NIST guidelines for cloud security, specified in SP-800-14 and listed in Table 16.3. Thus, the topic of cloud security is well beyond the scope of this chapter. In this section, we focus on one specific element of cloud security.

There are many ways to compromise data. Deletion or alteration of records without a backup of the original content is an obvious example. Unlinking a record from a larger context may render it unrecoverable, as can storage on unreliable media. Loss of an encoding key may result in effective destruction. Finally, unauthorized parties must be prevented from gaining access to sensitive data.

Table 16.3 NIST Guidelines on Security and Privacy Issues and Recommendations

Governance

Extend organizational practices pertaining to the policies, procedures, and standards used for application development and service provisioning in the cloud, as well as the design, implementation, testing, use, and monitoring of deployed or engaged services.

Put in place audit mechanisms and tools to ensure organizational practices are followed throughout the system life cycle.

Compliance

Understand the various types of laws and regulations that impose security and privacy obligations on the organization and potentially impact cloud computing initiatives, particularly those involving data location, privacy and security controls, records management, and electronic discovery requirements.

Review and assess the cloud provider's offerings with respect to the organizational requirements to be met and ensure that the contract terms adequately meet the requirements.

Ensure that the cloud provider's electronic discovery capabilities and processes do not compromise the privacy or security of data and applications.

Trust

Ensure that service arrangements have sufficient means to allow visibility into the security and privacy controls and processes employed by the cloud provider, and their performance over time.

Establish clear, exclusive ownership rights over data.

Institute a risk management program that is flexible enough to adapt to the constantly evolving and shifting risk landscape for the life cycle of the system.

Continuously monitor the security state of the information system to support ongoing risk management decisions.

Architecture

Understand the underlying technologies that the cloud provider uses to provision services, including the implications that the technical controls involved have on the security and privacy of the system, over the full system life cycle and across all system components.

Identity and access management

Ensure that adequate safeguards are in place to secure authentication, authorization, and other identity and access management functions, and are suitable for the organization.

Software isolation

Understand virtualization and other logical isolation techniques that the cloud provider employs in its multi-tenant software architecture, and assess the risks involved for the organization.

Data protection

Evaluate the suitability of the cloud provider's data management solutions for the organizational data concerned and the ability to control access to data, to secure data while at rest, in transit, and in use, and to sanitize data.

Take into consideration the risk of collating organizational data with those of other organizations whose threat profiles are high or whose data collectively represent significant concentrated value.

Fully understand and weigh the risks involved in cryptographic key management with the facilities available in the cloud environment and the processes established by the cloud provider.

Availability

Understand the contract provisions and procedures for availability, data backup and recovery, and disaster recovery, and ensure that they meet the organization's continuity and contingency planning requirements.

Ensure that during an intermediate or prolonged disruption or a serious disaster, critical operations can be immediately resumed, and that all operations can be eventually reinstituted in a timely and organized manner.

Incident response

Understand the contract provisions and procedures for incident response and ensure that they meet the requirements of the organization.

Table 16.3 Continued

Ensure that the cloud provider has a transparent response process in place and sufficient mechanisms to share information during and after an incident.
Ensure that the organization can respond to incidents in a coordinated fashion with the cloud provider in accordance with their respective roles and responsibilities for the computing environment.

The threat of data compromise increases in the cloud, due to the number of and interactions between risks and challenges that are either unique to the cloud or more dangerous because of the architectural or operational characteristics of the cloud environment.

Database environments used in cloud computing can vary significantly. Some providers support a **multi-instance model**, which provides a unique DBMS running on a virtual machine instance for each cloud subscriber. This gives the subscriber complete control over role definition, user authorization, and other administrative tasks related to security. Other providers support a **multi-tenant model**, which provides a predefined environment for the cloud subscriber that is shared with other tenants, typically through tagging data with a subscriber identifier. Tagging gives the appearance of exclusive use of the instance, but relies on the CP to establish and maintain a sound secure database environment.

Data must be secured while at rest, in transit, and in use, and access to the data must be controlled. The client can employ encryption to protect data in transit, though this involves key management responsibilities for the CP. The client can enforce access control techniques but, again, the CP is involved to some extent depending on the service model used.

For data at rest, the ideal security measure is for the client to encrypt the database and only store encrypted data in the cloud, with the CP having no access to the encryption key. So long as the key remains secure, the CP has no ability to read the data, although corruption and other denial-of-service attacks remain a risk.

A straightforward solution to the security problem in this context is to encrypt the entire database and not provide the encryption/decryption keys to the service provider. This solution by itself is inflexible. The user has little ability to access individual data items based on searches or indexing on key parameters, but rather would have to download entire tables from the database, decrypt the tables, and work with the results. To provide more flexibility, it must be possible to work with the database in its encrypted form.

An example of such an approach, depicted in Figure 16.10, is reported in [DAMI05] and [DAMI03]. A similar approach is described in [HACI02]. Four entities are involved:

- **Data owner:** An organization that produces data to be made available for controlled release, either within the organization or to external users.
- **User:** Human entity that presents requests (queries) to the system. The user could be an employee of the organization who is granted access to the database via the server, or a user external to the organization who, after authentication, is granted access.
- **Client:** Frontend that transforms user queries into queries on the encrypted data stored on the server.

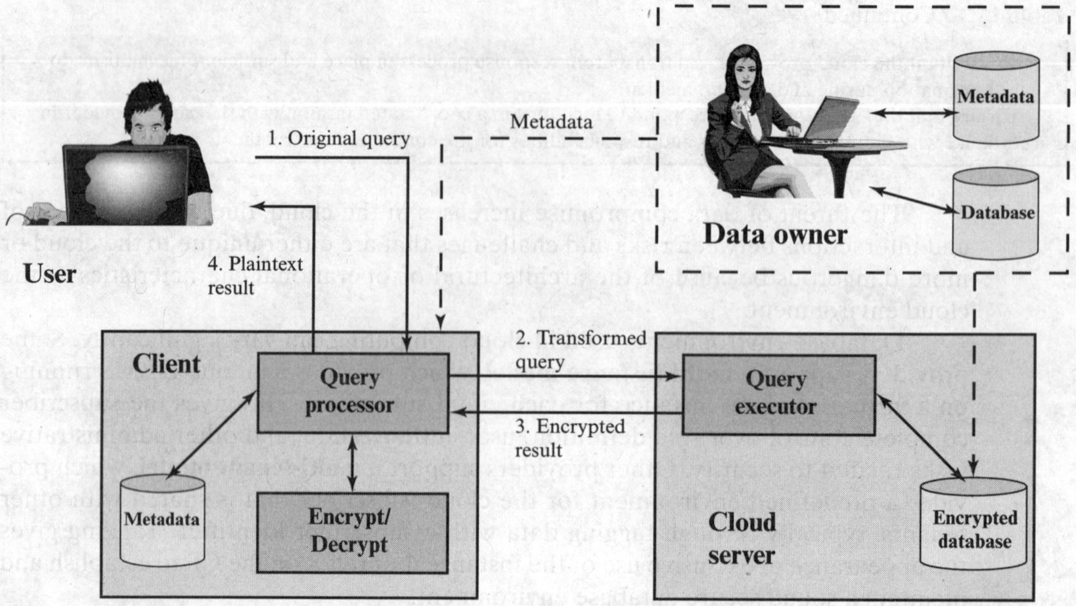

Figure 16.10 An Encryption Scheme for a Cloud-Based Database

- **Server:** An organization that receives the encrypted data from a data owner and makes them available for distribution to clients. The server could in fact be owned by the data owner but, more typically, is a facility owned and maintained by an external provider. For our discussion, the server is a cloud server.

Before continuing this discussion, we need to define some database terms. In relational database parlance, the basic building block is a **relation**, which is a flat table. Rows are referred to as **tuples**, and columns are referred to as **attributes**. A **primary key** is defined to be a portion of a row used to uniquely identify a row in a table; the primary key consists of one or more column names.[2] For example, in an employee table, the employee ID is sufficient to uniquely identify a row in a particular table.

Let us first examine the simplest possible arrangement based on this scenario. Suppose that each individual item in the database is encrypted separately, all using the same encryption key. The encrypted database is stored at the server, but the server does not have the encryption key. Thus, the data are secure at the server. Even if someone were able to hack into the server's system, all he or she would have access to is encrypted data. The client system does have a copy of the encryption key. A user at the client can retrieve a record from the database with the following sequence:

1. The user issues a query for fields from one or more records with a specific value of the primary key.

[2]Note that a primary key has nothing to do with cryptographic keys. A primary key in a database is a means of indexing into the database.

2. The query processor at the client encrypts the primary key, modifies the query accordingly, and transmits the query to the server.
3. The server processes the query using the encrypted value of the primary key and returns the appropriate record or records.
4. The query processor decrypts the data and returns the results.

This method is certainly straightforward but is quite limited. For example, suppose the Employee table contains a salary attribute and the user wishes to retrieve all records for salaries less than $70K. There is no obvious way to do this, because the attribute value for salary in each record is encrypted. The set of encrypted values does not preserve the ordering of values in the original attribute.

There are a number of ways to extend the functionality of this approach. For example, an unencrypted index value can be associated with a given attribute and the table can be partitioned based on these index values, enabling a user to retrieve a certain portion of the table. The details of such schemes are beyond our scope. See [STAL15] for more detail.

16.7 CLOUD SECURITY AS A SERVICE

The term **Security as a Service (SecaaS)** has generally meant a package of security services offered by a service provider that offloads much of the security responsibility from an enterprise to the security service provider. Among the services typically provided are authentication, antivirus, antimalware/-spyware, intrusion detection, and security event management. In the context of cloud computing, cloud security as a service, designated SecaaS, is a segment of the SaaS offering of a CP.

The Cloud Security Alliance defines SecaaS as the provision of security applications and services via the cloud either to cloud-based infrastructure and software or from the cloud to the customers' on-premise systems [CSA11b]. The Cloud Security Alliance has identified the following SecaaS categories of service:

- Identity and access management
- Data loss prevention
- Web security
- Email security
- Security assessments
- Intrusion management
- Security information and event management
- Encryption
- Business continuity and disaster recovery
- Network security

In this section, we examine these categories with a focus on security of the cloud-based infrastructure and services (Figure 16.11).

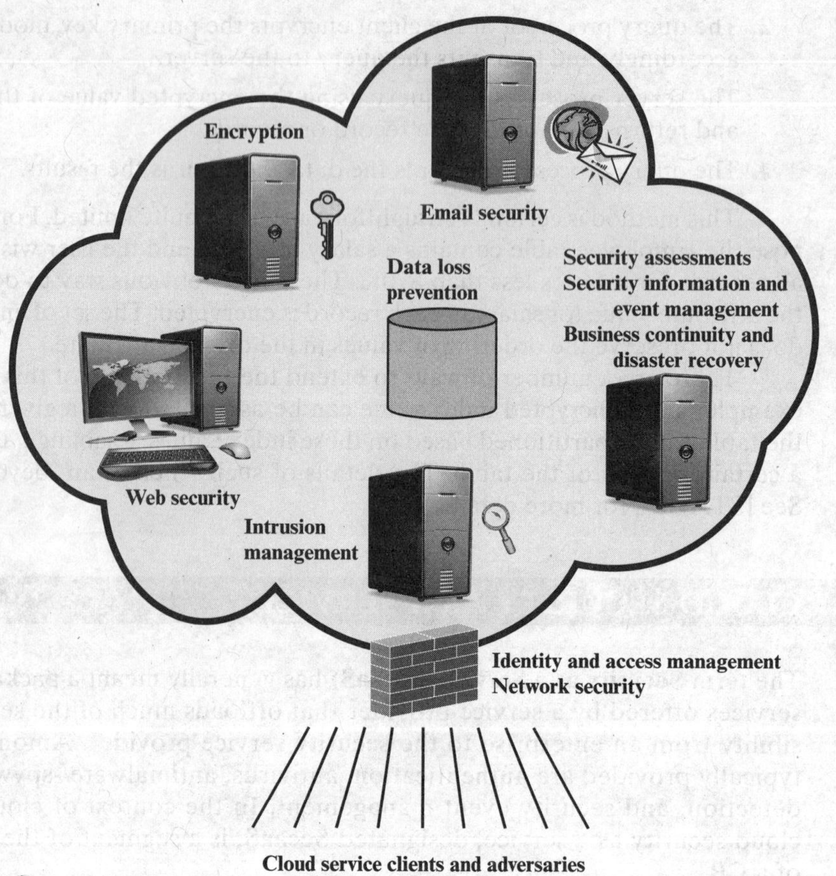

Figure 16.11 Elements of Cloud Security as a Service

Identity and access management (IAM) includes people, processes, and systems that are used to manage access to enterprise resources by assuring that the identity of an entity is verified, and then granting the correct level of access based on this assured identity. One aspect of identity management is identity provisioning, which has to do with providing access to identified users and subsequently deprovisioning, or deny access, to users when the client enterprise designates such users as no longer having access to enterprise resources in the cloud. Another aspect of identity management is for the cloud to participate in the federated identity management scheme (see Chapter 15) scheme used by the client enterprise. Among other requirements, the cloud service provider (CSP) must be able to exchange identity attributes with the enterprise's chosen identity provider.

The access management portion of IAM involves authentication and access control services. For example, the CSP must be able to authenticate users in a trustworthy manner. The access control requirements in SPI environments include establishing trusted user profile and policy information, using it to control access within the cloud service, and doing this in an auditable way.

Data loss prevention (DLP) is the monitoring, protecting, and verifying the security of data at rest, in motion, and in use. Much of DLP can be implemented by the cloud client, such as discussed in Section 16.6. The CSP can also provide DLP services, such as implementing rules about what functions can be performed on data in various contexts.

Web security is real-time protection offered either on premise through software/appliance installation or via the cloud by proxying or redirecting Web traffic to the CP. This provides an added layer of protection on top of things like antiviruses to prevent malware from entering the enterprise via activities such as Web browsing. In addition to protecting against malware, a cloud-based Web security service might include usage policy enforcement, data backup, traffic control, and Web access control.

A CSP may provide a Web-based email service, for which security measures are needed. **Email security** provides control over inbound and outbound email, protecting the organization from phishing, malicious attachments, enforcing corporate polices such as acceptable use and spam prevention. The CSP may also incorporate digital signatures on all email clients and provide optional email encryption.

Security assessments are third-part audits of cloud services. While this service is outside the province of the CSP, the CSP can provide tools and access points to facilitate various assessment activities.

Intrusion management encompasses intrusion detection, prevention, and response. The core of this service is the implementation of intrusion detection systems (IDSs) and intrusion prevention systems (IPSs) at entry points to the cloud and on servers in the cloud. An IDS is a set of automated tools designed to detect unauthorized access to a host system. We discuss this in Chapter 21. An IPS incorporates IDS functionality but also includes mechanisms designed to block traffic from intruders.

Security information and event management (SIEM) aggregates (via push or pull mechanisms) log and event data from virtual and real networks, applications, and systems. This information is then correlated and analyzed to provide real-time reporting and alerting on information/events that may require intervention or other type of response. The CSP typically provides an integrated service that can put together information from a variety of sources both within the cloud and within the client enterprise network.

Encryption is a pervasive service that can be provided for data at rest in the cloud, email traffic, client-specific network management information, and identity information. Encryption services provided by the CSP involve a range of complex issues, including key management, how to implement virtual private network (VPN) services in the cloud, application encryption, and data content access.

Business continuity and disaster recovery comprise measures and mechanisms to ensure operational resiliency in the event of any service interruptions. This is an area where the CSP, because of economies of scale, can offer obvious benefits to a cloud service client [WOOD10]. The CSP can provide backup at multiple locations, with reliable failover and disaster recovery facilities. This service must include a flexible infrastructure, redundancy of functions and hardware, monitored operations, geographically distributed data centers, and network survivability.

Network security consists of security services that allocate access, distribute, monitor, and protect the underlying resource services. Services include perimeter and server firewalls and denial-of-service protection. Many of the other services listed in this section, including intrusion management, identity and access management, data loss protection, and Web security, also contribute to the network security service.

16.8 ADDRESSING CLOUD COMPUTING SECURITY CONCERNS

Numerous documents have been developed to guide businesses thinking about the security issues associated with cloud computing. In addition to SP 800-144, which provides overall guidance, NIST has issued SP 800-146 (*Cloud Computing Synopsis and Recommendations,* May 2012). NIST's recommendations systematically consider each of the major types of cloud services consumed by businesses including Software as a Service (SaaS), Infrastructure as a Service (IaaS), and Platform as a Service (PaaS). While security issues vary somewhat depending on the type of cloud service, there are multiple NIST recommendations that are independent of service type. Not surprisingly, NIST recommends selecting cloud providers that support strong encryption, have appropriate redundancy mechanisms in place, employ authentication mechanisms, and offer subscribers sufficient visibility about mechanisms used to protect subscribers from other subscribers and the provider. SP 800-146 also lists the overall security controls that are relevant in a cloud computing environment and that must be assigned to the different cloud actors. These are shown in Table 16.4.

As more businesses incorporate cloud services into their enterprise network infrastructures, cloud computing security will persist as an important issue. Examples of cloud computing security failures have the potential to have a chilling effect on business interest in cloud services and this is inspiring service providers to be serious about incorporating security mechanisms that will allay concerns of potential subscribers. Some service providers have moved their operations to Tier 4 data centers to address user concerns about availability and redundancy. Because so many businesses remain reluctant to embrace cloud computing in a big way, cloud service providers will have to continue to work hard to convince potential customers that computing support for core business processes and mission critical applications can be moved safely and securely to the cloud.

Table 16.4 Control Functions and Classes

Technical	Operational	Management
Access Control	Awareness and Training	Certification, Accreditation, and Security Assessment
Audit and Accountability	Configuration and Management	Planning Risk Assessment
Identification and Authentication	Contingency Planning	System and Services Acquisition
System and Communication Protection	Incident Response	
	Maintenance	
	Media Protection	
	Physical and Environmental Protection	
	Personnel Security System and Information Integrity	

16.9 KEY TERMS, REVIEW QUESTIONS, AND PROBLEMS

Key Terms

access requestor (AR) authentication server cloud cloud auditor cloud broker cloud carrier cloud computing cloud consumer cloud provider community cloud Dynamic Host Configuration Protocol (DHCP) EAP authenticator EAP-GPSK	EAP-IKEv2 EAP over LAN (EAPOL) EAP method EAP pass-through mode EAP peer EAP-TLS EAP-TTLS Extensible Authentication Protocol (EAP) firewall IEEE 802.1X media gateway Network Access Control (NAC)	Network Access Server (NAS) Platform as a Service (PaaS) policy server private cloud public cloud Remote Access Server (RAS) Security as a Service (SecaaS) Software as a Service (SaaS) supplicant Virtual Local Area Network (VLAN)

Review Questions

16.1 What are the elements of a network access control system?

16.2 What is an EAP?

16.3 List and briefly define four EAP authentication methods.

16.4 What is DHCP? How useful is it to help achieve security of IP addresses?

16.5 List and briefly define common EAPOL frame types.

16.6 What are the essential characteristics of cloud computing?

16.7 List and briefly define the service models of cloud computing.

16.8 Discuss the five major actors defined by the cloud computing reference architecture.

16.9 Describe some of the main cloud-specific security threats.

Problems

16.1 Investigate the network access control scheme used at your school or place of employment. Draw a diagram and describe the principal components.

16.2 Figure 16.3 suggests that EAP can be described in the context of a four-layer model. Indicate the functions and formats of each of the four layers. You may need to refer to RFC 3748.

16.3 List some commonly used cloud-based data services. Explore and compare these services based on their use of encryption, flexibility, efficiency, speed, and ease of use. Study security breaches on these services in recent past. What changes were made by the services after these attacks?

CHAPTER 17

Transport-Level Security

LEARNING OBJECTIVES

After studying this chapter, you should be able to:

- ◆ Summarize Web security threats and Web traffic security approaches.
- ◆ Present an overview of Transport Layer Security (TLS).
- ◆ Understand the differences between Secure Sockets Layer and Transport Layer Security.
- ◆ Compare the pseudorandom function used in Transport Layer Security with those discussed earlier in the book.
- ◆ Present an overview of HTTPS (HTTP over SSL).
- ◆ Present an overview of Secure Shell (SSH).

Virtually all businesses, most government agencies, and many individuals now have Web sites. The number of individuals and companies with Internet access is expanding rapidly and all of these have graphical Web browsers. As a result, businesses are enthusiastic about setting up facilities on the Web for electronic commerce. But the reality is that the Internet and the Web are extremely vulnerable to compromises of various sorts. As businesses wake up to this reality, the demand for secure Web services grows.

The topic of Web security is a broad one and can easily fill a book. In this chapter, we begin with a discussion of the general requirements for Web security and then focus on three standardized schemes that are becoming increasingly important as part of Web commerce and that focus on security at the transport layer: SSL/TLS, HTTPS, and SSH.

17.1 WEB SECURITY CONSIDERATIONS

The World Wide Web is fundamentally a client/server application running over the Internet and TCP/IP intranets. As such, the security tools and approaches discussed so far in this book are relevant to the issue of Web security. However, the following characteristics of Web usage suggest the need for tailored security tools:

- ■ Although Web browsers are very easy to use, Web servers are relatively easy to configure and manage, and Web content is increasingly easy to develop, the underlying software is extraordinarily complex. This complex software may hide many potential security flaws. The short history of the Web is filled with examples of new and upgraded systems, properly installed, that are vulnerable to a variety of security attacks.
- ■ A Web server can be exploited as a launching pad into the corporation's or agency's entire computer complex. Once the Web server is subverted, an attacker may be able to gain access to data and systems not part of the Web itself but connected to the server at the local site.

- Casual and untrained (in security matters) users are common clients for Web-based services. Such users are not necessarily aware of the security risks that exist and do not have the tools or knowledge to take effective countermeasures.

Web Security Threats

Table 17.1 provides a summary of the types of security threats faced when using the Web. One way to group these threats is in terms of passive and active attacks. Passive attacks include eavesdropping on network traffic between browser and server and gaining access to information on a Web site that is supposed to be restricted. Active attacks include impersonating another user, altering messages in transit between client and server, and altering information on a Web site.

Another way to classify Web security threats is in terms of the location of the threat: Web server, Web browser, and network traffic between browser and server. Issues of server and browser security fall into the category of computer system security; Part Six of this book addresses the issue of system security in general but is also applicable to Web system security. Issues of traffic security fall into the category of network security and are addressed in this chapter.

Web Traffic Security Approaches

A number of approaches to providing Web security are possible. The various approaches that have been considered are similar in the services they provide and, to some extent, in the mechanisms that they use, but they differ with respect to their scope of applicability and their relative location within the TCP/IP protocol stack.

Table 17.1 A Comparison of Threats on the Web

	Threats	Consequences	Countermeasures
Integrity	• Modification of user data • Trojan horse browser • Modification of memory • Modification of message traffic in transit	• Loss of information • Compromise of machine • Vulnerability to all other threats	Cryptographic checksums
Confidentiality	• Eavesdropping on the net • Theft of info from server • Theft of data from client • Info about network configuration • Info about which client talks to server	• Loss of information • Loss of privacy	Encryption, Web proxies
Denial of Service	• Killing of user threads • Flooding machine with bogus requests • Filling up disk or memory • Isolating machine by DNS attacks	• Disruptive • Annoying • Prevent user from getting work done	Difficult to prevent
Authentication	• Impersonation of legitimate users • Data forgery	• Misrepresentation of user • Belief that false information is valid	Cryptographic techniques

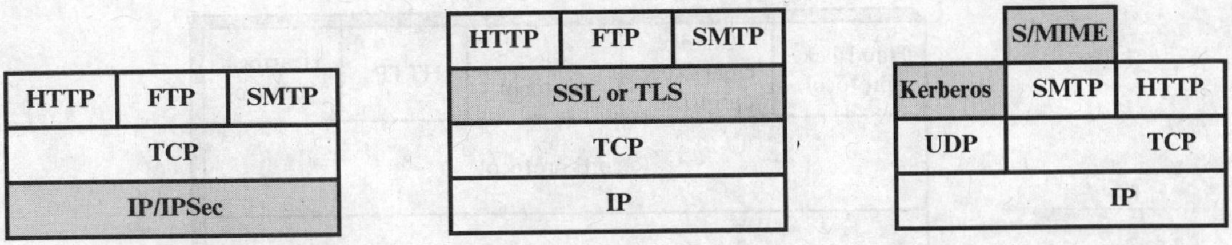

(a) Network level (b) Transport level (c) Application level

Figure 17.1 Relative Location of Security Facilities in the TCP/IP Protocol Stack

Figure 17.1 illustrates this difference. One way to provide Web security is to use IP security (IPsec) (Figure 17.1a). The advantage of using IPsec is that it is transparent to end users and applications and provides a general-purpose solution. Furthermore, IPsec includes a filtering capability so that only selected traffic need incur the overhead of IPsec processing.

Another relatively general-purpose solution is to implement security just above TCP (Figure 17.1b). The foremost example of this approach is the Secure Sockets Layer (SSL) and the follow-on Internet standard known as Transport Layer Security (TLS). At this level, there are two implementation choices. For full generality, SSL (or TLS) could be provided as part of the underlying protocol suite and therefore be transparent to applications. Alternatively, TLS can be embedded in specific packages. For example, virtually all browsers come equipped with TLS, and most Web servers have implemented the protocol.

Application-specific security services are embedded within the particular application. Figure 17.1c shows examples of this architecture. The advantage of this approach is that the service can be tailored to the specific needs of a given application.

17.2 TRANSPORT LAYER SECURITY

One of the most widely used security services is **Transport Layer Security (TSL)**; the current version is Version 1.2, defined in RFC 5246. TLS is an Internet standard that evolved from a commercial protocol known as **Secure Sockets Layer (SSL)**. Although SSL implementations are still around, it has been deprecated by IETF and is disabled by most corporations offering TLS software. TLS is a general-purpose service implemented as a set of protocols that rely on TCP. At this level, there are two implementation choices. For full generality, TLS could be provided as part of the underlying protocol suite and therefore be transparent to applications. Alternatively, TLS can be embedded in specific packages. For example, most browsers come equipped with TLS, and most Web servers have implemented the protocol.

TLS Architecture

TLS is designed to make use of TCP to provide a reliable end-to-end secure service. TLS is not a single protocol but rather two layers of protocols, as illustrated in Figure 17.2.

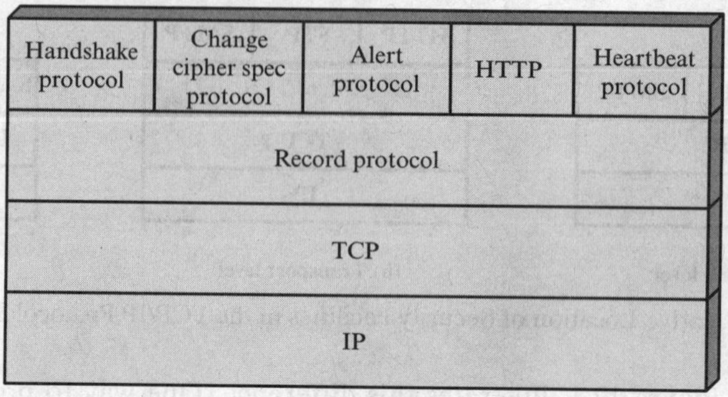

Figure 17.2 TLS Protocol Stack

The TLS Record Protocol provides basic security services to various higher-layer protocols. In particular, the **Hypertext Transfer Protocol (HTTP)**, which provides the transfer service for Web client/server interaction, can operate on top of TLS. Three higher-layer protocols are defined as part of TLS: the Handshake Protocol; the Change Cipher Spec Protocol; and the Alert Protocol. These TLS-specific protocols are used in the management of TLS exchanges and are examined later in this section. A fourth protocol, the Heartbeat Protocol, is defined in a separate RFC and is also discussed subsequently in this section.

Two important TLS concepts are the TLS session and the TLS connection, which are defined in the specification as follows:

- **Connection:** A connection is a transport (in the OSI layering model definition) that provides a suitable type of service. For TLS, such connections are peer-to-peer relationships. The connections are transient. Every connection is associated with one session.
- **Session:** A TLS session is an association between a client and a server. Sessions are created by the Handshake Protocol. Sessions define a set of cryptographic security parameters, which can be shared among multiple connections. Sessions are used to avoid the expensive negotiation of new security parameters for each connection.

Between any pair of parties (applications such as HTTP on client and server), there may be multiple secure connections. In theory, there may also be multiple simultaneous sessions between parties, but this feature is not used in practice.

There are a number of states associated with each session. Once a session is established, there is a current operating state for both read and write (i.e., receive and send). In addition, during the Handshake Protocol, pending read and write states are created. Upon successful conclusion of the Handshake Protocol, the pending states become the current states.

A session state is defined by the following parameters:

- **Session identifier:** An arbitrary byte sequence chosen by the server to identify an active or resumable session state.
- **Peer certificate:** An X509.v3 certificate of the peer. This element of the state may be null.

- **Compression method:** The algorithm used to compress data prior to encryption.
- **Cipher spec:** Specifies the bulk data encryption algorithm (such as null, AES, etc.) and a hash algorithm (such as MD5 or SHA-1) used for MAC calculation. It also defines cryptographic attributes such as the hash_size.
- **Master secret:** 48-byte secret shared between the client and server.
- **Is resumable:** A flag indicating whether the session can be used to initiate new connections.

A connection state is defined by the following parameters:

- **Server and client random:** Byte sequences that are chosen by the server and client for each connection.
- **Server write MAC secret:** The secret key used in MAC operations on data sent by the server.
- **Client write MAC secret:** The symmetric key used in MAC operations on data sent by the client.
- **Server write key:** The symmetric encryption key for data encrypted by the server and decrypted by the client.
- **Client write key:** The symmetric encryption key for data encrypted by the client and decrypted by the server.
- **Initialization vectors:** When a block cipher in CBC mode is used, an initialization vector (IV) is maintained for each key. This field is first initialized by the TLS Handshake Protocol. Thereafter, the final ciphertext block from each record is preserved for use as the IV with the following record.
- **Sequence numbers:** Each party maintains separate sequence numbers for transmitted and received messages for each connection. When a party sends or receives a "change cipher spec message," the appropriate sequence number is set to zero. Sequence numbers may not exceed $2^{64} - 1$.

TLS Record Protocol

The TLS Record Protocol provides two services for TLS connections:

- **Confidentiality:** The Handshake Protocol defines a shared secret key that is used for conventional encryption of TLS payloads.
- **Message Integrity:** The Handshake Protocol also defines a shared secret key that is used to form a message authentication code (MAC).

Figure 17.3 indicates the overall operation of the TLS Record Protocol. The Record Protocol takes an application message to be transmitted, fragments the data into manageable blocks, optionally compresses the data, applies a MAC, encrypts, adds a header, and transmits the resulting unit in a TCP segment. Received data are decrypted, verified, decompressed, and reassembled before being delivered to higher-level users.

The first step is **fragmentation**. Each upper-layer message is fragmented into blocks of 2^{14} bytes (16,384 bytes) or less. Next, **compression** is optionally applied. Compression must be lossless and may not increase the content length by more than

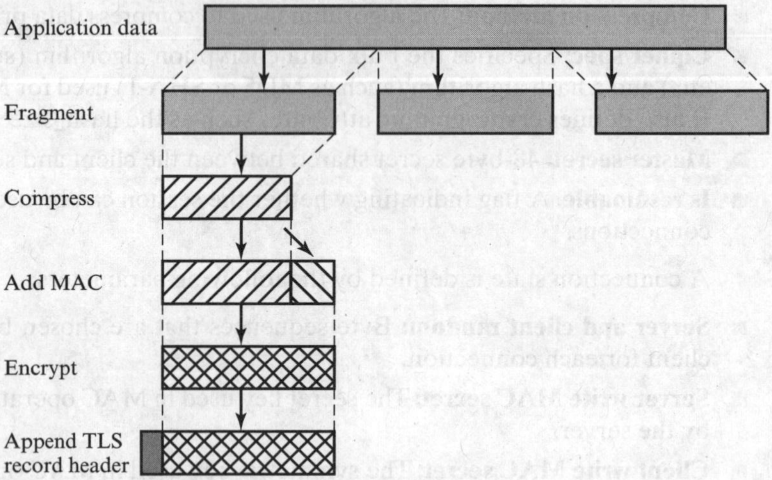

Figure 17.3 TLS Record Protocol Operation

1024 bytes.[1] In TLSv2, no compression algorithm is specified, so the default compression algorithm is null.

The next step in processing is to compute a **message authentication code** over the compressed data. TLS makes use of the HMAC algorithm defined in RFC 2104. Recall from Chapter 12 that HMAC is defined as

$$\text{HMAC}_K(M) = \text{H}[(K^+ \oplus \text{opad}) \| \text{H}[(K^+ \oplus \text{ipad}) \| M]]$$

where

H = embedded hash function (for TLS, either MD5 or SHA-1)

M = message input to HMAC

K^+ = secret key padded with zeros on the left so that the result is equal to the block length of the hash code (for MD5 and SHA-1, block length = 512 bits)

ipad = 00110110 (36 in hexadecimal) repeated 64 times (512 bits)
opad = 01011100 (5C in hexadecimal) repeated 64 times (512 bits)

For TLS, the MAC calculation encompasses the fields indicated in the following expression:

HMAC_hash(MAC_write_secret, seq_num || TLSCompressed.type || TLSCompressed.version || TLSCompressed.length || TLSCompressed.fragment)

The MAC calculation covers all of the fields XXX, plus the field `TLSCompressed.version`, which is the version of the protocol being employed.

Next, the compressed message plus the MAC are **encrypted** using symmetric encryption. Encryption may not increase the content length by more than 1024 bytes,

[1]Of course, one hopes that compression shrinks rather than expands the data. However, for very short blocks, it is possible, because of formatting conventions, that the compression algorithm will actually provide output that is longer than the input.

so that the total length may not exceed $2^{14} + 2048$. The following encryption algorithms are permitted:

Block Cipher		Stream Cipher	
Algorithm	Key Size	Algorithm	Key Size
AES 3DES	128, 256 168	RC4-128	128

For stream encryption, the compressed message plus the MAC are encrypted. Note that the MAC is computed before encryption takes place and that the MAC is then encrypted along with the plaintext or compressed plaintext.

For block encryption, padding may be added after the MAC prior to encryption. The padding is in the form of a number of padding bytes followed by a one-byte indication of the length of the padding. The padding can be any amount that results in a total that is a multiple of the cipher's block length, up to a maximum of 255 bytes. For example, if the cipher block length is 16 bytes (e.g., AES) and if the plaintext (or compressed text if compression is used) plus MAC plus padding length byte is 79 bytes long, then the padding length (in bytes) can be 1, 17, 33, and so on, up to 161. At a padding length of 161, the total length is $79 + 161 = 240$. A variable padding length may be used to frustrate attacks based on an analysis of the lengths of exchanged messages.

The final step of TLS Record Protocol processing is to prepend a header consisting of the following fields:

- **Content Type (8 bits)**: The higher-layer protocol used to process the enclosed fragment.
- **Major Version (8 bits):** Indicates major version of TLS in use. For TLSv2, the value is 3.
- **Minor Version (8 bits):** Indicates minor version in use. For TLSv2, the value is 1.
- **Compressed Length (16 bits):** The length in bytes of the plaintext fragment (or compressed fragment if compression is used). The maximum value is $2^{14} + 2048$.

The content types that have been defined are `change_cipher_spec`, `alert`, `handshake`, and `application_data`. The first three are the TLS-specific protocols, discussed next. Note that no distinction is made among the various applications (e.g., HTTP) that might use TLS; the content of the data created by such applications is opaque to TLS.

Figure 17.4 illustrates the TLS record format.

Change Cipher Spec Protocol

The Change Cipher Spec Protocol is one of the four TLS-specific protocols that use the TLS Record Protocol, and it is the simplest. This protocol consists of a single message (Figure 17.5a), which consists of a single byte with the value 1. The sole purpose of this message is to cause the pending state to be copied into the current state, which updates the cipher suite to be used on this connection.

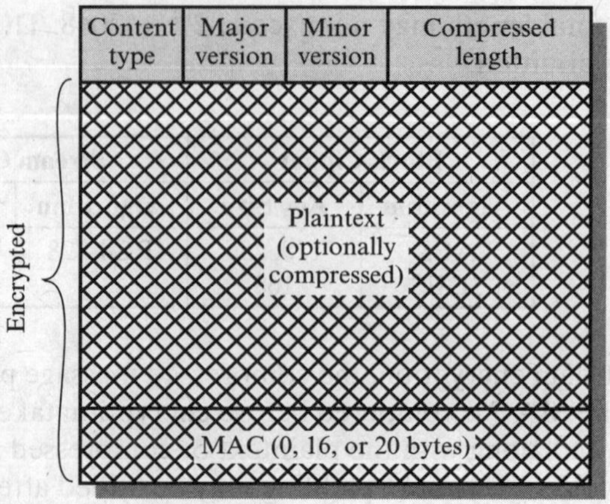

Figure 17.4 TLS Record Format

Alert Protocol

The Alert Protocol is used to convey TLS-related alerts to the peer entity. As with other applications that use TLS, alert messages are compressed and encrypted, as specified by the current state.

Each message in this protocol consists of two bytes (Figure 17.5b). The first byte takes the value warning (1) or fatal (2) to convey the severity of the message. If the level is fatal, TLS immediately terminates the connection. Other connections on the same session may continue, but no new connections on this session may be established. The second byte contains a code that indicates the specific alert. The following alerts are always fatal:

- **unexpected_message:** An inappropriate message was received.
- **bad_record_mac:** An incorrect MAC was received.
- **decompression_failure:** The decompression function received improper input (e.g., unable to decompress or decompress to greater than maximum allowable length).
- **handshake_failure:** Sender was unable to negotiate an acceptable set of security parameters given the options available.
- **illegal_parameter:** A field in a handshake message was out of range or inconsistent with other fields.

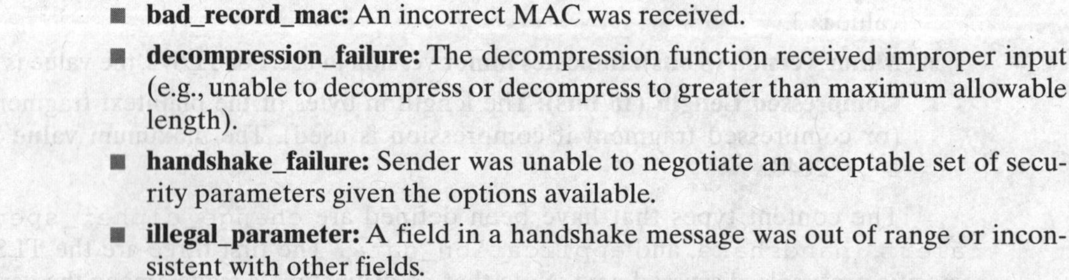

Figure 17.5 TLS Record Protocol Payload

- **decryption_failed:** A ciphertext decrypted in an invalid way; either it was not an even multiple of the block length or its padding values, when checked, were incorrect.
- **record_overflow:** A TLS record was received with a payload (ciphertext) whose length exceeds $2^{14} + 2048$ bytes, or the ciphertext decrypted to a length of greater than $2^{14} + 1024$ bytes.
- **unknown_ca:** A valid certificate chain or partial chain was received, but the certificate was not accepted because the CA certificate could not be located or could not be matched with a known, trusted CA.
- **access_denied:** A valid certificate was received, but when access control was applied, the sender decided not to proceed with the negotiation.
- **decode_error:** A message could not be decoded, because either a field was out of its specified range or the length of the message was incorrect.
- **export_restriction:** A negotiation not in compliance with export restrictions on key length was detected.
- **protocol_version:** The protocol version the client attempted to negotiate is recognized but not supported.
- **insufficient_security:** Returned instead of handshake_failure when a negotiation has failed specifically because the server requires ciphers more secure than those supported by the client.
- **internal_error:** An internal error unrelated to the peer or the correctness of the protocol makes it impossible to continue.

The remaining alerts are the following.

- **close_notify:** Notifies the recipient that the sender will not send any more messages on this connection. Each party is required to send a close_notify alert before closing the write side of a connection.
- **bad_certificate:** A received certificate was corrupt (e.g., contained a signature that did not verify).
- **unsupported_certificate:** The type of the received certificate is not supported.
- **certificate_revoked:** A certificate has been revoked by its signer.
- **certificate_expired:** A certificate has expired.
- **certificate_unknown:** Some other unspecified issue arose in processing the certificate, rendering it unacceptable.
- **decrypt_error:** A handshake cryptographic operation failed, including being unable to verify a signature, decrypt a key exchange, or validate a finished message.
- **user_canceled:** This handshake is being canceled for some reason unrelated to a protocol failure.
- **no_renegotiation:** Sent by a client in response to a hello request or by the server in response to a client hello after initial handshaking. Either of these messages would normally result in renegotiation, but this alert indicates that the sender is not able to renegotiate. This message is always a warning.

Handshake Protocol

The most complex part of TLS is the **Handshake Protocol**. This protocol allows the server and client to authenticate each other and to negotiate an encryption and MAC algorithm and cryptographic keys to be used to protect data sent in a TLS record. The Handshake Protocol is used before any application data is transmitted.

The Handshake Protocol consists of a series of messages exchanged by client and server. All of these have the format shown in Figure 17.5c . Each message has three fields:

- **Type (1 byte):** Indicates one of 10 messages. Table 17.2 lists the defined message types.
- **Length (3 bytes):** The length of the message in bytes.
- **Content (≥ 0 bytes):** The parameters associated with this message; these are listed in Table 17.2.

Figure 17.6 shows the initial exchange needed to establish a logical connection between client and server. The exchange can be viewed as having four phases.

PHASE 1. ESTABLISH SECURITY CAPABILITIES Phase 1 initiates a logical connection and establishes the security capabilities that will be associated with it. The exchange is initiated by the client, which sends a **client_hello message** with the following parameters:

- **Version:** The highest TLS version understood by the client.
- **Random:** A client-generated random structure consisting of a 32-bit timestamp and 28 bytes generated by a secure random number generator. These values serve as nonces and are used during key exchange to prevent replay attacks.
- **Session ID:** A variable-length session identifier. A nonzero value indicates that the client wishes to update the parameters of an existing connection or to create a new connection on this session. A zero value indicates that the client wishes to establish a new connection on a new session.

Table 17.2 TLS Handshake Protocol Message Types

Message Type	Parameters
hello_request	null
client_hello	version, random, session id, cipher suite, compression method
server_hello	version, random, session id, cipher suite, compression method
certificate	chain of X.509v3 certificates
server_key_exchange	parameters, signature
certificate_request	type, authorities
server_done	null
certificate_verify	signature
client_key_exchange	parameters, signature
finished	hash value

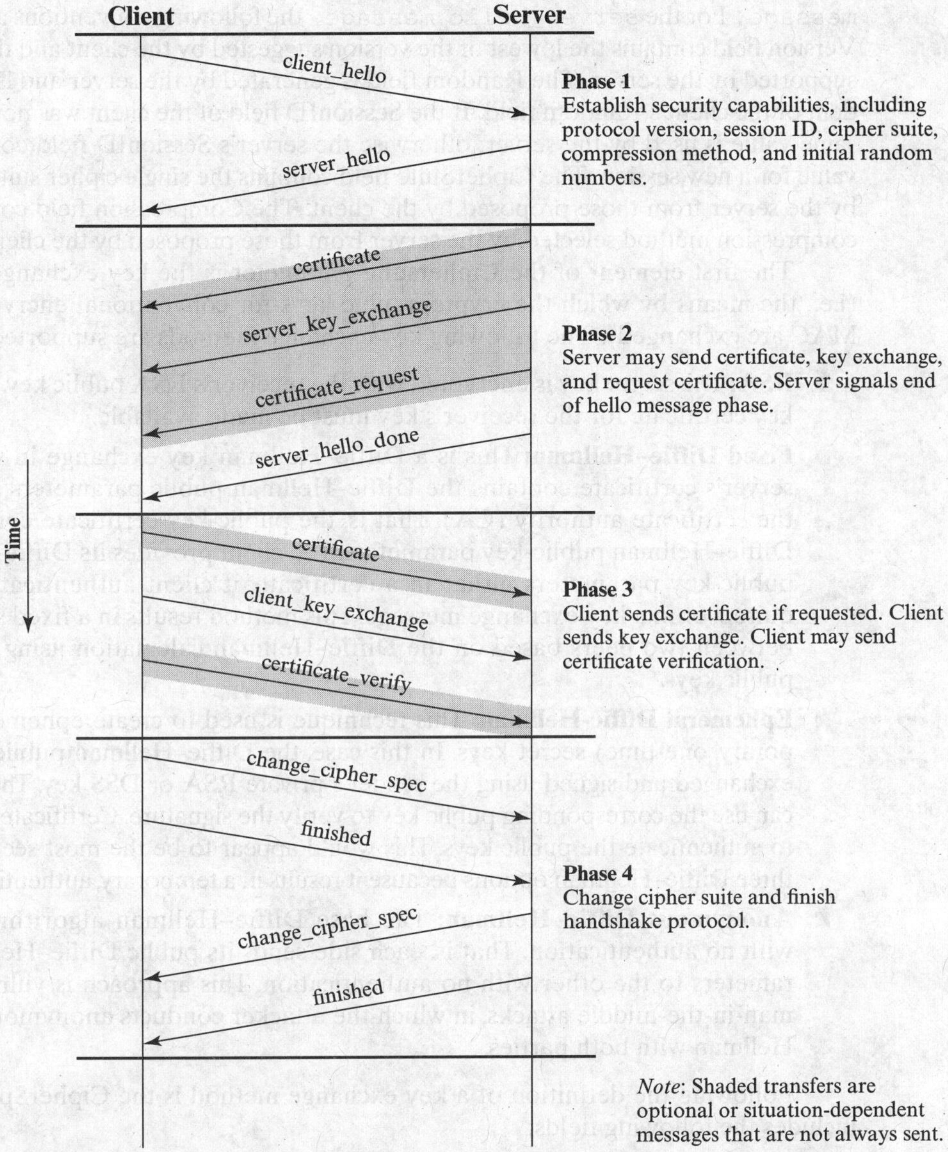

Figure 17.6 Handshake Protocol Action

- **CipherSuite:** This is a list that contains the combinations of cryptographic algorithms supported by the client, in decreasing order of preference. Each element of the list (each cipher suite) defines both a key exchange algorithm and a CipherSpec; these are discussed subsequently.
- **Compression Method:** This is a list of the compression methods the client supports.

After sending the `client_hello message`, the client waits for the **`server_hello message`**, which contains the same parameters as the `client_hello` `message`. For the `server_hello message`, the following conventions apply. The Version field contains the lowest of the version suggested by the client and the highest supported by the server. The Random field is generated by the server and is independent of the client's Random field. If the SessionID field of the client was nonzero, the same value is used by the server; otherwise the server's SessionID field contains the value for a new session. The CipherSuite field contains the single cipher suite selected by the server from those proposed by the client. The Compression field contains the compression method selected by the server from those proposed by the client.

The first element of the Ciphersuite parameter is the key exchange method (i.e., the means by which the cryptographic keys for conventional encryption and MAC are exchanged). The following key exchange methods are supported.

- **RSA:** The secret key is encrypted with the receiver's RSA public key. A public-key certificate for the receiver's key must be made available.
- **Fixed Diffie–Hellman:** This is a Diffie–Hellman key exchange in which the server's certificate contains the Diffie–Hellman public parameters signed by the certificate authority (CA). That is, the public-key certificate contains the Diffie–Hellman public-key parameters. The client provides its Diffie–Hellman public-key parameters either in a certificate, if client authentication is required, or in a key exchange message. This method results in a fixed secret key between two peers based on the Diffie–Hellman calculation using the fixed public keys.
- **Ephemeral Diffie-Hellman:** This technique is used to create ephemeral (temporary, one-time) secret keys. In this case, the Diffie–Hellman public keys are exchanged and signed using the sender's private RSA or DSS key. The receiver can use the corresponding public key to verify the signature. Certificates are used to authenticate the public keys. This would appear to be the most secure of the three Diffie–Hellman options because it results in a temporary, authenticated key.
- **Anonymous Diffie–Hellman:** The base Diffie–Hellman algorithm is used with no authentication. That is, each side sends its public Diffie–Hellman parameters to the other with no authentication. This approach is vulnerable to man-in-the-middle attacks, in which the attacker conducts anonymous Diffie–Hellman with both parties.

Following the definition of a key exchange method is the CipherSpec, which includes the following fields:

- **CipherAlgorithm:** Any of the algorithms mentioned earlier: RC4, RC2, DES, 3DES, DES40, or IDEA
- **MACAlgorithm:** MD5 or SHA-1
- **CipherType:** Stream or Block
- **IsExportable:** True or False
- **HashSize:** 0, 16 (for MD5), or 20 (for SHA-1) bytes
- **Key Material:** A sequence of bytes that contain data used in generating the write keys
- **IV Size:** The size of the Initialization Value for Cipher Block Chaining (CBC) encryption

Phase 2. Server Authentication and Key Exchange The server begins this phase by sending its certificate if it needs to be authenticated; the message contains one or a chain of X.509 certificates. The **certificate message** is required for any agreed-on key exchange method except anonymous Diffie–Hellman. Note that if fixed Diffie–Hellman is used, this certificate message functions as the server's key exchange message because it contains the server's public Diffie–Hellman parameters.

Next, a **server_key_exchange message** may be sent if it is required. It is not required in two instances: (1) The server has sent a certificate with fixed Diffie–Hellman parameters; or (2) RSA key exchange is to be used. The server_key_exchange message is needed for the following:

- **Anonymous Diffie–Hellman:** The message content consists of the two global Diffie–Hellman values (a prime number and a primitive root of that number) plus the server's public Diffie–Hellman key (see Figure 10.1).
- **Ephemeral Diffie–Hellman:** The message content includes the three Diffie–Hellman parameters provided for anonymous Diffie–Hellman plus a signature of those parameters.
- **RSA key exchange (in which the server is using RSA but has a signature-only RSA key):** Accordingly, the client cannot simply send a secret key encrypted with the server's public key. Instead, the server must create a temporary RSA public/private key pair and use the server_key_exchange message to send the public key. The message content includes the two parameters of the temporary RSA public key (exponent and modulus; see Figure 9.5) plus a signature of those parameters.

Some further details about the signatures are warranted. As usual, a signature is created by taking the hash of a message and encrypting it with the sender's private key. In this case, the hash is defined as

$$\text{hash(ClientHello.random} \,\|\, \text{ServerHello.random} \,\|\, \text{ServerParams)}$$

So the hash covers not only the Diffie–Hellman or RSA parameters but also the two nonces from the initial hello messages. This ensures against replay attacks and misrepresentation. In the case of a DSS signature, the hash is performed using the SHA-1 algorithm. In the case of an RSA signature, both an MD5 and an SHA-1 hash are calculated, and the concatenation of the two hashes (36 bytes) is encrypted with the server's private key.

Next, a nonanonymous server (server not using anonymous Diffie–Hellman) can request a certificate from the client. The **certificate_request message** includes two parameters: certificate_type and certificate_authorities. The certificate type indicates the public-key algorithm and its use:

- RSA, signature only
- DSS, signature only
- RSA for fixed Diffie–Hellman; in this case the signature is used only for authentication, by sending a certificate signed with RSA
- DSS for fixed Diffie–Hellman; again, used only for authentication

The second parameter in the certificate_request message is a list of the distinguished names of acceptable certificate authorities.

The final message in phase 2, and one that is always required, is the **server_done message**, which is sent by the server to indicate the end of the server hello and associated messages. After sending this message, the server will wait for a client response. This message has no parameters.

PHASE 3. CLIENT AUTHENTICATION AND KEY EXCHANGE Upon receipt of the `server_done` message, the client should verify that the server provided a valid certificate (if required) and check that the `server_hello` parameters are acceptable. If all is satisfactory, the client sends one or more messages back to the server.

If the server has requested a certificate, the client begins this phase by sending a **certificate message**. If no suitable certificate is available, the client sends a `no_certificate` alert instead.

Next is the **client_key_exchange message**, which must be sent in this phase. The content of the message depends on the type of key exchange, as follows:

- **RSA:** The client generates a 48-byte *pre-master secret* and encrypts with the public key from the server's certificate or temporary RSA key from a server_key_exchange message. Its use to compute a *master secret* is explained later.
- **Ephemeral or Anonymous Diffie–Hellman:** The client's public Diffie–Hellman parameters are sent.
- **Fixed Diffie–Hellman:** The client's public Diffie–Hellman parameters were sent in a certificate message, so the content of this message is null.

Finally, in this phase, the client may send a **certificate_verify message** to provide explicit verification of a client certificate. This message is only sent following any client certificate that has signing capability (i.e., all certificates except those containing fixed Diffie–Hellman parameters). This message signs a hash code based on the preceding messages, defined as

CertificateVerify.signature.md5_hash
  MD5(handshake_messages);
Certificate.signature.sha_hash
  SHA(handshake_messages);

where `handshake_messages` refers to all Handshake Protocol messages sent or received starting at `client_hello` but not including this message. If the user's private key is DSS, then it is used to encrypt the SHA-1 hash. If the user's private key is RSA, it is used to encrypt the concatenation of the MD5 and SHA-1 hashes. In either case, the purpose is to verify the client's ownership of the private key for the client certificate. Even if someone is misusing the client's certificate, he or she would be unable to send this message.

PHASE 4. FINISH Phase 4 completes the setting up of a secure connection. The client sends a **change_cipher_spec message** and copies the pending CipherSpec into the current CipherSpec. Note that this message is not considered part of the Handshake Protocol but is sent using the Change Cipher Spec Protocol. The client then immediately sends the **finished message** under the new algorithms, keys, and secrets.

The finished message verifies that the key exchange and authentication processes were successful. The content of the finished message is:

PRF(master_secret, finished_label, MD5(handshake_messages) || SHA-1 (handshake_messages))

where `finished_label` is the string "client finished" for the client and "server finished" for the server.

In response to these two messages, the server sends its own `change_cipher_spec` message, transfers the pending to the current CipherSpec, and sends its finished message. At this point, the handshake is complete and the client and server may begin to exchange application-layer data.

Cryptographic Computations

Two further items are of interest: (1) the creation of a shared master secret by means of the key exchange; and (2) the generation of cryptographic parameters from the master secret.

Master Secret Creation The shared master secret is a one-time 48-byte value (384 bits) generated for this session by means of secure key exchange. The creation is in two stages. First, a `pre_master_secret` is exchanged. Second, the `master_secret` is calculated by both parties. For `pre_master_secret` exchange, there are two possibilities.

- **RSA:** A 48-byte pre_master_secret is generated by the client, encrypted with the server's public RSA key, and sent to the server. The server decrypts the ciphertext using its private key to recover the pre_master_secret.
- **Diffie–Hellman:** Both client and server generate a Diffie–Hellman public key. After these are exchanged, each side performs the Diffie–Hellman calculation to create the shared pre_master_secret.

Both sides now compute the `master_secret` as

master_secret =
PRF(pre_master_secret, "master secret", ClientHello.random || ServerHello .random)

where `ClientHello.random` and `ServerHello.random` are the two nonce values exchanged in the initial hello messages.

The algorithm is performed until 48 bytes of pseudorandom output are produced. The calculation of the key block material (MAC secret keys, session encryption keys, and IVs) is defined as

key_block =
PRF(SecurityParameters.master_secret, "key expansion", SecurityParameters.server_random || SecurityParameters.client_random)

until enough output has been generated.

Generation of Cryptographic Parameters CipherSpecs require a client write MAC secret, a server write MAC secret, a client write key, a server write key, a client write IV, and a server write IV, which are generated from the master secret in that order. These parameters are generated from the master secret by hashing the master secret into a sequence of secure bytes of sufficient length for all needed parameters.

The generation of the key material from the master secret uses the same format for generation of the master secret from the pre-master secret as

$$\begin{aligned}\text{key\_block} = {} & \text{MD5(master\_secret} \parallel \text{SHA(`A'} \parallel \text{master\_secret} \parallel \\ & \quad \text{ServerHello.random} \parallel \text{ClientHello.random))} \parallel \\ & \text{MD5(master\_secret} \parallel \text{SHA(`BB'} \parallel \text{master\_secret} \parallel \\ & \quad \text{ServerHello.random} \parallel \text{ClientHello.random))} \parallel \\ & \text{MD5(master\_secret} \parallel \text{SHA(`CCC'} \parallel \text{master\_secret} \parallel \\ & \quad \text{ServerHello.random} \parallel \text{ClientHello.random))} \parallel \ldots\end{aligned}$$

until enough output has been generated. The result of this algorithmic structure is a pseudorandom function. We can view the `master_secret` as the pseudorandom seed value to the function. The client and server random numbers can be viewed as salt values to complicate cryptanalysis (see Chapter 21 for a discussion of the use of salt values).

Pseudorandom Function TLS makes use of a pseudorandom function referred to as PRF to expand secrets into blocks of data for purposes of key generation or validation. The objective is to make use of a relatively small, shared secret value but to generate longer blocks of data in a way that is secure from the kinds of attacks made on hash functions and MACs. The PRF is based on the data expansion function (Figure 17.7) given as

$$\begin{aligned}\text{P\_hash(secret, seed)} = {} & \text{HMAC\_hash(secret, A(1)} \parallel \text{seed)} \parallel \\ & \text{HMAC\_hash(secret, A(2)} \parallel \text{seed)} \parallel \\ & \text{HMAC\_hash(secret, A(3)} \parallel \text{seed)} \parallel\end{aligned}$$

where A() is defined as

$$\begin{aligned}A(0) &= \text{seed} \\ A(i) &= \text{HMAC\_hash(secret, } A(i-1))\end{aligned}$$

The data expansion function makes use of the HMAC algorithm with either MD5 or SHA-1 as the underlying hash function. As can be seen, `P_hash` can be iterated as many times as necessary to produce the required quantity of data. For example, if `P_SHA256` was used to generate 80 bytes of data, it would have to be iterated three times (through A(3)), producing 96 bytes of data of which the last 16 would be discarded. In this case, `P_MD5` would have to be iterated four times, producing exactly 64 bytes of data. Note that each iteration involves two executions of HMAC, each of which in turn involves two executions of the underlying hash algorithm.

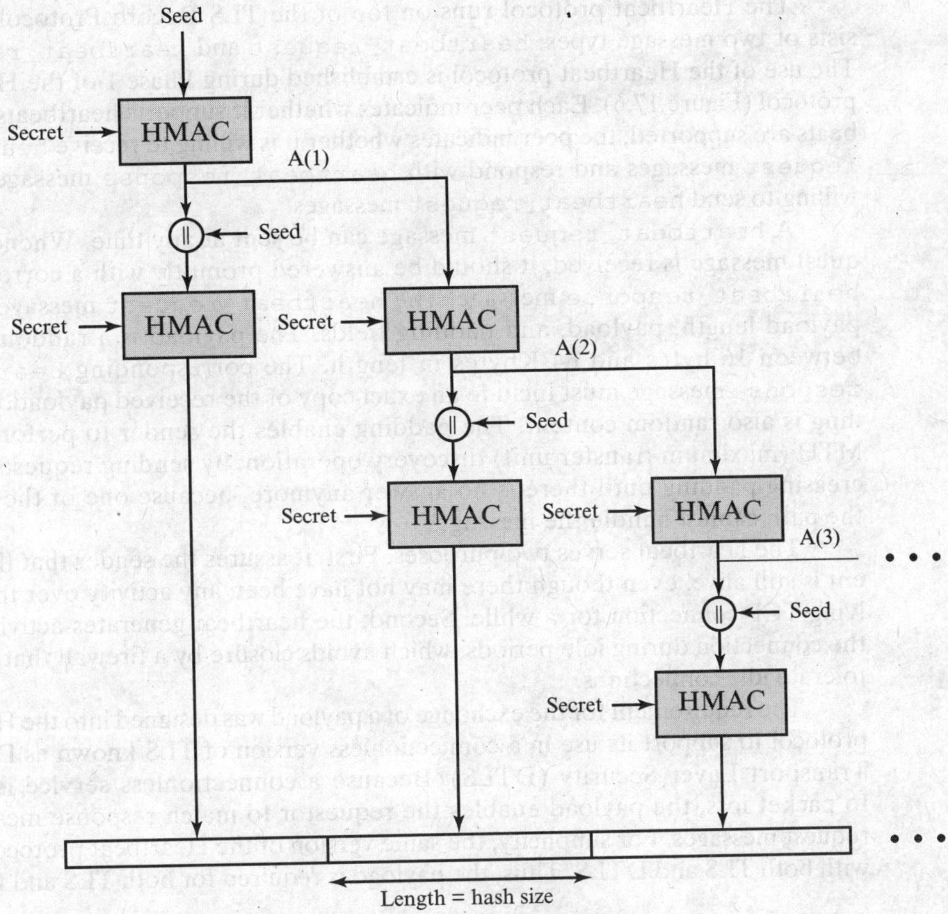

Figure 17.7 TLS Function `P_hash(secret, seed)`

To make PRF as secure as possible, it uses two hash algorithms in a way that should guarantee its security if either algorithm remains secure. PRF is defined as

PRF(secret, label, seed) = P_<hash>(secret, label || seed)

PRF takes as input a secret value, an identifying label, and a seed value and produces an output of arbitrary length.

Heartbeat Protocol

In the context of computer networks, a heartbeat is a periodic signal generated by hardware or software to indicate normal operation or to synchronize other parts of a system. A heartbeat protocol is typically used to monitor the availability of a protocol entity. In the specific case of TLS, a Heartbeat protocol was defined in 2012 in RFC 6250 (*Transport Layer Security (TLS) and Datagram Transport Layer Security (DTLS) Heartbeat Extension*).

The Heartbeat protocol runs on top of the TLS Record Protocol and consists of two message types: `heartbeat_request` and `heartbeat_response`. The use of the Heartbeat protocol is established during Phase 1 of the Handshake protocol (Figure 17.6). Each peer indicates whether it supports heartbeats. If heartbeats are supported, the peer indicates whether it is willing to receive `heartbeat_request` messages and respond with `heartbeat_response` messages or only willing to send `heartbeat_request` messages.

A `heartbeat_request` message can be sent at any time. Whenever a request message is received, it should be answered promptly with a corresponding `heartbeat_response` message. The `heartbeat_request` message includes payload length, payload, and padding fields. The payload is a random content between 16 bytes and 64 Kbytes in length. The corresponding `heartbeat_response` message must include an exact copy of the received payload. The padding is also random content. The padding enables the sender to perform a path MTU (maximum transfer unit) discovery operation, by sending requests with increasing padding until there is no answer anymore, because one of the hosts on the path cannot handle the message.

The heartbeat serves two purposes. First, it assures the sender that the recipient is still alive, even though there may not have been any activity over the underlying TCP connection for a while. Second, the heartbeat generates activity across the connection during idle periods, which avoids closure by a firewall that does not tolerate idle connections.

The requirement for the exchange of a payload was designed into the Heartbeat protocol to support its use in a connectionless version of TLS known as Datagram Transport Layer Security (DTLS). Because a connectionless service is subject to packet loss, the payload enables the requestor to match response messages to request messages. For simplicity, the same version of the Heartbeat protocol is used with both TLS and DTLS. Thus, the payload is required for both TLS and DTLS.

SSL/TLS ATTACKS

Since the first introduction of SSL in 1994, and the subsequent standardization of TLS, numerous attacks have been devised against these protocols. The appearance of each attack has necessitated changes in the protocol, the encryption tools used, or some aspect of the implementation of SSL and TLS to counter these threats.

Attack Categories We can group the attacks into four general categories:

- **Attacks on the handshake protocol:** As early as 1998, an approach to compromising the handshake protocol based on exploiting the formatting and implementation of the RSA encryption scheme was presented [BLEI98]. As countermeasures were implemented the attack was refined and adjusted to not only thwart the countermeasures but also speed up the attack [e.g., BARD12].
- **Attacks on the record and application data protocols:** A number of vulnerabilities have been discovered in these protocols, leading to patches to counter the new threats. As a recent example, in 2011, researchers Thai Duong and Juliano Rizzo demonstrated a proof of concept called BEAST (Browser Exploit Against SSL/TLS) that turned what had been considered only a theoretical vulnerability

into a practical attack [GOOD11]. BEAST leverages a type of cryptographic attack called a chosen-plaintext attack. The attacker mounts the attack by choosing a guess for the plaintext that is associated with a known ciphertext. The researchers developed a practical algorithm for launching successful attacks. Subsequent patches were able to thwart this attack. The authors of the BEAST attack are also the creators of the 2012 CRIME (Compression Ratio Info-leak Made Easy) attack, which can allow an attacker to recover the content of web cookies when data compression is used along with TLS [GOOD12]. When used to recover the content of secret authentication cookies, it allows an attacker to perform session hijacking on an authenticated web session.

- **Attacks on the PKI:** Checking the validity of X.509 certificates is an activity subject to a variety of attacks, both in the context of SSL/TLS and elsewhere. For example, [GEOR12] demonstrated that commonly used libraries for SSL/TLS suffer from vulnerable certificate validation implementations. The authors revealed weaknesses in the source code of OpenSSL, GnuTLS, JSSE, ApacheHttpClient, Weberknecht, cURL, PHP, Python and applications built upon or with these products.
- **Other attacks:** [MEYE13] lists a number of attacks that do not fit into any of the preceding categories. One example is an attack announced in 2011 by the German hacker group The Hackers Choice, which is a DoS attack [KUMA11]. The attack creates a heavy processing load on a server by overwhelming the target with SSL/TLS handshake requests. Boosting system load is done by establishing new connections or using renegotiation. Assuming that the majority of computation during a handshake is done by the server, the attack creates more system load on the server than on the source device, leading to a DoS. The server is forced to continuously recompute random numbers and keys.

The history of attacks and countermeasures for SSL/TLS is representative of that for other Internet-based protocols. A "perfect" protocol and a "perfect" implementation strategy are never achieved. A constant back-and-forth between threats and countermeasures determines the evolution of Internet-based protocols.

TLSv1.3

In 2014, the IETF TLS working group began work on a version 1.3 of TLS. The primary aim is to improve the security of TLS. As of this writing, TLSv1.3 is still in a draft stage, but the final standard is likely to be very close to the current draft. Among the significant changes from version 1.2 are the following:

- TLSv1.3 removes support for a number of options and functions. Removing code that implements functions no longer needed reduces the chances of potentially dangerous coding errors and reduces the attack surface. The deleted items include:

  –Compression
  –Ciphers that do not offer authenticated encryption
  –Static RSA and DH key exchange
  –32-bit timestamp as part of the Random parameter in the client_hello message

–Renegotiation
–Change Cipher Spec Protocol
–RC4
–Use of MD5 and SHA-224 hashes with signatures

- TLSv1.3 uses Diffie–Hellman or Elliptic Curve Diffie–Hellman for key exchange and does not permit RSA. The danger with RSA is that if the private key is compromised, all handshakes using these cipher suites will be compromised. With DH or ECDH, a new key is negotiated for each handshake.
- TLSv1.3 allows for a "1 round trip time" handshake by changing the order of message sent with establishing a secure connection. The client sends a Client Key Exchange message containing its cryptographic parameters for key establishment before a cipher suite has been negotiated. This enables a server to calculate keys for encryption and authentication before sending its first response. Reducing the number of packets sent during this handshake phase speeds up the process and reduces the attack surface.

These changes should improve the efficiency and security of TLS.

17.3 HTTPS

HTTPS (HTTP over SSL) refers to the combination of HTTP and SSL to implement secure communication between a Web browser and a Web server. The HTTPS capability is built into all modern Web browsers. Its use depends on the Web server supporting HTTPS communication. For example, some search engines do not support HTTPS.

The principal difference seen by a user of a Web browser is that URL (uniform resource locator) addresses begin with https:// rather than http://. A normal HTTP connection uses port 80. If HTTPS is specified, port 443 is used, which invokes SSL.

When HTTPS is used, the following elements of the communication are encrypted:

- URL of the requested document
- Contents of the document
- Contents of browser forms (filled in by browser user)
- Cookies sent from browser to server and from server to browser
- Contents of HTTP header

HTTPS is documented in RFC 2818, *HTTP Over TLS*. There is no fundamental change in using HTTP over either SSL or TLS, and both implementations are referred to as HTTPS.

Connection Initiation

For HTTPS, the agent acting as the HTTP client also acts as the TLS client. The client initiates a connection to the server on the appropriate port and then sends the TLS ClientHello to begin the TLS handshake. When the TLS handshake has finished, the client may then initiate the first HTTP request. All HTTP data is to be sent as TLS application data. Normal HTTP behavior, including retained connections, should be followed.

There are three levels of awareness of a connection in HTTPS. At the HTTP level, an HTTP client requests a connection to an HTTP server by sending a connection request to the next lowest layer. Typically, the next lowest layer is TCP, but it also may be TLS/SSL. At the level of TLS, a session is established between a TLS client and a TLS server. This session can support one or more connections at any time. As we have seen, a TLS request to establish a connection begins with the establishment of a TCP connection between the TCP entity on the client side and the TCP entity on the server side.

Connection Closure

An HTTP client or server can indicate the closing of a connection by including the following line in an HTTP record: `Connection: close`. This indicates that the connection will be closed after this record is delivered.

The closure of an HTTPS connection requires that TLS close the connection with the peer TLS entity on the remote side, which will involve closing the underlying TCP connection. At the TLS level, the proper way to close a connection is for each side to use the TLS alert protocol to send a `close_notify` alert. TLS implementations must initiate an exchange of closure alerts before closing a connection. A TLS implementation may, after sending a closure alert, close the connection without waiting for the peer to send its closure alert, generating an "incomplete close". Note that an implementation that does this may choose to reuse the session. This should only be done when the application knows (typically through detecting HTTP message boundaries) that it has received all the message data that it cares about.

HTTP clients also must be able to cope with a situation in which the underlying TCP connection is terminated without a prior `close_notify` alert and without a `Connection: close` indicator. Such a situation could be due to a programming error on the server or a communication error that causes the TCP connection to drop. However, the unannounced TCP closure could be evidence of some sort of attack. So the HTTPS client should issue some sort of security warning when this occurs.

17.4 SECURE SHELL (SSH)

Secure Shell (SSH) is a protocol for secure network communications designed to be relatively simple and inexpensive to implement. The initial version, SSH1 was focused on providing a secure remote logon facility to replace TELNET and other remote logon schemes that provided no security. SSH also provides a more general client/server capability and can be used for such network functions as file transfer and email. A new version, SSH2, fixes a number of security flaws in the original scheme. SSH2 is documented as a proposed standard in IETF RFCs 4250 through 4256.

SSH client and server applications are widely available for most operating systems. It has become the method of choice for remote login and X tunneling and

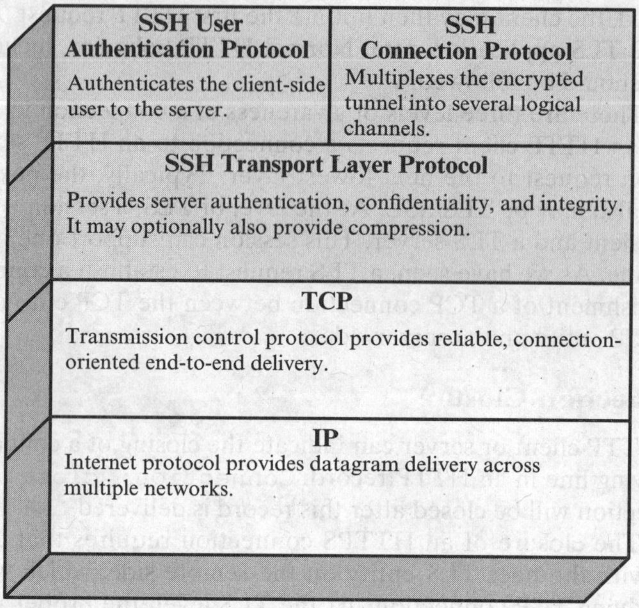

Figure 17.8 SSH Protocol Stack

is rapidly becoming one of the most pervasive applications for encryption technology outside of embedded systems.

SSH is organized as three protocols that typically run on top of TCP (Figure 17.8):

- **Transport Layer Protocol:** Provides server authentication, data confidentiality, and data integrity with forward secrecy (i.e., if a key is compromised during one session, the knowledge does not affect the security of earlier sessions). The transport layer may optionally provide compression.
- **User Authentication Protocol:** Authenticates the user to the server.
- **Connection Protocol:** Multiplexes multiple logical communications channels over a single, underlying SSH connection.

Transport Layer Protocol

HOST KEYS Server authentication occurs at the transport layer, based on the server possessing a public/private key pair. A server may have multiple host keys using multiple different asymmetric encryption algorithms. Multiple hosts may share the same host key. In any case, the server host key is used during key exchange to authenticate the identity of the host. For this to be possible, the client must have a priori knowledge of the server's public host key. RFC 4251 dictates two alternative trust models that can be used:

1. The client has a local database that associates each host name (as typed by the user) with the corresponding public host key. This method requires no centrally administered infrastructure and no third-party coordination. The downside is that the database of name-to-key associations may become burdensome to maintain.

2. The host name-to-key association is certified by a trusted certification authority (CA). The client only knows the CA root key and can verify the validity of all host keys certified by accepted CAs. This alternative eases the maintenance problem, since ideally, only a single CA key needs to be securely stored on the client. On the other hand, each host key must be appropriately certified by a central authority before authorization is possible.

PACKET EXCHANGE Figure 17.9 illustrates the sequence of events in the SSH Transport Layer Protocol. First, the client establishes a TCP connection to the server. This is done via the TCP protocol and is not part of the Transport Layer Protocol. Once the connection is established, the client and server exchange data, referred to as packets, in the data field of a TCP segment. Each packet is in the following format (Figure 17.10).

- **Packet length:** Length of the packet in bytes, not including the packet length and MAC fields.
- **Padding length:** Length of the random padding field.
- **Payload:** Useful contents of the packet. Prior to algorithm negotiation, this field is uncompressed. If compression is negotiated, then in subsequent packets, this field is compressed.

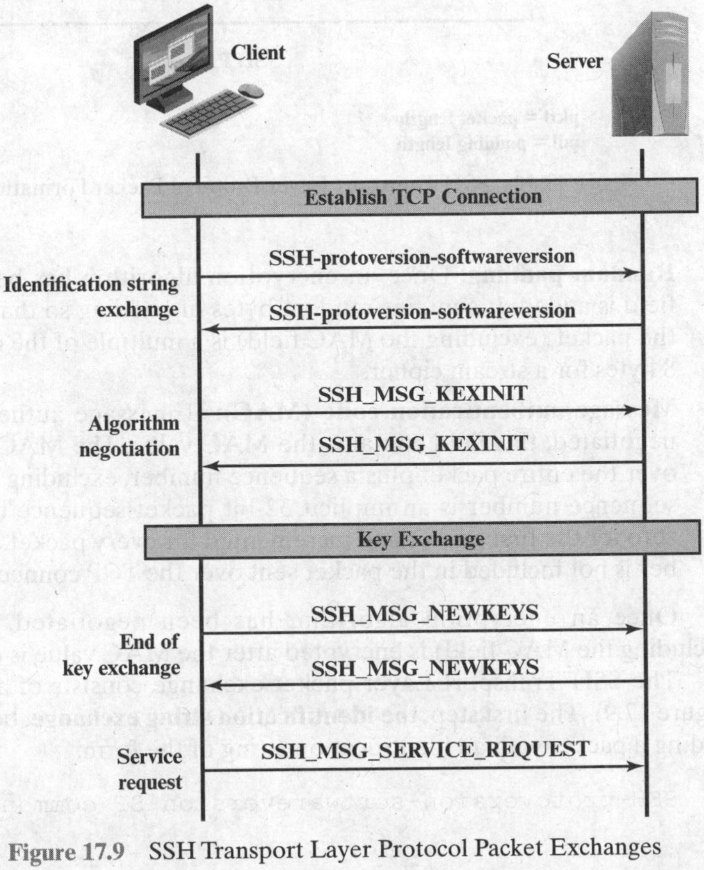

Figure 17.9 SSH Transport Layer Protocol Packet Exchanges

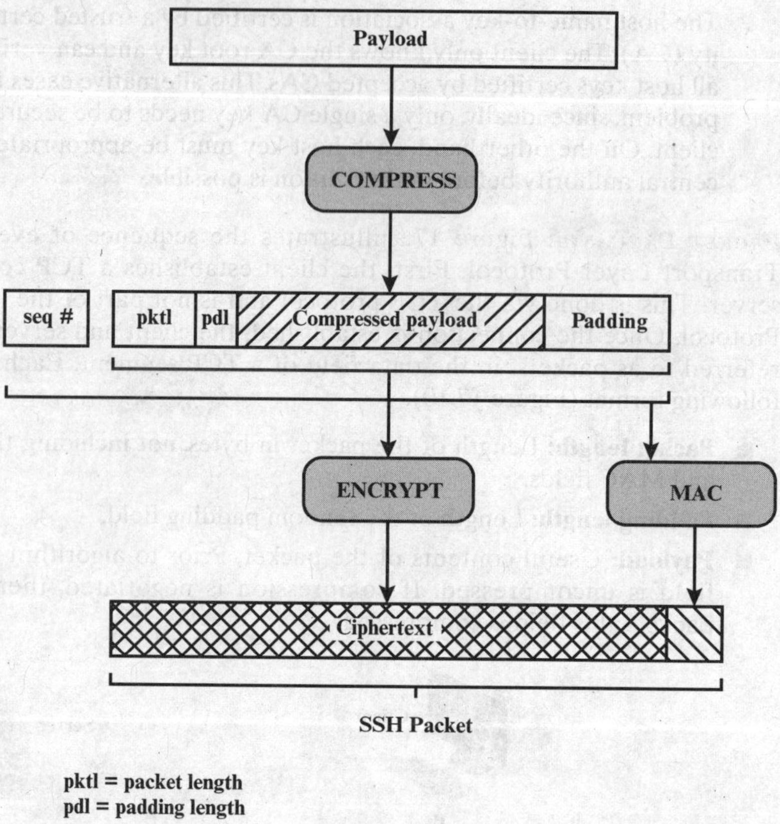

Figure 17.10 SSH Transport Layer Protocol Packet Formation

- **Random padding:** Once an encryption algorithm has been negotiated, this field is added. It contains random bytes of padding so that the total length of the packet (excluding the MAC field) is a multiple of the cipher block size, or 8 bytes for a stream cipher.
- **Message authentication code (MAC):** If message authentication has been negotiated, this field contains the MAC value. The MAC value is computed over the entire packet plus a sequence number, excluding the MAC field. The sequence number is an implicit 32-bit packet sequence that is initialized to zero for the first packet and incremented for every packet. The sequence number is not included in the packet sent over the TCP connection.

Once an encryption algorithm has been negotiated, the entire packet (excluding the MAC field) is encrypted after the MAC value is calculated.

The SSH Transport Layer packet exchange consists of a sequence of steps (Figure 17.9). The first step, the **identification string exchange**, begins with the client sending a packet with an identification string of the form:

```
SSH-protoversion-softwareversion SP comments CR LF
```

where SP, CR, and LF are space character, carriage return, and line feed, respectively. An example of a valid string is SSH-2.0-billsSSH_3.6.3q3<CR><LF>. The server responds with its own identification string. These strings are used in the Diffie–Hellman key exchange.

Next comes **algorithm negotiation**. Each side sends an SSH_MSG_KEXINIT containing lists of supported algorithms in the order of preference to the sender. There is one list for each type of cryptographic algorithm. The algorithms include key exchange, encryption, MAC algorithm, and compression algorithm. Table 17.3 shows the allowable options for encryption, MAC, and compression. For each category, the algorithm chosen is the first algorithm on the client's list that is also supported by the server.

The next step is **key exchange**. The specification allows for alternative methods of key exchange, but at present, only two versions of Diffie–Hellman key exchange are specified. Both versions are defined in RFC 2409 and require only one packet in each direction. The following steps are involved in the exchange. In this, C is the client; S is the server; *p* is a large safe prime; *g* is a generator for a subgroup of GF(*p*); *q* is the order of the subgroup; V_S is S's identification string; V_C is

Table 17.3 SSH Transport Layer Cryptographic Algorithms

Cipher	
3des-cbc*	Three-key 3DES in CBC mode
blowfish-cbc	Blowfish in CBC mode
twofish256-cbc	Twofish in CBC mode with a 256-bit key
twofish192-cbc	Twofish with a 192-bit key
twofish128-cbc	Twofish with a 128-bit key
aes256-cbc	AES in CBC mode with a 256-bit key
aes192-cbc	AES with a 192-bit key
aes128-cbc**	AES with a 128-bit key
Serpent256-cbc	Serpent in CBC mode with a 256-bit key
Serpent192-cbc	Serpent with a 192-bit key
Serpent128-cbc	Serpent with a 128-bit key
arcfour	RC4 with a 128-bit key
cast128-cbc	CAST-128 in CBC mode

MAC algorithm	
hmac-sha1*	HMAC-SHA1; digest length = key length = 20
hmac-sha1-96**	First 96 bits of HMAC-SHA1; digest length = 12; key length = 20
hmac-md5	HMAC-MD5; digest length = key length = 16
hmac-md5-96	First 96 bits of HMAC-MD5; digest length = 12; key length = 16

Compression algorithm	
none*	No compression
zlib	Defined in RFC 1950 and RFC 1951

* = Required
** = Recommended

C's identification string; `K_S` is S's public host key; `I_C` is C's `SSH_MSG_KEXINIT` message and `I_S` is S's `SSH_MSG_KEXINIT` message that have been exchanged before this part begins. The values of p, g, and q are known to both client and server as a result of the algorithm selection negotiation. The hash function `hash()` is also decided during algorithm negotiation.

1. C generates a random number $x(1 < x < q)$ and computes $e = g^x \bmod p$. C sends e to S.
2. S generates a random number $y(0 < y < q)$ and computes $f = g^y \bmod p$. S receives e. It computes $K = e^y \bmod p$, $H = \text{hash}(V\_C \| V\_S \| I\_C \| I\_S \| K\_S \| e \| f \| K)$, and signature s on H with its private host key. S sends $(K\_S \| f \| s)$ to C. The signing operation may involve a second hashing operation.
3. C verifies that K_S really is the host key for S (e.g., using certificates or a local database). C is also allowed to accept the key without verification; however, doing so will render the protocol insecure against active attacks (but may be desirable for practical reasons in the short term in many environments). C then computes $K = f^x \bmod p$, $H = \text{hash}(V\_C \| V\_S \| I\_C \| I\_S \| K\_S \| e \| f \| K)$, and verifies the signature s on H.

As a result of these steps, the two sides now share a master key K. In addition, the server has been authenticated to the client, because the server has used its private key to sign its half of the Diffie-Hellman exchange. Finally, the hash value H serves as a session identifier for this connection. Once computed, the session identifier is not changed, even if the key exchange is performed again for this connection to obtain fresh keys.

The **end of key exchange** is signaled by the exchange of `SSH_MSG_NEWKEYS` packets. At this point, both sides may start using the keys generated from K, as discussed subsequently.

The final step is **service request**. The client sends an `SSH_MSG_SERVICE_REQUEST` packet to request either the User Authentication or the Connection Protocol. Subsequent to this, all data is exchanged as the payload of an SSH Transport Layer packet, protected by encryption and MAC.

Key Generation The keys used for encryption and MAC (and any needed IVs) are generated from the shared secret key K, the hash value from the key exchange H, and the session identifier, which is equal to H unless there has been a subsequent key exchange after the initial key exchange. The values are computed as follows.

- Initial IV client to server: HASH($K \| H \|$ "A" $\|$ session_id)
- Initial IV server to client: HASH($K \| H \|$ "B" $\|$ session_id)
- Encryption key client to server: HASH($K \| H \|$ "C" $\|$ session_id)
- Encryption key server to client: HASH($K \| H \|$ "D" $\|$ session_id)
- Integrity key client to server: HASH($K \| H \|$ "E" $\|$ session_id)
- Integrity key server to client: HASH($K \| H \|$ "F" $\|$ session_id)

where `HASH()` is the hash function determined during algorithm negotiation.

User Authentication Protocol

The User Authentication Protocol provides the means by which the client is authenticated to the server.

Message Types and Formats Three types of messages are always used in the User Authentication Protocol. Authentication requests from the client have the format:

byte	`SSH_MSG_USERAUTH_REQUEST (50)`
string	user name
string	service name
string	method name
...	method specific fields

where user name is the authorization identity the client is claiming, service name is the facility to which the client is requesting access (typically the SSH Connection Protocol), and method name is the authentication method being used in this request. The first byte has decimal value 50, which is interpreted as `SSH_MSG_USERAUTH_REQUEST`.

If the server either (1) rejects the authentication request or (2) accepts the request but requires one or more additional authentication methods, the server sends a message with the format:

byte	`SSH_MSG_USERAUTH_FAILURE (51)`
name-list	authentications that can continue
boolean	partial success

where the name-list is a list of methods that may productively continue the dialog. If the server accepts authentication, it sends a single byte message: `SSH_MSG_USERAUTH_SUCCESS (52)`.

Message Exchange The message exchange involves the following steps.

1. The client sends a `SSH_MSG_USERAUTH_REQUEST` with a requested method of none.
2. The server checks to determine if the user name is valid. If not, the server returns `SSH_MSG_USERAUTH_FAILURE` with the partial success value of false. If the user name is valid, the server proceeds to step 3.
3. The server returns `SSH_MSG_USERAUTH_FAILURE` with a list of one or more authentication methods to be used.
4. The client selects one of the acceptable authentication methods and sends a `SSH_MSG_USERAUTH_REQUEST` with that method name and the required method-specific fields. At this point, there may be a sequence of exchanges to perform the method.

5. If the authentication succeeds and more authentication methods are required, the server proceeds to step 3, using a partial success value of true. If the authentication fails, the server proceeds to step 3, using a partial success value of false.
6. When all required authentication methods succeed, the server sends a `SSH_MSG_USERAUTH_SUCCESS` message, and the Authentication Protocol is over.

AUTHENTICATION METHODS The server may require one or more of the following authentication methods.

- **`publickey`**: The details of this method depend on the public-key algorithm chosen. In essence, the client sends a message to the server that contains the client's public key, with the message signed by the client's private key. When the server receives this message, it checks whether the supplied key is acceptable for authentication and, if so, it checks whether the signature is correct.
- **`password`**: The client sends a message containing a plaintext password, which is protected by encryption by the Transport Layer Protocol.
- **`hostbased`**: Authentication is performed on the client's host rather than the client itself. Thus, a host that supports multiple clients would provide authentication for all its clients. This method works by having the client send a signature created with the private key of the client host. Thus, rather than directly verifying the user's identity, the SSH server verifies the identity of the client host—and then believes the host when it says the user has already authenticated on the client side.

Connection Protocol

The SSH Connection Protocol runs on top of the SSH Transport Layer Protocol and assumes that a secure authentication connection is in use.[2] That secure authentication connection, referred to as a **tunnel,** is used by the Connection Protocol to multiplex a number of logical channels.

CHANNEL MECHANISM All types of communication using SSH, such as a terminal session, are supported using separate channels. Either side may open a channel. For each channel, each side associates a unique channel number, which need not be the same on both ends. Channels are flow controlled using a window mechanism. No data may be sent to a channel until a message is received to indicate that window space is available.

[2]RFC 4254, *The Secure Shell (SSH) Connection Protocol*, states that the Connection Protocol runs on top of the Transport Layer Protocol and the User Authentication Protocol. RFC 4251, *SSH Protocol Architecture*, states that the Connection Protocol runs over the User Authentication Protocol. In fact, the Connection Protocol runs over the Transport Layer Protocol, but assumes that the User Authentication Protocol has been previously invoked.

The life of a channel progresses through three stages: opening a channel, data transfer, and closing a channel.

When either side wishes to **open a new channel,** it allocates a local number for the channel and then sends a message of the form:

byte	SSH_MSG_CHANNEL_OPEN
string	channel type
uint32	sender channel
uint32	initial window size
uint32	maximum packet size
....	channel type specific data follows

where uint32 means unsigned 32-bit integer. The channel type identifies the application for this channel, as described subsequently. The sender channel is the local channel number. The initial window size specifies how many bytes of channel data can be sent to the sender of this message without adjusting the window. The maximum packet size specifies the maximum size of an individual data packet that can be sent to the sender. For example, one might want to use smaller packets for interactive connections to get better interactive response on slow links.

If the remote side is able to open the channel, it returns a SSH_MSG_CHANNEL_OPEN_CONFIRMATION message, which includes the sender channel number, the recipient channel number, and window and packet size values for incoming traffic. Otherwise, the remote side returns a SSH_MSG_CHANNEL_OPEN_FAILURE message with a reason code indicating the reason for failure.

Once a channel is open, **data transfer** is performed using a SSH_MSG_CHANNEL_DATA message, which includes the recipient channel number and a block of data. These messages, in both directions, may continue as long as the channel is open.

When either side wishes to **close a channel,** it sends a SSH_MSG_CHANNEL_CLOSE message, which includes the recipient channel number.

Figure 17.11 provides an example of Connection Protocol Message Exchange.

CHANNEL TYPES Four channel types are recognized in the SSH Connection Protocol specification.

- **session:** The remote execution of a program. The program may be a shell, an application such as file transfer or email, a system command, or some built-in subsystem. Once a session channel is opened, subsequent requests are used to start the remote program.
- **x11:** This refers to the X Window System, a computer software system and network protocol that provides a graphical user interface (GUI) for networked computers. X allows applications to run on a network server but to be displayed on a desktop machine.

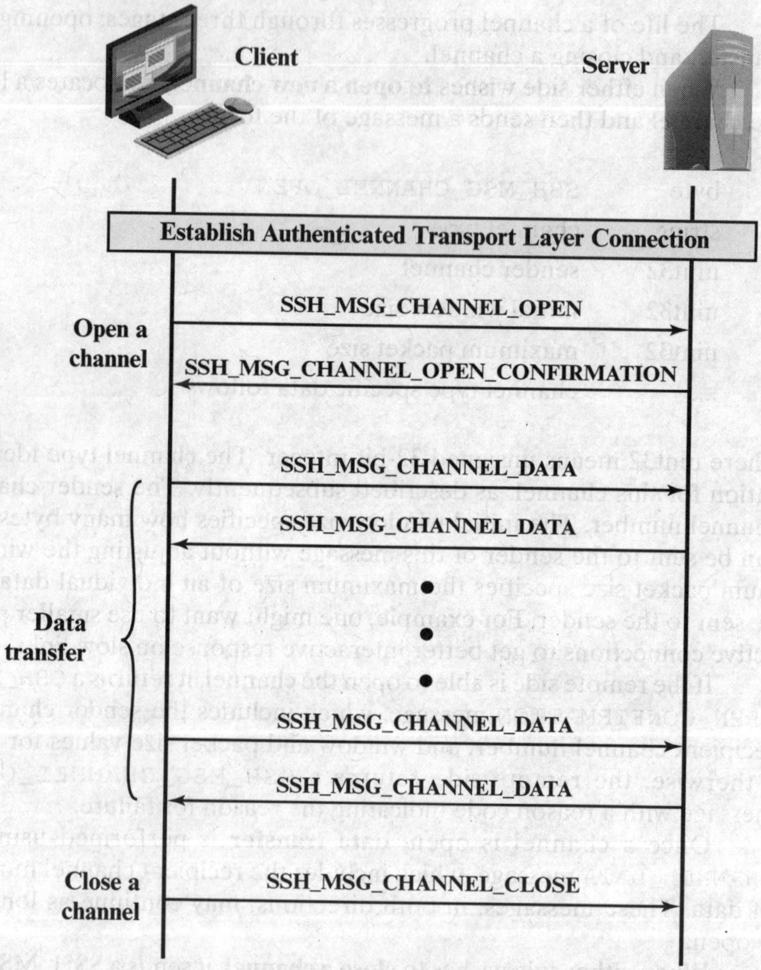

Figure 17.11 Example of SSH Connection Protocol Message Exchange

- **forwarded-tcpip:** This is remote port forwarding, as explained in the next subsection.
- **direct-tcpip:** This is local port forwarding, as explained in the next subsection.

PORT FORWARDING One of the most useful features of SSH is port forwarding. In essence, port forwarding provides the ability to convert any insecure TCP connection into a secure SSH connection. This is also referred to as SSH tunneling. We need to know what a port is in this context. A **port** is an identifier of a user of TCP. So, any application that runs on top of TCP has a port number. Incoming TCP traffic is delivered to the appropriate application on the basis of the port number. An application may employ multiple port numbers. For example, for the Simple Mail Transfer Protocol (SMTP), the server side generally listens on port 25, so an incoming SMTP request uses TCP and addresses the data to destination port 25. TCP recognizes that this is the SMTP server address and routes the data to the SMTP server application.

Figure 17.12 illustrates the basic concept behind port forwarding. We have a client application that is identified by port number *x* and a server application identified by port number *y*. At some point, the client application invokes the local TCP entity and requests a connection to the remote server on port *y*. The local TCP entity negotiates a TCP connection with the remote TCP entity, such that the connection links local port *x* to remote port *y*.

To secure this connection, SSH is configured so that the SSH Transport Layer Protocol establishes a TCP connection between the SSH client and server entities, with TCP port numbers *a* and *b*, respectively. A secure SSH tunnel is established

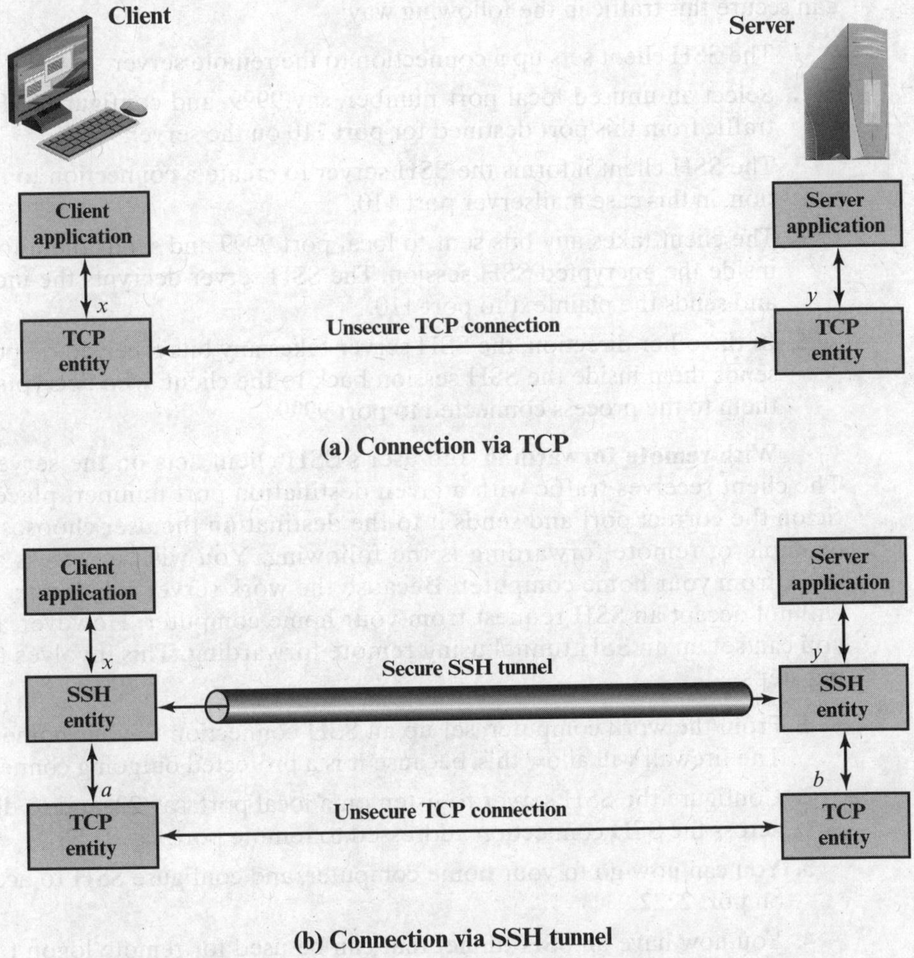

Figure 17.12 SSH Transport Layer Packet Exchanges

over this TCP connection. Traffic from the client at port x is redirected to the local SSH entity and travels through the tunnel where the remote SSH entity delivers the data to the server application on port y. Traffic in the other direction is similarly redirected.

SSH supports two types of port forwarding: local forwarding and remote forwarding. **Local forwarding** allows the client to set up a "hijacker" process. This will intercept selected application-level traffic and redirect it from an unsecured TCP connection to a secure SSH tunnel. SSH is configured to listen on selected ports. SSH grabs all traffic using a selected port and sends it through an SSH tunnel. On the other end, the SSH server sends the incoming traffic to the destination port dictated by the client application.

The following example should help clarify local forwarding. Suppose you have an email client on your desktop and use it to get email from your mail server via the Post Office Protocol (POP). The assigned port number for POP3 is port 110. We can secure this traffic in the following way:

1. The SSH client sets up a connection to the remote server.
2. Select an unused local port number, say 9999, and configure SSH to accept traffic from this port destined for port 110 on the server.
3. The SSH client informs the SSH server to create a connection to the destination, in this case mailserver port 110.
4. The client takes any bits sent to local port 9999 and sends them to the server inside the encrypted SSH session. The SSH server decrypts the incoming bits and sends the plaintext to port 110.
5. In the other direction, the SSH server takes any bits received on port 110 and sends them inside the SSH session back to the client, who decrypts and sends them to the process connected to port 9999.

With **remote forwarding**, the user's SSH client acts on the server's behalf. The client receives traffic with a given destination port number, places the traffic on the correct port and sends it to the destination the user chooses. A typical example of remote forwarding is the following. You wish to access a server at work from your home computer. Because the work server is behind a firewall, it will not accept an SSH request from your home computer. However, from work you can set up an SSH tunnel using remote forwarding. This involves the following steps.

1. From the work computer, set up an SSH connection to your home computer. The firewall will allow this, because it is a protected outgoing connection.
2. Configure the SSH server to listen on a local port, say 22, and to deliver data across the SSH connection addressed to remote port, say 2222.
3. You can now go to your home computer, and configure SSH to accept traffic on port 2222.
4. You now have an SSH tunnel that can be used for remote logon to the work server.

17.5 KEY TERMS, REVIEW QUESTIONS, AND PROBLEMS

Key Terms

Alert protocol Change Cipher Spec protocol Handshake protocol	HTTPS (HTTP over SSL) Master Secret Secure Shell (SSH)	Secure Socket Layer (SSL) Transport Layer Security (TLS)

Review Questions

17.1 What are the advantages of each of the three approaches shown in Figure 17.1?

17.2 Briefly describe about TLS.

17.3 What is the difference between a TLS connection and a TLS session?

17.4 List and briefly define the parameters that define a TLS session state.

17.5 List and briefly define the parameters that define a TLS session connection.

17.6 What services are provided by the TLS Record Protocol?

17.7 What steps are involved in the TLS Record Protocol transmission?

17.8 Which elements of the communication are encrypted when using HTTPS?

17.9 Which protocol was replaced by SSH and why? Which version is currently in the process of being standardized?

17.10 In context of SSH, what is port forwarding? What are its two types?

Problems

17.1 In SSL and TLS, why is there a separate Change Cipher Spec Protocol rather than including a `change_cipher_spec` message in the Handshake Protocol?

17.2 Consider the use of block encryption to encrypt the compressed message plus the MAC in the TLS Record Protocol. If the cipher block length is 16 bytes and the compressed plaintext plus MAC plus padding length byte is 92 bytes long, then what padding length (in bytes) can we use?

17.3 Consider the following threats to Web security and describe how each is countered by a particular feature of TLS.

a. Brute-Force Cryptanalytic Attack: An exhaustive search of the key space for a conventional encryption algorithm.

b. Known Plaintext Dictionary Attack: Many messages will contain predictable plaintext, such as the HTTP GET command. An attacker constructs a dictionary containing every possible encryption of the known-plaintext message. When an encrypted message is intercepted, the attacker takes the portion containing the encrypted known plaintext and looks up the ciphertext in the dictionary. The ciphertext should match against an entry that was encrypted with the same secret key. If there are several matches, each of these can be tried against the full ciphertext to determine the right one. This attack is especially effective against small key sizes (e.g., 40-bit keys).

c. Replay Attack: Earlier TLS handshake messages are replayed.

d. Man-in-the-Middle Attack: An attacker interposes during key exchange, acting as the client to the server and as the server to the client.

e. Password Sniffing: Passwords in HTTP or other application traffic are eavesdropped.
f. IP Spoofing: Uses forged IP addresses to fool a host into accepting bogus data.
g. IP Hijacking: An active, authenticated connection between two hosts is disrupted and the attacker takes the place of one of the hosts.
h. SYN Flooding: An attacker sends TCP SYN messages to request a connection but does not respond to the final message to establish the connection fully. The attacked TCP module typically leaves the "half-open connection" around for a few minutes. Repeated SYN messages can clog the TCP module.

17.4 Based on what you have learned in this chapter, is it possible in TLS for the receiver to reorder TLS record blocks that arrive out of order? If so, explain how it can be done. If not, why not?

17.5 SSH supports two types of port forwarding: local forwarding and remote forwarding. Discuss the differences between the two.

CHAPTER 18

WIRELESS NETWORK SECURITY

LEARNING OBJECTIVES

After studying this chapter, you should be able to:

- Present an overview of security threats and countermeasures for wireless networks.
- Understand the unique security threats posed by the use of mobile devices with enterprise networks.
- Describe the principal elements in a mobile device security strategy.
- Understand the essential elements of the IEEE 802.11 wireless LAN standard.
- Summarize the various components of the IEEE 802.11i wireless LAN security architecture.

This chapter begins with a general overview of wireless security issues. We then focus on the relatively new area of mobile device security, examining threats and countermeasures for mobile devices used in the enterprise. Then, we look at the IEEE 802.11i standard for wireless LAN security. This standard is part of IEEE 802.11, also referred to as Wi-Fi. We begin the discussion with an overview of IEEE 802.11, and then we look in some detail at IEEE 802.11i.

18.1 WIRELESS SECURITY

Wireless networks, and the wireless devices that use them, introduce a host of security problems over and above those found in wired networks. Some of the key factors contributing to the higher security risk of wireless networks compared to wired networks include the following [MA10]:

- **Channel:** Wireless networking typically involves broadcast communications, which is far more susceptible to eavesdropping and jamming than wired networks. Wireless networks are also more vulnerable to active attacks that exploit vulnerabilities in communications protocols.
- **Mobility:** Wireless devices are, in principal and usually in practice, far more portable and mobile than wired devices. This mobility results in a number of risks, described subsequently.
- **Resources:** Some wireless devices, such as smartphones and tablets, have sophisticated operating systems but limited memory and processing resources with which to counter threats, including denial of service and malware.
- **Accessibility:** Some wireless devices, such as sensors and robots, may be left unattended in remote and/or hostile locations. This greatly increases their vulnerability to physical attacks.

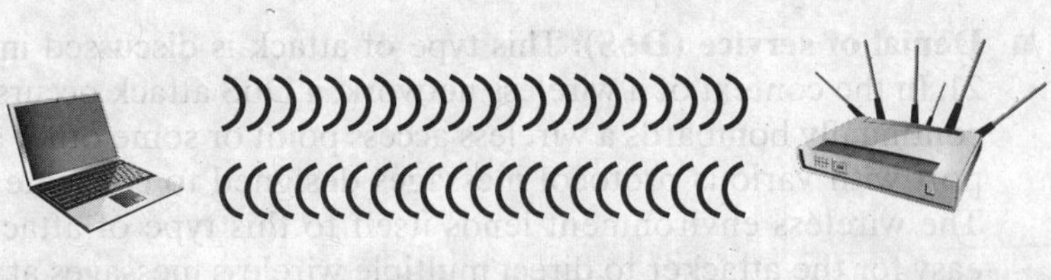

Figure 18.1 Wireless Networking Components

In simple terms, the wireless environment consists of three components that provide point of attack (Figure 18.1). The wireless client can be a cell phone, a Wi-Fi–enabled laptop or tablet, a wireless sensor, a Bluetooth device, and so on. The wireless access point provides a connection to the network or service. Examples of access points are cell towers, Wi-Fi hotspots, and wireless access points to wired local or wide area networks. The transmission medium, which carries the radio waves for data transfer, is also a source of vulnerability.

Wireless Network Threats

[CHOI08] lists the following security threats to wireless networks:

- **Accidental association:** Company wireless LANs or wireless access points to wired LANs in close proximity (e.g., in the same or neighboring buildings) may create overlapping transmission ranges. A user intending to connect to one LAN may unintentionally lock on to a wireless access point from a neighboring network. Although the security breach is accidental, it nevertheless exposes resources of one LAN to the accidental user.
- **Malicious association:** In this situation, a wireless device is configured to appear to be a legitimate access point, enabling the operator to steal passwords from legitimate users and then penetrate a wired network through a legitimate wireless access point.
- **Ad hoc networks:** These are peer-to-peer networks between wireless computers with no access point between them. Such networks can pose a security threat due to a lack of a central point of control.
- **Nontraditional networks:** Nontraditional networks and links, such as personal network Bluetooth devices, barcode readers, and handheld PDAs, pose a security risk in terms of both eavesdropping and spoofing.
- **Identity theft (MAC spoofing):** This occurs when an attacker is able to eavesdrop on network traffic and identify the MAC address of a computer with network privileges.
- **Man-in-the middle attacks:** This type of attack is described in Chapter 10 in the context of the Diffie–Hellman key exchange protocol. In a broader sense, this attack involves persuading a user and an access point to believe that they are talking to each other when in fact the communication is going through an intermediate attacking device. Wireless networks are particularly vulnerable to such attacks.

- **Denial of service (DoS):** This type of attack is discussed in detail in Chapter 21. In the context of a wireless network, a DoS attack occurs when an attacker continually bombards a wireless access point or some other accessible wireless port with various protocol messages designed to consume system resources. The wireless environment lends itself to this type of attack, because it is so easy for the attacker to direct multiple wireless messages at the target.
- **Network injection:** A network injection attack targets wireless access points that are exposed to nonfiltered network traffic, such as routing protocol messages or network management messages. An example of such an attack is one in which bogus reconfiguration commands are used to affect routers and switches to degrade network performance.

Wireless Security Measures

Following [CHOI08], we can group wireless security measures into those dealing with wireless transmissions, wireless access points, and wireless networks (consisting of wireless routers and endpoints).

Securing Wireless Transmissions The principal threats to wireless transmission are eavesdropping, altering or inserting messages, and disruption. To deal with eavesdropping, two types of countermeasures are appropriate:

- **Signal-hiding techniques:** Organizations can take a number of measures to make it more difficult for an attacker to locate their wireless access points, including turning off service set identifier (SSID) broadcasting by wireless access points; assigning cryptic names to SSIDs; reducing signal strength to the lowest level that still provides requisite coverage; and locating wireless access points in the interior of the building, away from windows and exterior walls. Greater security can be achieved by the use of directional antennas and of signal-shielding techniques.
- **Encryption:** Encryption of all wireless transmission is effective against eavesdropping to the extent that the encryption keys are secured.

The use of encryption and authentication protocols is the standard method of countering attempts to alter or insert transmissions.

The methods discussed in Chapter 21 for dealing with DoS apply to wireless transmissions. Organizations can also reduce the risk of unintentional DoS attacks. Site surveys can detect the existence of other devices using the same frequency range, to help determine where to locate wireless access points. Signal strengths can be adjusted and shielding used in an attempt to isolate a wireless environment from competing nearby transmissions.

Securing Wireless Access Points The main threat involving wireless access points is unauthorized access to the network. The principal approach for preventing such access is the IEEE 802.1X standard for port-based network access control. The standard provides an authentication mechanism for devices wishing to attach to a LAN or wireless network. The use of 802.1X can prevent rogue access points and other unauthorized devices from becoming insecure backdoors.

Section 16.3 provides an introduction to 802.1X.

Securing Wireless Networks [CHOI08] recommends the following techniques for wireless network security:

1. Use encryption. Wireless routers are typically equipped with built-in encryption mechanisms for router-to-router traffic.
2. Use antivirus and antispyware software, and a firewall. These facilities should be enabled on all wireless network endpoints.
3. Turn off identifier broadcasting. Wireless routers are typically configured to broadcast an identifying signal so that any device within range can learn of the router's existence. If a network is configured so that authorized devices know the identity of routers, this capability can be disabled, so as to thwart attackers.
4. Change the identifier on your router from the default. Again, this measure thwarts attackers who will attempt to gain access to a wireless network using default router identifiers.
5. Change your router's pre-set password for administration. This is another prudent step.
6. Allow only specific computers to access your wireless network. A router can be configured to only communicate with approved MAC addresses. Of course, MAC addresses can be spoofed, so this is just one element of a security strategy.

18.2 MOBILE DEVICE SECURITY

Prior to the widespread use of smartphones, the dominant paradigm for computer and network security in organizations was as follows. Corporate IT was tightly controlled. User devices were typically limited to Windows PCs. Business applications were controlled by IT and either run locally on endpoints or on physical servers in data centers. Network security was based upon clearly defined perimeters that separated trusted internal networks from the untrusted Internet. Today, there have been massive changes in each of these assumptions. An organization's networks must accommodate the following:

- **Growing use of new devices:** Organizations are experiencing significant growth in employee use of mobile devices. In many cases, employees are allowed to use a combination of endpoint devices as part of their day-to-day activities.
- **Cloud-based applications:** Applications no longer run solely on physical servers in corporate data centers. Quite the opposite, applications can run anywhere—on traditional physical servers, on mobile virtual servers, or in the cloud. Additionally, end users can now take advantage of a wide variety of cloud-based applications and IT services for personal and professional use. Facebook can be used for an employee's personal profiles or as a component of a corporate marketing campaign. Employees depend upon Skype to speak with friends abroad or for legitimate business video conferencing. Dropbox and Box can be used to distribute documents between corporate and personal devices for mobility and user productivity.

- **De-perimeterization:** Given new device proliferation, application mobility, and cloud-based consumer and corporate services, the notion of a static network perimeter is all but gone. Now there are a multitude of network perimeters around devices, applications, users, and data. These perimeters have also become quite dynamic as they must adapt to various environmental conditions such as user role, device type, server virtualization mobility, network location, and time-of-day.
- **External business requirements:** The enterprise must also provide guests, third-party contractors, and business partners network access using various devices from a multitude of locations.

The central element in all of these changes is the mobile computing device. Mobile devices have become an essential element for organizations as part of the overall network infrastructure. Mobile devices such as smartphones, tablets, and memory sticks provide increased convenience for individuals as well as the potential for increased productivity in the workplace. Because of their widespread use and unique characteristics, security for mobile devices is a pressing and complex issue. In essence, an organization needs to implement a security policy through a combination of security features built into the mobile devices and additional security controls provided by network components that regulate the use of the mobile devices.

Security Threats

Mobile devices need additional, specialized protection measures beyond those implemented for other client devices, such as desktop and laptop devices that are used only within the organization's facilities and on the organization's networks. SP 800-14 (*Guidelines for Managing and Securing Mobile Devices in the Enterprise*, July 2012) lists seven major security concerns for mobile devices. We examine each of these in turn.

Lack of Physical Security Controls Mobile devices are typically under the complete control of the user, and are used and kept in a variety of locations outside the organization's control, including off premises. Even if a device is required to remain on premises, the user may move the device within the organization between secure and nonsecured locations. Thus, theft and tampering are realistic threats.

The security policy for mobile devices must be based on the assumption that any mobile device may be stolen or at least accessed by a malicious party. The threat is twofold: A malicious party may attempt to recover sensitive data from the device itself, or may use the device to gain access to the organization's resources.

Use of Untrusted Mobile Devices In addition to company-issued and company-controlled mobile devices, virtually all employees will have personal smartphones and/or tablets. The organization must assume that these devices are not trustworthy. That is, the devices may not employ encryption and either the user or a third party may have installed a bypass to the built-in restrictions on security, operating system use, and so on.

Use of Untrusted Networks If a mobile device is used on premises, it can connect to organization resources over the organization's own in-house wireless networks. However, for off-premises use, the user will typically access organizational resources via Wi-Fi or cellular access to the Internet and from the Internet to the organization. Thus, traffic that includes an off-premises segment is potentially susceptible to eavesdropping or man-in-the-middle types of attacks. Thus, the security policy must be based on the assumption that the networks between the mobile device and the organization are not trustworthy.

Use of Applications Created by Unknown Parties By design, it is easy to find and install third-party applications on mobile devices. This poses the obvious risk of installing malicious software. An organization has several options for dealing with this threat, as described subsequently.

Interaction with Other Systems A common feature found on smartphones and tablets is the ability to automatically synchronize data, apps, contacts, photos, and so on with other computing devices and with cloud-based storage. Unless an organization has control of all the devices involved in synchronization, there is considerable risk of the organization's data being stored in an unsecured location, plus the risk of the introduction of malware.

Use of Untrusted Content Mobile devices may access and use content that other computing devices do not encounter. An example is the Quick Response (QR) code, which is a two-dimensional barcode. QR codes are designed to be captured by a mobile device camera and used by the mobile device. The QR code translates to a URL, so that a malicious QR code could direct the mobile device to malicious Web sites.

Use of Location Services The GPS capability on mobile devices can be used to maintain a knowledge of the physical location of the device. While this feature might be useful to an organization as part of a presence service, it creates security risks. An attacker can use the location information to determine where the device and user are located, which may be of use to the attacker.

Mobile Device Security Strategy

With the threats listed in the preceding discussion in mind, we outline the principal elements of a mobile device security strategy. They fall into three categories: device security, client/server traffic security, and barrier security (Figure 18.2).

Device Security A number of organizations will supply mobile devices for employee use and preconfigure those devices to conform to the enterprise security policy. However, many organizations will find it convenient or even necessary to adopt a bring-your-own-device (BYOD) policy that allows the personal mobile devices of employees to have access to corporate resources. IT managers should be able to inspect each device before allowing network access. IT will want to establish configuration guidelines for operating systems and applications. For example, "rooted" or "jail-broken" devices are not permitted on the network, and mobile

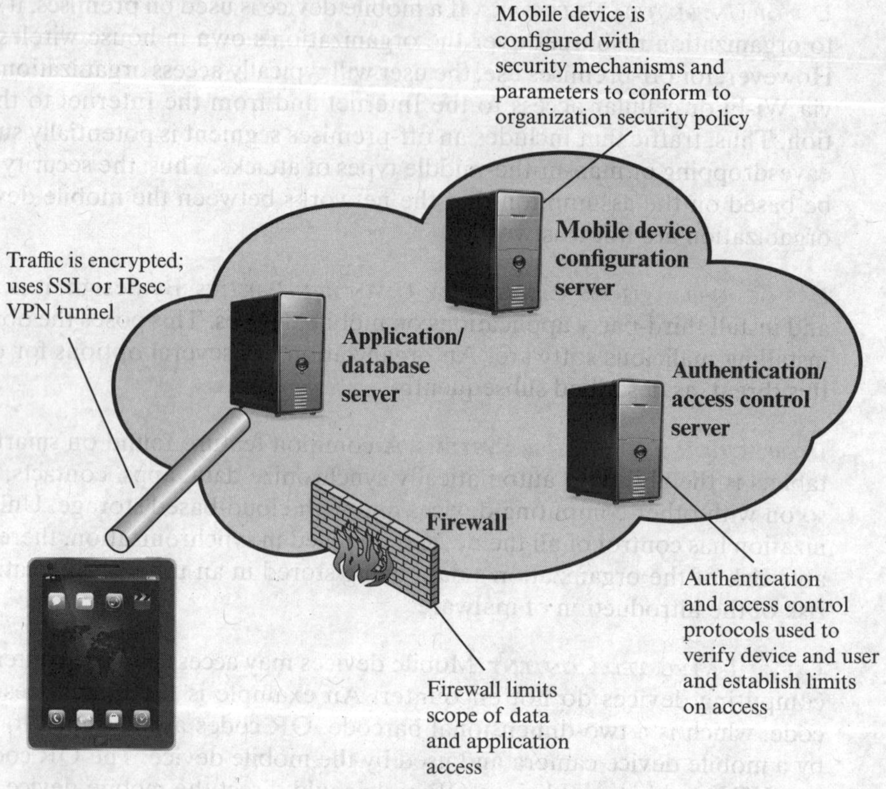

Figure 18.2 Mobile Device Security Elements

devices cannot store corporate contacts on local storage. Whether a device is owned by the organization or BYOD, the organization should configure the device with security controls, including the following:

- Enable auto-lock, which causes the device to lock if it has not been used for a given amount of time, requiring the user to re-enter a four-digit PIN or a password to re-activate the device.
- Enable password or PIN protection. The PIN or password is needed to unlock the device. In addition, it can be configured so that email and other data on the device are encrypted using the PIN or password and can only be retrieved with the PIN or password.
- Avoid using auto-complete features that remember user names or passwords.
- Enable remote wipe.
- Ensure that SSL protection is enabled, if available.
- Make sure that software, including operating systems and applications, is up to date.
- Install antivirus software as it becomes available.

- Either sensitive data should be prohibited from storage on the mobile device or it should be encrypted.
- IT staff should also have the ability to remotely access devices, wipe the device of all data, and then disable the device in the event of loss or theft.
- The organization may prohibit all installation of third-party applications, implement whitelisting to prohibit installation of all unapproved applications, or implement a secure sandbox that isolates the organization's data and applications from all other data and applications on the mobile device. Any application that is on an approved list should be accompanied by a digital signature and a public-key certificate from an approved authority.
- The organization can implement and enforce restrictions on what devices can synchronize and on the use of cloud-based storage.
- To deal with the threat of untrusted content, security responses can include training of personnel on the risks inherent in untrusted content and disabling camera use on corporate mobile devices.
- To counter the threat of malicious use of location services, the security policy can dictate that such service is disabled on all mobile devices.

Traffic Security Traffic security is based on the usual mechanisms for encryption and authentication. All traffic should be encrypted and travel by secure means, such as SSL or IPv6. Virtual private networks (VPNs) can be configured so that all traffic between the mobile device and the organization's network is via a VPN.

A strong authentication protocol should be used to limit the access from the device to the resources of the organization. Often, a mobile device has a single device-specific authenticator, because it is assumed that the device has only one user. A preferable strategy is to have a two-layer authentication mechanism, which involves authenticating the device and then authenticating the user of the device.

Barrier Security The organization should have security mechanisms to protect the network from unauthorized access. The security strategy can also include firewall policies specific to mobile device traffic. Firewall policies can limit the scope of data and application access for all mobile devices. Similarly, intrusion detection and intrusion prevention systems can be configured to have tighter rules for mobile device traffic.

18.3 IEEE 802.11 WIRELESS LAN OVERVIEW

IEEE 802 is a committee that has developed standards for a wide range of local area networks (LANs). In 1990, the IEEE 802 Committee formed a new working group, IEEE 802.11, with a charter to develop a protocol and transmission specifications for wireless LANs (WLANs). Since that time, the demand for WLANs at different frequencies and data rates has exploded. Keeping pace with this demand, the IEEE 802.11 working group has issued an ever-expanding list of standards. Table 18.1 briefly defines key terms used in the IEEE 802.11 standard.

Table 18.1 IEEE 802.11 Terminology

Access point (AP)	Any entity that has station functionality and provides access to the distribution system via the wireless medium for associated stations.
Basic service set (BSS)	A set of stations controlled by a single coordination function.
Coordination function	The logical function that determines when a station operating within a BSS is permitted to transmit and may be able to receive PDUs.
Distribution system (DS)	A system used to interconnect a set of BSSs and integrated LANs to create an ESS.
Extended service set (ESS)	A set of one or more interconnected BSSs and integrated LANs that appear as a single BSS to the LLC layer at any station associated with one of these BSSs.
MAC protocol data unit (MPDU)	The unit of data exchanged between two peer MAC entities using the services of the physical layer.
MAC service data unit (MSDU)	Information that is delivered as a unit between MAC users.
Station	Any device that contains an IEEE 802.11 conformant MAC and physical layer.

The Wi-Fi Alliance

The first 802.11 standard to gain broad industry acceptance was 802.11b. Although 802.11b products are all based on the same standard, there is always a concern whether products from different vendors will successfully interoperate. To meet this concern, the Wireless Ethernet Compatibility Alliance (WECA), an industry consortium, was formed in 1999. This organization, subsequently renamed the Wi-Fi (Wireless Fidelity) Alliance, created a test suite to certify interoperability for 802.11b products. The term used for certified 802.11b products is *Wi-Fi*. Wi-Fi certification has been extended to 802.11g products. The Wi-Fi Alliance has also developed a certification process for 802.11a products, called *Wi-Fi5*. The Wi-Fi Alliance is concerned with a range of market areas for WLANs, including enterprise, home, and hot spots.

More recently, the Wi-Fi Alliance has developed certification procedures for IEEE 802.11 security standards, referred to as Wi-Fi Protected Access (WPA). The most recent version of WPA, known as WPA2, incorporates all of the features of the IEEE 802.11i WLAN security specification.

IEEE 802 Protocol Architecture

Before proceeding, we need to briefly preview the IEEE 802 protocol architecture. IEEE 802.11 standards are defined within the structure of a layered set of protocols. This structure, used for all IEEE 802 standards, is illustrated in Figure 18.3.

Physical Layer The lowest layer of the IEEE 802 reference model is the **physical layer**, which includes such functions as encoding/decoding of signals and bit transmission/reception. In addition, the physical layer includes a specification of the transmission medium. In the case of IEEE 802.11, the physical layer also defines frequency bands and antenna characteristics.

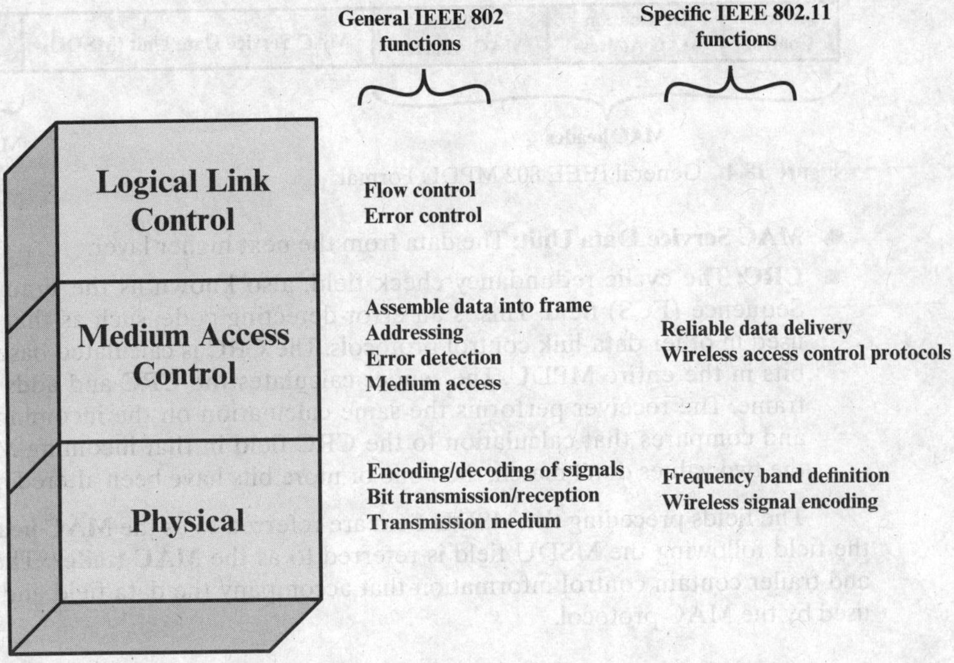

Figure 18.3 IEEE 802.11 Protocol Stack

MEDIA ACCESS CONTROL All LANs consist of collections of devices that share the network's transmission capacity. Some means of controlling access to the transmission medium is needed to provide an orderly and efficient use of that capacity. This is the function of a **media access control (MAC)** layer. The MAC layer receives data from a higher-layer protocol, typically the Logical Link Control (LLC) layer, in the form of a block of data known as the **MAC service data unit (MSDU)**. In general, the MAC layer performs the following functions:

- On transmission, assemble data into a frame, known as a **MAC protocol data unit (MPDU)** with address and error-detection fields.
- On reception, disassemble frame, and perform address recognition and error detection.
- Govern access to the LAN transmission medium.

The exact format of the MPDU differs somewhat for the various MAC protocols in use. In general, all of the MPDUs have a format similar to that of Figure 18.4. The fields of this frame are as follows.

- **MAC Control:** This field contains any protocol control information needed for the functioning of the MAC protocol. For example, a priority level could be indicated here.
- **Destination MAC Address:** The destination physical address on the LAN for this MPDU.
- **Source MAC Address:** The source physical address on the LAN for this MPDU.

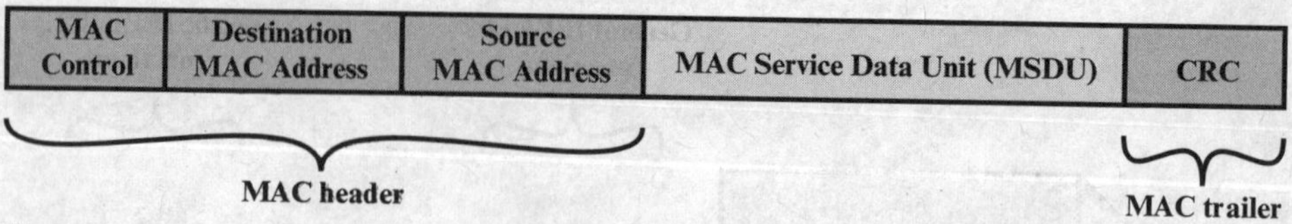

Figure 18.4 General IEEE 802 MPDU Format

- **MAC Service Data Unit:** The data from the next higher layer.
- **CRC:** The cyclic redundancy check field; also known as the Frame Check Sequence (FCS) field. This is an error-detecting code, such as that which is used in other data-link control protocols. The CRC is calculated based on the bits in the entire MPDU. The sender calculates the CRC and adds it to the frame. The receiver performs the same calculation on the incoming MPDU and compares that calculation to the CRC field in that incoming MPDU. If the two values don't match, then one or more bits have been altered in transit.

The fields preceding the MSDU field are referred to as the **MAC header**, and the field following the MSDU field is referred to as the **MAC trailer**. The header and trailer contain control information that accompany the data field and that are used by the MAC protocol.

Logical Link Control In most data-link control protocols, the data-link protocol entity is responsible not only for detecting errors using the CRC, but for recovering from those errors by retransmitting damaged frames. In the LAN protocol architecture, these two functions are split between the MAC and LLC layers. The MAC layer is responsible for detecting errors and discarding any frames that contain errors. The LLC layer optionally keeps track of which frames have been successfully received and retransmits unsuccessful frames.

IEEE 802.11 Network Components and Architectural Model

Figure 18.5 illustrates the model developed by the 802.11 working group. The smallest building block of a wireless LAN is a **basic service set (BSS)**, which consists of wireless stations executing the same MAC protocol and competing for access to the same shared wireless medium. A BSS may be isolated, or it may connect to a backbone **distribution system (DS)** through an **access point (AP)**. The AP functions as a bridge and a relay point. In a BSS, client stations do not communicate directly with one another. Rather, if one station in the BSS wants to communicate with another station in the same BSS, the MAC frame is first sent from the originating station to the AP and then from the AP to the destination station. Similarly, a MAC frame from a station in the BSS to a remote station is sent from the local station to the AP and then relayed by the AP over the DS on its way to the destination station. The BSS generally corresponds to what is referred to as a cell in the literature. The DS can be a switch, a wired network, or a wireless network.

When all the stations in the BSS are mobile stations that communicate directly with one another (not using an AP), the BSS is called an **independent BSS (IBSS)**. An IBSS is typically an ad hoc network. In an IBSS, the stations all communicate directly, and no AP is involved.

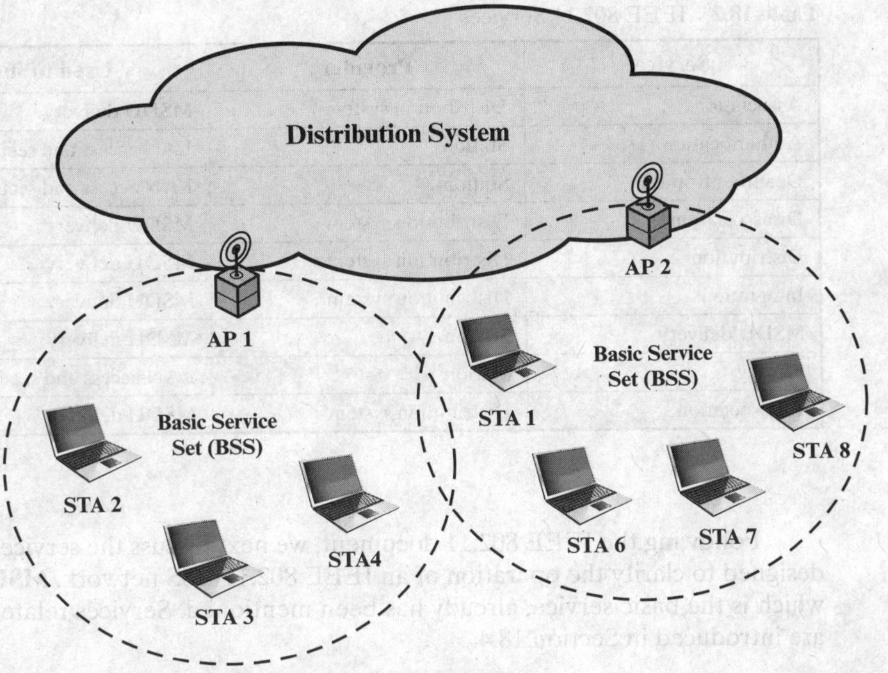

Figure 18.5 IEEE 802.11 Extended Service Set

A simple configuration is shown in Figure 18.5, in which each station belongs to a single BSS; that is, each station is within wireless range only of other stations within the same BSS. It is also possible for two BSSs to overlap geographically, so that a single station could participate in more than one BSS. Furthermore, the association between a station and a BSS is dynamic. Stations may turn off, come within range, and go out of range.

An **extended service set (ESS)** consists of two or more basic service sets interconnected by a distribution system. The extended service set appears as a single logical LAN to the logical link control (LLC) level.

IEEE 802.11 Services

IEEE 802.11 defines nine services that need to be provided by the wireless LAN to achieve functionality equivalent to that which is inherent to wired LANs. Table 18.2 lists the services and indicates two ways of categorizing them.

1. The service provider can be either the station or the DS. Station services are implemented in every 802.11 station, including AP stations. Distribution services are provided between BSSs; these services may be implemented in an AP or in another special-purpose device attached to the distribution system.
2. Three of the services are used to control IEEE 802.11 LAN access and confidentiality. Six of the services are used to support delivery of MSDUs between stations. If the MSDU is too large to be transmitted in a single MPDU, it may be fragmented and transmitted in a series of MPDUs.

Table 18.2 IEEE 802.11 Services

Service	Provider	Used to support
Association	Distribution system	MSDU delivery
Authentication	Station	LAN access and security
Deauthentication	Station	LAN access and security
Disassociation	Distribution system	MSDU delivery
Distribution	Distribution system	MSDU delivery
Integration	Distribution system	MSDU delivery
MSDU delivery	Station	MSDU delivery
Privacy	Station	LAN access and security
Reassociation	Distribution system	MSDU delivery

Following the IEEE 802.11 document, we next discuss the services in an order designed to clarify the operation of an IEEE 802.11 ESS network. **MSDU delivery**, which is the basic service, already has been mentioned. Services related to security are introduced in Section 18.4.

DISTRIBUTION OF MESSAGES WITHIN A DS The two services involved with the distribution of messages within a DS are distribution and integration. **Distribution** is the primary service used by stations to exchange MPDUs when the MPDUs must traverse the DS to get from a station in one BSS to a station in another BSS. For example, suppose a frame is to be sent from station 2 (STA 2) to station 7 (STA 7) in Figure 18.5. The frame is sent from STA 2 to AP 1, which is the AP for this BSS. The AP gives the frame to the DS, which has the job of directing the frame to the AP associated with STA 7 in the target BSS. AP 2 receives the frame and forwards it to STA 7. How the message is transported through the DS is beyond the scope of the IEEE 802.11 standard.

If the two stations that are communicating are within the same BSS, then the distribution service logically goes through the single AP of that BSS.

The **integration** service enables transfer of data between a station on an IEEE 802.11 LAN and a station on an integrated IEEE 802.x LAN. The term *integrated* refers to a wired LAN that is physically connected to the DS and whose stations may be logically connected to an IEEE 802.11 LAN via the integration service. The integration service takes care of any address translation and media conversion logic required for the exchange of data.

ASSOCIATION-RELATED SERVICES The primary purpose of the MAC layer is to transfer MSDUs between MAC entities; this purpose is fulfilled by the distribution service. For that service to function, it requires information about stations within the ESS that is provided by the association-related services. Before the distribution service can deliver data to or accept data from a station, that station must be *associated*. Before looking at the concept of association, we need to describe the concept of mobility. The standard defines three transition types, based on mobility:

- **No transition:** A station of this type is either stationary or moves only within the direct communication range of the communicating stations of a single BSS.
- **BSS transition:** This is defined as a station movement from one BSS to another BSS within the same ESS. In this case, delivery of data to the station requires that the addressing capability be able to recognize the new location of the station.
- **ESS transition:** This is defined as a station movement from a BSS in one ESS to a BSS within another ESS. This case is supported only in the sense that the station can move. Maintenance of upper-layer connections supported by 802.11 cannot be guaranteed. In fact, disruption of service is likely to occur.

To deliver a message within a DS, the distribution service needs to know where the destination station is located. Specifically, the DS needs to know the identity of the AP to which the message should be delivered in order for that message to reach the destination station. To meet this requirement, a station must maintain an association with the AP within its current BSS. Three services relate to this requirement:

- **Association:** Establishes an initial association between a station and an AP. Before a station can transmit or receive frames on a wireless LAN, its identity and address must be known. For this purpose, a station must establish an association with an AP within a particular BSS. The AP can then communicate this information to other APs within the ESS to facilitate routing and delivery of addressed frames.
- **Reassociation:** Enables an established association to be transferred from one AP to another, allowing a mobile station to move from one BSS to another.
- **Disassociation:** A notification from either a station or an AP that an existing association is terminated. A station should give this notification before leaving an ESS or shutting down. However, the MAC management facility protects itself against stations that disappear without notification.

18.4 IEEE 802.11i WIRELESS LAN SECURITY

There are two characteristics of a wired LAN that are not inherent in a wireless LAN.

1. In order to transmit over a wired LAN, a station must be physically connected to the LAN. On the other hand, with a wireless LAN, any station within radio range of the other devices on the LAN can transmit. In a sense, there is a form of authentication with a wired LAN in that it requires some positive and presumably observable action to connect a station to a wired LAN.
2. Similarly, in order to receive a transmission from a station that is part of a wired LAN, the receiving station also must be attached to the wired LAN. On the other hand, with a wireless LAN, any station within radio range can receive. Thus, a wired LAN provides a degree of privacy, limiting reception of data to stations connected to the LAN.

These differences between wired and wireless LANs suggest the increased need for robust security services and mechanisms for wireless LANs. The original 802.11 specification included a set of security features for privacy and authentication that were quite weak. For privacy, 802.11 defined the **Wired Equivalent Privacy (WEP)** algorithm. The privacy portion of the 802.11 standard contained major weaknesses. Subsequent to the development of WEP, the 802.11i task group has developed a set of capabilities to address the WLAN security issues. In order to accelerate the introduction of strong security into WLANs, the Wi-Fi Alliance promulgated **Wi-Fi Protected Access (WPA)** as a Wi-Fi standard. WPA is a set of security mechanisms that eliminates most 802.11 security issues and was based on the current state of the 802.11i standard. The final form of the 802.11i standard is referred to as **Robust Security Network (RSN)**. The Wi-Fi Alliance certifies vendors in compliance with the full 802.11i specification under the WPA2 program.

The RSN specification is quite complex, and occupies 145 pages of the 2012 IEEE 802.11 standard. In this section, we provide an overview.

IEEE 802.11i Services

The 802.11i RSN security specification defines the following services.

- **Authentication:** A protocol is used to define an exchange between a user and an AS that provides mutual authentication and generates temporary keys to be used between the client and the AP over the wireless link.
- **Access control:**[1] This function enforces the use of the authentication function, routes the messages properly, and facilitates key exchange. It can work with a variety of authentication protocols.
- **Privacy with message integrity:** MAC-level data (e.g., an LLC PDU) are encrypted along with a message integrity code that ensures that the data have not been altered.

Figure 18.6a indicates the security protocols used to support these services, while Figure 18.6b lists the cryptographic algorithms used for these services.

IEEE 802.11i Phases of Operation

The operation of an IEEE 802.11i RSN can be broken down into five distinct phases of operation. The exact nature of the phases will depend on the configuration and the end points of the communication. Possibilities include (see Figure 18.5):

1. Two wireless stations in the same BSS communicating via the access point (AP) for that BSS.
2. Two wireless stations (STAs) in the same ad hoc IBSS communicating directly with each other.

[1] In this context, we are discussing access control as a security function. This is a different function than media access control (MAC) as described in Section 18.3. Unfortunately, the literature and the standards use the term *access control* in both contexts.

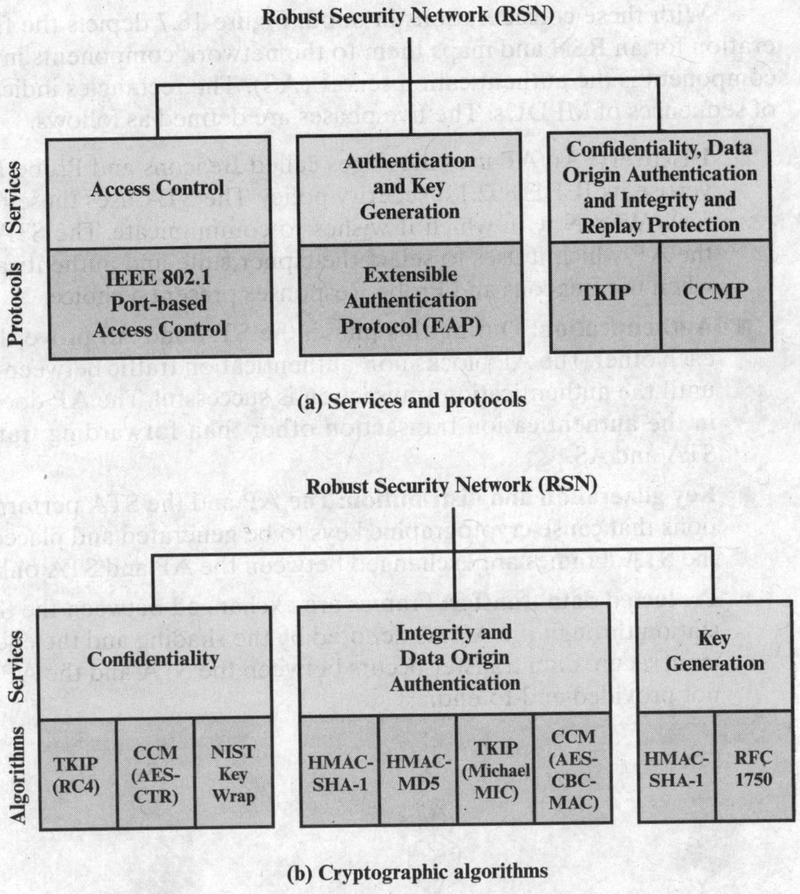

CBC-MAC	=	Cipher Block Chaining Message Authentication Code (MAC)
CCM	=	Counter Mode with Cipher Block Chaining Message Authentication Code
CCMP	=	Counter Mode with Cipher Block Chaining MAC Protocol
TKIP	=	Temporal Key Integrity Protocol

Figure 18.6 Elements of IEEE 802.11i

3. Two wireless stations in different BSSs communicating via their respective APs across a distribution system.
4. A wireless station communicating with an end station on a wired network via its AP and the distribution system.

IEEE 802.11i security is concerned only with secure communication between the STA and its AP. In case 1 in the preceding list, secure communication is assured if each STA establishes secure communications with the AP. Case 2 is similar, with the AP functionality residing in the STA. For case 3, security is not provided across the distribution system at the level of IEEE 802.11, but only within each BSS. End-to-end security (if required) must be provided at a higher layer. Similarly, in case 4, security is only provided between the STA and its AP.

With these considerations in mind, Figure 18.7 depicts the five phases of operation for an RSN and maps them to the network components involved. One new component is the authentication server (AS). The rectangles indicate the exchange of sequences of MPDUs. The five phases are defined as follows.

- **Discovery:** An AP uses messages called Beacons and Probe Responses to advertise its IEEE 802.11i security policy. The STA uses these to identify an AP for a WLAN with which it wishes to communicate. The STA associates with the AP, which it uses to select the cipher suite and authentication mechanism when the Beacons and Probe Responses present a choice.
- **Authentication:** During this phase, the STA and AS prove their identities to each other. The AP blocks non-authentication traffic between the STA and AS until the authentication transaction is successful. The AP does not participate in the authentication transaction other than forwarding traffic between the STA and AS.
- **Key generation and distribution:** The AP and the STA perform several operations that cause cryptographic keys to be generated and placed on the AP and the STA. Frames are exchanged between the AP and STA only.
- **Protected data transfer:** Frames are exchanged between the STA and the end station through the AP. As denoted by the shading and the encryption module icon, secure data transfer occurs between the STA and the AP only; security is not provided end-to-end.

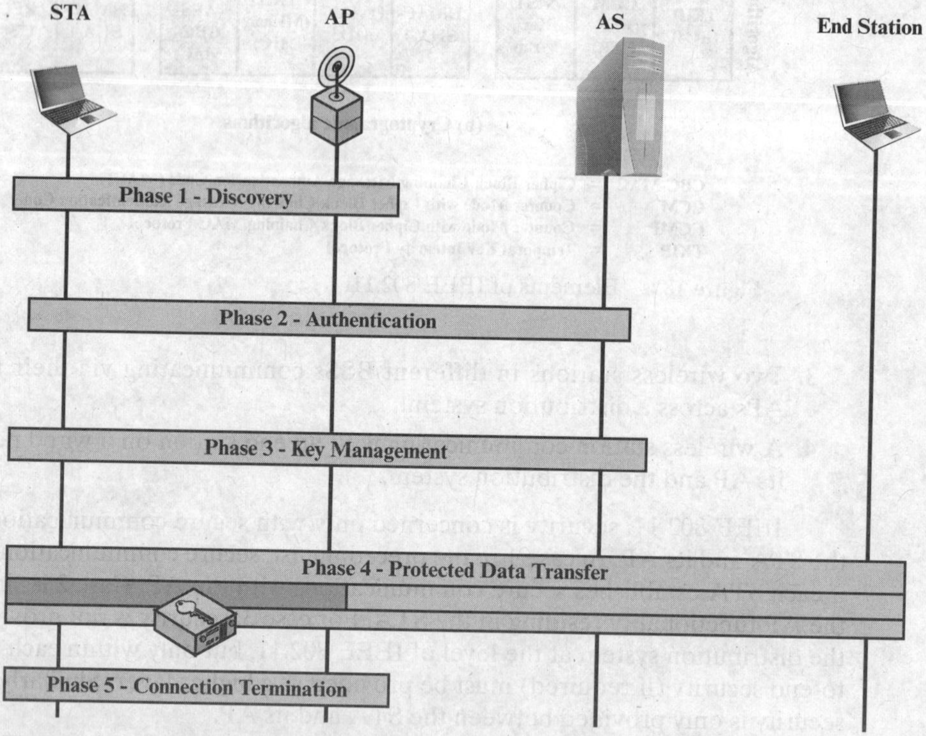

Figure 18.7 IEEE 802.11i Phases of Operation

- **Connection termination:** The AP and STA exchange frames. During this phase, the secure connection is torn down and the connection is restored to the original state.

Discovery Phase

We now look in more detail at the RSN phases of operation, beginning with the discovery phase, which is illustrated in the upper portion of Figure 18.8. The purpose of this phase is for an STA and an AP to recognize each other, agree on a set of security capabilities, and establish an association for future communication using those security capabilities.

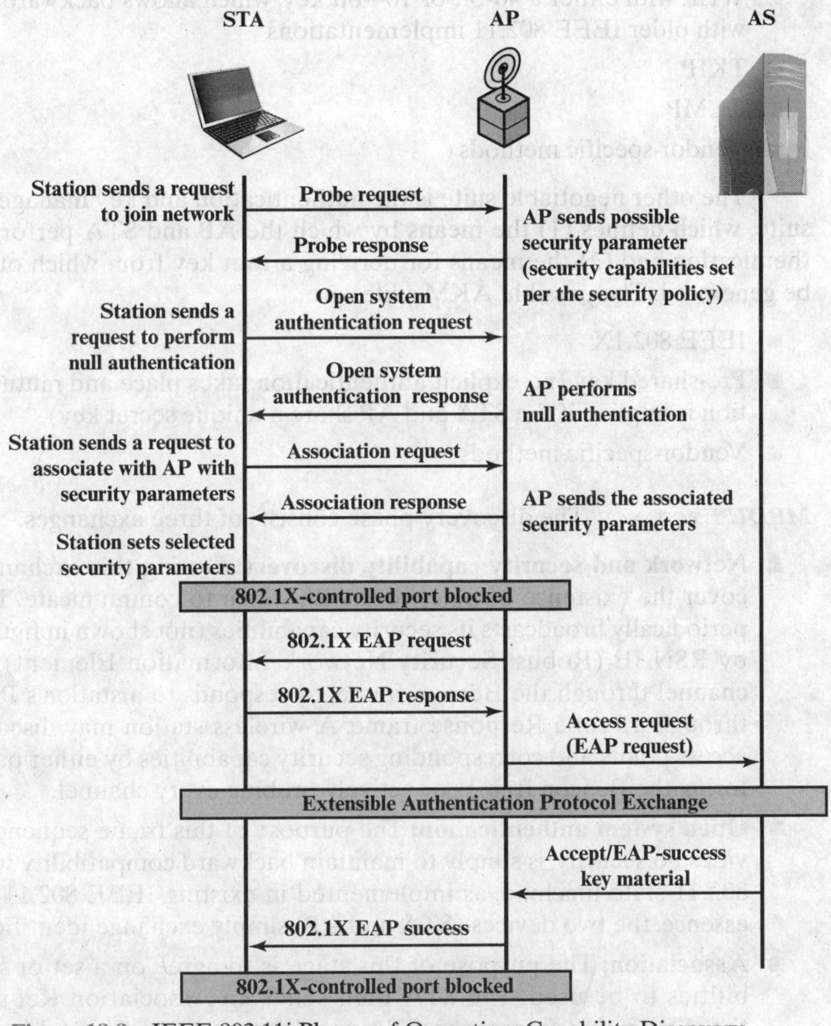

Figure 18.8 IEEE 802.11i Phases of Operation: Capability Discovery, Authentication, and Association

Security Capabilities During this phase, the STA and AP decide on specific techniques in the following areas:

- Confidentiality and MPDU integrity protocols for protecting unicast traffic (traffic only between this STA and AP)
- Authentication method
- Cryptography key management approach

Confidentiality and integrity protocols for protecting multicast/broadcast traffic are dictated by the AP, since all STAs in a multicast group must use the same protocols and ciphers. The specification of a protocol, along with the chosen key length (if variable) is known as a *cipher suite*. The options for the confidentiality and integrity cipher suite are

- WEP, with either a 40-bit or 104-bit key, which allows backward compatibility with older IEEE 802.11 implementations
- TKIP
- CCMP
- Vendor-specific methods

The other negotiable suite is the authentication and key management (AKM) suite, which defines (1) the means by which the AP and STA perform mutual authentication and (2) the means for deriving a root key from which other keys may be generated. The possible AKM suites are

- IEEE 802.1X
- Pre-shared key (no explicit authentication takes place and mutual authentication is implied if the STA and AP share a unique secret key)
- Vendor-specific methods

MPDU Exchange The discovery phase consists of three exchanges.

- **Network and security capability discovery:** During this exchange, STAs discover the existence of a network with which to communicate. The AP either periodically broadcasts its security capabilities (not shown in figure), indicated by RSN IE (Robust Security Network Information Element), in a specific channel through the Beacon frame; or responds to a station's Probe Request through a Probe Response frame. A wireless station may discover available access points and corresponding security capabilities by either passively monitoring the Beacon frames or actively probing every channel.
- **Open system authentication:** The purpose of this frame sequence, which provides no security, is simply to maintain backward compatibility with the IEEE 802.11 state machine, as implemented in existing IEEE 802.11 hardware. In essence, the two devices (STA and AP) simply exchange identifiers.
- **Association:** The purpose of this stage is to agree on a set of security capabilities to be used. The STA then sends an Association Request frame to the AP. In this frame, the STA specifies one set of matching capabilities

(one authentication and key management suite, one pairwise cipher suite, and one group-key cipher suite) from among those advertised by the AP. If there is no match in capabilities between the AP and the STA, the AP refuses the Association Request. The STA blocks it too, in case it has associated with a rogue AP or someone is inserting frames illicitly on its channel. As shown in Figure 18.8, the IEEE 802.1X controlled ports are blocked, and no user traffic goes beyond the AP. The concept of blocked ports is explained subsequently.

Authentication Phase

As was mentioned, the authentication phase enables mutual authentication between an STA and an authentication server (AS) located in the DS. Authentication is designed to allow only authorized stations to use the network and to provide the STA with assurance that it is communicating with a legitimate network.

IEEE 802.1X Access Control Approach IEEE 802.11i makes use of another standard that was designed to provide access control functions for LANs. The standard is IEEE 802.1X, Port-Based Network Access Control. The authentication protocol that is used, the Extensible Authentication Protocol (EAP), is defined in the IEEE 802.1X standard. IEEE 802.1X uses the terms *supplicant*, *authenticator*, and *authentication server* (AS). In the context of an 802.11 WLAN, the first two terms correspond to the wireless station and the AP. The AS is typically a separate device on the wired side of the network (i.e., accessible over the DS) but could also reside directly on the authenticator.

Before a supplicant is authenticated by the AS using an authentication protocol, the authenticator only passes control or authentication messages between the supplicant and the AS; the 802.1X control channel is unblocked, but the 802.11 data channel is blocked. Once a supplicant is authenticated and keys are provided, the authenticator can forward data from the supplicant, subject to predefined access control limitations for the supplicant to the network. Under these circumstances, the data channel is unblocked.

As indicated in Figure 16.5, 802.1X uses the concepts of controlled and uncontrolled ports. Ports are logical entities defined within the authenticator and refer to physical network connections. For a WLAN, the authenticator (the AP) may have only two physical ports: one connecting to the DS and one for wireless communication within its BSS. Each logical port is mapped to one of these two physical ports. An uncontrolled port allows the exchange of PDUs between the supplicant and the other AS, regardless of the authentication state of the supplicant. A controlled port allows the exchange of PDUs between a supplicant and other systems on the LAN only if the current state of the supplicant authorizes such an exchange. IEEE 802.1X is covered in more detail in Chapter 16.

The 802.1X framework, with an upper-layer authentication protocol, fits nicely with a BSS architecture that includes a number of wireless stations and an AP. However, for an IBSS, there is no AP. For an IBSS, 802.11i provides a more complex solution that, in essence, involves pairwise authentication between stations on the IBSS.

MPDU Exchange The lower part of Figure 18.8 shows the MPDU exchange dictated by IEEE 802.11 for the authentication phase. We can think of authentication phase as consisting of the following three phases.

- **Connect to AS:** The STA sends a request to its AP (the one with which it has an association) for connection to the AS. The AP acknowledges this request and sends an access request to the AS.
- **EAP exchange:** This exchange authenticates the STA and AS to each other. A number of alternative exchanges are possible, as explained subsequently.
- **Secure key delivery:** Once authentication is established, the AS generates a master session key (MSK), also known as the Authentication, Authorization, and Accounting (AAA) key and sends it to the STA. As explained subsequently, all the cryptographic keys needed by the STA for secure communication with its AP are generated from this MSK. IEEE 802.11i does not prescribe a method for secure delivery of the MSK but relies on EAP for this. Whatever method is used, it involves the transmission of an MPDU containing an encrypted MSK from the AS, via the AP, to the AS.

EAP Exchange As mentioned, there are a number of possible EAP exchanges that can be used during the authentication phase. Typically, the message flow between STA and AP employs the EAP over LAN (EAPOL) protocol, and the message flow between the AP and AS uses the Remote Authentication Dial In User Service (RADIUS) protocol, although other options are available for both STA-to-AP and AP-to-AS exchanges. [FRAN07] provides the following summary of the authentication exchange using EAPOL and RADIUS.

1. The EAP exchange begins with the AP issuing an EAP-Request/Identity frame to the STA.
2. The STA replies with an EAP-Response/Identity frame, which the AP receives over the uncontrolled port. The packet is then encapsulated in RADIUS over EAP and passed on to the RADIUS server as a RADIUS-Access-Request packet.
3. The AAA server replies with a RADIUS-Access-Challenge packet, which is passed on to the STA as an EAP-Request. This request is of the appropriate authentication type and contains relevant challenge information.
4. The STA formulates an EAP-Response message and sends it to the AS. The response is translated by the AP into a Radius-Access-Request with the response to the challenge as a data field. Steps 3 and 4 may be repeated multiple times, depending on the EAP method in use. For TLS tunneling methods, it is common for authentication to require 10 to 20 round trips.
5. The AAA server grants access with a Radius-Access-Accept packet. The AP issues an EAP-Success frame. (Some protocols require confirmation of the EAP success inside the TLS tunnel for authenticity validation.) The controlled port is authorized, and the user may begin to access the network.

Note from Figure 18.8 that the AP controlled port is still blocked to general user traffic. Although the authentication is successful, the ports remain blocked until the temporal keys are installed in the STA and AP, which occurs during the 4-Way Handshake.

Key Management Phase

During the key management phase, a variety of cryptographic keys are generated and distributed to STAs. There are two types of keys: pairwise keys used for communication between an STA and an AP and group keys used for multicast communication. Figure 18.9, based on [FRAN07], shows the two key hierarchies, and Table 18.3 defines the individual keys.

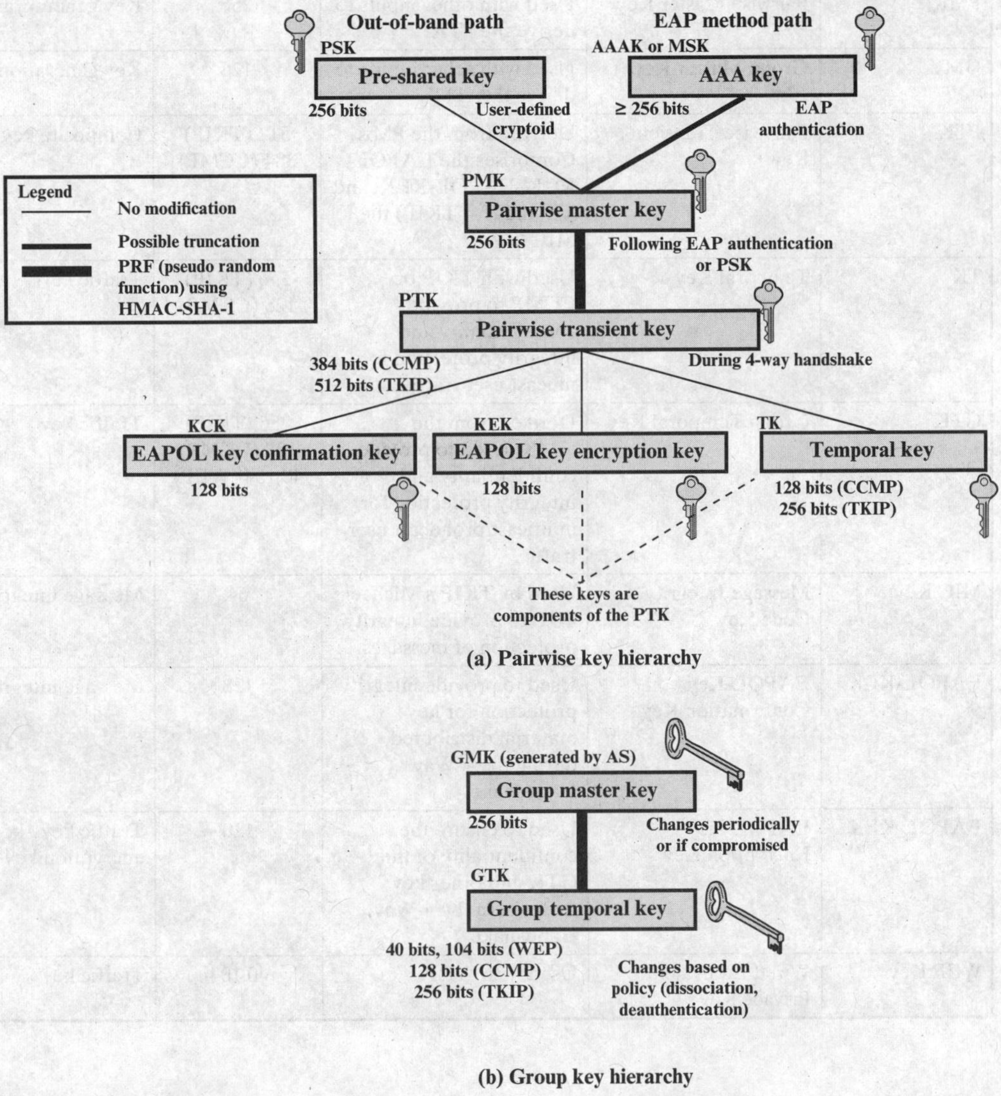

Figure 18.9 IEEE 802.11i Key Hierarchies

Table 18.3 IEEE 802.11i Keys for Data Confidentiality and Integrity Protocols

Abbreviation	Name	Description / Purpose	Size (bits)	Type
AAA Key	Authentication, Accounting, and Authorization Key	Used to derive the PMK. Used with the IEEE 802.1X authentication and key management approach. Same as MMSK.	≥ 256	Key generation key, root key
PSK	Pre-shared Key	Becomes the PMK in pre-shared key environments.	256	Key generation key, root key
PMK	Pairwise Master Key	Used with other inputs to derive the PTK.	256	Key generation key
GMK	Group Master Key	Used with other inputs to derive the GTK.	128	Key generation key
PTK	Pair-wise Transient Key	Derived from the PMK. Comprises the EAPOL-KCK, EAPOL-KEK, and TK and (for TKIP) the MIC key.	512 (TKIP) 384 (CCMP)	Composite key
TK	Temporal Key	Used with TKIP or CCMP to provide confidentiality and integrity protection for unicast user traffic.	256 (TKIP) 128 (CCMP)	Traffic key
GTK	Group Temporal Key	Derived from the GMK. Used to provide confidentiality and integrity protection for multicast/broadcast user traffic.	256 (TKIP) 128 (CCMP) 40,104 (WEP)	Traffic key
MIC Key	Message Integrity Code Key	Used by TKIP's Michael MIC to provide integrity protection of messages.	64	Message integrity key
EAPOL-KCK	EAPOL-Key Confirmation Key	Used to provide integrity protection for key material distributed during the 4-Way Handshake.	128	Message integrity key
EAPOL-KEK	EAPOL-Key Encryption Key	Used to ensure the confidentiality of the GTK and other key material in the 4-Way Handshake.	128	Traffic key / key encryption key
WEP Key	Wired Equivalent Privacy Key	Used with WEP.	40,104	Traffic key

Pairwise Keys Pairwise keys are used for communication between a pair of devices, typically between an STA and an AP. These keys form a hierarchy beginning with a master key from which other keys are derived dynamically and used for a limited period of time.

At the top level of the hierarchy are two possibilities. A **pre-shared key (PSK)** is a secret key shared by the AP and a STA and installed in some fashion outside the scope of IEEE 802.11i. The other alternative is the **master session key (MSK)**, also known as the AAAK, which is generated using the IEEE 802.1X protocol during the authentication phase, as described previously. The actual method of key generation depends on the details of the authentication protocol used. In either case (PSK or MSK), there is a unique key shared by the AP with each STA with which it communicates. All the other keys derived from this master key are also unique between an AP and an STA. Thus, each STA, at any time, has one set of keys, as depicted in the hierarchy of Figure 18.9a, while the AP has one set of such keys for each of its STAs.

The **pairwise master key (PMK)** is derived from the master key. If a PSK is used, then the PSK is used as the PMK; if a MSK is used, then the PMK is derived from the MSK by truncation (if necessary). By the end of the authentication phase, marked by the 802.1X EAP Success message (Figure 18.8), both the AP and the STA have a copy of their shared PMK.

The PMK is used to generate the **pairwise transient key (PTK)**, which in fact consists of three keys to be used for communication between an STA and AP after they have been mutually authenticated. To derive the PTK, the HMAC-SHA-1 function is applied to the PMK, the MAC addresses of the STA and AP, and nonces generated when needed. Using the STA and AP addresses in the generation of the PTK provides protection against session hijacking and impersonation; using nonces provides additional random keying material.

The three parts of the PTK are as follows.

- **EAP Over LAN (EAPOL) Key Confirmation Key (EAPOL-KCK):** Supports the integrity and data origin authenticity of STA-to-AP control frames during operational setup of an RSN. It also performs an access control function: proof-of-possession of the PMK. An entity that possesses the PMK is authorized to use the link.
- **EAPOL Key Encryption Key (EAPOL-KEK):** Protects the confidentiality of keys and other data during some RSN association procedures.
- **Temporal Key (TK):** Provides the actual protection for user traffic.

Group Keys Group keys are used for multicast communication in which one STA sends MPDU's to multiple STAs. At the top level of the group key hierarchy is the **group master key (GMK)**. The GMK is a key-generating key used with other inputs to derive the **group temporal key (GTK)**. Unlike the PTK, which is generated using material from both AP and STA, the GTK is generated by the AP and transmitted to its associated STAs. Exactly how this GTK is generated is undefined. IEEE 802.11i, however, requires that its value is computationally indistinguishable from random. The GTK is distributed securely using the pairwise keys that are already established. The GTK is changed every time a device leaves the network.

Pairwise Key Distribution The upper part of Figure 18.10 shows the MPDU exchange for distributing pairwise keys. This exchange is known as the **4-way handshake**. The STA and AP use this handshake to confirm the existence of the

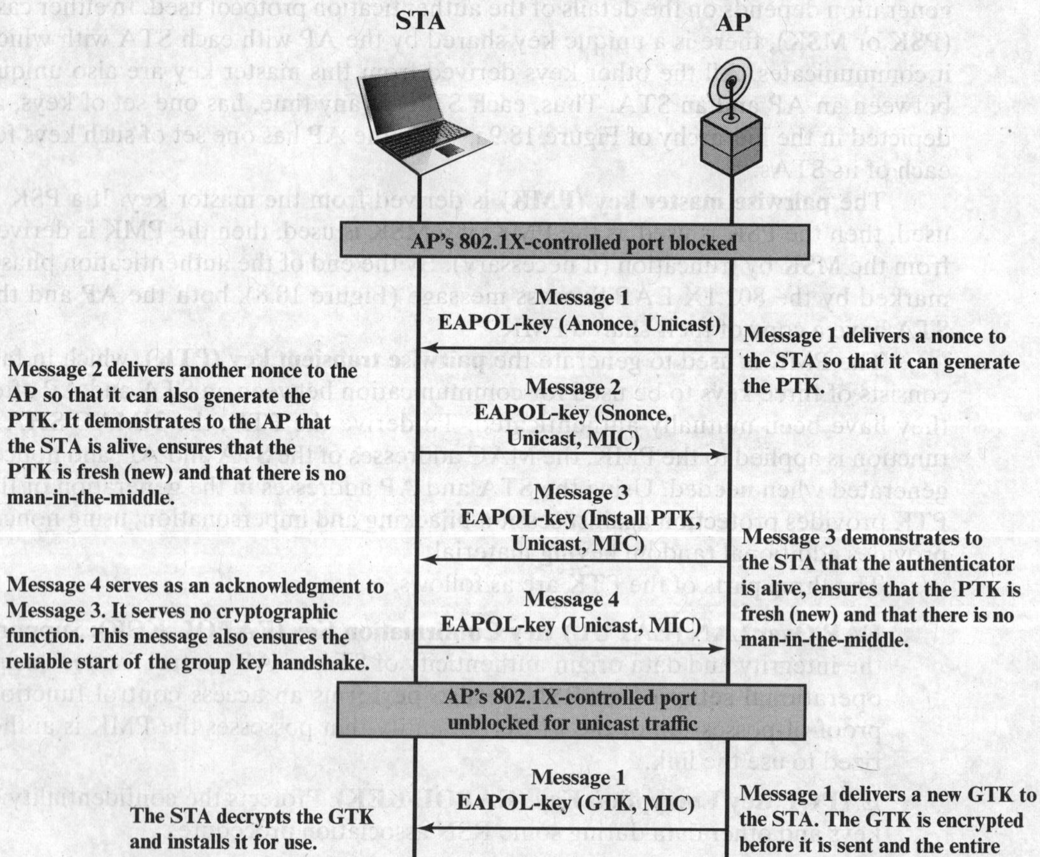

Figure 18.10 IEEE 802.11i Phases of Operation: Four-Way Handshake and Group Key Handshake

PMK, verify the selection of the cipher suite, and derive a fresh PTK for the following data session. The four parts of the exchange are as follows.

- **AP → STA:** Message includes the MAC address of the AP and a nonce (Anonce)
- **STA → AP:** The STA generates its own nonce (Snonce) and uses both nonces and both MAC addresses, plus the PMK, to generate a PTK. The STA then sends a message containing its MAC address and Snonce, enabling the AP to generate the same PTK. This message includes a message integrity code (MIC)[2] using HMAC-MD5 or HMAC-SHA-1-128. The key used with the MIC is KCK.
- **AP → STA:** The AP is now able to generate the PTK. The AP then sends a message to the STA, containing the same information as in the first message, but this time including a MIC.
- **STA → AP:** This is merely an acknowledgment message, again protected by a MIC.

Group Key Distribution For group key distribution, the AP generates a GTK and distributes it to each STA in a multicast group. The two-message exchange with each STA consists of the following:

- **AP → STA:** This message includes the GTK, encrypted either with RC4 or with AES. The key used for encryption is KEK, using a key wrapping algorithm (as discussed in Chapter 12). A MIC value is appended.
- **STA → AP:** The STA acknowledges receipt of the GTK. This message includes a MIC value.

Protected Data Transfer Phase

IEEE 802.11i defines two schemes for protecting data transmitted in 802.11 MPDUs: the Temporal Key Integrity Protocol (TKIP), and the Counter Mode-CBC MAC Protocol (CCMP).

TKIP TKIP is designed to require only software changes to devices that are implemented with the older wireless LAN security approach called Wired Equivalent Privacy (WEP). TKIP provides two services:

- **Message integrity:** TKIP adds a message integrity code (MIC) to the 802.11 MAC frame after the data field. The MIC is generated by an algorithm, called Michael, that computes a 64-bit value using as input the source and destination MAC address values and the Data field, plus key material.
- **Data confidentiality:** Data confidentiality is provided by encrypting the MPDU plus MIC value using RC4.

[2] While *MAC* is commonly used in cryptography to refer to a Message Authentication Code, the term *MIC* is used instead in connection with 802.11i because *MAC* has another standard meaning, Media Access Control, in networking.

The 256-bit TK (Figure 18.9) is employed as follows. Two 64-bit keys are used with the Michael message digest algorithm to produce a message integrity code. One key is used to protect STA-to-AP messages, and the other key is used to protect AP-to-STA messages. The remaining 128 bits are truncated to generate the RC4 key used to encrypt the transmitted data.

For additional protection, a monotonically increasing TKIP sequence counter (TSC) is assigned to each frame. The TSC serves two purposes. First, the TSC is included with each MPDU and is protected by the MIC to protect against replay attacks. Second, the TSC is combined with the session TK to produce a dynamic encryption key that changes with each transmitted MPDU, thus making cryptanalysis more difficult.

CCMP CCMP is intended for newer IEEE 802.11 devices that are equipped with the hardware to support this scheme. As with TKIP, CCMP provides two services:

- **Message integrity:** CCMP uses the cipher block chaining message authentication code (CBC-MAC), described in Chapter 12.
- **Data confidentiality:** CCMP uses the CTR block cipher mode of operation with AES for encryption. CTR is described in Chapter 7.

The same 128-bit AES key is used for both integrity and confidentiality. The scheme uses a 48-bit packet number to construct a nonce to prevent replay attacks.

The IEEE 802.11i Pseudorandom Function

At a number of places in the IEEE 802.11i scheme, a pseudorandom function (PRF) is used. For example, it is used to generate nonces, to expand pairwise keys, and to generate the GTK. Best security practice dictates that different pseudorandom number streams be used for these different purposes. However, for implementation efficiency, we would like to rely on a single pseudorandom number generator function.

The PRF is built on the use of HMAC-SHA-1 to generate a pseudorandom bit stream. Recall that HMAC-SHA-1 takes a message (block of data) and a key of length at least 160 bits and produces a 160-bit hash value. SHA-1 has the property that the change of a single bit of the input produces a new hash value with no apparent connection to the preceding hash value. This property is the basis for pseudorandom number generation.

The IEEE 802.11i PRF takes four parameters as input and produces the desired number of random bits. The function is of the form PRF(*K, A, B, Len*), where

K = a secret key
A = a text string specific to the application (e.g., nonce generation or pairwise key expansion)
B = some data specific to each case
Len = desired number of pseudorandom bits

For example, for the pairwise transient key for CCMP:

```
PTK = PRF (PMK, "Pairwise key expansion", min (AP-
      Addr, STA-Addr) || max (AP-Addr, STA-Addr) || min
      (Anonce, Snonce) || max (Anonce, Snonce), 384)
```

So, in this case, the parameters are

K = PMK

A = the text string "Pairwise key expansion"

B = a sequence of bytes formed by concatenating the two MAC addresses and the two nonces

Len = 384 bits

Similarly, a nonce is generated by

```
Nonce = PRF (Random Number, "InitCounter", MAC || Time, 256)
```

where **Time** is a measure of the network time known to the nonce generator.

The group temporal key is generated by

```
GTK = PRF (GMK, "Group key expansion", MAC || Gnonce, 256)
```

Figure 18.11 illustrates the function PRF(K, A, B, Len). The parameter K serves as the key input to HMAC. The message input consists of four items concatenated together: the parameter A, a byte with value 0, the parameter B, and a counter i. The counter is initialized to 0. The HMAC algorithm is run once, producing a 160-bit hash value. If more bits are required, HMAC is run again with the same inputs, except that i is incremented each time until the necessary number of bits is generated. We can express the logic as

```
PRF (K, A, B, Len)
R ← null string
for i ← 0 to ((Len + 159)/160 - 1) do
R ← R || HMAC-SHA-1 (K, A || 0 || B || i)
Return Truncate-to-Len (R, Len)
```

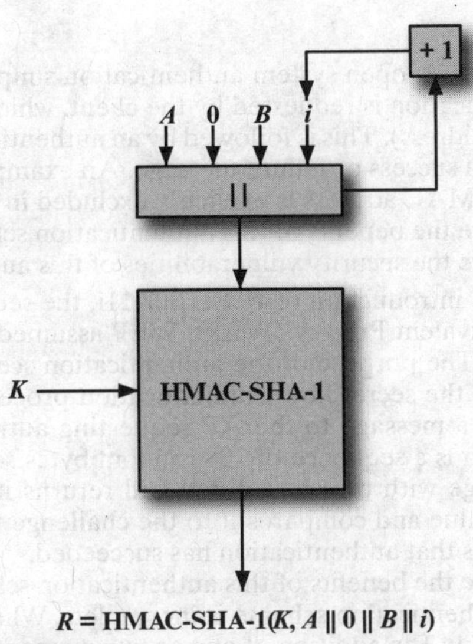

Figure 18.11 IEEE 802.11i Pseudorandom Function

18.5 KEY TERMS, REVIEW QUESTIONS, AND PROBLEMS

Key Terms

4-way handshake	independent BSS (IBSS)	pseudorandom function
access point (AP)	logical link control (LLC)	Robust Security Network (RSN)
basic service set (BSS)	media access control (MAC)	Temporal Key Integrity Protocol (TKIP)
Counter Mode-CBC MAC Protocol (CCMP)	MAC protocol data unit (MPDU)	Wi-Fi
distribution system (DS)	MAC service data unit (MSDU)	Wi-Fi Protected Access (WPA)
extended service set (ESS)	message integrity code (MIC)	Wired Equivalent Privacy (WEP)
group keys	Michael	Wireless LAN (WLAN)
IEEE 802.1X	pairwise keys	
IEEE 802.11		
IEEE 802.11i		

Review Questions

18.1 What is the basic building block of an 802.11 WLAN?

18.2 List and briefly define the key factors that contribute to the high security risk of wireless networks.

18.3 List and briefly define IEEE 802.11 services.

18.4 What are the principal elements of a mobile device security strategy?

18.5 How is the concept of an association related to that of mobility?

18.6 List and briefly define IEEE 802.11i services.

18.7 Briefly describe the five IEEE 802.11i phases of operation.

18.8 What is the difference between TKIP and CCMP?

Problems

18.1 In IEEE 802.11, open system authentication simply consists of two communications. An authentication is requested by the client, which contains the station ID (typically the MAC address). This is followed by an authentication response from the AP/router containing a success or failure message. An example of when a failure may occur is if the client's MAC address is explicitly excluded in the AP/router configuration.

a. What are the benefits of this authentication scheme?

b. What are the security vulnerabilities of this authentication scheme?

18.2 Prior to the introduction of IEEE 802.11i, the security scheme for IEEE 802.11 was Wired Equivalent Privacy (WEP). WEP assumed all devices in the network share a secret key. The purpose of the authentication scenario is for the STA to prove that it possesses the secret key. Authentication proceeds as shown in Figure 18.12. The STA sends a message to the AP requesting authentication. The AP issues a challenge, which is a sequence of 128 random bytes sent as plaintext. The STA encrypts the challenge with the shared key and returns it to the AP. The AP decrypts the incoming value and compares it to the challenge that it sent. If there is a match, the AP confirms that authentication has succeeded.

a. What are the benefits of this authentication scheme?

b. This authentication scheme is incomplete. What is missing and why is this important? *Hint:* The addition of one or two messages would fix the problem.

c. What is a cryptographic weakness of this scheme?

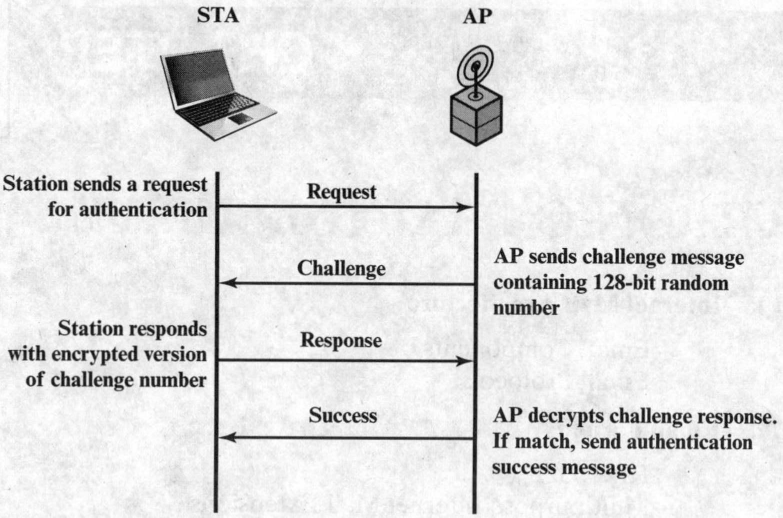

Figure 18.12 WEP Authentication; refer to Problem 18.2

18.3 For WEP, data integrity and data confidentiality are achieved using the RC4 stream encryption algorithm. The transmitter of an MPDU performs the following steps, referred to as encapsulation:

1. The transmitter selects an initial vector (IV) value.
2. The IV value is concatenated with the WEP key shared by transmitter and receiver to form the seed, or key input, to RC4.
3. A 32-bit cyclic redundancy check (CRC) is computed over all the bits of the MAC data field and appended to the data field. The CRC is a common error-detection code used in data link control protocols. In this case, the CRC serves as a integrity check value (ICV).
4. The result of step 3 is encrypted using RC4 to form the ciphertext block.
5. The plaintext IV is prepended to the ciphertext block to form the encapsulated MPDU for transmission.

   a. Draw a block diagram that illustrates the encapsulation process.
   b. Describe the steps at the receiver end to recover the plaintext and perform the integrity check.
   c. Draw a block diagram that illustrates part b.

18.4 A potential weakness of the CRC as an integrity check is that it is a linear function. This means that you can predict which bits of the CRC are changed if a single bit of the message is changed. Furthermore, it is possible to determine which combination of bits could be flipped in the message so that the net result is no change in the CRC. Thus, there are a number of combinations of bit flippings of the plaintext message that leave the CRC unchanged, so message integrity is defeated. However, in WEP, if an attacker does not know the encryption key, the attacker does not have access to the plaintext, only to the ciphertext block. Does this mean that the ICV is protected from the bit flipping attack? Explain.

CHAPTER 19

Electronic Mail Security

LEARNING OBJECTIVES

After studying this chapter, you should be able to:

- Summarize the key functional components of the Internet mail architecture.
- Explain the basic functionality of SMTP, POP3, and IMAP.
- Explain the need for MIME as an enhancement to ordinary email.
- Describe the key elements of MIME.
- Understand the functionality of S/MIME and the security threats it addresses.
- Understand the basic mechanisms of STARTTLS and its role in email security.
- Understand the basic mechanisms of DANE and its role in email security.
- Understand the basic mechanisms of SPF and its role in email security.
- Understand the basic mechanisms of DKIM and its role in email security.
- Understand the basic mechanisms of DMARC and its role in email security.

In virtually all distributed environments, electronic mail is the most heavily used network-based application. Users expect to be able to, and do, send email to others who are connected directly or indirectly to the Internet, regardless of host operating system or communications suite. With the explosively growing reliance on email, there grows a demand for authentication and confidentiality services. Two schemes stand out as approaches that enjoy widespread use: Pretty Good Privacy (PGP) and S/MIME. Both are examined in this chapter. This chapter concludes with a discussion of DomainKeys Identified Mail.

19.1 INTERNET MAIL ARCHITECTURE

For an understanding of the topics in this chapter, it is useful to have a basic grasp of the Internet mail architecture, which is currently defined in RFC 5598 (*Internet Mail Architecture*, July 2009). This section provides an overview of the basic concepts.

Email Components

At its most fundamental level, the Internet mail architecture consists of a user world in the form of Message User Agents (MUA), and the transfer world, in the form of the **Message Handling Service (MHS)**, which is composed of Message Transfer Agents (MTA). The MHS accepts a message from one user and delivers it to one or more other users, creating a virtual MUA-to-MUA exchange environment. This architecture involves three types of interoperability. One is directly between users: messages must be formatted by the MUA on behalf of the message author so that the message can be displayed to the message recipient by the destination MUA. There are also interoperability requirements between the MUA and the MHS—first when a message is posted from an MUA to the MHS and later when it is delivered from the MHS to the destination MUA. Interoperability is required among the MTA components along the transfer path through the MHS.

Figure 19.1 illustrates the key components of the Internet mail architecture, which include the following.

- **Message User Agent (MUA):** Operates on behalf of user actors and user applications. It is their representative within the email service. Typically, this function is housed in the user's computer and is referred to as a client email

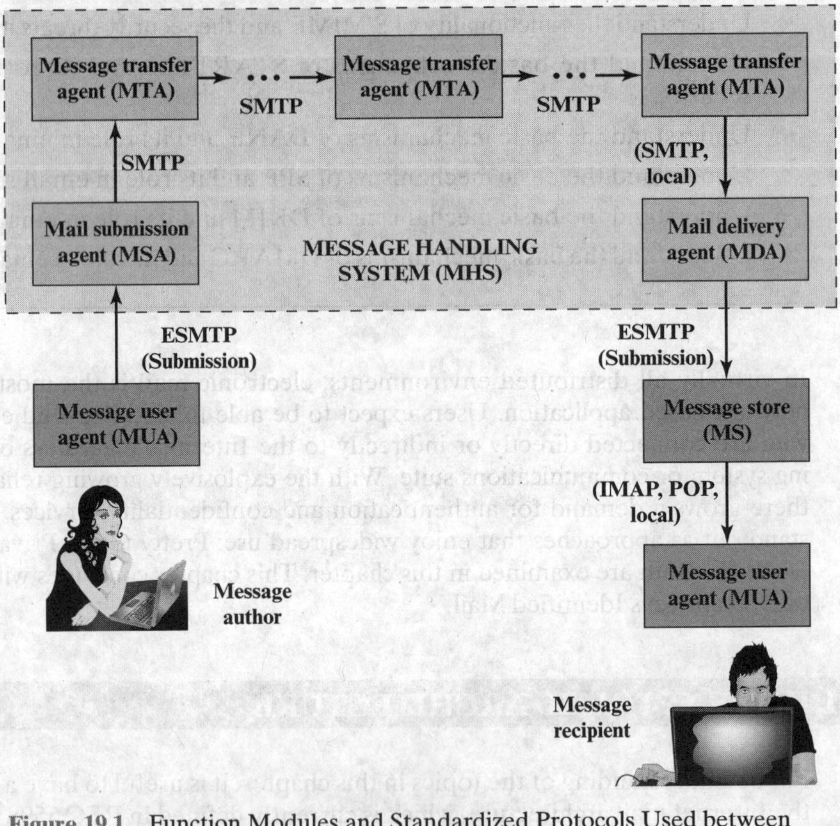

Figure 19.1 Function Modules and Standardized Protocols Used between them in the Internet Mail Architecture

program or a local network email server. The author MUA formats a message and performs initial submission into the MHS via a MSA. The recipient MUA processes received mail for storage and/or display to the recipient user.

- **Mail Submission Agent (MSA):** Accepts the message submitted by an MUA and enforces the policies of the hosting domain and the requirements of Internet standards. This function may be located together with the MUA or as a separate functional model. In the latter case, the Simple Mail Transfer Protocol (SMTP) is used between the MUA and the MSA.
- **Message Transfer Agent (MTA):** Relays mail for one application-level hop. It is like a packet switch or IP router in that its job is to make routing assessments and to move the message closer to the recipients. Relaying is performed by a sequence of MTAs until the message reaches a destination MDA. An MTA also adds trace information to the message header. SMTP is used between MTAs and between an MTA and an MSA or MDA.
- **Mail Delivery Agent (MDA):** Responsible for transferring the message from the MHS to the MS.
- **Message Store (MS):** An MUA can employ a long-term MS. An MS can be located on a remote server or on the same machine as the MUA. Typically, an MUA retrieves messages from a remote server using POP (Post Office Protocol) or IMAP (Internet Message Access Protocol).

Two other concepts need to be defined. An **administrative management domain (ADMD)** is an Internet email provider. Examples include a department that operates a local mail relay (MTA), an IT department that operates an enterprise mail relay, and an ISP that operates a public shared email service. Each ADMD can have different operating policies and trust-based decision making. One obvious example is the distinction between mail that is exchanged within an organization and mail that is exchanged between independent organizations. The rules for handling the two types of traffic tend to be quite different.

The **Domain Name System (DNS)** is a directory lookup service that provides a mapping between the name of a host on the Internet and its numerical address. DNS is discussed subsequently in this chapter.

Email Protocols

Two types of protocols are used for transferring email. The first type is used to move messages through the Internet from source to destination. The protocol used for this purpose is SMTP, with various extensions and in some cases restrictions. The second type consists of protocols used to transfer messages between mail servers, of which IMAP and POP are the most commonly used.

Simple Mail Transfer Protocol SMTP encapsulates an email message in an envelope and is used to relay the encapsulated messages from source to destination through multiple MTAs. SMTP was originally specified in 1982 as RFC 821 and has undergone several revisions, the most current being RFC 5321 (October 2008). These revisions have added additional commands and introduced extensions. The term Extended SMTP (ESMTP) is often used to refer to these later versions of SMTP.

SMTP is a text-based client-server protocol where the client (email sender) contacts the server (next-hop recipient) and issues a set of commands to tell the server about the message to be sent, then sending the message itself. The majority of these commands are ASCII text messages sent by the client and a resulting return code (and additional ASCII text) returned by the server.

The transfer of a message from a source to its ultimate destination can occur over a single SMTP client/server conversation over a single TCP connection. Alternatively, an SMTP server may be an intermediate relay that assumes the role of an SMTP client after receiving a message and then forwards that message to an SMTP server along a route to the ultimate destination.

The operation of SMTP consists of a series of commands and responses exchanged between the SMTP sender and receiver. The initiative is with the SMTP sender, who establishes the TCP connection. Once the connection is established, the SMTP sender sends commands over the connection to the receiver. Each command consists of a single line of text, beginning with a four-letter command code followed in some cases by an argument field. Each command generates exactly one reply from the SMTP receiver. Most replies are a single-line, although multiple-line replies are possible. Each reply begins with a three-digit code and may be followed by additional information.

Figure 19.2 illustrates the SMTP exchange between a client (C) and server (S). The interchange begins with the client establishing a TCP connection to TCP port 25 on the server (not shown in figure). This causes the server to activate SMTP

```
S: 220 foo.com Simple Mail Transfer Service Ready
C: HELO bar.com
S: 250 OK
C: MAIL FROM:<Smith@bar.com>
S: 250 OK
C: RCPT TO:<Jones@foo.com>
S: 250 OK
C: RCPT TO:<Green@foo.com>
S: 550 No such user here
C: RCPT TO:<Brown@foo.com>
S: 250 OK
C: DATA
S: 354 Start mail input; end with <crlf>.<crlf>
C: Blah blah blah . . .
C: . . . etc. etc. etc.
C: <crlf><crlf>
S: 250 OK
C: QUIT
S: 221 foo.com Service closing transmission channel
```

Figure 19.2 Example SMTP Transaction Scenario

and send a 220 reply to the client. The HELO command identifies the sending domain, which the server acknowledges and accepts with a 250 reply. The SMTP sender is transmitting mail that originates with the user Smith@bar.com. The MAIL command identifies the originator of the message. The message is addressed to three users on machine foo.com, namely, Jones, Green, and Brown. The client identifies each of these in a separate RCPT command. The SMTP receiver indicates that it has mailboxes for Jones and Brown but does not have information on Green. Because at least one of the intended recipients has been verified, the client proceeds to send the text message, by first sending a DATA command to ensure the server is ready for the data. After the server acknowledges receipt of all the data, it issues a 250 OK message. Then the client issues a QUIT command and the server closes the connection.

A significant security-related extension for SMTP, called STARTTLS, is defined in RFC 3207 (*SMTP Service Extension for Secure SMTP over Transport Layer Security*, February 2002). STARTTLS enables the addition of confidentiality and authentication in the exchange between SMTP agents. This gives SMTP agents the ability to protect some or all of their communications from eavesdroppers and attackers. If the client does initiate the connection over a TLS-enabled port (e.g., port 465 was previously used for SMTP over SSL), the server may prompt with a message indicating that the STARTTLS option is available. The client can then issue the STARTTLS command in the SMTP command stream, and the two parties proceed to establish a secure TLS connection. An advantage of using STARTTLS is that the server can offer SMTP service on a single port, rather than requiring separate port numbers for secure and cleartext operations. Similar mechanisms are available for running TLS over IMAP and POP protocols.

Historically, MUA/MSA message transfers have used SMTP. The standard currently preferred is SUBMISSION, defined in RFC 6409 (*Message Submission for Mail*, November 2011). Although SUBMISSION derives from SMTP, it uses a separate TCP port and imposes distinct requirements, such as access authorization.

Mail Access Protocols (POP3, IMAP) Post Office Protocol (POP3) allows an email client (user agent) to download an email from an email server (MTA). POP3 user agents connect via TCP to the server (typically port 110). The user agent enters a username and password (either stored internally for convenience or entered each time by the user for stronger security). After authorization, the UA can issue POP3 commands to retrieve and delete mail.

As with POP3, Internet Mail Access Protocol (IMAP) also enables an email client to access mail on an email server. IMAP also uses TCP, with server TCP port 143. IMAP is more complex than POP3. IMAP provides stronger authentication than POP3 and provides other functions not supported by POP3.

19.2 EMAIL FORMATS

To understand S/MIME, we need first to have a general understanding of the underlying email format that it uses, namely, MIME. But to understand the significance of MIME, we need to go back to the traditional email format standard,

RFC 822, which is still in common use. The most recent version of this format specification is RFC 5322 (*Internet Message Format*, October 2008). Accordingly, this section first provides an introduction to these two earlier standards and then moves on to a discussion of S/MIME.

RFC 5322

RFC 5322 defines a format for text messages that are sent using electronic mail. It has been the standard for Internet-based text mail messages and remains in common use. In the RFC 5322 context, messages are viewed as having an envelope and contents. The envelope contains whatever information is needed to accomplish transmission and delivery. The contents compose the object to be delivered to the recipient. The RFC 5322 standard applies only to the contents. However, the content standard includes a set of header fields that may be used by the mail system to create the envelope, and the standard is intended to facilitate the acquisition of such information by programs.

The overall structure of a message that conforms to RFC 5322 is very simple. A message consists of some number of header lines (*the header*) followed by unrestricted text (*the body*). The header is separated from the body by a blank line. Put differently, a message is ASCII text, and all lines up to the first blank line are assumed to be header lines used by the user agent part of the mail system.

A header line usually consists of a keyword, followed by a colon, followed by the keyword's arguments; the format allows a long line to be broken up into several lines. The most frequently used keywords are *From*, *To*, *Subject*, and *Date*. Here is an example message:

```
Date: October 8, 2009 2:15:49 PM EDT
From: "William Stallings" <ws@shore.net>
Subject: The Syntax in RFC 5322
To: Smith@Other-host.com
Cc: Jones@Yet-Another-Host.com

Hello. This section begins the actual
message body, which is delimited from the
message heading by a blank line.
```

Another field that is commonly found in RFC 5322 headers is *Message-ID*. This field contains a unique identifier associated with this message.

Multipurpose Internet Mail Extensions

Multipurpose Internet Mail Extension (MIME) is an extension to the RFC 5322 framework that is intended to address some of the problems and limitations of the use of Simple Mail Transfer Protocol (SMTP) or some other mail transfer protocol and RFC 5322 for electronic mail. RFCs 2045 through 2049 define MIME, and there have been a number of updating documents since then.

As justification for the use of MIME, [PARZ06] lists the following limitations of the SMTP/5322 scheme.

1. SMTP cannot transmit executable files or other binary objects. A number of schemes are in use for converting binary files into a text form that can be used by SMTP mail systems, including the popular UNIX UUencode/UUdecode scheme. However, none of these is a standard or even a *de facto* standard.
2. SMTP cannot transmit text data that includes national language characters, because these are represented by 8-bit codes with values of 128 decimal or higher, and SMTP is limited to 7-bit ASCII.
3. SMTP servers may reject mail message over a certain size.
4. SMTP gateways that translate between ASCII and the character code EBCDIC do not use a consistent set of mappings, resulting in translation problems.
5. SMTP gateways to X.400 electronic mail networks cannot handle nontextual data included in X.400 messages.
6. Some SMTP implementations do not adhere completely to the SMTP standards defined in RFC 821. Common problems include:
   - Deletion, addition, or reordering of carriage return and linefeed
   - Truncating or wrapping lines longer than 76 characters
   - Removal of trailing white space (tab and space characters)
   - Padding of lines in a message to the same length
   - Conversion of tab characters into multiple space characters

MIME is intended to resolve these problems in a manner that is compatible with existing RFC 5322 implementations.

Overview The MIME specification includes the following elements.

1. Five new message header fields are defined, which may be included in an RFC 5322 header. These fields provide information about the body of the message.
2. A number of content formats are defined, thus standardizing representations that support multimedia electronic mail.
3. Transfer encodings are defined that enable the conversion of any content format into a form that is protected from alteration by the mail system.

In this subsection, we introduce the five message header fields. The next two subsections deal with content formats and transfer encodings.

The five header fields defined in MIME are as follows:

- **MIME-Version:** Must have the parameter value 1.0. This field indicates that the message conforms to RFCs 2045 and 2046.
- **Content-Type:** Describes the data contained in the body with sufficient detail that the receiving user agent can pick an appropriate agent or mechanism to represent the data to the user or otherwise deal with the data in an appropriate manner.

- **Content-Transfer-Encoding:** Indicates the type of transformation that has been used to represent the body of the message in a way that is acceptable for mail transport.
- **Content-ID:** Used to identify MIME entities uniquely in multiple contexts.
- **Content-Description:** A text description of the object with the body; this is useful when the object is not readable (e.g., audio data).

Any or all of these fields may appear in a normal RFC 5322 header. A compliant implementation must support the MIME-Version, Content-Type, and Content-Transfer-Encoding fields; the Content-ID and Content-Description fields are optional and may be ignored by the recipient implementation.

MIME CONTENT TYPES The bulk of the MIME specification is concerned with the definition of a variety of content types. This reflects the need to provide standardized ways of dealing with a wide variety of information representations in a multimedia environment.

Table 19.1 lists the content types specified in RFC 2046. There are seven different major types of content and a total of 15 subtypes. In general, a content type declares the general type of data, and the subtype specifies a particular format for that type of data.

Table 19.1 MIME Content Types

Type	Subtype	Description
Text	Plain	Unformatted text; may be ASCII or ISO 8859.
	Enriched	Provides greater format flexibility.
Multipart	Mixed	The different parts are independent but are to be transmitted together. They should be presented to the receiver in the order that they appear in the mail message.
	Parallel	Differs from Mixed only in that no order is defined for delivering the parts to the receiver.
	Alternative	The different parts are alternative versions of the same information. They are ordered in increasing faithfulness to the original, and the recipient's mail system should display the "best" version to the user.
	Digest	Similar to Mixed, but the default type/subtype of each part is message/rfc822.
Message	rfc822	The body is itself an encapsulated message that conforms to RFC 822.
	Partial	Used to allow fragmentation of large mail items, in a way that is transparent to the recipient.
	External-body	Contains a pointer to an object that exists elsewhere.
Image	jpeg	The image is in JPEG format, JFIF encoding.
	gif	The image is in GIF format.
Video	mpeg	MPEG format.
Audio	Basic	Single-channel 8-bit ISDN μ-law encoding at a sample rate of 8 kHz.
Application	PostScript	Adobe Postscript format.
	octet-stream	General binary data consisting of 8-bit bytes.

For the **text type** of body, no special software is required to get the full meaning of the text aside from support of the indicated character set. The primary subtype is *plain text*, which is simply a string of ASCII characters or ISO 8859 characters. The *enriched* subtype allows greater formatting flexibility.

The **multipart type** indicates that the body contains multiple, independent parts. The Content-Type header field includes a parameter (called boundary) that defines the delimiter between body parts. This boundary should not appear in any parts of the message. Each boundary starts on a new line and consists of two hyphens followed by the boundary value. The final boundary, which indicates the end of the last part, also has a suffix of two hyphens. Within each part, there may be an optional ordinary MIME header.

Here is a simple example of a multipart message containing two parts—both consisting of simple text (taken from RFC 2046):

```
From: Nathaniel Borenstein <nsb@bellcore.com>
To: Ned Freed <ned@innosoft.com>
Subject: Sample message
MIME-Version: 1.0
Content-type: multipart/mixed; boundary="simple boundary"
This is the preamble. It is to be ignored, though it is a
handy place for mail composers to include an explanatory
note to non-MIME conformant readers.
—simple boundary
This is implicitly typed plain ASCII text. It does NOT end
with a linebreak.
—simple boundary
Content-type: text/plain; charset=us-ascii
This is explicitly typed plain ASCII text. It DOES end
with a linebreak.
—simple boundary—
This is the epilogue. It is also to be ignored.
```

There are four subtypes of the multipart type, all of which have the same overall syntax. The **multipart/mixed subtype** is used when there are multiple independent body parts that need to be bundled in a particular order. For the **multipart/parallel subtype**, the order of the parts is not significant. If the recipient's system is appropriate, the multiple parts can be presented in parallel. For example, a picture or text part could be accompanied by a voice commentary that is played while the picture or text is displayed.

For the **multipart/alternative subtype**, the various parts are different representations of the same information. The following is an example:

```
From: Nathaniel Borenstein <nsb@bellcore.com>
To: Ned Freed <ned@innosoft.com>
Subject: Formatted text mail
```

```
MIME-Version: 1.0
Content-Type: multipart/alternative;
boundary=boundary42

—boundary42

Content-Type: text/plain; charset=us-ascii
      . . . plain text version of message goes here. . . .

—boundary42
Content-Type: text/enriched

      . . . RFC 1896 text/enriched version of same message
goes here . . .

—boundary42—
```

In this subtype, the body parts are ordered in terms of increasing preference. For this example, if the recipient system is capable of displaying the message in the text/enriched format, this is done; otherwise, the plain text format is used.

The **multipart/digest subtype** is used when each of the body parts is interpreted as an RFC 5322 message with headers. This subtype enables the construction of a message whose parts are individual messages. For example, the moderator of a group might collect email messages from participants, bundle these messages, and send them out in one encapsulating MIME message.

The **message type** provides a number of important capabilities in MIME. The **message/rfc822 subtype** indicates that the body is an entire message, including header and body. Despite the name of this subtype, the encapsulated message may be not only a simple RFC 5322 message, but also any MIME message.

The **message/partial subtype** enables fragmentation of a large message into a number of parts, which must be reassembled at the destination. For this subtype, three parameters are specified in the Content-Type: Message/Partial field: an *id* common to all fragments of the same message, a *sequence number* unique to each fragment, and the *total* number of fragments.

The **message/external-body subtype** indicates that the actual data to be conveyed in this message are not contained in the body. Instead, the body contains the information needed to access the data. As with the other message types, the message/external-body subtype has an outer header and an encapsulated message with its own header. The only necessary field in the outer header is the Content-Type field, which identifies this as a message/external-body subtype. The inner header is the message header for the encapsulated message. The Content-Type field in the outer header must include an access-type parameter, which indicates the method of access, such as FTP (file transfer protocol).

The **application type** refers to other kinds of data, typically either uninterpreted binary data or information to be processed by a mail-based application.

MIME Transfer Encodings The other major component of the MIME specification, in addition to content type specification, is a definition of transfer encodings for message bodies. The objective is to provide reliable delivery across the largest range of environments.

The MIME standard defines two methods of encoding data. The Content-Transfer-Encoding field can actually take on six values, as listed in Table 19.2. However, three of these values (7-bit, 8-bit, and binary) indicate that no encoding has been done but provide some information about the nature of the data. For SMTP transfer, it is safe to use the 7-bit form. The 8-bit and binary forms may be usable in other mail transport contexts. Another Content-Transfer-Encoding value is x-token, which indicates that some other encoding scheme is used for which a name is to be supplied. This could be a vendor-specific or application-specific scheme. The two actual encoding schemes defined are quoted-printable and base64. Two schemes are defined to provide a choice between a transfer technique that is essentially human readable and one that is safe for all types of data in a way that is reasonably compact.

The **quoted-printable** transfer encoding is useful when the data consists largely of octets that correspond to printable ASCII characters. In essence, it represents nonsafe characters by the hexadecimal representation of their code and introduces reversible (soft) line breaks to limit message lines to 76 characters.

The **base64 transfer encoding**, also known as radix-64 encoding, is a common one for encoding arbitrary binary data in such a way as to be invulnerable to the processing by mail-transport programs. It is also used in PGP and is described in Appendix X.

A Multipart Example Figure 19.3, taken from RFC 2045, is the outline of a complex multipart message. The message has five parts to be displayed serially: two introductory plain text parts, an embedded multipart message, a richtext part, and a closing encapsulated text message in a non-ASCII character set. The embedded multipart message has two parts to be displayed in parallel: a picture and an audio fragment.

Canonical Form An important concept in MIME and S/MIME is that of canonical form. Canonical form is a format, appropriate to the content type, that is standardized for use between systems. This is in contrast to native form, which is a format that may be peculiar to a particular system. RFC 2049 defines these two forms as follows:

- **Native form:** The body to be transmitted is created in the system's native format. The native character set is used and, where appropriate, local end-of-line conventions are used as well. The body may be any format that corresponds to

Table 19.2 MIME Transfer Encodings

7 bit	The data are all represented by short lines of ASCII characters.
8 bit	The lines are short, but there may be non-ASCII characters (octets with the high-order bit set).
binary	Not only may non-ASCII characters be present but the lines are not necessarily short enough for SMTP transport.
quoted-printable	Encodes the data in such a way that if the data being encoded are mostly ASCII text, the encoded form of the data remains largely recognizable by humans.
base64	Encodes data by mapping 6-bit blocks of input to 8-bit blocks of output, all of which are printable ASCII characters.
x-token	A named nonstandard encoding.

```
MIME-Version: 1.0
    From: Nathaniel Borenstein <nsb@bellcore.com>
    To: Ned Freed <ned@innosoft.com>
    Subject: A multipart example
    Content-Type: multipart/mixed;
      boundary=unique-boundary-1
    This is the preamble area of a multipart message. Mail readers that
    understand multipart format should ignore this preamble. If you are reading
    this text, you might want to consider changing to a mail reader that
    understands how to properly display multipart messages.
    —unique-boundary-1
      . . . Some text appears here . . .
    [Note that the preceding blank line means no header fields were given and
    this is text, with charset US ASCII. It could have been done with explicit
    typing as in the next part.]
    —unique-boundary-1
    Content-type: text/plain; charset=US-ASCII
    This could have been part of the previous part, but illustrates explicit
    versus implicit typing of body parts.
    —unique-boundary-1
    Content-Type: multipart/parallel; boundary=unique-boundary-2
    —unique-boundary-2
    Content-Type: audio/basic
    Content-Transfer-Encoding: base64
      . . . base64-encoded 8000 Hz single-channel mu-law-format audio data goes
    here . . . .
    —unique-boundary-2
    Content-Type: image/jpeg
    Content-Transfer-Encoding: base64
      . . . base64-encoded image data goes here . . . .
    —unique-boundary-2—
    —unique-boundary-1
    Content-type: text/enriched

    This is richtext. as defined in RFC 1896
      Isn't it cool?

    —unique-boundary-1
    Content-Type: message/rfc822

    From: (mailbox in US-ASCII)
    To: (address in US-ASCII)
    Subject: (subject in US-ASCII)
    Content-Type: Text/plain; charset=ISO-8859-1
    Content-Transfer-Encoding: Quoted-printable
      . . . Additional text in ISO-8859-1 goes here . . .

    —unique-boundary-1—
```

Figure 19.3 Example MIME Message Structure

the local model for the representation of some form of information. Examples include a UNIX-style text file, or a Sun raster image, or a VMS indexed file, and audio data in a system-dependent format stored only in memory. In essence, the data are created in the native form that corresponds to the type specified by the media type.

- **Canonical form:** The entire body, including out-of-band information such as record lengths and possibly file attribute information, is converted to a universal canonical form. The specific media type of the body as well as its associated attributes dictates the nature of the canonical form that is used. Conversion to the proper canonical form may involve character set conversion, transformation of audio data, compression, or various other operations specific to the various media types.

19.3 EMAIL THREATS AND COMPREHENSIVE EMAIL SECURITY

For both organizations and individuals, email is both pervasive and especially vulnerable to a wide range of security threats. In general terms, email security threats can be classified as follows:

- **Authenticity-related threats:** Could result in unauthorized access to an enterprise's email system.
- **Integrity-related threats:** Could result in unauthorized modification of email content.
- **Confidentiality-related threats:** Could result in unauthorized disclosure of sensitive information.
- **Availability-related threats:** Could prevent end users from being able to send or receive email.

A useful list of specific email threats, together with approaches to mitigation, is provided in NIST SP 800-177 (*Trustworthy Email*, September 2015) and is shown in Table 19.3.

SP 800-177 recommends use of a variety of standardized protocols as a means for countering these threats. These include:

- **STARTTLS:** An SMTP security extension that provides authentication, integrity, non-repudiation (via digital signatures) and confidentiality (via encryption) for the entire SMTP message by running SMTP over TLS.
- **S/MIME:** Provides authentication, integrity, non-repudiation (via digital signatures) and confidentiality (via encryption) of the message body carried in SMTP messages.
- **DNS Security Extensions (DNSSEC):** Provides authentication and integrity protection of DNS data, and is an underlying tool used by various email security protocols.
- **DNS-based Authentication of Named Entities (DANE):** Is designed to overcome problems in the certificate authority (CA) system by providing an alternative channel for authenticating public keys based on DNSSEC, with the

Table 19.3 Email Threats and Mitigations

Threat	Impact on Purported Sender	Impact on Receiver	Mitigation
Email sent by unauthorized MTA in enterprise (e.g., malware botnet)	Loss of reputation, valid email from enterprise may be blocked as possible spam/phishing attack.	UBE and/or email containing malicious links may be delivered into user inboxes.	Deployment of domain-based authentication techniques. Use of digital signatures over email.
Email message sent using spoofed or unregistered sending domain	Loss of reputation, valid email from enterprise may be blocked as possible spam/phishing attack.	UBE and/or email containing malicious links may be delivered into user inboxes.	Deployment of domain-based authentication techniques. Use of digital signatures over email.
Email message sent using forged sending address or email address (i.e., phishing, spear phishing)	Loss of reputation, valid email from enterprise may be blocked as possible spam/phishing attack.	UBE and/or email containing malicious links may be delivered. Users may inadvertently divulge sensitive information or PII.	Deployment of domain-based authentication techniques. Use of digital signatures over email.
Email modified in transit	Leak of sensitive information or PII.	Leak of sensitive information, altered message may contain malicious information.	Use of TLS to encrypt email transfer between servers. Use of end-to-end email encryption.
Disclosure of sensitive information (e.g., PII) via monitoring and capturing of email traffic	Leak of sensitive information or PII.	Leak of sensitive information, altered message may contain malicious information.	Use of TLS to encrypt email transfer between servers. Use of end-to-end email encryption.
Unsolicited Bulk Email (UBE) (i.e., spam)	None, unless purported sender is spoofed.	UBE and/or email containing malicious links may be delivered into user inboxes.	Techniques to address UBE.
DoS/DDoS attack against an enterprises' email servers	Inability to send email.	Inability to receive email.	Multiple mail servers, use of cloud-based email providers.

result that the same trust relationships used to certify IP addresses are used to certify servers operating on those addresses.

- **Sender Policy Framework (SPF):** Uses the Domain Name System (DNS) to allow domain owners to create records that associate the domain name with a specific IP address range of authorized message senders. It is a simple matter for receivers to check the SPF TXT record in the DNS to confirm that the purported sender of a message is permitted to use that source address and reject mail that does not come from an authorized IP address.
- **DomainKeys Identified Mail (DKIM):** Enables an MTA to sign selected headers and the body of a message. This validates the source domain of the mail and provides message body integrity.
- **Domain-based Message Authentication, Reporting, and Conformance (DMARC):** Lets senders know the proportionate effectiveness of their SPF and DKIM policies, and signals to receivers what action should be taken in various individual and bulk attack scenarios.

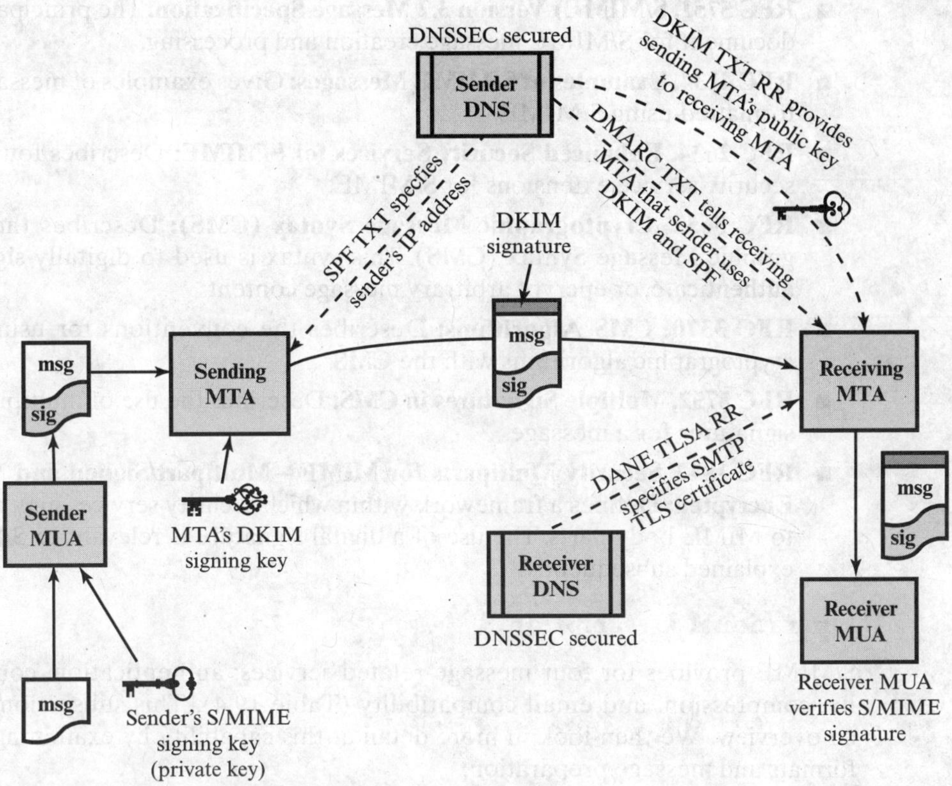

DANE = DNS-based Authentication of Named Entities
DKIM = DomainKeys Identified Mail
DMARC = Domain-based Message Authentication, Reporting, and Conformance
DNSSEC = Domain Name System Security Extensions
SPF = Sender Policy Framework
S/MIME = Secure Multi-Purpose Internet Mail Extensions
TLSA RR = Transport Layer Security Authentication Resource Record

Figure 19.4 The Interrelationship of DNSSEC, SPF, DKIM, DMARC, DANE, and S/MIME for Assuring Message Authenticity and Integrity

Figure 19.4 shows how these components interact to provide message authenticity and integrity. Not shown, for simplicity, is that S/MIME also provides message confidentiality by encrypting messages.

19.4 S/MIME

Secure/Multipurpose Internet Mail Extension (S/MIME) is a security enhancement to the MIME Internet email format standard based on technology from RSA Data Security. S/MIME is a complex capability that is defined in a number of documents. The most important documents relevant to S/MIME include the following:

- **RFC 5750, S/MIME Version 3.2 Certificate Handling:** Specifies conventions for X.509 certificate usage by (S/MIME) v3.2.

- **RFC 5751, S/MIME) Version 3.2 Message Specification:** The principal defining document for S/MIME message creation and processing.
- **RFC 4134, Examples of S/MIME Messages:** Gives examples of message bodies formatted using S/MIME.
- **RFC 2634, Enhanced Security Services for S/MIME:** Describes four optional security service extensions for S/MIME.
- **RFC 5652, Cryptographic Message Syntax (CMS):** Describes the Cryptographic Message Syntax (CMS). This syntax is used to digitally sign, digest, authenticate, or encrypt arbitrary message content.
- **RFC 3370, CMS Algorithms:** Describes the conventions for using several cryptographic algorithms with the CMS.
- **RFC 5752, Multiple Signatures in CMS:** Describes the use of multiple, parallel signatures for a message.
- **RFC 1847, Security Multiparts for MIME—Multipart/Signed and Multipart/Encrypted:** Defines a framework within which security services may be applied to MIME body parts. The use of a digital signature is relevant to S/MIME, as explained subsequently.

Operational Description

S/MIME provides for four message-related services: authentication, confidentiality, compression, and email compatibility (Table 19.4). This subsection provides an overview. We then look in more detail at this capability by examining message formats and message preparation.

Authentication Authentication is provided by means of a digital signature, using the general scheme discussed in Chapter 13 and illustrated in Figure 13.1. Most commonly RSA with SHA-256 is used. The sequence is as follows:

1. The sender creates a message.
2. SHA-256 is used to generate a 256-bit message digest of the message.

Table 19.4 Summary of S/MIME Services

Function	Typical Algorithm	Typical Action
Digital signature	RSA/SHA-256	A hash code of a message is created using SHA-256. This message digest is encrypted using SHA-256 with the sender's private key and included with the message.
Message encryption	AES-128 with CBC	A message is encrypted using AES-128 with CBC with a one-time session key generated by the sender. The session key is encrypted using RSA with the recipient's public key and included with the message.
Compression	unspecified	A message may be compressed for storage or transmission.
Email compatibility	Radix-64 conversion	To provide transparency for email applications, an encrypted message may be converted to an ASCII string using radix-64 conversion.

3. The message digest is encrypted with RSA using the sender's private key, and the result is appended to the message. Also appended is identifying information for the signer, which will enable the receiver to retrieve the signer's public key.
4. The receiver uses RSA with the sender's public key to decrypt and recover the message digest.
5. The receiver generates a new message digest for the message and compares it with the decrypted hash code. If the two match, the message is accepted as authentic.

The combination of SHA-256 and RSA provides an effective digital signature scheme. Because of the strength of RSA, the recipient is assured that only the possessor of the matching private key can generate the signature. Because of the strength of SHA-256, the recipient is assured that no one else could generate a new message that matches the hash code and, hence, the signature of the original message.

Although signatures normally are found attached to the message or file that they sign, this is not always the case: Detached signatures are supported. A detached signature may be stored and transmitted separately from the message it signs. This is useful in several contexts. A user may wish to maintain a separate signature log of all messages sent or received. A detached signature of an executable program can detect subsequent virus infection. Finally, detached signatures can be used when more than one party must sign a document, such as a legal contract. Each person's signature is independent and therefore is applied only to the document. Otherwise, signatures would have to be nested, with the second signer signing both the document and the first signature, and so on.

CONFIDENTIALITY S/MIME provides confidentiality by encrypting messages. Most commonly AES with a 128-bit key is used, with the cipher block chaining (CBC) mode. The key itself is also encrypted, typically with RSA, as explained below.

As always, one must address the problem of key distribution. In S/MIME, each symmetric key, referred to as a content-encryption key, is used only once. That is, a new key is generated as a random number for each message. Because it is to be used only once, the content-encryption key is bound to the message and transmitted with it. To protect the key, it is encrypted with the receiver's public key. The sequence can be described as follows:

1. The sender generates a message and a random 128-bit number to be used as a content-encryption key for this message only.
2. The message is encrypted using the content-encryption key.
3. The content-encryption key is encrypted with RSA using the recipient's public key and is attached to the message.
4. The receiver uses RSA with its private key to decrypt and recover the content-encryption key.
5. The content-encryption key is used to decrypt the message.

Several observations may be made. First, to reduce encryption time, the combination of symmetric and public-key encryption is used in preference to simply using public-key encryption to encrypt the message directly: Symmetric algorithms are substantially faster than asymmetric ones for a large block of content. Second, the use of the public-key algorithm solves the session-key distribution problem, because only the recipient is able to recover the session key that is bound to the message. Note that we do not need a session-key exchange protocol of the type discussed in Chapter 14, because we are not beginning an ongoing session. Rather, each message is a one-time independent event with its own key. Furthermore, given the store-and-forward nature of electronic mail, the use of handshaking to assure that both sides have the same session key is not practical. Finally, the use of one-time symmetric keys strengthens what is already a strong symmetric encryption approach. Only a small amount of plaintext is encrypted with each key, and there is no relationship among the keys. Thus, to the extent that the public-key algorithm is secure, the entire scheme is secure.

Confidentiality and Authentication As Figure 19.5 illustrates, both confidentiality and encryption may be used for the same message. The figure shows a sequence in which a signature is generated for the plaintext message and appended to the message. Then the plaintext message and signature are encrypted as a single block using symmetric encryption and the symmetric encryption key is encrypted using public-key encryption.

S/MIME allows the signing and message encryption operations to be performed in either order. If signing is done first, the identity of the signer is hidden by the encryption. Plus, it is generally more convenient to store a signature with a plaintext version of a message. Furthermore, for purposes of third-party verification, if the signature is performed first, a third party need not be concerned with the symmetric key when verifying the signature.

If encryption is done first, it is possible to verify a signature without exposing the message content. This can be useful in a context in which automatic signature verification is desired, as no private key material is required to verify a signature. However, in this case the recipient cannot determine any relationship between the signer and the unencrypted content of the message.

Email Compatibility When S/MIME is used, at least part of the block to be transmitted is encrypted. If only the signature service is used, then the message digest is encrypted (with the sender's private key). If the confidentiality service is used, the message plus signature (if present) are encrypted (with a one-time symmetric key). Thus, part or all of the resulting block consists of a stream of arbitrary 8-bit octets. However, many electronic mail systems only permit the use of blocks consisting of ASCII text. To accommodate this restriction, S/MIME provides the service of converting the raw 8-bit binary stream to a stream of printable ASCII characters, a process referred to as 7-bit encoding.

The scheme typically used for this purpose is Base64 conversion. Each group of three octets of binary data is mapped into four ASCII characters. See Appendix X for a description.

One noteworthy aspect of the Base64 algorithm is that it blindly converts the input stream to Base64 format regardless of content, even if the input happens to be ASCII text. Thus, if a message is signed but not encrypted and the conversion is applied to the entire block, the output will be unreadable to the casual observer, which provides a certain level of confidentiality.

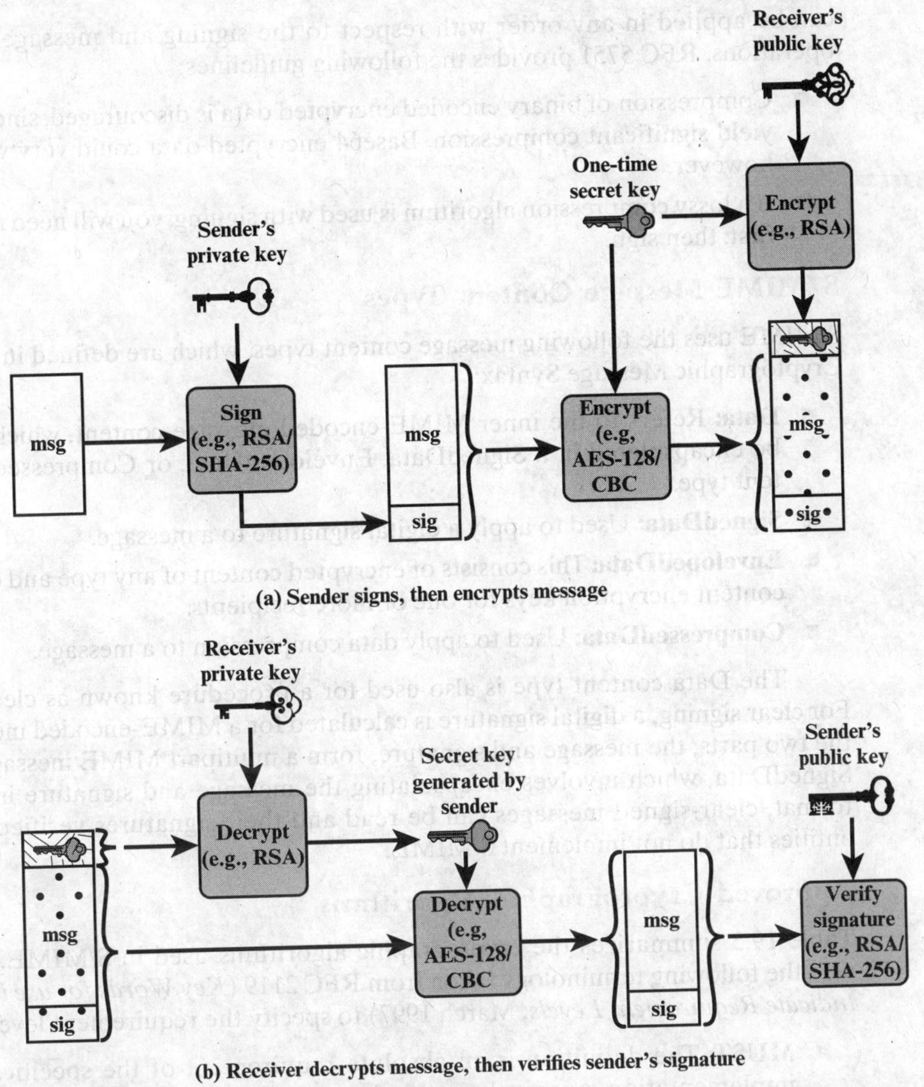

Figure 19.5 Simplified S/MIME Functional Flow

RFC 5751 also recommends that even if outer 7-bit encoding is not used, the original MIME content should be 7-bit encoded. The reason for this is that it allows the MIME entity to be handled in any environment without changing it. For example, a trusted gateway might remove the encryption, but not the signature, of a message, and then forward the signed message on to the end recipient so that they can verify the signatures directly. If the transport internal to the site is not 8-bit clean, such as on a wide area network with a single mail gateway, verifying the signature will not be possible unless the original MIME entity was only 7-bit data.

COMPRESSION S/MIME also offers the ability to compress a message. This has the benefit of saving space both for email transmission and for file storage. Compression can be applied in any order with respect to the signing and message encryption operations. RFC 5751 provides the following guidelines:

- Compression of binary encoded encrypted data is discouraged, since it will not yield significant compression. Base64 encrypted data could very well benefit, however.
- If a lossy compression algorithm is used with signing, you will need to compress first, then sign.

S/MIME Message Content Types

S/MIME uses the following message content types, which are defined in RFC 5652, Cryptographic Message Syntax:

- **Data:** Refers to the inner MIME-encoded message content, which may then be encapsulated in a SignedData, EnvelopedData, or CompressedData content type.
- **SignedData:** Used to apply a digital signature to a message.
- **EnvelopedData:** This consists of encrypted content of any type and encrypted-content encryption keys for one or more recipients.
- **CompressedData:** Used to apply data compression to a message.

The Data content type is also used for a procedure known as clear signing. For clear signing, a digital signature is calculated for a MIME-encoded message and the two parts, the message and signature, form a multipart MIME message. Unlike SignedData, which involves encapsulating the message and signature in a special format, clear-signed messages can be read and their signatures verified by email entities that do not implement S/MIME.

Approved Cryptographic Algorithms

Table 19.5 summarizes the cryptographic algorithms used in S/MIME. S/MIME uses the following terminology taken from RFC 2119 (*Key Words for use in RFCs to Indicate Requirement Levels*, March 1997) to specify the requirement level:

- **MUST:** The definition is an absolute requirement of the specification. An implementation must include this feature or function to be in conformance with the specification.
- **SHOULD:** There may exist valid reasons in particular circumstances to ignore this feature or function, but it is recommended that an implementation include the feature or function.

The S/MIME specification includes a discussion of the procedure for deciding which content encryption algorithm to use. In essence, a sending agent has two decisions to make. First, the sending agent must determine if the receiving agent is capable of decrypting using a given encryption algorithm. Second, if the receiving agent is only capable of accepting weakly encrypted content, the sending agent must decide if it is acceptable to send using weak encryption. To support this decision process, a sending agent may announce its decrypting capabilities in order of preference for any message that it sends out. A receiving agent may store that information for future use.

Table 19.5 Cryptographic Algorithms Used in S/MIME

Function	Requirement
Create a message digest to be used in forming a digital signature.	MUST support SHA-256 SHOULD support SHA-1 Receiver SHOULD support MD5 for backward compatibility
Use message digest to form a digital signature.	MUST support RSA with SHA-256 SHOULD support —DSA with SHA-256 —RSASSA-PSS with SHA-256 —RSA with SHA-1 —DSA with SHA-1 —RSA with MD5
Encrypt session key for transmission with a message.	MUST support RSA encryption SHOULD support —RSAES-OAEP —Diffie–Hellman ephemeral-static mode
Encrypt message for transmission with a one-time session key.	MUST support AES-128 with CBC SHOULD support —AES-192 CBC and AES-256 CBC —Triple DES CBC

The following rules, in the following order, should be followed by a sending agent.

1. If the sending agent has a list of preferred decrypting capabilities from an intended recipient, it SHOULD choose the first (highest preference) capability on the list that it is capable of using.
2. If the sending agent has no such list of capabilities from an intended recipient but has received one or more messages from the recipient, then the outgoing message SHOULD use the same encryption algorithm as was used on the last signed and encrypted message received from that intended recipient.
3. If the sending agent has no knowledge about the decryption capabilities of the intended recipient and is willing to risk that the recipient may not be able to decrypt the message, then the sending agent SHOULD use triple DES.
4. If the sending agent has no knowledge about the decryption capabilities of the intended recipient and is not willing to risk that the recipient may not be able to decrypt the message, then the sending agent MUST use RC2/40.

If a message is to be sent to multiple recipients and a common encryption algorithm cannot be selected for all, then the sending agent will need to send two messages. However, in that case, it is important to note that the security of the message is made vulnerable by the transmission of one copy with lower security.

S/MIME Messages

S/MIME makes use of a number of new MIME content types. All of the new application types use the designation PKCS. This refers to a set of public-key cryptography specifications issued by RSA Laboratories and made available for the S/MIME effort.

We examine each of these in turn after first looking at the general procedures for S/MIME message preparation.

Securing a MIME Entity S/MIME secures a MIME entity with a signature, encryption, or both. A MIME entity may be an entire message (except for the RFC 5322 headers), or if the MIME content type is multipart, then a MIME entity is one or more of the subparts of the message. The MIME entity is prepared according to the normal rules for MIME message preparation. Then the MIME entity plus some security-related data, such as algorithm identifiers and certificates, are processed by S/MIME to produce what is known as a PKCS object. A PKCS object is then treated as message content and wrapped in MIME (provided with appropriate MIME headers). This process should become clear as we look at specific objects and provide examples.

In all cases, the message to be sent is converted to canonical form. In particular, for a given type and subtype, the appropriate canonical form is used for the message content. For a multipart message, the appropriate canonical form is used for each subpart.

The use of transfer encoding requires special attention. For most cases, the result of applying the security algorithm will be to produce an object that is partially or totally represented in arbitrary binary data. This will then be wrapped in an outer MIME message and transfer encoding can be applied at that point, typically base64. However, in the case of a multipart signed message (described in more detail later), the message content in one of the subparts is unchanged by the security process. Unless that content is 7 bit, it should be transfer encoded using base64 or quoted-printable so that there is no danger of altering the content to which the signature was applied.

We now look at each of the S/MIME content types.

EnvelopedData An application/pkcs7-mime subtype is used for one of four categories of S/MIME processing, each with a unique smime-type parameter. In all cases, the resulting entity, (referred to as an *object*) is represented in a form known as Basic Encoding Rules (BER), which is defined in ITU-T Recommendation X.209. The BER format consists of arbitrary octet strings and is therefore binary data. Such an object should be transfer encoded with base64 in the outer MIME message. We first look at envelopedData.

The steps for preparing an envelopedData MIME entity are:

1. Generate a pseudorandom session key for a particular symmetric encryption algorithm (RC2/40 or triple DES).
2. For each recipient, encrypt the session key with the recipient's public RSA key.
3. For each recipient, prepare a block known as `RecipientInfo` that contains an identifier of the recipient's public-key certificate,[1] an identifier of the algorithm used to encrypt the session key, and the encrypted session key.
4. Encrypt the message content with the session key.

[1]This is an X.509 certificate, discussed later in this section.

The RecipientInfo blocks followed by the encrypted content constitute the `envelopedData`. This information is then encoded into base64. A sample message (excluding the RFC 5322 headers) is given below.

```
Content-Type: application/pkcs7-mime; smime-type=enveloped-
        data; name=smime.p7m
Content-Transfer-Encoding: base64
Content-Disposition: attachment; filename=smime.p7m
```

rfvbnj756tbBghyHhHUujhJhjH77n8HHGT9HG4VQpfyF467GhIGfHfYT6
7n8HHGghyHhHUujhJh4VQpfyF467GhIGfHfYGTrfvbnjT6jH7756tbB9H
f8HHGTrfvhJhjH776tbB9HG4VQbnj7567GhIGfHfYT6ghyHhHUujpfyF4
0GhIGfHfQbnj756YT64V

To recover the encrypted message, the recipient first strips off the base64 encoding. Then the recipient's private key is used to recover the session key. Finally, the message content is decrypted with the session key.

SIGNEDDATA The `signedData` smime-type can be used with one or more signers. For clarity, we confine our description to the case of a single digital signature. The steps for preparing a signedData MIME entity are as follows.

1. Select a message digest algorithm (SHA or MD5).
2. Compute the message digest (hash function) of the content to be signed.
3. Encrypt the message digest with the signer's private key.
4. Prepare a block known as `SignerInfo` that contains the signer's public-key certificate, an identifier of the message digest algorithm, an identifier of the algorithm used to encrypt the message digest, and the encrypted message digest.

The `signedData` entity consists of a series of blocks, including a message digest algorithm identifier, the message being signed, and `SignerInfo`. The `signedData` entity may also include a set of public-key certificates sufficient to constitute a chain from a recognized root or top-level certification authority to the signer. This information is then encoded into base64. A sample message (excluding the RFC 5322 headers) is the following.

```
Content-Type: application/pkcs7-mime; smime-type=signed-
        data; name=smime.p7m
Content-Transfer-Encoding: base64
Content-Disposition: attachment; filename=smime.p7m
```

567GhIGfHfYT6ghyHhHUujpfyF4f8HHGTrfvhJhjH776tbB9HG4VQbnj7
77n8HHGT9HG4VQpfyF467GhIGfHfYT6rfvbnj756tbBghyHhHUujhJhjH
HUujhJh4VQpfyF467GhIGfHfYGTrfvbnjT6jH7756tbB9H7n8HHGghyHh
6YT64V0GhIGfHfQbnj75

To recover the signed message and verify the signature, the recipient first strips off the base64 encoding. Then the signer's public key is used to decrypt the message digest. The recipient independently computes the message digest and compares it to the decrypted message digest to verify the signature.

Clear Signing Clear signing is achieved using the multipart content type with a signed subtype. As was mentioned, this signing process does not involve transforming the message to be signed, so that the message is sent "in the clear." Thus, recipients with MIME capability but not S/MIME capability are able to read the incoming message.

A multipart/signed message has two parts. The first part can be any MIME type but must be prepared so that it will not be altered during transfer from source to destination. This means that if the first part is not 7 bit, then it needs to be encoded using base64 or quoted-printable. Then this part is processed in the same manner as `signedData`, but in this case an object with `signedData` format is created that has an empty message content field. This object is a detached signature. It is then transfer encoded using base64 to become the second part of the multipart/signed message. This second part has a MIME content type of application and a subtype of pkcs7-signature. Here is a sample message:

```
Content-Type: multipart/signed;
   protocol="application/pkcs7-signature";
   micalg=sha1; boundary=boundary42
—boundary42
Content-Type: text/plain
This is a clear-signed message.
—boundary42
Content-Type: application/pkcs7-signature; name=smime.p7s
Content-Transfer-Encoding: base64
Content-Disposition: attachment; filename=smime.p7s
ghyHhHUujhJhjH77n8HHGTrfvbnj756tbB9HG4VQpfyF467GhIGfHfYT6
4VQpfyF467GhIGfHfYT6jH77n8HHGghyHhHUujhJh756tbB9HGTrfvbnj
n8HHGTrfvhJhjH776tbB9HG4VQbnj7567GhIGfHfYT6ghyHhHUujpfyF4
7GhIGfHfYT64VQbnj756
—boundary42—
```

The protocol parameter indicates that this is a two-part clear-signed entity. The `micalg` parameter indicates the type of message digest used. The receiver can verify the signature by taking the message digest of the first part and comparing this to the message digest recovered from the signature in the second part.

Registration Request Typically, an application or user will apply to a certification authority for a public-key certificate. The application/pkcs10 S/MIME entity is used to transfer a certification request. The certification request includes `certificationRequestInfo` block, followed by an identifier of the public-key encryption algorithm, followed by the signature of the `certificationRequestInfo` block, made using the sender's private key. The `certificationRequestInfo` block includes a name of the certificate subject (the entity whose public key is to be certified) and a bit-string representation of the user's public key.

Certificates-Only Message A message containing only certificates or a certificate revocation list (CRL) can be sent in response to a registration request. The message is an application/pkcs7-mime type/subtype with an smime-type parameter of degenerate. The steps involved are the same as those for creating a `signedData` message, except that there is no message content and the `signerInfo` field is empty.

S/MIME Certificate Processing

S/MIME uses public-key certificates that conform to version 3 of X.509 (see Chapter 14). S/MIME managers and/or users must configure each client with a list of trusted keys and with certificate revocation lists. That is, the responsibility is local for maintaining the certificates needed to verify incoming signatures and to encrypt outgoing messages. On the other hand, the certificates are signed by certification authorities.

User Agent Role An S/MIME user has several key management functions to perform.

- **Key generation:** The user of some related administrative utility (e.g., one associated with LAN management) MUST be capable of generating separate Diffie–Hellman and DSS key pairs and SHOULD be capable of generating RSA key pairs. Each key pair MUST be generated from a good source of nondeterministic random input and be protected in a secure fashion. A user agent SHOULD generate RSA key pairs with a length in the range of 768 to 1024 bits and MUST NOT generate a length of less than 512 bits.
- **Registration:** A user's public key must be registered with a certification authority in order to receive an X.509 public-key certificate.
- **Certificate storage and retrieval:** A user requires access to a local list of certificates in order to verify incoming signatures and to encrypt outgoing messages. Such a list could be maintained by the user or by some local administrative entity on behalf of a number of users.

Enhanced Security Services

RFC 2634 defines four enhanced security services for S/MIME:

- **Signed receipts:** A signed receipt may be requested in a `SignedData` object. Returning a signed receipt provides proof of delivery to the originator of a message and allows the originator to demonstrate to a third party that the recipient received the message. In essence, the recipient signs the entire original message plus the original (sender's) signature and appends the new signature to form a new S/MIME message.

- **Security labels:** A security label may be included in the authenticated attributes of a `SignedData` object. A security label is a set of security information regarding the sensitivity of the content that is protected by S/MIME encapsulation. The labels may be used for access control, by indicating which users are permitted access to an object. Other uses include priority (secret, confidential, restricted, and so on) or role based, describing which kind of people can see the information (e.g., patient's health-care team, medical billing agents).
- **Secure mailing lists:** When a user sends a message to multiple recipients, a certain amount of per-recipient processing is required, including the use of each recipient's public key. The user can be relieved of this work by employing the services of an S/MIME Mail List Agent (MLA). An MLA can take a single incoming message, perform the recipient-specific encryption for each recipient, and forward the message. The originator of a message need only send the message to the MLA with encryption performed using the MLA's public key.
- **Signing certificates:** This service is used to securely bind a sender's certificate to their signature through a signing certificate attribute.

19.5 PRETTY GOOD PRIVACY

An alternative email security protocol is Pretty Good Privacy (PGP), which has essentially the same functionality as S/MIME. PGP was created by Phil Zimmerman and implemented as a product first released in 1991. It was made available free of charge and became quite popular for personal use. The initial PGP protocol was proprietary and used some encryption algorithms with intellectual property restrictions. In 1996, version 5.x of PGP was defined in IETF RFC 1991, *PGP Message Exchange Formats*. Subsequently, OpenPGP was developed as a new standard protocol based on PGP version 5.x. OpenPGP is defined in RFC 4880 (*OpenPGP Message Format*, November 2007) and RFC 3156 (*MIME Security with OpenPGP*, August 2001).

There are two significant differences between S/MIME and OpenPGP:

- **Key Certification:** S/MIME uses X.509 certificates that are issued by Certificate Authorities (or local agencies that have been delegated authority by a CA to issue certificates). In OpenPGP, users generate their own OpenPGP public and private keys and then solicit signatures for their public keys from individuals or organizations to which they are known. Whereas X.509 certificates are trusted if there is a valid PKIX chain to a trusted root, an OpenPGP public key is trusted if it is signed by another OpenPGP public key that is trusted by the recipient. This is called the *Web-of-Trust*.
- **Key Distribution:** OpenPGP does not include the sender's public key with each message, so it is necessary for recipients of OpenPGP messages to separately obtain the sender's public key in order to verify the message. Many organizations post OpenPGP keys on TLS-protected websites: People who wish to verify digital signatures or send these organizations encrypted mail

need to manually download these keys and add them to their OpenPGP clients. Keys may also be registered with the OpenPGP public key servers, which are servers that maintain a database of PGP public keys organized by email address. Anyone may post a public key to the OpenPGP key servers, and that public key may contain any email address. There is no vetting of OpenPGP keys, so users must use the Web-of-Trust to decide whether to trust a given public key.

NIST 800-177 recommends the use of S/MIME rather than PGP because of the greater confidence in the CA system of verifying public keys.

Appendix P provides an overview of PGP.

19.6 DNSSEC

DNS Security Extensions (DNSSEC) are used by several protocols that provide email security. This section provides a brief overview of the Domain Name System (DNS) and then looks at DNSSEC.

Domain Name System

DNS is a directory lookup service that provides a mapping between the name of a host on the Internet and its numeric IP address. DNS is essential to the functioning of the Internet. The DNS is used by MUAs and MTAs to find the address of the next hop server for mail delivery. Sending MTAs query DNS for the Mail Exchange Resource Record (MX RR) of the recipient's domain (the right hand side of the "@" symbol) in order to find the receiving MTA to contact.

Four elements comprise the DNS:

- **Domain name space:** DNS uses a tree-structured name space to identify resources on the Internet.
- **DNS database:** Conceptually, each node and leaf in the name space tree structure names a set of information (e.g., IP address, name server for this domain name) that is contained in resource record. The collection of all RRs is organized into a distributed database.
- **Name servers:** These are server programs that hold information about a portion of the domain name tree structure and the associated RRs.
- **Resolvers:** These are programs that extract information from name servers in response to client requests. A typical client request is for an IP address corresponding to a given domain name.

The DNS Database DNS is based on a hierarchical database containing **resource records (RRs)** that include the name, IP address, and other information about hosts. The key features of the database are as follows:

- **Variable-depth hierarchy for names:** DNS allows essentially unlimited levels and uses the period (.) as the level delimiter in printed names, as described earlier.

Table 19.6 Resource Record Types

Type	Description
A	A host address. This RR type maps the name of a system to its IPv4 address. Some systems (e.g., routers) have multiple addresses, and there is a separate RR for each.
AAAA	Similar to A type, but for IPv6 addresses.
CNAME	Canonical name. Specifies an alias name for a host and maps this to the canonical (true) name.
HINFO	Host information. Designates the processor and operating system used by the host.
MINFO	Mailbox or mail list information. Maps a mailbox or mail list name to a host name.
MX	Mail exchange. Identifies the system(s) via which mail to the queried domain name should be relayed.
NS	Authoritative name server for this domain.
PTR	Domain name pointer. Points to another part of the domain name space.
SOA	Start of a zone of authority (which part of naming hierarchy is implemented). Includes parameters related to this zone.
SRV	For a given service provides name of server or servers in domain that provide that service.
TXT	Arbitrary text. Provides a way to add text comments to the database.
WKS	Well-known services. May list the application services available at this host.

- **Distributed database:** The database resides in DNS servers scattered throughout the Internet.
- **Distribution controlled by the database:** The DNS database is divided into thousands of separately managed zones, which are managed by separate administrators. Distribution and update of records is controlled by the database software.

Using this database, DNS servers provide a name-to-address directory service for network applications that need to locate specific servers. For example, every time an email message is sent or a Web page is accessed, there must be a DNS name lookup to determine the IP address of the email server or Web server.

Table 19.6 lists the various types of resource records.

DNS Operation DNS operation typically includes the following steps (Figure 19.6):

1. A user program requests an IP address for a domain name.
2. A resolver module in the local host or local ISP queries a local name server in the same domain as the resolver.
3. The local name server checks to see if the name is in its local database or cache, and, if so, returns the IP address to the requestor. Otherwise, the name server queries other available name servers, if necessary going to the root server, as explained subsequently.
4. When a response is received at the local name server, it stores the name/address mapping in its local cache and may maintain this entry for the amount of time specified in the time-to-live field of the retrieved RR.
5. The user program is given the IP address or an error message.

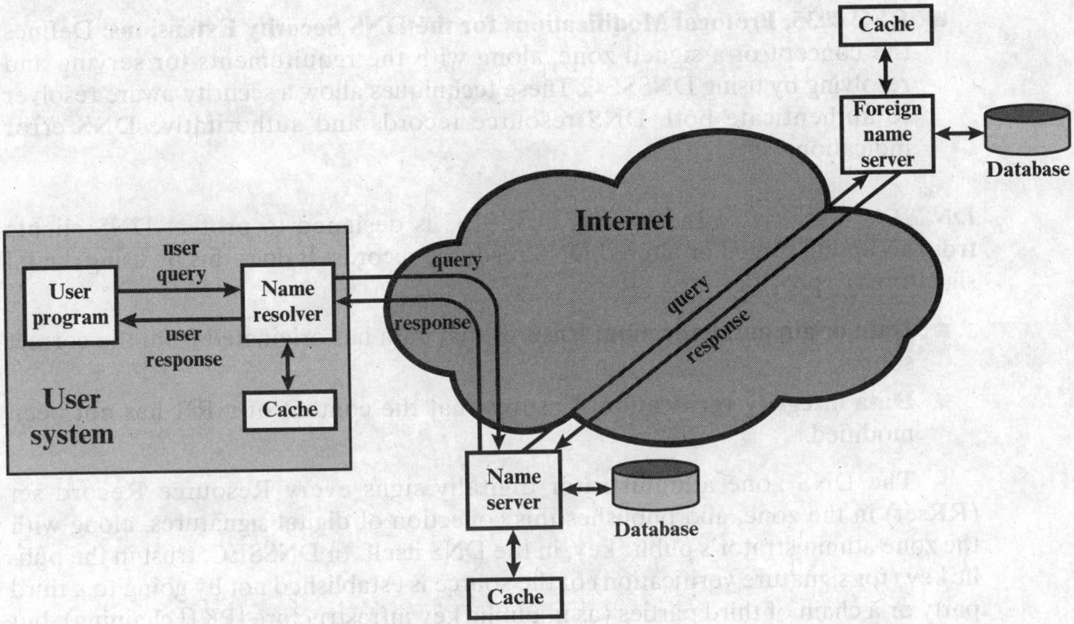

Figure 19.6 DNS Name Resolution

The distributed DNS database that supports the DNS functionality must be updated frequently because of the rapid and continued growth of the Internet. Further, the DNS must cope with dynamic assignment of IP addresses, such as is done for home DSL users by their ISP. Accordingly, dynamic updating functions for DNS have been defined. In essence, DNS name servers automatically send out updates to other relevant name servers as conditions warrant.

DNS Security Extensions

DNSSEC provides end-to-end protection through the use of digital signatures that are created by responding zone administrators and verified by a recipient's resolver software. In particular, DNSSEC avoids the need to trust intermediate name servers and resolvers that cache or route the DNS records originating from the responding zone administrator before they reach the source of the query. DNSSEC consists of a set of new resource record types and modifications to the existing DNS protocol, and is defined in the following documents:

- **RFC 4033, DNS Security Introduction and Requirements:** Introduces the DNS security extensions and describes their capabilities and limitations. The document also discusses the services that the DNS security extensions do and do not provide.
- **RFC 4034, Resource Records for the DNS Security Extensions:** Defines four new resource records that provide security for DNS.

- **RFC 4035, Protocol Modifications for the DNS Security Extensions:** Defines the concept of a signed zone, along with the requirements for serving and resolving by using DNSSEC. These techniques allow a security-aware resolver to authenticate both DNS resource records and authoritative DNS error indications.

DNSSEC Operation In essence, DNSSEC is designed to protect DNS clients from accepting forged or altered DNS resource records. It does this by using digital signatures to provide:

- **Data origin authentication:** Ensures that data has originated from the correct source.
- **Data integrity verification:** Ensures that the content of a RR has not been modified.

The DNS zone administrator digitally signs every Resource Record set (RRset) in the zone, and publishes this collection of digital signatures, along with the zone administrator's public key, in the DNS itself. In DNSSEC, trust in the public key (for signature verification) of the source is established not by going to a third party or a chain of third parties (as in public key infrastructure [PKI] chaining), but by starting from a trusted zone (such as the root zone) and establishing the chain of trust down to the current source of response through successive verifications of signature of the public key of a child by its parent. The public key of the trusted zone is called the *trust anchor*.

Resource Records for DNSSEC RFC 4034 defines four new DNS resource records:

- **DNSKEY:** Contains a public key.
- **RRSIG:** A resource record digital signature.
- **NSEC:** Authenticated denial of existence record.
- **DS:** Delegation signer.

An RRSIG is associated with each RRset, where an RRset is the set of resource records that have the same label, class, and type. When a client requests data, an RRset is returned, together with the associated digital signature in an RRSIG record. The client obtains the relevant DNSKEY public key and verifies the signature for this RRset.

DNSSEC depends on establishing the authenticity of the DNS hierarchy leading to the domain name in question, and thus its operation depends on beginning the use of cryptographic digital signatures in the root zone. The DS resource record facilitates key signing and authentication between DNS zones to create an authentication chain, or trusted sequence of signed data, from the root of the DNS tree down to a specific domain name. To secure all DNS lookups, including those for non-existent domain names and record types, DNSSEC uses the NSEC resource record to authenticate negative responses to queries. NSEC is used to identify the range of DNS names or resource record types that do not exist among the sequence of domain names in a zone.

19.7 DNS-BASED AUTHENTICATION OF NAMED ENTITIES

DANE is a protocol to allow X.509 certificates, commonly used for Transport Layer Security (TLS), to be bound to DNS names using DNSSEC. It is proposed in RFC 6698 as a way to authenticate TLS client and server entities without a certificate authority (CA).

The rationale for DANE is the vulnerability of the use of CAs in a global PKI system. Every browser developer and operating system supplier maintains a list of CA root certificates as trust anchors. These are called the software's root certificates and are stored in its root certificate store. The PKIX procedure allows a certificate recipient to trace a certificate back to the root. So long as the root certificate remains trustworthy, and the authentication concludes successfully, the client can proceed with the connection.

However, if any of the hundreds of CAs operating on the Internet is compromised, the effects can be widespread. The attacker can obtain the CA's private key, get issued certificates under a false name, or introduce new bogus root certificates into a root certificate store. There is no limitation of scope for the global PKI and a compromise of a single CA damages the integrity of the entire PKI system. In addition, some CAs have engaged in poor security practices. For example, some CAs have issued wildcard certificates that allow the holder to issue sub-certificates for any domain or entity, anywhere in the world.

The purpose of DANE is to replace reliance on the security of the CA system with reliance on the security provided by DNSSEC. Given that the DNS administrator for a domain name is authorized to give identifying information about the zone, it makes sense to allow that administrator to also make an authoritative binding between the domain name and a certificate that might be used by a host at that domain name.

TLSA Record

DANE defines a new DNS record type, TLSA, that can be used for a secure method of authenticating SSL/TLS certificates. The TLSA provides for:

- Specifying constraints on which CA can vouch for a certificate, or which specific PKIX end-entity certificate is valid.
- Specifying that a service certificate or a CA can be directly authenticated in the DNS itself.

The TLSA RR enables certificate issue and delivery to be tied to a given domain. A server domain owner creates a TLSA resource record that identifies the certificate and its public key. When a client receives an X.509 certificate in the TLS negotiation, it looks up the TLSA RR for that domain and matches the TLSA data against the certificate as part of the client's certificate validation procedure.

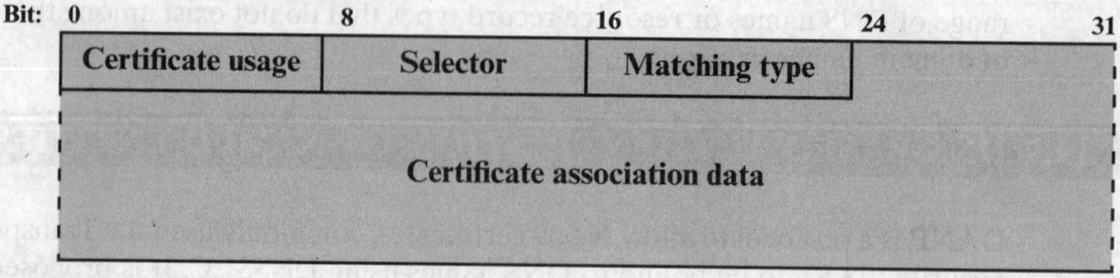

Figure 19.7 TLSA RR Transmission Format

Figure 19.7 shows the format of a TLSA RR as it is transmitted to a requesting entity. It contains four fields. The **Certificate Usage** field defines four different usage models, to accommodate users who require different forms of authentication. The usage models are:

- **PKIX-TA (CA constraint):** Specifies which CA should be trusted to authenticate the certificate for the service. This usage model limits which CA can be used to issue certificates for a given service on a host. The server certificate chain must pass PKIX validation that terminates with a trusted root certificate stored in the client.
- **PKIX-EE (service certificate constraint):** Defines which specific end entity service certificate should be trusted for the service. This usage model limits which end entity certificate can be used by a given service on a host. The server certificate chain must pass PKIX validation that terminates with a trusted root certificate stored in the client.
- **DANE-TA (trust anchor assertion):** Specifies a domain-operated CA to be used as a trust anchor. This usage model allows a domain name administrator to specify a new trust anchor—for example, if the domain issues its own certificates under its own CA that is not expected to be in the end users' collection of trust anchors. The server certificate chain is self-issued and does not need to verify against a trusted root stored in the client.
- **DANE-EE (domain-issued certificate):** Specifies a domain-operated CA to be used as a trust anchor. This certificate usage allows a domain name administrator to issue certificates for a domain without involving a third-party CA. The server certificate chain is self-issued and does not need to verify against a trusted root stored in the client.

The first two usage models are designed to co-exist with and strengthen the public CA system. The final two usage models operate without the use of public CAs.

The **Selector** field indicates whether the full certificate will be matched or just the value of the public key. The match is made between the certificate presented in TLS negotiation and the certificate in the TLSA RR. The **Matching Type** field indicates how the match of the certificate is made. The options are exact match, SHA-256 hash match, or SHA-512 hash match. The **Certificate Association Data** is the raw certificate data in hex format.

Use of DANE for SMTP

DANE can be used in conjunction with SMTP over TLS, as provided by STARTTLS, to more fully secure email delivery. DANE can authenticate the certificate of the SMTP submission server that the user's mail client (MUA) communicates with. It can also authenticate the TLS connections between SMTP servers (MTAs). The use of DANE with SMTP is documented in an Internet Draft (*SMTP Security via Opportunistic DANE TLS*, draft-ietf-dane-smtp-with-dane-19, May 29, 2015).

As discussed in Section 19.1, SMTP can use the STARTTLS extension to run SMTP over TLS, so that the entire email message plus SMTP envelope are encrypted. This is done opportunistically, that is, if both sides support STARTTLS. Even when TLS is used to provide confidentiality, it is vulnerable to attack in the following ways:

- Attackers can strip away the TLS capability advertisement and downgrade the connection to not use TLS.
- TLS connections are often unauthenticated (e.g., the use of self-signed certificates as well as mismatched certificates is common).

DANE can address both these vulnerabilities. A domain can use the presence of the TLSA RR as an indicator that encryption must be performed, thus preventing malicious downgrade. A domain can authenticate the certificate used in the TLS connection setup using a DNSSEC-signed TLSA RR.

Use of DNSSEC for S/MIME

DNSSEC can be used in conjunction with S/MIME to more fully secure email delivery, in a manner similar to the DANE functionality. This use is documented in an Internet Draft (*Using Secure DNS to Associate Certificates with Domain Names for S/MIME*, draft-ietf-dane-smime-09, August 27, 2015), which proposes a new SMIMEA DNS RR. The purpose of the SMIMEA RR is to associate certificates with DNS domain names.

As discussed in Section 19.4, S/MIME messages often contain certificates that can assist in authenticating the message sender and can be used in encrypting messages sent in reply. This feature requires that the receiving MUA validate the certificate associated with the purported sender. SMIMEA RRs can provide a secure means of doing this validation.

In essence, the SMIMEA RR will have the same format and content as the TLSA RR, with the same functionality. The difference is that it is geared to the needs of MUAs in dealing with domain names as specified in email addresses in the message body, rather than domain names specified in the outer SMTP envelope.

19.8 SENDER POLICY FRAMEWORK

SPF is the standardized way for a sending domain to identify and assert the mail senders for a given domain. The problem that SPF addresses is the following: With the current email infrastructure, any host can use any domain name for each of the various identifiers in the mail header, not just the domain name where the host is located. Two major drawbacks of this freedom are:

- It is a major obstacle to reducing unsolicited bulk email (UBE), also known as spam. It makes it difficult for mail handlers to filter out emails on the basis of known UBE sources.
- ADMDs (see Section 19.1) are understandably concerned about the ease with which other entities can make use of their domain names, often with malicious intent.

RFC 7208 defines the SPF. It provides a protocol by which ADMDs can authorize hosts to use their domain names in the "MAIL FROM" or "HELO" identities. Compliant ADMDs publish Sender Policy Framework (SPF) records in the DNS specifying which hosts are permitted to use their names, and compliant mail receivers use the published SPF records to test the authorization of sending Mail Transfer Agents (MTAs) using a given "HELO" or "MAIL FROM" identity during a mail transaction.

SPF works by checking a sender's IP address against the policy encoded in any SPF record found at the sending domain. The sending domain is the domain used in the SMTP connection, not the domain indicated in the message header as displayed in the MUA. This means that SPF checks can be applied before the message content is received from the sender.

Figure 19.8 is an example in which SPF would come into play. Assume that the sender's IP address is 192.168.0.1. The message arrives from the MTA with domain mta.example.net. The sender uses the MAIL FROM tag of alice@example.org, indicating that the message originates in the example.org domain. But the message header specifies alice.sender@example.net. The receiver uses SPF to query for the SPF RR that corresponds to example.com to check if the IP address 192.168.0.1 is

```
S: 220 foo.com Simple Mail Transfer Service Ready
C: HELO mta.example.net
S: 250 OK
C: MAIL FROM:<alice@example.org>
S: 250 OK
C: RCPT TO:<Jones@foo.com>
S: 250 OK
C: DATA
S: 354 Start mail input; end with <crlf>.<crlf>
C: To: bob@foo.com
C: From: alice.sender@example.net
C: Date: Today
C: Subject: Meeting Today
. . .
```

Figure 19.8 Example in which SMTP Envelope Header Does Not Match Message Header

listed as a valid sender, and then takes appropriate action based on the results of checking the RR.

SPF on the Sender Side

A sending domain needs to identify all the senders for a given domain and add that information into the DNS as a separate resource record. Next, the sending domain encodes the appropriate policy for each sender using the SPF syntax. The encoding is done in a TXT DNS resource record as a list of mechanisms and modifiers. Mechanisms are used to define an IP address or range of addresses to be matched, and modifiers indicate the policy for a given match. Table 19.7 lists the most important mechanisms and modifiers used in SPF.

The SPF syntax is fairly complex and can express complex relationships between senders. For more detail, see RFC 7208.

SPF on the Receiver Side

If SPF is implemented at a receiver, the SPF entity uses the SMTP envelope MAIL FROM: address domain and the IP address of the sender to query an SPF TXT RR. The SPF checks can be started before the body of the email message is received,

Table 19.7 Common SPF Mechanisms and Modifiers

Tag	Description
ip4	Specifies an IPv4 address or range of addresses that are authorized senders for a domain.
ip6	Specifies an IPv6 address or range of addresses that are authorized senders for a domain.
mx	Asserts that the listed hosts for the Mail Exchange RRs are also valid senders for the domain.
include	Lists another domain where the receiver should look for an SPF RR for further senders. This can be useful for large organizations with many domains or sub-domains that have a single set of shared senders. The include mechanism is recursive, in that the SPF check in the record found is tested in its entirety before proceeding. It is not simply a concatenation of the checks.
all	Matches every IP address that has not otherwise been matched.

(a) SPF Mechanisms

Modifier	Description
+	The given mechanism check must pass. This is the default mechanism and does not need to be explicitly listed.
–	The given mechanism is not allowed to send email on behalf of the domain.
~	The given mechanism is in transition and if an email is seen from the listed host/IP address, then it should be accepted but marked for closer inspection.
?	The SPF RR explicitly states nothing about the mechanism. In this case, the default behavior is to accept the email. (This makes it equivalent to '+' unless some sort of discrete or aggregate message review is conducted.)

(b) SPF Mechanism Modifiers

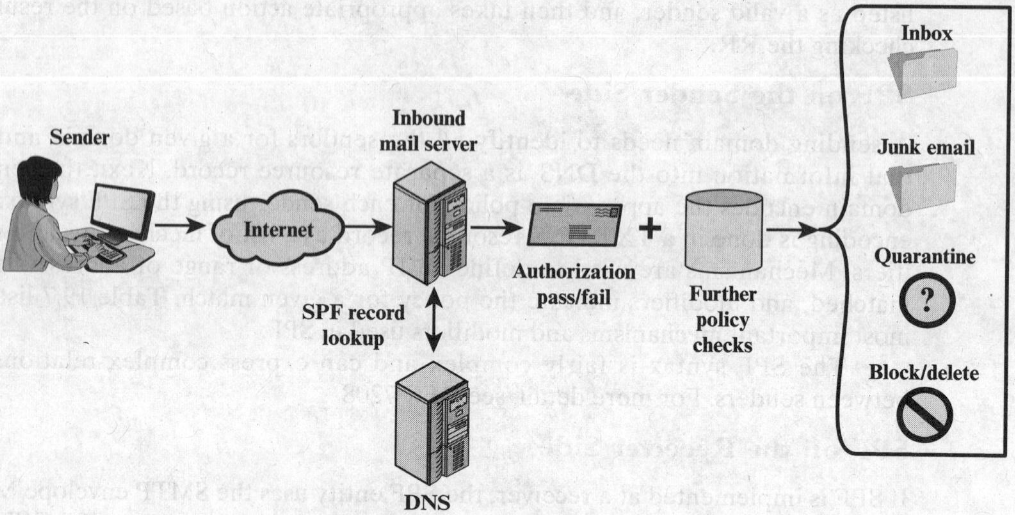

Figure 19.9 Sender Policy Framework Operation

which may result in blocking the transmission of the email content. Alternatively, the entire message can be absorbed and buffered until all the checks are finished. In either case, checks must be completed before the mail message is sent to the end user's inbox.

The checking involves the following rules:

1. If no SPF TXT RR is returned, the default behavior is to accept the message.
2. If the SPF TXT RR has formatting errors, the default behavior is to accept the message.
3. Otherwise the mechanisms and modifiers in the RR are used to determine disposition of the email message.

Figure 19.9 illustrates SPF operation.

19.9 DOMAINKEYS IDENTIFIED MAIL

DomainKeys Identified Mail (DKIM) is a specification for cryptographically signing email messages, permitting a signing domain to claim responsibility for a message in the mail stream. Message recipients (or agents acting in their behalf) can verify the signature by querying the signer's domain directly to retrieve the appropriate public key and thereby can confirm that the message was attested to by a party in possession of the private key for the signing domain. DKIM is an Internet Standard (RFC 6376: *DomainKeys Identified Mail (DKIM) Signatures*). DKIM has been widely adopted by a range of email providers, including corporations, government agencies, gmail, Yahoo!, and many Internet Service Providers (ISPs).

Email Threats

RFC 4686 (*Analysis of Threats Motivating DomainKeys Identified Mail*) describes the threats being addressed by DKIM in terms of the characteristics, capabilities, and location of potential attackers.

CHARACTERISTICS RFC 4686 characterizes the range of attackers on a spectrum of three levels of threat.

1. At the low end are attackers who simply want to send email that a recipient does not want to receive. The attacker can use one of a number of commercially available tools that allow the sender to falsify the origin address of messages. This makes it difficult for the receiver to filter spam on the basis of originating address or domain.
2. At the next level are professional senders of bulk spam mail. These attackers often operate as commercial enterprises and send messages on behalf of third parties. They employ more comprehensive tools for attack, including Mail Transfer Agents (MTAs) and registered domains and networks of compromised computers (zombies), to send messages and (in some cases) to harvest addresses to which to send.
3. The most sophisticated and financially motivated senders of messages are those who stand to receive substantial financial benefit, such as from an email-based fraud scheme. These attackers can be expected to employ all of the above mechanisms and additionally may attack the Internet infrastructure itself, including DNS cache-poisoning attacks and IP routing attacks.

CAPABILITIES RFC 4686 lists the following as capabilities that an attacker might have.

1. Submit messages to MTAs and Message Submission Agents (MSAs) at multiple locations in the Internet.
2. Construct arbitrary Message Header fields, including those claiming to be mailing lists, resenders, and other mail agents.
3. Sign messages on behalf of domains under their control.
4. Generate substantial numbers of either unsigned or apparently signed messages that might be used to attempt a denial-of-service attack.
5. Resend messages that may have been previously signed by the domain.
6. Transmit messages using any envelope information desired.
7. Act as an authorized submitter for messages from a compromised computer.
8. Manipulation of IP routing. This could be used to submit messages from specific IP addresses or difficult-to-trace addresses, or to cause diversion of messages to a specific domain.
9. Limited influence over portions of DNS using mechanisms such as cache poisoning. This might be used to influence message routing or to falsify advertisements of DNS-based keys or signing practices.

10. Access to significant computing resources, for example, through the conscription of worm-infected "zombie" computers. This could allow the "bad actor" to perform various types of brute-force attacks.
11. Ability to eavesdrop on existing traffic, perhaps from a wireless network.

Location DKIM focuses primarily on attackers located outside of the administrative units of the claimed originator and the recipient. These administrative units frequently correspond to the protected portions of the network adjacent to the originator and recipient. It is in this area that the trust relationships required for authenticated message submission do not exist and do not scale adequately to be practical. Conversely, within these administrative units, there are other mechanisms (such as authenticated message submission) that are easier to deploy and more likely to be used than DKIM. External bad actors are usually attempting to exploit the "any-to-any" nature of email that motivates most recipient MTAs to accept messages from anywhere for delivery to their local domain. They may generate messages without signatures, with incorrect signatures, or with correct signatures from domains with little traceability. They may also pose as mailing lists, greeting cards, or other agents that legitimately send or resend messages on behalf of others.

DKIM Strategy

DKIM is designed to provide an email authentication technique that is transparent to the end user. In essence, a user's email message is signed by a private key of the administrative domain from which the email originates. The signature covers all of the content of the message and some of the RFC 5322 message headers. At the receiving end, the MDA can access the corresponding public key via a DNS and verify the signature, thus authenticating that the message comes from the claimed administrative domain. Thus, mail that originates from somewhere else but claims to come from a given domain will not pass the authentication test and can be rejected. This approach differs from that of S/MIME and PGP, which use the originator's private key to sign the content of the message. The motivation for DKIM is based on the following reasoning:[2]

1. S/MIME depends on both the sending and receiving users employing S/MIME. For almost all users, the bulk of incoming mail does not use S/MIME, and the bulk of the mail the user wants to send is to recipients not using S/MIME.
2. S/MIME signs only the message content. Thus, RFC 5322 header information concerning origin can be compromised.
3. DKIM is not implemented in client programs (MUAs) and is therefore transparent to the user; the user need not take any action.
4. DKIM applies to all mail from cooperating domains.
5. DKIM allows good senders to prove that they did send a particular message and to prevent forgers from masquerading as good senders.

[2] The reasoning is expressed in terms of the use of S/MIME. The same argument applies to PGP.

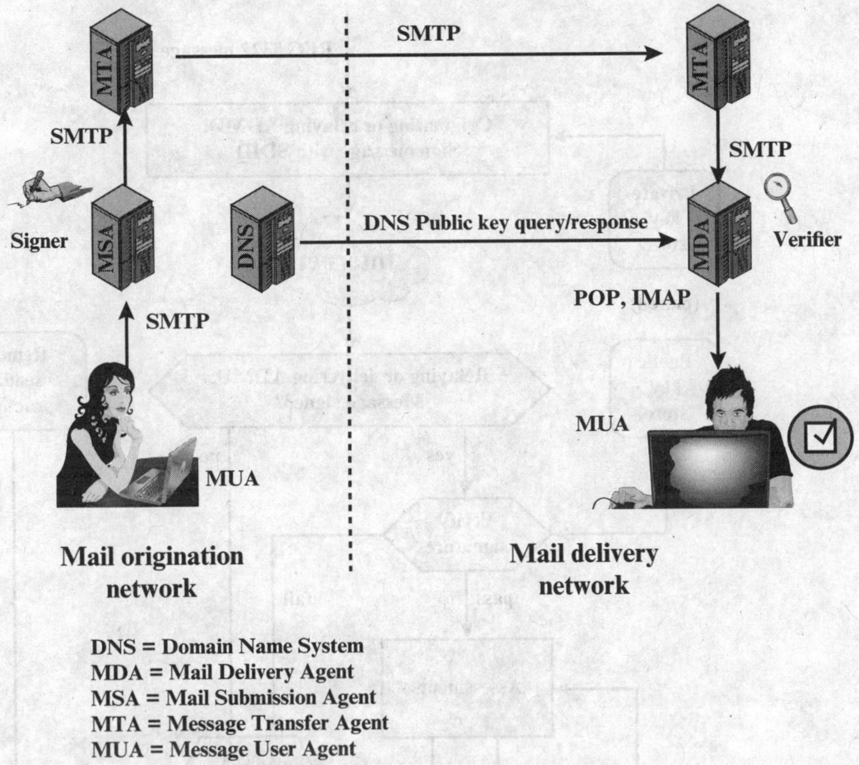

Figure 19.10 Simple Example of DKIM Deployment

Figure 19.10 is a simple example of the operation of DKIM. We begin with a message generated by a user and transmitted into the MHS to an MSA that is within the user's administrative domain. An email message is generated by an email client program. The content of the message, plus selected RFC 5322 headers, is signed by the email provider using the provider's private key. The signer is associated with a domain, which could be a corporate local network, an ISP, or a public email facility such as gmail. The signed message then passes through the Internet via a sequence of MTAs. At the destination, the MDA retrieves the public key for the incoming signature and verifies the signature before passing the message on to the destination email client. The default signing algorithm is RSA with SHA-256. RSA with SHA-1 also may be used.

DKIM Functional Flow

Figure 19.11 provides a more detailed look at the elements of DKIM operation. Basic message processing is divided between a signing Administrative Management Domain (ADMD) and a verifying ADMD. At its simplest, this is between the originating ADMD and the delivering ADMD, but it can involve other ADMDs in the handling path.

Signing is performed by an authorized module within the signing ADMD and uses private information from a Key Store. Within the originating ADMD,

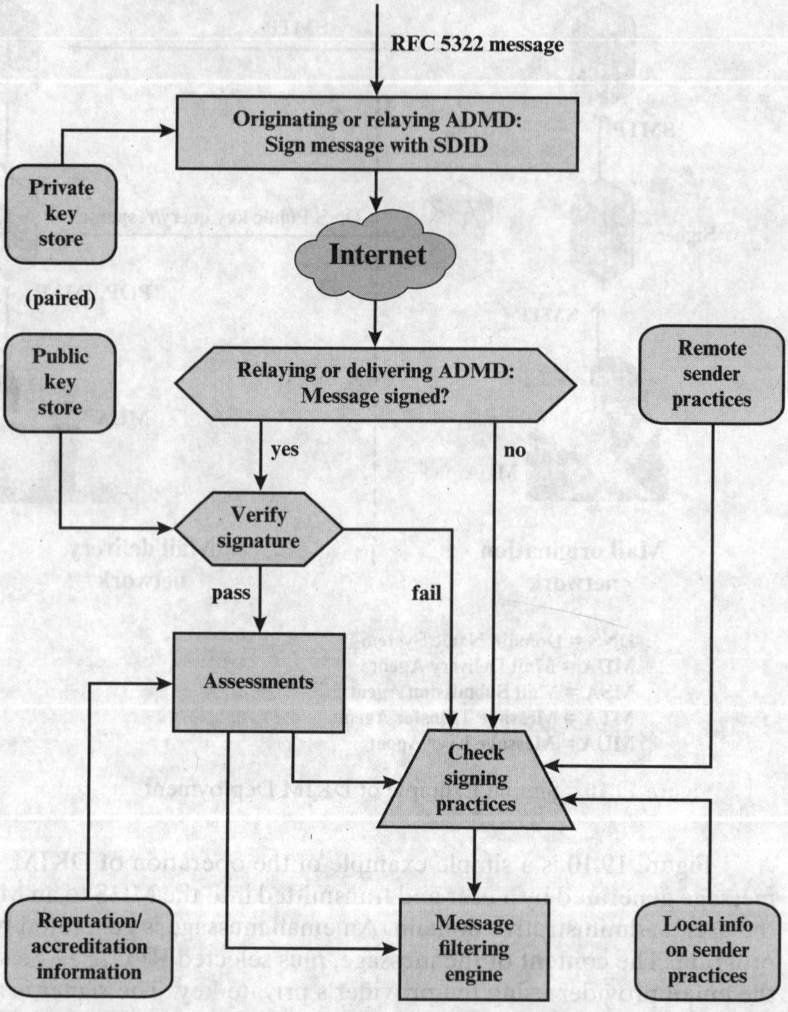

Figure 19.11 DKIM Functional Flow

this might be performed by the MUA, MSA, or an MTA. Verifying is performed by an authorized module within the verifying ADMD. Within a delivering ADMD, verifying might be performed by an MTA, MDA or MUA. The module verifies the signature or determines whether a particular signature was required. Verifying the signature uses public information from the Key Store. If the signature passes, reputation information is used to assess the signer and that information is passed to the message filtering system. If the signature fails or there is no signature using the author's domain, information about signing practices related to the author can be retrieved remotely and/or locally, and that information is passed to the message filtering system. For example, if the sender (e.g., gmail) uses DKIM but no DKIM signature is present, then the message may be considered fraudulent.

The signature is inserted into the RFC 5322 message as an additional header entry, starting with the keyword Dkim-Signature. You can view examples from your own incoming mail by using the View Long Headers (or similar wording) option for an incoming message. Here is an example:

```
Dkim-Signature:    v=1; a=rsa-sha256; c=relaxed/relaxed;
                   d=gmail.com; s=gamma; h=domainkey-
                   signature:mime-version:received:date:
                   message-id:subject :from:to:content-type:
                   content-transfer-encoding;
                   bh=5mZvQDyCRuyLb1Y28K4zgS2MPOemFToDBgvbJ
                   7GO90s=;
                   b=PcUvPSDygb4ya5Dyj1rbZGp/VyRiScuaz7TTG
                   J5qW5slM+klzv6kcfYdGDHzEVJW+Z
                   FetuPfF1ETOVhELtwH0zjSccOyPkEiblOf6gILO
                   bm3DDRm3Ys1/FVrbhVOlA+/jH9Aei
                   uIIw/5iFnRbSH6qPDVv/beDQqAWQfA/wF7O5k=
```

Before a message is signed, a process known as canonicalization is performed on both the header and body of the RFC 5322 message. Canonicalization is necessary to deal with the possibility of minor changes in the message made en route, including character encoding, treatment of trailing white space in message lines, and the "folding" and "unfolding" of header lines. The intent of canonicalization is to make a minimal transformation of the message (for the purpose of signing; the message itself is not changed, so the canonicalization must be performed again by the verifier) that will give it its best chance of producing the same canonical value at the receiving end. DKIM defines two header canonicalization algorithms ("simple" and "relaxed") and two for the body (with the same names). The simple algorithm tolerates almost no modification, while the relaxed algorithm tolerates common modifications.

The signature includes a number of fields. Each field begins with a tag consisting of a tag code followed by an equals sign and ends with a semicolon. The fields include the following:

- **v=** DKIM version/
- **a=** Algorithm used to generate the signature; must be either `rsa-sha1` or `rsa-sha256`
- **c=** Canonicalization method used on the header and the body.
- **d=** A domain name used as an identifier to refer to the identity of a responsible person or organization. In DKIM, this identifier is called the Signing Domain IDentifier (SDID). In our example, this field indicates that the sender is using a gmail address.
- **s=** In order that different keys may be used in different circumstances for the same signing domain (allowing expiration of old keys, separate departmental signing, or the like), DKIM defines a selector (a name associated with a key) that is used by the verifier to retrieve the proper key during signature verification.

- **h=** Signed Header fields. A colon-separated list of header field names that identify the header fields presented to the signing algorithm. Note that in our example above, the signature covers the domainkey-signature field. This refers to an older algorithm (since replaced by DKIM) that is still in use.
- **bh=** The hash of the canonicalized body part of the message. This provides additional information for diagnosing signature verification failures.
- **b=** The signature data in base64 format; this is the encrypted hash code.

19.10 DOMAIN-BASED MESSAGE AUTHENTICATION, REPORTING, AND CONFORMANCE

Domain-Based Message Authentication, Reporting, and Conformance (DMARC) allows email senders to specify policy on how their mail should be handled, the types of reports that receivers can send back, and the frequency those reports should be sent. It is defined in RFC 7489 (*Domain-based Message Authentication, Reporting, and Conformance*, March 2015).

DMARC works with SPF and DKIM. SPF and DKM enable senders to advise receivers, via DNS, whether mail purporting to come from the sender is valid, and whether it should be delivered, flagged, or discarded. However, neither SPF nor DKIM include a mechanism to tell receivers if SPF or DKIM are in use, nor do they have feedback mechanism to inform senders of the effectiveness of the anti-spam techniques. For example, if a message arrives at a receiver without a DKIM signature, DKIM provides no mechanism to allow the receiver to learn if the message is authentic but was sent from a sender that did not implement DKIM, or if the message is a spoof. DMARC addresses these issues essentially by standardizing how email receivers perform email authentication using SPF and DKIM mechanisms.

Identifier Alignment

DKIM, SPF, and DMARC authenticate various aspects of an individual message. DKIM authenticates the domain that affixed a signature to the message. SPF focuses on the SMTP envelope, defined in RFC 5321. It can authenticate either the domain that appears in the MAIL FROM portion of the SMTP envelope or the HELO domain, or both. These may be different domains, and they are typically not visible to the end user.

DMARC authentication deals with the From domain in the message header, as defined in RFC 5322. This field is used as the central identity of the DMARC mechanism because it is a required message header field and therefore guaranteed to be present in compliant messages, and most MUAs represent the RFC 5322 From field as the originator of the message and render some or all of this header field's content to end users. The email address in this field is the one used by end users to identify the source of the message and therefore is a prime target for abuse.

DMARC requires that From address match (be aligned with) an Authenticated Identifier from DKIM or SPF. In the case of DKIM, the match is made between the DKIM signing domain and the From domain. In the case of SPF, the match is between the SPF-authenticated domain and the From domain.

DMARC on the Sender Side

A mail sender that uses DMARC must also use SPF or DKIM, or both. The sender posts a DMARC policy in the DNS that advises receivers on how to treat messages that purport to originate from the sender's domain. The policy is in the form of a DNS TXT resource record. The sender also needs to establish email addresses to receive aggregate and forensic reports. As these email addresses are published unencrypted in the DNS TXT RR, they are easily discovered, leaving the poster subject to unsolicited bulk email. Thus, the poster of the DNS TXT RR needs to employ some kind of abuse countermeasures.

Similar to SPF and DKIM, the DMARC policy in the TXT RR is encoded in a series of `tag=value` pairs separated by semicolons. Table 19.8 describes the common tags.

Once the DMARC RR is posted, messages from the sender are typically processed as follows:

1. The domain owner constructs an SPF policy and publishes it in its DNS database. The domain owner also configures its system for DKIM signing. Finally, the domain owner publishes via the DNS a DMARC message-handling policy.
2. The author generates a message and hands the message to the domain owner's designated mail submission service.
3. The submission service passes relevant details to the DKIM signing module in order to generate a DKIM signature to be applied to the message.
4. The submission service relays the now-signed message to its designated transport service for routing to its intended recipient(s).

DMARC on the Receiver Side

A message generated on the sender side may pass through other relays but eventually arrives at a receiver's transport service. The typical processing order for DMARC on the receiving side is the following:

1. The receiver performs standard validation tests, such as checking against IP blocklists and domain reputation lists, as well as enforcing rate limits from a particular source.
2. The receiver extracts the RFC 5322 From address from the message. This must contain a single, valid address or else the mail is refused as an error.
3. The receiver queries for the DMARC DNS record based on the sending domain. If none exists, terminate DMARC processing.
4. The receiver performs DKIM signature checks. If more than one DKIM signature exists in the message, one must verify.
5. The receiver queries for the sending domain's SPF record and performs SPF validation checks.
6. The receiver conducts Identifier Alignment checks between the RFC 5321 From and the results of the SPF and DKIM records (if present).

Table 19.8 DMARC Tag and Value Descriptions

Tag (Name)	Description
v= (Version)	Version field that must be present as the first element. By default the value is always **DMARC1**.
p= (Policy)	Mandatory policy field. May take values **none** or **quarantine** or **reject**. This allows for a gradually tightening policy where the sender domain recommends no specific action on mail that fails DMARC checks **(p= none),** through treating failed mail as suspicious **(p= quarantine),** to rejecting all failed mail **(p= reject),** preferably at the SMTP transaction stage.
aspf= (SPF Policy)	Values are **r** (default) for relaxed and **s** for strict SPF domain enforcement. Strict alignment requires an exact match between the From address domain and the (passing) SPF check must exactly match the MailFrom address (HELO address). Relaxed requires that only the From and MailFrom address domains be in alignment. For example, the MailFrom address domain **smtp.example.org** and the From address **announce@example.org** are in alignment, but not a strict match.
adkim= (DKIM Policy)	Optional. Values are **r** (default) for relaxed and **s** for strict DKIM domain enforcement. Strict alignment requires an exact match between the From domain in the message header and the DKIM domain presented in the **(d=** DKIM), tag. Relaxed requires only that the domain part is in alignment (as in **aspf**).
fo= (Failure reporting options)	Optional. Ignore if a **ruf** argument is not also present. Value **0** indicates the receiver should generate a DMARC failure report if all underlying mechanisms fail to produce an aligned pass result. Value **1** means generate a DMARC failure report if any underlying mechanism produces something other than an aligned pass result. Other possible values are **d** (generate a DKIM failure report if a signature failed evaluation), and **s** (generate an SPF failure report if the message failed SPF evaluation). These values are not exclusive and may be combined.
ruf=	Optional, but requires the **fo** argument to be present. Lists a series of URIs (currently just **mailto:**<emailaddress>) that list where to send forensic feedback reports. This is for reports on message-specific failures.
rua=	Optional list of URIs (like in **ruf=**, using the **mailto:** URI) listing where to send aggregate feedback back to the sender. These reports are sent based on the interval requested using the **ri=** option with a default of 86400 seconds if not listed.
ri= (Reporting interval)	Optional with the default value of 86400 seconds. The value listed is the reporting interval desired by the sender.
pct= (Percent)	Optional with the default value of **100**. Expresses the percentage of a sender's mail that should be subject to the given DMARC policy. This allows senders to ramp up their policy enforcement gradually and prevent having to commit to a rigorous policy before getting feedback on their existing policy.
sp= (Receiver Policy)	Optional with a default value of **none**. Other values include the same range of values as the **p=** argument. This is the policy to be applied to mail from all identified subdomains of the given DMARC RR.

7. The results of these steps are passed to the DMARC module along with the Author's domain. The DMARC module attempts to retrieve a policy from the DNS for that domain. If none is found, the DMARC module determines the organizational domain and repeats the attempt to retrieve a policy from the DNS.
8. If a policy is found, it is combined with the Author's domain and the SPF and DKIM results to produce a DMARC policy result (a "pass" or "fail") and can optionally cause one of two kinds of reports to be generated.

9. Recipient transport service either delivers the message to the recipient inbox or takes other local policy action based on the DMARC result.
10. When requested, Recipient transport service collects data from the message delivery session to be used in providing feedback.

Figure 19.12, based on one at DMARC.org, summarizes the sending and receiving functional flow.

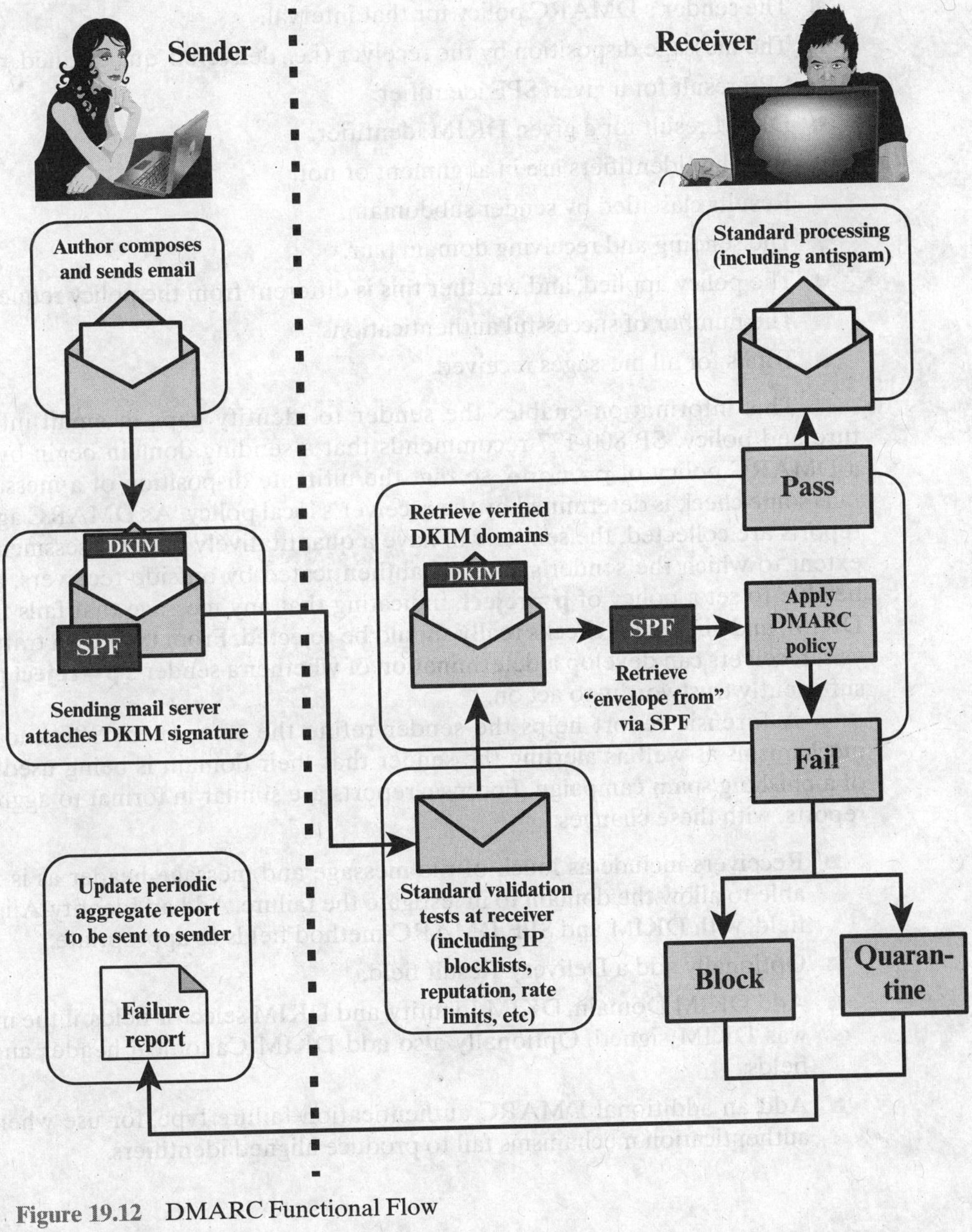

Figure 19.12 DMARC Functional Flow

DMARC Reports

DMARC reporting provides the sender's feedback on their SPF, DKIM, Identifier Alignment, and message disposition policies, which enable the sender to make these policies more effective. Two types of reports are sent: aggregate reports and forensic reports.

Aggregate reports are sent by receivers periodically and include aggregate figures for successful and unsuccessful message authentications, including:

- The sender's DMARC policy for that interval.
- The message disposition by the receiver (i.e., delivered, quarantined, rejected).
- SPF result for a given SPF identifier.
- DKIM result for a given DKIM identifier.
- Whether identifiers are in alignment or not.
- Results classified by sender subdomain.
- The sending and receiving domain pair.
- The policy applied, and whether this is different from the policy requested.
- The number of successful authentications.
- Totals for all messages received.

This information enables the sender to identify gaps in email infrastructure and policy. SP 800-177 recommends that a sending domain begin by setting a DMARC policy of **p= none**, so that the ultimate disposition of a message that fails some check is determined by the receiver's local policy. As DMARC aggregate reports are collected, the sender will have a quantitatively better assessment of the extent to which the sender's email is authenticated by outside receivers, and will be able to set a policy of **p=reject**, indicating that any message that fails the SPF, DKIM, and alignment checks really should be rejected. From their own traffic analysis, receivers can develop a determination of whether a sender's **p=reject** policy is sufficiently trustworthy to act on.

A forensic report helps the sender refine the component SPF and DKIM mechanisms as well as alerting the sender that their domain is being used as part of a phishing/spam campaign. Forensic reports are similar in format to aggregation reports, with these changes:

- Receivers include as much of the message and message header as is reasonable to allow the domain to investigate the failure. Add an Identity-Alignment field, with DKIM and SPF DMARC-method fields as appropriate.
- Optionally add a Delivery-Result field.
- Add DKIM Domain, DKIM Identity, and DKIM selector fields, if the message was DKIM signed. Optionally also add DKIM Canonical header and body fields.
- Add an additional DMARC authentication failure type, for use when some authentication mechanisms fail to produce aligned identifiers.

19.11 KEY TERMS, REVIEW QUESTIONS, AND PROBLEMS

Key Terms

administrative management domain (ADMD) base64 Cryptographic Message Syntax (CMS) detached signature DNS-based Authentication of Named Entities (DANE) DNS Security Extensions (DNSSEC) Domain-based Message Authentication, Reporting, and Conformance (DMARC)	Domain Name System (DNS) DomainKeys Identified Mail (DKIM) electronic mail Internet Mail Access Protocol (IMAP) Mail Delivery Agent (MDA) Mail Submission Agent (MSA) Message Handling Service (MHS) Message Store Message Transfer Agents (MTA)	Message User Agent (MUA) Multipurpose Internet Mail Extensions (MIME) Post Office Protocol (POP3) Pretty Good Privacy (PGP) Sender Policy Framework (SPF) session key Simple Mail Transfer Protocol (SMTP) STARTTLS SUBMISSION S/MIME trust

Review Questions

19.1 What are the two types of protocols used for transferring email?

19.2 What are the SMTP and MIME standards?

19.3 What is the difference between a MIME content type and a MIME transfer encoding?

19.4 Briefly explain quoted-printable encoding.

19.5 Why is base64 conversion useful for an email application?

19.6 What is S/MIME?

19.7 Briefly describe the S/MIME message content types.

19.8 What is the utility of a detached signature?

19.9 Discuss in brief the DKIM strategy.

Problems

19.1 The character sequence "<CR><LF>.<CR><LF>" indicates the end of mail data to a SMTP-server. What happens if the mail data itself contains that character sequence?

19.2 How compression of messages is achieved in S/MIME?

19.3 If a lossless compression algorithm, such as ZIP, is used with S/MIME, why is it preferable to generate a signature before applying compression?

19.4 Before the deployment of the Domain Name System, a simple text file (HOSTS.TXT) centrally maintained at the SRI Network Information Center was used to enable mapping between host names and addresses. Each host connected to the Internet had to have an updated local copy of it to be able to use host names instead of having to cope directly with their IP addresses. Discuss the main advantages of the DNS over the old centralized HOSTS.TXT system.

19.5 For this problem and the next few, consult Appendix P. In Figure P.2, each entry in the public-key ring contains an Owner Trust field that indicates the degree of trust associated with this public-key owner. Why is that not enough? That is, if this owner is trusted and this is supposed to be the owner's public key, why is that trust not enough to permit PGP to use this public key?

19.6 What is the basic difference between X.509 and PGP in terms of key hierarchies and key trust?

19.7 PGP makes use of the cipher feedback (CFB) mode of CAST-128, whereas most symmetric encryption applications (other than key encryption) use the cipher block chaining (CBC) mode. We have

CBC: $C_i = \mathrm{E}(K, [C_{i-1} \oplus P_i])$; $P_i = C_{i-1} \oplus \mathrm{D}(K, C_i)$

CFB: $C_i = P_i \oplus \mathrm{E}(K, C_{i-1})$; $P_i = C_i \oplus \mathrm{E}(K, C_{i-1})$

These two appear to provide equal security. Suggest a reason why PGP uses the CFB mode.

19.8 A PGP user may have multiple public keys. So that a recipient knows which public key is being used by a sender, a key ID, consisting of the least significant 64 bits of the public key, is sent with the message. What is the probability that a user with N public keys will have at least one duplicate key ID?

19.9 The first 16 bits of the message digest in a PGP signature are translated in the clear. This enables the recipient to determine if the correct public key was used to decrypt the message digest by comparing this plaintext copy of the first two octets with the first two octets of the decrypted digest.

a. To what extent does this compromise the security of the hash algorithm?

b. To what extent does it in fact perform its intended function, namely, to help determine if the correct RSA key was used to decrypt the digest?

19.10 Consider base64 conversion as a form of encryption. In this case, there is no key. But suppose that an opponent knew only that some form of substitution algorithm was being used to encrypt English text and did not guess that it was base64. How effective would this algorithm be against cryptanalysis?

19.11 Encode the text "plaintext" using the following techniques. Assume characters are stored in 8-bit ASCII with zero parity.

a. base64

b. Quoted-printable

19.12 Use a 2 × 2 matrix to categorize the properties of the four certificate usage models in DANE.

CHAPTER 20

IP SECURITY

LEARNING OBJECTIVES

After studying this chapter, you should be able to:

- Present an overview of IP security (IPsec).
- Explain the difference between transport mode and tunnel mode.
- Understand the concept of security association.
- Explain the difference between the security association database and the security policy database.
- Summarize the traffic processing functions performed by IPsec for outbound packets and for inbound packets.
- Present an overview of Encapsulating Security Payload.
- Discuss the alternatives for combining security associations.
- Present an overview of Internet Key Exchange.
- Summarize the alternative cryptographic suites approved for use with IPsec.

There are application-specific security mechanisms for a number of application areas, including electronic mail (S/MIME, PGP), client/server (Kerberos), Web access (Secure Sockets Layer), and others. However, users have security concerns that cut across protocol layers. For example, an enterprise can run a secure, private IP network by disallowing links to untrusted sites, encrypting packets that leave the premises, and authenticating packets that enter the premises. By implementing security at the IP level, an organization can ensure secure networking not only for applications that have security mechanisms but also for the many security-ignorant applications.

IP-level security encompasses three functional areas: authentication, confidentiality, and key management. The authentication mechanism assures that a received packet was, in fact, transmitted by the party identified as the source in the packet header. In addition, this mechanism assures that the packet has not been altered in transit. The confidentiality facility enables communicating nodes to encrypt messages to prevent eavesdropping by third parties. The key management facility is concerned with the secure exchange of keys.

We begin this chapter with an overview of IP security (IPsec) and an introduction to the IPsec architecture. We then look at each of the three functional areas in detail. Appendix L reviews Internet protocols.

20.1 IP SECURITY OVERVIEW

In 1994, the Internet Architecture Board (IAB) issued a report titled "Security in the Internet Architecture" (RFC 1636). The report identified key areas for security mechanisms. Among these were the need to secure the network infrastructure from unauthorized monitoring and control of network traffic and the need to secure end-user-to-end-user traffic using authentication and encryption mechanisms.

To provide security, the IAB included authentication and encryption as necessary security features in the next-generation IP, which has been issued as IPv6. Fortunately, these security capabilities were designed to be usable both with the current IPv4 and the future IPv6. This means that vendors can begin offering these features now, and many vendors now do have some IPsec capability in their products. The IPsec specification now exists as a set of Internet standards.

Applications of IPsec

IPsec provides the capability to secure communications across a LAN, across private and public WANs, and across the Internet. Examples of its use include:

- **Secure branch office connectivity over the Internet:** A company can build a secure virtual private network over the Internet or over a public WAN. This enables a business to rely heavily on the Internet and reduce its need for private networks, saving costs and network management overhead.
- **Secure remote access over the Internet:** An end user whose system is equipped with IP security protocols can make a local call to an Internet Service Provider (ISP) and gain secure access to a company network. This reduces the cost of toll charges for traveling employees and telecommuters.
- **Establishing extranet and intranet connectivity with partners:** IPsec can be used to secure communication with other organizations, ensuring authentication and confidentiality and providing a key exchange mechanism.
- **Enhancing electronic commerce security:** Even though some Web and electronic commerce applications have built-in security protocols, the use of IPsec enhances that security. IPsec guarantees that all traffic designated by the network administrator is both encrypted and authenticated, adding an additional layer of security to whatever is provided at the application layer.

The principal feature of IPsec that enables it to support these varied applications is that it can encrypt and/or authenticate *all* traffic at the IP level. Thus, all distributed applications (including remote logon, client/server, email, file transfer, Web access, and so on) can be secured. Figure 20.1a shows a simplified packet format for an IPsec option known as tunnel mode, described subsequently. Tunnel mode makes use of an IPsec function, a combined authentication/encryption function called Encapsulating Security Payload (ESP), and a key exchange function. For VPNs, both authentication and encryption are generally desired, because it is important both to (1) assure that unauthorized users do not penetrate the VPN, and (2) assure that eavesdroppers on the Internet cannot read messages sent over the VPN.

Figure 20.1b is a typical scenario of IPsec usage. An organization maintains LANs at dispersed locations. Nonsecure IP traffic is conducted on each LAN. For traffic offsite, through some sort of private or public WAN, IPsec protocols are used. These protocols operate in networking devices, such as a router or firewall, that connect each LAN to the outside world. The IPsec networking device will typically encrypt all traffic going into the WAN and decrypt traffic coming from the WAN; these operations are transparent to workstations and servers on the LAN. Secure

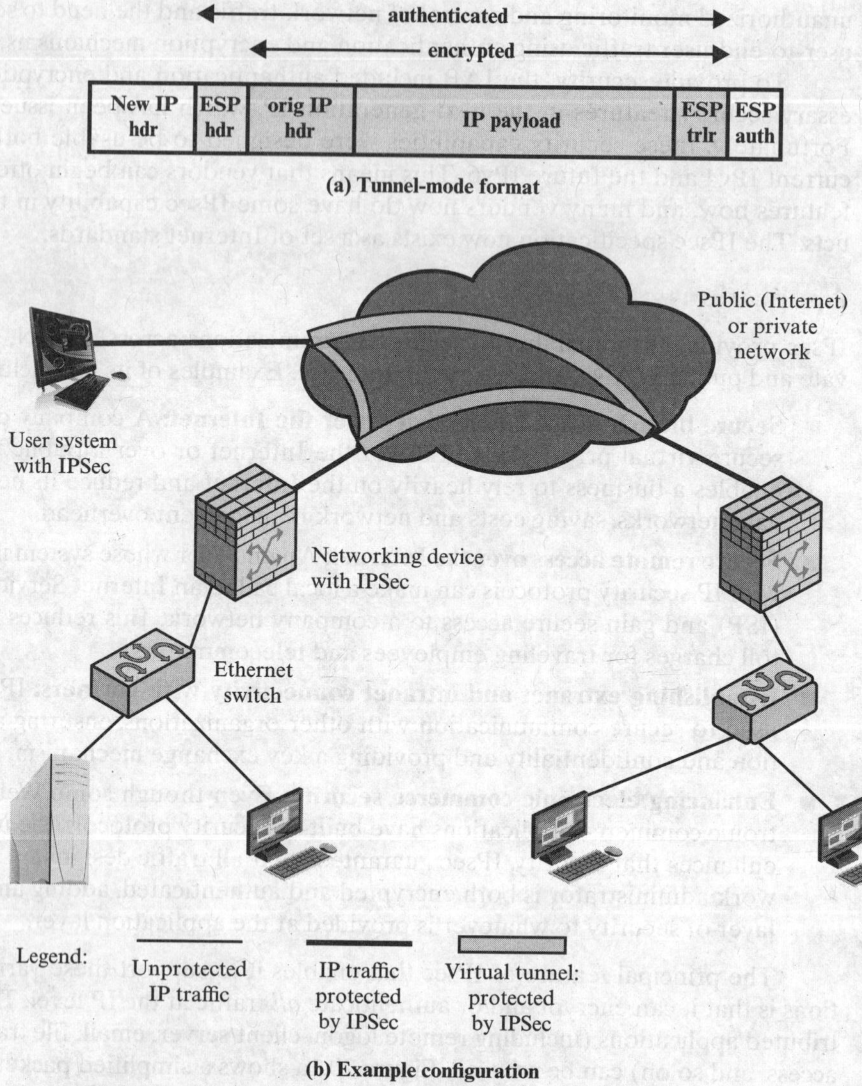

Figure 20.1 An IPSec VPN Scenario

transmission is also possible with individual users who dial into the WAN. Such user workstations must implement the IPsec protocols to provide security.

Benefits of IPsec

Some of the benefits of IPsec:

- When IPsec is implemented in a firewall or router, it provides strong security that can be applied to all traffic crossing the perimeter. Traffic within a company or workgroup does not incur the overhead of security-related processing.

- IPsec in a firewall is resistant to bypass if all traffic from the outside must use IP and the firewall is the only means of entrance from the Internet into the organization.
- IPsec is below the transport layer (TCP, UDP) and so is transparent to applications. There is no need to change software on a user or server system when IPsec is implemented in the firewall or router. Even if IPsec is implemented in end systems, upper-layer software, including applications, is not affected.
- IPsec can be transparent to end users. There is no need to train users on security mechanisms, issue keying material on a per-user basis, or revoke keying material when users leave the organization.
- IPsec can provide security for individual users if needed. This is useful for offsite workers and for setting up a secure virtual subnetwork within an organization for sensitive applications.

Routing Applications

In addition to supporting end users and protecting premises systems and networks, IPsec can play a vital role in the routing architecture required for internetworking. [HUIT98] lists the following examples of the use of IPsec. IPsec can assure that

- A router advertisement (a new router advertises its presence) comes from an authorized router.
- A neighbor advertisement (a router seeks to establish or maintain a neighbor relationship with a router in another routing domain) comes from an authorized router.
- A redirect message comes from the router to which the initial IP packet was sent.
- A routing update is not forged.

Without such security measures, an opponent can disrupt communications or divert some traffic. Routing protocols such as Open Shortest Path First (OSPF) should be run on top of security associations between routers that are defined by IPsec.

IPsec Documents

IPsec encompasses three functional areas: authentication, confidentiality, and key management. The totality of the IPsec specification is scattered across dozens of RFCs and draft IETF documents, making this the most complex and difficult to grasp of all IETF specifications. The best way to grasp the scope of IPsec is to consult the latest version of the IPsec document roadmap, which as of this writing is RFC 6071 [*IP Security (IPsec) and Internet Key Exchange (IKE) Document Roadmap*, February 2011]. The documents can be categorized into the following groups.

- **Architecture:** Covers the general concepts, security requirements, definitions, and mechanisms defining IPsec technology. The current specification is RFC 4301, *Security Architecture for the Internet Protocol*.

- **Authentication Header (AH):** AH is an extension header to provide message authentication. The current specification is RFC 4302, *IP Authentication Header*. Because message authentication is provided by ESP, the use of AH is deprecated. It is included in IPsecv3 for backward compatibility but should not be used in new applications. We do not discuss AH in this chapter.
- **Encapsulating Security Payload (ESP):** ESP consists of an encapsulating header and trailer used to provide encryption or combined encryption/authentication. The current specification is RFC 4303, *IP Encapsulating Security Payload (ESP)*.
- **Internet Key Exchange (IKE):** This is a collection of documents describing the key management schemes for use with IPsec. The main specification is RFC 7296, *Internet Key Exchange (IKEv2) Protocol*, but there are a number of related RFCs.
- **Cryptographic algorithms:** This category encompasses a large set of documents that define and describe cryptographic algorithms for encryption, message authentication, pseudorandom functions (PRFs), and cryptographic key exchange.
- **Other:** There are a variety of other IPsec-related RFCs, including those dealing with security policy and management information base (MIB) content.

IPsec Services

IPsec provides security services at the IP layer by enabling a system to select required security protocols, determine the algorithm(s) to use for the service(s), and put in place any cryptographic keys required to provide the requested services. Two protocols are used to provide security: an authentication protocol designated by the header of the protocol, Authentication Header (AH); and a combined encryption/authentication protocol designated by the format of the packet for that protocol, Encapsulating Security Payload (ESP). RFC 4301 lists the following services:

- Access control
- Connectionless integrity
- Data origin authentication
- Rejection of replayed packets (a form of partial sequence integrity)
- Confidentiality (encryption)
- Limited traffic flow confidentiality

Transport and Tunnel Modes

Both AH and ESP support two modes of use: transport and tunnel mode. The operation of these two modes is best understood in the context of a description of ESP, which is covered in Section 20.3. Here we provide a brief overview.

TRANSPORT MODE Transport mode provides protection primarily for upper-layer protocols. That is, transport mode protection extends to the payload of an IP packet.[1] Examples include a TCP or UDP segment or an ICMP packet, all of which operate directly above IP in a host protocol stack. Typically, transport mode is used for end-to-end communication between two hosts (e.g., a client and a server, or two workstations). When a host runs AH or ESP over IPv4, the payload is the data that normally follow the IP header. For IPv6, the payload is the data that normally follow both the IP header and any IPv6 extensions headers that are present, with the possible exception of the destination options header, which may be included in the protection.

ESP in transport mode encrypts and optionally authenticates the IP payload but not the IP header. AH in transport mode authenticates the IP payload and selected portions of the IP header.

TUNNEL MODE Tunnel mode provides protection to the entire IP packet. To achieve this, after the AH or ESP fields are added to the IP packet, the entire packet plus security fields is treated as the payload of new outer IP packet with a new outer IP header. The entire original, inner, packet travels through a tunnel from one point of an IP network to another; no routers along the way are able to examine the inner IP header. Because the original packet is encapsulated, the new, larger packet may have totally different source and destination addresses, adding to the security. Tunnel mode is used when one or both ends of a security association (SA) are a security gateway, such as a firewall or router that implements IPsec. With tunnel mode, a number of hosts on networks behind firewalls may engage in secure communications without implementing IPsec. The unprotected packets generated by such hosts are tunneled through external networks by tunnel mode SAs set up by the IPsec software in the firewall or secure router at the boundary of the local network.

Here is an example of how tunnel mode IPsec operates. Host A on a network generates an IP packet with the destination address of host B on another network. This packet is routed from the originating host to a firewall or secure router at the boundary of A's network. The firewall filters all outgoing packets to determine the need for IPsec processing. If this packet from A to B requires IPsec, the firewall performs IPsec processing and encapsulates the packet with an outer IP header. The source IP address of this outer IP packet is this firewall, and the destination address may be a firewall that forms the boundary to B's local network. This packet is now routed to B's firewall, with intermediate routers examining only the outer IP header. At B's firewall, the outer IP header is stripped off, and the inner packet is delivered to B.

ESP in tunnel mode encrypts and optionally authenticates the entire inner IP packet, including the inner IP header. AH in tunnel mode authenticates the entire inner IP packet and selected portions of the outer IP header.

Table 20.1 summarizes transport and tunnel mode functionality.

[1]In this chapter, the term *IP packet* refers to either an IPv4 datagram or an IPv6 packet.

Table 20.1 Tunnel Mode and Transport Mode Functionality

	Transport Mode SA	Tunnel Mode SA
AH	Authenticates IP payload and selected portions of IP header and IPv6 extension headers.	Authenticates entire inner IP packet (inner header plus IP payload) plus selected portions of outer IP header and outer IPv6 extension headers.
ESP	Encrypts IP payload and any IPv6 extension headers following the ESP header.	Encrypts entire inner IP packet.
ESP with Authentication	Encrypts IP payload and any IPv6 extension headers following the ESP header. Authenticates IP payload but not IP header.	Encrypts entire inner IP packet. Authenticates inner IP packet.

20.2 IP SECURITY POLICY

Fundamental to the operation of IPsec is the concept of a security policy applied to each IP packet that transits from a source to a destination. IPsec policy is determined primarily by the interaction of two databases, the **security association database (SAD)** and the **security policy database (SPD)**. This section provides an overview of these two databases and then summarizes their use during IPsec operation. Figure 20.2 illustrates the relevant relationships.

Security Associations

A key concept that appears in both the authentication and confidentiality mechanisms for IP is the security association (SA). An association is a one-way logical connection between a sender and a receiver that affords security services to the traffic carried on it. If a peer relationship is needed for two-way secure exchange, then two security associations are required.

A security association is uniquely identified by three parameters.

- **Security Parameters Index (SPI):** A 32-bit unsigned integer assigned to this SA and having local significance only. The SPI is carried in AH and ESP headers to enable the receiving system to select the SA under which a received packet will be processed.
- **IP Destination Address:** This is the address of the destination endpoint of the SA, which may be an end-user system or a network system such as a firewall or router.
- **Security Protocol Identifier:** This field from the outer IP header indicates whether the association is an AH or ESP security association.

Hence, in any IP packet, the security association is uniquely identified by the Destination Address in the IPv4 or IPv6 header and the SPI in the enclosed extension header (AH or ESP).

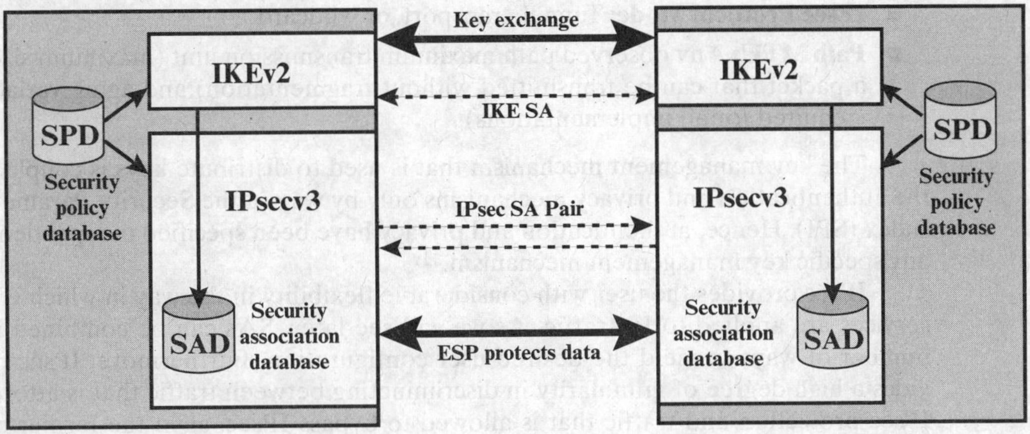

Figure 20.2 IPsec Architecture

Security Association Database

In each IPsec implementation, there is a nominal[2] Security Association Database that defines the parameters associated with each SA. A security association is normally defined by the following parameters in an SAD entry.

- **Security Parameter Index:** A 32-bit value selected by the receiving end of an SA to uniquely identify the SA. In an SAD entry for an outbound SA, the SPI is used to construct the packet's AH or ESP header. In an SAD entry for an inbound SA, the SPI is used to map traffic to the appropriate SA.
- **Sequence Number Counter:** A 32-bit value used to generate the Sequence Number field in AH or ESP headers, described in Section 20.3 (required for all implementations).
- **Sequence Counter Overflow:** A flag indicating whether overflow of the Sequence Number Counter should generate an auditable event and prevent further transmission of packets on this SA (required for all implementations).
- **Anti-Replay Window:** Used to determine whether an inbound AH or ESP packet is a replay, described in Section 20.3 (required for all implementations).
- **AH Information:** Authentication algorithm, keys, key lifetimes, and related parameters being used with AH (required for AH implementations).
- **ESP Information:** Encryption and authentication algorithm, keys, initialization values, key lifetimes, and related parameters being used with ESP (required for ESP implementations).
- **Lifetime of this Security Association:** A time interval or byte count after which an SA must be replaced with a new SA (and new SPI) or terminated, plus an indication of which of these actions should occur (required for all implementations).

[2]Nominal in the sense that the functionality provided by a Security Association Database must be present in any IPsec implementation, but the way in which that functionality is provided is up to the implementer.

- **IPsec Protocol Mode:** Tunnel, transport, or wildcard.
- **Path MTU:** Any observed path maximum transmission unit (maximum size of a packet that can be transmitted without fragmentation) and aging variables (required for all implementations).

The key management mechanism that is used to distribute keys is coupled to the authentication and privacy mechanisms only by way of the Security Parameters Index (SPI). Hence, authentication and privacy have been specified independent of any specific key management mechanism.

IPsec provides the user with considerable flexibility in the way in which IPsec services are applied to IP traffic. As we will see later, SAs can be combined in a number of ways to yield the desired user configuration. Furthermore, IPsec provides a high degree of granularity in discriminating between traffic that is afforded IPsec protection and traffic that is allowed to bypass IPsec, as in the former case relating IP traffic to specific SAs.

Security Policy Database

The means by which IP traffic is related to specific SAs (or no SA in the case of traffic allowed to bypass IPsec) is the nominal Security Policy Database (SPD). In its simplest form, an SPD contains entries, each of which defines a subset of IP traffic and points to an SA for that traffic. In more complex environments, there may be multiple entries that potentially relate to a single SA or multiple SAs associated with a single SPD entry. The reader is referred to the relevant IPsec documents for a full discussion.

Each SPD entry is defined by a set of IP and upper-layer protocol field values, called *selectors*. In effect, these selectors are used to filter outgoing traffic in order to map it into a particular SA. Outbound processing obeys the following general sequence for each IP packet.

1. Compare the values of the appropriate fields in the packet (the selector fields) against the SPD to find a matching SPD entry, which will point to zero or more SAs.
2. Determine the SA if any for this packet and its associated SPI.
3. Do the required IPsec processing (i.e., AH or ESP processing).

The following selectors determine an SPD entry:

- **Remote IP Address:** This may be a single IP address, an enumerated list or range of addresses, or a wildcard (mask) address. The latter two are required to support more than one destination system sharing the same SA (e.g., behind a firewall).
- **Local IP Address:** This may be a single IP address, an enumerated list or range of addresses, or a wildcard (mask) address. The latter two are required to support more than one source system sharing the same SA (e.g., behind a firewall).
- **Next Layer Protocol:** The IP protocol header (IPv4, IPv6, or IPv6 Extension) includes a field (Protocol for IPv4, Next Header for IPv6 or IPv6 Extension) that designates the protocol operating over IP. This is an individual protocol number, ANY, or for IPv6 only, OPAQUE. If AH or ESP is used, then this IP protocol header immediately precedes the AH or ESP header in the packet.

Table 20.2 Host SPD Example

Protocol	Local IP	Port	Remote IP	Port	Action	Comment
UDP	1.2.3.101	500	*	500	BYPASS	IKE
ICMP	1.2.3.101	*	*	*	BYPASS	Error messages
*	1.2.3.101	*	1.2.3.0/24	*	PROTECT: ESP intransport-mode	Encrypt intranet traffic
TCP	1.2.3.101	*	1.2.4.10	80	PROTECT: ESP intransport-mode	Encrypt to server
TCP	1.2.3.101	*	1.2.4.10	443	BYPASS	TLS: avoid double encryption
*	1.2.3.101	*	1.2.4.0/24	*	DISCARD	Others in DMZ
*	1.2.3.101	*	*	*	BYPASS	Internet

- **Name:** A user identifier from the operating system. This is not a field in the IP or upper-layer headers but is available if IPsec is running on the same operating system as the user.
- **Local and Remote Ports:** These may be individual TCP or UDP port values, an enumerated list of ports, or a wildcard port.

Table 20.2 provides an example of an SPD on a host system (as opposed to a network system such as a firewall or router). This table reflects the following configuration: A local network configuration consists of two networks. The basic corporate network configuration has the IP network number 1.2.3.0/24. The local configuration also includes a secure LAN, often known as a DMZ, that is identified as 1.2.4.0/24. The DMZ is protected from both the outside world and the rest of the corporate LAN by firewalls. The host in this example has the IP address 1.2.3.10, and it is authorized to connect to the server 1.2.4.10 in the DMZ.

The entries in the SPD should be self-explanatory. For example, UDP port 500 is the designated port for IKE. Any traffic from the local host to a remote host for purposes of an IKE exchange bypasses the IPsec processing.

IP Traffic Processing

IPsec is executed on a packet-by-packet basis. When IPsec is implemented, each outbound IP packet is processed by the IPsec logic before transmission, and each inbound packet is processed by the IPsec logic after reception and before passing the packet contents on to the next higher layer (e.g., TCP or UDP). We look at the logic of these two situations in turn.

Outbound Packets Figure 20.3 highlights the main elements of IPsec processing for outbound traffic. A block of data from a higher layer, such as TCP, is passed down to the IP layer and an IP packet is formed, consisting of an IP header and an IP body. Then the following steps occur:

1. IPsec searches the SPD for a match to this packet.
2. If no match is found, then the packet is discarded and an error message is generated.

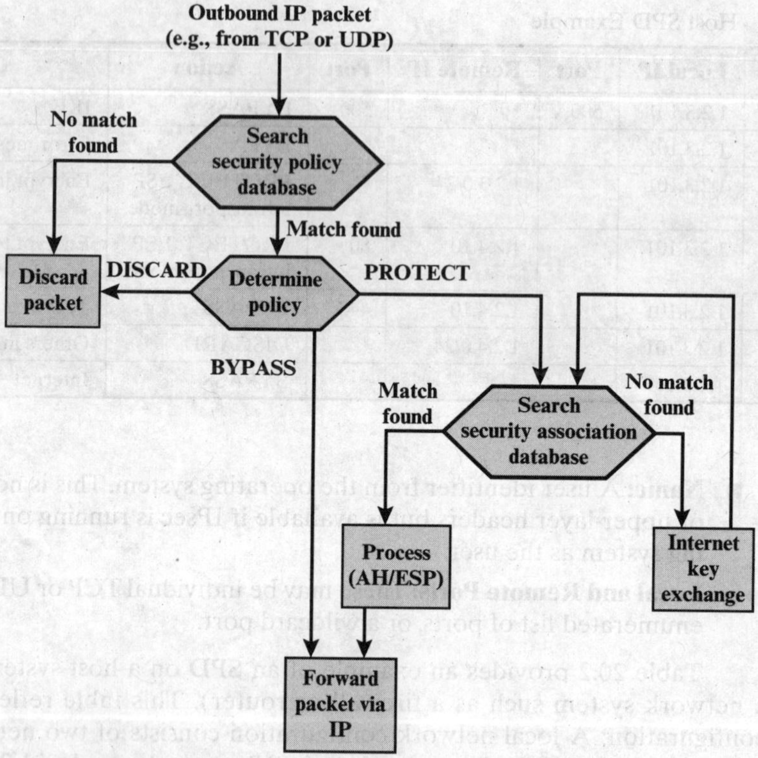

Figure 20.3 Processing Model for Outbound Packets

3. If a match is found, further processing is determined by the first matching entry in the SPD. If the policy for this packet is DISCARD, then the packet is discarded. If the policy is BYPASS, then there is no further IPsec processing; the packet is forwarded to the network for transmission.
4. If the policy is PROTECT, then a search is made of the SAD for a matching entry. If no entry is found, then IKE is invoked to create an SA with the appropriate keys and an entry is made in the SA.
5. The matching entry in the SAD determines the processing for this packet. Either encryption, authentication, or both can be performed, and either transport or tunnel mode can be used. The packet is then forwarded to the network for transmission.

Inbound Packets Figure 20.4 highlights the main elements of IPsec processing for inbound traffic. An incoming IP packet triggers the IPsec processing. The following steps occur:

1. IPsec determines whether this is an unsecured IP packet or one that has ESP or AH headers/trailers, by examining the IP Protocol field (IPv4) or Next Header field (IPv6).

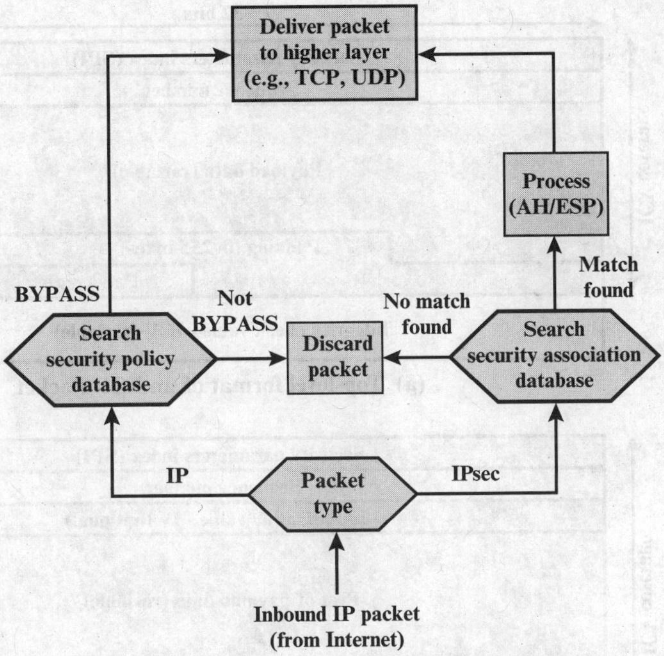

Figure 20.4 Processing Model for Inbound Packets

2. If the packet is unsecured, IPsec searches the SPD for a match to this packet. If the first matching entry has a policy of BYPASS, the IP header is processed and stripped off and the packet body is delivered to the next higher layer, such as TCP. If the first matching entry has a policy of PROTECT or DISCARD, or if there is no matching entry, the packet is discarded.
3. For a secured packet, IPsec searches the SAD. If no match is found, the packet is discarded. Otherwise, IPsec applies the appropriate ESP or AH processing. Then, the IP header is processed and stripped off and the packet body is delivered to the next higher layer, such as TCP.

20.3 ENCAPSULATING SECURITY PAYLOAD

ESP can be used to provide confidentiality, data origin authentication, connectionless integrity, an anti-replay service (a form of partial sequence integrity), and (limited) traffic flow confidentiality. The set of services provided depends on options selected at the time of Security Association (SA) establishment and on the location of the implementation in a network topology.

ESP can work with a variety of encryption and authentication algorithms, including authenticated encryption algorithms such as GCM.

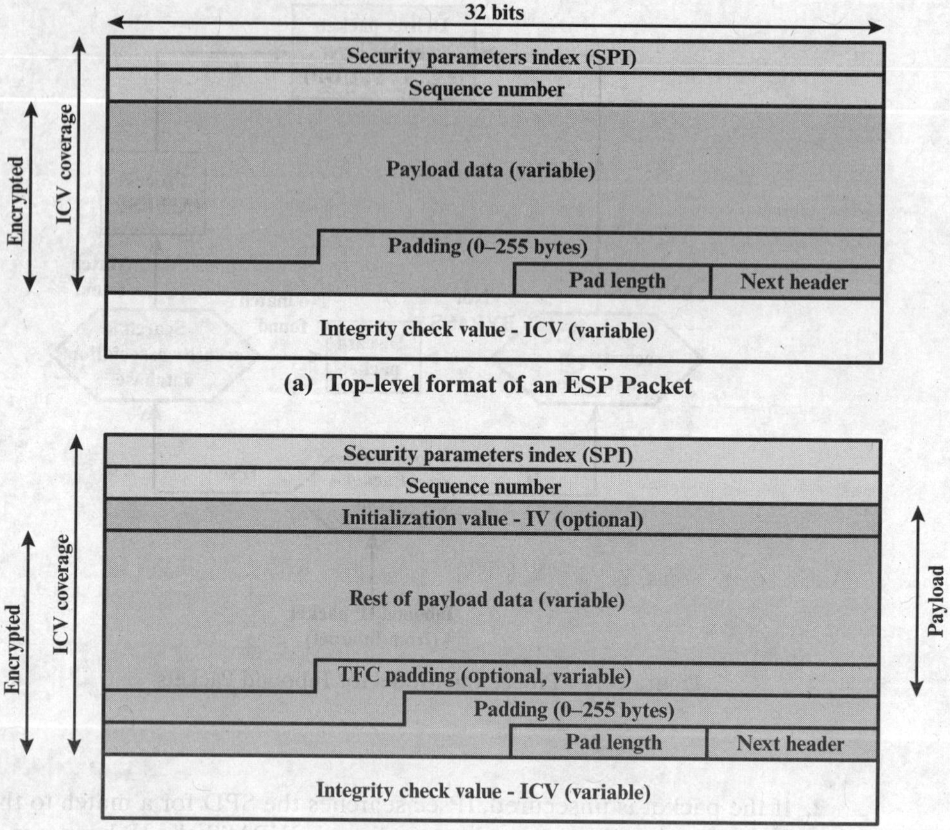

(b) Substructure of payload data

Figure 20.5 ESP Packet Format

ESP Format

Figure 20.5a shows the top-level format of an ESP packet. It contains the following fields.

- **Security Parameters Index (32 bits):** Identifies a security association.
- **Sequence Number (32 bits):** A monotonically increasing counter value; this provides an anti-replay function, as discussed for AH.
- **Payload Data (variable):** This is a transport-level segment (transport mode) or IP packet (tunnel mode) that is protected by encryption.
- **Padding (0–255 bytes):** The purpose of this field is discussed later.
- **Pad Length (8 bits):** Indicates the number of pad bytes immediately preceding this field.
- **Next Header (8 bits):** Identifies the type of data contained in the payload data field by identifying the first header in that payload (e.g., an extension header in IPv6, or an upper-layer protocol such as TCP).
- **Integrity Check Value (variable):** A variable-length field (must be an integral number of 32-bit words) that contains the Integrity Check Value computed over the ESP packet minus the Authentication Data field.

When any combined mode algorithm is employed, the algorithm itself is expected to return both decrypted plaintext and a pass/fail indication for the integrity check. For combined mode algorithms, the ICV that would normally appear at the end of the ESP packet (when integrity is selected) may be omitted. When the ICV is omitted and integrity is selected, it is the responsibility of the combined mode algorithm to encode within the Payload Data an ICV-equivalent means of verifying the integrity of the packet.

Two additional fields may be present in the payload (Figure 20.5b). An **initialization value (IV)**, or nonce, is present if this is required by the encryption or authenticated encryption algorithm used for ESP. If tunnel mode is being used, then the IPsec implementation may add **traffic flow confidentiality (TFC)** padding after the Payload Data and before the Padding field, as explained subsequently.

Encryption and Authentication Algorithms

The Payload Data, Padding, Pad Length, and Next Header fields are encrypted by the ESP service. If the algorithm used to encrypt the payload requires cryptographic synchronization data, such as an initialization vector (IV), then these data may be carried explicitly at the beginning of the Payload Data field. If included, an IV is usually not encrypted, although it is often referred to as being part of the ciphertext.

The ICV field is optional. It is present only if the integrity service is selected and is provided by either a separate integrity algorithm or a combined mode algorithm that uses an ICV. The ICV is computed after the encryption is performed. This order of processing facilitates rapid detection and rejection of replayed or bogus packets by the receiver prior to decrypting the packet, hence potentially reducing the impact of denial of service (DoS) attacks. It also allows for the possibility of parallel processing of packets at the receiver that is decryption can take place in parallel with integrity checking. Note that because the ICV is not protected by encryption, a keyed integrity algorithm must be employed to compute the ICV.

Padding

The Padding field serves several purposes:

- If an encryption algorithm requires the plaintext to be a multiple of some number of bytes (e.g., the multiple of a single block for a block cipher), the Padding field is used to expand the plaintext (consisting of the Payload Data, Padding, Pad Length, and Next Header fields) to the required length.
- The ESP format requires that the Pad Length and Next Header fields be right aligned within a 32-bit word. Equivalently, the ciphertext must be an integer multiple of 32 bits. The Padding field is used to assure this alignment.
- Additional padding may be added to provide partial traffic-flow confidentiality by concealing the actual length of the payload.

Anti-Replay Service

A **replay attack** is one in which an attacker obtains a copy of an authenticated packet and later transmits it to the intended destination. The receipt of duplicate, authenticated IP packets may disrupt service in some way or may have some other undesired consequence. The Sequence Number field is designed to thwart such attacks. First, we discuss sequence number generation by the sender, and then we look at how it is processed by the recipient.

When a new SA is established, the **sender** initializes a sequence number counter to 0. Each time that a packet is sent on this SA, the sender increments the counter and places the value in the Sequence Number field. Thus, the first value to be used is 1. If anti-replay is enabled (the default), the sender must not allow the sequence number to cycle past $2^{32} - 1$ back to zero. Otherwise, there would be multiple valid packets with the same sequence number. If the limit of $2^{32} - 1$ is reached, the sender should terminate this SA and negotiate a new SA with a new key.

Because IP is a connectionless, unreliable service, the protocol does not guarantee that packets will be delivered in order and does not guarantee that all packets will be delivered. Therefore, the IPsec authentication document dictates that the **receiver** should implement a window of size W, with a default of $W = 64$. The right edge of the window represents the highest sequence number, N, so far received for a valid packet. For any packet with a sequence number in the range from $N - W + 1$ to N that has been correctly received (i.e., properly authenticated), the corresponding slot in the window is marked (Figure 20.6). Inbound processing proceeds as follows when a packet is received:

1. If the received packet falls within the window and is new, the MAC is checked. If the packet is authenticated, the corresponding slot in the window is marked.
2. If the received packet is to the right of the window and is new, the MAC is checked. If the packet is authenticated, the window is advanced so that this sequence number is the right edge of the window, and the corresponding slot in the window is marked.
3. If the received packet is to the left of the window or if authentication fails, the packet is discarded; this is an auditable event.

Transport and Tunnel Modes

Figure 20.7 shows two ways in which the IPsec ESP service can be used. In the upper part of the figure, encryption (and optionally authentication) is provided directly between two hosts. Figure 20.7b shows how tunnel mode operation can be used to set up

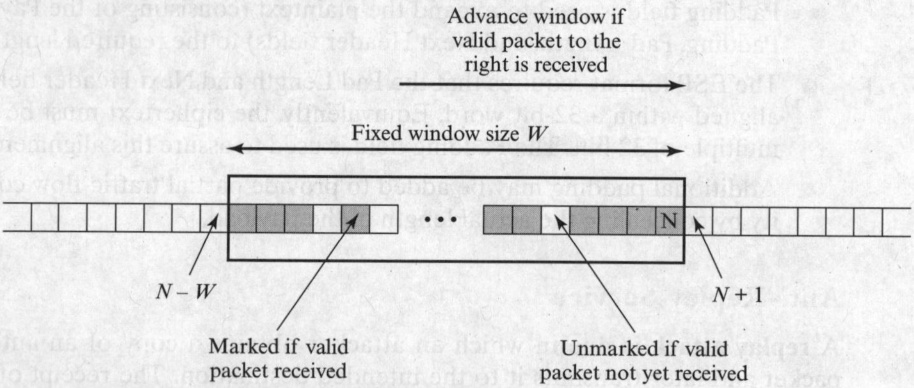

Figure 20.6 Anti-replay Mechanism

(a) Transport-level security

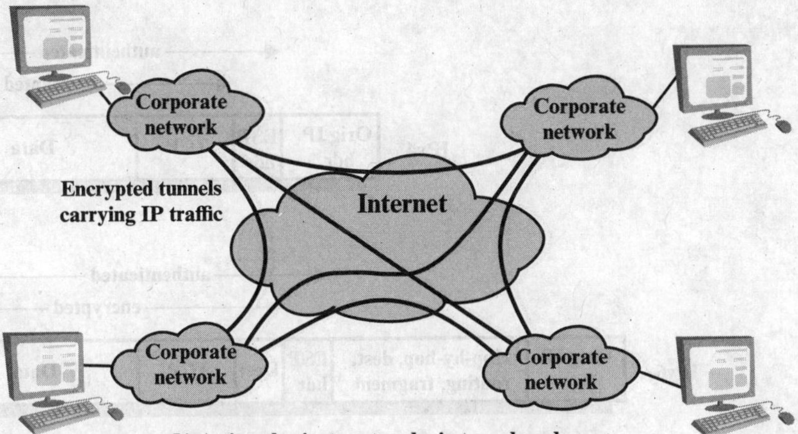

(b) A virtual private network via tunnel mode

Figure 20.7 Transport-Mode versus Tunnel-Mode Encryptionx

a **virtual private network**. In this example, an organization has four private networks interconnected across the Internet. Hosts on the internal networks use the Internet for transport of data but do not interact with other Internet-based hosts. By terminating the tunnels at the security gateway to each internal network, the configuration allows the hosts to avoid implementing the security capability. The former technique is supported by a transport mode SA, while the latter technique uses a tunnel mode SA.

In this section, we look at the scope of ESP for the two modes. The considerations are somewhat different for IPv4 and IPv6. We use the packet formats of Figure 20.8a as a starting point.

Transport Mode ESP Transport mode ESP is used to encrypt and optionally authenticate the data carried by IP (e.g., a TCP segment), as shown in Figure 20.8b. For this mode using IPv4, the ESP header is inserted into the IP packet immediately prior to the transport-layer header (e.g., TCP, UDP, ICMP), and an ESP trailer (Padding, Pad Length, and Next Header fields) is placed after the IP packet. If authentication is selected, the ESP Authentication Data field is added after the ESP trailer. The entire transport-level segment plus the ESP trailer are encrypted. Authentication covers all of the ciphertext plus the ESP header.

In the context of IPv6, ESP is viewed as an end-to-end payload; that is, it is not examined or processed by intermediate routers. Therefore, the ESP header appears after the IPv6 base header and the hop-by-hop, routing, and fragment extension headers. The destination options extension header could appear before or after the ESP header, depending on the semantics desired. For IPv6, encryption covers

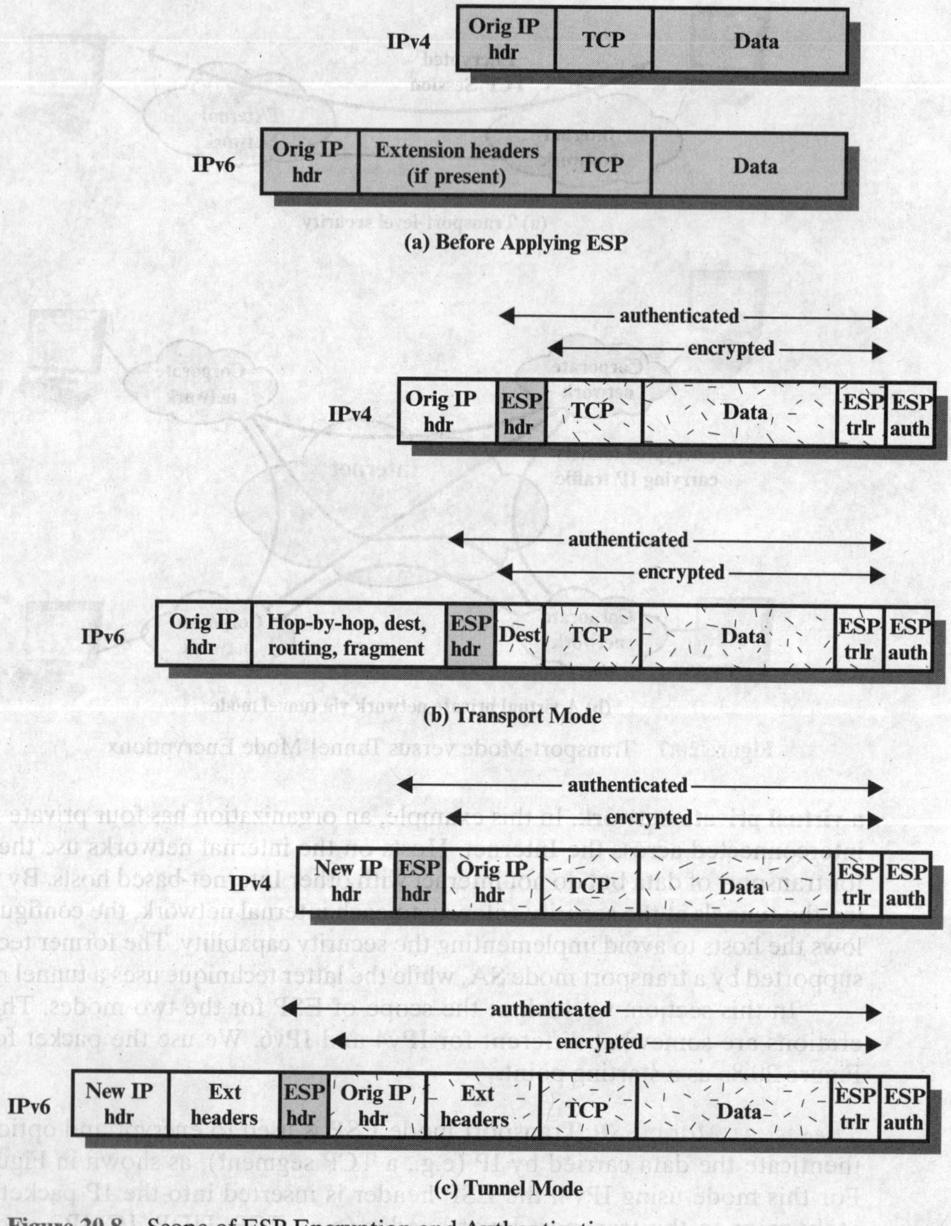

Figure 20.8 Scope of ESP Encryption and Authentication

the entire transport-level segment plus the ESP trailer plus the destination options extension header if it occurs after the ESP header. Again, authentication covers the ciphertext plus the ESP header.

Transport mode operation may be summarized as follows.

1. At the source, the block of data consisting of the ESP trailer plus the entire transport-layer segment is encrypted and the plaintext of this block is replaced

with its ciphertext to form the IP packet for transmission. Authentication is added if this option is selected.

2. The packet is then routed to the destination. Each intermediate router needs to examine and process the IP header plus any plaintext IP extension headers but does not need to examine the ciphertext.
3. The destination node examines and processes the IP header plus any plaintext IP extension headers. Then, on the basis of the SPI in the ESP header, the destination node decrypts the remainder of the packet to recover the plaintext transport-layer segment.

Transport mode operation provides confidentiality for any application that uses it, thus avoiding the need to implement confidentiality in every individual application. One drawback to this mode is that it is possible to do traffic analysis on the transmitted packets.

Tunnel Mode ESP Tunnel mode ESP is used to encrypt an entire IP packet (Figure 20.8c). For this mode, the ESP header is prefixed to the packet and then the packet plus the ESP trailer is encrypted. This method can be used to counter traffic analysis.

Because the IP header contains the destination address and possibly source routing directives and hop-by-hop option information, it is not possible simply to transmit the encrypted IP packet prefixed by the ESP header. Intermediate routers would be unable to process such a packet. Therefore, it is necessary to encapsulate the entire block (ESP header plus ciphertext plus Authentication Data, if present) with a new IP header that will contain sufficient information for routing but not for traffic analysis.

Whereas the transport mode is suitable for protecting connections between hosts that support the ESP feature, the tunnel mode is useful in a configuration that includes a firewall or other sort of security gateway that protects a trusted network from external networks. In this latter case, encryption occurs only between an external host and the security gateway or between two security gateways. This relieves hosts on the internal network of the processing burden of encryption and simplifies the key distribution task by reducing the number of needed keys. Further, it thwarts traffic analysis based on ultimate destination.

Consider a case in which an external host wishes to communicate with a host on an internal network protected by a firewall, and in which ESP is implemented in the external host and the firewalls. The following steps occur for transfer of a transport-layer segment from the external host to the internal host.

1. The source prepares an inner IP packet with a destination address of the target internal host. This packet is prefixed by an ESP header; then the packet and ESP trailer are encrypted and Authentication Data may be added. The resulting block is encapsulated with a new IP header (base header plus optional extensions such as routing and hop-by-hop options for IPv6) whose destination address is the firewall; this forms the outer IP packet.
2. The outer packet is routed to the destination firewall. Each intermediate router needs to examine and process the outer IP header plus any outer IP extension headers but does not need to examine the ciphertext.

3. The destination firewall examines and processes the outer IP header plus any outer IP extension headers. Then, on the basis of the SPI in the ESP header, the destination node decrypts the remainder of the packet to recover the plaintext inner IP packet. This packet is then transmitted in the internal network.
4. The inner packet is routed through zero or more routers in the internal network to the destination host.

Figure 20.9 shows the protocol architecture for the two modes.

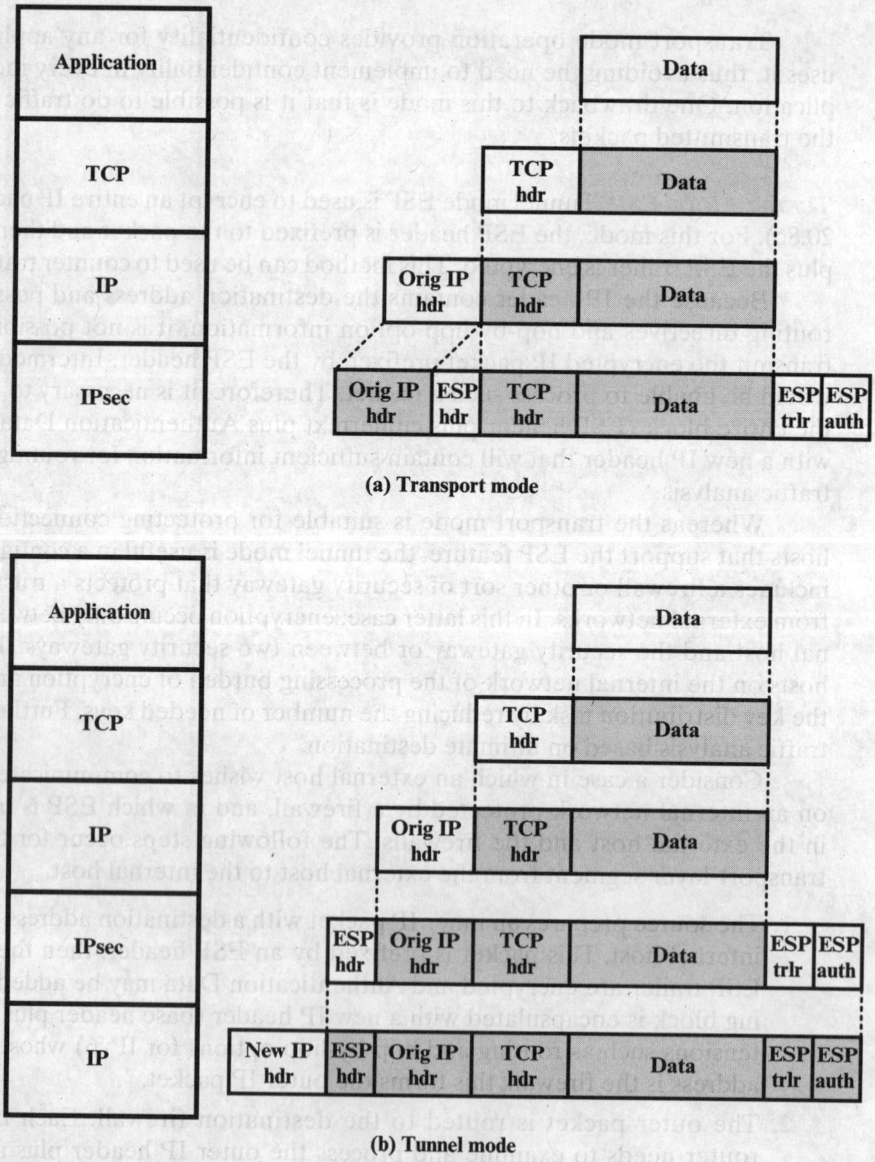

Figure 20.9 Protocol Operation for ESP

20.4 COMBINING SECURITY ASSOCIATIONS

An individual SA can implement either the AH or ESP protocol but not both. Sometimes a particular traffic flow will call for the services provided by both AH and ESP. Further, a particular traffic flow may require IPsec services between hosts and, for that same flow, separate services between security gateways, such as firewalls. In all of these cases, multiple SAs must be employed for the same traffic flow to achieve the desired IPsec services. The term *security association bundle* refers to a sequence of SAs through which traffic must be processed to provide a desired set of IPsec services. The SAs in a bundle may terminate at different endpoints or at the same endpoints.

Security associations may be combined into bundles in two ways:

- **Transport adjacency:** Refers to applying more than one security protocol to the same IP packet without invoking tunneling. This approach to combining AH and ESP allows for only one level of combination; further nesting yields no added benefit since the processing is performed at one IPsec instance: the (ultimate) destination.
- **Iterated tunneling:** Refers to the application of multiple layers of security protocols effected through IP tunneling. This approach allows for multiple levels of nesting, since each tunnel can originate or terminate at a different IPsec site along the path.

The two approaches can be combined, for example, by having a transport SA between hosts travel part of the way through a tunnel SA between security gateways.

One interesting issue that arises when considering SA bundles is the order in which authentication and encryption may be applied between a given pair of endpoints and the ways of doing so. We examine that issue next. Then we look at combinations of SAs that involve at least one tunnel.

Authentication Plus Confidentiality

Encryption and authentication can be combined in order to transmit an IP packet that has both confidentiality and authentication between hosts. We look at several approaches.

ESP with Authentication Option This approach is illustrated in Figure 20.8. In this approach, the user first applies ESP to the data to be protected and then appends the authentication data field. There are actually two subcases:

- **Transport mode ESP:** Authentication and encryption apply to the IP payload delivered to the host, but the IP header is not protected.
- **Tunnel mode ESP:** Authentication applies to the entire IP packet delivered to the outer IP destination address (e.g., a firewall), and authentication is performed at that destination. The entire inner IP packet is protected by the privacy mechanism for delivery to the inner IP destination.

For both cases, authentication applies to the ciphertext rather than the plaintext.

Transport Adjacency Another way to apply authentication after encryption is to use two bundled transport SAs, with the inner being an ESP SA and the outer being an AH SA. In this case, ESP is used without its authentication option. Because the inner SA is a transport SA, encryption is applied to the IP payload. The resulting packet consists of an IP header (and possibly IPv6 header extensions) followed by an ESP. AH is then applied in transport mode, so that authentication covers the ESP plus the original IP header (and extensions) except for mutable fields. The advantage of this approach over simply using a single ESP SA with the ESP authentication option is that the authentication covers more fields, including the source and destination IP addresses. The disadvantage is the overhead of two SAs versus one SA.

Transport–Tunnel Bundle The use of authentication prior to encryption might be preferable for several reasons. First, because the authentication data are protected by encryption, it is impossible for anyone to intercept the message and alter the authentication data without detection. Second, it may be desirable to store the authentication information with the message at the destination for later reference. It is more convenient to do this if the authentication information applies to the unencrypted message; otherwise the message would have to be reencrypted to verify the authentication information.

One approach to applying authentication before encryption between two hosts is to use a bundle consisting of an inner AH transport SA and an outer ESP tunnel SA. In this case, authentication is applied to the IP payload plus the IP header (and extensions) except for mutable fields. The resulting IP packet is then processed in tunnel mode by ESP; the result is that the entire, authenticated inner packet is encrypted and a new outer IP header (and extensions) is added.

Basic Combinations of Security Associations

The IPsec Architecture document lists four examples of combinations of SAs that must be supported by compliant IPsec hosts (e.g., workstation, server) or security gateways (e.g., firewall, router). These are illustrated in Figure 20.10. The lower part of each case in the figure represents the physical connectivity of the elements; the upper part represents logical connectivity via one or more nested SAs. Each SA can be either AH or ESP. For host-to-host SAs, the mode may be either transport or tunnel; otherwise it must be tunnel mode.

Case 1. All security is provided between end systems that implement IPsec. For any two end systems to communicate via an SA, they must share the appropriate secret keys. Among the possible combinations are

a. AH in transport mode

b. ESP in transport mode

c. ESP followed by AH in transport mode (an ESP SA inside an AH SA)

d. Any one of a, b, or c inside an AH or ESP in tunnel mode

We have already discussed how these various combinations can be used to support authentication, encryption, authentication before encryption, and authentication after encryption.

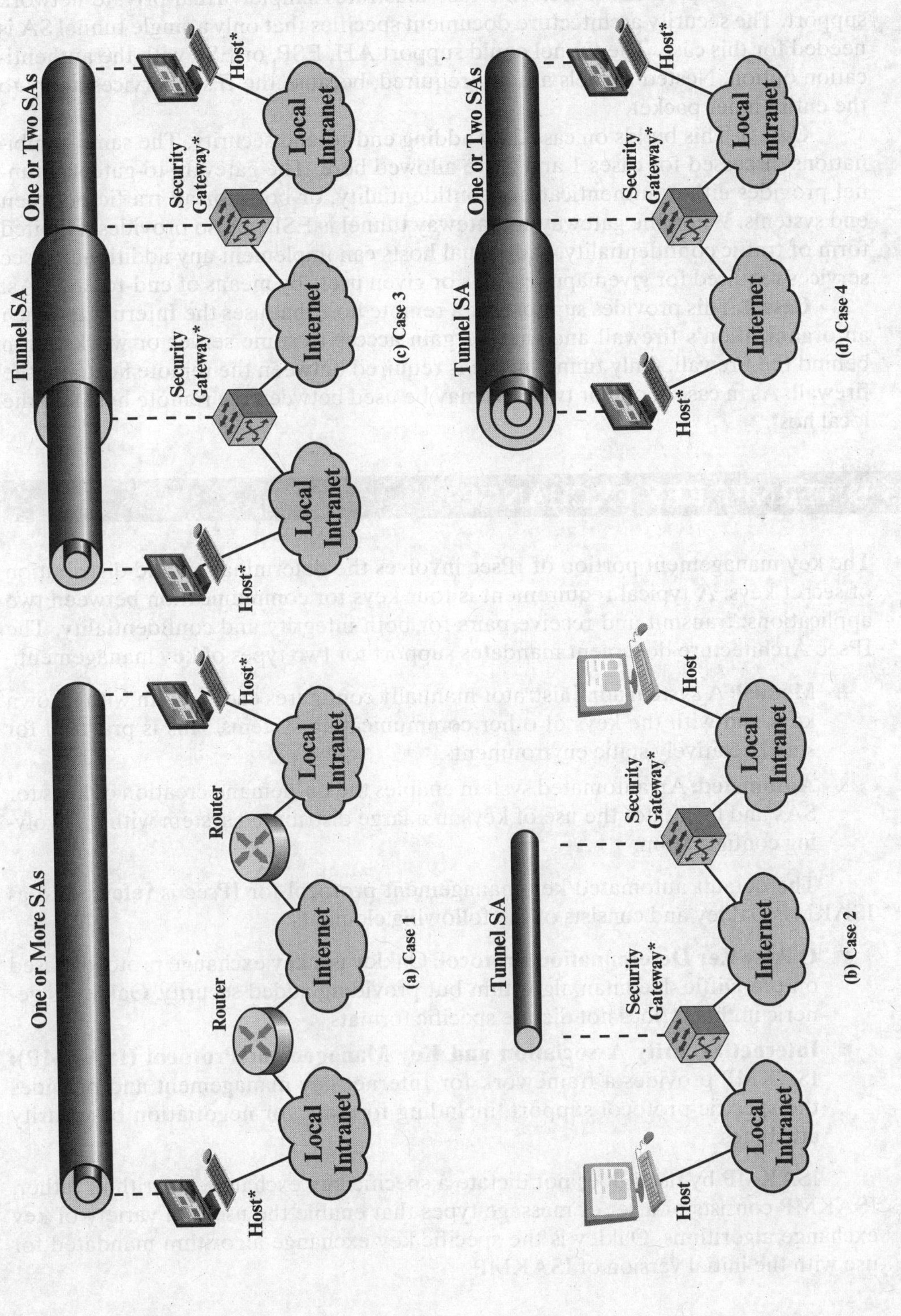

* = implements IPsec

Figure 20.10 Basic Combinations of Security Associations

Case 2. Security is provided only between gateways (routers, firewalls, etc.) and no hosts implement IPsec. This case illustrates simple virtual private network support. The security architecture document specifies that only a single tunnel SA is needed for this case. The tunnel could support AH, ESP, or ESP with the authentication option. Nested tunnels are not required, because the IPsec services apply to the entire inner packet.

Case 3. This builds on case 2 by adding end-to-end security. The same combinations discussed for cases 1 and 2 are allowed here. The gateway-to-gateway tunnel provides either authentication, confidentiality, or both for all traffic between end systems. When the gateway-to-gateway tunnel is ESP, it also provides a limited form of traffic confidentiality. Individual hosts can implement any additional IPsec services required for given applications or given users by means of end-to-end SAs.

Case 4. This provides support for a remote host that uses the Internet to reach an organization's firewall and then to gain access to some server or workstation behind the firewall. Only tunnel mode is required between the remote host and the firewall. As in case 1, one or two SAs may be used between the remote host and the local host.

20.5 INTERNET KEY EXCHANGE

The key management portion of IPsec involves the determination and distribution of secret keys. A typical requirement is four keys for communication between two applications: transmit and receive pairs for both integrity and confidentiality. The IPsec Architecture document mandates support for two types of key management:

- **Manual:** A system administrator manually configures each system with its own keys and with the keys of other communicating systems. This is practical for small, relatively static environments.
- **Automated:** An automated system enables the on-demand creation of keys for SAs and facilitates the use of keys in a large distributed system with an evolving configuration.

The default automated key management protocol for IPsec is referred to as ISAKMP/Oakley and consists of the following elements:

- **Oakley Key Determination Protocol:** Oakley is a key exchange protocol based on the Diffie–Hellman algorithm but providing added security. Oakley is generic in that it does not dictate specific formats.
- **Internet Security Association and Key Management Protocol (ISAKMP):** ISAKMP provides a framework for Internet key management and provides the specific protocol support, including formats, for negotiation of security attributes.

ISAKMP by itself does not dictate a specific key exchange algorithm; rather, ISAKMP consists of a set of message types that enable the use of a variety of key exchange algorithms. Oakley is the specific key exchange algorithm mandated for use with the initial version of ISAKMP.

In IKEv2, the terms Oakley and ISAKMP are no longer used, and there are significant differences from the use of Oakley and ISAKMP in IKEv1. Nevertheless, the basic functionality is the same. In this section, we describe the IKEv2 specification.

Key Determination Protocol

IKE key determination is a refinement of the Diffie–Hellman key exchange algorithm. Recall that Diffie–Hellman involves the following interaction between users A and B. There is prior agreement on two global parameters: q, a large prime number; and α, a primitive root of q. A selects a random integer X_A as its private key and transmits to B its public key $Y_A = \alpha^{X_A} \bmod q$. Similarly, B selects a random integer X_B as its private key and transmits to A its public key $Y_B = \alpha^{X_B} \bmod q$. Each side can now compute the secret session key:

$$K = (Y_B)^{X_A} \bmod q = (Y_A)^{X_B} \bmod q = \alpha^{X_A X_B} \bmod q$$

The Diffie–Hellman algorithm has two attractive features:

- Secret keys are created only when needed. There is no need to store secret keys for a long period of time, exposing them to increased vulnerability.
- The exchange requires no pre-existing infrastructure other than an agreement on the global parameters.

However, there are a number of weaknesses to Diffie–Hellman, as pointed out in [HUIT98].

- It does not provide any information about the identities of the parties.
- It is subject to a man-in-the-middle attack, in which a third party C impersonates B while communicating with A and impersonates A while communicating with B. Both A and B end up negotiating a key with C, which can then listen to and pass on traffic. The man-in-the-middle attack proceeds as
  1. B sends his public key Y_B in a message addressed to A (see Figure 10.2).
  2. The enemy (E) intercepts this message. E saves B's public key and sends a message to A that has B's User ID but E's public key Y_E. This message is sent in such a way that it appears as though it was sent from B's host system. A receives E's message and stores E's public key with B's User ID. Similarly, E sends a message to B with E's public key, purporting to come from A.
  3. B computes a secret key K_1 based on B's private key and Y_E. A computes a secret key K_2 based on A's private key and Y_E. E computes K_1 using E's secret key X_E and Y_B and computers K_2 using X_E and Y_A.
  4. From now on, E is able to relay messages from A to B and from B to A, appropriately changing their encipherment en route in such a way that neither A nor B will know that they share their communication with E.
- It is computationally intensive. As a result, it is vulnerable to a clogging attack, in which an opponent requests a high number of keys. The victim spends considerable computing resources doing useless modular exponentiation rather than real work.

IKE key determination is designed to retain the advantages of Diffie–Hellman, while countering its weaknesses.

Features of IKE Key Determination The IKE key determination algorithm is characterized by five important features:

1. It employs a mechanism known as cookies to thwart clogging attacks.
2. It enables the two parties to negotiate a *group*; this, in essence, specifies the global parameters of the Diffie–Hellman key exchange.
3. It uses nonces to ensure against replay attacks.
4. It enables the exchange of Diffie–Hellman public key values.
5. It authenticates the Diffie–Hellman exchange to thwart man-in-the-middle attacks.

We have already discussed Diffie–Hellman. Let us look at the remainder of these elements in turn. First, consider the problem of clogging attacks. In this attack, an opponent forges the source address of a legitimate user and sends a public Diffie–Hellman key to the victim. The victim then performs a modular exponentiation to compute the secret key. Repeated messages of this type can *clog* the victim's system with useless work. The **cookie exchange** requires that each side send a pseudorandom number, the cookie, in the initial message, which the other side acknowledges. This acknowledgment must be repeated in the first message of the Diffie–Hellman key exchange. If the source address was forged, the opponent gets no answer. Thus, an opponent can only force a user to generate acknowledgments and not to perform the Diffie–Hellman calculation.

IKE mandates that cookie generation satisfy three basic requirements:

1. The cookie must depend on the specific parties. This prevents an attacker from obtaining a cookie using a real IP address and UDP port and then using it to swamp the victim with requests from randomly chosen IP addresses or ports.
2. It must not be possible for anyone other than the issuing entity to generate cookies that will be accepted by that entity. This implies that the issuing entity will use local secret information in the generation and subsequent verification of a cookie. It must not be possible to deduce this secret information from any particular cookie. The point of this requirement is that the issuing entity need not save copies of its cookies, which are then more vulnerable to discovery, but can verify an incoming cookie acknowledgment when it needs to.
3. The cookie generation and verification methods must be fast to thwart attacks intended to sabotage processor resources.

The recommended method for creating the cookie is to perform a fast hash (e.g., MD5) over the IP Source and Destination addresses, the UDP Source and Destination ports, and a locally generated secret value.

IKE key determination supports the use of different groups for the Diffie–Hellman key exchange. Each group includes the definition of the two global parameters and the identity of the algorithm. The current specification includes the following groups.

- Modular exponentiation with a 768-bit modulus

$$q = 2^{768} - 2^{704} - 1 + 2^{64} \times (\lfloor 2^{638} \times \pi \rfloor + 149686)$$
$$\alpha = 2$$

- Modular exponentiation with a 1024-bit modulus

$$q = 2^{1024} - 2^{960} - 1 + 2^{64} \times (\lfloor 2^{894} \times \pi \rfloor + 129093)$$
$$\alpha = 2$$

- Modular exponentiation with a 1536-bit modulus
  - Parameters to be determined
- Elliptic curve group over 2^{155}
  - Generator (hexadecimal): X = 7B, Y = 1C8
  - Elliptic curve parameters (hexadecimal): A = 0, Y = 7338F
- Elliptic curve group over 2^{185}
  - Generator (hexadecimal): X = 18, Y = D
  - Elliptic curve parameters (hexadecimal): A = 0, Y = 1EE9

The first three groups are the classic Diffie–Hellman algorithm using modular exponentiation. The last two groups use the elliptic curve analog to Diffie–Hellman, which was described in Chapter 10.

IKE key determination employs **nonces** to ensure against replay attacks. Each nonce is a locally generated pseudorandom number. Nonces appear in responses and are encrypted during certain portions of the exchange to secure their use.

Three different **authentication** methods can be used with IKE key determination:

- **Digital signatures:** The exchange is authenticated by signing a mutually obtainable hash; each party encrypts the hash with its private key. The hash is generated over important parameters, such as user IDs and nonces.
- **Public-key encryption:** The exchange is authenticated by encrypting parameters such as IDs and nonces with the sender's private key.
- **Symmetric-key encryption:** A key derived by some out-of-band mechanism can be used to authenticate the exchange by symmetric encryption of exchange parameters.

IKEv2 EXCHANGES The IKEv2 protocol involves the exchange of messages in pairs. The first two pairs of exchanges are referred to as the **initial exchanges** (Figure 20.11a). In the first exchange, the two peers exchange information concerning cryptographic algorithms and other security parameters they are willing to use along with nonces and Diffie–Hellman (DH) values. The result of this exchange is to set up a special SA called the IKE SA (see Figure 20.2). This SA defines parameters for a secure channel between the peers over which subsequent message exchanges take place. Thus, all subsequent IKE message exchanges are protected by encryption and message authentication. In the second exchange, the two parties authenticate one another and set up a first IPsec SA to be placed in the SADB and used for

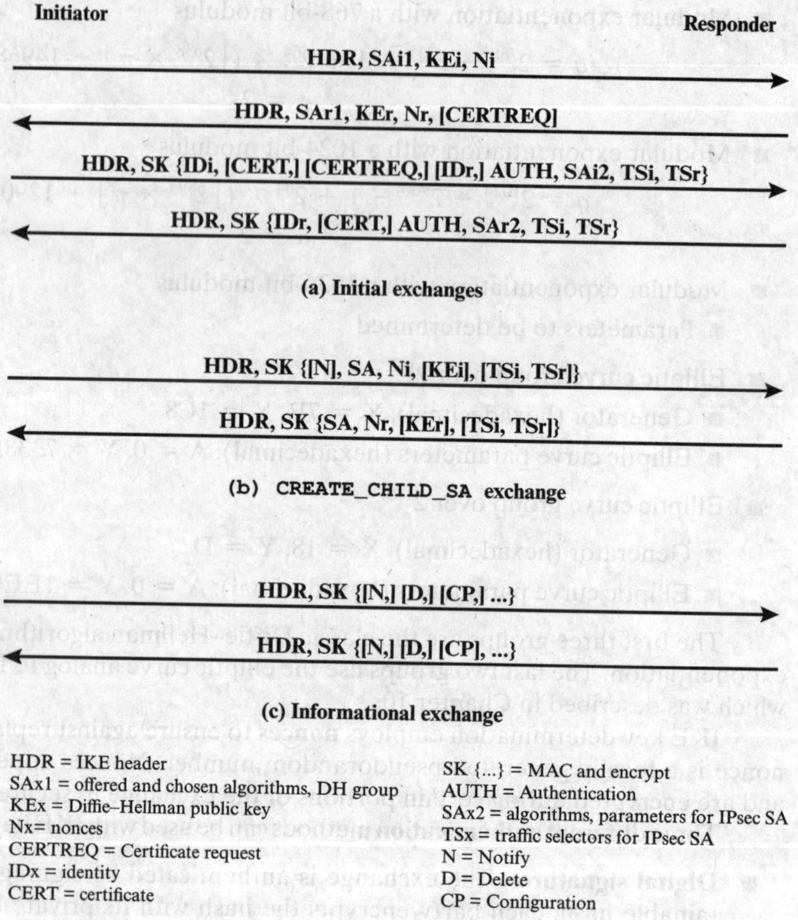

Figure 20.11 IKEv2 Exchanges

protecting ordinary (i.e. non-IKE) communications between the peers. Thus, four messages are needed to establish the first SA for general use.

The **CREATE_CHILD_SA exchange** can be used to establish further SAs for protecting traffic. The **informational exchange** is used to exchange management information, IKEv2 error messages, and other notifications.

Header and Payload Formats

IKE defines procedures and packet formats to establish, negotiate, modify, and delete security associations. As part of SA establishment, IKE defines payloads for exchanging key generation and authentication data. These payload formats provide a consistent framework independent of the specific key exchange protocol, encryption algorithm, and authentication mechanism.

IKE Header Format An IKE message consists of an IKE header followed by one or more payloads. All of this is carried in a transport protocol. The specification dictates that implementations must support the use of UDP for the transport protocol.

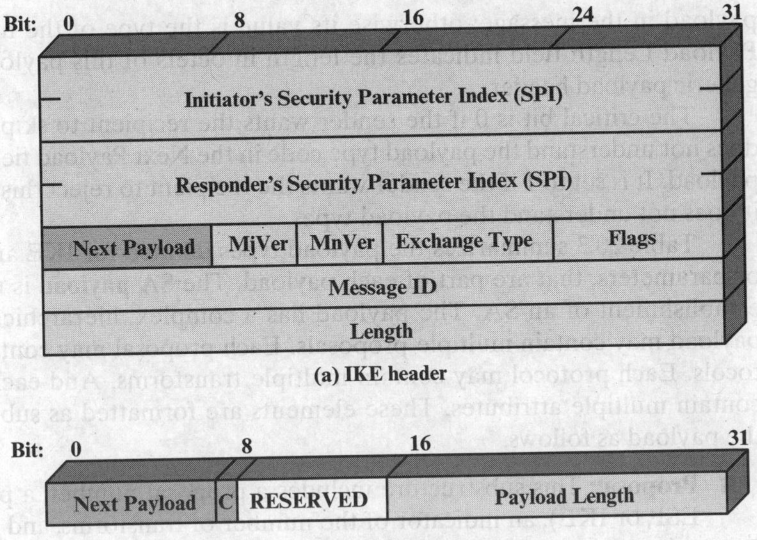

Figure 20.12 IKE Formats

Figure 20.12a shows the header format for an IKE message. It consists of the following fields.

- **Initiator SPI (64 bits):** A value chosen by the initiator to identify a unique IKE security association (SA).
- **Responder SPI (64 bits):** A value chosen by the responder to identify a unique IKE SA.
- **Next Payload (8 bits):** Indicates the type of the first payload in the message; payloads are discussed in the next subsection.
- **Major Version (4 bits):** Indicates major version of IKE in use.
- **Minor Version (4 bits):** Indicates minor version in use.
- **Exchange Type (8 bits):** Indicates the type of exchange; these are discussed later in this section.
- **Flags (8 bits):** Indicates specific options set for this IKE exchange. Three bits are defined so far. The initiator bit indicates whether this packet is sent by the SA initiator. The version bit indicates whether the transmitter is capable of using a higher major version number than the one currently indicated. The response bit indicates whether this is a response to a message containing the same message ID.
- **Message ID (32 bits):** Used to control retransmission of lost packets and matching of requests and responses.
- **Length (32 bits):** Length of total message (header plus all payloads) in octets.

IKE Payload Types All IKE payloads begin with the same generic payload header shown in Figure 20.12b. The Next Payload field has a value of 0 if this is the last payload in the message; otherwise its value is the type of the next payload. The Payload Length field indicates the length in octets of this payload, including the generic payload header.

The critical bit is 0 if the sender wants the recipient to skip this payload if it does not understand the payload type code in the Next Payload field of the previous payload. It is set to 1 if the sender wants the recipient to reject this entire message if it does not understand the payload type.

Table 20.3 summarizes the payload types defined for IKE and lists the fields, or parameters, that are part of each payload. The **SA payload** is used to begin the establishment of an SA. The payload has a complex, hierarchical structure. The payload may contain multiple proposals. Each proposal may contain multiple protocols. Each protocol may contain multiple transforms. And each transform may contain multiple attributes. These elements are formatted as substructures within the payload as follows.

- **Proposal:** This substructure includes a proposal number, a protocol ID (AH, ESP, or IKE), an indicator of the number of transforms, and then a transform substructure. If more than one protocol is to be included in a proposal, then there is a subsequent proposal substructure with the same proposal number.
- **Transform:** Different protocols support different transform types. The transforms are used primarily to define cryptographic algorithms to be used with a particular protocol.
- **Attribute:** Each transform may include attributes that modify or complete the specification of the transform. An example is key length.

Table 20.3 IKE Payload Types

Type	Parameters
Security Association	Proposals
Key Exchange	DH Group #, Key Exchange Data
Identification	ID Type, ID Data
Certificate	Cert Encoding, Certificate Data
Certificate Request	Cert Encoding, Certification Authority
Authentication	Auth Method, Authentication Data
Nonce	Nonce Data
Notify	Protocol-ID, SPI Size, Notify Message Type, SPI, Notification Data
Delete	Protocol-ID, SPI Size, # of SPIs, SPI (one or more)
Vendor ID	Vendor ID
Traffic Selector	Number of TSs, Traffic Selectors
Encrypted	IV, Encrypted IKE payloads, Padding, Pad Length, ICV
Configuration	CFG Type, Configuration Attributes
Extensible Authentication Protocol	EAP Message

The **Key Exchange payload** can be used for a variety of key exchange techniques, including Oakley, Diffie–Hellman, and the RSA-based key exchange used by PGP. The Key Exchange data field contains the data required to generate a session key and is dependent on the key exchange algorithm used.

The **Identification payload** is used to determine the identity of communicating peers and may be used for determining authenticity of information. Typically the ID Data field will contain an IPv4 or IPv6 address.

The **Certificate payload** transfers a public-key certificate. The Certificate Encoding field indicates the type of certificate or certificate-related information, which may include the following:

- PKCS #7 wrapped X.509 certificate
- PGP certificate
- DNS signed key
- X.509 certificate—signature
- X.509 certificate—key exchange
- Kerberos tokens
- Certificate Revocation List (CRL)
- Authority Revocation List (ARL)
- SPKI certificate

At any point in an IKE exchange, the sender may include a **Certificate Request** payload to request the certificate of the other communicating entity. The payload may list more than one certificate type that is acceptable and more than one certificate authority that is acceptable.

The **Authentication** payload contains data used for message authentication purposes. The authentication method types so far defined are RSA digital signature, shared-key message integrity code, and DSS digital signature.

The **Nonce** payload contains random data used to guarantee liveness during an exchange and to protect against replay attacks.

The **Notify** payload contains either error or status information associated with this SA or this SA negotiation. The following table lists the IKE notify messages.

Error Messages	Status Messages
Unsupported Critical	Initial Contact
Payload	Set Window Size
Invalid IKE SPI	Additional TS Possible
Invalid Major Version	IPCOMP Supported
Invalid Syntax	NAT Detection Source IP
Invalid Payload Type	NAT Detection Destination IP
Invalid Message ID	Cookie
Invalid SPI	Use Transport Mode

Error Messages	Status Messages
No Proposal Chosen	HTTP Cert Lookup Supported
Invalid KE Payload	Rekey SA
Authentication Failed	ESP TFC Padding Not Supported
Single Pair Required	Non First Fragments Also
No Additional SAS	
Internal Address Failure	
Failed CP Required	
TS Unacceptable	
Invalid Selectors	

The **Delete** payload indicates one or more SAs that the sender has deleted from its database and that therefore are no longer valid.

The **Vendor ID** payload contains a vendor-defined constant. The constant is used by vendors to identify and recognize remote instances of their implementations. This mechanism allows a vendor to experiment with new features while maintaining backward compatibility.

The **Traffic Selector** payload allows peers to identify packet flows for processing by IPsec services.

The **Encrypted** payload contains other payloads in encrypted form. The encrypted payload format is similar to that of ESP. It may include an IV if the encryption algorithm requires it and an ICV if authentication is selected.

The **Configuration** payload is used to exchange configuration information between IKE peers.

The **Extensible Authentication Protocol (EAP)** payload allows IKE SAs to be authenticated using EAP, which was discussed in Chapter 16.

20.6 CRYPTOGRAPHIC SUITES

The IPsecv3 and IKEv3 protocols rely on a variety of types of cryptographic algorithms. As we have seen in this book, there are many cryptographic algorithms of each type, each with a variety of parameters, such as key size. To promote interoperability, two RFCs define recommended suites of cryptographic algorithms and parameters for various applications.

RFC 4308 defines two cryptographic suites for establishing virtual private networks. Suite VPN-A matches the commonly used corporate VPN security used in older IKEv1 implementations at the time of the issuance of IKEv2 in 2005. Suite VPN-B provides stronger security and is recommended for new VPNs that implement IPsecv3 and IKEv2.

Table 20.4a lists the algorithms and parameters for the two suites. There are several points to note about these two suites. Note that for symmetric cryptography,

Table 20.4 Cryptographic Suites for IPsec

	VPN-A	VPN-B
ESP encryption	3DES-CBC	AES-CBC (128-bit key)
ESP integrity	HMAC-SHA1-96	AES-XCBC-MAC-96
IKE encryption	3DES-CBC	AES-CBC (128-bit key)
IKE PRF	HMAC-SHA1	AES-XCBC-PRF-128
IKE Integrity	HMAC-SHA1-96	AES-XCBC-MAC-96
IKE DH group	1024-bit MODP	2048-bit MODP

(a) Virtual private networks (RFC 4308)

	GCM-128	GCM-256	GMAC-128	GMAC-256
ESP encryption/ Integrity	AES-GCM (128-bit key)	AES-GCM (256-bit key)	Null	Null
ESP integrity	Null	Null	AES-GMAC (128-bit key)	AES-GMAC (256-bit key)
IKE encryption	AES-CBC (128-bit key)	AES-CBC (256-bit key)	AES-CBC (128-bit key)	AES-CBC (256-bit key)
IKE PRF	HMAC-SHA-256	HMAC-SHA-384	HMAC-SHA-256	HMAC-SHA-384
IKE Integrity	HMAC-SHA-256-128	HMAC-SHA-384-192	HMAC-SHA-256-128	HMAC-SHA-384-192
IKE DH group	256-bit random ECP	384-bit random ECP	256-bit random ECP	384-bit random ECP

(b) NSA Suite B (RFC 6379)

VPN-A relies on 3DES and HMAC, while VPN-B relies exclusively on AES. Three types of secret-key algorithms are used:

- **Encryption:** For encryption, the cipher block chaining (CBC) mode is used.
- **Message authentication:** For message authentication, VPN-A relies on HMAC with SHA-1 with the output truncated to 96 bits. VPN-B relies on a variant of CMAC with the output truncated to 96 bits.
- **Pseudorandom function:** IKEv2 generates pseudorandom bits by repeated use of the MAC used for message authentication.

RFC 6379 defines four optional cryptographic suites that are compatible with the United States National Security Agency's Suite B specifications. In 2005, the NSA issued Suite B, which defined the algorithms and strengths needed to protect both sensitive but unclassified (SBU) and classified information for use in its Cryptographic Modernization program [LATT09]. The four suites defined in RFC 6379 provide choices for ESP and IKE. The four suites are differentiated by the choice of cryptographic algorithm strengths and a choice of whether ESP is to provide both confidentiality and integrity or integrity only. All of the suites offer greater protection than the two VPN suites defined in RFC 4308.

Table 20.4b lists the algorithms and parameters for the two suites. As with RFC 4308, three categories of secret key algorithms are listed:

- **Encryption:** For ESP, authenticated encryption is provided using the GCM mode with either 128-bit or 256-bit AES keys. For IKE encryption, CBC is used, as it was for the VPN suites.
- **Message authentication:** For ESP, if only authentication is required, then GMAC is used. As discussed in Chapter 12, GMAC is simply the authentication portion of GMC. For IKE, message authentication is provided using HMAC with one of the SHA-3 hash functions.
- **Pseudorandom function:** As with the VPN suites, IKEv2 in these suites generates pseudorandom bits by repeated use of the MAC used for message authentication.

For the Diffie–Hellman algorithm, the use of elliptic curve groups modulo a prime is specified. For authentication, elliptic curve digital signatures are listed. The original IKEv2 documents used RSA-based digital signatures. Equivalent or greater strength can be achieved using ECC with fewer key bits.

20.7 KEY TERMS, REVIEW QUESTIONS, AND PROBLEMS

Key Terms

anti-replay service Authentication Header (AH) Encapsulating Security Payload (ESP) Internet Key Exchange (IKE)	Internet Security Association and Key Management Protocol (ISAKMP) IP Security (IPsec) IPv4 IPv6	Oakley key determination protocol replay attack security association (SA) transport mode tunnel mode

Review Questions

20.1 List and briefly describe some benefits of IPsec.

20.2 What services are provided by IPsec?

20.3 What parameters identify an SA and what parameters characterize the nature of a particular SA?

20.4 What is the difference between transport mode and tunnel mode?

20.5 Briefly describe the format of an ESP packet.

20.6 Why does ESP include a padding field?

20.7 What are the basic approaches to bundling SAs?

20.8 Which is the default key management protocol for IPsec?

Problems

20.1 Describe and explain each of the entries in Table 20.2.

20.2 Draw a figure similar to Figure 20.8 for AH.

20.3 List the major security services provided by AH and ESP, respectively.

20.4 In discussing AH processing, it was mentioned that not all of the fields in an IP header are included in MAC calculation.

a. For each of the fields in the IPv4 header, indicate whether the field is immutable, mutable but predictable, or mutable (zeroed prior to ICV calculation).

b. Do the same for the IPv6 header.

c. Do the same for the IPv6 extension headers.

In each case, justify your decision for each field.

20.5 Suppose that the current replay window spans from 120 to 530.

a. If the next incoming authenticated packet has sequence number 105, what will the receiver do with the packet, and what will be the parameters of the window after that?

b. If instead the next incoming authenticated packet has sequence number 440, what will the receiver do with the packet, and what will be the parameters of the window after that?

c. If instead the next incoming authenticated packet has sequence number 540, what will the receiver do with the packet, and what will be the parameters of the window after that?

20.6 When tunnel mode is used, a new outer IP header is constructed. For both IPv4 and IPv6, indicate the relationship of each outer IP header field and each extension header in the outer packet to the corresponding field or extension header of the inner IP packet. That is, indicate which outer values are derived from inner values and which are constructed independently of the inner values.

20.7 End-to-end authentication and encryption are desired between two hosts. Draw figures similar to Figure 20.8 that show each of the following.

a. Transport adjacency with encryption applied before authentication.

b. A transport SA bundled inside a tunnel SA with encryption applied before authentication.

c. A transport SA bundled inside a tunnel SA with authentication applied before encryption.

20.8 The sequence number in the ESP header in IPsec is used to prevent replay attacks: the receiver will only accept one packet with each sequence number, and reject a packet with a sequence number that has already been used. What then prevents an attacker from sending a packet with a higher sequence number to cause the original packet with this sequence number from being accepted?

20.9 In case of an error associated with SA or SA negotiation, indicate which parameters go in which IKE payload type?

20.10 Where does IPsec reside in a protocol stack?

Appendix A

Projects for Teaching Cryptography and Network Security

Analysis and observation, theory and experience must never disdain or exclude each other; on the contrary, they support each other.

—*On War,* Carl Von Clausewitz

Many instructors believe that research or implementation projects are crucial to the clear understanding of cryptography and network security. Without projects, it may be difficult for students to grasp some of the basic concepts and interactions among components. Projects reinforce the concepts introduced in the book, give the student a greater appreciation of how a cryptographic algorithm or protocol works, and can motivate students and give them confidence that they are capable of not only understanding but implementing the details of a security capability.

In this text, I have tried to present the concepts of cryptography and network security as clearly as possible and have provided numerous homework problems to reinforce those concepts. However, many instructors will wish to supplement this material with projects. This appendix provides some guidance in that regard and describes support material available in the **Instructor's Resource Center (IRC)** for this book, accessible to instructors from Pearson Education. The support material covers 12 types of projects and other student exercises:

- Sage computer algebra projects
- Hacking project
- Block cipher projects
- Laboratory exercises
- Research projects
- Programming projects
- Practical security assessments
- Firewall projects
- Case studies
- Writing assignments
- Reading/report assignments
- Discussion topics

A.1 SAGE COMPUTER ALGEBRA PROJECTS

One of the most important new features for this edition is the use of Sage for cryptographic examples and homework assignments. Sage is an open-source, multiplatform, freeware package that implements a very powerful, flexible, and easily learned mathematics and computer algebra system. A computer algebra system (CAS) is software that can perform symbolic as well as numerical calculations. CASs have been used for teaching since their inception some decades ago, and there is now a considerable literature on their use. A CAS is a natural tool for extending the learning experience in a cryptography course.

Unlike competing systems such as Mathematica, Maple, and MATLAB, there are no licensing agreements or fees involved with Sage. Thus, Sage can be made available on computers and networks at school, and students can individually download the software to their own personal computers for use at home. Another advantage of using Sage is that students learn a powerful, flexible tool that can be used for virtually any mathematical application, not just cryptography. The Sage Web site (http://www.sagemath.org) provides considerable documentation on how to install, set up, and use Sage on a variety of computers and how to use it online via the Web.

The use of Sage can make a significant difference to the teaching of the mathematics of cryptographic algorithms. Appendix B provides a large number of examples of the use of Sage covering many cryptographic concepts. Appendix C lists exercises in each of these topic areas to enable the student to gain hands-on experience with cryptographic algorithms. Copies of both appendices are available online so that students do not have to key in lines of code that are printed in the appendices.

The IRC contains solutions to all of the exercises in Appendix C.

Dan Shumow of Microsoft and the University of Washington developed all of the examples and assignments in Appendices B and C.

A.2 HACKING PROJECT

The aim of this project is to hack into a corporation's network through a series of steps. The corporation is named Extreme In Security Corporation. As the name indicates, the corporation has some security holes in it, and a clever hacker is able to access critical information by hacking into its network. The IRC includes what is needed to set up the Web site. The student's goal is to capture the secret information about the price on the quote the corporation is placing next week to obtain a contract for a governmental project.

The student should start at the Web site and find his or her way into the network. At each step, if the student succeeds, there are indications as to how to proceed on to the next step as well as the grade until that point.

The project can be attempted in three ways:

1. Without seeking any sort of help
2. Using some provided hints
3. Using exact directions

The IRC includes the files needed for this project:

1. Web Security project
2. Web Hacking exercises (XSS and Script-attacks) covering client-side and server-side vulnerability exploitations, respectively
3. Documentation for installation and use for the above
4. A PowerPoint file describing Web hacking. This file is crucial to understanding how to use the exercises since it clearly explains the operation using screen shots.

This project was designed and implemented by Professor Sreekanth Malladi of Dakota State University.

A.3 BLOCK CIPHER PROJECTS

This is a lab that explores the operation of the AES encryption algorithm by tracing its execution, computing one round by hand, and then exploring the various block cipher modes of use. The lab also covers DES. In both cases, an online Java applet is used (or can be downloaded) to execute AES or DES.

For both AES and DES, the lab is divided into three separate parts:

- **Block cipher internals:** This part involves encrypting plaintext and analyzing the intermediate results after each round. There is an online calculator for both AES and DES that provides the intermediate results and the final ciphertext.
- **Block cipher round:** This part involves calculating one round by hand and comparing the results to those produced by the calculator.
- **Block cipher modes of use:** Enables the student to compare the operation of CBC and CFB modes.

The IRC contains the `.html` and `.jar` files needed to set up these labs on your own Web site. Alternatively, the material is available from the Student Resources section of this book's Web site. Click on the rotating globe.

Lawrie Brown of the Australian Defence Force Academy developed these projects.

A.4 LABORATORY EXERCISES

Professor Sanjay Rao and Ruben Torres of Purdue University have prepared a set of laboratory exercises that are included in the IRC. These are implementation projects designed to be programmed on Linux but could be adapted for any Unix environment. These laboratory exercises provide realistic experience in implementing security functions and applications.

A.5 RESEARCH PROJECTS

An effective way of reinforcing basic concepts from the course and for teaching students research skills is to assign a research project. Such a project could involve a literature search as well as an Internet search of vendor products, research lab activities, and standardization efforts. Projects could be assigned to teams or, for smaller projects, to individuals. In any case, it is best to require some sort of project proposal early in the term, giving the instructor time to evaluate the proposal for appropriate topic and appropriate level of effort. Student handouts for research projects should include

- A format for the proposal
- A format for the final report
- A schedule with intermediate and final deadlines
- A list of possible project topics

The students can select one of the topics listed in the IRC or devise their own comparable project. The IRC includes a suggested format for the proposal and final report as well as a list of 15 possible research topics.

A.6 PROGRAMMING PROJECTS

The programming project is a useful pedagogical tool. There are several attractive features of stand-alone programming projects that are not part of an existing security facility:

1. The instructor can choose from a wide variety of cryptography and network security concepts to assign projects.
2. The projects are platform and language independent. Students can program the projects on any available computer and in any appropriate language.
3. The instructor need not download, install, and configure any particular infrastructure for stand-alone projects.

There is also flexibility in the size of projects. Larger projects give students more a sense of achievement, but students with less ability or fewer organizational skills can be left behind. Larger projects usually elicit more overall effort from the best students. Smaller projects can have a higher concepts-to-code ratio and, because more of them can be assigned, the opportunity exists to address a variety of different areas.

Again, as with research projects, the students should first submit a proposal. The student handout should include the same elements listed in the preceding section. The IRC includes a set of 12 possible programming projects.

The following individuals have supplied the research and programming projects suggested in the IRC: Henning Schulzrinne of Columbia University; Cetin Kaya Koc of Oregon State University; and David M. Balenson of Trusted Information Systems and George Washington University.

A.7 PRACTICAL SECURITY ASSESSMENTS

Examining the current infrastructure and practices of an existing organization is one of the best ways of developing skills in assessing its security posture. The IRC contains a list of such activities. Students, working either individually or in small groups, select a suitable small- to medium-sized organization. They then interview some key personnel in that organization in order to conduct a suitable selection of security risk assessment and review tasks as it relates to the organization's IT infrastructure and practices. As a result, they can then recommend suitable changes, which can improve the organization's IT security. These activities help students develop an appreciation of current security practices and the skills needed to review these and recommend changes.

Lawrie Brown of the Australian Defence Force Academy developed these projects.

A.8 FIREWALL PROJECTS

The implementation of network firewalls can be a difficult concept for students to grasp initially. The IRC includes a Network Firewall Visualization tool to convey and teach network security and firewall configuration. This tool is intended to teach and reinforce key concepts including the use and purpose of a perimeter firewall, the use of separated subnets, the purposes behind packet filtering, and the shortcomings of a simple packet filter firewall.

The IRC includes a `.jar` file that is fully portable, and a series of exercises. The tool and exercises were developed at U.S. Air Force Academy.

A.9 CASE STUDIES

Teaching with case studies engages students in active learning. The IRC includes case studies in the following areas:

- Disaster recovery
- Firewalls
- Incidence response
- Physical security
- Risk
- Security policy
- Virtualization

Each case study includes learning objectives, case description, and a series of case discussion questions. Each case study is based on real-world situations and includes papers or reports describing the case.

The case studies were developed at North Carolina A&T State University.

A.10 WRITING ASSIGNMENTS

Writing assignments can have a powerful multiplier effect in the learning process in a technical discipline such as cryptography and network security. Adherents of the Writing Across the Curriculum (WAC) movement (http://wac.colostate.edu/) report substantial benefits of writing assignments in facilitating learning. Writing assignments lead to more detailed and complete thinking about a particular topic. In addition, writing assignments help to overcome the tendency of students to pursue a subject with a minimum of personal engagement, just learning facts and problem-solving techniques without obtaining a deep understanding of the subject matter.

The IRC contains a number of suggested writing assignments, organized by chapter. Instructors may ultimately find that this is an important part of their approach to teaching the material. I would greatly appreciate any feedback on this area and any suggestions for additional writing assignments.

A.11 READING/REPORT ASSIGNMENTS

Another excellent way to reinforce concepts from the course and to give students research experience is to assign papers from the literature to be read and analyzed. The student is then asked to write a brief report on the assigned paper. The IRC includes a suggested list of papers, one or two per chapter, to be assigned. The IRC provides a PDF copy of each of the papers. The IRC also includes a suggested assignment wording.

A.12 DISCUSSION TOPICS

One way to provide a collaborative experience is discussion topics, a number of which are included in the IRC. Each topic relates to material in the book. The instructor can set it up so that students can discuss a topic either in a class setting, an online chat room, or a message board. Again, I would greatly appreciate any feedback on this area and any suggestions for additional discussion topics.

APPENDIX B

SAGE EXAMPLES

By Dan Shumow
University of Washington

This appendix contains a number of examples that illustrate cryptographic concepts, organized by the chapter in which those concepts were discussed. All the examples are in Sage.[1] See Appendix C for how to get started using Sage and for a brief introduction to Sage syntax and operations. We begin with a brief introduction to some basic Sage matrix and linear algebra operations.

You should be able to follow the examples in this section as written. However, if you have difficulty interpreting the Sage code, please refer to Section C.2 in Appendix C.

B.1 LINEAR ALGEBRA AND MATRIX FUNCTIONALITY

Sage includes linear algebra and matrix functionality. The following shows some of the basic functionality applicable to cryptography.

In Sage you specify a matrix as a list of lists of numbers, passed to the `matrix` function. For example, passing a list of lists of integers as follows:

```
sage: M = matrix([[1, 3], [7,9]]); M
[1 3]
[7 9]
```

Alternately, passing a list of lists of rationals as follows:

```
sage: M = matrix([[1/2, 2/3, 3/4],[5, 7, 8]]); M
[1/2 2/3 3/4]
[ 5 7 8]
```

You can specify that the input should be reduced by a modulus, using the IntegerModRing (functionality to be described later)

```
Sage: R = IntegerModRing(100)
sage: M = matrix(R, [[1],[102],[1003]]); M
[1]
[2]
[3]
```

Or that the input should be considered in a finite field (also to be described later).

```
sage: F = GF(2);
sage: M = matrix(F, [[1, 2, 0, 3]]); M
[1 0 0 1]
```

[1]All of the Sage code in this appendix is available at this book's Companion Web site in .sage files, so that you can load and execute the programs if you wish. See Preface for access information.

Sage also supports multiplication, addition, and inversion of matrices as follows:

```
sage: M1 = matrix([[1, 2],[3,4]]);
sage: M2 = matrix([[1,-1],[1, 1]]);
sage: M1*M2
[3 1]
[7 1]
sage: M1 + M2
[2 1]
[4 5]
sage: M2^-1
[ 1/2 1/2]
[-1/2 1/2]
```

B.2 CHAPTER 2: NUMBER THEORY

Example 1: Chinese Remainder Theorem.

```
def chinese_remainder_theorem(moduli, residues):
    r"""
    Function that implements the chinese remainder
    theorem.

    INPUT:

        moduli - list or positive integers.

        residues - list of remainders such that remainder
    at position j results when divided by the corresponding
    modulus at position j in moduli.

    OUTPUT:

        x - integer such that division by moduli[j] gives
    remainder residue[j].

    """

    if (len(moduli) != len(residues)):

    raise ValueError, "expected len(moduli) ==
    len(residues)"

    M = prod(moduli);

    x = 0;
```

```
    for j in xrange(len(moduli)):
        Mj = moduli[j]
        Mpr = M/Mj
         (Mj_Mpr_gcd, Mpr_inv, Mj_inv) = xgcd(Mpr, Mj)
        Mpr_inv = Mpr_inv
        if (Mj_Mpr_gcd != 1):
        raise ValueError, "Expected all moduli are
        coprime."
        x += residues[j]*Mpr*Mpr_inv;
    return x;
```

Example 2: Miller–Rabin Primality Test.

```
r"""
EXAMPLES:
    sage: MILLER_RABIN_TEST(101)
    False
    sage: MILLER_RABIN_TEST(592701729979)
    True
"""

def MILLER_RABIN_TEST(n):
    r"""
    This function implements the Miller-Rabin Test.
    It either returns "inconclusive" or "composite."
    INPUT:
        n - positive integer to probabilistically
        determine the primality of.
    OUTPUT:
    If the function returns False, then the test was
    inconclusive.
        If the function returns True, then the test was
    conclusive and n is composite.
    """
    R = IntegerModRing(n); # object for integers mod n
    # (1) Find integers k, q w/ k > 0 and q odd so that
    (n-1) == 2^k * q
    q = n-1
    k = 0
```

```
    while (1 == (q % 2)):
        k += 1
        q = q.quo_rem(2)[0] # q/2 but with result of type
        Integer

    # (2) select random a in 1 < a < n-1

    a = randint(1,n-1)
    a = R(a) # makes it so modular exponentiation is done
    fast

    # if a^q mod n == 1 then return inconclusive
    if (1 == a^q):
        return False
    # (3) for j = 0 to k-1 do: if a^(2^j * q) mod n = n-1
    return inconclusive

    e = q

    for j in xrange(k):
        if (n-1) == (a^e):
            return False
        e = 2*e

    # (4) if you've made it here return composite.
    return True
```

Example 3: Modular Exponentiation (Square and Multiply).

```
def ModExp(x,e,N):
    r"""
    Calculates x^e mod N using square and multiply.

    INPUT:

        x - an integer.
        e - a nonnegative integer.
        N - a positive integer modulus.

    OUTPUT:

        y - x^e mod N

    """

        e_bits = e.bits()
        e_bitlen = len(e_bits)

    y = 1

    for j in xrange(e_bitlen):

        y = y^2 % N
```

```
            if (1 == e_bits[e_bitlen-1-j]):
                y = x*y % N
    return y
```

Example 4: Using built-in Sage functionality for CRT.

Sage has built in functions to perform the Chinese Remainder Theorem. There are several functions that produce a wide array of CRT functionality. The simplest function performs the CRT with two modulii. Specifically CRT (or the lowercase crt) when called as:

```
crt(a,b,m,n)
```

will return a number that is simultaneously congruent to `a` mod `m` and `b` mod `n`. All parameters are assumed to be integers and the parameters `m`, `n` must be relatively prime. Some examples of this function are:

```
sage: CRT(8, 16, 17, 49)
-3120

sage: CRT(1,2,5,7)
16

sage: CRT(50,64,101,127)
-62166
```

If you want to perform the CRT with a list of residues and moduli, Sage includes the function CRT_list.

```
CRT_list(v, modulii)
```

requires that `v` and modulii be lists of integers of the same length. Furthermore, the elements of modulii must be relatively prime. Then the output is an integer that reduces to v[i] mod modulii[i] (for i in range(len(v))). For example, the last call to CRT would have been

```
sage: CRT_list([50,64],[101,127])
1969
```

Note that this answer is different. However, you can check that both answers satisfy the requirements of the CRT. Here are examples with longer lists:

```
sage: CRT_list([8, 20, 13], [49, 101, 127])
608343

sage: CRT_list([10,11,12,13,14],[29,31,37,41,43])
36657170
```

The function CRT_basis can be used to precompute the values associated to the given set of modulii. If modulii is a list of relatively prime modulii, then CRT_basis(modulii) returns a list `a`. This list a is such that if `x` is a list of residues of the modulii, then the output of the CRT can be found by summing:

```
a[0]*x[0] + a[1]*x[1] + ... + a[len(a)-1]*x[len(a)-1]
```

In the case of the modulii used in the last call to CRT_list this function returns as follows:

```
sage: CRT_basis([29,31,37,41,43])
[32354576, 20808689, 23774055, 17163708, 23184311]
```

The last CRT function that Sage provides is CRT_vectors. This function performs CRT_list on several different lists (with the same set of modulii) and returns a list of the simultaneous answers. It is efficient in that it uses CRT_basis and does not recompute those values for each list. For example:

```
sage:
CRT_vectors([[1,10],[2,11],[3,12],[4,13],[5,14]],
[29,31,37,41,43])
[36657161, 36657170]
```

Example 5: Using built-in Sage functionality for Modular Exponentiation.

Sage can perform modular exponentiation using fast algorithms (like square and multiply) and without allowing the intermediate computations to become huge. This is done through IntegerModRing objects. Specifically, creating an IntegerModRing object indicates that arithmetic should be done with a modulus. Then you cast your integers in this ring to indicate that all arithmetic should be done with the modulus. Then for elements of this ring, exponentiation is done efficiently. For example:

```
sage: R = IntegerModRing(101)
sage: x = R(10)
sage: x^99
91

sage: R = IntegerModRing(1024)
sage: x = R(111)
sage: x^345
751

sage: x = R(100)
sage: x^200
0

sage: N = 127*101
sage: R = IntegerModRing(N)
sage: x = R(54)
sage: x^95
9177
```

Creating an IntegerModRing is similar to creating a FiniteField with GF(...) except that the modulus can be a general composite.

Example 6: Using built-in Sage functionality for Euler's totient.

Sage has the Euler totient functionality built in. The function is called euler_phi because of the convention of using the Greek letter phi to represent this function. The operation of this function is simple. Just call euler_phi on an integer and it computes the totient function. This function factors the input, and hence requires exponential time.

```
sage: euler_phi(101)
100

sage: euler_phi(1024)
512

sage: euler_phi(333)
216

sage: euler_phi(125)
100

sage: euler_phi(423)
276
```

B.3 CHAPTER 3: CLASSICAL ENCRYPTION

The following functions are useful for classical cipher examples and exercises:

```
en_alphabet = "abcdefghijklmnopqrstuvwxyz"

#
# This function returns true if and only if the character
c is an
# alphabetic character
#
def is_alphabetic_char(c):
    return (c.lower() in en_alphabet)

#
# This function converts a single character into its
numeric value
#
def char_to_num(c):
    return en_alphabet.index(c.lower())

#
# This function returns the character corresponding to x
mod 26
# in the English alphabet
#
def num_to_char(x):
    return en_alphabet[x % 26]
```

Example 1: Implement Sage encryption/decryption functions that take a key (as an integer in 0, 1, 2, . . . , 25), and a string. The function should only operate on the characters 'a', 'b', . . . 'z' (both upper and lower case), and it should leave any other characters unchanged.

Solution:

```
def CaesarEncrypt(k, plaintext):
    ciphertext = ""
    for j in xrange(len(plaintext)):
        p = plaintext[j]
        if is_alphabetic_char(p):
            x = (k + char_to_num(p)) % 26
            c = num_to_char(x)
        else:
            c = p
        ciphertext += c
    return ciphertext
def CaesarDecrypt(k, ciphertext):
    plaintext = ""
    for j in xrange(len(ciphertext)):
        c = ciphertext[j]
        if is_alphabetic_char(c):
            x = (char_to_num(c) - k) % 26
            p = num_to_char(x)
        else:
            p = c
        plaintext += p
    return plaintext
```

Example 2: Implement a function that performs a brute force attack on a ciphertext, it should print a list of the keys and associated decryptions. It should also take an optional parameter that takes a substring and only prints out potential plaintexts that contain that decryption.

Solution:

```
def BruteForceAttack(ciphertext, keyword=None):
    for k in xrange(26):
        plaintext = CaesarDecrypt(k, ciphertext)
        if (None==keyword) or (keyword in plaintext):
            print "key", k, "decryption", plaintext
    return
```

Example 3: Show the output of your encrypt function (Example 1) on the following (key, plaintext) pairs:

- k = 16 plaintext = "Get me a vanilla ice cream, make it a double."
- k = 15 plaintext = "I don't much care for Leonard Cohen."
- k = 16 plaintext = "I like root beer floats."

Solution:

```
sage: k = 6; plaintext = 'Get me a vanilla ice
cream, make it a double.'
sage: CaesarEncrypt(k, plaintext)
'mkz sk g bgtorrg oik ixkgs, sgqk oz g juahrk.'

sage: k = 15; plaintext = "I don't much care for
Leonard Cohen."
sage: CaesarEncrypt(k, plaintext)
"x sdc'i bjrw rpgt udg atdcpgs rdwtc."

sage: k = 16; plaintext = "I like root beer floats."
sage: CaesarEncrypt(k, plaintext)
'y byau heej ruuh vbeqji.'
```

Example 4: Show the output of your decrypt function (Example 1) on the following (key, ciphertext) pairs:

- k = 12 ciphertext = 'nduzs ftq buzq oazqe.'
- k = 3 ciphertext = "fdhvdu qhhgv wr orvh zhljkw."
- k = 20 ciphertext = "ufgihxm uly numnys."

Solution:

```
sage: k = 12; ciphertext = "nduzs ftq buzq oazqe."
sage: CaesarDecrypt(k, ciphertext)
'bring the pine cones.'

sage: k = 3; ciphertext = "fdhvdu qhhgv wr orvh
zhljkw."
sage: CaesarDecrypt(k, ciphertext)
'caesar needs to lose weight.'

sage: k = 20; ciphertext = "ufgihxm uly numnys."
sage: CaesarDecrypt(k, ciphertext)
'almonds are tastey.'
```

Example 5: Show the output of your attack function (Example 4) on the following ciphertexts, if an optional keyword is specified, pass that to your attack function:

- ciphertext = 'gryy guru gob tab gb nzoebfr puncry.' keyword = 'chapel'
- ciphertext = 'wziv kyv jyfk nyve kyv tpdsrcj tirjy.' keyword = 'cymbal'
- ciphertext = 'baeeq klwosjl osk s esf ozg cfwo lgg emuz.' no keyword

Solution:

```
sage: ciphertext = 'gryy gurz gb tb gb nzoebfr puncry.'
sage: BruteForceAttack(ciphertext, 'chapel')
key 13 decryption tell them to go to ambrose chapel.

sage: ciphertext = 'wziv kyv jyfk nyve kyv tpdsrcj tirjy.'
sage: BruteForceAttack(ciphertext, 'cymbal')
key 17 decryption fire the shot when the cymbals crash.

sage: ciphertext = 'baeeq klwosjl osk s esf ozg cfwo lgg emuz.'
sage: BruteForceAttack(ciphertext)
key 0 decryption baeeq klwosjl osk s esf ozg cfwo lgg emuz.
key 1 decryption azddp jkvnrik nrj r dre nyf bevn kff dlty.
key 2 decryption zycco ijumqhj mqi q cqd mxe adum jee cksx.
key 3 decryption yxbbn hitlpgi lph p bpc lwd zctl idd bjrw.
key 4 decryption xwaam ghskofh kog o aob kvc ybsk hcc aiqv.
key 5 decryption wvzzl fgrjneg jnf n zna jub xarj gbb zhpu.
key 6 decryption vuyyk efqimdf ime m ymz ita wzqi faa ygot.
key 7 decryption utxxj dephlce hld l xly hsz vyph ezz xfns.
key 8 decryption tswwi cdogkbd gkc k wkx gry uxog dyy wemr.
key 9 decryption srvvh bcnfjac fjb j vjw fqx twnf cxx vdlq.
key 10 decryption rquug abmeizb eia i uiv epw svme bww uckp.
key 11 decryption qpttf zaldhya dhz h thu dov ruld avv tbjo.
key 12 decryption posse yzkcgxz cgy g sgt cnu qtkc zuu sain.
key 13 decryption onrrd xyjbfwy bfx f rfs bmt psjb ytt rzhm.
key 14 decryption nmqqc wxiaevx aew e qer als oria xss qygl.
key 15 decryption mlppb vwhzduw zdv d pdq zkr nqhz wrr pxfk.
key 16 decryption lkooa uvgyctv ycu c ocp yjq mpgy vqq owej.
key 17 decryption kjnnz tufxbsu xbt b nbo xip lofx upp nvdi.
key 18 decryption jimmy stewart was a man who knew too much.
key 19 decryption ihllx rsdvzqs vzr z lzm vgn jmdv snn ltbg.
key 20 decryption hgkkw qrcuypr uyq y kyl ufm ilcu rmm ksaf.
key 21 decryption gfjjv pqbtxoq txp x jxk tel hkbt qll jrze.
key 22 decryption feiiu opaswnp swo w iwj sdk gjas pkk iqyd.
key 23 decryption edhht nozrvmo rvn v hvi rcj fizr ojj hpxc.
key 24 decryption dcggs mnyquln qum u guh qbi ehyq nii gowb.
key 25 decryption cbffr lmxptkm ptl t ftg pah dgxp mhh fnva.
```

B.4 CHAPTER 4: BLOCK CIPHERS AND THE DATA ENCRYPTION STANDARD

Example 1: This example implements simplified DES, which is described in Appendix G.

```
#
# The Expansions/Permutations are stored as lists of
bit positions
#
```

```
    P10_data = [3, 5, 2, 7, 4, 10, 1, 9, 8, 6];
    P8_data = [6, 3, 7, 4, 8, 5, 10, 9];
    LS1_data = [2, 3, 4, 5, 1];
    LS2_data = [3, 4, 5, 1, 2];
    IP_data = [2, 6, 3, 1, 4, 8, 5, 7];
    IPinv_data = [4, 1, 3, 5, 7, 2, 8, 6];
    EP_data = [4, 1, 2, 3, 2, 3, 4, 1];
    P4_data = [2, 4, 3, 1];
    SW_data = [5, 6, 7, 8, 1, 2, 3, 4];
    #
    # SDES lookup tables
    #
    S0_data = [[1, 0, 3, 2],
               [3, 2, 1, 0],
               [0, 2, 1, 3],
               [3, 1, 3, 2]];
    S1_data = [[0, 1, 2, 3],
               [2, 0, 1, 3],
               [3, 0, 1, 0],
               [2, 1, 0, 3]];
    def ApplyPermutation(X, permutation):
        r"""
        This function takes a permutation list (list of
        bit positions.)
        And outputs a bit list with the bits taken from X.
        """

        # permute the list X
        l = len(permutation);
        return [X[permutation[j]-1] for j in xrange(l)];
    def ApplySBox(X, SBox):
        r"""
        This function Applies the SDES SBox (by table
        look up
        """

        r = 2*X[0] + X[3];
        c = 2*X[1] + X[2];
        o = SBox[r][c];
        return [o & 2, o & 1];
```

```
#
# Each of these functions uses ApplyPermutation
# and a permutation list to perform an SDES
# Expansion/Permutation
#
def P10(X):
    return ApplyPermutation(X, P10_data);

def P8(X):
    return ApplyPermutation(X, P8_data);

def IP(X):
    return ApplyPermutation(X, IP_data);

def IPinv(X):
    return ApplyPermutation(X, IPinv_data);

def EP(X):
    return ApplyPermutation(X, EP_data);

def P4(X):
    return ApplyPermutation(X, P4_data);

def SW(X):
    return ApplyPermutation(X, SW_data);

def LS1(X):
    return ApplyPermutation(X, LS1_data);

def LS2(X):
    return ApplyPermutation(X, LS2_data);

#
# These two functions perform the SBox substitutions
#

def S0(X):
    return ApplySBox(X, S0_data);

def S1(X):
    return ApplySBox(X, S1_data);

def concatenate(left, right):
    r"""
    Joins to bit lists together.
    """
    ret = [left[j] for j in xrange(len(left))];
    ret.extend(right);
    return ret;

def LeftHalfBits(block):
    r"""
    Returns the left half bits from block.
    """
```

```
        l = len(block);
        return [block[j] for j in xrange(l/2)];
    def RightHalfBits(block):
        r"""
        Returns the right half bits from block.
        """
        l = len(block);
        return [block[j] for j in xrange(l/2, l)];
    def XorBlock(block1, block2):
        r"""
        Xors two blocks together.
        """
        l = len(block1);
        if (l != len(block2)):
            raise ValueError, "XorBlock arguments must
            be same length"
        return [(block1[j]+block2[j]) % 2 for j in
        xrange(l)];
    def SDESKeySchedule(K):
        r"""
        Expands an SDES Key (bit list) into the two
        round keys.
        """
        temp_K = P10(K);
        left_temp_K = LeftHalfBits(temp_K);
        right_temp_K = RightHalfBits(temp_K);
        K1left = LS1(left_temp_K);
        K1right = LS1(right_temp_K);
        K1temp = concatenate(K1left, K1right);
        K1 = P8(K1temp);
        K2left = LS2(K1left);
        K2right = LS2(K1right);
        K2temp = concatenate(K2left, K2right);
        K2 = P8(K2temp);
        return (K1, K2);
    def f_K(block, K):
        r"""
        Performs the f_K function supplied block and K.
        """
        left_block = LeftHalfBits(block);
        right_block = RightHalfBits(block);
```

```
        temp_block1 = EP(right_block);
        temp_block2 = XorBlock(temp_block1, K);

        left_temp_block2 = LeftHalfBits(temp_block2);
        right_temp_block2 = RightHalfBits(temp_block2);

        S0_out = S0(left_temp_block2);
        S1_out = S1(right_temp_block2);

        temp_block3 = concatenate(S0_out, S1_out);

        temp_block4 = P4(temp_block3)

        temp_block5 = XorBlock(temp_block4, left_block);

        output_block = concatenate(temp_block5, right_
        block)

        return output_block;

    def SDESEncrypt(plaintext_block, K):
        r"""
        Performs a single SDES plaintext block encryption.
        (Given plaintext and key as bit lists.)
        """

        (K1, K2) = SDESKeySchedule(K);

        temp_block1 = IP(plaintext_block);

        temp_block2 = f_K(temp_block1, K1);

        temp_block3 = SW(temp_block2);

        temp_block4 = f_K(temp_block3, K2);

        output_block = IPinv(temp_block4);

        return output_block;
```

B.5 CHAPTER 5: BASIC CONCEPTS IN NUMBER THEORY AND FINITE FIELDS

Example 1: The Euclidean algorithm for the greatest common divisor.

```
def EUCLID(a,b):
    r"""
    The Euclidean algorithm for finding the gcd of a and b.
    This algorithm assumes that a > b => 0

    INPUT:
            a - positive integer
            b - nonnegative integer less than a
```

```
          OUTPUT:
              g - greatest common divisor of a and b
              """
              if (b < 0) or ( a <= b):
                  raise ValueError, "Expected 0 < a < b"
              (A, B) = (a,b);
              while (True):
                  if (0 == B):
                      return A;
                  R = A % B;
                  A = B;
                  B = R;
```

Example 2: The extended Euclidean algorithm for the greatest common divisor.

```
def EXTENDED_EUCLID(m,b):
r"""
The extended Euclidean algorithm to find gcd(m,b).
The input is expected to be such that 0 <= b < m.

INPUT:

    m - positive integer

    b - nonnegative integer less than m

OUTPUT:

(g, b_inv) - g is the gcd of m and b, b_inv is
the multiplicative inverse of b mod m.
"""

if (m < b) or (b < 0):

    raise ValueError, "Expected input (0 < b < m)"

(A1,A2,A3) = (1,0,m);
(B1,B2,B3) = (0,1,b);

while (True):

    if (0 == B3):
        return (A3, None)

    if (1 == B3):
        return (B3, B2)

    Q = floor(A3/B3)

    (T1,T2,T3) = (A1-Q*B1, A2-Q*B2, A3-Q*B3)
```

```
        (A1, A2, A3) = (B1, B2, B3)
        (B1, B2, B3) = (T1, T2, T3)
```

Example 3: Euclidean algorithm to find gcd of polynomials (with coefficients in a field).

```
def POLYNOMIAL_EUCLID(A, B):
    r"""
    Euclidian algorithm for polynomial GCD:
    Given two polynomials over the same base field,
    Assuming degree(A) => degree(B) => 0.

    INPUT:

        A - polynomial over a field.

        B - polynomial over the same field as A, and 0 <=
        degree(B) <= degree(A).

    OUTPUT:

        G - greatest common divisor of A and B.

    """
    degA = A.degree();
    degB = B.degree();

    if ((degB < 0) or (degA < degB)):
        raise ValueError, "Expected 0 <= degree(B) <=
        degree(A)"

    while(True):

        if (0 == B):
            return A;

        R = A % B;

        A = B;
        B = R;
```

Example 4: Extended Euclidean algorithm for the gcd of two polynomials (with coefficients in the same field).

```
def POLYNOMIAL_EXTENDED_EUCLID(m, b):
    r"""
    Extended Euclidian algorithm for polynomial GCD:
    Given two polynomials over the same base field,
    Assuming degree(m) => degree(b) => 0

    INPUT:

        m - polynomial over a field.
```

```
            b - polynomial over the same field as A, and 0 <=
            degree(B) <= degree(M).

        OUTPUT:

            (g,b_inv) - the pair where:

            g - greatest common divisor of m and b.

            m_inv - is None if G is not of degree 0, and
                    otherwise it is the polynomial such that
                    b(X)*b_inv(X) = 1 mod m(X)
        """
        degm = m.degree();
        degb = b.degree();

        if(degb < 0) or (degm < degb):
            raise ValueError, "expected 0 <= degree(b) <=
            degree(m)"

        (A1, A2, A3) = (1, 0, m);
        (B1, B2, B3) = (0, 1, b);

        while (True):

            if (0 == B3):
                return (A3, None);
            if (0 == B3.degree()):
                return (B3/B3, B2/B3);

            Q = A3.quo_rem(B3)[0];

            (T1, T2, T3) = (A1 - Q*B1, A2 - Q*B2, A3 - Q*B3);
            (A1, A2, A3) = (B1, B2, B3);
            (B1, B2, B3) = (T1, T2, T3);
```

Example 5: Sage has built in functionality for the gcd function. The regular greatest common divisor function can simply be called as:

```
sage: gcd(15,100)
5

sage: gcd(90,65311)
1
```

You can also call it as a method on Integer objects:

```
sage: x = 10456890
sage: x.gcd(100)
10
```

The extended Euclidean algorithm for the greatest common divisor is also built into Sage. Calling xgcd(a,b) returns a tuple, the first element is the gcd, the second and third elements are coefficients u, v such that gcd(a,b) = u* a + v* b. This can be called as:

```
sage: xgcd(17,31)
(1, 11, -6)
sage: xgcd(10, 115)
(5, -11, 1)
```

This can also be called as a method on Integer objects

```
sage: x = 300
sage: x.xgcd(36)
(12, 1, -8)
```

Example 6: Sage includes robust support for working with finite fields and performing finite field arithmetic. To initialize a finite field with prime order, use the GF command passing the order as the parameter.

```
sage: F = GF(2)
sage: F
Finite Field of size 2

sage: F = GF(37)
sage: F
Finite Field of size 37

sage: p = 95131
sage: K = GF(p)
sage: K
Finite Field of size 95131
```

To initialize a field with a prime power order use the GF command with the following syntax (to keep track of the primitive element of the extension field).

```
sage: F.<a> = GF(128)
sage: F
Finite Field in a of size 2^7
```

To do arithmetic in finite fields use the following syntax:

```
sage: K = GF(37)
sage: a = K(3)
sage: b = K(18)
sage: a - b
22
sage: a + b
21
sage: a * b
17
sage: a/b
31
```

```
sage: a^-1
25
sage: 1/a
25
```

To do arithmetic in a finite field with a prime power order, specify elements using the primitive element:

```
sage: F.<a> = GF(128)
sage: b = a^2 + 1
sage: c = a^5 + a^3 + 1
sage: b - c
a^5 + a^3 + a^2
sage: b + c
a^5 + a^3 + a^2
sage: b*c
a^3 + a^2 + a
sage: b/c
a^5 + a^3 + a^2 + a
sage: b^-1
a^5 + a^3 + a
sage: 1/b
a^5 + a^3 + a
```

Example 7: With Sage you can create rings of polynomials over finite fields and do arithmetic with them. To create polynomial rings over finite fields do the following:

```
sage: R.<x> = GF(2)[]
sage: R

Univariate Polynomial Ring in x over Finite Field of
size 2 (using NTL)
sage: R.<x> = GF(101)[]

sage: R
sage: R.<x> = F[]
sage: R
Univariate Polynomial Ring in x over Finite Field in
a of size 2^7
```

After initializing a polynomial ring, you can then just perform arithmetic as you would expect:

```
sage: R.<x> = GF(2)[]
sage: f = x^3 + x + 1
sage: g = x^5 + x
sage: f + g
x^5 + x^3 + 1
sage: f*g
x^8 + x^6 + x^5 + x^4 + x^2 + x
```

Division is accomplished by the quo_rem function:

```
sage: g.quo_rem(f)
(x^2 + 1, x^2 + 1)
```

You can also compute the greatest common divisor:

```
sage: f.gcd(g)
1

sage: g.gcd(g^2)
x^5 + x

sage: R.<x> = GF(17)[]
sage: f = 3*x^3 + 2*x^2 + x
sage: g = x^2 + 5
sage: f - g
3*x^3 + x^2 + x + 12
sage: f * g
3*x^5 + 2*x^4 + 16*x^3 + 10*x^2 + 5*x
sage: f.quo_rem(g)
(3*x + 2, 3*x + 7)
```

And computing gcds in this polynomial ring we see:

```
sage: f.gcd(g)
1
sage: f.gcd(x^2 + x)
x
```

When creating a Sage finite field with a prime power order, Sage finds an irreducible polynomial for you. For example:

```
sage: F.<a> = GF(32)
a^5 + a^2 + 1
```

However, there are many irreducible polynomials over GF(2) of degree 5, such as x^5 + x^3 + 1. Suppose that you want to create your own extension of the binary field with degree 5, and an irreducible polynomial of your choice. Then you can do so as follows:

```
sage: R.<x> = GF(2)[]
sage: F = GF(2).extension(x^5 + x^3 + 1, 'a')
sage: a = F.gen()
```

You need to do this last step to inject the primitive element into the interpreter's name space. This is done automatically when using the GF function to create an extension field, but not when you use the member function extension on a field object.

B.6 CHAPTER 6: ADVANCED ENCRYPTION STANDARD

Example 1: Simplified AES.

```
#
# These structures are the underlying
# Galois Field and corresponding Vector Space
# of the field used in the SAES algorithm
# These structures allow us to easily compute with these fields.
#
F = GF(2);
L.<a> = GF(2^4);
V = L.vector_space();
VF8 = VectorSpace(F, 8);
#
# The MixColumns and its Inverse matrices are stored
# as 2x2 matrices with elements in GF(2^4) (as are state
matrices.)
# The MixColumns operation (and its inverse) are performed by
# matrix multiplication.
#

MixColumns_matrix = Matrix(L, [[1,a^2],[a^2,1]]);

InverseMixColumns_matrix = MixColumns_matrix.inverse();

SBox_matrix = Matrix(L,
  [
  [       1 + a^3,           a^2,         a + a^3,1 + a + a^3],
  [ 1 + a^2 + a^3,             1,             a^3,    1 + a^2],
  [       a + a^2,             0,               a,      1 + a],
  [     a^2 + a^3, a + a^2 + a^3, 1 + a + a^2 + a^3, 1 + a + a^2]
  ]);

InverseSBox_matrix = Matrix(L,
  [
  [   a + a^3,     1 + a^2,           1 + a^3,      1 + a + a^3],
  [         1, 1 + a + a^2,               a^3, 1 + a + a^2 + a^3],
  [   a + a^2,           0,                 a,            1 + a],
  [ a^2 + a^3,         a^2,     1 + a^2 + a^3,      a + a^2 + a^3]
  ]);

RCON = [
 VF8([F(0), F(0), F(0), F(0), F(0), F(0), F(0), F(1)]),
 VF8([F(0), F(0), F(0), F(0), F(1), F(1), F(0), F(0)])
   ];
```

```
def SAES_ToStateMatrix(block):
    r"""
    Converts a bit list into an SAES state matrix.
    """

    B = block;

    # form the plaintext block into a matrix of GF(2^n)
    elements
    S00 = L(V([B[0], B[1], B[2], B[3]]));
    S01 = L(V([B[4], B[5], B[6], B[7]]));
    S10 = L(V([B[8], B[9], B[10], B[11]]));
    S11 = L(V([B[12], B[13], B[14], B[15]]));

    state_matrix = Matrix(L, [[S00,S01],[S10,S11]]);

    return state_matrix;

def SAES_FromStateMatrix(State Matrix):
    r"""
    Converts an SAES State Matrix to a bit list.
    """

    output = [];

    # convert State Matrix back into bit list
    for r in xrange(2):
        for c in xrange(2):
            v = V(State Matrix[r,c]);
            for j in xrange(4):
                output.append(Integer(v[j]));

    return output;

def SAES_AddRoundKey(state_matrix, K):
    r"""
    Adds a round key to an SAES state matrix.
    """

    K_matrix = SAES_ToStateMatrix(K);

    next_state_matrix = K_matrix + state_matrix;

    return next_state_matrix;

def SAES_MixColumns(state_matrix):
    r"""
    Performs the Mix Columns operation.
    """

    next_state_matrix = MixColumns_matrix*state_matrix;

    return next_state_matrix;
```

```
def SAES_InverseMixColumns(state_matrix):
    r"""
    Performs the Inverse Mix Columns operation.
    """

    next_state_matrix = InverseMixColumns_matrix*
    state_matrix;
    return next_state_matrix;

def SAES_ShiftRow(state_matrix):
    r"""
    Performs the Shift Row operation.
    """

    M = state_matrix;
    next_state_matrix = Matrix(L, [
                                    [M[0,0], M[0,1]],
                                    [M[1,1], M[1,0]]
                                   ]);
    return next_state_matrix;

def SAES_SBox(nibble):
    r"""
    Performs the SAES SBox look up in the SBox matrix
    (lookup table.)
    """

    v = nibble._vector_();
    c = Integer(v[0]) + 2*Integer(v[1]);
    r = Integer(v[2]) + 2*Integer(v[3]);
    return SBox_matrix[r,c];

def SAES_NibbleSubstitution(state_matrix):
    r"""
    Performs the SAES SBox on each element of an SAES
    state matrix.
    """

    M = state_matrix;
    next_state_matrix = Matrix(L,
              [ [ SAES_SBox(M[0,0]), SAES_SBox(M[0,1])],
                [ SAES_SBox(M[1,0]), SAES_SBox(M[1,1])] ]);
    return next_state_matrix;

def SAES_InvSBox(nibble):
    r"""
    Performs the SAES Inverse SBox look up in the SBox
    matrix (lookup table.)
    """

    v = nibble._vector_();
    c = Integer(v[0]) + 2*Integer(v[1]);
```

```
    r = Integer(v[2]) + 2*Integer(v[3]);
    return InverseSBox_matrix[r,c];

def SAES_InvNibbleSub(state_matrix):
    r"""
    Performs the SAES Inverse SBox on each element of an
    SAES state matrix.
    """

    M = state_matrix;
    next_state_matrix = Matrix(L,
    [ [ SAES_InvSBox(M[0,0]), SAES_InvSBox(M[0,1])],
      [ SAES_InvSBox(M[1,0]), SAES_InvSBox(M[1,1])] ]);
    return next_state_matrix;

def RotNib(w):
    r"""
    Splits an 8 bit list into two elements of GF(2^4)
    """
    N_0 = L(V([w[j] for j in xrange(4)]));
    N_1 = L(V([w[j] for j in xrange(4,8)]));
    return (N_1, N_0);

def SAES_g(w, i):
    r"""
    Performs the SAES g function on the 8 bit list w.
    """
    (N0, N1) = RotNib(w);
    N0 = V(SAES_SBox(N0));
    N1 = V(SAES_SBox(N1));
    temp1 = VF8( [ N0[0], N0[1], N0[2], N0[3],
                   N1[0], N1[1], N1[2], N1[3] ] );
    output = temp1 + RCON[i];
    return output;

def SAES_KeyExpansion(K):
    r"""
    Expands an SAES key into two round keys.
    """
    w0 = VF8([K[j] for j in xrange(8)]);
    w1 = VF8([K[j] for j in xrange(8,16)]);
    w2 = w0 + SAES_g(w1, 0);
    w3 = w1 + w2;
    w4 = w2 + SAES_g(w3, 1);
    w5 = w3 + w4;
    K0 = [w0[j] for j in xrange(8)];
    K0.extend([w1[j] for j in xrange(8)]);
    K1 = [w2[j] for j in xrange(8)];
    K1.extend([w3[j] for j in xrange(8)]);
```

```
        K2 = [w4[j] for j in xrange(8)];
        K2.extend([w4[j] for j in xrange(8)]);

        return (K0, K1, K2);

    #
    # Encrypts one plaintext block with key K
    #

    def SAES_Encrypt(plaintext, K):
        r"""
        Performs a SAES encryption on a single plaintext
        block.
        (Both block and key passed as bit lists.)
        """

        # get the key schedule
        (K0, K1, K2) = SAES_KeyExpansion(K);

        state_matrix0 = SAES_ToStateMatrix(plaintext);

        state_matrix1 = SAES_AddRoundKey(state_matrix0, K0);

        state_matrix2 = SAES_NibbleSubstitution
        (state_matrix1);

        state_matrix3 = SAES_ShiftRow(state_matrix2);

        state_matrix4 = SAES_MixColumns(state_matrix3);

        state_matrix5 = SAES_AddRoundKey(state_matrix4, K1);

        state_matrix6 = SAES_NibbleSubstitution
        (state_matrix5);

        state_matrix7 = SAES_ShiftRow(state_matrix6);

        state_matrix8 = SAES_AddRoundKey(state_matrix7, K2);

        output = SAES_FromStateMatrix(state_matrix8);
        return output;

    #
    # Decrypts one ciphertext block with key K
    #

    def SAES_Decrypt(ciphertext, K):
        r"""
        Performs a single SAES decryption operation on a -
        ciphertext block.
        (Both block and key passed as bit lists.)
        """

        # perform key expansion
        (K0, K1, K2) = SAES_KeyExpansion(K);
```

```
    # form the ciphertext block into a matrix of GF(2^n)
    elements
    state_matrix0 = SAES_ToStateMatrix(ciphertext);
    state_matrix1 = SAES_AddRoundKey(state_matrix0, K2);
    state_matrix2 = SAES_ShiftRow(state_matrix1);
    state_matrix3 = SAES_InvNibbleSub(state_matrix2);
    state_matrix4 = SAES_AddRoundKey(state_matrix3, K1);
    state_matrix5 = SAES_InverseMixColumns
    (state_matrix4);
    state_matrix6 = SAES_ShiftRow(state_matrix5);
    state_matrix7 = SAES_InvNibbleSub(state_matrix6);
    state_matrix8 = SAES_AddRoundKey(state_matrix7, K0);
    output = SAES_FromStateMatrix(state_matrix8);
    return output;
```

B.7 CHAPTER 8: PSEUDORANDOM NUMBER GENERATION AND STREAM CIPHERS

Example 1: Blum Blum Shub RNG.

```
def BlumBlumShub_Initialize(bitlen, seed):
    r"""
    Initializes a Blum-Blum-Shub RNG State.

    A BBS-RNG State is a list with two elements:
    [N, X]
    N is a 2*bitlen modulus (product of two primes)
    X is the current state of the PRNG.

    INPUT:
        bitlen - the bit length of each of the prime
        factors of n

        seed - a large random integer to start out the
        prng

    OUTPUT:

        state - a BBS-RNG internal state

    """
    # note that this is not the most cryptographically
    secure
```

```
    # way to generate primes, because we do not know how the
    # internal sage random_prime function works.

    p = 3;
    while (p < 2^(bitlen-1)) or (3 != (p % 4)):
        p = random_prime(2^bitlen);
    q = 3;
    while (q < 2^(bitlen-1)) or (3 != (q % 4)):
        q = random_prime(2^bitlen);
    N = p*q;
    X = (seed^2 % N)
    state = [N, X]
    return state;

def BlumBlumShub_Generate(num_bits, state):
    r"""
    Blum-Blum-Shum random number generation function.

    INPUT:

        num_bits - the number of bits (iterations) to
        generate with this RNG.

        state - an internal state of the BBS-RNG (a list
        [N, X].)

    OUTPUT:

        random_bits - a num_bits length list of random
        bits.
    """
    random_bits = [];
    N = state[0]
    X = state[1]

    for j in xrange(num_bits):
        X = X^2 % N
        random_bits.append(X % 2)
    # update the internal state
    state[1] = X;

    return random_bits;
```

Example 2: Linear Congruential RNG.

```
def LinearCongruential_Initialize(a, c, m, X0):
    r"""
```

```
    This functional initializes a linear congruential
    RNG state.

    This state is a list of four integers: [a, c, m, X]

    a,c,m are the parameters of the linear congruential
    instantiation X is the current state of the PRNG.

    INPUT:

        a - The coefficient
        c - The offset
        m - The modulus
       X0 - The initial state

    OUTPUT:

        state - The initial internal state of the RNG

    """
    return [a,c,m,X0]

def LinearCongruential_Generate(state):
    r"""
    Generates a single linear congruential RNG output
    and updates the state.

    INPUT:

        state - an internal RNG state.

    OUTPUT:

        X - a single output of the linear congruential RNG.

    """
    a = state[0]
    c = state[1]
    m = state[2]
    X = state[3]
    X_next = (a*X + c) % m
    state[3] = X_next
    return X_next
```

B.8 CHAPTER 9: PUBLIC-KEY CRYPTOGRAPHY AND RSA

Example 1: Using Sage we can simulate an RSA encryption and decryption.

```
sage: # randomly select some prime numbers
sage: p = random_prime(1000); p
191
```

```
sage: q = random_prime(1000); q
601
sage: # compute the modulus
sage: N = p*q
sage: R = IntegerModRing(N)
sage: phi_N = (p-1)*(q-1)
sage: # we can choose the encrypt key to be anything
sage: # relatively prime to phi_N
sage: e = 17
sage: gcd(d, phi_N)
1
sage: # the decrypt key is the multiplicative
inverse
sage: # of d mod phi_N
sage: d = xgcd(d, phi_N)[1] % phi_N
sage: d
60353
sage: # Now we will encrypt/decrypt some random 7
digit numbers
sage: P = randint(1,127); P
97
sage: # encrypt
sage: C = R(P)^e; C
46685
sage: # decrypt
sage: R(C)^d
97

sage: P = randint(1,127); P
46
sage: # encrypt
sage: C = R(P)^e; C
75843
sage: # decrypt
sage: R(C)^d
46

sage: P = randint(1,127); P
3
sage: # encrypt
sage: C = R(P)^e; C
288
sage: # decrypt
sage: R(C)^d
3
```

Also, Sage can just as easily do much larger numbers:

```
sage: p = random_prime(1000000000); p
```

```
114750751
sage: q = random_prime(1000000000); q
8916569
sage: N = p*q
sage: R = IntegerModRing(N)
sage: phi_N = (p-1)*(q-1)
sage: e = 2^16 + 1
sage: d = xgcd(e, phi_N)[1] % phi_N
sage: d
237150735093473

sage: P = randint(1,1000000); P
955802
sage: C = R(P)^e
sage: R(C)^d
955802
```

Example 2: In Sage, we can also see an example of RSA signing/verifying.

```
sage: p = random_prime(10000); p
1601
sage: q = random_prime(10000); q
4073
sage: N = p*q
sage: R = IntegerModRing(N)
sage: phi_N = (p-1)*(q-1)
sage: e = 47
sage: gcd(e, phi_N)
1
sage: d = xgcd(e,phi_N)[1] % phi_N
sage: # Now by exponentiating with the private key
sage: # we are effectively signing the data
sage: # a few examples of this

sage: to_sign = randint(2,2^10); to_sign
650
sage: # the signature is checked by exponentiating
sage: # and checking vs the to_sign value
sage: signed = R(to_sign)^d; signed
2910116
sage: to_sign == signed^e
True
sage: to_sign = randint(2,2^10); to_sign
362
sage: signed = R(to_sign)^d; signed
546132
sage: to_sign == signed^e
True
```

```
sage: # we can also see what happens if we try to
verify a bad signature

sage: to_sign = randint(2,2^10); to_sign
605
sage: signed = R(to_sign)^d; signed
1967793
sage: bad_signature = signed - randint(2,100)
sage: to_sign == bad_signature^e
False
```

B.9 CHAPTER 10: OTHER PUBLIC-KEY CRYPTOSYSTEMS

Example 1: Here is an example of Alice and Bob performing a Diffie–Hellman Key Exchange done in Sage:

```
sage: # Alice and Bob agree on the domain
parameters:
sage: p = 619
sage: F = GF(p)
sage: g = F(2)
sage: # Alice picks a random value x in 1 . . . 618
sage: x = randint(1,618); x
571
sage: # Alice computes X = g^x and sends this to Bob
sage: X = g^571; X
591
sage: # Bob picks a random value y in 1 . . . 618
sage: y = randint(1,618);y
356
sage: # Bob computes Y = g^y and sends this to Alice
sage: Y = g^y; Y
199
sage: # Alice computes Y^x
sage: Y^x
563
sage: # Bob computes X^y
sage: X^y
563
sage: # Alice and Bob now share a secret value
```

Example 2: In reality to prevent what is known as small subgroup attacks, the prime p is chosen so that $p - 2q + 1$ where p is a prime as well.

```
sage: q = 761
sage: p = 2*q + 1
sage: is_prime(q)
True
```

```
sage: is_prime(p)
True
sage: F = GF(p)
sage: g = F(3)
sage: g^q
1
sage: # note that g^q = 1 implies g is of order q
sage: # Alice picks a random value x in 2 . . . q-1
sage: x = randint(2,q-1); x
312
sage: # Alice computes X = g^x and sends it to Bob
sage: X = g^x; X
26
sage: # Bob computes a random value y in 2 . . . q-1
sage: y = randint(2,q-1); y
24
sage: # Bob computes Y = g^y and sends it to Alice
sage: Y = g^y; Y
1304
sage: # Alice computes Y^x
sage: Y^x
541
sage: # Bob computes X^y
sage: X^y
541
sage: # Alice and Bob now share the secret value 541
```

Example 3: Sage has a significant amount of support for elliptic curves. This functionality can be very useful when learning, because it allows you to easily calculate things and get the big picture. Doing the examples by hand may cause you to get mired in the details. First you instantiate an elliptic curve, by specifying the field that it is over, and the coefficients of the defining Weierstrass equation. For this purpose, we write the Weierstrass equation as

$$y^2 + a_1xy + a_3y = x^3 + a_2x^2 + a_4x + a_6$$

Then the Sage function EllipticCurve(R, [a1, a2, a3, a4, a6]) creates the elliptic curve over the ring R.

```
sage: E = EllipticCurve(GF(17), [1,2,3,4,5])
sage: E
Elliptic Curve defined by y^2 + x*y + 3*y = x^3 +
2*x^2 + 4*x + 5 over Finite Field of size 17

sage: E = EllipticCurve(GF(29), [0,0,0,1,1])
sage: E
Elliptic Curve defined by y^2 = x^3 + x + 1 over
Finite Field of size 29
```

```
sage: E = EllipticCurve(GF(127), [0,0,0,2,17])
sage: E
Elliptic Curve defined by y^2 = x^3 + 2*x + 17 over
Finite Field of size 127

sage: F.<theta> = GF(2^10)
sage: E = EllipticCurve(F, [1,0,0,1,0])
sage: E
Elliptic Curve defined by y^2 + x*y = x^3 + x over
Finite Field in theta of size 2^10
```

Example 4: Koblitz curves. A Koblitz curve is an elliptic curve over a binary field defined by an equation of the form

$$y^2 + xy = x^3 + ax^2 + 1$$

where $a = 0$ or 1. FIPS 186-3 recommends a number of Koblitz curves for use with the Digital Signature Standard (DSS). Here we give an example of a curve of similar form to the Koblitz curves:

```
sage: F.<theta> = GF(2^17)
sage: E = EllipticCurve(F,[1,0,0,theta,1])
sage: E
Elliptic Curve defined by y^2 + y = x^3 + theta*
x^2 = 1 over Finite Field in theta of size 2^17
```

Example 5: Sage can even easily instantiate curves of cryptographic sizes, like K163, which is one of the FIPS 186-3 curves.

```
sage: F.<theta> = GF(2^163)
sage: E = EllipticCurve(F, [1,0,0,1,1])
sage: E
Elliptic Curve defined by y^2 + x*y = x^3 + x^2 + 1
over Finite Field in theta of size 2^163
```

However, you should be careful that when instantiating a curve of cryptographic sizes, some of the functions on the curve object will not work because they require exponential time to run. While you can compute some things with these objects, it is best to leave your experimentation to the smaller sized curves.

You can calculate some values of the curve, such as the number of points:

```
sage: E = EllipticCurve(GF(107), [0,0,0,1,0])
sage: E.order()
108
```

You can also determine the generators of a curve:

```
sage: E = EllipticCurve(GF(101), [0,0,0,1,0])
sage: E.gens()
((7 : 42 : 1), (36 : 38 : 1))
```

Note that this output is printed (x : y : z). This is a minor technical consideration because Sage stores points in what is known as "projective coordinates." The precise meaning is not important, because for non-infinite points the value z will always be 1 and the first two values in a coordinate will be the x and y coordinates, exactly as you would expect. This representation is useful because it allows the point at infinity to be specified as a point with the z coordinate equal to 0:

```
sage: E(0)
(0 : 1 : 0)
```

This shows how you can recognize a point at infinity as well as specify it. If you want to get the x and y coordinates out of a point on the curve, you can do so as follows:

```
sage: P = E.random_point(); P
(62 : 38 : 1)
sage: (x,y) = P.xy(); (x,y)
(62, 38)
```

You can specify a point on the curve by casting an ordered pair to the curve as:

```
sage: P = E((62,-38)); P
(62 : 63 : 1)
```

Now that you can find the generators on a curve and specify points you can experiment with these points and do arithmetic as well. Continuing to use E as the curve instantiated in the previous example, we can set G1 and G2 to the generators:

```
sage: (G1, G2) = E.gens()
sage: P = E.random_point(); P
(49 : 29 : 1)
```

You can compute the sum of two points as in the following examples:

```
sage: G1 + G2 + P
(69 : 96 : 1)
sage: G1 + P
(40 : 62 : 1)
sage: P + P + G2
(84 : 25 : 1)
```

You can compute the inverse of a point using the unary minus (−) operator:

```
sage: -P
(49 : 72 : 1)
sage: -G1
(7 : 59 : 1)
```

You can also compute repeated point addition (adding a point to itself many times) with the * operator:

```
sage: 13*G1
(72 : 23 : 1)
```

```
sage: 2*G2
(9 : 58 : 1)
sage: 88*P
(87 : 75 : 1)
```

And for curves over small finite fields you can also compute the order (discrete log of the point at infinity with respect to that point).

```
sage: G1.order()
10

sage: G2.order()
10

sage: P.order()
10
```

Example 6: Using the Sage elliptic curve functionality to perform a simulated elliptic curve Diffie–Hellman (ECDH) key exchange.

```
sage: # calculate domain parameters
sage: F = GF(127)
sage: E = EllipticCurve(F, [0, 0, 0, 3, 4])
sage: G = E.gen(0); G
(94 : 6 : 1)
sage: q = E.order(); q
122

sage: # Alice computes a secret value x in
2 . . . q-1
sage: x = randint(2,q-1); x
33

sage: # Alice computes a public value X = x*G
sage: X = x*G; X
(55 : 89 : 1)

sage: # Bob computes a secret value y in 2 . . . q-1
sage: y = randint(2,q-1); y
55

sage: # Bob computes a public value Y = y*G
sage: Y = y*G; Y
(84 : 39 : 1)

sage: # Alice computes the shared value
sage: x*Y
(91 : 105 : 1)

sage: # Bob computes the shared value
sage: y*X
(91 : 105 : 1)
```

However, in practice most curves that are used have a prime order:

```
sage: # Calculate the domain parameters
sage: F = GF(101)
sage: E = EllipticCurve(F, [0, 0, 0, 25, 7])
sage: G = E((97,34))
sage: q = E.order()
sage: # Alice computes a secret values x in 2 . . . q-1
sage: x = randint(2,q-1)
sage: # Alice computes a public value X = x*G
sage: X = x*G
sage: # Bob computes a secret value y in 2 . . . q-1
sage: y = randint(2,q-1)
sage: # Bob computes a public value Y = y*G
sage: Y = y*G
sage: # Alice computes the shared secret value
sage: x*Y
(23 : 15 : 1)
sage: # Bob computes the shared secret value
sage: y*X
(23 : 15 : 1)
```

B.10 CHAPTER 11: CRYPTOGRAPHIC HASH FUNCTIONS

Example 1: The following is an example of the MASH hash function in Sage. MASH is a function based on the use of modular arithmetic. It involves use of an RSA-like modulus M, whose bit length affects the security. M should be difficult to factor, and for M of unknown factorization, the security is based in part on the difficulty of extracting modular roots. M also determines the block size for processing messages. In essence, MASH is defined as:

$$H_i = ((x_i \oplus H_{i-1})^2 \text{ OR } H_{i-1}) (\text{mod } M)$$

where

A = 0xFF00 . . . 00
H_{i-1} = the largest prime less than M
x_i = the ith digit of the base M expansion of input n. That is, we express n as a number of base M. Thus:

$$n = x_0 + x_1 M + x_2 M^2 + \ldots$$

The following is an example of the MASH hash function in Sage.

```
#
# This function generates a mash modulus
# takes a bit length, and returns a Mash
# modulus l or l-1 bits long (if n is odd)
```

```
# returns p, q, and the product N
#
def generate_mash_modulus(l):

    m = l.quo_rem(2)[0]

    p = 1
    while (p < 2^(m-1)):
    p = random_prime(2^m)

    q = 1
    while (q < 2^(m-1)):
    q = random_prime(2^m)

    N = p*q
    return (N, p, q)
#
# Mash Hash
# the value n is the data to be hashed.
# the value N is the modulus
# Returns the hash value.
#
def MASH(n, N):

    H = previous_prime(N)

    q = n

    while (0 != q):
        (q, a) = q.quo_rem(N)
        H = ((H+a)^2 + H) % N

    return H
```

The output of these functions running;

```
sage: data = ZZ(randint(1,2^1000))
sage: (N, p, q) = generate_mash_modulus(20)
sage: MASH(data, N)
220874
sage: (N, p, q) = generate_mash_modulus(50)
sage: MASH(data, N)
455794413217080
sage: (N, p, q) = generate_mash_modulus(100)
sage: MASH(data, N)
268864504538508517754648285037
sage: data = ZZ(randint(1,2^1000))
sage: MASH(data, N)
236862581074736881919296071248
sage: data = ZZ(randint(1,2^1000))
sage: MASH(data, N)
395463068716770866931052945515
```

B.11 CHAPTER 13: DIGITAL SIGNATURES

Example 1: Using Sage, we can perform a DSA sign and verify:

```
sage: # First we generate the domain parameters
sage: # Generate a 16 bit prime q
sage: q = 1;
sage: while (q < 2^15): q = random_prime(2^16)
. . . .:
sage: q
42697
sage: # Generate a 64 bit p, such that q divides
(p-1)
sage: p = 1
sage: while (not is_prime(p)):
. . . .: p = (2^48 + randint(1,2^46)*2)*q + 1
. . . .:
sage: p
12797003281321319017
sage: # Generate h and g
sage: h = randint(2,p-2)
sage: h
5751574539220326847
sage: F = GF(p)
sage: g = F(h)^((p-1)/q)
sage: g
9670562682258945855

sage: # Generate a user public / private key
sage: # private key
sage: x = randint(2,q-1)
sage: x
20499
sage: # public key
sage: y = F(g)^x
sage: y
7955052828197610751
sage: # Sign and verify a random value
sage: H = randint(2,p-1)
sage: # Signing
sage: # random blinding value
sage: k = randint(2,q-1)
sage: r = F(g)^k % q
sage: r = F(g)^k
sage: r = r.lift() % q
sage: r
6805
sage: kinv = xgcd(k,q)[1] % q
```

```
sage: s = kinv*(H + x*r) % q
sage: s
26026
sage: # Verifying
sage: w = xgcd(s,q)[1]; w
12250
sage: u1 = H*w % q; u1
6694
sage: u2 = r*w % q; u2
16706
sage: v = F(g)^u1 * F(y)^u2
sage: v = v.lift() % q
sage: v
6805
sage: v == r
True
sage: # Sign and verify another random value
sage: H = randint(2,p-1)
sage: k = randint(2,q-1)
sage: r = F(g)^k
sage: r = r.lift() % q
sage: r
3284
sage: kinv = xgcd(k,q)[1] % q
sage: s = kinv*(H + x*r) % q
sage: s
2330
sage: # Verifying
sage: w = xgcd(s,q)[1]; w
4343
sage: u1 = H*w % q; u1
32191
sage: u2 = r*w % q; u2
1614
sage: v = F(g)^u1 * F(y)^u2
sage: v = v.lift() % q
sage: v
3284
sage: v == r
True
```

Example 2: The following functions implement DSA domain parameter generation, key generation, and DSA Signing:

```
#
# Generates a 16 bit q and 64 bit p, both prime
# such that q divides p-1
#
```

```
def DSA_generate_domain_parameters():
    g = 1
    while (1 == g):
        # first find a q
        q = 1
        while (q < 2^15): q = random_prime(2^16)
        # next find a p
        p = 1
        while (not is_prime(p)):
            p = (2^47 + randint(1,2^45)*2)*q + 1
        F = GF(p)
        h = randint(2,p-1)
        g = (F(h)^((p-1)/q)).lift()
    return (p, q, g)
#
# Generates a users private and public key
# given domain parameters p, q, and g
#
def DSA_generate_keypair(p, q, g):
    x = randint(2,q-1)
    F = GF(p)
    y = F(g)^x
    y = y.lift()
    return (x,y)
#
# Given domain parameters p, q and g
# as well as a secret key x
# and a hash value H
# this performs the DSA signing algorithm
#
def DSA_sign(p, q, g, x, H):
    k = randint(2,q-1)
    F = GF(p)
    r = F(g)^k
    r = r.lift() % q
    kinv = xgcd(k,q)[1] % q
    s = kinv*(H + x*r) % q
    return (r, s)
```

REFERENCES

ABBREVIATIONS

ACM Association for Computing Machinery
IBM International Business Machines Corporation
IEEE Institute of Electrical and Electronics Engineers
NIST National Institute of Standards and Technology

ADAM94 Adams, C. "Simple and Effective Key Scheduling for Symmetric Ciphers." *Proceedings, Workshop on Selected Areas of Cryptography, SAC '94*, 1994.

AGRA04 Agrawal, M.; Kayal, N.; and Saxena, N. "PRIMES is in P." *IIT Kanpur, Annals of Mathematics*, September 2004.

AROR12 Arora, M. "How Secure is AES Against Brute-Force Attack?" *EE Times*, May 7, 2012.

ALFA13 Al Fardan, N., et al. "On the Security of RC4 in TLS and WPA." *USENIX Security Symposium*, July 2013.

BARD12 Bardou, R., et al. "Efficient Padding Oracle Attacks on Cryptographic Hardware," INRIA, Rapport de recherche RR-7944, Apr. 2012. http://hal.inria.fr/hal-00691958.

BASU12 Basu, A. *Intel AES-NI Performance Testing over Full Disk Encryption.* Intel Corp. May 2012.

BELL90 Bellovin, S., and Merritt, M. "Limitations of the Kerberos Authentication System." *Computer Communications Review*, October 1990.

BELL94 Bellare, M., and Rogaway, P. "Optimal Asymmetric Encryption—How to Encrypt with RSA." *Proceedings, Eurocrypt '94*, 1994.

BELL96a Bellare, M.; Canetti, R.; and Krawczyk, H. "Keying Hash Functions for Message Authentication." *Proceedings, CRYPTO '96*, August 1996; published by Springer-Verlag. An expanded version is available at http://www-cse.ucsd.edu/users/mihir.

BELL96b Bellare, M.; Canetti, R.; and Krawczyk, H. "The HMAC Construction." *CryptoBytes*, Spring 1996.

BELL96c Bellare, M., and Rogaway, P. "The Exact Security of Digital Signatures – How to Sign with RSA and Rabin." *Advances in Cryptology – Eurocrypt '96*, 1996.

BELL97 Bellare, M., and Rogaway, P. "Collision-Resistant Hashing: Towards Making UOWHF's Practical." *Proceedings, CRYPTO '97*, 1997; published by Springer-Verlag.

BELL98 Bellare, M., and Rogaway, P. "PSS: Provably Secure Encoding Method for Digital Signatures." *Submission to IEEE P1363*, August 1998. Available from http://grouper.ieee.org/groups/1363.

BELL00 Bellare, M.; Kilian, J.; and Rogaway, P. "The Security of the Cipher Block Chaining Message Authentication Code." *Journal of Computer and System Sciences*, December 2000.

BELL09 Bellare, M., et al. "Format Preserving Encryption". *Proceedings of SAC 2009 (Selected Areas in Cryptography)*, November 2009. Available at *Cryptology ePrint Archive* http://eprint.iacr.org/2009/.

BELL10a Bellare, M.; Rogaway, P.; and Spies, T. *The FFX Mode of Operation for Format-Preserving Encryption, Draft 1.1.* NIST, http://csrc.nist.gov/groups/ST/toolkit/BCM/documents/proposedmodes/ffx/ffx-spec.pdf, February, 2010.

BELL10b Bellare, M.; Rogaway, P.; and Spies, T. *Addendum to the FFX Mode of Operation for Format-Preserving Encryption: A Parameter Collection for Enciphering Strings of Arbitrary Radix and Length.* NIST, http://csrc.nist.gov/groups/ST/toolkit/BCM/documents/proposedmodes/ffx/ffx-spec2.pdf, September 2010.

BERT07 Bertoni, G., et al. "Sponge Functions." *Ecrypt Hash Workshop 2007*, May 2007.

BERT11 Bertoni, G., et al. "Cryptographic Sponge Functions." January 2011, http://sponge.noekeon.org/.

BETH91 Beth, T.; Frisch, M.; and Simmons, G., Eds. *Public-Key Cryptography: State of the Art and Future Directions.* New York: Springer-Verlag, 1991.

BLAC00 Black, J.; Rogaway, P.; and Shrimpton, T. "CBC MACs for Arbitrary-Length Messages: The Three-Key Constructions." *Advances in Cryptology – CRYPTO '00*, 2000.

BLAC05 Black, J. "Authenticated Encryption." *Encyclopedia of Cryptography and Security*, Springer, 2005.

BLEI98 Bleichenbacher, D. "Chosen ciphertext attacks against protocols based on the RSA encryption standard PKCS #1," *CRYPTO '98*, 1998.

BLUM86 Blum, L.; Blum, M.; and Shub, M. "A Simple Unpredictable Pseudo-Random Number Generator." *SIAM Journal on Computing*, No. 2, 1986.

BONE02 Boneh, D., and Shacham, H. "Fast Variants of RSA." *CryptoBytes*, Winter/Spring 2002. http://www.rsasecurity.com/rsalabs.

BRIE10 Brier, E.; Peyrin, T.; and Stern, J. *BPS: A Format-Preserving Encryption Proposal.* NIST, http://csrc.nist.gov/groups/ST/toolkit/BCM/documents/proposedmodes/bps/bps-spec.pdf, April 2010.

BRIG79 Bright, H., and Enison, R. "Quasi-Random Number Sequences from Long-Period TLP Generator with Remarks on Application to Cryptography." *Computing Surveys*, December 1979.

BROW07 Brown, D., and Gjosteen, K. "A Security Analysis of the NIST SP 800-90 Elliptic Curve Random Number Generator." *Proceedings, Crypto '07*, 2007.

BRYA88 Bryant, W. *Designing an Authentication System: A Dialogue in Four Scenes.* Project Athena document, February 1988. Available at http://web.mit.edu/kerberos/www/dialogue.html

CAMP92 Campbell, K., and Wiener, M. "Proof that DES is Not a Group." *Proceedings, Crypto '92*, 1992; published by Springer-Verlag.

CHOI08 Choi, M., et al. "Wireless Network Security: Vulnerabilities, Threats and Countermeasures." *International Journal of Multimedia and Ubiquitous Engineering*, July 2008.

COMP06 Computer Associates International. *The Business Value of Identity Federation.* White Paper, January 2006.

COPP94 Coppersmith, D. "The Data Encryption Standard (DES) and Its Strength Against Attacks." *IBM Journal of Research and Development*, May 1994.

CRAN01 Crandall, R., and Pomerance, C. *Prime Numbers: A Computational Perspective.* New York: Springer-Verlag, 2001.

CSA10 Cloud Security Alliance. *Top Threats to Cloud Computing V1.0.* CSA Report, March 2010.

CSA11a Cloud Security Alliance. *Security Guidance for Critical Areas of Focus in Cloud Computing V3.0.* CSA Report, 2011.

CSA11b Cloud Security Alliance. *Security as a Service (SecaaS).* CSA Report, 2011.

DAEM99 Daemen, J., and Rijmen, V. *AES Proposal: Rijndael, Version 2.* Submission to NIST, March 1999. http://csrc.nist.gov/archive/aes/index.html.

DAEM01 Daemen, J., and Rijmen, V. "Rijndael: The Advanced Encryption Standard." *Dr. Dobb's Journal*, March 2001.

DAMG89 Damgard, I. "A Design Principle for Hash Functions." *Proceedings, CRYPTO '89*, 1989; published by Springer-Verlag.

DAMI03 Damiani, E., et al. "Balancing Confidentiality and Efficiency in Untrusted Relational Databases." *Proceedings, Tenth ACM Conference on Computer and Communications Security*, 2003.

DAMI05 Damiani, E., et al. "Key Management for Multi-User Encrypted Databases." *Proceedings, 2005 ACM Workshop on Storage Security and Survivability*, 2005.

DAVI89 Davies, D., and Price, W. *Security for Computer Networks.* New York: Wiley, 1989.

DAWS96 Dawson, E., and Nielsen, L. "Automated Cryptoanalysis of XOR Plaintext Strings." *Cryptologia*, April 1996.

DENN81 Denning, D., and Sacco, G. "Timestamps in Key Distribution Protocols." *Communications of the ACM*, August 1981.

DENN82 Denning, D. *Cryptography and Data Security.* Reading, MA: Addison-Wesley, 1982.

DENN83 Denning, D. "Protecting Public Keys and Signature Keys." *Computer*, February 1983.

DIFF76a Diffie, W., and Hellman, M. "New Directions in Cryptography." *Proceedings of the AFIPS National Computer Conference*, June 1976.

DIFF76b Diffie, W., and Hellman, M. "Multiuser Cryptographic Techniques." *IEEE Transactions on Information Theory*, November 1976.

DIFF77 Diffie, W., and Hellman, M. "Exhaustive Cryptanalysis of the NBS Data Encryption Standard." *Computer*, June 1977.

DIFF79 Diffie, W., and Hellman, M. "Privacy and Authentication: An Introduction to Cryptography." *Proceedings of the IEEE*, March 1979.

DIFF88 Diffie, W. "The First Ten Years of Public-Key Cryptography." *Proceedings of the IEEE*, May 1988.

DIMI07 Dimitriadis, C. "Analyzing the Security of Internet Banking Authentication Mechanisms." *Information Systems Control Journal*, Vol. 3, 2007.

DOBB96 Dobbertin, H. "The Status of MD5 After a Recent Attack." *CryptoBytes*, Summer 1996.

ELGA84 Elgamal, T. "A Public Key Cryptosystem and a Signature Scheme Based on Discrete Logarithms." *Proceedings, Crypto 84*, 1984.

ELGA85 Elgamal, T. "A Public Key Cryptosystem and a Signature Scheme Based on Discrete Logarithms." *IEEE Transactions on Information Theory*, July 1985.

ENIS09 European Network and Information Security Agency. *Cloud Computing: Benefits, Risks and Recommendations for Information Security.* ENISA Report, November 2009.

FEIS73 Feistel, H. "Cryptography and Computer Privacy." *Scientific American*, May 1973.

FEIS75 Feistel, H.; Notz, W.; and Smith, J. "Some Cryptographic Techniques for Machine-to-Machine Data Communications." *Proceedings of the IEEE*, November 1975.

FERN99 Fernandes, A. "Elliptic Curve Cryptography." *Dr. Dobb's Journal*, December 1999.

FLUH00 Fluhrer, S., and McGrew, D. "Statistical Analysis of the Alleged RC4 Key Stream Generator." *Proceedings, Fast Software Encryption 2000*, 2000.

FLUH01 Fluhrer, S.; Mantin, I.; and Shamir, A. "Weakness in the Key Scheduling Algorithm of RC4." *Proceedings, Workshop in Selected Areas of Cryptography,* 2001.

FORD95 Ford, W. "Advances in Public-Key Certificate Standards." *ACM SIGSAC Review*, July 1995.

FRAN07 Frankel, S., et al. *Establishing Wireless Robust Security Networks: A Guide to IEEE 802.11i.* NIST Special Publication SP 800-97, February 2007.

GARD77 Gardner, M. "A New Kind of Cipher That Would Take Millions of Years to Break." *Scientific American*, August 1977.

GEOR12 Georgiev, M., et al. "The Most Dangerous Code in the World: Validating SSL Certificates in Non-Browser Software." *ACM Conference on Computer and Communications Security*, 2012.

GOLD88 Goldwasser, S.; Micali, S.; and Rivest, R. "A Digital Signature Scheme Secure Against Adaptive Chosen-Message Attacks." *SIAM Journal on Computing*, April 1988.

GONG92 Gong, L. "A Security Risk of Depending on Synchronized Clocks." *Operating Systems Review*, January 1992.

GONG93 Gong, L. "Variations on the Themes of Message Freshness and Replay." *Proceedings, IEEE Computer Security Foundations Workshop*, June 1993.

GOOD11 Goodin, D. "Hackers Break SSL Encryption Used by Millions of Sites." *The Register*, September 19, 2011.

GOOD12 Goodin, D. "Crack in Internet's Foundation of Trust Allows HTTPS Session Hijacking." *Ars Technica*, September 13, 2012.

GUTT06 Gutterman, Z.; Pinkas, B.; and Reinman, T. "Analysis of the Linux Random Number Generator." *Proceedings, 2006 IEEE Symposium on Security and Privacy*, 2006.

HACI02 Hacigumus, H., et al. "Executing SQL over Encrypted Data in the Database-Service-Provider Model." *Proceedings, 2002 ACM SIGMOD International Conference on Management of Data*, 2002.

HELL79 Hellman, M. "The Mathematics of Public-Key Cryptography." *Scientific American*, August 1970.

HEVI99 Hevia, A., and Kiwi, M. "Strength of Two Data Encryption Standard Implementations Under Timing Attacks." *ACM Transactions on Information and System Security*, November 1999.

HILT06 Hiltgen, A.; Kramp, T.; and Wiegold, T. "Secure Internet Banking Authentication." *IEEE Security and Privacy*, Vol. 4, No. 2, 2006.

HOWA03 Howard, M.; Pincus, J.; and Wing, J. "Measuring Relative Attack Surfaces." *Proceedings, Workshop on Advanced Developments in Software and Systems Security*, 2003.

HUIT98 Huitema, C. *IPv6: The New Internet Protocol.* Upper Saddle River, NJ: Prentice Hall, 1998.

IANS90 I'Anson, C., and Mitchell, C. "Security Defects in CCITT Recommendation X.509 – The Directory Authentication Framework." *Computer Communications Review*, April 1990.

INTE12 Intel Corp. *Intel® Digital Random Number Generator (DRNG) Software Implementation Guide*. August 7, 2012.

IWAT03 Iwata, T., and Kurosawa, K. "OMAC: One-Key CBC MAC." *Proceedings, Fast Software Encryption*, FSE '03, 2003.

JAIN91 Jain, R. *The Art of Computer Systems Performance Analysis: Techniques for Experimental Design, Measurement, Simulation, and Modeling.* New York: Wiley, 1991.

JAKO98 Jakobsson, M.; Shriver, E.; Hillyer, B.; and Juels, A. "A Practical Secure Physical Random Bit Generator." *Proceedings of the Fifth ACM Conference on Computer and Communications Security*, November 1998.

JANS11 Jansen, W., and Grance, T. *Guidelines on Security and Privacy in Public Cloud Computing.* NIST Special Publication 800-144, January 2011.

JOHN05 Johnson, D. "Hash Functions and Pseudorandomness." *Proceedings, First NIST Cryptographic Hash Workshop*, 2005.

JONE82 Jones, R. "Some Techniques for Handling Encipherment Keys." *ICL Technical Journal*, November 1982.

JUEN85 Jueneman, R.; Matyas, S.; and Meyer, C. "Message Authentication." *IEEE Communications Magazine*, September 1958.

JONS02 Jonsson, J. "On the Security of CTR + CBC-MAC." *Proceedings of Selected Areas in Cryptography – SAC 2002*, 2002.

JUEN87 Jueneman, R. "Electronic Document Authentication." *IEEE Network Magazine*, April 1987.

JURI97 Jurisic, A., and Menezes, A. "Elliptic Curves and Cryptography." *Dr. Dobb's Journal*, April 1997.

KALI95 Kaliski, B., and Robshaw, M. "The Secure Use of RSA." *CryptoBytes*, Autumn 1995.

KALI96a Kaliski, B., and Robshaw, M. "Multiple Encryption: Weighing Security and Performance." *Dr. Dobb's Journal*, January 1996.

KALI96b Kaliski, B. "Timing Attacks on Cryptosystems." *RSA Laboratories Bulletin*, January 1996. http://www.rsasecurity.com/rsalabs.

KALI01 Kaliski, B. "RSA Digital Signatures." *Dr. Dobb's Journal*, May 2001.

KEHN92 Kehne, A.; Schonwalder, J.; and Langendorfer, H. "A Nonce-Based Protocol for Multiple Authentications." *Operating Systems Review*, October 1992.

KLEI10 Kleinjung, T., et al. "Factorization of a 768-bit RSA modulus." Listing 2010/006, *Cryptology ePrint Archive*, February 18, 2010.

KNUD98 Knudsen, L., et al. "Analysis Method for Alleged RC4." *Proceedings, ASIACRYPT '98*, 1998.

KNUD00 Knudson, L. "Block Chaining Modes of Operation." *NIST First Modes of Operation Workshop*, October 2000. http://csrc.nist.gov/groups/ST/toolkit/BCM/workshops.html.

KNUT98 Knuth, D. *The Art of Computer Programming, Volume 2: Seminumerical Algorithms.* Reading, MA: Addison-Wesley, 1998.

KOCH96 Kocher, P. "Timing Attacks on Implementations of Diffie–Hellman, RSA, DSS, and Other Systems." *Proceedings, Crypto '96*, August 1996.

KOHL89 Kohl, J. "The Use of Encryption in Kerberos for Network Authentication." *Proceedings, Crypto '89*, 1989; published by Springer-Verlag.

KOHL94 Kohl, J.; Neuman, B.; and Ts'o, T. "The Evolution of the Kerberos Authentication Service." in Brazier, F., and Johansen, D. *Distributed Open Systems.* Los Alamitos, CA: IEEE Computer Society Press, 1994. Available at http://web.mit.edu/kerberos/www/papers.html.

KOHN78 Kohnfelder, L. *Towards a Practical Public Key Cryptosystem.* Bachelor's Thesis, M.I.T. 1978.

KUMA97 Kumar, I. *Cryptology.* Laguna Hills, CA: Aegean Park Press, 1997.

KUMA11 Kumar, M. "The Hacker's Choice Releases SSL DOS Tool." The *Hacker News*, October 24, 2011. http://thehackernews.com/2011/10/hackers-choice-releases-ssl-ddos-tool.html#.

LAM92a Lam, K., and Gollmann, D. "Freshness Assurance of Authentication Protocols." *Proceedings, ESORICS 92,* 1992; published by Springer-Verlag.

LAM92b Lam, K., and Beth, T. "Timely Authentication in Distributed Systems." *Proceedings, ESORICS 92,* 1992; published by Springer-Verlag.

LATT09 Lattin, B. "Upgrade to Suite B Security Algorithms." *Network World*, June 1, 2009.

LE93 Le, A., et al. "A Public Key Extension to the Common Cryptographic Architecture." *IBM Systems Journal*, No. 3, 1993.

LEHM51 Lehmer, D. "Mathematical Methods in Large-Scale Computing." *Proceedings, 2nd Symposium on Large-Scale Digital Calculating Machinery,* Cambridge: Harvard University Press, 1951.

LEUT94 Leutwyler, K. "Superhack." *Scientific American*, July 1994.

LEVE90 Leveque, W. *Elementary Theory of Numbers.* New York: Dover, 1990.

LEWA00 Lewand, R. *Cryptological Mathematics.* Washington, D.C.: Mathematical Association of America, 2000.

LEWI69 Lewis, P.; Goodman, A.; and Miller, J. "A Pseudo-Random Number Generator for the System/360." *IBM Systems Journal*, No. 2, 1969.

LIDL94 Lidl, R., and Niederreiter, H. *Introduction to Finite Fields and Their Applications.* Cambridge: Cambridge University Press, 1994.

LIPM00 Lipmaa, H.; Rogaway, P.; and Wagner, D. "CTR Mode Encryption." *NIST First Modes of Operation Workshop*, October 2000. http://csrc.nist.gov/groups/ST/toolkit/BCM/workshops.html.

LISK02 Liskov, M.; Rivest, R.; and Wagner, D. "Tweakable Block Ciphers. *Advances in Cryptology – CRYPTO 2002*, 2002.

MA10 Ma, D., and Tsudik, G. "Security and Privacy in Emerging Wireless Networks." *IEEE Wireless Communications*, October 2010.

MANA11 Manadhata, P., and Wing, J. "An Attack Surface Metric." *IEEE Transactions on Software Engineering*, Vol. 37, No. 3, 2011.

MANT01 Mantin, I., Shamir, A. "A Practical Attack on Broadcast RC4." *Proceedings, Fast Software Encryption*, 2001.

MATY91a Matyas, S. "Key Handling with Control Vectors." *IBM Systems Journal*, No. 2, 1991.

MATY91b Matyas, S.; Le, A.; and Abrahan, D. "A Key Management Scheme Based on Control Vectors." *IBM Systems Journal*, No. 2, 1991.

MAUW05 Mauw, S., and Oostdijk, M. "Foundations of Attack Trees." *International Conference on Information Security and Cryptology*, 2005.

MCGR04 McGrew, D., and Viega, J. "The Security and Performance of the Galois/Counter Mode (GCM) of Operation." *Proceedings, Indocrypt 2004*.

MCGR05 McGrew, D., and Viega, J. "Flexible and Efficient Message Authentication in Hardware and Software." 2005. Available at http://www.cryptobarn.com/gcm/gcm-paper.pdf.

MECH14 Mechalas, J. *Intel® Digital Random Number Generator (DRNG) Software Implementation Guide.* Intel Developer Zone, May 15, 2014. https://software.intel.com/en-us/articles/intel-digital-random-number-generator-drng-software-implementation-guide.

MENE97 Menezes, A.; Oorshcot, P.; and Vanstone, S. *Handbook of Applied Cryptography.* Boca Raton, FL: CRC Press, 1997. Available at http://cacr.uwaterloo.ca/hac/index.html.

MERK79 Merkle, R. *Secrecy, Authentication, and Public Key Systems.* Ph.D. Thesis, Stanford University, June 1979.

MERK81 Merkle, R., and Hellman, M. "On the Security of Multiple Encryption." *Communications of the ACM*, July 1981.

MERK89 Merkle, R. "One Way Hash Functions and DES." *Proceedings, CRYPTO '89*, 1989; published by Springer-Verlag.

MEYE88 Meyer, C., and Schilling, M. "Secure Program Load with Modification Detection Code." *Proceedings, SECURICOM 88*, 1988.

MEYE13 Meyer, C.; Schwenk, J.; and Gortz, H. "Lessons Learned From Previous SSL/TLS Attacks: A Brief Chronology of Attacks And Weaknesses." *Cryptology ePrint Archive*, 2013. http://eprint.iacr.org/2013/.

MICA91 Micali, S., and Schnorr, C. "Efficient, Perfect Polynomial Random Number Generators." *Journal of Cryptology*, January 1991.

MILL75 Miller, G. "Riemann's Hypothesis and Tests for Primality." *Proceedings of the Seventh Annual ACM Symposium on the Theory of Computing*, May 1975.

MILL88 Miller, S.; Neuman, B.; Schiller, J.; and Saltzer, J. "Kerberos Authentication and Authorization System." *Section E.2.1, Project Athena Technical Plan*, M.I.T. Project Athena, Cambridge, MA, 27 October 1988.

MITC90 Mitchell, C.; Walker, M.; and Rush, D. "CCITT/ISO Standards for Secure Message Handling." *IEEE Journal on Selected Areas in Communications*, May 1989.

MITC92 Mitchell, C.; Piper, F. ; and Wild, P. "Digital Signatures." in [SIMM92].

MOOR01 Moore, A.; Ellison, R.; and Linger, R. "Attack Modeling for Information Security and Survivability." *Carnegie–Mellon University Technical Note CMU/SEI-2001-TN-001*, March 2001.

MYER91 Myers, L. *Spycomm: Covert Communication Techniques of the Underground.* Boulder, CO: Paladin Press, 1991.

NCAE13 National Centers of Academic Excellence in Information Assurance/Cyber Defense. *NCAE IA/CD Knowledge Units.* June 2013.

NEED78 Needham, R., and Schroeder, M. "Using Encryption for Authentication in Large Networks of Computers." *Communications of the ACM*, December 1978.

NEUM93a Neuman, B., and Stubblebine, S. "A Note on the Use of Timestamps as Nonces." *Operating Systems Review*, April 1993.

NEUM93b Neuman, B. "Proxy-Based Authorization and Accounting for Distributed Systems." *Proceedings of the 13th International Conference on Distributed Computing Systems*, May 1993.

NIST95 National Institute of Standards and Technology. *An Introduction to Computer Security: The NIST Handbook*. Special Publication 800-12. October 1995.

ODLY95 Odlyzko, A. "The Future of Integer Factorization." *CryptoBytes*, Summer 1995.

ORE67 Ore, O. *Invitation to Number Theory*. Washington, D.C.: The Mathematical Association of America, 1967.

PARK88 Park, S., and Miller, K. "Random Number Generators: Good Ones are Hard to Find." *Communications of the ACM*, October 1988.

PARZ06 Parziale, L., et al. *TCP/IP Tutorial and Technical Overview*. ibm.com/redbooks, 2006.

PAUL07 Paul, G., and Maitra, S. "Permutation after RC4 Key Scheduling Reveals the Secret Key", *Selected Areas of Cryptography: SAC 2007, Lecture Notes on Computer Science*, Vol. 4876, pp. 360–337, 2007.

PELL10 Pellegrini, A.; Bertacco, V.; and Austin, A. "Fault-Based Attack of RSA Authentication." *DATE '10 Proceedings of the Conference on Design, Automation, and Test in Europe*, March 2010.

POIN02 Pointcheval, D. "How to Encrypt Properly with RSA." *CryptoBytes*, Winter/Spring 2002. http://www.rsasecurity.com/rsalabs.

POPE79 Popek, G., and Kline, C. "Encryption and Secure Computer Networks." *ACM Computing Surveys*, December 1979.

PREN96 Preneel, B., and Oorschot, P. "On the Security of Two MAC Algorithms." *Lecture Notes in Computer Science 1561; Lectures on Data Security*, 1999; published by Springer-Verlag.

RABI78 Rabin, M. "Digitalized Signatures." *Foundations of Secure Computation*, DeMillo, R.; Dobkin, D.; Jones, A.; and Lipton, R., Eds. New York: Academic Press, 1978.

RABI80 Rabin, M. "Probabilistic Algorithms for Primality Testing." *Journal of Number Theory*, December 1980.

RIBE96 Ribenboim, P. *The New Book of Prime Number Records*. New York: Springer-Verlag, 1996.

RIVE78 Rivest, R.; Shamir, A.; and Adleman, L. "A Method for Obtaining Digital Signatures and Public Key Cryptosystems." *Communications of the ACM*, February 1978.

RIVE84 Rivest, R., and Shamir, A. "How to Expose an Eavesdropper." *Communications of the ACM*, April 1984.

ROBS95a Robshaw, M. *Stream Ciphers*. RSA Laboratories Technical Report TR-701, July 1995. http://www.rsasecurity.com/rsalabs.

ROBS95b Robshaw, M. *Block Ciphers*. RSA Laboratories Technical Report TR-601, August 1995. http://www.rsasecurity.com/rsalabs.

ROGA03 Rogaway, P., and Wagner, A. "A Critique of CCM." *Cryptology ePrint Archive: Report 2003/070*, April 2003.

ROGA04 Rogaway, P. "Efficient Instantiations of Tweakable Blockciphers and Refinements to Modes OCB and PMAC." *Advances in Cryptology—Asiacrypt 2004. Lecture Notes in Computer Science*, Vol. 3329. Springer-Verlag, 2004.

ROGA10 Rogaway, P. "A Synopsis of Format-Preserving Encryption." *Unpublished Manuscript*, March 2010. http://web.cs.ucdavis.edu/~rogaway/papers.

ROS06 Ros, S. "Boosting the SOA with XML Networking." *The Internet Protocol Journal*, December 2006. cisco.com/ipj.

SALT75 Saltzer, J., and Schroeder, M. "The Protection of Information in Computer Systems." *Proceedings of the IEEE*, September 1975.

SCHN89 Schnorr, C. "Efficient Identification and Signatures for Smart Cards." *CRYPTO*, 1988.

SCHN91 Schnorr, C. "Efficient Signature Generation by Smart Cards." *Journal of Cryptology*, No. 3, 1991.

SCHN96 Schneier, B. *Applied Cryptography.* New York: Wiley, 1996.

SCHN99 Schneier, B. "Attack Trees: Modeling Security Threats." *Dr. Dobb's Journal*, December 1999.

SCHO06 Schoenmakers, B., and Sidorenki, A. "Cryptanalysis of the Dual Elliptic Curve Pseudorandom Generator." *Cryptology ePrint Archive*, Report 2006/190, 2006. eprint.iacr.org.

SEAG08 Seagate Technology. *128-Bit Versus 256-Bit AES Encryption.* Seagate Technology Paper, 2008.

SHAN49 Shannon, C. "Communication Theory of Secrecy Systems." *Bell Systems Technical Journal*, No. 4, 1949.

SIMM92 Simmons, G., Ed. *Contemporary Cryptology: The Science of Information Integrity.* Piscataway, NJ: IEEE Press, 1992.

SIMM93 Simmons, G. "Cryptology." *Encyclopaedia Britannica, Fifteenth Edition*, 1993.

SING99 Singh, S. *The Code Book: The Science of Secrecy from Ancient Egypt to Quantum Cryptography.* New York: Anchor Books, 1999.

SINK09 Sinkov, A., and Feil, T. *Elementary Cryptanalysis: A Mathematical Approach.* Washington, D.C.: The Mathematical Association of America, 2009.

SMIT71 Smith, J. "The Design of Lucifer: A Cryptographic Device for Data Communications." *IBM Research Report RC 3326*. April 15, 1971.

STAL15 Stallings, W., and Brown, L. *Computer Security.* Upper Saddle River, NJ: Pearson, 2015.

STAL16 Stallings, W. *Foundations of Modern Networking: SDN, NFV, QoE, IoT, and Cloud.* Upper Saddle River, NJ: Pearson, 2016.

STEI88 Steiner, J.; Neuman, C.; and Schiller, J. "Kerberos: An Authentication Service for Open Networked Systems." *Proceedings of the Winter 1988 USENIX Conference*, February 1988.

STIN06 Stinson, D. *Cryptography: Theory and Practice.* Boca Raton, FL: CRC Press, 2006.

TAYL11 Taylor, G., and Cox, G. "Digital Randomness." *IEEE Spectrum*, September 2011.

TSUD92 Tsudik, G. "Message Authentication with One-Way Hash Functions." *Proceedings, INFOCOM '92,* May 1992.

TUCH79 Tuchman, W. "Hellman Presents No Shortcut Solutions to DES." *IEEE Spectrum*, July 1979.

VANC11 Vance, J. *VAES3 Scheme for FFX.* NIST, http://csrc.nist.gov/groups/ST/toolkit/BCM/documents/proposedmodes/ffx/ffx-ad-VAES3.pdf, May 2011.

VANO90 van Oorschot, P., and Wiener, M. "A Known-Plaintext Attack on Two-Key Triple Encryption." *Proceedings, EUROCRYPT '90*, 1990; published by Springer-Verlag.

VANO94 van Oorschot, P., and Wiener, M. "Parallel Collision Search with Application to Hash Functions and Discrete Logarithms." *Proceedings, Second ACM Conference on Computer and Communications Security*, 1994.

VOYD83 Voydock, V., and Kent., S. "Security Mechanisms in High-Level Network Protocols." *Computing Surveys*, June 1983.

WANG05 Wang, X.; Yin, Y.; and Yu, H. "Finding Collisions in the Full SHA-1." *Proceedings, Crypto '05*, 2005; published by Springer-Verlag.

WAYN09 Wayner, P. *Disappearing Cryptography.* Boston: Burlington, MA: Morgan Kaufmann, 2009.

WEBS86 Webster, A., and Tavares, S. "On the Design of S-Boxes." *Proceedings, Crypto '85*, 1985; published by Springer-Verlag.

WIEN90 Wiener, M. "Cryptanalysis of Short RSA Secret Exponents." *IEEE Transactions on Information Theory*, Vol. 36, No. 3, 1990.

WOO92a Woo, T., and Lam, S. "Authentication for Distributed Systems." *Computer*, January 1992.

WOO92b Woo, T., and Lam, S. " 'Authentication' Revisited." *Computer*, April 1992.

WOOD10 Wood, T., et al. "Disaster Recovery as a Cloud Service: Economic Benefits & Deployment Challenges." *Proceedings, USENIX HotCloud '10*, 2010.

YUVA79 Yuval, G. "How to Swindle Rabin." *Cryptologia*, July 1979.

XU10 Xu, L. *Securing the Enterprise with Intel AES-NI.* Intel White Paper, September 2010.

CREDITS

Page 21: Definition of Computer Security from *An Introduction to Computer Security: The NIST Handbook* by Guttman, B. and Roback, E.A. Published by DIANE Publishing, © 1995.

Page 27: From RFC 4949 by Shirey, R. published by The IETF Trust, © 2007.

Page 29–30: Excerpt from Data Communication Networks: Open Systems Interconnection (OSI); Security, Structure and Applications, Permission provided by International Telecommunication Union (ITU).

Page 30: Excerpt from Data Communication Networks: Open Systems Interconnection (OSI); Security, Structure and Applications, Permission provided by International Telecommunication Union (ITU).

Page 32–33: Excerpt from Data Communication Networks: Open Systems Interconnection (OSI); Security, Structure and Applications, Permission provided by International Telecommunication Union (ITU).

Page 33: Recommendation X.800 - Data Communication Networks: Open Systems Interconnection (OSI); Security, Structure and Applications, Permission provided by International Telecommunication Union.

Page 111: Excerpt from The Silent World of Nicholas Quinn by Colin Dexter, published by Pan Macmillan, © 2011.

Page 239: Draft NIST Special Publication 800-38G, U.S. Department of Commerce.

Page 285: NIST IR 7298, Revision 2, U.S. Department of Commerce.

Page 333: Draft NIST Special Publication 800-57, Part 1, Revision 4, U.S. Department of Commerce.

Page 399: Data Authentication Algorithm Figure, William Stallings.

Page 414: Basic Structure of Hash-Based PRNGs Figure, William Stallings.

Page 471: Definition of Cryptoperiod from Recommendation for Key Management – Part 1: General (Revision 3), NIST Special Publication 800-57, U.S. Department of Commerce.

Page 510: Federal Information Processing Standards Publication, Personal Identity Verification (PIV) of Federal Employees and Contractors, U.S. Department of Commerce.

Page 527: Terminology Related to IEEE 802.1X Table, William Stallings.

Page 530: Definition of Cloud Computing from The NIST Definition of Cloud Computing: Recommendations of the National Institute of Standards and Technology, U.S. Department of Commerce.

Page 533: NIST Cloud Computing Reference Architecture: Recommendations of the National Institute of Standards and Technology, U.S. Department of Commerce.

Page 534: NIST Cloud Computing Reference Architecture: Recommendations of the National Institute of Standards and Technology, U.S. Department of Commerce.

Page 538–539: Guidelines on Security and Privacy in Public Cloud Computing, U.S. Department of Commerce.

Page 621: Excerpt from Multipurpose Internet Mail Extensions (MIME) Part Two by Ned Freed and Nathaniel S. Borenstein, published by Internet Engineering Task Force, © 1996.

Page 626: Trustworthy Email, U.S. Department of Commerce.

Page 632: Excerpt from Key words for use in RFCs to Indicate Requirement Levels by S. Bradner, published by Internet Engineering Task Force, © 1997.

Page 697: Quote from On War by Carl von Clausewitz edited by Michael Howard and Peter Paret, published by Princeton University Press, © 1989.

Page 703–743: Provided by Dan Shumow.

INDEX

N

Pearson

PEARSON TECH PACK

Decode the world of computers!

Only with **Pearson Tech Pack.**

Pearson brings you the world's best texts on computer science — books designed to completely transform your learning experience! Our series of books are **crisp, relevant** and contain **detailed notes** on all important topics, making them an **essential resource for all computer-science engineering students.** They not only help students excel in exams but also help them apply their knowledge to solve real-world problems. These books are widely **recommended by faculty members** and adopted in most of the major technical Indian universities.

HALLMARK FEATURES

- Well-written and error-free programming codes
- Self-explanatory flow-charts and algorithms
- Numerous examples and exercises

Computer Science Classics from Pearson

ISBN: 9788131700709
Author: M. Morris Mano

ISBN: 9788131792476
Author: Ramez Elmasri, Shamkant B. Navathe

ISBN: 9789332518667
Author: Alfred V. Aho, Monica S. Lam Ravi Sethi, Jeffrey D. Ullman

ISBN: 9789332550513
Author: Andrew S. Tanenbaum, Albert S. Woodhull

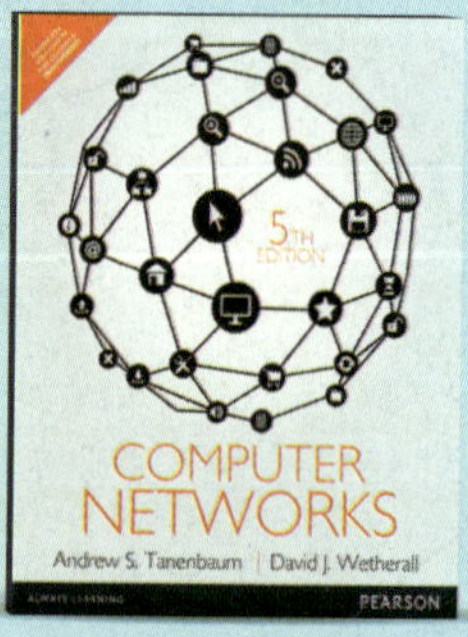

ISBN: 9789332518742
Author: Andrew S. Tanenbaum, David J. Wetherall

ISBN: 9789332518865
Author: William Stallings

ISBN: 9789332518858
Author: Ian Sommerville

ISBN: 9789332563292
Author: Paul Deitel, Harvey Deitel

ISBN: 9788131720479
Author: John E. Hopcroft, Rajeev Motwani, Jeffrey D. Ullman

ISBN: 9788177587654
Author: Donald D. Hearn, M. Pauline Baker

ISBN: 9789332543515
Author: Stuart J. Russell, Peter Norvig

ISBN: 9789332518773
Author: William Stallings

PEARSON TECH PACK

Hurry up! Grab a copy now.

To know more, visit www.pearson.co.in